P9-CTB-037

SHAKESPEARE SURVEY

ADVISORY BOARD

(1) Shakespeare and his Stage
(2) Shakespearian Production
(3) The Man and the Writer
(4) Interpretation
(5) Textual Criticism
(6) The Histories
(7) Style and Language
(8) The Comedies
(9) *Hamlet*
(10) The Roman Plays
(11) The Last Plays (with an index to *Surveys 1–10*)
(12) The Elizabethan Theatre
(13) *King Lear*
(14) Shakespeare and his Contemporaries
(15) The Poems and Music
(16) Shakespeare in the Modern World
(17) Shakespeare in his Own Age
(18) Shakespeare Then Till Now
(19) *Macbeth*
(20) Shakespearian and Other Tragedy
(21) *Othello* (with an index to *Surveys 11–20*)
(22) Aspects of Shakespearian Comedy
(23) Shakespeare's Language
(24) Shakespeare: Theatre Poet
(25) Shakespeare's Problem Plays
(26) Shakespeare's Jacobean Tragedies
(27) Shakespeare's Early Tragedies
(28) Shakespeare and the Ideas of his Time
(29) Shakespeare's Last Plays
(30) *Henry IV* to *Hamlet*
(31) Shakespeare and the Classical World (with an index to *Surveys 21–30*)
(32) The Middle Comedies
(33) *King Lear*
(34) Characterization in Shakespeare
(35) Shakespeare in the Nineteenth Century
(36) Shakespeare in the Twentieth Century
(37) Shakespeare's Earlier Comedies
(38) Shakespeare and History
(39) Shakespeare on Film and Television
(40) Current Approaches to Shakespeare through Language, Text and Theatre
(41) Shakespearian Stages and Staging (with an index to *Surveys 31–40*)
(42) Shakespeare and the Elizabethans
(43) *The Tempest* and After
(44) Shakespeare and Politics
(45) *Hamlet* and its Afterlife
(46) Shakespeare and Sexuality
(47) Playing Places for Shakespeare
(48) Shakespeare and Cultural Exchange
(49) *Romeo and Juliet* and its Afterlife
(50) Shakespeare and Language
(51) Shakespeare in the Eighteenth Century (with an index to *Surveys 41–50*)
(52) Shakespeare and the Globe
(53) Shakespeare and Narrative
(54) Shakespeare and Religions
(55) *King Lear* and its Afterlife
(56) Shakespeare and Comedy
(57) *Macbeth* and its Afterlife

Aspects of *Macbeth*
Aspects of *Othello*
Aspects of *Hamlet*
Aspects of *King Lear*
Aspects of Shakespeare's 'Problem Plays'

SHAKESPEARE SURVEY

AN ANNUAL SURVEY OF SHAKESPEARE STUDIES AND PRODUCTION

57

Macbeth and its Afterlife

EDITED BY

PETER HOLLAND

CAMBRIDGE
UNIVERSITY PRESS

PUBLISHED BY THE PRESS SYNDICATE OF THE UNIVERSITY OF CAMBRIDGE
The Pitt Building, Trumpington Street, Cambridge, United Kingdom

CAMBRIDGE UNIVERSITY PRESS
The Edinburgh Building, Cambridge, CB2 2RU, UK
40 West 20th Street, New York, NY 10011–4211, USA
477 Williamstown Road, Port Melbourne, VIC 3207, Australia
Ruiz de Alarcón 13, 28014 Madrid, Spain
Dock House, The Waterfront, Cape Town 8001, South Africa

http://www.cambridge.org

First published 2004

Printed in the United Kingdom at the University Press, Cambridge

Typeface Bembo 10/12pt. *System* LaTeX 2ε [TB]

A catalogue record for this book is available from the British Library

ISBN 0 521 84120 8 hardback

Shakespeare Survey was first published in 1948. Its first
eighteen volumes were edited by Allardyce Nicoll.
Kenneth Muir edited volumes 19 to 33.
Stanley Wells edited volumes 34 to 52.

EDITOR'S NOTE

It is with deep sadness that I note here the death in June 2004 of Inga-Stina Ewbank, a long-serving and much-loved member of *Shakespeare Survey*'s Advisory Board. Professor Ewbank was a great scholar and teacher; successive editors of *Survey* knew they could always call on her unfailingly wise advice and that her thoughts would be offered with kindness and generosity in the finest spirit of academic collegiality. We shall miss her.

Volume 58, on 'Writing About Shakespeare' and including papers from the 2004 International Shakespeare Conference, will be at press by the time this volume appears. The theme of Volume 59 will be 'Editing Shakespeare'.

Submissions should be addressed to the Editor at The Shakespeare Institute, Church Street, Stratford-upon-Avon, Warwickshire CV37 6HP, to arrive at the latest by 1 September 2005 for Volume 59. Pressures on space are heavy and priority is given to articles related to the theme of a particular volume. Please send a copy you do not wish to be returned. Submissions may also be made via e-mail attachment to pholland@nd.edu. All articles submitted are read by the Editor and at least one member of the Advisory Board, whose indispensable assistance the Editor gratefully acknowledges.

Unless otherwise indicated, Shakespeare quotations and references are keyed to *The Complete Works*, ed. Stanley Wells, Gary Taylor *et al.* (Oxford, 1986).

Review copies should be addressed to the Editor as above. In attempting to survey the ever-increasing bulk of Shakespeare publications our reviewers inevitably have to exercise some selection. We are pleased to receive offprints of articles which help to draw our reviewers' attention to relevant material.

P. D. H.

CONTRIBUTORS

Tom Blackburn, *Swarthmore College*
William C. Carroll, *Boston University*
†Frederick W. Clayton, *University of Exeter*
Natasha Distiller, *University of Cape Town*
Michael Dobson, *University of Surrey, Roehampton*
Beatrice Groves, *St John's College, Oxford University*
E. A. J. Honigmann, *University of Newcastle*
Arthur F. Kinney, *University of Massachusetts, Amherst*
Ruru Li, *University of Leeds*
Lynne Magnusson, *University of Toronto*
Richard C. McCoy, *Queens College, City University of New York*
Kathleen McLuskie, *University of Southampton*
Ruth Morse, *Université Paris 7, Denis-Diderot*
Simon Palfrey, *University of Liverpool*
Paul Prescott, *The Shakespeare Institute, University of Birmingham*
Eric Rasmussen, *University of Nevada*
Katherine Rowe, *Bryn Mawr College*
Carol Chillington Rutter, *University of Warwick*
James Shaw, *The Shakespeare Institute, University of Birmingham*
Lauren Shohet, *Villanova University*
Emma Smith, *Hertford College, University of Oxford*
Frances Teague, *University of Georgia*
Margaret Tudeau-Clayton, *University of Zürich*
Deanne Williams, *York University, Ontario*
Simon Williams, *University of California, Santa Barbara*

CONTENTS

CONTENTS

ILLUSTRATIONS

HUMANE STATUTE AND THE GENTLE WEAL: HISTORICAL READING AND HISTORICAL ALLEGORY

KATHLEEN McLUSKIE

I

Shakespeare's *Macbeth* has come in for some critical battering in recent times. The recurrent retreat from bardolatry has disconnected the play from its author, and the critical consensus is based on an acceptance that the Folio text of the play is a palimpsest of at least two versions: one from the time of the Gunpowder plot and one, with Middleton's additional songs, late enough to have been influenced by Jonson's *Masque of Queens*. The bibliographical uncertainties of the text (which are not many) have been used to endorse a freedom of interpretation that releases the play from historical particularity into wider speculation.

Stephen Orgel, for example, can assert that the Folio version was 'prepared for a single, special occasion' (p. 144),[1] a performance for King James VI and I, named as the 'great king' for whom the witches perform their antic round in Act 4. Orgel is too serious a scholar to hide the absence of any evidence for a court performance. However his historicist methodology allows him both to develop a political reading that depends upon the presence of the king and to reverse the argument by suggesting that the additional witch scenes constituted an effort, 'with uncertain success, to liven up an unpopular play' (p. 148).

Orgel's speculations are part of the background to an eloquently persuasive reading of the play's political ambiguity and its explicit exclusion of women. In fact, he seems to reject pedantic searching after the facts of the case in favour of a butterfly chase after 'the free-floating signifiers of post-modern theory, standing for an infinitely variable range of signifieds' (p. 143). The truth of the play's origins and the integrity of the text cannot be settled and so cannot act as any corrective to the free play of an imaginative critical reading. On the other hand, the indeterminacy of the play's historical existence cannot allow it to remain meaningless. The puzzling co-existence of the theatrical 'delights' of the witches' show and their terrible impact articulated by Macbeth must be resolved in a reading that insists on a political fable to do with the recurrent and dangerous instability brought about by the combination of a weak king and a powerful warrior.

The readings that result from this freedom do accumulate an authenticity of their own. Orgel's recent essay gains some of its authoritative impact from the prior existence of both Alan Sinfield's earlier work on the play's embodiment of oppositional early-modern politics and Janet Adelman's psychoanalytic account of the terror of maternity that runs through its action and language.[2] The methods of historical analogy and psychoanalytically informed close reading have replaced bibliography and positivist historicism as the building blocks of critical innovation. There is no longer

[1] Stephen Orgel, 'Macbeth and the Antic Round', *Shakespeare Survey 52* (Cambridge, 1999), pp. 143–54.

[2] Janet Adelman, 'Escaping the Matrix: The Construction of Masculinity in *Macbeth* and *Coriolanus*', in *Suffocating Mothers: Fantasies of Maternal Origin in Shakespeare's Plays* (London, 1992), pp. 130–64; Alan Sinfield, 'Macbeth: History, Ideology and Intellectuals', *Critical Quarterly*, 28 (1986), 63–77.

any need to find proof positive that 'the play as we have it derives from court performance' but where H. N. Paul used the connection with King James to valorize the contemporary cultural impact of Shakespeare's work,[3] more recent critics have used the same connection to denounce Shakespeare's creative use of his source materials as no more than cheap opportunism.

Diane Purkiss, for example, uses the connections between *Macbeth*, a contemporary newsbook account of James VI and I's trial of the witches of Berwick and *The Masque of Queens* to denounce Shakespeare's artistic integrity. She finds him 'unblushingly strip mining both popular culture and every learned text he can lay his hands on for the sake of creating an arresting stage event'.[4] Purkiss's Shakespeare is guilty of the same politically motivated insensitivity as James VI. James had forced Gillies Duncan to display her bewitching songs for the court as an entertainment in the course of his trial of the Berwick witches, accused of causing the storm at sea that had endangered the life of the king on his return from Denmark with his bride. Shakespeare in the theatre is seen as responsible only for 'unbridled sensationalism, which looks less appealing once the listener is conscious of the female voices suppressed' (p. 207).

In Purkiss's case, too, the history invoked offers a generalized chronological connection that cannot fully sustain her distinction between suppressed women's voices and the appropriating male artist. As Christina Larner has described, the language and references to legal processes in *News from Scotland* show that it must have been produced in England rather than Scotland, one of a series of news stories of witch trials published at the turn of the century.[5] What made the Berwick witch accusations special was that they turned on an alleged attempt on the life of the king himself. Local practice had become treason. Even more significant was the fact that James had returned from a visit to the Danish court. As well as collecting his bride there, he had spent time engaged in learned discussion with Danish theologians, expert in the continental demonology which had provided the intellectual rationale for the witch trials in Europe. The initial charges that witches had caused the gales which almost drowned the king and queen were initially made on the Danish side of the North Sea, but similar accusations were levelled at their Scottish counterparts, probably initiated by James himself. Unravelling the resulting murderous mix of local prejudice, clashing personalities, theological disputes and national politics is a daunting task for historical anthropologists: what it cannot do is to provide a simple line from a Scottish witch trial to the reception of an English play written nearly two decades later.

Both Orgel and Purkiss in different ways employ a method that Halpern has described as 'historical allegory'.[6] They elucidate meanings which were not necessarily identified in their originating moment but which nonetheless depend on a sense of history for their validation and critical weight. They offer fables that resonate with modern instances but are given their significance by their historical context. Although this context is only sketched in, it can stand for a contextualizing approach against which alternative decontextualizing approaches can be framed.[7]

Frank Kermode, for example, addresses his study of Shakespeare's language to the ever-elusive 'nonprofessional audience with an interest in Shakespeare'.[8] He acknowledges the quality of contemporary scholarship but explicitly chooses to ignore it, in favour of attention to the long-accepted superiority of Shakespeare's poetry. 'Language' here means poetry, not historical linguistics, and, in the account of *Macbeth*, other historical considerations of the provenance of the text, or the dating of the play are briskly dispatched. What follows

[3] Henry N. Paul, *The Royal Play of Macbeth* (New York, 1950)

[4] Daine Purkiss, *The Witch in History: Early Modern and Twentieth Century Representations* (London, 1996), p. 207.

[5] Christina Larner, 'James VI and I and Witchcraft' in Alan G. R. Smith, ed., *The Reign of James VI and I* (Basingstoke, 1973), pp. 74–90.

[6] Richard Halpern, *Shakespeare among the Moderns* (Ithaca, 1997), p. 12.

[7] See Halpern, *Shakespeare among the Moderns*, p. 40 on this 'oscillation within the critical dilemma of modernism'.

[8] Frank Kermode, *Shakespeare's Language* (London 2000), p. vii.

is a brilliantly eloquent explication of the play's central ethical paradoxes: that action cannot provide resolution; that the 'mere successiveness of time' (p. 215) is ultimately uncontrollable. Those observations about the action of *Macbeth* are partly commonplaces, but the quotations and the connection to the narrative of regicide and remorse give them a resonance that comes, at least in part, from their familiarity. Kermode builds on the resonance of that familiarity by connecting these ideas to a world older even than Shakespeare. He traces analogies between Shakespeare's ideas expressed in *Macbeth* and the deep past of St Augustine's confessions (p. 205) to create the sense that these are truths transcending time. Yet, in spite of this historical gesture, his interpretation ultimately depends upon assertion rather than proof:

> It is surely impossible to deny that certain words – 'time', 'man', 'done' – and certain themes – 'blood', 'darkness' – are the matrices of the language of Macbeth. In the period of the great tragedies these matrices appear to have been fundamental to Shakespeare's procedures. (p. 215)

His final statement acknowledges the open-endedness of his reading and its transcendence of history:

> We cannot assign them any limited significance. All may be said to equivocate, and on their equivocal variety we impose our limited interpretation. (p. 216)

Kermode would certainly not echo Orgel's statement about the postmodern condition that informs all modern criticism[9] but his open-ended conclusion suggests that the oscillation between contextualized and decontextualized criticism is becoming less pronounced. Whether critics focus on the history or the poetry, they are more willing to acknowledge the intellectual autonomy of their findings, the sense that they speak as much to our own preoccupations as to some essential character of the plays. Those preoccupations may be located in philosophical abstraction or in pressing contemporary concerns with tyranny or sexual difference but in either case they are addressed via aesthetic or imaginative appreciation.[10]

That aesthetic or imaginative appreciation, however, needs itself to be historicized. As Jonathan Bate has described, the 'genius' of Shakespeare is itself a product of historical contingency.[11] The passages chosen by Kermode, the illustrative historical texts chosen by Purkiss and Orgel, had already been selected by the individuals in the long list of famous and obscure commentators who preceded those critics. Reading the notes to the late nineteenth-century Variorum edition is a salutory reminder of how much work stands between the play and its modern reception and how that work, in theatre history, comparative quotation and source study, defines the limits of the editorial process. Moreover, the practice in early editions of marking fine passages and the collection of these in volumes of 'beauties' throughout the eighteenth and nineteenth centuries reveals a palimpset of the play that is more familiar even than that of the Folio text.[12] Editions of the Folio text themselves reinforce that tendency since they routinely smooth the uneven lineation into regular blank verse and retain emendations that support a view of Macbeth as a character poetically tormented by both his nature and his actions.

II

In the light of this critical consensus it is perhaps presumptuous to offer a corrective historicizing methodology, far less an alternative reading. It is perhaps inevitable that literary criticism should take the form of historical allegory. Its aim is to elucidate and thereby renew the meanings of the play. This process has been described as one that 'devalues its objects by subjecting them to a signifying intention. No longer meaningful in themselves, they can only point to a spiritual meaning

---

[9] See above p. 1.

[10] See Halpern, *Shakespeare among the Moderns*, p. 40 for an account of the origins of this process in early twentieth century modernism.

[11] 'Macbeth lives *because* he was reinvented as an icon of the romantic imagination.' Jonathan Bate, *The Genius of Shakespeare* (London, 1997), p. 286.

[12] See Rebecca Rogers, 'Eighteenth Century Macbeths: The English Poet and the Scottish Play', PhD Thesis (University of Southampton, 1999).

which does not inhabit their material realm.'[13] This critique of historical allegory is especially borne out by the literary critical treatment of the motif of equivocation in *Macbeth*. For the literary critic, equivocation becomes no more than another word for Macbeth's and the witches' statement of paradoxes: 'fair is foul and foul is fair'; 'nothing is but what is not'. This rhetorical trope is given an added resonance via the information that equivocation was associated with the gunpowder plotters whose connection with the play comes through the apparent reference in the porter scene to their trial and execution. The added resonance, however, is an effect of literary criticism, anxious to give signifying effect to a scene that in modern times has needed explication.

The Porter's reference to equivocation is an almost buried allusion which is not, at least in the Folio text, allowed to hold up the movement of the scene. It indicates no animus against the gunpowder plotters, except in commonplacely assigning them to hell, and it includes nothing to deflect the essentially comic tone of the speech. It makes no comment on the specifically *political* issues, such as James's tolerance of the loyal majority among Catholics, or the threat from Spain or Rome.

Historical analysis of the Gunpowder plot, on the other hand, provides an irritating excess of information: too much for a commentary note and spilling beyond what will explicate the scene. It presents a highly complex political and historical event which remains controversial to this day. The plotters seem to have been members of a radical group who harboured desperate frustration at the lack of progress in James's toleration of Catholics. In this, their political views were different from the majority of loyalist Catholics who accepted the separation of spiritual and temporal power and remained faithful to the English crown.[14] The Gunpowder plot was a disappointment to them, not because it failed to assassinate James and Members of Parliament, but because it provided a focus for anti-Catholic sentiments and justified further anti-Catholic penal laws. As Jenny Wormald has described:

> The Gunpowder plot takes us back beyond James's accession to the last years of Elizabeth's reign and the problem of her heir. It was a problem that emphasised the deep division within the English Catholic community, a division, roughly speaking, between the Jesuits and the non-jesuits, between those Catholics who looked to Spain for deliverance and those whose Englishness – and therefore anti-Spanishness – was as important in determining their political attitude as was their faith.[15]

Equivocation as a historical phenomenon similarly escapes the boundaries of the play. Its pejorative association, along with other forms of illusionism and prestidigitation, with Catholic theology and religious practice was a feature of Protestant polemic that dismissed the Catholic doctrine of the 'true presence' as a kind of sleight of hand, mocked as magic tricks and juggling. However, for Catholics this equivocation involved a genuine intellectual questioning of the relationship between abstract ideals of loyalty to the monarch and commitment to the policies of a particular king. As Alison Shell has shown,

> It does most of them a disservice to equate Catholicism with subversion . . . it was their aim to re-integrate tributes to Caesar with those to God, and most would have hoped that this could be accomplished by the conversion of the reigning monarch.[16]

This excess of information could produce an anxious awareness that Shakespeare may not have been entirely fair to Catholics, any more than he was entirely fair to women and witches. However, history does not require this *parti pris* and nor, in this post-bardolatrous moment, does literary criticism.

If we return to the historical analysis (as opposed to historical allegory), we might note that the Porter's speech provides a rather unusual example in Shakespeare of a clown who is given ample

[13] Halpern, *Shakespeare among the Moderns*, p. 12.

[14] See Alison Shell, *Catholicism, Controversy and the English Literary Imagination* (Cambridge, 1999), p. 142ff.

[15] Jenny Wormald, 'Gunpowder, Treason and Scots', *Journal of British Studies*, 24 (1985), p. 154.

[16] Shell, *Catholicism*, p. 111.

opportunity to speak more than is set down for him; more, perhaps, than the compilers of the First Folio wished or bothered to record for posterity. In the historical moment of the turn of the century, this might have served a commercial as well as a political agenda. As Leeds Barroll has argued most persuasively, the traditional association between Shakespeare's play and the arrival of King James in England is not sustained by the evidence of the King's Men's work at court in the early years of the century.[17] Rather, he suggests, the plague closures of those years may have been causing some anxiety to the proprietors and share-holders of the Globe and Shakespeare among them. The other volatile element in the commercial environment of the theatre in those years was the boys companies newly installed in the hall theatres of Blackfriars and Pauls. Between 1604 and 1608, the boy players took political topicality to extremes, producing *Philotas*, *The Isle of Gulls*, *Eastward Ho* and the *Biron* plays.[18] The resulting political brouhaha ended their brief theatrical career and possibly acted as a warning to the adult companies about the limits of political support. The Folio text, by contrast, shows Shakespeare and the King's Men flirting with topicality in *Macbeth*, touching on the Gunpowder plot, echoing the *News from Scotland* and bringing history right up to date in the vision of the 'twofold balls and treble sceptres' (4.1.137) of the witches' vision. The possible topicality of those episodes never amounts to an alternative political vision and can be entirely subsumed within the narrative coherence of the text – the very features that allow it to be carried forward into succeeding ages, free of its local meanings and available for interpretation.

III

Rejecting the factitious resonances of topicality may seem to leave the play a little bare. If it carries no freight of historical significance, how are we to claim significance for it at the present time? This anxiety is compounded when we turn to the rare and thus invaluable evidence of the 1611 account of the play provided by Simon Forman.[19]

In spite of the fact that Forman indicated that his notes on the plays he saw were 'for Common Pollicie', he seems little interested in their external meanings. Instead, he noted the relationships within the play between motivation and action. Macbeth and Lady Macbeth were apparently 'moch amazed & Affronted' by their inability to wash Duncan's blood from their hands and Macbeth's second murder was 'for feare of Banko, his old companion, that he should beget kinges but be no kinge him selfe'. He also notes particular theatrical moments, drawing attention to the bloody daggers and the sleepwalking scene and giving detailed attention to the appearance of Banquo's ghost. He causes further problems for modern readings by referring to '3 women feiries or Nimphes' rather than three witches as the bearers of the prophecy.

There is, of course, no need to regard Forman as a paradigmatic viewer, a native informant who will give us unproblematic access to the true history of *Macbeth*. However, the fact that he makes no mention either of the Porter or of the Act IV show of kings does open up the possibility of multiple versions of the play. The Gunpowder plot and equivocation may have disappeared in the 1611 performance for reasons of topicality. The absence of the show of kings requires a rather different kind of explanation.

Orgel's alternative accounts – that it was specially written for a command performance or that it was added to liven up a failing play – separate out topicality from the formal requirements of the play and closes both off from the wider historical context. Yet the show of kings does more than validate James's extended right to succession. That role was fulfilled by the sybils who greeted the King on his visit to St John's College Oxford on his way south

[17] J. Leeds Barroll, 'Shakespeare without King James', chapter 2 of *Politics, Plague and Shakespeare's Theatre* (Ithaca, 1991), pp. 22–69.

[18] Roslyn Knutson, 'Falconer to the Little Eyases: A New Date and Commercial Agenda for the "Little Eyases" Passage in *Hamlet*', *Shakespeare Quarterly*, 46 (1995), pp. 1–31.

[19] Quoted in *The Norton Shakespeare*, General Editor Stephen Greenblatt (London, 1997), p. 3336.

from Scotland. As Jonathan Bate observes, 'the sole function of the Oxford interlude was to flatter King James. That is why it has never been performed again.'[20] The show of kings has an equally important role in the narrative and emotional structure of the play. It provides a new set of prophecies and a new dramatic impetus for the conflict between Macbeth and Macduff. The magical stories of the moving wood and the bloody babe extend the story beyond questions of dynastic succession and develop the motifs of kinship and personal bonds.

Forman's account of the play gives us some idea of the nature of these changes. His description of the second half of the play has none of the vivid attention to detail of the earlier passages.

> Then Macduff fled to England to the King's son, and so they raised an army and came to Scotland, and at Dunsinane overthrew Macbeth. In the meantime, while Macduff was in England, Macbeth slew Macduff's wife and children, and after in the battle Macduff slew Macbeth.

This rather bald account of the action in the second half does not necessarily mean that the show of kings and the new prophecies were omitted from the version Forman saw. However they do give a sense of how flat the play would be without them. The show of kings does more than provide information about the dynastic connection between Banquo and James I. The pacing of the sequence and the parallel focus on Macbeth's reaction provides an opportunity for Macbeth to *enact* his horror at the realization of the succession that was to be denied to him. It directly connects the witches' initial conundrum that Banquo would 'beget kings though ye be none' with Macbeth's destructive rage that replaces the more anxious and remorseful character of the opening scenes.

Forman twice mentions the motif of succession, indicating that the death of Banquo was 'for fear of Banquo, his old companion, that he should beget kings but be no king himself'. The Folio text pays particular poetic as well as narrative attention to the question in ways that connect inheritance to murder and, paradoxically, call into question the connection between inheritance and kingship. The fact that Duncan names his son as his heir presents for Macbeth 'a step / On which I must fall down or else o'erleap, / For in my way it lies' (1.4.50–2). In the soliloquy that precedes the arrival of Banquo's murderers, Macbeth reflects on the second part of the witches' prophecy:

> Then, prophet-like,
> They hailed him father to a line of kings.
> Upon my head they placed a fruitless crown,
> And put a barren sceptre in my grip,
> Thence to be wrenched with an unlineal hand,
> No son of mine succeeding. If't be so,
> For Banquo's issue have I filed my mind,
> For them the gracious Duncan have I murdered,
> Put rancours in the vessel of my peace
> Only for them, and mine eternal jewel
> Given to the common enemy of man
> To make them kings, the seed of Banquo kings.
> (3.1.60–71)

The witches' prophecy had broken the connection between kin and kings. The murder of Banquo cannot restore it, which makes it a dead end for the emotional dynamic of the play. In the version Forman saw, Macbeth's fear at Banquo's ghost 'fronted him so, that he fell into a great passion of fear and fury, uttering many words about his murder, by which when they heard that Banquo was murdered, they suspected Macbeth'. The story of regicide is concluded by a story of restoration but the motivation for that restoration is left unexplored.

The poetry of the Folio version together with the show of kings links all this together by sustaining the interest from king to kin. The murder after the show of kings is not of a father but of his kin – his wife and children. In the murder scene itself and in Macduff's emotional reaction to it, we are presented with a different image of kin: the image of the affective, companionate family. It is tempting to sentimentalize Macduff's relations with his family in a modern world that has privatized familial relations. However, the play provides a different set of relationships that link kin and kingship. Macbeth's

[20] Bate, *Genius*, p. 221.

suspicion of Macduff begins when he remembers that Macduff was absent from the feast. The insult is not merely from a subject to a king but from a subject who, like Macbeth, has absented himself from the ceremony with which those relations are established and sustained.

Earlier, the language used to describe the relationship between Macbeth and his king emphasizes its ethical and personal nature. Macbeth's agonized contemplation of regicide insists on obligations which go beyond the political:

He's here in double trust:
First, as I am his kinsman and his subject,
Strong both against the deed; then, as his host,
Who should against his murderer shut the door,
Not bear the knife myself. Besides, this Duncan
Hath borne his faculties so meek, hath been
So clear in his great office, that his virtues
Will plead like angels, trumpet-tongued, against
The deep damnation of his taking off
(1.7. 12–20)

Being a subject is part of being a kinsman and those double relationships are reinforced by a culture of gifts and feasting which tie the participants into a network of obligation and recompense. When Duncan welcomes Macbeth to the Scottish camp each of them acknowledges their mutual obligation. Duncan begins:

O worthiest cousin,
The sin of my ingratitude even now
Was heavy on me! Thou art so far before
That swiftest wing of recompense is slow
To overtake thee. Would thou hadst less deserved,
That the proportion both of thanks and payment
Might have been mine. Only I have left to say,
More is thy due than more than all can pay.

Macbeth replies:

The service and the loyalty I owe,
In doing it, pays itself. Your highness' part
Is to receive our duties, and our duties
Are to your throne and state children and servants
Which do but what they should by doing everything
Safe toward your love and honour. (1.4.14–27)[21]

This ring of obligation is broken after Duncan comes to Macbeth's castle. Macbeth is absent from the feast and his isolation is marked by the contrast between his solitary figure and the preparation for the banquet which brings a '*Sewer, and divers servants with dishes and service over the stage*'. Immediately before Macbeth follows the dagger to Duncan's bedchamber, Banquo gives him the king's gift of a diamond, a symbolic sealing of a relationship between himself and Macbeth's household which is about to be irrevocably broken.

When Macbeth himself becomes king, he tries, in traditional fashion, to seal his authority with a feast for the thanes. The feast is, of course, poisoned by the murder of Banquo whose ghostly presence disrupts the harmony of the ceremonious occasion. As Lady Macbeth reminds him, the feast is more than the mere consumption of food:

the feast is sold
That is not often vouched, while 'tis a-making,
'Tis given with welcome. To feed were best at home.
From thence the sauce to meat is ceremony,
Meeting were bare without it. (3.4.32–6)

And when she fails to calm his hysterical response to the ghost, she chides him with

You have displaced the mirth, broke the good meeting
With most admired disorder. (108–9)

In spite of Macbeth's catastrophic rupture of the cycle of obligation, he himself remains locked in the culture of feudal relations.

These familiar relations of gifts and feasting are presented in the play as the necessary ceremonies which protect the culture from atavistic violence. This image of pre-feudal feasting recurs in the conversation between Lennox and the Lord which occurs between the banquet scene and Macbeth's return to the witches. The Lord speaks of Malcolm's plan to solicit aid from England. He hopes that the outcome of Malcolm's embassy will be such that, with Gods help,

[21] This exchange of formal statements of fealty is rhetorically similar to the exchange between Duncan and Lady Macbeth that Kermode calls an 'arithmetical measuring of gratitude'. Kermode, *Shakespeare's Language*, p. 207.

> we may again
> Give to our tables meat, sleep to our nights,
> Free from our feasts and banquets bloody knives,
> Do faithful homage, and receive free honours,
> All which we pine for now. (3.6.33–7)

There is no suggestion that Malcolm's return will produce a change in political or legal structures, merely that it will fulfil the deep desire for peace and the social harmony which is ensured by the familiar cycle of homage and honour and sealed by harmonious feasting.

These images of a world of feasting and extended kinship seem to have the effect of creating an explicitly historical framework for the action – a framework which puts the action beyond generalized political ideas about kingship and succession. Macbeth's reaction to Banquo's ghost, for example, describes it as an apparition which threatens the very foundations of his culture:

> If charnel-houses and our graves must send
> Those that we bury back, our monuments
> Shall be the maws of kites. (3.4.70–2)

He recognizes that his action returns his world to 'th'olden time / Ere humane statute purged the gentle weal' (74–5). His offence in killing both Banquo and the king is not merely the sin of murder but a disruption of the civilizing ties which keep his social world in one piece. That social world is located at a moment in the past when the possibilities for a coherent connection between kingship and kin are in the balance. Macbeth's regicide tips the balance back to the more primitive world 'ere humane statute purged the gentle weal'. The vengeful return of Macduff, on the other hand, brings with it the possibility of establishing the institutions of kingship that will ensure its peaceful continuity. He comes in support of the rightful patrilineal king Malcolm.

Malcolm's legitimacy as king is assured by his leadership of the army and his ability to draw to him the support of Siward's forces. At the end of the play, however, he disperses his power and shares it with the Scottish thanes. He declares that his thanes and kinsmen should 'Henceforth be earls, the first that ever Scotland / In such an honour named' (5.10.29–30). In returning peace to Scotland, he also ensured its continuity by establishing a new category of nobleman, an honour familiar to the English. The precarious and potentially bloody relations of kin are replaced by the legally endorsed social relations of formal institutions and the special kin relationship of patrilineal inheritance is assured.

It would, of course, be reductive to imagine that this finale or any of the other connections between the play and images of primitive kingship can close off the meanings of the play. However, it can perhaps act as a reminder that Shakespeare was himself involved in writing historical allegory. He is writing about a deep past that was even more distant from his time than he is from ours and making sense of it in terms that had gained a particular pressure because they had been re-opened by the succession debates and by the Scottishness of the new king. As James Pocock described many years ago, the constitutional debates in early modern England were part of a Europe-wide 'collision between the authority of kings and local or national privileges, liberties and constitutions'.[22] Those debates took place using 'all the subtleties of the common-law technique of reading history backwards'. The history in question consisted of the continued assertion of an ancient constitution that existed from 'time immemorial' and assured the rights of subjects over kings who were themselves subject to the law.[23] Even James himself, who has been seen as an uncompromising exponent of the doctrine of the 'Divine right of Kings', subtitled *The Trew Law of Free Monarchies* with *The Reciprock and Mutuell Duetie betwixt a Free King and his Naturall Subjects*.[24]

These issues of political theory were further inflected by the sense that the Scots represented a special case. The process of establishing James's legitimacy and authority was further compromised by endemic English hostility to the Scots. This hostility involved not only distrust of James as

[22] J. G. A. Pocock, *The Ancient Constitution and the Feudal Law* (Cambridge, 1957), p. 16.

[23] See Pocock, *Ancient Constitution*, p. 46.

[24] See Michael Hawkins, 'History, Politics and Macbeth', in John Russell Brown, ed., *Focus on Macbeth* (London, 1982), p. 163.

king but also a sense of the primitive character of Scottish kingship. A good deal of the resentment against a Scottish king arose from the fact that for many English people Scotland was regarded as backward and yet infuriatingly resistant to English imperialism.[25] In a notorious speech in Parliament, Sir Christopher Piggot alleged that the Scots 'have not suffered above two kings to die in their beds, these two hundred years'.[26] In reminding Parliament that murder had been a common mode of succession in Scotland, Piggot was calling into question not only the Scots' ethical authority but also the modernity of their ideas of kingship. His assertion was historically correct, but it also drew on long-standing historical debates which had been conditioned by the need to articulate the relative rights and strengths of Scots and English kingship in pursuit of the ancient conflict between the two nations. Nick Aitchison's account of the pre-history of the historical King Macbeth, for example, notes how Fordun's first complete narrative history of Scotland (*c.* 1336) 'emphasised the continuity of Scottish kingship to counter English claims of historical overlordship' and began the isolation of Macbeth as an exceptional murderous tyrant.[27]

Political theories of kingship, the debate about the balance between kings' and subjects' rights, are never explicitly argued in *Macbeth*. Like other historical allegorists, he is able to bring together quite contradictory ideas. In the show of kings, he was able, by theatrical fiat, to represent the dynasty of Scots and British kings as a single unbroken line, while the finale of the play presents a more familiar image of relations between English and Scots: the invasion of Scottish territories by border magnates, acting in the name of the English king and with the connivance of Scottish aspirants to the throne. Malcolm's creation of the loyal thanes as 'earls, the first thatever Scotland / In such an honour named' may have had a special resonance at the time when James was attempting to create a 'union of nobility' by giving titles to both English and Scots gentry as a way of binding their allegiance to him personally and to the United Kingdom.[28] What is more important dramatically is that the thanes have been given emotional credibility throughout the final act by their loyal fealty to their leaders in contrast to 'the wretched kerns whose arms / Are hired to bear their staves'. Historical knowledge is never a substitute for the theatrical, narrative and imaginative experience that the play affords. Indeed the critical challenge is to link that historical knowledge with those pleasures.

I have been arguing that the play's imagery of primitive kinship links it to the emergent establishment of patrilineal inheritance as the most legitimate source of royal authority. Nevertheless, it is also clear that the poetic discussions of patrilineal kingship deal with ethical and psychic as much as political considerations. When Macbeth considers the murder of his king he speaks of 'dark and deep desires', and the great soliloquy which opens 1.7 speaks in existential terms of an action which will, like all decisive and violent acts, be incapable of controlling its consequences. Though the vision of the line of kings is undoubtedly linked to the legitimation of the Stuart dynasty, Macbeth's reaction to it is emotionally powerful rather than politically analytical.

The poetic articulation of these essentially ethical and existential questions is one of the play's great strengths. It has allowed the play to be adapted and reproduced in cultures and circumstances in which the particular political significance of killing a king has very different resonances and for very different local political readings to be drawn from it. I would argue, nevertheless, that the resonance of these ethical questions depends upon their connection to the deep structures of the accounts of kinship that are invoked throughout the play and were possibly strengthened by the addition of the show of kings in Act 4.

---

[25] Wormald, 'Gunpowder, Treason and Scots', *Journal of British Studies*, 24 (1985), p. 158.

[26] Quoted in William C. Carroll, ed., *Macbeth: Texts and Contexts* (New York, 1999), p. 120. See also Brian P. Levack, *The Formation of the British State England, Scotland and the Union 1603–1707* (Oxford, 1987), p. 195.

[27] Nick Aitchison, *Macbeth, Man and Myth* (Stroud, 1999), p. 107.

[28] Levack, *Formation*, p. 188.

Ideas of kinship in the play were fundamentally linked to notions of a world before and outside culture. That world involved the fantasy of an Edenic perfection which had no need of law. However it also invoked the terror of a lawless world in which atavistic individualism was unconstrained and in which the witches could arbitrarily break the connection between kingship and kin. By locating his story in the primitive world of pre-modern Scotland, Shakespeare was able both to speak of the particular history of early modern kingship but also to articulate it in terms of the deeper emotional links which joined people into kin. Whether we call these relationships feudal or familial, whether we describe them in anthropological or ideological terms, they articulate a desired, fantasized, ideal of kinship which could provide emotional support and an almost magical assurance of security. That fantasy is, of course, always unstable and threatened: the gracious Duncan is murdered, Macduff's wife and child are killed, Lady Macbeth commits suicide and Banquo is assassinated. But Fleance gets away, Macduff avenges his children's death and Malcolm inherits.

Whether we are satisfied (either ethically or aesthetically) by this reassuring cycle of kinship depends on how far we are content to believe in the magical power of kings. In modern times when the understanding of different forms of kingship is subsumed in a generalized suspicion of political power and the extended relations of kin compromised by an awareness of the deformations of patriarchy, that belief is no longer possible. Instead history is invoked to undermine it or is ignored in order to claim a continuity of more generalized, poetically rendered human concerns as the heart of the play. Both of these processes are as inevitable in our version of the historical allegory as Shakespeare's was in his.

MACBETH'S KNOWLEDGE

ARTHUR F. KINNEY

The first duty of the historian who would understand and explain [sixteenth-century writers] will be to return them to their milieu, where they are immersed in the mental climate of their time. (Marc Bloch)

I

In an attempt to forge some kind of workable historical method of criticism in light of challenges from structuralism, semiotics, phenomenology, deconstruction, reader-response theory, New Historicism, and various psychological approaches to literature, Robert D. Hume some time ago set out as his first principle that 'Historicism at bottom implies the illumination of text by context',[1] arguing that

> No sensible interpreter should wish to ignore either text or context: the problem is that one cannot attend fully to both at the same time. One can do a bit of each; one can go back and forth – but one cannot fully carry out both textual and contextual enterprises simultaneously. (p. 70)

Thus extracted, the proposition seems almost commonplace, for much of the critical work since Hume wrote has excavated, dissected, and analysed contextual materials in Shakespeare's time to understand more reliably the cultural moment in which he wrote: the culture that formed his thinking and the culture of those who constituted his audiences. Such examinations, furthermore, have complicated the issue of combination (and occasionally also of simultaneity) by understanding the further issue of representation: that the 'objectivity' of past events and the records of past cultural beliefs when scrutinized provide no securely objective record at all, but rather the subjectivity of past documents and the necessary partiality of their observations, statements, and arguments. We cannot fully transcribe the past merely by transcribing any single record of it, for any record is more or less as perspectival and multivalent as any literary text we wish to lay alongside it. The significance of witchcraft in *Macbeth*, for instance, is difficult to address for it speaks of supernatural belief, the power of women (or fate, or both) and the use of political prophecy as just three of the many meanings that witchcraft, both as a faith and a practice, harbours. Moreover, such meanings are compounded if we recognize that they are enlisted, although never neatly correlated, in the events in Scottish history around 1040, the record of that past in Francis Thynne's contributions to Holinshed's *Chronicles*, and Shakespeare's play – and even that as it was written down, staged around 1606, and later published in a flawed text in 1623.

It should not be surprising, however, that Hayden White, who has spent a career working through various strategies of history as narrative and narrative as history, has also addressed such issues; nor, perhaps, is it entirely unexpected that he was invited to share his observations during a Presidential Forum at the Modern Language Association of America. There he remarked that

[1] Robert D. Hume, 'Texts Within Contexts: Notes Toward a Historical Method', *Philological Quarterly*, 71 (1992), p. 71.

Although historical discourse continually moves between the poles of the misrepresentation of reality given in the historical record and its own reconstructions of 'what really happened' (or what can be plausibly said really to have happened) in the past – and in the process provides reasons both for believing in these reconstructions and for understanding why reality was misrepresented in the way it is in the record – it remains blind to the extent to which its own reconstructions are, themselves, less defigurations than refigurations of the reality in question.[2]

Such reconfigurations are essentially, for both the historian and the literary critic, exercises in troping – in locating and analyzing those figures of speech or thought outlined by George Puttenham, images or image patterns, or controlling ideas or themes that are manifest and work as similes (or metaphors functioning as similes) joining together what Hume has called context and text. By isolating a particular facet of context (what I have elsewhere called the cultural moment) to defigure, correlate, and so refigure, the literary historian has pressed hard on an ideational node as a point of interrogation, reopening a text in the hopes of enlarging cognitive possibilities for comprehension and appreciation.

Such a methodology holds many risks for White but is nevertheless worth trying. He concluded his brief address noting that figurative thinking and writing can be 'a problem *for* interpreters, and they are a problem *of* interpreters. Figurations is a problem for interpreters because they must determine the literal meaning behind the figurative representation of reality; and it is a problem of interpreters insofar as they must guard against mistaking their own discourse for a speech free of any kind of figurative thought.'

This is why the master interpreters in the human and social sciences always bring to their work one or another version of a theory of tropology. For tropology is the theory of the relation between the figurative and the literalist dimensions of discourse and, as the basis of a method of inquiry, provides an instrument not only for the identification of misrepresentations in the thought of others but also for the construction of one's discourse to the extent it is a report of facts and also – and above all – an interpretation of their meaning. (p. 17)

What I propose here to do is test the axiomatic conjectures of both Hume and White by extracting a single, apparently offhanded, reassurance by Macbeth to his wife: 'There's not a one of them but in his house I keep a servant fee'd' (3.4.130–1). He tells us, in passing, that he has instituted a network of spies that will serve him as agents and protect him and his rule as King of Scotland and that he has them in the house of every thane that presents him with any real danger, and not simply the household of Macduff alone. He has, in addition, hired thugs to assassinate Banquo and Fleance that, in his mind, function as corollary servants following his particular plans: 'Your spirits shine through you', he tells the hired murderers. 'Within this hour at most / I will advise you where to plant yourselves, / Acquaint you with the perfect spy o'th' time, / The moment on't; for't must be done tonight, / And something from the palace' (3.1.129–33). His government is a government of surveillance. Such a remark may be a passing one to us, or merely a small constituent in the rule of any tyrant, but I want, contextually, to suggest that this plan had striking resonances for Shakespeare's Jacobean audiences and would not have gone unnoticed and that, tropically, it connects to a major concern throughout the play, the concern with Macbeth's knowledge.

II

Every second guest your table take
Is a fee'd spy, t'observe who goes, who comes,
What conference you have, with whom, where, when;
What the discourse is, what the looks, the thoughts
Of every person there, they do extract,
And make into a substance.

(*Sejanus His Fall*, 2.1.444–9)

Surveillance as a necessary strategy of rule was readily apparent to James I in 1603 with the 'Main Plot' in which Sir Walter Ralegh and his brother-in-law Baron Cobham along with several other

[2] Hayden White, 'The Real, the True, and the Figurative in the Human Sciences', *Profession*, 92 (New York, 1992), p. 15.

conspirators were convicted on weak and debatable evidence of plotting to put Arabella Stuart on the English throne rather than James following the death of Elizabeth. Closely connected was the 'Bye Plot' in which two seminary priests, William Watson and William Clarke, were accused of treason. Their plea – that they were concerned with assuring toleration for Catholics – was summarily dismissed; instead, it was argued that they belonged to a conspiracy which likewise threatened James's rule and therefore was exacerbated with the conjunction with the earlier 'plot' challenging James's right to the throne and his ability to rule. Such a shaky start to Jacobean rule would be registered in the conspiracies of Sejanus and Tiberius in Ben Jonson's *Sejanus His Fall* (1605) and Shakespeare's *Macbeth* (1606).

Nor did such threats cease after James's coronation. The Powder Plot on 5 November 1605, in which Fr. Henry Garnet and a number of co-conspirators were accused of attempting to blow up the government, the royal family, and the church leaders, was a flashpoint echoed (particularly) in the Porter's speech in *Macbeth* (2.3.1–18), but it inscribes a pervasive anxiety. Later that same month, on 25 November, Lord Chief Justice John Popham writes to the Earl of Salisbury,

> There is this night in Southwark a very notable outrage committed by certain insolent priests, such as the whole town was put in exceeding fear and uproar; yet the constable so handled the matter as he took three of them, who nevertheless continued in most insolent manner, threatening that they would not leave until they had fired them out; after which there came more, and gave great words and threats at the priest; the town pursued them also, but could not take them; and being searched for letters, one of them answered, if thou hadst searched me three weeks since, thou mightest have found a hundred about me.[3]

On 22 March the following year, villagers living just outside London thought that local constables chasing a man who had stolen a horse, with sword drawn, had committed regicide. According to a report of the incident recorded in the *Calendar of State Papers Venetian*,

> The people of the village joined in the hue and cry thinking that he must have attacked the King who had passed through a while before. The crowd grew from village to village, and also the rumor, until persons set off at full speed from London to tell the Queen and Council that the King was dead; this news was immediately confirmed by newcomers and was believed by the Court. The Council instantly took all necessary steps at the palace and summoned an extraordinary meeting. The news spread to the City and the uproar was amazing. Everyone flew to arms, the shops were shut . . . and had not the contradiction arrived some terrible accident would have happened to us all (x, 333)

Leeds Barroll, who first noticed this entry, adds that

> Meanwhile, outside that same village, King James and his [hunting] party knew nothing of all this and were returning to court in a leisurely fashion when the king's party encountered people who described the uproar. James immediately sent a messenger to court with the news that he was safe, but he also decided to return to the village and show himself in person. The villagers, who were now running to look at the place where the king had been killed, found James and fell on their knees with tears of joy. But their hysterical and confused behavior in turn caused James to think that perhaps some crucial event in London was ultimately causing all this fuss, so he quickly sent another messenger to the queen and the court to let them know that he was not only safe but also moving swiftly toward London with his entourage. On arriving at London, he entered to popular acclamation. Fireworks were set off and bells were rung.[4]

Even apart from the ongoing trials for the Powder Plot then underway, this must have made a considerable impression, lasting for some time. On 5 July, yet another plot was discovered when an English Catholic, Captain William Newce, was accused of conspiring with a brother of one of the Powder Plot conspirators and an Irish Catholic servant of the Spanish ambassador to England on the life of James.[5]

---

[3] *The Calendar of the MSS of . . . the Marquis of Salisbury . . . Part XVII*, ed. M. S. Guiseppi (London, 1938), p. 511.

[4] J. Leeds Barroll, *Politics, Plague, and Shakespeare's Theatre: The Stuart Years* (Ithaca, 1991), p. 139. The account from the Calendar of State Papers Venetian is also on p. 139.

[5] Barroll, *Politics*, p. 142.

As a consequence of such incidents – and there were many others – Parliament passed at its second session in the spring of 1606 'An acte the better discouering and repressing of Popish Recusants'. That act opens by noting that 'it is found by dayly experience, that many his Maiesties Suiects, that adhere in their hearts to the Popish Religion, by the infection drawen from thence, and by the wicked and Deuilish counsel of Iesuites, Seminaries, and other like persons dangerous to the church and State, are so farre peruerted in the point of their Loyalties and due allegieance with the Kings Maiestie, and the Crowne of England' that a test of loyalty was vital.[6] The act proceeds to establish a loyalty oath, especially for those at ports, havens, and creeks – both 'Customer and Controller' – to avoid charges of felony, that reads,

> That if the within bounden, &c. shall not at any time then after bee reconciled to the Pope or Sea of Rome, nor shall enter into or consent vnto any practice, plot, or conspiracie whatsoeuer against the Kings Maiesty, his Heires and Successours, or any his and their Estate and Estates, Realmes or Dominions: but shall within conuenient time after knowledge therof had, reueile and disclose to the Kings Maiestie, his Heires and Successours, or some of the Lords of his or their Honourable priuie Councell, all such practices, plots, and conspiracies, That then the said Obligation to be voyd. (fol. C4V)

To add to this tightening of authority, Chief Baron Fleming, issuing his 'Decision in the Bate's Case' of 1606, extended the king's prerogative, distinguishing between the king's will as it is revealed through his laws and as it is unrevealed through his will known only to himself, giving him both the constitutional power of common law and the extralegal power of sovereignty. 'As the constitution of this body [Parliament] varieth with time' Fleming wrote, 'so varieth this absolute law according to the wisdom of the King for the common good.'[7] In effect, though, Fleming was only concurring with an earlier tract on 'The Royall Prerogative' set down by Lord Chancellor Ellesmere in 1604, by which both the legal prerogative revealed by the king's laws and the private prerogative issued by the king's will and judgement came from the natural body of the sovereign and were absolute.[8]

Such perceptions and actions in collocation help us to sense the events hovering behind such representations, but such a charged atmosphere as produced them, only referred to in passing by Macbeth and his network of fee'd servants, was an inheritance of growing apprehension throughout the last three decades and more of Queen Elizabeth's rule. In a detailed study of this period, John Michael Archer points out that 'Intelligence in the sense of the sovereign's ideal knowledge became in practice intelligence as spying', adding that 'Sovereignty and intelligence were united in a culture of surveillance that was chiefly defined by a life at court.'[9] He cites Cesare Ripa's emblem of a spy in the *Iconologia* who is covered in a cloak displaying eyes, ears, and tongues and the (perhaps derivative) Rainbow portrait of the Queen which 'took up the eyes, ears, and tongues motif for the mantle that [she] wears, probably to indicate, in a less censorious vein, the many servants who provided her with intelligence'. He thus notes that 'Privy councilors and bishops alike employed pursuivants, special messengers with the power to execute warrants, in the hunt for Catholics' (p. 4).

Targeting Catholics as the agents of potential treason was instituted by the papal bull *Regnans in excelsis* (1570) in which Pius V excommunicated Elizabeth from the Roman Catholic church. In the fact that this papal condemnation initiated an active opposition, it was a failure, but it failed spectacularly in at least two other ways: it had no effect on Elizabeth's loyal Protestant subjects and it made her Catholic subjects feel increasingly insecure. The pope insisted that English Catholics persist in professing their Roman faith, and to aid them he established, within just four years, an

6 *Anno Regni Iacobi, Regis Angl. Scotiae, Franc. & Hybern* [*Statutes*] (1606), ch. 4, fol. B6v.

7 Chief Baron Fleming, 'Decision in the Bate's Case', in J. P. Kenyon, *The Stuart Constitution, 1603–1688: Documents and Commentary* (Cambridge, 1966), p. 63.

8 Ellesmere, 'The Royall Prerogative', in *Law and Politics in Jacobean England, The Tracts of Lord Chancellor Ellesmere*, ed. Louis A. Knalfa (Cambridge, 1977), p. 68.

9 John Michael Archer, *Sovereignty and Intelligence: Spying and Court Culture in the English Renaissance* (Stanford, 1993), p. 3.

English Catholic seminary at Douai, France (then located in the Catholic Spanish Netherlands) that would train priests to infiltrate England 'for the preservation and augmentation of the faith of the Catholics'.[10] Subsequently other missionaries were sent from Rome where an English pilgrim hospice had been converted into a second college run by the Jesuits. An English publication of 1582 by Anthony Munday, *The English Romayne Lyfe* – he identifies himself only as 'A.M. sometime the Popes Scollers in the Seminarie' on the title page – describes his experiences the previous year. The early chapters discuss the voyage from England to Rome with his Catholic guide:

Then he willed vs to walke with him, and he would bring vs where we should lodge that night, at this charges: all the way rehearsing vnto vs, how beneficiall the Pope was to our Countreymen, and howe highlie we might pleasure our selues, our friends and Countrey, if we would followe his councell. Beside, such horrible and vnnaturall speeches, he vsed against her Maiestie, her honourable Councell, and other persons that he named: as the verie remembraunce maketh me blushe, and my heart to bleede. (p. 5)

At the college itself, he follows Catholic regiment and instruction. He reports, in part, that

After Supper, if it be in winter time, they [his fellow scholars] goe with the *Iesuites*, and sit about a great fire talking, and in all their talke, they striue who shall speake wurst of her Maiesty, of some of her Councell, of some Bishop here [that is, in England], or such lyke: so that the *Iesuites* them selues, will often take vp their hands and blesse them selues, to heare what abhominable tales they will tell them. (p. 39)

Nor, back in England, do Catholics fare well in the roll call he supplies.

Sherwood, he ranne downe the Ladder, when death should arrest him, hauing killed one of his fellowe Papistes. *Campion*, their glorious Captaine, he looked dead in the face, so soone as he sawe the place of Execution, and remained quaking & trembling vnto the death. *Shert*, would have the people thinke, hee feared not death, and yet he catched holde on the halter, when the Cart was drawne away. *Kirbie*, quaking when he felt the Cart goe away, looked styll how nere the ende of it was, tyl he was quite beside. And *Cottom* dismaying, died trembling & in great feare. These are the Martirs of ye Romish Church, not one of them patient, penitent, nor endued with courage to the extremitie of death: but dismaying, treambling & fearfull, as ye eye witnesses can beare me record. (p. 66; see illustration 1)

As early as 1571, Parliament passed the Treasons Act which defined treason following the dictates of the papal bull and which imposed severe penalties on importing such bulls or other devotional objects.

Matters heated up a decade later. In 1581, a law made conversion to Catholicism with the intent of ending allegiance to the Queen an act of treason. Fines for nonattendance at church increased to £20 monthly; those failing to pay had their estates sequestered. An act of 1585 designated any apprehended Jesuit or seminary priest a traitor and those hiding them also liable for execution. One such hostess, the Yorkshire housewife Margaret Clitherow, refused to plead for mercy at her trial and was crushed to death. Through the reign, 123 priests were hanged, drawn, and quartered. While a discussion in Parliament in 1593 failed to take away from Catholics all their legal rights, a statute was passed that restricted all Catholics to within five miles of their homes. In addition to such measures, Sir Francis Walsingham, briefly Keeper of the Privy Seal and then co-Principal Secretary, established an international espionage system and, during a short time as English ambassador to France in 1572 (during the St Bartholomew Day Massacre), drafted a kind of manual, *The Compleat Ambassador* (not published until 1655) which set out methods, 'Means and Persons', for gathering intelligence.[11] Christopher Marlowe was one of his agents; another was Maliverny Catlyn, who offered his services to Walsingham in 1586 as someone who had infiltrated English Catholic circles in France and who later served him as a spy in Portsmouth before requesting a transfer to the Marshalsea where he spied on imprisoned priests.[12] Propaganda against Catholics

[10] Quoted in Patrick Collinson, *Elizabethans* (Hambledon, 2003), p. 231.

[11] Archer, *Sovereignty and Intelligence*, p. 47.

[12] Archer, *Sovereignty and Intelligence*, p. 69.

1
3

2
4

1 Anthony Munday, *The English Romayne Lyfe* (1582).

also poured from London presses, such as I. B.'s [John Baxter's] *A Toile for Two-Legged Foxes*, a combination of diatribe and satire, in 1600. The author identifies himself on the title page as '*Preacher of the word of God*', and notes that of

> Foxes infected with heresie, which do especially disturbe the church of England, there be two sorts; the one called recusants, because they haue forsaken our fellowship; the other church-haunts, who with false hearts frequent our assemblies, temporizing for feare of a fine, or further penaltie . . . Therefore haue they learned to temporize, and with double hearts to halt on both sides, hauing one for God, and another for Baal; one for the prince, and an other for the Pope; one for the Masse, and another for the communion. (pp. 105, 108)

Macbeth instructs Lady Macbeth that 'False face must hide what the false heart doth know' (1.7.82), but this phrase was frequently levied against papists and recusants. Baxter may also be alluding to Elizabeth's remark about looking into men's souls when he comments,

> If a window were framed in the brests of these discontented catholikes, that her maiestie and the state-guiding counsel, and all the true friends of this kingdome might know their secret intentions; or if their consciences were as deeply sounded, as they may be iustly doubted: then I know full well that many false hearts would be found lurking vnder painted hoodes and cakes of foule cancred malice, vnder meale mouthed protestations; neither would it bee troublesome to finde out a two-legged Foxe; or if the coles of the long festered choler were of that condition, as that being heaped together in their malicious minds, they could blister their tongues, or scald their lippes, we should neede no further search to finde out a Romain catholike. Howbeit although they haue no windowes in their brestes, wherethrough wee may see into euery corner of their consciences, how they packe and shuffle now; and (as it is greatly to be feared) meane to cut also if Poperie should get the upper hand; yea although they shrowd their wicked deuises with a vaile

> of obscuritie, and contriue their cruel crafts *in tenebris*: yet if that foresight and circumspection be had, which the subtiltie of such household enemies requireth, I doubt not but it shal be easie to espie the Woolfe, though he wander in sheepes clothing, by the manner of his howling; and the Asse, though he iet in the Lions skinne, by the length of his eares. (pp. 110–11)

Baxter concludes by asking, 'How many Iesuites in profession, Iscariots in practice, haue visited Tyburne? How many Foxe-priests haue taken their farewell at the gallowes? And although Rome hath lately beautified them with the title of Martyrs, whom either male-contentedness or malice, caused to be treacherous to their Prince; yet is it a thing euident, that rebellion not religion; treason not truth; hath brought them to the halter' (pp. 219–20). Meanwhile, Elizabeth took special precautions. Visiting St Paul's in London in 1588, 'shee was, under a rich canopie, brought through the long west isle to her travers in the quire, the clergie singing the Letanie: which being ended, she was brought to a closet of purpose made out of the north wall of the church'. We are likewise told that when she was received at Westminster in 1597, 'The Queen's Majestie [was] to come to the body of the churche, and soe to enter in at the weste dore of the quier, and so uppe to her travase by the communion table.' 'Despite her dependence upon the regime of pomp and display that is also evident in these passages,' Archer writes, 'there were already strong elements of surveilling power in Elizabeth's rule'.[13]

Increased danger and distress partly isolated the Queen as it will in time isolate Macbeth from Macduff (who refuses to attend his investiture at Scone), then Lady Macbeth and Banquo, and finally even Ross. Part of the atmosphere of distrust may be explained by Munday's remark that Jesuits were entering England by secret creeks and landing places disguised as merchants, soldiers, gentlemen, or sometimes even galley slaves; Macbeth is likewise fearful of a ghost that appears to be Banquo or, in time, of Birnam Woods moving towards Dunsinane Hille, Fife, a mere seven miles from Perth and closer yet to Scone Abbey. Such priests as arrived were smuggled into Catholic homes, many of them forming a geographical sweep across Warwickshire just a few miles north of Stratford-upon-Avon. In a recent study of places constructed to hide priests on their missions of celebrating the sacraments, teaching the faithful, and converting souls, Julian Yates learned of eleven priest-holes built in Hindlip Hall, Worcestershire, alone between 1580 and 1606.[14] He cites Michael Hodgetts who describes a priest-hole as 'usually an almost featureless space, perhaps 8 ft by 3 ft and 5 ft high, only identifiable by its flooring and by its entrance, which is most often a trapdoor in a garderobe closet or other dark corner', a place architecturally obscure and inconvenient, and so small one could hardly stand, but was forced to sit or lie down beside a few day's provisions.[15] Pursuivants for the government, highly suspicious, became highly trained. So did the government. Robert Cecil told his agents searching Hindlip Hall shortly after the discovery of the Powder Plot in 1605 to

> Observe in the parlour where they use to dyne and supp, in the east part of that parlour, it is conceived there is some vault, which to discover you must take care to drawe down the wanscott, whereby the entry into the vault may be discovered; and the lower parts of the house must be tryed with a broach [a pointed rod of wood or iron] by putting the same into the ground some foot or two, to try whether there may be perceived some timbers, which if be there must be some vault underneath it. For the upper roomes, you must observe whether they be more in breadth than the lower roomes, and look in which places the roomes be enlarged, by pulling up some boards you may discover some vault. Also, if it appears that there be some corners to chimneys, and the same boarded, yf the bordes may be taken away there will appear some. Yf the walls seem to be thicke and covered with waiscott, being tryed with a gymlet, yf it stick not on the wall, but go through, some suspicion is to be had thereof. Yf there be any double loft over two or three foot, one above another, in such places any may be harboured privately.

13 Archer, *Sovereignty and Intelligence*, p. 149. The two passages concerning Queen Elizabeth are also quoted by Archer on p. 149.

14 Julian Yates, *Error Misuse Failure: Object Lessons from the English Renaissance* (Minneapolis, 2003), p. 143.

15 Michael Hodgetts, *Secret Hiding-Places* (Dublin, 1985), p. 2, quoted in Yates, *Error Misuse Failure*, p. 145.

> Also, yf there be a loft towards the roof of the house in which there appears no entrance out of any oyther place or ledging, that must of necessity be opened and looked into, for these be ordinary places of leiving.[16]

Yates further notes two hiding places at Ufton Court in Berkshire in a space between the gables and the vertical partitions of the attic (p. 182) and one in Breccles Hall, East Anglia, in a chamber over the boltings house entered by way of the privy: 'The priest thus inhabited a space beneath the privy to one side of the flow of refuse but nevertheless within the symbolic space of the expelled debris' (p. 183). *The Apprehension of Henrie Garnet, Provinciall of the Jesuites, at the house of Mr. Thomas Abbington in Worcester Sheire*, a manuscript in the British Library composed at about the time Shakespeare was composing Macbeth, was read on two separate occasions by government officials who found nothing untoward (f. 108v) but in fact tells

> How, in the gallerie over the gate there were found two cunning and very arteficiall convayaunces, in the maine brickwall, so ingeniously framed and with such arte, as it cost much labour ere they could be found. Three other secret places, contained by no lesse skill and industrie, were likewise found in and about the chimnies, in one whereof, two of the traytours were close concealed.
>
> (f. 100v, quoted in Yates, p. 178)

A proclamation of 1591 established commissions to flush out such priests and to arrest them and to examine anyone providing for them, keeping their answers 'in a manner of a Register of Kalender' (quoted in Yates, p. 161). 'The state this intruded into the space of the household or home and demanded that everyone be accounted for and give account' Yates comments. 'In the process, queen and council redrew England as a map of anomalous or insufficient answers, of subjects whose hearts held "secrets"' (p. 161). Yates even locates a family pedigree of the Fitzherberts, related to Fr. Thomas Fitzherbert, which has a numbered circle with each family member's name, family relationship, location, and reasons for suspicion, isolating the one non-Catholic as the acceptable heir (pp. 163–5). Conversely, Katharine Eisaman Maus points out, 'The Jesuits [Robert] Persons and [William] Allen go so far as to claim that no Protestants possess genuine authority to question Catholics, "because a heretic queen is no legitimate queen".'[17]

This theatre of government was not lost on the playwrights and playgoers of the public theatres. Peregrine plays the pursuivant to Sir Pol in Ben Jonson's *Volpone*, making Sir Pol believe he is accused of treason and causing him to burn his papers even though 'I haue none, but notes, / Drawne out of play-bookes' (5.4.41–2). Silius tells Sabinus in Jonson's *Sejanus* that

> Every minist'ring spy
> That will accuse and swear is lord of you,
> Of me, of all, our fortunes, and our lives,
> Our looks are called to question, and our words,
> How innocent soever, are made crimes;
> We shall not shortly dare to tell our dreams,
> Or think, but 'twill be treason (1.64–70)

Tiberius is likewise suspicious:

> We have thought on thee,
> Amongst a field of Romans, worthiest Macro,
> To be our eye and ear; to keep strict watch
> On Agrippina, Nero, Drusus – ay,
> And on Sejanus. (3.679–83)

Such speeches anticipate that in the anonymous *Tragedy of Tiberius* (1607) – 'If though doost meane the Empire to obtaine, Sweare, flatter, lye, dissemble, cog & faine'; both of them draw ultimately on a common source, Suetonious' *Life of Tiberius*.[18] Jonson reiterates this same idea in *Timber:*

---

[16] Henry Foley, *Records of the English Province of the Society of Jesus* (London, 1878), vol. II, pp. 355–6, as quoted in Yates, *Error Misuse Failure*, p. 169.

[17] Katharine Eisaman Maus, *Inwardness and Theater in the English Renaissance* (Chicago, 1995), p. 28.

[18] 'Over and above his olde friends and familiars, hee had demaunded twenty out of the number of the best and principall Citizens, as Counsailours and Assistants unto him in publique affairs. Of all these, hee could hardly shewe twaine or three at the most alive: the rest, some for one cause and some for another he brought to confusion and killed: among whom (with the calamity and overthrow of many more) was AELIUS SEIANUS, whom hee had to the heightest place of authoritie advaunced.' 'Life of Tiberius' in Caius Suetonius Tranquillus, *The historie of twelve Caesars*, trans. Philemon Holland (1606), sig. L2v.

or Discoveries when he writes of tyrants that 'their fortune is often-times to draw a *Seianus*, to be neere about 'hem; who will at last affect to get above 'hem, and put them in a worthy feare' in contrast to more just rulers who need 'no Emissaries, Spies, Intelligencers, to intrap true Subjects'.[19]

Nor was Shakespeare exempt. His comedies show an interest in spying in what could be called eavesdropping if not surveillance. Such secret observations are the foundation of key scenes in *Love's Labour's Lost*, *Much Ado About Nothing* and *Twelfth Night*, growing somewhat darker with each successive comedy, until, in *King Lear*, the old king's final division of his kingdom, to join Cordelia 'As if we were Gods' spies' and 'take upon's the mystery of things' (conflated text, 5.3.17, 16), opens up the play's most tragic depth. But it is just what is a major focal point in this tragedy that is what all the tragedies share. Othello's need for ocular proof of Desdemona's infidelity leads to a fatal act of spying – 'Confine yourself but in a patient list', Iago tells him (4.1.73) – while the act of spying is repeatedly foundational throughout *Hamlet*, as Michael Neill has so persuasively shown. 'It is symbolically appropriate,' he points out,

> that the play should begin with a group of anxious watchers on the battlemented walls of the castle, for nothing and no one in Claudius's Denmark is allowed to go 'unwatched' . . . the treachery of [Rosencrantz and Guildenstern] illustrates how much, behind the mask of uncle Claudius's concern, his court is ruled by the prison-house customs of the stool pigeon and the informer [as we have already seen in the instance of Maliverny Catlyn]. How readily first Ophelia and then Gertrude allow themselves to become passive instruments of Polonius's and Claudius's spying upon the Prince; how easily Rosencrantz and Guildenstern are persuaded to put their friendship with Hamlet at the disposal of the state. Even Laertes's affectionate relationship with his sister is tainted by a desire to install himself as a kind of censor, a 'watch man' to the fortress of her heart (1.3.50). In this he is all too like his father, Polonius, [who is] the perfect inhabitant of this court: busily policing his children's sexuality, he has no scruple about prostituting his daughter in the interests of state security, for beneath his air of senile wordiness and fatherly anxiousness lies an ingrained cynicism that allows him both to spy on his son's imagined 'drabbing' in Paris and to 'loose' his daughter as a sexual decoy to entrap the Prince.

Hamlet's role as hero at once sets him apart from this prison-house world and yet leads him to become increasingly entangled in its web of surveillance,[20] spying directly (and as an audience to *The Mouse-Trap*) every bit as much as he is spied upon. Spying in this play stems from two causes: the desire to control through knowledge, and the fear of not knowing and of losing out. Lear's near-passivity turns desperate and lethal with Othello and Iago, Hamlet and nearly everyone else at Elsinore.

Such matters have not gone unnoticed; but what does seem to have gone unremarked is how closely much of this tracks events in *Macbeth*. The newly-elected King of Scotland is as anxious to know all he can as Claudius is, and for precisely the same reasons: to see if others perceive the election to the throne as an usurpation of the throne and to reassure himself that he is safely in power and able to maintain that power. Macbeth has his Polonius, too, in Ross, who begins with announcing to Macbeth his newly-awarded title as Thane of Cawdor to match his inherited title of Glamis, naturally derived from his father Sinel (1.3.69). Ross moves from Duncan's orbit into that of Macbeth, at first discovering Duncan's murder, then seeing if Macduff is still in the kingdom and so a threat to Macbeth's rule (for why else would he visit his cousin, warn his wife, and leave without taking her into his protection?) before, finally, going over to Malcolm. Ross is by his very nature a messenger, one who connects by his (temporary) superior knowledge; and he uses this information in much the same way Iago, Claudius and Macbeth do – to garner knowledge to assure his own safety. As for Neill's more passive Ophelia and Gertrude, who 'allow themselves' to become accomplices in the spying game, so Macbeth has his Banquo – whose knowledge of the witches'

[19] Ben Jonson, *Works*, ed. C. H. Herford [and] Percy and Evelyn Simpson (Oxford, 1947), vol. 8, pp. 601, 600.

[20] Michael Neill, '*Hamlet*: A Modern Perspective', in *Hamlet*, New Folger Library edition, ed. Barbara A. Mowat and Paul Werstine (New York, 1992), pp. 312–13.

prophecy and of Macbeth's response somehow remains inert after the regicide of Duncan so that he appears a silent accomplice to Macbeth, so that he arouses Macbeth's urgent need to know: 'I think not of [the 'three weird sisters']', Macbeth says to Banquo at their first opportunity to be alone, 'Yet, when we can entreat an hour to serve, / We would spend it in some words upon that business / If you would grant the time' (2.1.20–3). The hushed invitation is charged by the word *serve*, as king addresses thane; and the play's pointer has an eerie echo of Bacon's observation in his essay 'Of Discourse': 'If you dissemble sometimes your knowledge of that you are thought to knowe, you shall bee thought another time to know that you knowe not.'[21] Macbeth, however, is not content with the role of Claudius alone, but must compound it with the role of Hamlet. Just as the Prince of Denmark augments the play about *The Murder of Gonzago*, Macbeth would seek out his own play with the three weird sisters, travelling to them on the heath: 'I conjure you,' he tells them, 'by that which you profess, / Howe'er you come to know it, answer me' (4.1.66–7), *conjure* then having the primary meaning of *conspire*. As Hamlet conspires with the travelling players, Macbeth would conspire with the sisters, and each group presents a dumb show: the murder of a sleeping king, a '*show of eight kings, [the] last with a glass in his hand, and BANQUO*' (s.d. 4.1.127). To gain the knowledge spying on the show will provide, Hamlet isolates himself from the other spectators, spying on them in turn. Macbeth is already alone. Both plays turn on the masque-like dumb show that breathes freshly different life into their initially conventional revenge tragedy.

III

> By the gods,
> If I could guess he had but such a thought,
> My sword would cleave him down from head to heart.
> (*Sejanus His Fall*, 1.252–4)

Knowledge is difficult to determine. In that trial of Sir Walter Ralegh in 1603 in connection with the Main Plot, accused on what Maus calls a 'trumped-up treason charge', Ralegh protests that circumstantial evidence against him is insufficient in English common law. It is an interpretation of his case that Justice Warburton abruptly denies.

> I marvel, Sir Walter, that you being of such experience and wit, should stand on this point; for so many horse-stealers may escape, if they may not be condemned without witnesses. If one should rush into the king's privy chamber, whilst he is alone, and kill the king . . . and this man be met coming with his sword drawn all bloody: shall he not be condemned to death?[22]

Maus cites this retort and comments,

> Warburton's explication of English legal custom is correct. On the continent, the kinds and amount of evidence necessary for conviction were strictly prescribed. Two eyewitnesses, or a confession – which could be obtained under torture – were ordinarily required. In England, by contrast, evidentiary rules remained loose, almost chaotic. Under most circumstances torture was impermissible, but as John Langbein [in *Torture and the Law of Proof*] has pointed out, this apparent humanity was made possible by the fact that circumstantial evidence was all that was required for conviction. English courts made no rules about the admissibility of evidence, no qualitative distinction among kinds of proof, until well into the seventeenth century. The power to convince the jury was all that mattered. (p. 104)

The kind, number, and conflation of circumstances that could serve as admissible evidence could vary from case to case, from judge to judge, from jury to jury. It is a narrow instance of a wider cognitive issue: an event, Michel de Certeau has said, 'does not explain, but permits an intelligibility'; it is 'the postulate and the point of departure – but also the

[21] Quoted in Archer, *Sovereignty and Intelligence*, p. 130. Archer adds, 'It is hard fully to unpack this sentence: does it mean that we should pretend to know rather more than we do about something familiar, or that an element of fakery should be added to the style of our expertise so that our ignorance can't be told apart from it?' 'Of Studies', the first essay in the book, similarly cautions that studies 'teach not their owne vse, but that is a wisdome without them: and aboue them wonne by observation' (Archer, *Sovereignty and Intelligence*, p. 130).

[22] William Cobbett and Thomas Howell, *Cobbett's Complete Collection of State Trials* (London, 1809), vol. II, p. 15, quoted by Maus, *Inwardness*, p. 104.

blind spot – of comprehension',[23] signifying both the need to know and the frustration of never being sure you know.

This knotty problem of cognition was prevalent in Shakespeare's culture, in the context of the text of *Macbeth*. 'Persons and things inwardly *are*', Maus sums; 'persons and things outwardly only *seem*' (p. 5). It is Hamlet's very premise.

> Seems, madam? Nay, it *is*. I know not 'seems.'
> 'Tis not alone my inky cloak, good-mother,
> Nor customary suits of solemn black,
> Nor windy suspiration of forced breath,
> No, nor the fruitful river in the eye,
> Nor the dejected havior of the visage,
> Together with all forms, moods, shows of grief
> That can denote me truly. These indeed 'seem,'
> For they are actions that a man might play;
> But I have that within which passeth show –
> These but the trappings and the suits of woe.
> (1.2.76–86)

The speech could be taken right out of *The Passions of the Mind* by the English Jesuit Thomas Wright who claims that

> Every one may discover his fellow's natural inclinations not by philosophical demonstration, but only by natural conjectures and probabilities . . . For that we cannot enter into a man's heart, and view the passions or inclinations which there reside and lie hidden; therefore, as philosophers by effects find out causes, by properties essences, by rivers fountains, by boughs and flowers the core and roots; even so we must trace our passions and inclinations by some effects and external operations.[24]

Macbeth is keenly aware of this distinction from the start, for in the first scene he appears, his outer behaviour is consciously at odds with his inner thoughts, his speeches disjunctive with his soliloquies given as asides.

> MACBETH [*aside*] Glamis, and Thane of Cawdor,
> The greatest is behind. [*To* ROSS *and* ANGUS]
> Thanks for your pains.
> [*To* BANQUO] Do you not hope your children shall be kings
> When those that gave the thane of Cawdor to me
> Promised no less to them? (1.3.114–18)

His mind parses the inherent issues in the titles the three sisters award him; his public responses separate them out, sharing parts of them with a divided audience, keeping some of them to himself:

> MACBETH [*aside*] Two truths are told
> As happy prologues to the swelling act
> Of the imperial theme. [*To* ROSS *and* ANGUS] I thank you, gentlemen,
> [*Aside*] This supernatural soliciting
> Cannot be ill, cannot be good. If ill,
> Why hath it given me earnest of success
> Commencing in a truth? I am Thane of Cawdor.
> If good, why do I yield to that suggestion
> Whose horrid image doth unfix my hair
> And make my seated heart knock at my ribs
> Against the use of nature? (1.3.126–36)

As Thane of Cawdor he prepares for the kingship as James, in his *Basilicon Doron*, argued: outward actions and gestures – all that the public receives – can be put on display in a way that suggests they convey inward truths: 'they serve as trunch-men, to interpret the inward disposition of the mind, to the eyes of them that cannot see farther within him, and therefore must only judge of him by the outward appearance'.[25] Even if there is a disconnection between the knowledge conveyed and the knowledge retained, Wright, Macbeth and King James claim that both are important, even vital. This is not a matter of duplicity or of feigning a truth; both convey essential meanings functioning at different levels. Social interaction often requires translating the knowledge of thoughts into the full or partial knowledge revealed in a more public presentation. This leads the physician John Cotta in 1616 to propose the use of 'artificial conjecture',[26] what Maus

---

23 Michel de Certeau, *The Writing of History*, trans. Tom Conley (New York, 1988), p. 96.

24 Thomas Wright, *The Passions of the Minde in Generall*, ed. Thomas O. Sloan (Urbana, 1971), pp. 104–5, quoted in Maus, p. 5.

25 James I and VI, *The Basilicon Doron of King James VI*, ed. James Craigie (Edinburgh, 1944), p. 15, quoted in Maus, *Inwardness*, p. 5.

26 John Cotta, *The Triall of Witch-craft, Shewing the True Methode of the Discovery* (1616), p. 4, as quoted in Maus, *Inwardness*, p. 5.

interprets as 'reasoning from the superficial to the deep, from the effect to the cause, from seeming to being' (p. 5). Knowledge is thus a combination of knowing and speculating. Neither is sufficient alone, but the compound is made unstable because at least in the case of the knowledge withheld, the public knowledge is incomplete and can mislead, can even oppose that which is not disclosed. Knowledge is difficult to determine. Ralegh makes the problem more complicated still in his later work, *Skeptic, or Speculation*, first printed in 1651 but positing ideas realized much earlier: 'I may tell what the outward object seemeth to me; but what it seemeth to other creatures, or whether it be indeed that which it seemeth to me, or any other of them, I know not' (p. 4).[27] Macbeth shares this understanding, and this scepticism, when he divides his private response to the three sisters from his public response, and his public response is further divided among Banquo, Ross and Angus, and the sisters themselves.

We know that knowledge is a central issue in the play because Duncan announces the necessity of a king's knowledge before Lennox, Malcolm, Banquo and Donalbain as he apparently addresses Macbeth on their first meeting, just after the death of the previous Thane of Cawdor: 'There's no art / To find the mind's construction in the face. / He was a gentleman on whom I built / An absolute trust' (1.4.11–14). It is an astonishingly naive comment, sealed by his instant substitution of Macbeth (1.4.14–21), and naive as well in signalling to Macbeth the knowledge that Duncan can be blind to duplicity and surprised by betrayal. It is a knowledge Macbeth will put to almost immediate use. But Macbeth is a man helped and haunted by his interior knowledge, I think; the play's actions are consistently correlated to his soliloquies. Fifteen percent of the play is in monologue, compared with eight percent of *Hamlet*, and while the proportions are roughly the same, the sheer compactness of *Macbeth* makes the soliloquies more visible; they must carry more weight. Shakespeare, if not Macbeth, presses home the doubleness of knowledge by the doubleness of speech in dialogues with Lady Macbeth and with Banquo that miscarry, where the ideas and words of the characters slip past one another, rupturing fruitful conversation. The fullest break comes in 3.4 with the appearance of Banquo's ghost. Macbeth's accusations – first to his guests and then to Banquo: 'Which of you have done this?'; 'Thou canst not say I did it. Never shake / Thy gory locks at me' (3.4.48, 49–50) – are from his internal perspective part of a dialogue, while for those gathered for a coronation feast at his castle they appear to be soliloquies, lines Macbeth is addressing to himself. This striking dichotomy is made even more spectacular in the final act when Lady Macbeth provides a reprise with her own twist – sleepwalking, she addresses no one in particular (5.1) even as she does communicate at last with her husband, coalescing all their lives together into the one brief passage of time that is the bloody and inquisitive aftermath of their foul deed: 'The Thane of Fife had a Wife. Where is she now?' (5.1.40–1). Her absence is a synecdoche for the absence of Macbeth, Thane of Fife, too, and for all of Macbeth's thanes, for the kingdom that has slipped away from them both. The mind's construction is liberated; and the knowledge of it, for Macbeth, is dreadful.[28] For his 'dearest chuck', to 'Be innocent of the knowledge' was never possible (3.2.46).

Dame Helen Gardner has argued that the chief issue in *Othello* is not what, but 'How do you know?'[29] In *Macbeth*, the central question is 'What do you do with the knowledge you have?' recognizing, with 'servant[s] fee'd', that even that

---

27 As quoted in Maus, *Inwardness*, p. 7.

28 Stanley Cavell claims that 'More than any other Shakespearean tragedy, Macbeth thematically shows melodramatic responsiveness as a contest over interpretations, hence over whether an understanding is – or can be – intellectually adequate to its question, neither denying what is there, nor affirming what is not there (a deed, a dagger). As if what is at stake is the intelligibility of the human to itself.' *Disowning Knowledge in Seven Plays of Shakespeare*, updated edn (Cambridge, 2003), p. 223.

29 Helen Gardner, 'The Noble Moor', in *Interpretations of Shakespeare: British Academy Shakespeare Lectures*, ed. Kenneth Muir (Oxford, 1985), p. 170.

knowledge you do have is never enough. Harold Bloom has somewhat perversely suggested that 'Shakespeare grants little cognitive power to anyone in *Macbeth* and least of all to the protagonist himself',[30] but surely that cannot be true of a battlefield soldier and thane who throughout the play questions, schemes and assesses, who is haunted by the need for knowledge and the lack of certain knowing. Stanley Cavell has argued otherwise, that Macbeth's search for knowledge, like that of his wife's, is suicidal.

> Both he and Lady Macbeth associate doing, in addition to time, with thinking: 'I am afraid to think what I have done', he says (II,ii,50); and a few lines earlier she had said, 'These deeds must not be thought / After these ways; so, it will make us mad' (II, ii, 32.3). If there were nothing done or to do there would be nothing to think about. Before we come to ponder what it is they have to think about, I note that the opposite of thinking in Macbeth's mind is sleep ('sore labour's bath, / Balm of hurt minds' (II,ii, 37–8), and in acting to kill action and end time Macbeth 'does murther Sleep' (II,ii, 35); so that in acting metaphysically to end thought he consigns himself absolutely to thinking, to unending watchfulness. Lady Macbeth at last finds a solution to the problem of thinking how not to think, when there is no obvious way not to think, in sleepwalking, which her witness describes as a version of watchfulness. (pp. 234–5)

But like the apparently continual surveillance of his network of spies, Macbeth's mind, surely restless, is also concerned with action. The purpose, the inheritance, of spying is action: not only to scorch the enemy, but to kill them (3.2.15). The man of action, trained to kill and fearless in battle, 'Disdaining fortune, with his brandished steel / Which smoked with blood execution' is rightly 'valour's minion' (1.2.17–19). If he falters at the thought of forcing his own kingship out of the indeterminate time of the three sisters into the living presence of King Duncan as the guest in his castle, and needs his partner's encouragement to kill the king to make that possible – 'But screw your courage to the sticking-place / And we'll not fail' (1.7.60–1) – it is because in making Duncan vulnerable he will in turn make himself vulnerable, too. Lady Macbeth seems imprisoned in the moment; she cannot comprehend, and so cannot permit '"I dare not" wait upon "I would"' (1.7.44). But it is Macbeth's peculiar gift, despite his life on the battle field, to hold in his mind past, present and future all at once, as vital dimensions of knowing: the 'supernatural soliciting' (1.3.129) which he enlisted only after stumbling on the three sisters without premeditation or design looks back on the inherited title of Glamis, takes into account the current promise of Cawdor, argues for the future position of King. Such a sequence has potentially good and bad consequences (1.7.130–6). Such reasoning, such intellectual doubt is what keeps hesitation alive.

> If it were done when 'tis done, then 'twere well
> It were done quickly. If th'assassination
> Could trammel up the consequence, and catch
> With his surcease success: that but this blow
> Might be the be-all and the end-all, here,
> But here upon this bank and shoal of time,
> We'd jump the life to come. But in these cases
> We still have judgement here, that we but teach
> Bloody instructions which, being taught, return
> To plague th'inventor. This even-handed justice
> Commends th'ingredience of our poisoned chalice
> To our own lips. (1.7.1–12)

Neither a fighting machine nor a visionary, the thane who would plant spies in every house is one with an immense power of intellect. His thinking combines hypotheses ('If') and strategy that may or may not trammel up the consequence. The thinking here is not suicidal but its opposite.[31] Its complicated unfolding is remarkably different from that of Duncan's single use of knowing in proclaiming Malcolm Prince of Cumberland (1.4.35–42), and different too from Macbeth's knowing acts of hypocrisy ('False face must hide what the false heart doth know', 1.7.82).

---

30 Harold Bloom, *Shakespeare: The Invention of the Human* (New York, 1998), p. 526.

31 In the introduction to his Oxford World's Classics edition of *Macbeth* (Oxford, 1998), Nicholas Brooke lists ways in which the thinking of the audience is disparate from that of Macbeth or of other characters in the play (pp. 2–5).

The word *know* and its cognates have a relatively high frequency in this play, occurring 56 times with the preponderance of usage being that of Macbeth (15), followed by Ross (7), Malcolm (6), and Lady Macbeth (4).[32] More especially, Macbeth's use of the cognate words falls into a developmental pattern, moving from the interrogative at the start – 'Stay, you imperfect speakers, tell me more. / By Sinel's death I know I am Thane of Glamis, / But how of Cawdor?' (1.3.68–70) – to the instantly reflective just after the murder of Duncan: 'To know my deed 'twere best not know myself' (2.2.71). As the usurping king, Macbeth takes on, for the first time in the play, a language of command. To the hired murderers he is decisive: 'Know / That it was he in the times past which held you / So under fortune, which you thought had been / Our innocent self' (3.1.77–80); 'Know Banquo was your enemy' (3.1.116). He is equally in control at the start of the coronation banquet: 'You know your own degrees; sit down' (3.4.1). He has no difficulty with the political world. It is only with the interruption of another level of existence – with the appearance of the ghost of Banquo – that he is caught off guard, unsuspecting, uncertain, *un*knowing:

The time has been
That, when the brains were out, the man would die,
And there an end. But now they rise again
With twenty mortal murders on their crowns,
And push us from our stools. This is more strange
Than such a murder is. (3.4.77–82)

But even here he attempts to bring matters under the control of his knowing and those of the court: 'I have a strange infirmity which is nothing / To those that know me' (3.4.85–6).

Jarred loose now from the world of knowing, thrust into the world of the apparently hallucinatory, Macbeth will nevertheless seize control of that too. He deliberately links the two worlds, jamming their insights into connected aphorisms: 'It will have been blood, they say. Blood will have blood. / Stones have been known to move, and trees to speak' (3.4.121–2), bringing both into the single habitation of the 'known', thereby positing the next logical step, to consult the sisters to know more, not as a subject but as a co-conspirator ('I conjure you', 4.1.66). He wishes to learn not merely what they know ('that which you profess', 4.1.66) but the basis of such knowledge ('Howe'er you come to know it', 4.1.67), commanding that the visions they provide answer his need for further knowledge. He moves, with the aid of the sisters, from the present where he is ruler to the future which he has not yet inhabited. His military prowess, political ambition and savvy, and (presumably) even knowledge gained through surveillance all proven inadequate, he would expand his 'single state of man' (1.3.139) into the farthest stretches of the imagination.

Macbeth's cognitive powers have known that all along. Responding to the association of the sisters' prophecy and Ross's announcement – 'for an earnest of greater honor, / [Duncan] bade me from him call thee Thane of Cawdor, / In which addition, hail, most worthy thane, / For it is thine' (1.3.101–4) – Macbeth has turned from being an active soldier and surprised interrogator to being a man of reflection – 'Two truths are told', (1.3.126). When he is unable to reconcile the dilemma they provide, he moves into the range of his imagination:

This supernatural soliciting
Cannot be ill, cannot be good. If ill,
Why hath it given me earnest of success
Commencing in a truth? I am Thane of Cawdor.
If good, why do I yield to that suggestion
Whose horrid image doth unfix my hair
And make my seated heart knock at my ribs
Against the use of nature? Present fears
Are less than horrible imaginings,
My thought, whose murder yet is but fantastical,
Shakes so my single state of man that function
Is smothered in surmise, and nothing is
But what is not. (1.3.129–41)

Not the sisters nor Ross's report have unfixed his hair; the 'horrid image' they have given to him has

[32] All the other characters have two, one or no uses of *know* and its cognates.

and this image – what Sir Thomas Eliot notes in his dictionary is the root of imagination's meaning (sig. K4) – is Macbeth's own creation. The image results from 'that suggestion' which the sisters have anticipated, in calling him king, but which no one has yet proclaimed or described. It is the image of regicide, Macbeth's ability, given the power of his imagination, to foresee the murder of Duncan. It is the start of a line of associated images, surfacing once more in a floating dagger and again in the untrammeled consequence, the bloodied corpse of Banquo. This provides the reprise to the initial crime against nature, a reprise not on the actual regicide but of this very anticipatory vision of it. Pierre de Loier, in his *Treatise of Specters or straunge Sights, Visions, and Apparitions appearing sensibly unto men* (1605), translated from the French and printed by Shakespeare's printer, Valentine Simmes, notes that 'whatsoeuer the mind shall imagine & conceiue, the eye may presently see' (sig. H4) and it is in his mind's eye that Macbeth supplements his knowledge of the titles of Glamis and Cawdor with the imagined regicide and the title of king. Macbeth's 'horrible imaginings' may also acknowledge de Loier's next sentence, too: 'It must needes then followe, that some thinges shall present themselues to our eyes and sight, which neuer were in being, nor euer can be' (sig. H4). Macbeth forcing into the world of nature what cannot be, 'smothered in surmise', is what first makes his heart knock at his ribs. He has displaced *eikon* ('image', 'similitude', 'reflection') with its cognate *eidolon* ('mental image', 'likeness', 'fantasy', 'shadow', even 'ghost') which Bacon had proclaimed to be one of the false idols of the mind.[33]

Bacon's counter to the imagination, and a constituent of knowledge, is reason which Macbeth also understands early on. Macbeth's logic concerning the two truths and his 'thought' which he 'smother[s] in surmise' is initially countered by Banquo, who says of the three sisters, 'Were such things here as we do speak about, / Or have we eaten on the insane root / That takes the reason prisoner?' (1.3.81–3). But Macbeth knows that such reason is what, in the throes of realizing his imagination into being, he cannot allow. Later, in his key scene of self-confrontation,

> Had I but died an hour before this chance
> I had lived a blessed time, for from this instant
> There's nothing serious in mortality.
> All is but toys. Renown and grace are dead.
> (2.3.90–3)

he subjugates all reason and logic and truth to hypocrisy and surmise; he confesses to murder. But he does not confess to the regicide he imagined and accomplished but to the murders of the grooms which were none of his doing.

> Who can be wise, amazed, temp'rate and furious,
> Loyal and neutral in a moment? No man.
> Th'expedition of my violent love
> Outran the pauser, reason. Here lay Duncan,
> His silver skin laced with his golden blood,
> And his gashed stabs looked like a breach in nature
> For ruin's wasteful entrance; there the murderers,
> Steeped in the colours of their trade, their daggers
> Unmannerly breeched with gore. Who could refrain,
> That had a heart to love, and in that heart
> Courage to make's love known?
> (2.3.108–18)

The reason (and reasoning) on which he first based knowledge before he supplemented it with the imaging that unfixed his hair and made his heart to knock is outrun; it is replaced by the impossible sight – '*golden* blood', and the imaging makes him prisoner. The false image he conveys to the horrified Macduff, Lennox, Malcolm and Donalbain is its own gash into the side of nature, its own breaching of human nature, of the mind. His excuse is his emotion and loyalty to the king, but in ascribing courage to his heart and his deed, he makes courage the subject too of knowledge. This 'love known' corrupts all knowledge – the knowledge of what has happened, of what he would report, and of what his thanes are told. As a play, *Macbeth* deals not so much with 'How do you know?' but 'What do you do with the knowledge you have?' and how

[33] Kenneth Gross, *Spenserian Poetics* (Ithaca, 1985), pp. 29–30.

do you prevent the lure of the imagination when reason seems to fail.

IV

We have scorched the snake, not killed it.
She'll close and be herself, whilst our poor malice
Remains in danger of her former tooth.
But let the frame of things disjoint, both the worlds suffer,
Ere we will eat our meal in fear, and sleep
In the affliction of these terrible dreams
That shake us nightly. Better be with the dead.
(3.2.15–21)

When the basis of Macbeth's knowledge – observation, reason, logic, surveillance – turns to image-making, surrenders its powers of comprehension to the imagination, he loses direction, will and fortitude, and his days are given over to fears, his nights to dreams that shake him mightily. We can measure his greatness, and his loss, by Jonson's contemporary portrayal of Sejanus:

Swell, swell, my joys, and faint not to declare
Yourselves as ample as your causes are.
I did not live till now, this my first hour,
Wherein I see my thoughts reached by my power.
But this, and gripe my wishes. Great, and high,
The world knows only two, that's Rome, and I.
My roof receives me not; 'tis air I tread –
And, at each step, I feel my'advanced head
Knock out a star in heav'n! Reared to this height,
All my desires seem modest, poor, and slight,
That did before sound impudent. 'Tis place,
Not blood, discerns the noble and the base.[34]

The swelling act of Sejanus's imperial theme seems limp by comparison to Macbeth's, his self-knowledge lacking any means of self-doubt or self-correction. His very pride and ambition seem to him seals of approval and of success beyond any possibility of surcease. Macbeth's struggle to achieve such cognitive composure is what draws us to him, is both his strength and his failing. His mighty experience and knowledge are inadequate before his instincts and his 'horrible imaginings' (1.3.137); in the end, they corrupt him, realigning him with his 'partner of greatness' (1.3.9–10) in what he calls 'troubles of the brain', 'a mind diseased' (5.3.44, 42).

Maurice Morgann had some sense of this too in 1820 when he wrote that 'Macbeth changes under our eye: *the milk of human kindness is converted to gall; he has supped full of horrors*, and his *May of life is fallen into the sear, the yellow leaf*; whilst we, the fools of amazement, are insensible to the shifting of place and the lapse of time, and, till the curtain drops, never once wake to the truth of things, or recognize the laws of existence.'[35] His summary now seems almost incredibly romantic, but it still catches a certain truth of its own: that the failure of such potential makes its purchase on our attention. We can begin to appreciate the play's power in Shakespeare's day, too, when we recognize that the need to know coupled with the fear of not knowing, promoting an anxiety and a *mentalité* of surveillance, captures in an individual the whole crisis of an historical moment of English civilization. 'One cannot grasp the most profound logic of the social world', Pierre Bourdieu writes, 'unless one becomes immersed in the specificity of an empirical reality, historically situated and dated, but only in order to construct it as an instance (*cas de figure*) in a finite universe of possible configurations.'[36]

---

[34] My text for *Sejanus His Fall* throughout is the Revels text, ed. Philip J. Ayres (Manchester, 1990).

[35] Maurice Morgann, *An Essay on the Dramatic Character of Sir John Falstaff* (London, 1820), p. 73.

[36] Pierre Bourdieu in *Bourdieu: Critical Perspectives*, ed. Craig Calhoun, Edward LiPuma, and Moishe Postone (Chicago, 1993), p. 272.

'THE GRACE OF GRACE' AND DOUBLE-TALK IN *MACBETH*

RICHARD C. McCOY

Macbeth ends with a grisly flourish of the old king's severed head and the new king's invitation 'to see us crowned at Scone' (5.11.41). In its harshly literal juxtaposition of these two heads of state, the play's climax presents a truncated tableau of the king's two bodies. According to that ancient doctrine, the monarchy embodies the state and attains a kind of corporate immortality.[1] *Macbeth*'s final scene thus vividly dramatizes the traditional proclamation, 'The king is dead, long live the king'. In this paradoxical formula, continuity is assured from one reign to the next, even amidst the most brutal succession struggles. Still more reassuring is Malcolm's promise to govern 'by the grace of grace' (5.10.38), a prayerful allusion to monarchy's divine right and authority. *Macbeth* has been described as the consummate 'royal play' whose performance at court was intended to celebrate the reign of James I.[2] Yet Shakespeare's attitude towards monarchy here and elsewhere is ambiguous. Such ambiguity is typical of a playwright who, in *Hamlet*, places the claim that 'There's such divinity that doeth hedge a king / That treason can but peep to what it would' (4.5.122–3) in the mouth of Claudius, a regicide and usurper.[3] *Macbeth* presents even loftier visions of sacred kingship along with some of the ghastliest images of its violation. After murdering Duncan, Macbeth himself declares 'Renown and grace is dead' (2.3.93). By contrast, grace abounds at the English court of the sainted Edward the Confessor. There, Duncan's eldest son, Malcolm, finds refuge and support since 'sundry blessings hang about his throne / That speak him full of grace' (4.3.159–60). Intimations of royal 'grace' lost and found pervade the play, yet Malcolm's own state of grace is uncertain. Just before he pays tribute to Edward's many blessings, he renounces all the 'king-becoming graces' (4.3.92) in order to test Macduff's fidelity. After driving Macduff to despair, he then proceeds to 'Unspeak mine own detraction . . . [and] abjure / The taints and blames I laid upon myself' (4.3.124–5). Such a sudden, stunning reversal simply confuses Macduff who can only say 'Such welcome and unwelcome things at once / 'Tis hard to reconcile' (4.3.139–40).

Malcolm resorts in his exchange with Macduff to something like the equivocation that bedevils the entire play, and, for many, that insures Malcolm's fall from grace. 'Equivocation' is, of course, a major theme in *Macbeth*, surfacing explicitly in the Porter's speech (2.3.8–11) and again in Macbeth's recognition that the witches have misled him (5.5.40–2). Many critics think that equivocation is always bad,

[1] The classic study of this doctrine is Ernst Kantorowicz, *The King's Two Bodies: A Study in Medieval Political Theology* (Princeton, 1957).

[2] Henry N. Paul argues in *The Royal Play of Macbeth: When, Why, and How it was Written by Shakespeare* (New York, 1950) that it was a 'royal play for court performance as a compliment to' King James I performed at Hampton Court in 1606 to honor Christian IV's visit to England that summer (1). But see Michael Hawkings, 'History, Politics and Macbeth', in *Focus on Macbeth*, ed. John Russell Brown (London, 1982), who argues for the ambiguity of *Macbeth*'s royalism and disputes its status as a command performance (185).

[3] For a discussion of Shakespeare's ambivalence towards sacred kingship in *Hamlet*, see my *Alterations of State: Sacred Kingship in the English Reformation* (New York, 2002), pp. xii–xiv and 56–85.

and several object to Malcolm using such devious expedients to attain the throne.[4] More recent critics find these stratagems inevitable and exult in their display because they reveal the illegitimacy of all aspirations to power. Steven Mullaney says that Malcolm's prevarication taints him indelibly, exposing the 'family resemblance between authority and its Other', and he adds that equivocation or 'Amphibology marks an aspect of language that neither treason nor authority can control'.[5] Mullaney chooses the stranger and more sinister synonym to emphasize the dangerous unruliness of Shakespeare's language here and elsewhere.[6] Citing Samuel Johnson on Shakespeare's puns, Mullaney maintains that the playwright's wordplay can be seen as a '*malignant* power, seductive and alluring' that ultimately threatens to reduce all to chaos.[7] A deconstructive emphasis on the play's pervasive linguistic nihilism also marks several other recent approaches. As Russ McDonald notes, the 'unreliability and inadequacy of language have become familiar themes in Shakespeare studies'.[8] Malcolm Evans insists in *Signifying Nothing* that equivocation is 'a condition of language' that precipitates nothing short of a 'crisis of the sign'.[9] Karin S. Coddon argues that the play's pervasive 'semiotic instability' unleashes an 'anarchic play of unreason and its relentless deconstruction of boundaries'.[10] Jonathan Goldberg also contends that the play's discursive indeterminacy undermines any effort to articulate or construct 'absolute difference'.[11] 'Absolute difference' is probably only possible in melodrama or harangues against 'evildoers'. Shakespeare's tragedies are too complex to encourage such categorical distinctions. Nevertheless, one can forego moral absolutes and still differentiate between good and bad characters in *Macbeth*. Malcolm's equivocations, I would argue, can be a force for good and a source of grace. Indeed, it is precisely because he equivocates that Malcolm is my hero.

Malcolm is an unlikely hero in *Macbeth*, and he pales by comparison with other characters. Seeking the 'safest way' (2.3.141), he is neither a brave and brutal warrior like Macbeth or Macduff whom he manipulates to fight on his behalf. Nor is he a holy ruler like Edward or his 'royal father / . . . a most sainted King' (4.3.109–10). Indeed, when he becomes Scotland's new king, he does not unequivocally claim the supernatural grace possessed by these two. Instead, he begins his reign and concludes the play by swearing that whatever 'needful else / That calls upon us, by the grace of grace, / We will perform in measure, time and place' (5.11.37–9). The oddly doubled 'grace of grace' constitutes, in my view, Malcolm's most intriguing equivocation. The words recall the traditional proclamation of sovereignty's sacred authority '*Dei gratia*', and the line is usually glossed accordingly; Nicholas Brooke explains it as 'the grace of God, apostrophized as the essence of graciousness'.[12] Yet, the phrase's odd redundancy deviates from the standard formula, and its repetition recalls the portentous doubling – 'Double,

---

4 Richard Horwich sees Malcolm as a potential 'Macbeth in embryo' (372) in 'Integrity in *Macbeth*: The Search for the "Single State of Man"', *Shakespeare Quarterly*, 29 (1978), 365–73. See also Roy Walker, *The Time is Free: A Study of Macbeth* (London, 1949), p. 163.

5 Steven Mullaney, *The Place of the Stage: License, Play and Power in Renaissance England* (Chicago, 1988), pp. 125–6.

6 Mullaney, *Place of the Stage*, p. 120; the term is taken from George Puttenham's *Arte of English Poesie*.

7 Mullaney, *Place of the Stage*, pp. 127–8. In emphasizing amphibology's dangers, Mullaney argues for a link between Johnson's distress at Shakespeare's 'quibbles' and Thomas Hobbes's broader hostility to all 'Metaphors, and senslesse and ambiguous words' whose 'end [is] contention, and sedition' (p. 127).

8 Russ McDonald, *Shakespeare and the Arts of Language* (Oxford, 2001), p. 180; McDonald sees this radical linguistic scepticism as a form of 'presentism' in need of correction, and he objects to finding 'in Shakespeare the radical kind of linguistic skepticism that would appear in the work of Thomas Hobbes in the middle of the seventeenth century' (pp. 180–1).

9 Malcolm Evans, *Signifying Nothing: Truth's True Contents in Shakespeare's Texts* (Hemel Hempstead, 1989), p. 116.

10 Karin Coddon, '"Unreal Mockery": Reason and the Problem of Spectacle in *Macbeth*', *ELH*, 56 (1989), 497–8.

11 Jonathan Goldberg, 'Speculations: *Macbeth* and Source', in *Shakespeare Reproduced: The Text in History and Ideology*, eds. Jean E. Howard and Marion F. O'Connor (New York, 1987), p. 250.

12 *The Tragedy of Macbeth*, ed. Nicholas Brooke (Oxford, 1990), p. 211.

double' (4.1.10) – of the witches' incantations.[13] As Gary Wills notes, '"doubling" was another word for equivocation' or double-talk, and doubling the word certainly renders its meaning equivocal.[14] Grace can imply political favour or artful elegance as well as divine right. Malcolm's redoubled iteration attenuates our sense of a direct connection to God, and, combined with careful attention to 'measure, time, and place', his phrase suggests a notion of grace more poetic and performative than religious. For some of Shakespeare's contemporaries, secular artistic grace was morally suspect, and theatrical double-talk only increased their suspicions. Doubling was a charge frequently levelled against actors by their enemies. Men like Phillip Stubbes repeatedly attacked them as 'double-dealing ambidexters' whose role-playing made them liars.[15] But those less hostile to the theatre have long recognized that actors are, in words attributed to William Hazlitt, 'the only honest hypocrites' because they frankly admit the artifice of their role and performance.[16] As we shall see, Malcolm acknowledges and embraces his role as actor and player-king, a role rejected by Macbeth in his most famous soliloquy. Malcolm's recognition and acceptance of the actor's role permits the ascendant ruler more control over his equivocations. His double-talk is different from the witches' – less insidiously ruinous and more theatrically creative as well as politically astute. Even in this dark play, equivocation can be a form of graceful performance as well as pernicious deceit. Before attempting a thorough analysis of Malcolm's equivocal 'grace of grace', I want to examine the more traditional, one-dimensional ideas of grace that pervade *Macbeth* from the start. I also want to consider the equivocal nature of the evil forces opposing royal and religious grace.

Duncan is generally seen as a holy king. His vulnerability to Macbeth's machinations may raise doubts about his effectiveness, but even Macbeth regards him as a monarch whose 'virtues . . . plead like angels' (1.7.18–19) to forestall his murder.[17] For loyal subjects like Macduff, Duncan's killing is an act of religious desecration: 'Most sacrilegious Murder hath broke ope / The Lord's anointed Temple and stole thence / The life o'th'building!' (2.3.66–7). Macbeth brazenly joins in this shocked lament in order to deflect suspicion, proclaiming, 'Renown and grace is dead. / The wine of life is drawn, and the mere lees / Is left this vault to brag of' (2.3.93–5). Macbeth's hypocrisy does not diminish the desolation wrought by his bloody deed. In this play, the king's blood is clearly seen as the Eucharistic 'wine of life', now irretrievably spilt, staining the hands and faces of guilty and innocent alike. Regicide profanes the whole royal sacramental system and taints society's communion cup for all partakers. Even when merely contemplating his own 'Bloody instructions' (1.7.9) before the murder, Macbeth realizes his deed's toxic sacramental consequences: 'justice / Commends th'ingredience of our poisoned chalice / To our own lips' (1.7.10–12). The harrowing banquet at the play's midpoint vividly dramatizes this breakdown of social communion. Lady Macbeth urges her royal Lord to 'give the cheer' since 'the sauce to meat is ceremony' (3.4.32–5). Macbeth tries to drink 'to th'general joy of th'whole table / And to our dear friend Banquo, whom we miss. / Would he were here' (3.4.88–90), but the bloody re-appearance of Banquo's ghost thwarts that toast and aborts the festivities. Duncan's fulsome generosity aimed to inspire loyal devotion, and he said 'commendations' of his nobles were like 'a banquet to me' (1.4.57–8). Macbeth's murderous

[13] Jan H. Blits notes this deviation in *The Insufficiency of Virtue:* Macbeth *and the Natural Order* (Lanham, MD, 1996), p. 200.

[14] Gary Wills, *Witches and Jesuits: Shakespeare's* Macbeth (New York, 1995), p. 97. See also Frank Kermode on Shakespeare's predilection for various forms of doubling in *Hamlet* (pp. 100–14) and its tendency to 'introduce unease and mystery into an expression' (p. 102) in *Shakespeare's Language* (New York, 2000).

[15] Cited in Evans, *Signifying Nothing*, p. 135.

[16] Bert O. States, *Great Reckonings in Little Rooms: On the Phenomenology of Theater* (Berkeley, 1964), p. 200.

[17] Harry Berger says the old king's grip on his 'kingdom is no less shaky than his control of the facts or his subjects' loyalty' in 'The Early Scenes of *Macbeth*: Preface to a New Interpretation,' *ELH*, 47 (1980), p. 17. He sees Duncan as a 'good scapegoat' and mere foil to Macbeth's 'bad scapegoat' (28), who never achieves any genuine authority.

reign blights the reciprocity of all such 'feasts and banquets' (3.6.35) according to an anonymous lord, and, until they are delivered from this danger and distrust, Scotland's nobility cannot 'Do faithful homage, and receive free honours' (3.6.35–6).

While blasphemously violated in Scotland, sacred kingship still prevails in England. Duncan's son, Malcolm, finds a gracious reception there at the court 'Of the most pious Edward' (3.6.27). Macduff joins Malcolm 'to pray the holy King' for military aid (3.6.30). Later, Malcolm describes for Macduff 'A most miraculous work in this good King' (4.3.148) which the heir to the Scottish throne repeatedly witnesses. The miracle is the royal touch, the power to heal scrofula, a disease known as the 'King's Evil', and Malcolm recounts in graphic detail how:

> strangely-visited people,
> All swoll'n and ulcerous, pitiful to the eye,
> The mere despair of surgery, he cures,
> Hanging a golden stamp about their necks,
> Put on with holy prayers; and 'tis spoken,
> To the succeeding royalty he leaves
> The healing benediction. (4.3.151–7)

Malcolm adds that 'With this strange virtue, / He hath a heavenly gift of prophecy', and he says that the 'sundry blessings hang about his throne, / That speak him full of grace' (4.3.157–60). Edward the Confessor was the first English king to practise the royal touch. While church authorities questioned whether his healing powers derived from his status as saint or king, the belief that he left this 'healing benediction' to 'succeeding royalty' persisted through Shakespeare's time and beyond.[18] Queen Elizabeth touched her subjects for scrofula on ceremonial occasions, and, though initially sceptical, James continued doing it too; his son and grandson, Charles I and II, were both enthusiastic practitioners, the latter touching 'near half the nation', according to one contemporary.[19] Yet Shakespeare's treatment of the royal touch in *Macbeth* is somewhat wan and oblique because Edward remains offstage. The audience never actually sees the 'most miraculous work in this good king', nor does it hear any of the utterances inspired by his 'heavenly gift of prophecy'. Deborah Willis concludes that this most 'healing benediction' proves no match for the evil wrought by the witches or rebellion in this play.[20] Certainly the witches constitute a more vivid dramatic presence, easily upstaging a holy but absent king.

Even when the play stages grand royal spectacles, monarchy's image remains sketchy. The extraordinary 'show of eight Kings' in 4.1 is already compromised by its source, as Goldberg notes, since the witches produce it.[21] At court, it may have been staged as a grand pageant of the 'imperial theme', as Henry Paul suggests, alluding directly to James's reign as the ninth Stuart king in Scotland and flattering James's ancestral pride in a line stretching 'out to th' crack of doom' (4.1.133).[22] If the glass held by the eighth king in this solemn procession was a mirror, the king might even have caught a glimpse of himself in its reflection. Nevertheless, if he did, the image would be brief and wavering, and he would be seen in a glass darkly. In a courtly performance of this pageant, James might thus resemble the monarchs depicted by Velasquez in *Las Meninas* who are also dimly reflected in a mirror as the artist paints their portraits. Jonathan Brown has suggested that Velasquez's painting is 'structured like a representation of a court play which was attended by many, but intended for the king who was present both as a spectator and participant in the drama'.[23] As reflected in the 'show of eight kings',

---

[18] Barlow, 'The King's Evil', *English Historical Review*, 95 (1980), 17–18.

[19] Keith Thomas, *Religion and the Decline of Magic* (New York, 1971), pp. 192–8.

[20] Deborah Willis, 'The Monarch and the Sacred: Shakespeare and the Ceremony for the Healing of the King's Evil,' in *True Rites and Maimed Rites: Ritual and Anti-Ritual in Shakespeare and his Age*, eds. Linda Woodbridge and Edward Berry (Urbana, 1992), pp. 158–60. Andrew Hadfield suggests that Holinshed's account of Edward the Confessor may indicate that 'saintly kings were not necessarily good or effective kings' in '*Macbeth*, IV.iii.140–158, Edward the Confessor, and Holinshed's *Chronicles*', *Notes and Queries*, 49 (2002), p. 235.

[21] Goldberg, 'Speculations', p. 252.

[22] Paul, *The Royal Play*, pp. 168–182.

[23] Jonathan Brown, *Velasquez: Painter and Courtier* (New Haven, 1986), pp. 303 and 259.

the image of James is no less ambiguous. In Michel Foucault's famous description of the monarchs of *Las Meninas*, 'they are the palest, the most unreal, the most compromised of all the painting's images; a movement, a little light, would be sufficient to eclipse them . . . in so far as they are visible, they are the frailest and the most distant form of all reality. Inversely, in so far as they stand outside the picture and are therefore withdrawn from it in an essential invisibility, they provide the centre around which the entire representation is ordered.'[24] In Foucault's account, Velasquez's royal portrait is a 'pure representation of essential absence'.[25] As a 'royal play', *Macbeth* achieves a similar effect in its representation of the royal presence. Edward the Confessor and James I are certainly important figures in this drama, but each remains a remote and inscrutable if 'essential absence'. Neither has any real impact on the action, and their links to Malcolm are tenuous at best. Malcolm succeeds to the throne, but he has no place in the dynastic line that culminates in James. Similarly, while Edward may leave his 'healing benediction' to 'succeeding royalty' (4.3.156–7), there is no hint that he imparts this gift to Malcolm.[26] Even after witnessing the royal touch, Malcolm admits his ignorance of Edward's methods: 'How he solicits heaven / Himself best knows' (4.3.150–1). His perplexity suggests that he has not learned the secret.

The audience knows even less about how a holy king solicits heaven, seeing neither his miracles nor hearing any of his prophecies. However, we do hear plenty of 'supernatural soliciting' (1.3.129) by the three weird sisters, and we see their predictions confirmed. Their conjurations make up some of the play's most powerful scenes, and the witches are fearful, compelling, and plausible forces. Diabolical invocations clearly overshadow heavenly entreaties in *Macbeth*, and this is part of a larger pattern in Reformation Europe. As Walter Stephens explains in *Demon Lovers: Witchcraft, Sex and the Crisis of Belief*, much of the fascination with witchcraft during the Reformation derived from growing doubts about the sacraments and their practical efficacy.[27] For some Protestants, the exaltation of faith over works threatened to weaken their grip on the spiritual realm by arousing fears that 'one's religion was not "working"'.[28] If the Mass itself, among other rituals, no longer functioned as an *opus operatum* or efficacious work, divinity might seem for some more remote and inaccessible. Belief in witchcraft permitted a belief in ritual potency, however terrifying or malignant, because the 'supernatural soliciting' of witches seemed to work. Stephens describes both those who consort with and those who persecute witches as 'metaphysical voyeurs', determined to retain access to another spiritual dimension.[29] Marlowe's *Doctor Faustus* was certainly inspired by comparable impulses, and the popularity of such plays derived in part from their ability to arouse, gratify, and abate this spiritual voyeurism in their audience. In *Macbeth*, the witches stimulate a hunger for 'more . . . than mortal knowledge' (1.5.3) in both Macbeth and Lady Macbeth with their promise of 'metaphysical aid' (1.5.28). Even Banquo is allured by the power of those who 'can look into the seeds of time, / And say which grain will grow' (1.3.56–7).

Nonetheless, both Macbeth and Lady Macbeth are thwarted in their desires, and their own attempts at 'supernatural soliciting' fail them. In her first scene, Lady Macbeth invites infernal spirits to 'Come to my woman's breasts, / And take my milk

---

24 Michel Foucault, *The Order of Things: An Archaeology of the Human Sciences* (New York, 1973), p. 4. Foucault's brilliant analysis of this painting provides a point of departure for my discussion of the ghost of Hamlet's father in *Alterations of State*, p. xiv.

25 Foucault, *Order of Things*, p. 308. Cf. Franco Moretti who says that even though the king is supposed to be 'the point of equilibrium for the social order, the sovereign is the missing person, the impossible being in Shakespearian tragedy' in *Signs Taken for Wonders: Essays in the Sociology of Literary Forms*, trans. Susan Fischer, David Forgacs, David Miller (London, 1983), p. 68.

26 D. A. Traversi is certain that 'the holy Edward will impart to Malcolm the spiritual strength needed for this task' in *An Approach to Shakespeare* (Garden City, NY, 1956), p. 179, but I see no evidence for this.

27 Walter Stephens, *Demon Lovers: Witchcraft, Sex and the Crisis of Belief* (Chicago, 2002), pp. 231–40.

28 Stephens, *Demon Lovers*, p. 99.

29 Stephens, *Demon Lovers*, p. 32.

for gall' (1.5.46–7). Yet, despite her fierce resolve, none respond to her invocations. Reginald Scot's *Discoverie of Witchcraft* points out that a desire to consort with devils does not automatically produce miraculous results.[30] Like Glendower's spirits summoned 'from the vasty deep', these will not necessarily come when called. An ambivalent scepticism towards witchcraft in Shakespeare's time reduced it to a form of hysteria, and many see Lady Macbeth's collapse into insanity as confirmation of this attitude.[31] Although shakier at first than his wife, Macbeth proves firmer in his determination, and his conjurations actually work: the witches show up and do his bidding even after urging him 'to know no more' (4.1.119). But what does he learn from his bold pursuit of 'more . . . than mortal knowledge' (1.5.3)? Only, to his dismay, that 'th'equivocation of the fiend, / . . . lies like truth' (5.5.41–2), defeating both knowledge and desire. Deception was their intention from the start, as Hecate reveals: having snared him 'by the strength of their illusion', the witches succeed brilliantly in drawing 'him on to confusion' (3.5.28–9).

The disillusion that follows this discovery almost unhinges Macbeth. The witches have promised him safety 'Till Birnam wood remove to Dunsinane' (5.3.2) and add, 'No man that's born of woman / Shall e'er have power upon thee' (5.3.6–7). However, their assurances are full of figurative loopholes. They are designed to mislead by creating a false sense of 'security / . . . mortals' chiefest enemy' (3.5.32–3). Macbeth's literal-minded confidence in Birnam wood's stability overlooks the possibility of synecdoche, a possibility realized when Malcolm's soldiers cut down branches to conceal their numbers. He also forgets the fatal dangers of childbirth and is shocked by Macduff's announcement that his adversary 'was from his mother's womb / Untimely ripped' (5.10.15–16). Caught off guard, he bitterly attacks 'these juggling fiends . . . / That palter with us in a double sense' (5.10.19–20) in order to deceive him. Macbeth's bitter disappointment in the witches' double-talk suggests that he had previously been surprisingly naive and literal minded. He not only failed to allow for their evil intentions, but he was also oblivious to the inherent ambiguities of their promissory language. Jan Blits points out that what 'Macbeth calls paltering is, in fact, nothing but the Witches' figurative speech. Macbeth says that the Witches' prophecies "lie like the truth" (5.5.44), but they do so only in the way that all metaphors do.'[32] Donald Foster says of Macbeth, 'Although his imagination spawns timeless metaphors, his dull brain is, nevertheless, all too literalistic.'[33] The literal-minded Macbeth proves a vulnerable dupe for metaphoric double-talk.

Even before he realizes his grave errors, Macbeth despairs of all signification. In his notoriously bleak soliloquy, life is an illusion doomed to pointless repetition: 'Tomorrow, and tomorrow, and tomorrow, / Creeps in this petty pace from day to day / . . . And all our yesterdays have lighted fools / The way to dusty death' (5.5.18–22). When events initially confirmed both his hopes and the witches' prophecies, Macbeth saw them all 'As happy prologues to the swelling act / Of the imperial theme' (1.3.127–8). By the end, life becomes nothing more than 'a walking shadow' (5.5.24). The terms are still theatrical, but his conception of his role and the performance is much grimmer. He is appalled at the prospect of becoming 'a poor player, / That struts and frets his hour upon the stage' in 'a tale / Told by an idiot, full of sound and fury, / Signifying nothing' (5.5.23–7). Behind this dark soliloquy is a recoil from the stage itself.[34] Jacques Derrida

[30] Reginald Scot, *Discoverie of Witchcraft* (1584); cited by Joanna Levin, 'Lady Macbeth and the Daemonologie of Hysteria', *ELH*, 69 (2002), 39.

[31] Dympna Callaghan, 'Wicked Women in *Macbeth*: A Study of Power, Ideology, and the Production of Motherhood', in *Reconsidering the Renaissance*, ed. Mario A. Di Cesare (Binghamton, NY, 1992), pp. 355–69, Diana Purkiss, *The Witch in History: Early Modern and Twentieth-Century Representations* (London, 1996), pp. 242–7 and Levin all show how an equation of witchcraft with hysteria diminishes female power without completely containing it.

[32] Blits, *The Insufficiency of Virtue*, p. 193.

[33] Donald Foster, 'Macbeth's War on Time', *English Literary Renaissance*, 16 (1986), p. 337.

[34] Evans says that in Macbeth's last soliloquy, the stage 'negates itself' (134).

hints at the scope of that aversion in his discussion of Jean-Jacques Rousseau's anti-theatrical prejudice. In a glancing allusion to *Macbeth*, Derrida says that Rousseau objects not only to the actor who 'signifies nothing', but also to what Derrida calls 'the profound evil of representation' itself.[35] Rousseau contrasts the fraudulence of the actor with the sincerity of those who speak in their own name and say what they think and mean. As Jonas Barish shows in his classic study of the syndrome, the anti-theatrical prejudice has always been robust and persistent, often flourishing among playwrights disillusioned with the stage; Ben Jonson is perhaps the best-known example among Shakespeare's contemporaries.[36] Derrida also discerns a comparable antagonism towards representation and desire for authenticity in Antonin Artaud, playwright and proponent of the theatre of cruelty. Declaring himself 'the enemy of theater', Artaud strives to create plays that present reality itself rather than imitations of it.[37] He wants to move beyond the discursive ambiguity of 'the language of words' towards the semiotic stability of the 'objective' and 'directly communicative' 'language of *signs*'.[38] In Derrida's words, Artaud pushes drama to 'the inaccessible limit of a representation which is not repetition, of a *re*-presentation which is full presence, which does not carry its double within itself as its death, of a present which does not repeat itself, that is, of a present outside time, a nonpresent'.[39] Artaud shares Macbeth's disgust with shows whose doomed repetition and insignificance can only light the 'way to dusty death' (5.5.22).

By the play's last act, a general revulsion against illusion and equivocation sets in among many characters, and some are drawn to the harsh sign-systems of the theatre of cruelty. Macbeth describes his grim plight in terms that evoke the brutality of bear-baiting, another popular entertainment of the time: 'They have tied me to a stake: I cannot fly, / But bear-like, I must fight the course' (5.7.1–2). As Macduff moves in for the kill, he offers Macbeth ignominious surrender terms:

> Then yield thee, coward,
> And live to be the show and gaze o'th'time.
> We'll have thee as our rarer monsters are,
> Painted upon a pole, and underwrit,
> 'Here may you see the tyrant.'
>
> (5.10.23–27)

Macduff proposes to make an emblematic show of Macbeth vanquished. In fact, he would make the sign advertising the captive Macbeth into a classic emblematic device, combining painted *pictura* and 'underwrit' *subscriptio*. This lucid union of word and image seems intended to rule out any ambiguity by precisely defining and confining villainy: 'Here may you see the tyrant.' Macbeth refuses such terms and fights to the death, but Macduff defeats him anyway. After killing and decapitating him, he presents Malcolm with 'Th'usurper's cursèd head' (5.11.21) impaled upon his sword in the last scene. The severed head is brandished as a comparable symbol of treason's consequences, its significance as firmly fixed as the grisly object itself.[40] Like many spectacles in the play, Macbeth's head belongs to what Howard Felperin describes as a 'primitive and animistic world of portents and totems'.[41] In Felperin's view, Shakespeare neither mocks nor dismisses these signs and symbols, but he qualifies their impact by introducing 'an element of parody, of fallen repetition'.[42] In this instance, both the head and the sign 'Painted upon a pole' remind us of comparable images derided by Lady Macbeth: ''tis the eye of childhood / That fears a painted devil'

---

[35] Jacques Derrida, *Of Grammatology*, trans. Gayatri Chakravorty Spivak (Baltimore, 1976), pp. 304–5.

[36] Jonas Barish, *The Anti-Theatrical Prejudice* (Berkeley, 1981). Barish discusses both Jonson and Rousseau among others.

[37] Jacques Derrida, 'The Theater of Cruelty and the Closure of Representation', in *Writing and Difference*, trans. Alan Bass (Chicago, 1978), pp. 249 and 234.

[38] Antonin Artaud, *The Theater and Its Double*, trans. Mary Caroline Richards (New York, 1958), p. 107.

[39] Derrida, *Writing and Difference*, p. 248.

[40] Marjorie Garber, *Shakespeare's Ghost Writers: Literature as Uncanny Causality* (New York, 1987), p. 114.

[41] Howard Felperin, *Shakespearian Representation: Mimesis and Modernity in Elizabethan Tragedy* (Princeton, 1977), p. 138.

[42] Felperin, *Shakespearian Representation*, pp. 139 and 104.

(2.2.52–3). Her scorn may be too glib, but she still reminds us that these are only 'pictures' (2.2.52). What Felperin calls the 'essential doubleness' of these images reinforces the play's 'radical equivocation' even at its climax.[43]

In the end, Malcolm's denunciation of his predecessors as 'this dead butcher, and his fiend-like Queen' (5.11.35) seems to repeat similarly primitive polarities. Felperin denounces Malcolm's efforts, dismissing him as a vapid, unself-conscious, and presumptuous figurehead, only capable of an 'ingenuous repetition of convention'.[44] Yet, here and elsewhere, Malcolm is actually quite wary, self-conscious, and disingenuous. After his father's murder, he immediately sees through the duplicity of some of the mourners: 'To show an unfelt sorrow is an office / Which the false man does easy' (2.3.135–6). He declares his suspicions even more forcefully to Macduff, warning that he will only believe what he knows to be true (4.3.9) and responding cautiously to Macduff's exhortations: 'What you have spoke it may be so, perchance' (4.3.11). Malcolm is hardly mollified by Macduff's assurance that 'I am not treacherous' (4.3.18). Instead he eloquently asserts the impenetrability of others' intentions, the gap between appearance and character, and the need for defensive scrutiny:

> That which you are my thoughts cannot transpose.
> Angels are bright still, though the brightest fell.
> Though all things foul would wear the brows of grace,
> Yet grace must still look so. (4.3.22–5)

In the cryptic equivocation of his last phrase, 'grace' is both passive and active, and 'look' both transitive and intransitive. On the one hand, grace appears constant and 'looks so', appearing as it always should, amidst the dissimulations of 'all things foul'. On the other hand, by looking hard at 'all things foul' and seeing through their dissimulations, grace '*looks* so' and acts against them. In this equivocal formulation, grace shifts from an inherent but passive sanctity to a more aggressive hermeneutic strategy. Malcolm's 'royal father / was a most sainted King' (4.3.109), but Duncan had 'no art / To find the mind's construction in the face' (1.4.11–12). The son is more artful and discerning, determined to see through 'the brows of grace'. As a result, he regains the throne his father lost. His success is not attributable to sanctity; rather, he relies instead on a cunning stratagem of equivocation and careful scrutiny to test potential friends and adversaries alike. Malcolm aspires not to the God-given grace of sacred kingship. He aims instead for the shrewd poise of Machiavelli's prince.

In pursuing this canny strategy, Malcolm explicitly disclaims all 'the king-becoming graces' (4.3.92) and claims all 'particulars of vice' (4.3.52). In enumerating his alleged sins, Malcolm displays an imaginative exuberance for depravity that belies his otherwise innocuous demeanour:

> . . . there's no bottom, none,
> In my voluptuousness. Your wives, your daughters,
> Your matrons, and your maids could not fill up
> The cistern of my lust. (4.3.61–4)

Not satisfied with sexual rapine, he then warns that his 'staunchless avarice' will make him 'cut off the nobles for their lands; / . . . And my more-having would be as a sauce / To make me hunger more' (4.3.79–82). Macduff blanches at each of these alarming confessions but seems inclined to accept them reluctantly as tolerable occupational hazards of monarchy. So Malcolm presses on, vowing to 'Pour the sweet milk of concord into hell, / Uproar the universal peace, confound / All unity on earth' (4.3.99–101). As if this threat were not enough, he confirms his turpitude by adding, 'I am as I have spoken' (4.3.103). For Macduff this is the last straw, and he cannot help but denounce the heir who 'By his own interdiction stands accursed, / And does blaspheme his breed' (4.3.108–9). A life of exile is the only recourse remaining to him. Having forced Macduff to reveal his true feelings, Malcolm abruptly reverses course and proceeds to 'Unspeak mine own detraction . . . My first false-speaking / Was this upon myself' (4.3.124–32), reducing Macduff to a stupefied silence.

[43] Felperin, *Shakespearian Representation*, pp. 140–1. Cf. Karin Coddon who argues that all the spectacles in *Macbeth* prove 'unreal mockeries', p. 485.

[44] Felperin, *Shakespearian Representation*, p. 136.

Malcolm's equivocations are profoundly unsettling. Even if we allow for the exceptional nature of this 'first false-speaking', his speech still provokes suspicions not easily allayed. By contradicting his first categorical statement that, in all his viciousness, 'I am as I have spoken' (4.3.103), he undermines his subsequent claims that, in all his virtue, he 'never was forsworn' (4.3.127). As William O. Scott says in his probing essay on equivocation in *Macbeth*, all merely self-referential professions of truth are dubious to begin with, and Malcolm's directly contradict one another.[45] By doing so, they approximate the vertiginous illogicality of the liar's paradox, exemplified by the claim that 'This sentence is false.'[46] Scott sees this same philosophical conundrum informing Macbeth's final soliloquy inasmuch as 'It is the poor player acting Macbeth who tells, in words that signify that they signify nothing.'[47] As we have seen, Macbeth the character recoils from the prospect of becoming a poor player who 'struts and frets his hour upon the stage' (5.5.24), but both the actor playing his part and the audience watching him savor the desperate eloquence and profound import of his speech. In this instance, the contradictions of the liar paradox do not reduce it to illogical insignificance. On the contrary, Macbeth's recognition that all his exertions mean nothing becomes a powerfully moving *memento mori* and enhances our knowledge of his plight's broader significance. In sustaining this paradoxical perspective, Macbeth's last soliloquy allows the spectator the distinctive perspective that, Keats says, 'Shakespeare possessed so enormously – I mean *Negative Capability*, that is when man is capable of being in uncertainties, Mysteries, doubts, without any irritable reaching after fact & reason'.[48] Macbeth the character is incapable of living in such uncertainties, despite his own imaginative energies. He finds it a 'torture of the mind to lie / In restless ecstasy' (3.2.23–4) without some sort of resolution. Indeed, he wants to act without prior reflection because 'Strange things I have in head that will to hand, / Which must be acted ere they may be scanned' (3.4.138–9).

Malcolm, by contrast, devotes the play's longest scene to perpetrating 'uncertainties, Mysteries, [and] doubts' which defy 'fact & reason'. His equivocations are so intensely contradictory that they almost impose negative capability on the mind entangled in them. Malcolm also resembles his creator – and surpasses Macbeth – in his imaginative alacrity. In his eager description of his supposedly bottomless lust and 'staunchless avarice', he displays the same 'gusto' that Keats attributes to the 'poetical character'. In Keats's view, such a character may be disturbingly amoral and vacuous, but an essentially contemplative bias renders it less menacing: 'As to the poetical character itself . . . it is not itself – it has no self – it is every thing and nothing – It has no character – it enjoys light and shade; it lives in gusto, be it foul or fair, high or low, rich or poor, mean or elevated – It has as much delight in conceiving an Iago as an Imogen. What shocks the virtuous philosopher, delights the camelion Poet. It does no harm from its relish of the dark side of things any more than from its taste for the bright one; because they both end in speculation.'[49] Macbeth cannot speculate – 'I am afraid to think what I have done' (2.2.49) – but still must do what for him is unthinkable, whereas Malcolm relishes reflecting on the most heinous crimes without ever having to commit them. Indeed, he has no need to act because his eloquence and acuity enable him to persuade others to act on his behalf. At the beginning of their exchange, he tells Macduff, 'That which you are my thoughts cannot transpose' (4.3.22). However, as soon as Macduff learns of the murder of his wife and children, Malcolm does just that, urging him to 'make us medicines of our great revenge, / To cure this deadly grief'

[45] William O. Scott, 'Macbeth's – and Our – Self-Equivocations', *Shakespeare Quarterly*, 37 (1986), 162.

[46] Scott, 'Macbeth's – and Our – Self-Equivocations', p. 163. Strictly speaking, Malcolm's claim that his previous sentence is false, though suspect and unsettling, is not as tightly self-contradictory or illogical as 'This sentence is false.'

[47] Scott, 'Macbeth's – and Our – Self-Equivocations', p. 173.

[48] John Keats, 'To George and Thomas Keats' (21 December 1817), in *Selected Poems and Letters*, ed. Douglas Bush (Boston, 1959), p. 261.

[49] Keats, 'To Richard Woodhouse' (27 October 1818), in *Selected Poems and Letters*, p. 279.

(4.3.215) and to 'let grief / Convert to anger: blunt not the heart, enrage it' (4.3.230–231). Initially overwhelmed by grief, Macduff is gradually persuaded to seek revenge. Having orchestrated this transposition, Malcolm can proclaim, 'This tune goes manly', and confidently declare, 'our power is ready' (4.3.237–8). Malcolm's power derives not from action but acting, and skill in dissimulation as well as persuasion is an essential requirement for any actor. That requirement may explain Shakespeare's alteration of his source. In Holinshed's *Chronicles of Scotland*, Malcolm's final admission is that he is 'inclined to dissimulation . . . and all other kinds of deceit', and, for Macduff, this proves 'the worst of all, and there I leave thee'.[50] In the play, dissimulation is omitted and replaced by generic depravity 'In the division of each several crime' (4.3.97). Shakespeare may have dropped dissimulation not only because it can be a necessary evil for a monarch intent on retaining his throne but also because it is the stock-in-trade of the player. As we have seen, most recent criticism of *Macbeth* assumes that equivocation is always treacherous. From this perspective, Malcolm's victory is inevitably corrupted by what Rebecca Lemon calls 'the traitor's art'.[51] But equivocation is also an essential component of the actor's art because, as William O. Scott notes, it is 'the function of the player to lie like truth and of the audience to believe what it knows to be equivocation'.[52]

Malcolm embraces the player's role most dramatically in the play's conclusion, and his mastery of the part, I would argue, enhances his triumph rather than tainting it. In his final speech, he begins to assert his authority through a combination of careful political cost calculation and close attention to timing. He first tells his nobles that 'We shall not spend a large expense of time, / Before we reckon with your several loves, / And make us even with you' (5.11.26–8). He then bestows the new title of Earls upon his thanes, insisting that these honours are to be distributed equally. Malcolm also combines a sense of urgency about the tasks awaiting him with a determined composure. Included among the things 'to do / Which would be planted newly with the time' are the recall of 'our exiled friends abroad / That fled the snares of watchful tyranny' and the punishment of those 'cruel ministers' who served Macbeth (5.11.30–4). Malcolm's metaphor for his plans recalls his father's earlier promise to Macbeth with its scriptural allusion to Jeremiah 12.2: 'I have begun to plant thee, and will labour / To make thee full of growing' (1.4.28–9). Yet Malcolm's reference to new planting and new times reflects a resilient awareness of altered circumstances. In contrast to Malcolm's assurance, Macbeth's thoughts about the timing of what he must do seem frantically desperate. When Macbeth considers killing Duncan, he stands 'here upon this bank and shoal of time' and prepares to 'jump the life to come' (1.7.6–7), but he already anticipates the defeat of his 'Vaulting ambition, which o'erleaps itself / And falls on th'other' (1.7.27–8). Shortly afterwards, Lady Macbeth rebukes him for his defeatism which she links to bad timing: previously, when neither 'time, nor place / Did then adhere . . . yet you would make both' yield, but as soon as 'They have made themselves' amenable to his will, 'their fitness now / Does unmake you' (1.7.51–4). Malcolm, by contrast, can confidently assure himself and his audience that, whatever 'needful else / That calls upon us, by the grace of grace, / We will perform in measure, time, and place' (5.11.37–9).

As I have already noted, the phrase 'the grace of grace' is wonderfully equivocal. The invocation of 'grace' evokes all the traditional religious associations of sacred kingship, and yet the doubling of the term opens up other, more secular possibilities. Since royalty was frequently addressed as 'Your Grace', the phrase could also mean the grace or favour of the monarch. In a play performed at court before King James I, Malcolm's admission of his dependence on 'the grace of grace' (5.11.38) sounds a note of deference to the play's most eminent spectator and the company's royal patron, as

---

50 Holinshed, *Chronicle of Scotland*, Appendix A, in *Macbeth*, ed. Kenneth Muir (London, 1989), p. 177.

51 Rebecca Lemon, 'Scaffolds of Treason in *Macbeth*', *Theater Journal*, 54 (2002), 40.

52 Scott, 'Macbeth's – and Our – Self-Equivocations', p. 174.

Donald Foster notes.[53] The phrase could then stand as a final compliment by the player king to the real king and an implicit recognition of his own humbler, derivative status. Malcolm accepts his role as a stand-in and place-holder for the ruler whose reign was predicted in the fourth act. At the same time, 'the grace of grace' can imply, as I suggested earlier, an elegance or beauty of gesture and form. Gracious conduct entails a mastery of the social graces, and Malcolm exhibits these as well. His 'thanks to all at once, and to each one' restores a sense of grateful reciprocity and social communion long missing from the play (5.11.40). Moreover, his invitation 'to see us crowned at Scone' (5.11.41) may include both audience and players. These last notes of gratitude and humility resemble those sounded by another player-king and theatrical master of illusion, Prospero, in his epilogue. Malcolm's version of an epilogue certainly offers a more modest and inclusive contrast to the 'happy prologues to the swelling act / Of the imperial theme' (1.3.127–8) which are performed almost entirely within Macbeth's mind. Finally, as an accomplished player-king, Malcolm understands the importance of measure in speech and timing in performance. For both Malcolm and his creator, 'the grace of grace' depends on the artful and felicitous effect of words decorously arranged and gracefully performed 'in measure, time, and place'.

[53] Foster, 'Macbeth's War on Time', p. 342.

REMIND ME: HOW MANY CHILDREN HAD LADY MACBETH?

CAROL CHILLINGTON RUTTER

When L. C. Knights, prepped by F. R. Leavis, innocently dropped his question on an unsuspecting audience at a meeting of the Shakespeare Association in 1932, 'How Many Children Had Lady Macbeth?', he didn't expect an answer.[1] He expected a revolution. Comically self-deprecating, thirty years later he recalled the occasion, remembering himself as 'a comparatively young man, dissatisfied with the prevailing academic approach to Shakespeare', specifically, Bradley-ite 'character' criticism, the kind of criticism that observed the discrepancy between Lady Macbeth's Act 1 assertion, 'I have given suck and know / How tender 'tis to love the babe that milks me'(1.7.54–5), Macbeth's traumatized meditation on his childlessness in Act 3 (3.1.60–73), and Macduff's desolate cry in Act 4, 'He has no children'(4.3.217) and, worried by apparent inconsistencies, tried to account for the Macbeths' missing babies. Impatient with Bradley and his acolytes, Knights was 'excited by the glimpses I had obtained of new and it seemed more rewarding approaches' – modernist criticism, a criticism framed by Eliot and Wilson Knight that read Shakespeare's plays as dramatic poems, 'imaginative constructions mediated through the poetry', a criticism that found useful analogies with music, looking for *leitmotivs* and themes rather than motives and character-development, attempting to account for the complex structures of Shakespeare's verse and to find the plays' meanings in what Wilson Knight termed 'the logic of imaginative correspondence' rather than the 'logic of plot'. For young Lionel Knights this was bracing stuff. As he wrote, he 'welcomed the opportunity of proclaiming the new principles in the very home of Shakespearian orthodoxy, whilst at the same time having some fun with familiar irrelevancies of the kind parodied in my title, *How Many Children Had Lady Macbeth?*' Fired up for war, or at least a few bloody noses, he gave his paper 'and waited expectantly for the lively discussion that would follow this rousing challenge to the pundits'. Only, 'nothing happened':

> except that after a period of silence an elderly man got up at the back of the room and said that he was very glad to hear Mr Knights give this paper because it was what he had always thought.

'The revolution was over,' wrote Knights, 'and I went home.'[2]

Part of the 'fun' Knights' paper had with its original audience – and its subsequent readers – was its mandarin refusal to notice or address, never mind to answer, the question asked in its title. Like a beached whale (or red herring) 'How Many Children Had Lady Macbeth?' lay rhetorically stranded at the top of the paper, ignored, a huge joke, nothing further needed to demonstrate its concerns as among those 'familiar irrelevancies' modernist criticism wanted mocked.

But 'Jesters', as we know, 'do oft prove prophets' (*Lear* 5.3.64); one critic's 'familiar irrelevancy' turns

[1] L. C. Knights, 'How Many Children Had Lady Macbeth?', subtitled 'An Essay in the Theory and Practice of Shakespeare Criticism', the lecture was published in *Explorations* (London, 1946), pp. 1–39.

[2] 'The Question of Character in Shakespeare', in *Further Explorations* (London, 1965), pp. 186, 190–2.

out to be another's 'deepest consequence' (not least because such categories prove culturally sensitive, historically implicated); and 'the whirligig of time' unfailingly 'brings in his revenges'(*Twelfth Night* 5.1.373). Thus, while Knights in 1932 could see the urgent dramatic relevance of what, in 1912, the blockheaded editor of the Arden *Macbeth* called 'magnificently irrelevant' – the sleepwalking scene and Macbeth's Act 5 soliloquies[3] – it took Cleanth Brooks in 'The Naked Babe and the Cloak of Manliness', published in Great Britain in 1949, to show Knights why 'How Many Children Had Lady Macbeth?' was no irrelevancy but exactly the right question to be asking, why counting heads in Scotland's nurseries was not some 'pseudo-critical investigation'[4] but utterly to the point – and opened up the play's complex poetic structures to the very scrutiny of close reading that Knights was proposing.

For Cleanth Brooks, the child in *Macbeth* serves as 'perhaps the most powerful symbol in the tragedy'.[5] Framed sometimes as a character (Banquo's Fleance, Macduff's 'young fry'), sometimes as a materialized symbol (the 'bloody Child' and 'Child crowned' raised as apparitions by the Weird Sisters), sometimes as a metaphor ('pity' figured as 'a naked newborn babe / Striding the blast', or 'duties' to Duncan's 'throne and state' figured as 'children and servants' while murderous inspirations are 'firstlings' and 'noble passion' is integrity's 'child'), the image of the child draws together the play's stake in history, its yearning aspirations for 'tomorrow and tomorrow and tomorrow', its frustrated desires for 'blessed' yesterday, a time of grace before 'memory' came to figure as waste-ground rooted only with sorrow. From the Weird Sisters' opening utterance – 'When?' – *Macbeth* is concerned with futures, prophetic, dynastic, domestic, metaphysical, eternal, and the child is the material embodiment of these futures. But nostalgically the child represents a longing for the adult's past: his innocent selfhood, the time cited by Polixenes in *The Winter's Tale* as belonging to the 'boy eternal' (1.2.66), before corrupted nature in the grown man falls prey to 'cursed thoughts', invasive 'in repose'. Ironically, Macbeth wants both to possess the future – the one the Weird Sisters 'gave' him – and destroy it – the one they 'promised' Banquo. Calculating the relationship between 'surcease' and 'success' Macbeth is aware that 'consequence' always evades the 'trammel' of deceit and that 'Bloody instructions' 'return / To plague th'inventor' – but only much later that there is no 'success' without 'succession'. As children fail, so fails Macbeth's future: 'fruitless', 'barren', 'unlineal'. 'If't be so', he discovers, groping line by line after terrible knowledge,

> For Banquo's issue have I filed my mind;
> For them . . .
> Put rancours in the vessel of my peace
> Only for them . . .
> To make them kings, the seeds of Banquo kings.
> (3.1.66–71)

His recourse is to make war on the future – a 'war on children'.[6]

A. R. Braunmuller has observed that *Macbeth* is a play that thinks through metaphor,[7] and Lady Macbeth's claim to 'have given suck', to know 'How tender 'tis to love the babe that milks me' seems to have as much force as metaphor as personal history. It comes at the end of a pair of speeches whose objective is to make a man of Macbeth. He has decided against the 'business': honoured by Duncan, he is opinion's golden boy, dressed in glittering approval that is to be worn 'now', he says, in its 'newest gloss', not 'cast aside so soon' (1.7.31–5). She counters by turning the rhetorical tables on him, recasting his definitive statement, 'We will proceed no further', into a series of relentless questions, souring 'the hope . . . Wherein you dressed yourself' (35–6) as merely a drunkard's dream and the crown as an 'ornament' his valour mightily desires but his cowardice feebly fears to 'catch' even when it is thrown into his lap. She makes him a cat, a beast, a sot sick on ambition's fantasies. And a

[3] 'How Many Children', p. 18, n. 1.
[4] 'How Many Children', p. 37.
[5] Cleanth Brooks, *The Well Wrought Urn* (London, 1949), p. 31.
[6] Brooks, *The Well Wrought Urn*, p. 35.
[7] A. R. Braunmuller, ed., *Macbeth* (Cambridge, 1997), p. 17.

man? She constructs him manly – but only, tantalizingly, in one of those hypothetical past-futures this play is constantly imagining: 'When you durst do it, then you were a man' (1.7.49). Killing, it appears, is what makes a man a man. And it is as she is juggling these terms – 'make' and 'unmake', 'more', 'much more' – that she slips into the debate her stunning *non sequitur*, 'the babe that milks me'. Is a logic of association working here, analogizing gender? Does childbirth make a woman like killing makes a man? Or is the child instanced here as another degrading comparative – 'less than' a man as the beast or drunkard is 'less than' a man? Whatever the anecdote's status as 'real' history, its force here is rhetorical, to set up, through a syntax of conditionals, a terrifying equation on a hypothetical scale of committedness:

> I would, while it was smiling in my face,
> Have plucked my nipple from his boneless gums
> And dashed the brains out, had I so sworn
> As you have done to this. (1.7.56–9)

To make Macbeth a man, Lady Macbeth produces the death of the child.

But like Lionel Knights entitling Lady Macbeth's history then ignoring it, Cleanth Brooks read her poetry without enquiring its authority. For him, 'I have given suck' merely indexed Lady Macbeth's 'quite sincere' 'rationalism': 'She knows what she wants; and she is ruthless in her consideration of means.'[8] But consideration of her child or the self that might be de-formed by the loss of her child? Brooks did not make that enquiry.

Of course, it is possible that 'I have given suck' is one of those utterances, among many in this play, that 'palter with us in a double sense' (5.10.20) – an equivocation that 'lies like truth' (5.5.42). Be that as it may, the stubborn fact of the matter is that Lionel Knights' question refuses to go away – criticism continues to brood upon it, and in the theatre, it cannot be ducked: every actor who plays Lady Macbeth must interpret 'I have given suck'; and every actor who plays her husband must interpret what he hears.[9] Since 1986, when Sinead Cusack put 'How Many Children Had Lady Macbeth?', stripped of facetiousness, at the top of her performance agenda in an RSC production directed by Adrian Noble, subsequent Lady Macbeths have made it a matter of urgency to account for her missing children.

But something else has happened to *Macbeth* in performance since the 1980s. Its poetry has been politicized, its imaginative reference recruited to 'do' cultural work of the kind Martin Esslin alludes to when he writes that the theatre is the place 'where a nation thinks in public in front of itself'.[10] I want to argue by looking first at Noble's RSC *Macbeth* and then at Penny Woolcock's extraordinary contemporary film adaptation for television, *Macbeth on the Estate*, that *Macbeth* is the Shakespeare play our theatre has been using for the past twenty years to think through a cultural crisis in 'childness', to make us search our deep anxieties about relatedness and separation, about authority and autonomy, about locating the child in contemporary culture, about valuing the child's life – or not.[11] In the 1980s Britain became child-centred, the 1960s 'me' generation producing babies that absorbed them, 'mini-me's lavished with almost profligate care and attention. The royal family produced royal infants, the nation's 'future'; the politicians produced legislation that saw 'the value of children recognised in unprecedented ways' as the very concept of childhood was 'redefined' to emphasize

[8] Brooks, *The Well Wrought Urn*, p. 33.

[9] See for example in *The Masks of 'Macbeth'*, Marvin Rosenberg's speculations concerning 'Lady Macbeth's indispensable child' (Berkeley, 1978), Appendix pp. 671–6; and for contrast, Janet Adelman's 'Escaping the Matrix' in *Suffocating Mothers: Fantasies of Maternal Origin in Shakespeare's Plays, Hamlet to The Tempest* (London, 1992), p. 138. For actors' interpretations see Bernice W. Kliman, *Macbeth* (Manchester, 1992). In the Eric Porter/Janet Suzman production directed by John Gorrie for BBC television in 1970, for example, writes Kliman, the Macbeths 'have no children, they *had* no children'; Lady Macbeth's declaration is 'purely metaphoric, not historically accurate', p. 70.

[10] Martin Esslin, *An Anatomy of Drama* (London, 1976), p. 101.

[11] Noble's production opened at the RST on 6 November 1986; Woolcock's adaptation was screened on BBC2 in April 1997. I am extremely grateful to Michael Cordner and Susanne Greenhalgh for tracking down and supplying me with copies of Woolcock's films.

'its prerogatives and importance'.[12] Bastardy was removed from the law books, and caning from schools; child abuse entered public consciousness via the Cleveland crisis – and Victoria Gillick's case in the House of Lords. Between them, they provoked radical reforms that altered the status in law of Britain's children. But in the same year – 1989 – that Parliament passed the Children Act and the United Nations declared its Convention on the Rights of the Child, rights that could only be guarded by social responsibility, Britain's Prime Minister seemingly voided the very notion of social responsibility by declaring that there was 'no such thing as society': there were 'individual men and women' – and 'there [were] families'.[13] Her government's economic policies, however, were turning the screws on the family, impoverishing children and putting them – as the Opposition argued – at risk. After ten years of Thatcher government, the numbers of people living on Income Support had doubled, to nearly 4.5 million, piggy-backing another three million dependents, of whom two million were under sixteen.[14] Four major inquiries into child abuse and a number of sensational individual cases showed the traditional British family to be terminally dysfunctional, children its victims: the House of Windsor told this story at a national level. So did the working-class houses raided in Cleveland. And out of the tangled mass of accusation and counter-accusation published almost daily in the newspapers came national self-examination: what kind of adult could perpetrate child abuse, we wondered.[15] And, more anxiously, the question we almost didn't dare to ask: What kind of child could participate in it? What kind of child was its product? Were children innocents? Or delinquents? Virtuous – or iniquitous? For some of us, early modern Shakespeare converged with contemporary culture and politics to give us terms we could use to frame the debate – or at least keep our anxieties corralled. In Shakespeare, we could see 'childness' as a 'medicine' that 'cures' adults of 'thoughts that would thick [the] blood' (*Winter's Tale* 1.2.171–2) – equally, the child as a 'disease', a 'plague-sore' in the parent's flesh (*Lear* 2.4.217, 219), a reprobate needing 'the offending Adam' 'whipp'd . . . out of him' (*Henry V* 1.1.30). The redemptive child vs. the child of loss: at least there seemed to be two possibilities.

Then, in February 1993, the nation watched on the news replay after replay of some grainy CCTV footage, security images captured in a Liverpool shopping precinct that showed a small boy led away by two bigger boys, his little hand in one of theirs. That night, Jon Venables and Robert Thompson used bricks and an iron bar to batter two-year-old James Bulger to death; nine months later, they were convicted of his murder. Both were ten. Sitting in the courtroom, then writing about the Bulger case in a book called *As If*, Blake Morrison needed Shakespeare to supply a language big enough to comprehend the unimaginable 'deed that's done'; he set out lines from *Macbeth* as the book's epigraph:

---

[12] Marina Warner, *Into the Dangerous World: Some Reflections on Childhood and its Costs* (London, 1989), p. 9.

[13] Margaret Thatcher quoted in Warner, p. 16. The UN Convention was finally signed by the UK government in 1991.

[14] Income Support replaced the older social security provision, Supplementary Benefit. The actual figures, produced by the Secretary of State for Social Security in response to a question in the House of Commons at the end of 1988, were 4,354,000 claimants (against 2,855,000 on SB in 1979), 3,018,000 dependents (against 1.5 million) of whom 2,111,000 were under 16. The Secretary of State refused to talk about social 'poverty', insisting on calling it 'inequality' instead. Quoted in Warner, *Into the Dangerous World*, p. 3.

[15] I am conscious as I use it that 'we' in Britain is a conflicted term, referring on the one hand to the reserved pluralism of the 'royal' we, on the other to the mass response solicited in the headlines of tabloid newspapers. I use it, despite its difficulties and knowingly mobilizing its shades of irony, because it seems to me that over the past fifteen years a series of domestic events – from the soap operas of failed royal marriages to the melodrama of Princess Diana's death and funeral to the tragedies in Cleveland, Liverpool and Haringey that centred on the abuse and deaths of children – has involved the nation in a debate with itself about social cohesion and the future of the family, conducted with serious attention to issues like crime, social violence, childcare, education, single parents, race relations (and much more) in the broadsheet newspapers and on BBC television and radio. As I use it 'we' does not register easy consensus; rather, it serves metonymically to stand for the range of opinions and responses 'we' uttered as 'we' faced each new *Macbeth*-sized cultural gorgon.

. . . from this instant,
There's nothing serious in mortality.
All is but toys, renown and grace is dead,
The wine of life is drawn. (2.3.91–4)

And *Macbeth* kept surfacing in his writing, as if the play's language hung suspended in his imagination just below consciousness:

> In that spring of cold fear, it was as if there'd been a breach in nature: the tides frozen; stars nailed to the sky; the moon weeping far from sight. Those nameless boys had killed not just a child but the idea of childhood.[16]

As a nation, we agreed. From this instant, childhood was tainted, children evil. But demonising childhood as a way of making it possible for us adults to explain the inexplicable was an invention that returned to plague us. For demonizing the child was the very defence put up by the aunt and her boyfriend of eight-year-old Victoria Climbié to 'explain' why they'd tortured her to death in February 2000: she was 'possessed by witches', said the aunt; she must have been, said the boyfriend, for even when he beat her with a bicycle chain, she never cried. They had arranged an exorcism – but she died first.[17]

In William Worthen's terms, performance is 'an act of memory and an act of creation' that 'recalls and transforms the past in the form of the present'.[18] When it opened in late 1986 Adrian Noble's *Macbeth* seemed to be remembering Britain's recent collective past and, uncannily, to be anticipating 'horrible imaginings' we would wait a decade or more to see played out. This production took a long look at desecrated childhood, perverse parenting, assembling fragments from culture at large into a form that, resonating against the Shakespeare text, interrogated the present. The production poster, a cartoon by Pollock, was a Spitting Image portrait of the Macbeths (recognizably the actors, Jonathan Pryce and Sinead Cusack) as the (Un)Holy Family: Macbeth, his face lugubriously stretched like a Giacometti figure, his arm around his wife's shoulder; she, thin-lipped and hatchet-faced staring out of the frame; in her arms, a baby built by Dr Frankenstein: armless, neckless, its legs mismatched, seven strands of Adolf Hitler hair combed across its forehead; and below the folded fat of its blobby jowls, clearly visible, a line of sutures where the head was sewn on.[19] This monster infant with its *Rosemary's Baby* demon eyes looked like it might have emerged from the Weird Sisters' cauldron; indeed, this family portrait of 'We Three' weirdly anticipated the other three who would meet in the play's opening line. Somehow the baby looked both real and fake, a repulsive *putti* or fetish, or perhaps a *memento mori*, a doll dragged around by a deranged mother as a surrogate for a lost child. As the production's publicity 'image', it established, for spectators, a memory carried into the theatre of a past life for the Macbeths, he a father, she a mother – and the child a grotesque. As it quoted and mocked holy portraits by Michelangelo and Rafael, it was blasphemy. But it also, proleptically, inscribed the narrative with a back-story that would transform *Macbeth* into what Barbara Hodgdon calls a 'text of loss': only in the portrait could spectators see the 'complete' picture.[20] In the performance, the Macbeths were amputated, their arms empty of the absent child, their narrative pre-emptively cut. Of course, too, Pollock's poster offered an interpretive frame for reading *Macbeth*: it was, after all, a cartoon. It made a joke of sentimental family poses.

For Sinead Cusack the child-loss experienced in her fantasized, sub-textual history was the biological datum that directed her performance. Childless, indeed now barren, her Lady Macbeth invested all her energies in her husband, charging her obsessiveness with an eroticism that mocked its own redundancy. As Cusack came to understand 'the evil' her Lady Macbeth was 'drawn down into', she named it 'loss' – 'the loss of him', 'the loss of

---

[16] Blake Morrison, *As If* (London, 1997), p. 21.

[17] BBC News 01/10/2000 http://news.bbc.co.uk/1/hi/uk1035455.stm

[18] W. B. Worthen, *Shakespeare and the Force of Modern Performance* (Cambridge, 2003), p. 64.

[19] The effect was intensified by nail holes – stigmata – visibly perforating Lady Macbeth's hands.

[20] In Barbara Hodgdon, 'Two *King Lears*: Uncovering the Filmtext', *Literature/Film Quarterly*, 11 (1983), p. 88.

hope', 'And such a loss of innocence. But mainly the loss of hope of anything' – a loss she connected to the lost child: 'We [were] never going to have any more children'.[21] Paradoxically, then, her loss conflated innocence *and* evil in the symbolic body of the baby, since by a perverse logic the death of her child was the motivation for child-killing, the death of other mothers' children.

Like Cusack, Jonathan Pryce keyed his performance to a pre-text – but his came from 'real' history. He 'talked a lot to Adrian Noble' in the year before rehearsals began about 'an atrocity that [had] stayed with [him]' since he was a teenager – the Moors murders, committed between 1963 and 1965 by the 'butcher', Brady, and Myra Hindley, his 'fiendlike queen', whose 'gratification', thought Pryce, came 'through power over children'.[22] Their youngest victim was ten; the oldest, seventeen – the same age as Hindley's brother-in-law who shopped them; and only two years younger than Hindley, herself little more than a child when her partnership with Brady began. The children they abducted were sexually abused by the much older Brady before he killed them – gross acts of perverse parenting. But at least one of their victims, little Leslie Ann Downey, saw herself as a bad child. The tape recording of her last minutes, played in court, heard her pleading to be let go – she had to get home – she was late – her mother would kill her.[23]

Noble's production brooded upon these histories as a prompt, finding in them narratives to translate *Macbeth*'s evil, a metaphysical category largely unavailable to a culture formed by 1980s Thatcherite secularism, into scenarios to appal secular minds. The last taboo, the practice Britain still called 'evil', was the violation of the child, and it was the violation of a child that Noble staged as the originating action of his production. As the stage lights came up on a scene of carnage, dimly, through fog mixed with gun smoke made greasy with burning flesh, three shapeless figures toured a battlefield, looting bodies. Rolling one corpse over, they revealed what, falling, it had sheltered, the filthy half-naked body of a wild child, a bloody babe who rose from the dead, its hair knotted in 'glibs' – marking it as one of the 'meere' Irish, 'kerns and galloglasses', who had swarmed into Scotland 'from the Western Isles', swelling the rebellion against Duncan, 'in hope', according to Holinshed in the history that was Shakespeare's source, 'of the spoile'.[24] Described by William Harrison, the Scots were themselves originally Irish, 'a people mixed of the Scithian and Spanish blood', a 'barbarous nation, and longest without letters' 'which were given to the eating of mans flesh, and therefore called Anthropophagi': 'those Irish . . . are none other than those Scots . . . who used to feed on the buttocks of boies and womens paps, as delicate dishes'; they are kin, then, to Shakespeare's Weird Sisters.[25] Notoriously, among the 'meere Irish' was 'vsed a damnable superstition, leauing the right armes of their infants vnchristened (as they tearme it) to the intent it might giue a more vngratious and deadlie blow'.[26] The child on Noble's stage faced spectators as an oxymoron: a miracle, birthed from death as though 'untimely ripp'd' from mother-earth's womb; a survivor; hope-full.

But also an abomination. For, literally tainted by war's filth, and tainted by early modern racist 'history' that demonised him 'vngratious', the child scavenged by the Weird Sisters was hustled off, their booty, never seen again, unless, dismembered, he reappeared as body parts in the cauldron scene or as the blood that ringed the mouth of the Sister who answered 'Where hast thou been?' with dark irony, 'Killing swine' (1.3.1–2). His abduction located evil in *Macbeth*, fixed it on the archetypal moment of trust betrayed, taking the innocent child

---

21 *Guardian*, 7 November 1986.

22 *Guardian*, 7 November 1986.

23 See 'GO TO HELL', *Daily Express*, 16 November 2002; 'THE DEVIL: At last, Myra is where she belongs – HELL', *Sun*, 16 November 2002. See also obituary articles on Hindley in the *Mirror*, *Guardian*, *Independent* and *Daily Mail* for this date.

24 Raphael Holinshed *et al.*, 'Historie of Scotland' in *The . . . Second Volume of Chronicles* (1587), p. 169a. Quoted in Braunmuller, *Macbeth*, p. 104, n.13.

25 See Harrison's 'Description of Britaine' Chapter 4, in Holinshed *et al.*, *The First . . . Volume of Chronicles* (1587), p. 5b–6a. Quoted in Braunmuller, *Macbeth*, p. 11.

26 This 'record' of the barbaric practices of the 'meere Irish' appears on the last page of Richard Stanihurst's *The Description of Ireland* in Holished *et al.*, vol. v (London, 1808), p. 69.

in hand and leading him away. Only, the scene itself troubled any such obvious Manichean reading. *Was* the child good? If so, why didn't he recoil from the Weird Sisters? Instead, he was fascinated by the tinkling bell one of them produced from her sack and held out to him. He reached for it, a prize in a game or a seductive lure, a child-sized version of a bell Macbeth would later hear – a summons or an alarm, an invitation or a stay? Watching him turn to follow the bell, spectators saw the child enact a turn to evil.

In this production Macbeth enjoyed the company of children because he enjoyed clowning. When young Fleance, bored with all the hanging around waiting for the new king's entrance, perched himself on the big chair he didn't know was the throne and stared into space, blank to his father's urgent signals, Macbeth tip-toed up behind him, dropped his huge crown over the boy's head, watched it, ludicrously, land on his shoulders as Fleance's shocked face spun round to meet his grin – and roared with laughter. But the joke – and Macbeth's jokes were always edgy – strangely fulfilled the Weird Sister's prediction. In play, spectators saw the 'seeds of Banquo' king – but simultaneously saw Fleance contaminated with a future that put him suddenly at risk while ambiguously figuring him as dangerous, for he was, like Macbeth, in this moment the usurper. And in this moment, both potentially the wrecker and the wrecked. That the crown didn't fit merely emphasized the deferred punch-line to this joke: this Fleance was the infant prodigy who would ultimately strip 'the dwarfish thief' of those 'borrow'd' titles that hung 'loose about him like a giant's robe' (5.2.21–2).

Articulating evil through the body of the child, seeing the child recruited by 'the instruments of darkness' (1.3.122) and the sacred preserve of child's play contaminated by black jokers, this production saw children enlisted as foot soldiers in Macbeth's war on the future – and saboteurs. Chillingly, children took on the role of the apparitions in 4.1. At the end of the banquet (3.4), Macbeth was left smoothing the tablecloth, picking up cutlery to reset scattered places. As he exited, the Weird Sisters invaded his pitch, looting materials for a second sitting, a desecrated Lord's Supper that they weirdly fed back to him when he reappeared demanding to know, 'What is't you do? . . . answer me / To what I ask you' (4.1.64, 76–7).[27] Drenching a cloth in the mess they'd brewed in a chalice and thrusting him onto a chair, they blindfolded Macbeth. The hell-broth absorbed through the eyes went straight to the brain, producing hallucinations that walked and talked, 'sights' possessing the bodies of children. They entered giggling, three of them, in white nightgowns (dressed to 'murder sleep'?), carrying a basket of toys, playing a game of tig that changed to blind man's buff as they dodged Macbeth's blindly groping hands to deliver their predictions to his muffled ears. They looked like angels. The second, a little girl, popped up behind him like a jack-in-the-box; the third solemnly climbed up on Macbeth's knee, a pint-sized toy crown on his head, and whispered in the big man's ear what Macbeth, in a reversal of roles, scale and perspective, spoke aloud like the ventriloquist's dummy. They vanished when Macbeth tugged off the blindfold and started roaring after other children, those 'firstlings of [his] heart' that he would deliver as the 'firstlings of [his] hand' (4.1.163, 164). 'Be it thought and done' (line 165) he instructed himself, and it was. Weirdly, the 'firstlings' materialized in the space he'd just vacated: the apparitions returned in the next scene as Macduff's children, in those same nightgowns, with those same toys, to play at their mother's feet, golden-haired as if they wore halos. They *were* angels. Weren't they? And 'bright still', 'though the brightest fell'? But they couldn't help infecting this scene with toxic residues from the last. When the 'young fry' ran at the 'shag-haired villain' who called his father 'traitor', then flatly announced 'He has killed me, mother' (4.2.85), the audience laughed. This was a game; the child, tigged 'out'. Then they saw the blood. Lady Macduff's scream

[27] Noble cut 3.5 (the disputed Hecate scene) and moved 3.6 (Lennox's observation that 'Things have been strangely borne'[line 3]) so that 3.4 went straight into 4.1. This meant that Macbeth's exit, 'We are yet but young in deed' (line 144), was followed by the Weird Sisters' entrance, 'Thrice the brinded cat hath mewed' (4.1.1).

filled the theatre; blackout blinded spectators whose ears were filled with the sound of slaughter.

Abusing childhood, Noble's production put up onstage the representation of a violation that shocked to the core because it expressed 'present fears' contemporary Britain wanted denied and 'horrible imaginings' it wanted ignored, and it made a category many Britons thought obsolete terrifyingly present. It instantiated evil. And it understood fear. It forced spectators to look at culture's sentimental clichés, its standard tropes of innocence, as hypocritical cover-ups – whiteness, brightness, blondness. (Or maybe not. Because of course you really couldn't tell, there being 'no art to find the mind's construction in the face', 1.4.11–12.) It contaminated childhood's allotted space, the playground, poisoning it with the toxic image of the abuser's groping hands. It made children equivocal, saturated signs of the equivocations the *Macbeth* text everywhere produces: foul and fair; not ill, not good; 'honest trifles' who 'betray' the credulous 'in deepest consequence'. When the 'shag-haired villain' called Macduff's son an 'egg', spectators had to wonder whether it was the serpent's or the phoenix's.

Like Noble's *Macbeth* onstage, Penny Woolcock's 1997 television film, *Macbeth on the Estate*, opened on what looked like a battlefield. Across a grey expanse of cratered, rubble-strewn devastation walked a single man, not a looter, like Noble's Weird Sisters, but seemingly a war reporter, a huge man, Trevor MacDonald doubled in size, except that unlike MacDonald he wore trainers and an American football jersey, and when he turned to talk to the camera moving in for the close-up, he had a gold tooth and a West Indian Brummie accent – so, not just a reporter, but a combatant whom spectators would later recognise as Macduff (David Harewood). From the opening camera pan that took in grey tower blocks sticking up like amputated limbs in the distant background, spectators were aware that this urban landscape wasn't Bosnia. It was Birmingham. And it was now.[28] Macduff told 'of a time, not long past, when Duncan, de King, held d'power on dis estate – *and we loved him well.* We was men of war!' who 'punished offenders and gathered all finances due to de King' – 'offenders'; 'finances': a nice pair of euphemisms. But this perfect 'republic' didn't last. 'Duncan grew fat, slack, and many misrule men took occasion dereof to trouble d'peace wid seditious commotion.' Challenged by usurpers and 'Fearful of his crown, Duncan charged his cousin, de ever-loyal Macbeth, to take up arms and lead us into battle against de rebels.' From this first prologue, the film cuts to still shots, seven of them, that compose a second prologue, framing a portrait of 'dis estate' in exposures that educate the eye to urban blight: through a broken window, derelict flats; through a dank, water-puddled doorway, a rat nosing the sill; abandoned corridors and graffitied highrise balconies, a grass-stunted space, once a playground, now parking an industrial skip spilling junk. Over the images comes a high metallic sound and the cries of gulls – or maybe kids, calling something that sounds like 'Macbeth'. Then two children, in high long shot, run across the frame. In the next shot, catching up a third child to pass across the desolated open space, they vanish. As if triggering the action, the passing of these children throws the film footage into fast forward. A montage cut together of short clips shows bursts of violence stopped in freeze frames to pick out close-ups and name the players: Macbeth (James Frain) kicks down a front door and beats to a pulp a druggie he drags from sleep; Banquo (Andrew Tiernan) shoots aerosol into some guy's eyes then slams fists into his groin; Malcolm (Graham Bryan) leaps up and down like a gorilla with a baseball bat, smashing heads. Cuts from frenzy to inertia show Duncan, in mid-shot, counting time at his table in the community centre, chain smoking, ignoring his pint, massaging his forehead as though trying to keep his anxieties from cracking open his skull. Unlike the fit youths who do his dirty work, Duncan (Ray Winstone) is a bloated slob, a superannuated skinhead with

[28] Shot during the last full year of Conservative government, the TV film was broadcast less than a month before the May election that brought New Labour to power with a landslide victory.

'LOVE' tattooed on his knuckles and an unbuttoned Indian-dyed shirt that shows his beer belly draped with gold chains.

Shot on Birmingham's notoriously deprived Ladywood Estate by a director known as a documentary filmmaker who works in an experimental style that mixes realism with hyper-realism, even surrealism, and casts professional actors alongside local amateurs, *Macbeth on the Estate* taps into a language of violence that restores to Macbeth's story the primitiveness, rawness and thuggery recounted in Holinshed and dramatized by Shakespeare – though stripped out of the play that was subsequently captured for 'high' tragedy.[29] On the estate, Duncan is a gross parody of a Thatcherite entrepreneur running drugs, sex and protection rackets, and the estate is a dystopia, ugly, brutal and brutalizing, that functions as an 'Other' to the culture it despairingly mimics, but only mutely. 'Dis estate', unlike Scotland in Shakespeare, never gets a scene set, let's say, at Civic Hall, or Whitehall, where cultural difference (call it cultural supremacism) is interrogated, as in Shakespeare's England scene (4.3). Instead, the estate is a quarantined no-go area, a place, in Bea Campbell's terms, 'colonized' by male criminality, an anti-structure regulated by an illicit patriarchy that has put in place inverted versions of the same codes and hierarchies, including, of course, gender, that organize the licit world.[30] But that means that besides brutalizing its occupants the estate also, bizarrely, infantilizes them – it's a 'nanny' estate where grown men are stunted adolescents in dependency relationships with the 'father', and all the adults are needy children dependent on hand-outs, 'estate benefits' – or more pathetically (because more childishly credulous), dependent on the finger of fortune pointing at them. The lottery is big on the estate: watching the balls fall on the TV draw is what the junkies are doing when Macbeth smashes in the screen, and a billboard, promising 'More winners every week than seconds', sits on one of the estate's prime locations. The big fluffy cloud on the hoarding codes 'heaven', but the finger of fate stretching out from it belongs to the god of consumerism who's always, like Duncan on this estate, running a sleight-of-hand racket. Depressingly, the only hope this post-capitalist, post-scientific culture can put its money on is chance, fate, the come-on that 'It could be YOU'. In a place like this, people read palms. And Tarot cards. They 'look into the seeds of time'. And by the time viewers of the film see the billboard, they know that people on this estate are hooked in to witches.

In the film's first prologue and in the opening gang-war sequence that ends with the rebel Cawdor thrust into the driver's seat of a stolen car, doused with petrol through the broken window, and set alight, the estate looks like male territory, a war zone where hyped-up masculinity plays out over-determined rituals of aggression. What the adults don't know is that on this estate, they're only squatters. Their power structures have been infiltrated by fifth columnists. In Woolcock's version, Macbeth's 'war *on* children' is a guerrilla war conducted *by* children. The adults are only a front, a

[29] Woolcock's earlier films include *When the Dog Bites*, a profile of Consett after the closure of its steel mills, and her award-winning *Shakespeare on the Estate*, with Michael Bogdanov, for BBC2 (1994), shot in inner-city Birmingham. As Susanne Greenhalgh writes, these earlier 'performative documentaries' provided Woolcock a repertoire of practices that she re-used in her 'fiction film *Macbeth*': 'interview sequences (often filmed in a non-conventional *mise-en-scène*), observational footage with a clear symbolic as well as naturalistic force' and 'innovative and controversial use of dramatization in the form of scenarios improvised by some of the film's subjects'. See '"Alas poor country!": Documenting the Politics of Performance in Two British Television *Macbeths* since the 1980s' in Pascale Aebischer, Edward J. Esche and Nigel Wheale (eds), *Remaking Shakespeare: Performance Across Media, Genres and Cultures* (Basingstoke, 2003), p. 97. I am grateful to her for providing me a copy of her essay in advance of publication.

[30] See Beatrix Campbell, *Goliath: Britain's Dangerous Places* (London, 1993), pp. 319, 321. 'The word that embraced everything feared and loathed by the new orthodoxy about class and crime was *estate*: what was once the emblem of respectability, what once evoked the dignity and clamour of a powerful social constituency, part of the body politic, but which now described only the edge of a class and the end of the city. "Estate" evoked rookery, slum, ghetto – without the exotic energy of urbanity.' I owe this citation to Greenhalgh, 'Alas Poor Country!' p. 100.

puppet regime. The real government in this urban anarchy is not Duncan's in-yer-face totalitarianism. It's behind the scenes. Literally. To get to 'the man' you have to crawl under ventilation access shafts, duck through knocked-out partition walls. And when you get to him, 'the man' is three children.[31]

In *Macbeth on the Estate*, children overwhelm the visual text. They appear everywhere: on streets, at bus stops, on their father's knee as he plays poker, in their mother's arms as she crosses the estate. They watch grown-ups get out of their faces on hard stuff – then into each other's crotches. They bellow out the lyrics to 'Babylon's Burning' as the lurching Duncan, acting like a kid, leads the 'community singing' in a karaoke version of the Ruts' punk classic.[32] In the morning, they see the blood soaked sheets. They mimic adults. Fleance deals drugs in the community centre toilets and carries away loot from a raided flat. Macduff's boy questions his mother, 'Was my father a traitor?' (4.2.45) while he drags inexpertly on a fag. Two steps behind Macbeth and his baseball bat that magically opens the estate's locked doors to correction, tiny tots run along the same balconies, banging on the same doors with tiny tot baseball bats, chanting 'Hail Macbeth, hail Macbeth!' Children are not, in Woolcock's narrative, innocents initiated or implicated or even corrupted by the adults. They belong to the estate. The estate's norm is criminality, violence. They are 'good' estate children. And they watch adults constantly. But maybe that's what makes these knowing children seem unnaturally old. And in a world where adults behave like children and children, like adults, the idea of the child in the abstract vanishes – or becomes a disturbing inversion of itself.[33]

In this emotional consumer economy where homoeroticism codes heterosexist power relations, Duncan is a perverse parent who handles all his sons with a queasy tactility. A kind of one-man race relations drop-in centre, he has a black wife and a black girlfriend, and two mixed-race kids – the 'white' one, a swaggering yobbo skinhead who's dead chuffed at his unexpected promotion; and the barely noticed 'black' one. Racism, on this racially diverse estate, persists.[34] But Duncan also has his surrogate sons. And there's a nasty sexual undertow to his relations with them, the way he offers his own body as he embraces Macbeth, the way he incestuously touches up his victorious 'cousin', the exchange of glances between them as he tosses over the flashy diamond ring that codes – what, exactly? Nomination as Duncan's heir? Advance payment on another form of exchange? Watching in the background, Malcolm, in close-up, makes an obscene tongue gesture that Macbeth, catching, reads as 'arse licker' but shrugs off as the envy of the displaced weaker sibling. Then Malcolm is named 'prince' – and Macbeth turns away, clenching a fist around the meaningless ring on his finger, a 'lost son' who confirms rejection by the father by symbolically dropping out of male culture: Macbeth 'phones his wife.[35]

Leaving a message on the voicemail telling her what he'd been promised – 'more than mortal knowledge'; 'the coming on of time'; 'Hail, king that shalt be'(1.5.3, 9) – is both a compensation for what he's lost and a way of processing that loss. And loss is a psychic territory Susan Vidler's Lady

---

[31] In *Goliath*, writes Greenhalgh, 'Campbell suggests that a "new myth about children as criminals" displaced awareness of masculinity as a factor in the riots and estate crime of the early 1990s', 'Alas Poor Country!' p. 112.

[32] I owe this identification to Peter Balderstone, 'Who is Shakespeare? Who is Shakespeare? Nobody knows. Nobody cares. This is Ladywood', unpublished conference paper presented at the British Shakespeare Association meeting, August 2003, and I am grateful to him for sharing this work in progress with me.

[33] I am indebted for this observation – and for much stimulating conversation about the film that has shaped my thinking in this essay – to Naomi Everall in an unpublished seminar paper, 'Behold the Child', p. 9.

[34] Stereotypes of jealousy, violence and family neglect that attach to black masculinity are played out to complex ends in the Macduff plot line. Both the black Macduffs and the white Macbeths are racially 'pure' families.

[35] Banquo, too, will emerge as a 'lost son' when, later that night, at the fag end of the victory party hosted by the Macbeths, he recognizes Duncan as a loser. Watching his king attempt to stagger to bed and falling on his face, Banquo curls his lip, disgusted at the need to lackey to such clapped-out authority, snarling under his breath, 'Merciful powers, restrain in me the cursèd thoughts that nature gives way to in repose.'

Macbeth knows by heart. When the camera first finds her she's crossing the estate with her best mate, Lady Macduff (Patsi Fox), who's carrying her big-eyed baby daughter in her arms and manoeuvring the empty pushchair while Lady Macbeth holds the little Macduff boy by the hand. Lady Macbeth is good with kids – but these black babies clearly aren't hers. At home alone, as she listens to the voicemail message, the camera roams through rooms, compiling a visual text that fills in her lost narrative. There is a framed photograph of a laughing child beside the answerphone – who is nowhere physically present. As Lady Macbeth starts talking to her absent husband to herself, her soliloquies are overlaid with reminders of this missing child – ghostly laughter that comes from hide-and-seek brats who have buzzed the intercom and caught out the grown-up with 'knock down ginger'; a hesitation on the landing in front of a closed door. Behind that door is a blue room, a nursery, religiously preserved and meticulously ordered. Its mass-market clutter, though, belongs to a period of late capitalism that has emptied the commodity of its power to signify, except fetishistically; so it is impossible, in this place where every object is *à la mode retro* and codes both nostalgia and amnesia, to date the child or his exit securely.[36] (Did he die last week, last year, last decade? Men Macbeth's age have sons who are strapping teenagers, Banquo, for one.) In this nursery, though, time doesn't register. There's a cot with a Winnie-the-Pooh mobile playing a 1950s kids' radio signature tune, a duvet with an Aston Villa cover, posters of Noah's Ark and Mickey Mouse, a dresser draped with a Villa scarf, piled with stuffed animals – none of them worn. The room is a shrine, its atmosphere, dense with palpable absence. As Lady Macbeth picks up a photograph and traces her fingers around the image of her child's body, she weeps, but then regains stony composure, her back against the wall, sliding down it as she invokes the 'spirits who tend on mortal thoughts'(1.5.39). Her face is caught in a double exposure, full-on by the camera, and obliquely, reflected in a mirror on the dresser. The child's absence seems compounded in the doubled image of the mother, and as she dully calls upon evil's ministers to 'unsex me here' (39), she projects the sense that her child's absence has rendered a part of her, the mother, similarly absent, or caused a split that, cauterized, immunizes her to the violence she internalizes in these speeches.[37]

Killing Duncan will recuperate her loss, restore not just the lost son but the son lost when Duncan passed over Macbeth to make Malcolm his heir. So when he decides to 'proceed no further in this business', her rage expresses itself in sexual violence. Woolcock shot the marital row as a bedroom scene, Lady Macbeth remembering the 'babe that milk[ed] me' while Macbeth penetrates her, then straddling him, coercing him back into resolution by thrusting herself onto him, urging him to 'screw your courage to the sticking place' before bringing him to climax with 'What cannot you and I perform . . .?' When he whispers, 'Bring forth men-children only' (1.7.31, 55, 60, 69, 73) she slams face down the bedside photograph of their dead son – hiding the child's eyes.[38] Already absent, the child is doubly lost in the mother's gesture, as if the escalation of the parents' violence is reductive of the child – or the new 'baby', the murder they've just conceived, wipes out memories of the loss it's intended to compensate.

But this baby too is lost – figuratively, when killing brings no 'success' but rather the appalling realisation that 'Nought's had, all's spent' (3.2.6); but literally, too, in Woolcock's adaptation. Earlier,

[36] I am drawing on Fredric Jameson's theorizations in 'Postmodernism and Consumer Society', in *The Cultural Turn* (London, 1998), p. 7.

[37] More obviously, the sequence of mirror shots codes her duplicity – and worse. In the living room she brushes her hair before a circular mirror as she tells her absent husband, 'I fear your nature', twined around its circumference is a tangled pattern of leaves that produces her face as if wreathed with snakes, making her Medusa.

[38] The camera never moves in close enough to the photograph to establish whether the child is a boy or a girl; spectators perhaps assume a boy-child partly on the evidence of the furniture in the preserved bedroom. But plenty of fathers give their daughters football scarves. And on the Weird Children's altar the dolls that are being celebrated/sacrificed are girl-children, so reinforcing the final atrocity in the Macduff family killings, the stabbing of the baby girl.

plotting Banquo's death, Macbeth stood behind her at the kitchen sink, staring down at his fingers laced over his wife's flat belly, a look and gesture that coded pregnancy. Later, trying to sleep after the fiasco at the feast when he saw dead Banquo return among the living, Macbeth holds his wife – but she moans, rolls out of bed. A cut to the bathroom shows her reaching for the Tampax – then furiously grabbing the pregnancy kit that's sitting on the shelf next to them, wrenching it open, and trashing the testers. From now on, all of her energies go into cleaning – hoovering, dusting, more hoovering. She's picking imaginary fluff off the antiseptic sofa with a strip of Sellotape when Macbeth bursts through the front door, takes the stairs three at a time, grabs the baseball bat from under the bed and, businesslike, informs her that

From this moment,
The very firstlings of my heart shall be
The firstlings of my hand. And even now
To crown my thoughts with acts, be it thought and done.

But he's only half way through the rest of the plan –

The castle of Macduff I will surprise,
Seize upon Fife, give to th'edge o'th' sword
His wife, his babes, and all unfortunate souls
That trace him in his line. (4.1.162–9) –

when she is down the stairs and belting across the estate, flinging herself through the Macduffs' back door, babbling out Shakespeare's Messenger's speech, 'Be not found here. Hence with your little ones' (4.2.70), trying to herd the boys, assemble the push-chair, strap the baby into it, over Lady Macduff's bewildered protestations as Macbeth comes through the front door. The man himself commits these killings, and Lady Macbeth watches at the window as he pulps the mother and boys, then sinks to her haunches, rocking, covering her ears to deafen the baby's wailing. A close-up on the baby's face, her eyes magnified by tears and terror, cuts to a close-up on Ross, coming through the back gate, taking in the horror, turning and running, then to a close-up of Macbeth, gazing down at the baby girl, muttering 'you egg' (line 83) – and aiming his knife. Lady Macbeth tries to rise but her legs buckle. She moves back across the estate like someone walking in her sleep, traumatized by images of slaughtered children. She's standing at her own kitchen sink when she notices 'Yet' again, 'here's a spot', 'out damned spot'(5.1.30, 33), and scrubs and scrubs with the vegetable brush as clear water runs down the drain. In this mind-blown trance she plays out the night of the murder, pulling sheets off the guest bed, folding them into the washing machine, the camera angle shifting, as in a horror film, to show Macbeth leaning against the fridge, sullen, silent, watching. But when she urges 'To bed, to bed', (63) she turns – and sees her absent son in the doorway. Taking him by an invisible hand, she tucks him up in his empty bed in his vacant room. And sometime later that afternoon she stands on the roof of her tower block, lifts her head to survey a world beyond the estate – then walks over the edge.

Her hallucination is the last spasm of a hurt mind. Trying psychically to repair the extravagant damage of Macbeth's violence, to restore the lost children that represent an idea of a future, she feels her absent child most acutely present, presencing a 'blessed time' past. But the hallucination that makes the child heart-wrenchingly 'there' in mind and not there in matter works ironically to intensify his absence, an absence that reads as the annulling of the idea of childhood in the deaths of particular children. There is no bleaker moment in Woolcock's film.

When Macbeth finds his wife dead on the concrete she is ringed by children, little girls, a couple of mothers. He speaks 'tomorrow and tomorrow and tomorrow' (5.5.18) to them, close-ups cutting between his face and theirs, expressionless, maybe numb, or inoculated to horror that has no power any longer to shock their systems, certainly not demanding, just not reacting. They are beautiful, these little girls, but their folded arms across flat chests figure them also as ancient hags. It's appropriate that Macbeth is talking to them. For while his wife dealt with her childlessness by hoovering gullies into the carpet, Macbeth processed his grief by seeking the company of surrogate children – the 'Weird Children'.

The most disturbing decision this film makes is to see Shakespeare's Weird Sisters as children. Like the estate's children, they appear everywhere; but unlike them, they're unattached to adult culture. Adults push them away, threaten them with raised fists. They roam, a little feral pack of anarchists – doing, and undoing, estate business. But they almost always elude sighting, fugitives in a terrain that gives them hiding places. They are *literally* the estate's lost children. So it is only retrospectively that spectators realise it's the Weird Children they saw in distant long shot running through the estate in the second prologue sequence; it's they who triggered the action; they whose shapes appeared through the car window they smashed with a stone before standing back to observe Cawdor shoved inside and burned alive. After the gang battle, as he and Banquo are making their way across the estate to headquarters in the community centre, taking the back route through a condemned stretch of grey concrete and vandalized flats, Macbeth hears this blasted landscape weirdly calling out to him – voices, whispered, shouted, from an empty window, a dark doorway, a vacant hallway, voices like those hide-and-seek voices on Lady Macbeth's intercom, voices that can't be fixed to a source but keep shifting their ground with impossible speed; voices that call out 'Macbeth'. And then through a smashed pane, a child's head, caught long enough for Macbeth to focus on it, disappears; a foot flees down a corridor, a hand on a window frame vanishes. Undaunted by physical violence, Macbeth is spooked by this weird operation of the physical world – but intrigued. Shrugging off Banquo's cautioning hand he starts up the peeling switchback stairs – a replay of his assault on Cawdor, itself a take on countless suspense-driven action films. At the top, he stoops to peer through grey ventilation ducts that lead him to a hanging curtain, a grey membrane of builder's plastic. Lifting it, he gazes into something astonishing: a golden world illuminated by dazzling candlelight enclosing a bizarre shrine whose 'strange intelligence', impacting on Macbeth's eyes, makes him shift like a nervy horse while his 'seated heart knock[s] at [his] ribs'. For this shrine focuses strange energies. There's a voodoo mask on a wall, a clothes line pinned with Tarot cards, a curved, milky mirror that bends the images it reflects, the single arm of a mannequin holding up a grinning fetish, a sepia photograph, and at the centre, surrounded by votive candles, a seeming child, a white plastic doll, propped up and staring.

This shrine anticipates and inverts the other shrine, the blue room dedicated to the Macbeths' dead child, its antithesis, but also strangely its double. Both are set apart, perfect utopias, both beautiful, indeed, the only beauty spots on Macbeth's broken dystopian estate. Carefully assembled as memory spaces to fold time in on itself, they each fuse the future and the instant with the past. Bizarrely, too, like the nursery, this space looks like a kid's playground, an almost ludicrously excessive collection of mumbo-jumbo and Halloween frights. None of this stuff belongs to childhood – it's all hand-me-downs from the adults, like the stuffed toys in the nursery that aim to naturalize an adult-driven fantasy life for the child. Here it seems that objects captured from the grown-ups – the stopped clock, the rosary, Death in the Tarot pack – have been arranged to taunt those grown-ups with a parody of their own fantasy life, their inveterate superstitiousness, their willingness, as adults, to deceive themselves with lies. Or maybe what Macbeth is looking at isn't parody, but pastiche, in Fredric Jameson's terms, 'blank parody' that comes 'without parody's ulterior motive, without the satirical impulse, without laughter': 'parody that has lost its sense of humour'.[39] So maybe this scene isn't a laughing matter. Maybe it's for real – where the 'real' is evil.

Spectators see the scene from Macbeth's point of view. Then a cut shows us, like him, the rest of the picture; the high priests who officiate at this shrine are standing solemnly by. *And they're just kids.*[40] The biggest one has a beard coming on, but could still play Thisby. The littlest looks like he should be advertising Pears soap. The girl is bony, akimbo,

[39] In Jameson, 'Postmodernism and Consumer Society', p. 5.

[40] Played by Richard Chinn, Clare Dowling and Lee Williams.

odd, her over-sized National Health glasses on her angular cocked head making her look both earnest and old, like a studious tortoise. All of them weirdly fuse childness with a premature adultness, a sense of having grown 'instant old' (*Hamlet* 1.5.94): later, when she becomes the apparition and delivers the prediction that 'none of woman born / Shall harm Macbeth' (4.1.96–7), she's wearing a white headscarf and red lipstick erratically applied wide of the mark, dressing up like mother, perhaps, or strangely assimilating stereotypes of the virgin and the whore to interrogate the riddle of the child 'not born of woman' (5.3.4).

Like Macbeth, looking at these Weird Children – the name the estate knows them by – spectators are faced with a crisis of interpretation, a deep equivocation. Is the hocus-pocus objectified in this secret garden at the heart of Duncan's urban wasteland a bit of fun – like reading today's horoscope in the *Sun*? Or is what's going on here an initiation into occult practices that trap the neophyte in a parallel dark universe? Banquo scoffs. And his reaction is surely right. For there is something utterly ridiculous about the excessiveness of this scene that fits its interpretation into the orthodox understanding of evil as grotesque parody – and ultimately comic because doomed to failure. So much effort goes in to evil's bustling, futile projects that it's laughable. The inevitable tragic fall is always a pratfall, as Satan was the first to demonstrate.[41] Of course, this positivistic analysis of evil depends on other orthodoxies, faith in God's omnipotence, the willingness of the 'heavens' not just to 'look on' but to 'take [our] part' (4.3.225–6). So where is God on Duncan's estate?

And what if, on this God-forsaken estate, evil isn't a joke? What if the Weird Children aren't offering a parody of adult power that contains the parody while permitting it childishly to mimic adult power, but instead are operatives in an alternative system of power where the adults are the playthings and these children in control, 'our masters' (4.1.79)? We're on Macbeth's side when he searches the Weird Children's faces – for their intent. We need to know whether evil can be resident in the bodies of children. We need to know what evil looks like in the child's face – a need that has become urgent since the death of James Bulger. Looking at the police mug-shot of the peroxide blond from 1965 we recognise Myra as Medusa (don't we?).[42] But those chirpy little boys showing gap-toothed smiles in school photographs blown up into monsters on the front pages of the tabloids in 1993: who are they? How do we understand what they did, give 'A deed without a name' (4.1.65) a name? Was the abduction a playground game gone wrong – or is that a rationalist apology? Were Thompson and Venables intent on evil? After James Bulger, adults have needed to know more about knowing children – what they know, how they know it, how much of their knowledge they are responsible for.

These are things Macbeth wants to know too – but knowledge, in Shakespeare *and* Woolcock, is denied. And *ways* of knowing are catastrophically

---

41 See Arthur Lindley, 'The Unbeing of the Overreacher', *Modern Language Review*, 84 (1989), p. 1.

42 At her death, Jonathan Glancey wrote of the iconic status the photograph achieved in Hindley's lifetime: 'Myra, Medusa. Medusa, Myra. No matter what she looked like after she was sentenced to life imprisonment in 1966, Myra Hindley was fixed forever in the public eye as the peroxide-haired gorgon of that infamous police snapshot. Look at her defiant evil eyes, we are meant to say' (*Guardian*, 16 November 2002). In *The Tablet* a week later Peter Stanford (who, like Lord Longford, believed Hindley to be reformed and campaigned for her release) reflected on the same circulation of imagery. 'Britain's tabloid newspapers,' he wrote, 'faced with the enormity of their disgust' and knowing 'that they could not even begin to unravel why someone should do something so inhumane as to tape-record the murder of a 10-year-old girl calling out in despair for her mother', 'fell back on the Devil – the face of evil. Myra became the Devil, a shorthand way to sum up evil. That 1966 snapshot of her, taken at the time of the trial and showing her, Medusa-like, staring out defiantly from underneath her peroxide hair, has become the modern face of Satan, an icon of crime in the twentieth century' (23 November 2002). Evidently fascinated by the photographic image, Marcus Harvey used a cast of a child's hand to print a wall-sized acrylic version of it for the Royal Academy's 'Sensation' exhibition in 1997 – the same year as Woolcock's *Macbeth on the Estate*. In this portrait, 'Myra, Medusa' is composed entirely of children's handprints. When first shown, it was pelted with eggs and ink, and it remains one of the most controversial exhibits on permanent display at the Saatchi gallery in London.

destabilized. It turns out that these Weird Children are not explicable in mortal terms. They are not what they appear to be, victims of social deprivation and failed welfare programmes, trainee sociopaths whose 'weywardness' should be assigned to a case-worker for remedial action. For they are not finally knowable in socio-secular terms. They traffic in the metaphysical. They can vanish off the face of the estate. When Macbeth, wanting certainty from the Weird Children in 4.1, rips back the curtain that has separated spectator from spectacle and reaches out toward the apparitions, the shrine, its furniture, the candles and they themselves are simply gone, he, bewilderedly walking into their disappearance – and what they've left behind, a perfectly ordinary 'sight' on the estate, a vandalized, junk-littered room. If ontology is troubled in these children, so is teleology. They are not innocent of effect. Their child's play evidently produces images that simulate – and *stimulate* – terrible consequences. When Macbeth appears to them the second time they have rearranged their shrine. The icon at the centre – the white doll – has been replaced. With a black doll. Not sitting up, but lying sprawled on its back, eyes staring, while around it are posed dismembered, twisted limbs, an image that almost instantly translates into utterance – and execution. They imagine – or do they plant it? – what next comes into Macbeth's mind, the slaughter of Macduff's baby girl.

In these sequences, the bleak secularism of Duncan's estate is surprised by metaphysics. Ironically, though, Woolcock's Weird Children can deliver on the future not because they can predict it, but because, as children, they *are* it. And the temptation they offer James Frain's Macbeth is so potent because, as children, they complete the circuit that loops his desire through his loss by offering him both 'having' *and* 'hope'. Weirdly, in this film Macbeth's lost child and his dynastic aspirations come together in these lost children.

In the final condensed minutes of Woolcock's film Macbeth sits staring straight ahead, on his sofa, his dead wife sprawled beside him, his baseball bat between his knees, like a morbid re-vision of Grant Wood's 'American Gothic'. 'What's he / That was not born of woman?' (5.7.2–3) he asks the camera. It answers by cutting to Macduff, walking through Macbeth's front door. 'Despair thy charm,' he advises, and 'yield thee coward'(5.10.13, 23). Then he pulls out a gun and shoots. Macbeth, still on the sofa, in a slow zoom backwards is transported to a glade in Birnam Woods where his dead eyes stare up through the trees. A jump cut frames Macduff walking through another door, to the community centre. He tosses Duncan's ring on the table in front of Malcolm. 'Hail king,' he says (5.11.20). Then he turns on his heel and walks out. The 'boy' Malcolm self-importantly swaggers to his feet, delivering his stagy acceptance speech before turning to the bar to order rounds. The kid he elbows aside is Fleance – who, with his fingers, mimes a gun, lines up the sights on the back of Malcolm's skull, and pulls the imaginary trigger. Prediction proleptically fulfilled as the adolescent king is assassinated by the schoolboy usurper and violence passes down into ever smaller children's hands, the screen explodes to whiteout.

Like filmed *Macbeth*s before it (Welles's, Polanski's), Woolcock's *Macbeth on the Estate* ends with a return to its beginning. The imagined gunshot triggers a cut to Macduff. The reporter from the opening prologue is finally revealed as the survivor of these events who, all his children lost, has told this story 'of a time, not long past' as an effort of memory and an act of creation to put before spectators evidence they must process. Standing in long shot on the rubble-strewn waste-ground against the skyline of the estate – the estate that tropes the nation – Macduff has only this to say when the camera moves in to close-up: 'Alas, poor country. Almost afraid to know itself.' Then he turns and walks away. It isn't *Macbeth*'s last line. In Shakespeare it isn't Macduff's line. Spoken here, by him, the film's last words work like a zoom back, radically adjusting the final focus, opening up the ending, inviting spectators to read this performance as a kind of documentary and this film as a state of the nation address that wonders apocalyptically about the nation's future, a future equivocally predicted in its children. On the estate that is Britain, is childhood an alibi? Is it an 'elsewhere' invented by adults to locate (false) memory, nostalgia, and the seductive fantasy of innocence? Has the myth of childhood dissolved, childhood functioning only as a cultural placeholder for (adult) anxieties? Or is it rather that *adulthood* has dissolved, Woolcock's film documenting and critiquing a politics of abdication that spells the collapse of the myth of the grown-up? 'Alas, poor country. Almost afraid to know itself' speaks across this welter of questions. And Macduff's 'almost' is critical, for what Woolcock finally gives spectators is a version of *Macbeth* that is *unafraid* – a medium for this country to 'think in . . . front of itself', and by such thinking, 'to know itself'.[43]

[43] I am grateful to the Arts and Humanities Research Board for a grant that supported research on this project.

TAKING MACBETH OUT OF HIMSELF: DAVENANT, GARRICK, SCHILLER AND VERDI

SIMON WILLIAMS

Macbeth, it is widely recognized, has a dynamic unique among Shakespeare's tragedies. By-and-large we accept the premise that dramatic action on Shakespeare's stage serves as a surrogate for or a reflection of life in the world outside the theatre. Hamlet lives in the concrete reality of Elsinore and while his father's ghost may trouble his confidence in the reliability of his perceptions, we as his audience remain fairly confident that the world in which he lives can be understood as having a materiality equivalent to the physical surroundings in which we ourselves live. The same is true with *Othello*. Othello, with Iago's help, fills himself with the delusion of Desdemona's infidelity and comes to see the world through the grotesque forms and lurid colors of nightmare, but we as audience do not. In fact, the primary tension of the play lies between the world as Othello sees it through his inflamed imagination and our recognition that in actuality it is different from his vision of it. But in *Macbeth* our vision is as clouded, as coloured, and as mystified as that of Macbeth himself. He sees the world through his accumulating guilt and the terrible fears generated by his imagination; it is frightening, full of menace and we see it as he does. The main conflict is within him and not, as in *Othello*, between the hero and phenomenal reality. Because of this, Macbeth dominates the action of his play like no other Shakespearian hero does. In the other tragedies, not only is the 'real world' separate from the hero, it is also a region into which we can imaginatively retreat when we are overwhelmed by the intensity of the hero's tragic fate and from which we can observe him. In *Macbeth*, however, even when the 'real world' is made available to us, when the action, for example, moves to Macduff's castle or the English court, Macbeth is still the dominant presence onstage, because as the fate of every character is determined by him, they are entirely preoccupied with him. We can escape neither him nor the world he has made.

We often feel the hold Macbeth exercises over us to be more disturbing than with most other heroes in tragedy, because while he feeds our imagination, he also offends or even violates our moral sense, and yet while the enormity of this violation becomes more and more apparent, we find our sympathy for him intensifying. At the nadir of his degradation the sympathy we feel for him might even translate into admiration as it is at this point, as he contemplates his lonely old age and hears of Lady Macbeth's death, that he achieves sublime insights into the alienation of old age and the meaninglessness of human life, insights that we consider to be among the most penetrating statements on such matters in our culture. Not only do we feel more warmly toward this extreme criminal than we do for more overtly sympathetic tragic heroes, we find him to be a source of wisdom as well. Throughout the play Macbeth attracts an uncanny sympathy, even admiration, even though, by commonly accepted codes of norms, he is a regicide of unparalleled brutality. The disturbance implicit in our uncertain response to him arises from the lyrical nature of the tragedy, whose ultimate aim is to unfold Macbeth's emotional and imaginative being and the entire stage is employed to materialize this.

The ambivalent nature of Macbeth's appeal and the unconventional lyrical nature of the tragedy have created special problems for the staging of the play. *Macbeth*, we may intelligently speculate, was not especially suited to the ambience of the Globe theatre, where the ominous effect of dark imagery and the atmosphere of supernatural foreboding as a projection of Macbeth's horror over the consequences of his deeds would have been easily dispelled by the insistent daylight. It is a work that better suits the obscurity and claustrophobia of a dimly-lit indoor space such as that offered by the court theatre of the time[1] and, later, the public theatres in London after 1660; in such confines Macbeth's power to speak to the audience's imagination could work most effectively. But for centuries historical circumstances and cultural conditions resisted a full exploration of the uncanny and disquieting impact of Macbeth's appeal to our imagination. In England under Charles II, loyalty to the royal cause was the cue to political survival, and so a play like *Macbeth* should have had no place. Later, during the Enlightenment, theatre in both England and Europe was devoted, in intention at least, primarily to the moral improvement and genteel cultivation of its audiences. Here again it would be reasonable to assume that *Macbeth* would be more conspicuous by its absence from the repertoire. Only in the romantic age, when literature explored hidden strata of human emotion and evil came to be treated not as a vicious aberration from the norm but a necessary component of the human condition, would conditions seem to have been auspicious for a revival of *Macbeth*.

The performance history of *Macbeth*, however, confounds expectations. The play was central to the repertoire throughout the Restoration and the English Enlightenment and, once Shakespeare found his way onto the continent, it was among the first of his works to be staged in European theatres. Its prominence in the repertoire was due largely to the sheer quality of the work. While eighteenth-century critics expressed widespread disapproval of the bloodiness of Macbeth, the insinuating power of Lady Macbeth, and the affront to rationality offered by the witches, most of them, along with theatre practitioners and audience members, would have agreed with Elizabeth Montagu, when she described *Macbeth* as 'one of the greatest exertions of the tragic and poetic powers, that any age, or any country has produced'.[2] But the disturbing ambivalence of Macbeth's appeal could only be fully indulged in by those who read their Shakespeare; in the theatre matters were different. *Macbeth* was prominent in the repertoire, but, like many of Shakespeare's works, this was mainly through dint of adaptation. Onstage both the play's unique dramatic dynamic and the morally confusing, potentially subversive attraction exercised by Macbeth were substantially modified.

In this essay, I explore four cases of adaptation and stage interpretation of *Macbeth* over almost two hundred years of its performance history. During this time the play was moulded to redirect and readjust the audience's attitude toward Macbeth, his crimes, and the forces, be they psychological or supernatural, which impelled him to them. I begin with Sir William Davenant's adaptation of the 1660s, which was the version commonly seen in London until David Garrick's revival of the 1740s, during which he progressively returned to the play 'as written by Shakespeare', though with an interpretation of the leading role that substantially modified the disturbing aspects of the tragedy. The English theatre was as implicated in the Enlightenment project of cultivating and coercing audiences into the formation of a civil and civilized society as were its continental counterparts, but the court theatres of Central Europe were also actively engaged in the mission of validating the power of their royal patrons, a function that only disappeared with the unification of Germany in the latter part of the nineteenth century. Prior to that time, the version of *Macbeth* commonly seen on German stages was the one by Johann Friedrich Schiller, which

[1] Henry Paul, *The Royal Play of Macbeth* (New York, 1950), p. 3.

[2] Mrs Montagu, *An Essay on the Writings and Genius of Shakespeare*, 6th and Corrected Edition (London, 1810), p. 155.

was first staged at the Weimar Court Theatre in 1800. I conclude with a discussion of Verdi's operatic version of the play, first performed in Florence in 1847 and widely performed throughout Italy before it was rewritten and expanded for its premiere in Paris in 1865.

I have selected these four versions of *Macbeth* because they were widely regarded in their time as important versions and interpretations of Shakespeare's tragedy and consequently were performed for several decades, in some cases for over a century after their first performance. *Macbeth* had, for example, been given in several German theatres by the end of the eighteenth century, notably in adaptations by Christoph Martin Wieland and Friedrich Ludwig Schröder, but Schiller's version so clearly suited the function of theatre in Germany as an institution that furthered social cohesion that it soon became the standard version. All four versions of the play are also akin, if not identical, in their treatment of Macbeth and of the witches. Effectively, they take Macbeth out of himself so that we view the stage world around him not as a projection of his imagination or as a description of his inner world but as phenomenon independent of his consciousness. That this treatment was hard to cast off is demonstrated by Verdi's opera, which, while widely considered to be a prime specimen of romantic theatre and the first instance in which a serious attempt had been made in opera to capture the dramatic ambience of Shakespearian drama, is still conceptually related to the play as it was seen on the stages of eighteenth-century Europe.

DAVENANT: *MACBETH* AS MORALITY PLAY

Davenant's adaptation of *Macbeth*, first staged in London during the 1660s, has been treated with scant respect by scholars, most of whom consider it to be little more than a travesty of Shakespeare – Bartholomeusz considers Thomas Betterton's championing of this version as 'one of the disillusioning facts' of the play's stage-history.[3] But Davenant, it should be stressed, produced the play that his time needed. The royal warrant that assigned his company eleven plays of Shakespeare to perform required that he reform them, 'makeinge them, fitt' for the stage of his time.[4] Given the unstable political conditions following the restoration of the English monarchy, nothing was more likely to shake the stability of the nation than an act of regicide, as had been committed through the execution of the king's father, Charles I, in 1649. Whatever was attractive or even compelling in Shakespeare's representation of Macbeth, prior to the murder of Duncan or after it, was unlikely to find favour either with the authorities or the audiences of the London theatre.

In fact, the reduction of Macbeth's allure may well have been a principal aim of Davenant as he reworked Shakespeare's tragedy. From the start Macbeth is a less dangerous and volatile figure than he is in Shakespeare. The Captain's account of his heroic deeds in the battle against the Norwegians, delivered by Seaton, includes nothing to suggest that Macbeth's energies generate a violence that is vastly in excess of what the conflict itself might have required. Rather, the new Macbeth is a brave warrior, serving his king in a fairly unremarkable way. On hearing the prophecies of the witches, he is not troubled by any symptoms of fear and fascination at the supernatural; rather, he is intrigued, as if the witches have set a puzzling riddle to test his intelligence.

> This may be prologue to the name of King
> Less Titles shou'd the greater still forerun
> The Morning star do's usher in ye Sun
> This strange prediction in as strange a manner
> Deliver'd; neither can be good nor ill.
>
> (Davenant, 1.3.132–6)

Davenant's Macbeth is never torn apart by tormenting contradictions as Shakespeare's is, and though he may be something more than Mary

[3] Dennis Bartholomeusz, *Macbeth and the Players* (Cambridge, 1969), p. 15.

[4] Christopher Spencer, Introduction to *Davenant's Macbeth from the Yale Manuscript* (New Haven, 1961), pp. 1–2. All references to Davenant's adaptation are from this edition.

Edmonds' claim of 'an uncomplicated ambitious villain',[5] there is nothing heroic about his struggle against and complicity with the forces of darkness. As the thought of Duncan's murder grows upon him through conversations with his wife and in his soliloquies, there is little sense of him giving himself over to a dark world whose fascination he can do nothing to resist. As he debates the consequences of the murder – 'If it were well when done' (Davenant, 1.7.1) – he is exercised solely by the reasons why he should not murder Duncan, ones which he expounds upon with admirable clarity. Shakespeare's Macbeth is thrilled by the metaphysical catastrophe that will follow from the assassination of Duncan, almost as if he welcomes it, but although Davenant's Macbeth does see a dagger leading him to Duncan, he shows no awareness of the earth-shattering consequences of the deed he is about to commit.

Davenant's persistent tendency to favour clarity above metaphor gives Macbeth a transparency that Shakespeare's figure singularly lacks. He rewrites and simplifies whatever is obscure in Shakespeare and omits whatever might make the forces of darkness appear heroic or attractive. While Shakespeare's play has us feel with Macbeth and gather a visceral sense of his imaginative vision, Davenant, as Richard Kroll has demonstrated in such detail, 'works to expose the workings of figuration itself'.[6] Indeed, while political expedience may have been the first impetus in the adaptation, as Kroll argues, its more fundamental appeal to Davenant's contemporaries might have arisen from how it reflected the rational and empirical philosophy of Thomas Hobbes, which made little allowance for the presence of the irrational or supernatural in human life. Everything in Davenant's *Macbeth* is, therefore, explained, nothing left to speculation. The action accordingly acquires a moralistic perspective. A tragic one is impossible for the prime reality on Davenant's stage is social and political, not Shakespeare's quasi-expressionist realm in which all manifestations of physical and metaphysical planes of being may be extensions of Macbeth's subjectivity. Evil loses its compulsion as it no longer resides in Macbeth's giving way to his dark desires, and the world as we see it onstage is ontologically separate from him. The neo-classical tastes of the Restoration theatre, which Davenant observed in his adaptation,[7] aided him in specifying the social sphere. Not only is the plot tightened, but Shakespeare's long, unwieldy cast-list, which creates the effect of a world without boundary and interior coherence, is reduced. Davenant provides us with an environment that insists on its own reality, within which each character has a distinctive function. The roles of Lennox, Ross, Angus and Young Siward, for example, are compressed into one, so when this multiple character, called Lennox, is killed in battle by Macbeth, his death is unambiguously symbolic of the suffering Scotland has suffered at the hands of Macbeth. Seaton too is a composite of several of Shakespeare's smaller roles – the bleeding captain, the old man, multiple lords at the banquet, the messenger who tells Lady Macduff of the approaching murderers, and the doctor in the sleepwalking scene – and this too creates the illusion of a limited social reality within which Macbeth moves. Seaton's defection to the enemy at the end tells Macbeth more about his weakness than any internal promptings he might experience. The illusion that social and political retribution is the sole cause of Macbeth's downfall is strengthened by the return of Donalbain and Fleance to participate in the final victory. As the world around Macbeth increasingly presses in upon him, he declines in stature rather than grows, which is antithetical to what happens in Shakespeare's final act.

The removal of Macbeth from the centre of his play is most apparent in Davenant's celebrated reworking of the roles of Macduff and Lady Macduff, whose interpolated scenes are so prominent that they acquire the stature of antagonists. A moral polarity is thereby set up between the Macbeths and the Macduffs. Early on Macduff is

[5] Mary Edmond, *Rare Sir William Davenant*. The Revels Play Companion Library (Manchester, 1987), p. 193.

[6] Richard Kroll, 'Emblem and Empiricism in Davenant's *Macbeth*', *ELH* 57 (Winter 1990), 848.

[7] Edmond, *Davenant*, pp. 192–3.

put forward as the figure of virtue. For example, Banquo's confident avowal in the righteousness of his position

> In the great hand of God I stand and thence
> Against the undivulged pretence I fight
> Of treasonous malice
> (Shakespeare, 2.3.123–5)[8]

is transferred by Davenant to Macduff, whose view of himself with regard to the murder is far more secular,

> Guarded by vertue I am resolv'd to find
> The utmost of this business
> (Davenant, 2.3.103–4)

Wherever possible, Davenant augments the role of Macduff to make it clear that the field on which he and Macbeth will fight is that of civic order, not religious belief. In an interpolation in Act 1, Davenant has Lady Macduff take refuge with Lady Macbeth during the battle against the Norwegians, and here, in a conversation more appropriate for a polite soiree than a fearful refuge from battle, Lady Macduff insists that she loves her husband and disdains the glory of battle more than Lady Macbeth does. The Macduffs therefore become the dramatic counterweight to the Macbeths and the gravitational centre of the play shifts from Macbeth and his inner struggles to the conventional counterpoise of good and evil, virtue and ambition. In fact ambition, the vice that always becomes the whipping-boy when *Macbeth* is conceived of as a morality play, becomes the unifying theme of Davenant's play. Even Macduff is briefly tempted by ambition, when he considers wresting the sceptre from Macbeth and ruling in his place, but he is severely called back into line by his Lady who fears that he may lose his innocence (Davenant, 3.2.25–60) and from thenceforth he remains a model of virtue. The Macduffs also encounter the witches in a journey over the heath and they receive their own prophecies, which have no effect upon their plot; the purpose of their scene seems solely to grant the Macduffs equal stature to the Macbeths. In the concluding battle, Macduff's role as the avenger of outraged virtue is emphasized as he specifies how each blow he strikes is for one of Macbeth's victims:

> This for thy Royall Master Duncan
> This for my Dearest freind [sic] my wife
> This for those pledges of our Loves; my Children
> (Davenant, 5.7.76–8)

When *Macbeth* was revived at Dorset Garden Theatre in 1673, it was cause for a great spectacle with operatic choruses and dances.[9] Here the witches were clearly not figments of Macbeth's imagination, but beings with an independent existence, as tangible as the human characters. They did not arise, like the imaginary dagger, from the fumes of Macbeth's 'heat-oppressèd brain' (Shakespeare, 2.1.39). In the midst of their encounter with the Macduffs (Davenant, 2.5.54–91), the witches celebrate Duncan's death, which suggests that their purpose is not to confuse humans' sense of their own identity, but to overthrow order in the human state. Macbeth hears the three deceptive prophecies not from apparitions summoned up by the witches, but from the mouth of Hecate as if the supernatural world has acquired a hierarchical structure that parallels that of human politics. While the witches lack credibility as a serious entity, they still seem to be the origin of disorder, which comes from outside rather than within the pale of human life, but their threat can only work upon society through the conduit of the ambitious man, who is without virtue.[10]

The reduction of Macbeth from tragic hero to moral emblem is nowhere more apparent than in a scene with Lady Macbeth, interpolated by

8 William Shakespeare, *Macbeth*, ed. A. R. Braunmuller (Cambridge, 1997). All references to Shakespeare's *Macbeth* from this edition.

9 For a discussion of the initial performance history of Davenant's *Macbeth*, see Barbara E. Murray, *Restoration Shakespeare: Viewing the Voice* (Madison & Teaneck, 2001), pp. 51–5.

10 '[Davenant] has, wittingly or unwittingly, scaled down the moral universe of the play and made the nature of the evil therein more readily measurable to man; the metaphysical quality disappears.' Peter Dyson, 'Changes in Dramatic Perspective: From Shakespeare's *Macbeth* to Davenant's', *Shakespeare Quarterly*, 30 (Summer 1979), 404.

Davenant half-way through the scene at the English court (Davenant, 4.4.27–82). First, by bringing Macbeth onstage at this juncture in the action, Davenant eliminates any chance of his acquiring the potential grandeur that Shakespearian tragic heroes accumulate during their absence from stage at the end of Act 4 and the beginning of Act 5. In fact, Davenant devotes the scene to a display of Macbeth's weakness. The conversation between Macbeth and his Lady echoes the earlier discussion the Macduffs had about ambition. Picking up on the imagery of that scene, Lady Macbeth, who is pursued in her imagination by the ghost of Duncan, speaks of her dizziness now she has reached the height of fortune:

> I stand so high that I am giddy grown
> A mist do's cover me as clouds the Tops
> Of Hills; let us get down apace
> (Davenant, 4.4.49–51)

She urges Macbeth to give up the crown and lays the blame for their misery on his upsetting of the natural order of things because he, a man, failed to exercise his natural superiority over her as a woman:

> You were a man
> And by the charter of your sex you should
> Have govern'd me; there was more crime in you
> When you obeyed my Councells then I contracted by
> my giving it (Davenant, 4.4.62–6)

She continues by urging him to put off his crown and, the moment he does, he will also put off his guilt. Such transactions are easy in the world of the morality play; only in tragedy does guilt stick.

GARRICK AND THE INNOCENCE OF MACBETH

While Davenant's adaptation ruled the stage for the first part of the eighteenth century, Shakespeare's *Macbeth* was readily available to readers in the multiple editions of his plays that began to appear in the early eighteenth century. On the page, therefore, readers still encountered the supernatural and violent ambience that is inescapably part of *Macbeth*, but it is one they found difficult to validate. The philosophy of the play was faulty as well. Francis Gentleman was representative in his condemnation of the play 'for exhibiting the chimaeras of witchcraft and advancing the principles of fatalism'.[11] Any moral principle in the action was difficult to discover, Gentleman claimed, as Shakespeare pays too much attention to 'fate, necessity or predestination' and not enough to the capacity of the human mind to determine the destiny of the individual being. *Macbeth* was not, Gentleman insisted, a work to which 'young unsettled minds' should be exposed as 'whatever tends to weaken reason, to mislead the understanding, and intimidate the heart, should not be used as a subject for dramatic composition'.[12] Gentleman simply cannot accept the idea of blind fate. Nevertheless, while he insisted that the character of Macbeth was 'too disgraceful for nature to admit among her works', he had to acknowledge that 'there is not one personage to be found in our English drama which more strongly impresses an audience'.[13]

David Garrick would have agreed, as he considered Macbeth to be 'the most violent part I have'.[14] Nevertheless, when he revived the tragedy in 1744, he augmented rather than mitigated its savage and fatalistic atmosphere by largely rejecting Davenant's adaptation and returning to the work 'as written by Shakespeare'. Such claims of going back to the original were not always borne out in reality.[15] The introduction to the published text still had to object that in *Macbeth* 'the picture of the human

[11] Francis Gentleman, 'Notes to the Bell Edition of Garrick's Adaptation of *Macbeth*' (1773), quoted in *The Plays of David Garrick*, ed. Harry William Pedicord and Frederick Louis Bergmann, 7 vols. (Carbondale, 1982), vol. 3, p. 37. All references to Garrick's version from this edition.

[12] Francis Gentleman, *The Dramatic Censor*, 2 vols. (London, 1770; rep. New York, 1972), p. 104.

[13] Gentleman, *Censor*, pp. 106–7.

[14] Quoted in George Winchester Stone, Jr. and George M. Kahrl, *David Garrick: A Critical Biography* (Carbondale, 1980), pp. 557–8.

[15] It is possible that in early years of Garrick's *Macbeth* more passages from Davenant were included in performance than are found in his edition of the play. See Bartholomeusz, *Macbeth and the Players*, p. 59.

heart [is] rather too horrid'[16] but beyond cutting the actual representation of the murder of Lady Macduff and her family and trimming radically Malcolm's feigned self-accusations about his lust and cruelty, not much else that might have offended through its violence is omitted. The whole play is about 270 lines shorter than Shakespeare, with cuts made mainly in the interests of speeding up the action, omitting repetition, and clarifying obscure passages. Lady Macbeth is not present at the discovery of the murder as her fainting often elicited unsuitable laughter from the audience. Although the introduction claims that the witches are 'an insult to common sense', the only substantial part of Davenant that is retained are those passages relating to the witches, and Hecate still has a larger role than the Elizabethans gave her. The most celebrated interpolation comes at the end, where Garrick inserted an eight-line speech in which Macbeth moralizes upon the vanity of his ambitions and sinks, in his imagination, into the earth, in a manner reminiscent of Faustus or a repentant Don Juan.

> 'Tis done! the scene of life will quickly close.
> Ambition's vain, delusive dreams are fled,
> And now I wake to darkness, guilt and horror.
> I cannot bear it! Let me shake it off. –
> Twa' not be; my soul is clogged with blood.
> I cannot rise! I dare not ask for mercy.
> It is too late, hell drags me down. I sink,
> I sink – Oh! – my soul is lost forever!
> Oh! (*Dies*) (Garrick, 5.6.73–81)

This dying speech, combined with the retention of Davenant's avenging speech for Macduff, trenchantly emphasizes how the action ends with the restoration of the proper moral and political order.

Although Gentleman had problems with the play, he was full of praise for Garrick's performance of the leading role. Not only did Garrick counter the fatalistic tendency of the action, he even turned it to excellent effect. 'Mr Garrick's matchless genius', Gentleman wrote, 'not only captivates our sportive senses, but also furnishes highly relished substantial foods for our minds to strengthen by.'[17] This led him to attribute much nobleness to Macbeth in contrast to Lady Macbeth whom, in compensation, he regarded as an utter fiend. As Joseph Donohue has pointed out, the understanding of Macbeth's fundamental condition during the eighteenth century was that he was 'a figure for all virtuous men seduced and irredeemably betrayed by outside influences and, paradoxically, by their own innate sensibilities'.[18] This was a character paradigm that had been suggested at the end of the last century by Thomas Betterton, who, in Davenant's version, was never less than a gentleman in the role. Between him and Garrick, however, had come the portentous James Quin, whose brutal ranting Macbeth was the model against which Garrick had to work.

Garrick was aware that his Macbeth might not complement the taste of audiences who had been brought up on Quin's tragic style, something he tried to counter in the odd little pamphlet 'An Essay on Acting' published before he first acted the role. In this he treats his own style of acting satirically, describing the interpretation he will put onstage as 'the anti-climax, or rather the antipode of Shakespeare'.[19] For 'Shakespeare' one might more accurately read 'Quin'. Garrick's Macbeth, in contrast to Quin's, was more acted upon than acting. He was an urbane individual, an experienced general who is 'religiously humane', and he encounters an imaginative world of which he had previously no inkling. An innocent in a world of horror, he learnt about evil at the same time his audience did; hence he did not lead them like a confident villain into the depths of nightmare and bloodiness, rather the audience and the tragic king went hand in hand into an unknown world. Also, Garrick did not expend all his energies in the first two acts as did many for actors of the role – 'all the pith of it was [usually] exhausted', Thomas Davies commented, 'in the first and second acts of the

[16] Garrick, *Plays*, vol. 3, p. 4.

[17] Gentleman, *Censor*, p. 109.

[18] Joseph Donohue, *Dramatic Character in the English Romantic Age* (Princeton, 1970), p. 150.

[19] David Garrick, 'An Essay on Acting', *Actors on Acting*, ed. Toby Cole and Helen Krich Chinoy (New York, 1970), p. 133.

play'. Rather Garrick, with none of 'the drowsy and ineffectual manner' of his predecessors, strove 'to keep alive the attention of the spectators to the last syllable of so animated a character'.[20]

From the moment his Macbeth heard the witches' prophecy Garrick represented him in a state of possession, fascinated by possibilities that had never previously occurred to him. He did not eagerly leap toward Duncan's throne, but was driven there by steadily augmenting pressure, first from the unexpected kindling of his ambition, next from the persistent coercion of his wife, and then from a condition of satanic possession that seemed to overtake him as he contemplated the dagger. He stood helpless in the face of evil, a condition that reached its climax when he came face to face with the dreadful consequences of what he had done after the murder had been committed. Garrick's own words are most helpful here, as he gives a detailed description of Macbeth as a silent statue, petrified by the horror of the murder, so that his body seemed to occupy a different sphere from that of his soul. 'The murderer', he wrote, 'should be seen in every limb, and yet every member, at that instant, should be separated from his body, and his body from his soul. This is the picture of a complete regicide, and at that time the orb below should be hush as death.'[21] It is as if his soul dwells in the silent orb and his body, which has committed the murder, is elsewhere. This did not necessarily lead to exciting theatre; a member of the audience complained of Garrick's 'excessive dejectedness of his mind' and of his tendency to express 'grief more than horror',[22] but it was an attitude Garrick stuck by, for his Macbeth was never driven by active malice or confidence in his ambition.

Richard Cumberland, who considered Macbeth to be 'naturally noble', observed that, after he becomes king, he is forced to wade ever deeper into a sea of blood, acting 'more by desperation and dread than by any settled resolution or natural cruelty'.[23] This is what seems to have driven Garrick in the role. Terror possessed him with the appearance of Banquo's ghost, an obvious climax in the role, but one that had not been marked by previous Macbeths; indeed, it may have been at this point that the energy whose absence had been noted by the critical audience member erupted for the first time. In the final act, as Macbeth goes down, Garrick paid scant attention to his bodily pain but more to his inner agony so that Noverre, who wrote a wonderfully vivid account of how he acted the final speech, could claim that 'humanity triumphed over murder and barbarism'[24] as if the audience felt a touch of pity for a man who had found himself engaged with forces of the mind, nature, and the supernatural that were too large for him. Gentleman rejoiced at the moral lesson the ending taught the audience; it offered, he felt, the clearest instance in Shakespeare's plays of the workings of a moral order and therefore ultimately dispelled the deep reservations he had about the appeal of the work.

SCHILLER AND BENIGN FATE

The most widely performed version of *Macbeth* in Germany during the nineteenth century was the translation and adaptation by Johann Friedrich Schiller. The provenance of this version in Weimar Classicism is odd to say the least. Although Goethe and Schiller had been major figures in *Sturm und Drang* and associated with the nascent Romantic movement, the Weimar Court Theatre, which for a few years they both directed, was a model of late Enlightenment culture. Goethe, for example, did not regard its stage as a site for the existential torments of a Faust or the volatile outbursts of the heroes of *Sturm und Drang*. Instead Weimar Classicism articulated the optimistic outlook that humans are fundamentally noble and it is upon this assumption that social order is built. For Schiller especially, the end of tragic action was not the defeat of the

[20] Thomas Davies, *Dramatic Miscellanies*, 3 vols. (Dublin, 1784; rep. New York, 1971), vol. 2, p. 105.

[21] Garrick, *Actors on Acting*, p. 135.

[22] *The Private Correspondence of David Garrick*, ed. James Boaden, 2 vols. (London, 1831–2), vol. 1, p. 19.

[23] Richard Cumberland, *The Observer*, 8th edn, 3 vols. (London, 1808), vol. 2, p. 133.

[24] Jean Georges Noverre, *Letters on Dancing and Ballets*, trans. Cyril Beaumont (London, 1930), p. 84.

hero in the face of a hostile and inexplicable numen, but a victory for the human will in which 'a morally formed person' fights through to a detachment from life in which 'dissatisfaction with fate falls to the wayside'. At this point, the tragic hero achieves the recognition that there is 'a teleological connection among things, a sublime order, a benevolent will'.[25] In fact, few if any of Shakespeare's tragic heroes achieve this exalted condition, and none for any extended period of time. Macbeth might touch upon the sublime as he deplores the loneliness of his latter days and mourns the death of his wife, but he does not grow to recognize a benign order. In Schiller's version, Macbeth dies as defiant and confused as in Shakespeare, but the context of his fate is different. Schiller makes it clear that despite the destruction he has caused, Macbeth leaves a world that is in better order and less fragmented than it is at the close of Shakespeare's play.

One of the principal causes of the unease *Macbeth* created in the eighteenth century arose from the difficulty of distinguishing between the outer and inner worlds; how much are the supernatural forces impelling Macbeth the product of his own imagination and how much do they have an objective existence? If they are entirely the latter, how can the play accommodate itself to a view of the world that considers humanity to be fundamentally good? Garrick had solved the problem by sustaining the illusion that Macbeth has a basic innocence that remains untouched by all he encounters. Like Garrick, Schiller tried to maintain as much of the original play as he could. He was hampered by his poor English and was therefore overly reliant on previous prose translations by Wieland, Eschenburg and Heinrich Leopold Wagner,[26] so the simplification of complex metaphors in his text may have arisen as much from his difficulty in finding equivalents to the English in German than from an impulse to streamline Shakespeare's thought. Metaphors in Schiller's *Macbeth* are less particular and personal, characters address each other with greater formality, and Shakespeare's harsh humor and bitter irony have gone. Stylistically 'irregular' passages, such as Shakespeare's sudden switches to the intimacy of prose, are rewritten in verse, so that the majority of the play is delivered in stately decasyllabics. Cuts are relatively few, the only significant one being the usual omission of the murder of Lady Macduff and her son. There are, however, a number of passages that have been rewritten, not surprisingly in connection with the witches and Hecate.

That the universe is orderly is apparent from the opening scene in Schiller's *Macbeth*, which bears strikingly little resemblance to Shakespeare's. While the witches in Shakespeare's opening thirteen lines create a mood of anxiety and disturbing chill, in Schiller they have a frankly expositional function. They give specific information about the battle in which he has fought and they describe Macbeth in some detail. He is a noble hero whom they will bring down because of his good fortune, and, because he cannot protect his heart, it will be open to the power of the devil. They will destroy him because he is good and the powers of hell, for which they are mouthpieces, will thereby triumph. Schiller sets up a polarity different from that in Shakespeare, one that lies between the active malice of the witches and the passive goodness of Macbeth; Scotland will founder in the conflict between them. The witches, in fact, have a distinct purpose. If their accounts of their exploits are typical, they go through the world staging catastrophes that appear to have a moral end. They are not purely malicious like Shakespeare's. Rather than pointlessly torment the Master of the Tiger and his wife, they disturb the well-being of a poor but happy fisherman with vain dreams of gold, as if to preach, in the style of a moralistic fairy-tale, that to remain poor and happy one must not seek for riches (Schiller, 1.4, pp. 10–12).[27] They are not disgusting crones, but statuesque figures whom Banquo describes as

[25] Johann Friedrich Schiller, *Essays*, ed. Walter Hinderer and Daniel O. Dahlstrom, *The German Library*, 17 (New York, 1995), p. 9.

[26] *Schiller-Handbuch*, ed. Helmut Koopmann (Stuttgart, 1998), pp. 736–7.

[27] *Macbeth: Ein Trauerspiel von Shakespear zur Vorstellung auf dem Hoftheater zu Weimar, eingerichtet von Schiller* (Tübingen, 1801). All references to Schiller's adaptation from this edition.

'grau von Haaren, / . . . riesenhaft und schrecklich anzusehen!' ('grey of hair / . . . gigantic and terrible to look upon', Schiller, 1.5., p. 15).[28] Hecate does not have her own scene and only appears in the cave before Macbeth arrives to hear the prophecies. But when she is onstage, it is apparent that the supernatural world is ordered according to a strict hierarchy. The first half of her speech comes directly from Shakespeare (Schiller, 4.2, p. 101 and Shakespeare, 3.5.2–13), but the second half is original to Schiller. In it Hecate reveals that she knows the questions Macbeth will ask and how she will deliberately deceive him so that he becomes 'verwirrt und tollkühn' ('confused and foolhardy', Schiller, 2.4, p. 102), nothing more than a helpless victim with little responsibility for anything he does. Throughout the Cauldron scene, Hecate and the witches speak in regular rhyming octosyllabic couplets, an effect that highlights the artificiality of their show and makes it into a play within a play whose operations are transparent. In Schiller, as was largely the case in Davenant, the horrifying nightmare that Shakespeare's Macbeth experiences is objectified in a theatrical performance.

Although Schiller leaves the vast majority of Macbeth's role untouched, the sense that his fate is predetermined, his impersonality, and the regular, elevated tone of his language make him rather a dull character. As he is, according to the witches, a noble soul who is to be punished because he is fortunate, his dreadful fall does not seem to be the consequence of what he intrinsically is. The Captain's description of his bravery in battle has none of the savage excess that makes Shakespeare's Macbeth into such a fearsome figure, and when he first appears, he shows himself to be quite a rational individual. He is exercised less by fascination with the powers of darkness in himself as by external questions, interpolated by Schiller, over whether the murder of Duncan will really aid his ambition and not just serve the interests of Malcolm and Donalbain, whom he considers almost insuperable obstacles between him and the throne (Schiller, 1.15, p. 37). He is driven as much to the murder through observations made by Lady Macbeth that the thanes will never accept the child Malcolm as king as by any internal compulsion. Throughout, he displays a clear grasp of the objective political world in which he lives, so we never see it as we do in Shakespeare, coloured by Macbeth's feverish imagination, unruly ambition and abject fear. The downfall of Schiller's Macbeth is a matter of course, effected by machinery which had been set in motion early in the play.

The conflict of the play takes place therefore less within the mind of Macbeth, more within the society that suffers from his calamitous encounter with the witches. But even the devastation wreaked on Scotland is placed, as it were, at arm's length, most obviously through excising the death of Lady Macduff and her children because it is the most personal event in Shakespeare's play. In Shakespeare, the raw horror of Duncan's murder is also intensified by the apocalyptic drunkenness of the Porter, so that we may speculate that disorder at the level of the rulers is paralleled by disorder among the ruled. But Schiller uses the song of his sober Porter as genuine comic, though unfunny, relief, as he sings a *Morgenlied* in which the terrors of the night are banished by the rising of the sun and insists that he must complete his prayers prior to opening the gate to Ross and Macduff. Although Schiller does not cut subsequent references to the turbulent weather and the unnatural wildness of Duncan's horses, the eternal night that sets in in Shakespeare's play after Macbeth's murder of Duncan is mitigated in Schiller as the rays of the sun hailed by the Porter enlighten the following acts.

As we have seen above, English versions of *Macbeth*, Davenant's especially, emphasized the retribution brought on Macbeth's head by Malcolm's invasion of Scotland. Goethe rather than Schiller was responsible for structuring the play when it was performed at Weimar and, while he did

[28] In a revival of the play in Weimar in 1804, the three witches were beautiful young ladies. But in either case, they are phenomenologically separate from Macbeth, 'demons of nature who envy the happiness of mankind'. Hans Heinrich Borcherdt, 'Einführung: *Macbeth*, *Schillers Werke*, Nationalausgabe', 42 vols. (Weimar, 1943–2000), vol. 13, p. 312.

not cut much out of Act 5,[29] he followed neoclassical principles in sculpting the action so that the conflict between the warring troops was more clearly and unambiguously represented. Shakespeare's fragmentary scenes of Malcolm's invading forces and the Scottish troops led by Menteith and Caithness that join with them are combined into one extended scene in which the stage gradually fills with troops whose leaders successively declare their loyalty to Malcolm as if they are fulfilling a holy mission. The scene ends with the cutting of the boughs of Birnam Wood, as if these are the weapons that will overcome Macbeth. Schiller is almost as sparing of stage directions as Shakespeare, but he specifies that in the final scene the perspective stage on which the play was performed should be opened to its fullest depth and the invading army be seen advancing in slow steps toward the front of the stage. The attention to the ritual of battle more than to the individual agony of the fighters is characteristic of Schiller's *Macbeth* as a whole. At the end, there was more rejoicing over an order restored than the death of a bloody hero.

VERDI, LADY MACBETH AND GRAND OPERA

The Enlightenment view of *Macbeth* as a play in which an erring and ambitious monarch falls prey to forces of divine and social retribution that he has called upon himself is still more than vestigial in the operatic version by Giuseppe Verdi. On first sight this seems against historical sense. After all, Verdi's opera has all the trappings of romantic theatre and much of his music effectively actualizes those darker strata of the imagination that words can only allude to. In operatic guise Macbeth has all the potential of becoming a romantic hero whose personality has a potent and baleful influence on the world around him. But in Verdi this does not quite happen. There can be no doubt that he had a full, some might even say excessive appreciation of the tragic import of the action – 'The tragedy', he wrote, 'is one of the greatest creations of man!'[30] He claimed to have read Shakespeare since his youth and, as a dramatist in music, he welcomed the opportunity of adapting his plays because his characters were more complex and multilayered than the essentially melodramatic figures in most of the libretti he set. Because his adaptation of *Macbeth* is quite successful in realizing a greater subtlety in character, it has often been described as the first truly 'Shakespearian' opera. But it is not entirely successful. This has often been attributed to its stylistic inconsistencies, as it was first written for performance in Florence in 1847, at a point when Verdi was coming to the end of the first phase of his career in which he wrote operas structured primarily upon discrete musical numbers in the Rossinian bel canto tradition, the prime intention of which was the display of singers' voices. He was beginning to envision a mode of opera which attended instead to the needs of the dramatic action; in fact, he famously suggested that the singers playing Macbeth and Lady Macbeth should be less concerned with the beauty of their voices and more with their appropriateness to the emotions required by the dramatic moment. Hence, Lady Macbeth should not be beautiful but appear 'ugly and evil' and sing with 'a harsh, stifled, and hollow voice'.[31] If the initial version of *Macbeth* was stylistically mixed, such disparities became even more apparent when Verdi revised it for the first performance in Paris at the Théâtre-Lyrique in 1865, in which substantial new passages, written in the style of his mature middle period, coexisted with passages recalling the young, inexperienced composer.

But, as many critics have recently argued, stylistic irregularity does not mean that a work is weak.[32] The uncertainty *Macbeth* causes may arise from Verdi's own uncertainty as to where the dramatic centre of his work lay. While he insisted

[29] *Der Briefwechsel zwischen Schiller und Goethe*, ed. Hans Gerhard Gräf and Albert Leitzmann, 3 vols. (Leipzig, 1955), vol. 2, p. 310.

[30] Verdi to Francesco Piave, 4.9.1846, in *Verdi's Macbeth: A Sourcebook*, ed. David Rosen and Andrew Porter (New York & London, 1984), p. 8.

[31] Verdi to Salvatore Cammarano, *Sourcebook*, p. 67.

[32] Gary Schmidgall, *Literature as Opera* (New York, 1977), p. 208.

that there are only three characters in the work, Lady Macbeth, Macbeth, and the witches,[33] he also thought of it as a stage spectacle: 'in short', he wrote, 'the things that need special care in this work are: *Chorus and Machinery*'.[34] While most of the mechanic effects relate to the witches, their very presence encouraged audiences and critics in Florence in 1847 to think of it as a spectacular opera in the vein of Meyerbeer and Weber.[35] When Verdi revised *Macbeth* for its premiere in Paris, while he added an aria and duet for the principals, he also composed some effectively atmospheric ballet music and added choruses to the final act, which heightened the affinity of the work to French grand opera. Verdi considered this version to supercede the earlier work.[36] French grand opera, however, was a genre that, for all of its spectacle, presented an unheroic view of life, one in which any potential for heroic action on the part of an individual that might exercise either a malign or auspicious influence on social or political events was swept away by the forces of history. One of Verdi's signal achievements would be to counter this tendency by progressively representing the individual as a powerful agent in the social world, but in neither the 1847 or 1865 versions of *Macbeth* did he go the full course.

The nature of music as a dramatic medium requires that operas adapted from plays can never replicate the original action and dialogue in all their detail and intricacy, and Verdi's *Macbeth* is no exception. It is a stripped-down version of Shakespeare's tragedy, but it does not depart from the original that radically. Piave's libretto, much-maligned in its time, not only sticks close to the action, but the majority of it is taken directly from Shakespeare.[37] Some of Shakespeare is, surprisingly, passed over, notably almost the entire conversation between Macbeth and Lady Macbeth prior to the murder, and incidental scenes, such as the Porter, dialogues on the condition of Scotland, Macbeth's colloquy with the murderers, the murder of Lady Macduff, and the long scene between Malcolm and Macduff, are gone. The music is stylistically uneven to a degree that causes uncertainty as to how we are to understand the dramatic setting – the chorus of witches can sound tritely gleeful as well as threatening,[38] armies and royal processions materialize to buoyant, optimistic rhythms, the chorus of murderers awaiting Macbeth sounds comically bouncy, while the banquet scene begins with music more appropriate to a nineteenth-century soiree – but there is much powerful atmospheric writing as well. Not only can Verdi evoke an eerily Gothic atmosphere that produces some genuinely frightening moments, but when the libretto gives him the opportunity, his music provides access to levels of emotional confusion, mystery, and despair, which provide some of the most disturbing moments in romantic theatre.

Nevertheless, the dramatic polarity of Verdi's *Macbeth* belongs more to the Enlightenment than it does to romanticism. The witches are not three individual women but a triple chorus, reminiscent of Davenant, and they possess the same objective status as in Davenant and Schiller.[39] They can see into the future and although Hecate is absent as a singing character – she appears briefly in the ballet during the cauldron scene – they are clearly acting as agents of hell. The visions with which they confuse Macbeth are an elaborate theatrical show and the ballet written in 1865 skillfully intensifies the preternatural atmosphere. The

---

33 Verdi to Marie Escudier, 8.2.1865, *Sourcebook*, p. 99.

34 Verdi to Antonio Lanari, 15.10.1846, *Sourcebook*, p. 11.

35 Marcello Conati, 'Aspects of the Production of *Macbeth*', *Sourcebook*, pp. 231–4.

36 Roger Parker, '*Macbeth*', *The New Grove Dictionary of Opera*, ed. Stanley Sadie, 4 vols. (London, 1994), vol. 3, p. 111.

37 William Weaver discusses the Italian translations available to Verdi and his librettists in 'The Shakespeare Verdi Knew', *Sourcebook*, 144–7.

38 'Verdi's witches, like Shakespeare's, are out of St Trinians's.' Julian Budden, *The Operas of* Verdi, 2 vols. rev. edn (Oxford, 1992), vol. 1, p. 282. While I can agree with Budden on Verdi's witches, I am mystified as to why he would write this about Shakespeare's.

39 Frits Noske, *The Signifier and the Signified: Studies in the Operas of Mozart and Verdi* (Nijhoff, 1977), pp. 247–8. Noske suggests that Verdi would have known of Schiller's version as Count Maffei, a collaborator on the libretto, was familiar with Schiller's plays.

witches, who are unambiguously evil, do not find their thematic counterparts in the Macbeths, who are clearly swayed by them, but in the people of Scotland. The people are first heard at the end of Act 1, when, in the opera's most impressive ensemble, they call down heaven's vengeance on the head of Duncan's murderer. The subsequent action is no less than a fulfillment of that curse, which leads to the reaffirmation of an order whose durability will be guaranteed through a union of royalty and the divine guarding of the interests of a people who are bound by a sense of national identity. The ubiquity of the chorus in Verdi's *Macbeth*, be it as witches, murderers, members of the court, or exiles on the border of England and Scotland, gives the action a highly public profile and it was one that was greatly enhanced by the additions of 1865. While Shakespeare's *Macbeth* is a private tragedy with public ramifications, in Verdi's opera the public world does not so much serve as a background against which the private drama is played out, but becomes a presence that draws our attention away from conflict within individuals to its wider political and religious ramifications.

It is, however, difficult even within the tormented relationship of the Macbeths to find a point of gravity. Although Macbeth's career has the same disastrous trajectory in Verdi's opera as in Shakespeare's play, there are moments when he is oddly in danger of becoming a minor figure. Act 1, in this four-act work, covers the action to the discovery of the murder, climaxing with the mighty imprecations of the court upon the head of the murderer. But throughout the act, Macbeth strangely fails to establish himself as a dominant figure. A haunting duet, 'Due vaticini compiuti or sono' ('Two prophecies have come to pass', Verdi, 1.3, p. 63,[40] corresponding to Shakespeare, 1.3.126–41), in which Macbeth meditates on the witches' prophecies, provides a brief insight into how he is fascinated by evil, but Banquo invades his privacy with speculations on whether he is not already ambitious for the crown. The dagger speech – 'Ma si affaccia un pugnal?' ('Is this a dagger before me?' Verdi, 1.11, p. 66) – is one of those moments where Verdi abandons the melodically structured forms of Rossinian opera for a nascent music drama in which the music has no form of its own but fills out the meaning of the words and highlights their dramatic value. In the context of Verdi's work as a whole, it is an impressive advance, but the solo music in Act 1 that has the greatest impact is the more conventional scena and cavatina of Lady Macbeth, 'Vieni! t'affretta accendere' ('Hie thee hither', Verdi, 1.5, p. 64, corresponding to Shakespeare, 1.5.23–8), in which she envisages Macbeth ascending the throne. The brilliant cabaletta, which requires a dramatic soprano of uncommon agility and weightiness of voice, establishes Lady Macbeth as a vastly more dominant figure than her husband. She does not suffer from self-doubt and is driven by an overwhelming confidence. The great duet that follows the murder of Duncan is muted, a hurried colloquy in which Macbeth fights the growing terror and guilt at what he has done. It is intensely atmospheric; Verdi instructed that it should be sung 'sotto voce, but in a hollow voice such as to arouse terror',[41] so it requires no spectacular display of vocal prowess and flickers out uncannily in fear and confusion. But in opera, for good or ill, it is often volume and size that determine the final impression, and in the ensemble that brings the act to a rousing end, while the Macbeths have prominent parts in the larger vocal landscape, they do not exercise a commanding presence.

Macbeth never really does. One of the strangely moving aspects of Shakespeare's play is the mutual isolation that inserts itself between Macbeth and Lady Macbeth as soon as Macbeth ascends the throne; in Verdi's opera, however, they remain closely bound to each other, and Lady Macbeth grows rather than declines in stature, as she does in Shakespeare. This was clearly Verdi's intention, as in the Paris version he added an aria for Lady

---

40 Giuseppe Verdi, *Macbeth*, Opera Guide Series 41 (London, 1990), p. 63. All subsequent references are to the libretto in this edition, though I have translated the first lines myself as Jeremy Sams' translation in this edition was intended for the stage and does not always capture the literal meaning of the Italian.

41 Verdi to Felice Varesi, 7.1.1847, *Sourcebook* , p. 31.

Macbeth that is both eerie and violent, 'La luce langue', ('Light is fading', Verdi, 2.2, p. 72) based on lines that Shakespeare had used to convey the mesmeric power of Macbeth's imagination, 'Light thickens, /And the crow makes wing to the rooky wood' (Shakespeare, 3.2.50–1). It is Lady Macbeth, therefore, rather than her husband who is closer to being the central consciousness of the action. The aria's furious cabaletta, devoted to her anticipation of Banquo's murder, of which she has full knowledge, makes her into the driving force of the action just at the point where in Shakespeare she is going into decline. Because of this, Macbeth is scarcely the haunted figure he is in Shakespeare. He is not visited by nightmares and in contemplating Banquo's death is obsessed solely with questions of succession. In fact, the tragic heart of Verdi's Act 2 lies not with Macbeth at all, but with Banquo, whose brooding aria prior to his murder, 'Come dal ciel precipita' ('How the darkness falls', Verdi, 2.4, p. 73, corresponding to Shakespeare, 3.3.18), touches a level of anxious foreboding that Macbeth never reaches. Verdi's Macbeth does rise to impressive heights of terror and defiance in his confrontation with Banquo's ghost, but even here the banquet scene is held together by Lady Macbeth, whose 'brindisi' – drinking song – provides an upbeat rhythm that is impervious to Macbeth's outbursts and establishes her as unquestionably the more powerful dramatic agent. That she more than her husband is the protagonist was emphasized further in another addition for Paris, a perfunctory duet between Macbeth and Lady Macbeth after the cauldron scene (Verdi, 3.4, p. 83), which has no parallel in Shakespeare. In it the two swear to murder their way into total control of the crown of Scotland and its succession. Where Shakespeare represented Macbeth degenerating into a dangerously isolated despair, Verdi has him whipped into further action by his vengeful wife.

Even in the final act Macbeth has to struggle to occupy the centre of the action. Verdi bestows his most affecting music on the sleepwalking scene, in which a poignant extended melody that occupies the centre of the prelude to the opera returns and melodic fragments from earlier passages transform a character of unqualified villainy suddenly into a figure of immense pathos. Macbeth achieves some stature in his final aria, 'Pietà, rispetto, amore' ('Compassion, respect, love', Verdi, 4.5, p. 88, corresponding to Shakespeare, 5.3.22–8), after the news of Lady Macbeth's death. Here he reveals a capacity for nobility that has, perhaps, been latent in his character all along and it culminates in one of Verdi's characteristically broad melodies, accompanied by the strings in unison, which at last bestows upon him a heroic stature that he had previously never acquired. But it is a conventional declaration of heroism, with none of the searching pathos of Macbeth's philosophical farewell to life in Shakespeare. Verdi's Macbeth dies like Garrick's, in a brief aria,[42] in which he recognizes himself accursed by heaven and his death as a just retribution for his sins.

Some critics of Verdi have found the protagonists in *Macbeth* to be more central to the action than I do. Gilles De Van, citing Verdi's claim that the great duet of Act 1 and Lady Macbeth's sleepwalking scene are the central moments of the score, argues eloquently that Verdi 'beyond doubt . . . preferred to emphasize the scene of conscience rather than that of the outside world, psychological drama rather than epic conflict, the twilight within souls rather than clarity of actions'.[43] But while he may have preferred an action with more interiority, often the sheer impact of performance speaks differently and, with an effective chorus, in performance tragedy and redemption can seem to reside as much if not more in the public domain of the action than the private. Act 4 begins, not with the sleepwalking scene, but with an interpolated chorus, again added for Paris, in which Scottish exiles bewail their fate. This is an impressive addition and is no mere repetition of the famous chorus of the Hebrew slaves from *Nabucco* with which Verdi had

[42] Schmidgall, *Literature*, p. 210. Verdi cut Macbeth's death aria in the 1865 version, but today the 1865 score is the one most frequently performed, usually with Macbeth's death aria included.

[43] Gilles De Van, *Verdi's Theater*, trans. Gilda Roberts (Chicago, 1998), p. 218.

initially made his mark as an opera composer. It is a disturbing piece built on broken melodies to sparse accompaniment, a visceral representation of homelessness and lack of orientation. In contrast, the opera ends with a rousing chorus in which the buoyant rhythms of the victorious male army at first contrast and then unite with the women's hymn of praise for the transformation that Scotland is now celebrating. It is one of Verdi's strongest and most ecstatic finales, and one of his most uncharacteristic, as he normally ended his tragedies focused exclusively on the predicament of the tragic characters. But the closing chorus of his final version of *Macbeth* announces that the devastation caused by Macbeth's cataclysmic rule has been overcome and that the wounds that it opened will be healed. It is an ending that denies tragedy rather than dwelling, as Shakespeare's and most of Verdi's endings do, upon its persistence. In the celebration of a renewed national unity, the brutal career of Macbeth is entirely forgotten.

It is unlikely that the capacity of Macbeth to serve as the conduit through which we apprehend both the physical and metaphysical realms of the play was ever fully realized onstage for much longer than the first two hundred years after its first performance. There were many reasons for this. Censorship and conventions of performance from Davenant to Verdi would rarely allow the crime of regicide to be represented onstage and even the slightest possibility that audiences might identify with one who committed it would be suppressed.[44] Furthermore, neither the Enlightenment nor the romantic age believed in the inexorability of tragedy, so the dark universe we see through Macbeth's eyes does not serve as the sole determining force in human life. Then the fundamentally lyrical nature of the play was difficult to represent through the theatrical conventions of these times as the stage was normally regarded as symbolic of the objective world of the individual within which he lived, not of the subjective perspective through which he sees.

The fascination that Macbeth can exercise on his audience is, perhaps, a relatively recent theatrical phenomenon. Other actors of the romantic age, notably Edmund Kean and William Charles Macready, either represented him as an unrelieved villain akin to Richard III or with a distinct leaning toward nobility. Only at the end of the nineteenth century, with the performances of virtuosi actors such as Henry Irving, Friedrich Mitterwurzer, and Adalbert Matkowsky, did the violence and the vitality of Macbeth's imagination speak to audiences in contradictory yet strangely credible ways.[45] It may only have been with the coming of expressionism that the idea of the stage as a means of reflecting the inner consciousness of the character enabled performances of *Macbeth* that fully realized the disturbing dramaturgy of Shakespeare's tragedy and for the first time since the early seventeenth century returned Macbeth to himself.

---

[44] See 'A Note on Censorship' in *Sourcebook*, pp. 356–8, for an entertaining listing of the absurd alternatives the censors thought up for Macbeth's crime. In Palermo (1852) and Messina (1853) he did not murder King Duncan, but a wealthy retainer of the king, Count Walfred, whose position he coveted; in Rome (1852) the censors would allow nothing sacrilegious onstage, so the witches were turned into gypsies.

[45] See Simon Williams, 'The Tragic Actor', *The Cambridge Companion to Shakespeare on Stage*, ed. Stanley Wells and Sarah Stanton (Cambridge, 2002), pp. 128–30.

'TWO TRUTHS ARE TOLD': AFTERLIVES AND HISTORIES OF MACBETHS

WILLIAM C. CARROLL

Shakespeare's *Macbeth* made an immediate impression on his Jacobean contemporaries. Within a year or two of its first performance (late 1605 – early 1606, according to most scholars), one of the play's key scenes – the appearance of Banquo's ghost in 4.1 – had already been alluded to in Middleton's *The Puritan, or the Widow of Watling-Street*,[1] and parodied in Beaumont's *The Knight of the Burning Pestle*, when Jasper enters, '*his face mealed*' (5.1.4 SD).[2] Thomas Middleton seems to have been involved in making additions to Shakespeare's text – the songs in 3.5 and 4.1, and possibly more – after 1609.[3] In 1611, Simon Forman recorded details of a performance of the play at the Globe Theatre, including the evidently memorable scene of Banquo's ghost appearing, in addition to extensive commentary on the witches and their prophecies, and Lady Macbeth's sleepwalking scene.[4] After the Restoration, Davenant's adaptation of Shakespeare's *Macbeth* (1673) became highly successful[5] – Pepys recorded attending multiple performances – and inspired its own parody by Thomas Duffet in 1674.[6] A succession of the greatest actors and actresses of the late seventeenth and eighteenth centuries performed the lead roles. By the twentieth century, Shakespeare's *Macbeth* had become the sole origin of what might be called 'Macbeth-discourse', the only version of the story known to most readers and audiences; famous lines and scenes from the play had entered the general cultural lexicon as suitable for appropriation by commercial and other interests, and a feature film released in 2000, *Scotland, PA*, resituated the play to a fast-food restaurant in America.[7]

Yet it is worth noting that for centuries before Shakespeare's play, and for a century and a half after his play, another version of Macbeth – its afterlife significant in political as well as literary terms – continued in parallel to, and at times

[1] 'Instead of a jester, we'll have the ghost in the white sheet sit at the upper end of the table' (4.3), in *Disputed Plays of William Shakespeare*, ed. William Kozlenko (New York, 1974); the play is usually dated 1607.

[2] 'When thou art at thy table with thy friends, / Merry in heart, and filled with swelling wine, / I'll come in midst of all thy pride and mirth, / Invisible to all men but thyself' (5.1.22–5), in Francis Beaumont, *The Knight of the Burning Pestle*, ed. Michael Hattaway (London, 1995). See several other early allusions in *Macbeth*, ed. A. R. Braunmuller (Cambridge, 1997), pp. 58–60, and in the *Shakspere Allusion-Book*, ed. John Munro, 2 vols. (London, 1909).

[3] For a useful discussion of Middleton's contribution to the Folio text, see *Macbeth*, ed. Braunmuller, pp. 255–9, as well as Geoffrey Bullough, *Narrative and Dramatic Sources of Shakespeare*, vol. 7 (New York, 1973), pp. 424–5.

[4] E. K. Chambers, *William Shakespeare: A Study of Facts and Problems*, 2 vols. (Oxford, 1930), vol. 2, pp. 337–8. Forman's account of this production, like those of the other plays he visited, omits many key, even spectacular scenes, confuses others, at times seems to refer to stage actions he must have witnessed, and also seems to reflect his reading of Holinshed's account.

[5] Davenant greatly expanded the musical content as well as adding wholly new scenes concerning the Macduff family.

[6] Duffet's parody is the 'Epilogue' to his play *The Empress of Morocco. A Farce* (London, 1674); see the transcription in *Macbeth: Texts and Contexts*, ed. William C. Carroll (New York, 1999).

[7] A recent automobile ad heralded its new model with the words 'Something wicked this way comes', the writer perhaps not thinking that a demonic association might be off-putting to some drivers.

intersecting with, the Shakespearian version. This other version of the Macbeth narrative might be termed 'Buchanan's Macbeth', as it derives primarily though not entirely from the Scottish historian George Buchanan's account of Macbeth in his *Rerum Scoticarum historia*, published in Latin in 1582.[8] Buchanan's history was condemned by the Scottish Parliament in 1584 and termed a piece of 'infamous invective' by James himself in his *Basilikon Doron*.[9] To summarize all too briefly a well-known and complex story, Buchanan's history, along with his *De jure regni apud Scotos* ('The Powers of the Crown in Scotland'), 1579, provided important historical evidence for European writers seeking to advance a theory of royal succession based on election rather than inheritance, and to counter monarchical claims of absolute powers and prerogatives.[10] In justifying the deposition of Charles I in *The Tenure of Kings and Magistrates* (1649), John Milton quite logically returned to Buchanan (among others), who had justified the deposition of Mary Queen of Scots in the *De jure*, and whose *History* exemplified and continued the justification of his theories of succession. In his *Defensio pro populo Anglicano* ('A defence of the English people'), 1651, Milton simply replied to those who questioned the legality of a limited government, 'For Scotland I refer you to Buchanan'.[11] It might seem, in the years after the Restoration, that the Royalist position was victorious, and that the indefeasible right of inheritance would once again become the settled theory of succession for the British monarchy, but the constitutional crises of 1688–9 and at the end of Queen Anne's reign brought the same issues to the boil again. A full hundred years after his *History* was published posthumously, Buchanan's arguments and examples remained touchstones for polemicists on both sides of the question.[12]

For writers long before even Buchanan, the period of Scottish history just before and after Macbeth's reign was highly eventful in terms of contemporary issues of sovereignty and succession, as well as the links between England and Scotland; as Hector Boece noted in 1527, 'Be chance of sindry seasonis, specialy about the time of King Malcolme Canmore, al thingis began to change. For quhen oure nichtbouris the Britonis war maid effeminat be lang sleuth and doung out of Britane be the Saxonis in [i.e., into] Walis, we began to have alliance . . . with Inglismen.'[13] As Buchanan summarized in Book Seven of his *History*, the real problems in the Scottish monarchy began with King Kenneth III and his son Malcolm II, who 'did strive, to settle the Succession to the Crown in their Families, *That the Eldest Son might succeed the Father*' (7.205) – that is, in altering the traditional system of succession through alternation between parallel lines of descent (and sometimes to someone not related at all) to one of inherited lineal descent: from succession by election to succession by blood inheritance, as the terms would be simplified in debate through the next century and more.

---

[8] The text quoted here is the English translation by T. Page, London, 1690, hereafter cited in the text by book and page number.

[9] James connected Buchanan's history in this passage to John Knox's as well in his *Basilikon Doron* (*The Political Works of James I*, ed. C. H. McIlwain (Cambridge, Mass., 1918), p. 40).

[10] On these topics, see especially Quentin Skinner, *The Foundations of Modern Political Thought*, 2 vols. (Cambridge, 1978), and Howard Nenner, *The Right to Be King: The Succession to the Crown of England 1603–1714* (Chapel Hill, 1995).

[11] Don M. Wolfe, ed., *The Complete Prose Works of John Milton* (New Haven, 1966), vol. 4, p. 481.

[12] Buchanan was frequently paired with his Catholic parallel (but in every other way, his opposite), the Jesuit Robert Parsons, whose infamous work, *A Conference about the Next Succession to the Crown of England* (N. [Antwerp], 1594) appeared under the pseudonym, 'R. Doleman'. Parsons's and Buchanan's provocative books were still being quoted and reviled a century later, as is evident in the subtitles of works by the royalist supporter, Sir George Mackenzie: *Jus Regium: Or, the Just, and Solid Foundations of Monarchy . . . Maintain'd against Buchannan* [sic], *Naphtali, Dolman, Milton, &c.* (Edinburgh, 1684) and *That the Lawful Successor Cannot be Debarr'd From Succeeding to the Crown: Maintained against Dolman, Buchannan* [sic], *and others* (Edinburgh, 1684), and in William Assheton's *The Royal Apology or, An Answer to the Rebels Plea: Wherein, The Most Noted Anti-Monarchical Tenents, First Published by Doleman the Jesuit . . . Are distinctly consider'd* (London, 1684).

[13] Translation by John Bellenden, c. 1533; quoted in Arthur H. Williamson, *Scottish National Consciousness in the Age of James VI* (Edinburgh, 1979), p. 117. Malcolm Canmore is the Malcolm crowned at the end of Shakespeare's play.

The irony, Buchanan noted, was that this Malcolm did not leave a male heir, but had two daughters, one called Beatrix, married off to an important thane of the western islands, Abthane, while the other daughter, Doaca, was married to the Thane of Angus, 'by whom he begot *Mackbeth* or *Macbeda*' (7.206). When this Malcolm II died, the crown was worn by the nephew of the daughter Beatrix, one '*Donaldus*', or Duncan.

In Buchanan's narrative, Duncan is an 'effeminate and slothful King' (7.207), incapable of effective rule, as a result of which '*Mackbeth* . . . thereupon had conceived a secret Hope of the Kingdom in his Mind' (7.210). Moreover, Duncan made his son '*Malcolm*, scarce yet out of his Childhood, Governor of *Cumberland*. *Mackbeth* took this matter mighty Hainously; in regard, he look'd upon it as Obstacle of Delay to him, in his obtaining the Kingdom' since 'the Government of *Cumberland* was always look'd upon, as the first step to the Kingdom of *Scotland*' (7.210). Duncan's naming of Malcolm, an attempt to reinstitute Kenneth's change in the system of succession, is thus a prime but typical example of the perils of the new system, in which an incompetent could become king (Malcolm was 'scarce yet out of his Childhood', 7.210); moreover, the violation of the old system offends those who rest their belief in tradition. In Buchanan's version, Macbeth is certainly a violent warrior and an ambitious man, as he is in Shakespeare's, but he is also more clearly wronged, and in some ways had, as David Norbrook has noted in an important essay, 'half-buried associations with constitutionalist traditions', a figure in whom 'vestiges remain of a worldview in which regicide could be a noble rather than an evil act'.[14] Norbrook is referring here to the larger argument of Buchanan and others that the king derives his sovereign power from the consent of the people, in a contractural sense, and that it was not only possible but sometimes even necessary (as in the case of Mary Queen of Scots) for the monarch to be deposed or otherwise 'removed' from power. The history of the Scottish monarchy, Buchanan showed through example after example, was that tyranny resulted from such impulses as Kenneth's, and tyrannicide was not only possible, but virtually an obligation for a free people. Such arguments resonated throughout the seventeenth century, particularly in times of constitutional crisis, and the narrative of Macbeth would be continually appropriated and re-told by both royalists and their opponents, for the Macbeth narrative foregrounds the same problems of sovereign authority that were continually at stake. When Milton mused over five possible 'Scotch Stories' suitable as subjects for tragedy, one was the story of 'Kenneth who having privily poison'd Malcolm Duffe, that his own son might succeed is slain by Fenela', and the next the story of 'Macbeth beginning at the arrivall of Malcolm at Mackduffe. The matter of Duncan may be express't by the appearing of his ghost.'[15]

As popular as Shakespeare's *Macbeth* was, Buchanan's account also continued to be both available and widely quoted, and was more influential for some discourse, as we shall see, than Shakespeare's; at times, some writers merged aspects of both narratives, but the differences between the

[14] David Norbrook, '*Macbeth* and the Politics of Historiography', in *Politics of Discourse: The Literature and History of Seventeenth-Century England*, ed. Kevin Sharpe and Steven N. Zwicker (Berkeley, 1987), p. 116. Norbrook argues that Shakespeare seems to have been aware of Buchanan's account of Macbeth, perhaps through direct knowledge, perhaps through the 1587 edition of Holinshed's chronicles of Scotland, as the editor Francis Thynne had drawn 'on Buchanan to correct some points in earlier sections of the chronicle and to bring the narrative up to date beyond the point at which Boece [upon whose history Holinshed had drawn for the 1577 edition] had broken off' (p. 81), although, as Norbrook goes on to note, Thynne did so 'without enthusiasm' (p. 81), given Buchanan's controversial association with theories of deposition and regicide. Some of these 1587 additions were in any event ordered to be cut before publication.

[15] *The Works of John Milton* (New York, 1938), vol. 18, p. 245. Stories two and three in the list also concern the same period of Scottish history – 'Duffe & Donwald' and 'Haie the plowman'. Three of the five include a witch or a ghost – Scotland must have still seemed a bizarre place to the English. Milton of course also knew Shakespeare's play well (e.g. '*Adam* could not, but wept, / Though not of Woman born', *Paradise Lost* XI.496–7, *John Milton: Complete Poems and Major Prose*, ed. Merritt Y. Hughes (New York, 1957)).

two accounts are crucial. In Buchanan's version, the traitor Macdonwald commits suicide, and Macbeth then cuts off his head 'and hung up the rest of his Body, for all to behold, in a conspicuous place' (7.208). Sweno and the Norwegians are overcome not in open battle, but through the cunning administration of drugged wine ('made of Barly-Malt, mixed with the juice of a Poysonous Herb, whereof abundance grows in *Scotland*, called, *Somniferous Night-shade*', 7.209), sent by the Scots as part of a peace offering. There are no witches in Buchanan, as the prophecies appear to Macbeth in a dream; the prophetesses are not ugly hags, but 'Three Women, whose Beauty was more August and Surprizing than bare Womens useth to be' (7.210). In the dream, the women hail Macbeth first as '*Thane* of *Angus*', then '*Thane* of *Murray*', and then 'King of *Scotland*' (7.210). Lady Macbeth is mentioned only briefly, as spurring Macbeth on by 'daily Importunities' (7.210). Once king, Macbeth 'Enacted many good and useful' laws, and governed so well 'for ten years, that, if he had not obtained it by Violence, he might have been accounted inferior to none of the former Kings' (7.211). But eventually 'he converted his Government, got by Treachery, into a Cruel Tyranny' (7.211), and had Banquo murdered (whose own prophecy had been spread 'among the Vulgar' by 'Some ill Men', not witches). After the murder of Banquo, Macbeth 'broke forth into open Tyranny' (7.212) – hence justifying his overthrow, in Buchanan's thinking – and was overthrown by King Edward's 'Ten Thousand Men' (7.214); Malcolm's men 'stuck up green Boughs in their Helmets, representing an Army Triumphing' (7.214), but there is no second set of prophecies by the witches. Buchanan concludes his section on Macbeth by reminding his readers again that 'In the first Ten [years of Macbeth's rule], he performed the Duty of a very good King; in the last Seven, he equalled the Cruelty of the worst of Tyrants' (7.214). Shakespeare's version, derived substantially from Holinshed's account, itself deriving from Hector Boece's, includes much supernatural machinery, amplifies Macbeth's personal actions (e.g. Shakespeare's Macbeth slays Macdonwald himself), suppresses all reference to the ten years of Macbeth's good rule, and demotes Banquo from co-conspirator to conflicted but morally upright contrast. The slight reference to Lady Macbeth in Buchanan turns into the richly complex portrayal in Shakespeare (derived in part from Holinshed's account of the ambitious wife to Donwald in the account of King Duff's murder). To oversimplify, Shakespeare's version does not avoid the constitutional issues of succession and the origins of sovereign power; if anything, it mystifies them, multiplying the possibilities within the play (four different kings are shown or mentioned, each of whom has become king in a different way, each with different charismatic authority), and seeming not to choose among them; Buchanan's version, by contrast, presents a simpler, more admonitory narrative, stripped of the supernatural and other bizarre trappings that the Boece–Holinshed account had offered up – '*Milesian* Tales', as Buchanan dismissed them in his own uncannily accurate prophecy, 'and fitter for the Stage, than an History; and therefore I omit them' (7.214).

Near the end of James I's reign, Peter Heylyn published his *Microcosmus, Or A Little Description of the Great World*, dedicated to Prince Charles, which included a history of the Scottish monarchy. Heylyn began it, not with 'that rabble of kings mentoned by *Hector Boetius* [i.e., Boece] in his history of this kingdome and nation' but with Kenneth I. '*Machbed*' is simply the fourteenth king listed (whereas in Buchanan, who also dismissed the early kings as fable, he is the eighty-fifth king).[16] But in the second edition, printed in the year of James's death, 1625, Heylyn added an entirely new section, a two-page account of Macbeth before offering exactly the same list of kings again. The new material derives primarily from Holinshed's version – with the first set of prophecies made by 'three Fairies, or Witches (*Weirds* the *Scots* call them)', and with the Shakespearian

[16] Peter Heylyn, *Microcosmus, Or A Little Description of the Great World* (Oxford, 1621), p. 268. Heylyn was a royalist supporter and occasional polemicist; he is said 'to have had the chief part in passing seventeen new canons which asserted the divine right of kings'(*DNB*, 772).

sequence of titles: Glamis, Cawdor, then King. The second set of prophecies comes from 'certaine wizards' Macbeth consults, and includes not only the prophecy about Birnam Wood but also the promise that Macbeth could never 'be slaine by any man borne of a woman'. On the other hand, this account makes no reference to Lady Macbeth, and not only does not mention Macbeth's ten years of good rule, but insists that 'he omitted no kinde of libidinousnesse or cruelty for the space of 18 yeares, for so long he raigned, or to say better, tyrannized'. Macduff is joined by 'some fewe Patriots', not those ten thousand English soldiers, and with his slaying of Macbeth sees to it that Malcolm, 'the true heire of the Crowne, [is] seated in the throne'. In Heylyn's version, the Scottish constitutional questions have no place, and the narrative is about the restitution of lineal inheritance as the 'true heir' assumes the throne. The story thus reproduces some of the claims of the Stuarts, both in terms of their origin and in light of the succession of Charles I. Heylyn ends his narrative with the story of Fleance's flight to Wales, his son (by the Welsh princess) Walter returning to Scotland to become the Steward to King Edgar, and the descent from Walter to Robert Stewart, who became King, 'since which time there have been successively nine Soveraignes of this name [Stuart] in *Scotland*'.[17] Hector Boece had first invented Banquo, Fleance, and the mythical genealogy of the Stuart descent – thus staking out a Stuart claim to the English throne via the Welsh monarchy – and though some writers openly questioned this claim, most writers, even those as sceptical as Buchanan, repeated the account without comment.[18] Heylyn's work was extremely popular, and further editions in 1627, 1629, 1631, 1633, 1636, and 1639 simply repeated the 1625 account. For the Stuarts, this narrative was essential: a counter to Buchanan's history, a demonstration of the Stuarts' royal genealogy, and an object lesson in what 'Patriots' must see as the 'true heire of the Crowne'. Judging by his work here, one must conclude that Heylyn did not know Shakespeare's play at all.

Writers on both sides of the royal succession controversies in the seventeenth century continued to return to this key period of Scottish history. The restoration of the Stuart line had led to renewed genealogical claims about the antiquity of the house of Stuart; by re-asserting the purity and authenticity of the blood line, royalist supporters sought to enhance Stuart legitimacy and authority, a growing necessity as the crisis of 1688–9 came nearer. For Scottish royalist historians, like Sir George McKenzie (in his *A Defence of the Antiquity of the Royal Line of Scotland*, 1685), the legend of Fleance's founding of the Stuart line was long since settled fact; the Welsh connection was essential, since '*Henry* the 7th (to whom King *James* the 6th was the true Successor) was also the righteous Heir of *Cadwalloder* the last Prince of *Wales*', and therefore 'King *James* the 6th was upon all sides' – that is, Scottish as well as English – 'Heir to *William the Conquerour*, and to *Henry* the 7th'.[19] For English royalist historians like Edward Cooke,

[17] Peter Heylyn, *Microcosmus, A Little Description of the Great World. Augmented and revised* (Oxford, 1625), pp. 508–10. Heylyn's account of Macbeth was copied by an anonymous writer in 1670 into a handwritten book entitled *A Collection of Divers and Remarkable Stories* (Folger Shakespeare Library, v.a.81); the author extended the Stuart descent down to 1670. See the transcription in Carroll, *Macbeth: Texts and Contexts*, pp. 159–61.

[18] Sir George Buc, the deputy Master of the Revels in 1605, noted to James that 'some derive your Majesty's British race from a nameless, and a good nameless daughter of Griffith ap Leolhin (a prince of Wales about the year 1051) upon whom (as they pretend) Fleance thane, or Steward of Abria, flying into Wales for succor, begot unlawfully a son, who should be ancestor to all the chief Stewards to this day. But this being not acknowledged by the best Scottish historiographers, and the thing not honorable, I may well pretermit it' (*Daphis Polystephanos* (London, 1605)), A4v. On the invention of the Banquo-Fleance geneaology, see Murray G. H. Pittock, *The Invention of Scotland: The Stuart Myth and the Scottish Identity, 1638 to the Present* (London, 1991), passim, as well as Maurice Ashley, *The House of Stuart: Its Rise and Fall* (London, 1980), pp. 13–15, Caroline Bingham, *The Stewart Kingdom of Scotland 1371–1603* (London, 1974), pp. 20–3, and Gordon Donaldson, *Scottish Kings* (London, 1977), pp. 26–8. For a useful general account of Boece's additions to the narrative, see Nick Aitchison, *Macbeth: Man and Myth* (Thrupp, 1999), pp. 116–20.

[19] Sir George McKenzie, *A Defence of the Antiquity of the Royal Line of Scotland* (Edinburgh, 1685), pp. 189, 188.

however, the Scottish–Welsh line was irrelevant, often not even mentioned: that James I's 'Title was most just, no man can deny, being sprung from the United Roses of Lancaster and York, King Henry the Seventh, and Queen Elizabeth his Wife; whose Issue by the Male, failing in the late Deceased Queen Elizabeth of Blessed Memory, the Off-spring of Margaret their Eldest Daughter, was the next Heir, which Lady Married unto James, the Fourth King of Scotland, by him had Issue King James the Fifth, whose only Daughter Queen Mary, was Mother of this our Monarch.'[20] A world of political and constitutional problems is calmly smoothed over in such formulations.

The Revolution settlement that brought William and Mary to the throne in 1689 brought political stability for the moment but also led to continued debate between supporters of monarchical succession based upon hereditary right and those who, in light of the results of the Revolution, believed that the case had forever been made in favour of succession based upon election (through Parliament). As the reign of Queen Anne neared its end, uneasy, ironic parallels between her reign and the end of Queen Elizabeth's reign became evident, and the same constitutional issues, as Howard Nenner has shown, 'were referred to and played out again in the early eighteenth century'.[21] In many of these debates, the origins of the house of Stuart, and therefore the reign of Macbeth, were rhetorical touchstones. With an ageing queen on the throne and the end of a royal dynasty near (since it had become clear that the Pretender would not renounce his Catholicism), the story of Macbeth – not necessarily Shakespeare's version – still presented relevant issues of succession and sovereign power.

In 1708, as these succession questions were becoming ever more urgent, the London printer James Woodward published an anonymous work, *The Secret History of Mack-Beth, King of Scotland. Taken from a very Ancient Original Manuscript*.[22] The work evidently proved popular, or at least useful, because Woodward printed it again in the same year, this time as part of a book entitled *Hypolitus Earl of Douglas. Containing some Memoirs of the Court of Scotland; with the Secret History of Mack-Beth King of Scotland*. In this work, Woodward simply reprinted the *Secret History*.[23] The *Hypolitus* collection was reset and reprinted again in 1741; the text of the *Secret History* in this version is virtually identical to that of the 1708 edition. The *Secret History* was then anonymously reprinted again in 1768, in *A Key to the Drama . . . Containing the Life, Character, and secret History of Macbeth*.[24] Here the author/editor made substantial textual changes, to be discussed below, primarily to modernize the text and 'to purge . . . [it] of a number of indelicacies' (1768: iii). The *Secret History* made yet another appearance in 1828 as *The Secret History of Macbeth, King of Scotland;*

---

[20] Edward Cooke, *The History of the Successions of the Kings of England. From Canutus the First Monarch* . . . (London, 1682), p. 45 (sig. N1[r]).

[21] Nenner, *The Right to Be King*, p. 236. See also Mark A. Thomson, 'The Safeguarding of the Protestant Succession, 1702–18', in *William III and Louis XIV: Essays 1680–1720* (Toronto, 1968), ed. Ragnhild Hatton and J. S. Bromley, pp. 237–51.

[22] This edition of the *Secret History* is hereafter cited in the text as '1708'. The characters' names will be spelled 'Macbeth' and 'Lady Macbeth' in reference to Shakespeare's play, and 'Mack-Beth' and 'Lady Mack-Beth' in reference to the various editions of the *Secret History*.

[23] The 1708 *Hypolitus* was reprinted yet again in 1711. Authorship of the *Secret History* has frequently been attributed by bibliographers and librarians to the French author, Marie-Catherine D'Aulnoy (*c.* 1650/1–1705), on the grounds that she is the author of the *Hypolitus* (published in France in 1690). The seventeenth-century editions of the *Histoire d'Hypolite*, however, do not include the *Secret History*, which seems purely an English invention. Best known today for her collections of fairy-tales (*Les Contes des fées*, Paris, 1697 and *Contes nouveaux ou les Fées à la mode*, Paris, 1698), which were often reprinted and translated, Madame D'Aulnoy enjoyed a wave of popularity in England at this time. For her place in the genre of the memoir and travel-writing, and her influence on eighteenth-century English writers, see Melvin D. Palmer, 'Madame d'Aulnoy in England', *Comparative Literature*, 27 (1975), 237–53.

[24] *A Key to the Drama; or, Memoirs, Intrigues, and Atchievements, of Personages, who have been chosen by the most celebrated Poets, as the fittest Characters for Theatrical Representations. . . . Vol. I. Containing the Life, Character, and secret History of Macbeth. By a Gentleman, No professed Author, but a Lover of History, and of the Theatre* (London, 1768). Hereafter cited in the text as '1768'.

with interesting memoirs of the ancient thanes. (Originally from a very old MS.)[25] and again in 1841 as *Memoirs of the Court of Scotland . . . Containing the Secret History of Macbeth.*[26]

The textual history of the *Secret History* suggests the continuing fascination of Macbeth's story, even into the mid-nineteenth century, and the continuing relevance of Buchanan's version, which the *Secret History* primarily follows. The *Secret History* above all serves as an exemplary account of the dangers, on the one hand, of a weak king in a political culture of unbridled factionalism, and on the other, of an unchecked, hence tyrannical, monarchy. These situations reflect earlier Scottish narratives, Jacobean politics, and early eighteenth-century English history. At the end of the 1708 version, the Thane of Argyll makes a long speech to Malcolm upon his coronation, distilling his political wisdom.[27] The terms of Argyll's speech suggest how far the story's theory of sovereign power is from Shakespeare's play:

> The Prince therefore of any People shou'd reflect, that he is chose[n], and exalted to that high Post, not to indulge his Appetite, give a Loose to his Passions, and make ev'ry thing subservient to his Will, as if he were the Lord, not Ruler, of his People, and they his Slaves, not Subjects; that he is not only made to exalt a Favourite or two to vast Wealth, and excessive Power, and Sacrifice all things to his Avarice or Ambition. No, my Lord, a Prince has less Right to indulge, or give way to his Passions, than his Subjects . . . when a Subject gives way to his Passions so as to injure his Neighbour, he is liable to suffer by Law for making a breach in the Rules of Society. If therefore a private Man has a legal Remedy against the ungovern'd Passions of his Neighbour for a private Wrong, shall not the Publick have as just a Remedy against a Prince for indulging his Passions to the Injury of the Publick? the Reason is so much the stronger for the later, than the former, as the Publick is preferable to the Private.
>
> (1708: F8v)

The idea that the king is 'chose[n]' by the people, and that they have the right to a 'Remedy' – i.e., deposition – if the king becomes tyrannical, rests on a contractual theory of kingship derived from Buchanan (among others) that is far more openly articulated here than anywhere in Shakespeare's play.

The 1768 version of Argyll's speech makes the point about limited kingship even more explicitly:

> Let the voice of the *public* find, on all occasions, free access to your councils; and be ever suspicious of that favourite who shall endeavour to suppress their complaints, or poison your ears with the baneful sound of *prerogative* and *absolute power* . . . The affiance between a king and his subjects ought to be held as the most sacred compact . . . Like a contract between husband and wife, let the laws you assent to, and your coronation oath, be an inviolable contract between you and your people; then, my Liege, they will find it their supreme happiness to love and obey their Sovereign, as you, I hope, will find it yours, to cherish, support, and improve the rights of the Public. (1768: U6r, X1r)

The contractural language here, now even applicable to the sacrament of marriage, marks the eighteenth-century as opposed to Jacobean nature of the *Secret History*.

The *Secret History* relates the story of two powerful factions, one led by the Thane of Caithness and one by Ross, Thane of Gawry. Ross's followers (who were 'Affable, Courteous, but Rapacious and Niggardly') support Mack-Beth, while Caithness's followers (who were 'generally Hot-headed, but generous') stir the court against him (1708: B6r). Mack-Beth here is clearly the worthiest, most powerful and respected thane at the court, presided over by an ineffectual Duncan, who was 'A Prince of too sweet, and easie a disposition to be at the Head of

---

[25] Published in Peterhead, Scotland. I have not yet seen this edition, but James Cameron, *A Bibliography of Peter Buchan's Publications* (n.p., 1900) reported that it is 'printed verbatim from the original edition which appeared at London in 1708' (p. 110).

[26] Published in Edinburgh. I have not seen this edition.

[27] In *Macbeth: Man and Myth*, Aitchison suggests this is an allusion to Archibald, ninth Earl of Argyll, 'who was executed in 1685 for his opposition to the Test Act [of 1681] and the succession of the Catholic James VII and II' (p. 131). In the later reprints of *The Secret History* however, the impact of the historical Argyll must surely have been slight, if not unknown.

a Government so difficult to manage' (1708: A7[r]). The 1768 *Secret History* is even more direct on the subject of the weak king: '*Duncan* was of too soft and easy a disposition to be at the head of a government divided into a diversity of factions, every one of which making advantage of their monarch's inactivity, laboured to aggrandize their several families, without any sort of regard to the public-weal' and goes on to assert that Mack-Beth 'was himself of the blood royal' (1768: B1[v]).[28] Mack-Beth eventually leads a third faction, who call themselves the 'Patriots': 'they wanted a Man of Spirit, Bravery and Resolution to over-awe and quash all the Parties, that had got too great Head for the safety of *Scotland*' (1708: C5[r]); Duncan, in the meantime, names Malcolm Prince of Cumberland to head off the Patriots. Mack-Beth then kills Duncan – not personally, with Lady Mack-Beth's help, with daggers while he sleeps, as in Shakespeare; rather, as in Buchanan, 'he sent a party of Men, who joining *Bancho's*, and meeting the King on the Road in *Innerness*, fell on him from their Ambush, and having left him and some of his Train dead, separated without any Pursuit, so odious was the King grown to the People' (1708: C6[r]). The *Secret History* also follows Buchanan (and Holinshed) rather than Shakespeare's play in the beheading of Macdonwald, with additional sadistic touches: Macdonwald 'fell on his own Sword, expiring the very moment, the Fortress surrender'd. *Mack-Beth* was not satisfy'd with the Execution he had done on himself, but order'd his Head to be struck off on a Scaffold by the Provost Marshal in the sight of his army. Nor was he content with this Punishment of the Leader, but, contrary to the true Policy of sparing the Multitude, he hung up all the Prisoners he took, which drew the hatred of all the People on the King, as done by his Order' (1708: C3[r]).

The main outlines of the remainder of Mack-Beth's story in the *Secret History* play out as we know it from Buchanan, though also with some elements – primarily the aggressiveness of Lady Macbeth – that may have come from Shakespeare's play. Mack-Beth tries to escape from Dunsinane by donning a diguise, and is hardly brave at the end:

> Despair was to him Courage, wherefore he turns on his Enemies, and Fights with . . . Fury, and almost Madness, . . . he defended himself for a while against all; till *Mac-duff* coming up, and knowing him, notwithstanding this disguise, that he had put on for his secure Escape, encounter'd him with equal Force, and soon brought him to the Ground, with many Wounds, and frequent Exprobrations for the Murder of his Wife and Children. (1708: F7[v])[29]

Lady Mack-Beth, we are told with none of the ambiguity of Shakespeare's play, hanged herself (1708: F8[r]). 'Thus fell the Tyrant', the narrator sums up, 'who had rais'd himself by Virtues he had not, and fell by the Vices he cou'd not Master; after he had establish'd his doubtful Throne in Righteousness and Love, he forsook both, to destroy in Seven Years by his Folly, what he had built up in Ten by his Wisdom' (1708: F8[r]).

If the *Secret History* were no more than a transformation of Buchanan's *History* and Shakespeare's play into the terms of the eighteenth-century politics of faction, it would still be a remarkable testament to the centrality of the Macbeth narrative as an ideological instrument in political self-definition, from the beginning to the end of the Stuart dynasty. But the *Secret History* also follows Buchanan in suppressing the presence of the demonic, and it self-consciously revises the latent, malevolent power of sexuality in the Shakespearian narrative.[30]

---

[28] Although he shows Duncan to be a fatally passive king, Shakespeare suppresses the more openly contemptuous comments on Duncan in Holinshed – e.g. Macbeth spoke 'much against the kings softnes, and overmuch slacknesse in punishing offendors' (Bullough, *Narrative and Dramatic Sources of Shakespeare*, p. 490); Duncan was a 'dull coward and slouthfull person' (p. 492).

[29] As the 1768 redactor more melodramatically put it, 'the Tyrant fought with skill, but guiltiness enfeebling his nerves, he was unequal to the superior force of *Macduff's* unerring arm, which, after a few slighter passes, by one furious and well aimed blow, brought him, reeling, in mutterings unsanctified, to the ground!' (1768, U2[v]).

[30] The performance history of Shakespeare's play by contrast reflects a continuing *expansion* of the witches' roles, from Middleton's initial additions prior to 1623, to Davenant's extensive songs and additions and Thomas Duffett's parody of them (see note 5).

First, then, the *Secret History* resolutely banishes all traces of the supernatural. The prophecies Mack-Beth hears do not come from the weird sisters. Rather, he falls asleep one summer evening in his garden, as the Thane of Angus relates:

He had not been long asleep, but a Vision appear'd to him most surprising, and pleasing; three Women appear'd to him, with Faces shining with celestial Glory, and Garments like the Beams of the Sun. The first salutes him by the Name of *Thane* of *Angus*; the second by that of *Murray*, and the third by the Title of King of *Scotland*. I know very well, that there is a Story spread abroad since his evil Administration, that he met three Witches in a Forest, who visibly, and by Day-Light gave him those Salutations, but I had it from his own Mouth long before, and take the Dream to be nothing else but the Effect of his perpetual Thoughts, how to bring that ambitious Design about, and to which his Lady, whose Soul was nothing but Ambition, push'd him on incessantly. (1708: C4^{v})[31]

The 1768 revision is even more emphatic on this point, making even the dream a lie:

Macbeth himself communicated to me the account of a vision he pretended to have been visited with the preceding evening. 'Ruminating (said he) last night in my garden, upon the party distractions which divide the Chiefs of this kingdom . . . I was, by the gentle murmurs of that purling brook which glides through it, and the softening even songs of drowsy birds, invited to repose: I had slumbered but a short while, when methought, after a voice like distant thunder, not noisy but awful, and a prospect of lightening, not glancing nor frightful, but permanent and shining, there appeared before me three most angelic female figures, whose loose garments resembled the waving beams of the sun, and whose heads seemed encircled with crowns of celestial glory. The first, in passing, saluted me with – All hail to *Macbeth*, Thane of *Murray*! The second, All hail to *Macbeth*, Thane of *Glamis*! And the third, All hail to *Macbeth*, King of *Scotland*!' Whether there was any such vision or no, no body can determine, but his ambitious wife, to whom, as to me, he had related it, quickly raised upon it the diabolic structure, which from that moment she pressed him to execute with so much vehemence. It has been, I imagine, upon the foundation of that vision, that the ridiculous story was invented of his having been, in the same language, saluted by three witches, whom he visibly met in a forest in the middle of a day; and howsoever much the fiction of the witches may be better imagined, as better corresponding with the tyrannical conduct which followed it; yet I will vouch this dream, as now told by me, to be as it was related by himself, long before the story of the witches was ever heard of; and I now consider it to have been nothing else than the effects of his perpetual thoughts, which incited him to form such a dream, to the end that he might observe the impressions which these epithets carried with them upon the minds of those who heard them. (1768: I6^{r}–K1^{r})[32]

Banquo, on the other hand, neither dreamt nor made up his prophecy, as Lady Mack-Beth learns from her spies 'that some *Gypsies* had assur'd *Bancho*, on enquiring his Fortune, that his Posterity shou'd be Kings of *Scotland*, and keep Possession of the Throne, as long as the Nation remain'd. This tho' an idle Story, was sufficient to alarm a Woman of her Temper' (1708: D1^{r}), and so she proceeds to engineer his murder. The 1768 reviser, then, perceptively notes that 'the fiction of the witches' originated with Lady Mack-Beth; the demonization of the prophecies 'better correspond[s] with the tyrannical conduct which followed it', but the *Secret History* makes the same association in another way, through Lady Mack-Beth herself.

Lady Mack-Beth – absent in Buchanan but a terrifying enough figure in Shakespeare – is even more monstrous and unnatural in the *Secret Life*, motivated solely by a desperate ambition, and taking the lead in various schemes. More surprisingly – and we have now arrived at the most elaborate, even bizarre, revisionism in the entire Macbeth narrative – Lady Mack-Beth does not merely wish

31 The Angus-Murray-King sequence marks this material as deriving from Buchanan.

32 Cf. Holinshed's depiction of the 'three women in strange and wild apparell . . . the weird sisters, that is (as ye would say) the goddesses of destinie, or else some nymphs or feiries, indued with knowledge of prophesie by their necromanticall science' (Bullough, *Narrative and Dramatic Sources of Shakespeare*, pp. 494–5). The witches apparently first appeared in the history of Macbeth in Andrew of Wyntoun's verse *Orygynale Cronykil* (c. 1406–20) (Kenneth D. Farrow, 'The Historiographical Evolution of the Macbeth Narrative', *Scottish Literary Journal*, 21 (1994), pp. 18–20), were taken up by Boece, and thence appeared in Holinshed.

to 'unsex' herself, as Shakespeare's character does; rather, she is from the beginning blatantly a-sexual, yet willing to play the bawd for her husband: 'The Queen was a Woman, that took so little Delight in the Conjugal Embraces, that she had an utter Aversion to Man in that particular; and the better to engross her principal Delight, the governing of the Nation, she took care to amuse her Husband with the Chace of some Ladies of the Court, while she drew the Dispatch of all Affairs of State into her own Hands' (1708: C8^{v}–D1^{r}).[33] She thus exemplifies a pathological suppression of the 'natural' in the name of power, perhaps even with a hint of being lesbian.

Lady Mack-Beth's demonization in the *Secret History* drains off, as it were, the actual demonic powers present in the other Macbeth narratives. In Lady Mack-Beth's asexuality we find instead an equivalent unnaturalness, antithetical to but also ironically complementary to Mack-beth's 'secret' story: his insatiable sexual appetite. Angus's description of Mack-Beth initiates the narrative's move to the erotic:

> His Person was tall, and exactly proportion'd, a Masculine Beauty sate Enthron'd in his Face, and from his Eyes such a haughty and commanding Spirit shone out, as discover'd a Challenge of Soveraign sway. But his Manners were every way engaging to all he Convers'd with, never assuming to himself above his Company; Affable and Complaisant to all, and openly an Enemy to none. This won him the Hearts of all the Men of the Court, whilst his Person and Address, made an easy way for him to the Hearts of the Ladies. (1708: A7^{r-v})[34]

At ages 21 and 26 respectively, Mack-Beth and Angus, we are told, were more interested in sex than politics. 'Love chiefly employ'd our Industry; Intrigues with the Ladies took up more of our time, than Intrigues of State' (1708: A7^{v}). Perhaps the key move into factional politics, which leads to Mack-Beth's elevation to the kingship, occurs when Mack-Beth seduces Annabella, the beautiful young wife of the old Thane of Kyle.[35] The account of Mack-Beth's encounter with her, while the old husband is absent, features a pornographic voyeurism that amply fulfills the title's promise of the revelation of what has been 'secret' until this moment.[36] Admitted into her bed-chamber,

> I found her in a perfect Undress, but so adorn'd as might render her most agreeable to her Lover; a thin loose Robe, but ill conceal'd the Charming Proportion of her Limbs, and her snowy Bosom was all bare, and discover'd two such beautiful Breasts, as wou'd have tempted an Hermit to have press'd them with his consecrated Hands. They were White, Firm and Round, and heav'd with an agreeable Motion, that betray'd the soft Desires of her Heart; on her Face was spread a warm and conscious Blush, her Eyes darted Fire, and her curious Hair hung loosely down her Shoulders, in such Quantity as made her a Natural Veil for her Body.

---

33 The 1768 reviser is even more hostile to her: 'This lady, who had very little of either the temper of a *Venus* or of a *Juno* in her composition, was neither troublesome to her husband in respect of jealousy or of love. She was of a most uncommon turn of mind; her ruling passion was for Sway, and all the rest she made subservient to that of ambition: her thoughts were so totally bent upon that one object, that she never suffered herself to dissolve into the natural softness of her sex, and was truly incapable of making herself desireable in amorous enjoyments; insomuch, that as she well knew that *Macbeth*, with all the martial and aspiring genius which any man could possess, was nevertheless extremely devoted to the amorous, she was careful to give him no sort of interruption in these pursuits; on the contrary, that his mind might not be diverted from the Chace which she had in view, by employing too much of his time in the other scent, she herself would often procure for him!' (1768: K5^{v}).

34 Cf. Buchanan's description, which is more heroic and less decadent: 'This *Mackbeth* was of a sharp Wit, and of a very lofty Spirit; and, if Moderation had accompanied it, he had been worthy of a Command, tho' an eminent one' (7.208). An eleventh-century description of Macbeth, perhaps written by his own court poet, describes Macbeth as 'the red king', 'the red, tall, golden haired one' and 'the furious red one', according to Aitchison, *Macbeth: Man and Myth*, p. 47.

35 The son of Caithness, leader of one faction, will tell Kyle about the affair, leading to conflict with Mack-Beth and eventually the murder of Duncan.

36 The late seventeenth century witnessed a vogue for similar titles, promising (and sometimes delivering) revelations of royal scandal: e.g, *The Secret History of K. James I and K. Charles I* (1690), *The Secret History of the reigns of K. Charles II. and K. James II* (1690), *The Secret History of the Most Renowned Q. Elizabeth, and the E. of Essex* (2 parts, 1680 and 1695, and again in 1699).

> You may imagine this Sight was like Wild-fire in my Blood, and made me immediately throw my self down by her, throw aside the thin Garments that deny'd my Eyes the Beauties of her Naked Body, and discover such Symmetry, that all the Poets feign of *Venus* cou'd not come up to. I was now scarce got into Possession of this inestimable Treasure, when in the next Room we heard the *Thane*'s Voice, which made us start from all our Pleasures into the utmost Confusion.
>
> (1708: B1^{v}–B2^{r})

A bedroom farce worthy of Fielding now follows, as Mack-Beth, hiding under her bed, must listen to her and her husband – 'the old *Thane* by the Authority of a Husband made her submit to his Pleasure while I lay in a double Rack' (1708: B2^{r-v}). Still, after Annabella steps into a bath in order to cleanse herself of her husband's pollution, Mack-Beth becomes aroused again and joins her, with predictable consequences. The redactor of the 1768 version, who had promised 'to purge . . . a number of indelicacies' (1768: iii), in fact found himself unable to resist adding new details to this next scene from his own fevered imagination: 'She threw aside her loose attire, and plunged into a well prepared bath. The floating beauties which now inflamed my agitated soul, enhanced, if possible, the extacy I had felt before! – All patience left me; I rather tore than pulled off my clothes, and rushed into this new, this liquid scene of love!' (1768: E1^{v}).

Once Mack-Beth becomes king, his satyriasis abates for a period, but eventually returns. The people enjoy tranquility, and present no resistance to his rule: 'All Obstacles being remov'd, which kept awake the stirring Temper of *Mack-Beth*; he began to give way to that Amorous Inclination, which Hurry, and Ambition, and Business had along [sic] while lull'd asleep' (1708: C8^{v}). While his attention is diverted, through Lady Mack-Beth's procuring genius, she takes on more and more power to herself. The *Secret History*'s account of Mack-Beth, following Buchanan here, ends without a second set of prophecies. Macduff is *not* said to be 'not of woman born', though the English were 'marching from *Bernham*-Wood, with green Boughs all in their Hats, as in Triumph for a bloodless Conquest' (1708: F7^{v}). Mack-Beth thus falls because of his tyranny, his failure to suppress faction, and because of 'the Vices he cou'd not Master' (1708: F8^{r}).

This account of Mack-Beth, among its other attractions, reflects Malcolm's testing of Macduff in Shakespeare's version by claiming to be 'luxurious':

> But there's no bottom, none,
> In my voluptuousness. Your wives, your daughters,
> Your matrons, and your maids could not fill up
> The cistern of my lust, and my desire
> All continent impediments would o'erbear
> That did oppose my will. (4.3.60–5)[37]

Rebecca Bushnell has amply documented the 'association between femininity and tyranny . . . in two related images: the lustful and shrewish woman as the mirror image of tyrannical rule, and the "effeminated" prince subjected to his lust while he rules others tyrannically'. In most of these cases, she notes, the 'only vulnerability' of 'Renaissance stage tyrants' is 'their lust for women or their uxoriousness'. To the extent that the family was seen as analogous to the stage, Bushnell concludes, 'the shrew's "mannish" authority and her husband's submission to her served as a model of tyranny, the opposite of legitimate sovereignty. The image of "the woman on top" is not just a figure of a rebellion in the lower orders of society: it symbolizes a problem at the heart of sovereignty, located in reason's imperfect mastery of desire.'[38] The *Secret History* makes Mack-Beth not the least bit uxorious, at least in the sense of being under his wife's sexual powers; there is nothing here equivalent to Lady Macbeth's virtual seduction of Macbeth in Shakespeare. Rather, Mack-Beth's lechery and Lady Mack-Beth's wifely status are completely distinct. Neither seems jealous or concerned over the other's activities. Mack-Beth's pursuit of Annabella receives the greatest attention, but it is hardly his only such transgression: he eventually tires of Annabella, and casts his eye elsewhere in the court. Mack-Beth even falls for Banquo's beautiful nineteen-year-old

---

[37] William Shakespeare, *The Complete Works*, ed. Stanley Wells and Gary Taylor (Oxford, 1986).

[38] Rebecca W. Bushnell, *Tragedies of Tyrants: Political Thought and Theater in the English Renaissance* (Ithaca, 1990), pp. 68–9.

half-sister, Inetta; Lady Mack-Beth enables this pursuit, telling her husband how to view Inetta naked in her bath, but Inetta resists the king, telling him she would only consider a liaison if she could be queen (1708: D2^{v}). When Mack-Beth asks Banquo to intervene with Inetta on his behalf, Banquo is shocked, and the split between them, engineered by Lady Mack-Beth, leads to Banquo's death: Mack-Beth 'had a further Rage against him [in addition to the prophecy that his children would inherit], for designing to rob him of his Mistress, by sending away his Sister without any Warning' (1708: D4^{v}). In the meantime, as part of the plot, Mack-Beth has asked Banquo to sleep with Lady Mack-Beth in order to produce an heir; when Banquo crawls in bed with her, she stabs him to death, claiming he had attempted to rape her.[39] Mack-Beth then has his way with Inetta, who has been drugged, but when she awakens she continues to resist him. Eventually she and a number of other virtuous characters escape from the court. Mack-Beth himself goes to Lady Macduff (her husband has resisted the call to help build Dunsinane), and rapes her before killing her and the children (1708: E1^{r-v}). Mack-Beth even 'took fire' at Angus's (still to this point his ally) daughter, 'and made several Attempts on her Vertue' (E2^{r}), eventually leading to their flight and Angus's desertion (1708: F4^{v}).

Thus Mack-Beth as Caligula.[40] The conclusion to the *Secret History*, with the speeches on the responsibilities of sovereign power, offers a tone of high-philosophical seriousness; the 1768 version concludes with a listing of the twenty-five laws of King Kennethus II (printed in Boece and Holinshed but not in Buchanan), which Argyll gives to Malcolm as a guide to his kingship. But between the romance frame-story and the disquisitions on kingship theory, the *Secret History* offers a salacious vision of Mack-Beth, now an early eighteenth-century rake, as the tyrant of Stuart historiography and at the same time as a Buchanan-like example of the need for succession by election. The *Secret History* thus reflects the continuing influence of Buchanan's history of Macbeth into the early eighteenth century, and, at least in this case, the relative unimportance of Shakespeare's version. This relation between the two Macbeths was soon, and permanently, reversed.

39 The question now becomes, How many lovers had Lady Mack-Beth? and the answer is, None.

40 Indeed, in a digression within the *Secret History*, one character tells of his study of Roman tyrants, naming Caligula and Nero (1708: E3^{r}); see Bushnell, pp. 30–2, on invocations of Nero (in particular) and Caligula as ancient prototypes of the tyrant.

DOING ALL THAT BECOMES A MAN: THE RECEPTION AND AFTERLIFE OF THE MACBETH ACTOR, 1744–1889

PAUL PRESCOTT

MACBETH AND THE GHOST OF SUCCESS

The reputations of performers and performances have a marked tendency to ossify in the afterlife. The starting point for this discussion of the memory of six Macbeth actors is an assertion made by A. R. Braunmuller in the introduction to his Cambridge edition of the play. Braunmuller writes: 'David Garrick's performances as Macbeth were supported by those of Hannah Pritchard as Lady Macbeth – he effectively abandoned the rôle after her retirement – and he remains perhaps the only English actor to have conquered the part.'[1] There is some virtue in that 'perhaps', but the fundamental sentiment invites controversy. As if to substantiate his claim, Braunmuller continues:

> Almost two centuries later [after Garrick], a distinguished critic succinctly praised and faulted Laurence Olivier by comparing him to Garrick: 'Since it would seem that with the exception of Garrick a great Macbeth has never been in the calendar, it is reasonable to expect that the new one should be lacking in adequacy.'[2]

That distinguished critic was James Agate responding to Olivier's performance in 1937 and Braunmuller's citation affords a good example of how habits of thought are reinforced through intertextual reiteration. The authority of Agate's verdict and its value as evidence are not questioned, despite the fact that what Agate (like Braunmuller) knows of Garrick's Macbeth is only, can only be, via the body of texts the performance generated.

Braunmuller's rhetoric of exclusivity, of highly selective canonization, is common to discussions of *Macbeth* in performance. Nicholas Brooke writes in his 1990 Oxford Shakespeare introduction, that 'few leading actors have ever been distinctively identified with the role',[3] while, speaking for many journalistic critics of the play, Kenneth Tynan stated flatly in 1955 that 'nobody has ever succeeded as Macbeth',[4] although Tynan was in the process of revising that opinion in the light of Laurence Olivier's performance.

The idea that Macbeth is a nearly unplayable role, one that few if any actors have 'conquered', can be found in reviews and other responses to performance from Garrick's time to the present day. It has become almost a subdivision of the theatrical folklore that holds the play to be cursed in performance. More than any comparably important part in the canon, Macbeth has frequently been perceived to be beyond the scope of whichever actor is attempting the role. Theatre history is littered with the corpses of flop Macbeths: Charles Macklin, Kean (father and son), Henry Irving, Ralph Richardson, and, in this generation, Peter O'Toole, Derek Jacobi, Alan Howard, Mark Rylance: the line may well 'stretch out to th'crack of doom' (4.1.133). It is hard to imagine any serious critic writing, à la Braunmuller, that Olivier was the only English actor to have conquered Hamlet. Harder still, given the macho atmosphere of the statement, to imagine 'Peggy Ashcroft was the only

[1] A. R. Braunmuller, ed., *Macbeth* (Cambridge, 1997), p. 64.

[2] Braunmuller, *Macbeth*, p. 64.

[3] Nicholas Brooke, ed., *Macbeth* (Oxford, 1990), p. 44.

[4] Kenneth Tynan, *Tynan Right and Left* (London, 1967), p. 98.

English actress to conquer Rosalind.' Yet Braunmuller's verdict has further implications for Shakespearian performance criticism than simply what it reveals about widespread perceptions of Macbeth. It is a verdict that is not, of course, based on the critic's own empirical experience, but an opinion derived wholly from contemporary accounts of Garrick's performance, the textual traces his acting left behind. These traces may unanimously speak of Garrick's greatness, but what did it mean to be a great Macbeth in the mid-eighteenth century?

The placing of Garrick as the successful original performer who was succeeded only by failures propagates a postlapsarian narrative of performance. Herbert Blau's pregnant observation 'Where memory is, theatre is'[5] might here be reconfigured: where theatre is, selective memory is. Selective memory, as Roach writes in *Cities of the Dead*,

> requires public enactments of forgetting, either to blur the obvious discontinuities, misalliances, and ruptures or, more desperately, to exaggerate them in order to mystify a previous Golden Age, now lapsed [. . .] I believe that the process of trying out various candidates in different situations – the doomed search for originals by continuously auditioning stand-ins – is the most important of the many meanings that users intend when they say the word *performance*.[6]

In Roach's book, this auditioning of stand-ins, a process he coins 'surrogation', is brilliantly employed to explain a range of circum-Atlantic performances in which competing histories are remembered, forgotten or transfigured. But the public auditioning of stand-ins finds a more literal application in Shakespearian performance history, in which candidates sequentially or simultaneously undertake what is ostensibly the same role in the attempt to efface the memory of previous actors and, ideally, to acquire a possessive synonymity with the part. One thinks immediately – such is the power of the memories – of Betterton's Hamlet, Siddons's Lady Macbeth, Kean's Richard III, and so on. Most relevant here is Roach's discussion of the installation of Thomas Betterton as a cultural icon, and the links between Shakespearian tradition, cultural memory, and the structures of competition between the living and the dead that organize our responses to canonical performance. Roach writes:

> In a culture where memory has become saturated with written communication distributed and recorded by print, canon formation serves the function that 'ancestor worship' once did. Like voodoo and hoodoo, the English classics help control the dead to serve the interests of the living. The public performances of canonical works ritualizes these devotions under the guise of the aesthetic, reconfiguring the spirit world into a secular mystery consistent with the physical and mental segregation of the dead. In this reinvention of ritual, performers become the caretakers of memory.[7]

This has clear implications for any study of Shakespearian performance and reception, particularly of the pre-twentieth-century theatre. Entry into the Valhalla of collective memory depended to a large degree on the outcome of competitions between actors and theatres. The trying out of various candidates in the same role over a *longue durée* is central to canon formation, as is the notion of success or failure in that role as defined against past practice. Max Beerbohm wrote of seeing a succession of actors in the same role that in such circumstances:

> The play is dead. The stage is crowded with ghosts. Every head in the audience is a heavy casket of reminiscence. Play they never so wisely, the players cannot lay those circumambient ghosts nor charm those well-packed caskets to emptiness.[8]

Roach argues, in strikingly similar fashion, that even after death, actors' roles 'gather in the memory of audiences, like ghosts, as each new interpretation of a role sustains or upsets expectations derived from the previous ones'.[9] This theatrical competition between youth and age, the dead and the living, new role-playing and old, seems particularly

---

[5] Herbert Blau, *The Audience* (Baltimore, 1990), p. 382.

[6] Joseph Roach, *Cities of the Dead: Circum-Atlantic Performance* (New York, 1996), p. 3.

[7] Roach, *Cities of the Dead*, p. 77.

[8] Max Beerbohm, *Around Theatres* (London, 1953), pp. 8–9.

[9] Roach, *Cities of the Dead*, p. 78.

pertinent to *Macbeth*, a play which can be read as an Oedipal fantasy of surrogation; as Marvin Rosenberg writes, 'the youth versus age *agon* is acted out doubly: Macbeth against older Duncan, then Malcolm against older Macbeth who would destroy – does destroy – threatening younger men and children, until one destroys him'.[10] It is also a play in which the stage is inhabited by the living and the dead, where the latter irrupt into the present. Macbeth can no more vanquish the circumambient Banquo than the Macbeth-actor can put to rest the cumulative memories of past interpretation: 'The time has been / That, when the brains were out, the man would die, / And there an end. But now they rise again' (3.4.77–9). I will place the reception of the Macbeth actor from Garrick to Irving in the context of this spectral structure of reception. In doing so, I aim not only to describe an important interpretive pattern of pre-twentieth-century reception, but also to challenge one of the habits of thought through which we experience past (and present) Shakespearian performance. The habit of thought is canonical and competitive, and its rhetoric is one of success/conquering and failure/defeat. I want to complicate this depiction of past performance by drawing attention to the various colourful influences on the way the Shakespearian actor was received, but specifically the extent to which the protagonist's and actor's masculinity has been a source of concern for reviewers and has repeatedly inflected their evaluation (and thus our memory) of each performance.

Anthropologist David D. Gilmore argues in *Manhood in the Making* that being a man is more than a function of biology and is in most known cultures an acquisition rather than a birthright. Despite significant differences in economic structure, history and custom, 'most societies hold consensual ideals – guiding or admonitory images – for conventional masculinity and femininity by which individuals are judged worthy members of one or the other sex and are evaluated more generally as moral actors'.[11] Lady Macbeth clearly invokes and manipulates these consensual ideals of manhood in her attempts to prompt her husband to act. As social constructions of the feminine centre on ornamentation and passivity, it would be culturally unthinkable for Macbeth to reverse the argument that precedes Duncan's murder: 'You're a woman, why don't you do it?' is a non sequitur. 'An authentic femininity rarely involves tests or proofs of action, or confrontations with dangerous foes: win-or-lose contests dramatically played out on the public stage.'[12] Gilmore's language (actors, dramatically, public stage) reminds us that the site for these tests of masculinity is inherently theatrical, that doing all that becomes a man is a dramaturgical accomplishment.

In this exploration of the performance and reception of six major Macbeths, I follow Laurie E. Osborne in her argument that '[a]cknowledging the differences between text and performance requires that we attend to the rhetoric as well as the context of the textual attempts to capture performance'.[13] In the period under discussion, authority, legitimacy, canonization and competition, manliness, violence, and nationalism, all featured in the rhetoric and context of the textual responses to the Macbeth actor. Awareness of the presence of these preoccupations in the textual traces of performance should complicate the notion of success or failure in a Shakespearian role.

'ARE YOU A MAN?': MACBETH, KING DAVID AND THE IRISH JEW

Garrick was only three years into his London career when he decided to produce and star in a *Macbeth* that would (after decades of Davenant) substantially return to Shakespeare's text, although with certain crucial emendations and additions. That he was not confident of success, of passing the rite of passage,

---

[10] Marvin Rosenberg, *The Masks of Macbeth* (Berkeley, 1978), p. 81.

[11] David D. Gilmore, *Manhood in the Making: Cultural Concepts of Masculinity* (New Haven, 1990), p. 10.

[12] Gilmore, *Manhood in the Making*, p. 12.

[13] Laurie E. Osborne, 'The Rhetoric of Evidence: The Narration and Display of Viola and Olivia in the Nineteenth Century', in Edward Pechter, ed., *Textual and Theatrical Shakespeare: Questions of Evidence* (Iowa, 1996), pp. 124–43; p. 142.

is testified by his pre-performance publication of a pamphlet, the short title of which was *An Essay on Acting*. Such an intervention is indicative of the importance of widely circulated texts in the battle over theatrical authority and legitimacy. According to his first biographer, Arthur Murphy, 'a paper war [. . .] begun by the small wits' commenced at the moment Garrick announced his intention to play the part. Garrick, Murphy wrote,

> knew that his manner of representing Macbeth would be essentially different from that of all the actors who had played it for twenty or thirty years before; and he was therefore determined to attack himself ironically to blunt, if not prevent, the remarks of others.[14]

Garrick's performance and its textual pre-representation mark an important moment in the philosophy of lead performance. To offer a self-consciously new interpretation of a canonical role ran the risk of alienating an audience devoted to a genealogical tradition of interpretation. The mentality of this tradition in the early eighteenth century is best expressed in John Downes's *Roscius Anglicanus* (1708) where, in two instances, the authority of Betterton's performance is traced to Shakespearian instruction. Pre- and post-interregnum theatrical culture are umbilically linked in a fantasy of continuity that effaces the rupture of the Civil War:

> The Tragedy of *Hamlet*; *Hamlet* being Perform'd by Mr. *Betterton*, Sir *William* (having seen Mr. *Taylor* of the *Black-Fryars* Company Act it, who being Instructed by the Author Mr. *Shakespear*) taught Mr. *Betterton* in every Particle of it; which by the exact Performance of it, gain'd him Esteem and Reputation, Superlative to all other Plays.[15]

Garrick's bold gesture was to sacrifice the authority of this performance tradition, and instead to present his own authority as deriving, *despite* the intervening successions of *Macbeth*s, from Shakespeare, and specifically his text. The playbills announced that the production would be 'As written by Shakespeare', in implicit contradistinction to those based on Davenant's adaptation. But, as Stephen Orgel points out, 'the original text, in fact, was only marginally more satisfactory to Garrick's sense of the play than it had been to Davenant's. Why then the claim of authenticity?'[16] Chiefly, I would argue, the claim of textual authenticity was offered to justify, to a potentially hostile community of interpreters, Garrick's divergence from performance tradition and to locate the privileged origins of his originality.

The circulation of *An Essay on Acting* was likewise a pre-validating move. Garrick's pamphlet, anonymously put out and written in the persona of a fantastically demanding critic, was an attempt to win the first battle of what might be a long campaign. In persona, he objected to the propriety of such a diminutive actor presuming to play the six-foot Scotch warrior, suggesting that Fleance might be a more appropriate part for the vertically-challenged Garrick. (In performance, Garrick would cut the scene in which Macbeth is said to feel his title 'Hang loose about him, like a giant's robe / Upon a dwarfish thief' (5.2.20–2); 'dwarfish thief' was not an image Garrick, anxious of physicality and legitimacy, wanted to implant in his audience's imagination.) Clearly Garrick was acknowledging a cultural conception of Macbeth's physicality. Representing manhood, particularly courageous, heroic manhood, is an aesthetic problem. As William Ian Miller writes in *The Mystery of Courage*, 'we have no secure cultural rules of thumb about the shape and size of female courage',[17] yet men's bodies are consistently read for their predictive value. This issue of Macbeth's physicality will resurface in comparisons of Kemble and Kean's bodies and their relative appropriateness for the role. Garrick's comparison between

---

[14] Arthur Murphy, *The Life of David Garrick*, 2 vols. (London, 1801), vol. 1, p. 198.

[15] John Downes, *Roscius Anglicanus* (1708), eds. Judith Milhous and Robert D. Hume (London, 1987), pp. 51–2.

[16] Stephen Orgel, *The Authentic Shakespeare, and other Problems of the Early Modern Stage* (New York, 2002), p. 246.

[17] William Ian Miller, *The Mystery of Courage* (Cambridge, MA, 2000), p. 189.

the actor's body and that of the boy-character Fleance is humorously hyperbolic, but underscores performance anxieties: 'Are you a man?' indeed.

It has been widely recognized by a number of theatrical historians that Garrick altered Macbeth/*Macbeth* to suit the tastes of his time, tastes that are encapsulated in his friend Samuel Johnson's essay on the character which foregrounds 'the excellence and dignity of courage, a glittering idea which has dazzled mankind from age to age'.[18] The privileged guiding image of masculinity in mid-eighteenth century England was, of course, the man of sensibility, and Garrick assiduously assured that this was the man his audiences saw. Thomas Davies, who wrote that 'the genius of Garrick could alone comprehend and execute the complicated passions of Macbeth',[19] is a reliable guide to what was found valuable in Garrick's performance:

> In drawing the principal character of the play, the author has deviated somewhat from history; but, by abating the fierceness of Macbeth's disposition, he has rendered him a fuller subject for the drama. The rational and several delight, which the spectator feels from the representation of this piece, proceeds, in a great measure from the sensibility of the murderer, from his remorse and agonies, and from the torments he suffers in the midst of his successful villany.[20]

The ostentatious manifestation of remorse was a vital preoccupation of mid- to late-eighteenth-century criticism of dramatic villains. Davies claims that Shakespeare abated the violence of Macbeth's disposition in converting chronicle to play; Garrick's reworking of Shakespeare in turn vastly accentuated that abatement. It becomes easier for the critic to locate the play's meaning and value in the remorse of the protagonist if certain atrocities are airbrushed. Garrick, for example, removed most of Lady Macduff's scene with her son, including his murder. Furthermore, he appended a dying speech for Macbeth, an unhappy pastiche of Faustus's last gasps. The onstage death of the hero not only provides a moment of brilliant ostentation, of heightened display, it also, as A. C. Bradley would later argue after Hegel, aims to elicit from the audience 'a rush of passionate admiration, and a glory of the greatness of the soul'.[21]

Garrick's surgery on *Macbeth* thus produced a protagonist whose masculinity was less transgressive of contemporary decorum than Shakespeare's might have been. Dominated mentally and physically (if Johann Zoffany's portraits of the pair are accurate) by his wife, Macbeth was divested of responsibility for instigating evil. In a culture that privileged reaction over action,[22] it was appropriate if not desirable for Macbeth to reiterate ideals of masculine nobility through the expression of sensitive remorse. At the lines 'Pr'ythee, peace; / I dare do all that may become a man; / Who dares do more is none', *The Universal Museum* reported: 'The audience saluted him with a clap; which I could not help being much pleased with, as it not only showed a good judgement to applaud so fine a sentiment but at the same time a refin'd humanity' (9 January 1762).[23] It was in this fashion that Garrick 'conquered' Macbeth.

By the time Charles Macklin played Macbeth at Covent Garden in 1773, Garrick's performance in the part had achieved the status of a benchmark against which all competitors would be judged. This consensual benchmark is well represented by Francis Gentleman's passage on *Macbeth* in his *Dramatic Censor*, which was published anonymously in 1770. In Gentleman's opinion, there was 'not one personage to be found in English drama, which [sic] more strongly impresses an audience, which requires more judgment and greater powers to do

---

18 Samuel Johnson, *Johnson on Shakespeare*, ed. Walter Raleigh (Oxford, 1908), p. 170.

19 Thomas Davies, *Dramatic miscellanies: consisting of observations on Several plays* (1784, repr. New York, 1971), p. 83.

20 Davies, *Dramatic miscellanies*, p. 92.

21 A. C. Bradley, *Oxford Lectures on Poetry* (London, 1909), p. 77.

22 See Joseph Donohue, *Dramatic Character in the English Romantic Age* (Princeton, 1970), p. 222.

23 Repr. in Joseph C. Tardiff, ed., *Shakespearian Criticism Volume 20: Macbeth and Timon of Athens* (Detroit, 1993), p. 20.

it justice'[24] and this power to do justice to the role for Gentleman lay exclusively with Garrick. The performances of James Quin, Thomas Sheridan, Spranger Barry, William Powell, Charles Holland and William 'Gentleman' Smith (no relation) were all dismissed as multiply flawed, with Garrick alone, an '*immortal*' and 'matchless genius', endowed with the capacity to represent Macbeth. Macklin, like the would-be heirs to King David, the surrogate Macbeths in Gentleman's account, would now have to face a constituency of audiences and critics devoted to a canonical reading of the part. Roach writes:

> Because collective memory works selectively, imaginatively, and often perversely, surrogation rarely if ever succeeds. The process requires many trials and at least as many errors. The fit cannot be exact. The intended substitute either cannot fulfill expectations, creating a deficit, or actually exceeds them, creating a surplus. Then too the surrogate-elect may prove to be a decisive choice, one around whom factions polarize, or the prospective nominee may tap deep motives of prejudice and fear, so that even before the fact the unspoken possibility of his or her candidacy incites phobic anxiety.[25]

Garrick had last played the role four years before, in 1769, and it was now deemed to be the property of William 'Gentleman' Smith. The moniker 'Gentleman' resulted from Smith's affluent descent from a father who was a wholesale grocer and tea importer in the City of London, his attendance at Eton, his marriage to the sister of the Earl of Sandwich, and his lofty boast that he had never stooped to wearing a stage beard or disappearing through a trap-door. In a profession with historically tenuous ties to good breeding, Smith was no doubt keen to stress his social legitimacy, just as twentieth-century jazz musicians, with perhaps a greater sense of irony, would reinvent themselves as 'Duke' or 'Count'. When Macklin announced his intention to play Macbeth, squib warfare commenced with partisans of 'Gentleman' and 'King David' pitching in with criticisms of the projected performance. Such an energetic polarization and factionalism is entirely consonant with Roach's description of the atmosphere of attempted surrogation. The antagonism of Garrick's supporters, particularly, was based on long memories; it was thirty years since Garrick and Macklin's friendship had come to an acrimonious end when Garrick had broken an actor's strike at Drury Lane, and the theatre management subsequently refused to have Macklin back.[26] Macklin's defection to Covent Garden had then been followed by a series of head-to-head artistic clashes, such as the two houses' competing *Romeo and Juliet*s in the 1750 season. A retrospective account published in 1779 in the *Gentleman's Magazine* described this in typically agonistic terms:

> Mr. Garrick, not intimidated by the strength of the opposition, took the field on the 5th of Sept. with an occasional Prologue spoken by himself; which was answered by another delivered by Mr. Barry [at Covent Garden] . . . Those were only preludes to the trial of strength which was soon to follow . . . Both houses began [performances of *Romeo and Juliet*] on the first of October; and continued to perform it for 12 successive nights; when Covent Garden gave up the contention; and its rival kept the field one night more, with the credit of holding out longer than its opponent.[27]

Perhaps in an attempt to avoid a repetition of the attritional contest twenty-three years before, Macklin, after the opening night of his *Macbeth*, attempted to defuse the competitive atmosphere of Shakespearian acting and reception by writing that he wished '*only to please*, not to *conquer* [that verb again] or *defeat*' (*The Morning Chronicle*, 27 October 1773). It was to no avail. In Garrick's *Essay on Acting*, the actor had attached the disingenuous epigraph 'Macbeth hath murdered Garrick'. Garrick's supporters, three decades later, cracked an intertextual joke at Macklin's expense: 'In act the second, scene the first, Shakespeare has made Macbeth murder Duncan; now Mr Macklin, being

---

24 Francis Gentleman, *The Dramatic Censor: or, Critical Companion Volumes I and II* (1770; repr. Farnborough, 1969), p. 107.

25 Roach, *Cities of the Dead*, p. 2.

26 See Jean Benedetti, *David Garrick and the Birth of the Modern Theatre* (London, 2001), p. 75.

27 Repr. in John Adler, ed., *Responses to Shakespeare*, 8 vols. (London, 1997), vol. 2, pp. 172–3.

determined to copy from no man, reversed this incident and in the very first act, scene the second, murdered Macbeth' (*London Evening Post*, 23–6 October 1773).[28] A flurry of nasty impromptus were published in the press, many satirizing Macklin's presumption in attempting Macbeth, some on racial grounds: 'I learned tonight what ne'er before I knew, / That a Scotch monarch's like an Irish Jew'.[29] The *London Chronicle* (26–8 October 1773) carried the following stanza:

> 'Tis somewhere old *Dryden* has said or has sung,
> That *Vergil* with Majesty tosses his dung,
> And now if alive, he might sing or might say
> That with dignity *Garrick cuts throats* in a play:
> But Macklin appears so ungrateful a wretch
> His murders are done in the stile of Jack Ketch.[30]

'Jack Ketch' was the traditional name for any hangman, but the writer of the *Chronicle* verses may well have had the original Ketch in mind, a hangman of the 1670s and '80s who had a reputation both for savagery and colossal incompetence. If an actor had to cut throats (or at least order for them to be cut), it should be done elegantly, as Garrick had done.

After a series of physical skirmishes during and after Macklin's first two performances, the atmosphere became so riotous in the theatre that the management cancelled the run after the fourth night. Before what was to be his final performance as Macbeth, Macklin appeared before the audience 'with a sheaf of newsclippings in his hand', the paper bullets that had rained down on the very idea of his performance. He accused the actors Reddish and Sparks from Drury Lane of planning a hostile coalition against him; but affidavits sworn under oath by both men the next day 'brought the dispute to such a head in the newspaper[s] that a riot occurred the night of 18 Nov., when Macklin did Shylock (since Colman would not risk *Macbeth* after 13 Nov.) and announcement was made by Colman that Macklin had been dismissed'.[31] The tussle for canonicity, for the right to be thought of and remembered as a great Macbeth, was as much a question of off-stage events as of anything Macklin did during performance.

HEROIC ASSASSIN OR COMMON STABBER?: CLASS, MASCULINITY AND COURAGE

In his biography of John Philip Kemble, James Boaden summarized the acting and interpretative choices Macbeth was seen to demand of the actor in the late-eighteenth and early-nineteenth centuries:

> Does the actor [. . .] exhibit to us the noble nature absolutely sunk and depraved by the act, or a base one losing its very cunning in the fear of deduction? Is he a hero, who descends to become an assassin, or a common stabber, who rises to become a royal murderer?[32]

Whilst Boaden's binary far from exhausts the interpretive options of the role, it does reveal an important paradigm of contemporary critical attitudes. As with all binaries, a hierarchy is implied. Boaden's questions are rhetorical, not open-ended, and the privileged reading of the part, as it had been since Garrick, is that of 'the noble nature sunk and depraved by the act'. However he finishes the play, Macbeth begins it as an heroic example of ideal manhood. Boaden's opposites (noble/base, hero/common stabber, descends/rises) also have clear class connotations. Whether intentionally or not, he seems to me to be encapsulating the interpretive and professional rivalry of the two great Macbeths of his era: his subject, Kemble, and the actor who would eventually rise to displace him in popular esteem, an upstart crow if ever there was one, Edmund Kean. It is a nice coincidence, although not untypical of the play's contentious theatrical history, that the first encounter between

---

28 Quoted in William W. Appleton, *Charles Macklin: An Actor's Life* (Cambridge, MA, 1961), p. 180.

29 Repr. in Tardiff, *Shakespearian Criticism*, p. 51.

30 Quoted in Dennis Bartholomeusz, *Macbeth and the Players* (Cambridge, 1969), p. 80.

31 George Winchester Stone, Jr., ed., *The London Stage 1660–1800: Part 4: 1747–1776*, 3 vols. (Carbondale, IL, 1957), vol. 3, p. 1757.

32 Quoted in Joseph Donohue, 'Kemble and Mrs Siddons in "Macbeth": The Romantic Approach to Tragic Character'. Theatre Notebook, 22:2 (1967–8), 65–86; p. 71.

the two rivals took place during a performance of *Macbeth*. Kemble chose the play as the first drama to be staged at the newly reconstructed Covent Garden in April 1794. Unfortunately for him, the seven-year-old Edmund Carey (as he was then known) had been cast as one of a bevy of goblin-cum-spirits whose presence was intended to lend a haunting preternaturalism to Macbeth's confrontation with the weird sisters (4.1). At the moment when Kemble, as Macbeth, entered the cavern, Kean 'either accidentally or intentionally made a forward step which he was unable to recover'. In an attempt to get back in line, Kean somehow contrived to knock over his neighbour, who domino-like felled *his* neighbour, and so on, 'until the whole wicked company lay prostrate'[33] and irreparably compromised the integrity of the scene. Hecate's wish that the 'artificial sprites' might draw Macbeth 'on to his confusion' (3.5.27–9) was satisfied. The gods were standing up for bastards; Edmund the base topped the legitimate Kemble in a burlesque premonition of their future rivalry.

Kemble played Macbeth opposite his sister for over thirty years (1785–1816), and, Coleridge's complaint that 'these were not the Macbeths of Shakespeare' notwithstanding, the pair achieved a level of widespread critical approbation rare in the reception history of the play. When Kean opened his *Macbeth* in late 1814, he was challenging an established, already canonized production. In that year he had already excelled in playing a pair of Shakespearian misfits: Shylock, the part in which he made his London debut, and that other great outsider, Richard III. The qualities that had distinguished those performances – pace, energy, his unorthodox physicality – were now singled out as inappropriate for Macbeth. The issue of how an abstract principle can be embodied in the male physique resurfaced in performance reception. We have seen how Garrick worried that his small stature might count against him; for Kean, size did matter. Kemble was a taller and wider man than his new rival, and, according to contemporary cultural meanings ascribed to that brand of male physicality, Kemble's body was more predictive of such qualities as dignity and courage. A clear idea of these cultural meanings can be gleaned from Leigh Hunt's review (written in 1819) of Macready as Coriolanus:

> As far also as height and figure go, he will have no rival in the part: for though it is curious enough that heroes and great political chiefs have for the most part been short rather than tall (as in the instances of Alexander, Agesilaus, Caesar, Charles the 5th, Frederick the 2nd, and Bonaparte), yet this is not the poetical or sculptural ideal of a hero.[34]

The reception of Kean's Macbeth (as well as his Coriolanus) was influenced by his incompatibility with such a codified ideal. In his *The Life of Edmund Kean*, Bryan Waller Proctor admitted that Kean's 'small stature and incessant activity were the causes, perhaps, of his being generally less imposing than Mr. Kemble, who threw into the character [Macbeth] a more than regal dignity'.[35] The theatre critic of *The Examiner* watching Kean in his third year as Macbeth complained that 'his mouthing and mastication, in the quieter scenes, are as little contemplative, as his general appearance is heroic'.[36] (A more recent example of what could be called an homunculist critique of Kean's physicality can be found in Peter Thomson's essay on Kemble and Kean: '[h]owever vehement his gestures of defiance were, onstage or off it, he was a little man, onstage or off it, when the chips were down'.[37]) Macbeth was one of the few Shakespearian roles in which Kean suffered in comparison with Kemble; for Hazlitt, as for many reviewers, Kean was too close to the 'common stabber' Boaden described, too far from the ideal of the high-born hero presented by Kemble.

Kemble's conception of the role was clearly delineated in an offstage contest of interpretations

[33] J. Fitzgerald Molloy, *The Life and Adventures of Edmund Kean, Tragedian, 1787–1833*, 2 vols. (London, 1888), vol. 1, p. 13.

[34] Leigh Hunt, *Leigh Hunt's Dramatic Criticism 1808–1831*, eds. L. H. and C. W. Houtchens (New York, 1949), p. 244.

[35] Bryan Waller Proctor, *Life of Edmund Kean*, 2 vols. (1835, repr. NewYork, 1969), vol. 2, p. 106.

[36] Repr. in Tardiff, *Shakespearian Criticism*, p. 89.

[37] Peter Thomson, *On Actors and Acting* (Exeter, 2000), p. 126.

In his essay 'Macbeth and King Richard the Third: An Essay, in Answer to Remarks on Some Characters of Shakespeare' (1817), a vastly expanded version of his much earlier pamphlet 'Macbeth Reconsidered' (1786), Kemble sought to defend Macbeth's manhood against two previous critiques. Thomas Whately made his 'Remarks' on Shakespeare's characters in 1770, but they had to wait until 1785 to be published, and a further four decades to receive Kemble's final 'Answer'. What appears to have really provoked Kemble was the more recent recycling of Whately's arguments in Steevens's 1803 edition of the complete works. Whately, in making the by then conventional comparison of the characters of Richard and Macbeth, had argued that the latter was distinguished by a 'natural timidity', 'an acquired, though not a constitutional courage'. Questions of 'principled' and 'natural' courage and the degree to which a Shakespearian character possesses either were also central to that milestone of character criticism, Maurice Morgann's 'Essay on the Dramatic Character of Sir John Falstaff' (1777). Macbeth's ideas, Whately claimed, 'never rise above manliness of character, and he continually asserts his right to that character; which he would not do, if he did not take to himself a merit in supporting it'; Richard, on the other hand, 'never thinks of behaving like a man, or is proud of doing so, for he cannot behave otherwise'.[38] In this reading, Macbeth's self-consciousness of the gap between inherent and acquired manhood, his awareness that, in contrast to the uncomplicated Richard, he is capable of *not* behaving like a man, mark his masculinity as assailable and problematic.

Kemble would have none of this and chose to 'dispute it like a man' (4.3.221). His lengthy defence of Macbeth's manhood involved detailed denials of Whately's and Steevens's charges of timidity and cowardice. Kemble pointed to Banquo and Duncan's exchange near the opening of the play in which they extol Macbeth 'precisely for his being pre-eminently endowed with that very courage, which they [Whately and Steevens] have the temerity to deny him'.[39] Kemble's insistence on Macbeth's 'constitutional courage'[40] is obsessively reiterated and, as with all obsessions, could shade into inadvertent comedy. For Kemble, even Macbeth's ordering of Fleance's murder was not a cowardly act:

> Macbeth meditates the death of Fleance on motives unmixed with cowardice; for, allowing, for one moment, that he personally feared the father, it is absolutely impossible that he could have any *personal fear* of the son, who had not yet passed the term of boyhood.[41]

Indeed, such is Macbeth's fearlessness and bloody resolution, that Kemble took issue with the then current emendation of the line 'unseam'd him from the nave to the chops' (1.2.22) in which 'nape' had been substituted for 'nave'. Decapitation, however, was not sufficiently assertive for the intrepid hero Kemble believed Shakespeare to have presented. Arguing that the upward motion was entirely congruent with military reality, Kemble cited the example of Charles Ewart, a sergeant in the Scots Greys, who had 'bravely brought off a French eagle in the glorious battle won by the immortal Duke of Wellington at Waterloo'. Ewart, appropriately a Scottish warrior, reported that, on being attacked by a lancer, he had then sword-thrusted his assailant 'from the chin upwards, which went through his teeth'.[42] Kemble's essay began with an allusion to Anglo-French critical 'skirmishes' over Shakespeare, in particular Voltaire's 'paper bullets of the brain';[43] in his invocation of Waterloo in defence of Macbeth's warrior status, Kemble reinforced the links between nation, manhood and theatrical legitimacy.

---

38 Thomas Whately, *Remarks on Some of the Characters of Shakespeare* (1785), repr. in Adler, *Responses to Shakespeare*, vol. 3, p. 50.

39 J. P. Kemble, 'Macbeth and King Richard III: An Essay, in Answer to Remarks on Some Characters of Shakespeare' (1817), repr. in Adler, *Responses to Shakespeare*, vol. 5, p. 36.

40 Kemble, 'Macbeth', p. 120.

41 Kemble, 'Macbeth', pp. 58–9.

42 Kemble, 'Macbeth', p. 17.

43 Kemble, 'Macbeth', p. 5.

MID-CENTURY MACBETHS: RIVALRY AND RIOTING

An entry from the diary of William Charles Macready, 26 April 1841:

> I have improved Macbeth. The general tone of the character was lofty, manly, or indeed as it should be, heroic, that of one living to command. The whole view of the character was constantly in sight: the grief, the care, the doubt was not that of a weak person, but of a strong mind and of a strong man.[44]

Macready was pleased with these improvements because he felt that they pushed him closer to what Macbeth ought to be, and that desideratum consisted of the adjectives lofty, manly and heroic, concepts that Macready presents as more or less synonymous. Heroism is unthinkable without manliness or social and mental elevation. Macbeth was Macready's favourite Shakespearian lead and he played it for over three decades (1820–51) in front of a largely enthusiastic public but a succession of contrary critics. In another diary entry he records: 'I had taken a newspaper from Calcraft's table that gave me a very moderate praise for Macbeth, observing that though good, it was not so good as Kean's, which was a total failure.'[45] Professional vanity may be behind the description of 'total failure'; Kean was evidently widely praised for some moments in his interpretation. Yet Macready's blanket dismissal is symptomatic of the way in which the passage of time can simplify artistic reputation, of how balanced contemporary response can harden into unbalanced history.

'Manly', 'heroic', 'not that of a weak person, but of a strong mind and a strong man'. Was Macready protesting too much in his self-congratulatory diary entry? Macready's Macbeth was widely criticized, in fact, for its *lack* of manliness, for its passivity and moral cowardice. *The Spectator* wrote that 'Lady Macbeth always appeals to the bravery and manhood of her husband. These personal characteristics require to be made prominent to give due effect to the struggle between courage and conscience'; Macready, conversely, not only 'made Macbeth too passive an instrument of destiny, but degrades him into an ignoble craven, and an object of contempt rather than of pity' (9 April 1842).[46] In a review written to commemorate what was to be Macready's last performance in the role, the critic of *The London Illustrated News* wrote:

> We are of those who always saw a radical defect in the stage representations of this hero, and who require the nobility of character and the courage to be exhibited which Shakspeare predicates of him in the earlier scenes of the play [. . .] We therefore protest altogether against that prostration of soul and body with which Mr. Macready and others invest Macbeth throughout the first two acts of the play. It is a profane mistake, reducing the "noble, brave" and "peerless" ideal of Shakspeare to the level of a melo-dramatic murderer. It is too late now to call on Mr. Macready to amend his conception; but we record ours for the benefit of his successors.
>
> (13 October 1849)[47]

Kenneth Tynan once described theatre reviews as 'letters addressed to the future',[48] and this critic is clearly familiar with the notion that, although printed on ephemeral matter and recording an ephemeral art, reviews nonetheless have an afterlife that can shape cultural memory.

Macready's Macbeth offers one further example of the interface between performance, reception and masculinity. The newspaper on Calcraft's table placed Macready in diachronic competition with a deceased actor, just as Braunmuller implicitly creates a rivalry between Garrick and all subsequent attempts to 'conquer' the role. In the late 1840s, however, a more immediate and palpably dramatic rivalry formed between Macbeths. When the American actor Edwin Forrest toured to London, he was dismayed by elements in the audience who exhibited vocal dissatisfaction with his talents. As was the case when Macklin's Macbeth

---

44 W. C. Macready, *Macready's Reminiscences, and Selections from his Diaries and Letters*, ed. Frederick Pollock, 2 vols. (London, 1875), vol.2, p. 178.

45 W. C. Macready, *The Diaries of William Charles Macready 1833–1851*, ed. William Toynbee, 2 vols. (London, 1912), vol. 1, p. 112.

46 Repr. in Tardiff, *Shakespearian Criticism*, p. 101.

47 Repr. in Tardiff, *Shakespearian Criticism*, p. 102.

48 Kenneth Tynan, *Curtains* (London, 1961), p. 135.

was booed, it was assumed that this hostility was the result of audience loyalty to another actor, and Forrest apparently suspected that Macready was in some way responsible. When Macready embarked on an American tour in 1848 he was therefore prepared for some resistance. At first, his performances of Macbeth passed without much incident: the odd lobbed shrapnel of loose change, the occasional boo. But as the tour progressed, so did the disruptions, with ever larger missiles projected from the auditorium across the footlights. In Cincinnati, Macready was forced to compete with the onstage presence of half a dead sheep. When the show came to New York in the spring of 1849, the level of tension became so intense that by what turned out to be the last performance, there were only seven women in the audience, a sure sign of expected violence. Rioting did indeed break out, the militia were called, and, with their backs against the wall, opened fire, killing thirty-one of the rioters.

Richard Nelson's fine play *Two Shakespearian Actors* dramatizes the events of the Astor Place Riots by exploring the contrasts between English and American attitudes to life and art. Forrest is characterized as proto-Stanislavskian, a Method actor *avant la lettre*, while Macready represents the melodic, dignified and slightly stilted tendencies of the British theatre. The final scene of the play is a fantasia. Outside the theatre we hear raised voices, gunshots, while inside, alone at last, are the rival actors. Increasingly amicable, they compare notes on their profession, grow to admire each other's strengths, and finally bond over a series of Shakespearian soliloquies. I call this scene a fantasia not only because it never happened, but also because its premise, of two actors bonding over a Shakespearian lead role, is so at odds with the reality of performance and reception in the eighteenth- and nineteenth-century theatre.

A DOMESTIC COWARD: IRVING'S MACBETH AND THE MASCULINE ESTIMATE OF MAN

Towards the end of Macready's career an important intervention took place in the literary critical debate on Macbeth's character. In 1844 George Fletcher published an article in the *Westminster Review* entitled '*Macbeth*: Shakespearian Criticism and Acting', in which he became possibly the first critic to argue that Macbeth had planned to usurp and murder prior to the events dramatized in the play.[49] Similar interventions followed that, perhaps overstating the case to dent an existing critical hegemony, sought to replace the man of sensibility with the selfish criminal, whilst simultaneously suggesting that Lady Macbeth was more the devoted housewife than the amoral virago of theatrical tradition. Fletcher wrote of Helen Faucit's Lady, for example, that 'she was not the "fiend" that Mrs. Siddons presented to her most ardent admirers – but the far more interesting picture of a naturally generous woman, depraved by her very self-devotion to the ambitious purpose of a merely selfish man'.[50] The most controversial Macbeth of the late-nineteenth century sought to embody these new critical tendencies on the stage.

Henry Irving produced and starred in *Macbeth* in 1875, and then again in 1888–9. The first of these productions was far less successful, critically and certainly financially, than the second. Although literary critical discourse had changed in the interim, Irving was criticized in 1875 for many of the perceived shortcomings that Macready had exhibited three decades earlier. Theatrical critics were still, preponderantly, devoted to the noble and manly reading of the part that Macready had described as the ideal 'general tone of the character'. Like Macready, and every other unsuccessful actor of Macbeth since Garrick, Irving was widely criticized for portraying ignobility, moral cowardice and villainy. This despite the fact that Irving had wanted to strike a forceful keynote on his first entrance with his generals. In his study-book (the nearest we have to a prompt-book for the production) Irving had written that Macbeth should be:

> Lofty, manly, heroic. Living to command. The grief, the care, the doubt, not of a weak – but of a strong man, of

[49] See Braunmuller, *Macbeth*, p. 69n.

[50] John Fletcher, *Studies of Shakespeare* (London, 1847), p. 198.

a strong mind . . . A man of action – of overpowering strength and resolution.[51]

If this sounds familiar, it is worth again considering Macready's proud diary description of the performance in which he felt he had got the measure of Macbeth:

The general tone of the character was lofty, manly, or indeed as it should be, heroic, that of one living to command. The whole view of the character was constantly in sight: the grief, the care, the doubt was not that of a weak person, but of a strong mind and a strong man.[52]

The resemblance between the two passages is so astonishing that I think it probable that Irving had recently read Macready's account and internalized or even memorized the description of this ideal 'strong man' Macbeth. Sir Frederick Pollock's two-volume edition of *Macready's Reminiscences, and Selections from his Diaries and Letters* was, after all, published in the same year as Irving's production. If this study-book entry epitomized intention, it is clear that, as is frequently the case in cultural production, reception did not neatly mirror intention. Irving's most recent biographer summarized the response to the 1875 *Macbeth* as one in which

some journalists praised Irving's 'remorse, which looks like cowardice, perhaps, to an indolent and vulgar spectator' but the majority were vulgar enough to share Mr Punch's opinion that 'the exhibition of physical terror and cowering, shrieking remorse . . . becomes repulsive'.
(*Illustrated London News*, 15 December 1875; *Punch*, 9 November 1875)[53]

Clement Scott, a reviewer who would later become notorious for his comparison of Ibsen's *Ghosts* with an open drain, saw a certain legitimacy in Irving's conception of the part:

A moral coward, outwardly brave if you like, but full of treachery and deceit, plotting against those who have shown him most favour, and contriving his crimes so as still to curry favour with the world – such is Macbeth. The world thinks that Macbeth must be a good fellow because he is a brave soldier; but Shakespeare – who mirrors the conscience of Macbeth – tells us what a moral coward a brave soldier can be.[54]

Despite this concession to Irving's interpretation and rejection of what 'the world thinks', Scott ultimately realigned himself with a more orthodox response to the character. Although he praised Irving's intellect as a 'young student' of Shakespeare, he found the actor lacking the more traditional, muscular expressions of masculinity: 'no great actor has ever succeeded equally well in all the Shakespearian characters he has assumed. Many, indeed, like Mr. Irving, have not been gifted with the physical strength or robust vigour necessary to the trying demands of a tragedy like "Macbeth".'[55] The critic of *The London Illustrated News* agreed that Irving's 'style is somewhat too domestic for an heroic person of robust proportions' (2 October 1875).[56] The Macbeth-actor's body was once again the subject of the critical gaze, and on at least one occasion, ridicule. One periodical (*The Gentleman*) peddled the rumour that Irving was anxious about his physical suitability for the part, but that this fear was laid to rest when he came across the line 'Throw *physique* to the dogs'.[57]

Henry James, surveying Irving's negative critical reception, wrote, '[he] has been much criticized for his conception of his part – for making Macbeth so spiritless a plotter before his crime, and so arrant a coward afterward. But in the text, as he seeks to emphasize it, there is fair warrant for the line he follows'.[58] Textual fidelity may be the professed yardstick for theatrical evaluation, but, as is clear throughout the reception history of Macbeth, other factors – not least cultural definitions of heroism and masculinity – are equally constitutive of the

[51] Quoted in Alan Hughes, *Henry Irving, Shakespearian* (Cambridge, 1981), p. 95.

[52] Macready, *Reminiscences*, vol. 2, p. 178.

[53] Hughes, *Henry Irving*, p. 101.

[54] Clement Scott, *From "The Bells" to "King Arthur", a Critical Record of the First-Night Productions at the Lyceum Theatre from 1871 to 1895* (London, 1896), p. 74.

[55] Scott, *From "The Bells"*, p. 79.

[56] Repr. in Tardiff, *Shakespearian Criticism*, p. 134.

[57] Rosenberg, *Masks of Macbeth*, p. 88n.

[58] Henry James, *The Scenic Art, Notes on Acting and the Drama, 1872–1901*, ed. Allan Wade (Rutgers, 1948), p. 37.

process by which a performance is evaluated and remembered.

When Irving chose to revive *Macbeth* in December 1888, he sought literary means (like Garrick before him) to render his interpretation more acceptable to the reviewing community. Irving's pre-emptive strike was not, like Garrick's pamphlet, penned by the actor and anonymously circulated; rather it was the work of Comyns Carr, a friend of Irving's whose wife designed the dress that Ellen Terry would wear onstage and John Singer Sargent would immortalize on canvas. Carr's pamphlet condensed arguments about the natures of the Macbeths that had been current since Fletcher in the 1840s and, in so doing, offered a literary exegesis for the reading that Irving and Terry would present at the Lyceum. Carr's pamphlet differs from Garrick's in most respects. Garrick addressed himself to critics who habitually prescribed what movements an actor should make at certain key moments, their inflexions on individual words, and their appearance. Irving, ventriloquizing through Carr, sought to pre-empt a critical mindset more preoccupied with psychological plausibility, more thoroughly attuned to the idea of the actor as a three-dimensional character critic. Revealingly, perhaps the only continuity between the two texts (written roughly a century-and-a-half apart) is the concern, occasional in Garrick, pre-eminent in Carr, to address the vexed question of Macbeth's courage.

Although, as *The Athenaeum* put it, Irving's 1888 *Macbeth* was 'practically the same that thirteen years ago stirred eager controversy' (5 January 1889),[59] critical response was clearly and positively influenced by the pre-performance publication of Carr's monograph. Moreover, the production was successful commercially, running for 151 nights to capacity audiences, and was revived in 1895 for an American tour. Yet for all the apparent persuasiveness of Carr's argument of the inherent villainy of Macbeth and the innocence of his wife, reviewers still resisted the central interpretations. Ellen Terry's devoted Lady was too far from Siddons for most critics' comfort: 'the notion that this spiritual and ineffable creature could prompt to murder and assist at its committal is an insult to masculine estimate of woman', complained *The Athenaeum*. But the masculine estimate of man was also at stake. According to the *Saturday Review*, Irving's interpretation was persuasive enough to have 'proved that Macbeth has been too flatteringly portrayed in the past [. . .] It will no longer, we think, be quite so vehemently contended that Mr. Irving's conception of Macbeth is unduly heroic.' But, the reviewer continued,

> There is, on the other hand, plenty of room for the criticism that Mr. Irving's rendering of Macbeth is even more unheroic than his conception. It is impossible to deny that Macbeth is, on the whole, a poor creature. The very fact that one is compelled to insist so much on his mere physical courage is a tolerably clear indication that it is his only masculine virtue. He has no will, no nerve, no constancy of purpose, and his superstitious awe of the supernatural is excessive. (5 January 1889)[60]

Irving could nevertheless have still displayed 'more dignity of demeanour, and – at any rate occasionally – more self-control and self-respect'. Although, as we shall see, Irving was relatively successful in conveying physical courage in the play's final act, his perceived deficiency in other masculine virtues proved unpalatable to many critics. His lack of the masculine traits of nerve and self-possession became a leitmotif of reception. This would seem to be anticipated by the notes Ellen Terry made on Macbeth in the two bound copies of the play Irving had specially printed for her in preparation for the production. In one of the interleaved blank pages, she wrote of Macbeth:

> A man of great *physical* courage frightened at a *mouse*. A man who talks and talks and works himself up, rather in the style of an early Victorian hysterical heroine [. . .] M must have had a neglectful mother – who never taught him the importance of self-control. He has *none*! and is obsessed by the one thought *Himself*.[61]

Marvin Rosenberg writes that 'Irving's spectacular scoundrel evidently satisfied some need of the

[59] Repr. in Tardiff, *Shakespearian Criticism*, p. 136.

[60] Repr. in Tardiff, *Shakespearian Criticism*, pp. 138–9.

[61] Quoted in Roger Manvell, *Ellen Terry* (London, 1968), p. 194.

time'.[62] Given the largely negative critical response to his performance, it might be more accurate to say that Irving's characterization *failed* to satisfy some need of his time.

'LAY ON': THE MACBETH ACTOR EXITS FIGHTING

There is one moment in *Macbeth* when the protagonist's masculinity is orthodox and unproblematic. After the vacillations of the opening acts, then the murderous, insomniac villainy of the insecure king, Macbeth ends the play besieged and alone on the battlements of Dunsinane. When Macduff reveals that he is not of woman born, Macbeth and the audience know that he is doomed. Nevertheless, he will not yield: 'Before my body / I throw my warlike shield: lay on Macduff, / And damned be him that first cries "Hold enough!" (5.7.62–4). Our last impression of Macbeth is of a warrior, blindly courageous in the face of an unassailable fate. The fourth scene of the play has prepared us for the idea that facing death as if it were 'a careless trifle' can be the most becoming act of a man's life (1.4.8–11). For the first and last time we see Macbeth in action, and it is this active courage that makes his masculinity so unproblematic at the play's conclusion. Even for Thomas Whately, so critical of Macbeth's courage, the character is restored to a state of conventional and admirable masculinity at the play's conclusion: 'he summons all his fortitude; and, agreeably to the manliness of character to which he had always formed himself, behaves with more temper and spirit during the battle than he had before'.[63]

It therefore strikes me as more than coincidental that all the actors under discussion here, from Garrick to Irving, have been well received in their death scenes. Kean's death, for example, was so impressive as to alter perception of his stature: 'In the bustle of the fight, as may naturally be supposed Mr. KEAN becomes the very "giant of the scene"', wrote G. J. DeWilde in *The Drama* (March 1824).[64] John Forster wrote of Macready: 'But, unquestionably, Mr. Macready's greatest achievement in this tragedy is the fifth act [. . .] Nothing can probably be grander than his manner of returning, with that regal stride after he has received his mortal thrust, to fall again on Macduff's sword'.[65] Henry Irving's final act also seemed to compensate, in the eyes of some reviewers, for his performance's overall lack of masculine virtue. Clement Scott wrote of the 1875 production: 'Amidst all the varied pictures of this striking tragedy none will be better remembered than that of Macbeth, hunted down at last, and hacking with desperate energy at the firm sword of Macduff, with his suit of mail disordered, and his grizzled hair streaming in the wind'.[66] Frederick Wedmore in *The Academy* found the conclusion of the 1888 production of similar power: 'the play's end, as Mr. Irving interprets it, is of superb effectiveness, to summon our admiration for the courage [. . .] of its main character'.[67] Then, of course, there is Ellen Terry's account of the final moments in the last act after the battle: 'He looked like a great famished wolf, weak with the weakness of an exhausted giant, spent with exertions ten times as great as those of giants of coarser fibre, and stouter build'.[68] In the examples of Kean and Irving, the actor's body is presented as morphing from the mediocre to the gigantic. These and other responses celebrate the performance of great physical courage, *tableaux vivants* of conventional masculinity. Even after Garrick's death speech, or variation thereof, was cut from performance, almost nothing became the Macbeth-actor's stage-life like the leaving of it.

Macbeth, like all Shakespeare's protagonists, places a number of demands – physical, emotional

---

62 Marvin Rosenberg, 'Macbeth and Lady Macbeth in the Eighteenth and Nineteenth Centuries', in *Focus on Macbeth*, ed. John Russell Brown (London, 1982), pp. 73–86; p. 85.

63 Whately, *Remarks*, p. 73.

64 Repr. in Tardiff, *Shakespearian Criticism*, p. 90.

65 John Forster, *John Forster and George Henry Lewes: Dramatic Essays*, ed. R. W. Lowe and William Archer (London, 1896), p. 7.

66 Scott, *From "The Bells"*, pp. 77–8.

67 Repr. in Tardiff, *Shakespearian Criticism*, p. 144.

68 Ellen Terry, *Ellen Terry's Memoirs, with Preface, Notes and Additional Biographical Chapters by Edith Craig and Christopher St. John* (London, 1933), pp. 232–3.

and intellectual – on the actor. Yet the statistical likelihood of an actor flopping is far greater if he is playing Macbeth than if he is playing equally taxing roles such as Hamlet, Richard III or Lear. It is clear in reading the cultural subtexts of Macbeth reviews in the eighteenth and nineteenth centuries that other demands were being placed on the actor, demands that were as much constituted by perceptions of manhood as they were by any desire for textual fidelity. The 'difficulty' of the part does not inhere exclusively in Shakespeare (and Middleton's) text, but is partly the result of far broader societal conceptions of what is acceptable or laudable in human, specifically male, behaviour. Furthermore, if we accept that rivalry, competition and violence are traditionally 'masculine' traits, there is something inherently masculine and homosocial about the *conditions* of performance and reception. Bruce Smith, in summarizing the various types of masculine role in the canon, finds one factor common to them all: 'masculine identity of whatever kind is something men give to each other'.[69] Smith is talking about the attribution of identity between dramatic characters in the fictional world of each play, but his observation is equally valid for the relationship between actor and critic. Theatrical reviewing is a vital cultural activity that is performed almost exclusively by men. Currently there are only a handful of female critics employed by the British national newspapers; to the best of my knowledge, there were none in the eighteenth and nineteenth centuries, unless they were the female critics Max Beerbohm described in the late 1890s as being 'sent to first-nights to describe the millinery'.[70] When an actor plays a Shakespearian lead he unavoidably enters into a system of rivalry. If the play is one of the most frequently revived in the canon, this familiar canonicity creates competition, allowing – even necessitating – an evaluative process that is always longitudinal, and often synchronic. And the adjudicators of this competition between men have traditionally been men.

If we want to reassess the value of most cultural artifacts, whether novels, sculptures, piano sonatas, play-texts, or operettas, we can see, read or hear the original work in the present. This type of accessibility is the condition of reassessment and revision. Most theatrical productions are only accessible through the textual traces they left behind – in an important sense, these traces *become* the artifact. This is why the reputation of pre-twentieth-century actors' performances (that is, performances outside the memory of anyone alive today) have a habit of ossifying and are highly resistant to evaluative revisionism. Braunmuller calls Garrick the only actor to have conquered Macbeth because Garrick's contemporaries thought him magnificent in the part, and who are we to gainsay them? Yet Braunmuller's verdict implies that actors can be compared longitudinally, as if the conditions of theatrical performance were static, or as if the intensely variable dramatic sign that we call 'Macbeth' can be treated as a control in the comparative experiment. In *Cultural Selection*, Gary Taylor writes of how '[t]he living are measured by a standard set by the remembered achievements of the dead. Every maker is shaped and judged by the comparison with the memory of famous earlier makers'.[71] In reading traces of the theatrical past, we need to be sensitive to the circumstances – material and ideological – in which these memories are imprinted. In the case of *Macbeth*, this means considering the cultural pressures of masculinity, both as a performative ideal for dramatic character, and as a system of thought embedded in the act of reception.

[69] Bruce Smith, *Shakespeare and Masculinity* (Oxford, 2000), p. 60.

[70] Beerbohm, *Around Theatres*, p. 116.

[71] Gary Taylor, *Cultural Selection* (New York, 1996), p. 11.

MACBETH AND KIERKEGAARD

SIMON PALFREY

The art of writing lines, replies, that with full tone and all imaginative intensity sound out of one passion and in which there is nevertheless the resonance of the opposite – this art no poet has practiced except the one and only: Shakespeare. (Kierkegaard, 1848)

I

I want in this essay to read Kierkegaard and Macbeth as mutual illuminators, examining one in the light of the other. The ambition brings with it basic problems, although of a kind that Kierkegaard himself would dismiss as materialistic frippery. For Kierkegaard assumes – as we cannot – that the inwardness he locates in Macbeth is of the same essential kind as his own. As befits his imperative of urgently self-appropriative reading, his Macbeth is unapologetically *his*. Kierkegaard wasn't interested in historical differences between mid-nineteenth century Copenhagen and Jacobean England (and still less eleventh-century Scotland). Kierkegaard is interested only in 'subjective truth, the truth of appropriation': his reading always obeys this injunction. The young man's account in *Repetition* of how he reads Job might serve to describe all of Kierkegaard's most passionate textual engagements:

I do not read him as one reads another book, with the eyes, but I lay the book, as it were, on my heart and read it with the eyes of the heart, in a *clairvoyance* interpreting the specific points in the most diverse ways . . . Now a word by him arouses me from my lethargy and awakens new restlessness; now it calms the sterile raging within me, stops the dreadfulness in the mute nausea of my passion. Have you really read Job? Read him, read him again and again.[1]

There may well be some allusion here to the famous injunction at the end of the preface to Shakespeare's First Folio: 'Reade him, therefore; and againe, and againe: And then if you doe not like him, surely you are in some manifest danger, not to understand him.' Kierkegaard would lay yet greater stress upon the 'danger' of not understanding: appropriative reading is for him genuinely a rehearsal of the soul; his favourite characters are pioneers of inwardness, fighting 'the disputes at the boundaries of faith'. He *lives* them, and opens them to his peculiarly torturous, magnifying exposure because they rehearse or survive his own premonitory sense of ethical or existential possibility:

Every subject is an existing subject, and therefore this must be essentially expressed in all of his knowing and must be expressed by keeping his knowledge from an illusory termination in sensate certainty, in historical knowledge, in illusory results. In historical knowledge, he comes to know much about the world, nothing about himself; he is continually moving in the sphere of approximation-knowledge . . . Nothing historical can become infinitely certain to me except this: that I exist . . ., which is not something historical.[2]

[1] Søren Kierkegaard, *Fear and Trembling/Repetition*, ed. and trans. Howard V. Hong and Edna H. Hong (Princeton, 1983), p. 204.

[2] Søren Kierkegaard, *Concluding Unscientific Postscript to Philosophical Fragments*, ed. Hong and Hong (Princeton, 1992), p. 81.

But where is Shakespeare in this? It is true that Shakespeare's entrance-point into history often seems to be 'character', but he posits no such ontological divorce between the sensate and the infinite: his most metaphysical intimations are always tied to corporeal or political appetites. Indeed there is little evidence that Shakespeare shares Kierkegaard's concept of an essential self whose provenance and purpose reside in the God-relationship:

> Christianity is spirit; spirit is inwardness; inwardness is subjectivity; subjectivity is essentially passion, and at its maximum an infinite, personally interested passion for one's eternal happiness.[3]

This is not to dispute that God (or indeed God's absence) can powerfully inform the making or unmaking of the Shakespearian subject: but it does so in manifold and often tacit ways, difficult enough to pin down in relation to the traditions and conflicts of his own age, and certainly not equivalent to Kierkegaard's peculiarly friendless protestant individualism. Of course we could not 'read' the past or enjoy its art if we did not assume some sort of experiential commonality. This may be particularly pertinent in representations of spiritual confusion or psychological torment, the experience of which we might think often dwarfs specific contextual provocations, 'throwing' the sufferer into some anterior, culturally-abandoned state of abjection. But even if this is so, we cannot get access to such experience by facile appeal to compulsory reference-points or common languages (indeed if there were such things the experience would differ and perhaps even evaporate).[4] If we want to traverse such cross-cultural turf, we need to do so tenderly, with due attention both to shifting terrain and our own steps upon it.

Nevertheless, if difference is to be expected across and between cultures, it need be no less at work within a culture, and at times even within a single thinker or artefact of that culture. So it is that Shakespeare's 'party', political or religious, is notoriously elusive: consequent claims for his 'universalism' might just as easily be framed as *his* self-difference, or -discontinuity. His apprehension of subjectivity or soul-striving might be as constitutively punning and divided as the forms in which they are framed. Something similar holds for Kierkegaard. Never has there been a corpus more devoted to the 'anti-self', to voices that are never 'the author' but rather a 'stage' or 'shadow' on the path to a guiding self never yet reached. Furthermore, although Kierkegaard could only have written what he did when and where he did, his relation to every dominant idea, methodology, or institution of his age is one of opposition, whether mischievous or violent. Eventually mocked and ostracized by his contemporaries, he returned the disdain with interest:

> Out of love of humankind, out of despair over my awkward predicament of having achieved nothing and of being unable to make anything easier than it had already been made, out of genuine interest in those who make everything easy, I comprehended that it was my task: to make difficulties everywhere.[5]

One result is that terms of long use and common currency in religious, moral and aesthetic discourses – 'despair', 'demonic', 'spirit', 'ethical', 'comic' and many more – are given their own particular spin by Kierkegaard's dizzying dialectic. In a sense, Kierkegaard's very distinctiveness offers its own protection and almost pre-emptively wards off the danger of trans-historical assumptions. It is impossible to interpret Kierkegaard without being (almost) as neurotically reflexive about the terms we employ as he himself was:

> One who is existing is continually in the process of becoming; the actually existing subjective thinker, thinking, continually reproduces this in his existence and invests all his thinking in becoming. This is similar to having style. Only he really has style who is never finished with something but 'stirs the waters of language' whenever he begins, so that to him the most ordinary expression comes into existence with newborn originality.[6]

Clearly, Kierkegaard wouldn't get far in today's academy – indeed he didn't get far in his own.

---

[3] Kierkegaard, *Concluding Unscientific Postscript*, p. 33.

[4] See Elaine Scarry, *The Body in Pain* (Oxford, 1985).

[5] Kierkegaard, *Concluding Unscientific Postscript*, pp. 186–7.

[6] Kierkegaard, *Concluding Unscientific Postscript*, p. 86.

However, this was nothing to do with a naively essentialist or positivist understanding of the way words and actions represent inward subjectivity. Indeed, rather the opposite. Consider Kierkegaard's summary of his method: a 'doubly reflected ideality of a poetically actual author to dance with'; an 'evasive dialectical duplexity' of 'qualitative contrasts': there is no passage to 'inwardness' but through indirection; no 'truthful' revelation unless we imitate 'divine cunning'.[7] Here then is Kierkegaard's axial turning point: as ontological predicate, spiritual absolutism; as existential and aesthetic consequence, fold upon fold of irony.

It is this working paradox that allows Kierkegaard's approach to existential and communicative phenomena to remain so hermeneutically suggestive. For we can in a sense renounce Kierkegaard's God and still recognize much that Kierkegaard diagnoses. Because his self is a site of dialectical conflict – between what he calls the somatic and the pneumatic (spiritual), or finitude and infinitude – self-possession too must be a process of dialectical struggle. In this sense, the original ground of being – God – is more pertinently a point of departure. Kierkegaard is absolutely an existential 'essentialist': but the consequence of this is that he sees experience as a thing mediated almost entirely through varieties of screen, mask, indirection, and ventriloquism.[8] This in turn suggests how Kierkegaard's existentialism doubles – almost literally – as a form of drama criticism:

> There is probably no young person with any imagination who has not at some time been enthralled by the magic of the theatre and wished to be swept along into that artificial actuality in order like a double to see and hear himself and to split himself up into every possible variation of himself, and nevertheless in such a way that every variation is still himself . . . In such a self-vision of the imagination, the individual is not an actual shape but a shadow, or, more correctly, the actual shape is invisibly present and therefore is not satisfied to cast one shadow, but the individual has a variety of shadows, all of which resemble him and which momentarily have equal status as being himself. As yet the personality is not discerned, and its energy is betokened only in the passion of possibility . . . each of its possibilities is an audible shadow.[9]

Everything here – witness and witnessed – is a kind of dynamic metonym of the achieved self that is being sketched or intimated but which has definitively not yet been possessed. The existing self suffers and struggles in a penumbral 'cleft' between the gift and the loss of true inwardness. The only pathway to the self is through repeated self-simulacra, existential rehearsal, and the hypothetical inhabiting of alternative fictional narratives: but the path is, inevitably, a perilous one.

Consequently, if Shakespearian inwardness seems unproblematically familiar to Kierkegaard (and assuming for a moment that it doesn't to us), it is a familiarity rooted in dispossession, fracture, and above all *process*. Existence for Kierkegaard is no kind of achieved proper noun. It is always a verb, a subjunctive, and he retains in his percept of the moment the fullest narrative arc. 'Possibility' is never safely grounded, never without some latent power of ignition: *anything* might fall or return; if there has been a leap one way there might always be a recursive leap in the opposite direction. This means, for one thing, that he cannot dismiss criminality as the contemptible 'fate' of some 'criminal'. Hence the way Abraham is such a hero for the antinomian argument of *Fear and Trembling*: principally because 'the ethical' – refusing to kill his son at God's command – 'is the temptation' that the patriarch overcomes. This 'knight of faith' is a single delusion away from a sociopath. It is hardly surprising that Kierkegaard might be similarly magnetized by another inward-lurking, insomniac infanticide – Macbeth.

Consequently, I want in this essay to pursue my own little shadow-play. I want to trace Macbeth's presence in Kierkegaard's thought, and then to use the subsequent 'Shakespearian' repositioning

---

[7] 'No anonymous author can more slyly hide himself, and no maieutic can more carefully recede from a direct relation than God can.' Kierkegaard, *Concluding Unscientific Postscript*, pp. 243–5.

[8] 'The subjective *thinker's form*, the form of his communication, is his *style*. His form must be just as manifold as are the opposites that he holds together.' Kierkegaard, *Concluding Unscientific Postscript*, p. 357.

[9] Kierkegaard, *Repetition*, pp. 154–5.

of Kierkegaard as a key to re-interpreting the forms that figure any inwardness inferrable in or as Macbeth.[10] I am then proposing an alternative 'dialectical duplexity': not any straightforward mirroring or doubling between Kierkegaard's 'existing self' and Macbeth, but a 'doubly reflected' series of images of both. Crucial is the fact that neither side of the dialectic is at all formally static: it is not a relation of 'given' source to 'given' inheritor, but rather one of mutually constitutive ductility. There is no gainsaying the hermeneutic circle in this sort of project. The Kierkegaard here identified is inflected by the frame in which he is set; so too my sense of Macbeth precedes my search for traces of or clues to him in Kierkegaard. Nevertheless, any 'Macbeth' that emerges is also changed by the search, by turns burnished, magnified, and multiplied.

II

Shakespeare is for Kierkegaard 'the poet's poet', the one 'who stands unrivalled'.[11] The 'immortal' Shakespeare attends Kierkegaard's meditations, inheres in his multiple personae, as much more than a cast of quotable characters: 'the more one reads him, the more one learns'.[12] Shakespeare's characters have somehow got there first:

> Cudgel your brain, tear away every covering in your breast and expose the viscera of feeling, demolish every defense that separates you from the person you are reading about, and then read Shakespeare – and you will be appalled at the collisions.[13]

Here, then, is experience in the raw, the bare, forked thing of true self-exposure: the act of reading Shakespeare without protection or evasion, with a hyper-allergic sensitivity to his drama's inward intimacy. It is true that Kierkegaard does see a limit to Shakespeare's reach – he 'seems to have recoiled from essentially religious collisions'. This 'recoil' might have been fatal to the urgently appropriative reading that Kierkegaard recommends: after all, it does seem to presuppose a more profane model of selfhood than Kierkegaard's God-ordained hybrid of finitude and eternity. But Kierkegaard will not have it: it is as though Shakespeare is so eerily *right* about existence that he cannot have been deluded concerning the most essential matter of all. So, in pondering why Shakespeare did not treat of a terror quite like that suffered by Abraham when told by God to sacrifice his son Isaac, Kierkegaard (or his pseudonym Johannes de Silentio) suspects a secret sub-Faustian bargain, whereby Shakespeare keeps some '*horror religiosus*' entirely to himself, and in exchange receives his gifts of clairvoyance:

> Thanks, once again thanks, to a man who, to a person overwhelmed by life's sorrows and left behind naked, reaches out the words, the leafage of language by which he can conceal his misery. Thanks to you, great Shakespeare, you who can say everything, everything, everything just as it is – and yet, why did you never articulate this torment? Did you perhaps reserve it for yourself, like the beloved's name that one cannot bear to have the world utter, for with his little secret that he cannot divulge the

[10] A certain superstition has developed about 'character criticism', as though it necessarily implies a novelistic and bourgeois sentimentality. Certainly much such criticism is complacent, coercive, and spuriously naturalizing. As Catherine Belsey, Jonathan Goldberg and others have shown, there have been and remain strong political arguments for resisting the unifying seductions of empathetic character and insisting upon the construct's materiality, historicity and textuality. But one can agree about many of the objections to character criticism and yet still insist upon its validity and potential urgency. So: critical or popular ideas about characters are dictated by ethical predilection or political prejudice; there is no authentic Macbeth anterior to all appropriations, or one who survives all attempts at possession; Shakespeare does not present situationally transcendent and immanently coherent subjects. But this is no argument for junking the contingent 'reality' of dramatic personae: even the most 'discontinuous' character is only recognizable as such by a thoroughly old-fashioned process of inference. Although political meaning can be embodied in all kinds of forms and structures, the feelings of and consequences to 'characters' are among the most indispensable. Ultimately any proscription is itself anti-theatrical, ignoring much in the plays' provenance (e.g. writing in parts, typecasting) and the basic phenomenology of audience (or readerly) engagement.

[11] Kierkegaard, *Stages on Life's Way*, ed. and trans. Hong and Hong (Princeton, 1988), p. 454.

[12] Kierkegaard, *Stages*, pp. 220, 454.

[13] Kierkegaard, *The Sickness Unto Death*, trans. and ed. Hong and Hong (Princeton, 1980), p. 127.

> poet buys this power of the word to tell everybody else's dark secrets.[14]

Shakespeare is here both demonic and god-like: suspected of satanic voyeurism, thanked for providing the fig leaf for another's – the narrator's – primal shame. His plays, then, are almost Kierkegaard's original garden, as though populated symbiotically with temptation and omniscience, peril and knowledge, concealment and articulation. The reiterative hyperbole conveys an almost queasy sense in which no shame, no degradation, can escape Shakespeare's gaze: 'you who can say everything, everything, everything'. Kierkegaard's astonishment is palpable. It is as though the most buried desires are captured *in flagrante*; as though Shakespeare calls the bluff of 'inclosing reserve' and draws secret criminality blinking into light. Above all, to Shakespeare is granted the rarest capability of *saying*.

Kierkegaard's presentiment here is that Shakespeare writes at once forwards *and* backwards from his final vision. He doesn't write 'about' soteriological horror; he leaves the trap-door to salvation or perdition locked. But this all the more sharply focuses what he does represent, which is this, *now*, the existing subject in the moment. And here is the clue, I think, to Kierkegaard's reverence for Shakespeare's 'style', and more specifically Shakespeare's fabled power to hold contrary perspectives in tantalizing tension without sacrificing passion, control, or irony. That is, Kierkegaard's peculiar genealogy of the self means that a comi-tragic 'double-reflection' is the only way of doing justice to existence: Kierkegaard offers a 'metaphysical' explanation both for Shakespeare's generic hybridity and, consequently, for his plays' uncanny empathetic power:

> What lies at the root of both the comic and the pathos-filled is the misrelation, the contradiction between the infinite and the finite, the eternal and the becoming. A pathos that excludes the comic is therefore a misunderstanding, is not pathos at all. The subjectively existing thinker is therefore just as bifrontal as the existence-situation itself. The interpretation of the misrelation, viewed with the idea ahead, is pathos; the interpretation of the misrelation, viewed with the idea behind, is the comic.[15]

The 'idea' here is death, or whatever death screens, and the simple enormity that this mortal life must end and pass into *something* incommensurably other. If the idea is 'ahead' of the subject – in some sense seen or expected or the promised end – then the 'interpretation' is tragic. If it is 'behind' – if it is ignored, or if the subject pretends that it has been overcome or that it is somehow not – then we see more than the subject and the interpretation is comic. A joke is a tragedy averted; a tragedy is a joke that comes true. The thing about Shakespeare is that the two 'interpretations' again and again coalesce in a single moment. With no one is this truer than the 'bifrontal' Macbeth.

III

Macbeth is an intermittent presence in Kierkegaard's thought throughout the years of his greatest productivity, and the Macbeths among a few Shakespeare characters – Hamlet, Richard III and Lear are others – whose terms of existing guide or haunt him in his travels. Always he is re-making the play and – rather like Shakespeare, or indeed Macbeth – making the spectral palpable, or conflating one figure with another, or giving to erstwhile metaphorical relations an uncanny force of the real. Kierkegaard reads *Macbeth* 'romantically', as an imaginative resource of his own, and as far more of a poem of consciousness-in-process than a stage drama. Above all, the play's principals are assumed to inhabit the most hallowed and treacherous of existential grounds. So, a journal entry of 1843 has him suggest that Lady Macbeth's 'remorseful conscience' would have been more effectively presented if she 'never dared relax in sleep for fear of betraying herself'. Another entry from 1845 again extemporizes a different Lady Macbeth, one who 'does not dare sleep' and who curses both her 'excruciating wakefulness' and her need for sleep.[16]

---

[14] Kierkegaard, *Fear and Trembling*, p. 61.

[15] Kierkegaard, *Concluding Unscientific Postscript*, p. 89.

[16] Kierkegaard, *Journals and Papers*, vol. 4, ed. and trans. Hong and Hong (Bloomington and London, 1975), pp. 95–6.

The allusion is typical, not only because Kierkegaard often uses as a trope of dread (and seems himself to have suffered) such 'nocturnal anxiety',[17] but also because of the effective transference he makes between the known insomniac Macbeth and his wife. The various principals – Macbeth, Lady Macbeth, Kierkegaard, Kierkegaard's personae – mutate into and out of each other. Indeed Kierkegaard treats husband and wife almost as one. He frequently confuses or conflates one with the other. So, in *Concluding Unscientific Postscript* 'Johannes Climacus' suggests that 'Lady Macbeth's passion makes the blood spot so immensely large that the ocean cannot wash it away', and compares this to the empirical delusions that accompany the fear of committing to a 'leap' of faith. Here Kierkegaard conflates Macbeth's 'multitudinous seas incarnardine' with Lady Macbeth's 'out, damned spot' (2.2.60; 5.1.33). For Kierkegaard, Lady Macbeth has neither status nor interest as an example of womankind. She is instead at one with her husband, a twinned consciousness that he understands as a limit-case of existential probation, terror and bad faith.

Similarly, in '"Guilty?"/"Not Guilty?"' the suffering diarist compares Macbeth's fury at the servant's pale face (5.3) to his abandoned beloved's paleness, suggesting that in her case, unlike Macbeth's, 'paleness itself is the report'.[18] But so too it is, clearly enough, for Macbeth: the servant's 'Linnen cheeks' are horrifying because they are 'Counsailers to feare', like Banquo's ghost recalling to Macbeth's mind the 'great bond' whose severing keeps Macbeth 'pale'.[19] Even in this apparently casual and even incidental allusion, Kierkegaard touches the nerve where Macbeth's experience most chills him: basically, Macbeth's 'demonic' fear of the good and his desperate wish not to see what he sees. Furthermore, the diarist's misremembering of the scene, occluding his resemblance to Macbeth, in fact reinforces his affinity with Macbeth because of its evasive self-deflection. As 'Frater Taciturnus's' subsequent commentary on the diary ('Letter to the Reader') explains, this diary – rather like one of Macbeth's 'soliloquies' – is a 'frontier of understanding that posits the misunderstanding'.[20] The rather Bloomian 'misprision' of this allusion to *Macbeth* in fact concentrates the Kierkegaard-character's entire neurosis. Again and again this is how the play informs Kierkegaard: an adumbrating presence, or an off-stage lighting, garnering what Kierkegaard might call a 'subjunctive' rather than indicative quality, as Macbeth 'invisibly' guides a series of hypothetical self-supposings.[21]

Here then is another entry from Kierkegaard's journal (in fact cut from an early draft of *Anxiety*):

> Inwardness is earnestness – the remarkable words of Macbeth. When inwardness is missing, the spirit is finitized – inwardness is the eternal.[22]

Kierkegaard doesn't quote the lines to which he refers; he doesn't need to: he knows them well enough:

> Had I but dy'd an houre before this chance,
> I had liv'd a blessed time: for from this instant,
> There's nothing serious in Mortalitie:
> All is but Toyes: Renowne and Grace is dead,
> The Wine of Life is drawne, and the mere Lees
> Is left this Vault, to brag of. (2.3.90–5)

This journal jotting is contemporaneous with one of his most important works, *The Concept of Anxiety* (1844). Kierkegaard directly quotes these lines twice in *Anxiety* and again in *The Sickness Unto Death*, written a good four years later.[23] In

[17] 'When my mind is sleepless and the sight of my bed makes me more apprehensive than a torture machine does, even more than the operating table strikes fear in the sick person . . .' Kierkegaard, *Repetition*, p. 168.

[18] Kierkegaard, *Stages*, p. 242.

[19] 3.2.50–1. All quotations from *Macbeth* are taken from the First Folio. Act.scene.line references are in accordance with the Oxford Shakespeare.

[20] Kierkegaard, *Stages*, p. 428.

[21] 'It should be possible to write a whole novel in which the present subjunctive is the invisible soul, is what lighting is for painting.' Kierkegaard, *Journals*, III.2315.

[22] Kierkegaard, *Journals*, II. 460.

[23] There is no room here to do justice to Macbeth's presence in *Sickness*. Its subject is despair, and as 'Anti-Climacus' moves through gradations of self-loss the entire book can seem to be one long commentary upon Shakespeare's 'sick at heart' protagonist. For Macbeth occupies all stations: from primitive categories of 'immediate' desire ('in its craving, this self

'thinking' inwardness, Kierkegaard thinks of Macbeth, and appeals to Macbeth's 'remarkable words' as the most suggestive distillation of this most essential question. Kierkegaard's ultimate subject in both books is the loss of 'somatic-psychical' and 'pneumatic' (spiritual) freedom, and we can quickly see why the words might have so appealed: their sensitivity to the eternal load in the 'instant'; their knowledge of the inescapable freight of the self, as the seat of both worldly actuality ('Renowne') and eternal truth ('Grace'); and, not least, their ironic status as a public lie and private truth.[24] Macbeth's 'toys' speech is then used to fill out *Anxiety*'s refusal directly to define what is meant by 'earnestness' and 'inwardness':

> Some deny the eternal in man. At the same moment, 'the wine of life is drawn', and every such individuality is demonic. If the eternal is posited, the present becomes something different from what a person wants it to be. He fears this, and thus he is in anxiety about the good. He may continue to deny the eternal as long as he wants, but in doing so he will not be able to kill the eternal entirely . . . So they preach the moment, and just as the road to hell is paved with good intentions, so eternity is best annihilated by mere moments . . . But anxiety about the eternal turns the moment into an abstraction. Furthermore, this denial of the eternal may express itself directly or indirectly in various ways, as mockery, as prosaic intoxication with common sense, as busyness, as enthusiasm for the temporal, etc.[25]

Macbeth is present here in multi-form ways: his 'mockery' of the claims of mortality ('Swords I smile at, weapons laugh to scorn', 5.7.13); his 'prosaic intoxication' with (apparent) common sense in the form of misunderstood prophecy; the 'enthusiasm for the temporal' shown in his hopeless hankering for lost daily functions (friendships, sleep, good digestion, a harness on his back). But above all Macbeth suffers what Kierkegaard calls the 'demonic'. For all of his criminality, this is little to do with rip-roaring pacts with evil. It is instead a latent peril of individual existence ('there are traces of it in every man', 'it may happen to anyone').[26] It means, for Kierkegaard, 'fear of the good'.

There is a common seam running through all of Kierkegaard's descriptions of demonic form. It is characterized by 'two wills, one subordinate and impotent that wills revelation and one stronger that wills inclosing reserve'.[27] It then adopts the guise of 'inclosing reserve', 'the unfreely disclosed', 'the sudden', the 'trivial', the 'contentless'. The demonic requires indirection, a foreclosing of shared 'language games' or customary continuities.[28] Consider then Macbeth: his most characteristic words forge and dwell in a space of their own, outside *both* other characters and, perhaps uniquely, the normal taxonomies of dramatic speech. Invariably his speech is neither conversation nor soliloquy; his jokes appeal to no one, his insults fly above their target, his curses double as prayers, and so on. After the night of the murder, Macbeth speaks *to* basically no one, and consorts increasingly with self-ciphers. His speeches at best only nominally ever answer to the immediacies; each interlocutor, if there is one, is relevant mainly to the extent that Macbeth sees himself in their countenance. Macbeth's discourse then often connotes a *supra-referentiality* whose source and subject is what Kierkegaard would call Macbeth's demonic 'discontinuity'. This can be true even of those fleeting moments when he recognizes stilled or suffering life outside of himself: 'Curses, not lowd but deepe, Mouth-honor, breath / Which

is a dative, like the "me" of a child'), to more profound intimations of spiritual want ('if there were nothing eternal in man, he could not despair at all'), to the self-severance of 'despair over sin' and the ultimate 'mutiny' of wishing to be *nothing* other than one's own self-authored 'error'. Indeed the book culminates in a section, 'The Continuance of Sin', which is explicitly cued by Macbeth's 'toys' speech, and which can be read as a poetic 'riff' upon Macbeth's 'internal intensification' of despair.

[24] Kierkegaard, *The Sickness Unto Death*, p. 112 ff.

[25] Kierkegaard, *The Concept of Anxiety*, ed. and trans. Reidar Thomte (Princeton, 1980), p. 152.

[26] Kierkegaard, *The Concept of Anxiety*, pp. 120, 122.

[27] Kierkegaard, *The Concept of Anxiety*, p. 129.

[28] Cf. the play's suggestion of telepathic communication and shared minds: this vaporous boundary between one 'mind' and another inevitably requires a script, but the connection itself, the 'verb-al' energy, is silent. See Kent Cartwright, 'Scepticism and Theatre in *Macbeth*', *Shakespeare Survey 55* (Cambridge, 2002), pp. 219–36.

the poore heart would faine deny, and dare not' (5.3.29–30). Here he notes his subjects' hushed and cowering fear: but Macbeth might also be talking, at least along one shelf of his thought, about his own self-abrogation and the helpless, murmuring, almost inert style of discourse that consequently spills over, or that dwells 'deepe' within as the chilling reservoir of this self-sabotage. For his most characteristic self-representations, including even his beleaguered integrity, move precisely in-between 'mouth-honor' and 'breath'. The 'breath' that the 'poore heart would faine deny, and dare not', is then partly Macbeth's breath: the things that sneak out unbidden from his thoughts, fugitive things, wistful or accusatory easements within the blank fee simple of his nihilism.[29]

We might then see how demonic reserve decrees an 'emergency hiding-place' for the subject, which then provokes what Kierkegaard aptly names 'comic ventriloquism':

> The ventriloquism itself may be forthrightly declarative or indirect, as when an insane man betrays his insanity by pointing to another, saying, He is most disagreeable to me; he is no doubt insane . . . It may declare itself in facial expression, in a glance . . . an accusing glance that reveals what one is almost afraid to understand, a dejected, almost imploring glance that does not exactly tempt curiosity to gaze into the involuntary telegraphy. With respect to the content of inclosing reserve, all of this may in turn be almost comic, as when ridiculous things, trifles, vanities, puerilities, expressions of petty envy, petty medical follies, etc. in this way reveal themselves in involuntary anxiety.[30]

This well describes the 'glancing' dialogical methods of Macbeth, and particularly the way the most 'earnest' of inward struggles must overwhelmingly take comic form. Consider the compulsive locations of Macbeth's verbal hide-and-seek: grim wit ('what Purgatiue drugge / Would scowre these English hence', 5.3.57–8); mirthless puns ('Cow'd my better part of man', 5.10.18); ribald hyperbole ('had I three ears . . .', 4.1.94); fake-joyous incantations ('The minde I sway by, and the heart I beare, / Shall never sagge with doubt, nor shake with feare', 5.3.9–10; 'But Swords I smile at, Weapons laugh to scorne, / Brandish'd by a man that's of a Woman borne', 5.7.13–14); childish insults, childhood dichotomies, fable and fairy-tale and magic charm. Such is the case even when he vows a petrifying public singleness: 'To Crown my thoughts with Acts: be it thought & done'; 'Strange things I have in head, that will to hand, / Which must be acted, ere they may be scand' (3.4.138–9). These statements have an aura of cognitive endgame, as though declaring that he will now become simply an unreflective instrument (of 'power' or some such thing). But in fact semantics here oddly subvert mood: the thing he really wants to hold onto is exactly 'thought', the things 'in head' that he wishes could magically take effect. Rather than advocating some automaton zombie, Macbeth recommends a childlike field of imaginative possibility: in this world *anything* can come true. As so often, his mind – rendered here a kind of Midas – is nourished by fairy-tale and triggered to escape. The two resolves are utterly brutal, are trying to clear a path to the most efficient genocide: but they get their impetus from nostalgia for a more soothing, almost bedtime 'aesthetic', where prayer or superstition might not be so fiendishly tricky or untrustworthy. With mood and meaning, means and ends so at odds, it is a consummate instance of Kierkegaard's comic *and* pathos-filled 'misrelation'.

As a state of un-freedom, Kierkegaard's demonic implies an obscuring or evasion of the 'truth' that 'makes man free':

> Truth has always had many loud proclaimers, but the question is whether a person will in the deepest sense acknowledge the truth, will allow it to permeate his whole being, will accept all its consequences, and not have an emergency hiding place for himself and a Judas kiss for the consequences.[31]

The Judas kiss is for Kierkegaard the most demonic act imaginable, but less because it speaks of

---

[29] Compare 'Johannes Climacus's' analysis of the aesthete in *Either/Or*. 'Essentially it is depression, and so deep that, although autopathetic, it deceptively occupies itself with the sufferings of others.' Kierkegaard, *Concluding Unscientific Postscript*, p. 253.

[30] Kierkegaard, *The Concept of Anxiety*, p. 129.

[31] Kierkegaard, *The Concept of Anxiety*, p. 138.

cogitated evil than of self-loss. For the kiss is an act of (self-)departure, and a precipitous act of (self-) mourning. If it looks ahead to the desert and the hanging-tree, it equally looks behind to a once 'sincere' kiss and the openness before freedom thereby being paid homage. The kiss, then, is a sophistical piece of *language*. The refuge of a joke or a rhyme might be equally demonic:

> The demonic is . . . not dependent upon the variety of the intellectual content but upon the relation of freedom to the given content and to the possible content commensurate with the intellectuality, because the demonic is able to express itself as indolence that postpones thinking, as curiosity that never becomes more than curiosity, as dishonest self-deception, as effeminate weakness that constantly relies on others, as superior negligence, as stupid busyness, etc.[32]

Demonic symptoms, then, will be varieties of 'emergency hiding place' and 'Judas kiss': in other words, things that can marry self-delusion to malice aforethought; that can see the mendacity yet turn a blind eye to it; that can take refuge in sensual forgetfulness that is yet a knowing simulation of ceremonial form and of humility before the good. A typical example is Macbeth's toast at his feast:

> Sweet Remembrancer:
> Now good digestion waite on Appetite,
> And health on both. (3.4.35–7)

Macbeth here enacts command. At the same time, his main subject and addressee is himself. So, no one else is privy to the toast's hidden self-referent, to Macbeth's dry remembrance of 'Appetite' and wistful longing for 'digestion'. Macbeth is looking both behind and ahead, well beyond the purview of a feast to what he hopes will be more conclusive forms of 'digestion'. It truly is a silent kind of 'grace' for which he prays. But his control of the moment's ironies is decisively limited. The first mark of this is the grotesque comedy of Banquo's ghost, seated with silent and implacable knowledge just *behind* the ignorant host; the second is the dark comedy of Macbeth's own wit, splitting or rebounding in ways that he cannot forestall. The crucial touch is the pun upon 'waite'; as so often in this play it is the verb, the *doing*, which suffers the definitive dubiety. For 'waite' also means to serve: digestion then supplies appetite. This might seem an impossible inversion. But it is of course exactly Macbeth's suffering. Compulsively he leaps into the restful space where things have been 'done' before doing them; or he does the deed merely to achieve the 'digestion' that he lacks; or his 'Appetite' is never sated because digestion always precedes rather than succeeds the 'meate'. Similarly, Macbeth here leaps over any 'Ceremony' into the hope, or illusion, that commission is over: 'Now . . .', he says, as though recommencing the business of the hour having satisfied the claims of decorum: but there is no substance to his toast *except* this attempt to escape from it. The pathos of the verb-use, then, is in the way Macbeth at once so carefully lays down the ambiguity for himself alone, and yet cannot 'skarfe up' its portent (3.2.47). For the very things bleed out that, in turning the toast into a private joke, he had sought to damp down: the impossibility of 'good digestion' and the sleeplessness of 'Appetite'. As he says moments later, 'Augures, and understood Relations, have / By Maggot Pyes, & Choughes, & Rookes brought forth / The secret'st man of Blood' (3.4.123–4). Anything can be an agent of the moment's 'clairvoyance', and Macbeth's dark jokes – and barely a speech of his goes by without one – are like the dark birds of prey he here lists, the supra-sensory messengers of 'understood Relations'.

IV

We need to see here how one form of self-absence or evasiveness contains and colludes with another: linguistic secrecy, ethical sophistry, agential displacement and temporal shiftiness are each other's 'demonic' confidantes. Kierkegaard offers acute diagnoses of such angst-ridden attempts to fool eternity and 'turn the moment into an abstraction':

> Some bend eternity into time for the imagination . . . Some envision eternity apocalyptically, pretend to be

[32] Kierkegaard, *The Concept of Anxiety*, p. 138.

Dante, while Dante, no matter how much he conceded to the view of imagination, did not suspend the effect of ethical judgment. . . . Or eternity is conceived metaphysically in such a way that the temporal becomes comically preserved in it.[33]

Macbeth repeatedly rehearses just such evasions. For instance, he sees through to the 'eternal' judgement, while instantaneously eliding just such consequentiality:

For them, the gracious *Duncan* have I murther'd,
. . . and mine eternall Iewell
Given to the common Enemie of Man,
Rather then so, come Fate into the Lyst,
And champion me to th'utterance. (3.1.67–72)

As much as Macbeth knows that he has lost his 'eternall Iewell', he believes, or pretends to believe, that the gift is revocable. He will thus oppose 'Fate' in chivalrous battle and retrieve his name, his 'Peace', and his eternality. As Kierkegaard puts it, 'thoughts of the eternal become a fanciful pottering around': Macbeth imagines himself a character in his own after-life, dressed-up with absolutely nowhere to go. Kierkegaard characterizes such solipsistic delusion with appropriately withering irony:

A person says *Ich-Ich* [I-I] so long that it becomes the most ridiculous of all things: the pure I, the eternal self-consciousness . . . If eternity is conceived purely metaphysically and for some reason one wants to have the temporal included in it, then it certainly becomes quite comical that an eternal spirit retains the recollection that on several occasions he had been in financial difficulties, etc. . . . the recollection must become directly or indirectly comical – directly by recollecting ridiculous things or indirectly by transforming ridiculous things into essential decisions . . . [M]en are not willing to think eternity earnestly but are anxious about it, and anxiety can contrive a hundred evasions. And this is precisely the demonic.[34]

It is Macbeth who is here both inspiration and illustration. He is the man who says 'Ile see no more' when shown the glass of 'Doome', who purports to punish a 'pernitious houre' forever more through a curse (4.1.149), and who, knowing himself tied 'to a stake', immediately uses the evidence of prophecy – mocked if unpropitious, embraced if not – to scoff at all 'feare' (5.7.1–4). Indeed one might see the whole of Macbeth's role as an attempt to seize the after-life, to fashion what Kierkegaard calls a 'forward recollection' that might populate 'eternity' – preposterously – with all that he has lost.

Some such over-heated metaphysical mendacity helps explain Macbeth's luxurious iteration of sleep's prestige:

the innocent Sleepe,
Sleepe that knits vp the rauel'd Sleeue of care,
The death of each dayes Life, sore Labors Bath,
Balme of hurt Mindes, great natures second Course,
Chiefe nourisher in Life's Feast (2.2.34–8)

The point of this rapturous and almost lurid tribute is that Macbeth has precipitously seen over his own edge. He has committed the murder moments ago, and already he speaks wistfully of something he has not in fact yet lost; already he occupies a space of recollection even though everything might seem to be newly and unpredictably ahead of him. In other words, time itself has concertinaed. This is the context for the speech's curiously spurious nostalgia. He affects an egregious show of self-forgiveness ('sore labours Bath'), diminishing his crime in poeticizing ('the rauel'd Sleeue of care'), purporting to make *himself* its primary victim ('Balme of hurt Mindes'), and banalizing the act as though the kind of honest day's graft familiar to all such 'initiate' apprentices. But of course this sense of self-tribute is more powerfully a staging of absolute loss: he can never again deserve the reward he here so eulogizes.

Consequently, his paean to sleep is also an entrance – his insomnia like an ever-yawning curtain onto arctic wastes – into the post-murder Macbeth: unable to occupy his moment, unable to achieve forgetfulness, he experiences existence as eternal waking.[35] As Kierkegaard might have it, insomnia is grafted onto hypochondria. Narratives tumble out of the prostrate body, and in an awful

---

33 Kierkegaard, *The Concept of Anxiety*, p. 152–3.

34 Kierkegaard, *The Concept of Anxiety*, p. 153–4.

35 Cf. Stanley Cavell, *Disowning Knowledge in Seven Plays of Shakespeare*, updated edn (Cambridge, 2003), pp. 235ff.

way it doesn't matter to him what he does, because nothing he does, however vicious and massive, can catch up with his intimations:

> [W]hoever took possibility's course in misfortune lost all, all, as no one in actuality ever lost it . . . In actuality, no one ever sank so deep that he could not sink deeper . . . But he who sank in possibility – his eye became dizzy, his eye became confused, so he could not grasp the measuring stick that Tom, Dick, and Harry hold out as a saving straw to one sinking.[36]

This 'sleep' speech can then be seen as the retrospective partner to the prospective 'If it were done . . . done . . . done' speech. Both represent a mind captive to returning snapshots of experience (each 'done' supposes another tense, another moment before or after, another perspective upon the murder). Both exemplify Macbeth's favourite ruse of constructing more congenial self-tableaux in an alternative space and time. But both, inevitably, show how the ruse is pre-empted by its self-conscious illegitimacy. The single sleep in his mind – Duncan's – cues Macbeth's sudden flooding awareness of the full force of possibility: '*Macbeth* shall sleepe no more' (2.2.41).

Here as much as anywhere is where Kierkegaard's demonic describes Macbeth: the way he purports to compete with his temporal incarceration by proffering his own rival space-time continuum. Hence, as the above passage suggests, the immeasurable wistfulness in so many of Macbeth's speeches. He would construct a dimension parallel to 'fate', a bolt-hole of despair which works as virtual compensation for all he has sacrificed:

> If this which he avouches, do's appeare,
> There is nor flying hence, nor tarrying here.
> I 'ginne to be a-weary of the Sun,
> And wish th'estate o'th'world were now undon.
> Ring the Alarum Bell, blow Winde, come wracke,
> At least wee'l dye with Harnesse on our backe.
> (5.5.45–50)

Clearly this is a speech of resounding despair, of capitulation to and collusion in defeat. But the fact that the speech is a call for comprehensive annihilation makes its form, and its closing get-out clause, all the more suggestive. Basic to the effect here is a deadly earnest imitation of 'comic' form. So, rhyme usually suggests a purpose above and beyond the things said: a momentum and self-certainty that the rhyme-form itself conveys, and that is not dictated by the sense of the words. The rhyme in turn usually serves one of two moods: blithe comic confidence or implacable self-resolve. Usually, the 'rhymer' is in accord with the generic mood: it speaks through the speaker, but by the same token the speaker rolls happily along with it. Here, however, there is no such fit, and instead the speech brings to the surface a usually dormant tension concerning the possession of agency 'in' rhyme. So, these rhymes are absolutely Macbeth's, because so characteristically grim, mordant, self-mocking, and spoken as though with a choking grip upon rising hysteria; but then they are not his at all, because so redolent of over-determined impotence. Insofar as the rhymes remotely recall playfulness, or invoke escape from harshness or mundaneity, it is mainly a glum self-subverting joke, like swinging a pendulum over a stopped clock.[37] The use of rhyming couplets in this particular context, then, serves to mimic, even parody, the modes of escape or self-certainty that it at the same time invokes. In place of comic impregnability, we get tragic inescapability: the supra-subjective rhythm of rhyme here invokes existential repetition, meta-paralysis, and the 'supervision' of anterior form.

We see here how what Kierkegaard calls 'style' can embody a 'concretized' subjectivity. So, the rhyme-form at once reinforces Macbeth's distinctively hermetic sense of 'predestinate' doom and frames a detachment from the moment that (I want to suggest) is oddly *sculpturing*. Each couplet 'poses' a characteristic attitude: absolute over-determination and fatalism, and yet a gesture through which Macbeth would steal this

[36] Kierkegaard, *The Concept of Anxiety*, p. 158.

[37] 'If the comic power is cold and bleak, it is a sign there is no new immediacy sprouting; then there is no harvest, only the empty passion of a sterile wind storming over bare fields.' Kierkegaard, *Concluding Unscientific Postscript*, p. 282.

hopelessness as his own peculiar validation. The effect is at once of ruin and retrieval: as though successively petrifying the (falling) hero in a (disintegrating) strip of frieze, or building and then rebuilding a self-monument in chalk. There is then a plastic momentum, almost a meta-rhythm, to Macbeth's resolving and dissolving.[38] The point is a movement between repose and agitation: a 'statue' of the self that is at the same time abandoned or traduced by or into another. It is not one single sculpture, but a series of briefly captured attitudes, retrieving artistic consolation from his entropy. It is (to recall Wittgenstein's metaphor for Shakespeare's 'objectivity') a dance with his [anti-]selves, in a curious manner animating the promise the 'crack of doom' mirrors.[39]

How else to account for the superbly pointless relief of 'at least wee'l dye with harnesse on our backe'? Partly the effect comes from a knowing bathos: Macbeth is off to work, out to the killing fields; he will be buried in his work like a mad ploughman. But 'inside' this there is exultancy, a juvenile conviction that present function is somehow at one with old nostalgias. Hence the way his rhyme manages to join the self-deracinated sociopath with the young man who once upon a time admired heroes in tales; for is there not some whisper of 'georgic' redemption, as the 'Harnesse' invokes a distant but fleetingly *possible* alternative world? But this invocation of a more 'innocent', and certainly more regenerative, generic setting remains no more than what Kierkegaard might call a 'glance'. It testifies surely enough to the lingering or memorial presence of 'the good' in Macbeth. As a desperate return to childhood, a last-ditch tracking back through a suddenly wasted life, the words convey a terrible over-grown vulnerability. He pictures what he was, pays homage to lost hope. But at the same time as the memory is an act of mourning, it is equally one of almost sarcastic burial. As usual, Macbeth's honesty is in a lie; as usual, any 'earnestness' is located exactly in its sacrifice. In departing from the scene with knowingly false consolation, Macbeth epitomizes what Kierkegaard sees as the remorseless indirections of despair:

> When feeling becomes fantastic in this way, the self becomes only more and more volatilised and finally comes to be a kind of abstract sentimentality that inhumanly belongs to no human being . . . When feeling or knowing or willing has become fantastic, the entire self can eventually become that, whether in the more active form of plunging headlong into fantasy or in the more passive form of being carried away.[40]

Somewhat like Timon's shoreline monument – lashed by the waves, definitively dead, inviting ruin but resisting acquiescence – Macbeth's frozen image sustains its simulation of defiance in terminal symmetry with the reality of collapse. We might see, then, that this sculpturing temptation in Macbeth is a preparation for (even an expression of) posthumousness. He is rehearsing epitaphs or, perhaps more accurately, building a series of cenotaphs, monuments honouring the 'dead man' who, whether buried elsewhere or left disgracefully unburied, can claim in the cenotaph some appropriate remembrance. At the same time, the gestures have no more power of record than a joke.

V

I want to press here a little harder at the idea that Macbeth's speeches might embody some compact, in their peculiar 'supra-address', with the art-forms of dance, sculpture and mime. For it is fascinating

---

[38] Cf. Nietzsche's 'Apollonian' art in *Birth of Tragedy*, retrieving 'plastic' form from imminent torture and dissolution.

[39] *Culture and Value*, ed. G. H. Von Wright, trans. Peter Winch (Oxford, 1980), pp. 36–7. Also cf. Wittgenstein: 'Suppose someone said: every familiar word, in a book for example, actually carries an atmosphere with it in our minds, a 'corona' of lightly indicated uses. – Just as if each figure in a painting were surrounded by delicate shadowy drawings of scenes, as it were in another dimension, and in them we saw the figures in different contexts.' This seems uncannily like what Shakespeare does with Macbeth; even if as Wittgenstein suspects it cannot help account for ordinary language games, it may be quite appropriate for the scripted figurations of a play, where *everything* is in some basic sense at once palpably given and 'virtual'. *Philosophical Investigations*, trans. G. E. M. Anscombe (Oxford, 1958, repr. 1992), II. vi (p. 181).

[40] Kierkegaard, *The Sickness Unto Death*, pp. 30–2.

that perhaps Kierkegaard's most privileged form for representing the demonic is indeed what he calls 'the mimical':

> The most terrible words that sound from the abyss of evil would not be able to produce an effect like that of the suddenness of the leap that lies within the confines of the mimical. Even though the word were terrible, even though it were a Shakespeare, a Byron, or a Shelley who breaks the silence, the word always retains its redeeming power, because all the despair and all the horror of evil expressed in a word are not as terrible as silence . . . The horror that seizes one upon seeing Mephistopheles leap in through the window and remain stationary in the position of the leap! . . . This spring in the leap, reminding one of the leap of the bird of prey and of the wild beast, which doubly terrify because they commonly leap from a completely motionless position, has an infinite effect.[41]

This frozen leap is terrifying because it takes supposed 'incommensurables' hostage: being so 'sudden', it is estranged from all immediacy and mediation; but then, exactly *as* this abruptly seizing bestiality, it arrogates to itself eternality, as though paralysing all of possibility in its own image, or transfixing all witnesses with its Medusan self-confidence. Macbeth's mime of terror is never quite like this. While he sometimes assumes an attitude of monumental fearsomeness, it is time and again complicated by a sort of co-present 'self-gargoyle', dribbling the effluence of other dreams, other appetites, offering relief or hydration even from within the stony fixity of his misery. So, as much as his word-sculptures resemble the mimical, they do so as *movement* more than petrification, as one ghostly self-simulacrum 'floats' out after another. But the effect of this is indeed akin to Kierkegaard's mimical: Macbeth's most characteristic speaking evokes an estranged 'aporetic' dwelling, a mental space definitively outside both communal and temporal continuity. The things he actually performs develop a peculiarly sleepwalking quality, partly because of the language in which the actions couch: the mind that attends the actions is either elsewhere (following one or other trajectory of Macbeth's figuratively inscribed 'lines of becoming') or a ghostly servant of a thought already processed.[42] The tendency begins with *Macbeth*'s witches: they scramble all temporality, all succession, so much so that they render the 'future' a thing exactly of recollection. When Macbeth is made Cawdor it comes to him like the belated manifestation of a 'truth' already told, or like a memory. It is the same when he kills the king. Like Kierkegaard's 'forward recollection', Macbeth experiences the presentiment of a possibility that has, in the sense of a mental movement, already happened: 'Present Feares Are lesse then horrible Imaginings . . . Function is smother'd in surmise, And nothing is, but what is not' (1.3.136–41).

To call his speech and actions 'mimical' is not to minimize their devastating consequences. It is rather to acknowledge Macbeth's faithfulness to 'demonic' pathology: the suffering of others is to him little more than a hypothesis of his own possibilities; at best a silent shadow-play, or a barely heeded trompe l'oeil silhouette before his own all-and-nothing horizon. We might then see how he frames 'attitudes' toward his *own* experience that are again strangely mimical. After all, a mime is rarely in any copybook sense 'the thing' simulated. This thing (person, action, emotion, etc.) is abstracted, slowed down, turned into a thought *about* it. Mime then evokes a reflective repetition or rehearsal of an action or character that is usually *elsewhere*. The mime both expresses *and* elicits a certain contemplative super-charge, an aura of reappraisal. Something invariably seen as unproblematic or customary becomes, through the imitation and transvaluation of mime, a puzzle: it becomes quizzical, humorous, metaphysically in suspension. The thing 'imitated', then, is neither quite 'given' nor finished with. It is instead open for negotiation, as though a withdrawable presentiment, or a tracing of possibility, or a sketchy palpability.

---

41 Kierkegaard, *The Concept of Anxiety*, pp. 131–2.

42 Compare Cavell, *Disowning Knowledge*, p. 238: '"to receive at once the benefit of sleep, and do the effects of watching" – seems most literally a description of the conditions of a play's audience, and play-watching becomes, along with (or as an interpretation of) sleepwalking, exemplary of human action as such, as conceived in this play'.

Hence the way Macbeth cannot get at the reality of his acts *except* through one or another form of indirect leakage: the visual simulacra that pursue him everywhere (the dagger, Banquo's Ghost, professional murderers), or the phantoms that find form along his speech-acts' multiple shelves.[43] For instance, his incantation before the witches ('Though you untie the winds . . .' (4.1.68)) so generalizes destruction as to minimize its consequences, trivializing suffering and reducing even apocalypse to the momentary affect of his necessities. But this devastated future is also, of course, already here: it is *he* who has confounded and swallowed navigation, and who swoons and sickens from 'destruction'. At the same time as the words attend, with almost forensic accuracy, to Macbeth's flooding entropy, they are immeasurably displaced, imagining a scene aeons beyond his own immediacies. Another example comes after Macbeth has his prayer 'answered', and learns that Banquo's line will inherit the throne. He immediately orders everyone in *Macduff*'s line – not Banquo's – to be slaughtered, as though a vicarious convenience for his revenge. But it is no revenge at all to kill the wrong family: at best it is a rehearsal for something that will never happen. But if the act is almost 'by the way', an accidental compensation, then the satisfaction of the speech must come principally from its 'comic' pseudo-symmetry: pretending to exchange like for like (a Macduff for a Banquo) when really, of course, they are 'comically' incommensurable:

> [I]nclosing reserve maintains itself in the person as an abracadabra of continuity that communicates only with itself and therefore is always the sudden.[44]

Killing the Macduffs is a parody of 'overcoming' that mocks, through pleonastic repetition, Macbeth's impotence, loss and doom (hence too the half-buried, self-mocking 'jokes' through which he mimics renewed control over what he has just learned to be irrevocably lost: 'firstlings' (children) and 'Crown', 4.1.162–9). Like almost everything that Macbeth now performs, it is deadly real for everyone *except* Macbeth, for whom all words and action have become an ontologically hollowing, ethically etiolated 'Act'. For *him* this act is nothing, or nothing but derision: for it is not really the act at all, but a mirthlessly 'humorous', baroquely evacuated imitation of it:

> [I]t is not existence, but existence-possibility oriented toward existence . . . and holds existence at bay by the most subtle of all deceptions, by thinking. He has thought everything possible, and yet he has not existed at all.[45]

VI

I want to close by looking at a speech that concentrates many of the things that I have been exploring. It is when Macbeth hears the cry of women presaging the death of his wife (5.5). By now such 'interruptions' make him barely miss a beat. His thoughts keep their pattern, and the most dreadful news can be no more than a cue for another, almost desultory, turning of the page of his mental autobiography. But the consequent speech-acts are not simply expressions of desolation. They simultaneously re-enact the *process* of self-unravelling and project into hypotheses whose 'virtuality' or surreality at once retrieves, rehearses, and replaces all ethical and practicable possibility:

> I have almost forgot the taste of Feares:
> The time ha's beene, my sences would haue cool'd
> To hear a Night-shrieke, and my Fell of haire
> Would at a dismall Treatise rowze, and stirre
> As life were in't. (5.5.9–13)

As befits this peculiar supra-temporality, Macbeth is speaking as a kind of dead thing. Nothing can 'rowze' him now. He remembers how once upon a time it could seem that even the dead parts of him had life. It was a tactile illusion; there was *never* life in hair: there was never life at all, it was always a trick of the too-susceptible mind. The speech records the heaviest force of depression sinking home. All fullness now seems a bloated emptiness, all feeling a kind of fraudulence. The past too becomes subject

---

[43] I am grateful on these points for discussions with Bernard Beatty.

[44] Kierkegaard, *The Concept of Anxiety*, p. 130.

[45] Kierkegaard, *Concluding Unscientific Postscript*, p. 253.

to present euthanasia. But then the dual temporality of the speech is also a dual perspective upon the phenomena at issue. So, Macbeth is inhabiting his 'now', neutering what was then; he is also inhabiting 'then', and animating what is now. It is characteristic that Macbeth should be thus 'rowzed' through a cliché: so many of the life-thoughts that he allows briefly to flicker derive from or couch in just such almost child-like proverbiality. Furthermore, the speech creates a kind of meta-effect: just as it records a figure of speech coming true (my hair stood on end), so too it observes a prostrate mind drowsily rising, rather like the somnolent 'cow' with which Macbeth soon identifies, into a browsing form of sentience.

Accordingly, the speech is also playing with alternative biographies. Macbeth is nostalgic for a time when he could be scared half to death; it is a horrid enough joke, as though wishing himself Medusa's petrified victim. But the nostalgia is not so much for innocence as for *guilt*. Being so, it evokes a very specific past moment, the same one as so often: it describes the night of the regicide, or the simple image of it, when indeed Macbeth's hair stood on end and the smallest sound was an amplifying alarm.[46] Macbeth's saintliness was within his murderousness, never more present than it was that night, in his need for blessing and in his preternatural fears. But it is a night that is here not so much remembered as transfigured. As so often, the ironies run in both directions. Macbeth is replaying the murder both as it was and how he half-wishes it might have been. So, it becomes as though the last, lost night of his sensitive humanity. He killed, and he was *alive* to it all. The terror and pathos – indeed what Kierkegaard would perhaps see as the moment's comedy – is that Macbeth would hereby turn the murder into an act of fear and piety.

Hence that hint of monody, and of mourning for all he has murdered. A certain choked remorse here takes strangely speculative somatic form, like a rippled breathing upon Macbeth's stilled underground waters. Nowhere is there a more shivering embodiment of the 'fear of the good'. For just as Macbeth here is nostalgic for guilt, he is horrified by the thought of goodness, by the terrifying power of conscience. Characteristically, he at once reaches for and *refuses* both consolation and repair. The memory is absolutely poised, then, between a brewed and implacable brutality and a glimmer of possibility. Might he start again? Might he be there again, with a choice once more between feeling and anaesthesia, a choice for life or for death?

It is the most intimate, almost self-amazed confession, and a kind of recovery of the wondrousness of being. There could hardly be a more tactile thought than Macbeth's here, one more in touch with the inscrutable plumbing of a body, or the queasy surprise that we even belong to one. But the surprise is the point: *could that really have been me?* And so, as he acknowledges, 'the time ha's beene': it is over. Indeed perhaps the neurotic 'hypersensibility' he recalls was merely proof that he was always in some pre-frozen fashion written for guilt, and that he could thaw only into bloody terror. Even in innocence he was in dread; if he was waiting for or expecting something, perhaps it was merely for this fearful shiver truly to be worth it. For it is also a speech of horrible self-recognition: as though he somehow knows that a 'dismall Treatise' was his cue to rise; that he would 'stirre' into 'life' in the darkest hour.

The speech then represents, again, the evacuated mimicry of what Kierkegaard calls 'earnestness'. Redemption and despair may well turn on a knife-edge of 'possibility': but not for Macbeth, who witnesses endless possibility only as numbing, paralysing proof of *necessity*:

> To lack possibility means either that everything has become necessary for a person or that everything has become trivial . . . The determinist, the fatalist, is in despair . . . because everything for him has become necessity . . . Personhood is a synthesis of possibility and necessity . . . The self of the determinist cannot breathe, for it is impossible to breathe necessity exclusively, because that would utterly suffocate a person's self . . . Therefore the fatalist's worship of God is at most an interjection, and essentially it is a muteness, a mute capitulation: he

[46] In his first soliloquy Macbeth talks of the 'horrid image' which 'doth unfix my hair', suggesting the coalescence, again, of pre-image, act and remembrance (1.3.134).

> is unable to pray . . . Nevertheless, possibility alone or necessity alone can no more be the condition for the breathing of a prayer than oxygen alone or nitrogen alone can be that for breathing . . . if there is nothing but necessity, man is essentially as inarticulate as the animals.[47]

Consequently, if Macbeth is in such moments born into anything, it is only to *himself* as the sole imprimatur of being, and into an irreparable detachment from full humanity. Hence the way the pathos cohabits with mordancy, with a retrospective contempt, and with a uniquely Macbethian way of speaking that is in equal measures sarcastic and deadly earnest, as raw as a skinned beast and yet almost baroquely mannered. 'Comic ventriloquism' reaches here its demonic apogee. Macbeth quotes 'innocent' childlike transparencies (reprising his wife's early estimations and taunts) and invokes their contiguous sentimental faiths. Such faiths, we recall, characterized a 'dative' ingenuousness that could not long survive temptation. He now stares at this past self in scorn, as at an illusorily stirring corpse. But equally he does so nostalgically, in the full knowledge that here, now, in the meltdown of his fugal rage, such 'milky' consolations have never been more necessary. (Or if 'he' doesn't, the rhetoric does it for him, recalling and telescoping the stakes of his movement through the play.) The speech, like the play it encapsulates, vibrates upon its opening chords. To have 'almost forgot', and to concentrate all conceivable imaginative movement into the absurdity of that 'almost' – magnetized by amnesia, petrified by oblivion, suspended in the interim – is Macbeth's immanent comi-pathetic, comi-pathological cue.

---

47 Kierkegaard, *The Sickness Unto Death*, pp. 40–1.

MONSIEUR MACBETH: FROM JARRY TO IONESCO

RUTH MORSE

SHAKESPEARE EN FRANCE

The 'afterlife of *Macbeth*' in France raises issues which any study of 'Shakespeare offshoots'[1] must address, but extends them to a different linguistic and cultural situation: what constitutes 'adaptation' as it moves towards a new work; the intertextual status of the new work and reception by its audiences; the historical moment and contexts in which it is written and received, from theatrical fashions to national and world events; to politics broadly speaking; to its place in the developing *oeuvre* of its adaptor. In France, circumstances have coincided to make *this* play exceptionally intriguing, beyond the defamiliarization which anglophone readers may experience in considering a play beyond our own linguistic boundaries. As a case history, French *Macbeth*s require rather more history than may be necessary elsewhere: in order to draw the portrait I need the landscape, setting Alfred Jarry and Eugène Ionesco in a series of *conjonctures*, for however well established and confident French theatrical culture was in either period, it was always vulnerable to innovative attack. The treble, even quadruple content means beginning with a brief reminder of early French translations of Shakespeare; moving to how Shakespeare was known (not quite 'read' and 'seen'), via the French Opera composer, Verdi (whose second version of *Macbeth* was revised for Paris, with Paris conventions in mind); before concentrating on a schoolboy publicist and a Rumanian playwright. Two things above all: in France, as elsewhere in continental Europe, 'Shakespeare' never implied 'familiar', and, until the last two decades never implied 'known' at all. Concomitantly, unfamiliarity has allowed the erection of a genealogy which is widely accepted, and, as I shall demonstrate, false.

What passed for 'Shakespeare' was for many years so boldly adapted as to be not Shakespeare at all. The well-known history of Shakespeare translation from Voltaire's quarrels over correctness, or the adaptations of Ducis, to the accelerating number of versions which punctuate the nineteenth and twentieth centuries, gave 'Shakespeare' an instability quite unlike the dominance of the Johnson–Steevens 'received' text, whose availability in English always offered a contrast to the variety of acting versions. For all its critical quarrels, France, unlike Germany, never had a 'received' translation, a text which was known, or at least widely referred to.[2] This implied that knowledge of 'Shakespeare' also encompassed a kind of 'received familiarity', in which what is known may be what is *believed to be known*, which may not accord with any English-language edition of the play at all, but with ideas about it: in the case of *Macbeth*, as will become clear, with a 'recognized' plot cycle of political violence as well as 'remembered' visual icons of witches, daggers and sleepwalking. The dubiety

[1] I use the terminology of Ruby Cohn's pathbreaking book, *Modern Shakespeare Offshoots* (Princeton, 1976).

[2] Though even here it has to be remembered how constantly the Schlegel–Tieck translations were themselves modified by subsequent editors and translators. See Roger Paulin, *Native Literature and Foreign Genius: The Critical Reception of Shakespeare in Germany 1682–1914* (Hildesheim, 2003).

of 'received', 'recognized' and 'remembered' raises the problem that the inter-text, and, with it, audience experience of intertextuality, may evoke an original which is un-received, un-recognizable, or un-remembered, because unknown.

Definitions are notoriously difficult, so a hypothetical spectrum of referentiality is not just useful but may be the best we can do. Clearly, habits of translation were for many centuries more relaxed than would now be acceptable, and included modernization, rearrangement, suppression and improvement. Ducis, who 'corrected' Shakespeare, and whose corrected Shakespeare was used by the earliest Italian translators as if he represented Shakespeare, would be a clear example. At one limit, heavily adapted translation can scarcely be distinguished from new work based upon an older original, beyond the assertions of a 'translator' who may wish to smuggle his own work into being by attaching it to a high-status author: one might think of Voltaire's *La Mort de César* (1736) in this context.[3] There is a third term, which is a text explicitly adapted, not presented as a literal rendering, but nonetheless a version of an original. It is hard to draw lines; just as one generation's realism is rejected by the next, so what passed as 'translation' comes to be rejected as inaccurate, incorrect, insufficient, and one generation's 'adaptation' becomes another's 'offshoot'.

We might recognize three main variants as adaptation becomes offshoot: the slash and burn, the knock off, and the smash and grab. The first, 'slash and burn', includes the 'strong' or extreme adaptation which represents, corrects, and replaces (Voltaire is a stronger example than Dryden, because in English the constant alternative of a 'reading' Shakespeare survives); the 'knock off', as its name implies, imitates, usually by cataloguing what must be included, as it were with a checklist in hand (for example, the film *Men of Respect*). Thus far the categories parallel my first distinctions. But the third, 'smash and grab', which I have elsewhere called the 'satellite', takes ('extracts' might be better, but there is also the 'affiliative gesture' which deploys the original's authority for respectability or protection) one aspect out of a whole play and treats it as a new independent entity, such as Caliban, or Mary Cowden Clarke's Gruach-prequel, 'The Thane's Daughter', in her *Girlhoods*, or Shostakovich's 1934 'adaptation' of Nikolai Leskov's story for *Lady Macbeth of Mtsensk*.[4] My vernacular categories are far from denigration: Verdi's *Macbeth* is a 'slash and burn' and Shakespeare's own *The Merry Wives of Windsor* may be the earliest 'smash and grab'.[5] With the introduction of Hecate and her singing sisters as spectacle, it may be, of course, that *Macbeth* as we have it is itself a 'slash and burn'.

SHAKESPEARE: THE BOOK

In a larger sense, there are histories of habits of reading, histories of what is accepted as influence. In France *Macbeth* resembled a traditional plot: a king is betrayed and deposed by a faithful lieutenant who is subsequently betrayed and deposed in turn. Insofar as 'plot' exists as a distinctive and separable entity, *Macbeth* offered a political cycle ripe for allegorical application. French Shakespeare, continental Shakespeare, was – and continues to be – evidently a writer of *political* tragedies, for readers formed in a reading culture which has always proposed 'morals', and prompt to recognize what universal

[3] The complexities of this work are set out in Voltaire, *La mort de César*, ed. A.-M. Rousseau (Paris, 1964). Voltaire's own play is not to be confused with his translation (at the time considered literal) of part of Shakespeare's play (published 1764).

[4] In my 'Taking the Measure of *The Tempest*: *The Diviners* and *Mama Day*', in *Variations sur la lettre, le metre et la mesure*, ed. Dominique Goy-Blanquet (Amiens, 1996), pp. 41–54. Leskov's story may use *Macbeth*, but it is already far from Shakespeare's play, and Shostakovich's opera owes more to Dostoyevsky than to his so-called original. It is not insignificant that when Shostakovich rewrote the opera in 1958 (it had been condemned by Stalin and withdrawn in 1936), he called it *Katerina Ismailova*. Another test case would be the 'recognition' of Othello in a new story of extreme jealousy, where it is rather the tenuousness of the connection that is really extreme, as in Trollope's *He Knew He Was Right* or the film *Jubal*. 'Shakespearian' becomes an intensifier rather than a mark of influence.

[5] Von's wonderful cartoon (London, 1982) would count in my scheme as an edition (and Anne Tauté is credited as the editor).

message the lonely, prescient, genius shares about the eternal wheel of political fortune. This means that in following French afterlives we need to be aware that *Macbeth*'s ostensible resemblance to political 'cycle' tragedies of betrayal made plays which shared the 'cycle' plot 'resemble' *Macbeth*. 'Influence' is a tricky business. One other important generalization which can be made about Shakespeare in France is that he has always been a critical stick with which to beat the ever-presumed rule-bound decadence of French theatre.

This long preamble helps explain why, to understand Eugène Ionesco's *Macbett* of 1972, we must reach back almost a century, because the history of understanding Alfred Jarry's *Ubu roi* of 1896 intersects with *Macbeth*, with criticism, with ideas of the doomed artist, and with arguments within French theatrical production, including opera production for the Théâtre Lyrique. Only after building up layers of approach will I reach 1972: first, the diachronic melding of different kinds of 'theatre' which stretch back beyond the schoolboy Jarry, and from which, by the sixties, Anouilh and Beckett had already profited; second, how *Macbeth* could be read in France (and in Rumania); third, Ionesco's work at this moment in his career (he was sixty when the play was produced); fourth, Ionesco's politics, particularly his radical-conservative anti-communism; which, fifth, intersected with Jan Kott's insistent approach to *Macbeth* which identified in it a message: murder. Sixthly and lastly, as well as above all, *Macbeth* offers an unusual case, because, as I shall argue, for reasons which have to do with coincidence, criticism and legitimation, Jarry's play (if that is what it was), *Ubu roi, became* an adaptation.

One of the intriguing aspects to the afterlife of *Macbeth* in France is indirection. It is an acute distinction in the French case that, historically, a large number of Shakespeare translations were the work of men who knew little or no English. Thus the 're-'translating efforts which so marked the nineteenth century, made often with great fanfare, were equally often successive waves of modernizing or rewriting rather than a fresh look at an original. Those 'retranslations' sometimes became the bases from which other 'translators' worked across national linguistic boundaries, as was the case in Italy. Even those translators who had some English, who had even, perhaps, learned English in Britain, had no historical or philological training.[6] Not only did this encourage the 'recognition' of the plot or character types, it gave a certain urgency to the ambition to adapt. The history of French translation is one of varnishing the French of previous translations to create better 'replacement' texts, that is, translations which stood alone (as opposed to 'accompaniment' texts which function as aids or cribs). The very existence of prior translations was a competitive stimulus, but the presumption that there was a known source text, a stable edition, which one read across or through earlier efforts, repeated the history of translation elsewhere.[7] It need never, of course, have resulted in poor-quality texts, given talented writers. The problem of 'scholarship' (including problems of the stable edition) began to obtrude in the course of nineteenth-century arguments about nationalism (the origins of romance but also the origins of the European peoples, and, thus, the competition with German scholarly superiority). In France, therefore, the ground base of Shakespeare's political tragedies includes other kinds of argument.

[6] This certainly includes Ducis, the first French adaptor to treat complete plays and to stage his adaptations. LaPlace's *Théâtre anglois* (1746–9) extracts scenes. Ducis's *Macbeth*(ish) was performed in a first version in 1769, and finally collected in 1790 (*Oeuvres* II). He was well aware of LeTourneur's attempts to translate the plays for readers. By a historical irony, when Ducis was elected to the Académie française he succeeded Voltaire. See John Golder's indispensable *Shakespeare for the Age of Reason: The Earliest Stage Adaptations of Jean-François Duçis 1769–1792* (Oxford, 1992). It is of more than incidental interest that Ducis omitted Fortinbras from his *Hamlet*, that Mallarmé's famous comments on the play were written in the context of discussion of Ducis's decision, and that Peter Brook made the same choice for his two Paris *Hamlet*s (2000, 2002).

[7] Here my terminology follows earlier work on translation, in my *Truth and Convention in the Middle Ages: Rhetoric, Reality, and Representation* (Cambridge, 1995), ch. 5.

Germany had the famous Schlegel/Tieck version (as well as Luther's Bible), so an idea of 'received' translation and referential *loci communi*. France has never had translations with this kind of intense vernacular standing, which invite close attention to their verbal detail. Even when nineteenth-century 'scientific' ideas of accuracy began to hold sway, in theory if not in practice, Shakespeare translations continued to be overpainted versions 'after' Johnson-Steevens as previously rendered by Le Tourneur, Dumas, Montégut or Hugo *fils*. Neither Hugo *père*'s own *Cromwell* nor his *Préface* for his son's multi-volume translation was based on immediate engagement with English originals.

But immediate engagement (surely the tightest demonstration of influence), even with translations of the plays, was not the only 'engagement'. Familiarity can emerge elsewhere, and it is not clear what one ought to call the Lambs' *Tales*. Their *Contes de Shakespeare* were not only sold as beautifully illustrated children's books (individual, several, and sometimes complete), but towards the end of the nineteenth century individual tales were extracted, commented, and provided with pedagogic introductions for the use of schoolchildren learning English in the elite 'colleges' of the Third Republic.[8] One must imagine the republican English teacher, Mallarmé, not only writing briefly about the place of Fortinbras in the earliest translation of *Hamlet* by Ducis (no place, as Ducis had suppressed him altogether), but as using the Lambs' *Tales* as part of the academic syllabus. There were even special editions of the *Tales* for the Catholic private schools. The Shakespeare Gallery, too, had its own French incarnations. In 1844 Amadée Pichot, indefatigable entrepreneur, edited a *Galérie* which contained plot-summaries and bilingual 'beauties' extracted from each play, *molto brevissimo*. My own Montégut *Oeuvres Complètes* (1867–70) is *richement illustrées*, with engravings collected from numerous sources (the thirteen illustrations to *Macbeth* are those of F. Wentworth). The costumes are typical of the kind of Romantic exoticising of history which owes so much to Walter Scott, whose own presence and influence in France – not least as a reader of Shakespeare – I pass by.

STAGE AND SCENE

False familiarity grew from theatrical performance and reports of theatrical performance. If Garrick had already presented the 'dagger scene' on his Paris visits in the eighteenth century, and the famous tour of 1827/8 included *Macbeth*, we must remember that their adapted *Macbeth*s were not ours.[9] Shakespeare was also operatic. The story of Berlioz's fascination with things (and persons) Shakespearian requires no retelling here, but it is worth remembering that Berlioz's adored Miss Smithson was part of Macready's English-language troupe (playing Lady Macbeth to Macready's thane). The combination of mime and good theatrical programmes did much to convey plots and heightened emotion to francophone audiences. By then, of course, English was *chic*. But Shakespeare might not be played in English, and if he was performed in French, then French exigencies applied. It may seem eccentric to categorize Verdi's 1865 revision of his 1847 *Macbeth* as French, but so profoundly was it re-conceived for Paris, that it became a French opera.[10] The musical requirements of great roles plus the theatrical

[8] I have discussed the Lambs in more detail in 'From the Lambs to the Limelight: Shakespeare in French Education', in *Shifting the Scene: Shakespeare in European Culture*, ed. Ladina Bezzola Lambert and Balz Engler (Newark, Delaware, 2004). The bibliographical problem is complex, because editions varied in content and in illustrations without acknowledgement. Translations began to appear in 1842.

[9] See Marjorie Shaw, 'Shakespearian Performances in Paris in 1827–8' in *Studies in French Literature*, ed. J. C. Ireson, I. D. MacFarlane and Garnet Rees (Manchester, 1968), pp. 301–13. There is an excellent sketch of early French Shakespeare as well as of the tour of 1827/8 in Peter Raby, *Fair Ophelia: Harriet Smithson Berlioz* (Cambridge, 1982), ch. 4. For the availability of dual-language texts in the theatre, see p. 59.

[10] The critical literature on Verdi's *Macbeth* is extensive. I follow *A Verdi Companion*, ed. William Weaver (New York, 1979), and Weaver's essay, 'The Shakespeare Verdi Knew', in *Verdi's Macbeth: A Sourcebook*, ed. David Rosen and Andrew Porter (Cambridge, 1984).

conventions of great spectacle meant that chorus and ballet must be served (and there was a new second-act duet). Boito (librettist for *Otello* and *Falstaff*) read English, but Piave (librettist for *Macbeth*) did not, and, in any case, he was working from Verdi's own sketch, which concentrated on Macbeth, Lady Macbeth, and the weird sisters, what I have already referred to as the dagger, the sleepwalking, and the witches. Verdi instructed Varesi, his first Macbeth, to serve the poet rather than the composer, and sought hard to find a Lady Macbeth who would not prettify her role.[11]

The Paris opera was not a success, and, characteristically, contemporary reviews accused Verdi of ignorance. Verdi was hurt. I quote his reaction, because it illustrates the insistent claim that the original is palpable in the translation:

> [One French reviewer] states that I didn't know Shakespeare when I wrote *Macbeth*. Oh, in this they are very wrong. It may be that I have not rendered *Macbeth* well, but that I don't know, don't understand, and don't feel Shakespeare – no, by God, no. He is a favourite poet of mine, whom I have had in my hands from earliest youth, and whom I read and reread constantly.[12]

Verdi read Shakespeare in translation, and the available Italian translations were notoriously 'adaptations'.[13] What he found – despite them, and with the critical help, it must be remembered, of Schlegel – was character in conflict, character under pressure. Verdi provided the political background as a mute Duncan, as choruses moving upstage, against which his downstage principals could concentrate on individual psychological moments such as the imaginary dagger or the sleepwalking (the generic model for the traditional 'mad scene' reminds us of other stage requirements).[14] First, Verdi insists as readers did for centuries – upon his direct contact with Shakespeare's mind by reading through or across the translation; second, Verdi's exceptional psychological penetration is unquestionable; but third, by contrast, Verdi's achievement was strikingly limited, since subsequent writers significantly failed to follow his emphasis on Lady Macbeth.[15] Understandably enough, sopranos resist an instruction to make their singing ugly.[16] Verdi's choices about *Macbeth*, then, reinforce what was 'known' about the play without determining subsequent interpretation.

It would be safe to conclude, then, that in the nineteenth century, in France, there were ideas available of *Macbeth* and of the Macbeths which included, by plot, the political wheel; and, by character, the mix of supernatural and psychological (not yet so denominated) which excerpted the dagger and the sleepwalking. These two moments of vision were linked to the political plot in the micro-sense of individual guilt for treason, an emphasis which differs from a public macro-description of a cycle of power perpetually betrayed. The legitimacy of Duncan's authority was not in question, and there was no poetry. It is well worth reminding ourselves that 'Shakespeare' was thus identified with the macro-level of plot, character, and visual

---

[11] Weaver, *Companion*, pp. 184–5.

[12] Letter to Escudier, April 1865 (*Verdi's Macbeth*, p. 119). It is a striking feature of myths after Verdi that an article in the *Guardian* on Verdi's use of Schiller and Shakespeare repeats the old chestnut that 'Verdi kept copies of both writers on his bedside table'; as he read no English, quite what his *Shakespeare de chevet* was is a question (Tim Ashley, 'Three Giants', 18 April 2003, Review, p. 9).

[13] See James Hepkowski's two Cambridge Opera Handbooks: Giuseppi Verdi, *Falstaff* (Cambridge, 1983), p. 23 and Giuseppi Verdi, *Otello* (1987). Weaver thinks Verdi used more than one Italian translation, probably based upon pre-existing French ones, and dire. Later, in Verdi's library there was an unused copy of François–Victor Hugo's translation – which would have been rather later than his *Macbeth* (*Verdi's Macbeth*, p. 14[illegible]n).

[14] Jonas Barish deals succinctly with Verdi's 'Madness, Hallucination, and Sleepwalking' in the context of contemporary opera (*Verdi's Macbeth*, pp. 149–55). Ionesco, too, calls for upstage crowds of witness to the destructions of war.

[15] He even had trouble with his own Lady Macbeths, who wanted changes for their voices at the cost of his idea, as in the revival for Dublin in 1859 (*Verdi Companion*, p. 147). The failure of interiority where female characters are concerned only becomes more pronounced in Jarry and Ionesco.

[16] Though the historical recording of Callas's one complete (Italian) *Macbeth* is instructive in this instance.

icon, and never by micro-verbal attention.[17] It is against this background that I turn to Jarry and Ionesco.

ALFRED JARRY AND THE POLITICS OF PUBLICITY

Spectacle, and especially mime, comes at the heart of the theatrical text to which criticism always points when *Macbeth* is discussed in France. And here I reach a key methodological moment, because the reason for this association is *Ubu roi*, enshrined as the first, and most important, French offshoot of *Macbeth*. It is not. *Why* not, or perhaps better, *how* not, is a complicated matter. The association – in the minds of critics and in general culture – grew from that perceived plot resemblance with which I began, the wheel of fortune in which political power is a cycle of betrayal, usurpation and murder. The central figure, Père Ubu, began life as a parody of a much-detested teacher in a schoolboy play; by the time Jarry had rewritten it into something for the professional stage, Père and Mère Ubu had been transformed into a broad and vulgar farce which takes place in a 'nowhere' which is named 'Poland', just as 'Russia' is merely another kingdom. Characters have regional accents, including 'English', but the accents are part of the insistence upon no-place. Although the play begins with Mère Ubu urging her husband to become king by massacring the current king's whole family, her suggestion arises from her urgent need to distract his attention from murdering her. Above all, *Ubu* sends up the idea of legitimacy and authority. That is not a likeness to *Macbeth*.

Ubu was an extraordinary theatrical event, not only in 1896, but for years afterwards, not least because of the youth of its author/compiler. Jarry and his friends were children when they constructed something which later became the transfer of 'marionette theatre', or 'guignols' (in which puppets mime actors) to the Paris stage, with adult actors miming puppets. *Ubu* is such a mishmash of reworked motifs that one can all-too-easily claim to have found specific sources; but Jarry's original point was to parody and deride traditional theatrical devices in universal condemnation. *Ubu* was boldly, extravagantly, antipathetic to the conventions of 'bourgeois' theatre; it was about political murder; therefore, it was doubly revolutionary. It was one of the founding moments of what, before Martin Esslin gave us 'The Theatre of the Absurd', was already called by Rachilde (the pseudonym of Marguerite Valette) 'l'Ecole des démons de l'absurde', and therefore, left wing by definition. Jarry wrote, and persuaded his friends to write, the kinds of preliminary manifestos which prepare the way for a major cultural event, which he persuaded Lugné-Poe to produce. *Ubu* required defence, and it particularly required a defence which made it seriously unserious: assimilating Jarry to Shakespeare was one way of doing that, because, after all, Shakespeare famously (against French neo-classical norms) broke decorum. And Jarry, who had reached the age of twenty-three when *Ubu* was first performed in Paris, killed himself with a combination of drink and drugs by the time he was thirty-four, having produced a sequence, or a cycle, of Ubu-related plays, polemics and cartoons. But only the original *Ubu* seemed, even to supporters, *original*. The sequels had, wrote Albert Thibaudet, 'pas plus de rapport entre les deux styles qu'entre la *Tempête* shakespearienne et le *Caliban* de Renan. Jarry fit d'ailleurs mieux que d'avoir écrit *Ubu*. Il fut Ubu. Il se fit holocauste pour Ubu. Shakespeare acteur, cette fois, a mangé Shakespeare auteur.'[18]

---

[17] There is thus nothing, despite the welcoming retention of second- and third-person pronominal distinctions or the emphasis on rhetoric in French education, to compare to Adrian Poole's analysis in 'Macbeth and the Third Person', *Proceedings of the British Academy: Lectures and Memoirs*, 109 (Oxford, 1999), pp. 73–92.

[18] 'There is no more relation between the two styles than between the Shakespearian *Tempest* and Renan's *Caliban*. Besides, Jarry did better than just writing *Ubu*. He was Ubu. He made himself a sacrifice for Ubu. This time Shakespeare the actor has eaten Shakespeare the author.' This occurs, almost in passing, in a brief notice in *La Nouvelle Revue Française*, 30 (1 June 1928), 52–3, which was extracted for the blurb on the back cover of the popular paperback (Paris, 1962). This and other translations are mine.

That isn't 'like' either, but what is happening is that an idea of 'Shakespeare' is assuming false familiarity. Thibaudet elevates and legitimates the young man, doomed to repeat himself to death, and the association sticks.

Let me modify my denial slightly. If, in circumstances in which 'Shakespeare's *Macbeth*' is little known, and what *is* known is believed to be a familiar political plot, then what is believed to be *Macbeth* arguably replaces *Macbeth*. Critics, like translators, repeated each other and were believed. They associated Jarry's play with Shakespeare's, and thereby reinterpreted it, strengthening precisely the sense that *Macbeth* was a 'known' plot, and that resemblance through a married couple was enough, despite the lack of daggers, sleepwalking, ghosts or witches. Part of Jarry's brilliance as a publicist, or perhaps just his good luck, was the immediate association of Ubu with Macbeth. Ubu may not have started 'like' Macbeth, but he achieved the status of portraiture with the proviso 'parody'. In the first half of the last century the criteria for source-hunting were less stringent than they have since become; it is not surprising that readers – for *Ubu* was little revived – took traditional assertions as true. In the absence of familiarity with *Macbeth*, there remains a presumption of influence.[19]

Ubu is not 'like' Macbeth. He is one of those betraying traitors who is betrayed in turn. That is too tenuous an argument for influence. Ubu may have a wife, but she is not remotely like Lady Macbeth; their marriage is neither sexually charged nor childless.[20] There is no conscience, no agony of decision, no reflection upon action; no dagger; no sleepwalking. But the need to legitimate Jarry's scandalous puppet-show led his supporters to reach for Shakespeare, that stick with which to beat French theatrical decorum. Nobody had ever combined the *guignols* and the legitimate theatre before. It is hard to overemphasize this point for an anglophone audience, since the degree to which contemporary French theatre was restricted to 'heightened' language made it impossible for characters to speak in ordinary ways. *Ubu* opened with the nonce-word 'merdre' ('shite' might be close), which caused a riot, and Shakespeare was called in to legitimate indecorousness. It may further be said that the plays are not 'like' because there is nothing 'like' *Ubu*. By the institutional ironies we know well, *Ubu* has subsequently become an important reference, and sometimes a 'morceau choisi', one of those extracts schoolchildren have to memorize as part of culture. With time, not only has *Ubu* faded into sepia tradition and lost the shock of the new, but it has been reframed into ancestry, because of family resemblance to that Theatre of the Absurd which dominated the middle of the last century. Ionesco spoke for many when tracing theatrical lines of descent:

> Surtout, il y a eu Jarry. *Ubu roi* est une oeuvre sensationnelle où l'on parle pas de la tyrannie, où l'on *montre* la tyrannie sous la forme de ce bonhomme odieux, archétype de la goinfrerie matérielle, politique, morale qu'est le père Ubu.[21]

What has not faded is its kill-or-be-killed caricature: after events Jarry could not have conceived, they no longer seem caricatural, the excesses hardly excessive. In time's whirligig, Père Ubu's revenges

---

19 One disagrees with John Gross at one's peril, but his recent *After Shakespeare: Writing Inspired by the World's Greatest Author* (Oxford, 2002), pp. 295–6 assumes both this relationship and Jarry's detailed knowledge of Shakespeare, as does Curtis Perry in 'Vaulting Ambitions and Killing Machines: Jarry, Ionesco, and the Senecan Absurd', in Donald Hedrick and Bryan Reynolds, eds., *Shakespeare without Class: Misappropriations of Cultural Capital* (Houndsmill, 2000)

20 Even Keith Beaumont, writing about *Ubu*, hedges his comparison to *Macbeth* with multiple conditionals – it would be practically impossible, in France, to deny the connection. See his *Jarry: Ubu roi* (London, 1987), pp. 31–5. It is also a period feature of his criticism that he simply dismisses Mère Ubu without discussion. This may be period blindness, but it is also blind to the period under discussion, in which the wickedness and power of the idea of Lady Macbeth were problematic.

21 'Above all, there was Jarry. *Ubu Roi* is a sensational work where one doesn't speak of tyranny, but where one shows tyranny in the form of this odious bloke, this archetype of solid, political, ethical piggery we call Old Ubu.' This and the following quotations from Ionesco are taken from a book-length interview by Claude Bonnefoy, *Eugène Ionesco: Entre la Vie et le rêve. Entretiens avec Claude Bonnefoy* (Paris, 1966), p. 185.

make him a *père fondateur*. In retrospect, then, *Ubu* has become taken for granted as an adaptation of *Macbeth*.[22] It *became* one.

IONESCO, FIN DE PARTIE

Thus far I have evoked a series of contexts for the study of 'offshoots'. Here, I shall move from the landscape to the figure: one play in the career of one author. This is not the place to set any scene for a history of twentieth-century French theatre or the growth of what we now call 'the absurd' in plays, prose, and philosophy. It is well known how exceptionally rich was the post-war French stage. Ionesco's colleagues and competitors included Adamov, Anouilh, Artaud, Genet, Sartre the King, and, supremely, Beckett, whose English is suffused with memories of Shakespeare. One thinks additionally of Brecht, Miller, Pirandello. Nor am I going to rehearse the so-called 'London Controversy', which began with Kenneth Tynan taking exception to what he perceived as Ionesco's failure to continue his creative trajectory, except to stress how much incomprehension is due to inadequate translation. English critic and Franco-Rumanian playwright talk past each other: Ionesco thinks that Tynan wants socialist realism while Tynan thinks that the shock of Ionesco's new does not survive a second viewing precisely because the plays give us only

> isolated robots, conversing in cartoon-strip balloons of dialogue that are sometimes hilarious, sometimes evocative, and quite often neither, on which occasions they become profoundly tiresome. (As with shaggy dog stories, few of M. Ionesco's plays survive a second hearing . . .) This world is not mine, but I recognise it to be a valid personal vision, presented with great imaginative aplomb and verbal audacity. The peril arises when it is held up for general emulation as the gateway to the theatre of the future, that bleak new world from which the humanist heresies of faith in logic and belief in man will forever be banished.[23]

The high regard in which Ionesco was then held left him almost above criticism, but it also made it difficult for him – as, no doubt, for poor, doomed Jarry – to carry on without repeating himself.

By 1972, when *Macbett* was staged at the Théâtre de la Rive Gauche by Jacques Mauclair, Ionesco was renowned to the point of being a public institution.[24] He was also depressed, in the grip of writer's block. At this point, Ionesco was insisting that he was an a-political, as well as a non-psychological, non-realist, supra-generic writer. This fooled nobody. In the late sixties he was a constant angry contributor to the press, writing letters critical of contemporary political life.[25] He had accepted a mystical Catholicism, and in 1971 he succeeded Jean Paulhan as one of the forty immortals of the Académie française. This is neither the fastidiousness of an intellectual above the fray nor the political commitment characteristic of the 'engaged' writer. The hostility expressed by the Left was not new: satire of the fat cat Right was one thing, but lumping *all* political action together was retrograde. The French Left objected not to the subject (which appeared to be politics), nor to the style, but to the crudity which elided all power as tyranny and neglected to except the heroic historical struggle.[26]

But Ionesco also fooled everybody. In a kind of metatheatrical metonymy we can see the thing contained being taken for the container, as if the two were not inseparable (though far from

---

[22] As in Nancy Lane's passing comment that Ionesco's '*Macbett* is a grim clown show which lacks most of the spontaneity and verve of Jarry's Macbeth parody, *Ubu roi*', in her *Understanding Eugène Ionesco* (Columbia, SC, 1994), p. 150.

[23] The extract in *Notes and Counter Notes*, trans. Donald Watson (London, 1964 [orig. Paris, 1962]), pp. 91–2, is slightly truncated, but does not change the thrust of the original article, the *Observer* (22 June 1958), 15.

[24] Set and Costumes Jacques Noël, Music Francisco Semprum and Michel Christodoulidès, played by Roger Jacquet, Jacques Dannoville, Jacques Mauclair, Geneviève Fontanel, Brigitte Fossey, Alain Mottet.

[25] As recounted by Gilles Plazy, *Eugène Ionesco, le rire et l'espérance: une biographie* (Paris, 1994).

[26] It is the relationship with a badly understood Brecht which Edith Kern emphasizes in her 'Macbett in the Light of Verfremdung', in *The Two Faces of Ionesco*, ed. Rosette C. Lamont and Melvin J. Friedman (Troy, NY, 1978), pp. 215–44.

indistinguishable). It was one of the problems of Modernism that the most technically innovative writers turned out also to be the most conservative. Ionesco's new wineskins contained familiar flavours. With time, too, it becomes clear just how constrained his characters are by gender and class. At this distance he seems increasingly a Cold Warrior, whose politics react against the French Left's incomprehensions about what was happening in Central and Eastern Europe. In addition, I would go so far as to say that just as we reorient Ibsen, a century on, within the world of the well-made play, so, theatrically, Ionesco's similarity to Feydeau, his exploitation of the traditional techniques of farce, only becomes clearer as the years pass.

It is a feature of Ionesco's career that *La Cantatrice chauve* was written before he knew anything about staging or producing a play; one might argue that as in the course of his career he acquired more and better stage technique, so he found himself succumbing to precisely what he began by aiming to overturn. *La Cantatrice chauve* famously had no singer in it, bald or otherwise. Produced when Ionesco was already in his forties, its roots stretch twenty years further back, in Rumania, when Ionesco was failing to learn English from one of those 'made easy' readers which are characteristically constructed on the principle of useful vocabulary at whatever cost to sense. The play's title, by 1950, when it had become a play in French, was *L'Anglais sans peine* – but because a similarly-titled play had recently been produced the company chose something more startling. The Martins and the Smiths were apparently the characters in the Reader, whose sentence constructions so appealed to the illogical. To say that Ionesco depends increasingly on theatre technique (as modified, of course, by his own generation), that in his late period he reached further back to his theatrical ancestors, is perhaps only to recognize that his experience was not so exceptional after all. Like other playwrights in a fallow period, he adapted, and he returned to his own theatrical beginnings. Like other satirists he began as an *enfant terrible*, but grew into something much more conservative.

English may have remained beyond Ionesco's grasp, but he read, and reread, Shakespeare in translation. At least he said he did. Interviewing him, Claude Bonnefoy asked,

> 'Je reviens à Shakespeare. Que représente-t-il pour vous? Pour quelles raisons semblez-vous le considérer comme un dramaturge exceptionnel?'
>
> 'Exceptionnel, oui. Mais surtout, nous le comprenons bien. N'a-t-il pas dit, "Le monde est une histoire de fous racontée par un idiot", n'a-t-il pas dit que tout n'est que "bruit et fureur"? C'est l'ancêtre du théâtre de l'absurde. Il a tout dit, depuis bien longtemps. Beckett essaie de le répéter. Moi, même pas: puisqu'il a si bien dit ce qu'il a dit, que pouvons-nous ajouter?'[27]

The 'anti' position here, implicitly, is anti-French classicism, but in its critical position it is itself traditional: Shakespeare is ever the stick. That is one of the lights in which translations of Shakespeare have always been read. He is *the* contestatory playwright. Ionesco believed, equally traditionally, that all playwrights speak to us at some point in their own persons (here identifying Shakespeare himself with his character, as is apparent from the old-fashioned author-attribution in the quotation), whether this is popular with critics or not. In *Macbett* Ionesco's own most obvious direct address to the audience is Macbett's oration on the necessities of history, entirely out of character, but in a place not too distant from where *anglophone* readers might have expected something akin to 'Tomorrow and tomorrow'. Ionesco's view of that speech – that it

[27] 'I come back to Shakespeare. What does he represent for you? Why do you think of him as an exceptional dramatist?' 'Exceptional, yes. But, above all, we understand him so well. Didn't he say, 'The world is a story of madmen told by an idiot'?, didn't he say that everything is 'noise and rage'? He is the ancestor of the theatre of the absurd. He has already said everything, a long time ago. Beckett tries to repeat it, I, not even that. Since he's said what he had to say so well, what can we add?' [My translation has not assimilated Ionesco's quotations to the originals, and the 'madmen' are significantly misremembered and added] (Bonnefoy, *Eugène Ionesco*, p. 49). Shortly afterwards he returns to this point and again places Shakespeare in a line of ancestors, p. 129. For his insistence on recognizing Shakespeare in his characters, see pp. 164–5.

is Shakespeare speaking *in propria persona* – legitimates his placement of his own. In addition, the question of the necessary murders was a subject of Shakespeare criticism.

The French translation of Jan Kott's magisterial interpretation, *Shakespeare Our Contemporary*, what we would now call his 'Strong Reading', appeared in 1962.[28] The emphasis on 'critics', in Ionesco's Paris, with its own competing *maîtres à penser*, brings us to this critical event, which was more striking in France even than it was among Anglophone readers. The translation was fluent, in a period when translation of 'high popular' criticism was done in a rather different style than it would be now, as comparison with the English translation suggests, even to the non-Polish speaker. Within Kott's acknowledgement of the Hegelian/Marxist belief in historical necessity comes his reading that the killer must go on killing if only to escape being killed, mechanically; history is a machine, sometimes a steam roller (p. 103). When Kott hammered this home he 'conjugated' it as ambition = intention to murder, and fear = memory of past murders; for Kott there was a parallel equation, that 'history' and 'the history of this play' necessarily begin with the murder of the king.[29] Kott's critical authority is hard to recreate. England, for central Europe, did not fall; England fought on; nonetheless England's poet understood. Kott also found that Shakespeare added an 'Existential' nightmare quality, partly by setting many scenes in the dark, to discuss the paradox of man as a killing animal who cannot accept killing. The paradox, for Kott, was that once a man steps over the line, what he calls the 'Auschwitz experience', he is forever in the nightmare. Kott's Macbeth is a man trying to escape the machinery of Kott's world, but he cannot, for the world is a sealed unit.

Ionesco, who selected the historical machine rather than the world's nightmare, was prompt to acknowledge his debt.

> L'idée de faire une pièce d'après *Macbeth* m'a été donnée par la lecture de *Shakespeare notre contemporain*, le très beau livre de Jan Kott. Selon Kott, ce que voulait montrer Shakespeare c'est que le pouvoir absolu corrompt absolument, que tout pouvoir est criminel. Et parlant de Macbeth dans cette perspective, Kott pense à Staline . . . Evidemment, comme dans mes autres pièces, il y a un côté de dérision. Je me suis donc inspiré de son livre et, si j'ai fait cette pièce, c'est pour montrer une fois de plus que tout homme politique est un paranoïaque et que toute politique mène au crime. Sans doute, chez Shakespeare, dans l'ensemble de son théâtre, il y a beaucoup de bouffonnerie. Mais il a pris le personnage de Macbeth très au sérieux. Or, à y bien regarder, c'est aussi un personnage dérisoire. Tel que je l'ai traité, *Macbett* est inspiré, autant que par le héros shakespearien, que par le père Ubu. Ma pièce, c'est un mélange de Shakespeare et de Jarry. En conséquence, Macbett a été très mal accueilli par quelques critiques de l'intelligentsia qui l'ont considéré comme réactionnaire.[30]

---

[28] Trans. Anna Posner (Paris, 1962). The chapter which particularly concerns us is '"*Macbeth*" ou les contaminés par la mort', pp. 100–14. I quote Kott from this translation, which consistently used the Pléiàde translations of Shakespeare. The *Macbeth* is by Maurice Maeterlinck, *Oeuvres Complètes de Shakespeare*, ed. H. Fluchère (Paris, 1959).

[29] 'On a dit que *Macbeth* était la tragédie de l'ambition, on a dit aussi que c'était la tragédie de la peur. C'est faux. Dans *Macbeth*, il n'y a qu'un thème, un mono-thème. Ce thème, c'est le meurtre' [It has been said that *Macbeth* was the tragedy of ambition, and also that it was the tragedy of fear. It is false. There is only one theme in *Macbeth*, a mono-theme. This theme is murder] (Kott, *Shakespeare Our Contemporary*, p. 102). 'Conjuguer' in this sense is a word stronger, in argument, than 'variation' might be, because it gives a sense of a necessary structure – here, the mechanical structures of history.

[30] 'I got the idea of basing a play on *Macbeth* from reading Jan Kott's fine book, *Shakespeare Our Contemporary*. According to Kott, Shakespeare wanted to show that absolute power corrupts absolutely, that all power is criminal. Writing about Macbeth in that context, Kott thinks of Stalin. . . . So I was inspired by his book, and, if I wrote this play, it is to show one more time that all politicians are paranoids and all politics leads to crime. Obviously, as in my other plays, there's an aspect of derision ['le dérisoire' is technical in French, mockery with a pathetic aspect]. In Shakespeare's work as a whole there is undoubtedly a lot of clowning. But he took the character of Macbeth very seriously; however, if one looks closely, he is also a derisive character. In my version, *Macbett* is as much inspired by Père Ubu as by the Shakespearian hero. My play mixes Shakespeare and Jarry. Consequently, Macbett was very ill-received by some of the critics of the Intelligentsia [here,

So *Macbett* combines Ionesco's reading of Kott's reading of Shakespeare plus Jarry, where Jarry stands simultaneously for a kind of anti-theatrical style as well as false-familiar Shakespearian content (what 'is believed to be known'). Perhaps Ionesco meant to turn attention from the partiality of his reading of either. The two inspirations are closest in the mechanical repetitiveness of despotic slaughter, which might evoke Bergson's well-known idea of comedy as a kind of mechanical derision. The idea of Macbeth and Lady Macbeth as sexual partners in a nightmare of no place, with the world as the *tertium quid*, disappears. Although historically orientated, Kott's Macbeth belongs to the existential position in which the individual act of killing someone else is a manner of becoming oneself while at the same time rendering oneself unconditionally other. It is a personal choice underwritten by history which always implicates the murderer in history's necessities – and his own destruction. Kott's Macbeth is a man of imagination who cannot imagine his way out of his choice, because having chosen murder puts him beyond choice, and beyond what had been himself. He becomes 'the deed's creature'.[31] Ionesco will have none of this. Interior imagination was never one of his interests; nor were women, and, as has often been remarked, his misogyny reduces the women of the play to a pair of witches intent on the men's destruction. Kott's almost blasphemous Lady Macbeth burns because she is empty, unlike the Virgin, typologically the burning bush (which burned and was not consumed); Kott has an implicit subtext about murder as sex, which is as explicit in this chapter as he ever allows it to become. Ionesco's Lady Duncan is a Vamp and her servant a Sorcière's apprentice and dresser. To the machine of history she adds the devilish seduction of Woman. In Ionesco's anti-psychological theatre there can be no sleepwalking, but, in any case, he has no room for suffering women.

Ionesco offers a multiple misreading in the Bloomian sense, which conscripts Shakespeare via Kott to his own flag, his deeply pessimistic vision of the absolute corruption entailed by *political* power, his taste for farce to his view of Jarry. Criticism was not all, and the French post-war theatre had begun to conscript Shakespeare, who has remained a theatre-filler ever since. Nor was Ionesco an isolated case of recycling Shakespeare. We do well to notice that in 1964 Jean Anouilh's own relation to Shakespeare had produced both an adaptation of *Richard III* and *Ne réveillez pas Madame*, a play in which Anouilh's concentration upon childhood found expression in his character Julien's dream of playing *Hamlet*'s closet scene, what I categorized earlier as 'smash and grab', since it has nothing to do with Hamlet and everything to do with coding in Anouilh's anxieties and desires.[32] For Ionesco, reading beyond France and French tradition, beyond anything the authority of being *also* Rumanian could add, the discovery of the same plot, his idea of history, the cycle of betrayal–violence–betrayal reiterated somewhere else, in Jarry as well as by Kott, appeared further confirmation of his own vision at a time when Shakespeare's authority was also chic and when the aging Ionesco was depressed and short of inspiration. Ionesco told *Le Monde* that he wanted to write a piece against 'la folie de pouvoir'. 'Si on joue ma pièce dans vingt ans, dans un monde pacifié, ce ne seront pas les idées qui la maintiendront, ce sera sa construction particulière.'[33] By contrast, however, in

too, the word-choice is deliberate, politicized, and implies fastidious distaste] who understood it as reactionary' (Bonnefoy, *Eugène Ionescu*, pp. 161–2). No one seemed to remark Shakespeare's Duncan as an explicit counter-example to this universal law.

31 This is, of course, De Flores to Beatrice-Joanna in Middleton and Rowley's *The Changeling*, ed. Joost Daalder (London, 1990), III.iv.137.

32 Among others, 'Vercors' (Jean Bruller) attempted a *Hamlet* in 1977 and *Macbeth* later the same year. He published his 'rhythmic prose' (set out as a kind of blank verse) as *Pour Shakespeare: Hamlet, Macbeth* (Paris, 1978).

33 'If my play is acted in twenty years, in a world which has been pacified, it won't be its ideas which establish it, it will be its special construction', 3 February 1972 (quoted by Plazy, *Eugène Ionesco*, p. 223, who goes on to say that when the play was revived – once – at the Théâtre de la Colline in the early nineties, it was indeed a success).

Le Figaro he spoke not of construction but of genocide.[34]

Accuracy, sympathy, comprehension, even, are far from being the point – except in the sense of comprehending as a kind of ingestion. And by assimilating what he represents as *Shakespeare's* plot to the style we call absurd, by reorienting grandeur to guignol and the caricature of puppetry, he *reduces* what he touches. Not in Caxton's sense of reducing and translating, in the service of the source text and target language; not even in the sense in which a sauce can be reduced to intensify its aromas. The appearance of affiliation to Shakespeare attracts audiences; the apparent 'take' on Macbeth claims an interpretation for our time, an updated universalism; and the modest proposal to retell *Macbeth* legitimates the projection of his own ideas onto an almost blank screen. 'Almost' blank, because what Ionesco does depends upon the audience's relative distance from the plot, from knowledge of the play as a whole. And here we return to the special case of French innocence of Shakespeare.

Into his abstract décor, Ionesco places two pairs of interchangeable men: Glamiss and Candor, the original rebels, and Macbett and Banco. Each pair repeats in turn the same speeches, to illustrate their indistinguishable positions in the steam-roller of history. Lady Duncan has a moment of confusing the two, out of *Hamlet*. Ionesco has adopted Brechtian devices, such as a lemonade seller fluttering at the skirts of the battles. The Archduke – not king – Duncan is a coward who depends upon, then cheats, his noblemen, particularly Banco; this alludes to *Ubu* and to Kott rather than to *Macbeth*. It is his wife, Lady Duncan, who has the courage to ride to see how the war against the traitors is going, Lady Duncan who, with her servant, from time to time metamorphoses into a Witch. It is she who seduces Macbeth, puts him up to murdering her husband, then flies off, pretty much on her broomstick. Thus there is no point of contact either with the meek Scottish nor the saintly English king. This Duncan is a bloodthirsty coward whose mass executions take place upstage against a backdrop of guillotines. I am tempted to see Poulenc's *Dialogues des Carmelites* being recalled, but I would find it difficult to argue from a visual reminiscence. Opera does arise, but later. What is beyond question is that Macbett's last word, 'Merde', is Jarry's first, 'Merdre'.

The scene is geographically nowhere, as it was in *Ubu roi*; but unlike Jarry, Ionesco allows a degree of attractiveness to his main male characters. Like Jarry, he uses puppets, and, at one point, characters from current cartoons (Les Pieds nickelés), but here I confess myself sceptical of the mixed elements of farce and vaudeville. I except the moment when, after Banco, Macbett and Lady Duncan have conspired to kill the Archduke, one of the play's terrible moments of characters screaming 'assassin' at each other, she has a mood-changing curtain line which indeed assumes a parody of Shakespeare: 'C'était tout de même mon mari. Mort, il ressemble à mon père. Je n'aimais pas mon père'(180).[35]

Similarly, the play upon the names seems tired: 'Banco' as a gambling term, 'Candor' for Cawdor, 'Macol' for Malcolm. Macbett murders the unmarried Banco, having overheard Banco's ruminations about his own ambitions, his own possible future, thus nipping Shakespeare's prophecy, as Macbett thinks, in the bud. There is parody at the point of the banquet scene, and, once again, there is doubling, since Macbett's first vision is of Duncan's face replacing his own in a portrait – perhaps here, too, it is *Hamlet* which is an unexpected revenant. But Macbett's guests can see Duncan, too, as they can see Banco. They certainly ought to see Duncan, who reappears. Perhaps Ionesco plays with Kott's idea of killing the ghost. He characteristically addresses us directly through Macbett:

> Ah, si vous connaissierez . . . mais ne nous laissons pas aller. Une autre fois, les confidences. On voudrait faire des choses, on ne les fait pas. On en fait d'autres,

[34] *Le Figaro Littéraire*, 1355 (6 May 1972), pp. 15–18. He had also been interviewed for *Les Nouvelles Littéraires*, where he stressed that his play would be between Shakespeare and Jarry, 24 January 1972.

[35] 'All the same, he was my husband. Dead, he looks like my father. I never liked my father.'

qu'on n'aurait pas voulu accomplir. L'histoire est rusée. Tout vous échappe. Nous ne sommes pas les maîtres de ce que l'on a déclenché. Les choses se retournent contre vous. Tout ce qui se passe est le contraire de ce que vous vouliez qu'il arrivât. Régner, régner, ce sont les événements qui règnent sur l'homme, non point l'homme sur les événements. J'étais heureux du temps où je servais fidèlement Duncan. Je n'avais pas de soucis.[36]

I think we knew that. Given that this is parody, a farce upon *Macbeth*, there is no obvious way to end. What Ionesco does is to reach toward opera, or perhaps to operetta, to the preposterously complex plot-endings which tie everything up. Into this last scene, with its reminiscence of Shakespeare's banquet, walks not Lady Macbeth but Lady Duncan – the real one, she reveals – who has just escaped from the dungeons, into which she had been locked by the supposed Lady Duncan who seduced Macbeth and appeared to have married him. Macbeth's guests break into song, wondering if she is mad – a reference to all those operatic mad scenes to which Verdi, too, alluded. Are we back to Verdi? Yes, in a way we are, though really only insofar as Verdi shares opera's complex plots, as Jarry shared the political cycle. When Macol (Malcolm) now suddenly appears we hear in his aria that he is not Duncan's son at all, but Duncan's adopted son, the child of the murdered Banco and a gazelle – so, not of woman born.

Hosannas of triumph, of course, from a relieved and grateful populace. However, this is not the end. The end is a grim quotation from Shakespeare, displaced and taken as read: Macol suddenly reveals himself as the character of greed, avarice and lust whom Malcolm invents in order to test Macduff. It is Ionesco's longest direct borrowing. This time Ionesco speaks directly to the audience through Macol, using Malcolm's words to tell us that all power corrupts absolutely, that the paranoia of kings is inescapable, that no dictator who accepts the ring of power escapes the power of the ring.

And yet, like the purloined letter, which is too obvious to be visible, *Macbett* does offer more than opacity, more than a mirror. In the context of Ionesco's avowed reaction against the realist theatre, the conventions of stage comedy, above all his ambivalence about language itself, *Macbett* manages to be a satire almost entirely dependent upon overstatement, restatement, doubling and redoubling of word and action. Reviews at the time complained, as they always do, that he travestied Shakespeare, whom he had failed to understand, sparking the response I quoted above. I think they were right, but that that was not the point. For Ionesco, even writing as recently as thirty years ago, the Shakespearian terrain was emptier than it would soon come to be, with the extraordinary popularity of Shakespeare in French theatres and world cinemas. People still 'remembered' the Macbeth they thought they knew. He was a point of departure for Ionesco's own absurd machine. When the play was revived, in the nineties, it was treated not as anarchist satire, but respectfully, as the period piece it is. It has not been revived subsequently. As Shakespeare offshoots go, it is one of those which uses Shakespeare to legitimate its author's politics; with *Macbett* Ionesco announces his ability to struggle with greatness, but also his invitation, as Verdi put it, to fill the house.

BREF, EN CONCLUSION

Offshoots are never only shoots off the Shakespearian trunk. In tracing the history of Monsieur Macbeth I have tried to do justice to the complexity of Shakespeare in one country, in contexts of increasing familiarity with the idea of Shakespeare as well as with Shakespeares performed, translated

36 'Oh, if you only knew . . . but let's not let ourselves go. Another time for confidences. One wishes to do things, and doesn't do them; one does others that one wouldn't have wanted to finish. History is crafty. Everything escapes you. Things get away from you. We are not masters of what we set off. Things turn against you. Everything that happens turns out to be the opposite of what you had wanted to happen. Reign, reign, it's events which reign over man, not man over events. I was happy back when I served Duncan faithfully. I had no cares' (p. 190). Rosette C. Lamont, who sees much more detailed and specific intertextuality and allegory in the play than I do (and is more definite about Shakespeare than I am), attributes 'history is crafty' to Lenin, although without referring to this speech. See her *Ionesco's Imperatives: The Politics of Culture* (Ann Arbor, 1993), ch. 8.

and adapted. I believe I have uncovered, along the way, the curious case of a play which retrospectively *became* an offshoot, under the influence of source-hunting, and of criticism. I know of no other such example.

As parody has been the theme of both Jarry's theatrical and Ionesco's political satire, should we dare to ask whether Shakespeare's historical tragedy itself invites a kind of intertextuality rarely conceived? There was nothing arbitrary in my passing allusion to De Flores. Yet parody (comic or serious) is only one aspect of flattery as imitation: these French texts do invite us to turn again to Shakespeare's own understanding of his experience of the contexts of writing tragic history, both for the historical page and for the tragic stage. It is from this insight that we will return to *Macbeth* anew. *Macbeth* is ideal as an Absurd play because it combines a high proportion of talk with a high level of horror. To give Ionesco his due, *Macbeth* is Shakespeare's grotesque, his grandest guignol.[37]

---

[37] This paper was first drafted for a session at the Shakespeare Association of America in 2002. To my long-suffering readers, ever-due thanks: Professors Stefan Collini and Richard Marienstras.

THE POLITICS OF SLEEPWALKING: AMERICAN LADY MACBETHS

KATHERINE ROWE

More than any other aspect of Shakespeare's play, Lady Macbeth is understood in American discourse as impervious to change. The persistence and force of her character are illustrated especially well by the apparent distaste American audiences currently feel for innovation in her role. *The Wall Street Journal* reported several years ago, for example, on a failed attempt to revive the play for Hollywood. On 23 May 1996, the *Journal* described the frustrations of Scottish screenwriter Steven Simpson, then attempting to interest Hollywood in his new *Macbeth*, 'Throne of Destiny'. The screenplay dramatizes a Scottish nationalist *Macbeth*, in the mode of Rob Roy and William 'Braveheart' Wallace.[1] It inherits a cultural and nationalist revival that began in Scotland in the 1970s.[2] So it takes its history from George Buchanan, writing against the editorial revisions of Raphael Holinshed and Hector Boece that contributed to the 'imperial themes' of Shakespeare's play.[3] Simpson emphasizes the historical Macbeth's first ten years of peaceful rule and the proto-constitutionalism of the Scottish monarchy.[4] His Macbeth is obviously quite different from Shakespeare's ambitious usurper. In him, public action and the support of counselors overcome the bad rule of Buchanan's weaker King Duncan. This Macbeth restores the ancient liberties and rational political order that Duncan failed to maintain.

Given the success of contemporary films such as *Rob Roy* and *Braveheart* – which remake Scottish nationalist heroes into types of America's rebellious democratic character – Simpson's adaptation should have played well. However, as reporter Daniel Pearl points out, 'not everyone is buying Macbeth's rehabilitation'. Whoever Macbeth was, American film producers have always preferred his evil side. Cromwell Productions, for one, was offered the pro-Macbeth script for its upcoming film but it used Shakespeare's play instead. It's free,

[1] Daniel Pearl, 'Scots Toil and Trouble to Make *Macbeth* Into the Next Braveheart', *The Wall Street Journal*, 23 May 1996, B1. Since Scott's novel was adapted to the stage in 1818 (with William Charles Macready as Rob), *Rob Roy* and *Macbeth* have been perennial repertory pairings in Scotland. See James Dibdin, *Annals of the Edinburgh Stage* (Edinburgh, 1888), p. 435.

[2] See the recent 'excavation, rediscovery and re-examination of Scottish history' inaugurated by T. C. Smout's *A History of the Scottish People: 1560–1830* (New York, 1969). See also Ian Brown, 'Plugged into History: The Sense of the Past in Scottish Theatre', *Scottish Theatre since the Seventies*, eds. Randall Stevenson and Gavin Wallace (Edinburgh, 1996), pp. 84–99.

[3] On the politics of different versions of the *Macbeth* history see Sally Mapstone, 'Shakespeare and Scottish Kingship; A Case History', in *The Rose and the Thistle: Essays on the Culture of Late Medieval and Renaissance Scotland*, ed. Sally Mapstone and Juliette Wood (East Lothian, 1998), pp. 158–89; Arthur Kinney, 'Scottish History, the Union of the Crowns and the Issue of Right Rule: The Case of Shakespeare's *Macbeth*', in *Renaissance Culture in Context: Theory and Practice*, ed. Jean R. Brink and William F. Gentrup (Brookfield, VT, 1993), pp. 18–53; and David Norbrook, '*Macbeth* and the Politics of Historiography', in *Politics of Discourse: The Literature and History of Seventeenth Century England*, ed. Kevin Sharpe and Steven N. Zwicker (Berkeley, 1987), pp. 78–116.

[4] This revision is in keeping with recent experiments on the Edinburgh Stage: Ike Isakson's dramatic retelling of the Macbeth history in Gaelic and Scots in 1995, and rival Scots translations of Shakespeare's play, by R. L. C. Lorimer and David Purves, in 1992.

easy to stage and time-tested, explains producer Bob Carruthers. Moreover, Mr. Simpson says, even producers who have no problem with Macbeth as a good king find it hard to swallow a kind Lady Macbeth.[5]

There have been a number of revisions of *Macbeth* on the stage and screen, from the devoted wife of nineteenth-century sentimental revivals, to the vamps of recent BBC imports. If we accept that Mr. Simpson is not inventing a reluctant Hollywood audience, why is it that Americans especially resist a kinder, gentler Lady Macbeth? Or more precisely, what do we resist about her? One way to answer this question might be to survey and sort allusions to the play in contemporary American discourse, seeking patterns in the ubiquitous references to 'out, damned spot' (5.1.33) and other familiar quotations. This anecdotal activity would range widely: from feminist artists such as Elizabeth Layton, with her housewifely Lady Macbeth attempting to bleach out her 'damned spot' with Clorox, to the popular epithet for American First Ladies, regularly labelled 'Lady Macbeth' by critics hostile to the prospect of a powerful political woman.[6] Even a brief sampling seems to suggest that the burden of these allusions is the sexual politics of the tragedy, spun in ways that reflect how we like our women, powerful or obedient. A more complex view can be earned from taking a longitudinal approach, looking to earlier versions of Lady Macbeth in American popular culture and tracking specific strains of resistance and attachment to her figure.

The first observation to make is a simple one: the reluctance of Hollywood producers aside, American audiences have not always understood Lady Macbeth in exclusively negative terms. Indeed, her figure was for a long time tied to a model of assertive American femininity, familiar from Henry James novels but exported most successfully by the nineteenth-century actress Charlotte Cushman. Cushman made her career playing Lady Macbeth in a way that capitalized on the character's transgressive masculinity. Cushman's interpretation borrowed something of the hen-pecking wives of early minstrel shows and burlesques. Indeed, she was famous for bullying and cornering and 'pitching into' her husband onstage and was known to complain about the '*little* men' she had to play opposite.[7] Edwin Booth, for one, is supposed to have felt like telling her when she urged him to the murder, 'Why don't you kill him? You're a great deal bigger than I am.'[8] The roles of Macbeth and his Lady had already played an important part in the emerging culture of national celebrity and were instrumental in defining what it meant to be English or American.[9] When crossed with high Shakespearian art, the hen-pecking persona translated into a particularly American version of feminine sternness and resilience. Cushman revived the role throughout her career with tremendous success, in London as well as in the States. Her gender-bending brought equal acclaim in cross-dressed roles such as Romeo: glossed by contemporaries as a distinctively assertive, American femininity that reflected a successful vision of 'unsexing'.[10]

Cushman's interpretation popularized a version of Lady Macbeth as a woman whose exceptional virility finds effective uses. She made a lasting impression, to judge by the famous 1858 engraving of her in 2.2 (the scene Booth describes). Facing the audience with daggers in hand, she glares out of

---

5 Pearl, 'Scots Toil', p. B2

6 Anne Fadiman, 'Elizabeth Layton: Portrait of the Artist as an Old Woman', *Life*, March 1987, pp. 21–4.

7 Robert Falk, 'Shakespeare in America: A Survey to 1900', in *Shakespeare Survey 18* (Cambridge, 1969), p. 104; Charles Shattuck quoting contemporary actor and elocutionist George Vandenhoff, in *Shakespeare on the American Stage: From the Hallams to Edwin Booth* (Washington, 1976), p. 92.

8 Shattuck, quoting Booth, *American Stage*, p. 95.

9 Cushman's pioneering role followed the earlier pattern of Sarah Siddons who had used the role to establish the type of a dignified, loyal English wife. Concurrent productions starring Charles Macready and Edwin Forrest (rival English and American actors who defined a national Shakespearian style) helped spark the Astor Place Riots in New York City, in 1849.

10 For Cushman's success in exporting both the role and this version of assertive American femininity see Shattuck, *American Stage*, pp. 91–2 and Lisa Merrill, *When Romeo Was a Woman* (Ann Arbor, 1999), pp. 110–37.

the frame.[11] Yet for all the single-minded potency figured here, this scene in the play illustrates Lady Macbeth's complicity as much as her primacy in the crime. The paradox of the part, as critics since Coleridge have pointed out, is that by the close of the play Lady Macbeth famously fails to sustain the resilience of Acts 1 and 2. Repeated obsessively in the sleepwalking scene, 5.1, the moment with the daggers is reconfigured by the close of the play as the beginning of her destruction. (The two scenes appear to be the most frequently illustrated from the play.) Popular allusions to the character reflect this configuration, rarely straying far from the obsessive compulsion evoked by the phrase 'out, damned spot'. That line reminds us that while Lady Macbeth begins the play in Bradleyan terms, acting by 'sheer force of will', she ends in helpless perseveration.[12] What quotations of 'out, damned spot' code for, in other words, is a plot of inevitable regression: the transformation of an ambitious, persuasive and virile consort into a passive, guilty, self-divided and feminized sleepwalker. This plot has tremendous staying power in the theater. While dramatic interpretations of the role may change, few variations can be found in the imagination of Lady Macbeth's last scene. From the late eighteenth century on, sketches of her sleepwalking emphasize her trailing hair, and loose white gown, and blank face; these antedate Cushman's innovations and continue after her, reinforced by sentimental reincarnations of Lady Macbeth as a devoted wife.[13]

The figure of the independent American woman embodied by Lady Macbeth predates Cushman and continues long after. In its earliest versions that figure took a particular charge from the regressive arc of Lady Macbeth's plot. Her progress from potent ambition to feminine passivity is still, I want to hazard, what most resists reconstruction in American Lady Macbeths. It gains its force and persistence from late eighteenth-century debates about the nature and stability of the American republic. The play and Lady Macbeth in particular had a powerful claim on the imagination of pre- and post-revolutionary writers. It spoke to central problems in the construction of early American subjectivity, especially the notions of democratic consent and electoral voice at the heart of the constitutionalist debates. Read in this context, the significance of Lady Macbeth's regression has less to do with sexual politics (how Americans like their women) than with fundamental fears about the degree to which we enter a destructive complicity we cannot control when we cast our votes.

Macbeth was one of the most frequently staged Shakespeare plays in American repertory during the eighteenth century, from Lewis Hallam's first revival in 1759 to the spectacular 1795 production in Philadelphia.[14] With its plot of regicide and new order, the play had a lively but equivocal role in contemporary political discourse: as when, for example, John Adams denounced Mother England in the *Boston Gazette*, in 1765, as a 'Lady Macbeth' to the Colonies – for her un-maternal behaviour in imposing the Stamp Act. Adams charges the Colonies outright with childish timidity and invokes the 'horror' of a mother 'deaf to the cries of her children',

> Who 'had given suck, and knew'
> 'How tender 'twas to love the Babe that milk'd her,'
> But yet, who could
> 'Even while 'twas smiling in her Face,
> Have pluck'd her Nipple from the boneless Gums,
> And dash'd the Brains out.'[15]

---

[11] See the engraving of Cushman as Lady Macbeth, with daggers, from *The Complete Works of William Shakespeare, carefully collated by Halliwell, Knight, Collier, and others, illustrated with steel engraved portraits of characters portrayed by the most distinguished American Actors* (Johnson, Fry and Company, 1858)

[12] A. C. Bradley, *Shakespearean Tragedy: Lectures on Hamlet, Othello, King Lear, Macbeth*, 2nd ed. (London, 1926), p. 367.

[13] See *Shakespeare's Unruly Women*, ed. Georgianna Ziegler, with Frances E. Dolan and Jeanne Addison Roberts (Washington, 1997).

[14] E. Elandt, 'Puritan and Quaker Opposition to Performances of Shakespeare', in *Studia Anglica Posnaniensia: An International Review of English Studies*, 16 (1983), p. 251; Shattuck, *American Stage*, p. 29.

[15] John Adams, 'A Dissertation on the Canon and the Feudal Law', *The Boston Gazette*, 12 August, 19 August, 30 September, 21 October 1765, from the 21 October issue. Thomas Paine develops the figure of a maturing America in similar terms. 'I have heard it asserted by some, that as America hath

For all his resolute pragmatism, Adams's quotation is remarkably equivocal. If Mother England is Lady Macbeth and the colonies babes, silenced by our lack of representation, are we about to be plucked from her breast and dashed to the ground? Or are the Colonies Macbeth, urged to a reluctant regicide by her terrible insults? Then too, Adams plays Lady Macbeth, deploying the spectre of maternal infanticide to galvanize readers to action. Any of these readings introduces unwonted possibilities into the justification of Colonial independence. Either Americans are more helpless in our loss of European inheritance than Adams would allow, or we are guiltier of terrible transgression in making our new social institutions.[16] Adams's quotation epitomizes the mixed messages *Macbeth* delivered in this period. In this respect, the play seems to be exceptional. What we know about America's Shakespeare from Michael Bristol's work on the topic is that American writers tended to use Shakespeare to establish cultural continuity with the Old World. At the same time, they made him speak for the liberal individualism that required a political break with England.[17] The deep anxieties about prophetic voices and distributed agency in *Macbeth* work strongly against this trend. They undermine our confidence that Shakespearian texts (or any textual authorities we appeal to) can be made to speak in a predictable, instrumentalized way.

For this reason, *Macbeth* served, during and after the revolution, as a powerful resource for conservative warnings against the irrational foundations of consensual democracy and for arguments against a break with England. The most sustained and stinging of these warnings is delivered in 1798 by Charles Brockden Brown, in his gothic novel *Wieland; Or the Transformation: An American Tale*. *Wieland* was written during a particularly anxious moment in the federalist debates. Brown sent the novel to Thomas Jefferson, a gesture critics typically gloss as a warning or attempt to redirect those debates. Yet Brown's novel does more than attempt a topical intervention. It seeks to expose fundamental fractures within the expressive media – print, voice, public performance – which appear so stable in the pragmatist hands of writers such as Adams and Paine. For Brown, Shakespearian texts stand as much for the generic instability of literary voice *per se* as they do for the particular concerns they dramatize.

Macbeth in particular seems to saturate Brown's imagination. In both *Wieland* and his other novels, the play's vocabulary, atmosphere, scenes and dramatic conflicts appear an inexhaustible resource. *Wieland* might easily be read as an exercise in adapting dramatic conventions to those of epistolary fiction. But the relations between the novel and the play seem at once more organic and more self-reflective than we tend to assume adaptation will be. *Wieland* is better understood as a generic experiment in the variety and politics of literary quotation, updating *Macbeth's* concerns, osmotically assimilating its structures, but also quoting it clunkily out of context in much the same mode as Adams. To understand the political claims behind these diverse modes of quotation, it is worth exploring the novel at some length.

The Wieland family, Brown's central figures, model the precarious 'condition of a nation' founded on the principles of public persuasion and reasoned consent.[18] The novel opens with a

flourished under her former connexion with Great-Britain, that the same connexion is necessary towards her future happiness, and will always have the same effect. Nothing can be more fallacious than this kind of argument. We may as well assert that because a child has thrived upon milk, that it is never to have meat . . .', quoted in Thomas Paine, *Common Sense and Other Writings*, ed. Gordon Wood (New York, 2003), p. 20.

[16] Cf. Michael Bristol's discussion of Adams's use of Shakespeare, *Shakespeare's America, America's Shakespeare* (London and New York, 1990), p. 58 ff.

[17] Bristol, *Shakespeare's America*, p. 123. Post-revolutionary American references to *Macbeth* can sound more like the Tory Shakespeare of late eighteenth and early ninetheenth-century England. See Nicola Watson on Walter Scott's use of Shakespeare Histories, 'Kemble, Scott and the Mantle of the Bard', in Jean Marsden, ed., *The Appropriation of Shakespeare: Post-Renaissance Reconstructions of the Works and the Myth* (New York, 1991), pp. 73–92.

[18] Quotations from the novel reference Charles Brockden Brown, *Wieland and Memoirs of Carwin the Biloquist*, ed. Jay Fliegelman (New York, 1991).

nostalgic family idyll, set between the French and Revolutionary wars. Clara, the central character, narrates the story in a long letter. She, her brother Theodore, her sister-in-law, and their friend Henry Pleyel live outside of Philadelphia, a community of siblings deracinated from their European connections. The shadow of their father's mysterious and occult death hangs over the family. Still, they confidently pursue a life of scholarly debates in which reasoned analysis appears to hold sway and all voices carry equal weight. This model Jeffersonian society is threatened by the arrival of a stranger named Carwin, a ventriloquist whose mysterious voice (perhaps inadvertently) leads Theodore to believe he hears divine commands to kill his family. Theodore obeys, in a terrible scene reminiscent of the murder of Lady Macduff and her son.

Writing three years after these events, in distress so deep she is certain she will die as soon as she lays down her pen, Clara cannot stop reliving the scenes she recounts. Her story unfolds with the kind of manic repetition compulsion one would expect to find in a narrative written by Lady Macbeth. The central problem figured in this obsessive remembering is also *Macbeth*'s problem – a political and cultural one as well as a familial one – how to guarantee continuity when everyone who might pass on what needs to be known is dead or dying. The manic style and Brown's turn to theatrical texts (Shakespeare in particular) mount a specific challenge to the kind of expressive pragmatism found in Adams and Paine. For Brown, the loss of family history, of inherited political institutions, and of time-tested religious ceremony makes the Wielands vulnerable to Carwin's deceptions. These losses cannot be compensated by the rule of rational law and individual choice. To paraphrase Christopher Looby's reading, order that is sustained through argument and persuasion rather than by customary authority – as it is in the Wieland family, and was in the deeply contested republican debates of this period – makes the new democratic institutions especially vulnerable to verbal assault.[19] Carwin's dangerous ventriloquism challenges the foundations of American expressive individualism: the efficacy of rational discourse and the essential tie between political intent and election figured in the metaphor of a popular voice. The novel systematically undermines the republican formula, *Vox Populi, Vox Dei* – the voice of the people is the voice of God.[20] And it challenges any stable connection between what one intends to say and the effects of one's speech. In this way, it questions the moral autonomy of individuals in a state (such as the emerging electoral state) in which one person speaks for another.[21]

More than this, however, the novel challenges some of the fundamental pragmatist assumptions of early republican print exchanges, assimilating prose – by way of its Shakespearian subtext – to the more equivocal arts of theatre. Capitalizing on the popularity of the play, Brown seems particularly interested in the theatrical model of moral complicity *Macbeth* offers, as it directs our attention to the psychological experiences that attend political choices. The exchange of bloody daggers after Duncan's murder, in 2.2, is (as with Cushman) the theatrical moment that best captures the shift from powerful autonomy to moral complicity which preoccupies Brown. Complicity is vividly conveyed, in this scene, by its central gestures and striking dialogue. In Shakespeare's version (and in David Garrick's, Brown's likely source text) the scene begins with a sequence of interlaced lines in which Lady Macbeth and Macbeth finish each other's fractured thoughts. The fractured thinking represented in stichomythic dialogue here is highly unusual in Shakespeare, rarely used before this play. It adumbrates the fragmented speech that marks later scenes, when Lady Macbeth sleepwalks and Macbeth approaches his phantom dagger.

The stichomythic lines in this scene offer Brown a verbal corollary, at the level of address, for the way

[19] Christopher Looby, *Voicing America: Language, Literary Form, and the Origins of the United States* (Chicago and London, 1996), p. 147.

[20] Jay Fliegelman, *Declaring Independence: Jefferson, Natural Language & the Culture of Performance* (Stanford, 1993), p. xi.

[21] Looby, *Voicing America*, p. 147.

one's mind can penetrate into and place thoughts, intentions and expectations in another. That he finds these resources in Shakespeare, in particular, is a point he wants us not to miss. The borrowings work at several levels, but in the interests of clarity it is helpful to begin with plot. For his main actions, particularly events that befall the narrator, Clara, Brown integrates this scene with the two others that bracket Lady Macbeth's action: the 'murthering ministers' soliloquy, in 1.5, and the sleepwalking scene, 5.1.[22] Brown brings these scenes together early in the novel, in an episode that offers a good example of the way Lady Macbeth's plot allegorizes the progress of a subject that is distinctly anti-Adamsian and anti-Jeffersonian. Resting on a bench after a long walk in the woods, Clara falls half-asleep, unwittingly preventing Carwin from keeping an assignation. In her phantasmagoric state, she dreams that she is sleepwalking. Carwin, hoping to wake her and scare her off, creeps up behind like a stalker and throws his voice out suddenly, shouting 'Hold! Hold!' (*Wieland*, p. 71). The phrase will be familiar to Shakespearians as Lady Macbeth's:

> . . . Come, thick night,
> And pall thee in the dunnest smoke of hell,
> That my keen knife see not the wound it makes,
> Nor heaven peep through the blanket of the dark
> To cry 'Hold, hold!' (1.5.49–53)

In her half-waking state, Clara hears Carwin's call as a divine voice and imagines that it catches her at the brink of a terrible fall. She remembers vividly, she tells us, what she was dreaming at that moment. She dreamed she was walking towards her brother's estate. Carelessly ignorant of a pit in her path, she looked up to see her brother beckoning her across a terrible precipice:

> I mended my pace, and one step more would have plunged me into this abyss, had not some one from behind caught suddenly my arm, and exclaimed, in a voice of eagerness and terror, 'Hold! hold!' The sound broke my sleep, and I found myself at the next moment, standing on my feet, and surrounded by the deepest darkness. Images so terrific and forcible disabled me, for a time, from distinguishing between sleep and wakefulness, and withheld from me knowledge of my actual condition. (*Wieland*, pp. 71–2)

The pitfall Clara faces here is an excessive belief in her own powers of rational analysis and in the evidence of her senses. These are established early in the novel as the foundations of her sense of herself as a reasonable social agent. They are shaken even more seriously as the narrative continues. Like Lady Macbeth, Clara begins as a decisive, rational actor but ends in a state of helpless horror: unable to trust the evidence of her senses, certain only of her own complicity in her destruction. Like Lady Macbeth all she can do in this state of horror is manically replay the scene.

When Carwin explains his purpose in haunting Clara, he claims that his intentions were never evil, despite their results. And he justifies himself, weirdly, by claiming Shakespearian authority. He likes to use the phrase 'Hold, hold', he says, because 'The mode in which heaven is said by the poet to interfere for the prevention of crimes, was somewhat analogous to my province, and never failed to occur to me at seasons like this' (p. 232). At the bottom of this page, Brown footnotes the quotation, citing part of the line that precedes it in Lady Macbeth's soliloquy: ' – Peeps through the blanket of the dark, and cries Hold! Hold! – SHAKESPEARE.' By being so archly explicit here, Brown means to counter the kind of Shakespearian quotation that revolutionaries such as Adams were using to justify what were for him dangerous experiments. The quotation captures the essence of a conservative warning: stop, hold on, conserve, retain what you have. Yet peculiarly, this warning comes in the voice of the least reliable character in the novel. To make sense of this puzzle, we need to unravel the several voices and modes of address quoted in Lady Macbeth's phrase.

22 Brown used David Garrick's edition, followed here. There are no differences between Garrick's version of the soliloquy and F, only minor differences in 5.1.

What 'peeps' in Lady Macbeth's speech is heaven, following the keen glance of her knife. By having Carwin gloss the quotation, Brown underlines the ironic and profane nature of Carwin's pompous analogy between his own actions and divine intervention. The footnote emphasizes the loss of a real, governing, divinity in this community: Carwin fakes it, but there is no moral or spiritual principle animating his voice. Instead, Carwin's analogy is the basis for his own self-deception, which lets him continue his terrible program. Notably, in footnoting Lady Macbeth's speech, Brown expands Carwin's quotation only slightly, stopping just short of pointing out the parallel deceptions. Indeed, he abbreviates the line so as to reverse its meaning, eliding Shakespeare's negative subjunctive: '*that* my keen knife see *not* . . . *nor* heaven peep . . .' (*Macbeth* 1.5.51–3). Any careful reader going back to the text (such as Theodore Wieland himself, whom we learn is a textual purist) will catch this decontextualization. What the footnote quotes, in other words, is not only Shakespeare's play but the characteristic mode of breezy, pragmatist quotation, here translated into Carwin's opportunistic, selective memory.

Tellingly, the negatives Brown drops out mark Lady Macbeth's failure to internalize heaven's voice, her active repression, rationalization and occulting of the 'compunctious visitings' of conscience. Her impious 'inner voice' exemplifies Brown's particular unease with the adaptation of Puritan models of conscience to the new metaphor of popular voice. For Brown, the slippage from individual to collective, from inner to public voice invites profound self-deceit. This deception calls into question the key assumptions behind individual suffrage and rational consent: the notion that one can know one's own intentions and, by speaking, bring those intentions to pass. Accordingly, the Shakespearian allusion thematizes so many internal displacements of divine warning that one cannot trace them to an originary voice. Brown quotes Shakespeare by way of Garrick; Carwin ventriloquizes the poet by way of Lady Macbeth, ventriloquizing the voice of God; she does so only in imagination, profanely, to evade or repress that voice. The voice of the people in this tangle of attributions is very clearly not the voice of God. Moreover, any quoted authority – even and especially Shakespeare – appears here likely to be quoting someone else of uncertain authority, for occulted reasons, in infinite regression. Theodore Wieland, the novel's literalist, may be 'diligent in settling and restoring the purity of the text', as we learn he is with Cicero; but textual scrupulousness helps him not at all in discerning true and dissembling voices of authority.[23]

Lady Macbeth personifies her knife in order to displace moral responsibility and prevent self-reflection. Her lines paradoxically call attention to this displacement. The attention alerted and deferred in this way is hers, ours, and heaven's: and it is this simultaneous failure of internal, social and divine governance that draws Brown to these lines. For it is not just the heedlessness of his speakers – both Carwin and Clara, with her own epistolary ventriloquism – but their *wilful* heedlessness, that Lady Macbeth models. If she brought her intentions into line with their terrible consequences, to acknowledge the two as an ethical unit and see the wound she makes, she could not act. So she conjures intention and act, instrument and will apart.[24] Carwin's apparently neutral arguments follow the same pattern: they hide a genuinely immoral self-interest that willfully refuses to calculate effects into its operation. His self-deceit echoes the self-deceptions into which he lures the Wielands. Over and over in the novel, Carwin repeats what he implies here: that he knows at some level his actions are wrong yet his addiction to the power of ventriloquism is such that he cannot stop using it, although he tries. The protestations capture the essence of the repetition compulsion in *Macbeth*; once you begin assuming the power of other voices you cannot stop. The terrible consequences of these vocal deceptions underline the weaknesses of the

[23] See Brown, *Wieland*, p. 27.

[24] On the humoral logic of this self-discipline see Katherine Rowe, 'Minds in Company: Shakespearean Tragic Emotions' in *A Blackwell Companion to Shakespeare's Works Vol. 1*, ed. Richard Dutton and Jean Howard (Oxford, 2003), pp. 47–72.

republican formula, *Vox Populi, Vox Dei*, as scholars such as Looby, Fliegelman and others observe.[25] However, Brown's scepticism about the instability of voice as an agent force in human activities goes beyond the concerns of his contemporary political scene. For the infinite regress of Carwin's quotation disables even the warning that the text itself delivers. Tellingly, the looming darkness and terrible events of the novel cannot (any more than in *Macbeth*) be attributed exclusively to Carwin or explained by his debunking.

Murky questions of agency tied in Shakespeare's play to the witches re-appear in Brown's novel not only as a gothic apparatus (a father dying by spontaneous combustion) but in its formal structures, particularly its relentless use of the passive voice. Passive voice stands as a kind of formal analogue, in address, for the fundamental detachment between voice and authority that Brown finds in a culture that deliberately deracinates itself. The passage immediately following the footnote to Shakespeare, in which Carwin glosses his actions, provides a typical example:

> It was requisite to break your slumbers, and for this end I uttered the powerful monosyllable, 'hold! hold!' My purpose *was not prescribed* by duty, yet surely it was far from being atrocious and inexpiable. To effect it, I uttered what was false, but it was well suited to my purpose. Nothing less *was intended* than to injure you.
>
> (*Wieland*, p. 233; my italics)

Such wilful false-consciousness is less frightening in Carwin, it turns out, than in Clara herself. Brown makes this clear at the end of the novel, in a scene that recalls Lady Macbeth's dagger more pointedly. Having murdered his wife and children, still inflamed by religious enthusiasm, Theodore returns to kill Clara as well. She calls for Carwin's help, and he speaks to Theodore in her defense: calling 'hold!' in his divine voice for the last time and then revealing himself. When she asks him to speak for her, Clara begins to collude with rather than resist Carwin's deceptions and this collusion clarifies Brown's concern about the electoral process. To ask or authorize another to speak for you, he fears, is never to be sure whose interests are expressed.

Worse, to speak for another or be spoken for makes it impossible to set limits on ones complicity in the inevitably violent results. When Theodore learns that his fantasies of divine inspiration are false, he despairs and kills himself. But it is Clara who provides him with the suicide weapon. Recounting their exchange of the knife, she describes a remarkable series of cognitive displacements. 'Having received the knife from his hand', she tells us, 'I held it loosely and without regard; but now it seized again my attention, and I grasped it with force' (p. 260). A few lines later Brown repeats the quiet allusion: 'my right hand, grasping the unseen knife, was still disengaged [by Theodore]. It was lifted to strike' (p. 261). The unseen knife that seizes her attention, before she wilfully grasps it, clearly takes its cue from Shakespeare's keen blade. It reverses the relation of agent and instrument so that its holder may not attend nor claim the wound it makes.

The self-deception figured by this knife connects the early, potent and murderous Lady Macbeth of 1.5 and the sleepwalking Queen. In this revision, a sleepwalking Lady Macbeth suffers the consequences of a self-deception – through 'willed submission to demonic powers' – that made her powerful.[26] In this extraordinary moment, Clara's and Theodore's thoughts interlace in the same fragmented, complicit way as in Shakespeare's 2.2. The slow buildup of their complicity is explored at some length in this scene. Reacting to the news that he was deceived, Theodore is seized by a 'spirit of tempestuous but undesigning activity':

---

[25] Looby draws the connection between Carwin's mimicry and the raging contemporary debate about the validity of the electoral process: 'are the constituents making their delegate speak for them, or is the delegate making his constituents accept his speech as their own?' (172). For Brown, the problem with the electoral model is not which direction intention (and therefore responsibility) flows; as Looby points out, it must flow both ways. But the ambiguity that permits this flow also dissolves the connection between intent and ethical analysis.

[26] The phrase is W. Moelwyn Merchant's, 'His Fiend-Like Queen', *Shakespeare Survey 19* (Cambridge, 1966), pp. 75–81 (p. 80).

He rose from his place and strode across the floor, tottering and at random. His eyes were without moisture, and gleamed with the fire that consumed his vitals. The muscles of his face were agitated by convulsion. His lips moved, but no sound escaped him. That nature should long sustain this conflict was not to be believed. (p. 263)

Clara identifies closely with this internal conflict, falling into second-person address:

My state was little different from that of my brother. I entered, as it were, into his thought. My heart was visited and rent by his pangs – Oh that thy phrenzy had never been cured! that thy madness, with its blissful visions, would return! or, if that must not be, that thy scene would hasten to a close! that death would cover thee with his oblivion!

What can I wish for thee? Thou who hast vied with the great preacher of thy faith in sanctity of motives, and in elevation above sensual and selfish! Thou whom thy fate has changed into parricide and savage! Can I wish for the continuance of thy being? No. (p. 263)

As if sleepwalking, Theodore runs through a series of theatrical poses for overwhelming grief, wringing his hands like Lady Macbeth and clutching his head.

For a time his movements seemed destitute of purpose. If he walked; if he turned; if his fingers were entwined with each other; if his hands were pressed against opposite sides of his head with a force sufficient to crush it into pieces; it was to tear his mind from self-contemplation; to waste his thoughts on external objects. (p. 264)

Finally, identifying with Theodore, knowing his thoughts by voicing them, Clara crosses the moral precipice that separated her from her brother in that first walking nightmare. Here, she participates in both his thoughts and his actions:

Speedily this train was broken. A beam appeared to be darted into his mind, which gave a purpose to his efforts. An avenue to escape presented itself; and now he eagerly gazed about him: when my thoughts became engaged by his demeanour, my fingers were stretched as by a mechanical force, and the knife, no longer heeded or of use, escaped from my grasp, and fell unperceived on the floor. His eye now lighted upon it, he seized it with the quickness of a thought. (p. 264)

The passive way her attention becomes 'engaged' here and the 'unperceived' release of the dagger are belied by the verbal echoes that tie Theodore's intention with hers: the darting beam and his lighting eye, her thoughts and his grasp 'with the quickness of a thought'. These implicit accusations are confirmed by the bloody hands and guilty impressions that obsess Clara, *pace* Lady Macbeth, ever after:

I shrieked aloud, but it was too late. He plunged it to the hilt in his neck; and his life instantly escaped with the stream that gushed from the wound. He was stretched at my feet; and my hands were sprinkled with his blood as he fell.

Such was thy last deed, my brother! For a spectacle like this was it my fate to be reserved! Thy eyes were closed – thy face ghastly with death – thy arms, and the spot where thou liedest, floated in thy life's blood! These images have not, for a moment, forsaken me. Till I am breathless and cold, they must continue to hover in my sight. (p. 264)

Brown uses the passive voice throughout the novel as verbal parallel to the waking trance that increasingly overtakes his narrator. It is a great perturbation of nature, to receive at once the benefits of a sleeping conscience and do the murderous effects of watching. Thus, this final violent scene is explicitly theatrical and didactic – designed to communicate Clara's state of horrified suspension and half-conscious action to the reader, projecting onto us the progressive, enervating feminization that overtakes this representative democratic subject. In contemporary productions of the play, as reviews suggest, the sleepwalking scene was often the most compelling dramatic moment, precisely for this combination of sensationalism and didacticism.[27]

---

[27] Analysing the physiology of fear in *Macbeth*, David Garrick writes in the *Essay on Acting* (1744) of the 'spasmodic paralysis of the limbs as the spirits rush to the head' when Macbeth sees the daggers. The actor 'should at that time, be a moving statue, or indeed a petrified man; his eyes must speak, and his tongue be metaphorically silent; his ears must be sensible of imaginary noises, and deaf to the present and audible voice of his wife; . . . every member, at that instant should seem

Brown identifies Clara's willfully induced helplessness and self-division as a specifically feminine condition. The novel builds her reputation as a formidable and independent woman. But these qualities are directly contradicted by her attachment to the passive voice, which relays the self-division produced by trauma. Her initial vigour of mind, resoluteness, and rationality mirror her brother's tragic overconfidence. Indeed, these are the very qualities that entice Carwin, who begins his ventriloquist experiments explicitly to test her prodigious autonomy and self-possession. His interventions are meant to scare away an inconvenience but also to prove Clara's vulnerability and feminine emotions. Accordingly, he stages his faux threats in such a way that Clara will interpret them according to the familiar literary conventions (from novels like *Clarissa*) of a rape plot. Beyond scaring her off, however, Carwin has a clinical interest in testing her psychologically, and Brown frames this testing as a true, psychological rape, the results of which prove deeply traumatic. As scholars such as Fliegelman and Looby have noted, the narrative of rape and trauma allegorizes threats to the ethical and political safety of the citizen-subject, figured as a self-possessed American woman. As Clara's friend Pleyel tells her (too late, after the fact), Carwin's success will make 'you a confederate in your own destruction, to make your will the instrument by which he might bereave you of liberty and honor' (pp. 150–1).

We risk that confederacy, Brown claims, whenever we make the pragmatic assumption that true authority is constituted in its citation. Without the crucial help of right interpretations – learned, taught, handed down – we lose the educated scepticism that allows us to discriminate and interpret rightly, in a medium that is inherently unstable. The novel needs to quote the play not so much because it offers received wisdom in support of these claims but because Brown imagines literary fiction – and theatrical fictions in particular – as the expressive medium that can best expose the constructedness of voice. Yet having exposed the positivist pragmatism of the constitutional debates, the novel has no resources to answer its own deeply conservative scepticism. How can we guarantee continuity when everyone who might provide it is dead? This intractable problem is also *Macbeth's*, of course. And in this respect the novel reads as a kind of repetition compulsion of the play, its claim on us still urgent precisely because it is not worked through.

Because *Wieland* is usually read in the local context of early republican debates, the lasting resonance of the novel's repetitions of the play tend to be missed by Americanist scholars. Brown's vision of a narrator dreaming Lady Macbeth sleepwalking adumbrates an anxiety that will continue to haunt American politics: the fear that a dishonourable instrumentality lies at the heart of the Jeffersonian notion of consent and feminizes each democratic subject in disabling ways. This is the danger embodied in the transformation of Lady Macbeth from ambitious, self-possessed Queen to helpless sleepwalker. And it helps explain why later incarnations of Lady Macbeth continue to offer such compelling, resonantly ambivalent figures. They resist reconstruction in part because they recall this willful alienation of self so powerfully. They are most likely to do so, paradoxically, in the context of a reconstructed, nationalist *Macbeth* such as Steven Simpson's. By rights, Simpson's revisions ought to appeal to the Jeffersonian rebel in US audiences. Scottish nationalist revivals work in the US because we read back onto them our old anti-monarchical politics (even when, as in the case of *Rob Roy*, they are not in fact anti-monarchical). In keeping with this trend, Simpson's 'Throne of Destiny' apparently defends the '"last king of a truly independent Scotland" who was *elected* to replace Duncan'. Yet

separated from his body, and his body from his soul', quoted in Joseph Roach, *The Player's Passion: Studies in the Science of Acting* (Newark, 1985), p. 90. It seems likely, from the similarities between Garrick's theory of fear and Wieland's actions in his final scene that Brown was familiar with the *Essay*; in any case, the dramatic principles advanced here were certainly commonplace by the end of the eighteenth century. In his introduction Fliegelman notes Brown's deep suspicion of Garrick's theories of naturalistic acting, evident in his later novel, *Ormond* (1799) (pp. xxiii–xxxiv).

it is precisely this republican subtext that fixes the figure of Lady Macbeth most firmly in place.

That something of the anxieties articulated in Brown's novel remain urgent and still to be worked through is suggested by the powerful hold Lady Macbeth's plot of transgressive virility and punitive feminization has on our democratic unconscious, at least as it pertains to American First Ladies. The label 'Lady Macbeth' has been applied to political wives with some regularity: Lady 'Macbird' Johnson, Nancy Reagan and Cora Masters Barry to name a few. The well-travelled epithet stuck particularly strongly to Hillary Clinton through the early 1990s. It was launched most recently by Daniel Wattenberg's 1992 essay in *The American Spectator*, 'The Lady Macbeth of Little Rock', speculating on the extent of Clinton's political influence over her husband.[28] Wattenberg's headline harks back to the hen-pecking wives of early American burlesques, as well as Charlotte Cushman's career-making, masculine, aggressive Queen. The epithet epitomized popular suspicion of Clinton's unwomanly ambition, something that surely contributed to the public conversion of her image in the second campaign. This progress from demonized consort to gentler spouse – bleaching the story of her own cuckolding in memoir – uncomfortably recalls Elizabeth Layton's vision of Lady Macbeth and eerily recapitulates Brown's. Yet, as with the anxieties articulated in Clara Wieland's story, the sexual politics of this conversion cover for other fundamental concerns. In running for her Senate seat, Clinton effectively ran against her own iconographic inertia as a figure that activates electoral scepticism about the efficacy of the popular voice. One early anxiety raised by Clinton's politically forceful presence was that she was not elected. The *vox populi* was not represented by her voice in the President's ear (Nancy Reagan kept *her* prompting *sotto voce*). The fantasy of pillow talk was all but dispelled by the Lewinsky scandal,[29] then put to rest by Clinton's own election to the US Senate. But these eventualities obscure in retrospect what made the epithet stick for so long: the fear that Lady Macbeth articulates for the American political imagination, that we deceive ourselves that we have that ear as we cast our votes. This fear may have seemed a theoretical one in 1992. But it feels both more timely, and more urgent, after the US elections of 2000 in Florida. Those elections turned finally on the balance of only nine voices (on the Supreme Court) and exposed failed polling procedures that may have disenfranchized tens of thousands of voters. Such failures, still to redress in more states than Florida, put acute pressure on the national perception of an organic connection between the electoral college and the popular vote.

Reading *Macbeth* along the axis of a single thread in its reception history, as this essay does, reminds us to remember the play as a composite 'work': in Jerome McGann's definition, the sum of all its iterations, retellings, additions, revivals, adaptations and translations into multiple genres and media.[30] Defined widely, a history of reception can illuminate the ways dramatic fictions shape as well as reflect their contemporary political scenes. Reading Hillary Clinton's incarnation as Lady Macbeth in the light of Brown's adaptation, in this longitudinal way, we can understand them as part of a surprisingly persistent pattern of allusion. As 'Lady Macbeth', Clinton represented for a time a nightmare version of our own doubleness as democratic subjects. At once complicit and helpless, giving away our voices to be ventriloquized and quoted as absent authorities, made responsible for actions we cannot control and did not imagine we intended, she figures ourselves consenting to our own loss of consent.

---

28 Daniel Wattenberg, 'The Lady Macbeth of Little Rock', *The American Spectator*, 25–8 August 1992, pp. 25–32.

29 During and after the Lewinsky scandal, Shakespearian pastiches in the editorial sections of American newspapers typically allocated Lady Macbeth's taglines to Bill Clinton, rather than Hillary, drawing an off-colour connection between stained dresses and 'out, damned spot'. See for example, 'The Next Two Years', *The Christian Science Monitor*, 19 August 1998, p. 12 and John O'Sullivan, 'All's Well that Ends Ill', *The New York Times*, 19 September 1998, A15.

30 Jerome McGann, 'The Case of The Ambassadors and the Textual Condition', in George Bornstein and Ralph G. Williams, eds., *Palimpsest: Editorial Theory in the Humanities* (Ann Arbor, 1993), pp. 151–66.

MACBIRD! AND *MACBETH*: TOPICALITY AND IMITATION IN BARBARA GARSON'S SATIRICAL PASTICHE

TOM BLACKBURN

Once one has seen or read a play like *Macbeth*, it has perforce an afterlife in memory, in imaginative and emotional recollections of the experience of the performance or the reading. That sort of afterlife remains private and is as varied in content as readers are in nature and number. The sort of afterlife on which this paper focuses, however, is of a different sort, a public afterlife captured in literary, graphic or cinematic artefacts, or in any or all of the theatrical productions that have followed since the play's first staging by the King's Men. I have coined the term, 'afterfact'– conflated from 'artefacts of the afterlife' – as a convenient label for this second sort of survival.

Macbeth afterfacts can be divided into two classes. The first consists of those productions on stage or film that purport to represent the original, ranging from reverent attempts to reproduce a simulacrum of the historical original, to the '30 Minute Macbeth' chanted almost entirely by the witches staged at Oxford in the mid 1950s. The second group of afterfacts clearly has a relationship to the original, but does not claim to represent it in anything like its entirety. Films like Kurosawa's *Throne of Blood*, or *Men of Respect* may be somewhere on a borderline between the two classes, but *Gruach, Ubu Roi, Macbett*, and *Cahoot's Macbeth*, as well as Barbara Garson's *Macbird!*, my topic, are clearly members of the second class.

As teachers, scholars and critics engaged with the Shakespeare texts, the reasons why we pay attention to the first class of afterfacts are mainly connected, I would venture, to a desire to supplement or complement reading with theatrical experience, and to an impulse to extend and enhance the varieties of interpretive approaches brought to bear on our own readings of the plays (and those of our students). Interest in the second class may be more difficult to justify pedagogically or as a topic for scholarship. Most directly, these afterfacts may suggest a reading of *Macbeth*, or some aspects of it, that leads us to enhance or revise how we read the original. The afterfact itself may be judged to possess intrinsic merit, either from a dramatic or literary perspective, or as a particularly witty, accurate or effective commentary on its own times. By the reformulation or recontextualizing of plot, theme or language from the original, the afterfact may at once reveal to us something about the historical particularity of the political, cultural or moral climates in which both the original and the afterfact were produced. *MacBird!*, I believe, repays scrutiny in all of these categories.

As Stephen Greenblatt reminds us in his preface to *Macbeth* in *The Norton Shakespeare*, the play was written not long after the Gunpowder Plot of 1605 had provoked fears of attempts to assassinate the King. As Greenblatt puts it, 'Of Shakespeare's great tragedies, *Macbeth* has always seemed the most topical, cannily alert not only to contemporary events, but to King James's political beliefs and personal obsessions. Not surprisingly for someone whose mother and father had both been killed, James had a horror of assassination and a powerful conviction that a king was a sacred figure.'[1] Killing a king is at

[1] *The Norton Shakespeare*, ed. Stephen Greenblatt *et al.* (New York, 1997), p. 2256.

the centre of the *Macbeth* plot (as it is in most of the English historical plays, in *Hamlet* and in *Julius Caesar*, all plays to which there are frequent allusions in *MacBird!*). Neither that aspect of the plot, nor the political topicality of the play, however, seems to have been the first reason why Barbara Garson selected *Macbeth* as the base for her own topical satire. In the 'Foreword' to the Grove edition of *Macbird!*, Lisa Lyons recounts that

> *Macbird!* originated in August 1965, as a slip of the tongue when Barbara Garson, speaking at an anti-war rally in Berkeley, California, quite accidentally referred to the First Lady of the United States as Lady MacBird Johnson. Since it was just a few weeks after the Watts insurrection and the Berkeley troop-train demonstrations, the opening lines of a play suggested themselves immediately: 'When shall we three meet again / In riot, strike, or stopping train?' (XI)[2]

First conceived as a sixteen-minute satirical sketch, the play evolved into the three-act piece published by Garson's own Grassy Knoll Press (Berkeley and New York) in 1966, and then into the extended version that opened Off Broadway in January 1967 and provided the text for the Grove Press Edition.

To set the topical context for *MacBird!* we need first to recall that John F. Kennedy was assassinated in the fall of 1963 and succeeded by Lyndon Baines Johnson. In the summer of 1965 when Garson was rallying in Berkeley, headline stories in the *New York Times* on 12 August included Johnson's assertion, 'US in Vietnam on Saigon's Plea', as well as news that a second US jet was downed by missiles south of Hanoi and that Martin Luther King, Jr. was planning to appeal directly to President Ho Chi Minh of North Vietnam, to President Johnson, to the Vietcong and to the Saigon government to halt the war in Southeast Asia. On 13 August *The Times* front page carried an account of 'new Negro riots' erupting in South Los Angeles. On an inside page of the 11 August paper, a United Press story told of 'Stiff penalties voted in House for burning draft registrations'. The story quoted Representative William G. Bray, Republican of Indiana, describing such protestors as 'generally filthy beatniks', and Representative L. Mendell Rivers of South Carolina stating that 'This bill places these birds where they belong – behind bars.' On the other side, earlier in August, *The Times* published a letter from Dr Benjamin Spock in which he protested that 'The photograph of US marines burning 150 dwellings in a South Vietnam village because of a burst of sniper fire makes me sick with shame for my country' and that such deeds will 'increasingly earn for us their hatred and the scorn of the world' (5 August).

On 19 January 1967, the day on which previews of *MacBird!* opened at the Village Gate Theater, *The Times* reported that US casualties during the prior week were the war's highest, with 144 killed, 1044 wounded, and six missing. B-52s dropped thousands of tons of incendiary bombs in an attempt to defoliate a forest believed to be hiding Vietcong camps. A South Vietnamese effort to negotiate a truce for the Lunar New Year celebrations in February appeared to have been rejected by the enemy in Hanoi, while Gerald Ford and Everett McKinley, in a Republican State of the Union talk, alleged that President Johnson's foreign and domestic policies were leading America into 'frustration and failure, bafflement and boredom'. Johnson himself had increasingly become the target of anti-war forces (we may recall the taunting chant 'Hey, hey LBJ, how many kids did you kill today') and the personal and external forces that eventually led him to decline to run in the 1968 race were gathering power.

Out of, and into, this political and policy maelstrom, Garson launched what was widely hailed, as Robert Brustein put it, 'as one of the most brutally provocative works in the American theatre, as well as one of the most grimly amusing'.[3] Perhaps moved by the Lady MacBird slip to look at *Macbeth* as a model for political satire, Garson seems

[2] Barbara Garson, *MacBird!* (New York, 1967), p. ix. All further quotations from this edition will be identified parenthetically in my text by page number. For a substantial amount of *MacBird!* material, see the website of Dennis Brumm: www.brumm.com./MacBird/index.html. Brumm's site includes audio cuts from the original cast album.

[3] Quoted in Garson, *MacBird!*, p. i.

to have recognized both the possibilities in the plot for development of the alleged rivalry between LBJ and the 'upstart' Kennedy clan, and the likeness between the unhappy state of Scotland under Macbeth's reign and the terrible unrest in America. In the vast web of conspiracy theories surrounding the assassination of JFK, Garson also found what became the most outrageous piece of the plot, the suspicion that LBJ had succeeded to the 'throne' by complicity in the killing of his predecessor. Lest one think that Garson manufactured that suspicion out of general opposition to LBJ's policies, we need only look to a website such as the 'JFK Assassination Homepage' where one finds:

> Who Killed JFK?
> Answer these questions:
>
> 1. Whose sole obsession in life was to become a U.S. president?
> 2. What U.S. Vice-president had a short expected life span?
> 3. Who 'forced' his way to be JFK's running mate?
> 4. Who disliked JFK and hated Robert Kennedy?
> 5. Who knew he would be dumped from the 1964 ticket?
> 6. Who had several strong motives to kill President Kennedy?
> 7. Who was among the few people involved in the intimate planning of JFK's Dallas trip?
> 8. Who ordered the seizure of all evidence after the assassination?
> 9. Who created the Warren Commission and who did it report to?
> 10. Whose Commission decided not to release much of the assassination evidence for are [sic] lifetime?
> 11. Who gained the most from President Kennedy's death?
> 12. Who was the principal culprit in the murder of President John F. Kennedy
>
> ANSWER
> LYNDON B. JOHNSON

Choosing *Macbeth* as her reference text at once reflected Garson's awareness of the public suspicions about LBJ, and obligated her to deal with the central event in the play's plot, the murder of Duncan. Shaping LBJ as a Macbeth to JFK's 'Ken O'Dunc' seemed to most of the original commentators on the play its 'most disturbing and "controversial" aspect'.[4]

When we look closely at *MacBird!*, however, we find that Garson's treatment of the murder is one of the principal differences between the parody and its model. The *MacBird!* witches do prophesy to MacBird the ascent from leader of the Senate to Vice-President and thence to the Presidency. The first scene of the play is set at a Democratic nominating convention. The witches, all male, represent a spectrum of protestors: '*The* 1st witch *is dressed as a student demonstrator, beatnik stereotype. The* 2nd witch *is a Negro with the impeccable grooming and attire of a* Muhammed Speaks *salesman. The* 3rd witch *is an old leftist, wearing a worker's cap and overalls. He carries a lunch pail and a lantern*' (p. 5).

The witches confront MacBird and his 'Crony' at the convention. MacBird challenges the apparitions (first describing them as 'a nigra and a filthy beatnik', while his crony calls the Third Witch 'a bum done up in worker's duds'.(p. 9)): 'Come on, speak up, now what in thunder are you?' (p. 10). The witches reply, their prophecies interspersed with responses by the Crony and then MacBird:

1st Witch: All hail Macbird! All hail the Senate's leader!
2nd Witch: All hail Macbird, Vice-President thou art!
3rd Witch: All hail MacBird, that shall be President!
All Witches: All Hail MacBird, that shall be President!
Crony:
Hey boss, how come you gulp and seem to fear?
It has a kind of pretty sound I think.
(to Witches:) If you can look into your crystal ball
And say who'll get ahead and who'll go down,
Speak then to me.
When he becomes the chief
What will I be?
1st Witch: You'll be his leading hack.
2nd Witch: It's not so high, but so much less to fall:
For you shall share the fate of his career.
MacBird shall be the mightiest of all,
But Ken O'Dunc alone shall leave an heir.

---

[4] Dwight Macdonald, quoted from *The New York Review of Books*, in Garson, *MacBird!*, p. ii.

3rd Witch:
An heir who'll play a king, like other kings.
He too shall be an extra on our set.
He'll strut and fret his hour on the boards
And be applauded wildly from the pit.
But if you skip and read a later page,
We take the final bow upon this stage.
MacBird (*who has been absorbed in his thoughts*):
The Senate leader, that I *know* I am.
But how Vice-President, when Ken O'Dunc
Despises me like dirt? And to be chief –
Unthinkable while Ken O'Dunc holds sway!
(pp. 10–11)

This immediate response and his 'gulp', however, can be read as based on an ambition already conceived only by reference back to *Macbeth*. When MacBird writes to Lady MacBird ('Lady M') to announce the Ken O'Dunc visit, however, he notes 'two down and one to go', but it is Lady M who translates his desire to 'expose' Ken to his Texan power base into the ambiguous threat to '*expose* him to the fury of his foes' (pp. 19, 21). When MacBird queries her emphasis, she replies, with a further ominous quibble on 'force',

Just expose him. Nothing more
I mean but what you meant, but what you want.
Your broad dominions shelter not a few
Who'd show great force of feeling for their chief.
(p. 22)

MacBird counters with one of the play's relatively few direct quotations from *Macbeth*, 'I dare do all that may become a man. / Who dares do more is none' (p.22, *Macbeth* 1.7.45–7), and Lady M, after protesting that she is not a man, but 'a lady and a Southern hostess', concludes the scene with another direct quotation, 'you shall put / This day's great business into my dispatch / Which shall to all our days and nights to come / Give solely sovereign sway and masterdom' (p. 22, *Macbeth* 1.6.65–8).[5]

Alhough MacBird later anticipates John Ken O'Dunc's visit to Dallas with words again drawn almost directly from Macbeth's – 'but let that be / Which the eye fears, when the hand has done, to see' (p. 27, *Macbeth* 1.5.52–3) – his own hand is never directly involved in the shooting of John. Garson elsewhere rewrites history by implying that the gunman from the Book Depository was killed by MacBird, as Macbeth murdered Duncan's guards to forestall inquiry into their guilt. The question, 'Who did it', is put by a '1st Voice' but not answered directly. MacBird, echoing MacBeth more ambiguously, replies:

Who could refrain when Ken O'Dunc lies dead?
Who could be calm when he saw that scoundrel grin?
Who could be loyal yet neutral? I tell thee, no man.
(p. 36)

Throughout, MacBird's complicity in the killing of Ken O'Dunc, and in the elimination of the actual assassin, thus remains, as it was in history, a matter of innuendo and suspicion, not the theatrical (and historical) fact the killings were in *Macbeth*. These suspicions, as treated in Garson's play, seem less directed at any real claim that LBJ was guilty in the assassination – the business of the conspiracy fringe as represented on the website above – than part of an overall critique of American domestic and foreign policy carried out in *ad hominem* terms, and a commentary on the duplicity and self-interest of all politicians.

Though LBJ is the principal parodic target of the play, neither the Kennedy brothers nor other Democratic politicians fare much better. As the play begins, John and Robert, perhaps echoing Duncan's designation of Malcolm as his successor, are looking ahead to a dynastic future for the family in a monarchical presidency. Reassuring Robert the cynical bid for party unity in offering MacBird the office of Vice-President will not undermine his brother's future, John proclaims his vision for the country, borrowing in part from John of Gaunt's address to Richard II,

Enough is said! At least we need to ask.
He won't accept and, even if he does,
His name will just stand second on the ticket.
You, Bob, are still the second in succession.

[5] Hereafter, when exact or nearly exact quotations from Shakespeare are incorporated into Garson's text, page references to Garson's play will be followed by act, scene and line reference to *Macbeth*.

And Ted is next . . . and princes yet unborn . . .
And for this land, this crowned continent,
This earth of majesty, this seat of Mars,
This forceful breed of men, this mighty world,
I see a . . . *New Frontier* beyond her seas.
She shall o'erflow her shores and burst her banks,
Eastward extend till East does meet with West,
And West until the West does touch the East
And o'er this hot and plagued earth descend
The Pox [sic] Americana, a sweet haze,
Shelt'ring all the world in its deep shade.
And our descendants, locking link to link,
Shall lay a lofty line of loved kings
To serve the faithful, laying low the foe;
Guiding, guarding, governing this folk.

Teddy's reaction immediately undercuts this vision (already partially vitiated by the 'Pox' and the suggestion that the 'sweet haze' may be partly pharmacological):

Ted: Gee, that's keen (*counting on his fingers*)
So let's see . . . That means Jack in '60 and '64, then Bobby in '68 and '72, then me in . . . what would that make it . . .'76 and '80 and then in 1984 it could be . . . (p. 6)

Teddy's childish folly is hit on again near the end of the play when Robert is about to be nominated for the Presidency, and Ted asks, 'Can I head up the Navy? I love boats' (p. 101).

Lady MacBird's justification for MacBird's use of the 'biggest lie' in dealing with Ken O'Dunc rests on JFK's own suppression of the truth in regard to his responsibility for the failed invasion of Cuba at the Bay of Pigs in 1961: 'Remember he attacked that rebel isle, / Denied he did it, then announced: "'Twas I?"' (p. 28). The legendary political ambition of the Kennedys as propelled by Joe Kennedy is finally attacked as genuinely inhuman in Robert's revelation of a parallel to MacDuff's riddling birth 'not of woman'. Faced with MacBird's proud, witch-inspired boast that 'No man with beating heart or human blood / Can ever harm MacBird or touch his throne', Robert replies:

Your charm is cursed. Prepare to hear the worst.
At each male birth, my father in his wisdom
Prepared his sons for their envisioned greatness.
Our first gasped cries as moist, inverted infants
Confirmed for him our place as lords and leaders.
To free his sons from paralyzing scruples
And temper us for roles of world authority
Our pulpy human hearts were cut away.
And in their place precision apparatus
Of steel and plastic tubing was inserted.
The sticky human blood was drained and then
A tepid antiseptic brine injected.
Although poor Teddy suffered complications,
The operation worked on all the others,
Thus steeling us to rule as more than men.
And so, MacBird, that very man you fear,
Your heartless, bloodless foe now lifts his spear.
(p. 107)

Before the spear can fall, MacBird, already shaken by the news that 'burning wood has come to Washington' (in the form of cherry trees set on fire by black rioters), drops dead of a heart attack. Robert Ken O'Dunc takes on the Presidency with precisely the same words used by MacBird after John's death: 'A tragic twist of fateful sorrow, friends, / Makes me your president this fearful day' (p. 108). His conduct, and his pledge to adopt MacBird's 'Smooth Society', simply confirm the insight of the Third Witch a scene earlier that the 'Bob-cat' is 'just like all the rest. They're all alike' (p. 98).

Others in the liberal Democratic ranks prove equally corrupt or easily manipulated. Adlai Stevenson, as the 'Egg of Head', eulogizes John Ken O'Dunc in terms borrowed from Ophelia's lament on what she perceives to be Hamlet's disordered mind:

Oh, what a noble mind was here brought down!
The statesman's, soldier's, scholar's eye, tongue, sword,
The expectancy and rose of this fair state,
The glass of fashion and mold of form,
Supreme in war and thus our hope for peace,
The believed of all believers – quite, quite dead.
And I, of statesman most deject and wretched,
That sucked the honey of his many vows,
Now see that most noble and most sovereign leader
His silver skin laced with his own bright blood,
That unmatched form and future of grown youth,
Blasted with a rifle. Woe is me!
To see what I have seen; see what I shall see. (p. 41)

This passage nicely illustrates Garson's mode of emendation and pastiche. Ophelia's speech is modified by changing 'quite, quite down' to 'quite, quite dead', and 'blasted with an ecstasy' to 'blasted with a rifle' (*Hamlet* 3.1.153–64). Having paid tribute to the public image of the youthful and vigorous John, she further adapts the source passage to her plot by adding a slightly changed version of a line from Macbeth's hypocritical description of the dead Duncan: 'His silver skin laced with his golden blood' (*Macbeth* 3.1.114).

Despite this eulogy for the dead John, the 'Egg of Head' finally temporizes, again in a parody of the Hamlet 'To be or not to be' soliloquy, and decides weakly that 'Security makes cowards of us all' and that he will 'work within for change' under a MacBird presidency (pp. 41–2). The 'Earl of Warren' proves no more steadfast as he agrees to investigate the killing of John even though he knows MacBird is looking for a cover-up (p. 49).

The play's central critique, however, remains directed at LBJ's 'Smooth Society' programs and his understanding and conduct of the Vietnam war. He emerges as a kind of Texas redneck, racist in his assumptions, insensitive to the implications and effects of the conflict in Vietnam, and jealous of the polish and power of the Kennedy family.

At the first press conference after his 'coronation', MacBird appropriates Ken O'Dunc's earlier rhetoric:

A tragic twist of fateful sorrow, friends,
Made me your President that fearful day.
And I shall be the President of all:
Not just the rich, not just the fortunate
Not just the folks that vote for me,
(*Ominous or emphatic*) but *all*
And stretching out beyond our nation's shores,
To east and West around this seething globe,
Where constant conflagrations blaze and rage,
We mean to be the fireman of peace,
Dousing flames with freedom's forceful flow.
Our highest goal is peace, but in its quest
We shall not fear to use our righteous might.
In short we seek that Pox Americana
That all the freedom-loving world desires.
The unity of *all* alone contents us,
We plan to guide this planet by consensus.

When a reporter then intervenes to ask the new ruler how he plans 'to deal / With rebel groups which thrive in Viet land?' Mac Bird immediately gives the lie to his own vision. The responses by MacBird and 'Lord MacNamara' initiate the liberal attack on the motives and miscalculations of the war:

MacBird:
What rebel groups? Where is this Viet land?
Who gave them folks permission to rebel?
Lord MacNamara, valiant chief of war,
What is the place I've just been asked about?
MacNamara:
It's way off to the East, eight thousand miles.
A little land we're trying to subdue.
MacBird:
What crap is this 'we're *trying* to subdue'?
Since when do we permit an open challenge
To all the world's security and peace?
Rip out those Reds! Destroy them, root and branch!
Deploy whatever force you think we need!
Eradicate this noxious, spreading weed!
MacNamara:
Your word is my command. Your will is done.
That land will be subdued ere set of sun. (pp. 54–5)

The actual horrors of that conflict are most vividly presented by the Third Witch in Garson's version of Macbeth's second visit to the weird sisters:

Taylor's tongue and Goldberg's slime,
MacNamara's bloody crime
Sizzling skin of napalmed child,
Roasted eyeballs, sweet and mild
Now we add a fiery chunk
From a burning Buddhist monk.
Flaming field and blazing hut,
Infant fingers cooked and cut,
Young man's heart and old man's gut,
Groin and gall and gore of gook
In our caldrons churn and cook.
(p. 79)

In the same scene, the Second Witch's chant conjures up the riotous unrest in the black community with its current and historic suffering, perhaps unfairly linked to LBJ on the basis of his southern background, and in this play by his casual use of 'nigra':

> Around the caldron chant and sing,
> Arson rape and rioting.
> Bombed-out church and burning cross
> In the boiling caldron toss.
> Club and gas and whip and gun,
> Niggers strung up just for fun.
> Black men beat and burnt and shot,
> Bake within our melting pot. (p. 78)

Every protest theme of the mid-sixties has its moment in the play, and no prominent figure of the time really escapes the satiric whip, whether Republican or Democrat (including Reagan, blamed as Governor of California for part of the problems energizing protests at Berkeley (p. 78)).

As in the most Swiftian of satires, or, indeed, in Shakespeare's own bitter drama of universal corruption, *Troilus and Cressida*, no character in *MacBird!* stands for or stands by any normative vision of an ideal society. Positive values can only be intuited from their absence and their opposites.[6] Perhaps that is why Garson's play seems so true to much of the protest movement of the sixties, to an anger propelled in large part by frustration at finding no established authority that seemed capable of rescuing the country from the apparent abysses of Viet Nam and racial strife. The depth or complexity of awareness as Garson's cartoon-like characters demonstrate (see the illustrations by Lisa Lyons) depends mainly on lines borrowed from *Macbeth*, *Hamlet*, *Richard II*, *Richard III* or *Julius Caesar*. In the parodic adaptation of those lines, however, heroic or tragic allusions are undercut by awkward contemporary references or near laughable shifts into exaggerated colloquialism. Neither MacBird nor the Ken O'Duncs can match up to their Shakespearian originals, nor, like Eliot's Prufrock, are they meant to. They inhabit a world devoid of tragedy or heroism, and of the values that make either possible.

Garson's skilful pastiche turns the tragedy of *Macbeth* into darkly comic satire, but reading the Scottish Play through it may lead us to reflect on one possible implication of the crowning of Malcolm at the end of the play. Not only may the bizarre charade of Malcolm assuming Macbeth's faults in 4.3 leave a doubt in the reader's mind of the depth of his moral superiority, but MacDuff's leadership in deposing Macbeth places him in such a position of power that we may begin to wonder if the kingmaker will remain satisfied in a secondary role. Does Garson's imagined cycle of endless corruption and disloyalty indeed mirror a counter-text in Macbeth? A counter-text in which Macbeth's disillusioned vision of the world as an idiot's tale may be as true, or as possible, as Macduff's closing promise of a time set free by the ascent of Malcolm? The meaninglessness of the shifts of rulers and the sacrifices of life involved in *MacBird!* is not implied by the silent presence of MacDuff but in the sheer hypocrisy, already alluded to, of Robert Ken O'Dunc's final speech. Having managed the confrontation that leads to MacBird's death, Robert doffs his armour and over the body proclaims:

> My lords, black sorrow hovers o'er the land,
> MacBird, our brilliant leader, lives no more.
> The plotters of his downfall, now obscure,
> I vow to bring to light, to bring to trial.
> *Crowd gathers round.*
> A tragic twist of fateful sorrow, friends,
> Make me your President this fearful day.
> And though I never sought it, history
> Assigned to me her most demanding task,
> To follow my great predecessor's path
> In hewing out the Smooth Society.
> So choked with grief, I pledge my solemn word
> To lift aloft the banner of MacBird. (p. 108)

As a text that may be provocatively read against its sources, *MacBird!* should endure, at least

[6] Reading Garson's work as a sociologist of labour, e.g. *All the Livelong Day* (New York, 1977) and *The Electronic Sweatshop* (New York, 1988), one might infer that her own political and social ideals incorporate a classic Marxist revulsion from the dehumanization of labour with mildly anarchist leanings, both of which evince a deep distrust of both big buisiness and big government. Her more recent reflections on anti-globalism and anti-war action in the aftermath of September 11 2001 continue those themes (see http://zmag.org/garsoncalam.htm).

peripherally, in Shakespeare studies. As political drama, however, the play, despite its verve, wit, and propelling anger, finally suffers from one difficulty that relegates it to the category of ephemera occupied by most topical satires. Garson wrote in the midst of the history she critiques. The history of Shakespeare's *Macbeth* was already written when the playwright came to craft his political and personal tragedy; no speculative plot after the assassination of Duncan and Macbeth's ascent to the throne needed to be invented, and the vision of Banquo's succession had its validation in the sitting monarch. Within a year after *MacBird!* had its moment onstage, events had outrun Garson's plot inventions. Though Lyndon B. Johnson's death was still a few years in the future, his political career was about to end with his decision not to run for reelection. The possibility of Robert F. Kennedy succeeding his assassinated brother's office ended with his murder in Los Angeles in the midst of a promising campaign. As an afterfact of *Macbeth* with a brief but bright life of its own, *MacBird!* earns a place in the history of the 1960s not for the accuracy of its political projections, nor for its literary quality, but as a striking record of the mood and tenor of the protest culture of the times.

MICK JAGGER MACBETH

DEANNE WILLIAMS

With opening credits that announce the film as 'A Playboy Production', and list Hugh Hefner as Executive Producer, Roman Polanski's *Macbeth* is nothing if not a period piece. In his autobiography, *Roman, by Polanski*, Polanski recalls his creative collaboration with Kenneth Tynan (who also wrote for *Playboy*) in terms that situate it within the sybaritic world of the late sixties and early seventies. As they rehearsed the murder of Duncan in a Belgravia flat, with Tynan reclining on the bed and Polanski, as Macbeth, bent over him, an open window allowed their game to be witnessed by a clique of fascinated elderly residents who stared, 'transfixed, sherry glasses frozen in midair'.[1] Polanski concludes, 'they doubtless assumed that our actions were all part of the swinging London scene'. Along with its association with the international party crowd, Polanski's *Macbeth* was mired in controversy from its inception. While its graphic depiction of violence and nudity earned the film an 'X' rating before its release in autumn 1971, the grisly murder of Polanski's pregnant wife, Sharon Tate, by Charles Manson and his followers in August of 1969 made it impossible to view the film, and, in particular, its obsessive return to visual images of hanging and stabbing, without recalling the events of that terrible summer. Queried by Tynan about the amount of blood shed by the injured and dying bodies in the film, Polanski referred to his own experiences to authorize his directorial choices: 'You didn't see my house last summer. I know about bleeding.'[2]

Yet Polanski has complained about the extent to which critics fastened upon the obvious parallels between life and art, insisting that the film must have served him with 'some cathartic purpose'.[3] Indeed, many of Polanski's directorial choices seem to draw upon the Manson murders: the domestic space of the Macduff household 'surprised', and his 'wife and children savagely slaughtered' (4.3.206–7) is depicted in gruesome detail, with multiple dead

---

I would like to thank Stephen Orgel, Adrian Kiernander, Anthony Miller, Seth Lerer, Simon Palfrey and the comments of an anonymous reader for their most helpful contributions to this essay. Special thanks are due to Terry Goldie for his willingness to act as 'native informant'. I have made use of the three versions of the film's screenplay generously deposited at the Folger Shakespeare Library by Bernice Kliman. A fellowship at the Folger Shakespeare Library made it possible to complete this essay in ideal circumstances.

[1] Roman Polanski, *Roman, by Polanski* (New York, 1984), p. 333.

[2] John Parker, *Polanski* (London, 1995), p. 178.

[3] Polanski, *Roman*, p. 331.

Each critical discussion of Polanski's *Macbeth* calls attention, in some way, to the parallels. See Kenneth Rothwell, 'Roman Polanski's Macbeth: Golgotha Triumphant', *Literature/Film Quarterly*, 1 (1973), 71–5; Normand Berlin, '*Macbeth*: Polanski and Shakespeare', *Literature/Film Quarterly* 1 (1973), 291–8; Jack J. Jorgens, *Shakespeare on Film* (Bloomington, 1977), pp. 161–74; William P. Shaw, 'Violence and Vision in Polanski's *Macbeth* and Brook's *Lear*' *Literature/Film Quarterly*, 14 (1986), 211–13; E. Pearlman, '*Macbeth* on Film: Politics', *Shakespeare Survey 39* (Cambridge, 1986), pp. 67–74. Bryan Reynolds's article, 'Untimely Ripped: Mediating Witchcraft in Polanski and Shakespeare', in *The Reel Shakespeare: Alternative Cinema and Theory*, ed. Lisa S. Starks and Courtney Lehmann (Madison, 2002), pp. 143–64, compares the atmosphere of the Elizabethan/Jacobean witchtrials to the Manson murders.

bodies splayed in the hall.[4] In an early scene, when a soldier on the battlefield nudges a body to check for life, the body squirms, and the soldier bludgeons it, just as the Manson murderers made sure that they did not leave behind any survivors.[5] Particularly stunning is the extent to which specific events and lines from Shakespeare's *Macbeth* seem to apply directly to the Manson murders. For example, in each case, women are active participants in the violence: in *Macbeth*, the three witches' prophesy instigates Lady Macbeth's murderous plan, whereas the Manson murders were accomplished by three female members of the Manson 'family' and their lone male companion. Lady Macbeth's impulse to wash the blood from her hands was shared by Manson's followers, who tried to wash their own bloodstained hands with a garden hose; the observation, 'Yet who would have thought the old man to have so much blood in him' (5.1.34) was echoed by the testimony of the cult members at the trial. The idea of Macduff having been 'from his mother's womb / Untimely ripped' (5.10.15–16); and Malcolm's evocation of Scotland's political vulnerability 'each new day a gash / Is added to her wounds' (4.3.41–2), are eerily consistent with the horrifying fate of Sharon Tate.

As much as it represents a specific response to his own personal tragedy, Polanski's *Macbeth* offers a wide-ranging meditation upon the larger political and social events of the sixties, when events such as the assassinations of Martin Luther King, Jr and Robert Kennedy, the riots of 1968, and the Vietnam war brought a decade which had advocated racial tolerance, sexual liberation and civil rights to a violent, bloody conclusion. Dubbed 'the most distinguished cinematic version of the play' by A. R. Braunmuller, the editor of the New Cambridge *Macbeth*, Polanski's *Macbeth* explores the dark side of the combination of boundless individualism and a powerful sense of collective purpose that characterized the youth culture of the sixties.[6] Polanski's relentless depiction of violence produces a kind of jaded nausea, through overexposure, that lends itself to a reading of the Macbeths as representatives of sixties optimism: supremely confident in their own moral superiority, but also the unreflective instigators of an unexpected tragedy. In this respect, Polanski's *Macbeth* does more than hold a mirror up to the nature of sixties culture; it also offers a powerful, personal study of its excesses.

THE SEASON OF THE WITCH

Polanski had been eager to try his hand at Shakespeare ever since he was a student in acting school in postwar Krakow. The idea for a *Macbeth* film occurred to him while he was on the slopes of Gstaad, where he spent the winter of 1970 recovering from the murders in the company of martial arts actor Bruce Lee and an assortment of students from one of the local finishing schools. His batteries recharged by the promise of a new project, Polanski flew to London, holing up in the Belgravia flat with his friend Tynan (the producer of *Oh! Calcutta*, literary director of the National Theatre, and the first person ever to say 'fuck' on television). There they acted out scenes, dreamed up swordfights and produced the screenplay for *Macbeth*. What impressed Polanski most about Kenneth Tynan was his 'encyclopedic knowledge of Shakespeare and uncanny knack of extemporizing Shakespearian blank verse to fit any occasion'.[7] Flying to Hollywood to promote the script, Polanski was introduced to Hefner by his friend Victor Lownes, head of the British division of Playboy, Inc. As Polanski recalls, Hef 'flew in in his black bunny DC-9, with a retinue of girls and courtiers, played a lot of backgammon, and gave the go-ahead'.[8]

Polanski considered *Macbeth* fair game because he felt that the technical shortcomings of Orson Welles's 1948 film version of the play (which he described as 'a sort of universal sewer filled with

[4] See *Macbeth*, ed. A. R. Braunmuller, The New Cambridge Shakespeare (Cambridge, 1997). All quotations from *Macbeth* are from this edition.

[5] My sources on the Manson murders are Vincent Bugliosi with Curt Gentry, *Helter Skelter* (New York, 1974), and John Gilmore and Ron Kenner, *The Garbage People: The Trip to Helter-Skelter and Beyond* (Los Angeles, 1978, rpt. 1995).

[6] See Braunmuller, *Macbeth*, p. 86.

[7] Polanski, *Roman*, p. 332.

[8] Polanski, *Roman*, p. 334.

a bunch of incestuous warlocks'), and the artistic shortcomings of George Schaefer's 1961 version, left much to be desired.[9] While landmark theatrical productions of *King Lear* in the forties and fifties starring John Gielgud, Alan Badel, Laurence Olivier and Donald Wolfit (among others), and culminating in Peter Brook's 1962 production with Paul Scofield, reflected overwhelming feelings of loss and destruction in the aftermath of World War Two, the moral ambiguities of *Macbeth* – with its topsy-turvy sense of 'fair is foul and foul is fair' (1.1.12), and its rapid movement from a spirit of possibility and entitlement to one of decadence and disillusionment – had more to say to the sixties generation. Thus, Polanski deliberately cast the Macbeths as 'young and good-looking – not, as in most stage productions, middle-aged and doom-laden'.[10] Tynan defended their choice of Francesca Annis and Jon Finch, both in their twenties, with characteristic bluntness: 'It makes nonsense to have Macbeth and Lady Macbeth performed by 60 year-olds and menopausals. It's too late for them to be ambitious. Much more plausible for them to be young, sexy with their lives ahead.'[11] For both Polanski and Tynan, *Macbeth* is not the story of middle-aged aspirants seizing their last chance, but instead, of an untimely decline from starry-eyed youth to disillusioned maturity, the movement from high hopes and great expectations to jaded dissipation.

Annis was initially hesitant about accepting the part of Lady Macbeth: 'I thought Lady Macbeth should have been older, but Roman didn't have to do much arm-twisting to persuade me.' Finch, best known for his work in Hammer Studios horror films such as the lesbian-themed *The Vampire Lovers* and *The Horror of Frankenstein*, who was cast as Macbeth, bears an uncanny resemblance to Mick Jagger, lead singer of the Rolling Stones (see illustration 2).[12] Finch's Macbeth seems to draw particular inspiration from Turner, the autobiographical character Jagger plays in *Performance* (1970) directed by Nicholas Roeg and Donald Cammell (see illustration 3). Jagger is cast as a debauched rock-star who provides refuge to a gangster on the run (played by James Fox), giving

©CP-MAC-14
2 Jon Finch as Macbeth in Roman Polanski's *Macbeth* (1971).

him a sartorial and sexual makeover. The film's examination of the theme of performance – the fluidity of gender and sexual identities, and the appeal of surfaces and the spectacle – pushed the buttons of many critics, who considered it a self-indulgent star vehicle. A key example of sixties theatricality, with its emphasis upon the performative quality of everyday life (or 'living theatre'), *Performance* was embraced by younger audiences, for whom it represented the cutting-edge of cool at a time when 'art films' were just beginning to reach the mainstream. As it charts, in a leisurely manner, the burnout and murder of its self-destructive hero,

[9] See Roman Polanski, interview with Francis Wyndham, 'The Young Macbeth', *Sunday Times Magazine* 28 February 1971, pp. 16–19. For discussion of these versions, Michael Mullin, 'Macbeth on Film', *Literature/Film Quarterly*, 1 (1973), 332–42.

[10] Polanski, *Roman*, p. 332.

[11] Mark Shivas, 'They're Young, They're in Love, They're the Macbeths', *New York Times*, 28 February 1971, Section D 13.

[12] He later starred in Alfred Hitchcock's *Frenzy* (1972).

3 Mick Jagger in Donald Cammell and Nicolas Roeg's *Performance* (1970).

Performance glamorizes the sixties mandate of peace and love as well as its more destructive aspects, thus anticipating Polanski's reading of Macbeth as a charismatic sixties anti-hero, abandoned to the pursuit of satisfaction.

Annis and Finch were unpopular with the critics. Although each was a seasoned actor (Annis had played Ophelia, Miranda and Juliet, and Finch augmented his B-movie career with appearances in upwards of fifty plays), many read their youth as inexperience. Pauline Kael found a lack of depth to their performances, complaining that 'the murder of Duncan does not change Macbeth or awaken anything in him', while a critic for the *Daily Mirror* dismissed Lady Macbeth as a mere 'spot-crazy Playboy bunny'.[13] But this is precisely the point. As a study in the loss of the ideals of sixties youth culture, the film uses the twenty-something Macbeths to convey a sense of naivety, even superficiality, as opposed to corruption or even self-awareness. For Polanski, the choice was consistent with his personal theories about evil: 'people who do ghastly things in life, they are not grim, like a horror movie'.[14] As with Mick Jagger's performance in *Performance*, the contrast between their youthful guises and their diabolical actions highlights the sense of moral disconnection from their actions. As Tynan observes (in words that could apply to the sixties generation as a whole), 'they don't know they're involved in a tragedy; they think they're on the verge of a triumph predicted by the witches'.[15] Accordingly, their murder of Duncan evokes the kind of Oedipalized struggles that motivated many of the anti-establishment activities of the sixties in the spirit of the credo, 'Never trust anyone over thirty'. The plan is presented by Lady Macbeth in a spirit of puckish mischief and, when she faces opposition, offended innocence that seems better suited to such harmless acts of civil disobedience as putting cut flowers in gun barrels. As the film progresses, and Annis becomes glassy-eyed and jittery, and Finch, with a more than a few days' beard, is hard-eyed and surly, Polanski reveals (as Duncan puts it) 'the mind's construction in the face' (1.4.12), dramatizing the extent to which the party is over.

If the film's casting supplied easily identifiable characters to its intended audience (those old enough to gain admittance to an X-rated film, and young enough not to be alienated by its affiliations with *Playboy*), its bleak, blank landscape places it firmly in the theatrical and critical avant-garde of the sixties. The 'grey, desolate muddy seashore, with heavy clouds hanging over it' which opens the film evokes the hopeless, miserable world of Samuel Beckett and absurdist drama.[16] Polanski and Tynan came up with the ghastly detail of the severed hand in the first scene: the Blind Witch 'places the handle of the dagger in the palm of the severed hand, and tries to force the fingers to grasp it. Rigor mortis prevents her from succeeding.' This scene of ritualized violence establishes a

---

[13] Pauline Kael, *Deeper into Movies* (Boston, 1972), p. 400 and Polanski, *Roman*, p. 297.

[14] Polanski, 'The Young Macbeth', p. 19.

[15] See Kathleen Tynan, *The Life of Kenneth Tynan* (London, 1987), p. 292.

[16] *The Tragedy of Macbeth by William Shakespeare*. Screenplay by Roman Polanski and Kenneth Tynan (1970), p. 1.

On the three versions of the screenplay, see Bernice W. Kliman, 'Gleanings: the Residue of Difference in Scripts: the Case of Polanski's Macbeth', in *Shakespearian Illuminations. Essays in Honor of Marvin Rosenberg*, ed. Jay L. Halio and Hugh Richmond (Newark, 1998), pp. 130–46.

continuity with Peter Brook's landmark production of *King Lear* at Stratford-upon-Avon: a production in which many critics located, and criticized, the influence of Jan Kott, the Polish intellectual whose controversial *Shakespeare Our Contemporary* (1964) made waves in the scholarly community. As Kott argues, 'a reader or spectator in the mid-twentieth century . . . is not terrified – or, rather, not amazed – at Shakespeare's cruelty. He views the struggle for power and mutual slaughter of the characters far more calmly than did many generations of spectators and critics in the nineteenth century'.[17] Finch's portrayal of Macbeth as morally vacuous and spiritually vacant is of a piece with Kott's sense that 'Macbeth has reached the limits of human experience. All he has left is contempt'.[18] Like his countryman, Polanski obsessively lingers over violence, challenging the viewer to connect the violence in Shakespeare to the atrocities of twentieth-century history.

Polanski mines the play for every trace of violence. As Kott insists, 'a production of *Macbeth* not evoking a picture of the world flooded with blood, would inevitably be false'.[19] Hangings are taking place in the background as we see Macbeth for the first time, fresh from battle. While the film eliminates so many of the vivid, lyrical speeches that distinguish the language of the play, it allows Polanski's trademark technique, voyeuristic set pieces without dialogue, to present an interpretation of *Macbeth* through the preponderance of action. Polanski adds to the violence that already exists in the play, actualizing events that are implicit in the text, but are either not part of its action or not explicitly mentioned. He adds a scene in which Cawdor ('nothing in his life / Became him like the leaving of it' (1.3.7–8)) is hanged, showing his feet dangling for a little while afterwards. The scene is preceded by a spectacularly Foucauldian moment in which the traitor is shown, hands cuffed, wearing an iron collar that secures him, with four chains emanating out from it, attached to iron rings embedded in the stone floor, creating a kind of 'X' shape. The murder of Duncan goes on at great length. The screenplay reads: 'After a long pause he slowly removes the coverlet from the KING's naked chest with the tip of a dagger. Gently he extends the dagger towards the KING's heart, not touching the skin. He hesitates . . .'[20] The scene concludes with Duncan awakening, which startles Macbeth into plunging the dagger repeatedly into his chest. Even Lady Macbeth has her moment: having evidently thrown herself from the balcony, her body is inspected by Macbeth and his attendants. It is as if Polanski wants to excavate every trace of violence in the play, in order to present the full story: while he does not wish to praise it, clearly, neither will he bury it. Instead, the desire to uncover and to foreground violence that is inchoate in what is already an extremely violent play seems to aim for a kind of exorcism: the audience witnesses these acts of violence directly in an effort to rid the play of it altogether, not through repression or excision but through exposure.

In the spirit of Artaud's Theatre of Cruelty, Polanski makes the audience complicit in the film's violence by placing it in dialogue with apparent normalcy. Polanski's childhood memories of the Krakow ghetto inspired his direction of Macbeth's henchmen in the Macduff household: 'the SS officer had searched our room in the ghetto, swishing his riding crop to and fro, toying with my teddy bear, nonchalantly emptying out the hatbox full of forbidden bread'.[21] Polanski locates the greatest terror in domestic details: the naked young Macduff in the bath emphasizes the fragility and vulnerability of the inhabitants, as the murderers chuck

---

17 *Shakespeare Our Contemporary*, trans. Boleslaw Taborski (New York, 1964), p. 3. On the connections between Kott's and Polanski's work, and their Polish roots, see Per Serritslev Petersen, 'The Bloody Business of Roman Polanski's Macbeth: A Case Study of the Dynamics of Modern Shakespeare Appropriation', *Screen Shakespeare*, ed. Michael Skovmand (Aarhus, 1994), pp. 38–53. On Artaud, see Reynolds, 'Untimely Ripped'.

18 See Kott, *Shakespeare Our Contemporary*, p. 77.

19 See Kott, *Shakespeare Our Contemporary*, p. 86.

20 Polanski and Tynan, *The Tragedy of Macbeth*, p. 27.

21 See Polanski, *Roman*, p. 291. See Herbert Eagle, 'Roman Polanski', in *Five Filmmakers: Tarkovsky, Forman, Polanski, Szabo, Makavejev*, ed. Daniel J. Goulding (Bloomington, 1994), pp. 92–155.

the pet falcon under the chin, smash the milk jug, and murder the little boy, the escalating violence accrues greater horror through its intrusion into the quotidian. By contrast, the final fight scenes, in which Macbeth kills a sequence of soldiers in hand-to-hand combat, before Macduff finally gets to him, possesses a two-dimensional, iterative, *Monty-Python-and-the-Holy-Grail*-esque quality. It is like reading Malory: one soldier is killed after the other, a variety of methods (dagger, sword, battleaxe, clubs) produce a myriad of flesh wounds, and the climax occurs only with Macbeth's beheading. The violence is unrepentant, unremarkable, and relentless, precisely because it seems so offhand and everyday. In both scenes, Polanski manipulates the tension between the violence and death, which take place at the outer limits of experience, and the mindset and frame of reference of the normal.

Polanski's use of violence participates in the rebellion, among his theatrical contemporaries, against the tendency in eighteenth and nineteenth-century productions of Shakespeare to minimize or overlook violence: a tendency which allowed Macbeth to be celebrated as a pathetic, tragic hero.[22] Yet at the same time, Polanski's sharp sense of historical accuracy seems a throwback to the detail-driven antiquarianism of Charles Kean and his followers. Polanski and Tynan were not as concerned with avoiding what Brook called the 'operatic hangover' of nineteenth-century tradition. While they were filming in North Wales, Polanski shot medieval castles, costumes, and catapults with an almost Victorian fascination with historical accuracy. He had an enormous amount of trouble with the fireballs that are sent crashing into Dunsinane at the end of the film, which prompted him to dub his crew the 'special defects' team. Just as the Victorian stage used medieval history, filtered through Shakespeare, to dramatize the historical roots of English nationhood, Polanski locates, in the play's medieval Scottish setting, a resolutely contemporary sense of the godless universe. As with Peter Brook's 1971 *King Lear* (a film version of his stage production), Polanski's medieval setting uses furs and pelts, primitive wagons and enormous stone fireplaces to convey the sense of chill and isolation connoted by 'the Dark Ages' that dovetails neatly with the absurdist void.

While Polanski's historicism, like that of Charles Kean, was effective at conveying an overarching visual sense of the Middle Ages, it left him vulnerable to criticism from scholars. Frank Kermode objected vociferously to the anachronism of Fleance's 'sad song of love', performed just before Duncan retires to bed. As Kermode argues, the lyric, entitled 'Merciles Beaute', was 'written by Chaucer for the court of Richard II three hundred years later, and in another country' (actually, the poem was not ascribed to Chaucer in the manuscript, and scholars continue to debate its authenticity).[23] Yet anachronism is hardly a valid criticism given Shakespeare's own presentation of history. And while a fourteenth-century lyric may be anachronistic for eleventh-century Scotland, it is a perfectly viable indicator of Shakespearian notions of the medieval: lyrics such as these were well-known to Shakespeare. The complexities of historicism aside, this medieval English lyric offers a poignant commentary on Macbeth's conundrum: as Fleance sings, 'Oh, your two eyes will slay me suddenly', he makes a complaint about ensnarement, even victimization by the beloved. Lines such as 'I may the beauty of them not sustain. / So pierceth it throughout my heart keen' offer a pithy commentary on Macbeth's manipulation by Lady M, as well as anticipate the murder which is about to take place. Lines from the lyric that the film does not include, such as 'For Daunger halt your mercy in his cheyne' and 'Giltles my deeth thus han ye me purchaced', shed thematic light on why Tynan may have thought of the lyric in the first place.[24]

[22] On the Victorian Shakespeare, see Richard Schoch, *Shakespeare's Victorian Stage* (Cambridge, 1998).

[23] Polanski and Tynan, *The Tragedy of Macbeth*, p. 18. On the Chaucer lyric, see the *Riverside Chaucer*, ed. Larry Benson (Boston, 1987), p. 1090 and Frank Kermode, 'Shakespeare in the Movies', in *Film Theory and Film Criticism*, ed. Gerald Mast and Marshall Cohen (New York, 1974), p. 326.

[24] *Riverside Chaucer*, ed. Benson, p. 659. I am citing the screenplay's modernized version of lines which appear in the film, and the *Riverside Chaucer* for those that do not.

4 Francesca Annis as Lady Macbeth in Roman Polanski's *Macbeth* (1971).

The film's self-conscious medievalism, from suits of armour to bearbaiting (a popular medieval sport also associated with the Elizabethan theatre, which Polanski uses to great effect to communicate the heartlessness of the Macbeths in the wake of their rise to prominence), extends beyond the desire for historical verisimilitude. Sixties medievalism, like that of its nineteenth-century predecessors, had as much to do with adaptation and appropriation as it did with acts of historical recovery. At the same time that medieval studies was offering scholars an opportunity to locate a system of solid structures of belief and community, as well as an alternative and antidote to the violence and misery of the modern, the popular idea of the 'medieval' gave sixties culture a place on which to focus its aspirations for a kind of uncultivated, 'natural' simplicity, even innocence. Indeed, the sixties was the time of the genesis of the Society for Creative Anachronism (founded in Berkeley in 1966), of the worldwide medieval and Renaissance 'fayres', and of the recuperation of the traditions of medieval drama through performance of the Corpus Christi plays in Leeds, Toronto, York and elsewhere. The scene in which Lady Macbeth awaits the return of her husband recalls the visual conventions associated with Guenevere (see illustration 4). Similarly, the ludic performativity of the banquet scene, in which Lady

Macbeth, dressed in an ermine-trimmed gown with a veil and circlet, eats delicately with her hands, while surrounded by a court jester, minstrels, and sword-dancers, all in brightly-coloured, flowing clothes, playing period instruments, seems to have been inspired by the sixties musical *Camelot*: the Broadway hit that provided the soundtrack for the John F. Kennedy administration, and is frequently invoked in its memorialization.[25] The film's musical soundtrack is in keeping with the sixties spirit of popular medievalism, and with a vogue for traditional folk ballads and instruments represented by Donovan, Steeleye Span and Fairport Convention. Jagger and Richards were inspired by this trend in their love song to marijuana, Lady Jane, composed in what Keith Richards describes as 'Chaucer English', and using an Elizabethan-inspired melody and dulcimer.

In keeping with sixties discourse about Shakespeare, however, Polanski draws upon medieval culture only as far as it contributes to his own reading of the play, not hesitating to substitute a more contemporary sound or semiotic where necessary. Along with his academic and theatrical counterparts such as Kott and Joseph Papp, creator of the New York Shakespeare festival, Polanski's priority was to make *Macbeth* speak directly to the concerns and experience of his late twentieth-century audience. As Papp exhorts, 'If you have loved wisely but too well, if you have felt the unkindest cut of all, if you have held the mirror up to nature and asked what's in a name, you are thinking Shakespeare.'[26] Rather than appreciating the play as a piece of medieval history or as a Jacobean artifact, Polanski wanted his audience to relate *Macbeth* to their current preoccupations. Polanski justified his decision to present a young Macbeth not with reference to historical verisimilitude or authorial intention, but because he is 'easier for *me* to identify with' [italics my own].[27] The Third Ear Band, which composed the original music for the film, and which became popular with the release of their 1969 album, *Alchemy* (they also produced the soundtrack for a German television version of *Abelard and Heloise*) superimposes electronic instruments over hand drums, woodwinds and strings, producing a hurdy-gurdy effect that is described by one critic as 'a baleful but strangely beautiful interweaving of modern and medieval music'.[28] When the situation calls for it, as in the murders of Duncan and Macbeth, the film's soundtrack dispenses with medievalism altogether, and adopts instead the qualities of contemporary aleatory or chance music, as in the work of John Cage, to express its themes of moral dissolution and disorder.

This interplay between historicism and contemporaneity is best illustrated by the film's portrayal of Lady Macbeth. Polanski's decision to depict the sleepwalking Lady Macbeth in the nude was ostensibly a gesture to authenticity (and theatre history). As Polanski observes, 'everyone slept naked in her day. The wearing of nightclothes was a social and theatrical convention, not least because women's parts in Shakespeare's time were played by young boys.'[29] *The Times*, brilliantly, declared her 'Lady MacBuff'. While we may applaud Polanski for his rejection of bourgeois convention in order to remain faithful to the historical realities of medieval culture and the early modern stage, the nude Lady Macbeth also illustrates the freedom with which Polanski moves between Shakespeare (and medieval Scotland), and personal and political

[25] The connection apparently started with Jacqueline Kennedy, who gave Theodore H. White an interview shortly after John F. Kennedy's assassination, in which she explained that the Kennedys would listen to the soundtrack on the Victrola each night before bed, and that Jack's favourite song concluded with the following lines: 'Don't let it be forgot / That once there was a spot / For one, brief, shining moment / That was known as Camelot'.

[26] See Helen Epstein, *Joseph Papp. An American Life* (Boston, 1994), p. 84. Kott makes a similar argument: 'by discovering in Shakespeare's plays problems that are relevant to our own time, modern audiences often, unexpectedly, find themselves near to the Elizabethans; or at least are in the position to understand them well'. See Kott, *Shakespeare*, p. 3.

[27] See Polanski, 'The Young Macbeth', p. 19.

[28] Their music for *Macbeth* was nominated for a BAFTA (though they lost to Nino Rota's score for *The Godfather*). The quotation is from critic Debora Thomas's citation for the award, quoted in: www.forcedexposure.com/artists/thirdearband.html.

[29] Polanski, *Roman*, p. 333.

preoccupations that reflect the cusp period between the sixties and the seventies. When the film was released, Lady Macbeth's mad scene in which, as Polanski and Tynan ordain, 'she is naked', caused quite a stir.[30] Although the viewer is treated to little more than a bare bottom, it was this brief scene, as much as the endless violence, that instigated the film's 'X' rating.

If Lady Macbeth's nudity is true to history, it is also utterly co-existent with her status, throughout the film, as a kind of naughty-angelic 'bunny': Playboy underwrites the film in more than just the financial sense. Annis's handling of Macbeth in their first scene together, from her seductive delivery of 'O never shall sun that morrow see' (1.5.59–60); to the Stepford-wifely domestic competence exuded by 'leave all the rest to me' (72); to the tearfully girlish petulance of her subsequent 'When you durst do it, then you were a man' (1.7.49), offers an interpretation of the character as a perfect blend of the contradictions inherent in the Playboy *mythos*: the smiling acquiescence of the sex symbol, the persistent acceptance of helpful domesticity, and the transparent emotional manipulations of the *femme fatale*. Yet the nude Lady Macbeth would be as at home at a party at the Playboy Mansion as she would at a nudist beach: with her Lady Godiva-like hair and naturalistic pallor, we can imagine the naked Lady M in a sixties commune, her hand-wringing dementia the result of a bad trip.

Filtering the play's female characters through the lens of contemporary gender politics, Polanski removes all references to Lady Macbeth's motherhood ('I have given suck, and know / How tender 'tis to love the babe that milks me', 1.7.54–5). While Lady Macbeth's image of a murdered baby ('I would . . . / Have plucked my nipple from his boneless gums and dashed his brains out' 1.7.56–9) may have given the grieving Polanski pause, its absence, along with the excision of such lines as 'Come to my woman's breasts / And take my milk for gall' (1.5.46–7), suggest how motherhood is at odds with the film's conception of her character. The physical realities of maternity and lactation contradict the Playboy vision of femininity: high voice, golden tresses, slender figure. If Lady Macbeth represents one side of Swinging Sixties sexual liberation, the witches evoke its other side, offering an unappealing image of first-wave feminist sisterhood. The scene in which Macbeth visits the witches appears to contain hundreds of topless witches (though Polanski had a hard time finding extras for this scene, and had to rely on cardboard dummies). Although the witches seem as likely to be throwing their bras into the cauldron as newts' eyes, their opposition to the kind of conventional female behaviour displayed by Lady Macbeth does not extend to embracing hirsutism. Beards are as much at odds with the film's characterization of the witches as motherhood is with Lady Macbeth. While they may be 'so withered, and so wild' (1.3.38), and in another dimension entirely from Lady Macbeth's Guenevere-esque chic, the witches still don't get to have beards. Banquo does not get to speak the lines that convey a typically early modern confusion about the witches' gender: 'You should be women, / And yet your beards forbid to interpret / That you are so' (43–5). Contrary to the transvestite conventions of the Shakespearian stage, then, in Polanski's *Macbeth*, the women are *always* 'women'.

LADY MACDEATH

Polanski's *Macbeth* is a product of its time: a reflection of, and meditation upon, sixties culture and its dialogue with the past. Yet this is not to leave the Manson murders entirely out of the picture. For Polanski's personal tragedy was a potent symbol that heralded the end of the sixties. As Joan Didion recalls in her memoir, *The White Album*, 'Many people I know in Los Angeles believe that the Sixties ended abruptly on August 9, 1969, ended at the exact moment when word of the murders on Cielo Drive traveled like brushfire through the community, and in a sense this was true.'[31] Richard Sylbert, the art director of *Rosemary's Baby*, reflects, 'You could hear the toilets flushing all

[30] Polanski and Tynan, *The Tragedy of Macbeth*, p. 71.

[31] Joan Didion, *The White Album* (New York, 1979), p. 41.

over Beverly Hills. Everybody became Presbyterian. That marked the end of the fun and games of the 60s . . . it was the end of the joke.'[32]

As people tried to make sense of the carnage, Polanski's involvement with Satanism and the dark aspects of the occult was read almost as an incitation. As Didion puts it, 'black masses were imagined, and bad trips blamed. I remember all of the day's misinformation very clearly, and I also remember this, and I wish I did not: I remember that no one was surprised.'[33] Yet Polanski's films, such as *The Fearless Vampire Killers Or, Pardon Me But Your Teeth are in My Neck* (1967), a spoof on horror films complete with fake blood, bulbs of garlic and a haunted castle, and *Rosemary's Baby* (1968), in which the eponymous heroine is carrying the devil's child, were firmly tongue-in-cheek. They participated in, as well as poked fun at, the popular vogue for Satanism in sixties counterculture, ranging from albums such as the Rolling Stones' *Their Satanic Majesties Request*, and their song 'Sympathy for the Devil', to the goofy Gothicism of Billy Van's popular children's television show, *The Hilarious House of Frightenstein* (in which Vincent Price made a regular guest appearance), and from the feminist activism of WITCH (Women's International Terrorist Conspiracy from Hell), to the more sinister doings of the Hell's Angels and the Manson Family.[34] In fact, the three Manson girls who committed the murders 'had assumed new names and were known as witches'.[35] And, as Charles 'Tex' Watson claimed on the night of the murders, 'I am the Devil. I'm here to do the Devil's purpose.'

In its more benign form, sixties Satanism exhibited a playful kind of rejection of traditional structures of belief and categories of right and wrong prompted by the seriously cataclysmic events of the earlier part of the century. Polanski's personal experiences as a child, in wartime Krakow, living in the Jewish ghetto, his parents sent to concentration camps; his adolescence as a kind of abandoned street-child in the immediate post-war years; and his young adulthood in the repressive atmosphere of Communist Poland, gave him immediate, lived access to the violent extremes of twentieth-century depravity – a subject which he explores more directly in his acclaimed recent film, *The Pianist* (2001). In his memoir, Polanski quotes a childhood friend on the subject of God: 'if there is a God, he's a rotten old whore who watched what went on at Auschwitz and Hiroshima – who watched say millions of innocent people murdered – and what kind of God is that? No, my friend, there isn't any God'.[36] A confirmed atheist, Polanski uses Satanism in *Rosemary's Baby* to poke fun at a mentality that looks to a higher supernatural power to explain mundane events. As Polanski reflects, 'I no more believed in Satan as evil incarnate than I believed in a personal god; the whole idea conflicted with my rational view of the world'.[37] Thus, *Rosemary's Baby* depicts the foolish credulity of Rosemary (played by Mia Farrow), a wide-eyed innocent who slowly interprets a series of stereotypical signs and portents to signify Satan's involvement in her pregnancy. The film sets the terms for the audiences not to believe her: it all seems a silly set of coincidences.

However, as *Rosemary's Baby* concludes, Rosemary was right. What appears, at first glance, to be a foolish delusion prompted by the hormonal fluctuations of pregnancy, suddenly turns deadly serious: the film concludes with a cameo by a real-life Satanist, Anton LaVey, Manson's former mentor and the self-designated Black Pope and head of the Church of Satan.[38] Polanski's *Macbeth* presents a similar sense of casual dabbling gone horribly wrong, and of its proximity to genuine malefactors.

32 See the New York State Writers Institute Film Notes, posted at www.albany.edu/writers-inst/fns98n3.html

33 Didion, *The White Album*, p. 42.

34 For an interesting web site that develops the hypothesis that Mick Jagger is Satan, see www.spin.com/new/koolthing/recentkool.html.

35 See Gilmore and Kenner, *The Garbage People*, p. 74.

36 Polanski, *Roman*, p. 106.

37 Polanski, *Roman*, p. 265.

38 Note the confluence of Satanism with medievalism: Anton LaVey's Church of Satan uses a goat's head emblem associated with the Knights Templar, and Latin prayer that parodies Catholic liturgy: 'in nomine Dei nostri Satanas Luciferi excelsi'. See Parker, *Polanski*, p. 122.

Macbeth's involvement with the witches gives him more than he bargained for. Like a neophyte involved in some kind of sixties cult, he is at first fascinated, and then mildly disgusted by them. Sitting around a fire, singing songs, spattered with folk-festival-esque mud, the witches evoke the earthy communalism of Manson's cult members that was, at the same time, shared by the harmless, idealistic, hippie fringe. Macbeth has no idea what he is getting into with the witches: but how was he to know? Yet their prophecy, with its rhetoric of personal freedom and possibility ('thou shalt be king hereafter' (1.3.48)), reaches something deep inside of him: you can do your own thing![39] That it should involve rebellion against, and even replacement of, authority figures such as Duncan is even more intoxicating. Nevertheless, there is a particularly chilling quality about the youngest witch, played by Noelle Rimmington, who exudes a kind of dishevelled flower-child innocence, and spaced-out credulity, much in the manner of a Manson follower, like 'Suki' or 'Sadie Mae Glutz': she's the witch who suddenly flashes herself at Macbeth and Banquo, with a grotesque squawk. Things can go wrong very quickly.[40]

As a detective working on the Manson case commented, 'this is weirder than *Rosemary's Baby*'.[41] Yet Manson's followers had no knowledge of Polanski's work. While his films' depiction of the dark arts, and his personal involvement with a high-flying 'sex, drugs and rock'n'roll' lifestyle, gave the media ample material for pontification and sermonizing, Polanski had given the Manson 'family' absolutely no provocation. They didn't even know whom they had killed until they watched the reports on television. An aspiring folk musician and one-time minor celebrity, Manson was expecting the music producer Terry Melcher, Doris Day's son, who owned 10050 Cielo Drive, to be at home that night: Melcher had been introduced to Manson by Dennis Wilson of the Beach Boys, but he distanced himself from Manson soon after expressing a tepid interest in his music. Manson, angered by what he had perceived as a broken record contract, had left a bullet with a note attached at the doorstep of the Cielo Drive house a short time before. But Melcher was out of town, and Polanski was partying with the Playboy crowd in London. Instead, that night, the house contained Sharon Tate, Polanski's wife and budding starlet (who starred in Polanski's *The Fearless Vampire Killers* and a film about witchcraft, *The Eye of the Devil*); Abigail Folger, a coffee heiress; her boyfriend, the Polish writer Voityek Frykowski; and Jay Sebring, hairdresser to the stars.

Manson was motivated more by professional resentment than by political or ideological principles. Terms such as 'pig', which he scrawled in blood on the walls of the house (or worse), borrowed from the Beatles' *White Album*, do not so much express a rejection of the star system as an indignant fury at having been rejected by it. Like Mark David Chapman, who shot John Lennon, Manson was resentful of the disconnect between the classic sixties rhetoric of free-form tolerance and equality ('anything goes', or, to avoid the anachronistic Cole Porter associations, 'let it all hang out') and the realities of the entertainment business, its economic bottom line, its enormous class divide between fans, groupies and celebrities, and its endorsement of an exclusive coterie of 'beautiful people'. Manson's list of future hits included Elizabeth Taylor, Frank Sinatra and Tom Jones. The language of anti-capitalism and anti-authoritarianism (expressed, by Chapman, in a Holden Caulfield-inspired hatred of 'phonies') thus provides only a flaccid pretext for a self-absorbed, Malvolio-like jealousy motivated by the sting of personal rejection. It wasn't that Manson wanted to reject hierarchy and achieve equality instead: he was just miffed that he wasn't on top. His ultimate goal was that the murders would incite a race riot that would result in the installation of an all-white elite.

---

39 As Pearlman observes, 'Polanski has devised a population which is naively attractive (though violent and irreligious) but prey to a powerful and supernaturally sanctioned cult.' See 'Macbeth on Film', p. 70.

40 As Polanski puts it, 'What I like is a realistic situation where things don't quite fit in', quoted in Jorgens, p. 170.

41 Barbara Leaming, *Polanski: His Life and Film* (London, 1982), p. 71.

With his followers, he envisioned the day when he would rule the world, as a fifth angel, accompanied by the Beatles. Of course, the irony is that Charles Manson ultimately did succeed in becoming, however grotesquely, a 'star'.[42]

As an unavoidable subtext of Polanski's *Macbeth*, the Manson murders invite reflections upon the paradoxes of sixties celebrity culture. Like John Lennon, or Mick Jagger, or even Polanski himself, Polanski's Macbeth is a kind of *enfant terrible*, achieving tremendous success, or 'star status', for the wrong reasons, and at a time when he is too immature to handle it. Kenneth Rothwell picks up on this aspect of the film when he describes it as 'cocksure'.[43] However, the conclusion of the ill-fated Rolling Stones concert at Altamont Raceway near San Francisco in December 1969 (an event which was seen, like the Manson murders a few months before, to herald the end of the 'Summer of Love') sheds light on why a self-proclaimed 'loser' such as Manson, unknown and untalented, may have felt so betrayed by his celebrity idols.[44] One of the many myths that swirled about this concert was that an audience member, Meredith Hunter, was stabbed to death by the Hell's Angels while the Stones played 'Sympathy for the Devil'. As the documentary *Gimme Shelter* depicts, the song was actually 'Under My Thumb' – perhaps equally appropriate, as it is a paean to male domination, female obedience, and, most importantly, the violent vindication of the resentful dismissed. As the song reveals, old habits die hard: while mayhem broke out in the crowds, and the Hell's Angels, who had been hired for security for the concert, used brutal and deadly means to attempt to keep them in check, a young black man was their victim. Manson hoped that the murders would instigate precisely this kind of racial violence. But this is the realm of the common man. Mick Jagger, in his long, beautiful, pink silk scarf, simply got into his helicopter with the rest of his band and flew away.

If Polanski's *Macbeth* charts the widespread disenchantment that took place at the end of the sixties, as idealistic hopes for personal freedom and positive collective action were answered by violence and conspiracy, it also charts a more personal sense of disappointment. Polanski emigrated to America in the wake of the success of his 1962 film, *A Knife in the Water*, which received a 1963 Academy Award nomination for Best Foreign Film. While the United States provided the backdrop to his professional triumphs, he was not an unreflective apologist for it. As Polanski recalls, 'prior to the murders, I'd never thought of hippies as potentially dangerous. On the contrary, I'd found them an attractive social phenomenon – one that had influenced us all and affected our outlook on life.'[45] His depiction of the witches, giving each other backrubs and engaged in reciprocal grooming, makes them seem less-than-human, like monkeys or apes, and the scene in which Macbeth visits their overpopulated coven, suggests not only a kind of nausea about the perversion of hippie culture represented by the Mansons, but also a distaste for the collective.

Polanski's jaundiced attitude toward the continuum of sixties communalism – from hippies to feminists to murderous cult members – is consistent with his suspicion for collective initiatives of any sort (his right-wing sympathies ultimately led to a

[42] As Gilmore observes, 'These killers are not so special as killers of humans. They just became famous from it. Others have killed but the chemical ingredients to make them stars just wasn't on the menu. We're in a "star system" and being a star is what it's all about. Jimmy Dean and Janis Joplin and Lenny Bruce became stars in other ways. Manson is a star.' See *The Garbage People*, iv.

[43] Kenneth Rothwell, 'Roman Polanski's *Macbeth*: Golgotha Triumphant', *Literature/Film Quarterly*, 1 (1973), 71–5, p. 71.

[44] The following lines from Don Maclean's 'American Pie' have been interpreted as a reference to Altamont and the Stones's great escape: 'Oh, and there we were all in one place / A generation Lost in Space / With no time left to start again / So come on, Jack be nimble, Jack be quick / Jack Flash sat on a candlestick / 'Cause fire is the Devil's only friend / Oh, and as I watched him on the stage / My hands were clenched in fists of rage / No angel born in hell / Could break that Satan's spell / And as the planes climbed high into the night / To light the sacrificial rite / I saw Satan laughing with delight / The day the music died'.

[45] See Polanski, *Roman*, p. 323.

falling-out with Tynan). His experiences in Communist Poland led him to despise even unions, suspecting them of seeking to limit individual freedom and talent. Thus it comes as no surprise that his *Macbeth* should present the sinister side of a prevailing sixties fantasy of a cooperative, communal lifestyle that expressed itself in a kind of nostalgia for a medieval 'deserted village', as it was precisely the sort of thing that Polanski loathed. While Polanski's *Macbeth* may be read, in this way, as a story of the devastating effects of a collective and its powers of suggestion upon Macbeth, it may also be taken as a kind of homage to Macbeth's own haphazard heroism, and his willing embracement, by the end of the film, of spectacular failure. It implies, as well, a sense of history that is peppered with geniuses, with individuals, and that celebrates the contributions of a name, a personality, instead of the progress of an identity-erasing collectivity. The film's extremely dark visual effects (it was filmed almost entirely using natural light, during an unusually wet Welsh autumn) owe more to Rembrandt, the virtuoso of the self-portrait, than to the kaleidoscopic decorations of the medieval altarpiece. Its rich black-and-brown palette is mitigated by the occasionally stunning tableau: Polanski's evocation of Lady Macbeth in the dagger scene and the mad scene, for example, seems to be a deliberate homage to the dazzlingly ghoulish paintings of Henry Fuseli: her wild, black-circled eyes and striking posture recalling the chiaroscuro effects of characterological paintings such as 'Lady Macbeth Sleepwalking' and 'Lady Macbeth Seizing the Daggers'.[46]

Polanski's *Macbeth* reflects a series of sixties preoccupations – medievalism, folk music, hippies, the occult, B-movie horror flicks – that expressed and responded to a widespread sense of disorientation and disruption, not only in the aftermath of the Second World War, but also in response to the polarized mendacities of the fifties. Polanski mines the depths of violence in his Shakespearian source, and the highly charged theatricality that defines *Macbeth* (from crowd-pleasers such as the witches and the murders, to set pieces such as the daggers and Lady Macbeth's mad scene), to produce a meditation upon the sixties, and upon sixties theatricality, after the end of the sixties had happened, one might say, to him personally. Through the sixties, television had broadcast war, sex, death, murder, even Tynan's paradigm-shifting 'fuck' into the nation's living rooms, and films and plays experimented with the idea that social life was to be played out before an audience (an idea confirmed by the current vogue for reality TV). Polanski's Kottian quest for an honest, unmediated Macbeth thus returns to the idea of performance that lies at the heart of sixties culture, exploring the limits of representation and of decency that were stretched when the most private and painful parts of his own life were lived, and scrutinized, in public.

Strenuously disavowed by Polanski himself, the connection between Manson and Polanski's *Macbeth* at the very least resists an easy one-to-one correlation. The film challenges the viewer to locate Manson and his followers not only in the witches, but also in Macbeth himself, just as it prompts us to view Macbeth as well as Macduff through the lens of Polanski's biography. Thus, Polanski's *Macbeth* resists any vision of order restored: in this film, there are no sides that remain untarnished. Polanski's Macbeth is unable to detach himself fully from his complicity with violence, and from its effects and final outcome. As the film closes, with Donalbain paying his own little visit to the witches, Polanski confirms that no one, not the bright young things, not the self-proclaimed agents of liberation and salvation, is a saint. Ultimately, the film's oblique yet essential connection to Polanski's personal history suggests that, regardless of the position that the historical players may or may not occupy in the film, it is impossible to adopt the position of the detached spectator, relishing the spectacle. It is no longer possible to dabble, to satirize, and to luxuriate in postmodern detachment. Nor is it

[46] While a full treatment of this subject lies outside the scope of this essay, the corpus of eighteenth and nineteenth-century paintings of *Macbeth* had a major influence on Polanski and Tynan's visual conception of the play.

possible to laugh with the gods at human credulity, and to undermine recklessly the strong and stark distinctions between good and evil. Polanski's subsequent films, from *Tess* (1979) through *The Pianist*, achieve an increasingly psychological sense of personal responsibility and individual ethics. His is a filmic universe in which witches are not just a campy convention: they exist, they are malevolent, and they offer bad advice. And so it is necessary to take individual action. This is because, for Polanski, the real evil isn't out there: it is in the weak and impressionable human heart and soul.

'THE ZULU MACBETH': THE VALUE OF AN 'AFRICAN SHAKESPEARE'

NATASHA DISTILLER

I

Shakespeare, as a literary influence and as a powerful icon of education, culture and civility, has a fruitful history in South African creative writing. Published texts initially emerged from the mission schools in the early 1840s;[1] thus, South Africa's first writers were informed and influenced by an education in English Literature. Shakespeare was available not only as a series of texts, but as a cultural icon whose authority could be invoked for purposes other than the purely literary. The most well-known example of an early South African use of Shakespeare which is both literary and political is the work of Solomon Plaatje, the first translator of Shakespeare in Southern Africa. Plaatje's translations into Setswana of five of the plays was meant in part to demonstrate Setswana's worth as a language, in order to make a plea for its protection and survival.[2] In addition, Plaatje wrote of his love and appreciation of Shakespeare, both to mark them as such, and to protest against the increasingly uncivilized behaviour of the colonisers in South Africa.[3] From Plaatje onwards, Shakespeare has been available to South African writers to use for purposes simultaneously cultural and political, as both creative influence and as cultural capital.[4]

This multidimensional use of Shakespeare as both text and icon, as cultural and political referent, can be traced in the life of Welcome Msomi's play *uMabatha*, 'The Zulu Macbeth'. The reception history of *uMabatha* demonstrates one use of Shakespeare in the context of apartheid, and a related use of Shakespeare in post-apartheid South Africa, where *Macbeth*'s afterlife is characterized by the intersection of culture, economics, and the politics of representation. Msomi's presentation of the 'Zulu Macbeth' needs to be placed in the context of Shakespeare's mobilization in South African writing, in a framework where the use of Shakespeare's play functions as a claim on an available notion of culture. This kind of culture, signified by Shakespeare, is seen to have self-evident and intrinsic worth; cultural (and commercial) value. In tandem with the play's literal performance, Msomi is offering specific performances of 'Shakespeare', of a notion of the 'Zulu', and, indeed, of 'African', in the initial run of *uMabatha* and in its subsequent revivals. A complex performance of cultural worth is being enacted alongside the commodification of the play's various performances.

Initially in part a tool to promote the worth of a tribalized 'Zuluness' and counter racist dehumanization by performing 'Zulu culture' in Shakespearian (that is, recognisable and elevated) terms, *uMabatha* drew particular responses from

[1] Kelwyn Sole, 'Class, Continuity and Change in Black South African Literature 1948–1960', *Labour, Townships and Protest: Studies in the Social History of the Witwatersrand*, ed. Belinda Bozzoli (Johannesburg, 2001), pp. 143–82, esp. 146–7; and A. C. Jordan, *Towards an African literature: The Emergence of Literary Form in Xhosa* (Berkeley, 1973).

[2] Sol Plaatje, *Sol Plaatje: Selected Writings*, ed. Brian Willan (Johannesburg, 1996), esp. pp. 381–2.

[3] Plaatje, *Selected Writings*, esp. pp. 211–2.

[4] Natasha Distiller, 'The Presence of the Past: Shakespeare in South Africa', *Quidditas*, 24 (2003), forthcoming.

white reviewers in apartheid South Africa during its original runs. Subsequently, through the ways the play has been written about during its recent revivals, we can suggest implications for the nature of a specific performance of culture in post-apartheid South Africa. The 'Zulu Macbeth' is thus a vehicle to trace constructions of, first, 'Zuluness' in the apartheid arena, and then 'Africanness' on the world stage. But it is not only the construction of types of Africanness which can be investigated. The spaces of reception – first, a section of apartheid South Africa, and later, a section of global cultural space, within which post-apartheid South Africa is creating a niche – also become available for comment. Ultimately, this article will argue, the discursive and economic spaces of the revived *uMabatha* reveal some of the ways in which the commodification of Shakespeare and the commodification of Africanness work together in the realm of culture in the 'new' South Africa.

In 1974, *uMabatha* had its first extended South African run, at the Maynardville Open-Air Shakespearian theatre in Cape Town. *uMabatha* was unusual in a space which had been specifically constructed for English-speaking whites.[5] Indeed, despite the all-black cast, in keeping with apartheid legislation governmental permission had to be sought to allow a special performance for black South Africans.[6] Limited, and partial, access to the Zulu Macbeth for South Africans who were not white is addressed in a letter to the Editor of the daily *The Argus* on 14 January, entitled 'Seating Plans unfair to Blacks':

> I booked four tickets for the play UmaBatha at Maynardville. As a Black man, I feel very annoyed at the way the seats are situated for Black patrons. In fact, it is outrageous the way our people are culturally exploited . . . [W]hy [are] our seats . . . situated at the back of the theatre . . . Culture cannot be divided by a rope, separate sections or characteristic 'black smells' . . . Umabatha is a drama of common human emotions. Therefore there must be no barrier which has a psychological effect on the Black members of the audience, preventing them from becoming emotionally involved in the play. This is a drama of great cultural value and it is staged by Black players who are native to this country. It must not be staged before a divided audience. It should draw us together and be appreciated and criticised as an entity.[7]

The writer of this letter, D. C. October, expresses a hope that the power of 'cultural value' implicit in a play that bears a relation to Shakespeare and that thus speaks of 'common human emotions' will overcome the cultural exploitation of 'our people'. The racial separation he concedes in this phrase is complicated by his insistence that black audience members respond to the same cultural stimuli as white audiences. Shakespeare's putative commonsensical universality is invoked to insist on the shared humanity of black and white theatre-goers.

October's identification of black audiences with black performers, in an attempt to make his point about the insult that unequal access embodies, is undermined by the response printed underneath the letter, which refuses October's self-definition. Enforcing apartheid categories as emphatically as he enforces apartheid laws, a 'spokesman for the Town Clerk's office' replies:

> To enable Coloured people to attend the show at Maynardville the lessees . . . had to apply to the Department of Community Development for a permit in terms of the Act. In granting the permit the department would impose certain conditions in regard to seating.

---

5 In 1964 Maynardville produced a booklet to mark its tenth anniversary, *Maynardville 1955–1964* (Pamphlet. National Library of South Africa, Cape Town. A.Q. 792.0968712 MAY). This booklet constructs a history for the theatre and its land, as well as a space for Maynardville in apartheid South Africa's cultural life. In 'The Magic of Maynardville', a cultured, white, English speaking ideal spectator is constructed for the theatre.

6 The difficulty in staging the production is mentioned a number of times in the newspaper reports of the time; for example the *Cape Times* of 7 January 1974 reported that it took two years of negotiations to get the play to Cape Town ('Zulu play begins run', p. 9). In an interview with *The Argus* Rene Ahrenson, one of the two white actresses who founded Maynardville, confirms that 'We have just obtained all the necessary permission and co-operation to stage the play again next year' ('uMabatha tickets all sold' ['City Late', 25 January 1974], p. 8).

7 *The Argus* (14 January 1974), p. 10. The spelling variations are in the original.

Responding presumably to his name (although the fact that October is not referring to the 'special performance for Africans' as is obvious by the letter's date might also have lead to the assumption that the writer of the letter was 'coloured' and not 'black'), the 'spokesman' refuses October's assertion of blackness. He ignores October's appeal to universal humanity, and the concomitant right to equal access to 'culture'; instead, the spokesman relies on the inviolability of the law of separate seating. He thus counters October's challenge to separation by insisting on the boundaries between racial categories.

The relationship between racial and spatial boundaries, and the resulting issues of access, arise again in reports of the show's Maynardville run. The repeated references to the 'real' work done by *uMabatha*'s cast members make it clear that African labour belongs to a specific arena, which cannot include full-time theatrical performance. This allocation of African labour to a different sphere than the professionally theatrical is linked to a putative authentically 'African' cultural difference. In one instance, this is manifest in the play's stage management needs (what is being performed is not skillfully crafted theatre, but authentic African cultural expression):

> All in all the backstage scene at Maynardville is as uncomplicated as any producer could wish for. Instead of a clutter of greasepaint make-up and clothes there are only neat little rows of black cloth – the cowhide skirts . . . and bundles of bead trimmings. Nothing more. When the cast is onstage there's nothing happening backstage either – no call boys, no prompt, no stage manager, no conductor. Everyone knows where to move and when, Mrs Stuart said. 'They have a wonderful sense of theatre and timing. There's no script and if anyone changes his or her lines there's no panicking. They simply carry on.'[8]

These performers, it is implied, are not actors in what is understood to be the Shakespearian sense. They are doing what comes 'naturally'. A photograph of Ntombi Nkosi Mhlongo, 'Lady MacDuff', which accompanies the article, is captioned, 'In real life Mrs Mhlongo is an assistant in a Durban shop.' Mrs. Mhlongo's 'real life' does not include Shakespeare; she is not 'really' an actor. 'African' life is naturalized as different, as something other to the lives of those whose everyday culture includes access to Shakespearian theatre. The placement of the 'real life' of blacks outside of the borders of Maynardville reserves the Shakespeare performed inside its borders for whites. The 'Zulu Macbeth' becomes available to be used to emphasize Zulu (and from there, black South African) Otherness. *uMabatha* is used by white reviewers to construct discursively an 'authentic' picturesque Zuluness. Instead of functioning to illustrate shared and thus equal cultural value, instead of a performance which is simultaneously and equally 'African' and 'Shakespearian', what results is a whites-only Shakespeare who is entertained by the performance of African tribal exoticism enacted in homage to a notion of Shakespearian culture which it can only ever mimic in its free time.

During the month that *uMabatha* began its Maynardville performances, January, the two longest-running Cape Town dailies ran reviews of the play, as well as a number of features about its players. Ian Forsyth, reviewing the play for *The Cape Times*, calls it a 'vibrant theatrical experience' but seems to have experienced the spectacle as unnerving. He finds the 'sound of Zulu . . . terrifyingly harsh', the 'Sangomas (Witch Doctors) . . . evil and frightening'; 'one suspects that UmaBatha played in a smallish theatre, with its dancers – quite magnificent they were – could become really quite frightening'.[9] His rave review reassures 'anybody who has the remotest doubt about what has been described . . . as a Zulu Macbeth . . . because the language happens to be Zulu should rapidly lose this doubt . . . It is unnecessary to be able to understand Zulu.' The universality of Shakespeare's themes (and thus of 'European' culture) is affirmed, while what 'happens to be Zulu' is what gives the experience its frisson of excitement, its slightly alarming exoticism. Throughout its review history, the accessibility of *uMabatha* is constantly inscribed as

---

[8] *Cape Times* (10 January 1974), p. 5.

[9] *Cape Times* (9 January 1974), p. 6.

evidence of the universality of 'Shakespeare's themes'. Ambition, greed, love, all human traits originate with and belong to Shakespeare. The Africans who enact these emotions are demonstrating Shakespeare's fundamental humanity, not their own. This weighting in favour of a version of 'Shakespearian' fundamental humanity which is defined as culturally 'European',[10] that is, different to 'African', cannot be comfortably consigned to the apartheid past, as the discussion of more recent reviews of *uMabatha* demonstrates below.

In 1974, the stress on how naturally *Macbeth* translates into a Zulu version is at once proof of Shakespeare's genius, and reflective of white reviewers' concern with the authenticity of their experience of the 'Zulu culture' on offer.[11] *The Argus* reviewer at the time, like his *Cape Times* counterpart, similarly considers the play a 'theatrical triumph'; 'exotic and startling'. His adjectives are telling:

> [T]he story of Macbeth, who was a primitive, warring, bloodthirsty and ambitious Scottish chief, transposes easily and *naturally* to the days of the tribal Zulu warrior. Ambition, revenge, blood, courage, nobility, a strong belief in a hierarchical society and traditional values . . . – these fit themselves *naturally* into noble Zulu folklore . . . It all sounds very fine and stirring . . . with rolling cadences of a *natural* euphony . . . There is a tremendous cast . . . they all play together with what must be an *instinctive* sense of ensemble . . . Macduff . . . was a little masterpiece of . . . *genuine* anguish . . .The Weird Sisters are very weird and very *credible*, crouching half-naked over their pot . . .[12]

The stress on nature serves to confirm the authenticity of the offered performance of Zuluness: the 'half naked' women are 'very credible'; the play is both 'exotic' and 'genuine'. This description ascribes to homogenized 'black culture' a 'natural euphony', an 'instinctive sense of ensemble', which stresses two stereotypes: that 'blacks have rhythm', and that 'they' operate communally.

There is another sense in which *Macbeth* supposedly 'naturally' translates into the Zulu. It is not coincidental that *Macbeth*, of all Shakespeare's plays, should so successfully and enduringly function as an 'African' cultural export. *Macbeth* is a drama of warriors, battles, bloodshed and black magic. This is in contrast to the more insistently cerebral context of, for example, *Hamlet*. David Schalkwyk suggests that the enormously popular 'Zulu Macbeth' has never been packaged together with a 'Zulu Hamlet' because the associations of bloodthirstiness, superstition, violence and clannishness that accrue to *Macbeth* suit 'Western' stereotypes of the 'African'.[13] These translate easily into the kind of physical and aural spectacle of Africanness that Msomi continues to offer in the revived *uMabatha*. That such associations are indeed widespread is suggested in Maurice Gilmour's 1996 account of his production of *Macbeth* with the Highfields Action Theatre Group, a Community College group for young people in Leicester. *Macbeth* was selected, and staged with a Masai 'theme', because,

> Since the likelihood was that the majority in the group would be Afro-Carribean, we looked for a parallel in Africa . . . comparisons with mediaeval Scotland held up well. Like the Scots of that period, the present-day Masai depend very much on cattle . . . They live in extended families which are even referred to . . . as clans. Fiercely independent and proud, the Masai will fight to preserve their freedoms . . . it meant too that . . . the witches could be depicted as the magicians or witch doctors who still hold sway in some areas of Africa. Thus . . . the use of black magic could make sense . . .[14]

The assumption here is that 'Africa' is tribal, clannish, proud, warlike and superstitious – just like Macbeth's Scotland. An additional implication is that the 'Africans' who currently occupy such a cultural space exist in a different time; as is appropriate to their authentic Africanness, they, like Macbeth, are pre-modern: 'In setting the play among the Masai . . . [we] could give a flavour of the past,

[10] In apartheid parlance, 'European' designated 'white'.

[11] The concern with authenticity is not reflected in a sustained attempt to spell the name of the play correctly, as will be clear in the quoted extracts.

[12] Emphasis added. *The Argus* (9 January 1974), p. 12.

[13] Personal conversation.

[14] Maurice Gilmour, 'Shakespeare in a Society of Diverse Cultures', *Shakespeare for All in Secondary Schools*, ed. Maurice Gilmour (London, 1996), pp. 88–95, esp. p. 90.

yet stay rooted in the present'.[15] Despite the 'Afro-Caribbean' 'origins' of the group of British youth, their blackness ensures that a generic 'African' connection can be made with a specific society in central Africa, a point not lost to the actors: ' "Why are we doing this in Africa? Macbeth's Scottish." And the answer came back from Patsy. "Because we're black, stupid".'[16]

Similarly, as in 1974 it was not necessary to understand the language to enjoy the spectacle of Africanness (which is assumed to be physical, not verbal or cerebral), so too does Gilmour's troupe replace Shakespeare's difficult and obscure 'funny talk' with dance, so that 'we [could] explore African dance movement and sound'. The result is a *Macbeth* with 'more choreography than dialogue'.[17] It is not coincidental that an 'Africanized' *Macbeth* should forego dialogue in favour of physical performance. Pointing to the representational strategies available to 'Africa' after centuries of Western Othering, South African performance poet Lesego Rampolokeng prefaces his recent play *Fanon's Children* (2002) with the epitaph: 'Beyond the song and dance, and the sound of gunfire, the African continent is inarticulate.'[18]

The voyeurism implicit in the Maynardville reviewers' 1974 attempt to observe Zulu authenticity is reflected in the debate the play caused about the morality of bare African breasts onstage. In a *Cape Times* article entitled, 'Bare breasts culture, say UmaBatha cast', 'black' breasts metonymically stand for Zulu Otherness; they implicitly demonstrate the un-Western(ized), 'uncivilized', nature of the 'authentic Zuluness' the writer understands the play to be performing. Msomi is quoted as saying, 'We have our values which we treasure greatly and bare breasts are highly valued by the Zulu people.' The article continues:

> Thembi Mtshali, a member of the chorus, told me: 'Bare breasts are our custom and so they don't worry us.' When I spoke to her she was dressed in trendy gear which included a fashionable denim jacket . . .
>
> NO CONFLICT
>
> She admitted that, although she saw herself as a Westernized or urbanized African woman (when not acting in UmaBatha she works as a shop assistant in a department store in Durban), she felt no moral conflict about performing before a White South African audience in the costume of her tribal ancestors . . .
>
> Mrs. Mhlongo said the UmaBatha cast were 'deeply interested' in presenting their history and customs in their purity for White South Africans to see.[19]

In Msomi's quote, breasts become 'Zulu values'; here they become symbolic of 'Zulu culture'. Later in the same article, in a verbal slippage, breasts become a 'form of dress', highlighting the exoticisim of primitive and naked 'Zulu culture': 'A prominent Cape Town academic, Dr David Welsh, who is senior lecturer in Comparative African Government and Law at the University of Cape Town, said that bare breasts had never been considered erotic among Bantu-speaking people. They were traditionally a natural form of dress among the Zulu people.'[20] 'Pure' Zulu culture, reified into something to be presented for the edification of white audiences both in *uMabatha* and in this *Cape Times* article, becomes a comment on the difference of Africans. This is explicit in the way the article's intention, to educate white audiences on how to 'read' the women's bare breasts, facilitates a display of exoticized female Otherness in its accompanying photograph of Daisy Dumakude (she is captioned 'Lady Macbeth'; her character's name is Kamadonsela) 'in full traditional regalia', bare breasted.

Patricia Williams, journalist for *The Argus*, takes up the debate in an article headlined, 'Censors have two views on nudity': 'The anomalies of South African censorship are being shown up pointedly by the bare-breasted frolicking of ten women before affluent White audiences':

> Because they are Black (the badly reasoned excuse that this is the traditional way of African tribal life is ridiculous when considering the Westernisation of many of the

[15] Gilmour, *Shakespeare for All*, p. 90.
[16] Gilmour, *Shakespeare for All*, p. 91.
[17] Gilmour, *Shakespeare for All*, pp. 93; 92; 94.
[18] www.allafrica.com/stories/200211060320.html.
[19] *Cape Times* (26 January 1974), p. 11.
[20] *Cape Times* (26 January 1974), p. 11.

Zulu women in the cast), these women may perform in the most vigorous and exotic manner while the audience, including a number of prominent Nationalists when I saw it, applauded enthusiastically. The tribal dances are fulsome and natural, but it could be argued that they are erotic.[21]

This article is accompanied by a picture of Daisy Dumakude, with the caption: 'A beaded and bare-breasted Lady Macbeth was perhaps not what Shakespeare intended.' According to the logic of this comment, authentic Zuluness is in fact not always appropriate to Shakespeare's *Macbeth*.[22] When it slips out of control (and out of Western clothing), it threatens overtly to titillate its white viewers.

While many of the articles that discuss *uMabatha*'s development stress its white benefactor, Elizabeth Sneddon,[23] Msomi's didactic intentions for his production are also represented. Mid-way through the play's extremely successful run (it played to sold-out houses as early as from 9 January, the day after it opened and by 23 January it was sold out until the 28th, with only a 'few seats left' until 2 February[24]), the *Weekend Argus* ran a story which focused on Welcome Msomi:

'uMabatha,' he says 'proves that the things we have got, such as our cultural background, music and so on are not inferior . . . this is something people in this country never thought we could do . . .' Mr Msomi says uMabatha . . . 'might cause more people to learn Zulu. There are surely parts in uMabatha where a person will say to himself: "I wish I knew what he said then", and wished he had a Zulu sitting next to him to tell him what it was all about'.

Msomi uses Shakespeare's status as a cultural icon to legitimate the worth of an Other culture, making it clear that the performance of Zuluness is meant to demonstrate something to its mostly white audiences which is of more than simply entertainment value. Given the separate performances for some blacks, and separate seating for others, Msomi's imaginative construction of a white audience member desiring a Zulu neighbour is pointed. Despite Msomi's hopes that the performance of a 'Zulu Macbeth' would educate about, and demonstrate the equal worth of, 'Zulu culture', 'Shakespeare's' capacity to express Zuluness ultimately demonstrated the universality of 'Western' culture while reinforcing apartheid notions of African difference to these 'Western' norms.

II

The relationship between a Shakespeare recognized as belonging to the 'West', and Africanness as embodied by *uMabatha*, continues to be vexed. In its more recent revivals, the ways *uMabatha* represents 'Zulu tradition' in order to commodify a brand of 'Africanness' is more complex than the original binary formulation implicit in the responses of the white press in 1974.

After the Maynardville production, *uMabatha* toured America, where Msomi remained in exile for thirteen years. *uMabatha* was revived in Johannesburg in 1995, ran in Durban in 1996, and went to the new Globe Theatre in London, after which it toured America in 1997. Most recently, it opened the Celebrate South Africa festival in London in 2001. Welcome Msomi's career subsequent to the Maynardville staging of *uMabatha* illustrates the potential for economic advancement made possible in part by tourism in the 'new' South

[21] *The Argus* (14 January 1974), p. 5. This debate simultaneously manages to construct the exotic black woman as sexualized and therefore threatening to white viewers, and to deny any expression of adult sexuality to the Zuluness it is so concerned to morally quantify; for Williams, 'tribal dances' cannot be *both* 'natural' (that is, 'authentically tribal') and 'erotic'.

[22] The debate continued into the following week. A reader wrote a 'Letter to the Editor' in response to Williams's article, occasioning a further reponse from the journalist. The reader insists, 'The whole point is that the difference between Europeans and Zulus cannot merely be allied to the colour of their skin'; Williams replies that a play set in the garden of Eden with a topless white Eve had been banned, and 'where could nakedness be more traditional than there [the garden of Eden]?' (*The Argus* (14 January 1974), p. 5).

[23] For example, *Women's Argus Supplement*, 'UmaBatha' (3 January 1974), p. 2; *Weekend Argus*, 'The Secret Story Behind Umabatha' (26 January 1974), p. 2.

[24] *The Argus* (23 January 1974), p. 14.

Africa, for those who can package 'authentic' South Africanness. For Msomi, *uMabatha* has lead to a successful career in cultural performances.[25] As well as continuing to produce theatre, Msomi organized Mandela's presidential inauguration ceremony, and was communications advisor to the ANC during the 1994 elections. In 1997 he launched Sasani Investments, where, as CEO, his task was to 'carry on ideas to market the richness of our culture both here and overseas, much like Hollywood has marketed America to the rest of the world'.[26] His ability to combine producing, politics and finance culminated in his being named chair of the board of the Pretoria State Theatre by Minister of Arts and Culture Ben Ngubane in 2000.

The approval with which Msomi's branding has been met by both journalists and the ANC[27] can be explained in more than simply economic terms. Msomi's sense that South Africanness is something worth selling is significant. In 1974, as we have seen, he told the *Weekend Argus*, '*uMabatha* . . . proves that the things we have got, such as our cultural background, music and so on are not inferior'. In 2001, the endorsement of the cultural value of 'Africanness' still has resonance. Msomi told *The Sunday Times*: 'It is all about changing people's mindsets about themselves, about their language. Why should we be ashamed of what we are?'[28]; elsewhere he said, 'It dawned on me what we had was something rich and that it needed to be marketed and preserved.'[29] Marketability is one way to understand cultural worth.

Msomi's equation of commodity value and pride is significant given the construction of 'African tradition' as something Other to (something worth less than) 'European Culture'. He told Malala, 'We need to . . . appeal to overseas markets . . . There is a huge potential and all we have to do is . . . tap our own uniqueness.' Despite the constant billing of *uMabatha* as 'the Zulu Macbeth', Msomi doesn't seem to understand his work as primarily derivative: *uMabatha* is an expression of 'our own uniqueness'. Without appearing to view the commodification of South Africanness negatively, or commodification as a primarily acquisitive enterprise, Msomi is explicit about his intention to brand 'South Africanness'. Instead, the marketability of this uniquely South African Shakespearian product is a cultural asset. *uMabatha* has become a vehicle for the performance of 'South Africanness' to the world cultural market.

'South Africanness', particularly in its recent embodiment as 'new South Africanness', is often authorized to represent a form of 'Africanness'. In its recent international runs, 'The Zulu Macbeth' seamlessly becomes 'the African Macbeth'.[30] Both UCLA and Binghamton University included the play in cultural studies courses, because 'This really shows how Shakespeare was experienced in Africa and also gives us a chance . . . to share the African experience.'[31]

---

[25] For a much less cynical reading of the ways in which *uMabatha* uses culture, one which relies on undefined notions of 'authentic' 'tradition', and of struggle in South Africa, see Edith Hallberg, 'Shakespeare's *Macbeth* Crossing Borders: Violence and Reconciliation in Welcome Msomi's *UMabatha*' in *Crossing Borders: Contemporary Drama in English 8*, ed. Bernhard Rentz and A. Von Rothkirch (Trier, 2001), pp. 75–88.

[26] 'All the world's a stage for Welcome Msomi's business', *Business Times*, www.btimes.co.za/97/0302/newsm/newsm.htm.

[27] See, for an example of the former, Justice Malala, 'MacZulu creates a stir in Britain's cultural cauldron', *Sunday Times* (29 April 2001); and for an example of the latter, see the press release for the 'Celebrate South Africa' festival in London in 2001 mentioned later ('London explodes with a fusion of South African Talent', www.music.org.za/news/celebrateSA.htm). Nelson Mandela's involvement in promoting the revivals of *uMabatha* also suggests active ANC endorsement.

[28] Justice Malala, 'MacZulu'.

[29] Quoted in Edith Hallberg, 'Shakespeare's *Macbeth*', p. 84.

[30] A reviewer at UCLA, where Msomi was invited to lecture on the origins of what programme notes call 'South Africa's only cultural classic', commented: 'When South African playwright/director Welcome Msomi set out to write an ambitious drama about the history of his people, the Zulus, he was bluntly told that a play focusing on the African nations would never succeed' ('Center Kicks Off With "Zulu Macbeth"' www.today.ucla.edu/html/70929 CentreKicks.html).

[31] 'Zulu Macbeth performance to highlight general education focus on global perspective' (inside.binghamton.edu/September-October/Sept-4-97/Zulu.html).

As implicit proof of the play's authentic Africanness, Msomi invokes its ability to 'remind' people of who they are, as he provides details of plans to present to real Africans the authentic Africanness they have lost, implicitly through colonial and apartheid abuses: 'We plan to go to the more rural areas of Africa . . . to share this culture and history. I believe when a nation loses its soul, it loses its foundation. People lose something about themselves.'[32] This construction of what Msomi goes on to describe as the play's 'legacy' allows an Africanized Shakespeare to transmit pre-colonial 'African values'. In this formulation, the 'Zulu Macbeth' carries African cultural purity. Such a 'legacy' also allows the play's American audiences (to whom this comment was addressed) to feel that they are contributing to post-colonial redress, to the renewal of African pride, by supporting the show.

As well as standing for a commodification of Africanness in general, this commodification of Zuluness becomes a commodification of 'new' South Africanness in particular. There is political as well as cultural investment in successfully branding a Shakespearian-inflected new South African cultural worth. In the light of the colonial and apartheid history to which Msomi implicitly refers in his assertion of African cultural worth through Shakespearizing Zulu history, the assertion of the worth of South African culture has affective importance beyond the economic implications of the play's international success. In its press release launching the 2001 'Celebrate South Africa' festival in London, the South African government promised to present the 'new nation' on the 'world stage' by showcasing examples of its cultural expression.[33] In addition to the political and cultural investments of this performance of the 'new' South Africa, there is also an economic benefit; indeed, as Msomi's didactic project suggests, economic and cultural worth serve to authorize each other. The day after the press release, the 'ANC Daily News' of 6 April 2001 reported that the Celebrate South Africa campaign was 'aimed at creating markets for rural artists'.[34]

Billed as a 'highlight' of the festival is 'classic Shakespeare in the form of Welcome Msomi's critically acclaimed production Umabatha – the Zulu Macbeth at Shakespeare's Globe'. A booklet produced for Maynardville's 20-year anniversary, which documents each season's performances, carefully controls the apportioning of authority and ownership of *uMabatha*, ensuring that those responsible for the play are all white, and all English-speaking. Msomi himself is not mentioned in the *Maynardville Chronicle*'s piece on *uMabatha*, despite the fact that he was both writer and main actor. The production is billed as 'Originally produced . . . by Professor Elizabeth Sneddon with artistic direction by Professor Pieter Scholz'.[35] By 2001, in a reversal of the ownership ascribed in the 1974 Maynardville production, Msomi's role in the play's existence is part of its authenticity as a South African artifact.

Despite the renewed potential for cultural capital available to the revived *uMabatha*, and the ways in which Zuluness becomes South Africanness, becomes proud, valuable Africanness in this process, for many reviewers Shakespeare's universal themes remain emotions that Shakespeare demonstrates Africans can also feel. Shakespeare's universality is invoked to prove not only that humanity is shared across 'races', as Msomi hoped when he wrote the play, but that the nature of the humanity that is shared is defined by Shakespeare, the voice of Western culture, which is splendidly augmented by the spectacle of African tradition. Shakespeare brings the universal themes, and the Africans bring the music and the energetic mass of bodies: 'Incorporating Shakespeare's timeless themes of ambition, deceit, love, hate and fear, "Umabatha" dramatizes the history of 19th-century Africa during the

[32] www.dailybruin.ucla.edu/DB/issues/97/10.01/ae.Umabatha.html.

[33] 'London explodes with a fusion of South African Talent' (5 April 2001), www.music.org.za/news/celebrateSA.htm.

[34] www.anc.org.za/anc/newsbrief/2001/news0406.txt.

[35] *The Maynardville Chronicle 1956–1976* (Pamphlet. National Library of South Africa, Cape Town. AF. 1981 – 355), p. 51.

Scottish thane Shaka Zulu's reign through song and dance'; 'Welcome Msomi has transported Shakespeare's universal story of ambition, greed and fear from the Moors of Scotland to the vast plains of the African continent.'[36] Msomi is not seen as contributing to Western culture through his South African use of Shakespeare; instead, 'Shakespeare's universal themes' are manifest in what can be reduced to the generically 'African', to the single cultural and geographic landscape shared by all Africans, 'the vast plains of the African continent'. These themes, in their African manifestation, are expressed through 'song, and dance', not through words: '[J]oyous exuberance prevails . . . [in] authentic songs and chants . . . authentic tribal ceremonies and customs'.[37]

Kathleen McKluskie comments on the levels of cultural reductionism and commodification that adhere to the play's more recent performances when she notes her post-colonial critic's response to the spectacle.

> *Umabatha*['s] . . . style of performance was too firmly tied to Zulu drumming and dancing to demystify the social relations of Shakespeare performance in the post-colonial world . . . Bare-breasted women with beaded hair and dancing warriors in furry leggings are a slightly embarrassing image of Africa for the sophisticated consumer of post-colonial Shakespeare . . .[38]

McKluskie is pointing to the problematic 'tribal' image of 'Africa' that Msomi could be described as selling back to the West. Part of McKluskie's point is that the play's commodification of 'African cultural expression' reduces or negates its espoused capacity to represent an ideal(ized) 'Zuluness'. Part of the problem is how to approach 'Zuluness' at all, given the discursive histories of colonialism, apartheid, nationalism, and post-colonialism. McKluskie suggests that

> the artifacts of traditional culture are so overlaid with the history of their appropriation, and so implicated in the global market, that they have become 'neo-traditional'. Their celebration involves a denial of modernity, an obfuscation of the real cultural and economic relations of the contemporary African world.[39]

South Africans 'doing' Shakespeare at the Globe in the twenty-first century will inevitably also be 'doing' Africanness. There are many ironies in this use of, and profit from, *Macbeth* and Shakespeare's continued positioning as the essentially human, as the reviews of *uMabatha* make clear. The ironies are encapsulated in the following promotional blurb, provided in the Shakespeare's Globe News Bulletin review of the 1997 production:

> Welcome Msomi's transposition of Shakespeare's story of ambition, greed and fear from the Moors of Scotland to the plains of the African continent was an unmitigated success, displaying both the flexibility of the Globe space and the incredible talent of this visiting company. Welcome Msomi concluded the opening night by declaring: 'Shakespeare is African', to which the multinational audience cheered enthusiastically.[40]

The play, necessarily for its authenticity and concomitant performance value, is ascribed to its African creator, even as the universal elements of the story remain Shakespeare's. The specificities of Zulu history become an undifferentiated African landscape, in phrasing that is repeated in various reviews of the show. Such a 'transposition' demonstrates the 'flexibility' of Shakespearian space, its ability to hold an almost infinite range of meaning-making practices. At the same time, this triumphant space, the new Globe, is a theatre whose vexed status in modern Britain has been noted.[41] Msomi's transposition also demonstrates the 'incredible talent', the abilities of the Africans who have engaged with the English heritage represented by 'Shakespeare'. Finally, Msomi's

---

[36] www.dailybruin.ucla.edu/DB/issues/97/10.01/ae.Umabatha.html; www.rdg.ac.uk/globe/research/1997/OpenSeasonProg.htm.

[37] Edith Hallberg, 'Shakespeare's *Macbeth*', pp. 80, 81; 86.

[38] Kathleen McKluskie, '*Macbeth/UMabatha*: Global Shakespeare in a Post-Colonial Market', *Shakespeare Survey 52* (Cambridge, 1999), pp. 154–65, esp. p. 155.

[39] Kathleen McKluskie, '*Macbeth/ UMabatha*', p. 164.

[40] www.rdg.ac.uk/globe/research/BackIssues.htm.

[41] See, for example, Graham Holderness, ed., *The Shakespeare Myth* (New York, 1988).

statement, and the fact of an enthusiastic response from the audience, are presented on a website which promotes international theatre trade with the professional authority of 'Shakespeare's' Globe. The declaration 'Shakespeare is African' relies on an understanding of, an acquiescence to, and most importantly makes use of, Shakespeare's value in the world cultural market. At the same time as Msomi is claiming access to essential humanity for 'Africa', he is claiming access to the commodity value of culture within a world market, for whom the concepts 'Shakespeare', 'African', and indeed, the 'Zulu Macbeth', denote a range of performances for various kinds of profit.

'A DRUM, A DRUM – MACBETH DOTH COME': WHEN BIRNAM WOOD MOVED TO CHINA

RURU LI

To the sound of strident percussion and martial music, an army emerged onto the stage in a swirl of colourful costumes and flags. The soldiers and generals with their elaborate acrobatic movements drew the audience's attention to the entrance of Ma Pei, the Chinese Macbeth in the 1986 version. In Chinese productions of the play Macbeth's entrance is always accompanied by the sound of percussion.

Few transformations of Shakespeare seem to Western eyes as extreme as the transfers into Chinese theatre. Strikingly, most Shakespeare performances in mainland China are of the comedies and romantic plays.[1] Among the few Shakespeare tragedies ever staged, *Macbeth* has been by far the most performed. The predominant mode for staging Shakespeare is *huaju*, or spoken drama, a theatrical form devised at the beginning of the twentieth century on the basis of the Western dramatic tradition. However, among the nine mainland *Macbeth* productions, only three are spoken drama (including a radio play), while six are adaptations into different genres of the traditional Chinese music theatre.[2]

The first spoken drama *Macbeth*, Huang Zuolin's 1945 production entitled *The Hero of the Turmoil*, was an adaptation into an episode from Chinese history. By contrast, the 1980 *Macbeth* staged by a Moscow-trained director, Xu Xiaozhong, used Stanislavski's Method and a straight translation of the play, together with costumes and make-up (including wigs, prosthetic noses, false eyelashes and blue colour on the eyelids) that were deliberately aimed at presenting an exotic

[1] For a general study of Shakespeare productions in China see my book *Shashibiya: Staging Shakespeare in China* (Hong Kong, 2003); Xiaoyang Zhang, 'Shakespeare on the Chinese Stage', in *Shakespeare in China: A Comparative Study of Two Traditions and Cultures* (Newark and London, 1996), pp. 130–72; Antony Tatlow, '*Macbeth* and *Kunju* Opera', in *Shakespeare in Comparison* (Hong Kong, 1995), pp. 169–201; Weijie Yu, 'Topicality and Typicality – the Acceptance of Shakespeare in China', in *The Dramatic Touch of Difference: Theatre, Own and Foreign*, ed. Erika Fischer-Lichte, Josephine Riley and Michael Gissenwehrer (Gunter Narr Verlag, 1990), pp. 161–7.

[2] The nine *Macbeth* productions on the mainland are:

Heroes of the Turmoil (*Luan shi yingxiong*), spoken drama adaptation, Bitter Toilers Drama School, 1945.

Macbeth, spoken drama, Central Academy of Drama, 1980.

Macbeth, radio play, Shanghai People's Broadcasting Station, 1986.

Blood-stained Hands (*Xie shou ji*), *kunju* adaptation, Shanghai *Kunju* Company, 1986.

The King of the Turmoil (*Luanshi wang*), *jingju* adaptation, Wuhan City *Jingju* Company, 1986.

The Bloody Sword (*Xie jian*), *wuju* adaptation, *Wuju* Small Hundred Flowers, Dongyang Company, 1987.

King Dian's Dream (*Dianwang meng*), *dianju* adaptation, Kunming City *Dianju* Company, 2000.

General Ma Long (*Ma Long jiangjun*), *yueju* adaptation, Zhejiang Shaoxing Small Hundred Flowers *Yueju* Company, 2001.

Lady Macbeth (*Makebaisi furen*), *chuanju* adaptation, Sichuan *Chuanju* School, Youth Company, 2001.

Among the Chinese operatic adaptations, six regional genres are featured. Traditional Chinese theatre is a musical theatre, known in the West as 'Chinese Opera'. There are over three hundred varieties of local performance styles in China today, some over four hundred years old, like *kunju*, a genre used by *Blood-Stained Hands*, and some formed as recently as the 1950s. Fifteen regional theatres have staged Shakespeare plays.

medieval Scottish setting to the Chinese audience. Nonetheless, in this work, the sole Chinese staging of *Macbeth* to strive for absolute authenticity in conveying the original, Xu also intended to create a new 'stage vocabulary' based on the aesthetic concepts of traditional Chinese theatre. When David Jiang directed *Macbeth* with a group of British performers for the 1994 Shanghai International Shakespeare Festival, this intercultural production incorporated stage techniques from both traditional Chinese and contemporary English theatres.

These three Chinese practitioners perceived that an especial affinity existed between *Macbeth* as a play and their indigenous theatrical tradition. Might this simply be dismissed as novelty-seeking? Or rather, might such cross-cultural work yield significant insights into the art of Shakespeare and of the traditional Chinese theatre? To explore the issue fully would require the analysis not just of the original English text and its protagonist, but also of a wide range of historical, social, political, cultural and theatrical factors respective to the playwright and to the modern-day practitioners – translators, adapters, directors, stage-designers and performers – as well as to the audiences.[3]

Bourdieu, in his theory of the cultural field, offers a useful model to investigate such complex cultural processes. It constructs 'the space of positions and the space of position-takings [*prises de position*]', and argues: 'The literary or artistic field is a *field of forces*, but it is also a *field of struggles* tending to transform or conserve this field of forces.'[4] The concept of 'struggle' put forward by Bourdieu recognizes that each cultural component has its own inner logic and its own strength, so that, when two cultures encounter, both fight in order to preserve their own nature and particular features. Thus cross-cultural performance is an art of compromise and negotiation. This will be exemplified below in the examination of four Chinese productions of *Macbeth* in spoken drama and traditional operatic forms. From the outset of each project, the participants at each level sought their own position in the future work and attempted to balance the positions between the different cultures involved. As we will see, for stage productions of this type to succeed depends crucially on the outcome of the negotiating and positioning.

The positioning process starts at the very beginning of the cultural exchange: the selection of a suitable play. One reason why *Macbeth* has attracted the attention of Chinese artists is that

> many archetypes like Macbeth can be found in Chinese history, especially during the 'Spring and Autumn Period' (770–476 BC), the 'Warring States' period (468–221 BC) and the 'Five Dynasties and Ten Countries' period (AD 907–960). Quite a number of former heroes had become villains and were doomed to destruction due to their ever-enlarging egomaniac desires.[5]

Hence the 1945 spoken drama adaptation chose to replace Macbeth with a historical figure, Wang Deming, from the Five Dynasties and Ten Countries period, a figure who briefly usurped the throne before being killed by other rebels. Li Jianwu, the adapter of this production, noted moreover a 'resonance between souls'[6] whereby Chinese people identified a spiritual kinship with the moral principles suffusing Shakespeare's writing. Similarly, Zheng Shifeng, the script-writer of the 1986 *kunju* adaptation argued that 'the humanism of Shakespeare, which is broad and universal, such as that goodness is rewarded, wrongs are redressed and evils punished, the small and weak are sympathetic

---

3 In my book *Shashibiya: Staging Shakespeare in China*, p. 116, I offer readers a diagram to illustrate how at each successive level the practitioners in the target culture, using their understanding of Shakespeare's works and of their own culture and theatrical genre, choose what in the original text is to remain, what is to be filtered out and what added or changed. At the final level, the stage presentation is interpreted by audiences according to their own perspectives. All these decisions made by practitioners and by spectators are fundamentally influenced by the social, political and cultural contexts in which the adaptation is made and seen.

4 Pierre Bourdieu, *The Field of Cultural Production* (Cambridge, 2000), p. 30.

5 'A Hard Step with Pride' by Zheng Shifeng (the script-writer of *Blood-Stained Hands*, the 1986 *kunju* adaptation of *Macbeth*), *Shanghai Kunju Theatre Programme Notes*, Autumn 1987, p. 16.

6 'Preface' (*Qianyan*) to *A Shi Na*, a spoken drama adaptation of *Othello* by Li Jianwu, *Literature Journal* (*Wenxue zazhi*), 2.1 (June 1947), p. 63.

while the mean and repulsive are castigated, is the common heritage of all human beings far beyond time and space'.[7] Yet the clear parallels between *Macbeth* and events in Chinese politics also contributed to the absence of the play from the Chinese stage for decades after the 1945 production.

It has been commented that 'much of Shakespeare's history is in fact the history of assimilation within the People's Republic of China'.[8] Since 1949, when Mao drove the National Party out of the mainland, Communist ideology has impinged upon all facets of life in China, including the theatre. Furthermore, Shakespeare performance became particularly influenced by the work of the Soviet experts who were invited by the Chinese government to assist in developing spoken drama during the 1950s. The Russians' choice of comedies and romances, and their teaching on interpretation and stage presentation, were followed unquestioningly by most Chinese practitioners over the next four decades. None of Shakespeare's political tragedies was performed publicly between 1949 and 1980,[9] a little over three years after Mao's death and the end of the Cultural Revolution, when *Macbeth* was staged by Xu Xiaozhong in Beijing and was subsequently broadcast on national television.

While rigorously applying Stanislavski's Method in rehearsing this production, Xu nevertheless considered that the orthodox style of spoken drama performance was inadequate to express the supernatural aspect and the symbolism inherent in *Macbeth*. Chinese spoken drama, following the Western theatrical conventions of the late-nineteenth and early-twentieth centuries, tends to focus on illusion and to run each unit as a relatively stable fragment of the real world. Xu felt that only by creating a new stage vocabulary would he be able to present this 'open text', and to do so he drew on ideas and stage techniques from the traditional Chinese theatre.

Xu's idea is also reflected in Huang Zuolin's long-held ambition of staging *Macbeth* in an authentic Chinese music theatre. Having directed the 1945 *huaju* (spoken drama) version, Huang in 1986 adapted *Macbeth* into *kunju*, a centuries-old operatic genre. As Huang observed, *Macbeth* 'possesses the wildest imaginative power among all of Shakespeare's thirty-seven plays . . . What bewildered Goethe and Hazlitt about the difficulties of putting Shakespeare on the European stage is exactly the reason why *kunju* can do it.'[10] *Kunju*, and traditional theatre in general, runs a flexible and fluid sign-system, enabling the actors to present any time and any place and to move easily between them. It never attempts to represent a truthful external world, but instead embodies the subjective and expressive. Such a stage is like the human mind itself in that it gives limitless freedom to the imagination. The Chinese term for the traditional theatre is *xiqu*, literally meaning 'theatre melody'. Singing is essential, but dance and body movements are also vital features of this theatre, and *Macbeth* naturally furnishes opportunities for arranging battle scenes in which the performers' acrobatic skills can be displayed.

Notwithstanding such ways in which the traditional theatre appears compatible with Shakespeare, profound differences also exist. For example, the feelings that Derek Jacobi described when he played Macbeth in 1993 reveal something that characters in Chinese theatre do not often possess: 'He knows where he's reached, he knows what he's lost, and he knows what it entails . . . I have given

---

7 'A Hard Step with Pride' by Zheng Shifeng, *Shanghai Kunju Theatre Programme Notes*, Autumn 1987, p. 16.

8 'Shakespeare on the Stage of Asia' by J. Gillies, R. Minami, R. Li and P. Trivedi, in *The Cambridge Companion to Shakespeare on Stage*, ed. Stanley Wells and Sarah Stanton (Cambridge, 2002), pp. 259–83, p. 266.

9 In 1959, Jiao Juyin worked with an Advanced Directing Class at the Central Academy of Drama on *Hamlet*, a play he directed in 1942. However, there is virtually no record surviving of the production. Given the status of Jiao, who had already become China's number one director and his rehearsals were always recorded in detail, the staging is much under-discussed. I suspect that the low-key publicity of Jiao's *Hamlet* in the 1950s was caused by the fact that the authorities did not like an ambiguous historical play on the Chinese stage or at least a Shakespeare historical play did not go along with the current propaganda purpose.

10 Quotation taken from my 1992 interview with Huang Zuolin.

in to the evil that I fought not to give in to and it has grown like a cancer within me'.[11] In order to portray Macbeth's inner conflict – suffering from knowing that he does wrong and must ceaselessly sink ever deeper – it has been necessary for artists in the traditional theatre to develop skills beyond the rigid conventions of their genres. In consequence, local theatres develop. Thus many have argued that Shakespeare is the 'new blood' needed to transform the traditional theatre if it is to survive in a rapidly changing world.

The seven adaptations of *Macbeth* into Chinese settings have all given special prominence to the role of Lady Macbeth. Indeed, the 2001 adaptation into the regional genre called *chuanju* is entitled *Lady Macbeth* and concentrates entirely upon her. The 'fiend-like queen', as Malcolm calls her, is 'the most commanding and perhaps the most awe-inspiring figure that Shakespeare drew'.[12] However, it is Macbeth who is given a third of the lines in Shakespeare's play, while Lady Macbeth remains off-stage after 3.4 until her final brief appearance in her madness at the beginning of Act 5. What then particularly interests Chinese artists in this character?

The powerful and inflexible will demonstrated by Lady Macbeth in the first half of the play is something scarcely seen in female roles on the Chinese stage. For most Chinese practitioners, with a respect for authority instilled through Confucian tradition and reinforced by Communist ideology, it is important to strive for authenticity when adapting Shakespeare. But the adapters cannot remain entirely uninfluenced by their own cultural background and by the theatrical conventions of the genre for which the adaptation is being written. In terms of Bourdieu's 'field of struggles', the target culture of the local theatre is here so strong that it tends to dominate the source culture of the foreign play. Confronted with the complicated psychological dimension of the original Macbeth, as a noble man who cannot resist pursuing a course he knows is evil, Chinese adapters have inevitably opted to exploit Lady Macbeth – the peculiar, strange and fiend-like woman – as a convenient 'short-cut' to explain Macbeth's development from a hero to a villain. She at least fits one traditional Chinese concept that 'Women are the bane of men [literally: women are the disastrous flood]', and the archetypal storyline in which honourable generals or emperors are seduced by beautiful women and neglect their duties to the state with catastrophic consequences.

It should be observed, moreover, that most of these adaptations appeared at a time of widespread hatred for the 'Gang of Four', referring to the political alliance between Jiang Qing (Mao's wife) and three men. They were arrested in October 1976, following Mao's death, and the official position is that the 'Gang' effectively ruled China in the closing years of the Cultural Revolution and was directly responsible for the afflictions suffered by the Chinese people.[13] The adapters could hardly avoid reflecting the parallel in Lady Macbeth.

Another relevant factor is that in the aftermath of the Cultural Revolution it became permissible to import selected foreign literature and films, and people were very eager to view works that had been banned from mainland China for decades. One such was Akira Kurosawa's version of *Macbeth* in his 1957 film *Cobweb Castle* (English title: *The Throne of Blood*). The image of Asaji (the Japanese Lady Macbeth) as the real motivator behind her husband in Kurosawa's film often appears to have shaped the portrayal of Lady Macbeth in the Chinese stage adaptations.

Having outlined the main cultural elements underlying the interpretation of *Macbeth*, we will now look in greater detail at four of the productions to illustrate the intriguing cross-cultural processes by which Chinese audiences see a Shakespeare

[11] 'Derek Jacobi – Macbeth', in *Players of Shakespeare 4*, ed. Robert Smallwood (Cambridge, 1998), pp. 193–210 (p. 207).

[12] *Shakespearean Tragedy* by A. C. Bradley (Houndmills and London, 1992), p. 322.

[13] During the Cultural Revolution, more than 700,000 people were purged, some 35,000 had died either from gross maltreatment or suicide. Many more were physically or mentally disabled. Education halted, and students were sent to the countryside and factories to be re-educated. Many theatrical genres were banned because of the 'decadent feudal and bourgeois influence'. The economy of the whole country stagnated and living standards declined.

performance, and through which the Chinese theatrical traditions have evolved in dealing with this foreign play.

MACBETH IN SPOKEN DRAMA

As mentioned earlier, there have been only two stage productions of *Macbeth* in *huaju*, or spoken drama. Huang Zuolin's 1945 version, on which I shall concentrate, was an adaptation into a Chinese historical plot; whereas Xu Xiaozhong's staging in 1980 aimed to convey Shakespeare's vision of Medieval Scotland. It is noteworthy that both productions occurred at crucial moments in modern Chinese history. The former was performed in Shanghai when the city was still under Japanese occupation four months before the end of the Second World War. The title chosen by Huang for his stage work was *The Hero of the Turmoil*, and as the reviewer wrote in the *China Weekly News* (*Zhongguo zhou bao*): 'Having experienced the turmoil and chaos of the War, *The Hero of the Turmoil* really shocks us! What a sigh of emotion!'[14] Thirty-five years later, the 1980 *Macbeth* came in the aftermath of the Cultural Revolution, when the whole nation still bore the painful 'scar'[15] of the chaotic and traumatic Cultural Revolution which had been instigated by Mao in 1966 and did not end until after his death in 1976.

Within the context of modern Chinese theatre, Xu Xiaozhong's 1980 *Macbeth* proved a landmark. Although the production was strongly politicized, Xu rejected the notion of treating Shakespeare as 'our contemporary', or of using the performance to make direct political comments on recent events. As a committed revolutionary artist, Xu was concerned to develop Shakespeare's original character, emphasizing that Macbeth could have become a revered national hero, a 'giant' in Engels's term,[16] were it not for his unbridled ambition. Xu further stated: '*Macbeth* is also a tragedy of the people. Shakespeare reveals that a careerist and tyrant like Macbeth can bring disaster to his ancestral land and its people.'[17] The 1980 *Macbeth* presented a striking image of a man who might have become the saviour of his country, but who now 'wanders,

5 The conspiracy scene in *huaju Macbeth* (1980). Lady Macbeth: 'Look like the innocent flower, / But be the serpent under't.'

stumbles and eventually drowns in . . . whirlpools of blood'.[18] The question that Xu urged the audience to think about was: 'Our times needed giants and displayed the conditions for the appearance of giants. But why, on the contrary, did those

14 Cited in *My 'Xieyi' Conception of Theatre and I* (*Wo yu xieyi xiju guan*) by Huang Zuolin, ed. Jiang Liu (Beijing, 1990), p. 59.

15 During this period, 'scar literature' appeared which focused on people's experiences through the Cultural Revolution.

16 Since the early 1950s, commentaries on Shakespeare by Marx and Engels have dominated Shakespeare studies on mainland China. The concept of 'Renaissance giant' that Engels put forward in the 'Introduction' to his *Dialectics of Nature* crystallized the Chinese attitude towards Shakespeare and his works. Engels wrote: 'It [the Renaissance] was the greatest progressive revolution that mankind has so far experienced, a time which called for giants and produced giants – giants in power of thought, passion, and character, in universality and learning.' Ed. and trans. Clemens Dutt (New York, 1960), pp. 2–3.

17 'Elementary Explorations: My Rehearsals and Teaching of Macbeth' (*Makebaisi chu tan – Makebaisi de paiyan yu jiaoxue*), in *Arts of Directing and Aesthetics of Expression* (*Xiang biaoxian meixue tuokuan de daoyan yishu*) by Xu Xiaozhong (Beijing, 1996), pp. 239–357 (p. 243).

18 Xu Xiaozhong, *Arts of Directing and Aesthetics of Expression*, p. 242.

who could have become giants let their minds get warped?'[19] There was no need to make Shakespeare 'contemporary', since a truthful presentation of Macbeth's story would enable audiences to perceive the parallels and the relevance to their own reality and experiences.[20]

This essential attitude towards Shakespeare, that 'he was not of an age, but for all time', was likewise evident in Huang Zuolin's work in 1945.

THE HERO OF THE TURMOIL (*LUAN SHI YINGXIONG*), 1945: REFLECTING THE CONTEMPORARY CHAOS DURING THE SINO-JAPANESE WAR

The adapter of this production, Li Jianwu, had a profound knowledge of Chinese, English and French literature. At university he had been inspired by French Symbolism, although when he went to live in France between 1931 and 1933 he concentrated on the study of Gustave Flaubert, since he thought it was 'realism that China needed most'[21] and he had to put his country's interests ahead of his own.

During the Sino-Japanese War (1937–45), Li Jianwu joined the many Chinese literati and artists who gathered in Shanghai under the shelter of the French Concession and International Settlement. Despite the fact that by the end of 1941 these foreign concessions had, like the rest of Shanghai, fallen under the control of the Japanese military, the activities of professional and amateur theatres continued to flourish. Ironically, with the prohibition of American films after Japan attacked the USA, stage work was even stimulated. Under these abnormal conditions, theatres had an urgent need for new plays, and adaptations of foreign plays proved a fertile source of scripts. Indeed, such adaptations became singularly acceptable: firstly, because strict censorship effectively excluded any work that conveyed the slightest patriotic feeling; and secondly, most literati refused to be accomplices with the Japanese invaders and the puppet government, and adopted 'stop-creating-Chinese-original-plays' as a form of protest.[22] Thus, in a further irony, Shakespeare's universally acknowledged literary greatness proved useful for Chinese artists as they struggled against the foreign occupying powers for some degree of artistic freedom and independence.[23]

Li Jianwu adapted two Shakespeare tragedies in the 1940s: *Macbeth* and *Othello*. 'Learn from Shakespeare': this was the first as well as the final sentence of Li Jianwu's preface to *A Shi Na*,[24] the adaptation of *Othello* which appeared three years after his work on *Macbeth*. To Li, 'agreeing with Shakespeare mentally' was more important than a close resemblance in the appearance. He identified two objectives for himself: 'Seeking Shakespeare's sublimity through history; refining Shakespeare's poetry through language.' From French Realism he deduced that he should 'set the story, action and characters against a realistic historical background' and could manipulate Shakespeare's text to help 'reinforce the impression of right and wrong'. The re-writing was to be 'hundred percent Chinese', yet 'Shakespeare should have the same weight'. Li insisted that fulfilling these principles was not a simple process: 'On the contrary, for the adapter, it was creative work like a ten-month pregnancy. He had worn himself out to accomplish his work. They are words, sentences, structure and techniques, but

[19] *Research on Xu Xiaozhong's Art of Directing* (*Xu Xiaozhong daoyan yishu yanjiu*) by Lin Yinyu (Beijing, 1991), p. 355.

[20] Xu Xiaozhong and the 1980 *Macbeth* are discussed in greater depth in *Shashibiya: Staging Shakespeare in China*, pp. 69–81.

[21] 'My Path in the Translation World' (*Wo zou guo de fanyi daolu*) by Li Jianwu, cited in *Biography of Li Jianwu* (*Li Jianwu zhuan*) by Han Shishan (Taiyuan, 1997), p. 98.

[22] *Biography of Li Jianwu* (*Li Jianwu zhuan*) by Han Shishan (Taiyuan, 1997), p. 270.

[23] Xing Yunfei's *Romeo and Juliet* in 1938 provides a good example to show how Chinese left-wing artists used Shakespeare as a canonical figure to fight against interference by the authorities in the theatre. For details see *Shashibiya: Staging Shakespeare in China*, pp. 30–1.

[24] *A Shi Na* with its 'Preface' was published in *Literature Journal* (Wenxue zazhi), 2.1 and 2.2. 'Preface' in Issue 1, (Shanghai, 1947) pp. 63–64. The following quotations are all from the same source unless otherwise noted.

also blood and flesh. They are lives.' Following his guidelines, Li used the Chinese historical figure Wang Deming as the new protagonist in his version of *Macbeth*. The Shanghai audience in 1945 might readily appreciate the underlying connection between the tragedy of a Medieval Scottish tyrant, the chaos in China in the days of Wang Deming, and their own problematic situation in the eighth year of the Sino-Japanese War. However, the choice of historical setting also posed a difficulty for the adapter, since his script had both to express 'Shakespeare's sublimity' and to convince audiences that the characters and their behaviour were true to life for tenth-century China.

Most traditional Chinese plays and literary works are concerned with the relationships between parents and children, husbands and wives, sovereigns and officials. The plots typically focus on the protagonist's actions in the outside world rather than dwelling on any inner strife in his psychology. Protagonists have definite antagonists to fight against, with the good and the bad distinguished unambiguously. By contrast, in adapting *Macbeth*, Li wished to preserve from the original the psychology of evil evinced in the protagonist. Like Macbeth, Wang Deming has a conscience which speaks against his crimes, but despite his ever-present fear he feels compelled to continue to commit them. Afterwards, he is fully aware of what he has lost and where he now stands.

In order to convey the profound psychological conflicts in Wang Deming, Li carefully elaborated the background to his characterization. In particular, the adapter put a heavier moral burden on Wang Deming by presenting him as the adopted son of King Wang Rong (the Chinese Duncan), with his original birth-name, Zhang Wenli, having been changed to accord with the King's family name of Wang. Confucianism, the backbone of Chinese culture for 2500 years, was structured on the fundamental and unalterable obligations of the individual to the family and to the state: 'Heaven will not change, so the way of nature will not change either.' Order in the universe required the absolute obedience of the child to the father, and of the subject to the king. Wang Deming is thus doubly a transgressor since he not only usurps the throne but also kills his own foster father, the man who has given him his identity.

This close personal relationship makes it harder for Wang Deming to perpetrate the assassination and exacerbates his sense of fear at violating the sacred bonds to his king and father. Yet Wang Deming immediately proceeds to kill the legitimate heir, whom he accuses of having plotted the king's assassination and orders the pursuit of the king's younger son who has escaped his clutches. In the adaptation, the Chinese Donalbain is described as a young child and does not appear on-stage, although he provides the rationale for the insertion of a new act (Act 5 in the six-act adaptation) and two new characters: Li Zhen and his son.

These new characters take the place of Macduff and his family, but have a very different function in the storyline. Li Zhen, a Confucian scholar, is a court official who is the only noble to express his allegiance to Wang Deming after the latter has seized power. Li is despised by his peers for his seeming disloyalty to the assassinated Wang Rong. However, his real intention is eventually revealed as pretending to serve the new regime while actually seeking the legitimate successor of Wang Rong to lead the fight against the usurper.

The new Act 5 comes after the banquet scene where Wang Deming has been traumatized by the ghost of Fu Tong (Banquo). As Wang Deming's fear and insecurity deepen he becomes ever more desperate to eliminate Wang Rong's surviving son, and he orders his soldiers to kill every boy they find between eight and ten years old. In fact, Fu Xi (Fleance), who is organizing an attack on the regime, has brought the young prince to Li Zhen's ancestral hall. Act 5 opens with Li Zhen at home giving a lesson to his ten-year-old son Li Quan on Confucian teachings. He explains to his son that life is more important than death: 'People all die. So death is nothing. But if you live, you must do something worthwhile.' Furthermore, 'a man must be strong and resolute, because he shoulders heavy responsibilities over the long road ahead. Men like this are trustworthy to look after an orphan or anyone's life.'[25]

When Wang Deming's soldiers arrive at Li's home searching for the prince, Li Zhen faces a cruel dilemma. Finally, to protect the rightful successor of King Wang Rong, Li Zhen pretends once again to be loyal to the usurper and hands over his own son Li Quan to the soldiers, telling them this child is the prince. The episode is touching and tense, because in order to convince the soldiers that he is betraying the true prince, Li Zhen must suffer being misunderstood by everyone else, most painfully of all by his own son. The ambiguity in his words to the soldiers hints at his real distress: 'Even if I could deceive you, can I deceive the King?[26] Can I deceive my own conscience?' Half weeping and half laughing, he continues: 'Oh, heart! Heart is made of flesh. It knows how to shiver and it aches. But conscience![27] Oh, innocent and pure conscience, you have harmed my heart which is made of flesh and blood.' Just before his son is taken away, he holds the child tightly: 'Oh, no, good child. You can call me daddy. You poor child! You ask for help from Heaven, but there is no response. Your father is deaf. He has ears but he cannot hear. Your father's heart is made of iron, even if he can hear your voice, he pretends not to hear anything. Don't cry. Do not cry!' Act 5 ends with Li Zhen returning to the solace of *The Confucian Analects*: 'A man must be strong and resolute, because he shoulders heavy responsibilities over the long road ahead. Benevolence is one's responsibility. Isn't it too heavy for him? One should carry this out all his life till he dies. Isn't there too long a way to go?'

The insertion of this scene provides a further illustration of Bourdieu's 'field of struggles' in the process of cultural transformation, and the power of the local culture to interpose itself in a foreign play. The concept of sacrificing one's own son to the villain to save the heir of a good man is an archetype of classical Chinese drama, and to this day many local theatres still perform their own versions of *The Orphan of the Zhao Family* [*Zhao shi gu'er*], originally written in the fourteenth century by Ji Junxiang. (Voltaire's *The Chinese Orphan* quarried materials from this play.) Whereas Shakespeare's Macbeth expresses his sleepless torment through exquisite poetry, Wang Deming is less inclined to introspection, and sleeplessness just motivates him to kill more people. As Li Zhen comments in the play: 'If among ten thousand only one did not bend to him, he will simply slaughter nine thousand nine hundred and ninety-nine people to keep the rebel company.' Due to the different expectations of theatre, the Chinese adapter felt that his audiences needed to see more concrete events onstage, and added Li Zhen's story to serve as a visualization of Wang Deming's psychology.

As has been seen, the adapter, Li Jianwu, was a liberal artist greatly influenced by French philosophy and literature. He was inspired by the ideals of freedom and democracy advocated by the French Revolution. Nevertheless, consciously or subconsciously, he rewrote a tragedy of a 'great terrible figure'[28] torn by the guilt and evil in his soul into a tragedy that eulogizes the loyalty a subject owes to his king, one of the fundamental virtues according to Confucianism and feudal society. Perhaps, given the situation of China under Japanese occupation, there was a subliminal imperative to depict the traditional heroism of a father sacrificing his son for the sake of the country.

MACBETH IN THE TRADITIONAL OPERATIC FORM

Traditional Chinese music theatre is a total theatre with aria singing, dance, mime and acrobatics.

---

25 *Wang Deming* in *Selected Plays by Li Jianwu* (*Li Jianwu juzuo xuan*) (Beijing, 1982), pp. 415–88, (Act Five, pp. 466–79). All the citations of the play in this article are from the same source. Li Zhen's lines here are also quotations from *The Confucian Analects* (*Lun yu*).

26 In the original Chinese text, Wang Deming is addressed as Bing Ma Liu Hou. I translate this title as 'king' for convenience.

27 'Heart' in Chinese is *xin* while conscience is *liangxin*; both words share the same character *xin* (heart). Li Zhen's lines make a pun of 'heart'.

28 *Shakespearean Tragedy* by A. C. Bradley (Houndmills and London, 1992), p. 306.

Thus, after seeing Wu Hsing-Kuo's[29] *The Kingdom of Desire*, Benedict Nightingale's observation from a Western perspective was: 'To be an actor in China is also to be a singer, dancer, gymnast and, for all I know, juggler and trapeze artist as well. Match that, Kemble, Macready, Gielgud, anyone.'[30] A theatrical form that focuses to such an extent on the performers' skills and artistry does not easily accommodate a Shakespeare play. Yet if the adapters and artists are able to overcome the challenges, the resulting performances can be outstandingly successful.

An immediate issue for the adapters is how to create suitable situations for arias, because the Chinese traditional form is *xiqu*, or 'theatre melody', and singing is its most important component. Looking at the adaptations of *Macbeth*, the principal arias tend to be arranged at the following points: the conspiracy scene, with either a soliloquy sung by Macbeth expressing his inner conflicts or a duet between the couple; before or after the assassination; the banquet scene; and Lady Macbeth's final hand-washing scene. The rule by which singing is organized in a play derives from the ancient theory of poetry: 'The affections are stirred within and take on form in words. If words alone are inadequate, we speak them out in sighs. If sighing is inadequate, we sing them. If singing them is inadequate, unconsciously our hands dance them and our feet tap them.'[31] Hence the singing has to originate in the character's inner emotions.

Arias are sung in a very different way from Western opera. Apart from the musical instruments and the use of percussion, Chinese operatic performers always accompany their arias with sequences of spectacular body movements. These movements typically exploit traditional features of the costumes: such as long sleeves, boots with high platforms, plumes or pompoms on the helmets, as well as the make-up, beards and hair, and props such as fans and swords. It is worth noting that all the adaptations changed Macbeth's dagger to a Chinese sword. Perhaps because the shape and smallness of a dagger offer performers little opportunity for dances or gestures, daggers rarely appear on the traditional stage. Swords, on the contrary, are widely employed and there are numerous sets of conventional body movements and dances for using swords in both male and female roles.

To deal with the more profound questions regarding the psychological dimension of the original play and the characterization – for instance, the relationship between the couple, Macbeth's motivation, and his hesitation and fear at carrying out the assassination – the operatic adaptations each followed a distinct approach. The adapters were evidently attracted to different aspects of the play, reflecting their individual personalities and experiences as Chinese artists, their theatrical backgrounds and the local forms for which they were now working. As a result, in the 'field of struggles', as defined by Bourdieu, the processes of negotiation and compromise led to diverse conclusions. However, all the adapters shared a belief that through their versions of *Macbeth* they were helping to transfuse the 'new blood' to revitalize the indigenous music theatre.

By reviewing certain aspects of three operatic adaptations, the analysis below examines how essential meanings may metamorphose in such intercultural productions of *Macbeth*.

BLOOD-STAINED HANDS (*XIE SHOU JI*), 1986: EXPLORING AND EXPLOITING SHAKESPEARE'S POETRY

Huang Zuolin, the director of the 1945 spoken drama adaptation *The Hero of the Turmoil*, had long dreamed of staging Shakespeare in a Chinese operatic form. For decades, his idea was criticized as a bizarre notion and a bad effect of his education in the decadent West (in the 1930s, Huang had studied at Cambridge and the London Theatre Studio). Yet in 1986, when the first Shakespeare Festival was organized as an official showcase for

[29] I follow the conventional spelling in the press for the names of Wu Hsing-Kuo and Lin Hsiu-Wei.

[30] 'Macbeth as Martial Art', *The Times*, 16 November 1990.

[31] 'Great Preface' (*Ta-hsü*) to *Book of Songs* (*Shi Ching*): *Readings in Chinese Literary Thought*, by Stephen Owen (Cambridge, MA, 1992), p. 41.

the government's open-door policy to Western culture, the octogenarian director was at last offered an opportunity to realize his forty-year-old project.

Huang considered that the most appropriate form to convey Shakespeare's poetry was *kunju*, one of the oldest extant genres of Chinese theatre, which flourished in the sixteenth and seventeenth centuries and is regarded as 'the wet nurse' for all younger genres. *Kunju* is noted for its poetry and contributed significantly to classical Chinese literature. Huang also believed that an interpretation of Shakespeare by Chinese theatre would add another dimension to the understanding of Shakespeare's works. This 1986 *kunju* adaptation, entitled *Blood-Stained Hands*, demonstrated Huang's boldness and originality as a director.[32]

A remarkable feature of this adaptation was the portrayal of the three witches. In the traditional theatre, roles are strictly categorized and performers specialize in a particular role-type. As there is no convention for playing witches, the parts were assigned to performers of an acrobatic sub-type of the clown role. Shakespeare's lines: 'When shall we three meet again? / In thunder, lighting, or in rain? / . . . Fair is foul, and foul is fair' (1.1.1–12) gave Huang the idea how to present the three creatures. On a dark stage clouded with smoke, accompanied by conventional *kunju* music and using percussion for the thunder, a figure with a grotesque mask emerged. Gradually, audiences realized that the mask was attached to the back of the performer's head. On his face, there was no white patch on the nose – the conventional symbol for a clown. Instead, his light pink make-up was closer to a female role. 'I am true and false', said the first witch in a voice pitched between that of a man and a woman. At a swirl of the first witch's cloak, following the rhythmic percussion, the second witch rolled out from under the cloak, as did the third witch. Two of them used crouching steps – a conventional clown routine – to appear dwarf-like in a choreographic arrangement for one tall and two short figures. They were all made 'double faced' by having masks on the backs of their heads, so that they showed the audience calm and smiling female faces and then turned round to display the hideous visages. The use of masks was a theatrical device externalizing Shakespeare's 'fair/foul' antithesis. It also echoed their new lines in rhyme:

Witch A I am true and false.
Witch B I am benevolent and malevolent.
Witch C I am beautiful and ugly.
Witch A [We] keep each other company floating in the air of the Phantom Beach.
Witches [We] keep each other company floating in the air of the Phantom Beach.
Witch C The cold wind is blowing, I am hot and sweating.
Witch B The bright sun is shining, my heart is freezing.

The three witches glided smoothly along the stage, exuding an atmosphere of mystery and menace. An intriguing counterpoint to this opening scene came at the close of the production, reflecting Huang's interest in the Brechtian theory of alienation and contrasts with the 'historical' ending of the original.

Witch A How splendid the battle was.
Witch B How tumultuous it was here.
Witch C But now everything is silent.
Witch A *Sheng, dan, jing, mo, chou,*[33] all the character types in the opera are now hurriedly removing their make-up.
Witch B The story is true but not really true; [it] is false but not really false.
Witch C [Do you] want to know what happens afterwards?
Witches Of course something may happen afterwards.
Witch A A play can continue forever.
Witch B But the curtain has to fall.
Witch C [May I] give you some advice: never take it all as a true story.
Witches We sisters will now be gone with the wind![34]

[32] This production is analysed in greater detail in *Shashibiya: Staging Shakespeare in China*, pp. 118–35.

[33] Chinese terms for different role types in *kunju*.

[34] The translation is based on the script kindly offered by the Shanghai *Kunju* Theatre.

6 The Banquet scene in *Blood-Stained Hands* (1986). The figure at the back is Banquo played by a painted-face role type (*jing*). He is in the same costume as when he was alive, but two white strips are now on the sides of his helmet to mark his 'ghost' status. The Macbeths are in the front.

The witches' scenes highlight the power of the theatricality that Huang was able to achieve by expanding on the *kunju* conventions. Similarly, in staging the banquet scene, Macbeth's lines in 3.4 and images like 'the rugged Russian bear, / The arm'd rhinoceros, or the Hyrcan tiger' could be given effective expression through the theatricality of *kunju*, illuminating the dramatic tension and the inner conflicts of the characters. Initially, Ma Pei (Macbeth) is carefree, relaxed and proud. The nervous crisis that he suffers on seeing the ghost is dramatized in an episode involving long arias sung by Ma Pei and the ghost, music and percussion, together with beautifully arranged choreography for everyone on the stage including Lady Macbeth and the courtiers. While singing, Ma Pei adroitly threw his crown off his head, his tightly bound long hair now loosened and dishevelled. The highly skilled technique of turning the head to make the long hair swing through the air in a wide circle rendered the situation even more appalling. The loud clashing of cymbals, in time with Ma Pei's swaying dance, seemed to strike his body like physical blows, and his movements demonstrated the reaction to each blow. The scene formed an astounding synthesis of the rich and powerfully externalized Chinese stage conventions and the Shakespearian psychological dimension. As Francis King observed after seeing the performance at the Edinburgh Festival in 1987: 'The verbal indications of guilty agony in the original are given thrilling visual form.'[35]

35 'Strange Union of Farce and Tragedy', *Sunday Times*, 30 August 1987.

7 The conspiracy scene in *The Kingdom of Desire* (1986). The actors wear costumes altered from the traditional ones appropriate to their roles and status, lacking, for instance, the usual long sleeves beyond the cuffs and the conventional headdresses.

THE KINGDOM OF DESIRE (*YUWANG CHENG GUO*), 1986: A REBELLION ON THE *JINGJU* STAGE

Careful examination and bold exploitation of Shakespeare's text helped Huang Zuolin make *Blood-Stained Hands* 'conform to *kunju*'s own rules' and present both '*kunju* and Shakespeare'.[36] Conversely, in the same year, 1986, the young Taiwanese artist Wu Hsing-Kuo was attempting to use a 'foreign play' to get rid of 'the burden of tradition' so a 'new theatrical form could therefore emerge'[37] in his production in Taipei of *The Kingdom of Desire*.

Without any communication between them, Chinese artists from both sides of the straits simultaneously produced exceptional sinified versions of *Macbeth*. Wu Hsing-Kuo, like Huang Zuolin, loved the traditional theatre and was anxious about its future. But as a rebel, Wu Hsing-Kuo was not interested in 'innovating the tradition', and in *The Kingdom of Desire* he refused to conform to the conventions of *jingju* (Peking Opera).[38] Instead, he intended it to be an entirely new production based on both Shakespeare and *jingju*.

[36] 'Huang Zuolin's Talk on *Kunju* and Shakespeare' (*Huang Zuolin tan kunju yu Sha ju*) by Ye Zhongmin, *Wenhui bao*, Hong Kong edition, 20 May 1986.

[37] 'The Contemporary Legend Theatre Strides Towards Its Tour in France' (*Dangdai Chuanqi xiang Faguo zhi xing nuli*) by Huang Fumei, *Culture and Arts* (*Wen xin yi fang*), 115 (January 1994).

[38] *Jingju* has been known as Peking Opera or Chinese Opera in the West. In Taiwan, it is called *guoju*, or national theatre. In this article, I have used the transliteration of original Chinese terms. Following Chinese generic terminology, *jingju* means 'the drama of the capital', i.e. Beijing.

Having trained at the Fuxing Drama School in Taipei for eight years, Wu is a specialist in the male warrior types in the *jingju* theatre. After a few years of stage experience, however, Wu felt that his creativity was limited by the restrictive conventions of the genre and wished to break free from them. In 1986 the Contemporary Legend Theatre was founded by Wu, together with his wife Lin Hsiu-Wei and two other colleagues. Its manifesto declared that only those who were under thirty years old could join the company, and its first work was *The Kingdom of Desire*. Attending the first performance, Zhong Mingde, a critic in Taipei, recorded the following anecdote. Three people were sitting together. After the first act, the person on the right walked out, saying 'This is not *jingju*.' After the second act, the person on the left remarked 'This is not spoken drama', and also walked out. The person who sat in the middle remained to the end of the performance and then departed in silence. Such perplexity was echoed at the Taiwan National Council for Cultural Planning and Development because the company's approach could not be categorized as either *jingju* or *huaju* but has always striven to be bold and experimental.[39]

'*Jingju* has died, it's been deeply buried under too many conventions and rules. I'm a *jingju* actor and how can I let it go like this?' Wu stated passionately.[40] He loved *jingju* because his career was part of his being, and he hated *jingju* because it suppressed his originality. So Wu deliberately set out in his work to break open the boundaries of the role types and ultimately alter the nature of *jingju*. Role categorization is central to the traditional theatrical system, with the different role types each having specific sets of formulae governing the performers' use of voice, gesture, body movements, make-up and costumes. Basically, the characters in the traditional repertoire are divided into four main types: male role (*sheng*), female role (*dan*), male painted-face (*jing*)[41] and the clown (*chou*), all of which have their own sub-types. Each performer usually specializes in one such sub-type.

However, in Wu Hsing-Kuo's *The Kingdom of Desire*, the complex character of the protagonist Aoshu Zheng (Macbeth) went far beyond the capacity of any of the orthodox male role types. For his performance as Aoshu, Wu learned different steps, gestures and body movements from other role types, and even from other forms of theatre such as spoken drama and modern dance. Moreover, the manipulation of the traditional categories was not limited solely to the protagonist's role. Throughout the whole production, the structure of the plot and the arrangements for costumes, make-up, stage techniques and blocking, all evinced a hybridity of styles.

With excellent performing skills, Wu brought home to his audiences the protagonist's tragedy. Towards the end of the production, Aoshu was isolated on a towering rock, surrounded by his enemies. His armour was torn and his helmet missing. Like Ma Pei in the *kunju* production, his tightly-bound long hair became loosened and dishevelled, a stage convention expressing desperation, fear or horror. Using his limbs, hands and feet, Aoshu agilely twisted and turned to avoid the volleys of arrows shot by the soldiers. When he was finally hit, he reeled and stumbled, then plunged twenty feet, performing a double back-somersault, to land skilfully on the stage while wearing traditional boots with platforms as high as two inches. Finally, the audience was left struck by the poignant and compelling image of Aoshu's staring eyes and his arm pointing aloft for a whole minute, as he staggered round through the ranks of his enemies before toppling backwards like a felled tree to the ground. This remarkable scene blended *jingju* conventions, such as the long hair, the somersaults and the final fall ('*jiangshi*' or 'stiff body'), with non-stylized gestures, in particular, the frozen arm.

---

[39] 'The Contemporary Legend and Continuing Revolution' (*Dangdai Chuanqi yu jixu geming*) by Zhong Mingde, *The Ten Years of the Contemporary Theatre* (*Dangdai Chuanqi shi nian*) (Taipei, 1996).

[40] 'The Contemporary Legend Theatre Strides Towards Its Tour in France' (*Dangdai Chuanqi xiang Faguo zhi xing nuli*) by Huang Fumei, *Culture and Arts* (*Wen xin yi fang*), 115 (January 1994).

[41] *Jing*, or painted face, has a varied terminology in different theatrical genres.

Aoshu died more disturbingly than any other Chinese Macbeth, although those who remember Kurosawa's film *The Throne of Blood* would have found Aoshu's death scene familiar. The producer of *The Kingdom of Desire*, Lin Hsiu-Wei, pointed out to me that they found it easier to sinify Kurosawa's version than the original English play.[42] However, there has been no discussion of the source materials in the reviews or articles – practitioners and critics alike accepted that the *Kingdom* was an adaptation of Shakespeare's *Macbeth*.

The conspiracy scene similarly follows the Kurosawa storyline, with a 'Mountain Spirit' taking after the image of the Japanese Kurozuka (a hag figure in Noh plays) to replace the original witches. Despite the fulfilment of his predicted promotion, Aoshu remains uneasy about the prediction that he will one day gain the throne. 'I'm a loyal general, honest and upright. I won't be a greedy villain insulting the King's trust', he tells his wife.[43] But on hearing of the unexpected arrival of the King and his army, Lady Aoshu convinces her husband that Meng Ting (Banquo) must have informed the King about the predictions of the Mountain Spirit. She thus argues that the King will slaughter them all, unless Aoshu strikes first and kills the King. Aoshu is gradually persuaded by his wife but still hesitates between loyalty and treachery, subservience and ambition. He sings:

> I have been a giant pole that can hold up the sky,
> I am magnificent and never afraid of anything.
> I have been under other people's eaves, being a subordinate, I have no security.
> Nobody would not admire colourful embroidered gowns and the crown decorated with invaluable pearls
> But I am also worried. If it is exposed, my crime and guilt will be as high as the sky, and everything I have now will become an empty dream in the world.

After these four lines, the tempo of the aria increases, as Aoshu recalls the renown he has won and the service he has given the country. This leads into a nineteen-line duet with his wife, in which Lady Aoshu settles the question that he must assassinate the King without delay: 'The dragon is now on the sandy beach and the water is shallow. / He will never escape your sharp steel broadsword.'

Immediately, Lady Aoshu hurries off to ply the guards with drugged wine. Aoshu is left on his own. His eyes move rapidly from side to side, and the conflict in his emotions is revealed in his face and his steps – fast and slow, backward and forward – as well as the movements of his wide sleeves (a modification of the traditional long-sleeved *jingju* costumes). He has been seduced by the idea of seizing the throne, but his resolve to usurp power is also paralysed by his sense that this is evil. His wife returns and throws a sword to her husband, but seeing his hesitation she groans: 'Every day, you boast that you are a real man and a genuine hero. But in fact you are a coward. You are discouraged! All right. From today on, do not mention your aspiration any more and do not tell me that you will be overlord controlling the whole world. You will be just laughed at by everyone!' Shamed by his wife, Aoshu proceeds directly to execute the deed, as this adaptation (in contrast to *Blood-Stained Hands*) omits the dagger scene. Wu Hsing-Kuo's aptitude to explore and exploit the wealth of theatrical resources beyond the traditional confines generated a much more externalized *Macbeth* than even Shakespeare might have envisaged. The production marked a momentous opening step in Wu's ongoing personal and professional struggle both to achieve his own reconciliation with his strong theatrical heritage and to accommodate particular Western canonical works within the Chinese tradition.

LADY MACBETH (MAKEBAI FUREN), 2001: EXHIBITING A STAR'S TALENTS

Tian Mansha, the principal performer of *Lady Macbeth* as well as the adapter and director, is an artist in *chuanju* (literally: the drama of the Sichuan area), a centuries-old genre in southwestern China.

42 I saw the play in London at the Royal National Theatre in November 1990 and interviewed Lin.

43 The translation is based on the script kindly offered to me by Wu Hsing-Kuo and his Contemporary Legend Theatre.

8 The coronation scene in *Lady Macbeth* (2001).

For reasons of geography and dialect, the cultures that developed in this region were quite distinct from the dominant culture originating around the Yellow River and the Central Plains. Whereas traditional theatres in most of China have been facing problems of declining audiences since the mid-1980s, *chuanju* has retained its popularity in its heartland.

The fifty-minute presentation of *Lady Macbeth* was virtually a solo performance, although Macbeth and attending ladies also appeared. The ladies created a court atmosphere and, at a practical level, they helped Lady Macbeth change costumes on-stage. For the 'hand-washing' scene, twelve attendants were choreographed to form the outline of three big washing bowls. Using different arrangements and stage blocking for each group, interweaved with Lady Macbeth's hand-washing dance, Tian generated a beautiful scene. Macbeth was a non-speaking part, and the conversation between the couple was understood from Lady Macbeth's replies. For example, Lady Macbeth says: 'Oh, you met the spirit on your way home.'[44] Then the next line is: 'Don't believe any spirit. What it said is in fact what you have thought to yourself!'

The performance provided an excellent display of Tian's unique skills in singing, reciting, acting, dancing and acrobatics. As an actress, Tian was attracted to the broad scope of the psychology and the different facets of the character that Shakespeare's Lady Macbeth afforded. Moreover, not unlike the artists in other *Macbeth* adaptations, Tian used the production to develop her own career and skills by borrowing and absorbing techniques from other role-types and theatrical genres. Not only has this added to her personal reputation as an

[44] The translation is based on a transcript from the videotape kindly supplied by Renate Heitmann, Bremer Shakespeare Company, Germany.

actress, but it also promoted *chuanju* as a theatrical genre. Indeed, media attention and controversy has surrounded Tian since 1993 when she organized the first private *chuanju* theatre in Chengdu, the capital city of Sichuan province, and performed in a four-star hotel. On one side she was accused of being greedy by raking in money from foreign tourists, on the other she was praised for her boldness and innovation in attracting new audiences to her traditional theatre. In 1995, she personally bought the copyright of a spoken drama script *Ripples in the Stagnant Water* (*si shui wei lan*)[45] direct from the playwright, bypassing the official channels and again subverting the Communist ideology of value, organization and regulation. Yet its *chuanju* premiere won Tian the 'Plum Blossom Award', which is the highest national award in the traditional theatrical circles.

Tian Mansha's production, *Lady Macbeth*, took as its starting point the final appearance of the character in Shakespeare's original play, opening with her mad scene and ending with her death. The performance began in darkness. A spotlight picked out a white object at the centre of the stage. Suddenly, without musical accompaniment, an extremely high-pitched female voice could be heard singing: 'Oh, the enormous palace! The pitch-dark night! The ominous dream!' This shriek, followed by silence, accentuated the mysterious and menacing atmosphere in the auditorium. Then, with two sharp beats from the percussion, the lighting came on and immediately Lady Macbeth jumped up wearing a white dress, half-covered by a light purple coloured gown, which is the conventional style of costume signifying a person in a mad state. Her hair was also unkempt. 'Who is at the gate?' No answer. 'Who is knocking at the door?' she repeated three times. Her sleeves were unusually long, about three feet each, and as she swirled, her whole body appeared wrapped under the white and purple sleeves. 'The ghost is coming. The spirit is coming!' She turned her head quickly and her long tousled hair traced a circle through the air. Following her thought, the performance then flashed back to the scenes preceding the assassination.

In this production, the assassination was completed by Lady Macbeth after she had taunted her husband: 'What? Not dead yet? . . . You cannot do it again?! You coward! Go away and stand there. Let your wife add one more thrust for you.' Tian arranged three attempts to stab the emperor. After the first hesitation, Lady Macbeth rushed to the left side of the stage as if the emperor were lying behind the side curtains. She raised her broadsword high above her head, but suddenly stopped. She was frozen, and the female chorus interjected 'Oh, no, it's wrong.'

Very few forms of local theatre include a chorus, but it plays an important role in *chuanju*. The chorus has different functions depending on the precise circumstances, and it can give comments, asides, or represent a voice from the inmost core of the character. Throwing down her sword, Lady Macbeth sang:

> The wounded old man is groaning.
> His white hair and wrinkled face just look like my father.
> Blood is spurting out, flowing in front of my eyes.
> My father is injured, and I, his daughter, am taking his life.
> The scene is too horrid to look at.
> It is the feeling between bone and flesh that has made my heart . . .
> CHORUS That has made my heart, my heart . . .
> LADY MACBETH *Walks towards the left-side curtains.* Father! *Suddenly awake.* He is not my father. He is the emperor.

To recover her determination, she recapitulated the reasons to kill the old man: 'For my husband. He wants to be the emperor. So we must give him another thrust!' Having steeled herself mentally and physically, Lady Macbeth grasped the broadsword, jumped into the air, swirled, then knelt down to pray to heaven to give her courage, before finally proceeding to the killing.

[45] The play concerns the impact of the economic reforms on the lives of local peasants.

The above scene illustrates some aspects of the appropriation. On the structural level, it switches the focus of the play. On the acting level, the creation of the three attempts before the final stabbing points to the aesthetic ideation of the indigenous Chinese performing system. As seen in the other two adaptations, Chinese music theatre is not concerned with offering audiences an illusion of realism. The emphasis is laid on the expression of a character's inner world and the display of the performer's unique skills.

Presenting 'guilt that arises as a consequence of the struggle for power',[46] *Lady Macbeth* is a short, violent and tense production. It is fascinating to compare the reactions this adaptation has aroused. John Russell Brown,[47] having seen it performed at the Shakespeare festival in Bremen in 2001, strongly recommended it at the conference on 'Shakespeare Performance in the New Asias' (held in Singapore, 2002). Conversely, Wei Minglun, a *chuanju* playwright who has contributed greatly to contemporary Chinese theatre since the end of the Cultural Revolution, did not think this was a good approach to presenting Shakespeare on the Chinese stage. 'I can only see Tian Mansha, but no Shakespeare', Wei commented, and concluded that if Shakespeare is adapted in this way, he will cease to have any interest.[48] Such contrasting responses from different cultural perspectives point to an essential question of what and whom Shakespeare is for. As a Western Shakespearian, Professor Brown is intrigued by any unique interpretation of a Shakespeare play, whereas Wei, a Chinese playwright with less opportunity to become familiar with Shakespeare's works, may view the pursuit of novelty in such productions as diminishing and trivializing the experience of seeing the play. This is an issue practitioners of intercultural theatre need to ponder over.

Inspired by Shakespeare's lines, the Chinese appearance of Macbeth is always associated with a heavy drum. The four productions considered in this article illustrate a diversity of approaches to the interpretation and presentation of *Macbeth*. As China continues its increasingly rapid transition towards an uncertain future, we can anticipate that in any further staging of *Macbeth* the beat of the drum will be different again.

---

46 *Shakespeare aus Asien, Ein Theaterfestival 2001*, translated by Heidi Frances.

47 It was Professor Brown who told me of this production which he saw in Bremen. I am most grateful to him for giving me the contact information.

48 Quoted from a telephone conversation in September 2002.

THE BANQUET OF SCOTLAND (PA)

LAUREN SHOHET

he is full so valiant,
And in his commendations I am fed;
It is a banquet to me . . . (*Macbeth* 1.4.56–8)

Commending the victorious Macbeth with these lines, King Duncan sets up a model of mutual nourishment between lord and vassal, between political father and son. Duncan's praise is commodiously ambiguous, potentially pointing both to other thanes' reports of Macbeth's valour as nourishment for Duncan and to Duncan's advancement of Macbeth as itself a source of nourishment: by praising *him*, *I* am fed; *his* valour and *my* remarking that valour constitute the *mise en place* for concocting the comedic feast of successful community. 'Banquet' evokes both social and natural, both festive celebration and quotidian requirement. Being 'fed' – here in provocatively passive construction – also signals the way that food functions as a liminal substance that is both part and not part of the individual who ingests it, the way eating enacts both agency (the eater masticating, consuming, metabolizing the foodstuff) and dependence (without sustenance, no agent survives). All these resonances accrue to the dramatic logic of food as a leitmotif in *Macbeth*.

Billy Morissette's film *Scotland, PA* (premiered at the 2001 Sundance festival and commercially released by Lot 47 films in 2002) playfully literalizes Duncan's 'banquet', exploring these questions of agency and identity in the context of depressed – if officially only 'recessed' – 1970s rural America. This black comedy, Morissette's first feature film, offers a surprisingly detailed and nuanced set of ways to think about identity and agency in both *Macbeth* and the 1970s. Setting *Macbeth* in a greasy spoon, *Scotland, PA* makes burgers the foundation of Joe McBeth's ('Mac's') grab for power; the advent of the drive-through service window is here the opportunity that catalyzes Mac's, and particularly his wife Pat's, ambition. Mac (James LeGros) and Pat (Maura Tierney) are former high-school sweethearts, in their thirties and still passionately in love at the time of the film, who work as a line cook and a waitress in the drab local eatery, 'Duncan's', whose dull, prosperous and well-meaning proprietor (James Rebhorn) seems invested in keeping the diner as staid as possible. When the restaurant's manager is revealed as an embezzler, Norm Duncan elevates his elder son Malcolm (Tom Guiry) to the title, promoting Mac only to Assistant Manager, although neither the aspiring rock musician Malcolm nor his younger, tentatively gay brother Donald (Geoff Dunsworth) has any interest in the business.

Upon Mac's ascension, Duncan confides an astonishing innovation he plans for the restaurant: a drive-through service window. This vision is not so novel for Mac, however, because the three stoned hippies (Andy Dick, Timothy Speed Levitch and Amy Smart) who frequent a local carnival have predicted it to him privately. Pat and Mac murder Duncan in a deep-fat fryer, buy the restaurant with funds stolen from Duncan's safe, open

My thanks to Katherine Rowe, Scott Black, Laura McGrane, Edmund Campos, Jane Hedley and participants in the 'Shakespeare and the Movies' seminar at the 2003 SAA meeting for helpful comments on earlier drafts of this essay.

the drive-through themselves, and luxuriate in the fruits of their prosperity until police lieutenant Ernie McDuff (Christopher Walken) is called in to help local law enforcement investigate the murder. With quirky, indeterminably strategic oddity, McDuff puts increasing pressure on the McBeths, leading Mac to murder potential witnesses, including his friend Banco (Kevin Corrigan). As Mac becomes more brutal, Pat succumbs to hallucinations of a severe grease burn on her hand, and their good fortune collapses when the ghost of Banco appears to Mac during the local television station's filming of a story on their drive-through. Mac lures McDuff to a final confrontation on the restaurant roof, which culminates in Mac's being fatally impaled on the longhorns mounted on the front of his car. Pat kills herself by cutting off her offending hand. The film is equally saturated by thoroughgoing engagement with details of the Shakespearian text and with textures of the 1970s: Bad Company songs, white lipstick, polyester prints, large jewelry, domestic wall murals, marijuana haze, rural unemployment.

Since the 1970s were the time when fast food permeated fully into the more remote areas of the US – with an enormous range of consequences, as Eric Schlosser's *Fast Food Nation* has recently brought to popular attention – the crisis instigated by Scotland's new drive-through offers a window into larger American issues of the decade.[1] With fast food comes a new commodification of the 'eating experience', a homogenization of locales that both en-franchises and erases them, a transformation of individuals into consumers. In *Scotland, PA*, the witches' prophecy upon their first encounter with Mac wonderfully encapsulates these transactions, evoking the commodification of food when the fortune-teller momentarily mistakes her vision of the restaurant drive-through for a bank window ('a bank . . . for food?'), signalling the permeation and erasure of locale when the witches, intoning Dave Banconi's nickname 'Banco', puzzle 'A Spanish bank?' only to discern eventually that there's nothing Spanish at stake, and pointing up how individuals flatten into cashpoints when the witches misrecognize Banco's personal name for the word 'bank'. The 1970s are also, of course, the era of Watergate, of Vietnam, of cultural confrontation between 'square' inheritors of the 1950s and 'hip' heirs of the 1960s. *Scotland, PA*, I shall show, illuminates how these phenomena come together to make agency – what Lady Macbeth would call 'acting like a man' – fraught to the point of impossibility.

Exploring the ways *Scotland, PA* figures agency, which it often undertakes through relation to *Macbeth*'s models, unfolds both what the 1970s can offer as a setting for *Macbeth*, and what the play can offer as a lens for thinking about the decade. Both film and play mine ways that spectacle and patrimony provide rich grounds for negotiating what counts as agency: for whether and how individuals can effectively act. Reading the film against the play reveals just how dark *Scotland, PA*'s vision of the possibilities for individual action is; reading the play against the film reveals just how intelligent – if far from pious – a take on *Macbeth Scotland, PA* offers. *Macbeth* is a play that ponders the origins of action: do the witches foresee or instigate? Do they corrupt the valiant or are they drawn to a target predisposed to err? Once the prophecy is spoken, how much responsibility for his ensuing actions can Macbeth deflect onto it? How much culpability accrues to Lady Macbeth's urging Duncan's murder, how much to Macbeth's executing it? In *Scotland, PA* characters explicitly argue about the fraught ambiguities of what agents know, do not know, prefer not to know, of their own intentions. The McBeths plan Duncan's murder the evening after Mac accidentally knocks Duncan unconscious with a refrigerator door. Driving home from work, Pat exults to Mac, 'It was like I could read your mind in there . . . I knew exactly what you were thinking'; when Mac demurs '*I* didn't know what I was thinking', Pat remonstrates 'Mac, look at me. Yes, you did. You *did*.' Later in the film, as Mac secretly begins planning Banco's murder and Pat begs, 'Mac! What are you doing? You have to tell

---

1 Eric Schlosser, *Fast Food Nation: The Dark Side of the All-American Meal* (New York, 2001).

me what you're doing!' Mac erupts, 'I don't know! It's a surprise.' In such scenes that draw together how characters in both 1970s movies and Jacobean tragedy avoid confronting their choices, *Scotland, PA* lets us consider how well Harry Berger's remark that *Macbeth* 'dramatiz[es] failures or evasions of responsibility correlated with problematic structural tendencies that *seem* benign because it is in the interest of self-deceiving characters to view them that way' might gloss Richard Nixon's brilliantly passive gloss on Watergate, 'mistakes were made'; how well it might gloss Lyndon Johnson's strategically mystifying Vietnam policy of 'peace with honor'.[2]

Scotland, PA moves food from the margins to the centre of the drama. Mac's ambition first shows itself when, leaving his grill, he vaults o'erleaping the service counter to rout unruly thanes engaged in a food fight in one of the best glosses on 'minion' ever dramatized: the fortuitous opportunity shows Mac as fortune's darling, perhaps, but also stages his subservience to facilitating the post-game restaurant rush that benefits the boss and the customers, never the line cook. The film transliterates the play's negotiations of Scottish and English power into negotiations between carnivorous and vegetarian culture. Just as *Macbeth* imagines remedy 'from gracious England' (4.3.44) for Scotland's 'nation miserable / With an untitled tyrant bloody-sceptered' (4.3.104–5), so too does *Scotland, PA* bring in an outsider police lieutenant McDuff to investigate Duncan's murder. What the play figures as English, the film makes 1970s downmarket urbane: McDuff arrives in town as a vegetarian, in a beige suit, bearing a plate of baba ghanouj to Duncan's wake and driving an olive-green Audi filled with transcendental meditation tapes.[3] By contrast, the forlornly, claustrophobically backwater Scotland socializes over burgers and its men hunt deer. Mac draws attention to diet as the figure for cultural difference in his penultimate confrontation with McDuff after Banco's murder, asking nastily whether McDuff is 'gracing our home with a vegetable dish' upon this occasion (as he had at Duncan's wake) as a sign of 'how the better half lives'.

The divide between the 'better' and lesser 'halves' is rigidly confining, in no way altered by the amelioration in individuals' local circumstances offered by the successful drive-through. In Mac and Pat McBeths' moment of ascendancy, they make over Duncan's staid restaurant into the cheerfully gaudy formica McBeth's. This brings happy crowds to the restaurant, and the newly prosperous McBeths move from a trailer to a ranch house. They cast their lot with meat, seizing a chance to improve themselves within the rural/carnivorous gestalt, but the McBeths' grab for agency is circumscribed by their apparent inability to escape their town. Although there are no clear financial or family barriers to their leaving Scotland after stealing money from Duncan's safe, their agency seems limited to becoming the bosses of the pre-existing business, not leaving the system entirely. The film emphasizes this systemic continuity when lowly restaurant employee Robert/Richard (Pat cannot remember his name) gives Pat the finger in a scene that mirrors her earlier response to her erstwhile manager. Escape seems out of the question, despite Pat's complaints about Scotland's limitations ('this town is too fucking small') – limitations emphasized by soundtrack selections invoking a larger world, as when Pat resolves upon suicide to the Three Dog Night track 'Never been to Spain'.

Although the McBeths seem firmly trapped in the 'Scottish half', the sociocultural divisions figured by vegetarianism, particularly the fantasies McDuff projects onto Scotland, are complex. Just

---

[2] Berger, '*Macbeth*: Preface to a New Interpretation', *ELH*, 47 (1980), 1–31; p. 3.

[3] My term 'English' here somewhat oversimplifies Jacobean distinctions among already Anglicized, potentially civilizable, and intractably barbarian (northern) Scots; the play allies actual English and the first category of Scots. See Mary Floyd-Wilson, *English Ethnicity and Race in Early Modern Drama* (Cambridge, 2003); Arthur Kinney, 'Scottish History, the Union of the Crowns, and the Issue of Right Rule: The Case of Shakespeare's Macbeth', in *Renaissance Culture in Context: Theory and Practice*, eds. J. R. Brink and William Gentrup (Aldershot, 1993); and Kinney, 'Shakespeare's Macbeth and the Question of Nationalism', in *Literature and Nationalism*, eds. Vincent Newey and Ann Thompson (Liverpool, 1991).

as the politics of ethnicity are not straightforward in early Jacobean England, where a newly Scottish court intersects with English traditions casting Scots as barbarians, the politics of diet are not entirely straightforward in Scotland, PA. McDuff is firmly vegetarian ('oh yes, the whole family') and jokes about greasy food killing Duncan's/McBeth's customers. But McDuff's vegetarianism does not offer any clear-cut positive alternative to the problems of Scotland. McDuff misperceives Scotland as pastoral, or perhaps more properly georgic, romanticizing the capacity of Scotland's restaurant to nurture its citizens ('do not underestimate what you do, sir! Workin' the grill, fryin' the fries, feeding hungry people'). He demonstrates an hilarious fascination with the workings of the restaurant whenever his investigations take him there, cooking an order on the line and puzzling over Mac's innovations (' "French . . . fry . . . truck": is that right?'). McDuff is bemused by the apparent warmth of Scotland's community: for instance, witnesses hug him after he interviews them in his murder investigation. The viewer, however, knows that this apparent sincerity is an effect brought about by layers of confused imitation: the first witness hugs McDuff in gratitude for the lieutenant's willingness to conceal the witness's adultery, then other witnesses assume this to be 'standard procedure', as the jaded waitress Mrs. Lennox drawls. Not genuine connection, but something like its opposite – serial imitation based on collusion to conceal betrayal – underlies this emergent 'ritual'. The uncogency of McDuff's misrecognition of Scotland becomes clearer when he comes to inherit the restaurant and the film's final shot shows him standing in a stylized Birnham-Woods apron covered with tiny trees, holding a carrot, in an empty parking lot that we know never will be filled by Scotland customers hankering after a 'garden burger'. That final scene closes with a streaker flashing past McDuff, the 1970s leaving the McDuff who seemed so effective in his professional capacity ludicrous, isolated and befuddled when he seeks to fulfill his own dream.

The final scenes of both *Macbeth* and *Scotland, PA* depict what remains when the toil and trouble's done; *Macbeth*'s counterpart to McDuff's vigil on the asphalt of his newly acquired restaurant is Malcolm inviting the assembly 'to see us crowned at Scone' (5.11.41). Indeed, *Macbeth* might be read in broader terms as a play about what survives: what remains of political order after catastrophic disruption; what remains of prophecy (or suggestion or curse) after the forecasting apparitions vanish; what remains of folk drama and ritual into the Renaissance; what remains of morality plays upon the Shakespearian stage. In *Macbeth*, Malcolm's survival and return to claim his rightful throne affirm dramatic catharsis and political hope.

Scotland, PA is likewise intrigued by questions of remains; less solemn than *Macbeth*, *Scotland PA*'s primary kind of 'remain' is the leftover. With an a-posteriori gesture befitting a remake, the film's first two scenes open with leftovers. In the first, seated on an after-hours Ferris wheel (as wheel of fortune), the pothead witches accidentally drop their bag of leftover chicken. A dead bird dropping from the sky, their fried chicken echoes evil omens (the ritual remains of Rome, the dramatic remains of *Macbeth*). Furthermore, this moment serves as a pretext to cite the pre-text: 'the fowl was fair', bemoan the witches upon its loss, in a giggly, stoned riff on 'fair' and 'foul' that opens *Scotland, PA* with what remains of another play. Equally understated, and just as provocative, is the opening shot of the film's second scene, inside Duncan's diner. This begins with tight focus on a half-eaten burger; into the frame then comes the waitress's hand, which we watch clearing the tray. (Thus the first two scenes bring into the frame the two major fast-food products of the early franchise era: fried chicken and burgers.) As she takes it to the kitchen, the waitress (who later shows herself to be both self-righteously judgemental in condemning Malcolm and hypocritically light-fingered in stealing the restaurant's paper products) furtively takes a bite of the leftover meat. Satisfyingly disgusting, this image offers a ripe figure for intertextual borrowing, for what it means for a text to avail itself of sources. The snatched gulp of pre-possessed meat is unhygienic, cheap, aesthetically unpleasing – but this is how *Macbeth* can be chewed over.

Like the waitress nibbling the leftover burger, *Scotland, PA* invokes its sources, which extend well beyond *Macbeth*, as a not-fully-integrated series of borrowings that enable both formal and psychological response. Concurring with Lady Macbeth's 'when you durst do it, then you were a man' (1.7.49), *Scotland, PA* links problems of agency with problems of masculinity. By inundating the viewer with diverse spectacles of masculinity that wonder what it is to be a man (an undrafted man, at that) in a depressed coal valley in the era of Vietnam, the film emphasizes questions of modelling, of theatricality, and of imitation within the rubric of 'acting as a man' – what Macbeth with rich ambiguity calls 'do[ing] all that may *become* a man' (1.7.46, emphasis added). Serial, fragmentary images create a pastiche of manhood: Duncan's assertion 'every young man likes [American] football' cuts to the posters of Joe Namath and Liza Minelli, followed by Superman shirts and Mark Spitz fitness videos, that mark a campily gay sensibility. The adulterous local tanning-salon operator offers one, 'swinging', model of fulfilment (open Hawaiian shirt, sideburns, necklace); Donald and his boyfriend Tommy's quiet suaveness, in matching crimson silk bathrobes, another.

Spectacles of masculinity in *Scotland, PA* intercut citation with action that tries (and fails) to imitate it. Perhaps most prominently, clips from the television detective show *McCloud* bracket the film's action with their image of an impossibly effectual good detective. Immediately after the opening shots of the Ferris wheel, *Scotland, PA* cuts to a *McCloud* clip that shows the detective dangling from a helicopter, sustaining the dizzying height that Mac will not, before riding the vehicle back to earth and forcing the bad guy to surrender with a gesture that Mac precisely recapitulates when he feigns surrender to McDuff at the end of the film. During the investigation, the hapless local police officer watches *McCloud* in the station, unable to drag his eyes away from the episode in order to talk with an informant, too absorbed by the didactic *image* of effective policing to *act* as a police officer. Other sources are offered more allusively or fragmentarily. McDuff's character evokes the television detective Columbo as much as it does McCloud: McDuff's apparent (or genuine?) digressiveness, his allusions to a never-seen wife and family, his eventual success in solving his case all echo Columbo. In another example unavailable to characters, but very present for viewers, several hunting and drinking scenes allude to Michael Cimino's 1978 film *Deer Hunter* – a film similarly set in depressed 1970s western Pennsylvania, a film for which the same actor who here plays McDuff, Christopher Walken, won an Oscar. Such borrowing from other texts not only produces the formal texture of the film but also defines affective and psychological response: affect here originates in outside sources. When Banco offers Mac the information required to begin Mac's advancement at the restaurant, for instance, Mac's decision to take his fate into his own hands is accompanied by his pointedly crossing the room (of the local bar 'The Witches' Brew') and kicking the jukebox, which changes the soundtrack to Bad Company's 'Bad Company'.

The relationship between *Scotland, PA* and the various images, sounds and genres it cites underscores the affective and psychological vacuum its characters experience. Most pointedly unavailable, and most longingly sought, are workable ways to define 1970s masculinity. Columbo is inimitably enigmatic; McCloud is impossibly effective. Whereas the deer hunters in *Deer Hunter* are variously emasculated by having gone or not gone to Vietnam, the deer hunters in *Scotland, PA* seem to have merely failed at life (despite bagging a doe). The photo of Nixon, on the wall behind McDuff in the big-city-police-station interview scene that turns the murder investigation in the right direction, provides a backdrop of corrupt political order. The film's pointedly ethical character, Officer Ed (so reluctant to open a letter addressed to another, even when instructed to do so by the addressee, that he pulls the shades before complying), is professionally incompetent. Malcolm pursues his dream of touring with a rock band but is booked only at forlorn strip clubs; Donald seems admirably ungrasping (and generously nurturing with his fondue), but withdrawn to the point of apathy from the world beyond his house ('we're rich, right? Then I don't care'). McDuff is professionally effective but otherwise hapless. Unlike Macbeth, Mac seems to have no legitimate options at all for advancing himself: where King Duncan 'plants' Macbeth, Norm Duncan insultingly makes Mac *assistant* manager, subordinated to Duncan's disinterested teenaged son. There are no models to be found here.

Both *Scotland, PA* and *Macbeth* figure effective action as paternal, and both show how cultures can use father figures to imagine ways of acting in the world. Like *Macbeth*, *Scotland, PA* depicts a culture yearning for fathers while killing off the ones it has. *Macbeth* draws upon James I's iconography of himself as the 'nursing father' of *Ecclesiastes* in its portrayal of Duncan as the head of the political order desired by nature, as the paternal source of bounty for his subjects ('I have begun to plant thee, and will labour / To make thee full of growing' (1.4.28–9), Duncan tells Macbeth), and as the image of Lady Macbeth's own father (2.2.12–13).[4] Once Macbeth slays his political benefactor, of course, all of nature runs backwards, and Macbeth himself works as the opposite of a nurturing father, the 'butcher' of Scotland (5.11.35) who recounts a ghostly masque vision of himself with 'a fruitless crown, / And . . . barren sceptre in my grip, / Thence to be wrenched with an unlineal hand, / No son of mine succeeding' (3.1.62–5). *Macbeth* is not prodigal of good and effective fathers: the benevolent Duncan and Banquo both are killed, while conflicting duties tear Macduff from his family and earn him the teasing but evocative name of 'traitor' from his wife (4.2.46). Siward's Stoic reception of news that his son is dead ('Had I as many sons as I have hairs, / I would not wish them to a fairer death' (5.11.14–15)) might raise some questions about his paternal commitments as well. Effective fathers await the fulfilment of Banquo's masque of lineage, presumably, not to appear until 1603. Until then, the play has no wellspring of paternal authority once Duncan is dispatched, and seekers must flutter unsatisfied from England back to Scotland, from the future (the masque of Banquo's heirs) to the present, from the military to the domestic (Macduff).

Scotland, PA seeks effective fathers at least as intensely as *Macbeth*, and the ambivalence of its conclusions echoes a larger ambivalence in the patrimony of the 1970s. Characters seek fathers both explicitly and in the film's broader explorations of paternal models of agency. McDuff comes into town as a good father – the competent and effectual detective who throws into relief the patricidal turpitude (the McBeths) and unintentionally complicit incompetence (Officer Ed) of Scotland. As the investigation draws to a close, both Mac and Ed explicitly remark upon McDuff's paternal qualities. Mac chooses Tab as a mixer for his bourbon with the snide remark that he wants to 'eat healthy' 'like big Daddy McDuff and all the little McDuffs'; Officer Ed, queried whether he finds McDuff 'pushy', forlornly remarks that McDuff (who protectively does not allow Ed to keep real bullets in his gun) is 'really nice; I kind of wish he would always be around'. Images of fathers and children play out in the margins of many of the films most important scenes. In the peripeteian scene where the First Class track 'Beach Baby' undergirds both the McBeths' exulting in their successful reinvention of the restaurant and McDuff's ominous appearance to reopen investigation of Duncan's murder, the camera pans past the first witness's carbon-copy son (a tanned, Hawaiian-shirted, mini-Burt Lancaster) on its way to the interview. McLeary's children play with and around Banco's shrouded corpse as it is removed from the garage where Mac murdered his friend; furthermore, evoking MacDuff's vulnerable progeny of 'pretty chickens' (4.3.219), Ed changes his order from a burger to 'little chicken McBeths' when he arrives at the restaurant the night of Mac's death.

Most chilling, perhaps, is the paternal dimension of Mac's transformation from erotically passionate if economically under-achieving companionate husband to a 'father' who is powerful but brutal.

[4] On Duncan's nurturing qualities, see Janet Adelman, *Suffocating Mothers: Fantasies of Maternal Origin in Shakespeare's Plays, 'Hamlet' to 'The Tempest'* (New York, 1992); on James I and images of paternal nurture, see Elizabeth Spiller, 'The Counsel of Fulke Greville: Transforming the Jacobean "Nourish Father" through Sidney's "Nursing Father" ', *Studies in Philology*, 97 (2000), 433–53.

The film's seeds of action are planted when, in Mac's first encounter with the witches, the female witch urges, 'Screw management! You can do better. Don't you think you deserve better? Don't you think . . . [Mac's own voice suddenly coming out of the witch's mouth] *she* deserves better?' Mac does come to provide better for Pat, but the frighteningly paternalist dimensions of this emerge three murders later, when Mac, believing he receives further instructions from the witches via a ringing phone that Pat cannot hear, abruptly departs without answering Pat's questions about his plans. He promises, 'Everything's going to be all right. I'm going to take care of *everything*, Pat. I'm going to take care of *you*!' Pat recoils, and the ambiguity about whether her horror indicates that Mac's 'taking care' of Pat refers to his seizing the directive role she always has played in their marriage (the interpretation offered in the director's DVD commentary) or whether 'taking care' of business here has an ominously gangland ring signals how dangerous paternalistic agency can be.

Other invocations of father figures in *Scotland, PA* are mediated by formal and generic shifts, reminding us that 'fathers' are image as much as flesh. Dropping the inaudible 'a' from 'Mac' to make 'Mc' telegraphs how consumer culture replaces the patronymic prefix with a branding prefix: 'Macbeths' and 'Macduffs' become McMeals and McProducts – without even a ripple in the surface of pronunciation. The ineffectualness of paternal inheritance in *Scotland, PA* evokes the cultural crisis of the 1970s: what, if anything, will America take forward from previous generations? Duncan's own sons do not want the restaurant; the McBeths are patricides; McDuff's garden burgers will find no custom. In *Macbeth*, the failure of paternal inheritance internal to the play can serve to affirm James I, Banquo's descendant, as a resolution to the problem. It's worth remarking, though, that even in *Macbeth* this is shown as distant and mediated. The vision of lineal descent comes in a masque, drawing attention to the importance of formal representation in 'naturalizing' political inheritance, and only Macbeth even witnesses the spectacle. The film's quite nuanced version of the masque of Banquo's heirs suggests the even greater tenuousness of inheritance – is there anything worth inheriting in, or from, the 1970s? – in *Scotland, PA*. The movie's inheritance masque is fragmented and subtle. In an aside, early in the film, the stoned witches call out 'Anthony! Anthony!' and then, upon establishing that Mac's friend Dave Banconi is called 'Banco', one witch remarks 'sounds Italian'. Halfway through the film, the source of the witches' citation comes on the television Mac is watching in the McBeths' new ranch house: a commercial that opens with a mother calling 'Anthony! Anthony!' out her apartment window to bring her son in for lunch. The commercial voiceover sets the scene 'in Boston's Italian North End, home of the Prince [n.b.] Spaghetti Company'. This has the same effect as the masque in *Macbeth*: soon after watching the commercial, Mac remarks to Pat, 'Banco's a problem'. Lineage is here attenuated to the word 'prince'; dynasty attenuated to corporation; ethnic inheritance attenuated to a marketing device (for food, no less).

As the brief television image of Anthony's mother offering spaghetti perhaps highlights through contrast, maternal nourishment is even less effective in *Scotland, PA* than paternal succour. In the film's first scene in the diner, the sound fades in to the corrupt manager Douglas McKenna drilling Pat in making soft-serve ice cream cones: 'The tip of that mountain's going to go right into our customer's mouth, and make him happy.' Called to 'get out here, and have a look at your wife's beautiful cones' after Pat's thirteenth try, Mac deadpans, 'I love your cones, baby.' McKenna's leering at Pat's breasts in the next diner scene consolidates the cones' figuration as breasts, offering the soft-serve cone as Pat's counter gesture to Lady Macbeth's 'I have given suck' (1.7.54). But where Lady Macbeth once offered maternal milk from her own body, Pat provides only the frozen, vastly artificial concoction of soft-serve from a metal nozzle. The next scene, at the Scotland football game, shows another woman ineffectively staffing a dairy dispenser: the heavily made-up Joan, who sighs that Malcolm 'is just crying out for a new Momma'. Delighted to serve Duncan, Joan tears up when her cocoa dispenser proves empty and she cannot fulfil his request ('Damn this cocoa! *Damn* this cocoa! We're out of cocoa, Norm'). As in the play, Pat is the only female character to get any substantial screen time; as for bit parts, *Scotland, PA* offers no counterpart to Lady Macduff. The other women, briefly glimpsed, pointedly fail to nourish: Peg the nurse abandons her shift at the hospital to play Yahtzee; the stripper at the Atlantic City club where Malcolm's band plays offers the most sterile model of sexuality; the Statue of Liberty statuette incongruously trotted out for the drive-through celebration reveals just how cynically the US invokes its symbols ('just put the bitch in the corner, guys'). Mrs McDuff sends baba ghanouj but is never seen; the sad, passive, alcoholic Pat Nixon is perhaps evoked in Pat McBeth's first name and her martini-soaked silent vigils late in the film. Mothers provide no more hope here than fathers do.

Scotland, PA's characters experience the difficulty of either articulating identity or acting effectively in a depressed rural economy, in a strongly patriarchal nation corrupt at the top, during the selective service draft, as the McDonalds spread across the land. No wonder the witches have the munchies. They are hungry for action, but caught – like the film's human characters – between eras. ('I know! Mac should kill McDuff's entire family!' proposes one witch; 'Oh that'd work great! . . . about a thousand years ago', sneers another.) *Scotland, PA*'s witches share with *Macbeth*'s a somewhat ambiguous ontological status that arguments the blurriness of agency and instigation in the texts. *Macbeth* lets us ask to what extent the witches direct intention and to what extent they reflect it. Similarly, *Scotland, PA*'s witches have access to knowledge beyond Mac's horizons, indicating that they are not mere displacements of his psyche, but the film queries the extent to which the witches project Mac's desires when the female witch sometimes speaks in Mac's voice. The first encounter between Mac and the witches dramatizes the slipperiness with which characters flip-flop recognition and precognition. Two of the witches hail Mac from behind a carnival screen with fragments of his name – fragments that also draw attention to the linguistic play of prefix that acquires such import in a film about failed patrimony and all-too-successful commercialization – 'Mac!' 'Beth!' 'Beth!' 'Mac!' 'Mac!' 'Fleetwood Mac!' 'Macramé!' When Mac asks how they know his name, the witches exclaim 'you mean your name really is Mac? I thought we were just saying it like you say it . . . like "Watch your step, Mac!", "Up yours, Mac!", "Fuck you, Mac!".' Like Macbeth, Mac seems to have been all too easily interpellated by a hail he need not have embraced; at the same time, the witches' disclaimer of foreknowledge is disingenuous insofar as 'Beth' was indeed part of their initial appeal for Mac's attention.

In both film and play, the witches' relationship to characters' actions is only a small part of the complexity surrounding characters' relationship to their *own* actions: the problem of where action comes from. Indeed, Macbeth and Lady Macbeth consistently mystify questions of agency. Upon conceiving his first nefarious act, murdering the Prince of Cumberland, Macbeth intones 'Let not light see my black and deep desires; / The eye wink at the hand; yet let that be / Which the eye fears, when it is done, to see' (1.4.53–5). The 'winking' eye both sees and does not see, perceives what is seen and unseen, seen in fragments, uncannily perceived through Banco's thick dirty glasses, chattered over through the witches' haze of marijuana smoke. Furthermore, divorcing the eye and hand to worry about whether the *tool* knows what it is doing (here, the metonymic hand; later, Lady Macbeth's invoking hell smoke 'that my keen knife see not the wound it makes' (1.5.51)), these characters strategically beg the question of agency – whether *they* know what they are doing.

The liminality of the hand – as Marx notes, part of the body, but the part that grasps external tools, a prosthetic link, inscribed by culture as much as nature – makes it a rich figure for thinking through complexities of agency. What the eye winks at in *Macbeth* is the hand, and *Scotland, PA* makes full use of the ambiguities about agency internal to this corporeal figure in addition to the ambiguities in the relation between hand and eye. In *Macbeth*, of course, the hand serves as central site for the expression of the repressed: after the deeds have been executed that the eye was to wink upon, Lady Macbeth's 'damned spot' appears upon her hand (although, winkingly, only to her). *Scotland, PA* makes Lady Macbeth's spot more prominent, and draws out the ambivalent agency of the hand, when Pat redresses her spectral burn by fatally chopping off her own hand. When one of her hands seizes a cleaver to chop off her other hand, clad in a Scottish plaid potholder, upon a cutting board, the potholder emphasizes the hand's potential to grasp at the same time that the cutting board emphasizes its disintegration from the body. Inter-cut with the scene of Pat (clad in Birnham-woods-print polyester) chopping off her own hand is the scene of Mac (clad in damned polka dots) attempting to choke McDuff with a burger – an effort foreclosed by McDuff biting Mac's hand. Both Pat's hand on the cutting board and Mac's hand in McDuff's teeth emphasize flesh as mere foodstuff, the opposite of corporeal agency. Moreover, these hands recall the prominent shots of Duncan's tied hands hanging out of the fryer upon his murder. Stretching one's grasp in this film – exercising agency to open a drive-through window, to become more than assistant manager – turns the member that grasped into mere mortal meat.

Indeed, the film's final shots of both Mac and Pat show only their hands. Pat's severed hand on the cutting board is grotesquely large because of its potholder, evoking her overreaching grasp. The final view of Mac shows only his hand sticking out of the blanket that covers his corpse, propped upon the longhorn welded to the front of his car. Thereby Mac's grasp at the burger empire concludes supported by an animal part that is not even food but rather stylized decoration, ludicrously dated. This offers far less hope than what even bloodily butchered Scotland, UK offers Malcolm in *Macbeth*. In the play, Malcolm attests that when he comes to assert his inherited privilege of rule, 'I think withal / There would be hands uplifted in my right' (4.3.42–3). Mac's 'uplifted' hand, by contrast, can exercise nothing. Transliterated to the capitalist politics of carnivorism, the huge horns on Mac's car signal something more complex than the symbols of cuckoldry they evoke. The hypermasculine car ornament emasculates the erstwhile driver; the beast bites back with its impaling horn, but after its own death has rendered its aggression moot. The steer's flesh already has been consumed by an anonymous customer; the hungry burger industry has bagged both the longhorn and the franchise operator.[5]

In *Scotland, PA* the groggy sleep of McDonaldsification doth murder all. Paternal somnolence pervades the film: Malcolm chides Duncan for habitually falling asleep in his office; Officer Ed dozes at the police desk. Perhaps the sole genuinely poignant moment in the film comes just after Duncan's murder, when the McBeths silently listen to Malcolm pounding on his father's office door, shouting 'wake up, Dad!' But even when awakening is possible in this film, it only illuminates confinement. Here, Duncan is not murdered in his sleep, but rather when he tries to seize initiative: the provocatively named 'Norm' Duncan catalyses his murder when he unveils his homemade blueprints to the McBeths ('tonight, you two are going to witness history'). In another of the film's explorations of how spectacle and imitation produce action, Duncan glosses the blueprints for the mystified McBeths by abruptly putting Pat and Mac into a mock rehearsal, seizing the role of a Method director who has the McBeths develop a scene of discovering their need for drive-through takeout. Indeed, Duncan coaches the McBeths to feign yawning to signal that they're too exhausted for any other alternative. And Mac recapitulates this very yawn in his final fight with McDuff, turning feigned surrender into feigned sleepiness to get McDuff off balance. As it turns out, of course, the imitated gesture of sleep quickly becomes the permanent sleep

[5] For related interpretations of ways that Almereyda's *Hamlet* critiques capitalist modes of both production and representation, see Mark Thornton Burnett,' "To Hear and See the Matter": Communicating Technology in Michael Almereyda's *Hamlet*', *Cinema Journal*, 42 (2003), 48–69; and Katherine Rowe, '"Remember Me": Technologies of Memory in Michael Almereyda's *Hamlet*', in *Shakespeare, the Movie, II: Popularizing the Plays on Film, Television, and DVD*, ed. Richard Burt and Lynda Boose (New York, 2003).

of death. Duncan and all the rest of Scotland also 'sleep' in their belief that fast food will mitigate rather than exacerbate their passivity. The audience knows that global McDonalds, not the local McBeth's, is the Big Mac here. The McBeths' retitling of their menu encapsulates this when it names their offerings the 'Big McBeth', 'Little McBeth', 'Fishy McBeth', 'McBeth McBeth'. The leftover burger Mrs Lennox chewed as the film opens now carries the McBeths name. This seems a victorious assertion of agency when they re-make the restaurant. But in the end, 'the McBeth' is what's consumed. The 'bitch' statue of liberty stays stashed in the corner of a fast food nation.

SCOFF POWER IN *LOVE'S LABOUR'S LOST* AND THE INNS OF COURT: LANGUAGE IN CONTEXT

LYNNE MAGNUSSON

Although recent criticism has made claims to bridge the gap between the linguistic criticism of Shakespeare and the new historicism, between close reading and cultural poetics, many questions still remain about what a historicized study of Shakespeare's language or style should look like.[1] Should it attend primarily to how sociohistorical contexts motivate verbal exchanges, showing how – in Bakhtin's words – 'the internal politics of style (how the elements are put together) is determined by [the] external politics'[2] of historically specific social relationships, class structures, and gender or racial ideologies? Should it depend upon a historical tool-kit for analysis, deriving, for example, from classical and Elizabethan rhetoric, or can a historicized study of language draw effectively upon modern-day discourse analysis? Should it engage seriously with the sociohistory of the English language itself, taking, for example, as work by Jonathan Hope and Sylvia Adamson does, research into period-specific grammatical changes as its starting point?[3] Might it perhaps focus on how Shakespeare's linguistic capital has functioned in the historical contexts of this canonical author's reception and reproduction? These methodological questions are important ones, and each one of these directions is potentially fruitful. If, as Frank Kermode has asserted, much of 'the life of [Shakespeare's] plays is in the language',[4] then we should not be ignoring their linguistic texture or failing to provide our students with tools that can allow them to engage with its complexity and interest. Yet Kermode's own book, *Shakespeare's Language*, scornful of recent critical developments, proceeds as if the study of Shakespeare's language should start up once again where it paused thirty years ago, before it retreated into a defensive backwater of the discipline and came to function principally as a defining other in historicist platforms. Even though this essay is most immediately concerned with what I want to call scoff power in early modern linguistic interaction, its more general point is that a renewed criticism of Shakespeare's language should find ways to proceed not in scoffing confrontation but in fruitful

[1] See, for example, Patricia Parker, *Shakespeare from the Margins: Language, Culture, Context* (Chicago, 1996); Russ McDonald, ed., *Shakespeare Reread: The Texts in New Contexts* (Ithaca, NY, 1994); Lynne Magnusson, *Shakespeare and Social Dialogue: Dramatic Language and Elizabethan Letters* (Cambridge, 1999); Bruce R. Smith, *The Acoustic World of Early Modern England: Attending to the O-Factor* (Chicago, 1999). Sylvia Adamson and Russ McDonald offered complementary approaches to this topic at the plenary session of the Shakespeare Association of America on 'Historicizing Shakespeare's Language' in 2001 at which this paper originated. I am grateful to the Social Sciences and Humanities Research Council of Canada for research support and to Paul Stevens for helpful suggestions.

[2] M. M. Bakhtin, *The Dialogic Imagination: Four Essays*, ed. Michael Holquist, trans. Caryl Emerson and Michael Holquist (Austin, Texas, 1981), p. 284.

[3] See Jonathan Hope, 'Shakespeare's "Natiue English"', in *A Companion to Shakespeare*, ed. David Scott Kastan (Oxford, 1999), pp. 239–55 and Sylvia Adamson, 'Understanding Shakespeare's Grammar: Studies in Small Words', in *Reading Shakespeare's Dramatic Language: A Guide*, ed. Sylvia Adamson et al. (London, 2001), pp. 210–36.

[4] Frank Kermode, *Shakespeare's Language* (London, 2000), p. 4 (quoting English director Richard Eyre).

conversation with the socially and politically oriented historicism that has reinvigorated early modern studies.

This chapter is intended to illustrate one approach among many possible ways of proceeding with this conversation. *Love's Labour's Lost* is treated here as a case study of ways to read the 'external politics' of a play's linguistic style, or – to adapt Bakhtin's formulation further – to see how the play's language 'lives . . . on the boundary between its own context and another, alien context'.[5] Focusing on the play's related uses of language for social discrimination and for the production of wit, I treat the context of the play's own imagined speech community in relation to two 'alien' and historically specific contexts. A first brief section considers difference-making in the language of the play in relation to the context of nationalist linguistic polemic invoked by the play's allusions to inkhornism and spelling reform. Explaining how injurious speech reception can contribute to a politics of social differentiation even at the moment when a unifying national language is being conceived, this first section establishes the overarching principle for showing how the speech dynamics of *Love's Labour's Lost* may be rooted in experience of such elitist speech communities as the London Inns of Court. The second, longer section extends the analysis of linguistic mechanisms for social discrimination by exploring 'scoff power' in *Love's Labour's Lost* in relation to the context of an Inns of Court speech community. In doing so, I introduce a pedagogic tool from speech ethnography that is potentially helpful for mapping interrelations between social context and linguistic orientation in order to profile this elite male speech community, which I will be analysing as a site for the production of wit as verbal injury and social classification.

'MAKING A DIFFERENCE OF ENGLISHE'

The allusions in *Love's Labour's Lost* to the inkhorn debate and to English spelling reform invoke the context of polemical writings like Thomas Wilson's *The Arte of Rhetorique* (1553) and Richard Mulcaster's *The First Part of the Elementarie* (1582) that made a nationalist 'call for *English*': 'whatsoeuer shall becom of the English state, the English tung cannot proue fairer, then it is at this daie', writes Mulcaster.[6] 'But why not all in *English*?' (p. 274), he demands, promoting the coming of age of the English tongue, its readiness to cast off 'the thraldom & bondage' (p. 269) of subjugation to Latin, to supply all the linguistic needs of an English commonwealth – in learning, in religion, in state business and in commerce, in law and in poetry, and to share out the treasures of language more equitably among all English people. *Love's Labour's Lost* may be set in Navarre, but its 'great feast'[7] is of the English language: with its 'fire-new words' (1.1.176), wealth of puns, rhetorical copiousness, and linguistic variety, it showcases and extends the newly elaborated resources of the English vernacular and could be read as an enthusiastic seconding of Spenser's question, made newly fresh by Richard Helgerson, 'why a Gods name may not we, as else the Greekes, haue the kingdome of oure owne Language?'[8]

Yet *Love's Labour's Lost* brings into clear focus some troubling contradictions in the politics of this newly liberated and seemingly democratizing English. The inkhorn letter discussion in Thomas Wilson's *The Arte of Rhetorique*, a likely source of inspiration for Armado's epistolary extravagances, symptomizes the tension. While Wilson complains of the 'foolishe phantasticall, that . . . will so latine

5 Bakhtin, *Dialogic Imagination*, p. 284.

6 Quoted from *Mulcaster's Elementarie*, ed. E. T. Campagnac (Oxford, 1925), pp. 270, 179. The inkhorn debate is evoked in the play especially by Armado's overblown letters and spelling reform by Holofernes's critique of Armado's pronunciation (5.1.17–25).

7 *Love's Labour's Lost*, ed. H. R. Woudhuysen, Arden Third Series (Walton-on-Thames, Surrey, 1998), 5.1.36. Hereafter this text is quoted parenthetically.

8 Letter to Gabriel Harvey, in *The Works of Edmund Spenser: A Variorum Edition*, ed. Edwin Greenlaw *et al.*, 11 vols. (Baltimore, 1949), vol. 10, p. 16; quoted in Richard Helgerson, *Forms of Nationhood: The Elizabethan Writing of England* (London, 1992), p. 1.

their tongues, that the simple cannot but wonder at their talke',[9] he nonetheless regards the admission of Latin and Greek words into English as an important resource for amending its 'lacke of store' and 'enrich[ing] the language' (sig. y3v). His satire of 'he that can catche an ynke horne terme by the taile' (sig. y2v) in order to 'get a good personage' (sig. y3r) and be accounted 'a fine Englishe man' (sig. y2v) makes the measure of linguistic overkill, or inauthentic English, the understanding of the 'vnlearned man', who will not be able to 'tell, what half this [inkhorn] letter signifieth' (sig. y3r). For, according to Wilson, 'either we must make a difference of Englishe, and saie some is learned Englishe, and other some is rude Englishe, or the one is courte talke, the other is countrey speache, or els we must of necessitee, banishe al such affected Rhetorique, and vse altogether one maner of language' (sig. y3r). Thus, Wilson sees affected 'ynkepot termes' as borrowed words which are potentially injurious, because they are not shared in common: their use 'make[s] a difference of Englishe' (sig. y3r). By contrast, if a borrowed Latin word, like 'Communion' or 'the Kynges *prerogatiue*' or 'letters *patentes*' 'signifieth open to all men', then, says Wilson, 'I knowe no man greued for these termes' (sig. y3v, emphasis added). In other words, Wilson suggests that a kind of symbolic violence occurs when 'we . . . make a difference of Englishe'. It is this kind of violence that Shakespeare exposes in the 'envoy' exchange between Armado and Costard, where Armado's words seem to lead Costard to fear the forced anal administration of a purgative, or some other hurtful treatment for his broken shin:

MOTH
A wonder, master! Here's a costard broken in a shin.

ARMADO
Some enigma, some riddle. Come, thy l'envoy – begin.

COSTARD No egma, no riddle, no l'envoy, no salve in the mail, sir! O, sir, plantain, a plain plantain! No l'envoy, no l'envoy, no salve, sir, but a plantain!

ARMADO By virtue, thou enforcest laughter; thy silly thought, my spleen; the heaving of my lungs provokes me to ridiculous smiling. O, pardon me, my stars! Doth the inconsiderate take *salve* for l'envoy, and the word 'l'envoy' for a salve?

(3.1.67–76)[10]

Armado, in turn, takes Costard's discomfiture in a self-congratulatory way, as a marker of status difference between them. Act 3, scene 1 of *Love's Labour's Lost* proceeds as a language lesson *within* English comparable to the Latin lesson of Act 4, scene 1 of *The Merry Wives of Windsor*. The Latin lesson, with a boy and his tutor's Latin learning set against an uneducated woman's bawdy englishing of words, makes it clear that Shakespeare saw the practice of bilingualism in England as a social divider. The English lesson in *Love's Labour's Lost*, with Costard's comic misappropriations of 'l'envoy', 'remuneration' and 'guerdon', shows how readily the cultivation of eloquent English, and specifically the use of foreign loan-words, can function as social dividers within English, multiplying the possibility for potentially injurious social discrimination.

More often in *Love's Labour's Lost*, however, the emphasis is on how the reception practices of the play's speech communities make injurious differences in English. In his *Elementarie*, Richard Mulcaster looks back with momentary nostalgia to what he regards as the more level linguistic playing field of republican Rome, where 'publik orations were in ordinarie trade, and the verie tung alone made a chariot to honor': 'Our state is a *Monarchie*', he laments, 'which mastereth language, & teacheth it to please' (p. 272). An exchange in *Love's Labour's Lost* between the Princess of France and a Forester provides a quiet and innocuous illustration of Shakespeare's emphasis in this play on the injurious reception of speech:

9 Thomas Wilson, *The Arte of Rhetorique* (London, 1553), sig. y2v; cited hereafter parenthetically.

10 For illuminating close readings of the Costard-Armado exchange, see Patricia Parker, 'Preposterous Reversals: *Love's Labor's Lost*', *Modern Language Quarterly*, 54 (1993), 435–82 (pp. 447–53) and also Stephen Booth, *'King Lear', 'Macbeth', Indefinition, and Tragedy* (New Haven, Connecticut, 1983), pp. 68–9.

PRINCESS
Then, forester, my friend, where is the bush
That we must stand and play the murderer in?
FORESTER
Hereby, upon the edge of yonder coppice,
A stand where you may make the fairest shoot.
PRINCESS
I thank my beauty, I am fair that shoot,
And thereupon thou speak'st 'the fairest shoot'.
FORESTER
Pardon me, madam, for I meant not so.
PRINCESS
What, what? First praise me, and again say no?
O, short-lived pride! Not fair? Alack for woe!
FORESTER
Yes, madam, fair. (4.1.7–16)

Here the forester offers competent advice, using words as if in the ordinary trade of the commonwealth of a shared language. The princess's response refuses to acknowledge the skilled man's competent but non-deferential words as legitimate exchange. Her supposedly playful insistence on hearing the language of compliment turns his straightforward words into courtship, making a difference of English by teaching his language how to please.

Most of the instances of injurious difference-making in linguistic reception so prevalent in *Love's Labour's Lost* are far less subtle. 'Most barbarous intimation!', Holofernes responds to Dull's efforts at conversation, 'after his undressed, unpolished, uneducated, unpruned, untrained, or rather unlettered, or ratherest unconfirmed fashion, to insert again my *haud credo* for a deer' (4.2.13, 16–9). 'This is abhominable, which he would call "abominable"' (5.1.23–4), remarks Holofernes of Armado's pronunciation, making differences between Armado's 'too picked, too spruce, too affected' style and his own picked, spruce, and affected style (5.1.12–3). '*Judas I am* –' (5.2.589), Holofernes begins his part in the pageant of Worthies with a display of learned reference – language for which he might expect to draw praise, to ride, in Mulcaster's words, as 'a chariot to honor'. He is greeted by perhaps the ugliest and most crushing example of difference-making in reception, as the lords twist his words and heap what they regard as witty insults on him:

HOLOFERNES *Judas I am, ycleped Maccabaeus.*
DUMAINE Judas Maccabaeus clipped is plain Judas.
BEROWNE A kissing traitor. How, art thou proved Judas?

...

HOLOFERNES I will not be put out of countenance.
BEROWNE Because thou hast no face.
HOLOFERNES What is this?
BOYET A cittern-head.
DUMAINE The head of a bodkin.
BEROWNE A death's face in a ring.
LONGAVILLE The face of an old Roman coin, scarce seen.
BOYET The pommel of Caesar's falchion.
DUMAINE The carved-bone face on a flask.
BEROWNE Saint George's half-cheek in a brooch.

...

HOLOFERNES You have put me out of countenance.
BEROWNE False! We have given thee faces.
HOLOFERNES But you have outfaced them all.
(5.2.592–4, 601–11, 615–17)

As so often in the play, the language in which speakers are asserting their high social credentials has a low or scatological aspect,[11] and the long exchange concludes with Berowne's jeering and abusive return, 'For the ass to the Jude? Give it him. Jud-as, away!' (line 622).

In the criticism of this play, emphasis has often been placed on speech varieties: 'One of the play's strengths', William C. Carroll wrote in his seminal book, 'is its variety of style'.[12] In the tradition of stylistic criticism thirty years ago, when Carroll made this comment, it was usual to emphasize Shakespeare's use of stylistic variation to individuate character; today we might be more likely to emphasize the use of varieties to demarcate social groups and classes. But the point has occasionally, and I think rightly, been made, for

[11] Parker, 'Preposterous Reversals', explores uses of the 'preposterous', including the scatological, and how routinely in *Love's Labour's Lost* 'the language of the "high" . . . is contaminated or brought low by the "low matter" of the bodily and sexual' (p. 437). As a gloss to 'given thee faces' in the Judas exchange, she suggests an interlingual pun 'with French buttocks or *fesses*' (p. 468).

[12] William C. Carroll, *The Great Feast of Language in 'Love's Labour's Lost'* (Princeton, NJ, 1976), p. 25.

example by Camille Wells Slights, that the linguistic distinction-making among characters practised by commentators underplays some very significant continuities among the speech profiles of the characters. It is not hard to demonstrate, instead, the considerable stylistic continuities: the ladies and the lords both delight in wit combats composed of volleys of puns; Costard's clever punning on 'manner and form' at his first entrance can be seen as imitating and overgoing Berowne's punning on 'style' (1.1.196–210); Holofernes shares Armado's trick of amplifying his expression through *synonymia*; and Berowne's 'Three-piled hyperboles' (5.2.407) are not that easily separated from Armado's. Slights goes so far as to say that 'the primary effect is stylistic similarity rather than variety'.[13] My point is that Shakespeare's play is doing a number of things. First, it brings out a contradiction not fully explicit in Wilson when he worries over making 'a difference of Englishe' (sig. y3r): that is, a tension between constructing a national English as heterogeneous, copious with possibilities for functional variation within the language, and, at the same time, constructing a national English as homogenous, its language capital shared out equitably among an English-speaking people who are using 'altogether one maner of language' (sig. y3r). Second, and more important, it emphasizes the reception of difference. What *Love's Labour's Lost* emphasizes is not how people of different social status speak differently, but how the reception tactics of the characters operate to construct, exaggerate, and organize differences within English usage in order to index and enhance the critical listener's own social capital. Thus, the play critiques and exposes the politics of linguistic differentiation, reflecting on how listeners as social agents play out a struggle for superiority and distinction and are themselves, in Pierre Bourdieu's words, 'producers' of 'acts of classification', makers of social division.[14] It is this principle that best explains how the play may be rooted in the experience of socially advantaged speech communities that heighten linguistic difference-making such as the London Inns of Court.

SCOFF POWER AND THE INNS OF COURT

Love's Labour's Lost stands out among Shakespeare's plays not only for its accent on linguistic display; it also stands out in subjecting virtually every character to experiences where his or her words are turned back, both twisted and derogatively classified or classed, with mocking derision. I have been discussing examples of nationalist linguistic polemic as one context directly invoked by the play that may help to illuminate why pride in one English language for a nation might go hand in hand with linguistic dividing practices. But such an abstract context does little to tell us whether the verbal injuries represented evoke historically specific experiences within speech communities or contexts that might have been recognizable to early modern Londoners. Let me come at this indirectly by explaining the discourse reception in the early 1590s of one elderly widow among the smart young men at Gray's Inn, the most socially upscale of those London training grounds in law and would-be courtiership, the Inns of Court.

Lady Anne Bacon, whose knowledge of Latin and Greek far outstripped both Holofernes's and Shakespeare's, and whose linguistic skill in translation won rich praise from Archbishop Parker in her century and C. S. Lewis in ours, regularly wrote letters of news and advice to her sons Anthony and Francis Bacon, both resident (Anthony more temporarily than Francis) at Gray's Inn.[15] In the

[13] Camille Wells Slights, *Shakespeare's Comic Commonwealths* (London, 1993), p. 82.

[14] Pierre Bourdieu, *Distinction: A Social Critique of the Judgement of Taste*, trans. Richard Nice (Cambridge, Mass., 1984), p. 467. On uses of rhetoric for social division in *Love's Labour's Lost*, see also Lynne Magnusson, 'Language and Comedy', in *The Cambridge Companion to Shakespearean Comedy*, ed. Alexander Leggatt (Cambridge, 2002), pp. 156–78 (pp. 160–2).

[15] Matthew Parker's comments occur in his prefatory letter to Anne Bacon's translation of John Jewel, *An Apologie or answere in defence of the Churche of Englande* (1564), and C. S. Lewis's in *Poetry and Prose in the Sixteenth Century* (Oxford, 1954), p. 307. On her correspondence with her sons, see Lynne

annals of English drama, Lady Bacon's letters have occasionally been quoted as representative of puritan anti-theatrical prejudice: 'I trust they will not mum nor mask nor sinfully revel at Gray's Inn', she writes to Anthony on 5 December 1594, just before the start of what was to be among their most extravagant and extended Christmas revels.[16] Her letters are also, however, remarkable for how forcefully they reveal her anxieties about how they will be read and received among her sons' male companions. Her wish is that the letters will be read privately by Anthony and Francis; her fear is that her words will be read in company and circulated among the throngs of young men she habitually pictures hanging about her sons and contaminating their judgement – and being read in this company that they will be subjected to derision and mockery, and set at nought: 'Let not your men see my letters', she instructs, 'I write to you, and not to them'[17]; 'Read not my letters either scoffingly or carelessly, which hath been used so much'[18]; 'Let not Lawson, that fox, be acquainted with my letters . . . He commonly opened underminingly all letters sent to you from counsel or friends'[19]; 'Observe I pray burn my letter. Your men and your brother's pry into every matter and listen.'[20] I believe that Lady Bacon had good reason to imagine she was being caricatured and classified by self-assured packs of scornful young men who were being made privy to her letters. As one male companion made privy to her correspondence from an earlier period had written to her son Anthony, 'altho' I well know, my lady, your mother, to be one of the sufficientest without comparison of that sex, yet, at the end of the career *il y a tousjours de la femme*', 'a woman, which is a vessel so frail and variable, as every wind wavereth, as you know'.[21]

The scoffing putdowns that Lady Bacon anticipates for letters delivered and communally read out at Gray's Inn typify much of the speech action of *Love's Labour's Lost*. The display of wit charged by critique of other people's words begins in the first scene with Berowne's mockery of the King's decrees and accompanying penalties, quickly followed up by the use of Armado's letter as entertainment. Within the play, the dynamics of witty but injurious linguistic reception intensify in their ferocity, with many of the most extreme examples occurring in the lengthy final act of the play, especially in relation to contexts of formal performance. Not only is Berowne characterized and blamed for his general speech habit as 'a man replete with mocks . . . and wounding flouts' (5.2.831–2), but the visiting ladies, when presented a masque of Muscovites, have been forearmed to treat the men as they anticipate being treated by them – 'mock for mock' (5.2.140). The ladies have advance notice of the foresworn lords' intent to woo them in exotic disguise and, on the principle that 'There's no such sport as sport by sport o'erthrown' (5.2.153), make a deliberate plan to 'cross' (5.2.139) their suitors' intent, so that 'they, well mocked' will 'depart away with shame' (156). From the outset, the ladies overturn the very conditions for establishing communication upon which a performance and its positive reception depend. First, they turn their backs, disabling face-to-face communication, as the boy Moth begins his prefatory speech. Second, masked and, having switched favours received earlier from the men, so that they are wearing misleading identity markers, they confound the intended direction of address, so that each lord woos the wrong woman. And, finally, they frustrate communication

Magnusson, 'Widowhood and Linguistic Capital: The Rhetoric and Reception of Anne Bacon's Epistolary Advice', *English Literary Renaissance*, 31 (2001), 3–33.

16 Lambeth Palace Library MS 650.222 (hereafter LPL MS); quoted from James Spedding, ed., *The Letters and the Life of Francis Bacon* in *The Works of Francis Bacon* (London, 1861), vol. 8, p. 326.

17 24 May 1592, LPL MS 648.106; quoted from Spedding, *Works*, vol. 8, p. 114.

18 n.d., LPL MS 653.183. I modernise spelling here for consistency with the selected letters as edited by Spedding.

19 3 February 1592, LPL MS 653.192; quoted from Spedding, *Works*, vol. 8, p. 113.

20 [5 December 1594], LPL MS 650.224.

21 Anthony Standen to Anthony Bacon, 1 September 1591, LPL MS 648.58; quoted from Thomas Birch, *Memoirs of the Reign of Queen Elizabeth, From the Year 1581 till her Death*, 2 vols. (1754), vol. 1, p. 68.

by insisting on a literal reception of the words spoken, as where Berowne asks 'White-handed mistress, one sweet word with thee' (230) and the Princess, his misrecognized love object, answers 'Honey, and milk, and sugar: there is three' (231). The lords are further humiliated for their spoiled performance, when it is described back to them as a show of 'fools' (371) when they return to the women's camp as themselves.

Yet the injured lords subject the commoners and men of learning to still worse mocks and injuries (including the 'Jude-Ass' wound) in the crushing reception of their Pageant of Worthies: they interrupt, they refuse to yield performance space or quiet hearing, and they hijack the proceedings with their own commentary, corrections, and self-displaying performances of injurious wit. These entertainments within *Love's Labour's Lost* are, in the words of the play, 'dash[ed] . . . like a Christmas comedy' (5.2.462) – indeed, they are dashed like a particular Christmas comedy performed before an upscale audience of student revellers and their eminent guests at Gray's Inn on 28 December 1594: *The Comedy of Errors*.

A familiar feature of the Christmas season at the London Inns of Court in the late sixteenth and early seventeenth centuries were extended revels, expensive and elaborate occasions involving mock coronations and mock ceremonies, pseudo-forensic orations and wit displays, plays (especially comedies), processions and masques, by which the law students entertained themselves, important court dignitaries, including peers and noblewomen, their own student counterparts at the other Inns, and civic authorities of the City of London.[22] Most of the celebrations took place in the Inns' Halls, the usual site not only of the students' obligatory 'commons', or residence meals, but also of the legal training exercises in argumentation referred to as 'moots' and 'bolting'.[23] But the season typically included processions to the Lord Mayor's and masquing before the Queen or King at Court, so the students' sports spilled over into the London streets and would have been widely known and talked of. Detailed accounts survive of two Christmas revels of the 1590s. The *Gesta Grayorum*, published in 1688, gives an account of the Prince of Purpoole's reign at Gray's Inn in December 1594 through February 1595, in which Francis Bacon had a hand, and *Le Prince d'Amour*, published in 1660, describes revels at the Middle Temple extending from 24 December 1597 to Candlemas Night on 2 February 1598. This period coincides with the likely period of composition and early performance of *Love's Labour's Lost*, which is often dated 1594/5 and was published in Quarto in 1598, with the title page claiming performance before 'her Highnes this last Christmas'.

It is the *Gesta Grayorum* that describes a performance of *The Comedy of Errors*, almost certainly Shakespeare's play, in chaotic circumstances on 28 December 1594. The players performed late on what the Grayians afterwards dubbed '*The Night of Errors*' before an audience – or perhaps more accurately, given the recorded difficulty of securing performance space due to 'a disordered Tumult and Crowd upon the Stage'[24] – *amidst* an audience of rowdy Inn's Men together with their elite guests. The Hall had been from early evening the scene

[22] For detailed histories of the Inns of Court in early modern times, see W. C. Richardson, *A History of the Inns of Court: With Special Reference to the Period of the Renaissance* (Baton Rouge, Louisiana, 1975) and Wilfrid R. Prest, *The Inns of Court under Elizabeth I and the Early Stuarts, 1590–1640* (London, 1972). On the Inns of Court revels and the overall Inns' socioliterary culture, see Philip J. Finkelpearl, *John Marston of the Middle Temple* (Cambridge, Mass., 1969), pp. 3–80, esp. pp. 32–61; Arthur Marotti, *John Donne, Coterie Poet* (Madison, Wisconsin, 1986), pp. 25–95; Desmond Bland's Preface and Introduction to *Gesta Grayorum* (Liverpool, 1968), pp. v–xxv; Basil Brown, *Law Sports at Gray's Inn* (New York, 1921); A. Wigfall Green, *The Inns of Court and Early English Drama* (New York, 1931). For recent arguments about links to Shakespeare's plays, see Anthony Arlidge, *Shakespeare and the Prince of Love: The Feast of Misrule in the Middle Temple* (London, 2000) and W. R. Elton, *Shakespeare's 'Troilus and Cressida' and the Inns of Court Revels* (Aldershot, 2000). I am grateful to Edward Gieskes for sharing his bibliography on Elizabethan lawyers.

[23] On these legal exercises, see Richardson, *History of the Inns of Court*, pp. 128–66 and Prest, *Inns of Court*, pp. 115–36.

[24] W. W. Greg, ed., *Gesta Grayorum* 1688, Malone Society Reprints (Oxford, 1914), p. 22. Hereafter cited parenthetically in the text.

of an enormous gathering, with the Prince of Purpoole's 'court' honouring a mock Ambassador and his retinue from the Inner Temple at the same time as they entertained 'a great Presence of Lords, Ladies, and worshipful Personages' (p. 20). The crowded conditions, combined with a propensity among the worshipful company for self-display and social distinction-making – that is, a demand to be placed on platforms as high as the mock-prince of Purpoole and his retinue – delayed the evening's planned entertainments, creating impossible conditions for play-acting:

When the Ambassador was placed, . . . and that there was something to be performed for the Delight of the Beholders, there arose such a disordered Tumult and Crowd upon the Stage, that there was no Opportunity to effect that which was intended: There came so great a number of worshipful Personages upon the Stage, that might not be displaced; and Gentlewomen, whose Sex did privilege them from Violence. (p. 22)

The contingent from the Inner Temple registered the general disorder as an insult to their own entertainment and status, and departed in disgust, causing 'the Throngs and Tumults' to 'somewhat cease, although so much of them continued' that the Gray's Inn Men resolved not to go forward with 'any thing of Account'. Instead, 'Dancing and Revelling with Gentlewomen' followed, the writer of *Gesta Grayorum* tells us, 'and after such Sports, a Comedy of Errors (like to *Plautus* his *Menechmus*) was played by the Players. So that Night was begun, and continued to the end, in nothing but Confusion and Errors; whereupon, it was ever afterwards called, *The Night of Errors*' (p. 22). The players mentioned in this account were derisively classified during the Grayians' follow-up sports and jests of the next day as 'a Company of base and common Fellows' (p. 23), despite the seemingly high-toned classical manner of their dramatic offering. They were almost certainly the newly constituted Lord Chamberlain's Men. And either Shakespeare was among them, or, almost certainly, he would have heard all about a reception which probably vied with that of the Worthies for condescending interruption and shaming disrespect.

It may very well be that the 1594–5 Gray's Inn revels, or the general pattern of Inns of Court revels that they exemplified, had a greater influence on the invention of situations for Shakespeare's sourceless play, *Love's Labour's Lost*, than is generally acknowledged. Most usually accepted is an isolated connection between a Russian embassy to Purpoole's court in the revels and Shakespeare's masque of Muscovites.[25] Frances A. Yates speculated on a number of related links, suggesting, for example, that the play's phrase, 'a mess of Russians' (5.2.361), may be a joking allusion to the Gray's Inn revels, since a usual contemporary referent of the word 'mess' would have been the party of four Inns of Court benchers or law students who dined together and debated points from legal cases after meals.[26] But might not the players' experiences of linguistic injury and humiliation so accented in *Love's Labour's Lost* also be coloured by Shakespeare's own, or his friends', experience of uncivil or mocking reception at Gray's Inn?

Before developing further this similarity to an Inns' culture of wit and scoffing, let me sketch briefly how the general situation of the play may resemble the standard template for Inns of Court revels. *Love's Labour's Lost* begins with a satirical scene of oath-taking. Navarre's men are required to subscribe their names to a number of articles which they are certain to break and which contravene common sense: foregoing the sustenance of sleep or adequate diet and renouncing the sight and conversation of women. Similarly, at the Christmas revels, once a mock-court has been set up through the coronation of a mock-prince – the Prince of Purpoole at Gray's Inn or the Prince d'Amour at the Middle Temple, the wit of the Inns' men is displayed by multiplying the satirical articles to which knights of the newly constituted Order must swear: for example,

---

[25] See, for example, G. R. Hibbard, 'Introduction', *Love's Labour's Lost* (Oxford, 1990), pp. 45–7.

[26] *A Study of 'Love's Labour's Lost'* (Cambridge, 1936), p. 156. Berowne also uses the word 'mess' of the male foursome at 4.3.203: 'you three fools lacked me fool to make up the mess'.

> '*Item*, No Knight of this Order shall, in point of Honour, resort to any Grammar-rules out of the Books *De Dullo*, or such like; but shall out of his own brave Mind, and natural Courage, deliver himself from Scorns, as to his own Discretion shall seem convenient.
>
> '*Item*, No Knight of this Order shall be inquisitive towards any Lady or Gentlewoman, whether her Beauty be *English* or *Italian*, or whether, with Care taking, she have added half a Foot to her Stature; but shall take all to the best.' (*Gesta Grayorum*, p. 28)

In keeping with the Christmas season of misrule and student habits of mocking regulations, these orders echo the form and parody the content of the Benchers' rules and orders governing Inns of Court behaviour. The '*Item, That*' form framing Navarre's decree that '*no woman shall come within a mile of my court*' (1.1.119–20) precisely echoes the wording of such orders, and the wording of the penalty, '*On pain of losing her tongue*' (1.1.122–3), exaggerates penalties for such offences as wearing 'feathers or ribbens on . . . caps, upon pain to forfeit, for the first default iii *s.* iiii *d.* and the second, expulsion without redemption'.[27] Both in the revels and in the play, the inverted 'orders' are closely connected with the law students' favoured device of 'paradox' – the defence of propositions that apparently oppose common sense, as in Berowne's claims that study dulls the brain and that women's eyes are the best books or the favourite Inns of Court example, that foul-looking women are the most desirable. The men of *Love's Labour's Lost* seem to act out one satirical edict laid out for the Knights of the Helmet in *Gesta Grayorum*, '*Item* . . . that no Knight of this Order shall take upon him the person of a Male-content, . . . saying, that His Highness's Sports were well sorted with a Play of Errors' (p. 31). When the King of Navarre expresses fear that the Pageant of Worthies 'will shame us' (5.2.509), and Berowne responds 'We are shame-proof, my lord; and 'tis some policy / To have one show worse than the King's and his company' (510–1), the Princess of France proposes 'That sport best pleases that doth least know how – . . . When great things labouring perish in their birth' (514, 518). 'A right description of our sport, my lord' (519), Berowne comments. In general, the princely students' academic purposes having been discarded from as early as the first scene, *Love's Labour's Lost* dwells on some of the same kinds of sports, verbal displays and jests, scornful distinction-making, and performance situations that are typical of Inns of Court society, especially during revels but also while engaged in their everyday pursuits. Indeed, even the play's link to the refinements of Spanish culture in the person of Armado, a 'traveller of Spain . . . in all the world's new fashion planted' (1.1.161–2) has a parallel in the Gray's Inn revels, in that Henry Helmes, crowned Prince of Purpoole, together with such friends as Frances Davison who wrote the concluding masque, studied Spanish during the 1590s with John Minsheu and incorporated Spanish-sounding names such as '*Amarillo de Paddington*' (*Gesta Grayorum*, p. 12) into their entertainment. Dedicating his *Spanish Grammar* to 'the right worshipfull gentlemen students of Grayes Inne', Minsheu may have captured something of the quality of this discourse community in his ironic injunction to the dedicatees: 'if a man have any learning or qualitie, let him bring it to you, and if it be too tedious unto you, or hinder your sport, rather then be troubled with him, bob him or flout and scoffe him away'.[28]

Such parallels between Inns entertainments and *Love's Labour's Lost* may deserve fuller attention, despite the uncertain dating of the play. My primary purpose in this essay, however, is not to advance arguments about sources or analogues but instead to read the speech community of the London Inns of Court as one fruitful context among other possible historically specific contexts for illuminating what cross class and intra-class group-intensified speech exchange and reception might have felt like in early modern London. I am suggesting that it illuminates

---

[27] For a useful sampling of the language of these orders, see Appendices IV and V of Richardson, *History of the Inns of Court*, pp. 409–62 (p. 434). The phrase 'In manner and form' that Costard plays upon (1.1.202) is also part of the legalese of the orders (for an example, see Richardson, p. 434).

[28] *Spanish Grammar* (1599) is described as 'first collected' by Richard Percival and 'augmented and increased' by John Minsheu. See sig. i2r.

the phenomenon of 'scoff power' in *Love's Labour's Lost*.

In the interests of making good my suggestion that we try to find manageable teaching tools to enable students to participate in a contextualized and historicized approach to Shakespeare's language, in Table 1 I have adapted a paradigm from speech ethnography (S-P-E-A-K) for identifying linguistic behaviour particular to a specific community in order to profile the speech community of Gray's Inn.[29] By accenting the salient features of this discourse community, it should, I hope, suggest why linguistic aggression and scoff power (accented under ACTS in Table 1) might be a pervasive fact of life in such a context.

It would be a mistake to imagine – given the examples of Lady Bacon and of Shakespeare's playing company – that scoff power in the play and at Gray's Inn was deployed primarily to put down outsiders, injurious reception thus primarily framing acts of exclusion. With the young lords in *Love's Labour's Lost* as at the Inns of Court, there is strong evidence that mockery and verbal shaming also played an important role in shaping identity in their in-group communication. The first major scene of exposure in *Love's Labour's Lost*, where each lord is 'discovered' as a lover, is between men. In an inversion of the accustomed notion of how manuscript poetry circulates to the *admiration* of 'private friends' within courtly or what Arthur Marotti calls 'satellite-courtly environments, like the Inns of Court',[30] the male friends overhear, quote, critique, and deride one another's amorous verses. Beyond this in-group mockery, letters and poems also circulate outside the social group in which they originated: at one remove, the lords and commoners read and mock the letters Armado intended them to see, by which he meant to win insider status. At a further remove, letters and poems end up in the hands of the middle-class characters, Holofernes and Nathaniel, whose critique of verses such as Berowne's to Rosaline serves to set up their own cultural capital in competition with that of the courtiers.[31] Repeatedly, the play highlights the parodic quotation of others' speech and writing and the reception of others' written compositions in critical and discriminatory contexts, both within and across groups. It is clear that the Inns of Court was a similar site for discourse production: as we shall see, for example, the diary of John Manningham of the Middle Temple, from 1602–3, is full of admiring quotations in which one Inns' member holds up for ridicule, distortion, and critique the words or sayings of another member. Within the noblemen's group in the play, even for Berowne, who stands out as an alternative leader amidst the scoffing companions, a high-flying verbal performer whose influence is secured by his highly developed linguistic capital, speech performance among his friends and in his wider social environment is high risk. He is always in danger himself of being turned into the caricature into which he and his friends turn Armado. We can see this in how often his friends mock him from the outset. The king's critique of 'How well he's read, to reason against reading' (1.1.94), for example, quickly turns into a verbal competition amongst the men highlighting rhymes in which Berowne works to regain the ascendancy in wit and criticism. Berowne's speech performance (both serious and jesting) tends to be self-consciously framed and strategized in anticipation of the threat of put-downs and scoffs.

The habitual speech events engaged in by Inns of Court men, like Navarre's men, were occasions where they were subjected to criticism, censure,

[29] S-P-E-A-K as a device for profiling a speech community is adapted and abbreviated from the ethnographic mnemonic S-P-E-A-K-I-N-G developed by Dell Hymes, 'Models of the Interaction of Language and Social Life', in John J. Gumperz and Dell Hymes, eds., *Directions in Sociolinguistics: The Ethnography of Communication*, 2nd edn (Oxford, 1986), pp. 35–71 and from Vimala Herman, who developed it as a tool for analysing dramatic discourse in *Dramatic Discourse: Dialogue as Interaction in Plays* (London, 1995), pp. 18–26. To simplify, I have collapsed 'instrumentalities' (I), including spoken and written modes, into 'key' (K).

[30] Marotti, *John Donne, Coterie Poet*, p. 9.

[31] For an excellent analysis of the circulation and critique of sonnets in *Love's Labour's Lost*, see David Schalkwyk, *Speech and Performance in Shakespeare's Sonnets and Plays* (Cambridge, 2002), pp. 60–4.

Table 1 *Gray's Inn in 1590s profiled as a speech community*

S SPACE: elements of social space for this community
- Inn hall is a primary site of social and speech interaction: site of conversation at hall tables during meals; site of legal academic exercises after meals; with constructed stage and scaffolding, site during Christmas revels of Prince of Purpoole's court and sports
- geographically and socially situated 'between' City and Court; imagined as 'third university'
- rooms and chambers are occasional sites of private entertainment, especially for those of greater privilege, including readers and ancients
- visits made to 'better' ordinaries and to theatres

P PARTICIPANTS: members of community
- predominantly young men, aged 16 to 20 on admission, loosed from tight controls of universities, studying law according to little fixed curriculum or openly cultivating other interests; status of entrants (1590–1639): peer-esquire 40.2%, gentlemen 45.4% (Prest 30)
- senior members, including readers, ancients, occasional members from amongst peerage with greater privileges (free wine, exemptions from commons, governing committees, supervision of moots and other legal exercises, right to service of live-in clerk)
- women excluded, except on occasion by invitation, when their access to various spaces would be limited and regulated (e.g., 'gentlewomen' present for revels on 28 December 1594)
- Inn servants and a limited number of clerks and servants permitted to senior members; visitors such as messengers

E EVENTS: principal speech or discourse events
- conversation at table – with performative element emphasized both in *Gesta Grayorum* and John Hoskins's *Directions*: premium on being 'able to govern a Table with Discourse'
- legal academic exercises – case-putting, bolts (moots without pleading), moots, readings: importance of anticipating and answering arguments and criticism, premium on performance skills
- letter-writing, letter-reading
- exercise of 'literary' skills, including verse and speeches for revels; composition and circulation of sonnets, epigrams, libellous verses, satires, caricaturing put-downs
- performance of masks and revels, listening to plays, etc.

A ACTS
- speech acts within the community tend to be performances at varying (but sometimes intense) levels of risk, regularly subjected to critique, censure, and mockery (SCOFF POWER) – applies to legal exercises, table talk, coterie poetry, various revels
- given heightened speech risk, danger of having one's words twisted, misrepresented, classed and caricatured: speakers within the group develop SCOFF PROOFING strategies – tactics for surviving linguistic aggression

K KEY: channels, codes
- speech and writing; other codes including semiotics of clothing, song, dance, fencing
- 'speaking in print' – permeable boundary between speech and writing evident in many discourse events: memorization for oral academic exercises; reading letters, sonnets, or epigrams in company; reciting speeches at sports and revels; forming models in writings by Sidney, Guazzo, etc. for talk

and threatened mockery. Legal academic exercises – the 'case-putting', 'bolts', and moots – represented rigorous and recurring institutional occasions of testing and censuring speech. We know that the more literary among the Inns of Court men, such as Sir John Davies, aimed satiric epigrams and caricaturing satires at one another,[32] many of which circulated among acquaintances in

[32] See, for example, Sir John Davies's *Epigrammes, The Poems of Sir John Davies*, ed. Robert Krueger (Oxford, 1975), pp. 129–51.

manuscript. There is also evidence that the table talk in hall preceding after-meal academic exercises was highly performative, in the sense of always being open to the risk of censure. The *Gesta Grayorum* itself, in a mock catalogue of reading requisite for Purpoole's Knights, including '*Guizo* [probably Steven Guazzo's *Civile Conversation*], the *French* Academy, *Galiatto* the Courtier, *Plutarch*, the *Arcadia*, and the Neoterical Writers', bears witness to how high a premium was placed on becoming 'accomplished with Civil Conversations, and able to govern a Table with Discourse' (pp. 29–30).[33] John Hoskins' *Directions for Speech and Style*, a manuscript rhetoric book illustrated from the *Arcadia*, bears out the idea that Inns of Court conversation held out a high risk of injury and required sophisticated forearming against potential mockery. Hoskins recommends his art of rhetoric to the young Inner Temple dedicatee in the hopes it 'may benefit' his 'Conversation': he warns the young man against 'The shame of speaking unskilfully', for 'Careless speech doth not only discredit the personage of the speaker but it doth discredit the opinion of his reason and judgment.' Hoskins extends the potential risk in verbal performance from speech to writing: if words in conversation 'fly and escape censure . . . how shall he be thought wise whose penning is thin and shallow?': 'now methinks I terrify and threaten you, for you see my opinion of you if you should not write well'.[34]

That Inns of Court men took pastime, delight and hurt in shaming performances of one another's words can be illustrated from the Bacon family correspondence I invoked earlier. Equal social status, friendship, intimacy or even brotherhood did not protect against parodic public performances of one's private communications. Anthony Bacon's manuscript commonplace book contains the draft or copy of a letter to Francis at Gray's Inn in which he accuses his brother of being party to the mocking recital of his correspondence from the Continent: 'Truly brother it was no lesse troublesome then strange unto me to heare that he [Mr Phillipps] had so farre abused your trust and familiarity as to make a playne song of some of my letters to you to deskant upon in bed and at bord according to his quipping and fantasticall humour.'[35] Prodding his brother's memory to forestall his denial of wrongdoing, Anthony gives us a good sense of what elements of his own linguistic performance might have occasioned the travesty:

> and to the end you may the better Call to mynde when and where you Communicated any such matter unto him the subiect of his quips was the Italien prouerbes which sometimes I enterlace in my letters namely where I sayd that when Kings cary hornes on their foreheads pore gentlemen had neede to looke before they leape [for feare] they should cary some in their bosome and [such lyke] free discourse.[36]

'[A]nd yet not so free', Anthony continues, making it abundantly clear how grievous verbal injuries of this kind could indeed feel, 'but that [I] thought yt as close in your [hand] as in myne owne head and (with the gentlemans leaue be it spoken) I wrote nothing but that I might write to a brother neither otherwise then I thought . . . well brother you may make your profit of this'.[37] The circulation of letters out of the sender's control and their parodic performance in *Love's Labour's Lost* is usually regarded as a purely theatrical convention, but the Bacon correspondence makes it clear that the quipping recitation of private letters was a recognizable social practice within this community of young men, a prime occasion for the production of lacerating wit.

---

33 H. R. Woudhuysen in his Introduction mentions Sidney's work, including the *Arcadia*, and Pierre de la Primaudaye's *L'Académie française* as likely sources for situations in *Love's Labour's Lost* (pp. 2–7 and 66–7).

34 *Directions for Speech and Style*, ed. Hoyt H. Hudson (Princeton, 1935), pp. 1–2.

35 Edinburgh University Library Laing MS iii.193, fo. 142v (hereafter abbreviated EUL Laing MS). I am grateful to Andrew Gordon and Alan Stewart of the Francis Bacon Correspondence Project for the transcript of this material from which I quote, and to Alan Stewart for drawing the example to my attention. I have silently expanded abbreviations and omitted words crossed out. The letter is quoted in part in Lisa Jardine and Alan Stewart, *Hostage to Fortune: The Troubled Life of Francis Bacon* (London, 1998), p. 103; the identification of Mr Phillipps is theirs.

36 EUL Laing MS iii.193, fos. 142v–143r.

37 EUL Laing MS iii.193, fo. 143r.

That responses to verbal injuries administered as witty critique could escalate to aggression and outright violence is clear from the infamous incident at the Middle Temple, days after the revels of the Christmas season 1597–8, when John Davies, the satiric figure Stradilax mocked at and scorned during the revels described in *Le Prince d'Amour*, cudgelled and bludgeoned Richard Martin, his former friend and the revels' Lord of Misrule, and was expelled from the Middle Temple, to recover his standing only three years later. The same witty denunciation, arranged as an anagram rather than a pun, is applied to the expelled Davies in Manningham's diary that is applied to Holofernes as Judas Maccabeus in the Masque of Worthies: quoting Martin's wit, Manningham records, January 1601: 'Dauis. Aduis. Iudas. (Martin.)'[38] Moreover, just as the lords' wit, like some Inns of Court epigrams, descends to a devastating caricature of Holofernes's 'face' in the reductive and shaming series – 'A cittern-head', 'The head of a bodkin', 'A death's face in a ring', 'The pommel of Caesar's falchion', 'The carved-bone face on a flask', 'Saint George's half-cheek in a brooch' (5.2.604–611) – the Manningham diary produces wit by quoting the in-crowd's caricature of Davies's ass and gait: 'Jo[hn] Davys goes wadling with his arse out behinde as though he were about to make every one that he meetes a wall to pisse against. (B. Rudyerd, or Th. Overb[ur]y). He never walkes but he carries a clokebag behinde him, his arse stickes out soe farr.'[39]

But more usually, within-group scoff power at the Inns of Court or in Shakespeare's related kingdom of Navarre went hand in hand with scoff proofing: that is, the inculcation of routinized performance skills in order that the young man of privilege might, in the words of *Gesta Grayorum*, 'deliver himself from Scorns' (p. 28). Outsiders, subjected to the scoff power of elite collectivities of young men like the Inns' Men, had to endure unprotected by institutional drills and cliquish solidarity the twisting of their words and distorting of their names: Jude-Ass for some, 'vpstart Crow . . . with his *Tygers hart wrapt in a Players hyde*' or 'Shake-scene' for others.[40] At least one of them, nonetheless, found the means to show scorn its own image and to make of his tongue, using the commonwealth of the English language, 'a chariot to honor'.[41]

---

38 *The Diary of John Manningham of the Middle Temple, 1602–1603*, ed. Robert Parker Sorlien (Hanover, New Hampshire, 1976), p. 48.

39 *Diary of John Manningham*, p. 235.

40 Robert Greene, *Greenes Groatsworth of Wit* (1592), sig. F1v. The injury here came, of course, from a 'University Wit' rather than an Inns of Court man.

41 Mulcaster, *Elementarie*, p. 272.

MERCURY, BOY YET AND THE 'HARSH' WORDS OF *LOVE'S LABOUR'S LOST*

FREDERICK W. CLAYTON AND MARGARET TUDEAU-CLAYTON

If there is a god who might challenge Cupid's place as the presiding deity of *Love's Labour's Lost* it has to be Mercury. Obsessed with the use, and abuse of words, the play closes with the gnomic utterance, 'The words of Mercury are harsh after the songs of Apollo' (5.2.914–15), which, as they appear in the Folio, may be taken proleptically to refer to the announcement of separation which follows: 'You that way, we this way' (line 915).[1] The utterance has attracted a diversity of interpretations, predictably given its enigmatic and sentential character, but there is a more or less general consensus that Mercury and his harsh words represent some form of reality principle which breaks up the Arcadian fantasy world of (the) play, and which is embodied in the figure of Marcade, the messenger who brings the news of the death of the princess's father. Not only does Marcade correspond to contemporary versions of the god's name, as several critics have pointed out, but his function corresponds to Mercury's functions as messenger and psychopomp.[2] There is, however, a more prominent figure that the play invites spectators to associate with Mercury. Linked to Marcade by his dramatic function as well as by his office – he is sometimes grouped with Marcade in the 'persons of the play' – 'honey-tongued' (5.2.335) Boyet, the only major male figure at the princess's court, is associated with 'sweet tong'd' Mercury[3] both through more general features and, more importantly, through the specific features attributed to him in the two portraits by Berowne, especially the first (5.2.316–35). Some of these features are particularly striking in this respect: Boyet as 'the ape of form . . . / That . . . chides the dice' (326–7), for instance, corresponds closely to Nathaniel Baxter's description of Mercury as '[w]ittie, as an Ape, to follow/ . . . /At dice, . . . all the day long'.[4] Though not always so striking, almost all the features strengthen the association, and, taken together, furnish convincing evidence that the speech was inserted primarily in order to advertise the likeness of Boyet to Mercury in the last act of the play. It is, moreover, a likeness

What follows is a truly collaborative effort. At his death, my father, Professor F. W. Clayton (1913–99), a brilliantly original classicist, left a vast amount of unpublished research including notes on Berowne's speech on Boyet and the 'harsh' words of Mercury in *Love's Labour's Lost*. To these I have added research of my own and arguments that I trust are in the spirit of his work. But the piece could never have been written without the assistance of Vicky Stevens, honorary research fellow of the Department of Classics at the University of Exeter, who sifted through piles of papers and chased up references with exemplary generosity and efficiency. The Clayton family is deeply indebted to her.

[1] To save space, citations from classical texts will be taken in all cases fom the Loeb editions, which will not be specifically identified. In quoting from early modern texts I have modernized i/j u/v spellings.

[2] Anne Barton, 'A Source for *Love's Labour's Lost*', *TLS*, 24 November 1978, 1373–4; J. M. Nosworthy, 'The importance of being Marcadé', *Shakespeare Survey 32* (1979), pp. 105–14; Joseph A. Porter, *Shakespeare's Mercutio: His History and Drama* (Chapel Hill and London, 1988), pp. 208–9.

[3] Giles Fletcher, *The English Works of Giles Fletcher*, ed. Lloyd E. Berry (Madison, 1964), p. 94 (Sonnet XXV, line 5); 'sweet-tongued Mercury' is evoked too in John Marston, *Entertainment of Alice, Dowager Countess of Derby*, in *The Works*, ed. A. H. Bullen (London, 1887), vol. 3, p. 397.

[4] Nathaniel Baxter, *Sir Philip Sydneys Ourania* (London, 1606), n.pag.

that was recognised by contemporaries, as we shall see from traces of its afterlife in two plays by Ben Jonson, first, in the figure of the 'bright-shining gallant' 'humourous as quicksilver' 'monsieur Fastidious Brisk, otherwise cal'd the fresh Frenchefied courtier' in *Every Man Out of His Humour* (performed 1599, published 1600), second, in the figure of Mercury disguised as a '*Monsieur*, or *french*-behav'd gentleman' in *Cynthia's Revels* (performed 1600, published 1601). John Florio too recalls the likeness in a self-portrait as Mercury, which is of particular interest given Florio's supposed implication in the topical significance of the play.[5] Indeed, this is one of several citations featuring the figure of Mercury which come from texts that scholars have agreed belong to the play's complex intertextual and topical matrix. In conclusion, however, I would like to propose another set of intertextual relations, which emerges in the light of what follows and which suggests a significance at once local and more general, related as it is to the topos of paternal-authorial 'untimely death' and the unfinished business of cultural production which follows in/as its wake.

BOYET AND MERCURY

In his discussion of the attitudes to language explored through various groups in the play Ralph Berry comments in passing that the group of the princess's court should include 'epicene Boyet',[6] an epithet hinted at in the closing lines of Berowne's second, more vituperative portrait: 'Die when you will, a smock shall be your shroud' (5.2.480). According to Joseph Porter, epicene is how Mercury 'with his newly problematic gender and sexuality' came to be represented in the Renaissance, as an illustration from the sixteenth-century mythographer Cartari, in which the god 'seems a bit of a transsexual', shows.[7] Echoed in astrological discourse – 'Mercury is masculine and feminine according to the nature of the planet with whom it is joined'[8] – a corresponding image in the English literary tradition is found in John Gower's *Confessio Amantis,* where Mercury is described as a transvestite, if not as a transsexual: a 'gret spekere in all thinges / . . . and of lesinges' (i.e. lies),[9] 'whanne he wolde himself transforme' he '[f]ulofte time . . . tok the forme / Of womman'.[10]

This sexual ambiguity may grow out of representations in the classical tradition according to which Mercury is, again ambiguously, still a boy or a boy yet, that is, at the liminal moment at which so many of Shakespeare's ambiguously gendered figures – the young man of the Sonnets, the boys playing girls playing boys in the comedies – are located: '[a] yong man's likenesse, of the first flowr'd chin, / Whose forme hath all the grace of one so yong'; 'comely youth of beauty new'.[11] Moreover, the collocation 'boy yet' recurs, if tantalizingly, in association with Elizabethan figures of Mercury. In one of her progresses, for instance, Elizabeth is met by a boy playing Mercury and is told a narrative which includes this exchange between Jove and himself: 'Abide, *boy* . . . /Thou goest not *yet*'.[12] Habituated as she

[5] Francis Yates, *A Study of Love's Labour's Lost* (Cambridge, 1936), pp. 27–49.

[6] Ralph Berry, 'The Words of Mercury', *Shakespeare Survey 22* (1969), pp. 69–77 (p. 73).

[7] Porter, *Shakespeare's Mercutio,* p. 53 and fig. 6.

[8] W. Eland, *A Tutor to Astrology,* 7th edn (London, 1694), p. 16.

[9] Cf. 'Now Mercury indue thee with leasing.' *Twelfth Night* 1.5.93.

[10] John Gower, *Confessio Amantis*, Book 5, lines 945–6, 941–3 in *The English Works of John Gower*, ed. G. C. Macaulay, 2 vols. (London, 1957), vol. 1, pp. 427–8.

[11] *Chapman's Homer*, ed. A. Nicoll, 2 vols., 2nd edn (New York, 1967), vol. 2, p. 178 (lines 371–2); *The Aeneid of Thomas Phaer and Thomas Twyne*, ed. Steven Lally (London, 1987), p. 89 (line 616). Compare 'te . . . puerum' in Horace, *Odes* 1, x (lines 9–10), which might be translated as 'You, a mere boy yet . . .' (F. W. Clayton).

[12] J. Nichols, *The Progresses, and Public Processions of Queen Elizabeth,* 2 vols. (London, 1788), vol. 2, p. 61 (emphasis added). More important still are the two instances in *Cynthia's Revels* discussed below. This is not to deny the possibility that Shakespeare picked up the name from the list of French courtiers attendant on Henry of Navarre as Lefranc suggested (A. Lefranc, *Sous le Masque de William Shakespeare*, 2 vols. (Paris, 1919), vol. 2, p. 60). Given, however, the cultural habit of hearing/seeing homophonic relations we may suppose that the name stuck because it rhymed with representations of Mercury as a 'boy yet', rather as the name of Marcade stuck because of its resonance with versions of the god's name (or perhaps, as Stephen Orgel and H. R. Woudhuysen

9 'Qua dii vocant, eundum' in Geffrey Whitney, *A Choice of Emblemes, and other Devises* (Leyden, 1584).

was to being met by such figures and even to being 'conducted to her privy-chamber by Mercury' as gentleman usher,[13] Elizabeth – before whom the play was performed in the Christmas season of 1597/8 – must surely be included amongst those spectators who would have recognized the relation of the princess's ambiguously gendered gentleman usher to Mercury, the boy yet.[14]

Engaging in erotically charged exchanges of wit with both groups – the princess and her ladies, on the one hand, and the king and his lords, on the other – Boyet is, like Mercury, a go-between, conveying messages from one to the other.[15] But he also comes between the two groups, notably in Act 5, when he betrays to the princess and her ladies the lords' plot to come wooing disguised as Muscovites (5.2.89–126). This thwarting of their design is represented by Berowne as like the dashing of 'a Christmas comedy' (5.2.463) brought about by Boyet whom he then describes in his second more vituperative portrait (lines 464–82). *Love's Labour's Lost* is of course itself a Christmas comedy which is dashed by the news of the death of the princess's father brought by Marcade. The thwarting of consummation, at once sexual and artistic, is thus staged twice, the first a mock version, occasioned by the 'news' brought by Boyet ('Thy news, Boyet?' (5.2.81)), proleptically shadowing the second, occasioned by the 'news' brought by Marcade

have suggested, because of the resonance with Mar-Arcadie). The homophone Boyet/boy-yet is, moreover, exact since the name rhymes with debt (5.2.334–5). This is not, of course, how the French courtier mentioned by Lefranc would have pronounced his name.

13 Thomas Warton, *History of English Poetry*, ed. W. Carew Hazlitt (1871) repr. 4 vols. (New York, 1970), vol. 4, p. 356.

14 The occasional suggestions of Boyet's relative seniority (e.g. 'you are my elder' (5.2.600)) may be taken as theatrical irony, playing on a discrepancy between such suggestions and his youthful appearance (as a Mercurial boy yet), or between his apparent age and the implications of his name and Mercurial character.

15 Compare Mistress Quickly, the go-between in *The Merry Wives of Windsor* described by Falstaff as a 'she-Mercury' (2.2.79) – a comic take on the epicene god.

('the news I bring' (5.2.712)). The structural parallel as well as the relation to the figure of Mercury of these newsbringers, agents of the thwarting of sexual/artistic consummation, is pointed up by the phrase 'harsh indignity' which Boyet himself uses of the mockery to which he has exposed the lords: 'it can never be / They will digest this harsh indignity' (5.2.289–90). This anticipates the closing utterance, 'the words of Mercury are harsh', which itself not only looks back to the news brought by Marcade, but also looks forward, in the Folio, to the words announcing the separation occasioned by the news: 'You that way, we this way.' This is effectively a stage direction, and stage directions are what Boyet has been giving throughout Act 5 from the moment he enters with *his* 'news': 'Prepare, madam, prepare' (5.2.81); 'The trumpets sound, be masked' (156); 'change favours' (293); 'Ladies, withdraw' (309). As the god who guides it is Mercury, we might say, who issues stage directions in the *theatrum mundi*. More specifically, as Mercury *in trivio* (the crossroads), he guides at the junction of 'divers wayes' as Geffrey Whitney's emblem puts it (illustration 9).[16] But, as we shall see, it is only when, in his guidance, he announces the separation of friends or lovers in 'divers wayes' that he is specifically represented as harsh. It is then to assume this 'harsh' aspect of Mercury that the princess bids Boyet 'prepare' (5.2.720), echoing his own earlier instructions and so underscoring his role as agent of the reiterated frustration of sexual/aesthetic consummation. Assuming this 'harsh' aspect Boyet becomes a more sombre figure, shedding those aspects of Mercury, including the contrary aspect of the sweet or honey tongue, attributed to him by Berowne in the verbal portraits, which, as I indicated earlier, serve primarily to advertise the likeness of Boyet to the multifaceted god.

BOYET AND MERCURY: BEROWNE'S VERBAL PORTRAITS

> This fellow pecks up wit as pigeons peas,
> And utters it again when God doth please.
> (5.2.316–17)[17]

Whether pecking up (Q) or picking up (F) wit the implication is clearly that Boyet is something of a 'pick-purse' of others' wit, or a plagiarist.[18] Mercury is of course the god of theft as well as of wit as John Donne recalls in an epigram on one of the earliest, notoriously unreliable, continental newsheets, *Mercurius Gallo Belgicus*: 'Thou art like Mercury in stealing.'[19] More specifically, in *Quip for an Upstart Courtier* (1592), a widely circulated text by Robert Greene, who elsewhere attacks Shakespeare as a plagiarist, there is a dinner scene in which tailors, 'eatinge their pease with theyr needels pointes, one by one', i.e. picking up peas, are joined by Mercury who, in his hunger, turns the needle flat side up to pick up more peas and is accused of bad manners: 'what fellow' (cf. Berowne's 'this fellow') 'a showell and a spaede, to buttred pease?'[20]

Though Greene does not mention pigeons, he might well have done so as pigeons are consistently associated with Mercury in Western European culture from antiquity to the eighteenth century. In Latin designated by the phrase 'nuntius ales' – winged messenger or messenger bird – both are regularly represented as celestial messengers: Rabelais calls the bird 'celeste messaiger', while Dryden calls the god 'the Coelestial Messenger' and Diderot brings the two together in his description

[16] Geffrey Whitney, *A Choice Of Emblemes, and other Devises* (Leyden, 1584), p. 2.

[17] What follows represents perhaps a fifth of the material collected by F. W. Clayton on Berowne's portrait of Boyet; we have aimed to select the most convincing arguments and illustrations.

[18] This is how Sidney represents the plagiarist in *Astrophel and Stella* (sonnet 74, line 8) in *The Poems of Sir Philip Sidney*, ed. William A. Ringler (Oxford, 1962); see Jonson 'On Poet Ape': 'would pick and glean, . . . / makes each man's wit his owne' (Epigram LVI, lines 5, 8) in *The Works*, ed. C. H. Herford, Percy and Evelyn Simpson, 11 vols. (Oxford, 1925–42), vol. 8, pp. 44–5. All citations from Jonson's works are from this edition.

[19] John Donne, *Poems*, ed. Hugh I'Anson Faussett (London, 1958), p. 55.

[20] Robert Greene, *A Quip for an Upstart Courtier* in *Life and Complete Works of Robert Greene*, ed. Alexander B. Grosart (repr. New York, 1964), vol. 11, p. 264.

of the pigeon as 'l'oiseau Mercure'.[21] Pigeons were also believed to feed their young by regurgitating food into their beaks – uttering or retailing food as the *Mercurius Gallo Belgicus* retails news, and as the pedlar Autolycus 'littered under Mercury' (*The Winter's Tale* 4.3.25), 'sings several tunes faster than you'll tell money. He *utters them as he had eaten ballads*' (4.4.184–6, emphasis added).

This association of pigeons with retelling/retailing food/news returns in *As You Like It* (?1599/1600) at the entry of a figure who, in several senses including the phonetic, is a faint echo of Boyet: Monsieur Le Beau.

CELIA Here comes Monsieur Le Beau.
ROSALIND With his mouth full of news.
CELIA Which he will put on us as pigeons feed their young.
ROSALIND Then shall we be news-crammed.
CELIA All the better: we shall be the more marketable. *Bonjour*, Monsieur Le Beau, what's the news? (1.2.86–93)

With this description of Celia and Rosalind as 'marketable' (because crammed with news to retail/retell) and with the figure of Autolycus, the pedlar, who sings 'Money's a meddler, / That doth *utter* all men's ware-a' (4.4.320–1, emphasis added) we enter the field of associations evoked in Berowne's next lines:

He is wit's pedlar, and retails his wares
At wakes and wassails, meetings, markets, fairs.
And we that sell by gross, the Lord doth know,
Have not the grace to grace it with such show.
(5.2.318–21)

Mercury is god of trade as well as of wit – a combination suggested earlier by the princess's denigration of Boyet's praise as '*uttered* by base sale of *chapmen's* tongues' (2.1.16, emphasis added).[22] Mercury is also, as we have seen, the god of travellers, a function that is given a specifically English inflection by Thomas Overbury, who describes the Almanac Maker as 'a dumb *Mercury* to poynt out High-wayes, and a Bayliffe of all Marts and Faires in England'.[23] Doing the rounds of the very English occasions listed by Berowne hardly fits with the figure of a French courtier, which itself indicates that the association with Mercury is more important here than consistency of characterization. Indeed, the first two lines would be more appropriate for the anglicized son of Mercury, Autolycus the pedlar, who 'haunts wakes, fairs, and bear-baitings' (4.3.100–1), retailing his wares, a 'snapper-up of unconsidered trifles' like his father (4.3.25–6). Deriving ultimately from the denigratory epithet παλιγκάπηλος which is used of the god in Aristophanes' *The Plutus* (line 1156) and which denotes precisely a retailer, this character of Mercury persists in the English literary tradition: in Dryden's *Amphitryon* (1690), for instance, the god, in disguise, suggests to Phaedra: 'Suppose I were Mercury, the God of Merchandise?' to which she replies, 'What, the God of small Wares, and Fripperies, of Pedlars and Pilferers?'[24] Associated with the round of English festive occasions by Autolycus, who congratulates himself on having 'cut most of their festival purses' (4.4.615), this character of Mercury is evoked too by the figure of the cutpurse who haunts the English fair in Jonson's *Bartholmew Fair* and who is called, if ironically, 'our Mercury'.[25]

[21] F. Rabelais, *Gargantua et Pantagruel*, 2 vols. (Paris, 1993), vol. 1, p. 471 (book 4, chapter iii); John Dryden's translation of *Aeneid* 4, 571 (where there is no equivalent in the Latin); D. Diderot, *Oeuvres*, ed. E. M. Butdahl et al., 25 vols. (Paris, 1984), vol. 14, p. 63.

[22] The god of trade is combined with the god of eloquence in Renaissance emblems featuring Mercury. See C. Balavoine, 'L'Emblematisation de Mercure à la Renaissance', in *Mercure à la Renaissance* (Paris, 1988), pp. 55–67 (64–5).

[23] Thomas Overbury, *New and Choise characters* (London, 1615), sig. H3r.

[24] John Dryden, *Amphitryon* II.ii.134–6 in *The Works*, ed. H. T. Swedenberg Jr *et al.*, vols. 20 (Berkeley, 1956–2000), vol. 15, p. 260.

[25] *Bartholomew Fair* in *The Works*, vol. 6, 4.3.105. Note too that Mercury is the patron god of wrestling (as Jonson recalls in *Cynthia's Revels* 1.1.32), a traditional feature of English wakes (and the news brought by Le Beau in *As You Like It* is of a wrestling match). Also, in a poem to Sir Robert Wroth, Jonson places Hermes and his lyre in the English rural context of the nobleman's country house where 'the jolly wassall walkes the often round' ('To Sir Robert Wroth' in *The Forrest* in *The Works*, vol. 8, pp. 96–100, lines 51, 59).

10 Mercury leading the Graces in V. Cartari, *Le imagini de i dei degli antichi* . . . (Padua, 1603) [*By permission of the Syndics of Cambridge University Library*]

While Autolycus receives 'by th' gross' the goods he then retails (4.4.207–8), Berowne draws an ironic contrast between the retailing pedlar Boyet-Mercury and those like himself who sell their wit 'by gross', an ironic contrast which tends to backfire given the princess's recent denigration of the lords' wit as 'gross, gross' (5.2.268). The main point of the contrast, however, is the wordplay it introduces on gross/grace, a word play which we find elsewhere, for instance in William Browne's description of a 'lovely Boy' '[w]hose body all the Graces hath ingrosst'.[26] Mercury might well be said to have engrossed the graces not only on account of his own beauty, but also on account of his persistent association with the (plural) Graces, as in the illustration from Cartari (illustration 10), an association which is evoked in the very first speech by Boyet when he seeks to persuade the princess: 'Be now as prodigal of all dear grace / As nature was in making graces dear' (2.1.9–10). This association of Mercury with the Graces is explained by Robert Burton in a passage particularly suggestive of Berowne's portrait of Boyet: referring to the 'grace' of 'good discourse, eloquence, wit', which renders a man 'gracious', Burton writes, 'our old poets . . . made Mercury the gentleman *usher* to the graces' because 'a *sweet* voice causeth admiration; and he that can *utter* himself in good words . . . is called . . . a divine spirit'.[27] Mercury seems indeed to be almost automatically associated with grace or graces: the boy Mercury, for instance, who addresses Elizabeth on her progress, says 'I kiss hir steppes . . . And leave with hir such graces from above, . . . So with this grace, good Queene, now heere adue'.[28] Crites too, in Jonson's *Cynthia's Revels*, talks of the 'grace divinest *Mercurie* hath done me' (5.1.2). The word 'grace' even creeps into translations where there is no equivalent in the original. Thus Chapman: 'Then tooke he up his rod, that hath the grace / To shut what eyes he list', where there is nothing in the Greek to justify the word 'grace', as there is nothing to justify the periphrastic description 'this Grace of men' seven lines later.[29]

Surrounded by Graces – a girl on each arm as it were – 'this gallant' Mercury may well be said, as Berowne says of Boyet, to 'pin the wenches on his sleeve' (line 322).[30] 'Had he been Adam', Berowne goes on, 'he had tempted Eve' (line 323), a curious inversion of the biblical narrative, which may be explained by the association of Mercury

26 William Browne, *Britannia's Pastorals* (repr. Menston, 1969), p. 53 (Book 2, song 3).

27 Robert Burton, *The Anatomy of Melancholy*, 3 vols. (New York and London, 1932), vol. 3, p. 25 (emphasis added).

28 Nichols, *The Progresses*, vol. 2, p. 62.

29 *Chapman's Homer*, ed. Nicoll, vol. 1, p. 486 (translating *Illiad*, 24.343–4, 353).

30 Clayton suggests a more specific, if tenuous, connection to Mercury: in a published sermon (1585) Archbishop Sandys uses the phrase 'pinning themselves upon men's sleeves' of those who identify with particular apostles, namely, Apollos or Paul, the latter being called Mercury by the people of Lystra and a 'Christian Mercury' by Gabriel Harvey, as we shall see.

with both Adam and the tempting serpent. The association with Adam is most explicit in alchemical discourse: 'the matter of the philosophers stone is nothing else but a fiery and perfect *Mercury* . . . the true *Hermaphrodite, Adam*' and 'the Composition of this sacred *Adamick* Stone, is made after the *Adamick Mercury* of the wise men'.[31] On the other hand, Mercury as tempter dates from classical antiquity – Ovid uses 'seduxit' of Mercury's persuasion of Battus (*Metamorphoses* 2, 691) – and the snakes of the caduceus readily lent themselves to association with the diabolic serpent in Christian culture. Thus, following the story of Battus, Golding translates 'caducifer' (*Metamorphoses* 2, 708), 'The Bearer of the charmed Rod, the suttle Mercurie', using the biblical epithet for the serpent of Eden ('more subtil than any beast of the field' (Genesis 3.1)).[32] Marlowe too describes how Mercury, seeking to seduce a country maid, 'with his snakie rod / Did charme her nimble feet', while Shakespeare's Thersites, in *Troilus and Cressida*, addresses Mercury by invoking 'the serpentine craft of thy caduceus'.[33] Finally, Mercury often appears in visual representations as nude or nearly nude, like Adam and Eve. More specifically, in *The Golden Ass*, a theatrical performance of the judgement of Paris is described in which Mercury appears as a 'young man all naked' 'with his rodde called Caduceus' and 'in his right hand an apple of gold'.[34] A nearly naked Mercury similarly offers the apple to Paris in an Italian ceiling panel exactly contemporary with Shakespeare's play.[35] When, one wonders, does the apple of Eden acquire a golden tinge?

The ideas of temptation/seduction continue as Boyet's courtly manners are specified: 'A can carve too, and lisp, why, this is he / That kissed his hand away in courtesy' (5.2.324–5). While carving was associated with Mercury in classical literature – it is one of the skills bestowed by Hermes in *Odyssey* 15 (lines 319–23) – it is a specifically courtly skill by the time of Chaucer whose Knight's son could 'carf biforn his fader at the table'.[36] Jonson brings the skill and the god together in Cupid's caustic description of Mercury's ability to 'wait mannerly at a table with a trencher' (i.e. a knife to cut meat) in *Cynthia's Revels* (1.2.25–6). (Compare 'trencher-knight', which Berowne uses in his second portrait of Boyet (5.2.465).) 'How daintly he carves', says the citizen's wife Fallace of Sir Fastidious Brisk, the Mercury-Boyet imitation in *Every Man Out of His Humour* (4.1.36; see below). As this example suggests, carving could also imply seduction, as when Falstaff says of Mrs Ford, 'she carves, she gives the leer of invitation' (*Merry Wives* 1.3.39–40). Seduction may be implied too when the princess requests of Boyet that he apply his skill in carving to the opening of a love letter: 'Boyet, you can carve. / Break up this capon' (4.1.55–6).

According to astrologists, lisping was a defect that could afflict those born under Mercury.[37] It tended, however, to be treated rather as an affectation 'to make . . . English sweet upon his tongue', as Chaucer says of the Friar who 'lipsed' (sic).[38] In *Merry Wives* it is associated with the seductive eloquence of ambiguously gendered young men, who are likened to buds of May (the month named after Maia, mother of Mercury): 'these lisping hawthorn-buds that come like women in men's apparel' (3.3.66–7) (cf. Berowne: 'This is the flower that smiles on everyone' (5.2.332)). Lisping was also associated specifically with the '*Mercuriall*' nation,

31 *Paracelsus*, trans. R. Turner (London, 1657), pp. 27, 32.

32 *Ovid's Metamorphoses, The Arthur Golding Translation*, ed. J. F. Nims (repr. Philadelphia, 2000), book 2, line 880 (p. 55). All biblical citations are from the Authorized King James version. According to Ludwig Schrader Mercury is even represented as a devil in the Middle Ages, although he gives no specific examples. Ludwig Schrader, 'Diversité des Fonctions de Mercure: l'exemple de Pontanus', in *Mercure à la Renaissance* (cited n. 22), pp. 45–54 (46).

33 *Hero and Leander*, lines 398–9, in *The Complete Works of Christopher Marlowe*, ed. Roma Gill, 4 vols. (Oxford, 1987–96), vol. 1, p. 199; *Troilus and Cressida*, 2.3.11–12.

34 *The xi Bookes of the Golden Asse*, trans. W. Adlington (London, 1566), sig Ggiir–Ggiiv (translating Book 10, section 30).

35 Panel from the ceiling of the Farnese Gallery 1597–8, by A. Carraci, reproduced in John Rupert Martin, *The Farnese Gallery* (Princeton, 1965), fig. 66.

36 Geoffrey Chaucer, 'General prologue' line 100 in *The Works*, ed. F. N. Robinson, 2nd edn (London, 1968), p. 18.

37 Eland, *A Tutor to Astrology*, p. 16.

38 Chaucer,'General prologue', lines 265, 264 in *The Works*, p. 19.

the French,[39] and with English travellers who picked up the affectation (*As You Like It* 4.1.31–2; *Romeo and Juliet* 2.3.26–7). Kissing one's hand in courtesy was associated with the Italians as well as with the French: in Nashe's *Lenten Stuffe* (1599) the Pope's caterer 'flew as swift as Mercury' and 'kissed his hand thrice'.[40] Elsewhere Nashe associates the gesture with affected behaviour picked up in Italy, which 'formes our yong master' by making him 'to kis his hand like an ape'.[41] For Robert Burton, more generally, '[t]o see a man protest friendship kiss his hand . . . smile' illustrates how men 'act variety of parts', 'temporize and vary, like Mercury the planet' and 'like apes follow the fashions'.[42]

Drawing on the same network of associations Berowne's speech continues:

> This is the ape of form, Monsieur the Nice,
> That when he plays at tables chides the dice
> In honourable terms. (5.2.326–8)

'*Mercurie*' writes Nathaniel Baxter, '[w]ittie, as an Ape, to follow / . . . / At dice, Cards, and gaming, all the day long'.[43] God of games of chance Mercury is also linguistically associated specifically with dice: in Latin dice are *tali* (from the word for ankle bones, originally used as dice) and the game is *talarius ludus*, while *talaria* is the word for the winged ankles/sandals of Mercury. These associations might have been pointed out by a well-read schoolmaster commenting on *talaria* in the most well known description of Mercury, in *Aeneid* 4.238–58 (line 239). Indeed the god here comes precisely to 'chide' Aeneas, as the ghost of Hamlet's father, likened to the god as he appears in the Virgilian passage – 'the herald Mercury / New lighted on a heaven-kissing hill' (*Hamlet* 3.4.57–8) – comes his 'tardy son to chide' (line 97).[44]

Mercury is described by Robert Henryson as 'full of rethorie / With polite terms',[45] but 'honourable terms', which editors often gloss 'polite', is unusual. Yet it too is associated with Mercury and in a text that has been recognized as belonging to the play's contextual matrix, namely the published quarrels between Gabriel Harvey and Thomas Nashe (to which of course Robert Greene's *Quip for an Upstart Courtier,* cited earlier, also belongs).[46] In *Pierces Supererogation* (1593) (to which Shakespeare may allude in 4.2.81–8) Harvey holds the apostle Paul up as a model of proper behaviour who, like 'a Christian Mercury', 'demeaned himself' well 'not only before the king Agrippa, but also before the twoo (sic) Romane Procuratours of that Province, Felix and Festus: whom he entreated in honourable terms'.[47] With the striking and unusual phrase 'honourable terms' Harvey seeks to draw a contrast with Nashe who, in *Pierce Penilesse* (1592), had warned: 'I have tearmes (if I be vext) laid in steepe in *Aquafortis*, & Gunpowder.'[48]

Associations with Mercury in the context of the Harvey–Nashe dispute continue to be evoked in the next lines: 'Nay, he can sing / A mean most meanly, and in ushering / Mend him who can' (5.2.328–30). Linked to music and song from classical antiquity on, Mercury is described as 'singand merilie' by Henryson.[49] There is, however,

39 James Howell, *Instructions and Directions for Forren Travell* (London, 1650), p. 34 (a contrast of the '*Mercuriall*' French with the '*Saturnine*' Spanish).

40 Thomas Nashe, *Works*, ed. R. B. McKerrow, 5 vols. (London, 1904–10), vol. 3, pp. 207–8.

41 Nashe, *Works*, vol. 2, p. 301 (*The Unfortunate Traveller).*

42 Burton, *The Anatomy of Melancholy*, vol. 1, pp. 65, 66.

43 Baxter, *Sir Philip Sydneys Ourania*, n. pag. (cited above, note 4).

44 Shakespeare here conflates the figure of Mercury with the ghost of Aeneas's father who, as Aeneas tells Dido, haunts his dreams with warnings (*Aeneid* 4, lines 351–3) reinforcing the words of the god.

45 Robert Henryson, *Testament of Cresseid*, ed. Denton Fox (London, 1968), p. 69.

46 See W. Schrickx, *Shakespeare's Early Contemporaries. The Background of the Harvey-Nashe Polemic and Love's Labour's Lost* (Antwerp, 1956).

47 Gabriel Harvey, *Pierces Supererogation* (London, 1593), p. 81. The biblical passages to which Harvey refers come some ten chapters after the story of the healing at Lystra for which Paul was called 'Mercurius, because he was the chief speaker' (Acts 14.12).

48 Thomas Nashe, *Pierce Penilesse* in *Works*, vol. 1, p. 195; cf. Gabriel Harvey, *Foure Letters* (1592), ed. G. B. Harrison, (London, 1922), p. 66.

49 Henryson, *Testament of Cresseid*, p. 69 (line 243).

a more specific allusion here to the description of Mercury in *Aeneid* 4, as this had been translated by Richard Stanyhurst, who was one of the objects of the Harvey-Nashe quarrels, praised as he was by Harvey and damned by Nashe. Translating Virgil's comparison of Mercury to a bird, Stanyhurst writes, 'Not to the sky maynely, but neere sea *meanely* she flickreth / So with a *mean* passadge twixt sky and sea Mercury slideth'.[50] In his preface to Robert Greene's *Menaphon* (1589), which is at the origin of his quarrel with the Harvey brothers, Nashe comments that had Stanyhurst not risen to fame, Phaer would have enjoyed just celebrity for his translation and '*corrigat qui potest*' would have been 'subscribed to his workes' – a Latin tag very exactly rendered by 'Mend him who can'.[51] It is, moreover, the description of Mercury in *Aeneid* 4, specifically his role as guide or usher, to the dead that Stanyhurst himself had mentioned in the preface to his translation as a place where Phaer's translation required, precisely, correction.[52]

Ushering is of course one of Mercury's primary functions, whether as psychopomp – 'By Mercury the Wooers' soules / Are usher'd to th'Infernall Pooles' – or as usher to the gods – 'thus the Mercury of heaven, / Ushers th' ambrosiate banquet of the Gods'.[53] As we have seen, he is also 'gentleman usher to the graces' (Burton), a role assumed by figures of Mercury in relation to Elizabeth and her retinue on progresses as it is assumed by Boyet in relation to the princess and her ladies (see illustration 10). Boyet, however, is not called 'sweet' by the princess or her ladies, as Berowne goes on to suggest that he might be: 'The ladies call him sweet' (line 330). 'Sweet' is, on the other hand, repeatedly used by an enamoured Fallace of the Mercurial Fastidious Brisk (see below), while it is used of Mercury himself by John Donne who, invoking the god's power to seduce ladies, asserts that '[h]e that charm'd *Argus*' eyes, sweet *Mercury*, / Works not' on the pure soul of Elizabeth Drury in its progress to heaven.[54]

'The stairs', continues Berowne, 'as he treads on them kiss his feet' (5.2.331). As usher and messenger the stairs are a place to find Boyet, like Mercury, who was noted for his light and nimble feet not only as an usher but also as a dancer.[55] Jonson, for instance, compares Pan to Hermes as leader of the Naiads and Dryads 'to their daunces', while Milton describes Mercury as the first deviser of the 'court guise' of 'trippings' 'with the mincing Dryades'.[56] It is, moreover, with an usher of a dancing school that Nashe – again in his quarrels with Harvey – associates the kissing of feet: 'No Usher of a dauncing Schoole was ever yet such . . . a kisser of the shadow of your feetes shadow'.[57] Although it is the usher who does the kissing here, as it is the boy Mercury who declares of Elizabeth that he will 'kiss hir steppes' (see above), and as it is Fastidious Brisk who is described as 'kissing ladies pumps' (see below), the network of associations – of Mercurial ushers with kissing feet – remains the same.

From feet to face the portrait concludes with a close-up of smiling features and a complimentary acknowledgement of the principal skill of 'sweet' or 'honey' 'tongued' Boyet-Mercury:

---

[50] Richard Stanyhurst, *The First Foure Bookes of Virgil His Aeneis* (Leyden, 1582), p. 72 (emphasis added). The translation is playing on the sense of Virgil's 'humilis' (*Aeneid* 4, line 255) as this is used in relation to style, including the 'mean' style of Virgil's *Eclogues*.

[51] Thomas Nashe, 'To the Gentlemen Students' in *Works*, vol. 3, p. 319. Towards the close of this letter Nashe uses the phrase 'taffety fooles' (p. 324), which may be echoed in Berowne's 'Taffeta phrases' (5.2.407).

[52] Stanyhurst, *The First Foure Bookes*, sig Aiiir.

[53] 'The Argument' in *Chapman's Homer*, ed. Nichol, vol. 2, p. 404 (*Odyssey* 24); Thomas Dekker, *Satiromastix*, 5.2.1–2, in *The Works*, ed. F. Bowers, 4 vols. (Cambridge, 1953–61), vol. 1. The association of Mercury with ushering is noted by H. R. Woudhuysen in the third Arden edition of the play (1998) (note to 5.2.328).

[54] Donne, *Poems*, p. 198 ('The Progress of the Soul').

[55] Clayton suggests that 'stairs' might be emended to 'stars', which Mercury is said to tread, for instance in Claudian's *The Rape of Proserpine*. For reasons of space we have chosen to omit this densely illustrated part of his argument.

[56] Ben Jonson, *Pan's Anniversary*, line 178 in *The Works*, vol. 7, p. 535; John Milton, *Comus* in *Complete Shorter Poems*, ed. John Carey (London, 1968), p. 224.

[57] Nashe, 'Have with you to Saffron Walden' in *The Works*, vol. 3, p. 92 (referring to Gabriel Harvey).

This is the flower that smiles on everyone
To show his teeth as white as whalës bone,
And consciences that will not die in debt
Pay him the due of 'honey-tongued' Boyet.
(5.2.332–5)

Though it may be as a 'flower' of courtesy that Boyet is described here it is worth noting that Mercury was the name of several plants, and of one in particular which existed in 'three kinds', as Randall Cotgrave points out in his French-English dictionary (1612), including a 'male' and a 'female' kind, called, according to the *OED*, boy's Mercury and girl's Mercury, the boy's being the female plant and the girl's the male, an intriguing botanical echo of the image of the epicene god. Mercury too smiles, like Boyet (and this feature is mentioned again in Berowne's second speech (line 465)): 'what a nice smile he has for everyone' is how Lucian's description of the newborn son of Maia – προσγελα πάσι – is rendered in the Loeb translation.[58] According to Natalis Comes too the god was regularly represented 'vultu hilari'[59] or 'glad of contynaunce and chere' as John Lydgate puts it in a long description of Mercury which, four lines earlier, specifically mentions 'His tethe eke white as evory, / Wel set in ordre'.[60] Finally, as Ben Jonson recalls in his opening 'catalogue' of Mercury's functions in *Cynthia's Revels*, Mercury as psychopomp might claim a share of the fee owed to Charon by the souls of the dead (*Cynthia's Revels* 1.1.35–7). What Boyet is paid, here, however, is a debt of praise due to the seductive power of his eloquence, which he shares with Mercury (see note 3). It is a power that, as editors have often noted, is also attributed to 'hony tongued' Shakespeare by Francis Meres in his pantheon of English authors, *Palladis Tamia* published, like the quarto of the play, by Cuthbert Burby and in the same year (1598).[61] Nothing, however, has been made of the echo, presumably because editors and critics have been reluctant to associate Shakespeare with this particular creature of his imagination. What they have missed is the implicit third term – the figure of Mercury – which was to be made explicit by Jonson after Shakespeare's death, as we shall see. For Meres this third term was no doubt self-evident from the portrait of Boyet from which he quotes, and which is effectively a catalogue of traits of the multifaceted god, inflected at times by local contexts in which they feature, notably, the Greene/Nashe–Harvey quarrels. Certainly, as we shall now see, it was as Mercury that Boyet was recognized by Shakespeare's contemporaries, Ben Jonson and John Florio.

THE IMMEDIATE AFTERLIFE OF BOYET-MERCURY

John Florio's 'epistle dedicatory' to the third volume of his translation of Montaigne – addressed to noblewomen who are his pupils of French as well as his patronesses – opens with an elaborate comparison of himself as their French teacher to a man leading a dance, specifically a French *branle* – the dance which is Englished (correctly) as 'brawl' in Shakespeare's play (3.1.8).[62] In this role he likens himself to Mercury at once as planet and as gentleman usher to the Graces. The passage reproduces several of the associations evoked in the portrait of Boyet–Mercury, which it may recall:

Your Honorable Ladieships, excelling in Musike, . . . can tell me of a French branle . . . wherein one man, *like Mercurie betweene the radiant orbes of Venus and Moone,*

[58] *Dialogues of the Gods* in *Lucian*, vol. 7, pp. 292–3.

[59] Natalis Comes, *Mythologiae* (Venice 1567), (repr. New York, 1976), fol. 134v.

[60] John Lydgate, *Reson and Sensuallyte*, ed. E. Sieper, 2 vols. (repr. London, 1965), vol. 1, p. 46 (lines 1721, 1717). The line is echoed by George Turbeville, who, in a poem in 'Praise of his Love', describes 'teeth as white as Whale his bone / each one in order due'. George Turbeville, *Epitaphes, Epigrams, Songs and Sonets* (London, 1567), fol.129v.

[61] Woudhuysen, n. to 5.2.334 and 'Introduction', pp. 78–9. As Woudhuysen helpfully reminds us, the play, which is included in Meres' list of Shakespeare's comedies, is the only one Meres could have read in print.

[62] Cotgrave glosses 'Bransle' 'a brawle, or daunce'. For Francis Yates this was one of the indications of the play's satiric treatment of the foreign language teachers in London, including Florio. Yates, *A Study*, pp. 65–9.

> *leadeth a daunce to two women.* In resemblance whereof; though much I want *the eloquence of Mercurie* to move you, much more *his abilitie to guide you,* most of all his nobilitie to comfort you, yet, as for your exercise . . . sometime you practise with *meaner* than a teacher, or a teacher much *meaner* than your selves: vouchsafe me your unworthie, but herein happy teacher, joyntly to *usher* you to this French motion.[63]

Particularly striking here is the phrase 'nobilitie to comfort', since this is not an office or aspect of Mercury. It is, however, an office that might have been performed by Lord Boyet as he ushered the mourning princess and her ladies offstage in contemporary performances of the play. At any rate it would appear that Florio chose to identify with this figure, perhaps as a way of distracting attention from his possible implication in other less flattering figures in the play.

If Florio chooses to foreground the noble and courtly character of Mercury–Boyet, in *Every Man Out of His Humour* (performed 1599, published 1600) Jonson chooses rather to develop the portrait's satirical edge in his figure of the 'bright-shining *gallant*' '*Monsieur* Fastidious Brisk, otherwise cal'd the fresh *Frenchefied courtier*' 'humourous as *quicksilver*' (1.3.192, 194–5, 197, emphasis added). Attributed in the formal description of characters specifically with a 'wand' and a jingling 'spurre' that attracts the attention of the would-be gallant Fungoso, Fastidious is described by Fallace, the enamoured citizen's wife, as having a 'face like a *Cherubin*' 'a body like an angell' (? a boy yet) 'and a tongue able to ravish any woman i'the earth' (2.6.123, 126–7, 130). Characterized by smiles (2.1.11), he is repeatedly described as 'sweet', especially by Fallace whose speech in praise of his courtly manners – including 'how daintily he carves! how sweetly he talks, and tels newes' – contains no less than three rapturous exclamations of 'Oh, sweete Fastidius' (4.1.29–41). He is also repeatedly associated with grace or graces. 'Let thy words ever sound in mine eares and thy graces disperse contentment through all my senses' (2.6.115–16), cries Fallace, who earlier brings sweetness and grace together in another rapture: 'Ah, the sweet grace of a courtier!'(2.6.40). This is in response to Fastidius's own account of his success at court: 'in grace, . . . both of the noble masculine, and feminine' (5–7) (a hint at Mercurial sexual ambiguity?), 'grac't . . . beyond all aime of affection' (24), 'by the grace of god' (31).

This flattering view is undercut by the scholar Macilente, who, when asked by the citizen Deliro about his visit with Fastidius to his mistress at court – 'no doubt you have beene grac't exceedingly' (4.2.26) – replies with a caustic exposure of the real case. Far from being 'graced' Fastidius is an object of scorn at court:

> Though he but *apishly* doth imitate
> The *gallant'st* courtiers, *kissing ladies pumps,*
> Holding the cloth for them, praising their wits,
> And serviley observing every one,
> May do them *pleasure*: fearefull to be seene
> With any man . . .
> That's not *in grace*, . . .
> Thus courtiers doe, and these he counterfeits.
> (4.2.34–40, emphasis added)

A counterpoint to Fallace's speech of praise, which closes the previous scene, Macilente's speech likewise takes up elements of the portraits of Boyet, especially those with a satirical edge. Compare, for instance, Macilente's 'may do them pleasure' with Berowne's 'please-man' (5.2.464), from his second, more sarcastic speech. Compare too how Berowne goes on to liken Boyet to 'some slight zany' that 'knows the trick / To make my lady laugh' (464, 466–7) with Macilente's concluding lines: 'Hee's like the *Zani*, to a tumbler, / That tries tricks after him, to make men laugh' (44–5). A self-conscious English imitation of a French Mercurial 'ape of form' Jonson's remake of Boyet–Mercury serves, finally, his satiric purpose of exposing the affected behaviour of English courtiers.[64]

---

[63] John Florio, *Essays*, 3 vols. (repr. London, 1946), vol. 3, p. 1 (emphasis added).

[64] Fastidious Brisk himself has an afterlife: he is explicitly mentioned by Richard Burton and by John Marston in ways which point up the association with Mercury-Boyet, as we hope to explore elsewhere.

The same purpose is served by Jonson's second, more complex remake of the figure in *Cynthia's Revels* (performed 1600, published 1601). This features Mercury himself who, towards the end of the play, assumes the disguise of a '*Monsieur*, or *french*-behav'd gentleman' (5.4.12) in a contest of 'behaviour' with those he has earlier condemned as 'ridiculous heads, / Who with their *apish* customes, and forc'd garbes, / Would bring the name of courtier in contempt' (5.1.34–6, emphasis added). The contest of 'behaviour' at moments clearly recalls Berowne's portrait of Boyet as, for instance, when the french-behaved gentleman speaks in praise of one of the court ladies: 'Sweet Madam . . . all the Graces smile in your cheeks; . . . you have a tongue steep't in honie . . .' (5.4.429, 431–2, 433). However, although Mercury wins the contest, his purpose is not to promote the model of behaviour he represents as the french-behaved gentleman but rather to 'correct, / And punish' (5.1.17–18) the apish courtiers, and their obsession with form or 'behaviour' as the criterion of nobility.[65]

This role as the agent of a (harsh) satirical purpose is in sharp contrast with the first appearance of Mercury, when he is himself the object of a satiric description by Cupid whose detailed 'catalogue' (1.1.33) of Mercury's functions, which occasionally echoes Berowne's portrait of Boyet, as we have seen, serves no obvious purpose except perhaps to demonstrate a more thorough knowledge of the classical representations of the god (the subtext being that Jonson has actually read Aristophanes, Lucian, etc.). Acted by a boy, Mercury here is very much the mischievous, light-fingered boy (yet), as Jonson signals in the opening exchange between Mercury, in his first disguise as page, and his master the courtier Hedon.

HEDON *Boy*!
MERCURY Sir.
HEDON Are any of the ladies in the presence?
MERCURY None *yet,* sir. (2.2.1–4, emphasis added)

The collocation – boy yet – returns in the closing scene, when Mercury has assumed again the disguise of a page (after playing the french-behaved gentleman) and the sovereign authority Cynthia proceeds to make her 'discoveries'. Unmasking 'the boy', Cupid, she then exclaims:

Dear Mercurie, our brother, like a page,
To countenance the ambush of the *boy*?
Nor endeth our discoverie as *yet*.
(5.11.76–8, emphasis added)

Significantly, boy-yet is 'discovered' when Mercury is represented specifically as the agent of the thwarting or blocking of the designs of the boy Cupid/Eros. Cupid had indeed planned a 'comeodie toward, that would not be lost for a kingdome' (5.10.7–8), specifically, a romantic comedy to 'match' the courtiers (line 10) by 'shaking . . . a shaft' (line 27) (as in a comedy by Shake-speare). Mercury had offered to save him 'a labour' (line 77) by reminding him of the blocking of eros caused by the courtiers' drinking from the fountain of selflove (a theme taken up in *Twelfth Night*). Though for Cupid an 'indignitie not to be borne' (line 91; compare Boyet's 'harsh indignity'), this frustration of his aesthetic and sexual design is appropriate to the court of chaste Cynthia who, in her final speech, bids Cupid vanish even as she requests Mercury to oversee the purgatorial penances imposed on the courtiers in order to bring about her intended 'reformation' of the court (5.5.46; compare the 'reformation' imposed on Berowne's wit (5.2.856) and the purgatorial tone of the close of *Love's Labour's Lost*). It is to Mercury, then, that the courtiers appeal in a closing palinode, which is modelled on a supplication in the prayerbook Litany and which carries the refrain: 'Good Mercury defend us.'

In a transformation more radical than that of Boyet, Mercury here has entirely shed his character as mischievous boy to assume the role of psychopomp, the god who with his 'wand / Charmes the disorders of tumultuous ghosts' (5.5.15–16), as the virtuous Arete puts it when encouraging Crites to organize the masque for Cynthia. Her image aligns the figure of the psychopomp with the agent

[65] Cf. Berowne's exclamation on seeing Boyet: 'Behaviour what wert thou / Till this madman showed thee' (5.2.338–9). Mercury was, of course, the god said to have civilized the manners of men, as in Horace's Hymn to Mercury (*Ode*, 1, 10)

of the satiric plot which, blocking the romantic or erotic plot, brings about the purgatorial penance of the close. Crites himself underscores the alignment when he represents the corrective aim of their '*ironicall* confederacie' (5.1.29) in terms of making '[t]hose whom our sports taxe in these *apish graces,* / Kisse (like the fighting snakes) your peacefull rod' (5.4.613–14, emphasis added). Most significantly perhaps, when Mercury outlines their purpose to 'inflict just paines' and so 'to correct, / And punish' (5.1.10, 17–18), he draws a distinction between false courtiers and the 'better race in court' who 'have the true nobilitie, call'd vertue' (lines 30–1) and who will approve the 'fit rebuke' (line 34). He then goes on to represent this distinction in terms of the hierarchy between those few loved by a just Jove who gain the upper air and those who are destined to remain with the 'inferi' below (*Aeneid* 6, lines 129–31 to which Mercury alludes in lines 38–9).[66] As psychopomp it is Mercury who ushers souls this way or that, as Virgil indicates in *Aeneid* 4 (lines 242–3). In Jonson's closing act this office becomes the office of a Mercury whose 'harsh' words are the words of judgement – the 'fit rebuke' – through which the satiric plot seeks at once to thwart the erotic or romantic plot and to 'correct' not only the moral deviations of a corrupt court obsessed with 'behaviour', but the structuring of the social hierarchy according to the criterion of birth rather than the (bourgeois) criteria of virtue and merit. This then, is the inflection Jonson gives in his remaking of Mercury–Boyet as a figure of the thwarting of sexual/artistic consummation through the 'harsh' words of separation: you (the damned) that way, we (the righteous) this way.

WHEN THE WORDS OF SWEET-TONGUED MERCURY ARE 'HARSH'

Usually sweet or honey tongued Mercury is then harsh only when he is the agent of the separation of loved ones (friends/lovers).[67] In the classical tradition this is illustrated crucially by two passages. The first, and more familiar, is from Virgil's *Aeneid* 4, which itself echoes Homeric passages and which, as we have seen, is evoked in Berowne's portrait of Boyet. Described as a lovely boy Mercury is sent (twice) to chide Aeneas for his affair with Dido, which is consequently ended. Cupid/Eros is thus thwarted by Mercury, romance by epic. But, although implied, Mercury is not actually described as 'harsh' here, as he is in the second passage, from one of the odes of Horace – an author who is named by Shakespeare only in *Titus Andronicus* (4.2.20–4) and *Love's Labour's Lost*.[68] Addressed to Virgil (and in compliment to its addressee alluding to *Aeneid* 4) the ode (1, 24) laments the death of their common friend Quintilius: such is the harshness of the irreversible end of death that Virgil's appeals to the gods are in vain (*frustra*), to no avail, even should he play his lyre more seductively than Orpheus

[66] For further discussion of Jonson's use of these lines from *Aeneid* 6 throughout his work, see Margaret Tudeau-Clayton, '"Underwor(l)ds" l'ancien et le nouveau: de Virgile à Ben Jonson', in F. Laroque and F. Lessay, eds., *Esthétiques de la Nouveauté à la Renaissance* (Paris, 2001), pp. 59–76 (64–8).

[67] In his discussion of the figure of Mercutio Porter confines the god's role 'to end[ing]. . . romantic entanglement' (Porter, *Shakespeare's Mercutio*, p. 23). But the harshness of Mercury is linked too, as we shall see, to the separation of same-sex friends by death. The association of the guidance of Mercury with separation is signalled in the image, if not the text, of Whitney's emblem (illustration 9) (taken from Christopher Plantin's 1577 Leyden edition of Alciati's *Emblemata*): in the right background a traveller is walking in the direction indicated by Mercury and away from another figure whose gesture evokes the pathos of separation even as it indicates an alternative (wrong) direction. (My thanks to Dieter Bitterli for help in elucidating this emblem.)

[68] Astonishingly, the wordplay around the reference has gone unnoticed, or at least unrecorded: Holofernes (Nathaniel in Q/F) asks of the letter brought by Jacquenetta, 'what are the contents?' (4.2.100), continuing 'Or rather, as Horace says in his'. At this point there is a pause, which the minimally educated Elizabethan spectator/reader would have filled with the commonly abbreviated title of the poet's best-known work – *Ars*. Together with the words which follow the pause, 'what, my soul – verses?', this furnishes an explicit advertisement of 'arsieversie', the topos which, as Patricia Parker has brilliantly shown, informs the play, although she does not notice this explicit illustration. Patricia Parker, 'Preposterous Reversals: *Love's Labour's Lost*', *Modern Language Quarterly*, 54 (1993), 435–82.

(lines 9–20). It is as the agent of the irreversible separation of death that the figure of Mercury is invoked in what is perhaps the only place in the classical tradition where he is explicitly described as *non lenis*, i.e. harsh (and the negative form invites recognition that this is contrary to his usual character) and his *virga* or caduceus as *horrida* (lines 17, 16). An ode of mourning, the poem not only laments the loss of a common friend, but the futility of verse in the face of death. Or rather death is at once invoked as origin of and obstacle to lyric utterance, summoned and defeated by the loss of the beloved. Love's labour is lost as it was for Orpheus whose 'effusus labor' (Virgil, *Georgics* 4, 492) is surely a *locus classicus* of love's labour lost – the labour being at once that of the lover and of the poet whose song, though consolatory, fails to restore to union those separated by death. What *Love's Labour's Lost* shares with the ode is, at a general level, a reflection on the relation of cultural production to the irreversible rupture that is death, and, on a more specific level, the metonymic figure for this rupture, namely a Mercury who is 'harsh' in his separation of friends/lovers and who is represented at the close of the play by the princess's gentleman usher Boyet. As we shall now see, both theme and figure had a local resonance in the year of the publication of the Quarto of Shakespeare's play.

OF UNTIMELY DEATHS AND UNFINISHED LABOUR: THE 'HARSH' WORDS OF MERCURY IN 1598

As Woudhuysen points out in his recent edition of the play, the year in which the Quarto text was published saw the publication of a substantial collection of texts by Philip Sidney who, Woudhuysen argues, is the 'presiding spirit' of the play.[69] I think he is right, although it is not only Sidney's writings that haunt the play, but what Hugh Sanford, referring to Sidney, describes as 'the fathers untimely death' in his preface to the second edition of the *Arcadia* published in 1593 with the title page advertisement 'now since the first edition augmented and *ended*' (emphasis added), the first edition, published in 1590, having come to a stop in mid-sentence.[70] In the very year that this edition of the *Arcadia* was published the other figure whose untimely end haunted the 1590s – Christopher Marlowe – died, leaving his 'Historie of *Hero and Leander*' 'not finished (being prevented by sodaine death)', as Henry Petowe puts it in the dedication of his completion, published in the same year as the collection of Sidney's writings and the Quarto of Shakespeare's play – 1598.[71] The pathos of artistic endeavour thwarted by sudden/untimely death is thus prominently illustrated in the 1590s by the figures of Marlowe and Sidney, who both left what Edward Blunt calls, in the dedication to his first edition of *Hero and Leander* (1598 again), an 'unfinished Tragedy' of love, both having been 'snatcht . . . too soone', as Nashe puts it in his preface to the first edition of Sidney's sonnet sequence *Astrophel and Stella* (1591).[72] Itself a tale of love's labour lost, which resonates throughout Shakespeare's play, as Woudhuysen has underscored, the sequence is described by Nashe as a 'tragicommody of love', 'the Prologue hope, the Epilogue dispaire', its presiding muse Melpomene, the muse invoked by Horace at the beginning of his ode of mourning for Quintilius.[73]

Whether or not the ode is at the back of his mind, Nashe goes on to represent Astrophel/Sidney in terms of the figures of Apollo, Mercury and Orpheus, just as Henry Petowe will do in an idealisation of Marlowe in prefatory lines to his completion of *Hero and Leander*. While both authors are likened to Apollo and Orpheus, Sidney/Astrophel is also likened by Nashe to Mercury, whose place as prolocutor to the gods he is claimed to have taken.[74] In Petowe's prefatory lines, however, it is not Marlowe – 'th'admired Marlo [illegible] whose

69 Woudhuysen, 'Introduction', pp. 2–7.

70 'To the Reader', *The Countess of Pembrokes Arcadia* (London, 1593), n. pag.

71 Henry Petowe, *The Second Part of Hero and Leander* (London, 1598), sig. A3v.

72 *Hero and Leander by Christopher Marlowe* (London, 1598), sig. A3v; Thomas Nashe, 'Preface to Sidney's *Astrophel and Stella*' in *Works*, vol. 3, pp. 327–33 (p. 331).

73 Nashe, 'Preface', p. 329.

74 Nashe, 'Preface', pp. 330–1.

honney flowing vaine, / No English writer can as yet attaine'[75] – but Petowe himself who is likened to Mercury and in a contrastive comparison with Apollo which is clearly reminiscent of the closing words of Shakespeare's play:[76]

> *Apollo*'s Lute bereav'd of silver string,
> Fond *Mercury* doth harshly gin to sing.
> (lines 91–2)

With the adverb 'harshly' Petowe here acknowledges the inferiority of his verse to the verse of Marlowe/Apollo. A few lines later he uses the adjective 'harsh' in a reiteration of the comparison which, in addition to underscoring this inferiority, points to the contrasting *content* of their respective narratives.

> Why should harsh *Mercury* recount again
> What sweet *Apollo* (living) did maintaine?
> (lines 109–10)

Since 'sweet *Apollo*' has told of the 'pleasing faire', complains Petowe, he has 'left me nothing pleasing to recite,' (lines 111, 119) '[b]ut of unconstant chance, and fortunes spight . . . / Faire *Hero*, and *Leanders* miserie' (lines 120, 122), the misery, specifically, of their enforced separation (before their eventual reunion and the 'happy end' of what we might call love's labours won; see note 79). The words of Mercury are once again harsh in telling of the separation of lovers and the deferral of their union. In his dedication Petowe links this deferral explicitly to the deferred completion of Marlowe's 'unfinished tragedy' on account of 'sodaine death' by representing the incomplete poem as a separation of (authorial) head from body, a separation announced by the '*harsh* sentence: *Dessunt Nonnulla*'.[77] The 'harsh' words cited here are of course those appended to Marlowe's poem in the first edition published by Edward Blunt earlier in 1598. At once doom and gnomic utterance this 'harsh sentence' – set apart from the poem by larger italic typeface, as the last lines on the 'harsh' words of Mercury are set apart by larger typeface in the 1598 Quarto text of the play – announces the lack occasioned by the rupture of sudden or untimely death. Far from producing the sense of an ending that aesthetic and especially dramatic convention would have us believe, untimely death – and when is death anything but untimely? – produces a sense of unfinished business, calling forth 'farther obsequies due unto the deceased', as Edward Blunt puts it.[78] In the case of Sidney, these obsequies take the form of the completion of the *Arcadia* and republications, and, in the case of Marlowe, publication, then sequels, like Henry Petowe's 'first labor', as he calls it, the '[s]econd part of Hero and Leander'. Shakespeare's labour of love, or cultural wake, takes the form at once of intertextual negotiations, especially with the writings of Sidney, and a rehearsal of the drama of artistic as well as sexual consummation deferred by the 'harsh' words of Mercury, a drama exemplified by the lives and writings of his two dominant predecessors, whose sudden/untimely deaths and unfinished stories of love's labour lost haunted English literary culture in the 1590s.[79]

---

75 Henry Petowe, *The Second Part of Hero and Leander*, in *Elizabethan Narrative Verse*, ed. Nigel Alexander (London, 1967), pp. 120–36 (lines 58–60). Citations will be from this edition.

76 Alexander notes the parallel without commenting on its significance (*Elizabethan Narrative Verse*, p. 325).

77 Henry Petowe, *The Second Part of Hero and Leander* (London, 1598), sig. A3v (emphasis added).

78 *Hero and Leander by Christopher Marlowe*, sig. A3r.

79 Inevitably, of course, *Love's Labour's Lost* calls for its own sequel, which is assumed to have been supplied by *Love's Labour Won*, the play mentioned by Francis Meres in 1598, but apparently 'lost', in what might be another, poignantly ironic, illustration of 'fortune's spight'. Yet if I am right about the local dimension to the drama of *Love's Labour's Lost* it might be worth reconsidering the case of *Much Ado about Nothing* (?1598–9; published 1600) as *Love's Labours Won*. For if the Hero of Shakespeare's drama bears little resemblance to her namesake in Marlowe's poem (apart from fidelity in love), her story echoes the fate of Hero in the sequel by Henry Petowe (which might well be called 'Love's Labour's Won'). Most strikingly, when the lovers have been separated on account of the tyrants Archilaus and Euristippus, Leander is warned by an oracle that 'upon suspect she (i.e. Hero) shal be slaine, / Unles thou do returne again' (lines 467–8). Having returned in disguise and having overcome her enemies, Leander reveals himself to her: 'When Hero all amazd gan revive, / And she that then seem'd dead, was now alive' (lines 595–6). Shakespeare's Hero too seems dead, doomed by 'suspect', but revives for the required 'happy end' of aesthetic and sexual consummation.

It is hardly surprising then that the same cultural paradigm should return with the posthumous publication of the works of Shakespeare in 1623, represented again as what Heminge and Condell call 'an office' 'done' 'to the dead', 'to procure' 'Guardians' for the 'Orphanes' of this father-author, who, like his predecessors, has been prematurely snatched – taken 'so soone' 'from the Worlds-Stage', as one of the prefatory verses of tribute puts it.[80] In his own prefatory verses – his due to the deceased – Ben Jonson places Shakespeare at the head of a pantheon of English poets and dramatists, including Marlowe, then goes on to assert his universality – 'He was not of an age, but for all time' – as Petowe does for Marlowe and Nashe for Sidney through their comparisons with Apollo and Mercury – a secular form of canonization which had already been implied for Shakespeare by Meres in 1598 and which is now made explicit by Jonson:

And all the Muses still were in their prime,
When like Apollo he came forth to warme
Our eares, or like a Mercury to charme!

Snatched by untimely death, this honey-tongued English Mercury, like his predecessors,[81] leaves a sense of indebtedness, a 'due' to be 'paid' from those whose cultural productions follow in/as their wake, which is one way of describing what we all do.

[80] *Mr William Shakespeares Comedies, Histories, & Tragedies*, facsimile repr., ed. H. Kökeritz (New Haven and London, 1954), sig. A2v and n. pag. The lines from Jonson's prefatory poem are quoted as they are given in this edition.

[81] Petowe in 1598 mentions the 'silver charming toung' (line 79) as well as the 'honney flowing vaine' (line 59) of Marlowe; as Woudhuysen notes 'hony-flowing Vaine' is also used of Shakespeare by Richard Barnfield in 1598 (note to 5.2.334).

SHAKESPEARE, *SIR THOMAS MORE* AND ASYLUM SEEKERS

E. A. J. HONIGMANN

All over the world the problems created by asylum seekers, and the hostility aroused by legal and illegal immigrants, grow more acute. Shakespeare dramatized these problems – the anti-alien feeling that flared up at various times in London, and a wonderfully compassionate statement on behalf of refugees, in a scene of three pages that he added to the play of *Sir Thomas More*. As a former asylum seeker, some of whose relatives perished in concentration camps, I would like to comment on the originality of a scene that is sometimes described as hastily written, 'with the remaining ink of a pen otherwise employed', to explain why Shakespeare wrote it and why no one else could have written it.

Let us consider first how Shakespeare's Sir Thomas rebukes the anti-alien rioters in London, remembering that his speech 'was intended to reflect the crisis over aliens that was troubling the City'[1] at the very time (1593) when the play is thought to have been composed.

> Imagine that you see the wretched strangers,
> Their babies at their backs, with their poor luggage
> Plodding to th' ports and coasts for transportation,
> And that you sit as kings in your desires,
> Authority quite silenced by your brawl,
> And you in ruff of your opinions clothed:
> What had you got? I'll tell you: you had taught
> How insolence and strong hand should prevail,
> How order should be quelled, and by this pattern
> Not one of you should live an aged man,
> For other ruffians, as their fancies wrought,
> With selfsame hand, self reasons and self right
> Would shark on you, and men like ravenous fishes
> Would feed on one another. (2.3.80–93)

This is writing of high quality. Like some of Shakespeare's most celebrated speeches it proceeds from a vivid picture to an argument and then to an irresistible conclusion.

Sir Thomas tells the rioters that their insurrection is an act of defiance against God, since St Paul urged 'obedience to authority' (Romans 13.1 ff.) and the king represents God on Earth. He asks the rioters to imagine that they themselves are asylum seekers –

> Say now the king,
> As he is clement if th'offender mourn,
> Should so much come too short of your great trespass
> As but to banish you, whither would you go?
> What country, by the nature of your error,
> Should give you harbour? Go you to France or Flanders,
> To any German province, Spain or Portugal,
> Nay, anywhere that not adheres to England,
> Why, you must needs be strangers. Would you be pleased
> To find a nation of such barbarous temper
> That breaking out in hideous violence
> Would not afford you an abode on earth,
> Whet their detested knives against your throats
> Spurn you like dogs, and like as if that God
> Owed not nor made not you, nor that the elements
> Were not all appropriate to your comforts,

[1] See *Sir Thomas More*, ed. V. Gabrieli and G. Melchiori (Manchester, 1990), p. 12. Modern-spelling quotations from the play are from this edition; old-spelling quotations are from the text prepared by W. W. Greg for *William Shakespeare: The Complete Works*, ed. Peter Alexander (London, 1951).

But chartered unto them? What would you think
To be thus used? This is the strangers' case,
And this your mountanish inhumanity.
(2.3.133–51)

Again, an argument that moves irresistibly to its conclusion.

It was one of the triumphs of the 'New Bibliography' that the essays included in *Shakespeare's Hand in the Play of Sir Thomas More*, edited by A. W. Pollard (Cambridge, 1923), persuaded just about every specialist in the field that the scene I have quoted must be the work of William Shakespeare. This view, if correct – as I think it undoubtedly is, though it has been challenged (see below, p. 227) – carries important implications: being his most moving plea in defence of foreigners, it has a bearing on our interpretation of Othello, Shylock and others – and, being so unmistakably sympathetic to Sir Thomas, who later refused to save his life by accepting the Oath of Supremacy and thus in effect became a Catholic martyr, the 'Three Pages' prove that Shakespeare was as open-minded about religion as about foreigners. In short, whether or not the play was ever performed, the writing of the Three Pages was an act of considerable courage.

Before I present new evidence for Shakespeare's authorship of the scene, I want to glance at the Londoners who clamour to kill or expel the asylum seekers.

LINCOLN Peace, hear me: he that will not see a red herring at a Harry groat, butter at elevenpence a pound, meal at nine shillings a bushel, and beef at four nobles a stone, list to me.

ANOTHER CITIZEN It will come to that pass, if strangers be suffered: mark him.

LINCOLN Our country is a great eating country, *argo* they eat more in our country than they do in their own.

CLOWN By a halfpenny loaf a day troy weight.

LINCOLN They bring in strange roots, which is merely to the undoing of poor prentices, for what's a sorry parsnip to a good heart?

ANOTHER Trash, trash! They breed sore eyes, and 'tis enough to infect the city with the palsy.

LINCOLN Nay, it has infected it with the palsy, for these bastards of dung – as you know they grow in dung – have infected us, and it is our infection will make the city shake, which partly comes through the eating of parsnips.

CLOWN True, and pumpions together.

SERGEANT What say you to the mercy of the king? Do you refuse it?

LINCOLN You would have us upon th'hip, would you? No, marry, do we not; we accept of the king's mercy, but we will show no mercy upon the strangers.

SERGEANT You are the simplest things
That ever stood in such a question. (2.3.1–26)

The rioters – Lincoln, Doll, the Clown, Betts and Williamson – had already appeared in previous scenes. Shakespeare clearly knew how they had been characterized and introduced an important change of tone. In the earlier scenes the rioters repeatedly urge each other to fire the houses of the hated foreigners:

LINCOLN Then gallant bloods, you, whose free souls do scorn
To bear th'enforcèd wrongs of aliens,
Add rage to resolution, fire the houses
Of these audacious strangers . . . (2.1.19–22)

and the Clown echoes these words, 'fire the houses. / Brave captain courageous / Fire me their houses.'

DOLL Ay, for we may as well make bonfires on May day as at midsummer; we'll alter the day in the calendar, and set it down in flaming letters.
(2.1.36–8)

Lincoln explains his strategy.

LINCOLN
Then fire the houses, that the mayor being busy
About the quenching of them, we may 'scape.
(2.1.70–1)

and the Clown again echoes him. 'Fire, fire! I'll be the first'. In the next scene the earls of Shrewsbury and Surrey stress that 'this most dangerous insurrection' is almost out of control, 'I hear they mean to fire the Lombards' houses', and then the next scene, Shakespeare's scene, switches to a much less savage tone, omitting all references to firing the strangers' houses and dwelling, instead, on the humour of simplicity. As in so many other plays where we find the same tone (the Cade scenes in *2 Henry VI*, the 'mechanicals' in *A Midsummer Night's Dream*, the watchmen in *Much Ado*, the plebeians in *Julius Caesar* and *Coriolanus*) the humour sits below the verbal surface, as it were; simplicity is quite unselfconscious of itself: this send-up of 'working-class' thinking is so characteristic of Shakespeare that, quite apart from all the other evidence, it should itself count as a valuable clue to the scene's authorship.

Shakespeare, it seems, toned down the rage of the rioters in order to prepare for the mood-swing when Sir Thomas addresses them: the two things are connected, just as Sir Thomas's urging of 'obedience to authority' (101) must be connected with his own disobedience to authority later in the play (see below p. 231). Even though the handwriting of the Three Pages suggests a dramatist in a hurry, I believe that Shakespeare gave some thought to the play as a whole, before he decided how he might help to rescue it. If so, it is all the more remarkable that he, and his fellow dramatists, thought it possible that so dangerous a play, with its anti-alien rioting and its saintly and heroic Catholic martyr, would ever be performed. Would they dare to proceed without a powerful protector? From the actors' point of view the situation resembled others that followed – in 1601, when the Earl of Essex's supporters persuaded the Lord Chamberlain's Men to revive *Richard II*, and in 1624, when they performed *A Game at Chess*.

Scott McMillin has argued that Strange's Men, 'on theatrical evidence alone . . . appear to have been the company that possessed the unusual combination of resources reflected in the original *Sir Thomas More*'. Gabrieli and Melchiori, the editors of the play in the Revels series, agree.[2] I believe that Ferdinando, Lord Strange, may have been more deeply involved than others have suspected. This gifted man, only five years older than Shakespeare, may well have been the protector of *Sir Thomas More* and also the most important influence on the youthful dramatist, and deserves more attention than he has so far received.

Even if A. W. Pollard edited *Shakespeare's Hand in The Play of Sir Thomas More*, W. W. Greg, another founding father of the New Bibliography, played an at least equally crucial part in establishing Shakespeare's authorship of the Three Pages. Greg edited the Malone Society Reprint of the play (1911), supplied three of the seven chapters in *Shakespeare's Hand*, and later commented repeatedly on this and related problems. Paul Werstine, who now rejects Shakespeare's hand, thinks that Pollard stage-managed his collaborators in 1923, especially Greg, and presented them as more unanimous than they were. 'Unlike the other contributors to the book, Greg refused to commit himself to the identification of Shakespeare as the writer of the Three Pages.'[3] Werstine cites Dover Wilson's much later recollection (1956) that Greg 'was at first inclined to reserve his verdict'. The truth of the matter is that Greg described himself in 1927, in his cautious way, as a 'moderate believer' in Shakespeare's authorship,[4] later spoke of the evidence as quite conclusive, and welcomed Shakespeare's hand as early as 1919:

> By one of those almost unbelievable pieces of good fortune which sometimes seem to set the approbation of providence upon an undertaking, Sir Edward Maunde Thompson . . . produced, in his remarkable monograph on *Shakespeare's Handwriting*, a palaeographical analysis which, when taken in conjunction with other lines of

---

[2] *Sir Thomas More*, ed. Gabrieli and Melchiori, p. 12; Scott McMillin, *The Elizabethan Theatre & The Book of Sir Thomas More* (Ithaca,1987), p. 72.

[3] See P. Werstine, 'Shakespeare, More or Less: A. W. Pollard and Twentieth-Century Shakespeare Editing', *Florilegium*, 16 (1999), 125–45. I am indebted to Professor Werstine for sending me this article. Also Arthur F. Kinney, 'Text, Context, and Authorship of *The Booke of Sir Thomas Moore*', in *Pilgrimage for Love*, ed. Sigrid King (Tempe, Arizona, 1999), pp. 134–60.

[4] *The Collected Papers of Sir Walter W. Greg*, ed. J. C. Maxwell (Oxford, 1966), p. 200, and *TLS*, 24 November, 1 December 1927.

argument, must be held to establish at least the probability that we have, in the manuscript play of *Sir Thomas More*, three foolscap pages of dramatic composition in Shakespeare's own handwriting.[5]

Did Greg really refuse 'to commit himself'? Pollard could not have opened his Introduction in 1923 with the claim that his contributors, on 'various grounds and with various degrees of confidence', believe in the book's thesis if Greg had 'refused to commit himself'.

Most of the arguments for 'Shakespeare's hand' have survived the passage of eighty years remarkably well. Werstine, seeking to demolish them, concentrates on the stylistic or literary approach, 'because [R. W.] Chambers' argument has been found by many readers to be so much more accessible and appealing', and I shall do the same. He thinks Chambers's chief example to be the parallel between *More* 31–87 and *Troilus and Cressida* 1.3.85 ff., and repeats what others have said, that the same image clusters 'could also be detected in the canonical works of other dramatists'. I would reply that image clusters are only a small part of the evidence. More's speeches must also be compared with other plays where a 'friend of the people' addresses his simple followers – scolding, grieving, predicting, advising submission and at the same time impressing us as a superior intelligence with its own hidden agenda. For instance, *Julius Caesar* 1.1.52–3 ('Be gone! / Run to your houses, fall upon your knees') and 3.2.74–252, or *Coriolanus* 1.1. The marvel is that while More's speeches belong to a recognizable Shakespearian type, the speaker's voice is as sharply individualized as the voices of Mark Antony and Menenius, and modulates as naturally from one tone to another, a characteristic Shakespearian ripple-effect.

Chambers also cited other parallels, more compelling than an image cluster that later turned out to be traditional – for instance, the scene of rioting quoted above.[6] Comparing this passage with the Jack Cade scenes in *2 Henry VI* (4.2 etc.), Chambers said that *argo* (for *ergo*) occurs in only three plays between 1580 and 1610, namely *More*, *Hamlet* 5.1.12, 19 (*argal*) and *2 Henry VI*. 'Jack Cade and his men chop their logic, and all the time the author is poking fun at them' with his characteristic good-nature. 'The point is that the thought is the same: we have the same type of false argument, mingled with false economics, and discussion of the diet of the poor. The *argo* and the *halfpenny loaf* are merely, as it were, signposts which attract our attention.'

Even though Chambers missed at least one *argo* (in Middleton's *The Phoenix*, 1607, sig. $H4^b$, probably an echo of Shakespeare), we may say that *argo* and *argal* were extremely rare, as was the spelling *scilens* (*More* 50, and *2 Henry IV*, Q, 18 times), once claimed as unique to Shakespeare. And these very rare usages, together with literary echoes in similar contexts, make up 'the extreme complexity of the combinations common to the "Three Pages" of *Sir Thomas More* and to Shakespeare'. (Chambers identified seven different components that link the 'Three Pages' by Hand D and the Jack Cade scenes in *2 Henry VI*). To pursue these combinations for a moment, let us not forget that humour also involves combinations and can be very personal, and that Lincoln and Jack Cade are related to bully Bottom, who similarly domineers over his simple followers. The humour of simplicity supporting simplicity, as in the opening pages by Hand D, is also Shakespearian: compare Dogberry, Verges and the watchmen and, again, Bottom and his mechanicals. In each case Shakespeare contrasts the social and intellectual gulf between a 'working class' out of its depth and the critical voices of authority.

Rhythm, sentence-structure, line-structure and the placing of a climax can also be very personal, as Chambers noted. Compare *More* 93, 'Would feed on one another' and *Coriolanus* 1.1.184–6:

[5] W. W. Greg, 'The "Hamlet" Texts and Recent Work in Shakespearian Bibliography', *MLR*, 14 (1919), 380–5, and *The Collected Papers*, p. 192.

[6] R. W. Chambers discussed the 'Three Pages' in *Sir Thomas More* three times: (1) in *Shakespeare's Hand in the Play of Sir Thomas More*, ed. A. W. Pollard (Cambridge,1923); (2) in *MLR*, 26 (1931), 251–80; and (3), in greatest detail, in 'Shakespeare and the play of *More*' (printed in his *Man's Unconquerable Mind*, (London, 1939)).

> You cry against the noble Senate, who,
> Under the gods, keep you in awe, which else
> *Would feed on one another.* [emphasis added]

'What matters is that, in each case, [the half-line] occupies the same position as the conclusion to the same train of thought.'[7]

I have quoted some of Chambers's more telling points, much abbreviated; readers would do well to refer to the original. What can we add to his third and most detailed statement of the case (1939) for Shakespeare's hand (now known as 'Hand D') which was thought convincing for so long by the large majority of competent critics? Most of what follows, I believe, is new.

I *Speech prefixes.*

(i) In Hand D and some of the good quartos, speech prefixes are shortened when repeated, and sometimes they taper off to a single letter. Thus in *Romeo and Juliet*, Q2, Lady Capulet is *Mother, La., Mo., M., M., M.* (H3[b] ff., where there is plenty of space for a longer speech prefix). Compare *M.* for Mercutio (F3[b]) and for Minstrel (K3[b]); and, in Hand D, *other, other, oth, o.*

(ii) The rare speech prefix *other* occurs nowhere else in the *More* manuscript (*Another* occurs once, line 272). It is also found in *Hamlet*, Q2, 5.1 (11 times).

(iii) The speech prefix *all* occurs 10 times in Hand D (147 lines) and only 9 times in the rest of the *More* manuscript (1986 lines, plus additions), where there are many crowd scenes. *All* speeches are common in other Shakespeare texts.[8]

(iv) Hand D seems to have written the dialogue first, then added speech prefixes, omitting and misplacing some. This habit could explain omitted and misplaced speech prefixes in Shakespeare's 'good' texts.

II *Punctuation.*

As E. K. Chambers noted, Hand D punctuated very lightly.[9] In 77 lines (More's long speech), D 'has only 25 commas and 2 semi-colons, none of either at line-ends. There are 4 full-stops, 3 at line-ends. There are no colons. Interruptions have no stops. Many necessary pauses are unstopped.' Similar very light punctuation is found in some of the good quartos.

III *Echoes.*

The 147 lines resort to many words and phrases that, while not unique to Shakespeare, remind us again and again of his plays. R. W. Chambers drew attention to several, such as 'And you in ruff of your opinions clothed' (79) and 'dressed in an opinion' (*Merchant of Venice* 1.1.91), or 'to slip him like a hound' (122) and 'like a fawning greyhound in the leash, / To let him slip at will' (*Coriolanus* 1.7.38). Many more Shakespearian echoes could be added.

(i) And 'twere no error if I told you all
You were in arms 'gainst God.
All. Marry, God forbid that!
More. Nay certainly you are
For to the king God hath his office lent . . .
(*More*, 95 ff., my emphasis)

Compare *Merchant of Venice* 2.2.30 ff.: Launcelot meets his blind father, Old Gobbo, and tells him that Launcelot is deceased (*Gobbo. Marry, God forbid!*), with a lot of ergos thrown in. And again, also smiling at simplicity, *Shrew* 4.2.79, 'Of Mantua, sir? *Marry, God forbid!*' Compare also *Pericles*, 12.76, '*Nay, certainly* tonight, / *For* look how fresh she looks.'

(ii) peace how (= peace ho!); peace I say; peace peace (*More* 28, 35, 60): compare 'Peace how' (*Merchant of Venice*, Q, 5.1.109), *Romeo and Juliet* 4.4.92, *Julius Caesar* 3.2.55, etc; *Antony and Cleopatra* 4.3.12, *Twelfth Night* 2.5.32 (peace I say); *Coriolanus* 3.1.216, 4.2.13 (peace peace).

(iii) list to me (3): compare *Shrew* 2.1.359, 'Sir, list to me.'

---

[7] R. W. Chambers, *Man's Unconquerable Mind*, p. 246. The MS reads 'woold feed on on another': 'on on' could also be modernized as 'one on'.

[8] Cf. Honigmann, 'Re-Enter the Stage Direction', *Shakespeare Survey 29* (Cambridge, 1976), pp. 117–25 ('"All" speeches' (pp. 120–2)).

[9] E. K. Chambers, *William Shakespeare: A Study of Facts and Problems*, 2 vols. (Oxford, 1930), vol.1, p. 510 n.

(iv) even by the rule you have among yourselves (46): compare *Julius Caesar* 5.1.100, 'Even by the rule of that philosophy.'

(v) I thank thy good worship for my brother (59): compare *Measure for Measure* 2.1.176, 'I thank your good worship for it.'

(vi) although we grant you get the thing you seek (69): compare *Lucrece* 211, 'if I gain the thing I seek'.

(vii) which cannot choose but much help (70): compare *1 Henry IV* 5.2.44, 'which cannot choose but bring him', *Sonnets* 64.13.

(viii) before God (88): compare *Much Ado* 2.3.177, *1 Henry IV* 5.3.50.

(ix) power and command (99): compare *Othello* 5.2.340: 'Your power and your command is taken off.'

(x) wash your foul minds with tears (108): compare *Much Ado* 4.1.154, 'speaking of her foulness, / Washed it with tears'.

(xi) safer wars than ever you can make (112): compare *Cymbeline* 2.2.40, 'stronger than ever law could make'.

(xii) alas, alas (122): compare *Measure for Measure* 2.2.74, 3.1.133.

It turns out that Shakespeare and Hand D agree in their use of very unusual images, phrases, spellings and speech prefixes, and they also agree in a large number of more common words and phrases: their syntax, stock of words and mind-set, we may say, are remarkably similar. Thus (xiii) 'what's a sorry parsnip to a good heart?' (9) is infused with the same whimsy as 'What's a joint of mutton or two in a whole Lent?' (*2 Henry IV* 2.4.350), viz. 'what's a small mouthful to a hungry man?'

IV *Repetition.*

To give coherence to longer speeches, and to make an argument easier to follow, Shakespeare sometimes resorts to rhetorical repetition.

what do you then,
Rising 'gainst him that God Himself installs
But rise 'gainst God? What do you to your souls
In doing this, O desperate as you are?
Wash your foul minds with tears, and those same hands
That you like rebels lift against the peace,
Lift up for peace, and your unreverent knees
Make them your feet. To kneel to be forgiven . . .
(*More*, 112–19)

Force should be right – or rather, right and wrong,
Between whose endless jar justice resides,
Should lose their names, and so should justice too.
Then everything includes itself in power,
Power into will, will into appetite:
And appetite, an universal wolf
So doubly seconded with will and power,
Must make perforce an universal prey,
And last eat up himself.
(*Troilus and Cressida* 1.3.116–24)

The image of disorder as a self-devouring cannibalism, I need hardly add, repeats *More* 87, 'Would feed on one another', which is itself repeated in *Coriolanus*.

A series of imperatives can also operate as rhetorical repetition. '*Look what* you do offend you cry upon . . . *Imagine* that you see the wretched strangers . . . Let me set up before your thoughts, good friends, / *One supposition*' (*More*, 67, 80, 96): compare *Richard II* 1.3.286 ff.:

Look what thy soul holds dear, *imagine* it
To lie that way thou goest, not whence thou com'st.
Suppose the singing birds musicians . . .

V *Structure.*

In the Three Pages the howling and silences of the mob are integrated, and supporting voices mediate between the main speaker and '*All*'; the rhythms of the verse, of prose speeches and of 'scenic structure', are as authentic as in any other 147 lines in Shakespeare.

The first fifty lines of comic prose in the Three Pages remind us not only of very similar episodes in Shakespeare's other work, such as *2 Henry VI*, they also link up with the deeply felt hortatory verses of More's speech, preparing for the mood-swing that he achieves. And this combination of comic prose leading into verse speeches with a more serious purpose is itself Shakespearian, as in *Julius Caesar* and *Coriolanus*; indeed, the gradual acceleration and climaxing of More's speeches, so beautifully controlled, no less than 'Friends, masters, countrymen' (*More*, 30), point forward to 'Friends, Romans, countrymen' and to some of the greatest speeches in Shakespeare, if we have ears to hear.

In addition, More's address to the rebels points forward to a scene that Shakespeare did not write but must have known about. As in *Troilus and Cressida* 1.3.74 ff. (Ulysses on degree), *Henry V* 1.2.183 (Canterbury on the honey bees) and *Coriolanus* 1.1.94 ff. (Menenius on the fable of the belly), More preaches the gospel of obedience to authority to simple listeners, who are easily persuaded. Later it transpires in all these plays that social-political roles are not so straightforward, authority may be abused: Ulysses praises emulation (3.3.139 ff.); Henry, unlike the emperor of the bees, announces that 'France being ours, we'll bend it to our awe, / *Or break it all to pieces*' (1.2.224–5); and it suits Coriolanus to choose his own social role, i.e. not to be the leader but only second-in-command (1.1.263 ff.). So, too, while More, like the other preachers of 'obedience', appears to speak in good faith, his simple platitudes let him down when he discovers that the king may command what God forbids, and he himself has to refuse to obey the magistrate. Understandably, the play is not too explicit about More's later position but it says enough to make his tragic dilemma clear:

> 'Tis strange that my lord chancellor should refuse
> The duty that the law of God bequeaths
> Unto the King. (4.1.106–8)

It is hard to believe that Hand D did not know the end of More's story – his refusal to accept the Oath of Supremacy, which led directly to his death. Accordingly we may conclude that the dramatic irony of his address to the rebels links Hand D to all the other Shakespeare plays that insist on 'obedience' and then show that in the real world we may have to answer to very different imperatives.

The case for Shakespeare's hand in *Sir Thomas More* is more formidable than readers of Werstine's essay will suppose. Very unusual images, phrases, spellings and speech prefixes are only part of the evidence: the halfpenny loaf, chop-logic about the diet of the poor, *argo*, 'scilens', 'Would feed on one another', the speech prefix *other*, simplicity supporting simplicity, dramatic irony about obedience – these very different kinds of evidence, and a common stock of phrases, all reinforce one another. Werstine alleges that Greg argued for 'Shakespeare's hand' from nothing more than 'cumulative evidence'. Suffice it to say that R. W. Chambers already considered this possible counter-argument in 1939, and replied that the case for Shakespeare lies in the interlocking of the evidence, 'in the whole combination of combinations' (p. 211). I hope that I have helped to confirm this view and Greg's summing-up of 1955: the argument for Shakespeare 'comes as near to formal proof as its nature allows, and is likely to be held conclusive by anyone capable of judging evidence'.[10]

Years ago I suggested that Marlowe may have had something to do with the planning, if not the writing, of *Sir Thomas More*.[11] This possibility, which cannot be proved or disproved, would explain some unexplained anomalies. Why were five dramatists involved in the play's writing and revision? How many other dramatists would dare to propose a play that made so much of scenes of rioting and of the 'good Sir Thomas's' steadfast refusal to obey his sovereign? Who else would dare to celebrate the heroism of a Catholic martyr? Was it not reported that Marlowe said, 'in almost every company', that 'if there be any god or any good religion, then it is in the papists because the service of God is performed with more ceremonies . . . That all Protestants are hypocritical asses'?[12] Whereas other dramatists would realize that a sympathetic treatment of More would lead to trouble, big trouble, such a subject was bound to appeal to the iconoclast Marlowe,

[10] W. W. Greg, *The Shakespeare First Folio* (Oxford, 1955), p. 99.

[11] Honigmann, 'The Play of *Sir Thomas More* and some Contemporary Events', *Shakespeare Survey 42* (Cambridge, 1990), pp. 77–84.

[12] See J. B. Steane, *Marlowe: A Critical Study* (London, 1964), p. 363.

and indeed fits neatly into the trajectory of his previous career. *Sir Thomas More* follows on from *Dr Faustus* – again, the tragedy of a scholar, admired by other scholars, who trusts his own judgement (too much?) and rejects the advice of all the world. Intellectual pride leads to the death of both men – horrible pride in Faustus, admirable pride in More. Both men love 'low' humour and practical jokes, spring surprises on others, take part in dramatic entertainments. And, though they differ from each other as well, particularly in More's devotion to his family and Faustus's uneasy relationship with his family of devils, they also resemble each other in their aloofness, one might almost say in their sense of their own superiority, a Marlovian touch.

Yes, I hear the reply, *More* resembles *Dr Faustus* – should we not add, too much so? No writer repeats himself as closely as this. Well, few other writers do but Marlowe did, from Tamburlaine to Barabas to Faustus, and Sir Thomas, though more sympathetic and mature than these predecessors, fits into the Marlovian scheme. And, let me repeat, I am not arguing that Marlowe wrote *Sir Thomas More* (except, perhaps, some of the prose scenes), only that he proposed the play and, it may be, prepared a scenario.

It is now pretty generally agreed that *More* was first written in 1593, whatever the date of the 'revisions'. The play seems to me to connect with many events of the year from May 1593 to May 1594, some of which are well known, others matters of speculation. I would like to offer some speculations – I think I see possible connections that others may have missed. Several major figures are involved, and that makes a brief digression worthwhile.

First, the general picture: 1593 was a year of almost continuous plague[13] as well as anti-alien riots. Dramatists and actors had to survive as best they could, the London theatres being closed. On 6 May the Privy Council issued a licence to Edward Alleyn (normally a member of the Lord Admiral's Men, the company that performed most of Marlowe's plays) and W. Kempe, T. Pope, J. Heminges, A. Phillips and G. Brian, 'being all one company, servants to our very good . . . Lord the Lord Strange', to exercise their quality 'so it be not within seven miles of London or of the court'.[14] Strange's Men toured the provinces, other companies 'broke', and dramatists looked for alternative employment: Shakespeare published *Venus and Adonis* (S. R. 18 April) and Marlowe's death (30 May) prevented him from completing *Hero and Leander*. At very much the same time (5 May and on other dates) anti-alien libels were posted on the wall of the Dutch churchyard and anti-alien rioters were stocked, carted and whipped.[15] This was the general picture when, I suggest, Marlowe mooted the idea of a play on the life and death of Sir Thomas More.

As already stated, I believe that *Sir Thomas More* was written for Strange's Men. In addition I believe that the play ought to be placed in the context of Lord Strange's own activities in 1593 and 1594. I quote from Camden's *Annals*:[16]

> For all this yeere [1593] *London* was most grievously afflicted with the Pestilence . . . insomuch, as there dyed this yeere of the pestilence and other diseases within the City and the Suburbs, 17890. persons . . . *Bartholomew* Fayre was not kept, and *Michaelmasse* Terme was holden at S. Albones, twenty myles from the City: Where *Richard Hasket* [Hesketh, related to the Hesketh of Rufford] was condemned and executed for treason, who being secretly sent by the *English* fugitives, perswaded *Ferdinand* Earle of *Darby*, (whose father *Henry* was lately [25 September] deceased) to take upon him the title of the Crowne, fetching his pedegree from his great Grandmother *Mary*, the daughter of King *Henry* the seventh, and made him large promises of men and money from the *Spaniard*, threatening the Earle with assured destruction, unlesse he would do it, and conceale the matter. But the Earle fearing lest some trappe were layed for him, accused the man, who by his owne confession acknowledged the crime at the barre, detesting those which had given him counsell.

Hesketh was executed on 29 November. Then, on 16 April 1594,

[13] See William Camden's *Annals*, 3rd edn (London, 1635), p. 423.

[14] See E. K. Chambers, *The Elizabethan Stage*, 4 vols. (Oxford, 1923), vol. 2, p. 123.

[15] See A. W. Pollard's introduction to *Shakespeare's Hand*, p. 40.

[16] Camden, *Annals*, p. 423.

> *Ferdinand Stanley* Earle of *Darby* . . . expired in the flowre of his youth, not without suspition of poison, being tormented with cruell paines by frequent vomitings of colour like rusty iron. There was found in his chamber an image of waxe, the belley pierced thorow with haires of the same colour that his were, put there (as the wiser sort have judged) to remove the suspition of poyson.
>
> (p. 436)

Ferdinando, a poet and friend and patron of poets, most of whose followers were Catholics, paid the penalty for not committing himself unambiguously to either the Catholic or the Protestant cause. In the 1580s he secretly accused his father of leniency to recusants; in the 1590s, trapped in a power struggle between different political factions, he evidently regarded Hesketh as an *agent provocateur*.[17] A dangerous situation, which almost certainly led to his death. Whether Ferdinando was poisoned by Catholics or by Protestants, the year from May 1593 was not a good time for Strange's Men to produce *Sir Thomas More*, even though Edward Alleyn, the ideal actor for the part of Sir Thomas, who had triumphed in other plays by Marlowe, now led the company.

Did Strange's Men intend to perform *Sir Thomas More* in public? It would seem so, since they submitted the manuscript to the Master of the Revels. Or was the play intended for private, Catholic audiences, to test the political temperature? We do not know. Nevertheless I feel that there could be a connection between the dangerous game played by Lord Strange and that of his Men if they commissioned *Sir Thomas More*. The extraordinary fact that five different dramatists (Munday, Chettle, Shakespeare, Dekker, and probably Heywood) took part in the writing and revision of *More* also requires an explanation. I do not see Munday, whose anti-Catholic activities were no secret, as the author of a play so dedicated to the praise (we might almost say, the rehabilitation) of More, but why should he not help out as its scribe to oblige the actors, his paymasters? The reason why five dramatists were needed, I think, was that the original proposer or author was not available, was dead, and therefore a team of hacks had to be assembled to finish the job.

Why did Shakespeare agree to be one of the team? I can imagine a number of reasons (loyalty to Lord Strange or his actors, or to Marlowe); we believe, however, that it was not his habit to offer or beg scenes (*vide* Leonard Digges), so why did he make an exception? One scene needed to be written with particular care – the central scene of the play, where Sir Thomas's good service brings him to the notice of the king, to a knighthood, a place on the Privy Council and ultimately to his appointment as Lord Chancellor. Shakespeare, 'in his own conceit the only Shakescene in a country', chose to write the Three Pages because they dramatize the most important event in the upward movement of More's career: they demonstrate the quality of More's mind and personality.

But Shakespeare could also have had a very personal reason for writing in defence of asylum seekers.[18] His friends and acquaintances included an unusual number of foreigners, some of them certainly refugees. In 1593, the year to which *Sir Thomas More* is usually assigned, his fellow Stratfordian, Richard Field, issued *Venus and Adonis*, Shakespeare's first publication. Field had married the widow of his master, Thomas Vautrollier, and 'Vautrollier and his wife Jacqueline, or Jaklin, were Huguenot fugitives from France.'[19] In 1599 the Globe theatre was built by one Peter Street, a carpenter: the old *Dictionary of National Biography* had no entry for Street, but the *Publications of the Huguenot Society of London* inform us that Peter Street, a joiner of Dutch origin, lived in St Olave's, Southwark, in 1583. Closer in time to the building of the Globe, a suit in the Court of Requests (42 Elizabeth: Req 2, 174/67, J. Buckler v. Cicely

---

[17] See particularly Christopher Devlin, 'The Earl and the Alchemist' in Devlin, *Hamlet's Divinity and Other Essays* (Carbondale, Ill., 1963); also Park Honan, *Shakespeare: A Life* (Oxford, 1998), pp. 66–7.

[18] Compare also *Edward III*, 3.2, where 'two French men, a woman and two little children', with bag and baggage, fly from the English invaders. They are not strictly asylum seekers (i.e. refugees from another country), but Shakespeare knew and, it is thought, helped to write this play.

[19] *A Dictionary of Printers and Booksellers (1557–1640)* ed. R. B. McKerrow (London, 1910), p. 272.

Colmer) reveals that 'five messuages or tenements' were in the tenure of Peter Street, carpenter, or his assigns, from which I deduce that Street was no mere odd-job carpenter. Though he or his forebears had probably arrived in England as refugees, he had gone up in the world: he secured the contract to build the Globe theatre in 1599 and the Fortune in 1600. In 1604 Shakespeare lived as a lodger with Christopher Mountjoy, a Huguenot tire-maker, whose apprentices (Stephen Belott, Gui Asture and Ufranke de la Coles)[20] seem to have been Huguenots as well; Shakespeare helped to persuade Belott to marry his master's daughter, Mary. In 1616 or later Gheerart Janssen (also known as Gerard Johnson) was the stonemason responsible for Shakespeare's monument in Holy Trinity Church, Stratford. Why was Janssen entrusted with this commission, when his workshop was situated so far away, in Southwark, near the Globe Theatre? Janssen had previously supplied the effigy for the tomb of Shakespeare's friend John Combe (1614), perhaps at Shakespeare's instigation: it seems probable enough that he knew Shakespeare by sight – which, however, need not inspire confidence in his likeness of the dramatist with its expressionless face.

I think more highly of Martin Droeshout's engraving of Shakespeare's face in the First Folio. Schoenbaum did not care for it:

> An apparently neckless head sits on its platter of a wired-band . . . The mouth has wandered off to the right, the ear lobe defies anatomy . . . Proportions are awry: the head is much too big for the torso . . . In all, a lamentable performance

and the vapid face also confirms 'the artist's ineptitude'.[21] The Droeshout family worshipped at the same Dutch church as Janssen; it seems that the First Folio engraving was commissioned before young Martin (born 1601) had made a name for himself. How is it that so important a commission went to an unknown artist? I believe the explanation may be that the Droeshouts, who included other artists and engravers, possessed the only available sketch of Shakespeare's face, that they refused to lend this unless Martin was given the commission, and that an inexperienced engraver was then asked to fit together the face, the torso and clothes. Is it fair to describe the Folio face as vapid? It lacks the sparkle that one expects from anecdotes about Shakespeare's quickness in repartee. Nevertheless, its abstracted, thoughtful expression gives us the other side of the man: it catches not the Falstaff but the Hamlet in Shakespeare.[22]

Apart from the foreigners discussed above, and other possible foreigners who are mere names to us, such as 'Dorothy Soer, wife of John Soer' bracketed with Shakespeare in 1596,[23] others known to the dramatist may well have had foreign ancestors. Of the two dramatists who sided with him in the War of the Theatres, Dekker, though born in London, is thought to have belonged to a Dutch immigrant family, and Marston's mother was the daughter of an Italian doctor. Thousands of immigrants settled in London,[24] or with English patrons in their country residences (e.g. John Florio, who joined the entourage of Shakespeare's patron, the Earl of Southampton).

Is it not surprising that so many of Shakespeare's professional and casual acquaintances in London came from immigrant families, and does it not follow that he must have known many more? What they told him about wretched strangers,

> Their babies at their backs, with their poor luggage
> Plodding to th' ports and coasts for transportation,

lingered in his mind, and bore fruit when he chose to help out with the re-writing of *Sir Thomas More*.

[20] See S. Schoenbaum, *William Shakespeare: A Documentary Life* (Oxford, 1975), p. 211.

[21] S. Schoenbaum, *William Shakespeare: Records and Images* (London, 1981), pp. 169–70.

[22] See also my paper, 'Shakespeare and London's Immigrant Community circa 1600', in *Elizabethan and Modern Studies*, ed. J. P. Vander Motten (Gent, Seminarie voor Engelse en Amerikaanse Literatuur, R.U.G., 1985), pp. 143–53.

[23] Leslie Hotson, *Shakespeare versus Shallow* (London, 1931), p. 9.

[24] Pollard, *Shakespeare's Hand*, p. 39.

Four hundred years later we can salute this gesture as typical of Shakespeare's generosity of spirit, one that linked him for all time with the only other Englishman of the sixteenth century whose genius in many ways equalled his own. He had already encountered More's mind when he wrote *Richard III.* In the Three Pages their geniuses again converged: the dramatist, living in 'a London crowded with refugees, and full of anti-alien prejudice',[25] was inspired by More to write a 'noble plea for toleration' that still speaks home today.[26]

[25] R. W. Chambers, *Man's Unconquerable Mind*, p. 249. On Shakespeare's debts to More, see also the Arden edition of *King Richard III*, ed. Antony Hammond (London, 1981), p. 75.

[26] See also my defence of Shakespeare's 'foul papers' and 'good quartos' and their relevance to the Three Pages in *Textual Performances*, ed. Lukas Erne and M. J. Kidnie (Cambridge, 2004), pp. 77–91.

HAL AS SELF-STYLED REDEEMER: THE HARROWING OF HELL AND *HENRY IV PART 1*

BEATRICE GROVES

The second tetralogy begins with a king who, by calling those who condemn him 'Pilates' and his betrayers 'Judases', overtly styles himself as the Christ. This article will consider how one of Richard II's successors revives his overt and inept imagery with subtlety and political insight and argue that Hal creates an implied, and thoroughgoing, symbolic connection between his and Christ's redeeming action, while never explicitly equating his own power and mission with Christ's.[1] Henry's stratagem of glittering Christian rhetoric, piety that has been questioned by a number of recent critics of *Henry V*, begins in *Henry IV Part 1*. Hal stages his own redemption in Christian terms: a Lenten period of expectant, self-imposed exile is followed by a reconciliation between a father and son through a decisive single combat which is staged with a resonant allusion to the harrowing of hell. The text contains reminiscences of the dramatic form of the Easter liturgy, the biblical story and the mystery plays which invest Hal's history with their power. These allusions place Hal in the position of Christ but the connections are not simple analogies. Hal needs to redeem England and himself, but there is an uneasiness with both the glory and the humility he stages.[2]

The harrowing of hell is the name given to a non-biblical episode in which Christ went down into limbo between his Crucifixion and Resurrection and rescued the souls of the dead. This doctrine remained the teaching of the Church of England in Shakespeare's day and would have been well known to his audience. Some of Shakespeare's audience may even have retained a visual image of the event from the survival of pre-Reformation images. Despite the statute against wall paintings, not all were destroyed at the Reformation – famously the guild chapel paintings in Stratford were not whitewashed until the year of Shakespeare's birth, and some survived even longer. In the medieval religious college at Ashridge, for example, which was converted into a royal residence under Edward VI, forty biblical frescoes, including a harrowing, were only defaced in 1800.[3] The life of Christ was by far the most popular subject for church decoration, and the number of images still surviving of the harrowing illustrate its popularity.[4]

---

[1] Richard's self-styling as the Christ has been widely recognized, see Peter Ure, ed., *King Richard II* (London, 1994), pp. xlviii, lxii. See also *Richard II* 3.2.128; 4.1.161; 4.1.229–32.

[2] For a revisionist approach to *Henry V* see Norman Rabkin, *Shakespeare and the Problem of Meaning* (London, 1981), pp. 49, 55–62. For evidence that Shakespeare knew the mystery plays see Emrys Jones, *The Origins of Shakespeare* (Oxford, 1977), p. 31; and Michael O'Connell, 'Vital Cultural Practices: Shakespeare and the Mysteries', *Journal of Medieval and Early Modern Studies*, 29.1 (1999), 149–68.

[3] Henry John Todd, *The History of the College of Bonhommes, at Ashridge, in the County of Buckingham, Founded in the Year 1276, by Edmund, Earl of Cornwall* (London, 1823), pp. 28, 59.

[4] C. E. Keyser, *A List of Buildings in Great Britain and Ireland having Mural and other Painted Decorations, of Dates Prior to the Latter part of the Sixteenth Century*, 3rd edn (London, 1883), pp. 10, 60, 126, 154, 158, 236, 279, 285. For surviving representations of the harrowing in Shakespeare's home county see Clifford Davidson and Jennifer Alexander, *The Early Art of Coventry, Stratford-upon-Avon, Warwick and Lesser Sites in Warwickshire: A Subject List of Extant and Lost Art Including Items Relevant to Early Drama* (Kalamazoo, Michigan, 1985), pp. 131–2, 32.

Glass representations, such as the fifteenth-century stained glass harrowing in St Michael's, Coventry, frequently survived into the late sixteenth and early seventeenth centuries.[5]

Churchgoers would have read of the harrowing in the thirty-nine articles and recited the words of the Apostle's creed at morning and evening prayer: 'he descended into hell'. Alexander Nowell's *Catechism* (1570), the official catechism of the Elizabethan church and one of the most read books of the late sixteenth century, declares that 'as Christ in his bodie descended into the bowels of the earth, so in hys soule seuered from the bodie he descended into hell'.[6] The homilies likewise taught that Christ 'passed through death & hell . . . He destroyed the devill and all his tyranny, and openly triumphed over him, and tooke away from him all his captives'.[7]

Some early versions of the Easter liturgy placed great emphasis on the harrowing. In the monastery of Barking, near London, a fourteenth-century abbess greatly extended the *elevatio* – the celebration of Christ's Resurrection enacted through the elevation of the cross and host from the Easter sepulchre – to include an elaborate, symbolic harrowing. All the members of the convent were shut into a side chapel, a priest uttered the *tollite portas* three times, and the door was flung open and all the imprisoned spirits, carrying palms of victory departed singing. Some German service books give examples of such liturgical dramas of the harrowing continuing into the 1590s.[8] The *tollite portas* was the triumphal end of Psalm 24 which became associated with Christ at hell's gates early in the medieval period: 'lift vp your heads ye gates, and be ye lift vp ye euerlasting doores, and the King of glory shall come in. Who is this King of glorie? the Lord strong and mightie euer the Lord mightie in battell'.[9]

The harrowing of hell would also have been in the general consciousness in the 1590s because of a heated debate about it at that time. Mainstream theology in the Church of England accepted the literal understanding of the article of the creed 'he descended into hell'. Luther's Torgau sermon of 1533 describes Christ as entering hell as a 'victorious hero' and argues that this article of the creed is best understood as it is shown in the 'children's play presented at Easter'.[10] Calvin, however, did not wish to retain Luther's 'crude pictures' and interpreted the creed as referring to Christ suffering hell's pains on the cross, not a literal descent. Calvin's interpretation gained ground quickly and was widely accepted among Puritan circles by the 1580s and 1590s.[11] The Martin Marprelate tracts accused the established church of taking a Catholic line on Christ's descent into hell, and this was followed by a war of sermons and books on the subject between Alexander Hume and Adam Hill in

[5] For the survival of stained glass in Elizabethan England see Paul L. Hughes and James F. Larkin, eds., *Tudor Royal Proclamations*, 3 vols. (London, 1964–9), vol. 2, p. 147; Frederick J. Furnivall, ed., *Harrison's Description of England in Shakespere's Youth*, 3 vols. (London, 1877), vol. 1, p. 31; Trevor Cooper, ed., *The Journal of William Dowsing: Iconoclasm in East Anglia during the Civil War* (Woodbridge, 2001), pp. 232, 260, 295, 302, 89–106.

[6] Alexander Nowell, *A Catechisme, or first Instruction and Learning of Christian Religion* (London, 1570), sigs. K3^{v}–4^{r}.

[7] Mary Ellen Riches and Thomas B. Stroup, eds., *Certaine Sermons or Homilies Appointed to be Read in Churches In the Time of Queen Elizabeth I (1547–71)* (Gainesville, Florida, 1968), p. 192.

[8] Karl Young, *The Drama of the Medieval Church*, 2 vols. (Oxford, 1962), vol. 1, pp. 102–4, 167; Karl Young, 'The Harrowing of Hell in Liturgical Drama', *Transactions of the Wisconsin Academy of Sciences, Arts and Letters*, 16.2 (1909), 889–947, esp. 910; E. K. Chambers, *The Mediaeval Stage*, 2 vols. (Oxford, 1948), vol. 2, pp. 4–5.

[9] Young, *Drama*, vol. 1, pp. 149–50. All biblical quotations are from the Geneva Bible unless otherwise stated. For Shakespeare's knowledge of this and other versions see Naseeb Shaheen, *Biblical References in Shakespeare's Plays* (London, 1999), pp. 17–50.

[10] This sermon was a seminal text for the Lutheran doctrine of the descent. For a translation see Robert Kolb and James A. Nestingen, ed., *Sources and Contexts of The Book of Concord* (Minneapolis, 2001), pp. 246–9.

[11] John Calvin, *Institutes of the Christian Religion*, ed. John T. McNeill, translated by Ford Lewis Battles, *The Library of Christian Classics*, vol. 20 (Philadelphia, 1960), bk II, chap. xvi, sections 8–12; Dewey D. Wallace, 'Puritan and Anglican: The Interpretation of Christ's Descent Into Hell in Elizabethan Theology', *Archiv fur Reformations-Geschichte*, 69 (1978), 248–87, esp. 266.

1589–94.[12] The established church responded with a sermon by Thomas Bilson, the bishop of Winchester, preached at St Paul's cross during Lent, 1597 (a possible dating for the composition of *Henry IV Part 1*) which argued that Christ '*personallie conquered* and disarmed' the devil.[13]

The harrowing of hell would have been known to Shakespeare and his audience through books, pamphlets, sermons, church-going and, in some cases, drama.[14] Mystery cycles were performed until the 1570s in a number of places, and the harrowing play was central to them. Its popularity in the Coventry cycle – staged only fourteen miles from Shakespeare's home until 1579 – is attested by a joke in John Heywood's *The Foure PP* (1547), in which the porter of hell's gates turns out to have 'played the deuyll at Couentry'.[15] Those members of Shakespeare's audience who had not seen mystery plays may have had memories of liturgy, wall-paintings or stained glass windows which would have given colour to the recitation of the creed or perhaps supplied a mental picture when listening to the martial words of the homilies. It seems therefore at least possible that the Elizabethan audience could have recognized, at least subconsciously, that Hal was appropriating a role that belonged to a different, and divine, king.

Christ prepared himself for his Passion by going out into the wilderness to be tempted by the devil. The liturgical season that remembers and re-enacts this time of trial is Lent, and this is the season that governs *Henry IV Part 1*. Just as Christ was tempted by Satan, Hal is tempted by the 'reverend Vice' Falstaff (2.5.458).[16] Such at least is the schema. But Hal is not really tempted. He allows himself to be drawn into idleness, play fighting with his friends while his father prepares for war, but he had always intended to 'throw off' this 'loose behaviour' so that

> My reformation, glitt'ring o'er my fault,
> Shall show more goodly, and attract more eyes
> Than that which hath no foil to set it off.
>
> (1.2.210–12)

This is a staged Lenten period, not a genuine time of temptation and self-searching, but in an inverted manner it contains the characteristics of the season: fish, leanness, biblical quotations and repentance. Falstaff, both the diabolical tempter in the desert and the carnival figure of Shrove Tuesday, carries the preponderance of the Lenten imagery.[17] The war of words between him and the prince is a battle between fat and lean, a leitmotif of the play:

---

[12] William Pierce, ed., *The Marprelate Tracts 1588, 1589* (London, 1911), pp. 56, 186, 271–2, 280; Adam Hill, *The Defence of the Article: Christ descended into Hell* (London, 1592); Alexander Hume, *A reioynder to doctor Hil concerning the descente of Christ into Hell, wherein the answere to his sermon is justlie defended, and the roust of his reply scraped from those arguments as cleanlie, as if they had never bene touched with that canker* (Edinburgh, 1594).

[13] The Oxford edition argues that evidence from the Oldcastle debate suggests that it was written and performed while Cobham was Lord Chamberlain (August 1596–March 1597). Lent fell in February/March in 1597. Cf. David Bevington, ed., *Henry IV Part One* (Oxford, 1987), p. 9; Thomas Bilson, *The effect of certaine Sermons tovching The Fvll redemption of mankind by the death and bloud of Christ Jesvs: Wherein Besides the merite of Christs svffering, the manner of his offering, the power of his death, the comfort of his Crosse, the glorie of his resvrrection, Are handled, what paines Christ suffered in his sovle on the Crosse: Together, With the place and pvrpose of his descent to hel after death* (London, 1599), sig. A4r.

[14] For the evidence that sermon and theatre audience overlapped, which supports the argument that a playwright might make use of a theological debate, see Martha Tuck Rozett, *The Doctrine of Election and the Emergence of Elizabethan Tragedy* (Princeton, 1984), pp. 15ff.

[15] See R. W. Ingram, ed., *Coventry*, Records of Early English Drama (Manchester, 1981), pp. 294, xvii–xix. The harrowing of hell play, like most of the Coventry cycle, is now lost but it is the focus for one of the best pieces of criticism linking Shakespeare's dramaturgy with that of the mystery cycles: Glynne Wickham, *Shakespeare's Dramatic Heritage: Collected Studies in Mediaeval, Tudor and Shakespearean Drama* (London, 1969), pp. 214–31. For the continuation of mystery plays throughout England in the Elizabethan period, and up to 1605 in Kendal, see the other REED project volumes.

[16] Cf. J. Dover Wilson, *The Fortunes of Falstaff* (Cambridge, 1970), pp. 17–23 and Willard Farnham, 'Falstaff and the Grotesque', in Harold Bloom, ed., *Falstaff* (New York, 1992), pp. 155–70, esp. 166–8.

[17] Francois Laroque, 'Shakespeare's Battle of Carnival and Lent: The Falstaff Scenes Reconsidered (1 & 2 Henry IV)', in Ronald Knowles, ed., *Shakespeare and Carnival: After Bakhtin* (London, 1998), pp. 83–96.

PRINCE HARRY I'll be no longer guilty of this sin. This sanguine coward, this bed-presser, this horse-back-breaker, this huge hill of flesh –
SIR JOHN 'Sblood, you starveling, you elf-skin, you dried neat's tongue, you bull's pizzle, you stock-fish. (2.5.245–9)

This skirmish of wit is a prelude to the single combat with Hotspur, and its dramatic function of anticipation is similar to the narrative function of Christ's temptation in the wilderness, which is likewise a verbal trial of strength that anticipates the main action of the Passion. Contemporary sermons about the temptation in the desert borrowed the martial language of the devil's final destruction for this preliminary tussle. Lancelot Andrewes, for example, in a 1592 sermon series described Christ and Satan as 'the two Champions' and the holy spirit as 'the leader of Iesus into the lists'.[18]

The terms of Falstaff and Hal's argument quoted above are those of the battle of Lent: the popular enactment of the financial rivalry between fishmongers and butchers during this season. Falstaff counters the Prince's meaty criticism – 'sanguine', 'horse', 'flesh' – with the piscine barb 'stock-fish' (and perhaps a particularly thin 'ling', a staple Lenten fish, could have been heard in 'starveling').[19] Nashe's *Praise of the Red Herring* (1599), composed close to *Henry VI Part 1*, makes reference to this martial Lenten imagery in a literal battle of fish and flesh, which parallels his support for the Yarmouth fishermen against 'their bloudy adversaries, the butchers'.[20] It is also possible that *Lenten Stuffe* shares with *Henry IV* a submerged satire against the Cobham family.[21] In Nashe, Scoufos argues, Oldcastle is parodied as the Lenten fish par excellence, the herring. In Shakespeare the Falstaff/Oldcastle jibes have Lenten associations too, except here the 'roasted Manningtree ox with the pudding in his belly' (2.5.457) is definitely on the meaty side of the war. The Puritan ancestry of Falstaff seems surprising, but Puritans were not always parodied as abstainers from the pleasures of the flesh. Poole has argued convincingly that Shakespeare's presentation of Falstaff is fully in keeping with the tenor of late-sixteenth-century anti-Puritan literature. She has shown how the anti-Marprelate tracts and the burlesque stage performances of the Marprelate controversy created a grotesque, fleshy Puritan who could have been the dramatic antecedent of Falstaff.[22]

Falstaff, like a Puritan, objects to the strictures of Lent. Protestants did not observe Lent rigorously because it was based on the tradition of the Church, rather than Scriptural authority.[23] Taylor's Protestant satire *Jack-a-Lent* ends with the assertion 'I am persuaded that a man may go to heaven as well with a leg of a capon, as with a red herring.'[24] A capon leg is part of Falstaff's avoidance of the most solemn fast of Lent – Poins asks him 'how agrees the devil and thee about thy soul, that thou soldest him on Good Friday last, for a . . . cold capon's leg?' (1.2.113–15). The religious language highlights the fact that this broken fast is not merely

[18] Lancelot Andrewes, *The Wonderfvll Combate (for Gods glorie and Mans saluation) betweene Christ and Satan* (London, 1592), sig. A3^{r}; for another contemporary example see Robert Holland, *The holie history of our Lord Jesus Christs natiuitie, life, resurrection a. acsension: gathered into English meeter* (1594), sig. C2^{v}.

[19] The Arden editor, through his emendation of 'elf-skin' to 'eel-skin', adds another fish to the list: cf. A. R. Humphreys, ed., *King Henry IV Part 1* (London, 1960), p. 69.

[20] Ronald B. McKerrow, ed., *The Works of Thomas Nashe*, 5 vols. (London, 1904–10), vol. 3, pp. 183, 201–4.

[21] Charles Nicholl, *A Cup of News: The Life of Thomas Nashe* (London, 1984), pp. 249–53; Alice Lyle Scoufos, 'Nashe, Jonson and the Oldcastle Problem', *Modern Philology*, 65 (1968), 307–24, esp. 249–53.

[22] Kristen Poole, *Radical Religion from Shakespeare to Milton: Figures of Nonconformity in Early Modern England* (Cambridge, 2000), p. 34.

[23] For example in John Bale's *Temptacyon of Our Lorde and Saver Jesus Christ by Sathan in the Desart* (1538) Jesus is at pains to point out that his forty-day fast is not a model for man to follow: in Peter Happé, ed., *The Complete Plays of John Bale* (Cambridge, 1986), lines 74–5.

[24] John Taylor, 'Jacke A Lent His Beginning and Entertainment with the mad prankes of his Gentleman Vsher Shrove Tuesday that goes before him, and his Footman hunger attending (1630)' in Charles Hindley, ed., *The Old Book Collector's Miscellany* (London, 1872), p. 22. The opposition between herring and capons was so marked that by the late seventeenth century the joke had become linguistically enshrined and a red herring was known as a 'Yarmouth capon', *Oxford English Dictionary* herring 3.

the act of a humorously greedy clown, but also in keeping with the image of the grotesque Puritan.

Falstaff's refusal to keep fasts is in keeping with his original incarnation as a Puritan martyr, but used in the pursuit of greed rather than holiness. Likewise his constant Puritan idiom (he calls himself a 'saint' whom Hal has led astray (1.2.91)) is used in the pursuit of vice. He encourages Poins with 'God give thee the spirit of persuasion and him the ears of profiting' (1.2.150–1), hoping that Poins will persuade Hal to commit a robbery, and in preparation for his impersonation of the king in a tavern play says, 'an the fire of grace be not quite out of thee, now shalt thou be moved' (2.5.386).[25] The mismatching is very funny, and Falstaff intends it to be so. He creates comedy by using high moral language for a low moral purpose. The use of such phraseology by Falstaff can be read as a parody of Puritanism, but it is also something more engaging – the parodic Puritan's hypocrisy in twisting biblical phrases to his own use becomes innocent in Falstaff who does not intend to be misunderstood.

This open, humorous vice can seem more captivating than Hal's masked virtue, and draws it into question. Hal understands, as Machiavelli put it, that 'it is necessary to know well how to colour this nature, and to be a great pretender and dissembler . . . [for] everyone sees how you appear, few touch what you are'.[26] Later Christianizers of Machiavelli were to understand this principle of the necessary participation in evil and dissimulation by the Prince as an imitation of the Incarnation, when divinity becomes fused with fallen humanity.[27] Hal attempts to infuse his Machiavellian dissimulation of his true nature with an aura of the Incarnation, a descent to the mortal world of the tavern, employed in order to hide his true royalty. In both parts of *Henry IV* there is an early cozening scene in the sub-plot which holds in microcosm the Incarnational allusion of Hal's dissimulation. In *Henry IV Part 2* Hal tricks Falstaff by putting on the leather jerkin and apron of a servant, and says: 'From a god to a bull – A heavy declension – it was Jove's case. From a prince to a prentice – a low transformation' (2.2.165–7). This jest of a prince becoming a serving man is couched in pagan terms, although the ubiquitous use of 'Jove' for the Christian God at this time alerts the audience to the possibility that held within the joke is the story of a god who did not scorn to stoop so low, Jesus Christ 'who being in the forme of God thought it no robberie to be equal with God: But he made himself of no reputation & tooke on him the forme of a seruant'.[28] Hal alludes to the Incarnation, but although willing for the moment to play at being a servant, he grows dissatisfied with the game and shortly after it has begun leaves the tavern never to return.

Lent, the time when *Henry IV Part 2* is set (2.4.346–51), and the season that governs *Henry IV Part 1*, draws to a close in holy week. As the Crucifixion, and the battle, approach, the protagonist withdraws from his usual companions to be alone with his father. Prior to the Crucifixion Christ goes to Gethsemane to pray. It is a time of pain and absolute submission; but Hal's apparent capitulation to his father's will prior to the battle (the position of the reconciliation is Shakespeare's invention: in the sources it does not happen until after the rebellion has been crushed) is similar only in outward appearances. For Hal there is no struggle because for him there will be no suffering. Hal's appropriation of the Passion narrative contains parallels with the time in the wilderness, Gethsemane and the harrowing of hell, but lacks the crucial central event. There is no Crucifixion.

Hal addresses his father in the language of Isaiah 63 (the epistle for the Monday before Easter in the Book of Common Prayer) to invest his

[25] Tom McAlindon has argued suggestively that Falstaff's quicksilver wit might come from Bale's description of Oldcastle as a man with verbal dexterity: cf. 'Perfect Answers: Religious Inquisition, Falstaffian wit', *Shakespeare Survey 54* (Cambridge, 2001), pp. 100–7.

[26] Niccolo Machiavelli, *The Prince*, trans. Harvey C. Mansfield (London, 1998), pp. 70–1.

[27] Peter S. Donaldson, *Machiavelli and the Mystery of State* (Cambridge, 1971), pp. 213–16.

[28] Philippians 2.6 (Geneva Bible). This is a central biblical text for the understanding of the Incarnation.

reformation with overtones of the messiah returning triumphant to heaven:

I will redeem all this on Percy's head,
And in the closing of some glorious day
Be bold to tell you that I am your son;
When I will wear a garment all of blood,
And stain my favours in a bloody mask,
Which, washed away, shall scour my shame with it.
(3.2.132–7)

Hal's emphatic 'I am your son' resonates with Christian reworking of Isaiah 63 in which the Son's submission to the Father leads to his Crucifixion.[29] The relationship between father and son is a crux of *Henry IV Part 1*. Psychoanalytic critics have long argued that Hal can be considered as having two fathers: 'in a sense Falstaff *is* his father; certainly he is a "father-substitute" in the psychologist's word'.[30] But in this speech Hal's proud statement of kinship with Bolingbroke marks his rejection of Falstaff and his world. Hal's filial obedience is the more striking because in Shakespeare's source play *The Famous Victories of Henry V* the reconciliation between the king and his son carries with it a genuine threat of danger to Henry IV: '*enters the Prince with a dagger in his hand*'.[31] Shakespeare has inverted this for now the reconciliation will come through the shedding of the son's blood instead: 'I will wear a garment all of blood, / And stain my favours in a bloody mask, / Which, washed away, shall scour my shame with it.'

Hal's conflation of blood with cleansing borrows a ubiquitous image from the Atonement, used in the prayer of humble access in the Book of Common Prayer's order for Holy Communion: 'that our sinful bodies may be made clean by his body, and our souls washed through his most precious blood'.[32] The dominant biblical image of Hal's speech, however, comes from Isaiah 63.1–10:

Who is this that cometh from Edom, with red *garments* from Bozrah? hee that is *glorious* in his apparel . . . Wherefore is thine apparel red, and thy *garments* like him that treadeth in ye winepresse? I have trodden the winepresse alone, and of all people there was none with mee: for I will treade them in mine anger, and tread them underfoote in my wrath and their *blood shal be sprinkled upon my garments*, and I will *staine* all my raiment . . . in his love and in his mercie he *redeemed* them.[33]

One interpretation of Christ's fulfilment of Isaiah 63 was the Anselmian view that only God himself, in the person of Christ, was capable of making a complete satisfaction for the infinite offence of sin. In the new dispensation therefore, the person who comes from Edom has borne the wrath of God for us, and his clothes are stained with his own blood instead of the blood of his enemies. The Book of Revelation describes Christ's fulfilment of Isaiah 63: 'and he was clothed with a garment dipt in blood and his name is called *the worde of God* . . . for he it is that treadeth the wine presse of the fiercenesse and wrath of almightie God' (19.13–15). The New Testament transforms the aggressive triumph of God in Isaiah into the passion of the suffering, blood-soaked redeemer; and the two

---

29 See Christ's similarly bold claim in the York cycle that his obedience makes him worthy to be recognized as his father's son: Richard Beadle, ed., *The York Plays* (London, 1982), p. 374.

30 J. I. M. Stewart, *Character and Motive in Shakespeare: Some Recent Appraisals Examined* (London, 1949), p. 138; see also Ernst Kris, *Psychoanalytic Explorations in Art* (London, 1953), pp. 277–9. For a more recent and subtler approach see James L. Calderwood in Bloom, *Falstaff*, p. 55.

31 Geoffrey Bullough, ed., *Narrative and Dramatic Sources of Shakespeare*, 8 vols. (London, 1964–75), vol. 4, p. 315. Psychoanalytic critics explain the lack of this undercurrent in Shakespeare's play by arguing that Hal's 'parricidal impulses' find their outlet in his treatment of Falstaff and in the rebellion of his alter-ego Hotspur: Stewart, *Character and Motive*, pp. 137–8 and Kris, *Psychoanalytic Explorations*, p. 278.

32 Cf. John Andrewes, *Christ his Crosse or The Most Comfortable Doctrine of Christ Crucified, and ioyfull tidings of his Passion, teaching us to love, and imbrace his Crosse, as the most sweete and celestiall doctrine unto his soule, and how we should behave ourselves therein according to the word of God* (Oxford, 1614), p. 13; William Keatinge Clay, ed., *Liturgies and Occasional Forms of Prayers set forth in the Reign of Queen Elizabeth* (Cambridge, 1847), p. 194.

33 The verbal parallels of the Geneva version are highlighted. Naseeb Shaheen also notes the 'similar thought' of this passage to Hal's speech: *Biblical References in Shakespeare's Histories* (London, 1989), p. 146.

interpretations become one in the cross that is both God's humiliation and his glory.

Isaiah 63 was seen as a messianic prophecy both of Christ's suffering on the cross and of his final victory. As Lancelot Andrewes preached, using this as his text for Easter day, 1623, 'His *coming* heer from Edom, will fall out to be *His rising from the dead*. His returne from Bozra nothing but his vanquishing of *hell*.'[34] In this interpretation of Isaiah the risen Christ retains the blood-soaked clothes, the badge of his Crucifixion, when he comes in glory. The suffering is remembered at the moment of triumph because it is through suffering that Christ has triumphed. Likewise in the mystery plays Christ's red clothes are used after his Resurrection. In the Chester cycle's play of Christ's Ascension the tailors clothe Christ in his blood-stained robes of Bozrah. The angels greet the ascending redeemer with the cry of Isaiah:

> Who ys this that cometh within
> the blysse of heaven that neuer shall blynne,
> bloodye, owt of the world of synne –
> and harrowed hell hath hee?[35]

In Hal's reworking of Isaiah he will 'wear a garment all of blood' and answer the question 'who is this?' with a triumphal 'I am your son' (3.2.134). Hal uses Isaiah in the same way as the book of Revelation and the authors of the mystery plays, to look forward to the time when the battle has been won and the son and father will be reunited.

In both the popular *Christus victor* model of the Atonement, and in the mystery plays, the climax of salvation is imagined as a battle. Christ-as-victor-knight became ubiquitous in medieval piety, and most lyrics about the Passion had some reference to it.[36] *Christus victor* as an image for the harrowing survived the Reformation, both in medieval texts that remained popular, and in the language of reformers who used the old metaphor to couch their new concept of the event. The apocryphal *Gospel of Nicodemus*, where the imagery originates, might itself have been known to Shakespeare's audience as it was printed at least eight times in English during the sixteenth century. A recent commentator on a manuscript of the apocryphal gospel written after 1564 suggests that it 'retained a deep-rooted fascination which even the Reformation could not destroy'.[37] *Piers Plowman*, which relies strongly on the *Christus victor* image for both the Crucifixion and harrowing, was enthusiastically championed, and printed, by Protestant dissenters throughout the Tudor period.[38] Protestant writers who avoid any suggestion of a literal descent still retain the *Christus victor* imagery. John Foxe, for example, in *Christ Jesus Triumphant* (1579) supports a metaphorical understanding of the descent but still calls Christ 'our heauenly Champion' and the verso of the title page carries a full-page picture of Christ rising out of the tomb, trampling on death and carrying a victor's palm.[39] As demonstrated earlier, most writing on the harrowing – such as the homilies, the official catechism and Luther's Torgau sermon – uses the traditional *Christus victor* imagery. Even Calvin retains the martial language for describing the metaphorical descent to hell, Christ's battle with hell's pains on the cross: 'he must also grapple hand to hand with the armies of hell'.[40]

The *Christus victor* as an image for the harrowing of hell can also be found in the literature of the 1590s. Spenser's Easter sonnet, Amoretti 68, begins triumphantly:

---

34 Lancelot Andrewes, *XCVI Sermons* (London, 1629), p. 567.

35 R. M. Lumiansky and David Mills, ed., *The Chester Mystery Cycle*, Early English Text Society [EETS], ss 3 and 9, (Oxford, 1974–86), vol. 1, pp. 373–4.

36 For examples see Douglas Gray, ed., *English Medieval Religious Lyrics* (Exeter, [illegible]), pp. [illegible].

37 C. W. Marx, 'The *Gospel of Nicodemus* in Old English and Middle English', in Zbigniew Izydorczyk, ed., *The Medieval Gospel of Nicodemus: Texts, Intertexts, and Contexts in Western Europe* (Tempe, Arizona, 1997), pp. 256–9.

38 Barbara A. Johnson, *Reading Piers Plowman and The Pilgrim's Progress: Reception and the Protestant Reader* (Carbondale, Southern Illinois, 1992), p. 99.

39 John Foxe, *Christ Iesvs Triumphant* (London, 1579), sig. B1^{r}.

40 Calvin, *Institutes*, vol. 20, p. 515. For a full discussion of this image in Christian thought see Gustaf Aulen, *Christus Victor: An Historical Study of the Three Main Types of the Idea of the Atonement*, trans. A. G. Herbert (London, 1931).

> Most glorious Lord of life! that, on this day,
> Didst make Thy triumph over death and sin;
> And, having harrowed hell, didst bring away
> Captivity thence captive, us to win.

In this biblical image of enslaving death and leading it in triumph like a victorious general, Spenser is making a numerological pun as it is Psalm 68, the same number as his sonnet, from which the quote 'thou hast led captivity captive' (v.18) comes.[41] Spenser also uses harrowing imagery repeatedly in *The Faerie Queene* when Arthur breaks into the plot to save beleaguered knights, most clearly in Book 1, canto 8.[42]

Hal's martial encounter with Hotspur, like the harrowing play of the mystery cycles, is the climax of the dramatic action. Hal wins back all the glory that Hotspur had taken from him. There are a number of small parallels between Hotspur's behaviour and the devil's that enable Hal to claim a symbolic connection to the salvation of the world in his small victory. Hotspur, as a rebel, is automatically linked in royalist Tudor rhetoric to the first rebel, Lucifer. The *Homilie Against Disobedience and Wilfull Rebellion* – which was read at least once a year in every church – makes a striking comparison between rebels and the devil:

> Where most rebellions and rebelles bee, there is the expresse similitude of hell, and the rebelles themselves are the verie figures of fiendes and devils, and their captaine the vngratious patterne of Lucifer and Satan, the prince of darkenesse, of whose rebellion as they bee followers, so shall they of his damnation in hell vndoubtedly bee partakers.[43]

This connection between a rebel leader and the devil is particularly pertinent as there is strong evidence that Shakespeare drew on this homily when writing his second tetralogy.[44]

Another connection between Hotspur and satanic forces is that he is extremely unwilling to let his captives go. When the king demands them he impetuously declares 'I'll keep them all' (1.3.212). A desire to keep his prisoners is a strong part of the characterization of the devil, both in *Piers Plowman* and in the mystery plays. When Satan, in the Chester play, suddenly realizes that he is not strong enough to fight Christ, he cries out:

> Owt, alas, I am shente!
> My might fayles, veramente.
> This prynce that ys nowe present
> Will pull from me my praye.[45]

The freeing of souls is a crucial event in the iconography of the harrowing, and most depictions of it focus on this event.[46] Hal's first act after his victory, in his final speech of the play, is to free a prisoner: 'go to the Douglas and deliver him / Up to his pleasure, ransomless and free' (5.5.28–9).[47] Hal's final action of this play could be an attempt to imitate the largesse inherent in Christ's deliverance of mankind, the action that ends the harrowing plays, but Hal's chivalrous behaviour is crucially different from Christ's salvation of all virtuous captive souls. Not only has the number of freed men become severely curtailed, but Douglas was *his* prisoner, not Hotspur's.

It is praise, however, not 'praye', that Hotspur has kept from Hal, but he dies regretting it as much as Satan does his souls:

> O Harry, thou hast robbed me of my youth.
> I better brook the loss of brittle life
> Than those proud titles thou hast won of me.
> (5.4.76–8)

41 Kenneth J. Larsen's excellent edition, which shows how the sonnets correspond with the daily order of scriptural readings in the Church of England, references the Psalm but does not draw attention to the pun. Cf. *Edmund Spenser's Amoretti and Epithalamion: A Critical Edition* (Tempe, Arizona, 1997). For another possible *Christus victor* image cf. Giorgio Melchiori, ed., *King Edward III* (Cambridge, 1998), 3.4.30–61.

42 Discussed further below.

43 *Certaine Sermons or Homilies*, pp. 296–7.

44 See Alfred Hart, *Shakespeare and the Homilies: And Other Pieces of Research into the Elizabethan Drama* (London, 1934), pp. 38–61.

45 William Langland, *The Vision of Piers Plowman: A Critical Edition of the B-Text based Trinity College Cambridge MSB.15.17*, ed. A. V. C. Schmidt, 2nd edn (London, 1995), passus xviii.276–351; *Chester Mystery Cycle*, vol. 1, p. 332.

46 Gertrude Schiller, *Iconography of Christian Art*, 2 vols. (London, 1972) vol. 2, plates 12, 15, 22, 379, 476, 539, 767.

47 Cf. the liberation of the patriarchs in *York Plays*, p. 342.

Shakespeare makes Hotspur a noble rather than a devilish figure, and the characteristics which he shares with medieval and early modern dramatizations of the devil are attractive rather than Satanic. The most fundamental of these is that Hotspur, like the devil, belongs to an outmoded world order. Satan is part of the old dispensation, who clings to the idea that Christ will not be able to take his prey because he is bound to fight according to the old law of justice. In *Piers Plowman* Lucifer says:

> If he reve me of my right, he robbeth me by maistrie;
> For by right and by reson the renkes that ben here
> Body and soule beth myne, bothe goode and ille.
> For hymself seide, that sire is of hevene,
> That if Adam ete the appul, alle sholde deye . . .
> And sithen he that Soothnesse is seide thise wordes . . .
> I leeve that lawe nyl noght lete hym the leeste.
> (passus xviii.276–84)

Hotspur likewise fights according to old rules, in his case outmoded models of chivalry and honour. When the king's servant approaches him on the battlefield and demands he give over his prisoners to the king, Hotspur refuses. The King says of Hotspur's behaviour:

> KING What think you, coz,
> Of this young Percy's pride? The prisoners
> Which he in this adventure hath surprised
> To his own use he keeps, and sends me word
> I shall have none but Mordake Earl of Fife.
> (1.1.90–4)

But in fact according to the law of arms Hotspur is entitled to retain all the prisoners, except for the Earl of Fife who has royal blood.[48] They are his by right, according to the old system.

In common with other similar characters who Shakespeare portrays as relics within their own cultures, such as Antony and Hector, Hotspur is sympathetic and the values he stands for are not cast aside. However, unlike their opponents, Caesar and Achilles, both of whom refuse to fight them in single combat – a method of fighting that represents everything these figures of the heroic past stand for – Hal meets and overcomes Hotspur on the latter's own terms.[49] Hal speaks to the drawer in his own language and beats Hotspur according to his own rules.

Likewise Christ, when he enters hell in his glory, comes not to destroy the old law but to fulfil it. In *Piers Plowman* Christ replies to the devil's fears with the answer:

> Al that man hath mysdo, I man, wole amende it.
> Membre for membre was amendes by the Old
> Lawe . . .
> So leve it noght, Lucifer, ayein the lawe I feeche
> hem,
> But by right and by reson raunsone here my liges . . .
> I in liknesse of a leode, that Lord am of hevene,
> Graciousliche thi gile have quyt – go gile ayein gile!
> (passus xviii.343–58)

Lucifer believes that he is invincible fought according to the old law of justice, but through the Incarnation, man – as Jesus here explains – as been able to make satisfaction for man.

In an interpretation of the Atonement, popular in medieval times, known as the 'guiler beguiled' theory, Satan was cozened by the Incarnation and so remained ignorant of God's plan for the salvation of mankind until his power had been destroyed. Gregory of Nyssa famously used the metaphor of Christ's human nature being the worm that concealed the hook of his divinity, and tempted the devil to impale himself on it:

> For since . . . it was not in the nature of the opposing power to come in contact with the undiluted presence of God . . . the Deity was hidden under the veil of our nature, that so, as with a ravenous fish, the hook of the Deity might be gulped down along with the bait of flesh.[50]

---

[48] Humphreys, ed., *King Henry IV Part 1*, note to 1.1.91–4.

[49] Cf. *Troilus and Cressida* 5.9.9–14, and *Antony and Cleopatra* 3.13.24–30; 4.1.1–6.

[50] Gregory of Nyssa *Dogmatic Treatises etc.*, in *A Select Library of Nicene and Post-Nicene fathers of the Christian Church*, 2nd series, 14 vols. (Oxford, 1893), vol. 5, p. 494. For a use of Gregory's metaphor by one of Shakespeare's contemporaries see William Perkins, *Satans Sophostrie Answered by Ovr Saviovr Christ* (London, 1604), sig. B7v. Roy Battenhouse presents a speculative case for the use of it in Shakespeare's own work in 'Measure for Measure and Christian Doctrine of the Atonement', *PMLA*, 61 (1946), 1029–59.

This divine deception of the devil is a fundamental part of the 'abuse of power' model of the Atonement. Pope Leo the Great explained that when Christ hid 'the power of His Godhead which was inseparable from His manhood under the veil of our weakness, the crafty foe was taken off his guard'.[51] Satan tries to punish Christ with damnation, as he justly does with all other men, but because Christ is sinless Satan has no jurisdiction over him and, for this abuse of his power, has all his other captives taken from him. It is fundamental to this model of the Atonement that Satan does not recognize Jesus as God and hence does not understand what is happening when at Christ's approach hell is flooded with light. Christ has deliberately concealed his divine nature in order to deceive the infernal powers.[52] Hal's strategy of redemption, and his ability to take on Hotspur in single combat which the latter thinks he will win is likewise based on his concealment of his true nature.

Early in *Henry IV Part 1* there is a microcosm of this central deception in the sub-plot. The Gad's Hill incident belongs to the folk tradition of royalty concealing itself in the clothes of common man, an image which had itself been used by Origen as a description of the concealed Christ in the 'guiler beguiled' model of the Atonement.[53] Origen's image is drawn from a wider, and ubiquitous, metaphor for the Incarnation which involves Christ 'clothing' himself in humanity.[54] Hal's deeper disguise of himself as a prodigal son is literalized in the clothes of buckram that he puts on to fight Falstaff: 'I have cases of buckram for the nonce, to immask our noted outward garments' (1.2.174).[55] Hal's comic subterfuge holds in miniature the masking of his nobility which is the central plot of the play. This deeper design is revealed twenty lines after the Gad's Hill plot is hatched:

> Yet herein will I imitate the sun,
> Who doth permit the base contagious clouds
> To smother up his beauty from the world . . .
> [so that] My reformation, glitt'ring o'er my fault,
> Shall show more goodly, and attract more eyes
> Than that which hath no foil to set it off.
>
> (1.2.194–6, 210–12)

Hal's dissimulation at Gad's Hill is in pursuit of the same goal as his central deception: a combat with someone who does not comprehend his true nature. The hidden royalty of Hal at Gad's Hill reveals the most important parallel between his later duel and the combat between Christ and Satan. Christ, according to the myth, concealed his divinity and Hal conceals his royalty, that part of himself which could in Elizabethan times be considered quasi-divine. Hal hides that fact that he is his father's son in martial might and kingliness under a cloak of dissipation.

The moment that Hal first starts to win back praise to himself is when Vernon sees him before the battle and reports what he has seen to Hotspur in language that glisters with light and the rhetoric of deification. Vernon describes seeing Hal and his comrades:

> Glittering in golden coats like images,
> As full of spirit as the month of May,
> And gorgeous as the sun at midsummer; . . .
> I saw young Harry with his beaver on,
> His cuishes on his thighs, gallantly armed,
> Rise from the ground like feathered Mercury,
> And vaulted with such ease into his seat
> As if an angel dropped down from the clouds
> To turn and wind a fiery Pegasus.
>
> (4.1.100–10)

Christ in the harrowing play would have been similarly bright, dressed in white and gold, and possibly

---

[51] *Leo the Great*, in *A Select Library of Nicene and Post-Nicene Fathers*, vol.12, p. 131.

[52] Alan H. Nelson, 'The Temptation of Christ; or, The Temptation of Satan', in Jerome Taylor and Alan H. Nelson, eds., *Medieval English Drama: Essays Critical and Contextual* (London, 1972), pp. 218–29; see also David L. Wee, 'The Temptation of Christ and the Motif of Divine Duplicity in the Corpus Christi Cycle Drama', *Modern Philology*, 72 (1974), 1–16.

[53] Aulen, *Christus Victor*, p. 68.

[54] Cf. Langland, *Piers Plowman*, xviii.22.

[55] Buckram also has connections with disguise. *Oxford English Dictionary*, 4b states that buckram, as an adjective, meant 'a false appearance of strength'.

also attired as a knight.[56] The bright clothes in the staging of the mystery plays were a symbol for the light which at Christ's approach broke in upon hell and threw it into confusion.

At this point in most of the harrowing narratives the other devils recognize the light as a sign of Christ's divinity and scatter in despair, while Satan, like Hotspur, remains obdurate. In the mystery plays Satan is the last to realize that a superior adversary has entered hell. The Towneley play has a particularly strong dramatization of this as first Rybald and then Belzabub realize the truth and flee, while Satan remains arrogantly self-assured until he is beaten. In the Towneley play Satan does not understand how the man he has killed can come to hell not as a captive but calling himself king, and demands to know more from those who have seen him: 'what page is there that makes prees, / And callis hym kyng of vs in fere?' David replies that he is 'full fers in fight' and 'worthi to wyn honoure'.[57] In the York and Towneley plays Satan does not think his challenger is worthy of him. He brushes David's commendation aside and lays the charge on his adversary that he has led a wild and foolish life:

> Nay, faitour, ther-of schall he faile,
> For alle his fare I hym deffie,
> I knowe his trantis fro toppe to taile,
> He levys with gaudis and with gilery.[58]

Hotspur, likewise, is incredulous about this new, reformed Hal, surprised by his princely challenge to single combat and questions those who are better informed:

> WORCESTER The Prince of Wales stepped forth before the King
> And, nephew, challenged you to single fight . .
> HOTSPUR . . . Tell me, tell me,
> How showed his tasking? Seem'd it in contempt?
> VERNON No, by my soul, I never in my life
> Did hear a challenge urg'd more modestly, . . .
> HOTSPUR Cousin, I think thou art enamourèd
> On his follies. Never did I hear
> Of any prince so wild a liberty. (5.2.45–71)

Vernon and Worcester have understood Hal's true nobility at this point, while the leader of the rebellion is still ignorant of it. Hotspur's questions, his incredulity and his belief in Hal's foolish wildness follows the pattern of the mystery plays. Hotspur, like Satan, is blind to his adversary's true nature and does not know his strength. Hotspur still thinks of Hal as the Cheapside rogue, calls him 'the nimble-footed madcap Prince of Wales' (4.1.95), and is cozened by his guise as an ordinary young man. Hotspur has been duped into understanding only one side of Hal's nature. Hotspur's own forthright character is unable to grasp Hal's strategy of deception and he remains ignorant of Hal's character as both apparent commoner and true prince until Hal destroys him.

In the battle at Shrewsbury there is a general confusion about who people are, illustrated most clearly by the killing of Blunt while dressed as the king (5.3.1–28). When Hotspur finally faces Hal, he seems slightly unsure about whether he has indeed found the prince:

> HOTSPUR If I mistake not, thou art Harry Monmouth.
> PRINCE HARRY Thou speak'st as if I would deny my name.
> HOTSPUR My name is Harry Percy . . .
> PRINCE HARRY I am the Prince of Wales.
> (5.4.58–62)

Even Falstaff fails to recognize Hal during the battle and asks 'but who comes here?' (5.3.39). This recalls the questioning of both Psalm 24 and Isaiah 63: 'who is this that cometh?'; it is the question that the demonic forces ask at the harrowing of hell and the angels ask when Christ ascends in glory. In the *Piers Plowman* harrowing Langland retains the Latin (which in this text is a sign of scriptural or liturgical

[56] Peter Stuart Macaulay, 'The Play of the Harrowing of Hell as a Climax in the English Mystery Cycles', *Studia Germanica Gandensia*, 8 (1966), 115–34, esp. 129. For the possible religious reference of 'like images' see M. St. Clare Byrne, 'Like Images', *Times Literary Supplement*, 2313 (1946), 259.

[57] Martin Stevens and A. C. Cawley, ed., *The Towneley Plays*, EETS, ss 13, 2 vols. (Oxford, 1994), vol. 1, p. 331. Cf. the similar play in *York Plays*, p. 336.

[58] *York Plays*, p. 337. 'Trantis', 'gaudis' and 'gilery' are deceitful tricks, cheats and games.

quotation): '*Quis est iste*?' The Chester playwright translates and embellishes the passage, but the allusion to Isaiah is still clear: 'who ys he so styffe and stronge / that so maysterlyke comes us amonge?'[59] The devil does not recognize Christ because he bursts open hell in his divine nature, and he had been tricked into believing that he was just a man.

Elizabethan versions of the harrowing of hell preserved the medieval sense of a veiled godhead. The battle between Arthur and Duessa's forces over the Redcross knight in book one of the *Faerie Queene* is an allegorical harrowing. The allusion is made clear in such details as the fast-shut gates that open miraculously at Arthur's bidding, and the fact that the dungeon in which Redcross languishes is 'as darke as hell'.[60] Less generally recognized, but as important a parallel, is the fact that the inmates of the castle are ignorant of who Arthur is because his shield is covered. Ostensibly the covered shield means that Arthur's enemies are unable to read his heraldry and find out who he is; allegorically it finds a parallel in the demons who do not comprehend Christ's divine nature while it is shrouded by his humanity. During the battle the veil is dislodged, and his enemies are blinded and vanquished, as the devils are in the harrowing when Christ comes in the full glory of his divinity. Spenser underlines the allusion by adding that the shield's dazzling light could only be compared to divine brightness 'as where th'Almighties lightning brond does light / It dimmes the dazed eyen, and daunts the senses quight' (1.8.21).

The analogy of divinity and majesty is an ancient and thoroughgoing one, and a central idea within it is the parallel between twin-natured kingship – a mortal man and an immortal office – and the two natures of the God-man Christ. Some advocates of the theory of the King's two bodies argued that for this reason the king presents 'on the terrestrial stage the living image of the two-natured God'.[61] The *Homilie Against Disobedience and Wilfull Rebellion* proclaimed that

> As the name of the king is very often attributed and given unto God in the holy scripture; so doth God himself in the same scriptures sometime vouchsafe to communicate his name with earthly princes, terming them gods.

This is in essence the same statement of divine sanction for divine right as James's less carefully worded 'kings are not only God's lieutenants upon earth and sit upon God's throne, but even by God himself they are called gods'.[62] James's accession has been taken by some historians as the beginning of absolutist and divine right thinking in England, but in fact a number of works were published during the 1590s (such as Richard Bancroft's *Daungerous Positions and proceedings* (1593) and Hadrian Saravia's *De Imperandi authoriate et Christiana obedientia* (1593)) that enthusiastically championed the divine power of the monarch. James VI's *True Law of Free Monarchies* was also published during the 1590s and ends by describing the king as 'our God in earth'.[63] Such rhetoric gained strength in England from the need to assert, after the break with Rome, the English monarch's divine right to rule both Church and state. Divine right monarchy became a nationalist agenda, constructing a God-given right for England to rule herself without the intervention of the Pope. The more divine the monarch appeared, the more obvious her right to govern in God's stead. Christopher Hill states that 'religion is a sixteenth century word for nationalism', a dictum that Hal espouses as he invests himself with numinous imagery that will carry him through to his triumph over the French.[64]

---

59 *Piers Plowman*, xviii.316; *Chester Mystery Cycle*, vol. 1, p. 330.

60 Edmund Spenser, *The Faerie Queene*, ed. A. C. Hamilton (London, 2001), 1.viii.3; 1.viii.5; 1.viii.39. See also Matthew A. Fike, 'Prince Arthur and Christ's Descent into Hell: *The Faerie Queene*, 1.viii and II.viii', *ANQ: A Quarterly Journal of Short Articles, Notes, and Reviews*, 7.2 (1997), 6–13.

61 Ernst H. Kantorowicz, *The King's Two Bodies: A Study in Medieval Political Theology* (Princeton, 1957), p. 47.

62 *Certaine Sermons and Homilies*, p. 279; J. R. Tanner, ed., *Constitutional Documents of the Reign of James I* (Cambridge, 1960), p. 15.

63 J. P. Sommerville, 'Richard Hooker, Hadrian Saravia, and the Advent of the Divine Right of Kings', *History of Political Thought*, 4 (1983), 229–45, esp. 231; James I, *The True Law of Free Monarchies and Basilikon Doron*, ed. Daniel Fischlin and Mark Fortier (Toronto, 1996), p. 82.

64 Christopher Hill, *Religion and Politics in 17th Century England*, 2 vols. (Brighton, 1986), vol. 2, p. 20.

Hal has constructed a pattern in which, after his Lenten period in the wilderness, he will return and overcome the opposing forces and rise as England's glorious new hope. After Hal has thrown off his disguise as a dissolute youth at Shrewsbury, and defeated Hotspur, he is ready to rise again to the new life of a courtly prince and heir apparent. However at just the moment that Hal brings to fruition the actions that were to bring about his own carefully orchestrated resurrection, rising from the harrowed hell like the messiah into the glory of privileged fatherly affection, Falstaff pre-empts him: '*Sir John rises up*' (5.4.109). Falstaff's resuscitation is a perfectly timed parody and postpones Hal's rebirth because it destabilizes the imagery that he has so carefully created. Throughout the play Falstaff's actions and speeches comment through comparison, and Hal's redemptive scheme cannot withstand the ironic force of Falstaff's rising from a feigned death, and unchivalric wounding of Hotspur in the (euphemistic) thigh. Falstaff jumps up and Hal's Christ-like stance collapses under the pressure. This is perhaps why he allows Falstaff's claim that he has killed Percy himself. The design has gone awry and before Hal can become the victorious king of *Henry V* he must wait through another play. In the second part of *Henry IV* there is once again Lenten imagery, the early comic subplot parody of the Incarnation, and the climactic battle, but this time Hal will not allow Falstaff to steal his thunder.

In *Henry IV Part 1* the allusion to the harrowing of hell might seem of a piece with the rhetoric of Tudor monarchist propaganda by placing the royal prince in the position of Christ. However the play shows that the divine analogy is an artifice created by Hal for his own ends, and something which he cannot completely fulfil. The nuance which the allusions to the Passion narrative gives to these plays has been overlooked in the critical controversy surrounding Hal, and where biblical echoes have been noticed they have often been enlisted in a simplistic way as implying support for him as a holy ruler. Critics have long been aware that despite the glittering surface of *Henry V* and the jingoistic portrayal of Henry as a triumphant king, there might be a disjunction between the apparent sympathies of the play and what it actually endorses. Henry V uses rousing rhetoric and wins Agincourt, but undercurrents in the play detract from the king's portrayal of himself as a perfect leader. Throughout the last three plays of the tetralogy Henry constructs a redemptive curve by which he intends that the wrong done by his father can be expiated, and England, the Lancastrians and the crown become numinous once more. *Henry V* is not only the glorious zenith of Hal's redeeming mission, but also the play in which Henry's characterization is darkest. The failure of Hal's attempt to save England from the civil war which threatens it is made clear by the already written, already staged, horror of the Wars of the Roses, recalled in the epilogue of *Henry V*. The religious imagery of *Henry IV Part 1*, the first play with Henry as its hero, likewise appears to give Hal quasi-divine status, but the allusions are skewed and do not act as simple endorsements. Hal is an extremely successful king, but the illusion of divinity is part of his masterful manipulation of appearance, not the result of his Christian kingship.

MR HAMLET OF BROADWAY

FRANCES TEAGUE

In 1908, rumours began to circulate in New York's theatrical circles that the variety stage comedian Eddie Foy planned to change his name to Mr Edwin Fitzgerald, because he felt he required a more distinguished moniker before venturing into the legit by undertaking the role of Hamlet. When asked about the rumour, Foy would answer:

> I have long known that I have the artistic temperament for those roles. I am really a Shakespearian actor, but the managers have kidded me out of it. I shall start with Hamlet, and after that play Touchstone, Lear, and other roles. Of course no artist can be sure of success in Shakespearian drama, but if, as I expect, I do succeed, none will ever hear of me in a comedy as Eddie Foy again.[1]

Despite the remark that 'no artist can be sure of success in Shakespearian drama', Eddie Foy could be sure of success on the variety stage, where he had long enjoyed starring roles across the country as a comedian in musical shows and vaudeville. Whether playing a comic chef (*Hotel Topsey Turvey*), jailer (*The Strollers*), or sandman (*Piff Paff Pouf*), a travelling hypnotist (Paracelsus Noodle in *The Wild Rose*), a dog-trainer and would-be earl (Jim Cheese in *The Earl and the Girl*), a head gardener (Artie Choke in *The Orchid*), or Sister Anne in *Mr Bluebeard, Jr*, Eddie Foy was a godsend to management because his shows made money. And Foy required money since he and his third wife (his first two wives had died) were raising a large family: eight children in all. (Later Foy and his family formed a famously successful vaudeville act, called the Seven Little Foys.) When Eddie Foy played on a vaudeville bill, he was a well-paid headliner. Why, then, would Foy leave the variety stage for the legitimate stage to try his hand at a role so risky and unremunerative as Shakespeare's Hamlet?

He wouldn't. He couldn't. He didn't. In fact, the rumours were planted during the publicity campaign for his next show, *Mr Hamlet of Broadway*. In this musical comedy, Foy played Joey Wheeze, a circus clown who winds up at Starvation Inn in Lake Putrid, where he is hired at the last minute to play Hamlet in the place of a non-appearing tragedian. Produced by the Shubert organization and staged by Ned Wayburn, *Mr Hamlet of Broadway* began touring in September 1908, opened at New York's Casino Theatre on 23 December 1908 and ran for fifty-four performances during that season. The show then toured from February to April 1909, again toured in a revised form from August 1909 to April 1910, ending with a week in Brooklyn's Majestic Theater.[2] The book was by Edgar Smith, with lyrics by Edward Madden and music by Ben M. Jerome. Musical numbers included 'The Dusky Salome', 'Under the Honeymoon', 'The Hornpipe Rag', 'When I Was a Kid like You', 'Good-bye Mollie Brown', 'Waltz Me Away with You Dearie', 'A Poor Little Girl like Me', 'Mr Hamlet of Broadway', 'Nimble Symbaline', 'When We Made the Gallant Charge at Bunker Hill', and 'The Man Who Built the Summer Hotel'. (Two of

[1] Information about Foy's life comes from two sources: Eddie Foy and Alvin F. Harlow, *Clowning through Life* (New York, 1929), and Armond Fields, *Eddie Foy: A Biography* (Jefferson, N. C., 1999). The quotation is from Foy and Harlow, p. 298.

[2] Fields, *Eddie Foy*, pp. 242–3.

these songs have been recorded.) Throughout the tour of the production, songs were altered, dropped or added. Thus the song 'Hamlet's Ghost', which was in the show in 1908, had disappeared by 1909. When the show was revived for the 1909 season, it had additional songs, including 'Beautiful Rose', with lyrics by George Whiting and Carter De Haven and music by Ted Snyder; other added songs were Madden and Jerome's 'Everything Depends on Money' and 'Down Where the Watermelon Grows'.[3]

At first the use of Shakespeare in this musical comedy seems incidental, simply offering Eddie Foy a chance to fool around in his characteristic style. To be sure, the names Hamlet and Cymbeline provide song hooks for 'Mr Hamlet of Broadway' and 'Nimble Symbaline', but little more. Numbers like 'Dusky Salome' or 'When We Made the Gallant Charge at Bunker Hill' are substantially less Shakespearian. From Foy's autobiography, however, as well as Armond Fields's recent biography, one learns that the show integrated Shakespeare, that centrepiece of the legit stage, into what would be the most successful musical in which Foy ever starred.[4] Although *Mr Hamlet of Broadway* uses a Shakespearian burlesque, its unconventional tone makes it arguably the first Shakespearian musical comedy.

Such an argument rests on understanding the distinction between Shakespearian burlesque and musical comedy. Shakespearian burlesques generally take for their subject one of the histories or tragedies. Such a choice heightens the contrast between the original serious work and the burlesque itself that mocks that original, often by incorporating topical satire. Shakespeare burlesques were common in English and American variety performances (including vaudeville, minstrel shows, music halls, and so forth).[5] A musical comedy has a book that is, generally, just as important as the musical numbers, which are often slight (unlike opera, in which the musical score is far more important than the libretto). A musical may use incongruity, as a burlesque does, but it does not as a rule mock its source text. Thus burlesques of Shakespeare have tended to make fun of his tragedies or histories (or, as Schoch suggests, to make fun of performances of such plays), but musical comedies can consider less serious genres (as *Boys from Syracuse* does *Comedy of Errors*) or treat the source text with some respect (as *West Side Story* treats *Romeo and Juliet*).[6] Every discussion of

[3] Thanks to the Shubert Archive, particularly Mark Schwarz, for allowing me to examine scripts, programmes, and other documents relating to the production and its tours. I have also used Fields's detailed discussion and Foy's comments in Foy and Harlow, *Clowning through Life*.

The two recorded songs, are 'Goodbye, Mollie Brown', and 'Dusky Salome', *Music from the New York Stage*, volume 2: 1908–1913 (Sussex, England, 1993). This record is quite hard to locate, and I am grateful to music historians at Indiana University, Thomas Mathiesen, Jeff Magee, and Peter Schimpf, who sent me information about the recording. Information about 'Beautiful Rose' is from The Tunesmiths Database, http://nfo.net/.CAL/ts6.html, consulted on 17 January 2001. The other added songs are named in Fields, *Eddie Foy*, p. 179.

[4] Shakespeare's central position in the legitimate theatre is underscored by the *OED*'s definition of 'the legitimate drama: the body of plays, Shakespearian or other, that have a recognized theatrical and literary merit . . . Also in other collocations. So as sb., an actor of legitimate drama.' The first instance the *OED* offers is from the late eighteenth century.

[5] I am using 'variety' as an inclusive theatrical form, not as the predecessor of vaudeville. Again, the *OED* is helpful: its definition of variety is 'Used to designate music-hall or theatrical entertainments of a mixed character (songs, dances, impersonations, etc.). Also applied to things or persons connected with such entertainments'. I should note, however, that some writers use variety to mean an older and cruder form of entertainment than vaudeville. For American performance history, Lawrence Levine's generative essay, 'High Brow, Low Brow' is useful, as is Ray B. Browne's 'Shakespeare in American Vaudeville and Negro Minstrelsy', *American Quarterly* 12 (1960), 374–91. For the English performance history, see Richard Schoch's book, *Not Shakespeare* (Cambridge, 2002); Stanley Wells has collected examples of both English and American burlesques in six volumes. I have also found *American Vaudeville as Seen by its Contemporaries*, ed. Charles W. Stein (New York, 1984), a collection of first-person recollections, an invaluable resource for understanding early twentieth-century variety performers.

[6] I have argued elsewhere that burlesque, like parody, travesty, or pastiche, is a comedy of imitation; all 'assume a canon of literature exists, that it can be mocked by irreverent imitation, and that its readers will recognize and welcome such mockery. A burlesque may implicitly criticize its target, but it also

Shakespearian musicals has claimed *The Boys from Syracuse* (1938) as the first one: to claim *Mr Hamlet of Broadway* would push that date back thirty years. I think that it is a show structured much like *Kiss Me, Kate* (1947) in that it uses a Shakespearian burlesque within a frame plot that echoes the inset Shakespearian material. Even if one refuses to see the show as a Shakespearian musical comedy, however, its affectionate treatment of *Hamlet* inside a book that does not simply mock Shakespeare makes it an interesting example of how Shakespeare's presence was received on the popular stage at the beginning of the twentieth century.

Mr Hamlet of Broadway opens at Starvation Inn on Putrid Lake, a sad resort hotel that is going broke, to the chagrin of the inn's landlord Jonathan Cheatam. Indeed, the residents at the hotel are so disgusted that they are ready to leave, but they settle down after Cheatam promises them anything they ask for. In particular, Cheatam promises a guest, Mrs Barnaby Bustle, that a well-known New York tragedian will come and play Hamlet to her Gertrude. The peaceful moment allows the Bustles' daughter, Cymbeline (or Symbaline), to enjoy her courtship by Tom Manleigh, who belongs to the local militia company known as the Utica Reds. After word arrives that the great tragedian cannot come, Jonathan Cheatam thinks quickly and engages Joey Wheeze (Eddie Foy), a clown with a trick bear whose circus is stranded nearby, to fill in as Hamlet. Barnaby Bustle, reluctant to play Claudius, tries to bribe Wheeze to back out of the show, but negotiations fail when Mrs Bustle bribes the actor to stay. Wheeze remains loyal to the role of Danish prince as the first act ends.

In Act 2, the action shifts to Mount Kalish, where the production of *Hamlet* is being guarded by the Utica Reds. In the course of rehearsing and performing *Hamlet*, Foy found many gags. The show became a series of sketches that featured his comic abilities to entertain the audience: he drilled the militia company, performed a novelty song about nursery rhymes, fought a mock duel, and presented a burlesque version of *Hamlet*, which included this soliloquy's musings on the life of a small-time actor:

To flee, or not to flee, that is the question
Whether 'tis nobler in the sun to suffer
The slings and arrows of outrageous scorching
Or to fling his claims against a sea of critics
And, I suppose, offend them;
To fly, to sneak, to 'blow' and by that sneak
To say, I end the headshakes and the thousand
Natural wrongs the profesh is heir to.
To fly, to sneak, and when that sneak I make –
What meals may come? For where's the grub?
Oh, who could bear the trips to one-night stands,
The press' wrongs, the crowds' damned contumely,
The trains delay, the prongs of despised hotels,
The insolvency of managers, and the spurn of waiting
    sheriff
When your trunk he takes with a bare suitcase;
This makes me rather play the part I have than fly
To authors that I know not of.
What! Ho! Some music!

Using the form of Hamlet's metaphysical contemplation on being, the burlesque substitutes observations about the difficulties that a variety actor faces: critical sneers, constant travelling and financial chicanery. To be a Shakespearian actor is to hold a distinguished place in the legit theatre, worthy of critical praise, but to be Joey Wheeze, taking the place of that distinguished actor as Hamlet, means facing contempt, a sea of sneering critics. He considers escape, not via a bare bodkin, but by sneaking off, 'blowing' the engagement, to escape the acting 'profesh's' innate difficulties. The slang he uses here continues with 'grub' and 'prongs', the insider's language for the bad food and inconveniences of life on the road as an actor. As Schoch points out, 'In looking . . . at the burlesque's relentless use of slang, we are looking not at a gratuitous recitation of vulgarities, but rather at the public performance of a sociocultural identity through a particular mode of speech'.[7] While what he says is true, it is equally true that American variety performers, who were often highly sensitive about professional gradations of status, struggled with slang in the theatre. (I am

thereby reasserts, implicitly, the target's importance', in Alex Preminger and T. V. F. Brogan, *The New Princeton Encyclopedia of Poetry and Poetics* (Princeton, 1993), s.v. burlesque, 152.

[7] Schoch, *Not Shakespeare*, p. 130.

here treating burlesque and vaudeville as forms that have similar approaches to social propriety; Foy's training was certainly in vaudeville, although his success in this soliloquy is in a burlesque.) The legit actor and playwright, Edwin Royle, recalled a season he had spent in vaudeville, particularly the prohibition on vulgar slang as defined by the management, viz., 'Such words as Liar, Slob, Son-of-a-Gun, Devil, Sucker, Damn, and all other words unfit for the ears of ladies and children'.[8] Royle reports that he was caught violating that prohibition, and he was not alone. Despite the desire of managers and some performers to escape being labelled vulgar, others knew perfectly well that they were vulgar and that they could use that vulgarity to good effect in getting laughs. In the instance of Foy's burlesque soliloquy, the use of such colloquial terms as 'grub' and 'profesh' or the mild profanity 'damned' elicits laughter because the diction is at odds with the grandeur of the source text, the 'to be or not to be' soliloquy. The language also serves to establish Foy's character as a small-time actor who would ordinarily be kept well away from any Shakespearian role.

This humour is unsophisticated, in keeping with the rest of the play. Indeed, it is superior wit compared to some gags. For instance, Joey Wheeze is sad because he has lost his trained bear Amelia, but announces,

> I'm a clown, an actor, a bear trainer, and a tin soldier, all in twenty four hours. I think I had better study up this part if I am going to play it. (Reading) Who can bear . . . There's a bear in this. Who can foredells bear when he himself can this quie[t]us make with a bear . . . Holy Smoke, there's a lot of bears in this . . . if Amelia hadn't escaped last night she could have had a swell part in Hamlet.[9]

And Fields points to other such jokes: 'At the end of his soliloquy, the King remarked, "Our Ham is cured", while Ophelia, with garlands of carrots and turnips in her hair, made it difficult for Hamlet to "plant" her after she died.'[10] The burlesque production of *Hamlet* succeeds, however, and saves the inn, which means the lovers can marry and all live happily ever after.

While a burlesque of *Hamlet* is hardly unusual, Foy's treatment of Shakespeare in *Mr Hamlet of Broadway* was rather reverential. For instance, the publicity stunt about changing his name was a fair representation of Foy's actual interests: he says in his autobiography that he would have enjoyed playing a straight Shakespearian role. That desire stems from his early days in Chicago, when he had served as a supernumerary for Shakespeare productions. He reports that as a beginning performer, 'I appeared as citizen, ruffian, soldier, peasant, or brigand in *Julius Caesar, Coriolanus*, *Macbeth*,' and in Edwin Booth's 1876 Chicago appearances as Hamlet.[11] Later in vaudeville, Foy would imitate Booth's Macbeth as part of a comedy act in vaudeville: 'he'd [i.e. Foy] swing a sword menacingly over his head, only to crack himself in the skull, the sword flying offstage. Staggering onto the boards, sword embedded in his body, would be an impaled, astonished "stagehand".'[12] Foy also told, with considerable relish, of a production of *Julius Caesar* in which he was persuaded to take part after he had enjoyed some success, but before he became a vaudeville headliner. Unfortunately during the assassination of Caesar, one of the actors looked at Foy and got the giggles, and the infectious laughter spread uncontrollably, ruining the performance. There was enough affection in Foy's feelings toward Shakespeare that he could claim, 'I knew Hamlet's lines backwards and forwards, and had . . . often been heard off the stage reciting not only that but other Shakespearian parts by the yard'.[13]

Foy had a lifelong fondness for Shakespeare and a fair knowledge of the canon. Moreover in the first

[8] Edwin Milton Royle, 'The Vaudeville Theatre', in Stein, *American Vaudeville*, p. 24.
[9] Script from the Shubert Archive, Act 2, page 5.
[10] Fields, *Eddie Foy*, pp. 176–7.
[11] Foy and Harlow, *Clowning through Life*, p. 71 and ch. 8 *passim*; Fields, *Eddie Foy*, pp. 21–2.
[12] Fields, *Eddie Foy*, pp. 45.
[13] Foy and Harlow, *Clowning through Life*, p. 298.

decade of the twentieth century, Foy might well have considered a move away from clowning. In December 1903, he had starred in *Mr Bluebeard, Jr* at Chicago's Iroquois Theater. A defective light set the playhouse on fire, and 'Of the 1,900 people in the audience, mostly women and children, at least 600 perished.'[14] Foy was backstage with one of his young children as the alarm was given. When Foy realized what was happening, he handed his child to a stagehand and went out on the stage despite his own danger to plead with the audience not to panic, but to exit carefully. Nevertheless, afterwards 'trampled bodies were piled ten high in the stairwell area where exits from the balcony met the exit from the main floor'. Horrified by the event, Foy left Chicago, performing in vaudeville for a while before moving to New York and signing with the Shuberts to do musical comedies. One unexpected result of the Iroquois Theater fire, as Fields suggests, is that Eddie Foy's gallantry had made him a public hero: had he chosen a different path as a performer, he might well have enjoyed success (155–6). Instead he chose to continue with comedy.

He did claim to feel some regret when he played *Mr Hamlet of Broadway*:

> In the [Hamlet] burlesque . . . I dressed and made up the part with scrupulous care as to tradition. I used all the grace of voice and gesture that I could command, but the words I spoke were ridiculous parodies of the original lines. At the very last minute I longed – oh, how wistfully! – to play just one scene in the original words, as I had longed to do it thirty years before.[15]

Foy then reports, with great satisfaction, that the critics praised his Hamlet and he quotes a Philadelphia critic, 'For once we see the comedian becomingly garbed, and it was to be noted that he has an admirable stage presence, that his reading is good when he wanted it to be so, and that he has a grace of movement and an authority which are quite compelling' (p. 303). Indeed, the production's poster (also used as the cover for the sheet music) uses a caricature of Foy in the costume that he thought closely resembled Booth's presentation of Hamlet (see illustration 11). To my eye there is little resemblance to portraits of Booth, but that is hardly the point. What matters is not the uncanny resemblance (which there's not), but that Foy dreamed of himself as being like Booth, although his wonderfully comic appearance led him away from the legit stage. His anecdote about how laughter at his looks spoiled the production of *Julius Caesar* suggests that he was well aware that he would not be taken seriously as a Shakespearian and that he made the best of his features. Usually burlesques from this period are pointed, even hostile toward the legit theatre's production of Shakespeare; Foy made more fun of himself than anyone else.

Were Foy's regrets simply the conceit of a nostalgic comedian convinced he is able to do serious work, a sort of Pagliacci Syndrome or a King of Comedy Crisis? More may be going on in this case than the daydreaming of a clown. As the 'To flee or not to flee' soliloquy suggests, burlesque was very much part of the larger plot line, which one might see as an extended consideration of where a performer (whether Joey Wheeze or Eddie Foy) registered in the cultural range that stretched from the legit stage's productions of Shakespeare's tragedy and the variety stage's burlesques of such drama.

Initially American theatrical practice was to mix material from either end of that range. Lawrence Levine remarks, 'the play may have been the thing, but it was not the only thing. It was the centerpiece, the main attraction, but an entire evening generally consisted of a long play, an afterpiece (usually a farce), and a variety of between-act specialties', in a clear anticipation of a vaudeville bill. By the mid-nineteenth century, however, a play and a farce afterpiece formed the bill in the legit theatre, while the comic sketches, singing and dancing, and animal acts that had once accompanied the plays

[14] My information on the fire is from Foy's autobiography, checked with Marshall Everett, *The Great Chicago Theater Disaster* (Chicago, 1904), as well as the splendid Chicago Public Library website on the Iroquois Theatrical Fire: http://cpl.lib.uic.edu/004chicago/disasters/iroquois fire. html, consulted 25 September, 2002.

[15] Foy and Harlow, *Clowning through Life*, p. 302.

"'TIS A PRETTY THING"
SAM S. and LEE SHUBERT INC. OFFER :-
EDDIE FOY
IN
MR. HAMLET
OF
BROADWAY.
PRODUCED BY NED WAYBURN.
BOOK BY . . . EDGAR SMITH.
LYRICS BY
EDWARD MADDEN.
MUSIC BY
BEN M. JEROME
Musical Numbers
1 The Dusky Salome . . . . . 60c.
2 Under The Honeymoon . . . . 60c.
3 The Hornpipe Rag . . . . . 60c.
4 When I Was a Kid Like You . . . 60c.
5 Good-bye Molly Brown . . . . 60c.
6 Waltz Me Away With You Dearie . 60c.
7 A Poor Little Girl Like Me . . . 60c.
8 Mr. Hamlet of Broadway . . . . 60c.
10 When We Made the Gallant Charge of Bunker Hill . . . . . . 60c.
11 The Man Who Built The Summer Hotel 60c.
12 Selection $1.00
ALL THEATRICAL & PUBLISHING RIGHTS FOR ALL COUNTRIES STRICTLY RESERVED.
ELBEL BROS. MUSIC DEALERS SOUTH BEND, IND.
The TREBUHS PUBLISHING Co., INC.
NEW YORK CITY

11 Caricature of Eddie Foy in *Mr Hamlet of Broadway*, in a costume modelled on that of Edwin Booth.

were performed in variety theater (a label that covers minstrel shows, vaudeville, and burlesque, the forms that contributed so much to the development of the Broadway musical).[16] Douglas Gilbert notes the opposition between variety and the legit:

> Variety was a curious hit-or-miss activity, a theatrical shot in the dark. It was of the stage, yet distinct from the legitimate theater whose 'Harolds and Arthurs' regarded variety performers as low persons of no moment.[17]

Gilbert overstates the situation somewhat, especially in 1908 when *Mr Hamlet of Broadway* was performed. There was traffic between legit and variety stages, although no one would deny that the legit performer had a higher social rank than the variety performer. Dramatic critic Norman Hapgood told this story to illustrate the distinction in 1901:

> A famous American actress, now one of our most popular stars, was, a few years ago, in decided need of money. A vaudeville manager offered her eight thousand dollars to play eight weeks in his houses. She refused.[18]

Hapgood goes on, however, to say that 'the lines between the legitimate and vaudeville have been shattered of late', although he insists that movement between the two is almost exclusively legit actors stepping down to vaudeville:

> Of course, the great majority of vaudeville players have no opportunity to decide which stage they will appear on. They usually lack talent sufficient for success in the drama.[19]

A contemporary, Acton Davies, contributed an essay to the first issue of *Variety* (1905) declaring that between the legit and vaudeville, 'there is a wide gulf fixed – one of those gulfs which no suspension can ever span. The actor in nearly every instance regards his dip into vaudeville as a vast condescension on his part', and regards vaudevillians as 'belonging to an essentially lower orbit, a being of a distinctly cruder grade'.[20] That oppositional nature of legit and variety is important to the way that Shakespeare is treated in Foy's musical comedy because the traditional hostility shown by variety burlesques of Shakespeare here gives way to an implicit claim that even the variety performer – who must 'fly, sneak, and "blow" ' in his performance – can reasonably play in the Shakespearian dramas that Harolds and Arthurs customarily guarded. A variety comic may even be a weak performer, and 'fling his claims against a sea of critics' knowing he'll offend them, but nevertheless he decides to go on as Hamlet, however inadequately, and by so doing achieves a happy ending for the musical comedy. The idea that *Hamlet*, a mighty mainstay of the legit, has the power to enable lovers to marry, a resort to succeed, and a career to be launched is not the usual sort of message that one might expect from the American variety stage.

Another important feature is that two topics occurring regularly in variety are central to musical comedies, even Shakespearian ones: sex and ethnicity. As Gilbert notes, before 1880 'in beer halls and for-men-only dives, roughhouse turns and afterpieces were smuttily "blued" to amuse the tosspots, strumpets, dark-alley lads, and slummers who in those days made up variety audiences', while Levine, Browne and Gilbert all comment how variety performers depended on ethnic and racist jokes for laughs. Royle's comments on the prohibition against slang suggest the anxiety many vaudeville managements felt about the wide perception of their shows as vulgar. Despite impresario B. F. Keith's insistence on such rigid social rules in the vaudeville circuit that he ran, most managements were less fussy.[21] Those jokes – whether dirty or ethnic – survive in American musical comedy.

In *Mr Hamlet of Broadway* we can see both elements of bawdiness and ethnicity. The song

---

16 William Gould remarked in 1907, 'seven-eighths of the musical comedy stars received their theatrical education and training in vaudeville', in Stein, *American Vaudeville*, p. 78.

17 Douglas Gilbert, *American Vaudeville: Its Life and Times* (New York, 1963, reprint of 1940 edition), p. 24.

18 Norman Hapgood, 'The Life of a Vaudeville Artiste', in Stein, *American Vaudeville*, p. 34.

19 Hapgood in Stein, *American Vaudeville*, p. 39.

20 Acton Davies, 'What I Don't Know about Vaudeville', in Stein, *American Vaudeville*, p. 84.

21 See, for example, the anonymous lament about the passing away of Keith's standards and the risqué nature of vaudeville shows in Stein, *American Vaudeville*, pp. 60–7.

'Goodbye, Mollie Brown' is a comic song that mocks people who are French and English, for example,[22] while Maude Raymond claiming to be the 'Dusky Salome' brags about her 'Oriental style' and announces in the song's chorus that, 'I want a coon who can spoon to the tune of Salomy, / I'll make him giggle with a brand new wiggle' (Act 2, 9). Neither song refers to Shakespeare.[23] Even a Shakespearian reference could be made into an ethnic joke, however. When Ophelia does her mad scene, she sings

> Tomorrow is St Patrick's Day
> And in the morning time
> I'll wear my old plug hat and sash
> And be my valentine,

transforming herself into a stereotypical Irish joke. The authors seem to have felt the need for a ghost story that Foy could perform. In some versions of the script, there is a ghost song by Jerome and Madden called 'De Ebony Spook', in which we learn of a 'Niggar spook' [sic] and how he frightened a preacher so much that 'Black Parson Green turned white'. Another ghost song sometimes used in the second act, 'Hamlet's Ghost', includes clear references to the play:

> He's a most important factor to the young ambitious actor
> He will say the part of Hamlet fits you most
> And he said to one comedian, 'Why you're a born tragedian'
> 'I ought to know for I am Hamlet's ghost.'

The ghost explains that

> As I flit about first-nighting I have heard you oft reciting
> Those immortal lines 'tis such a pretty thing.
> Shakespeare said I'd recognize you, you're the man he put me wise to
> He had you in mind when he wrote Hamlet's part.

But although the ghost pretends to welcome the actor who (like Foy himself) recites Hamlet's lines so often, he is playing a trick. Despite his encouragement for the actor, the ghost shows a malicious streak in the song's chorus:

> When Hamlet says, 'To be or not to be'
> The ghost cries out in fiendish glee
> 'I'm hid behind the scenery
> Where the eggs cannot reach me.'

The actor who dares attempt Hamlet is greeted with derision and eggs. This song illustrates the dangers inherent in a variety performer attempting the legit role. Others include explicit intrusions of ethnicity and sexuality that may highlight the way that legitimate theatres suppressed the topics, sometimes by erasing them, sometimes by rendering them implicitly. It seems valuable to remember that only two seasons before, Shaw's *Caesar and Cleopatra* had had its premiere in New York, where it was more successful than it would be in the West End of London. While the highly respectable E. H. Sothern and Julia Marlowe or Robert Mantell struggled to make their Shakespeare productions pay in New York, Foy's comedy was highly successful.[24] Moreover in the years to come, Shakespearian musicals would be daringly risqué, to judge from the reviews for *The Boys from Syracuse*, *Kiss Me, Kate*, *Your Own Thing*, or John Guare's *Two Gents* suggest, or would engage with ethnicity as in *Swingin' the Dream*, *West Side Story*, *Two Gents*, or *Play On!*. *Mr Hamlet of Broadway* is an early instance of what occurs when the musical comedy looks toward the legitimate stage; like earlier burlesques, the Shakespearian musical will insist that Shakespeare's work must include sexuality and racial identity.

Because book musicals grew out of variety theatre, operating in opposition to the legit from mid-nineteenth century on, the place of Shakespearian musicals is tricky from the outset, for in a

[22] Shubert Archive script, Act 1, 25–6.

[23] Doug Lanier has pointed out to me another variety stage song, 'When Mister Shakespeare Comes to Town, or, I Don't Like Them Minstrel Folks', which can be found at the Library of Congress website: http://memory.loc.gov/ammem/award97/rpbhtml/aasmTitles10.html as of 16 February 2001. Self-described as a coon song, it praises Shakespeare, but is principally about minstrel shows.

[24] Gerald Bordman, *American Theatre*, vol. 1, 1869–1914 (Oxford, 1994), pp. 594–5, 648–9. Bordman includes only the legit stage, so Foy and his show goes unmentioned.

Shakespearian musical, the creators take over a legit text, then use that play to overtake legit's 'Harolds and Arthurs' as performers. What starts out in vaudeville as performers mocking another theatrical style to celebrate their own theatrical form becomes direct competition when book musicals use Shakespeare. In the musical, a show invokes Shakespeare, yet dismisses most aspects of the legit, including the text; moreover, a musical's descent from variety theatre means it usually employs sex and race, partly to sell the show, partly because those topics are more interesting than conventional Shakespearian productions. The Eddie Foy show *Mr Hamlet of Broadway* fits this pattern, although it is far from the sort of book musical that we recognize today. The credit for the first Shakespearian musical has always gone to *The Boys from Syracuse* (1938), and perhaps knowing what is the 'first' is unlikely to alter theatre history in any significant way. Yet Shakespearian musicals offer an index to the way that variety theatre regards its rival, the legit stage. If that be the case, then the cheerful way in which *Boys from Syracuse* acknowledges Shakespeare only to dismiss him suggests impertinent self-confidence. This earlier show, with the leading comedian's wistful longing (the diction is Foy's), shows us a theatrical world that may be less self-confident about the priority of comedy, but that sees no obstacle to claiming Shakespeare as part of its own.

SHAKESPEARE PERFORMANCES IN ENGLAND, 2003

MICHAEL DOBSON

If Shakespeare were still alive to collect performance fees, 2003 would have been a lucrative year for the Bard, with some thirty revivals of his plays staged by major professional companies in England alone: unless, that is, a large part of the plays' continuing appeal to the cash-strapped theatres of this country lies in the fact that they are safely out of copyright. Had Shakespeare been a current paid-up member of the Authors' Licensing and Collecting Society in 2003, for example, it is quite possible that the Royal Shakespeare Company would have avoided his work altogether. With budgetary shortfalls for once restraining the exuberance even of their designers (except Colin Peters, of whose adventures with *As You Like It* more later), and with the company's management still in the uncertain interregnum between Adrian Noble's Project Fleet (see *Survey* 55 and 56), and the full assumption of the Artistic Directorship by his successor Michael Boyd, the RSC announced only towards the end of 2003 that it would be performing new plays again (for the first time since 2001) late in the 2004 season. Despite reports in the summer that negotiations towards the establishment of a new London home for the company were on the verge of a successful outcome, and despite the news that the company's forthcoming Swan productions of *All's Well That Ends Well* and *Othello* would each transfer briefly to the Gielgud in spring 2004, only two RSC shows from its summer 2003 repertory, Gregory Doran's interlinked revivals of *The Taming of the Shrew* and Fletcher's *The Woman's Prize; or, The Tamer Tamed* will be transferring to London (for a short run at the Queen's in early spring 2004). The bulk of the company's 2003 repertoire closed at the end of its late autumn run in Newcastle, never reaching metropolitan audiences at all. In short, instead of having five theatres, including two studios – the Barbican Theatre and the Pit in London, in addition to the Royal Shakespeare Theatre, the Swan and the Other Place in Stratford – as it did at the beginning of the twenty-first century, the RSC currently has only two theatres of its own, the RST and the Swan, both of them in Stratford and neither of them studios, and in 2003 it was looking like a very provincial company indeed.

Whatever the economic factors behind managements' decisions to stage Shakespeare's public-domain (albeit large-cast) scripts, and where to do it, the year's profuse harvest of revivals – some of the most interesting of which were imported from other countries – necessitates a particularly ruthless distinction in what follows between those shows that can be recorded in any detail and those that considerations of space must relegate to a few sentences. Considerations of tact, too, for if 2003 saw several productions that were probably as good as anything this journal has ever sought to record – most conspicuously Nicholas Hytner's first production as artistic director of the National, *Henry V*, with Adrian Lester in the title role – then it also saw certain companies achieve new lows, probably best forgotten. The fact that it was authored by John Fletcher, for example, spares me from saying very much about Doran's *The Woman's Prize; or, The Tamer Tamed* at the Swan, though it is not the show itself I am thinking of here but its interval, during which members of the cast, in Elizabethan costume, came and sang merrie English songs among the audience outside. Only one other theatre in Britain, surely, could match this level of dumbing-down for the tourists, and sure enough the Globe did, with Phyllida Lloyd's strenuously jolly all-female *Taming of the Shrew* in August. Lloyd, for example, adorned her rendition of 4.1 by making one member of the cast dress up in a dog suit and take part in an interpolated slapstick sequence, to the screaming delight of most of the audience, in answer to Petruccio's question at line 136, 'Where's my spaniel Troilus?' (If ever there was a Troilus who *deserved* to have his brains dashed out with a Grecian club, this was surely he.) If I structure this article by genre, as always, and move in roughly chronological order through Shakespeare's career within each category, we'll be able to get that particular show out of the way fairly soon and move on towards productions memorable for better things, among them Yukio Ninagawa's *Pericles* at the National, Dominic Cooke's *Cymbeline* at the Swan, Hytner's *Henry V*, the Icelandic company Vesturport's *Romeo and Juliet* at the Young Vic, and Jonathan Kent's Japanese *Hamlet* at Sadler's Wells.

COMEDIES

The Woman's Prize, Fletcher's account of Petruccio's second marriage (after Katharina's death) to the seemingly demure Maria, ran at the Swan in the summer in tandem with *The Taming of the Shrew* in the RST, and in Gregory Doran's hands the two plays were made to match each other even more thoroughly than Fletcher's script suggests: a couple of Fletcher's character names were changed, for example, to allow Hortensio and Gremio to reappear in the sequel, Jasper Britton played Petruccio in both plays, and Alexandra Gilbreath played both Katharine (very well) and her young and hitherto harmless-looking successor Maria (very incongruously). Although Shakespeare's play was still nominally set in Padua and Fletcher's in London, both shows shared the same costumes and general look, which even before the arrival at Petruccio's manor in Act 4 of *Shrew* was predominantly sixteenth-century rustic, as if the Induction (which was in fact cut) had taken over the whole enterprise. In other words, the costumes were stock Elizabethan ones, the incidental music was folksy, and many of the cast, especially Nicolas Tennant as Grumio, wore implausible quantities of pretend mud all over their hands and faces in compliance with the popular and entirely mistaken belief, much-cherished by television costume drama, that nobody outside the aristocracy ever bothered to wash before about 1860. The only factor by which Stephen Brimson Lewis's design distinguished this *Taming of the Shrew* from any other provincial revival of the play over the last century was the great number of wooden doors – something like eighteen of them, no two the same – which stood in their free-standing frames around the bare stage and its wooden gallery upper level, so that the cast, perpetually negotiating with one another around a series of invisible walls, always had something by which to shut one another out or let one another in.

These insistently delineated thresholds turned out to be largely personal rather than social, since this was a *Shrew* played less for any resonance it might have with contemporary concerns about the role of women either within or beyond the family than for whatever laughs might be had with a clear conscience during an upbeat account of how two interestingly eccentric individuals, neither of them happy with the social expectations within which they had to operate at the beginning of the play, achieved a separate peace with one another by the end of it. Gilbreath's Katharine had something of the air of a pirate *manquée*, furiously kicking the doors which kept being closed behind her in her father's house as if experienced in the martial arts, and for the last movement of the play – after her brief excursion into a more conventional and surprisingly unbecoming wedding dress for 3.3 – she reverted to the strangely tatty outfit in which she apparently felt most comfortable, regardless of the dress codes which the occasion imposed on those around her, like an outspoken and uncoventional Cinderella allowed a happy ending without being obliged by her newly reconciled husband to dress up for it. (In keeping with the economic conditions of this season, this outfit mainly consisted of items mixed and matched from stock, including the cardigan Peggy Ashcroft wore in *All's Well That Ends Well* twenty years ago). The main distinguishing feature of this production, though, was its determination to palliate or excuse Petruccio's violence towards this attractively militant frump by portraying him throughout as a man just as troubled about his own masculinity as Katharine ever was about her status as a marital commodity. As if subsuming the lost role of Christopher Sly, Britton's Petruccio arrived in Padua unshaven and with a serious drink problem, and his swaggering boasts about being in quest of a rich wife and fearless of Kate's shrewish reputation served only, as we gathered from his tremulous, distressed, half-embarrassed delivery of 1.2.53–6 ('Antonio, my father, is deceased'), to cover a profound sense of uncertainty over how to take on his late father's authoritative male role in the world. At his house, at the end of 4.1 – having left Kate out in the snow at the rear of the stage throughout his initial tirade against the servants, 106–25, and then well-nigh brained her against his ancestral threshold when carrying her belatedly in – he addressed the bulk of 'Thus have I politicly begun my reign' (4.1.174–97). not to the audience but to the portrait of his father which had dominated the scene, which he took down from the wall and almost cradled. In the picture his father had a falcon on his wrist, and Britton stressed the word 'my' in the first line of the speech, as if to suggest that his adoption of the methods of falconry in order to deal with his new wife was directly imitated from the one set of skills which his father had either valued or passed on.

This was a distinctly strange moment, a glimpse into the troubled mind of a very mixed-up bridegroom indeed, but then given the way in which this production had staged the 'wooing' scene, 2.1, it had a great deal to explain: Petruccio had to suggest here that he had relapsed into some sort of overwhelming personal neurosis since successfully and cheerfully betrothing himself to Kate, because otherwise his humiliation of her on her wedding day and thereafter looked, in this show, entirely unnecessary and unmotivated. Over the course of 2.1, which was as beautifully worked-up, timed and played for comedy as I've ever seen it, the two fell visibly in love as thoroughly as the more sentimental readings of this play could ever have wished them to do by the end of Act 5. The turning-point of the scene (and of the production, though it was a turning which then had to be reversed for much of what followed) came when this unusually earthy Katharine, instead of being affronted by Petruccio's obscene joke at line 216 – 'What, with my tongue in your tail?' – paused in delighted disbelief and then burst out laughing, clearly as game for a forbidden rude laugh as any Sid James. As Petruccio here began to recognize, she had always been at least as playfully rough as the comparatively fragile bravado of his exterior all along, and like him she had a concealed vulnerability too, looking pathetically and touchingly grateful for his surprised and eventually genuine praise, especially at 2.1.267, 'Thy beauty that doth make me like thee well'. From this moment on, all was an elaborate and delightful game, no more coercive or lacking in mutuality than the bout of foot-tickling by which Petruccio reduced a floored Kate to further delighted giggles; a game which was resumed, after its long and puzzling interruption, in the final scene. Thus at the close of her submission speech (its content belied by her distinctly non-Stepford outfit), Kate stated her willingness to place her hand beneath her husband's foot in jubilant defiance of the conventional women around her, not expecting to be taken literally at all; Petruccio then briefly shocked and disconcerted her by indicating, with a contemptuous, imperious point of his finger, that she should indeed do so; but then, after her momentary dismay, she realized that he was only winding her up for fun, and she complied, all smiles, to the understandable horror of the respectable society which Petruccio and Katharine seemed to be looking forward to defying together for the rest of their natural lives. This was a production carried by two very charismatic and expert performers rather than by any very strenuous rereading of the text – in essence, merely a post-Men's Movement variation on the old 'it's not sexist, it's just about two mutually therapeutic individuals finding each other' line – but it was easily

12 *The Taming of the Shrew*, directed by Gregory Doran, RSC, Royal Shakespeare Theatre (2003). The wooing scene: Petruccio (Jasper Britton) experiments with reflexology on Katharine (Alexandra Gilbreath).

the strongest show in the RST this year, even if I for one might have singled out a different Stratford production for a London transfer. It was at very least far more interesting than its pendant production of *The Tamer Tamed*, a much triter piece of work anyway, in which Fletcher's whimsical 'wouldn't it be funny *if* women successfully defied their husbands' plot appeared in performance to take the plight of women far less seriously than does Shakespeare's display of how husbands *can* subdue their wives; the press department's attempts to sell Fletcher's play as feminist *avant la lettre* looked either dim or disingenuous as a result.

London audiences desperate to see *The Taming of the Shrew* at all costs and unwilling to wait until 2004 to see Gilbreath and Britton's vigorous if ultimately rather cosy double act had to content themselves, if they could, with Phyllida Lloyd's all-female production at the Globe (a show she took over at short notice after Barry Kyle, finding the position of male director untenable, resigned a fortnight into rehearsal with the words 'Thus have I politicly ended my reign'; politicly indeed, as he was well off out of it). I've already given this show more space than it really deserves, but I should probably just record the fact that the spectacle of women inanely aping, rather than even parodying, the conventional brainless machismo of an old-style Burton/Taylor *Shrew* turns out to be remarkably depressing. As Petruccio, Janet McTeer, having mimed relieving herself all over one of the Globe's pillars soon after her first entrance in 1.2 (and if that had been the cheapest laugh of the evening, we'd have been spared a great deal), spent much of the wooing scene throwing Kathryn Hunter's ugly rag-doll stooge of a Kate all over the stage, and

13 *Love's Labour's Lost*, directed by Trevor Nunn, National Theatre Company, Olivier auditorium (2003). Longueville (Tam Mutu), Navarre (Simon Day), Boyet (Philip Voss) before the French princess (Olivia Williams) and her entourage.

the fact that both performers were women, instead of ironizing or mitigating the play's potential for a pretty brutal and misogynistic sort of baiting farce, apparently just licensed the audience to laugh as gleefully and uncritically at the assaults and battery that continued to follow as they might have done at a Punch and Judy show. In fact you would never have guessed from either of these two productions of *The Taming of the Shrew* that forced marriages and domestic violence were dominating British newspaper headlines in 2003 to anything like the extent that they were: it may be that a director will have to do something as unsubtle as setting this play among the present-day Asian community before audiences will allow themselves to remember that its central subject matter is still sufficiently serious to be worth making jokes about at all.

The other early comedies had a quieter year. Rachel Kavanaugh directed *The Two Gentlemen of Verona* at the Open Air Theatre in Regent's Park in the summer, in a bland, Merchant-Ivoryesque production in pretty Regency clothes (not unlike her *Love's Labour's Lost* the previous season), throughout which the principals seemed slightly too old and dignified for the behaviour the play depicts. The only member of the company funny enough to upstage the director's own dog Josie's performance as Crab was John Hodgkinson as Speed, and any production of this play in which Speed is the best thing going is surely missing something. Trevor Nunn's last production as artistic director of the National, an expensive-looking *Love's Labour's Lost* in the Olivier in the spring, ought to have been far more impressive, but despite a strong cast – particularly Joseph Fiennes (as Biron), Simon Day (as Navarre), and Philip Voss (as Boyet, giving the first of two impeccable and exquisitely cast performances this year) – the evening foundered on Nunn's fussy unwillingness either to trust the play or even, apparently, to notice much of what it had to say. In conception, the production seemed to be an attempt to go further and less subtly down the road indicated by Ian Judge's *Zuleika Dobson*-influenced revival of the play for the RSC nine years earlier (see *Survey 48*), in which a nostalgic Edwardian setting was given poignancy by the ominous distant rumbling of the guns of Flanders at the very end. Nunn placed his courtly lovers in the same period, but, with the invasion of Iraq impending while his show was rehearsed and staged, he couldn't wait until the end of the evening before bringing the shadow of war into the play. Hence this *Love's Labour's Lost* opened abruptly, and to the audience's great surprise, with a noisy skirmish across the no man's land of First World War France, during which one officer appeared to be fatally wounded; as he lay on the mud, left behind by his comrades beneath the blasted remains of an immense tree, the sounds of combat faded, and a figure in black with a top hat (looking rather like a professional mourner) arrived like an apparition, to deliver the penultimate line of the play as its first: 'The words of Mercury are harsh after the songs of Apollo' (5.2.914–15). This, it turned out, was not Armado (to whom Shakespeare originally gave the line) but Mercadé, the messenger of death, and the dying officer was Biron, and the whole play to follow was to be understood as his last memory, a long and intense flashback to the carefree days of peace. The lighting changed, and by the theatrical miracle of gauzes and filters the blasted tree resumed its foliage and the ground its greenness; the wounded soldier disappeared; taped pre-war birdsong faded up over the sound system, and there were Ferdinand of Navarre, Longueville and Dumaine, about to forswear their cream linen suits in favour of academic robes. Presently they were joined by Biron's younger self, with a little moustache and a pepper-and-salt suit that made him faintly resemble Basil Fawlty, and the play as we have hitherto known it could begin.

This was an effective enough conceit by which to frame the play, if a little heavy-handed, but it was ultimately spoiled by an epilogue which gave the story a far more sentimental closure than Shakespeare himself was willing to provide: at the end of Act 5, after the lords and the ladies had gone their separate ways (with Biron and Rosaline's final dialogue here postponed until after the song of the cuckoo and the owl, and with Mercadé again poaching Armado's line), we abruptly cut back to the battlefield, and the same skirmish that opened the show was replayed – except that this time, instead of Mercadé arriving to indicate Biron's impending death, a party of paramedics arrived to rescue him, and who should that young female volunteer in the Red Cross uniform turn out to be but – Rosaline? (Fade on cinematic tableau of their poignant dumbstruck mutual recognition. Applause. Curtain call.) So instead of leaving its Biron separated, probably forever, from Rosaline, this *Love's Labour's Lost* left him with the prospect of a happy convalescence in her company, jesting in a hospital only from the comfort of his own bed; not so much a sadder and wiser French satirist as an English patient. (The relationship between Armado and Jacquenetta, amazingly, was equally sentimentalized: here Annette McLaughlin's generic country wench, complete with picturesque milk pails, swooningly and genuinely fell for the Spaniard, occasioning a surprising amount of romantic jealousy in the usually pragmatic Costard, and she was thus obliged somehow to deliver the line 'With that face?', 1.2.132, as if it indicated a blossoming infatuation.) All this might have been more touching had Fiennes' Biron shown more sign of earning his unwontedly happy ending by properly learning his lessons against affectation and showing-off and in favour of sincerity and simplicity, but even his speeches of recantation in 5.2 (especially 'Thus pour the stars down plagues for perjury', 395–416) still seemed to be played to amuse and impress his male comrades rather than to convince his mistress. But then this was never a show which valued simplicity, in form any more than in content: the actors were conspicuously and boxily miked-up throughout; the stage was continually busied between and sometimes during scenes with elaborately choreographed, well-pressed non-speaking villagers, looking like volunteers at some themed National Trust Edwardian

Country-House Weekend Event; a whole classroomful of winsome Edwardian schoolchildren, some cutely clutching jam-jars and fishing nets, gathered around Holofernes and Nathaniel in 4.2 so that the audience wouldn't feel obliged to try to understand their dialogue; and any opportunity for musical set-pieces was grabbed with both hands. Mote (here a top-hatted blackamoor minstrel, played by Akiya Henry) got to sing to the musing Armado much more thoroughly than usual in 3.1; the poems recited by the successive covertly lovestruck scholars in 4.3 became light-comedy ragtime musical numbers, miraculously performed under the tree to full orchestral accompaniment; and the song of the cuckoo and the owl – the still and perfect moment to which all the bustle has been leading us, precisely the exemplar of that delicately poised combination of the lyrical and the debunking, spring and winter, towards which the whole play has been moving – was here massacred by an entire chorus of villagers and schoolchildren, in a hideously flippant and over-elaborate setting, complete with comedy bobbings-up-and-down, for which Steven Edis, its composer, deserves to be officially banished from coming within a ten-mile radius of any of Shakespeare's lyrics. The lingering effect was of a production which patronized its audience and Shakespeare's play in about equal measure; but perhaps Nunn was being deliberately generous, departing on an uncharacteristically low note so that he might be an easier act for Nicholas Hytner to follow.

Of 2003's crop of *A Midsummer Night's Dreams*, the closest in spirit to Nunn's *Love's Labour's Lost* was probably Michael Grandage's at the Crucible in Sheffield during the autumn, in that it was drastically over-directed and above all over-designed, although the overall tendency here was to push the play towards the cold and the portentous rather than the twee and the middlebrow. The penchant for imposing visual effects which Grandage and his designer Christopher Oram displayed to such good effect in their *Tempest* in 2002 – where they could be focused, owned and animated by two warm central performances, from Derek Jacobi and Daniel Evans – rather buried this earlier, busier play: Shakespeare's egalitarian distribution of authority among *Dream*'s cast apparently left no member of the company in a position to question or take charge of the succession of mildly sinister, clinical-looking special effects which Grandage and Oram projected onto this show from without. Ray Fearon and Samantha Spiro made a handsome and well-spoken duke and duchess / fairy king and queen, but in common with the rest of the cast – with the possible exception of the spotlessly white-clad lovers, who kept dashing unpredictably forwards at the end of scenes to exit arbitrarily from one side or other of stage front – they were kept so far towards the back of the stage (dominated, in the wood, by the backdrop of an immense stylized science-fiction moon, ringed with what looked like spiky palm fronds) that there was never much risk of their engaging the audience. Even the mechanicals shared this disadvantage, more noticeable for the tastefully co-ordinating shades of khaki, cream and green in which they had been dressed than for anything they were doing (until, that is, Bottom was fitted with a revolting electric-blue ass-head with light-up red eyes), and they too were largely dwarfed by the solemn, sci-fi lighting and chill, clean, reverberating sci-fi sound effects which in practice dominated the evening, often at the expense of the text. (For all her hard work as an affectingly willowy Helena, for example, Nancy Carroll was robbed of what should have been one of her best lines, 'And I have found Demetrius like a jewel, / Mine own and not mine own', 4.1.190–1, when the awakening scene was cut to ribbons.) Michael Pennington's production of the play in Regent's Park was slightly funnier, if rather sporadically so, looking strangely amateur in its apparently random accretion of good and bad pieces of unrelated business. Theseus and Hippolyta were dressed in the style of the Greece of the Colonels, both of them looking bored and rather lugubrious, while Dale Rapley's Oberon seemed to have stepped out of a low-budget heavy metal video, and the mechanicals were an odd mixture of Scots, Irish and Welsh (though a hitherto Irish Quince decided to perform his prologue to 'Pyramus and Thisbe' as an impersonation of Noel Coward: it was probably quite funny in rehearsal, the first time). The one revival of the play to do anything like justice to this play's combination of joyous invention and flawless discipline of structure was Edward Hall's for the Watermill theatre near Reading, using the same all-male company who performed his adaptation of the *Henry VI* plays, *Rose Rage*, a couple of seasons earlier: this show played in the round at its home venue, then toured to theatres of all shapes and sizes around England, in Barbados, in Germany and in Italy, before settling for a deservedly successful run in the West End. This was *A Midsummer Night's Dream* via *Coppélia*, via rumours of Peter Brook's production (which Hall is surely too young to have seen, regardless of his family background), and via 1970s camp: its keynote was struck by the dyed-blonde, shop-soiled waif Simon Scardifield, who trebled the roles of Philostrate, Puck and Starveling in clownish make-up, tutu and stripey stockings, and who opened the proceedings by being the first of the cast to emerge from under white dust-sheets, as if from sleep, to distribute costumes from a magic, mirrored box (into which Bottom was later placed by Titania at the end of the first half, at the close of 3.1). There was nothing very mimetic about any of the female impersonations in this production – as Helena, Robert Hands, with white face and round dots of red for cheeks, looked like Bob Hope impersonating a marionette, and Richard Clothier made a gloriously beefy Titania, able to carry Tony Bell's Bottom in his arms in the manner of Rhett Butler with Scarlett O'Hara – but the play forgave them all, and even if Guy Williams's Oberon gabbled his verse in that self-important, actorish manner best parodied by Peter Cook in 'So That's The Way You Like It' in *Beyond the Fringe*, this was a consistently energetic, inventive account of the play, sweaty, kitsch and magical by turns.

The mature and darker comedies fared less well in 2003. Rachel Kavanaugh directed an RSC production of *The Merry Wives of Windsor* at the Swan at the end of 2002, a show which, together with David Farr's *Coriolanus* (played by the same cast), toured extensively in 2003, finishing up with a summer run at the Old Vic in London. Like much of Kavanaugh's work, this was an efficient, harmless production, consistently and undemandingly entertaining: it will perhaps be best remembered for its setting, in an Ealing Comedy version of the late 1940s, where Page and Ford were bowler-hatted commuters and Mistress Quickly (Alison Fiske) was a high-voiced, sing-song Cockney daily reminiscent of Dot Cotton from *EastEnders.* Pistol and Bardolph, though apparently demobbed, still wore army uniforms, and Fenton, implausibly enough, was a black US airman in a bomber jacket, so that Page's professed objection to him as a son-in-law – 'He is of too high a region' (3.2.67) – was accompanied by a hand-gesture indicating an aeroplane, and an embarrassed look, as though this were merely a cover for a genteelly unexpressed racism. The production was most notable, though, for a disproportionate, virtuoso comic performance by Greg Hicks as Dr Caius – a role allotted to him, presumably, as a sort of pun, since in the other show on this tour he was playing Caius Martius Coriolanus. Hicks played the Frenchman as a twitching, self-important mass of offended dignity in a slightly undersized suit and overtight bow tie, all elbows and nervously adjusted lapels, part Jacques Tati and part Inspector Clouseau. Every other performance on the stage, even Richard Cordery's amiably lazy Falstaff, seemed tiny and flat by comparison, and an unscripted final happy tableau of the two wives linking hands with Anne Page to run off after the rest of the cast just before the curtain call – Anne's acceptance, in effect, as a third merry wife – seemed a mere afterthought after his glorious discomfiture at 5.5.200–3: no one this year worked harder or more fussily for a laugh than Hicks did on 'I ha' married *un garçon*, a boy, *un paysan*, by Gar', or was more deservedly rewarded.

Slight as this production was, it seemed positively deep compared to the year's only *Merchant of Venice*, directed by Gale Edwards as part of the Chichester festival season, a monochrome modern-dress affair which was set nowhere in particular on a stage whose shallow covering of water, partly covered by wooden platforms which unfortunate stagehands had to paddle about rearranging between scenes, suggested a swimming pool showroom rather than the canals of Venice. Edwards' ranks as one of the least intelligent productions of this play I can remember: Desmond Barritt's Shylock, for example, sleepwalking through the play in standard stage-Jew manner like a depressed Topol with a Welsh accent, was obliged actually to perform the outbursts attributed to him in mockery by Solanio and Salerio in 2.8 ('My daughter! O, my ducats! O, my daughter . . .', 15–22) while splashing about the stage in an interpolated display of his discovery of Jessica's flight after 2.6, and both this strangely unenlightened directorial decision and the scimitar-wielding caricature of a performance given by Ricky Fearon as Morocco sat oddly with Edwards's censorship of Portia's prejudice against her only black suitor: 'Let all of his complexion choose me so' (2.7.79) became 'Let all that are so gilded choose me so', an awkward emendation which Niamh Cusack, at the performance I saw, at least had the decency almost to forget. Cusack's usual manner – as if she is struggling to be especially cheerful and bright because not far underneath the surface she is actually furious about something – suited the Portia of the early acts quite well, but then she had to try to look pleased to have been won by Patrick Robinson's inert Bassanio, and given how few among the rest of the cast could even speak their lines intelligibly (as Antonio, Philip Quast couldn't have chosen less appropriate words to stress had he tried) Cusack stood little chance of lifting this show out of the baffled, polite indifference with which the ageing Chichester audience understandably received it.

The year's two revivals of *As You Like It* – one by Gregory Thompson for the RSC at the Swan, and one by Sir Peter Hall for his own company, which opened at the Theatre Royal in Bath and then toured – were both considerably more enjoyable than this, but the remarkable amount which they had in common demonstrated the extent to which this play is currently languishing in something of an interpretative rut. Both dropped fake snow onto an uncomfortable-looking Arden during 2.1, for example, and then changed to dappled-green idyllic spring for the second half of the play; both had the same actor, unhelpfully, doubling both Dukes (so that both characters in effect disappeared, replaced only by the effect of a single performer busily distinguishing them from one another); both had Orlando kiss Ganymede and then look shocked at himself during the mock-wedding in 4.1; both treated the uncomplicatedly time-filling 4.2, 'What shall he have that killed the deer?', as a nonsensically portentous dream-sequence-cum-pagan-ritual; and neither seemed able to take Audrey, Silvius or Phoebe at all seriously, with Hall in particular having all three played as standard dumb comedy rustics. To his credit, Thompson at least made some effort to take the realities of agricultural life into consideration – his production opened, for example, with Orlando and Adam tediously sawing logs in the de Boys family orchard, and his Adam found life sufficiently hard out in the country to die at the end of 2.7 (an event which seemed every bit as gratuitous here as it did when Stephen Pimlott introduced the same strangely unmentioned incident in his own production back in 1996). Indeed Thompson's *As You Like It* was at first an expensive exercise in period setting, supposedly all about rural social disruption after the Napoleonic wars, with the cast wearing frock coats and occupying an elaborate set by Colin Peters which represented early industrial machinery but then miraculously transformed itself into forest trees for the move to Arden. This huge creation, though, quite inappropriate to the Swan, was built only to be scrapped a few weeks into the production (built and scrapped not once, but twice, since the show briefly visited Washington DC in May and the American crew had already built a version of Peters' folly before being told it wouldn't be needed after all), and the centre of this warm-hearted evening became in the event its post-interval emancipation from any such set-and-costume orientation. In the second half, the cast relaxed and played nice rehearsal games, with all of them except David Fielder's incongruous and unimposing Jaques remaining on stage for most of the time to impersonate trees for the love scenes or pretend to be Silvius's sheep or Audrey's goats, and instead of getting the usual Corin merely impersonating Hymen during the last scene, as if pre-rehearsed by Rosalind (as we did from Hall), we were treated to a nice, non-realist goddess (Amy Finegan), singing from the gallery above the stage. In keeping with Thompson's sense of ensemble playing, none of the performances particularly stood out (not even Nina Sosanya's competent if slightly monotonous Rosalind), and in keeping with the slight feeling of a Sunday School picnic which haunted his well-meaning Arden, he originally had his cast interrupt the applause during the curtain call to sing the 23rd Psalm together: but this innovation, though it delighted some, occasioned so many complaints from the unpious that it was eventually dropped.

Hall's production, which also visited the States, though very similar in many respects and of a similar calibre, attracted a great deal more publicity, partly because this was the first time he had ever directed the play, and partly because he had cast his own daughter, the twenty-one-year-old Rebecca Hall, as Rosalind. As I've already suggested, he certainly didn't seem to have chosen to direct *As You Like It* at long last because he had suddenly had a new idea about the play: the main distinguishing ideas visible in this show were a determination to showcase his daughter at all costs and a pedantic insistence that all the cast should pause audibly at the end of every line of verse, regardless of the demands of the syntax, as though Shakespeare had never discovered enjambment. (This rendered Oliver's narrative of his rescue by Orlando, for example, well-nigh incomprehensible, and it's a good thing that so much of this play is written in prose.) In the event, though, Hall senior's direction of the play primarily as a star vehicle for Hall junior did produce some unexpected and intriguing effects, not all of them deliberate: certainly this was the first *As You Like It* I've ever seen in which Rosalind looked much more like a problem than like a solution. Tall, dark, slightly gawky and with an arrestingly low, hard-edged voice – in overall effect somewhere between Nigella Lawson and a youthful Frances de la Tour – Rebecca Hall easily commanded the audience's attention, but her curiously shifty, offhand manner never quite engaged its collective trust. I don't think she met Celia's eye once during the entire play, and given the fact that Rebecca Callard seemed to have been cast and directed solely to make Hall look better by comparison, you could see why not. A petite actress, Callard looked dumpy in the half-Elizabethan formal dress she wore in the opening court scenes and a positive fright in the more modern countrified outfit she was given in Arden, and she seemed to have been told to stay near the back of the stage and look as inconspicuous as possible throughout. For once, Duke Frederick seemed to be perfectly right about the supposed friendship between Rosalind and her cousin – 'She is too subtle for thee', 1.3.76–81 – and Rosalind's defiant insistence that neither she nor her father were traitors sounded less like a courageous assertion of the truth regardless of her own interests than simply the petulant outburst of a girl so spoiled that the idea that her uncle or anyone else might actually have the nerve to harm her was completely beyond her grasp. Joseph Millson made a strong, interestingly vulnerable Orlando during the early scenes of the play, genuinely and touchingly half-suicidal before the wrestling match in 1.2, but in his scenes with Ganymede in Arden he was demoted to a mere conventional love-struck stooge: this was a production only interested in Rosalind's feelings, and furthermore this was a Rosalind only interested in Rosalind's feelings too. Wearing a fedora hat, and a man's white shirt over trousers, Hall as Rosalind as Ganymede resembled nothing so much as an over-indulged Wycombe Abbey sixth-former keeping herself from boredom during the summer holidays by trying out a few emotional experiments on the locals, and of the whole cast only Philip Voss – a superb, deliberate, blinkered but estimable Jaques – seemed able or willing to try to exert some moral authority over her. Insisting on fixing her eye during their little dialogue in 4.1, he stood resolutely up to her glib, rude dismissal of him as a bankrupted and boring old ex-traveller, and his reply, 'Yes, I have gained my experience' (4.1.24), with a strong emphasis on the last word, here expressed not self-importance but an amply justified attempt to point out to this youth that s/he didn't in fact know it all. Who did she think she was? It was an interesting question, certainly, but not quite interesting enough to sustain a whole production.

Endless gags, no matter how ingenious or well executed, won't always do it either, though in Lucy Bailey's *Twelfth Night* in the autumn, at the Royal Exchange in Manchester, they had a good try. Illyria here became a grandiose but run-down hotel, complete with extra galleries and even tiny bedrooms fitted ingeniously around the circular auditorium's own upper levels, and a wrought-iron staircase that led down to a stage proper which was set out as the lobby, with Fabian as desk clerk. As this piece of staffing suggests, this Illyria, surprisingly, was not Orsino's property. The first two scenes, as they so often are, were thoughtlessly swapped around (so that Illyria became initially something that happened to Viola, rather than vice versa, which does make a difference), but when we did get to 'If music be the food of love, play on' it was not an imperious command from a self-indulgent aristocrat but a plaintive appeal from a has-been glam-rock star, waking still half-intoxicated in the hotel lobby and moaning to his backing musicians, Valentine and Curio. The ownership of this hotel did not become finally clear until the following scene, when a Garboesque Olivia descended proprietorially from her boudoir in sunglasses, straw hat and silk dressing gown, attended by, among others, a petty-minded under-manager with a Bobby Charlton hairstyle and pencil moustache, Malvolio. This unexplained and unhelpful reversal of relative status between Orsino and Olivia was partly compensated for, it is true, by the Count's unusual relative presence. In his boxer shorts, eye liner and gold devoré dressing gown, Mark Bonnar cut a splendidly ruined figure, if less Illyrian than bohemian, and he was probably the ablest bass guitarist to have played Orsino in the play's history: this debauchee's evident bisexuality, furthermore, allowed the mandatory kiss with Emma Cunniffe's trendily cropped-blonde Cesario to be got inconsequently out of the way during their first scene together (on 'And all is semblative the woman's part', 1.4.34), and his recovering-addict's unpredictability helped his various emotional outbursts to sound genuinely dangerous, with a note of real, shrill misogyny at 2.4.92–103 ('There is no woman's sides', a sentiment further glossed by a fierce New Order-style thrash with his band after Cesario's departure) and a murderous hysteria in 5.1 ('a savage jealousy' indeed at 5.1.117). Furthermore, the presence of some rock musicians (complete with drum kit and amplifiers) forever loitering around the lobby in which most of the action took place allowed for some enjoyable elaborations of scenes in which Valentine and Curio don't usually feature at all, notably the catch scene, during which 'There dwelt a man in Babylon' was growled into a microphone by Sir Toby to their accompaniment, to the tune of 'The House of the Rising Sun', so that the dressing-gowned Malvolio could only make his presence known to the revellers, as the jam grew ever more clamorous, by pulling the plug from Valentine's guitar amplifier. But if Orsino gained in emotional conviction from this treatment, most of the other characters lost out, reduced by Bailey's endless hyperactive provision of intricate business to mere situation comedy types. Having Sir Toby and Aguecheek disguise themselves as *Charlie's Aunt* dowagers for the forged letter scene instead of hiding behind a box tree, for example, as if Malvolio would read the letter aloud in the lobby in front of a pair of strange guests any more than he would in front of people he knew and loathed, was merely distracting, and the rest of the business piled onto this scene – far too elaborate to be described here, but involving cushions, tea trays, a sofa, and misplaced sugar cubes – only served to prevent Malvolio becoming anything more interesting than a deservedly humiliated jobsworth. Bailey's baroque exuberance served *A Midsummer Night's Dream* extremely well here in 2002, but a good *Twelfth Night* needs to achieve a more complex and intimate engagement with the characters if even the plot is to work to any effect; there isn't the same invincible scenic structure to carry the piece's movement and thematics, and here most of the more tentative and ambiguous side of this later play was lost completely. It has to be admitted, though, that the schools matinee audience among whom I saw this show didn't seem to be missing it very much, and the play was undeniably very funny, if rarely anything else. It has to be admitted, too, that it was far more enjoyable than the year's other production of a darker comedy, Sean Holmes's RSC *Measure for Measure* in the Stratford main house in the summer, which didn't even have elaborate gags to recommend it, but relied solely on a half-thought-out concept which in the event did less than nothing for the play. All Holmes did, with the help of his designer Anthony Lamble, was to try to make *Measure for Measure* resemble *Schindler's List*: nearly all the male characters wore double-breasted suits and trench-coats, Emma Fielding's Isabella wore a red coat throughout and looked like a refugee rather than a novice, Daniel Evans's transparently lascivious and over-susceptible Angelo (a sad piece of miscasting; he is a terrific actor, but he doesn't do coldness) wore Dr Goebbels metal-framed glasses, there was irrelevant klezmer music between scenes which still, alas, made no reference to the Holocaust at all, and for the prison scenes there were large quantities of barbed wire stretched across the stage which still didn't seem to prevent a spivvish Lucio from wandering in and out at will without anyone even checking his papers. To answer the main question asked of productions of this play, Paul Higgins's hypocritical Duke (who intermittently swigged bootleg schnapps from a hip-flask) didn't receive any explicit refusal to his proposal at the end, and he shepherded a weary but just-about willing-looking Isabella off towards his palace before anyone else left the stage, but by then it was difficult to care either way.

As all of the above may suggest, social realism wasn't a very strong element in the presentation of the comedies in 2003, even in productions which gestured towards it: Edwards's modern-dress Venice, for example, looked more like an animated department-store window display than a real society in action, Kavanaugh's post-war Windsor was a period fantasy in inverted commas and, though Peter Hall's courtiers wore clothes from contemporary wardrobes once they got to Arden, his *As You Like It* was no more interested in contemporary social behaviour than Thompson's really was in the agricultural depression of the 1820s. While the cynical may attribute all this to a desire not to puzzle or offend corporate sponsors or the middlebrow priorities they are assumed to favour, it seems to reflect a more general sense that what people really want from Shakespearian comedy nowadays is romance, or escapism, or archetypes, and it has to be relevant here that 2003 saw no fewer than three revivals of *Pericles*, a play which before Adrian Noble's Arabian Nights-influenced production in 2002 seemed to be completely out of favour. With Sir Ian McKellen occupying the world's cinema screens as Gandalf rather than pacing the stage as Lear, and Dame Maggie Smith apparently confined to Hogwarts for the remainder of her natural life, fantasy seems to be the preferred mode of the moment, and this year's three wildly differing versions of Shakespeare's nostalgic play about disorientation and dispossession were in their different ways, and with different degrees of self-consciousness, more than willing to provide it.

Yukio Ninagawa's beautiful production, staged by his own company, visited the Olivier for just a week at the end of March after a successful run in Tokyo, and its transfer to a venue just across the Thames from the Ministry of Defence just before the invasion of Iraq can only have increased its poignant intensity. Like Nunn's *Love's Labour's Lost*, which preceded it in this space, it began with the sounds of war, but this was a war made the more sinister and effective for being kept offstage. To the sounds of distant gunfire, lights came up on a stage empty but for silent tubs, each fitted with a single tap, and into this space, shambling and broken, arrived Ninagawa's company through the auditorium, as refugees: one had lost a leg, perhaps to a land mine: some clutched shapeless baggages that might have been the cereclothed corpses of children: only one older couple wore clothes that could just be recognized, dirty and tattered as they were, as the traditional robes of kabuki. Miraculously, there came a lull in the firing, and still more miraculously the taps all began to run in unison; and the refugees fell on the tubs, drinking, washing, laying down their burdens. With the stage space now simply and elegantly defined as a place of respite

14 *Pericles*, directed by Yukio Ninagawa, HoriPro Inc, National Theatre, Olivier auditorium (2003). Masachika Ichimura and Kayoko Shiraishi as Gower.

from war, a place of recuperation and even consolation, the play could begin; all save the old couple dispersed, and these two impoverished and disreputable ballad-singers (Masachika Ichimura and Kayoko Shiraishi) began to recite Gower's prologue by turns, the old man drawing out a triangular-bodied Japanese lute on which to accompany himself. These proxies for Shakespeare thereby identified themselves as revenants from a more ceremonial age, and in defiance of the suffering all around them and in prospect they promised a story that lords and ladies had read for restoratives. (The cast worked in Japanese throughout, with Shakespeare's text – which clearly had been translated pretty much in its entirety – projected as surtitles on screens on either side of the stage.) One by one, as the play progressed, the cast returned to act it out, now transformed by the traditional sanctity and loveliness of formal Samurai-period dress; and the first to arrive, now whole and magnificently robed, was Masaaki Ukino, previously the refugee who had lacked one leg, but now a proud Pericles undauntedly surveying the severed heads which had come dangling down on ropes to indicate Antiochus's court.

Watching a play performed in a language one does not understand is always liable to lead one to take a more than usually close interest in the visual design, but this production would surely have been an overwhelming series of intelligent delights to the optic nerves even for those fluent in Japanese. The mock-medieval idiom of *Pericles* lent itself to a far more successful fusion of Japanese and Western elements than had Ninagawa's previous Shakespearian production, the *King Lear* he produced in collaboration with the RSC in 1999, and he and his designer Tsukasa Nakagoshi managed a series of dazzling and often very simple effects which for once convincingly filled the Olivier stage. Masachika Ichimura and Kayoko

15 *Pericles*, directed by Yukio Ninagawa, HoriPro Inc, National Theatre, Olivier auditorium (2003). Masaaki Ukino as Pericles.

Shiraishi doubled their roles as Gower with Cleon and Dionyza, establishing the famished state of their city by the simple means of immensely tall, ragged grey banners; a team of nine *kuroko* (the back-clad technicians who manipulate puppets in bunraku) operated an entire silvery ocean of strips of textile for the storm scenes, through which at first a puppet of Pericles, washed overboard from a sinking cardboard ship, and then Pericles himself struggled towards the shore of Pentapolis; the dumb shows were performed as pure bunraku, with masked puppets of the characters performing in an immense mirrored box, about fifty feet wide and ten high, that served as a theatre within the theatre (a tableau vivant of Marina's rivalry with Philoten at embroidery was especially charming); Simonides's court was opulently decorated with immense glowing lotus blossoms; Marina (a delicate Yuko Tanaka) was abducted by pirates who resembled rogue sumo wrestlers, their ringleader with a huge rose tattooed on one buttock, and she later mimed the fate of a trapped bird while trying to reclaim Lysimachus (Masachika Ichimura in yet another guise) in the brothel (which was run by Kayoko Shiraishi, transformed again, as a memorably crooked and caustic Bawd). The acting favoured eminently readable, graceful gestures: Marina's ultimate escape from the brothel, for example, was signalled, at the close of her dialogue with Boult, once she had persuaded him not to rape her, with a slow and solemn taking of his hand, as if exacting a formal promise. During the recognition scene, which here was every bit as moving as it should be, Pericles lifted Marina up horizontally in his arms to show her in joy to Helicanus: it looked, of course, like the end of *King Lear*, except that this beloved daughter was alive, and there was still the vision of silver Diana and the reunion with Thaisa at her temple to come.

All of this exquisite and touching art, however, was perpetually framed for us by the pressure of what was still happening offstage; during intervals in the action, we again heard the sounds of warfare, and they were growing ever closer. The triumph and closure of Gower's last speech broke off into sorrow and renewed desperate flight, as, with the invading army (complete with jet aircraft and helicopters) now audibly close to the boundaries of the acting area, the whole company resumed their guises as refugees, returning to the stage, reshouldering their burdens and this time shambling onwards exhausted and away through its rear. Our last image was thus not of Pericles's restored and regal family in Diana's temple, but of that same solitary refugee with only one leg, hobbling on crutches behind his fellows. For Ninagawa, apparently, *Pericles* offered a consoling but ultimately impotent fantasy, its text speaking less *about* our own world of war and displacement than *to* that world's sad craving for an escape. The play was at once ennobled and diminished by this all-but explicit acknowledgement of the slight guilt which many in its audience felt about being powerlessly at the theatre at all, just a few weeks after the National's very building had itself supplied one of the foci for the all-too-futile two-million strong anti-war demonstrations of 15 February. It was a remarkable and very charged occasion, and its curtain call, most unusually in this theatre and indeed this city, found many of the audience standing, their faces wet with tears.

A very different attempt to politicize the play, again by reference to the plight of refugees, was offered at another South London venue (the Warehouse on Mandela Way, just off the Old Kent Road in east Southwark) by the Cardboard Citizens, 'the UK's only homeless people's professional theatre company'. (The name alludes to the 1980s nickname of the colony of rough sleepers who lived in the big underpass between Waterloo Station and the National Theatre, 'Cardboard City'.) This show, directed by Adrian Jackson, was produced in alliance with the RSC (principally its education department, then headed by the late Clare Venables), in a clear bid to preserve – albeit somewhere well away from Stratford – something of that company's older reputation as an organization committed to making Shakespeare relevant to present-day Britain. But if this were an attempt to delegate the RSC's social conscience to the Cardboard Citizens, the transaction oddly left out Shakespeare's text, which remained strangely incidental to what was in fact the central purpose of the performance. Both the *mise-en-scène* and the framing device of this production, which were in their own way rather magnificent, utterly dwarfed what the company were in the event able to do with Shakespeare's play proper. The whole vast complex of warehouses in which the show took place, which had been used only the previous Christmas to house a large number of London's rough sleepers, had been converted for this occasion into a series of spaces imitating those that might be encountered by refugees and asylum seekers. On arrival at the venue, the audience was made to queue up behind a series of ugly wooden desks, where surly front-of-house staff impersonating minor Home Office officials made them complete forms and issued them with identity badges to wear from a chain around their necks for the remainder of the proceedings. We were issued, too, with a grubby brown manila envelope each, containing a programme consisting largely of separate xeroxed sheets bearing information about the plight of asylum seekers, with an essay by Hanif Kureishi, relevant cuttings from the *Guardian*, and so on. The individual actor biographies, instead of providing the usual list of previous roles in Shakespeare, musicals and *The Bill*, were pastiche Home Office identity forms, giving family name, date and place of birth, nationality, whether and when they had ever lived in another country, how they had entered the UK, names and nationalities of parents and grandparents. (One effect of this was to obfuscate quite what the company means when it claims to be 'the UK's only homeless people's professional theatre company', working with 'homeless and ex-homeless people, including asylum seekers and refugees, as creators, participants and audiences', since it camouflaged exactly how many of the cast were in fact perfectly ordinary professional actors, and ex-RSC play-as-cast ones at that, homeless only in so far as they weren't in Stratford this season.)

We were then ushered into the first of a series of nightmarish, agoraphobic, neon-lit spaces, this one set up as an immense examination hall, where each audience member sat behind an individual desk bearing yet more forms to complete: it was explained from a platform at the front that we would be seeing a production of a play by William Shakespeare to contribute to our assimilation within British culture, something which would be helpful to us should our applications for political asylum eventually be granted. This, in effect, identified Shakespeare as a tool of the oppressive state apparatus, and the performance which ensued never quite managed to get him to change sides. For the successive acts of the play, we were ushered – with greater and lesser degrees of politeness, by staff members often representing detention camp guards – into further cavernous rooms: a collective industrial-scale laundry room, a camp full of line on line of tents, and so on, ending at last in a raked space approximating more closely to a conventional theatre. The actors moved through and around the audience throughout, and they punctuated their account of *Pericles* by performing bits of another script entirely: each member of the company sooner or later stopped the action to recite the first-person narrative of a real-life asylum seeker. In the middle of Gower's last speech, with the whole company on stage, each completed his or her story, and one of the real-life refugees who had been described even appeared on a video screen behind the cast, completing her own narrative to the accompaniment of generically heartwarming music.

The odd thing about this massive and often thoroughly engaging exercise in promenade agitprop theatre was that the evening's preoccupation with the immediate cause of refugees and asylum seekers actually had the effect of draining *Pericles* of topical energy rather than harnessing that energy through the play itself. To be blunt, the play proper wasn't particularly well acted, or well directed – dividing the role of Pericles between two actors, for example, one taking over from Act 4 onwards, pretty much abolished whatever emotional hold his wanderings might have retained; representing the temple of Diana by piles of withered flowers in front of a portrait of the late Princess of Wales seemed both dated and irrelevant; and only Marina's misadventures in the sex industry at Mytilene seemed to take place in the same present-day universe as that inhabited by the asylum seekers whose stories kept interrupting hers. Boult's attempted rape of Marina here took place inside a nasty little office whose windows were blanked out save for a few small apertures: the scene was relayed onto a video screen for most of the audience, but a few likely voyeurs were singled out by attendants and handed 'Tickets for the Peepshow' which entitled them to gaze uncomfortably in, their faces pressed against the glass. I blush to confess that they spotted me as an obvious potential client for this dubious entertainment, perhaps in part because for once – and this is much to Jackson's credit – I found myself one of the oldest people in a Shakespeare audience rather than one of the youngest. But a fairly perfunctory modern-dress production of *Pericles*, surprisingly uninformed by any very detailed or vivid sense of how the play's story might actually play out in a world of immigration controls and border police, was apparently serving only to lure audiences to the Warehouse so that they could be proselytized about asylum seekers by other means. Putting refugees centre stage seemed to involve pushing Shakespeare to the margins – often literally, as the actors struggled to make themselves heard from the edges of successive echoing spaces – and denying his text any active participation in the humanitarian project of the show. It was an impressive and worthy undertaking, but it found little to say either to or through the play.

Soon afterwards, in September, yet another *Pericles* appeared in London, this one directed by Neil Bartlett at the Lyric, Hammersmith. If Gower had hitherto been a refugee, indulging nostalgic Shakespearian fantasies, here he was another humble and excluded figure, played by Bette Bourne as a crankish hospital orderly who kept telling us the story of Pericles, with which he was nerdishly obsessed, in the intervals of his menial job. The whole stage, inexplicably, represented the corridor of a present-day hospital, and most of the play used only props which might have been found in one: this can't be said to have helped it very much, and it even sabotaged the play's chief instance of medical drama, the revival of Thaisa by Cerimon, since Angela Down's white-coated Cerimon simply injected a prone Sarah Malin in as businesslike, effective and unmagical way as any NHS trainee might have administered a tetanus vaccine. Down later reappeared as the Bawd, which she played as a standard stylized Cockney comedy turn, and apart from reminding its audience of the theatre's proximity to the Royal Hammersmith Infirmary this production made no connection to the world outside at all: the main thing it offered its audience was the spectacle of Will Keen, as Pericles, emoting, something which this actor invariably does by staying absolutely still and quivering and bleating. (To be fair to the full extent of his range, he sometimes does these things separately or in succession instead of all at once.) For the recognition of his daughter at Mytilene, Keen was wheeled onto the stage comatose on a hospital trolley, and Pascale Burgess's Marina had to insist, as if maliciously, on waking him violently up to hear her sing: but for all the emotional impact which Bartlett was able to generate from the remainder of the scene (which he scarcely seemed to have read, leaving Marina and Pericles far apart and stock still even for the line 'But, good sir, / What will you of me?', 21.163–4), she might as well have let him sleep on. This was a leaden production, but it was very warmly received by an audience clearly in the mood for comforting emotion and fantasy without too much content. Shakespeare was here just a romantic and sentimental old outcast, telling a very simple and undemanding story to pass the time, and that's how these people liked it: I suspect we will be seeing more revivals of *Pericles* next year.

A much more intelligent, lively and illuminating approach to a hitherto neglected late play, mercifully, was taken by Dominic Cooke's RSC *Cymbeline* in the Swan during the summer, which for my money was the little gem of the year's otherwise undistinguished Stratford season. I hesitate to categorize this play among the comedies, since the Folio didn't, and this was a production which did ample justice to the text's competing affinities with history and with tragedy, but then again Paul Chahidi did give what was certainly one of the year's funniest (and nastiest) performances as a Cloten sufficiently vain and aesthetically challenged to wear diamante jewellery among the flaunted hairs of his chest. As this detail may suggest, this was not a *Cymbeline* trapped in the furs, leathers and vaguely Celtic motifs of the stage's standard version of Ancient Britain, but one which boasted designs (by Rae Smith) which were as eclectic as Shakespeare's script, dramatizing that curious offshore tribe the Britons (who seem in this script to be simultaneously on the edge of the Roman empire and of contemporary Europe) in terms which similarly mingled and counterpointed the present and the past. Cymbeline's courtiers wore bowler hats on their heads but also false horse tails projecting from their breeches, and held a symbolic umbrella above the wheelchair cum throne in which their king was confined until the last act (partly, it was made clear, thanks to the drugs by which his queen was slowly poisoning him). Emma Fielding's Imogen looked like a nubile designer Boadicea or perhaps Diana, with extra false blonde hair extending her own in a pony tail that flowed down her back almost to her knees, a quiver of arrows slung over one shoulder, and a golden satin dress just short of knee-length, in shape reminiscent of the tunic traditionally worn by Peter Pan in the pantomime, beneath which leather cross-garterings adorned white stockings (as Fidele, she swapped all this, disappointingly, for a well-nigh shapeless boiler suit). The Queen, too, wore false hair, though in a more overtly Cruella de Vil style; Anton Lesser's coldly suave Jachimo wore a sharp white and wholly contemporary Italian suit; the Romans, as opposed to the Italians, looked like Romans, in golden breastplates compared to which Cymbeline's colourful but improvised-looking court appeared suitably provincial (Rory Kinnear's gracious but pained Caius Lucius amply lived up to Shaw's description of his behaviour as 'urbanity among barbarians', looking as though he had been almost certain of a posting to Athens before being told he was being sent to Lud's town); and Jupiter, surprisingly, looked like a cross between Jehovah and Father Time, a white-bearded old man in a white loincloth who had immense white feathery wings (less eagle than dove) and was dangled vertically down above the ghosts of Posthumus's family on a single hawser to deliver the rebukes and promises that initiate the play's miraculous final movement.

Nor was this production's style of acting and direction confined to the more-or-less naturalism-with-metre which has become the RSC's normal house manner: Cooke experimented, for example, with several versions of what one might call freeze frame – as at the opening, where the whole of Cymbeline's court stood immobile about the stage while the two Gentlemen walked among them, the informative First indicating the characters in his story as he spoke, or during the stroboscope-enhanced, stylized renditions of the battle scenes – and he used one trick borrowed from the repertoire of the Shared Experience company, a sequence depicting Imogen's tedious progress through the Welsh countryside in which she was followed, as she plodded wearily around the stage, by most of the rest of the cast, notably Posthumus, joining and leaving the little procession in turn as if representing her own exhausted and circling thoughts about them. The production's soundscape, by Paul Arditti, ranged from percussive wooden clashes and pings for scenes like this (half high modernist, half primitive) to a naturalistic roaring, alternating with

16 *Cymbeline*, directed by Dominic Cooke, RSC, Swan Theatre, 2003. 'The bird is dead': Daniel Hawksford (Guiderius), Simon Trinder (Arviragus), Emma Fielding (Imogen), Christopher Godwin (Belarius).

uncanny silence, for the battle scenes. The performances, too, worked across a considerable scope of effects. As Imogen, Emma Fielding could be as touching as any Victorian critic of the play might have desired, but she was also very, very angry at the treatment she received from her father, from her husband and from her stepbrother; in the last scene, after all, Cymbeline only recognizes her voice by the rage with which she accuses Pisanio of having tried to poison her, and his line 'The tune of Imogen!' (5.6.140) was here greeted with appropriate and supportive laughter. The one point at which Fielding shied away from any of the emotional extremes through which the play puts Imogen came during her speech over the headless body of Cloten, when instead of deliberately and savagely defacing her beauty with blood on 'O, / Give horror to my pale cheek with thy blood, / That we may seem the horrider' (4.2.332–4) she decorously cradled the corpse and got a little bloodstained as if by accident: the audience was in fact wholly with her here, their initial giggles at the arrival of the dummy cadaver long passed even before what was here a very capable account of the funeral dirge (as ever, the scenes between Belarius and the two princes worked beautifully in performance, however absurd they can look on the page), and Fielding could have afforded to go a lot further into hysteria than she did before her very moving, almost lethargic surrender of herself to Caius Lucius. Daniel Evans, however, did not hold back at all from the ugliness and violence of 'Is there no way for women to be . . .?' (2.5), standing on the bench at which he had sat to dine with Philario and ranting directly at specific women in the Swan's intimate auditorium, and it is a great tribute to his skill that he was able to move back from here and become someone capable of receiving the audience's forgiveness as well as that of his fellow characters by the end of the play. They made a fetchingly and fascinatingly troubled couple, and as Cymbeline, David Horovitch matched them in expertise, playing the diplomacy scene, 3.1, so often skimped or simplified, as though the relations between Britain and Europe actually mattered (as, incidentally, they do), and steering the astonishing last scene adroitly between comedy and tragedy and sometimes across both at once, convincing me for the first time that Cymbeline may actually be a role worth playing. All in all, this was a production that was usually willing to trust the play to make sense of all its own disparate styles and contents, and the play did not let it down. My only regret is that the cuts which Cooke and Roger Warren made in quest of a running time below four hours fell disproportionately on the later scenes: the wonderfully lugubrious jailer of 5.5, for example, practically vanished (and, played in an executioner's mask, he couldn't even *look* very depressed), and in the same scene Posthumus's spectral family was abbreviated by one character, his mother, a cut which any psychoanalytically inclined critic interested in the restoration of his psychic wholeness would surely deplore. But this was a stimulating, inventive piece of theatre, and the twists and turns of *Cymbeline*'s narrative were more than sufficient to keep its cast from the sorts of introverted, method-oriented declamation – verse-speaking designed to convince you that the actor is feeling a great deal about the language, without making the content of the language clear at all – which was otherwise heard rather too much around Stratford this year.

HISTORIES

That curious sound of English actors trying very hard to convince you that they are living in the moment through Shakespeare's language – a process which seems to involve their underlining most of the words in any given sentence, to minimize the risk of your being distracted from their emotion by the sentence's actual subject-matter or movement, and then pausing artlessly before the 'action' words which they have decided are the most important ones, as if these are not only underlined but printed in bold – was often audible around the Globe in 2003 too, during a season glibly and controversially labelled, well before the Iraq war began, 'The Season of Regime Change'. Tim Carroll's production of *Richard II*, as well as being seen on Bankside during the summer, was performed in the hall at Middle Temple in April, using the same traverse-shaped acting area as 2002's *Twelfth Night* (see *Survey 56*). Once I have recorded the fact that Mark Rylance played Richard, I probably need say little more, save to mention that the show opened with Richard's court singing a jolly catch while out hunting somewhere, so that Bolingbroke and Mowbray appeared to have had to pursue the King deep into the New Forest in order to insist on getting him to consider their dispute at all. (This first scene starred the sort of very dead deer which used to be reserved for pre-war Stratford revivals of *As You Like It*, and Rylance occasionally stroked it pensively in order to distract the audience while other actors were speaking.) I should also report, in the interests of stage historians, that 3.3, the Flint Castle scene, worked perfectly practicably using an upper level above the hall's dais and screen for Richard's appearance on the walls: the wait for him to arrive downstairs after he agrees to descend (between lines 182 and 184) was not excessive and made perfect dramatic sense in its context. Rylance, for what it may be worth, wore a white Elizabethan outfit with puffed hose that looked like rompers (as Bolingbroke, Liam Brennan wore black, and seemed to be doing his best to be invisible), an appropriate enough resemblance given that he offered the usual whimsical, petulant, self-indulgent, little-boy-lost performance which he always does unless he is working with a director able to exert rather more authority than Carroll seemed to have been able to muster. Even the experience of being deposed didn't change or modulate this Richard's infantile act in any way: some of the greatest lines in the English language went on being thrown away or half-mumbled at random, and the play, so far from occasioning any profound reflections on the nature of political allegiance or the ethics of regime change, seemed to be about nothing at all. The more interesting shows at the Globe this year were both by Marlowe, *Edward II* and *Dido, Queen of Carthage.* The other Shakespearian history in its repertory, *Richard III*, directed by Barry Kyle, ought to have been a good deal more interesting than it was, if only because this was one of the first recorded professional all-female productions of the play in this country: having women act out this story in which grieving women attempt to assert their own right to narrate the sufferings which its central male egotist has inflicted upon them should have made a difference; but no. Kathryn Hunter's performance as Richard consisted almost entirely of her leaning back almost horizontally, holding her right arm stiffly, bending her right knee and pointing her right toes and then skipping across the stage on her left heel, and over five acts it got pretty boring. As Buckingham, Amanda Harris, though she had plenty of presence, projected little except her evident pleasure about what a dashing Principal Boy she looked in her black Elizabethan outfit (leading the crowd in the yard in completely inappropriate panto-like cheers for Richard during 3.7), and the rest of a lacklustre cast looked and sounded much like a French and Saunders skit or a girls' school play. The worst aspect of the production, though, was its treatment of the little princes, who were played as crude and horrid caricatures of children by two grown actresses, Liza Hayden and Laura Rogers: this skewed the play's morality entirely by making the audience actively want Richard to get rid of them at his earliest possible opportunity, by whatever means, and seemed a particularly incongruous way of casting these small but important roles for a theatre which prides itself on having such close and mutually beneficial relations with local schools. Southwark must be full of children willing and able to do a far better job.

The year's other *Richard III*, by contrast, Sean Holmes's RSC production, which ran in the Stratford main house at the same time, boasted even more real children than usual, and they were among the best things in it. Henry Goodman's Richard – his first Shakespearian role since his brilliant Shylock at the National in 1999 – was so closely in touch with his inner child that he was often accompanied by an outer child too, the page whose role is usually confined to fetching Tyrrell in 4.2. This boy, ably played at alternate performances by David Jowett and Jack Snell, was dressed as a little replica of Richard, right down to a caliper on one leg, in what seemed like a deliberate allusion to Dr Evil's Mini-Me in the *Austin Powers* films: the effect, though, was not so much to make the page look like a diminutive Richard as to make Richard look like an overgrown child, especially when his chosen throne, in the fourth act, sat him at his court's head height like an enormous highchair. Goodman, unusually, seemed far more at home in this second half of the play than in the first, far better at childish tantrums and despair than at gleeful machiavellian ambition, but this may simply have been a side-effect of a production which, with an unimpressive supporting cast and a comparatively inexperienced director, seemed to have forced him to fall back far too heavily on his own accustomed armoury of movements and gestures: there was a definite sense that Goodman's performance, too, was by now desperately and insecurely flailing about in a solitary vacuum. Holmes chose to dress the play in Victorian costumes, thereby neatly cutting it off from either fifteenth-century or modern resonances, but this did have the potentially beneficial effect of allowing Goodman's performance to draw on the conventions of music hall, melodrama, and Punch and Judy. Certainly it allowed Holmes to use something very rarely seen in the RST nowadays, a red curtain, from behind which Goodman emerged for his first soliloquy into a follow-spot, dressed like a nineteenth-century compere or ringmaster in grey suit, gloves, spats and top hat. As this smiling and at first able-bodied Mr Showbiz spoke, though (from line 14 onwards, 'But I, that am not shaped for sportive tricks'), he abruptly began to remove items of the outfit to reveal his caliper, deformed leg, claw hand and deformed arm, his speech increasingly snarling. It was all very elaborate, and long too: taken slowly and with grinning pauses, the speech was even extended, as in the days of the Victorian actor-managers, with added

17 *Richard III*, directed by Sean Holmes, RSC, Royal Shakespeare Theatre (2003). Richard (Henry Goodman) on his cart in 4.4.

material from Richard's soliloquies in *3 Henry VI*. Richard periodically resumed this compere role on the forestage for asides and soliloquies, complete with follow-spot and abruptly drawn red curtain, throughout the first half of the play, but he had already exhausted most of his repertoire of tricks by the end of his first speech, and seemed, as I have suggested, increasingly uneasy and over-emphatic in his straining after the same effects during the remainder of the play. An ammunition chest on wheels, ridden round and round the stage in 4.4 like a toy chariot pulled by human horses for his confrontation with his mother and Queen Elizabeth, provided one new idea, but it was soon overused, and the collapse into conscience and defeat at Bosworth – to make way for the triumph of a completely cardboard Richmond (the wonderfully-named Bradley Freegard) – came almost as a relief. For all Goodman's evident interest in Richard's psychology as a damaged child, Holmes's production seemed in the main to be repeating effects explored just as monotonously in Stephen Pimlott's production, with David Troughton, in 1996: an explicitly show-business Richard who behaves like Mr Punch comes to much the same thing as one who dresses throughout as a jester, and leaves much of this play – which is set in a much more carefully delineated real world of real victims than this production was able to dramatize – completely untouched.

The Shakespeare history play for this difficult year of warfare and its discontents, surprisingly to those who continue to regard it as parochial and jingoistic, turned out to be *Henry V*, which was seen in two contrasting productions during the build-up to the war in Iraq and during its aftermath. Barrie Rutter's Northern Broadsides production, together with his revival of Heywood's *A Woman*

Killed With Kindness, toured the North extensively between February and June and even ventured briefly into the wicked metropolitan South to play for five nights in late March at the unfinished Kingston Theatre in West London. Here, in a freezing unheated structure of still-bare concrete, for the moment resembling a hybrid between a roofed Globe and a multi-storey car park, the show seemed oddly dated and irrelevant, largely because this production was in fact more or less a scaled-down recreation of Terry Hands's famous revival of 1975, in which Rutter played MacMorris: now he was the Chorus, an enthusiastic host excited by the verse and the heroism, and surprisingly similar in effect to Emrys James a quarter of a century earlier. Cut to a playing time of two and a half hours, the play was here primarily an exercise in highly competent narrative; Conrad Nelson's muscular Henry scarcely had time to have much in the way of interiority, and the main emphasis of a muddy Agincourt – played on a surface of crumpled tarpaulin, as per 1975 – was on the unambiguous celebration of brotherhood. This was all very well, but you might just as well have got it from Hull Kingston Rovers rugby team, and in London in March, on the very brink of the American-led invasion, it seemed at best worryingly off the point: unlike the Falklands conflict, which had reanimated the play for Adrian Noble and for Michael Bogdanov in the 1980s, the one preoccupying this audience's minds wasn't even primarily a British war, and there seemed no useful or energizing parallels to be found between Shakespeare's account of Henry's war and the newspapers' continual speculations about Blair's.

Nicholas Hytner, though, had absolutely insisted that his first production as artistic director of the National – rehearsed, in the event, before and during the main phase of the conflict, but performed after it – should be of this play, and, with Rutter's production and its lukewarm reception comparatively fresh in my mind, I arrived for its first night on 13 May in some trepidation as to whether *Henry V* could possibly speak to this particular moment. Even the sponsorship of the National's whole spring and summer repertory by a foreign currency exchange company, Travelex, which kept the price of almost every seat in the Olivier down to £10, seemed ominous: surely they must only have subsidized the show to this extent in anticipation of a simple-minded exercise in Francophobia, in the hopes of thereby holding off still further the adoption by the British of the euro? But in the event I need not have worried. The pressure of offstage events and concerns was so great on this production, the desire of its audience to see a public debate about whether an invasive war can ever be justified so overwhelming, that even the points at which the story did not match the tale of Bush and Blair's selling of their attack on Baghdad became themselves perversely topical – as the production now seemed to be showing us Blair's fantasy about himself as a war leader (a glimpse of a world in which dissenting Cabinet colleagues such as Scroop, Grey and Masham could be taken out and shot, and the enemy was the French), and now projecting his nightmares (of finding himself on a battlefield in person, outnumbered by the enemy and surrounded by sceptical squaddies). In any event, Shakespeare's play turned out to be perfectly able to hold its own as a penetrating examination of the ethics of war.

What Hytner did, to make this extraordinary achievement sound simple and easy, was just stage the play in high-gloss modern dress, and see what happened: and if his production did not carry quite the frisson it might have enjoyed had British troops still been in full-scale action when it opened, its early scenes were given a phenomenal boost by the debate which continued to rage all summer about the extent to which the famous dossier in which Blair had set out his reasons for supporting an invasion had been artificially and deliberately 'sexed up'. Onto a polished, hyperclean-looking open stage, bearing a long black table set out with glasses and smart little individual bottles of mineral water, arrived Penny Downie as the Chorus, bearing a few heavy books, wearing her hair imperfectly tied up and the sort of clothes in which a female academic might choose to face a television camera (right down to costly red shoes that co-ordinated beautifully with the bottle tops). Casting such a woman as the Chorus, interestingly if a little worryingly,

18 *Henry V*, directed by Nicholas Hytner, National Theatre Company, Olivier auditorium (2003). Adrian Lester as Henry.

placed her attitude to Henry under suspicion from the first: there was little risk of the audience taking this cloistered presenter's gushing enthusiasm for the king as an authoritative statement of what either the play or the production would be seeking to show us, and indeed as the play progressed, especially after Agincourt, this expert herself seemed increasingly to doubt her own earlier uncomplicated pleasure in recounting Henry's victories, as if the whole performance had represented her thinking through the evidence once more and reaching some more disquieting conclusions. As her first speech reached its own conclusion, two entirely modern-looking senior clerics arrived at the table: and, deliciously, one of them, William Gaunt's worldly Canterbury, was carrying not just one dossier but a whole pile of them. During his cynical dialogue with Ely, in between lighting an expensive slim cigar, he distributed these folders around the table, and it became clear – to the knowing, mischievous delight of the audience – that what we were watching was the preparation for a Cabinet meeting, a meeting which as far as this particular minister was concerned had already been carefully engineered to ratify a pre-ordained outcome. Sure enough, 1.1 ran continuously into 1.2, with the King and his peers arriving in pin-striped suits (save for a couple of senior military uniforms, most importantly, that of Peter Blythe's sensitive Exeter) and taking their places around the table. In their centre sat Adrian Lester's Henry, like a young, unnaturally handsome and unnaturally authoritative prime minister, sternly and carefully cueing Canterbury to explain the contents of the folder.

The Salique Law speech (1.2.33–95), surely, can never have been so electrifying. As the archbishop spoke (with definite self-satisfaction, until brought up short by Henry's 'May I with right and conscience make this claim?', a question which here sounded more like a demand for a more explicit brief sound-bite than the urgent prompting of conscience), different cabinet members around the table puzzled over the sexed-up dossier's contents, turning the xeroxed family trees this way and that and trying, often belatedly, to follow Canterbury as he indicated the whereabouts of Salic ('twixt Elbe and Saale') on his own copy of a brightly coloured map. Remote and deliberate, it was not entirely clear which way Henry intended to make his decision until the message from an apprehensive French ambassador – superbly played by Rupert Wickham in just such a suit as is seen on Brussels's civil servants – succeeded in almost rousing his temper, and tipped him into committing himself and his country to a war which clearly had not quite been a foregone conclusion. After this inescapably topical, well-nigh voyeuristic recreation of what a Cabinet meeting about a decision to open hostilities might have looked like in a more articulate parallel universe, Hytner's production never looked back: the audience were hooked on the possibility of direct, sceptical comment on the present situation, and they weren't disappointed. At the end of 1.2, for example, Henry called in a small television crew to videotape the resolute, sincere delivery of his speech urging his government to prepare for war (lines 300–10), and the production's interest in this piece of spin and its reception, perfectly grounded in the script's own interest in Henry's legendary status and how it was achieved, flowed over into the beginning of 2.1. A bank of television screens descended behind the stage, onto which part of Henry's performance of the speech was projected – until, that is, a bored Bardolph, revealed at a pub table holding a TV remote control, channel-hopped first to a snooker game, then back, and then off. The ingenious re-imagining of this play into a world of television news management, indeed, was one of the production's most striking and successful features. In direct parallel to this little broadcast, for example, Ian Hogg's King of France delivered his speech of defiance in 3.5 as a live address to his nation via the camera, from a little podium in the production's elegant facsimile of an Elysée Palace reception room (in which an aggressive Dauphin, played by Adam Levy in Italian suit and greased-back ponytail, resembled nothing so much as the sort of French football star more usually seen playing for Chelsea); and the pointed placing of the French princess's English lesson naming the parts of her body, directly after Henry's threats that his soldiers would commit rape unless Harfleur surrendered, was beautifully underscored when the opening of 3.4 found Catherine and Alice gloomily watching footage of Henry making this speech on the television news, complete with French subtitles. Throughout his French campaign, indeed – staged as a reassuringly expensive facsimile of genuine modern combat, complete with off-line naturalistic military asides such as 'At ease, men, three minutes' from Exeter to the army and 'Fuck off!' from the army to Mountjoy, and featuring no fewer than two armoured jeeps – we watched Henry signalling, whenever a camera crew was present, which of his utterances were to be filmed and which not. Surprisingly, the Crispin Crispian speech, delivered in front of one of the jeeps, was not among the rhetorical performances recorded in this way, perhaps because this Henry seemed at that point to have given up all hope of victory or even survival, and was enabled to make the speech's gracious gestures only by a sense that he now had nothing to lose. But he was careful to reassume the management of his image and reputation thereafter; after the war, at the end of Act 4, we saw much of the more flattering earlier footage of Henry among his army edited together with swirling Union Jacks, serving as the video accompanying just the sort of ghastly cockneyfied rap novelty record which English tabloid newspapers might give away free on such an occasion, 'We thank you, Lord, for victory', a piece which stood in for much of the 5.0 chorus describing the victory celebrations.

Nor was all the camerawork in this production professional: at the opening of 2.3, Pistol, Nym, Bardolph and Mistress Quickly and the Boy were discovered as if at Falstaff's wake in the pub, nostalgically watching an old videotape of the mock-play of Hal and his father from *1 Henry IV*. The younger Henry sported dreadlocks, and Desmond Barritt's Sir John a disreputable old mackintosh: this was a useful way of incorporating much the same flashback as does Branagh's film, and it helped to make Henry's subsequent execution of Bardolph all the more shocking. In a dramatic trumping of the odd modern convention by which Bardolph's reported death sentence for looting is almost invariably carried out on stage at Henry's nod (on 'We would have all such offenders so cut off', 3.6.108), Henry, in another allusion to television news footage (this time from Vietnam) here took his own pistol and held it to Bardolph's head; anxiously trying to convince himself that his old drinking companion was only joking, a shaking Bardolph grinned straight into the king's eyes, but Henry, as if as desperate to prove his resolution to himself as to his subordinates, pulled the trigger after only a momentary hesitation.

It is appropriate to this production, though, that we should have seen Lester's Henry kill one of his own army: the moments at which this careful, warily impassive king (who usually seemed serenely confident of having no need to work too hard to seduce either his inferiors or the audience) was roused into unconcealed emotion were generally those he spent among his own soldiers. Perhaps predictably, the heart of this production was its staging of the night before Agincourt, from Henry's encounter with Pistol onwards. (Pistol was played by another of the cast's black actors, Jude Akuwudike, so that Henry's announcement of his alias 'Le Roy' occasioned a gleeful, spurious moment of hand-slapping bonding when Pistol brightly repeated it as 'Leeroy!'). Bates, Court and Williams were a knot of authentically fed-up Tommies, whose refusal to accept that the war was a matter for anyone's conscience but the king's was beautifully articulated, and whose undisguised boredom and discontent when their newly-met comrade turned out to be a mere God-botherer, as the disguised king anxiously and lengthily tried to justify his own actions ('So, if a son that is by his father sent about merchandise', 4.1.146–84), filled Henry with such unmixed anger that the subsequent 'Upon the King' speech (227–81) was entirely fuelled by pique at their perceived ingratitude. The king's setting of Fluellen to denounce and attack the wearer of the glove after the battle (which briefly occasioned a full-scale brawl in the victorious camp in 4.8) was here actively vindictive rather than playful, and only the avuncular intervention of Exeter (who in this production served, interestingly, as Henry's external conscience) saved Williams from at least a severe beating. The French prisoners in 4.6, needless to say, were less lucky: despite Exeter's visible concern, Henry gave the order that this line of about eight blindfolded, kneeling figures across the back of the stage should be killed, and then he and Exeter both left the stage; at this the individual private soldiers who were guarding them, horrified, refused to obey the order, and the sorry little mass execution had to be carried out with a machine gun by the only officer now present, Fluellen. Actors playing Fluellen have often had the apparently lightweight dialogue with Gower in the following scene, 4.7, in which Fluellen expounds on Henry's resemblance to Alexander the Great, made very difficult by their having just discovered the onstage corpse of the Boy, but Robert Blythe had an even trickier task here, obliged to play this scene as if in post-traumatic shock about the war crime he has just committed and desperate to convince himself that his King is still a hero: it was an astonishing feat of acting, and Fluellen's failure to contradict Gower's account of the killing of the prisoners – reported to have been executed in reprisal for the killing of the boys, when we have in fact seen that it took place before this incident, as Fluellen knows only too well – became part of this production's searching look at how the reputation of a war hero comes into being. These soldiers were neither simply heroes, nor simply criminals, nor simply victims, but were fully shown by the play to behave, under the pressures of combat, as a compound of all three: it was only Henry who had the task of turning all these contingent accidents, misadventures and deaths into a coherent story about the needs of State, and only the Chorus who, albeit with growing misgivings, had the task of endowing it all with the glamour of epic.

The unprecedented vividness of this production's rendering of the usually tedious Salic Law speech was matched by an unusually gripping and

19 *Henry V*, directed by Nicholas Hytner, National Theatre Company, Olivier auditorium (2003). The English delegation at the 5.2 peace talks, including Exeter (Peter Blythe), Gloucester (Tom McKay) and Henry (Adrian Lester).

affecting delivery – by the same actor, William Gaunt, as if he had been transformed from hawk to dove over the course of the performance – of Burgundy's long speech lamenting the consequences of war in 5.2, which Gaunt played rather in the manner of a humane and tearful Harold Macmillan. 5.1, the forcing of Pistol to eat Fluellen's leek, was cut entirely to make way for this very full and careful presentation of the peace talks in 5.2, a scene which this production had the courage not to play, at any point, for reassuringly easy laughs. The French king and queen were in deep mourning and deep shock (in this production, we saw the Dauphin killed at Agincourt during the French attack on the boys and the luggage, though his name was as always puzzlingly absent from the list of casualties), and there was no pretence that Felicité du Jeu's Princess Catherine was in any way pleased to be getting married off to her country's conqueror. (She held Henry's eyes only once, to demand 'Is it possible that I should love the enemy of France?', an earnestly serious question rather than a coy one.) Equally, there was no pretence that Henry's 'wooing' was anything other than the proper diplomatic gesture to be made before a dynastic marriage which he had no more power to avoid than did she: all his flatteries were just a relentless, more or less courteous insistence: look, I have to marry you now, and neither of us can get out of it, can't we put the expected brave, happy face on it? But she wouldn't, seriously affronted by a kiss which here, like the whole interview, was just a sort of diplomatic rape: 'that is as it shall please *le roi mon père*' was as much as a shruggingly rueful Henry, with a fairly dismal marriage to look forward to, was ever going to get. It made for an unusually sombre vision of what the war had finally achieved – the French king's eventual acceptance of the condition that he should adopt Henry as his heir in place of the dead Dauphin visibly horrified both his wife and his daughter – and the Chorus, concluding, sounded equally unconvinced that the whole enterprise had been worth its cost, leaving the stage looking anxiously as though she had realized that she needed to do a good deal more thinking about the man to whose biography she had been dedicating her career. There was nothing puzzled or tentative about the response that greeted this production, though – the curtain call found many of the audience standing every time I saw it – and it must rank as the most successful attempt to get Shakespeare back into the centre of serious public discourse in England for many years. It is to be hoped that Hytner will repeat the experiment on another work by this acute political commentator at his earliest opportunity.

20 *Titus Andronicus*, directed by Bill Alexander, RSC, Royal Shakespeare Theatre (2003). Titus (David Bradley) emerges to welcome his guests to the banquet in 5.3, before hastily going to change his bloodstained apron.

TRAGEDIES

Surprisingly, there is far less to report under this heading this year than is usually the case, though with the RSC planning to revive practically nothing else in 2004 – with productions of *Romeo and Juliet*, *Hamlet*, *Othello*, *Macbeth* and *King Lear* all scheduled before the end of the summer – this situation won't last. That organization's contribution to this genre in 2003 was confined to comparatively unexciting productions of Shakespeare's first and last Roman plays, though Bill Alexander's *Titus Andronicus*, the last play to join the Stratford summer repertory, at least had the distinction of being the first incarnation of this play to have graced the main house in many years. In common with many others, I suffer from the great disadvantage in relation to this play of having seen Deborah Warner's Swan production in 1987, which still ranks as one of the best productions of Shakespeare or of anything else I've ever seen, and which is likely to go on overshadowing all other attempts on this difficult play for some time to come. Alexander's, sadly, achieved nothing like the same effect of an ensemble working cogently and unflinchingly through the text's horrors and its humanity. David Bradley, it is true, was extremely well cast as Titus – looking rather like Willie Nelson, and with a face which one can easily believe might have witnessed the burials of fifty sons, he is particularly skilled at moving with only the minimum of facial expression between grief and wry comedy, and his first, Tamburlaine-like entrance, holding five Gothic prisoners on the ends of chains like a pack of tamed dogs, was splendid. But his nuanced, precise performance found little support from the rest of the show. The cutting of his killing of Mutius after this disobedient son intervenes in defence of Lavinia's elopement with Bassianus in 1.1 – a cut presumably intended to make Titus a more readily sympathetic victim thereafter, despite his sacrifice of Alarbus – rather spoiled the play's pendulum-like movement from one atrocity back to another, and in any case it was hard to distinguish, in Alexander's economically empty version of Rome, quite how much of this sort of behaviour was normal and what would constitute an unaccustomed instance of barbarism. The real problem, though, was with this production's villains: Bradley's subtle underplaying, part stoicism and part sarcasm, had little or nothing to play against, since there was little emotional intensity being aroused or sustained around his sufferings by his antagonists. As Tamora, Maureen Beattie looked nasty but sounded merely indistinct; Joe Dixon's Aaron seemed a cheerful, laddish sort of character rather than a figure of satanic malignity, so that his reappearance in captivity in 5.1 seemed irrelevant and uninteresting; and John Lloyd Fillingham's Saturninus just seemed like a camp impersonation of Nicholas Woodeson. Martin Hutson and Daniel Brocklebank did what they could to compensate, it's true, as a memorably repulsive Demetrius and Chiron, and the killing of Lavinia, at least, was as shocking as ever – the cracking sound effect as Titus unceremoniously stood behind her at the dinner table and snapped her neck was perhaps this production's highlight – but Alexander didn't seem to have any very clear idea as to what he wanted to do with the play, and he did it few favours as a result.

The Rome of David Farr's *Coriolanus* also suffered from underpopulation; in today's economic climate in the theatre, when two is a retinue and three is a crowd, this play's inclusion of an angry mob as a main character can make it extremely difficult to stage with the sort of naturalistic violence for which its street scenes call. Farr resorted to stylization, dressing the play in Japanese costumes and half-imitating some of the conventions of kabuki (so that Michael Cordery's Menenius looked like a fugitive from *The Mikado*), but this strategy tended to backfire, leaving the whole odd spectacle both robbed of any political valence and starved of energy. Again, the central character was superbly cast – you couldn't ask for a more natural Coriolanus than Greg Hicks, an actor who specializes in behaving as though he is under such unbearable internal tension that his sinews might snap at any moment, and who couldn't look like someone capable of being assimilated inconspicuously into normal human society if he tried. But this production's decision to make everyone else behave in a curiously deliberate, stylized manner too meant that he didn't stand out as a problem to nearly the extent that he should have done, and the scant, harmless-looking group of uniform-looking plebeians who signalled their discontent in 1.1 primarily by harmlessly formal ritual gestures never looked like much of an antagonist. (As Volumnia, Alison Fiske wasn't up to Hicks's weight either, so that he couldn't even meet a worthy foil in the bosom of his own family.) Addressing public speeches directly to a bemused audience, furthermore – speeches written neither as asides nor soliloquies but as pieces of rhetoric whose reception we should be watching as intently as their delivery – never works, and it certainly didn't here: having Hicks perform 'O' me alone, make you a sword of me?' (1.7.76–84) while completely alone on the stage, for example, was quite absurd, if undeniably economical. Hicks's harsh and eccentric central performance certainly held and rewarded the audience's attention – his departure from Rome at the end of 3.3, scornfully dictating the phrase 'There is a world elsewhere' syllable by syllable to the two clerks who, incongruously, were minuting his trial on typewriters, was magnificent – but it deserved a larger and more courageous production than this one: I hope he'll have the chance to play the role again.

The year's two principal productions of the ever-popular *Romeo and Juliet* made far more of a contrast. The English Touring Theatre's version, directed by Stephen Unwin, was entirely characteristic of this company's work: full of energy, played on as bare a stage as possible with a minimum of intrusive design (the costumes were 1940s, but only because Unwin felt that he didn't have a big enough budget to afford Renaissance clothes that wouldn't look distractingly silly), and cut almost to the bare bones of the text to ensure a rapid and easily comprehensible pace for the provincial audiences to which it tirelessly played. It was expert, moving, and almost entirely predictable. Far more striking, and far more responsive to the play's own youthful excitement and spirit of playful improvisation, was the production brought to the

Young Vic in the autumn by the Icelandic company Vesturport, directed by Gisli Orn Gardarsson, a performer young and strong enough to have also played Romeo. A cast of only fourteen here played Shakespeare's text in an idiom which combined orthodox classical theatre with circus and ballet. On a narrow traverse stage placed diagonally across the Young Vic auditorium, the opening chorus was spoken not, as so often is the case, by either the actor who reappears as the Prince or the one who plays the Friar, but by a clownish Peter (Vikingur Kristjansson), who appointed himself as compere and bantered with the audience at some length about the company's temerity in performing Shakespeare in English to an English audience (he later humiliated what appeared to be a German tourist arriving late, but who turned out, to the audience's relief, to be a plant). This was novel enough, but more so were the wires which ran directly above the acting area between two raised platforms: and as the narrative got under way, it turned out that most of this cast, as well as possessing excellent English (and since they were primarily interested in conveying the grammatical sense of what they were saying, this Icelandic company, shamingly, spoke Shakespeare's text far more lucidly than do many native ones), were accomplished trapeze artists. After a spectacular opening brawl that resembled a duel between rival teams of tumblers (featuring a Tybalt, face bedaubed with leonine whiskers, who could literally breathe fire), the production settled to making wonderfully literal the play's own interest in the imagery of up and down – not just in the balcony scene, or the aubade, but everywhere. Falling in love, in this show as in much of the play's poetry, meant defying gravity. At the close of their sonnet duet at the ball – a ball animated by some dazzling communal break-dancing, to a pounding piece of funk (by Karl Olgeirsson) that became only slowly and delightfully recognizable as a variation on Prokofiev's Dance of the Knights – Romeo, unforgettably, kissed Juliet while hanging upside-down by his feet from a chandelier and lifting her, still vertical, up to meet him. Shakespeare's dialogue flowed in and out of such balletic, acrobatic enactments of its conceits throughout the show: Mercutio's banter with Romeo in 2.3, for example, was accompanied and dramatized by their virtuoso pas-de-deux on a single trapeze. In the balcony scene Romeo literally walked on air towards Juliet on 'With love's light wings did I o'erperch these walls' (2.1.108), and the more mutual their dialogue became, the more both soared above the ground, deftly steering their hands on runners along the wires. From here onwards, Nina Dogg Filippsdottir's brave, wonderfully undrippy Juliet generally hung suspended above the action in a hoop to await their next meeting, as if floating on her own emotional excitement, and at her clandestine wedding to Romeo just before the interval – a kitsch and joyous occasion, complete with a tacky interpolated gospel song of 'Yea, though I speak with the tongues of angels' – Friar Laurence invited the audience to reach under their seats, where we found bubble-blowing tubs and were able further to gloss the couple's love by suspending ephemeral bubbles in the air above the stage (so light is vanity). The play's catastrophes were ultimately signalled by terrible reassertions of gravity: Tybalt killed Mercutio, for example, by hurtling viciously down onto him head-first, arm outstretched to hit his throat, along a streamer; and in the tomb – Shakespeare's dialogue, by now occasionally lapsing back into Icelandic under the pressure of emotion and otherwise almost entirely supplanted by choreography – Juliet hanged herself, to die dangling head-down on another streamer just above Romeo's prone and fallen body. This was at once a funny, inventive, playful elaboration from the play and a very faithful and surprisingly upsetting translation of it into a rich, popular idiom, and it received as warm and moved a response from its primarily youthful audience as anything I saw all year.

Just in case anyone was beginning to think that all imported Shakespearian productions are more interesting than the current native product, however, along came Calixto Bieito, a Barcelona-based director who for the last decade has enjoyed the status of being one of the most overrated figures in the European theatre. Bieito had two Shakespeare productions in England in 2003, a *Macbeth*

21 *Romeo and Juliet*, directed by Gisli Orn Gardarrson, Vesturport, Young Vic Theatre (2003). Juliet (Nina Dogg Filippsdottir).

performed at the Barbican (in alternating Catalan and Spanish) by his own Teatre Romea company in April, and a *Hamlet*, produced by Birmingham Rep (in English), which was seen first at the Edinburgh Festival and then in Birmingham in the late summer. The chief difference between the two was that in *Macbeth* the leather sofa was black and occupied a sleazy haunt of gangland villains and in *Hamlet* it was white and occupied a sleazy nightclub, and in *Macbeth* the cast were primarily drinking beer and taking tablets in between violating one another and masturbating while in *Hamlet* they drank spirits and snorted cocaine; also in *Macbeth* Banquo played a ghastly Hammond organ while in *Hamlet* Horatio played a white nightclub piano. Both productions resembled in overall effect those performances staged by sixth-formers for audiences of polite parents in which all the cast smoke and swear continually to show how adult they are: nasty, brutish and short, they were performed without intervals, but plenty of people left before their respective promised ends anyway. It was just about possible to believe that there might be Catalan-speaking gangsters as crass and tasteless as the ones who thrashed their way meaninglessly through something approximating to the plot of *Macbeth*, but the English cast of *Hamlet* seemed related to no imaginable reality at all, and at least one of them admitted it, albeit fleetingly; when Rachel Pickup's floozily-clad Ophelia began narrating her shocking visit from Hamlet, here to both Polonius and the king, 'My lord, as I was sewing in my closet' (2.1.78), Claudius (George Costigan) interrupted her with a snort of amused disbelief, '*Sewing*??' But apart from this welcome moment of self-irony, this was pure Eurotrash Shakespeare, Shakespeare retold by an idiot, full of sound and fury, signifying nothing.

However, to remind us that *Hamlet* is actually an astoundingly good play, whatever some directors may be prepared to do to conceal the fact, there was Jonathan Kent's production at Sadler's Wells, for only one precious week at the end of August and beginning of September, with which I will briefly conclude this account of the year's Shakespeares, native and foreign, on a very high note indeed. Produced in collaboration with the same organization who mounted Ninagawa's *Pericles*, HoriPro Inc. this too was a visually stunning and compellingly direct production, though the designs here, albeit in a partly Japanese idiom, were by the English designer Paul Brown. An immense, lacquered box, at least twenty feet high, rotated in the centre of an almost dark stage to the sounds of distant surf as the audience (very heavily composed of Japanese expatriates) filed into the auditorium; on its front were

22 *Hamlet*, directed by Jonathan Kent, HoriPro Inc, at Sadler's Wells, 2003. Hamlet (Mansai Nomura) taunting Gertrude (Eisuke Sasai) and Claudius (Kohtaro Yoshida) during 'The Mousetrap' in 3.2.

nine symmetrically-placed panels bearing Renaissance motifs (a tree, an embryo, a nymph; a chalice, a skull, a pestle; weapons, a piazza, an astrolabe). Presently fire became visible high up on its top as it stopped rotating, and a brazier appeared, around which the sentries of 1.1 were trying to keep warm, awaiting a ghost who eventually crossed the stage far below them. Again, the costumes were Samurai-period Japanese but the stage technology was modern: for 1.2, stunningly, the box opened, and the nine figured panels turned out to have been concealing nine human-sized pigeonholes, in each of which was placed one of Claudius's court, with the king and queen in the central compartment. Only Mansai Nomura's feral, cat-like Hamlet paced among the shadows of the stage in front of it, occupying the same space where he would subsequently meet his father's white-haired, exhortatory ghost before a gilded Japanese pine tree. The box continued to produce this sort of surprise throughout the performance: Ophelia, for example, had a silvery compartment of her own filled with stylized dolls from which she emerged for her interview with Laertes; hauntingly, she was left to turn the huge revolve alone at her exit after the nunnery scene, ignored by her father as he resumed his discussion with Claudius about the violence they had witnessed. The players, dressed in more Westernized clothes at their arrival in Elsinore but in full kabuki dress for their show, brought their own box within-a-box and acted the Mousetrap around it in front of the court's, while Hamlet climbed eagerly up and down the front of the larger box to taunt his uncle and mother. In Act 4 the area in front of the box became a beach, on which the mad Ophelia gathered driftwood to distribute as supposed herbs; eerily, four blindfolded figures, transitional between this world and the next, would lower her body into its grave, and would at the chilling close of the performance lift Hamlet's body and deliver it into the waiting arms of his father's ghost. Can it only be because this production wasn't in English that it seemed, like Vesturport's *Romeo and Juliet*, so fresh, so unhampered by psychologizing, so comfortable with the play's own movements between naturalism and metaphor? And that the sympathetic, intense performances by males of Gertrude (Eisuke Sasai) and Ophelia (Shinobu Nakamura) were so uncluttered by the giggly campiness that afflicts most English stage transvestism? I do hope not. In any case, all *Hamlets* next year have a great deal to live up to. This one would have been worth a trip to Kyoto, never mind Sadler's Wells, and would alone have been enough to single out 2003 as a very good year for Shakespearian performance in England.

PROFESSIONAL SHAKESPEARE PRODUCTIONS IN THE BRITISH ISLES JANUARY–DECEMBER 2002

JAMES SHAW

Most of the productions listed are by professional companies, but some amateur productions are included. The information is taken from *Touchstone* (www.touchstone.bham.ac.uk), a Shakespeare website maintained by the Shakespeare Institute Library. *Touchstone* includes a monthly list of current and forthcoming UK Shakespeare productions from listings information. *The Traffic of the Stage* database, also available on *Touchstone*, archives UK Shakespeare production information since January 1993, correlating information from listings with reviews held in the Shakespeare Institute Library. The websites provided for theatre companies were accurate at the time of going to press.

ANTONY AND CLEOPATRA

Royal Shakespeare Company. The Royal Shakespeare Theatre, Stratford-upon-Avon, 11 April–13 July; Theatre Royal Haymarket, London, 28 August–21 September; Theatre Royal, Newcastle-upon-Tyne, 8–12 October.
www.rsc.org.uk
Director: Michael Attenborough
Antony: Stuart Wilson
Cleopatra: Sinead Cusack

AS YOU LIKE IT

New Shakespeare Company. Open Air Theatre, Regent's Park, London, 30 May–7 September.
www.openairtheatre.org
Director: Rachel Kavanaugh
Rosalind: Rebecca Johnson

Theatre Set-up. Touring production, June-August. www.ts-u.co.uk
Director: Wendy Macphee
Open-air Shakespeare company.

Illyria Company. Open-air touring production, summer 2002. www.illyria.uk.com
Director: Oliver Gray
Open-air touring Shakespeare company with a cast of five actors.

Natural Perspectives Theatre Company. Royal Observatory, London, 28 July–11 August.
Director: Adam Megiddo

THE COMEDY OF ERRORS

Adaptation

The Bomb-itty of Errors

Edinburgh Fringe Festival, August.
Rap version with cast of four and DJ.

CORIOLANUS

Southend Shakespeare Company. Palace Theatre, Westcliff, 23–7 April.
www.southendshakespeare.co.uk
Amateur company.

Royal Shakespeare Company. The Swan Theatre, 14 November 2002–25 January 2003.
www.rsc.org.uk

Director: David Farr
Coriolanus: Greg Hicks

EDWARD III

Royal Shakespeare Company. The Swan Theatre, Stratford-upon-Avon, 23 April–14 September. www.rsc.org.uk
Director: Edward Hall

HAMLET

Royal Shakespeare Company. Barbican, London, 6 December 2001–2 April 2002. Transfer from the Royal Shakespeare Theatre. www.rsc.org.uk
Director: Steven Pimlott
Designer: Alison Chitty
Hamlet: Sam West

British Touring Shakespeare Productions. Westminster Theatre, London, 10 December 2001–2 February 2002.
www.britishtouringshakespeare.co.uk
Director: Miles Gregory
Hamlet: Tom Mallaburn

West Yorkshire Playhouse, 25 October–30 November. www.wyplayhouse.com
Director: Ian Brown
Hamlet: Christopher Eccleston

Adaptations

Ophelia

SPID Theatre Company. Arcola Theatre, London, 12–16 February; Candid Gallery, London, 20–7 February.
Playwright/Director: Helena Thompson
A radical reworking viewing the play from Ophelia's perspective.

Rosencrantz and Guildenstern are Dead

Clwyd Theatr Cymru, Mold, 7 February–2 March and tour. www.clwyd-theatr-cymru.co.uk
Playwright: Tom Stoppard
Director: Terry Hands

Quarry Theatre, West Yorkshire Playhouse. 19 September–19 October.
www.wyplayhouse.com
Playwright: Tom Stoppard
Director: Gemma Bodinetz

Who Goes There?

Dreamthinkspeak. Battersea Arts Centre, London. 12 June–7 July. www.dreamthinkspeak.com
Directors: Tristan Sharps and Henk Schut
Promenade production incorporating film and video techniques.

Humble Boy

Royal National Theatre Company. Gielgud Theatre, June. Transfer from Cottesloe Theatre.
www.nationaltheatre.org.uk
Playwright: Charlotte Jones
Director: John Caird
A reworking of *Hamlet* themes, set in Cambridge University.

Gertrude–The Cry

The Wrestling School. Riverside, London, 23 October–2 November and tour.
Playwright: Howard Barker
Director: Howard Barker
A radical adaptation focusing on Gertrude. Barker's programme notes describe her as 'passionate, defiant and more authentically tragic than the adolescent prince'.

HENRY IV PART 1

Bristol Old Vic, 14 October–30 November.
bristol-old-vic.co.uk
Director: Gareth Machlin
Falstaff: Gerard Murphy
Prince Hal: Jamie Barber

HENRY IV PART 2

Bristol Old Vic, 11–30 November.
bristol-old-vic.co.uk
Director: Gareth Machlin

Falstaff: Gerard Murphy
Prince Hal: Jamie Barber

HENRY V

Maddermarket Theatre. The Maddermarket, Norwich, 21 February–2 March. www.maddermarket.co.uk
Director: John Dane
Henry V: Tom Mallaburn

British Touring Shakespeare Productions. The Shaw Theatre, London, 21 April–4 June. www.britishtouringshakespeare.co.uk
Director: Miles Gregory

Adaptation

The Battle of Agincourt

Generator Theatre Company. The Dream Factory, Warwick, 27 February–2 March and tour until July.
Adaptor: John Barton
Director: Stuart McGill

HENRY VI PARTS 1–3

Adaptation

Rose Rage (Parts 1 and 2)

Propeller Productions. Haymarket, Theatre Royal, London, 16 June–21 July. Revival of 2001 Watermill Theatre production.
Director: Edward Hall
Adaptors: Edward Hall and Roger Warren
Adaptation of the Henry VI trilogy, with all-male cast. Script published by Oberon Books, London, 2001.

HENRY VIII

Adaptation

Suzanna Rosenthal Ltd in Association with Steam Industry. Bridewell Theatre, London, 5–29 June. http://freespace.virgin.net/s.rosenthal
Adaptor and Director: Phil Willmott
Henry VIII: Simon Merrells
An adaptation that retained the text but included liberal cuts, reallocated speeches and transposed scenes.

JULIUS CAESAR

Royal Shakespeare Company. Barbican, London, 24 January–6 April. Transfer from Royal Shakespeare Theatre. www.rsc.org.uk
Director: Edward Hall
Julius Caesar: Ian Hogg
Mark Antony: Tom Mannion
Brutus: Greg Hicks
Played without an interval.

Adaptation

SeZaR

Oxford Playhouse in association with Arcadia Productions from South Africa, UK tour September–November.
Adaptor: Yael Farber
SeZaR: Hope Sprinter Sekgobela
Set in the fictional African state of Azania.

KING JOHN

Royal Shakespeare Company. The Pit, London, 6 December 2001–19 February 2002. Transfer from Swan Theatre. www.rsc.org.uk
Director: Gregory Doran
Designer: Stephen Brimson Lewis
King John: Guy Henry
Bastard: Jo Stone-Fewings

KING LEAR

Almeida Theatre at King's Cross, London, 31 January–30 March. www.almeida.co.uk
Director: Jonathan Kent
King Lear: Oliver Ford Davies

English Touring Theatre. September–December tour. www.englishtouringtheatre.co.uk
Director: Stephen Unwin
King Lear: Timothy West

Royal Shakespeare Company Academy 2002. The Swan Theatre, 23 September–12 October with transfers to Newcastle Haymarket Playhouse and Young Vic. www.rsc.org.uk
Director: Declan Donnellan

Adaptations

Lear

SPID Company. Jacksons Lane Theatre, London, 19–22 June and transfer to Camden People's Theatre, 2–24 July.
Author and Director: Helena Thompson
Liberal adaptation involving a power struggle in a tabloid newspaper office.

Lear

Glasgow Repertory Company. Glimorehill G12, Glasgow, 21–30 November. www.glasgowrep.org
Director: Scot Palmer
Two-hour adaptation with five roles; Lear, three daughters and Perilus, an attendant lord.

Opera

Vision of Lear

Royal Opera House, London, 31 January–2 February.
Composer: Toshio Hosokawa
Director: Harry Ross
King Lear: Nicholas Garrett
An office worker experiences a nervous breakdown in a corporation undergoing restructuring.

MACBETH

Southwark Playhouse, London, 25 January–8 February.
Director: Thomas Hestcott

Creation Theatre Company. BMW Group Plant, Oxford, 31 January–23 March.
www.creationtheatre.co.uk
Director: Zoe Seaton

The Marlowe Dramatic Society. Cambridge Arts Theatre, 26 February–2 March.
Director: Ben Naylor

Clwyd Theatr Cymru. Theatr Clwyd, Mold, 7–30 March. www.clywd-theatr-cymru.co.uk
Director: Terry Hands

Northern Broadsides. Touring production, March–June. www.northern-broadsides.co.uk
Director: Barrie Rutter
Macbeth: Andrew Vincent
Lady Macbeth: Helen Sheals

Arcola Theatre, London, 2 May–1 June.
www.arcolatheatre.com
Directors: Jack Shepherd and Mehmet Ergen
Macbeth: Jack Shepherd
Lady Macbeth: Amanda Boxer

Richmond Theatre, Richmond, 28 October–2 November, transfer to Albery Theatre, November.
Director: Edward Hall
Macbeth: Sean Bean
Lady Macbeth: Samantha Bond

Adaptation

RO Theatre (Rotterdam) at Royal Lyceum, Edinburgh, 20–2 August.
Adaptor and Director: Alize Zandwijk
In Dutch with English subtitles. Performed as part of the Edinburgh International Festival.

Opera

Macbeth

Royal Opera Company. Royal Opera House, London, 13 June–5 July.
Director: Phyllida Lloyd
Opera by Verdi.

MEASURE FOR MEASURE

Dundee Rep Resident Company. Dundee Repertory Theatre, Dundee, 13–30 March.
www.dundeerep.co.uk
Directors: Hamish Glen and Stephen Stenning

Royal National Theatre Education Department & London Bubble Theatre Company. Cottesloe Theatre, London, 8–10 April and national tour. www.nationaltheatre.org.uk
Director: Jonathan Petherbridge

Adaptation

Measure for Measure Malaya

Suzanna Rosenthal Ltd in association with Steam Industry. Riverside Studios, 4–30 November. http://freespace.virgin.net/s.rosenthal
Adaptor and Director: Phil Willmott

THE MERCHANT OF VENICE

Royal Shakespeare Company. The Swan Theatre, Stratford-upon-Avon, 28 November 2001–19 January 2002 and national tour until May. www.rsc.org.uk
Director: Loveday Ingram

THE MERRY WIVES OF WINDSOR

Ludlow Festival. Ludlow Castle, 24 June–6 July. www.ludlowfestival.co.uk
Director: Michael Bogdanov
Falstaff: Philip Madoc

The Royal Shakespeare Company. The Swan Theatre, Stratford-upon-Avon, 23 October 2002–25 January 2003. www.rsc.org.uk
Director: Rachel Kavanaugh
Falstaff: Richard Cordery

Opera

Falstaff

London Opera Players. Swan Theatre, Stratford-upon-Avon, 29–30 March. www.operaplayers.co.uk
Director: John Ramster
Opera by Verdi.

A MIDSUMMER NIGHT'S DREAM

Royal Shakespeare Company. Royal Shakespeare Theatre, 1 February–23 March and national tour until June.
www.rsc.org.uk
Director: Richard Jones

Brunton Theatre Company. Brunton Theatre, Musselburgh, 1–16 February.
www.bruntontheatre.com
Director: David Mark Thomson

Royal Exchange Theatre Company. Royal Exchange Theatre, Manchester, 6 March–20 April. www.royalexchange.co.uk
Director: Lucy Bailey

Shakespeare's Globe Theatre, London, 26 May–27 September. www.shakespeares-globe.org
Director: Mike Alfreds
Hippolyta/Titania: Geraldine Alexander
Theseus/Oberon: Paul Higgins

Chapterhouse Theatre Company. National tour June–August. www.chapterhouse.org
Directed by Karen Crow

Opera

The Fairy Queen

English National Opera. Coliseum, London, 12 June–6 July 2002. www.eno.org
Directors: David Pountney and Quinney Sacks
Opera by Henry Purcell.

MUCH ADO ABOUT NOTHING

Royal Shakespeare Company. The Royal Shakespeare Theatre, Stratford-upon-Avon, 30 April–13 July; transfer to Theatre Royal Haymarket, 1–22 August. www.rsc.org.uk
Director: Gregory Doran
Benedick: Nicholas Le Prevost
Beatrice: Harriet Walter

OTHELLO

Theatre Unlimited. UK tour 30 January–30 March.
Director: Christopher Geelan
Othello: Nicholas Monu
Iago: Rupert Wickham

Traffic of the Stage. Pentameters, London, 22 February–17 March.
Director: Judy Bowker

Southwark Playhouse, London, 11 June–6 July.
www.southwarkplayhouse.co.uk
Director: Spencer Hinton
Othello: Leo Wringer
Iago: Christopher Hunter

Royal Exchange, Manchester, 16 September–2 November. www.royalexchange.co.uk
Director: Braham Murray
Othello: Paterson Joseph
Iago: Andy Serkis

Adaptation

Crazyblackmuthafuckin'self

Theatre Upstairs, Royal Court, London, 3–21 December.
Playwright: Deobia Oparei
Director: Josie Rourke
The lead character rehearses as Othello in a street-wise production called *Y'Othello*.

Opera

Otello

Royal Opera Company. Royal Opera House, London, 28 June–12 July.
www.royaloperahouse.org
Opera by Verdi.

PERICLES

Royal Shakespeare Company. The Roundhouse, London, 28 June–13 July; transferred to Royal Shakespeare Theatre, Stratford-upon-Avon 12 August–2 November. www.rsc.org.uk
Director: Adrian Noble
Pericles: Ray Fearon

London Bubble. 25 July–14 August tour of London venues. www.londonbubble.org.uk
Director: Jonathan Petherbridge
Pericles: Simon Startin
Open-air promenade production.

RICHARD III

Sheffield Crucible Theatre Company. Crucible Theatre, Sheffield, 13 March–6 April.
www.sheffieldtheatres.co.uk
Director: Michael Grandage
Richard III: Kenneth Branagh

Heartbreak Productions. UK tour 18 June–18 August. www.heartbreakproductions.co.uk
Director: Peter Mimmack

Rapture Theatre. Cottier Theatre, Glasgow, 23–30 November.
Director: Michael Emans
Richard III: Michael Tibbetts

ROMEO AND JULIET

Logos Theatre Company. Wimbledon Theatre, London, 16 April–4 May.

New Shakespeare Company. Open Air Theatre, Regent's Park, London, 5 June–5 September.
www.openairtheatre.org
Director: Dominic Hill
Romeo: Alan Westaway
Juliet: Laura Main

Heartbreak Productions. UK tour 8 June–18 August. www.heartbreakproductions.co.uk
Director: Marcus Fernando

British Touring Shakespeare Productions. The Shaw Theatre, London, 20 April–2 June.
www.britishtouringshakespeare.co.uk

Director: Miles Gregory
Romeo: Mike Rogers
Juliet: Lucia Latimer
Nurse: Tobias Beer

Cutting Edge Theatre Company. Production touring Scotland, 11 July–10 August.

Northcott Theatre Company. Rougemont Gardens, Exeter, 19 July–24 August.
www.northcott-theatre.co.uk
Director: Ben Crocker
Romeo: Daniel Hawksford
Juliet: Eva Bartley

Chichester Festival Theatre, Chichester, 21 August–5 October. www.cft.org.uk
Director: Indhu Rubasingham
Romeo: Lex Shrapnel
Juliet: Emily Blunt

Mercury Theatre, Colchester, 30 September–19 October. www.mercurytheatre.co.uk
Director: David Hunt

Adaptations

Romeo and Juliet: The Musical

Piccadilly Theatre, London, November.
Music: Gerard Presgurvic
Lyrics: Don Black

Forbidden Love–Romeo and Juliet

Blue Mountain Theatre Company. The Broadway Theatre, Catford Bridge, London, 26 April–5 May.
www.bluemountaintheatre.com

Rome and Jewels

Rennie Harris Puremovement. Peacock Theatre, London, 28 May–22 June.
www.puremovement.net
Director and Choreographer: Rennie Harris
A hip-hop dance adaptation.

Ballet

Royal Ballet. Royal Opera House, London, 26 April–23 May.
Ballet by Prokofiev
Choreographer: Kenneth MacMillan.

THE TAMING OF THE SHREW

Nottingham Playhouse Company. Nottingham Playhouse, Nottingham, 8 February–2 March.
www.nottinghamplayhouse.co.uk
Director: David Farr
Petruccio: David Partridge
Kate: Phillipa Peak

Lincoln Shakespeare Company. Lincoln Medieval Bishop's Palace, Lincoln, 23 July–4 August.
www.lincolnshakespeare.co.uk

Salisbury Playhouse, Salisbury, 5–28 September.
www.salisburyplayhouse.com
Director: Douglas Rintoul
Petruccio: Jay Villiers
Katherine: Katia Caballero

Royal Lyceum, Edinburgh, 26 October–16 November.
Director: Tony Cownie
Petruccio: Jimmy Chisholm
Katherine: Meg Fraser

Adaptation

Ballet

The Independent Ballet Wales. UK tour 20 April–17 June.
www.welshballet.co.uk
Director: Darius James

THE TEMPEST

Royal Shakespeare Company. The Roundhouse, London, 19 April–22 June; transferred to Stratford-upon-Avon.
www.rsc.org.uk
Director: Michael Boyd
Prospero: Malcolm Storry

Derby Shakespeare Theatre Company. Minack Theatre, Penzance, 12–16 August.

Sheffield Crucible Theatre Company. Crucible Theatre, Sheffield, 2–9 October.
Director: Michael Grandage
Prospero: Derek Jacobi

Plymouth Theatre Royal and Thelma Holt. October tour.
Director: Patrick Mason
Prospero: Richard Briers

Adaptation

Full of Noises

Citizen's Theatre, Glasgow, 11–14 September.
www.citz.co.uk
Adaptor: Peter Arnott
Directors: Guy Hollands and Neil Packham

TITUS ANDRONICUS

Adaptation

The Kaos Titus Andronicus

Kaos Theatre, UK tour, 1 February–5 March.
www.kaostheatre.com
Director: Xavier Leret
Titus: Lee Beagley

TWELFTH NIGHT

Royal Shakespeare Company. Barbican, 18 December 2001–9 March.
www.rsc.org.uk
Director: Lindsay Posner
Malvolio: Guy Henry

British Touring Shakespeare Company. Westminster Theatre, London, 14 January–2 February. www.britishtouringshakespeare.co.uk
Director: Miles Lattimer-Gregory

New Globe Theatre Company. Middle Temple Hall, London, 25 January–10 February.
www.shakespeares-globe.org
Director: Mark Rylance

Shakespeare at the Tobacco Factory. The Tobacco Factory, Bristol, 21 March–27 April.
www.shakespeareatthetobaccofactory.co.uk
Director: Andrew Hilton

Shakespeare's Globe, London, 11 May–28 September. www.shakespeares-globe.org
Director: Tim Carroll
All-male production.

Chapterhouse Theatre Company. UK tour 14 June–31 August. www.chapterhouse.org
Director: Karen Crow

Donmar Warehouse, London, 22 October–30 November. www.donmar-warehouse.com
Director: Sam Mendes
Malvolio: Simon Russell Beale

Adaptations

Malvolio's Revenge

Works Well Productions. Touring production, October.
www.workswellproductions.co.uk
Playwright: Jonathan Shelley
Director: Simon Neal

Twelfth Night

Manweb Studio, Gateway Theatre, Chester, December.
Director: Russ Tunney
75-minute version.

THE WINTER'S TALE

Shakespeare at the Tobacco Factory. The Tobacco Factory, Bristol. 7 February–16 March.
www.shakespeareatthetobaccofactory.co.uk
Director: Andrew Hilton
Hermione/Perdita: Lisa Kay
Leontes: John Mackay

Royal Shakespeare Company. The Roundhouse, London, 28 March–19 June; transferred to the

Royal Shakespeare Theatre, 31 July–2 November.
www.rsc.org.uk
Director: Matthew Warchus
Leontes: Douglas Hodge
Hermione: Anastasia Hille

MISCELLANEOUS

Elizabeth Rex

Birmingham Repertory Theatre, Birmingham, 3–18 May.
www.birmingham-rep.co.uk
Playwright: Timothy Findley
Elizabeth: Stephanie Beacham

A play about Elizabeth I, on the eve of the execution of Essex. Includes Shakespeare as a character.

The Hollow Crown

Royal Shakespeare Company. Royal Shakespeare Theatre, Stratford-upon-Avon, 16–20 July and UK tour. www.rsc.org.uk
Devised by John Barton.

The Loves of Shakespeare's Women

UK tour, 31 January–2 May.
Susannah York's one-woman show.

THE YEAR'S CONTRIBUTIONS TO SHAKESPEARE STUDIES

1. CRITICAL STUDIES

reviewed by Ruth Morse

Last year I began with the crisis in publishing, and the difficulties young scholars now face with first monographs. Nothing suggests that the situation has eased; rather, the monograph itself is threatened. The consequences can be severe in academic cultures which require the production – I am choosing my words with care – of extended, continuous arguments between hard covers, not once but repeatedly. As publishers change their lists in the direction of 'Companions' and 'Guides', 'Topics' and 'Accents', and other collections targeted at student markets, good new work appears increasingly in formats once disdained by committees reviewing dossiers for appointment, tenure, promotion, merit awards, all the armature of careers. Increasingly, the wider publication in journals and reviews becomes necessary, and no longer simply to try out ideas which will be discussed and modified later, or which may not contribute to a larger argument. The Net offers potential alternatives, but resistance to Net publication is no doubt in part fuelled by the wild freedom which has given a disreputable glow to much that happens there. The uploading of journals is to be welcomed – for much of the wide world of scholarship, it revolutionizes access, although the prices of subscriptions remain a problem. A free site, such as Shaksper (www.shaksper.net, edited by Professor Hardy M. Cook), has the advantages and disadvantages typical of all discussion groups: above all, for better or for worse, quantity. The phenomenon is hardly restricted to the Net: the proliferation of journals, and of the ephemeral appearance of conference papers, raises questions about just how much the world of scholarship can sustain. We all depend increasingly on judgements recorded in annotated surveys and bibliographies, none of which can ever be comprehensive, all of which are soon out of date (some nonetheless listed below) – which brings us back to the need for publishers to send out copies of their books, or, failing that, for authors to do so. Last year I worried about subsidy presses, and increasing pressure to subsidize covertly; this year I was less aware of the problem. In this year's chapter, as in last year's, I observe special interest groups, schools and styles of critical orientation, that threaten to create intellectual enclaves which discourage us from reading around, let alone buying or subscribing to a physical object. I once again notice currently popular subjects, from history and religion, to rhetoric, the resurgence of character analysis, the arts of language, film and other adaptations, with, this year, increased attention to the poems, to literary and popular romances, and a marked attraction to philosophical terms and positions. There was work directly focused on tragedy, the problem of evil, and the place of gender within systematic cruelty. And there

Note: full details of titles and publishers will be found in the bibliography which follows this essay.

is always *The Merchant of Venice*. However, I must signal from the outset a worrying amount of dicey over-interpretation in which resemblance becomes analogy and analogy a demonstration. One possibility is that we are in a period of methodological exhaustion, leading to over-reading, as people seek something new to sell, but that surely is contradicted by the excitement of new, or renewed, attention to, for example, religion. Just as I worried last year that disagreements about 'history' threaten to become the new divide about 'theory', so this year it strikes me that a certain number of questionable assertions are perhaps being washed in on the wave. Over-interpretations and strong readings have their place; but there are certain constraints which invite respect, otherwise the salmon in Monmouth and Macedon threaten to perfume our arguments.

Let me begin with a big book by an established scholar, Brian Vickers, which he himself characterizes as 'unnecessary' and overlong. Would that it were so. This is a work more significant than its focus on author-attribution might suggest. As it happens, Gilles Monsarrat had simultaneously, elegantly, refuted the case for Shakespeare's authorship of 'A Funeral Elegye' and established Ford as the likeliest candidate, as computer tests run by Hugh Craig (whose essay on grammatical modality I praised last year) have statistically confirmed. The first word in Vickers's subtitle, 'evidence', is relevant to everything we argue, and the combination of skills Vickers brings to bear on the problems amount to a master class in statistical analysis, in rhetoric and style, demonstrating the 'What is *pourquoi*? Do or not do?' which we ignore at our peril. Vickers is particularly good on the importance of tests by negative evidence, not just the use of statistics, and his book is by no means unnecessary, if nonetheless a Vickeriorum of exasperated instruction, which could be used to great effect in many an advanced class to introduce a large number of ideas, skills, and disciplines. The implications of his demonstrations ought to be felt elsewhere. Anyone who prefers the short course should read Gilles Monsarrat's concise article in *RES*, which compresses a lifetime's scholarship into a brief proof. He bases his analysis of the parallel passages on a textual corpus appropriate to the period of composition and not arbitrarily inflated (i.e. by using all of Shakespeare); he understands the religious orientation of elegy and banishes the idea of God modelling his son on the deceased William Peter. He is sensible about plausibility; biography; diffusion; ghost-writing. No one should now argue that the 'Funeral Elegie' is by anyone but John Ford. The techniques of statistical analysis will reappear below in the section on the poems, with MacDonald P. Jackson's equally exemplary demonstration of the 'rare words' tests. Exemplary, too, this year, is Lukas Erne's account, based on broad reading and careful analysis, and with the evidence clearly presented in tabular form, of the ways playwrights thought of their scripts as books for readers. It is another positive example of what constitutes a good argument. And no one should now fear to assume that Shakespeare may have anticipated readers as well as spectators. The analytical tables and impressive statistical grip of these four contributions are exceptional in any year.

The weak arguments are too often the result of a passion to prove something, such as Shakespeare's religion, and it is a gloomy prospect to think that sectarian strife may be re-emerging under the guise of ostensibly new historical analysis. John Klause's insistence on Southwell remembered in *King John* has more than a whiff of burnt Bacon about it. His specious argument for influence depends upon assumed dating, on difficult and iffy circumstantial non-evidence of Shakespeare's relationship to Southwell, but, above all, on *loci communi* of expression which both authors no doubt shared with traditional poetry. These questions, including authorship, were controversial in medieval studies over the long period in which the corpus of alliterative poetry was submitted to similar analyses; it is a pity that the impermeable borders of contemporary study now require much of that work to be learned again. Given a large enough corpus, you can find abundance of likenesses, as Vickers points out. That does not make likeness significant. The weasel in these meretricious 'proofs' is the recourse to rhetorical questions, which too often transmogrify into assumptions. 'Could it be mere coincidence, then, that Lewis's lines, so much like Southwell's and perhaps written in 1595, are succeeded by mention of the drawing, hanging, and quartering that had killed the "traitor" priest himself near the beginning of that same year?' There is often a double problem of context and cloth-ears about these assertions. Given, here, that the context is Lewis's clichéd reaction to the beauty of his newly presented fiancée, there is a degree of bad taste in addition to the dodgy critical claims which injure the argument. Nor are the clichés in would-be parallel passages any more convincing, when they are entirely decontextualized, and truncated to make Southwell's ostensible source passages seem more of a match. In any study of influence one has to look outside the two juxtaposed texts: could two authors have derived their similarities (if similarities they be) from other texts (e.g. the evolving discourses of courtly love)? Do enough other writers of the period use the material enough to make it commonplace? The answer in both cases is 'yes'. There are further tell-tale weaknesses in bad arguments, first, when vague gestures substitute for precision: what exactly might 'verbal stimulants' mean, or, for that matter, 'mere coincidence'? Or, when authors footnote articles written largely by themselves, as if the oft-expressed were ne'er so well thought. In this case, what is most implausible is the claim that Shakespeare's mind, suffused with Southwell's writings, took them to heart for a play whose politics so oppose questions of a universal church under the Roman pontiff.

But this is not the worst, as long as we can say 'this is the worst', and not all Richard Wilson's undeniable brilliance and copious reading can make his British Academy lecture convincing. As one would expect from the pope of papistry, the claims for Shakespeare the militant Catholic are woven into the texture of a lecture which begins with gazes into the distance. The argument is a similar tissue of assertions then taken as true, where point after point is hypothetical, circumstantial, exaggerated and hyberbolically sparkling – but dubious, time and again. Quotations out of context abound, and the display of erudition itself attempts to bludgeon the reader into submission. Wilson has argued before that Shakespeare's works are full of Catholic allegory, and now he insists that we know 'where Shakespeare was coming from', that he 'must have dismayed his [Catholic] controllers when he did not sail for France'. It is a long time since scholars have discovered such allegory and autobiography encrypted in the plays and poems. The passive voice abounds in Wilson's work, and paragraph-long sentences heap up lists which disappear into syntactical sands, confusing the authority and agency of his claims. Cordelia's 'nothing' as church papist? *Love's Labour's Lost* as resistance to sectarian extremes? Titus's Virgo as Elizabeth in a shared Puritan meditation? Even the samphire gatherer perceived from the distance of Dover Cliff turns out to be a reference to the pope, because Douer=Douai and samphire=St Peter's herb.

Paul Dean has familiar problems in his attempt to relate *Twelfth Night* to the Trinity. His argument is that the play's interest in threes is somehow related to both neo-Platonism and the Trinity, but it might just as well be a logical solution, where the strength of three examples unified as one is a rhetorical move. The so-called liturgical echoes are far-fetched (e.g. twin and twain hardly make one think immediately of the New Testament), as is the desire to identify 'we three' with the angels who come to Abraham. As often elsewhere this year, the over-interpretation arises from thin collocation – there's a degree of claimed resemblance which depends upon words and phrases which belong to commonplace repertoires; or repertoires characteristic of an author outside special circumstances; or too far apart; or numerous but not significant, for example, the contrast between common words or *loci communi* and nonce-words which reappear, or hard words, or unusual lexical appearances. One has to allow for characterisation's weighting of repeated words, for characters at particular points speaking to specific interlocutors, and to consider how Shakespeare's language changed over his lifetime. There is often too little sensitivity to the dramatic moment, and to what literary criticism is supposed to teach us to control. Nor is Aaron Landau more convincing as he over-interprets what he calls

Hamlet's 'confession' to claim both that Hamlet moves from Catholic to Protestant, and that the play is contradictory; ditto Horatio. 'Confessions', in the sectarian sense, were not monoliths; they were evolving throughout the sixteenth and seventeenth centuries. Landau wants the play to be a consideration of religion, and claims that other critics have not taken its 'historico-religious context of the Reformation' seriously enough; the multiple 'Reformation*s*' weren't monoliths, either.

Not religion alone, but also politics, can lead to strained analogies. Andrew Hadfield seems to be arguing that in *The Rape of Lucrece* and *Titus Andronicus* we can see Shakespeare dabbling with republican ideas, like his patron, because they were both fed up with the ageing queen – so that we find throughout the 1590s coded proposals of the possibility of alternative government for England, not just for Rome. '[*Lucrece*] would appear to foreshadow the aims of the Essex rebellion five years later, obliquely enough to escape official censure and any possibility of censorship, but clearly enough to signal this message to the initiated'. Frankie Rubenstein combines 'Religion and Politics in *King Lear*'. There are certainly dangers inherent in too much professional agreement, especially in our tendency to cite the same authors or texts, often as a flag of affiliation. Nonetheless, some engagement with the current conversations is a good antidote towards over-reading. If you begin by thinking of the Britain of *King Lear* as a 'mismanaged kingdom in which immorality was rampant, betrayal omnipresent, and civil strife among princes heightened expectation of foreign intervention' and that this is (also) Shakespeare's world, then you might well want to argue for the play as a grotesquely parodied morality drama with a divine dénouement. If you are using Clark and Wright's *Complete Works*; and the recent criticism you cite is twelve years old, and contradicted by 'an unpublished note'; and your argument turns on 'Shakespeare may also have been reflecting', then there is going to be trouble.

Now, take *Macbeth*, please, as the stand-up comedians cited elsewhere in this year's *Survey* might say. Jane Wilkinson analyses 'the' historical and nationalist issue ('Anglo-Scottish DissemiNations') in the light of Homi Babha's post-colonial work. '*Macbeth* restages recent historiographical reconstructions of imaginings and questionings of the collective self in eleventh-century Scotland, construing them in a future preterite temporality as a pre-text to contemporary issues.' Recent? Eleventh-century? Collective self? Once more there is over-interpretation: of Malcolm's failure to recognize Ross (evidently 'loss of community'). But 'community' is not defined, and the essay is full of signifying juxtapositions and the use of the verb 'to be' rather than closely argued from the text; Wilkinson works from anachronisms of nationhood imagined in what Shakespeare could not have conceptualized as a medieval period, because that kind of periodization was not yet available.

'Influence' hunting, even when not religious, tended to over-read likeness, such as Robert Leach's attempt to argue for *As You Like It* as a 'Robin Hood' play by noticing certain putative resemblances. But once again there is loose collocation, and no engagement with what is not there (e.g. no outlaw band loyal to an absent monarch and committing crimes, no bower, no Maid Marian, no Friar, no Lincoln-green uniform), or even an acknowledgement of different Robins in various traditions. Nor does Leach consider just how many plays have country dancing or sports: *The Winter's Tale*, for instance. But influence studies also offered intriguing possibilities, such as Pamela Royston Macfie's detailed consideration of a passing moment in *Othello*, where she finds possible memories of Ovid's *Tristia* (rather than Seneca), as well as Marlowe's *Hero and Leander* particularly interesting in the association of Othello's violent nature and Marlowe's association of love and blood in the Hellespont. Influence also comprehends imaginary visuals, in a study of the descent (literary) of the 'yellow leaf', which Robert E. Jungman traces back to Virgil, *Aeneid* VI. I'm not sure that tracing ancestry also demonstrates unbroken lines of influence, especially in climates with similar autumns, but it is worth remembering how often and how likely it is that what we see may be mediated by what we read.

Then there is sodomitical special pleading. Richard Halpern plays fast and loose with a series of undefined and anachronistic assertions, including a claim that medieval theologians considered the idea that same-sex acts are the counterpart of an unrepresentable God. (He eventually mentions one book.) He focuses on a very few sonnets to look at a tension of 'use' in order to discuss an unspeakable sublime which denies the attraction to homoerotic sex. Much hangs on 'glass' as pure and crystalline, for the 'perfume bottle' of Sonnet 5 – but neither in the middle ages nor in Shakespeare's day was glass necessarily clear, and he pulls his interpretations out of balance. No single misunderstanding would make that much difference, and he is aware of the anachronism of his ideas, but he, too, takes things out of context and without weighing the sonnets as a whole. I think it worth mentioning that here, as elsewhere, many of the supposed 'same-sex' generalizations mean 'men'.

By contrast, Paul Hammond's collection of essays on the representations of (male) homosexuality from Shakespeare to Rochester is an old-fashioned book which applies practical-critical skills to homoerotic texts. That it should now be acceptable simply to write openly about once-closed subjects is to be welcomed. However, many of the readings here, too, strike me as over-interpreted, or interpreted as if homosexuality were unique in its needs for rhetorically covering physical sexual expression. There isn't really a lot of 'figuring'; instead, there is a lot of decoding of coded desire. There is some unclarity in the problem of whether love is love which alteration finds, or if such love should be different from other loves because it is between men; or whether desire was more rhetorically euphemized when its object was of the same sex. Why should we expect the language of love to be different if the love is between men, when it isn't different for parents and children, souls and god, women and men, and perhaps even women and women? The idea that *paradiastole* is especially characteristic of this love poetry doesn't stand up, since metaphors of the unsaid appear whenever the poet-lover seeks what it is immoral to achieve, that is, illicit sexual intercourse. Hammond has some difficulties with the question of risk in friendship's varieties, and at times seems to evoke a nostalgically-imagined period of sexual tolerance under Elizabeth, followed by a rather uninflected seventeenth century – surprising from a scholar whose work in that period is usually so very precise. In his own desire to make homosexuality special, he removes poetic expression from its many contexts: he ignores the concatenation of political criticism of sexual deviance from Martial to the middle ages, he seems unconcerned with the language of prayer and the desire for possession by god (gender unspecified), where similar imagery plays dangerously upon an erotic agape. Hammond is a prolific writer, and the speed with which this book has been written is betrayed by the repetition of sentences which, in the cutting and pasting, were not cancelled. For those interested in secondary sexual characteristics, Will Fisher's article on beards as a marker of adult maleness, complicated by the stage 'false beard', will appeal. Shakespeare has only a walk-on part here, but the use of the beard beyond its place as a prop is a subject which deserves attention. (And an article on 'hair' in Shakespeare by Jonathan Gil Harris suggests an intriguing interest in excrescences.)

'Use' has clearly become something of a key concept. There is an exemplary discussion in Charles Edelman's 'Which is the Jew that Shakespeare knew?' in *Shakespeare Survey 52* (Cambridge, 1999), pp. 99–106. At greater length, this year, David Hawkes has difficulties with his definitions because he begins from *mis*use, that is, the pathological before the normal. Interpretation depends upon definition: right use is different from wrong use is different from financial misuse of interest: paradoxically, usury is the *opposite* of sodomy, because it makes money breed unnaturally, but sodomy approaches usury because it is associated with the sterile. So, of course, is stubborn chastity, but one seldom hears about that refusal to put oneself into circulation through progeny – the right 'use' of the body. He has the problem, often associated with the abuse of new historicist approaches, of quoting chronologically distant texts as if there had been no change. As Edelman has shown, right financial 'use' could indeed include reasonable interest – so it's wrong to criticize the right use of sexuality to breed children. There's always a problem in these arguments with the metaphoric fecundity and immortality of art. In addition, as with so much of the vocabulary of exchange/value, this is a period in which there was monetarizing of imagery – but the imagery is not in and of itself monetarized. As Richard Halpern acknowledges in his chapter on the Sonnets, this was noticed by Eliot in his Clark lectures. We are always in danger of over-interpretation if we reach back to recognize an exact moment when 'capital', say, became money, or 'exchange' was equated with it. Halpern identifies the youth of the first seventeen sonnets with 'the beloved friend', and assumes that the sonnets are contemporaneous with *The Merchant of Venice*, so his association of 'misuse', like Hawkes's, leads him to look for error, rather than to play even more with the dangers of 'right use'. I shall return to use, coins, and the 'capital' questions below.

It is rare for a scholar to vaunt his ambition for fame and money. Although Bruce Boehrer acknowledges a number of books which engage with animals, he largely prefers to take his own way. His 'readings', in *Shakespeare among the Animals*, are neither new nor startling (though often eccentric), and he moves so breathlessly through possible associations that there is no time to consider what he does quote. He erects three 'inevitably reductive', admittedly contradictory, categories of 'imagining animals', but then reifies them as if they functioned unproblematically. There are many unspecified references to putative early-modern practices (exactly who lynched Jews upside down between dogs as a crucifixion parody? when and where and how often? with what reactions from bystanders, readers or authorities?) which he juxtaposes to plays as though that were a demonstration: this is a book full of 'arguably's', marred by vague gestures towards widely separated countries, languages and chronologies. The fundamental problem is that this is not a book about plays, but a would-be introduction to thinking with animals, which is better done elsewhere. As a kind of bottoming out, let me instance Lisa Hopkins's argument that *Lear* is about the Leicesters. The etymology of Leicester is Leir's castle, as Leir was supposed to have founded it. This leads to a link between the play and Robert Dudley, Earl of Leicester. Dudley was loved by two sisters, and there were rumours of poisoning, which Hopkins labels 'parallel plots'. Leicester had the right to maintain 100 knights; used 'bear' as his crest – and there is bear imagery in Lear; the Leicester *impresa* resembled Edmund's 'I grow, I prosper'; the misogynistic libels of Leicester after his death parallel Lear's misogyny; Gloucester's fall parallels Amy Robsart's (Leicester's inconvenient wife whose death was potentially so opportune). And, of course, Leicester had opposed Elizabeth's possible French marriage.

Sometimes, it must be remembered, weak arguments can strike us as the wrong end of the right stick. Nicholas Crawford asks if more means less, in an article which is based on a series of shaky premises, but which uses them to put questions well worth asking. (Post-modern paronomasia, especially around etymology – which was also characteristically medieval, but with less excuse – gives rise to associations of 'dilation' and 'dilution' in a study of 'copia', which never meant mere repetition: the plenty of rhetorical *copia* meant variation upon something, some *thing*.) Crawford is on the way to posing the question whether repetition, traditionally assumed to be the rhetorical effect of greatest force, may weaken rather than strengthen. He articulates this as tension between 'dilution' and 'dilation' (the etymologies are unsound); and he moves from words to things via a loose application of 'multiplied signifiers'. The counterfeit kings of *1 Henry IV* are neither counterfeit nor kings: they are decoys; Harry does not 'play' with his father's crown, but assumes it metonymically and verily when he believes his father dead; he is ontologically wrong, as he is the second to recognize. Crawford confuses the distinction between token and type. Neither the decoys nor the crowns ramify or discredit either king or kingship, and the real question about two kings is not the father and son Harry (for as long as the monarch lives his son is only 'apparent'); but whether the status of 'king' is abrogated, for example, during the brief period of Lancastrian victory while the Plantagenet Richard still lived (two appearances or two substances?). And this does appear to be true, since one usurpation encourages the next, and the rebel magnates have a precedent for social mobility which was certainly a threat throughout the sixteenth century. Rhetoric is indeed stylistic play, but it has always had a serious intent: moving and persuading. Despite my reservations, I think Crawford's central issues make this a fruitful essay. Can one repeat something without weakening its standing (he calls it 'authenticity'), is there an idea which links, even equates, increase or exaggeration with diminution, and, how much of a special case can a king be as *fons et origo* of legitimacy? In the same collection of conference papers, Robert Reeder titles his talk as a 'performance of precocity', but that isn't quite what he means. He looks at how Shakespeare used children and adolescents, and shows not precocity *per se* but a tendency to display rhetorical wit from what, in rhetoric, was called the *puer senex*. His examples include *Richard III*, but not Arthur in *King John*; *Twelfth Night* but not *The Merry Wives of Windsor*. Children are an up-and-coming subject, and this is a promising line of enquiry, but it lacks that comprehensiveness which encourages assent.

Vickers's points about looking at more evidence, over a wider span, than may suit the particularities of one's argument, applies to Alison A. Chapman's discussion of the stereotype 'shoemaker'. She writes about holidays and the 'Politics of Memory', an ambitious attempt to look at who designated and controlled festival days, taking King Henry's new emphasis on St Crispin's Day as her case study. She wants to see Henry as grabbing control 'from above' of traditions which had arisen 'from below'. To do this, she surveys *topoi* of tradesmen in prose fiction and drama, opening out into reflections on historical memory. It's a pity that she seems to have missed the 'Chaucerian' collection, *The Cobbler of Canterbury*; and here, too, there's a shaky assumption about what holidays are and where they come from, since on any day a choice of saints was available without concomitantly creating holy- or holi-days. Henry isn't declaring the day '*feria*', work-free, but associating it with reminiscence. Nonetheless, this is a fascinating perception about ideas of responsibility for social unrest and the technique of projection onto 'ordinary' speakers (like *Richard II*'s gardeners) which goes right back to Bede's 'vera lex historiae'. I am not sure I am convinced by Wendy Wall's attempts to find social struggle in fairy lore, by juxtaposing Puck and the fairies of *A Midsummer Night's Dream* with the *charade* of fairies in *The Merry Wives of Windsor*, to argue that the Ford household 'presents a domestic-national ideology in which housewifery never has to be renounced at all'. The essay covers laundresses and penises, with a degree of analogy hunting which I find tempting, above all, in her focus on domesticity in the sense of care for a *domus*. There is certainly a lurking argument there which promises a 'from below' look at good governance; even with the consent of the governed. She might be surprised to find herself in the company of Leo Salingar's much more old-fashioned exploration of 'Englishness' in the same play. His nationalism is linguistic nationalism, and he is interested in a variety of pretensions as butts for social satire.

Interpretations should be consistent, coherent and comprehensive. Wearied readers may ask why I include these farragos of wrenched interpretations, inconsistent in every way except in their assurance, and their insistence upon infinite paronomasia (when sex, history or religion are revealed), constructed on the shifting sands of textual incoherence? Because I take them to signify something extremely worrying about a loss of nerve over what constitutes an argument. There is also, as I complained last year, a worrying erasure of the Middle Ages, the more worrying as so invisible to so many. The failure of memory makes it all too possible to return to a romantic reminiscence of a Merrie England, associated in sensibility, under one idea of Catholicism, and unchanging over centuries.

Sometimes, more optimistically, what may seem to be anachronism can be wonderfully enlightening. In Laurie Maguire's 'Anatomy of Abuse(s) in *Troilus and Cressida*', she means 'abuse' as in child-abuse, sexual abuse, and insists on taking the deed as existing whether or not the behaviour could have been so articulated in the sixteenth century. Hers is a clever example of the ways that changes in our understanding of the world can illuminate earlier representations of character and action (inaugurated, perhaps, by Freud and Jones), in this instance, by rethinking Cressida as manipulated by an abuser. The heuristic case proposes an alternative to arguments of defence or condemnation, by transforming the traditionally unfaithful Cressida to a victim (readers of Henryson will reflect that at least she doesn't seem to have abused others in her turn). The argument comes with acute consciousness about different periods, and an accommodation with Freudian as well as those 'post-' approaches which comprehend character by another name. Here, too, the risk is that the concept of 'abuse' is too thin, in the philosophical sense. But Maguire is precise about what she means, and along the way illuminates Emilia and Iago, as well as putting some of the year's gentler approaches to Katherine and Petruccio in their place. If abuse, at last, is the true 'universal', we are back to perceptions of 'aggression' and 'passivity', not to mention 'violence', which solicit further thought. R. A. Foakes gives us further thought, which I shall discuss in detail below.

Permutation and combination are the heart of much medieval and renaissance structural patterning, and Shakespeare's thrifty penchant for repetition and variation is not news: multiplication can suggest dilution, but also imitation. Mark Taylor's study of *Shakespeare's Imitations* concentrates upon Shakespeare borrowing from himself, in the broad sense of absorbing and reusing: copies, replicas, duplicates, distortions, caricatures, parodies. Taylor suggests that, where the changes are so great that we recognize something new, we should promote 'imitation' to 'translation', and claims that imitation is to translation as simile is to metaphor. Imitation becomes everything which is repeated, where the repetition draws attention to the importance of the thing/word imitated. There are no constraints upon Taylor's argument, and he moves quickly through what are sometimes no more than associations. Offering a label, 'proleptic mimesis', is one of those moves which appears to legitimate something by renaming it in ostensibly technical language: he means 'anticipation'. What could imitating forwards possibly mean? No one disputes the skill of any author in forward planning, in the architectonic achievement of setting up from the beginning what will be needed later on. Shakespeare always introduces themes before we can know what they are going to mean. Taylor's analysis of *A Midsummer Night's Dream* is more to do with Ovid than Shakespeare's own earlier work, although there is some comparison to *Romeo and Juliet*, on the assumption that it came first. The idea that Henry and Sir Walter Blunt resemble Achilles and Patroclus is hard to entertain, and the *topos* of disguised armour may indeed be very old, but a direct link is unconvincing. Some of the resemblances are commonplaces of epic literature on war (Patroclus, Turnus, Aeneas). There could be an interesting argument here that Shakespeare finds himself in a line of epic writers, but then one might do better to look at, say, Froissart. He argues that the doubles in *Hamlet* include the obscene ravings of Ophelia which make her resemble the lustful Gertrude; that the Ghost is trying to place Hamlet in a revenge tragedy. This is a wasted opportunity, because, if he'd wanted an imitation, he could have used Pyrrhus, since Pyrrhus killed Priam at the altar, precisely what Hamlet declines to do. In the discussion of *The Tempest*, he asserts that Claribel is 'exiled' from her own play; he forgets that Prospero and Miranda are not 'exiled' to the island, but sent out into the open sea, in a leaky boat, to drown. 'Imitation', throughout this book, is too thin.

Too thin, too, is Jeremy Tambling's chapter on *Cymbeline* in his ambitiously titled *Becoming Posthumous: Life and Death in Literary and Cultural Studies*. In an energetic consideration of deaths and afterlives, there is rapid display of what 'after death' (after replacement? after drugs? after substitution?) might mean in the play (*any* erasure or disappearance, or reappearance or replacement, come to that), which may be to the taste of those who admire fertile free assertiation. Like this: 'When the posthumous becomes integral, involving resurrection before death in the case of Iachimo and his trunk, and being capable of repetition, it cuts out narrative order.' Another instance of 'proleptic mimesis', perhaps. Tambling thinks Posthumus Leonatus was born by Caesarian and that *therefore* he evokes Macduff. There is a promising opening in the throwaway observation that *Cymbeline* is both a colonial play and a celebration of British history (although incoherent), but the historical implications are not worked out in any detail. I wonder if some combination of romance and reconciliation might not be helpful here, as well as in some of the work on *Cymbeline* I shall mention below.

Sometimes philosophical positioning appears to be more historically orientated, as in Ellen Spolsky's consideration of scepticism. Beginning from the cognitive proposition that scepticism is hard-wired in the human brain, Spolsky considers what writers and artists have done with the 'sceptical dilemmas' they inevitably face. I have to say that I find myself sceptical in the face of the initial idea, not just because of the unsubstantiated claim that the human brain is built sceptical, but because the idea of 'doubt' seems so broad (why not 'curiosity', for example?), and reversing it just as satisfactory: human experience of dilemma teaches human beings to be sceptical. The period attraction to formal, philosophical scepticism, whether it be traced to the work of Cornelius Agrippa, Rabelais or Montaigne, has been previously studied by Sukanta Chaudhuri (*Infirm Glory*, 1981), among others. But Spolsky's is a much bolder claim, because she seeks to demonstrate that artists, by expanding our minds, also physically expand our brains, and that, concomitantly, a sixteenth-century Protestant brain will, by its cultural upbringing, differ markedly from contemporaneous brains elsewhere, in the ways that it confronts, and sometimes surmounts, the existential doubts which everyone, everywhere, experiences. This position accounts for the satisfactions we feel in art, because art negotiates the discomforts of the hard-wired scepticism. I don't see why this claim should not be vulnerable to accusations of Lamarckianism, but the sub-title, 'Embodied Knowledge', thus itself embodies the paradox which grows by what it feeds on. Cognitive anxiety eventually becomes the key to the collapse of Catholicism in England. It seems to me that there are three subjects here: doubt or curiosity or scepticism and how we experience them; how the experiences are portrayed in art, either as, second, someone searching for knowledge (which may be unattainable); or, third, as someone in the throes of doubt about knowledge in the abstract. So Thomas might doubt that Christ was risen, but he was wrong, and paintings depict his knowledge assuaging that doubt and, thus, ours. There are two substantive chapters which use Shakespeare to illustrate kinds of scepticism. To take Coriolanus as a parallel to the risen Jesus, and his refusal to display his wounds as a reference to Thomas seems to me perverse. What would Spolsky make of Henry's invitation to the proto-veterans of Agincourt to display *their* wounds? or Portia's wounded thigh? Can we really see in Volumnia's kneeling plea to her son Mary with hers? And how is this an illustration of scepticism? The chapter on *Othello* attempts to attach knowledge to visibility, imaginability, a step onward (or backward) from Thomas's physical intimacy with the resurrected body. Do we really think that the handkerchief is a holy relic (if so, is the *Spanish Tragedy*'s, too)? Othello is faced with cognitive dissonance, but it is hard to see his experience as scepticism, either. Red Crosse 'saw' Una misbehaving, and had to learn what Beatrice knows beyond doubt: the Holmesian hypothesis (proleptic) that once the impossible has been excluded, one must prefer the improbable. Now that would have been an exercise in ratiocinative scepticism.

My evocation of a philosophical reservation about the concepts for good argument leads me to the most philosophically impressive of this year's books, David Schalkwyk's use of twentieth-century ordinary-language philosophy to analyse the speaker of the Sonnets – not just as *persona*, but as poet, to argue that the mask is the man. This intelligent and sophisticated book looks not only at the poetry, but at the habit of sonneteering in the plays (and, less exhaustively, in Sidney), at exchanges between subjects and objects of love (especially where they are divided by social status or sexual orientation). His context is the social significance of utterance, embodied by the variety of speakers of different ages, social standings or statuses (not just class, after all, but married or single), and gender. Power, the leave to speak and to speak in what ways, are integral to the analysis. He is alert to the ways that poetry as epistle, that is, as speaking message, may look different and act differently, depending on who is reading in what contexts, with what assumptions about who is writing. The huge variety of message and voice is cogently explored, as is the problem of the unrecoverable speaking voice and literary representation of the spoken voice. The problem to be solved is to deduce what kind of speaker could voice the sonnets, and the speaker turns out to be a sixteenth-century actor, probably named Shakespeare. Wittgenstein gives the most important philosophical matrix, and the sociological theorist Goffman is striking as an absence in a discussion of role-playing. As in Crawford's article, there is an underlying problem about authenticity. The circularity of the argument begins from the assumption that there is a connection between Shakespeare and the poems, and that that can be best demonstrated by looking at similar language games in the plays, supplemented by what we know of the social situation of Shakespeare-the-player in a position of hierarchical inferiority which he tries to overcome when finding a position from which to address the recipients of the sonnets. I rather think this is convincing, I want it to be, but it is deep in Leo Spitzer's hermeneutic circle, where the quality of the reading is underwritten by the hypotheses the reading is attempting to prove. As Vickers insists, negative evidence, comparative evidence, is always required. One could look, for contrast, at who voices other sonnet cycles, or at characters who write or speak poetry in other kinds of literature of the period. There the answer (the authentic voice of a possible poet-actor) is less comfortable, because one has to take account of satire and parody which ridicules would-be poets. By extension, too, the speaker of songs is often 'acted' by the singer of the song, so that the lyrics require im-personation (the 'I' I sing may represent an 'I' like me, or I may speak for an 'I' I resemble, or only voice for the duration of the song). Schalkwyk's philosophical underpinnings engage with real force in setting previous sonnet criticism straight by recontextualizing the rhetorical activities of the sonnets. He imagines them as acted, spoken by a deducible body, with illocutionary force in J. L. Austin's sense. An initial chapter sets the philosophical and critical stage, indicating what the trends in criticism of the sonnets have been, and how one might rethink the historico-formalist divide. Subsequent chapters range from embodiment to interiority, names and naming, and transformations. The chapter which concentrates upon the desired and repudiated marriage between Bertram and Helena is particularly gripping, though I think the limitations of the comparison to the sonnets may be even more fascinating than the similarities in the unresolvable question of recognizing true nobility. The permutations seem endless: one might, after all, admire outstanding virtue without loving it, or wanting to be married to it; or, ultimately, accept marriage to it without feeling desire or admiration; or feel desire without accepting marriage to it. Or, in the circumstances of the French knight, Launcelot, the discovery that one has been all-too-publicly revealed as the victim of a bedtrick may sully *and* elevate one's name, turning betrayed intention to something undreamt of and transcendent. Launcelot's immediate reaction, however, is to retreat from trauma into madness. The poet of the Sonnets sanely metamorphoses madness into poems of the most immediate rhetoric. In that sense we can have autobiographical anonymity if we wish, but, in our own words, or voices, we may read them otherwise. If this book stimulates multiple interpretations, then it has already performed its engagement to rethink what we might now see as speech *acting* in the Sonnets.

Schalkwyk's pre-publication influence is already palpable: as in Patrick Cheney's exploration of the theatrical matrix of the sonnets, although it isn't clear to me whether it's useful to ask if Shakespeare was a poet or a dramatist. Performatives move into performance in Ramie Targoff's essay on intention and the eliciting of consent from the governed (this follows, I think, Targoff's earlier work on opposition to the theatre in the context of public utterance). Targoff goes back and looks at the etymology of 'amen' (which would be a performative if we were indeed saying, 'Let it be so', although that also raises the problem of the false imperative where we have no power or authority to add our voices to letting it so be) and the Protestant insistence on 'informed consent', More's Richard (not, however, protestant), and the combination of different confessions' ideas. The essay ends with a clever observation about applause and feudal allegiance being related gestures (but which allows for only one gesture of applause, with fingers extended).

However, the hermeneutic circle problem is a serious obstacle to these approaches, though perhaps not one that cannot be overcome, as MacDonald P. Jackson does in his study of 'Vocabulary and Chronology' in the Sonnets. For anyone new to the 'rare words' argument, it runs, briefly, as follows: most of the time most of Shakespeare's vocabulary is the same, but as he aged small groups of words unusual for him clustered and then passed from his habitual use. For example, as Jackson points out, 'particular' is rare at the beginning of Shakespeare's career, but frequent in the period of the great tragedies, so clustered appearances elsewhere suggest we rethink chronology. The implications for dating are clear, as is the circularity of any such arguments, unless they are buttressed by broad research and correlations external to the poems. In Jackson's work, they are. Jackson's impressive statistics are also basic to Brian Vickers's book, as they should be to the work of Donald Foster (who makes a brief appearance in Jackson's final note, which politely emphasizes that Foster has not published his evidence). These arguments have been used before, and Jackson builds upon, and refines, the 1991 article of Hieatt, Hieatt and Prescott (*Studies in Philology*, 88). Briefly, his analyses suggest that sequences *within* the sonnets correspond to different periods (i.e. that the chronology of the 'story' does not correspond to order of composition), that the cycle as we have it was not essentially completed in 1593–6, as is often assumed, and that sonnets were still being written in the seventeenth century. Taken together, the two articles have important repercussions on any attempt to identify the recipients or actors of *The Sonnets*, and no writer either on the poem's inception or on Shakespeare's biography can afford to neglect their tough and demanding arguments.

Attention to individual sonnets, or to sonnets typical of the cycle, occupy Kenji Go and Joyce Sutphen. The former article goes back to Malone to reconsider a received emendation and restore a *lectio durior*; the latter isolates Sonnets 5, 94, 116 and 129 as representing Shakespeare's major concerns in the sequence. Reading our reading of Shakespeare's poems involves not just the editorial tradition but a historical sense of how reading itself has evolved. Once again let me recommend a short, elegant article and a longer, elegant book. Katherine Duncan-Jones's article looks at the presentation of the 1616 print of *Lucrece*, and shows how its editorial division into 12 narrative sections appears to be an attempt to make it easier to read; Harvey's famous marginal annotation about who preferred which Shakespeare texts encourages the idea that readers found *Lucrece* hard, less a narrative than a mix of 'speech, introspection, and complaint', so there's no voyeurism. She makes an interesting comparison to Heywood's 1614 play. Sasha Roberts's *Reading Shakespeare's Poems in Early Modern England* is surely one of the outstanding books of the year, but readers should be warned that it is about reception, as its title says, and not directly about Shakespeare as *we* read him in current editions. On the other hand, although its chapters revolve around the sonnets and narrative poems, it encompasses more than the poems alone. Roberts has devilled in the archives, examining the marginalia in folios and quartos of Shakespeare, in miscellanies and commonplace books, on plays and parodies. Her book is a powerful antidote to generalizations about moralists, hegemonic patriarchy and centralizing powers; her many readers, many of them women, read in manifold ways, with irony, amusement, or even with an erotic charge. She is sympathetic and tentative about what they say about reading, and what was said about their reading, and always alert to the power of extracts and of old poems arranged in new contexts. The notes offer what is in effect a course description of early modern reading which could be applied to later periods. This is a book likely to be pillaged by those looking for research topics.

As the sonnets attract attention taken alone, so do the narrative poems. Christa Jansohn describes German readers finding a degree of theatricality in *Venus and Adonis* that became an imaginary drama, and then a staged one, up to and including Henze's opera – which can send us back to one of the least read of Shakespeare's creations. Lauren Shohet's 'Eager Adonis' is a less ambitious piece, with desire transferred to pursuit, whereas Venus's desire is expressed in contradictory, yet analogical, arguments. Thus, she argues, some of the humour results from the logical, metamorphic and poetic contradictions.

This year there was, unusually, a book on the poems for students, a difficult brief. But almost a third of Peter Hyland's Introduction is an introduction to the period, beginning with ideology from a very basic perspective, and limited social and critical distinctions. It is a pity to find yet another book which writes off the survival of what we think of as medieval, as if the Bible did not preserve both the language and the poetry of late Middle English in its archaising and conservative texts. Nor is there much about the Latin poetry male readers memorized at school. When we finally get to *Venus and Adonis* Hyland has only a brief view of historical interpretations of the poem to offer, then a character analysis of a kind of dramatic two-hander – perhaps like Jansohn's German readers of Shakespeare. Curiously, he doesn't see the way that one attempt to explain the unexplainable, in *Lucrece*, is to refer to history, to stories from which one can draw the comfort of recognition. The politics of a poem such as *Lucrece* depend upon the openness of the representation, which itself includes the openness of Lucrece's choice as one of the greatest *loci communi* of suicide, not, surely, 'a disclosure of patriarchal self-regard and irresponsibility'. Hyland wants the narrative poems to be about power, and the abuse of power, but there is in both of them a sense of what compulsion feels like, even for the oppressor, Tarquin, in the grip of the madness the gods use to destroy. In the section on the sonnets, too, we get an introduction to what sonnets are, to Sidney, and then a narrative story of the poems. What Hyland never manages to do is to convey why we might want to read the poems at all.

At the outset of this year's survey I mentioned work on the tragedies and ideas of evil. In Cristina León Alfar's fashionably titled *Fantasies of Female Evil: The Dynamics of Gender and Power in Shakespearean Tragedy*, the question of the messenger and the message is at the centre. She takes the question of how and why we categorize evil as particular to women in the context of gender anxieties and male projections of dis-ease and disease. Her book has the virtue of attempting to offer counter-factuals, if not always negative evidence. The approach is resolutely feminist. She focuses on Lady Macbeth, Goneril and Regan, and, to drive home the male fantasy in accusations of corruption, not Hermione so much as Leontes's mistaken view of Hermione, as adulteress, traitor and rebel. The argument stresses the ways that paternity and property rights of succession underpin patriarchal categories of masculinized/evil women, so that Cleopatra appears guilty of women's first disobedience, lust (rather than guilty of being a prince). Of course there were societal presumptions of women's guilt, particularly where men privileged the advice of other men (Iachimo/Posthumus, or Iago/Othello). As so often with wide moral labels, there are complex problems in the categories. We might consider, as a parallel example, Kant's refusal to allow that lying can ever be moral in any circumstances – perhaps an instance of the limits of philosophy in the cold light of day, given how many kinds and degrees of 'lying' we might want to agree upon. I use this example because it seems to me important not to reify (or make into monoliths) categories or concepts which may join what we should keep asunder. Female evil – like lying – invites delicate distinctions: first, here, in kinds and degrees of transgression (are certain acts only evil sometimes? or depending upon the gender of the agent?); then, in who is guilty of what acts of which degree of culpability; third, not trivially, where the accusers are wrong and the presumption of guilt is shown for what it is, a fantasy, projection, or just a mistake. It is important to remember that no one underwrites Othello's murder; condemnation from the within-play society itself brings apparent 'rights' into question. Political ambition, for example, is a difficult trait: it can be questionable in men when misplaced (betraying one's monarch, breaking a vow which betrays one's self), but must it be evil in women? In Joan, for her king; in *Henry VI*'s Duchess of Gloucester for her husband; or Emilia's imaginary 'all the world'? Is social ambition evil? Gender needs to be inflected, additionally, by status: is *Much Ado*'s Margaret better or worse than the Capulet parents, with their desires for upward social mobility through marriage?

Tragedy is also in play in Marina Favila's 'Mortal Thoughts' in *Macbeth*, ambiguously as thoughts of killing but also as thoughts which can kill (as in conscience), which are therefore magic. One might argue that they are not magic, but rather *inwit* as remorse – unless one insists that any access to conscience as a religious instinct be thought of as magical. Favila's is a psychoanalytic reading which uses mortal thoughts to unify what is otherwise, in the play, kept separate, a 'life cycle' reading, in which Macbeth regresses to childhood in the desire to kill the father without being caught, although it is Lady Macbeth who thinks about fathers. This is a contemplative essay, but it staggers each time 'magical' arises: it seems to mean fantasy, as in a child's desire; wishing; but also an error of thought which mistakes desire for omnipotence. 'Magic' as a word for the imagination reaches a limit when she claims that the murder of Duncan 'creates for the audience the same illusion of magical thinking'. It is not magic: the king has been murdered by his relative (not son), his host, his subject. And the onstage murder of a king could not be like the murder of any other person onstage. The assertion that the witches 'resemble the dark mirror of Winnicott's "good-enough mother"' suggests that this essay is more concerned with enlisting Shakespeare to talk about psychoanalysis than it is focused on the play in its own complex dramatic structures.

Given the number of assertions now made about patriarchy and the law, Kathryn Jacobs's short study of the history of marriage contracts is to be welcomed. Jacobs surveys relations between literature and the practices, laws and expectations which governed marriage in England from the late fourteenth to the early seventeenth centuries. She crosses genres and centuries, compares court cases and courtly writing. Perhaps because her scope is so large, however, the final effect is curiously unsatisfactory, even disjointed. It is always a good idea to ask questions so obvious that we may not previously have noticed them, but one expects more originality in the analysis of individual works. To conclude that the relations between law and literature are complex, or that literature changes along with the laws of marriage and reveals the holes, contradictions and difficulties in social practices, is unsurprising. The greater part of the book is about Chaucer, and towards the end of this first section Jacobs begins an analysis of widows (but not widowers), which resurfaces later in the book, and is almost a different subject. The attempt to link changes on the stage to legal changes in England as opposed to continental Europe is not altogether successful, partly because of the great difficulty of tying literature to social change without allowing for genre. She might have made more allowance for the rhetoric of the stage, which encouraged the tendency of renaissance literature to take 'elsewhere' as a place (often a Catholic place) where ferocious foreign laws could be imagined to provide appropriately dangerous circumstances. She is mainly concerned with non-Shakespearian plays, which offer an intriguing context for reconsidering Shakespeare's marriages. Nonetheless, it is surprising to find Claudius mentioned only as a usurping second husband (not quite a wicked step-father), rather than in the context of *Hamlet*'s emphasis on forbidden degrees. The vocabulary and register of land tenure occupy William O. Scott in a brief study of *Richard II*. In a discussion which also remarks what Shakespeare doesn't write about (land tenure lower down the social scale), he makes an interesting suggestion about the ways vocabulary can be extended, polemically, to cover non-'real' property, for example, when men begin to encompass skills, say, or trade (as in good-will) as possessable things with negotiable value. This may be the place to signal the appearance of an important book on the confluence of law, commerce and religion, in the treatment of property, Robert C. Palmer's *Selling the Church*. Given that Palmer's span (1350–1550) covers the period of Shakespeare's English histories, his exploration of how the law worked in practice, and changed, proposes a series of correctives to common assumptions about how things functioned and intertwined, from economics to belief.

Contemporary law gives way to legal/medical analysis in Joanna Levin's article on Lady Macbeth, which is about the categories 'witch' and 'hysteric', building upon the work of Janet Adelman and Michael MacDonald, and testing and refining Dympna Callaghan's proposition that Lady Macbeth moves from witch to hysteric. In its wider ambitions, it is another look at the 'hystery' of psychoanalytic and medical (but not religious-conscience) categories. Although Levin seems clear that the extent to which Lady Macbeth might be labelled 'witch' is limited, she sees aspects of both secular witchcraft and hysteria in Shakespeare's depiction, and turns *Macbeth* once more towards a play for James. In recognizing that being (or not) a mother is part of the play's deep structures, Levin thickens the description, though I would not myself follow her in finding a pun on female sexuality in Macbeth's despairing 'nothing' (a word of moment, this year). Perhaps Levin would be intrigued to consider that Lear's opening exchange with Cordelia might be proto-hysteric, focused on what *he* fears and loathes.

More acute, in terms of terms, is Catherine Belsey's exploration of 'possession' in *The Rape of Lucrece*, in which she plays with various meanings and ideas of possession, including the desiring subject possessed by his own desire, and therefore incapable of possessing anything. Possession is a deeply ironic concept, since the things, goods, services we 'possess' our very mortality limits to a metaphor of lease-hold or loan; Lucrece 'possesses' honour, as Collatine's most honourable 'possession', both bestowing and receiving it. We might ask what it means to be a possession, if one is mortal, or consenting, or reciprocal: for what Christian marriage stressed is that mysteriously the couple possess each other to the point of identification. Collatine may see his wife as a possession, but she is nothing like a slave. (Indeed, it might be argued that a slave is not like the idea of a slave, or land, or a business.) She is honourable, and, whatever is said – and always allowing for changes in perception which give us new vocabulary – not dishonoured, but polluted.

I shall come back to the poems, but let me continue with some other articles about women in their family contexts, particularly Kate the shrew. Attempts to 'save the appearances' this year started from different positions, but ended up quite close. Anne Blake tries to recontextualize *The Taming of the Shrew* generically, by first categorizing objections to farce as antedating objections to misogyny. She then asks what is the dynamic between farce and underlying serious themes such as good marriage and domestic tranquility, to defend farce's 'innocent [sic!] if unsubtle pleasures'. Aggression becomes knockabout *farce* rather than knocking about. Blake argues that to find the play funny one has to rescue 'farce' from too much literal-mindedness, but that one also needs to acknowledge that Kate has to learn, that she begins as a dupe, one of those 'deformed creatures' at whom we laugh, as, indeed, actresses who have played her report. Wouldn't it be nice to imagine that one day we could, indeed, have a sense of humour about taming, or other kinds of prejudice? For the time being, though, Kate isn't just a dupe, such as Sir Andrew, she's a woman; Sir Andrew knows Olivia is not for him, but Kate has no escape. Jay Halio attempts to demonstrate that Sly's conviction that he isn't who he is points to acting elsewhere, so that Kate is simultaneously only pretending to be a shrew and has to discover that Petruccio isn't similarly antisocial. Under this interpretation, he frees her from an unnecessary pose, wakes her to a new reality, and happiness. The implications of such an argument are more worrying than Halio realizes, and I suspect a bad dose of D. H. Lawrence may have something to answer for (he knows she wants it, really, she does). I think he means to save the play for love by freeing Kate from misery, but it depends completely on an implicit communication from an Induction which explicitly suggests a fantasy of wife-taming rather than an evolution in understanding; it flies in the face of the play's many references to curbing Kate's humour. I have to say that I should prefer to see what Laurie Maguire could make of Kate the abused. Perhaps we may need to acknowledge that this is one of those jokes which aren't funny any more.

Often scholarship on women has been scholarship on young women. Lisa Hopkins's study of the *Female Hero in English Renaissance Tragedy* is not primarily about Shakespeare, but his influence on later women *writers*, who, she argues, found Shakespeare's heroines empowering. By contrast, Jeanne Addison Roberts opens an original and fruitful subject: the Crone. This is a suggestive overview, balancing history, demography and literary conventions, beginning with traditions of the old woman from the classical period, and the assumption that once procreation is over, women are otiose. Roberts is impressive on the power of non-reproductive women in Greek Tragedy (though I would exempt Medea and Clytemnestra). She then glances at changes in demography in early modern Italy, where dowagers may have continued to hold property, and wonders about the closing of convents as retreats for older women. In English drama crones tend to be 'trivialized or absent', sometimes demonized, where it looks as if literary convention was stronger than demographic experience, since women were running their defunct husbands' businesses. Men haven't noticed these characters as worthy of attention. She is good on widows, nurses, bawds (in a way the bawd is the female equivalent of the Eunuch), and includes some benign examples which are exceptions to the general trend of the crone as a *memento mori*. This is a timely essay, which reminds us of our tendency to identify with the coming generation, not that Grey Power which appears to be withering out a young man's revenue.

Contrastive Italy occupied a number of this year's writers. I shall mention Peter Parolin's Rome below, but here let me mention the question of Italy as a place of paradox, or at least Venice as an exotic space, in Peter G. Platt's essay, which moves from paradox as rhetoric, to agreed places of paradox, to the stage as a destabilizing locus which forces its audience to rethink themselves (out of Brecht, perhaps?). He sports a series of 'theorists' from Lacan to Quine to run together a concatenation of real paradoxes and binary polarities, which I am not sure I follow. This is an exciting essay, but the emphasis on Venice as place or space raises numerous questions, among them the problem that Othello isn't 'in' Venice when he is deceived – and that Cassio is a Florentine. Italy is present in Christoph Clausen's look at gender issues in opera generally, and *Otello* specifically, using Verdi as a test case, thinking about the shift to women in Catholic Italy, voiced by a composer and a librettist who were far from pious. Not only are great adaptations always fertile for thinking about their originals but, in addition, in the context of post-colonial study, looking at an example from old Europe offers rich fields for thought. Clausen engages with the binary polarity that characters are either 'voiced or silenced' to ask us to think again. In the same number of *Shakespeare Jahrbuch*, Tobias Doering uses Derek Walcott's 1983 *A Branch of the Blue Nile* to move back and forth between Jacobean fantasies of exoticism (in Walcott's meta-text, *Antony and Cleopatra*) and current critical positioning of 'post-colonial' cultural specificity.

In this space one can find the protean mode of 'romance', with its own exoticisms. Lori Humphrey Newcomb's work is an impressively gestated book-of-the-thesis, which has grown from an interest in *Pandosto* into an interest in reading habits. Much of it covers well-known ground, but its juxtapositions create new insights, both more and less than the title suggests: a comparison of popular reading in Ireland (but not France) which extends well into the eighteenth century. Her range is useful, if constrained by a sense of outrage at the ways the rich and powerful attempted to legislate for the under-privileged. She has also contributed an essay to *Ovid and the Renaissance Body* on 'monumentality' and 'loss' in a 'Butlerian' reading of gender. Helen Hackett, too, focuses on women as readers as well as characters in *Women and Romance Fiction in the English Renaissance*. The book is a clear survey and recapitulation of well-known ideas about romance readers and writers in the sixteenth century. Part of the challenge in any such compendium is what 'romance' meant, because of the range from oracy to literacy, classical, English historical, contemporary continental, and more recent attempts to recuperate an amalgam of romance traditions for new ambitions. Spenser and Sidney, to take the best-known as well as the best, examples, were not addressing maidens in their bowers. Greek romances were both literary and erotic; many tales associated with Chaucer or Gower were literate but, because their English had become 'quaint', appeared naive; Arthurian romances, which included Caxton's Malory, rightly enjoyed reputations for immorality in violence as well as sexual transgression; continental pastorals were more political but also potentially more libertine. As the old romances were reduced to the back-packery of chapmen's stocks, social derogation further eroded a once courtly reputation, as is celebrated in *The Knight of the Burning Pestle*. But there was also the definitional problem of the *novelle* imported ultimately from Italy. Hackett asks if the ostensible address to women readers was not in practice a way of denigrating-to-defend the 'trifles' written almost exclusively by men. Her chapter on Shakespeare's romances emphasizes the idea of the 'old wives' tales' and the plays' language of maternity, with images of birth and fecundity upholding themes of regeneration and redemption, while mothers are conspicuous by their absence, another way of feminizing writing which was nonetheless masculine. Historically, romances were considered to eroticize the exotica they described, as if associating them with the private reading of women or the domestic story-telling of mothers and grandmothers were simultaneously a way to recuperate and dignify the *nugae* of oracy, or the inter-referentiality of a genre not always textual. This book usefully brings together texts often studied separately.

In the territory of painting, Alan Young creates a kind of virtual exhibition, which pays tribute to the wonderful holdings of the Folger Library, in a study of *Hamlet and the Visual Arts, 1709–1900*. Visual representations of *Hamlet* and Hamlet probably began in the mind's eye, like any ghost, but they soon took more solid flesh. This book surveys the history of such representations, and amasses a mountain of detail, from accompanying illustrations to stand-alone Hamlet-reference objects and images. Organization is, perhaps unavoidably, a problem, and the book often strays beyond Hamlet to Shakespeare interpretation generally, and loses itself in the rich labyrinthine lists of its subject. Young would like to demonstrate that Hamlet could be as well known by images as by actual contact with the play; this certainly seems possible, but remains hard to prove, although Young spends time on the material base of textual and artistic reproduction. That artistic representation partook of Romantic 'psychologizing' in characterization also seems plausible, but also remains asserted rather than discussed at any length: that artists hesitated to depict Hamlet killing Polonius and not-killing Claudius remains a mention in passing rather than a subject for discussion. So it is with the promising topics which recur: how far the gestures of depiction (such as the famous stage business, the 'Hamlet start' on seeing the Ghost) are related to the gestures of the stage, or of actual bodily expression; the illustration of scenes from the imagined or implied 'story' outside the action of the stage (such as Millais's drowned Ophelia); the growth in a kind of painterly 'dramatic moment'; the choices of costume and what that might say about 'history' painting; what paintings might say about painting, as artists use composition to refer to other artists; the changes which came with photography; the pressure of portraiture, concomitantly, on a thespian's or writer's or politician's (even) use of the imagery of Hamlet to make a statement of his or her own. For the ambitious artist, of course, seeking fame in the contests of exhibition, pictorial Shakespeare came to offer a repertoire which was neither religious nor classical and which had the further advantage of a kind of non-historical national story. Among other subjects I should have liked to see discussed is the question of whether non-anglophone artists (in countries where, to follow Young's own idea, images would have had advantages over reading or watching the play) took more liberties with received interpretations of the play and its characters; or gendered inclusions (the paucity of Gertrudes, for example) or representations (Delacroix, as Young mentions only in passing, made use of a woman for his Hamlet's face, a question dealt with at greater length by Catherine Belsey in an article I mentioned last year). And, as I finish this report, there is a fine exhibition at the Dulwich College Picture Gallery, with a stunning and informative catalogue on *Shakespeare in Art*, edited by Jane Martineau, an ideal coffee-table-cum-gift-book which scholars will want to own and use. Here, too, the bibliography is a cornucopia. A series of short illustrated essays is followed by colour reproductions of the exhibits. Readers will find some old friends but plenty of surprises, too, especially in the juxtapositions. The publishers (www.merrellpublishers.com) have an electronic picture archive.

Historical recontextualization, when texts can be re-placed within the intellectual milieu of long-dead arguments or controversies, has been one of the most powerful currents in intellectual history in the last thirty years and has illuminated – in our neck of the woods – complex questions of intention. Tracing the sources of inspiration, type or stereotype can tell us how things were used, how they were expected to be used, how differently – or similarly – they are used – or omitted, when omitted means something rather more aggressive. The explanatory power such histories convey are only as eloquent as the historical and critical grip of the explicator 'mere coincidence' tells us not very much. Sometimes just a detail adds, just, to our knowledge, as with the indefatigable Maurice Hunt's reconsideration of 'stewards' and other servants, Chapman's more complex work on shoemakers, Fisher on beards, or Harris on hair, all mentioned earlier. Sometimes erudition results in assuring us that we cannot resolve something complex, that 'perhaps', in all its glorious ambiguity, is the order of the day. Barbara Mowat looks at 'Prospero's Book' in a detailed historical exploration of magic and magicians, before coming back to Prospero with the conclusion that we don't know much more than we did at the start; but we don't know in rather different ways, much more informed ways. This reorientation might help us understand more about Shakespeare's world, and will certainly make us more careful, as well as more curious, in characterizing both the wronged Duke as well as other 'magicians'.

So 'history' is no magic bullet, but it is one of our most powerful necessaries. In this year's *Shakespeare Studies* Dympna Callaghan organizes a group of essays on 'the idea of history in Renaissance studies'. But, as so often, we have a serious problem in the neglect of the middle ages. Callaghan's introduction itself, describing a period negotiating between Antiquity and a nascent modernity, makes a fascinating comparison between historiography and an archaeology of individualism. 'Literature perhaps records at the level of culture what Freud described at the level of the individual psyche, and as such literature resists and even contradicts the claims of empiricism.' Although only one of her contributors is a card-carrying historian, the five pithy pieces in thirty suggestive pages cover interesting ground. The focus of the 'position papers' is emphatically aesthetic, whether, like Frances Dolan, one argues against the existence of the category altogether or, like Chris Kyle, one imports it into the 'archive' to redescribe records as made not born. John Parker succumbs, warily, to the romantic lure of the past, what I have elsewhere described as the new exoticism, and there are two substantive glances at Jonson as retrograde in retrospect and on the renaissance Lucretius. The expertise of literary criticism is crucial to the understanding of historiography, because it is so alert to the structure of story and the rhetoric of recording.

Elsewhere, a more political focus is visible, especially in work on the English history plays. Derek Cohen meditates on history in the making, as the characters of *Richard II* and *Henry IV* reflect on it, and how that reflection itself 'makes' history, and history makes a nation. Alison Thorne looks at the politics of *Henry V*, beginning by reflecting on Helgerson's ideas about history to situate *Henry V* in relation to (largely unnamed, except for Heywood) chronicle plays. Benjamin Griffin's *Playing the Past: Approaches to English Historical Drama 1385–1600*, which I praised here last year, offers a longer, more detailed examination of some of these issues. Here, as elsewhere, a good subject can be hobbled by a failure to think about its fundamental terms: when Gregory M. Colón Semenza argues that, with the waning of 'sport' as preparation for battle, the prestige of sport fell to triviality. So sometimes does war. But what counted as sport, and sport for whom, with what conventions, rules, or even laws? How can one leap from the idea that the biggest blow to 'sport' was the replacement of archery by gunpowder, when 'archery' has such a long literary, as well as historical, past? War was not suddenly 'debased' because 'chivalry' was suddenly passing. I have already worried about Peter A. Parolin's assertions about historical Italy. If you maintain that *Cymbeline* claims Rome's imperial legacy, appropriates the mantle of Roman civilization, celebrates a Roman alliance, and 'foregrounds the fact that once on the historical stage no nation can control the way it is written into the historical record', then you are going to run into difficulties. Parolin further argues that the play engages with, indeed criticizes, James's failures in foreign policy and alliance-forging. The problem is that Parolin's article is working at such a high level of abstraction that it leaves the play's plot out of account. Is it not more likely that this, like *Lear*, is a play which takes advantage of remote 'British' history to raise the tone of a domestic romance? The return of interest in romance is, I think, a trend which is being enriched by more political orientation than has perhaps been traditional, and a combination of politics and exotic imaginings seems to be making a comeback, as work such as that of Newcomb and Hackett suggests, or as Richard McCoy explored in the writing of Sidney years ago.

James, the historical king, continues to be a focus of historical speculation. Alex Garganigo wants to see in Menenius's fable in *Coriolanus* coded references both to a political Britain and to James's own body. More powerful, and more convincing, is what one cannot call a 'recontextualization' of a play we haven't yet contextualized. We are starting to read *Edward III* with the attention due its recent promotion. Leslie Thomson has a clear eye on its 'Theatrical Rhetoric', both verbal and visual, including weapons, kneeling, exits. I mention this here because of the great difficulty of noticing what isn't there that one might expect, and Thomson is particularly good on what this play lacks: deaths (which is impressive in a history play), but also battles, pageants, or dumb shows of any kind, though to some extent these are made good by noises off. The cumulative effect is dynastic celebration, appropriate in the post-Armada period.

Close attention can be 'close reading', but 'close reading' can include much more than words on pages. Richard A. Levin explores a theatrical *topos* he calls 'Secret Schemers', the dramatic devices by which characters express intention without revealing it to other characters, by protesting, urging, flattering, affirming, attacking others, calling something into question by reiterating an idea or by using equivocal terms, or, conversely, clarifying by allusion; criticizing; or withholding information. He doesn't use the modern philosophical terms 'perlocutionary' or 'illocutionary', but he might have done. The interest of his book lies not simply in its morphology of 'policy' but in the fine grain of the analyses of how characters assert their wills by excesses in speech, which should modify generalizations about 'machiavels'. Chapters are devoted to *Richard II*, *Hamlet*, *All's Well That Ends Well* and *Antony and Cleopatra*, and there is an extremely useful schematic exposition of 'expository prompts' in an appendix which may make us think again about characters' good wishes, pious hopes, and chivalric assertions. In addition, just as we have now begun to go back to the early editors in order to understand the evolution of the 'received text', so this book returns to the received wisdom of character criticism by beginning with Morgann, in order to take another look at inwardness and subjectivity.

Close attention combines with a life-time of close reading, editing, play-going and reflection in a new book from R. A Foakes, *Shakespeare and Violence*. Foakes begins with the idea that Shakespeare was concerned with a first act of violence, between (adult) men, which has no cause or reason. He derives this primal act from Cain (who, however, might be thought to have had all too much reason). One added complexity at the heart of the book is that the model of Cain appears to presuppose the identity of the first murderer as also the first founder of cities, and therefore of civilization. Foakes almost addresses a more worrying question, which is the violence of the Old Testament God himself: although there is little reflection on God's emotion (aside from his boasting about his justice), there is every reason to think that his actions imply some degree of pleasure in the violence he metes out. I am not sure that Foakes fully takes up the suggestive association with Cain and Abel; no doubt in each generation, each child (even each only child) is still faced with a traditional crisis of acquiring the will to subordinate his own desires to act out his fantasies. There is perhaps an unheard musical bourdon here from Freud's *Civilisation and its Discontents*.

This is an old-fashioned book, inflected by new fashions for more personal writing, and by a willingness to think about Shakespeare in our time (and film violence, too, with its constant ratcheting up of what can be shown, including a disturbing example from Anthony Hopkins), and the fruit of many years of watching individual productions grapple with the expression of violence of many kinds. It is recognizable in its opening statement of a thesis, which may be little more than a question (how does Shakespeare think about violence?), which is then explored in a series of readings, whose quality justifies the enterprise, exploring this violence between men. That such violence is innate in men (I'd have said in humans) hardly needs demonstrating, but some degree of differentiation and distinction among kinds or degrees of aggressivity might be expected. Blinding Arthur is not the same as blinding Gloucester, and not acted out by the principal concerned. The correction of children or subordinates leads us into the territory addressed by Laurie Maguire. Foakes is deep in the problem of excess, the moment when we cannot explain what we might construe as the *subjective* correlative, the need or desire for pleasure in and by the infliction of pain. In this sense the logical conclusion is that violence is one thing when we grimly agree its necessity, but quite other if we dare enjoy it. In the long term, societies have to find ways of agreeing to transfer aggression from a private right to a public system of justice (which opens another question about judicial or institutionalized violence, and how far its authorities might be individually answerable for their administration of it). There is a deeply pessimistic observation, fundamental to the rejection of tragic understanding, that we retrospectively provide meaning for the meaningless.

Why we hurt each other, as well as how, can be distinguished, and the distinctions matter. Although Foakes announces that the book will be about male violence to other men, some of his more striking passages are about female violence to men, where it seems clear that from Aeschylus to Shakespeare there is at least a double problem: men have access to a degree of physical action which they may use or misuse, but women must never appropriate, because their access to physical action is forbidden as a defining feature of what it might be to be a woman. And here there is a curious silence in Foakes's argument: does he or does he not think the 'excess' of which he treats is available to all human beings at all times? or does he find himself caught in the same dilemma he opened with, that violence is largely associated with men, and high-status men, that it is and remains a prerogative which defines masculinity, but also status, from Cain onwards, if not from God onwards, and that violent women are multiply horrifying when they masculinize themselves into monstrosity?

Shakespeare's tragedies always inspire good work, none more than *Hamlet*, of course. This year there is a lovely exhibition of what close hearing can do in an essay by Stephen Booth, which plays mightily with physics, starting from one soliloquy and reaching out. As with the books by Foakes and Levin, paraphrase kills, but, if I say that Booth reveals the doubleness of metaphor as a trope of necessity expressed as place, and then turns, pretzelly, toward actors and visages and double business, that may at least whet appetites. It should be emphasized that every meaning or implication or shadow of a doubt is supported by reference to other features of the play. One cannot précis such unpacking. And there is another fine instance of what this technique can reveal in Ruth Stevenson's exploration of mice, motes, moles and minching malecho. Taking *Hamlet* as a book to be read, Stevenson elucidates the 'old mole' metaphor, beloved of idealist as of psychoanalytic philosophers, and traces its permutations through the play. She is defensive about *Hamlet* read, but now that we have Lukas Erne's authoritative enquiry into *Shakespeare as Literary Dramatist*, no apologies should be necessary. Her emphasis is on the way paronomasia can offer cohesion in addition to semantic coherence. She presses the case for case, as well, emphasizing present participles and gerunds in 'ing'. She reaches out towards allusion and what she calls 'eruption', as breakdown becomes breaking out. Insisting that Hamlet's imagination, as ours, follows the verbal trajectory she traces, her essay is a *tour de force* of forcing. Claude-Gilbert Dubois's more historically-minded recapturing of physic in the sense of medicine concentrates on *Hamlet*'s ghost as a manifestation of 'pneuma', following Aristotle, to speak of an astral 'third way', a kind of envelope for the soul, which can continue to suffer, but which remains mysterious. The trouble is that in a brief exploration there is no evidence for the idea of 'pneuma' anywhere else in Shakespeare. Nor any discussion of how the witnesses categorize the ghost (which he assumes is Hamlet senior's). I wonder if ailing ectoplasm would demand revenge?

Metaphors and money, including reward and revenge, inspired some outstanding work this year. Let me signal a series of essays which follow the money. First, there was money in *The Merchant of Venice*. Phyllis Rackin looks at the ways that ambivalences about foreign trade, a world shifting to a monetary scheme of value, and the hopes and fears that the expanding globe presented to Elizabethans, inform Venice both as celebration and as anxiety. She is well aware that plays are dynamic, and that characters are not personification allegories. She sees audience-expectations that are constantly undercut, and two points of view about weddings: from one, great wealth is promised for a small, if dangerous, investment, but from another, the risks are just as great, but begin later, after the cargo is hoist. She is thinking that the gamble of foreign adventure helped monetarize cultures whose exchange and value had earlier had different bases (I take it that that is what credit does to cash). This is a very suggestive reading for the possibilities of one great social change which was nevertheless perceived for different places at different speeds and different times. Peter Holland does sums, focusing on the four figures actually specified in the play. He includes some arithmetic calculations which are shocking in their grotesque exactitude (converted into the price of meat by the kilo, Shylock's pound of flesh would work out at 6600 ducats a kilo, for example). Not 'what' so much as 'how' exactly are the ducats worth? The four sums concentrate the play's monetary language for value; identify characters' ascription of value to actions; invite us to reflect upon representations of our own financial criteria. Holland looks carefully at laws about lending, which helped define usury, so that the metaphors are less metaphoric, less like poetry and more immediate. Lisa Hopkins prefers the polarities in the idea of exchange, and argues that Portia learns about exchange in the course of the play, in ways she wants to be 'not entirely dissimilar to that by which the Old World is modified and inflected by its encounter with the New'. At this high level of abstraction, she seems to be running a number of things together: exchange, money, loyalty, difference, similarities of thought and taste between Portia herself and Bassanio, and then she asserts that Portia acquires a knowledge of 'cultural relativism'.

Thoughts about financial exchange have been the focus of others of the outstanding essays this year, and I want to continue, just for a moment, to follow the money into the history plays, where reward can be a sign of class patronage. Taking it, or not, is William Leahy's question about the moment in *Henry V*, when Williams either does or doesn't. Leahy considers the ways that critics have tried to understand what happens at that moment: if Williams doesn't take the money, why doesn't he? Are we meant to see Fluellen as mindlessly loyal? Why have critics insisted on ignoring Williams's resistance? And is this a case where the temptation to read the common soldier as evidence of subaltern opinion evaporates in the impossibility of representing any 'below'? Status always complicates things, because superiors may consider that their inferiors are putting on airs, or forgetting their place, or just being touchy. Perhaps the value of value changes with point of view. When Jesse M. Lander looks at the value of money, that is, coins as money, he takes the artefacts as a symbol of value through the language of numismatic reference. *Henry IV* becomes an example of arguments and anxieties current elsewhere not only in England, but on the continent, racked by inflation and the stresses it engendered. Lander has read widely and thought hard about relations among the metaphors and metonymies the characters exploit; he is very good on the impossibility of reducing the play to a single discourse, let alone a binary polarity. Although he wants to conclude that the play 'attempts to manage' both the inflationary and numismatic crises of early Tudor society, the thrust of the article is rather to explore the ramifications of characters' manipulations of numismatic possibility. As he so clearly demonstrates, what Shakespeare 'manages' is an incoherent and eloquent series of possibilities (including arrant anachronism) which tell us about characters by virtue of the imageries they employ. It dovetails well with Rackin's and Holland's work, and with Charles Edelman's. This is an excellent and ambitious use of close linguistic attention and analysis of Shakespeare's imagination and imagery of worth. We may hope that the article tries out material for a book to come. The common assumption that Venice is special in some way that is defined by its (anachronistic) trading position requires some modification in the light of these explorations.

As I mentioned earlier, the play which has had exceptional interest this year is not *Hamlet* but *The Merchant of Venice*. This year the 'new critical essays' series was expanded by a volume on *Merchant*, but I'm sorry to have to report that this is not the strongest volume in this useful series, although overall these essays survey prior study with comprehensive bibliographies and notes. The contributors seem to have been overwhelmed by new interests in religion, almost as if, should we turn the play to an allegory of Christian magnanimity, its anti-semitism would go away. The opening essay tracing the history of reception is straightforward, and careful about the play's complex and difficult distastefulnesses. Unresolved questions of Shakespeare's relations to Marlowe reappear throughout. But then we have a series of claims that the play is redemptively allegorical in ways simply hard to believe. M. J. Levith wants Antonio and Portia to figure Christ, as if any filial obedience, any offer of succour, were susceptible to being an *imitatio Christi*. The argument proceeds by juxtaposition and assertion, including a guilt-by-association reference to *The Tempest*. Is *The Merchant of Venice* really a Faustian comedy (Faust once visited Venice, asserts Levith portentously), with Shylock as overreacher and symbolic Catholic/Puritan (this is not exaggeration on my part)?

From an opening reference to Spielberg's *Schindler's List* which asks us to think about desire across boundaries, Joan Ozark Holmer's essay asks us to wonder if the demarcations of Lorenzo's world were 'like' Nazi Germany. The idea that Scott's Rebecca is 'denied intermarriage in *Ivanhoe*' reveals a curious insensitivity to her autonomy or Ivanhoe's love for Rowena, as well as a failure to think about social mobility and the circulation of women. She discovers 'good Jews' in previous plays and literature, then asks why good Jewish daughters disappear after *The Merchant of Venice*. Do they? On the problem of religion and race she is confused about the limitations of hatred: one could simultaneously hate someone as both foreign *and* Catholic, say, let alone hate threats from different social classes or wealth. Where Others are concerned, one must remember that sometimes Venetian Catholics are not 'us', but that sometimes they most certainly are, as, for example, in the closing of Western-European Christianity's ranks after the victory at Lepanto. She veers toward the Bible and Bible study, emphasizing the allegory in names such as Abigail's (do we really see Ophelia influenced by Abigail?) or Jessica's, surely not in relation to the tree of Jesse, to an idea of 'gift' or/as sacrifice? But Jessica and Lorenzo are so irresponsible that their inherited money is put in trust for them. Maryellen Keefe, too, piously conflates everything with the celestial banquet and *Isaiah* to try to make a kind of social 'communion' justify Venetian demands. And then John Cunningham and Stephen Slimp rediscover *figura* and typology in emblems in order to encourage a Christian allegorical reading in which Shylock, the old man, the Jew, the character 'most in need of redemption', conflates metamorphosis and transformation. For them Emblem is 'a mystery'. Antonio and Portia become emblems for Christ, and Shylock for Judas. But they do nothing with the unattractive side of the Christians, nor with how the 'emblems' might function and for whom (who says Shylock 'is' Judas, for example?). They argue for Gobbo in *psychomachia* – but in denying any realism they forget what the play is like onstage. All the speeches turn out to be one repertoire, generally interpretable as Christian allusion, rather than words spoken by characters in particular circumstances at particular times in the play. The evident anti-semitism of the text is denied in their notes. This is a very long, very footnoted essay, but very ham fisted in its insistence on allegorical identification. It reminds me of the kinds of patristic analysis which did so much to inhibit Chaucer studies in the sixties and seventies. Grace Tiffany's essay on names emphasizes etymologies without a glance at sources, or at Anne Barton on the names of comedy, and she repeats the identification of Antonio with St Antony.

As if this religious distortion were not enough, R. W. Desai hales back to retrograde views of women and 'race'. His *Merchant* is a play full of 'Others', including Portia as a successfully threatening wife whom it is good to have escaped, where points of view are multiple and contradictory (Portia is northern if you're Morocco but southern if you're Faulconbridge). Thus, geographically, there's a north–south dichotomy; religiously, he sees Judah and Tamar in *the* ring; aesthetically, he adduces a problem no one else has noticed about the significance of Golden Hair; biographically, speculates that Shakespeare's knowledge of India (Titania's boy is obviously from Kerela) and Shakespeare's own tastes in complexion (for dark women) must be surfacing from time to time. Desai asserts that Morocco must be played as 'uncompromisingly black', to make Shakespeare's colour palate more consistent and more definite than it was. In finding no source for Morocco or Aragon, he ignores national character/ethnic stereotypes elsewhere in literature or on the stage. He hangs part of his argument on the Englishness of the name 'Launcelot', that most French of knights.

Portia gets an unusually hard time in this collection. Corinne S. Abate argues that Nerissa as 'helper' arranges things for Portia, but then (without explanation) Portia takes her life in hand and retains dominance. At the same time, her Portia is a corrupt manipulator in early Capitalist society. There is no attention to traditions of literary or confidential servants as helpers; or about recent work which suggests the advantages for wealthy or powerful women of choosing a husband of lower status, trading at an advantage in order to keep some autonomy. By contrast, Karoline Szatek's Belmont is no fairytale world but, like other pastoral areas in Shakespeare, 'a borderline contact zone', and her Belmont participates in mercantilism, including 'marketing' Portia. Szatek seems to take Venetian law as a possible statute, rather than as one of those heuristic devices from which rhetorical speeches and plots were derived.

As I wondered at the beginning of this essay, we may be seeing a double release of historical and religious interest, not yet fully integrated, so it is a pleasure to signal two essays in this collection which are exceptionally good. At last a fine exploration of the Gobbos, and the question of parents and children, which takes the play as a play, structured as a series of permutations and combinations which resolve little, but suggest much. John Drakakis is sensitive about the Jessica plot, which 'is one of a number of mirrors in the play, each of which refracts the dominant values of Venice. It is neither direct contrast nor a mimetic double.' In discussing the play's three fathers he contextualizes its comedy: 'at issue is the power of patriarchy to impose limits and obligations upon its subjects, particularly its female subjects, and this is a tension that informs a number of Shakespeare's comedies', and points out the doubled caskets and doubled rings. Freud used Shakespeare, and Drakakis uses Freud – I've never been a fan of the inevitable relation with the third woman who destroys a man, but perhaps male mythology will always be with us; Drakakis calls Jessica 'uncanny' in her relation to Portia, because in effect Portia kills her father. There is always slippage in these assertions about the Law of the Father, when one is dealing with real progenitors, with laws rather than Imaginaries. Insofar as it is identified with the will of a particular paternity (and can thus be opposed and disobeyed), Lacanian Law is a long way from the social hierarchies of a singular patriarchy: Shylock as a father is subject to rebellion. But that does not make Jessica feel less guilty at the cost of her transfer of her affections. Drakakis sees how Jessica's rebellion instaurs a reapportionment of blame, and uses the law to attack the now-guilty father (except that it isn't Jessica or Lorenzo who attacks Shylock, but Antonio – who has more creditors than Shylock, as we also learn from the Tubal's report of Jessica's monkey).

The Gobbos also figure in John F. Andrews's fascinating, problematic, analysis of the names Shakespeare wrote. Given what we know, or think we know, about printers and printing houses, Andrews's presumption that Q represents Shakespeare's own spelling and punctuation seems doubtful at best, but as with some of the articles with which I started, I include it for the sake of the argument that the spellings and speech prefixes give nuances of meaning, e.g. Launcelet Gobbo and not Lancelot; Iobbe and not Gobbo (except, of course, that speech prefixes are silent). I am not sure that all his connections are phonologically irreproachable – nor that his proposal that Shakespeare cued pronunciation for his original actors could overcome the practice of scrivener fair-copying. He appears to turn Shakespeare into a post-modernist using typography/orthography/phonology to suggest multiple meaning, but I think that, as with re-viewing Rowe's editorial decisions, this is an area which invites more attention.

Last year I urged readers to buy and give away John Gross's Oxford Anthology, *After Shakespeare: Writing Inspired by the World's Greatest Author*; this year I have already mentioned the beautiful *Shakespeare in Art*. Let me recommend Stanley Wells's *Shakespeare for all Time*, which is a broadly conceived and also beautifully illustrated century-by-century survey of Shakespeare's text, stage and cultural presence among readers, spectators, and us, critics, from then till now. By the time this issue of *Shakespeare Survey* arrives, Oxford will, I hope, have corrected some howlers (the illustration which says 'secretary hand' is no such thing, for example). And for readers inclined to curl up with, even to use, interesting cookery books, let me end with a contribution beginning with Z: Betty and Sonia Zyvatkauskas's *Eating Shakespeare: Recipes and more from the Bard's Kitchen*. I include it for two other reasons: first, it illustrates the way that, as Stanley Wells would recognize, hooking something onto Shakespeare's name is a strong sales pitch, but second, because, although it is a 'trade' book, its descriptions of food and eating from period books (much depends upon Gervase Markham) are useful – though it isn't a manual for neophytes. Armchair cooks will find side notes along the way with period references and quotations. The authors' suggestions about suspending candles from the ceiling with hidden wire obviously inspired the special effects for Hogwarts School.

WORKS REVIEWED

Abate, Corinne S., '"Nerissa teaches me what to believe": Portia's Wifely Empowerment in *The*

Merchant of Venice', in *The Merchant of Venice: New Critical Essays*, ed. John W. Mahon and Ellen Macleod Mahon (New York and London, 2002), pp. 283–304.

Alfar, Cristina León, *Fantasies of Female Evil: The Dynamics of Gender and Power in Shakespearean Tragedy* (Newark and London, 2003).

Andrews, John F., 'Textual Deviancy in *The Merchant of Venice*', in *The Merchant of Venice: New Critical Essays*, ed. John W. Mahon and Ellen Macleod Mahon (New York and London, 2002), pp. 165–78.

Belsey, Catherine, 'Tarquin Dispossessed: Expropriation and Consent in *The Rape of Lucrece*' (315–35), *Shakespeare Quarterly*, 52 (2001).

Blake, Anne, '*The Taming of the Shrew*: Making Fun of Katherine', *The Cambridge Quarterly*, 31 (2002), 237–52.

Boehrer, Bruce, *Shakespeare among the Animals: Nature and Society in the Drama of Early Modern England* (Basingstoke, 2002).

Booth, Stephen, 'The Physics of Hamlet's "Rogue and Peasant Slave" Speech', in *"A Certain Text": Close Readings and Textual Studies on Shakespeare and Others*, ed. Linda Anderson and Janis Lull (Newark and London, 2002), pp. 75–93.

W. Bushnell, Rebecca, *King Lear and Macbeth: An Annotated Bibliography of Shakespeare Studies 1774–1995* (Asheville, NC, 1996).

Callaghan, Dympna *et al.*, 'Forum: The Idea of History in Renaissance Studies', *Shakespeare Studies*, 30 (2002), 23–55.

Candido, Joseph, *Richard II, Henry IV, I and II & Henry V: An Annotated Bibliography of Shakespeare Studies 1777–1997* (Asheville, NC, 1998).

Chapman, Alison A., 'Whose Saint Crispin's Day Is It?: Shoemaking, Holiday Making, and the Politics of Memory in Early Modern England', *Renaissance Quarterly*, 54 (2001), 1467–94.

Cheney, Patrick, '"O, let my books be . . . dumb presagers": Poetry and Theater in Shakespeare's Sonnets', *Shakespeare Quarterly*, 52 (2001), 222–54.

Cohen, Derek, 'History and the Nation in *Richard II* and *Henry IV*', *Studies in English Literature*, 42 (2002), 293–315.

Collington, Philip D., '"I Would Thy Husband Were Dead": *The Merry Wives of Windsor* as Mock Domestic Tragedy', *English Literary Renaissance*, 30 (2000), 184–212.

Colón Semenza, Gregory M., 'Sport, War, and Contest in Shakespeare's *Henry VI*', *Renaissance Quarterly*, 54 (2001), 1251–72.

Cunningham, John and Slimp, Stephen, 'The Less into the Greater: Emblem, Analogue, and Deification in *The Merchant of Venice*', in *The Merchant of Venice: New Critical Essays*, ed. John W. Mahon and Ellen Macleod Mahon (New York and London, 2002), pp. 225–82.

Dean, Paul, '"Comfortable Doctrine": *Twelfth Night* and the Trinity', *Review of English Studies*, 52 (2001), 500–16.

Desai, R. W., '"Mislike me not for my complexion": Whose mislike? Portia's? Shakespeare's? or that of his Age?', in *The Merchant of Venice: New Critical Essays*, ed. John W. Mahon and Ellen Macleod Mahon (New York and London, 2002), pp. 305–24.

Drakakis, John, 'Jessica', in *The Merchant of Venice: New Critical Essays*, ed. John W. Mahon and Ellen Macleod Mahon (New York and London, 2002), pp. 145–64.

Dubois, Claude-Gilbert, 'Pathologie du corps spectral a la Renaissance', *Cahiers élisabethains*, 59 (2001), 45–58.

Duncan-Jones, Katherine, 'Ravished and Revised: The 1616 Lucrece', *Review of English Studies*, 52 (2001), 516–23.

Erne, Lukas, *Shakespeare as Literary Dramatist* (Cambridge, 2003).

Favila, Marina, '"Mortal Thoughts" and Magical thinking in Macbeth', *Modern Philology*, 99 (2001), 1–25.

Fisher, Will, 'The Renaissance Beard: Masculinity in Early Modern England', *Renaissance Quarterly*, 54 (2001), 155–87.

Foakes, R. A., *Shakespeare & Violence* (Cambridge, 2003).

Garganigo, Alex, 'Coriolanus, the Union Controversy, and Access to the Royal Person', *Studies in English Literature*, 42 (2002), 335–59.

Gaskill, Gayle, 'Making *The Merchant of Venice* Palatable for U.S. Audiences', in *The Merchant of Venice: New Critical Essays*, ed. John W. Mahon and Ellen Macleod Mahon (New York and London, 2002), pp. 375–86.

Gay, Penny, 'Portia Performs: Playing the Role in the Twentieth-Century English Theatre', in *The*

Merchant of Venice: New Critical Essays, ed. John W. Mahon and Ellen Macleod Mahon (New York and London, 2002), pp. 431–54.

Go, Kenji, 'Unemending the emendation of "still" in Shakespeare's Sonnet 106', *Studies in Philology*, 98 (2001), 114–42.

Hackett, Helen, *Women and Romance Fiction in the English Renaissance* (Cambridge, 2000).

Hadfield, Andrew, 'Tarquin's Everlasting Banishment: Republicanism and Constitutionalism in *The Rape of Lucrece* and *Titus Andronicus*', *Parergon*, 19 (2002), 77–104.

Halio, Jay, 'The Induction as Clue in *The Taming of the Shrew*', in *"A Certain Text": Close Readings and Textual Studies on Shakespeare and Others*, ed. Linda Anderson and Janis Lull (Newark and London, 2002), pp. 94–106.

Halpern, Richard, *Shakespeare's Perfume: Sodomy and Sublimity in the Sonnets, Wilde, Freud, and Lacan* (Philadelphia, 2002).

Hammond, Paul, *Figuring Sex between Men from Shakespeare to Rochester* (Oxford, 2002).

Harris, Jonathan Gil, 'Shakespeare's Hair: Staging the Object of Material Culture' (479–91), *Shakespeare Quarterly*, 52 (2001).

Holland, Peter D., 'The Merchant of Venice and the Value of Money', *Cahiers élisabethains*, 60 (2001), 13–30.

Holmer, Joan Ozark, 'Jewish Daughters: the Question of Philosemitism in Elizabethan Drama', in *The Merchant of Venice: New Critical Essays*, ed. John W. Mahon and Ellen Macleod Mahon (New York and London, 2002), pp. 107–44.

Hopkins, Lisa, 'Lear's Castle', *Cahiers élisabethains*, 62 (2002), 25–32.

The Female Hero in English Renaissance Tragedy (Basingstoke, 2002).

'"Like parrots at a bagpiper"; The Polarities of Exchange in *The Merchant of Venice*', *Parergon*, 19 (2002), 105–20.

Huffman, Clifford Chalmers, *Love's Labor's Lost. Midsummer Night's Dream. The Merchant of Venice* (Binghamton, New York, 1995).

Hunt, Maurice, 'Qualifying the Good Steward of Shakespeare's Timon of Athens', *English Studies*, 82 (2001), 507–20.

Hyland, Peter, *An Introduction to Shakespeare's Poems* (Basingstoke, 2003).

Jackson, MacDonald P., 'Vocabulary and Chronology: The Case of Shakespeare's Sonnets', *Review of English Studies*, 52 (2001), 59–75.

Jacobs, Kathryn, *Marriage Contracts from Chaucer to the Renaissance Stage* (Gainesville, 2001).

Jansohn, Christa, 'Theatricality in *Venus and Adonis* and its Staging in Germany (1994–1998)', *Cahiers élisabethains*, 61 (2002), 31–41.

Keefe, Maryellen, O. S. U., 'Isolation to Communion: A Reading of *The Merchant of Venice*', in *The Merchant of Venice: New Critical Essays*, ed. John W. Mahon and Ellen Macleod Mahon (New York and London, 2002), pp. 213–24.

Klause, John, 'New Sources for Shakespeare's King John: The Writings of Robert Southwell', *Studies in Philology*, 98 (2001), 401–27.

Lander, Jesse M., '"Crack'd Crowns" and Counterfeit Sovereigns: The Crisis of Value in *1 Henry IV*', *Shakespeare Studies*, 30 (2002), 137–61.

Laundau, Aaron, '"Let me not burst in ignorance": Skepticism and Anxiety in Hamlet', *English Studies*, 82 (2001), 218–30.

Leach, Robert, '*As You Like It* – A "Robin Hood" Play', *English Studies*, 82 (2001), 393–400.

Leahy, William, '"All Would be Royal": The Effacement of Disunity in Shakespeare's *Henry V*', *Shakespeare Jahrbuch*, 138 (2002), 89–98.

Levin, Joanna, 'Lady Macbeth and the Daemonologie of Hysteria', *ELH*, 69 (2002), 21–55.

Levin, Richard A., *Shakespeare's Secret Schemers: The Study of an Early Modern Dramatic Device* (University of Delaware, 2001).

Levith, Murray J., 'Shakespeare's *The Merchant of Venice* and Marlowe's Other Play', in *The Merchant of Venice: New Critical Essays*, ed. John W. Mahon and Ellen Macleod Mahon (New York and London, 2002), pp. 95–106.

Mahon, John W., 'The Fortunes of *The Merchant of Venice* from 1596 to 2001', in *The Merchant of Venice: New Critical Essays*, ed. John W. Mahon and Ellen Macleod Mahon (New York and London, 2002), pp. 1–94.

Macfie, Pamela Royston, 'The Ovidian Underworld in *Othello* 3.3', *Renaissance Papers*, 59 (2002), 45–60.

Maguire, Laurie E., 'Performing Anger: The Anatomy of Abuse(s) in *Troilus and Cressida*', *Renaissance Drama*, 31 (2002), 153–83.

Martineau, Jane *et al.*, *Shakespeare in Art* (London, 2003).

Monsarrat, Gilles, '*A Funeral Elegy*: Ford, W. S., and Shakespeare', *Review of English Studies*, 53 (2002), 186–203.

Mooney, Michael E., *Hamlet: An Annotated Bibliography of Shakespeare Studies 1604–1998* (Asheville, NC, 1999).

Mowat, Barbara, 'Prospero's Book', *Shakespeare Quarterly*, 52 (2001), 1–33.

Newcomb, Lori Humphrey, *Reading Popular Romance in Early Modern England* (New York, 2002).

O'Connor, John, 'Shylock in Performance', in *The Merchant of Venice: New Critical Essays*, ed. John W. Mahon and Ellen Macleod Mahon (New York and London, 2002), pp. 317–30.

Palmer, Robert C., *Selling the Church: The English Parish in Law, Commerce, and Religion, 1350–1550* (Chapel Hill and London, 2002).

Parolin, Peter A., 'Anachronistic Italy: Cultural Alliances and National Identity in *Cymbeline*', *Shakespeare Studies*, 30 (2002), 188–215.

Platt, Peter G., '"The Meruailouse Site": Shakespeare, Venice, and Paradoxical Stages', *Renaissance Quarterly*, 54 (2001), 121–54.

Rackin, Phyllis, 'The Impact of Global Trade in *The Merchant of Venice*', *Shakespeare Jahrbuch*, 138 (2002), 73–88.

Reeder, Robert, '"You are now out of your text": The Performance of Precocity on the Early Modern Stage', *Renaissance Papers*, 58 (2001), 35–44.

Richmond, Hugh Macrae, *Shakespeare & the Renaissance Stage to 1616 and Shakespean Stage History 1616 to 1998: An Annotated Bibliography of Shakespeare Studies 1576–1998* (Asheville, NC, 1999).

Roberts, Jeanne Addison, 'The Crone in English Renaissance Drama', *Medieval and Renaissance Drama*, 15 (2003), 116–37.

Roberts, Sasha, *Reading Shakespeare's Poems in Early Modern England* (Basingstoke, 2003).

Rubenstein, Frankie, 'Speculating on Mysteries: Religion and Politics in *King Lear*', *Renaissance Studies*, 16 (2002), 234–62.

Salingar, Leo, 'The Englishness of the Merry Wives of Windsor', *Cahiers élisabethains*, 59 (2001), 9–26.

Schalkwyk, David, *Speech and Performance in Shakespeare's Sonnets and Plays* (Cambridge, 2002).

Scott, William O., 'Landholding, Leasing, and Inheritance in *Richard II*', *Studies in English Literature*, 42 (2002), 275–92.

Shohet, Lauren, 'Shakespeare's Eager Adonis', *Studies in English Literature*, 42 (2002), 85–102.

Short, Hugh, 'Shylock is Content: a Study in Salvation', in *The Merchant of Venice: New Critical Essays*, ed. John W. Mahon and Ellen Macleod Mahon (New York and London, 2002), 199–212.

Spolsky, Ellen, *Satisfying Skepticism: Embodied Knowledge in the Early Modern World* (Ashgate, 2001).

Stevenson, Ruth, '*Hamlet*'s Mice, Motes, Moles, and Minching Malecho', *New Literary History*, 33 (2002), 435–59.

Szatek, Karoline, '*The Merchant of Venice* and the Politics of Commerce', in *The Merchant of Venice: New Critical Essays*, ed. John W. Mahon and Ellen Macleod Mahon (New York and London, 2002), pp. 325–52.

Tambling, Jeremy, *Becoming Posthumous: Life and Death in Literary and Cultural Studies* (Edinburgh, 2001).

Targoff, Ramie, '"Dirty" Amens: Devotion, Applause, and Consent in *Richard III*', *Renaissance Drama*, 31 (2002), 61–84.

Taylor, Mark, *Shakespeare's Imitations* (Newark and London, 2002).

Thomson, Leslie, 'The Theatrical Rhetoric of Edward III', *Medieval and Renaissance Drama*, 15 (2003), 43–56.

Thorne, Alison, '"Awake Remembrance of these Valiant Dead": *Henry V* and the Politics of the English History Play', *Shakespeare Studies*, 30 (2002), 162–87.

Tiffany, Grace, 'Names in *The Merchant of Venice*', in *The Merchant of Venice: New Critical Essays*, ed. John W. Mahon and Ellen Macleod Mahon (New York and London, 2002), 333–67.

Velz, John W., 'Portia and the Ovidian Grotesque', in *The Merchant of Venice: New Critical Essays*, ed. John W. Mahon and Ellen Macleod Mahon (New York and London, 2002), 179–86.

Vickers, Brian, *'Counterfeiting' Shakespeare: Evidence, Authorship, and John Ford's Funeral Elegye* (Cambridge, 2002).

Wall, Wendy, 'Why does Puck Sweep?: Fairylore, Merry Wives, and Social Struggle', *Shakespeare Quarterly*, 52 (2001), 67–106.

Wells, Stanley, *Shakespeare for all Time* (Basingstoke, 2002).

Wilkinson, Jane, 'The Sickly Weal: Anglo-Scottish DissemiNations in Macbeth', *Anglistica*, 4 (2000), 103–29.

Young, Alan R., *Hamlet and the Visual Arts, 1709–1900* (Newark and London, 2002).

Zyvatkauskas, Betty and Sonia, *Eating Shakespeare: Recipes and more from the Bard's Kitchen* (Toronto, 2000).

COLLECTIONS

"A Certain Text": Close Readings and Textual Studies on Shakespeare and others in Honor of Thomas Clayton, ed. Linda Anderson and Janis Lull (Newark and London, 2002).

The Merchant of Venice: New Critical Essays, ed. John W. Mahon and Ellen Macleod Mahon (London, 2002).

Ovid and the Renaissance Body, ed. Goran V. Stanivukovic (Toronto, 2001).

2. SHAKESPEARE IN PERFORMANCE

reviewed by EMMA SMITH

That Shakespeare in performance has come of critical age seems to be signalled by the volume dedicated to it in Cambridge University Press's Companion series. *The Cambridge Companion to Shakespeare on Stage* edited by Stanley Wells and Sarah Stanton joins Companions to 'Shakespeare', 'Shakespeare on Film', 'Shakespearian Comedy', 'Shakespeare's History Plays' and, forthcoming, 'Shakespeare's Tragedies'. The asymmetry of this taxonomic division may seem rather like Foucault's report of the Chinese encyclopaedia's distribution of the animal kingdom: the rationale offered in the volume is a response to 'the increasing number of courses devoted to the history of Shakespeare in performance' (p. xv). Something more explicit on the demands, opportunities and theory of this pedagogical shift might have been useful – a curious lack of reflection on methodological issues emerges as a dominant theme of writing on Shakespeare in performance – but the contributions map an elegant conspectus of approaches to the subject. The collection opens with 'Shakespeare's Plays on Renaissance Stages', and then there are chapters on Restoration, Romantic, Victorian, neo-Elizabethan and twentieth-century production trends. A clutch of chapters consider non-English stage traditions, in North America, Asia and Africa, and there are chapters on political Shakespeare, on women, on touring, and on comic and tragic actors. The collection's international focus is a welcome and distinctive one, although probably not one that many of those target courses on Shakespeare in production have the resources realistically to share. Gary Taylor's opening chapter argues that, rather than being a secondary manifestation of a pre-existent text, theatricality is in fact the ur-state of a play: 'For Shakespeare, a play began life in the theatre' (p. 1). Subsequent chapters open up more temporal space between increasingly distinct categories of 'text' and 'performance'. Constructing the volume historically and thematically gives it conceptual clarity, but makes few concessions to those readers concerned with a specific play rather than a performance issue or era.

These two approaches – the historical and the geographical – are amplified in a range of other publications. First, the historical. Katherine West Scheil's *The Taste of the Town: Shakespearian Comedy and the Early Eighteenth-Century Theater* argues that the reception and reproduction of comedies in the eighteenth century highlights the uneven progress of Shakespeare's reputation in the period. She considers adaptations not primarily in connection with their Shakespearian source but as reflections of local performance conditions, arguing persuasively that the label 'Shakespearian adaptations' has unhelpfully and anachronistically tethered these new theatrical texts to their sixteenth-century author. Scheil argues, for example, that few spectators would have recognized that Davenant's *The Law Against Lovers* was taken from *Measure for Measure* and *Much Ado About Nothing*, given that there were no performances and no newly reprinted texts during the Interregnum; instead of judging the play in connection with its Shakespearian sources, spectators compared it with contemporary offerings in other theatres. Shakespeare's name, Scheil concludes, was of little value in the market for comic entertainment; even the introduction of actresses did not stimulate interest in Shakespeare's comedies; 'adaptations' have most to tell us about the conditions of theatre writing and production in the period.

The relative importance of the signifier 'Shakespearian' is also of interest in Richard W. Schoch's *Not Shakespeare*, an account of Shakespeare burlesques which identifies their crucial role in puncturing the earnest pretensions of Victorian bardolatry. In the spring of 1853 no fewer than six Shakespearian parody shows were playing in London: 'we are done to death with burlesques', wrote the *Spectator* (p. 6). Drawing on a range of wonderfully named texts, from *A Thin Slice of Ham Let!* to *Macbeth Somewhat Removed from the Text of Shakespeare*, the study traces the development of a set of consistent burlesque attributes, including rhyming couplets paraphrasing Shakespeare's text, the transposition of characters into ludicrously mundane settings, classic scenes made risible by stage business, topical references, and set pieces rearranged to opera, minstrel or popular songs. A number of burlesques appear promptly as parodies of the high seriousness of performances by Kean and others, although the repertoire of playtexts burlesqued is surprisingly limited, with *Hamlet*, *Romeo and Juliet* and *Richard III* accounting for almost half the total examples. There are no burlesques of *Henry V* despite its popularity in the Victorian theatre, and none of the comedies, other than *The Merchant of Venice*, proved amenable to burlesque treatment. Schoch deals with his material with a light touch – his descriptions of Henry Hall as King John wearing a helmet topped with a weather-vane, for example – but his tone is sober and conceptually rigorous. Parody functions to reinvigorate canonical forms once they have become rigid or mechanistic, and thus parody preserves rather than undermines its original. Distinguishing between adaptation, which '*is* the play which it adapts', and burlesque, which '*represents* the play it burlesques', Schoch argues for burlesques as interpretations rather than iterations of Shakespeare (p. 21), and traces their multiple ambivalences to their originating texts. Burlesques often claimed the authentic connection to Shakespeare which they accused their targets in the legitimate theatre of having forfeited, but they were also, as Schoch illustrates, energetic and popular vehicles for the revived, topical and politicised theatrical culture of the nineteenth century.

Schoch's study of burlesque identifies it as a contributor, rather than a threat, to Shakespeare's cultural prestige during the nineteenth century. Richard Foulkes's *Performing Shakespeare in the Age of Empire* also identifies performance as fundamental to 'Shakespeare's cultural preeminence' (p. 1): his book serves as the flipside of Schoch's in tracing the impact of the abolition of the patent theatres' monopoly on productions of Shakespeare's plays. Macready's 1837 prospectus for his Covent Garden theatre proclaimed 'his strenuous endeavours to advance the drama as a branch of national literature and art' (p. 10) gave Shakespeare a starring role in this national cultural project, in which royal patronage, changing theatre regulation and a new realism in acting style all played their part. Subsequent chapters in Foulkes's study pass Macready's mantle to Phelps, Kean, Calvert, Rignold and the other dominant actor-managers of the Victorian theatre. There is an excellent discussion of the professional and national rivalries which dogged arrangements for the 1864 Tercentenary celebrations: both Schoch and Foulkes reprint a *Punch* cartoon from 1864 entitled 'Shakespeare and the Pigmies' in which Shakespeare's monument in Holy Trinity Church, with the playwright's eyes blinded, is assailed by Lilliputian figures in top hats attempting to carve their own names alongside his and flypost advertisements for the tercentenary programme. For Foulkes, this bathetic epitaph registers the failure of the celebrations and a nadir in Shakespeare's reception; for Schoch the cartoon 'captures the essence of the burlesque critique' (p. 75) in its restorative anti-bardolater energies. Shakespeare's rise and fall due to changing theatrical tastes and an increasing association of the bard with education rather than entertainment meant that the next tercentenary, of Shakespeare's death in 1916, was organized by literary and academic figures rather than theatrical ones. Foulkes's argument that the vitality of Victorian Shakespeare was on the stage rather than page is thus triumphantly endorsed: in the hands of the scholars this etiolated celebration had neither the commercial nor the ideological impetus to make much impact.

Turning from studies structured around a historical moment to studies taking geography as their lens, Aimara da Cunha Resenda has edited the first book in English on Brazilian readings of Shakespeare, *Foreign Accents*. Resenda's own introductory essay outlines a history of theatrical, fictional and televisual appropriations, anchored around the theme, so fruitful for anti- and post-colonial Latin American Shakespeares, of Caliban's use of language. There is a compelling account of a sharply hierarchical version of *Othello* directed by Afonso Grisolli for Brazilian television. Marlene Soares dos Santos takes a rather apologetic tone in discussing Augusto Boal's *A Tempestade* as a play which needs to be performed to be appreciated; Anna Stegh Camati's discussion of a version of *Hamlet* called *Hamletrash* makes suggestive parallels between Brazilian recycling, post-modern pastiche, and the self-reflexivity of the play itself. Other essays give the perspective of Brazilian scholars on a range of questions, not all of them connected with performance. Altogether the collection is uneven – the descriptions of Brazilian theatre and of recent stagings of Shakespeare are more arresting than the unexceptionable but rather deracinated scholarly essays on more general topics. Like all good books on performance, however, it has the capacity to make the reader simultaneously regret and idealize the impermanence and irrecoverability of the productions it describes. *Four Hundred Years of Shakespeare in Europe* edited by A. Luis Pujante and Ton Hoenselaars shares some of the same strengths and weaknesses. The major strength is to reconfigure the performance hotspots: too often our map of Shakespeare in performance seems, like a medieval map's wilful centring on Jerusalem and, with similar insularity, to have as its epicentre the theatres of Stratford-upon-Avon. Here Berlin, Avignon, Sofia and Basel also draw the eye. Balz Engler begins by reminding us that one of the first eye-witnesses of performed Shakespeare was the Swiss Thomas Platter; Dennis Kennedy discusses the role of Shakespearian production in post-war Europe 'as a site for the recovery and reconstruction of values that were perceived to be under threat, or already lost' (p. 163); Isabelle Schwartz-Gastine discusses nineteenth-century French productions. The book gives the sense that this must have been a wonderful conference to attend – at Murcia in 1999 – it's a kind of reverse page-stage problem that this sense of intellectual cohesion and excitement cannot come over quite so well in print.

One problem with both historical and regional Shakespeare is that particular plays crop up only randomly. The theatrical fortunes of individual plays are, however, amply traced in a number of other series. One, Cambridge University Press's Shakespeare in Production series (I should declare an interest here, since I edited the volume on *King Henry V*, 2002), offers the New Cambridge version of the text annotated not with details of etymology or historical context but with information from the stage history of the play. The New Cambridge editors have been traditionally attentive to matters of staging: the Shakespeare in Production series develops this as its *raison d'être*, and is the only one of the current batch of stage histories not to be conducted entirely through critical narrative but through the annotation of individual lines. One of the advantages of this method is an explication of those aspects of a play which modern readers are likely to find most difficult. For example, Ann Thompson's excellent edition of *The Taming of the Shrew* (1984) properly glosses the references in Induction 2 to classical figures Semiramis, Io, Daphne and Cytherea with reference to mythology. There are no such pointers in Elizabeth Schafer's *The Taming of the Shrew* in the Shakespeare in Production series, but instead, the note tells us about the tendency of twentieth-century productions to brandish here 'a portfolio of smutty photographs'. This note doesn't tell us who Semiramis *et al.* were, rather as, in the theatre, we could not reach for a reference book to look up an unfamiliar name. Instead it suggests that what is significant about the classical figures in dramatic terms is not who they were or who raped them, but rather the atmosphere of sexual licence and *Ars Amatoria* lubricity created for the hapless Christopher Sly in the Induction. Since the names may not automatically conjure this atmosphere for a modern audience, a prop is employed as an adjunct: the pornographic pictures function as the theatre's material equivalent of the footnote.

This is a method that can work well for puns and jokes, enabling readers to imagine the comic effect of wordplay that can remain resolutely leaden on the page. It is hard to be fleet of editorial foot when glossing a sequence of puns such as those between Katherine and Petruccio in 2.1: Thompson's clear account – 'movable (1) portable item of furniture, (2) inconsistent or changeable person'; 'burden (1) lie heavy on (in the act of sexual intercourse and hence 'make pregnant'), (2) makes accusations against (*OED* sv *v* 2)' – gives readers all the information, but cannot make the exchange funny. We might expect that Schafer's research would bring the scene to life, but actually her annotations to this sequence admit that the very heaviness of the punning texture of the language has led directors to favour physical rather than verbal comedy at this point. Promptbooks tell of Petruccios goosing Katherines, of Katherines kicking Petruccios in the crotch, of missiles including fruit, books and a chair flying across the room. Here production history seems to indicate that, *OED* citations and editorial legwork notwithstanding, the sparkling verbal humour cannot be recreated theatrically, only translated into the rough slapstick of sexualized violence on the stage.

This, too, is a useful insight, since it offers a challenge to the levelling effect of traditional editorial glossing. It is very hard to know, for example, when looking at the heavily annotated servants' quarrel in *Romeo and Juliet* (1.1), whether editorial footnotes present scholarly ingenuity about a line which was always obscure, or whether the gloss retrieves for us a state of easy comprehension as experienced by the play's first audiences. Annotating tends to place difficult material all at the same pitch – in the altercations between Sampson and Gregory, for example, 'colliers', 'take the wall', and 'poor-John'; by contrast the 'Shakespeare in Production' annotations in James Loehlin's volume tell us where the burden of cutting falls, as when eighteenth-century performances suppressed the lines for their bawdy innuendo and twentieth-century directors for their incomprehensibility. In *Rescripting Shakespeare*, Alan Dessen's study of textual choices involved in compiling playscripts for modern Shakespearian performances (discussed in more detail below), Dessen gives a range of examples of complicated phrasing or textual cruces which editors have expended much energy in elucidating but which directors almost always cut anyway in the theatre.

There are also points at which performance tradition makes a quite different emphasis from editorial tradition. M. M. Mahood, in her New Cambridge edition of *The Merchant of Venice*, notes that the endwords of each line in the song 'Tell me where is fancy bred' (3.2) rhyme with 'lead' and that this may therefore be intended as a clue to Bassanio about which casket he should choose. She goes on, however, to discount this as a real possibility, since it contravenes their moral characters as, presumably, already and unassailably established: it 'belittles Portia's integrity and Bassanio's insight' (p. 127). In performance, of course, Portia may or may not have integrity and Bassanio may or may not be blessed with particular insight. The notes to Edelman's 'Shakespeare in Production' volume on the play are accordingly more permissive than Mahood's: Edelman discusses various directors from Komisarjevsky to Sellars, and the response of reviewers to what the *Daily Telegraph* in 1932 called 'this uncommonly dirty trick'. Strikingly, however, Edelman still draws on an authority located within the text itself, rather than refracted in its multiple stage realizations, asserting that 'what many directors,

John Barton a worthy exception, seem unwilling to accept is that 'Fancy bred' is indeed a hint, but a serious one that depends on Bassanio giving careful attention to all its words, not just the rhymes' (pp. 188–9). So there is an intrinsic and correct meaning after all – perhaps, though Edelman is too sophisticated to use this phrasing, 'Shakespeare's intention' – to which directors must remain faithful in order to earn the critical approbation of that epithet 'worthy'. Both Cambridge editions of the play, therefore, know what the play means us to think at this point, and both see the job of the notes to fix meaning rather than to record possibilities. Perhaps the selectivity of the production history cited in the 'Shakespeare in Production' series serves to endorse certain theatrical interpretations and silently to discount others. The authority of the editor, albeit the editor of a stage history, dominates over the dispersed and ventriloquized authorities of the director or reviewer.

Of course, using information from performance as a supplementary (rather than an alternative) form of editorial authority has been an increasing feature of mainstream editions, and this has tended to become more integrated than previously. Here, though, series do not seem to have a consistent practice: Roger Warren and Stanley Wells's 1994 *Twelfth Night* for the Oxford Shakespeare draws extensively on performance history throughout the introduction and notes, whereas John Jowett has a separate section, 'On stage', in his recent *Richard III* (2000). Despite, or perhaps because of, the outpouring of critical works on stage history, this approach has maintained a kind of separateness within academic criticism of Shakespeare. It is still often perceived as methodologically unsophisticated, a matter either of trawling through reviews and promptbooks, or of describing subjective recollections of theatre performances, or watching a few films on video and writing about them. To some extent the books published in this area this year confirm this suspicion. In the discipline of literary criticism which elsewhere may be unhelpfully fraught with methodological questions, few of the performance studies books under consideration seem to be overtly troubled by their own procedures or assumptions. What performance studies *is* goes without elaboration. Is it play-specific and longitudinal – the project of the 'Shakespeare in Production' series? Should it be placed historically and geographically, as the semesterized contents of the *Companion to Shakespeare on Stage* suggest? How does it relate to its disparate contiguous discourses of theatre studies, theatre reviewing, literary criticism, cultural history and theatre history? In his book on *As You Like It* in the 'Shakespeare at Stratford' series, Robert Smallwood talks about the difficulties of sifting 'the informative from the merely opinionated' (p. 10): this may be a laudable principle, but how these categories might be arrived at is less certain. Crucially, this information records both theatrical production and reception: performance history, as it inhabits a grey disciplinary space between 'English Literature' and 'Theatre Studies', draws both on the intentionalism of author/practitioner-centred approaches and on the affective aspects of a kind of reader/audience-response criticism. It is an apparent feature of stage histories that their evaluations are hidden. Of course there is a process of selection, of which productions to include and which, silently, to leave out. The 'Shakespeare in Production' volumes serve to gather up the scattered and fragmented commentary which can enable theatrical pasts to be reconstructed. By sifting information from promptbooks, reviews, interviews, memoirs, photographs and film, their editors provide and make intelligible information from a wide range of sources. The main method is, however, descriptive rather than analytical: there are rarely evaluative comments. Differences of interpretation are scrupulously recorded, reviewers who did and did not like a certain piece of business are quoted, but the question of theatrical or artistic merit is neatly sidestepped.

The language of much performance criticism, in contrast to its parent disciplines, is apparently transparent, unspecialized. There is very little to choose between the register of, say, the academic Smallwood on *As You Like It* or the actor Oliver Ford Davies on *King Lear*. It is its great strength that performance studies can claim a non-professional readership, particularly given the increasing specialization and esotericism of academic prose, but this may be the very reason why it is not more highly regarded within the academic institution. Sometimes this absence of explicit critical self-consciousness is in fact a suppressed presence in the argument. Jay Halio warns readers at the beginning of his *Shakespeare in Performance: A Midsummer Night's Dream* that 'though critics sometimes forget it, the theatre is not the study'. He goes on to assert, in an apparent theoretical contradiction that would bear some further meditation, both that 'it is only in the theatre that the text achieves realisation' *and* that 'regard for Shakespeare's text has been constant, particularly as various productions have played it, adapted it, rewritten it, and in other ways celebrated or distorted the *Dream*'s comic achievement' (p. 1). Halio's apparent obeisance to the study rather than the theatre, to the 'text' rather than the performance, to a 'comic achievement' independent of theatrical life, is a curiously tacit modesty topos, in which performance criticism is at the service of something else. In the words of the general editors of the 'Shakespeare in Performance' series, this 'something else' is the portable, book-format Shakespearian text, what they call the 'play in hand'. Writing on Shakespeare on film, partly because of the highly theorized nature of much of film studies, is an exception to the transparency of much performance criticism. Contributors to Lisa Starks and Courtney Lehmann's *The Reel Shakespeare: Alternative Cinema and Theory* discuss a range of Shakespearian films including Godard's *King Lear*, Taymor's *Titus*, Greenaway's *Prospero's Books*, and Welles's *Chimes at Midnight*. Since the developments in the scholarship on filmed Shakespeare can be attributed to influence from the institution of cinema on the one hand and the institution of liberal arts education on the other, it is good to see a section on pedagogy. Douglas Green discusses the representation of homosocial bonds in Branagh's films and how classroom discussions in his particular institutional context are a negotiation between different humanist, historicist and presentist voices. John Brett Mischio takes up films of *The Taming of the Shrew* as an example of performance-based pedagogy in high school classrooms.

Contributors to *Shakespeare in Performance*, edited by Frank Occhiogrosso, are more reflective about methodology. John Russell Brown proposes that performance criticism is 'not a territory for bookworms and, since little is indisputable, not for dogmatists either' (p. 16), and suggests, radically for most performance critics, that more would be gained from seeing the same production several times than from seeing a number of different productions. James C. Bulman discusses the intersections between performance criticism and post-structuralism in relation to *The Merchant of Venice*, arguing for a more ambiguous presentation of Shylock than the tragic scapegoat/comic villain dichotomy allows. Jay Halio considers a nuanced concept of authenticity in historical or modern versions of *Romeo and Juliet*. The volume ends with a heartfelt contribution from Marvin Rosenberg about the possibilities of performance criticism to 'enrich our students, our colleagues, our lives' (p. 136): perhaps a sentiment few critics of other persuasions would feel so comfortable with, but one which appeals to the uniquely affective power of the theatre.

Academic engagement with performance practitioners does tend towards the admiring. Even by these standards, however, there is something hagiographic about the 'Shakespeare at Stratford' series, in which the theatrical *mappa mundi* still focuses defiantly on the Cotswolds. When Smallwood, writing as the series' General Editor, asserts that productions at Stratford since 1945 provide 'a representative cross-section of the main trends in [. . .] theatrical interpretation in the second half of the twentieth century' (p. xii), we might wonder whether this history tells us something rather more institutionally specific about the changing fortunes of a high-profile subsidized theatre under royal patronage. Smallwood's tone on *As You Like It* is affectionate. From designer Kaffe Fassett's imprint on the jumpers and cushions of Greg Doran's 2000 production, to the 'Irish sense of mischief and energy' (p. 85) brought by Sinead Cusack (1980) and then Fiona Shaw (1985) to the part of Rosalind, considered but contagious enthusiasm for the theatre gives his prose a personable energy. Smallwood draws effectively on the soundbite idiolect of newspaper reviewers, so that memorable and summary short phrases sum up different production styles. 'Jung ones in Arden' represents Adrian Noble's 1985 production; Michael Billington recalls Sophie Thompson's Rosalind as 'the life and soul of the Arden Junior Lacrosse team' (p. 126); Robert Speaight records a Jaques departing like 'Marcel Proust retiring to a monastery' (p. 197). This is theatre history as enjoyment, both the enjoyment of the productions discussed and the enjoyment of writing about them, and enjoyment, sadly, is not necessarily the dominant impression of much academic criticism. But while this enjoyment is necessarily personal, the role of the first person in the discourse of performance criticism seems unclear. For some reason, Smallwood goes through considerable stylistic contortions to avoid the use of the personal pronoun at the end of his *As You Like It* study as he alludes to the current debates about a new theatre building for Stratford: 'one found oneself wondering, as one watched this thirteenth in the extraordinarily various, and distinguished, sequence with which this book has been concerned, how many more Rosalinds there might be, before a new building came along' (p. 214). Why not say 'I found myself wondering'? Smallwood's credentials for explicitly offering his own opinion or response, are, after all, unquestionable.

This question of the place from which to speak authoritatively about performance seems (perhaps I should add, self-consciously, 'to me') a collective issue arising from these books. When Oliver Ford Davies talks about *Playing Lear* – subtitled *An Insider's Guide from Text to Performance* – it is obvious that he writes as a particular kind of insider: an actor. Indeed, in the space on the back cover usually reserved for testimonials for the book, there are two quotations from reviewers about his stage performance: the authority for the book's insights, its success or failure as a book, is elided with that of his already over, but here fossilized, 'moving and intelligent' characterization of Lear on the Almeida stage. Davies's style is readable, if at times banal. His opening, describing his preparations for Act 1, scene 1, begins ingenuously: 'I know this scene is a big problem, so I read it very carefully' (p. 14). But there are some interesting points about diachronic readings. Plays in the theatre move forward from start to finish. We cannot flick back to a previous scene to check our recollection or follow some thematic or structural niceties. Davies outlines how rehearsal towards this teleological presentation of the play is recursive and circular: he cannot decide how to play 1.1 until he has decided how to play the whole. The section on 'First Reading' is full of unanswered questions, mostly ones familiar from critical debates about the play – where is the Fool in the opening scene? What happened to Lear's wife? Why does Shakespeare's ending go against all his sources? What does Q offer that F doesn't? – but Davies places them unpompously, unencumbered with critical footnotes, arising from the play rather than being brought from elsewhere to it. Lots of different voices advise and shape Davies's work on the play: critics including Eagleton, Kott, Bloom, Bate, and Ted Hughes; Miranda, his English Literature graduate daughter; previous Lears; the director and fellow actors, often drawing on the dynamics of their own family relationships. On the question 'do you play what the text seems to indicate or do you use the text as a springboard for further interpretation' (p. 92), Davies's phrasing may be different but his position is rather similar to that of the performance critics already discussed above: yes, acting is always reinterpretation, but there's no need to do anything 'plainly contrary to Shakespeare's intentions' (p. 93). *Playing Lear* has modest intellectual and chronicle ambitions and fulfils them in readable style. Also concerned with the specific insights of performers is the second edition of Mary Maher's *Modern Hamlets and their Soliloquies*. Maher adds Kenneth Branagh and Simon Russell Beale to her list of twentieth-century Hamlets, most of whom she has interviewed, but a couple, Richard Burton and Laurence Olivier, have their thoughts articulated through careful interrogation of their filmed performances. Maher's tone is sympathetic rather than challenging, allowing her Hamlets to have their head and restricting her own voice to that of narrator. The book offers a valuable record of some iconic productions, although in its focus on their central protagonist rather than on the production as a whole, it might be seen to endorse Hamlet's tendency towards solipsism. For Maher's study, *Hamlet* is Hamlet, just as Davies's Lear is *King Lear*. This is the new wine of performance criticism in the old bottles of character study, laced with the genuflection of academics at the specific creative energies of theatre practitioners.

Alan Dessen's methodology is based instead on close analysis of the promptbook texts of Shakespeare productions, a study of their scripts rather than their characters. *Rescripting Shakespeare: The Text, the Director, and Modern Productions* employs two terms for the range of activities involved in turning Shakespeare's text into an acting script for a modern performance: 'rescripting', which involves smaller-scale changes to streamline, eliminate obscurity or reduce the number of actors required, and 'rewrighting', in which the director takes on some of the roles of the playwright in a major artistic reconfiguration, such as, for example, combining parts 1 and 2 of *Henry IV* into a single play. Dessen's acute theatrical sense is paired with a refreshing willingness to evaluate directorial textual choices, using the economic vocabulary of 'price-tags' and 'trade-offs'. Clarity, fluidity or psychological consistency may be achieved by reshaping Shakespeare's texts, but Dessen's interest is in the costs of, for example, Trevor Nunn's textual work for his *Troilus and Cressida* (National Theatre, 1999), which created a 'clearer narrative' but 'reduced the ironic or deflationary effects built into the script' (p. 73). One of Dessen's most engaging chapters is about the role and placement of the interval in modern productions. Describing the placing of the interval in David Thacker's promenade production of *Julius Caesar* in 1993, Dessen notes that it gained the powerful effect of having patrons walk round the body of Cinna the poet as they left for their drinks, but forfeited the close parallels between this scene of mob violence and the 'more insidious pricking of names' that begins 4.1 (p. 95). Breaking *Much Ado About Nothing* after 3.2, Matthew Warchus was able to make connections not only between the tricking of Benedick and the tricking of Beatrice, as is more usual, but also to associate with this apparently benign deceit the darker tricking of Claudio and Don Pedro on which the first half closed. Dessen's investigation of directorial authority is interrogative rather than submissive. He distances himself from point-scoring academic reviewers of Shakespeare productions in journals as a 'version of Falstaff wounding a dead Hotspur in the thigh' (p. 236), an image it is pleasantly difficult to paraphrase, but which still manages to prioritize the 'academic' approach to the text as a worthy partner to the theatrical.

At the end of his book, Alan Dessen makes a confession: 'I am painfully aware of the theatre historian's dirty little secret – how little we actually know about how these plays were first conceived and performed' (p. 237). Perhaps this mystery is getting less and less dirty, less and less secret. Certainly a number of books consider and illuminate further aspects of the early modern stage. Arthur F. Kinney's *Shakespeare by Stages: An Historical Introduction* works to synthesize much recent scholarship on the material conditions of performance in Shakespeare's day. He offers judicious and measured commentary on the extant documentary evidence including de Witt's drawing of the Swan and recent archaeological investigations on London's South Bank. More detailed is Mariko Ichikawa's valuable study *Shakespearian Entrances*, which analyses the meanings of the stage directions *exit/exeunt* as actions of a certain duration rather than single, complete movements. It is the beginning of overlapping or extended exits that are usually marked by the stage direction, rather than their completion, and thus characters may still be onstage to hear two or three lines after the direction which apparently indicates their departure. Presumably, Ichikawa argues, 'some convention operated on the Shakespearian stage concerning the relationship between onstage characters and entering or exiting characters' (p. 54), rather in the manner of the non-naturalistic conventions governing what are anachronistically called 'asides'. For entrances, Ichikawa cites a number of uses of the adverbial phrase 'afar off' or 'aloof', as when

Hamlet and Horatio enter the grave-diggers' scene in the Folio text of *Hamlet*. Throughout, Ichikawa's concern is for stage directions as depictions of performance actions: it would be interesting to consolidate this work with a sense of stage directions as information for readers – in, for example, Jonson's plays.

It is well known that collections of essays are generally remembered for one or two outstanding contributions rather than a cumulative sense of the whole. Two recent collections on early modern staging practices challenge this rule. In *Staged Properties in Early Modern English Drama*, the editors Jonathan Gil Harris and Natasha Korda gather together significant contributions towards a material history of stage properties and their thematic and emblematic relevance. Harris and Korda argue that even material histories have tended to endorse Romantic priorities of character and text over object – certainly this is probably true of the stage histories in the 'Shakespeare in Production' series. Harris's own likeable and stimulating essay considers early modern 'product placement', in which metatheatrical advertisements for consumer goods, including the shoes made in Eyre's workshop in Dekker's *The Shoemaker's Holiday* or the gilded enamelled belt given by William Revetour to the Girdlers of York for their pageant wagon in 1446, pique consumerist demands and engage with a historical dialectic of capitalist production and artisanal skill. Lena Cowen Orlin discusses the difficulties of Henslowe's props list, and its inscription of complicated social and commercial functions including ownership, accountability and fungibility. One feature of her argument is to reawaken the connection between 'playhouse' and 'house' as part of a wider cultural dynamic of 'property'. Other essays consider specific metonymic props: the bed, the table in domestic tragedy, the handkerchief in *Othello*, the prosthetic beard as a property of gender, clothing and costumes, props associated with women.

Another notable collection of essays is Paul Whitfield White and Suzanne Westfall's *Shakespeare and Theatrical Patronage in Early Modern England*. Here twelve individually and collectively coherent contributions fill out complex interactions between the early modern theatre and specific patrons as well as with the institutions of cultural and theatrical patronage. White's own essay discusses the mess into which the Lord Chamberlain's Men stumbled around the Oldcastle affair, arguing that Cobham's antitheatricality has been overstated by previous accounts and that rather the controversy was animated by a clash between major factions within the patronage system. David Bergeron makes the link between the patronage of performance and the patronage of publication through an analysis of the dedicatees of the First Folio, William and Philip Herbert, and their role as patrons for Jonson's 1616 *Works*. A number of essays focus on aristocratic entertainments and the political functions of patronage in the context of the drama of the Elizabethan and Jacobean court. Patronage relations are considered more laterally in Alexandra Johnston's work on the city of York as a patron of drama during the heyday and decline of the city's sponsorship of the Corpus Christi cycle and, in the final essay in the collection, Alexander Leggatt on 'The audience as patron'. Leggatt discusses the market concept of playwrighting and performance in the public theatres, Jonson's distaste, and the complex inscription of audience members in the burlesque *The Knight of the Burning Pestle*.

Jonson's ambivalence to paying theatrical customers is absorbed by Rosalyn Knutson into a more thoroughgoing investigation of the commercial aspects of the wars of the theatres, particularly Jonson's rivalry with Marston. Her study is explicitly and compellingly revisionist: in reassessing the traditional stress on authorial personality as the driving force of the so-called poetomachia, she sketches out the dynamics of industrial competition existing between entrepreneurs, companies, theatres and other stakeholders, rather than between playwrights. Guilds offered a contemporary model in which similarly skilled professionals, who might otherwise be commercial rivals, could work cooperatively: Knutson argues that while the theatre industry never organized itself into such a formal professional alliance, it developed ways of working to the overall benefit of the theatre rather than the exclusive gain of a particular company or venue. She suggests that an undue emphasis on 'theatre history as personality' – the title of her opening chapter reviewing existing critical approaches to the subject – has distorted the narrative of theatrical commerce in the years either side of 1600 and, by casting her net more widely to include, for example, the Oldcastle plays, the revived *Spanish Tragedy* and books of satires and epigrams, she recasts the significance of author-based critiques. Instead she argues that the so-called 'war' was rather a cooperative entrepreneurial strategy designed to whet audience appetite for new plays and to extend the market of the London theatre. Knutson's work is based on extensive archival research. She traces networks of kinship, friendship and proximity which connect players from different companies; she identifies Shakespeare's unrepresentative singularity in being associated exclusively with one company throughout his career and shows how theatrical entrepreneurs depended on a large number of mobile and cooperative writers who could operate within fashionable genres and themes; she demolishes some of the assumptions around *Histrio-Mastix* and downplays its significance in the commercial relations of the Elizabethan theatre. Perhaps most controversially, Knutson redates the 'little eyases' passage in the Folio text of *Hamlet* 2.2, usually located by commentators as part of the Wars of the Theatres in 1601 with particular reference to the alleged rivalry between men's and children's playhouses. Instead, Knutson marshals convincing evidence that this passage should be seen as a later rewriting in response to intra-theatrical relations in the period 1606–8, when plays such as *The Isle of Gulls* transgressed the fragile protocols about political engagement and satire on the stage and threatened the whole industry with increased regulation.

Finally, Stephen Orgel's stimulating and wide-ranging *Imagining Shakespeare* proposes to focus 'not on the texts but on the history of performance because that is really all there is' (p. xiv). What a Shakespearian text represents is 'an anthology of productions' (p. 2), and so-called 'bad quartos' come good if we look at them from the point of view of production. In the absence of those productions, however, Orgel's argument is of necessity textual: promptbooks, illustrations of theatres, woodcuts from play title pages, illustrations to Shakespeare and other playwrights in print. Ranging from contemporary accounts through a long history of stage and print reception, Orgel's chapters take particular prompts – Shakespeare's portrait, Mrs Charles Kean as Clio the Muse of History, alias the Chorus to *Henry V*, Giulio Romano's pornographic engravings known as *I Modi* – to develop a densely argued web of allusive commentary. It is heavily illustrated but it is a shame that the pictures from *I Modi* are so pixellated, although the blurriness of these images of buggery does add the connotations of internet pornography to their illicit thrill. The chapter on *A Midsummer Night's Dream* engages most directly with questions of Shakespeare in performance: here Orgel's analysis is breathtaking in its interweaving of royal influence, stories of witchcraft, *The Masque of Queens*, the question of the plays' marriages and the role of magic, and the ominously allusive mythological context for Theseus and Hippolyta. In engaging performance criticism with historicism, with a strong awareness of visual culture including the theatre, and in the histories of Shakespeare's ongoing reception of Shakespeare, Orgel's book is a fine example of the power of Shakespeare in performance to interrogate and enrich the whole critical project.

WORKS REVIEWED

Davies, Oliver Ford, *Playing Lear: An Insider's Guide from Text to Performance* (London, 2003).

Dessen, Alan C., *Rescripting Shakespeare: The Text, the Director, and Modern Productions* (Cambridge, 2002).

Edelman, Charles, *Shakespeare in Production: The Merchant of Venice* (Cambridge, 2002).

Foulkes, Richard, *Performing Shakespeare in the Age of Empire* (Cambridge, 2002).

Halio, Jay L., *Shakespeare in Performance: A Midsummer Night's Dream*, Second Edition (Manchester and New York, 2003).

Harris, Jonathan Gil and Natasha Korda, eds., *Staged Properties in Early Modern Drama* (Cambridge, 2002).
Ichikawa, Mariko, *Shakespearean Entrances* (Basingstoke, 2002).
Kinney, Arthur F., *Shakespeare by Stages: An Historical Introduction* (Oxford, 2003).
Knutson, Roslyn Lander, *Playing Companies and Commerce in Shakespeare's Time* (Cambridge, 2001).
Loehlin, James N., *Shakespeare in Production: Romeo and Juliet* (Cambridge, 2002).
Maher, Mary Z., *Modern Hamlets and their Soliloquies: An Expanded Edition* (Iowa, 2003).
Ochiogrosso, Frank, ed., *Shakespeare in Performance: A Collection of Essays* (Cranbury NJ and London, 2003).
Orgel, Stephen, *Imagining Shakespeare: A History of Texts and Visions* (Basingstoke and New York, 2003).
Resende, Aimara da Cunha, ed., *Foreign Accents: Brazilian Readings of Shakespeare* (Newark and London, 2002).
Schafer, Elizabeth, ed., *Shakespeare in Production: The Taming of the Shrew* (Cambridge, 2002).
Scheil, Katherine West, *The Taste of the Town: Shakespearian Comedy and the Early Eighteenth-Century Theater* (Cranbury NJ and London, 2003).
Schoch, Richard W., *Not Shakespeare: Bardolatry and Burlesque in the Nineteenth Century* (Cambridge, 2002).
Smallwood, Robert, *Shakespeare at Stratford: As You Like It* (London, 2003).
Smith, Emma, ed., *Shakespeare in Production: King Henry V* (Cambridge, 2002).
Starks, Lisa S. and Courtney Lehmann, eds., *The Reel Shakespeare* (Cranbury NJ and London, 2002).
Wells, Stanley and Sarah Stanton, *The Cambridge Companion to Shakespeare on Stage* (Cambridge, 2002).
White, Paul Whitfield and Suzanne R. Westfall, eds., *Shakespeare and Theatrical Patronage in Early Modern England* (Cambridge, 2002).

3. EDITIONS AND TEXTUAL STUDIES

reviewed by Eric Rasmussen

Brian Vickers's *Shakespeare, Co-Author: A Historical Study of Five Collaborative Plays* makes a case for George Peele's authorship of part of *Titus Andronicus* that has rocked the profession – or at least sent palpable tremors through it, with the Arden 3 editor of the play publicly recanting his argument that 'the play was wholly by Shakespeare'.[1] The study's other conclusions – that Middleton co-wrote *Timon of Athens*, Wilkins co-wrote *Pericles*, and Fletcher co-wrote *Henry VIII* and *The Two Noble Kinsmen* – have had less of an impact, since the attributions in question are already widely accepted by Shakespearians. But Vickers – determined to confound what he views as a lingering 'orthodoxy of Shakespeare the Non-Collaborator' – has performed a valuable service by assembling an impressive array of evidence for his claims, including stylistic and verse tests put forward in the nineteenth and early twentieth centuries, corroborating results from more sophisticated statistical tests undertaken in recent attribution studies, and some original evidence of his own.

Indeed, *Shakespeare, Co-Author* may be seen as a culmination of the growing interest in Shakespeare as collaborator, which perhaps had its beginnings in Kenneth Muir's book on the subject in 1960. It was further fuelled in the 1980s by the editors of the Oxford Shakespeare (who presented detailed cases for collaborative authorship of several plays), and has most recently been made manifest on the title pages of critical editions, such as the Oxford (1999) and Arden 3 (2000) editions of *Henry VIII*, which feature other authors' names alongside Shakespeare's. *Shakespeare, Co-Author* now provides a compendium of the relevant evidence pointing to collaborative authorship, a treasure-trove of data that future editors of *Titus*, *Timon*, *Pericles*, *Henry VIII*, and *The Two Noble Kinsmen* will be bound to acknowledge.

My thanks to Arthur Evenchik for editorial suggestions throughout.

[1] See Jonathan Bate, *TLS*, 18 April 2003.

Given the sheer volume of evidence in this 558-page book, it is not surprising that one would find occasional slips. In his introductory discussion of the methodology of authorship studies, Vickers champions the Chadwyck-Healey database of literature online (LION) as a new tool 'of potentially great importance to attribution studies', noting that it helped him refute (in his previous book, *'Counterfeiting' Shakespeare*) Donald Foster's Shakespearian attribution of *A Funerall Elegye* by identifying John Ford as the true author. According to Vickers, his search of the database revealed that 'the word "over-passe", used in the *Elegye* (316), occurs elsewhere only in Ford's play *Perkin Warbeck* and in his poem *Christes Bloodie Sweat*'. Unfortunately, this supposed instance of the database's utility is actually a demonstration of error. 'Over-pass' is not unique to Ford: the word appears throughout the early modern period. But in searching the database – where texts are in original spelling – Vickers apparently neglected to check for variant spellings. Thus, while a search for 'over-passe' in the drama database turns up only Ford's use of the word, a search for 'ouerpasse' in all works published between 1578 and 1642 (the span that Vickers examines) yields twenty-four hits in prose, twenty in poetry, and four in drama other than Ford's; a search for 'ouer passe' yields an additional twelve hits in poetry and six in prose; and a search for 'overpasse' yields a further eleven hits in poetry and one in prose.

Similarly, Vickers observes that 'successful' appears three times in the first scene of *Titus* and four times in Peele's *Battle of Alcazar*: 'In both plays we find the word "successful" (used by Shakespeare only four times outside this play) being applied to victory in battle, with a further idiosyncrasy, its combination with the preposition *in* . . . This usage seems to be unique to Peele: I find it nowhere [else] in the Chadwyck-Healey databases.' A search of those databases, however, reveals two other instances in the drama of the period in which 'successful in' appears and is applied to victory in battle: Middleton's *More Dissemblers besides Women* ('General of the field, successful in his fortunes') and *The Return from Parnassus* ('thou canst not be successful in the fray').

Although Vickers is right to insist that 'collaborative authorship was standard practice in Elizabethan, Jacobean, and Caroline drama', and that 'it would be extremely surprising if Shakespeare had not shared this form of composition', the generalization that 'every major playwright in the period worked collaboratively at some point in his career' is not correct. John Lyly wrote eight plays entirely on his own and, so far as we know, never collaborated with anyone.

Lukas Erne has a wonderful knack for discerning patterns in publication histories that have been unaccountably overlooked by previous investigators. In the wake of his groundbreaking article on 'Shakespeare and the Publication of his Plays' (reviewed last year), *Shakespeare as Literary Dramatist* now brings even further revelations. Erne observes, for example, that the practice of acknowledging authorship on the title pages of printed plays begins to take hold only in 1594. Of the eighteen play quartos published that year, seven feature the author's name thus prominently, whereas of the twenty-three quartos of plays written for the professional theatre and published between 1584 and 1593, only three acknowledge the author at all, and none bears the full name on the title page. (George Peele's name appears at the end of the text in the so-called 'explicit' of *Edward I* [1593] and the title pages of two of Robert Wilson's plays bear his initials.)

1594 was, of course, the year in which the first quartos of Shakespeare's plays were published, although it was not until 1598 that his name appeared on a title page. Erne devotes a substantial portion of his narrative, along with four full-page illustrations, to disproving Douglas Brooks's mistaken claim that the 1600 quarto of *2 Henry IV* was the first to give evidence on the title page of Shakespeare's authorship, explaining that 'there would be no need to rehearse Brooks's argument at such length if its publication by a reputed press did not grant it wide circulation'. As it happens, I drew attention to Brooks's error several years ago in this space – in the same reputed press – observing that the title pages of Q2 *Richard III* and Q3 *Richard II* both featured Shakespeare's name in

1598. Erne now makes the additional point that whereas all previous Shakespearian quartos were printed anonymously, those printed late in 1598 and in 1599 all bear his name.

Something seems to have happened in 1598 that bolstered Shakespeare's marketability. Erne provocatively suggests that this event may have been the publication of Francis Meres's *Palladis Tamia*, which places Shakespeare among the literary giants of the day, 'the most excellent in both kinds for the stage'. He concludes that 'Meres's promotion of Shakespeare to the top of the canon of recent and contemporary English poets is responsible for his name's appearance on the title pages of his plays'. Erne then traces the arc of Shakespeare's growing popularity as manifested in the literary anthologies *England's Parnassus* (1600) and *Belvedere, or the Garden of the Muses* (1600). He makes the fascinating observation, which came as news to me, that both of these anthologies contain more excerpts from Shakespeare than from any other playwright.

Looking at the history of Shakespearian reprints, Erne deduces that 'comedies were less popular reading matter than tragedies or histories'. Of the five comedies published during Shakespeare's lifetime, only *Love's Labour's Lost* was reprinted before 1619. Conversely, Erne points out that most of the histories and tragedies were reprinted multiple times, with *1 Henry IV* going through a remarkable seven known editions before the publication of the First Folio. But the assertion that '*2 Henry IV* is in fact the only one of the twelve histories or tragedies printed during Shakespeare's lifetime which appeared in a single quarto edition' seems to overlook *Troilus and Cressida* (1609), which was never reprinted in quarto. Also, it is unclear where *Pericles* fits into the picture: it was the only romance to be published in quarto and was a popular one at that, going through four reprintings before 1623.

In the second part of the book, Erne explores the evidence for the average length of theatrical performances in the early modern period and concludes that about a dozen of Shakespeare's texts are too long to have been performed in their entirety. His extended concluding discussion of the ways in which the short (née 'bad') quartos have been wrongly linked with provincial touring should have attended to Paul Werstine's essay on the same subject which reaches similar conclusions.[2]

David Lindley's New Cambridge edition casts *The Tempest* in a brave new light, not so much 'a grand finale to a writing life' as an 'experimental' play that 'breaks new Shakespearian ground'. Lindley argues that the play's use of music and spectacle was radically new: 'In mounting a tempest complete with a shipwreck before the spectators' eyes, Shakespeare was . . . attempting an unprecedented theatrical coup'. This fresh approach to the novel features of *The Tempest*, which Lindley views as Shakespeare's response to the opportunities presented by the newly acquired indoor theatre at Blackfriars, sets the tone for a lively edition that will no doubt re-energize study of this major play.

In his critical introduction, Lindley explores a broad range of 'readings and stagings', deftly weaving his observations about various productions into a larger evaluation of the play itself. (The absence of a separate section on 'the play in performance' may, however, diminish somewhat the edition's usefulness to students specifically interested in performance history.) The photos in Lindley's edition are superbly chosen to illustrate the 'other-worldliness' of the play, from the strangeness of G. Wilson Knight's Caliban in 1938, complete with green body-paint and purple highlights, to the eroticism of Rachel Sanderson's Ariel in 1996 'stripping off her costume of white tabard with long sleeves to reveal the female body beneath'. Lindley notes a historical trend to make Caliban less and less monstrous, especially when the actor is black: 'an audience properly sensitive to endemic racism would see a black actor playing a grotesque Caliban as unacceptable stereotyping'.

[2] See Werstine, 'Touring and the Construction of Shakespeare Textual Criticism', *Textual Formations and Reformations*, ed. Laurie E. Maguire and Thomas L. Berger (Newark and London, 1998), pp. 45–66.

But, disappointingly, the edition provides no illustration of a black actor in the role.

Discussion of the play's most famous crux, 'wise'/'wife' at 4.1.123, has tended to focus on whether the piece of type in question is a long 's' or a broken 'f'. It now seems clear that the letter is an 's', but Lindley, noting that a misreading of 'wife' as 'wise' would be an easy error for a compositor to make, argues that 'everything turns on editorial judgement of the more persuasive reading in context'. In this edition, he opts for 'wife', but mentions that a recent director chose to retain 'wise' because 'she felt that "and a wife" sounded too much like including Miranda as an afterthought'.

Lindley emends the text in a few key instances, and the rationale for each change is admirably detailed in his 'textual analysis'. Considering that no previous editor had thought to challenge Ferdinand's 'put it to the foile' at 3.1.47, Lindley's proposed emendation 'put it to the soil' (with the sense of 'moral stain or tarnish') is bold as well as persuasive. He also makes a compelling case for re-assigning, to Antonio, the second awkward sentence of Sebastian's 'What if he had said widower Aeneas too? / Good Lord, how you take it' at 2.1.75–6.

The emendation of the Boatswain's insistence that Gonzalo go below unless he can 'work the peace of the present' – Lindley emends to 'work a peace of the present' (1.1.19) – is more questionable. Lindley asserts that 'there are no contemporary parallels for the F reading "work the peace", whereas "work a peace" occurs in many places, including, for example, Milton's "Ode on the Morning of Christ's Nativity"'. However, this parallel from Milton ('And with his Father work us a perpetual peace') does not seem exactly on point. In searching several electronic databases, I find only two occurrences of 'work a peace' – in Henry Burnell's *Landgartha* (1641): 'see if that benefit may worke a peace betwixt us'; and in a diplomatic missive from 1583: 'He laboureth under-hand to work a peace between the duke and Gowrie' – in both of which the meaning is 'broker a peace treaty' (with 'between' forming part of the phrase), a usage somewhat different from that in *The Tempest*. Moreover, changing 'the peace of the present' weakens the parallel in the Boatswain's following sentence: 'the mischance of the hour' (1.1.22).

There are a few minor errors in Lindley's text. 'I'm' for 'I am' at 3.1.76 is probably an intentional emendation for the meter's sake (like Lindley's emendation of F's 'is it' to 'is't' at 1.2.48) but is not collated as such. At 2.1.227, 'throes' is Pope's emendation of F's 'throwes' and needs a note. Lindley renders F's 'chaps' as 'chops' at 2.2.75, which should have been noted, although 'chaps' – which the *OED* (n^2 2. pl) defines as 'used of animals, and only applied contemptuously or humorously to humans' – may be the better reading for Stephano's instruction to Caliban ('open your chaps').

Finally, convention dictates that collation notes flagging departures from the control text provide the rejected Folio readings in original spelling, punctuation and font. Casual readers may not care that the dogs in Ariel's song bark with a '*bowgh-wawgh*' in the Folio (1.2.383) rather than the 'bowgh waugh' in Lindley's collation (which, rather remarkably, gets the spelling, punctuation, and font all wrong) but the most careful scholars should be aware that there are errors of this sort throughout.[3]

---

[3] Errors in the collations include: 1.1.0 SD.2 for '*mariners*' read '*Mariners*'; 1.1.48–50 for 'drown- / ing' read 'drow- / ning'; 1.2 for '*Scena Secunda*' read 'Scena Secunda'; 1.2.193–5 for 'Performed' read 'Performd'; 1.2.380 for 'beare / the burthen' read '*beare / the burthen*'; 1.2.381–3 for 'Harke, harke . . . bowgh waugh' read '*Harke, harke . . . bowgh-wawgh*'; 1.2.383 for '*Burthen dispersedly*' read 'Burthen dispersedly'; 1.2.429 for 'The best' read 'the best'; 2.1.129–31 for 'them' read 'them:'; 2.1.129–31 for 'fault's' read 'faults'; 2.1.129–31 for 'owne' read 'owne.'; 2.1.129–31 for 'losse' read 'losse.'; 2.1.129–31 for 'Sebastian' read '*Sebastian*'; 2.1.134–5 for 'chirugeonly' read 'Chirurgeonly'; 2.1.165–8 for 'Gonzalo' read '*Gonzalo.*'; 2.1.165–8 for 'sir' read 'Sir?'; 2.1.187–8 for 'so' read 'so.'; 2.1.191–3 for 'person' read 'person,'; 2.1.191–3 for 'safety' read 'safety.'; 2.1.240–1 for 'Naples' read '*Naples*?'; 2.2.159 for 'trenchering' read '*trenchering*'; 3.2.37–8 for 'Island' read 'Island.'; 3.3.13–14 for 'throughly' read 'throughly.'; 3.3.102–4 for 'mudded' read 'mudded.'; 3.3.102–4 for 'Second' read 'Second.'; 4.1.12 for 'oracle' read 'Oracle.'; 4.1.74 for 'Here'

The New Cambridge Shakespeare has issued several 'updated editions' of volumes it originally published in the mid 1980s. Each now features a new introductory section highlighting noteworthy recent productions and critical developments. In the updated *A Midsummer Night's Dream*, R. A. Foakes presents Louis Montrose's now-famous argument that Elizabeth's 'pervasive *cultural presence* was a condition of the play's imaginative possibility', then counters it by arguing that although 'we tend to see the reign of Elizabeth through the perspective of her court and power, there is no reason to think the Globe audience was equally obsessed by her'. In the updated *Romeo and Juliet*, Thomas Moisan takes the opportunity to discuss important works by Coppélia Kahn and Marjorie Garber that were, in fact, published in the early 1980s but not mentioned in G. Blakemore Evans's original edition in 1984. Angela Stock's new introductory section to *Much Ado About Nothing* offers a thought-provoking detail about Beatrice's age-on-stage: 'since the 1970s she . . . has several times been played as considerably older than Hero and Claudio, even middle-aged'.

Ann Thompson's updated *Taming of the Shrew* offers a re-appraisal of 'pre-feminist' approaches to the play and concludes by wondering – given recent Shakespearian productions with actresses playing Richard II, Lear, Hamlet and Prospero – 'could we be ready for a masculine Kate?' Robert Hapgood's update to *Hamlet* nicely critiques Branagh's 1996 motion picture ('reaching for grandeur, his film can become merely grandiose'), alerts readers to John Updike's prequel novel *Gertrude and Claudius* (albeit with the slip 'Updyke'), and gives appropriate notice of influential studies by Janet Adelman and Elaine Showalter. Andrew Gurr observes that over the last twenty years '*Richard II*'s context has received far more attention than its text'; he discusses the importance to historicist/materialist criticism of the play's production on the eve of the Essex rebellion and provides several new examples illustrating the connection that the Elizabethans found between Richard's misrule and Elizabeth's. Regrettably, Gurr's updated discussion of the play's sources does not mention Macdonald Jackson's discovery that *Thomas of Woodstock* almost certainly post-dates *Richard II*.[4]

The seemingly simple task of inserting a new introductory section of some dozen or sixteen pages into an otherwise unchanged edition can prove a nightmare for publishers: not just the subsequent page numbers, but also the original cross-references throughout, must be revised. Although most of the updated Cambridge editions have attended to this, two of the cross-references in *Romeo and Juliet* and *Much Ado About Nothing* are now inaccurate.[5]

Roger Warren is a man of the theatre, and his rich discussion of recent productions of *Henry VI, Part 2* is worth the price of his new Oxford edition. Unlike the stage histories in most critical editions, which rely upon the observations of other reviewers, Warren's focuses exclusively on productions he himself has seen. In place of derivative summaries, then, Warren provides a wealth of original insights. Moreover, he realizes that actors' and directors' interpretations have every right to stand alongside those of critics in commentary notes. Glossing 'and York' at 3.1.39, for instance, Warren writes that 'Peggy Ashcroft paused slightly before this phrase, subtly seeking the approval of someone who was not an ally, and demonstrating that lists of names in Shakespeare can yield more dramatic point than might at first appear.' Brewster Mason brought out the variety of 'Madam be still, with reverence may I say' (3.2.207), 'modulating from a snapped *be still* ("shut up") to a delivery of *with reverence* (i.e. with respect) that exposed the perfunctoriness of Warwick's courtesy; by contrast, Geff Francis

read 'here'; 4.1.142 SD for '*After*' read '*after*'; 4.1.165–6 for 'Caliban' read '*Caliban.*'; 4.1.168 for 'have' read 'haue'; 4.1.196–201 for 'you' read 'you.'; 5.1.172–3 for 'loue' read 'loue,'; 5.1.172–3 for 'world' read 'world.'; 5.1.179 for 'have' read 'haue'; 5.1.277 for 'now' read 'now;'. The collation notes for 2.1.304, and 305–6 belong on the following page.

4 See Jackson, 'Shakespeare's *Richard II* and the Anonymous *Thomas of Woodstock*', *Medieval and Renaissance Drama in England*, 14 (2001), 17–65.

5 In the cross-reference on page 63 of *Romeo and Juliet*, for 'pp. 206–12' read 'pp. 222–8'; in the commentary note to 2.1.0 of *Much Ado About Nothing*, for 'p. 148' read 'p. 160'.

at Stratford in 2000 spoke the line with smiling courtesy, conscious of his moral superiority'. An actor's interpretation can even be brought to bear on textual issues: in asserting that F's irregular verse line at 3.1.98, 'Well, Suffolk, thou shalt not see me blush', may not require emendation, Warren notes that Paul Hardwick turned its irregularity to dramatic advantage by following 'his aggressive delivery of "Suffolk" with an emphatic pause, equivalent to one beat of the five-stress line'.

Warren's textual work is careful throughout, and his original emendations are often compelling. His explanation for Buckingham's line in the Folio, 'Or thou, or I Somerset will be Protectors' (1.1.177) – which has metrical problems as well as the apparent error of 'Protectors' for 'Protector' – is particularly clever: Warren suggests that 'Somerset' was marked to be moved or added to the manuscript, and an 's' written at the end of the line to flag the place where the name was to be inserted: 'Or thou or I will be Protector, Somerset.' In the event, however, the compositor misunderstood the revision marks in the manuscript, failing to move the name and inserting the 's' after 'Protector' to produce the Folio reading.

There are a few slips: the emendation 'Gaunt's' for 'his' at 2.2.56, proposed by the editors of the Oxford Complete Works and now claimed to be adopted for the first time in Warren's text, was, in fact, anticipated by Ronald Knowles's Arden 3 edition. In the additional passages from Q1, a collation note should have alerted readers that line 26 in passage 'D' is printed after line 29 in Q1; at line 6 of passage 'B', a note that 'Zounds' is spelled 'Sonnes' in Q1 might have been appropriate. Warren's remarkable claim that 'so far as I know, *Henry VI, Part 2* has not been staged on its own, as an independent work, since it was given at the Birmingham Repertory Theatre in 1951' is rendered untenable by the archives of at least one professional company: the Oregon Shakespeare Festival's 1976 season included *Henry VI Part 2, Much Ado, Lear* and *Errors*. Most seriously, Warren's extensive argument for Q1 as a reported text unaccountably fails to address Barbara Kreps's important article and thus does not fully enter into recent debate on the subject.[6]

Charles Whitworth's new Oxford edition of *The Comedy of Errors* argues that the play was written specifically for private performance and presented only on special occasions (at Gray's Inn in 1594 and at court during the 1604 Christmas season), thus never figuring in the commercial repertoire of Shakespeare's company. Pointing out that *Errors* is nearly twenty per cent shorter than the next shortest play in the Folio, Whitworth concludes that it 'was just not substantial enough to provide a full afternoon's entertainment for paying customers at the Theatre'. The limited stage history that Whitworth proposes helps to explain the fact that the authorial foul papers were apparently available to be used as printer's copy for the Folio, nearly thirty years after the play's composition. He argues that the authorial manuscript served as the playbook for those rare performances and remained otherwise 'unrevised, untranscribed, and unmarked-up' in the company's keeping until it was brought out for printing in the Folio.

Whitworth finely observes that *Errors* is unique among the Folio comedies in that it has 'comedy' in its title, whereas nearly every play in the third section begins with the formulaic '*The Tragedie of* . . .'. Whitworth's convincing argument that the source for the framing plot was not Gower's *Confessio Amantis* but Lawrence Twine's *Pattern of Painful Adventures* may well prove to be this edition's most lasting contribution to the study of the play.

This edition is alive to the smallest details of the text. For example, it punctuates 'I am invited, sir, to certain merchants'' (1.2.24) with a possessive apostrophe, so that the line refers to the merchants' establishments rather than to the merchants themselves. Whitworth is the first editor to ask how it is that the Second Merchant, obviously a stranger in Ephesus, knows about 'the laws and statutes of this town' (5.1.126).

6 See Kreps, 'Bad Memories of Margaret? Memorial Reconstruction versus Revision in *The First Part of the Contention* and *2 Henry VI*', *Shakespeare Quarterly*, 51 (2000), 154–80.

He emends the short passage by swapping the speech headings for the merchant and Angelo the goldsmith (5.1.118–28), so that the stranger now asks the questions ('Upon what cause?') and the local resident provides the details.

Whitworth's commentary makes frequent recourse to the habits of individual compositors as the basis for textual emendation. He emends 'face' to 'place' at 3.1.47, observing that Compositor D 'sometimes added or substituted words in verse passages and may have done so here'; he emends 'iollitie' to 'policy' at 2.2.90, noting that such an error 'would be typical of Compositor C who set this page (H2v), and whose errors tend to be more serious and more subtle than Compositor D's'. Readers who are primarily interested in glosses on the text may not welcome this level of specialized information in the commentary (e.g. the note that begins 'In F, the column break on page H3v comes after line 46, the long fifteen-syllable line 47 and its weak rhyme coming at the top of column b. This break may have distracted Compositor D, who set both columns'). Moreover, the controlling assumption that one can distinguish between the serious/subtle errors characteristic of one compositor and the distracted substitutions of another misrepresents the more limited and more modest conclusions that can be reached through compositor analysis.

Whitworth's text is relatively error-free: at 2.2.12, 'thou didst answer me' needs a collation note recording the F reading 'did didst'; the extra 'sir' in 4.1.87 was presumably intentionally omitted, following Capell, but needs a note to that effect; at 5.1.33 the text silently adopts F3's 'God's' where F1 reads 'God'.

In Arden: Editing Shakespeare – Essays in Honour of Richard Proudfoot, edited by Ann Thompson and Gordon McMullan, is an unusual festschrift in that all of the contributors (myself included) are Arden editors.[7] One of the highlights of this collection is R. A. Foakes's 'Cautionary Note on Stage Directions', which points to the marginal note in *The Battle of Alcazar* calling for '3. viols of blood & a sheeps gather' and wryly asks 'Does this mean that whenever this play was performed, the bookkeeper, Edward Alleyn, or someone sent one of the lads round to a nearby butcher?'

In 'Shakespeares Various', A. R. Braunmuller investigates the question of how the present format of scholarly Shakespeare editions evolved and provides some tentative answers: the Cambridge Shakespeare (1863–6) may have been the first edition to adopt the now-standard line numbering by 5s, and Howard Staunton's edition in the late 1850s seems to have been the first to be formatted in the now-common three-layer system (text/collation/commentary). Braunmuller's findings may be supplemented by observing, as Bernice W. Kliman has pointed out to me, that Samuel Ayscough's 1807 edition included a rudimentary line-numbering system by 5s in the gutter between the two columns of text, with the numbers going from 5–50 on each page. Also, Kliman has elsewhere drawn attention to the five Shakespearian tragedies Charles Jennens edited in the 1770s; Jennens published each in a separate volume, and provided, at the foot of each page, a collation of variant readings, thereby setting a precedent for modern single-volume critical editions.[8]

In 'Early Play Texts: Forms and Formes' (which might have been more descriptively titled 'Early Printers Draw a Blank'), H. R. Woudhuysen brilliantly observes that the presence of final blank leaves in play quartos, which would protect the print when folded or stitched copies were stored

[7] Although I have in the past recused myself from reviewing collections to which I contributed, I have included *In Arden: Editing Shakespeare* and *Stage Directions in 'Hamlet'* in this review. A truly objective reviewer would probably note that my contributions to each of these volumes both begin in a cloyingly familiar tone ('Let's be honest: most Shakespearians don't care very much about stage directions' and 'Let's face it, textual collations . . . are often incomprehensible to the average reader') and end with the identical example of a variant stage direction in *Hamlet*.

[8] See Kliman, 'Charles Jennens' Shakespeare and his Eighteenth-Century Competitors', *Cahiers Elisabethains: Late Medieval and Renaissance English Studies*, 58 (2000), 59–71.

without wrappers, may challenge received ideas about the relative value of printed plays. 'If they were the unconsidered trifles they are generally taken to have been, it is strange that printers or publishers were so often willing to leave blank paper in them.' Woudhuysen demonstrates that printers of play quartos often apparently tried to consolidate space at the end of the text in order to leave the final verso blank. The last three pages of Q1 *Lear* (1608), for instance, contain fourteen examples of continuous printing (short speeches of two or three words tucked in on the same line as the end of the previous speech), 'suggesting a decision to avoid using the verso of the final leaf'.

George Walton Williams ruminates on what Proudfoot terms 'advanced exits', the kind that an editor sometimes supplies for a character in the middle of a scene, before the general exeunt. Williams observes that by reducing the number of actors onstage, advanced exits have the effect of 'decreasing the busyness of the scene and replacing it with a diminution of *foci* of activity'. Editors who insert such directions give proof that they have visualized the stage action. One might also point out the usefulness of doubling charts (an often overlooked feature of critical editions, but standard in the Arden 3 series) as a means of discovering where early exits are required – as when a Messenger must leave the stage so that the actor can return in another role at the opening of the following scene.

The more theoretical essays in this collection reflect contemporary concerns, with Anthony B. Dawson exploring 'the ways in which one's political desires can colour all philosophical position-taking' and Suzanne Gossett's 'Feminist Inflections in Editing *Pericles*' trenchantly concluding that 'all our commitments, including our sexual politics, may have textual consequences'.

Meanwhile, the honorand of *In Arden* continues to refine our understanding of early dramatic texts. Proudfoot's contribution to *'A Certain Text': Close Readings and Textual Studies on Shakespeare and Others in Honor of Thomas Clayton* identifies a new edition of *Mucedorus*, printed between 1615 and 1618. Analysing the eight editions of the play that were printed between 1606 and 1621, Proudfoot detects a subtle but observable process of modernization, such that 'the Jacobean reprints appear to a twentieth-century reader to be more "modern" than the first quarto of 1598'.

Similar attention to textual changes in seventeenth-century reprints is evident in Sonia Massai's essay in *Shakespeare Survey* 55. Marshalling a compelling array of evidence, Massai argues that the scope and consistency of the changes made in the Shakespeare Fourth Folio reflect an underlying set of editorial guidelines followed by the three printing houses that each produced a section of the book. Although Massai is careful not to use the anachronistic term 'editor' to describe the agent responsible for establishing these conventions, her study ably demonstrates that what we would now call *editorship* 'was already perceived as a specific and crucial function'.

Elsewhere in *Shakespeare Survey* 55, Michael Cordner observes that 'the work of annotation . . . remains effectively unscrutinized'. This deficit of critical attention to the theory behind annotation has now been substantially remedied by Cordner's essay and by two in the Proudfoot festschrift, G. K. Hunter's 'The Social Function of Annotation' and Helen Wilcox's 'The Character of a Footnote . . . or, Annotation Revisited'.

There's long been a double standard in the editorial treatment of dialogue and stage directions. Although editors tend to treat Shakespeare's text as relatively sacrosanct, stage directions are often freely rewritten and emended in critical editions, sometimes within square brackets or 'broken brackets', sometimes with no brackets at all. *Stage Directions in 'Hamlet': New Essays and New Directions*, edited by Hardin L. Aasand, is intended to re-focus attention on stage directions as *text*. Ann Thompson and Neil Taylor report that in preparing their forthcoming Arden 3 *Hamlet*, they initially considered creating a 'framework' of editorially invented stage directions ('providing explanations for readers and actors of just what is going on on stage') that would have remained more or less constant throughout the edited texts of Q1, Q2 and F1. But they subsequently abandoned that idea in favour of affirming each text, and its stage directions, as a separate entity, such that 'Q1's SDs belong to Q1 alone, Q2's to Q2 alone, and F's to F alone'. The importance of preserving the textual differences of stage directions is splendidly illustrated by Pamela Mason's discussion of the interpretative possibilities of Laertes's entrance at the tail end of the Q2 direction in 5.2, '*A table prepared, Trumpets, Drums, and officers with Cushions, King, Queene, and all the state, Foiles, daggers, and Laertes*' ('it might suggest that he is hanging back, indicating a degree of reluctance, shame, trepidation, or anxiety on his part. Alternatively it could grant him a position of prominence'), all of which vanish in the more regularized F direction: '*Enter King, Queene, Laertes, and Lords, with other Attendants*'.

Bernice W. Kliman provocatively suggests that graphics (parentheses and dashes) in original texts, which are seldom retained in modern editions, may function as subtle stage directions. The possibility that the F parentheses in ''Tis not alone my Inky Cloake (good Mother)' may 'encourage actors playing Hamlet to adopt a mocking or ironic tone' is genuine food for thought. George Walton Williams – whose chapter's title, 'Exit by Indirection, Finding Directions Out', plays on *directions* rather more felicitously than does the title of the collection – offers further musings upon early exits. Steven Urkowitz's characteristically spirited defense of Q1 *Hamlet*'s much-maligned 'I there's the point' examines the swift actions and halting rhythms in the Q1 text before and after it. James Hirsh contextualizes the incongruous presumption of Hamlet's advice to the players by imagining 'how members of the Royal Shakespeare Company would feel if Prince Charles stopped by one day to instruct them on the craft of acting'.

Frank Nicholas Clary offers a lively exploration of early prompt books, critical commentaries and illustrations of the closet scene in order to address the perennial question of whether Hamlet's 'look here upon this picture, and on this' (3.4.53) refers to miniatures or to wall portraits. Alan R. Young's richly illustrated tour of eighteenth- and nineteenth-century visual representations of Hamlet holding Yorick's skull – Young has identified an astounding 140 works of art that take this moment as their subject – certainly whets the appetite for Young's electronic database containing thousands of images from the Folger Shakespeare Library. Aasand contributes an amusing examination of the directions that editors have appended to Hamlet's exclamation to the skull – 'pah'(Q2) or 'Puh' (F1) – variously instructing the actor to smell the skull curiously, set it down gracefully or throw it to the ground in disgust.

In closing, I would like to suggest that future essayists refrain, in their titles, from attempts to play upon Hamlet's most famous line. In the collection under review, 'To Soliloquize or Not to Soliloquize' and 'To See or Not to See' aspire to be clever, but are not.

WORKS REVIEWED

Aasand, Hardin L., ed., *Stage Directions in 'Hamlet': New Essays and New Directions* (Madison and London, 2003).

Braunmuller, A. R., 'Shakespeares Various', in Thompson and McMullan, *In Arden: Editing Shakespeare* (London, 2003), pp. 3–16.

Clary, Frank Nicholas, 'Pictures in the Closet: Properties and Stage Business in *Hamlet* 3.4', in Aasand, *Stage Directions in 'Hamlet'* (Madison and London, 2003), pp. 170–88.

Cordner, Michael, 'Actors, Editors, and the Annotation of Shakespearian Playscripts', *Shakespeare Survey 55* (2002), pp. 181–98.

Dawson, Anthony B., 'Correct Impressions: Editing and Evidence in the Wake of Post-modernism', in Thompson and McMullan, *In Arden: Editing Shakespeare* (London, 2003), pp. 31–47.

Erne, Lukas, *Shakespeare as Literary Dramatist* (Cambridge, 2003).

Foakes, R. A., 'Raw flesh/lion's flesh: a Cautionary Note on Stage Directions', in Thompson and McMullan, *In Arden: Editing Shakespeare* (London, 2003), pp. 125–37.

Gossett, Suzanne, '"To foster is not always to preserve": Feminist Inflections in Editing *Pericles*', in Thompson and McMullan, *In Arden: Editing Shakespeare* (London, 2003), pp. 65–80.

Hirsh, James, 'Hamlet's Stage Directions to the Players', in Aasand, *Stage Directions in 'Hamlet'* (Madison and London, 2003), pp. 47–73.

Hunter, G. K., 'The Social Function of Annotation', in Thompson and McMullan, *In Arden: Editing Shakespeare* (London, 2003), pp. 177–93.

Kliman, Bernice W., 'Explicit Stage Directions (Especially Graphics) in *Hamlet*', in Aasand, *Stage Directions in 'Hamlet'* (Madison and London, 2003), pp. 74–91.

Mason, Pamela, '". . . *and Laertes*" The Case against Tidiness', in Aasand, *Stage Directions in 'Hamlet'* (Madison and London, 2003), pp. 92–100.

Massai, Sonia, '"Taking just care of the impression": Editorial Intervention in Shakespeare's Fourth Folio, 1685', *Shakespeare Survey 55* (2002), pp. 257–70.

Proudfoot, Richard, '"Modernizing" the Printed Play-Text in Jacobean London: Some Early Reprints of *Mucedorus*', in Linda Anderson and Janis Lull, eds., *'A Certain Text': Close Readings and Textual Studies on Shakespeare and Others in Honor of Thomas Clayton* (Newark and London, 2002), pp. 18–28.

Shakespeare, William, *The Comedy of Errors*, ed. Charles Whitworth, Oxford Shakespeare (Oxford, 2002).

Hamlet, Prince of Denmark, ed. Philip Edwards, updated edition with new introductory section by Robert Hapgood, New Cambridge Shakespeare (Cambridge, 2003).

Henry VI, Part 2, ed. Roger Warren, Oxford Shakespeare (Oxford, 2002).

King Richard II, ed. Andrew Gurr, updated edition, New Cambridge Shakespeare (Cambridge, 2003).

A Midsummer Night's Dream, ed. R. A. Foakes, updated edition, New Cambridge Shakespeare (Cambridge, 2003).

Much Ado About Nothing, ed. F. H. Mares, updated edition with new introductory section by Angela Stock, New Cambridge Shakespeare (Cambridge, 2003).

Romeo and Juliet, ed. G. Blakemore Evans, updated edition with new introductory section by Thomas Moisan, New Cambridge Shakespeare (Cambridge, 2003).

The Taming of the Shrew, ed. Ann Thompson, updated edition, New Cambridge Shakespeare (Cambridge, 2003).

The Tempest, ed. David Lindley, New Cambridge Shakespeare (Cambridge, 2002).

Thompson, Ann and Gordon McMullan, eds., *In Arden: Editing Shakespeare: Essays in Honour of Richard Proudfoot* (London, 2003).

Thompson, Ann and Neil Taylor, 'Variable Texts: Stage Directions in Arden 3 *Hamlet*', in Aasand, *Stage Directions in 'Hamlet'* (Madison and London, 2003), pp. 19–32.

Urkowitz, Steven, '"I there's the point" in Context: Theatricality and Authorship', in Aasand, *Stage Directions in 'Hamlet'* (Madison and London, 2003), pp. 134–9.

Vickers, Brian, *Shakespeare, Co-Author: A Historical Study of Five Collaborative Plays* (Oxford, 2002).

Wilcox, Helen, 'The Character of a Footnote . . . or, Annotation Revisited', in Thompson and McMullan, *In Arden: Editing Shakespeare* (London, 2003), pp. 194–208.

Williams, George Walton, 'Exit by Indirection, Finding Directions Out', in Aasand, *Stage Directions in 'Hamlet'* (Madison and London, 2003), pp. 42–6.

'To Edit? To Direct? – Ay, there's the rub', in Thompson and McMullan, *In Arden: Editing Shakespeare* (London, 2003), pp. 111–24.

Woudhuysen, H. R., 'Early Play Texts: Forms and Formes', in Thompson and McMullan, *In Arden: Editing Shakespeare* (London, 2003), pp. 48–61.

Young, Alan R., 'Eighteenth- and Nineteenth-Century Visual Representations of the Graveyard Scene in *Hamlet*', in Aasand, *Stage Directions in 'Hamlet'* (Madison and London, 2003), pp. 189–213.

BOOKS RECEIVED

This list includes all books received between September 2002 and September 2003 which are not reviewed in this volume of *Shakespeare Survey*. The appearance of a book in this list does not preclude its review in a subsequent volume.

Benabu, Isaac, *Reading for the Stage: Calderón and his Contemporaries* (Woodbridge, Suffolk, 2003).

Chamberlain, Franc, *Routledge Performance Practitioners: Michael Chekhov* (London, 2004).

Hope, Jonathan, *Shakespeare's Grammar* (London, 2003).

Kinney, Arthur, ed., *The Blackwell Companion to Renaissance Drama* (Oxford, 2002).

Knight, W. Nicholas, *Autobiography in Shakespeare's Plays: 'Lands so by his father lost'* (Frankfurt, 2002).

Mebane, John S., ed., *Pegasus Shakespeare Bibliographies: Cymbeline, The Winter's Tale*, and *The Tempest* (Fairview, NC, 2002).

Merlin, Bella, *Routledge Performance Practitioners: Konstantin Stanislavsky* (London, 2003).

Murray, Simon, *Routledge Performance Practitioners: Jacques Lecoq* (London, 2003).

Olsen, Kirstin, *All Things Shakespeare: An Encyclopedia of Shakespeare's World*, 2 vols. (Westport, CT, 2002).

Pitches, Jonathan, *Routledge Performance Practitioners: Vsevolod Meyerhold* (London, 2003).

Stubbes, Philip, *The Anatomie of Abuses*, ed. Margaret Jane Kidnie (Tempe, Arizona, 2002).

Thorne, Alison, ed., *New Casebooks: Shakespeare's Romances* (Basingstoke, 2003).

Warren, Michael, ed., *Pegasus Shakespeare Bibliographies: Shakespeare: Life, Language and Linguistics, Textual Studies, and the Canon* (Fairview, NC, 2002).

Wiedle, Roland, *Shakespeares Dramaturgische Perspektive* (Heidelberg, 2002).

Williamson, Marilyn N., ed., *Pegasus Shakespeare Bibliographies: As You Like It, Much Ado About Nothing, and Twelfth Night* (Fairview, NC, 2003).

Wynne-Davies, Marion, *Siney to Milton, 1580–1660* (Basingstoke, 2003).

INDEX

No book titles or play titles, other than Shakespeare's, are included in this index, but the names of the authors are given. Book titles in review articles are listed alphabetically at the end of each section.

INDEX

INDEX

INDEX

INDEX

INDEX

INDEX

P9-EGK-656

WITHDRAWN

AMERICAN HYMNS OLD AND NEW

American Hymns Old and New

ALBERT CHRIST-JANER
CHARLES W. HUGHES
CARLETON SPRAGUE SMITH

New York 1980
COLUMBIA UNIVERSITY PRESS

Library of Congress Cataloging in Publication Data

Main entry under title:

American hymns old and new.

With music.
Bibliography: p.
Includes index.
1. Hymns, English. I. Christ-Janer, Albert, 1910–1973. II. Hughes, Charles William, 1900– III. Smith, Carleton Sprague, 1905–
M2117.A573 783.9'52 79-4630
ISBN 0-231-03458-X

Music engraving by Lloyd Johnson and Karen Sayers of Publishers' MusiComp, Wilmington, Delaware

Columbia University Press
New York Guildford, Surrey

Printed in the United States of America

Contents

Preface

THE PSALMIST of old urges, "Sing a new song unto the Lord." Yet during the twentieth century not many have been sung. Therefore one of the two main purposes of this hymn book is to offer new songs to God.

The idea of such an offering grew out of conversations with my father, a Lutheran choirmaster and church organist, when I sang under his baton during the 1920s. Later at Saint Olaf College my choir director and teacher, Oscar Overby, supported it with his inimitable enthusiasm.

But it was not until Roy Harris, completing his eventful Pittsburgh Music Festival in 1952, learned of my plan to commission hymns that this work got under way. He offered two of his tunes and asked other composers to participate.

A list of poets was prepared; they were asked to write verses. Each of the interested composers was sent a selection of these poems, suited to his conviction and style. The composers were also encouraged to set music to older verses that fired their imaginations. By the time the selected words and music were united, over a decade had gone by. But forty hymns by American composers and a new garnering of American religious verse had been assembled to be presented for the first time. The Psalmist's new songs had finally been created.

Meanwhile, a second purpose of this book developed. Roy Harris introduced me to Carleton Sprague Smith, then chief of the Music Division of the New York Public Library. Having a special interest in American music, Dr. Smith proposed that the commissioned work be displayed against the rich background of hymns which the colonies and the United States could supply. As a result, this book has been rounded out with the historical sections covering four centuries, outlined and sketched in with the skill and taste acquired from years of American musicology.

In the initial years of the development of this second purpose, Dr. Smith designed the form of the assembled material. His enthusiasm for the psalters of the seventeenth century and knowledge of the lyrics of those earliest American poets qualified him to choose in this vast field. His familiarity with the contemporary music world enabled us to add those twentieth-century hymns which supplement the commissioned works.

Burdened by administrative duties at the library, Dr. Smith turned for help in filling in the outline to Charles W. Hughes, professor at Hunter College (and later at Lehman College, when the uptown campus at which he taught became a separate college under that name). Soon Dr. Hughes, devoting all of his energy to this task, was deep in research. Gradually he took up the whole burden alone and for a decade combed through the details, all the while reshaping them to their present condition. His work produced this book.

As the administrative editor, I pay tribute to these colleagues. The hymnbook could not have had a beginning without the expertise of Dr. Smith; it would not have had an end but for Dr. Hughes's faithful professional labor.

These volumes would not exist but for the constant interest and support of Martha Baird Rockefeller, whose enthusiasm for the plan of the work and whose zeal for its completion buoyed the editors' confidence and determination over many years. Mrs. Rockefeller met the expense of commissioning hymns, made possible the collection of materials and research, and ensured publication by her generous gifts. Her aid was indispensable, her professional understanding invaluable.

Supporting Mrs. Rockefeller's wishes Dana S. Creel, president of the Rockefeller Brothers Fund, has been a mainstay. A mediator in times of stress, an adjudicator when vital decisions were necessary, he never failed us with his helping hand.

Abundant gratitude also flows to those who, working for love, made valued contributions. These ranged from frequent and fundamental services to fractional offerings, but each was important in the development of various sections of the hymnbook.

For the years when the editors and their helpers were allowed space in the New York Public Library's Music Division, special thanks are given to Edward B. Freehafer for his permission and to Philip Miller for his constant cooperation.

The President and the Director of the Budget of New York University allowed use of staff time, legal depository, and technical aid to develop this publication. For her continuous help, over the years, Nancy Greenberg deserves high praise.

The Reverend Charles L. Atkins, consultant for over a decade, checked all the biographies, music notes, and prefaces. Without his index, his life work, many historical questions could not have been answered. With patient skill he wove into the warp and woof many enriching threads.

Fannie L. Hughes copied and scored music, wrote critical comments on doubtful passages. No commendation can say how her steady strength sustained her husband through the years.

Virginia Christ-Janer and Elsie Christie worked for months on end doing research for biographies, writing them, and typing them. Lorraine Lerner, Marie C. Reilly, Barbara Delany Buermeyer, and Virginia Ball typed page after page, editing as they went along, and Virginia Ball handled the obtaining of permissions.

Finally, the completion of this hymnbook owes much to the combined efforts of specialized scholars, libraries, translators, editors, and proofreaders. Noteworthy assistance from the following is gratefully acknowledged: Richard Appel, Sydney Beck, Lee H. Bristol, Jr., J. H. Brouwer, Annabel Morris Buchanan, Sheema Z. Buehne, Gilbert Chase, Rev. Pablo Cotto, Dan Crena de Iongh, S. Foster Damon, Hans David, Clarence Dickinson, Margaret Dodd, Leonard Ellinwood, Theodore M. Finney, Alfred Frankenstein, Rev. Marvin Halverson, J. Vincent Higginson, H. Wiley Hitchcock, Wiley Lee Housewright, Hilda G. P. Hutchinson, George Pullen Jackson, Harold Jantz, Elizabeth Jarratt, Raymond Kendall, John Kirkpatrick, Rev. George L. Knight, Arthur Loesser, Irving Lowens, Donald M. McCorkle, Ruth Messenger, Luther Noss, Hugh Porter, John Powell, Rev. Luther Dotterer Reed, Rev. E. E. Ryden, Robert L. Sanders, Charles L. Seeger, Mary B. Slade, John Joseph Stoudt, Richard J. Wolf, and G. Wallace Woodworth.

Special mention must be made of the contributions of Henry Wilder Foote. Professor Edward K. Kravitt, chairman of the Music Department of Lehman College, CUNY, from which Dr. Hughes has since retired, did everything in his power to facilitate this work.

To the Hymn Society of America for aids too numerous to name because of the helpful magazine *The Hymn,* heartfelt thanks are given. And to Robert Stevens Baker of the Union Theological Seminary School of Sacred Music and his conscientious examination of the total work, many thanks are due.

At the Columbia University Press, Henry H. Wiggins, Joan McQuary, and Susan Bishop are commended for help beyond the call of duty. In fact, they made possible the completion of the final stages of preparation of these two volumes.

Because their contributions are included in the section of contemporary hymns, the names of the poets and composers whose talents enhanced this publication need not be listed here. Nonetheless, the gratitude of the editors and, more important, the thanks of the genera-

tions who will sing these hymns are forthcoming. Theirs is one of the most significant additions to religious literature in this century.

Albert Christ-Janer
Fuller E. Callaway Professor of Art
The University of Georgia

July 9, 1973

Introduction

"IT IS TO BE a historical singing book, and what can give a better history of church music in America than the exact music itself." This statement, which might well have been written to describe *American Hymns Old and New* was actually written almost a century ago by Moses Ela Cheney, a Vermont singing master. It is probable that Cheney's book was never finished; certainly it was not published. If we have been more fortunate, it has been due to the sustained support of Albert Christ-Janer. A productive artist, a teacher, and for much of the time a busy administrator, he always found time to confer, to advise, to mediate. He was the persuasive advocate who sought and found the financial support without which this book could neither have been completed nor published. He enlisted the aid of the American composers and poets whose hymns form the final section of this collection. It is a source of deep regret that he did not live to see the completion of a book which he initiated.

We have also been most fortunate in our publisher, the Columbia University Press, and are particularly indebted to Henry Wiggins, Joan McQuary, Gustave Niles, and Audrey Smith for patient, understanding, and helpful cooperation. Beyond this we have been assisted by clergymen of many denominations, hymnologists, archivists, ethnologists, linguists, librarians, scholars, composers, poets, and friends who have provided information, edited texts in foreign languages, provided translations, given or lent books, and sent us poems or hymn tunes. To name them all would extend this introduction beyond reasonable limits, but their assistance is gratefully acknowledged.

What we have produced is a "historical singing book." We have sought a historical panorama showing what Americans were singing at different times, in different parts of the country, and in different places of worship. Thus *American Hymns Old and New* is inter-denominational in scope, and it has been compiled and organized in a fashion which differs considerably from the hymnals in the hands of a singing congregation. A hymnbook compiler will seek or adopt a felicitous union of hymn and tune, but he need not be especially concerned that they are of the same period or the same country. A denominational hymnal is a very complex association of music and religious verse from many periods and many countries.

In separating out one strand of this web, the American hymn, we

seek native texts and native tunes. Since we follow the progress of the hymn through three centuries and a substantial part of the fourth, the arrangement is chronological. To associate literary and musical styles the text and music for each hymn are of the same period and frequently from the same region and denomination. We have sought tunes by American composers which were originally set to American texts as well as hymns written by American poets and set by musicians in their circle. In a number of cases the poet and the musician were the same person. Where such associations were not found, we have not hesitated to do as other editors have done before us, choosing suitable tunes for desirable texts and suitable texts for famous American tunes.

The attempt has been to include as wide a selection as the generous scope of the work permitted, welcoming both popular and traditional folk melodies as well as composed tunes. Even so it has not been possible to represent nearly all of the sects and denominations that flourished here. The Amish, for example, though long established in this country, have continued to sing from the hymnal they brought here. They appear to have created no new songs in a new land. Since our primary focus is on hymns sung in the vernacular and by the congregation, the Latin hymns which formed a part of the Roman Catholic liturgy and the Hebrew chants of the orthodox synagogue do not fall within our scope. We do however include Catholic hymns in English, and hymns sung in English by the congregation in Reformed Synagogues.

It is especially regrettable that early Indian psalm singing could not be presented in this collection. That John Eliot's "praying Indians" used the metrical psalms which he translated for them is clear from a letter dated August 27, 1651, which describes them as singing a psalm in their own language to an English tune "chearefully and prettie tuneably." In the next century Experience Mayhew, minister to the Indians on Martha's Vineyard, also made translations into their language. His pathetic *Narrative of the lives of pious Indian children* (London, 1727) contains an account of little Joseph Peag, who died when four years and twenty-one days old. "Whenever he heard persons singing of Psalms . . . the child would slip away thither and with great solemnity attend that exercise to the conclusion; and did also frequently attempt to sing by himself." Still, there seemed little to be gained by presenting an English tune with a text in a language which no living Indian and very few scholars could read. However see Jean de Brebeuf's Huron carol, "Jesous Ahatonhia," the tune Osceola by Thomas Commuck, "When shall we all meet again" (which was said to have been sung by three Indians on graduating from Dartmouth

College), "Waked by the Gospel's Powerful Sound" by Samson Occom, a Mohegan Indian, and "Que Preciosas Mananitas" from the Southwest.

In editing the hymns we have tried to make them as accessible as possible without sacrificing authenticity. The texts are modernized in capitalization, spelling, and punctuation, but obsolete words are retained. A study of seventeenth-century psalms paraphrases in English seemed to show that at that time certain words were pronounced with an extra syllable. See for example Ainsworth's version of Psalm 77, "I minded God," where the tune seems to require that "ancient" be pronounced with three, and meditation with five syllables. In this and similar instances the music has been adjusted to accommodate the word in its modern pronunciation, since what may have sounded normal in the seventeenth century would certainly seem artificial if not incorrect to us.

In most congregational hymnals all of the tunes are presented in four parts and many have been reharmonized. From a historian's point of view this produces a certain uniformity in style and texture in tunes that were originally much more varied. Since our aim is to show how the hymns were originally sung our hymns appear as unaccompanied melodies, in three, four, and six parts as they were published and with unaltered harmonies. Yet, since we hope that readers will both play and sing these hymns, we present them in a simple and familiar form.

Music published as separate parts has been transcribed into close score on two staves, soprano and alto above in the treble clef, tenor and bass below in the bass clef. However in certain psalm tunes for three voices where the upper parts cross frequently it seemed clearer to use a separate staff for each voice. Obsolete clefs and time signatures have been replaced by forms in current use.

In seventeenth century psalmody the poetic line was the unit, and the line is organized on the basis of its metric structure rather than in measures of equal length as in the later hymn tune. We have therefore printed these settings without bars, except at the end of a line, and without time signatures, both of which lead singers to make accents at regular time intervals rather than to respond to the natural accents of the text and the metric patterns.

In the seventeenth and eighteenth centuries the tenor frequently sang the tune rather than the soprano. Where such tunes survive in modern books these parts are inverted, giving the soprano the melody. Here again it seemed better to preserve the original arrangement. Those who sing these tunes at the organ (or piano) will note the

direction "Tune in tenor" above the music. In such cases we recommend singing the tenor part and playing the others. Many tunes have been transposed to bring the music within the range of the ordinary voice. Those who wish to know the original key should turn to the appropriate note.

We would have preferred to make no changes at all in the harmonizations of these tunes, yet obvious misprints are not uncommon in the earlier books. There are cases where the composer himself made changes in a later edition. There are passages so rude as to obscure the good qualities of the tune. In most cases the original edition was consulted and in difficult cases several editions, where they were available, in the hope of establishing a good reading. We have made a distinction between the effects natural to an early New England singing master or a Southern folk hymn arranger and those sought by a composer skilled in harmony and counterpoint. The general principle has been to avoid alterations. Where changes have been made they are indicated in the notes.

Many German chorales were published in the form of a melody with a figured bass. The figures represented musical intervals, and musicians of the baroque period were taught to interpret them at sight at the organ. This skill became obsolete except as an academic exercise but has been revived to some extent as the performance of baroque music has become more general. In such chorales the harmonies have been filled in but the figures have been retained. We have also supplied optional accompanying parts where the original was a melody or a melody with an unfigured bass.

A number of the tunes presented here are in a mode rather than in a major or minor scale. The modes were a series of arrangements of tones which formed the basis for Western music before the development of the major/minor system. There are various ways of naming them but we have used the following method: the Dorian scale is from D to D, the Phrygian from E to E, the Lydian from F to F, the mixolydian from G to G, and the Aeolian from A to A. They are without sharps or flats and may be represented by the white notes on the piano keyboard. However from relatively early times sharps were sung and then notated in certain situations. It is easy to see that an Aeolian scale differs from one form of the minor scale (the harmonic minor) only in the fact that the seventh note of the minor scale is G♯ where the Aeolian scale has G. Yet where an Aeolian melody moved from G to A at a close or cadence, it was usual to sharp the G. If this was done whenever G moved to A the character of the melody would become minor rather than Aeolian. Something of this kind frequently hap-

pened when an early New England tune was reprinted over a period of time, and accidentals are sometimes used even in first editions in a way calculated to inspire doubt.

Where a hymn tune existed both in folk tradition and in print, the folk sometimes clung to the older scale while the printed version followed the modern scale. The crucial difference between the Dorian mode and the minor scale is B♮ where the minor scale on D has B♭. In the case of "Wondrous Love" (q.v.) both Annabel Morris Buchanan and George Pullen Jackson have found that traditional singers sing the raised sixth where the printed score has the lowered form. In both examples we see an older practice yielding to a more recent one.

However the present popularity of folk music, the influence of Gregorian chant, and the works of recent composers who have found new and effective ways to use the modes, have invested such melodies with a new charm. There are instances in this collection where we have assumed that a melody printed in minor was originally modal. WAY TO CANAAN, for example seemed stronger and better as a modal tune and we have presented it in that form.

The problems of the editor diminish with the progress of the nineteenth century. Though some hymn composers (and particularly composers of gospel hymns) studied music as best they might, competent music teachers were more available and more organists and choir directors pursued theoretical studies. The result was a general mastery of the simple musical elements used in the hymn tune, but also a greater uniformity of style.

But as editorial problems diminished the problem of choice became more difficult. Most of the successful teachers of vocal music and organizers of musical conventions published at least one singing book which contained original hymn tunes, and some published a series of them. Lowell Mason is said to have composed well over sixteen hundred tunes. This is less remarkable than the fact that many of them were reprinted in book after book. Even today, in a period when tastes have so markedly changed, a substantial number of his tunes are still sung.

Thetford Center, Vermont — Charles W. Hughes

AMERICAN HYMNS OLD AND NEW

THE SEVENTEENTH CENTURY

THE SEVENTEENTH century for North America was an age of settlement. Each shipload of settlers brought with them the songs of their native land and of their church and, if they were Protestants, their sea chests contained Bibles and psalmbooks. The various settlements on the new continent might well have been distinguished by their songs.

Our search in *American Hymns* is for an "American voice," but obviously this was something which took shape gradually as characteristic modes of thinking and feeling appeared. The very existence of a new land with the hopes it inspired influenced both our own poets and those who remained in Europe. Yet clearly we cannot expect anything like a single voice. What was eventually to take on something of a native aspect had to develop from what was brought here from Europe.

Nor was our progress equal. It is clear that text-making must precede tune-making. From the earliest period the learned pastor was likely to settle with his flock and many a pastor could and did write verses. Yet the creation of music is by its nature a more specialized gift requiring a knowledge of musical notation to write down if not to conceive a melody. Religious verse flows here with some freedom by the middle of the seventeenth century, but we must wait a century more before a school of American composers appears. Thus we follow the course of history when first we reproduce the texts and tunes brought here by the early settlers, next set native texts to tunes of European origin, and finally set American texts to American tunes.

It is easy to see that extemporaneous prayer might take account of local and even personal concerns, while prescribed forms of prayer must deal with the needs and aspirations of humanity in general. In the same manner hymns by an individual, once they were permitted to be sung, might illustrate divine truths with local examples. Obviously the degree to which sacred songs could assume an American character varied according to two factors: the extent to which the elements of a religious service were subject to change, and the closely related question of the degree of centralized control within the religious group. However, it is not difficult to find instances where the language of the psalms assumes a British or an American character according to the nationality of the poet.

Just as the idea of "passing over Jordan" was frequent in nine-

teenth-century hymnody, the pilgrim hymn appears in the seventeenth century, even in the work of poets who did not come to America. George Wither, who wrote hymns for men in all manner of situations, included one for those settling in a new land, "Lord, Many Times Thou Pleased Art." When Edwin Sandys wrote "In Pilgrim Life Our Rest," he may have been thinking of life as a pilgrimage, but he may also have been thinking of those who crossed the Atlantic to seek a place where they might worship undisturbed. William Bradford and Thomas Tillam, who actually went to the New World, express the same hope in more specific terms ("And Truly It Is a Most Glorious Thing" and "Hail, Holy Land"). When Jacob Steendam wrote "God set us here despite the savage wild," he was comparing the American Indians with the hostile tribes who warred on King David. A different note is sounded by Roger Williams. In a day when Indians and their culture were despised and feared, he wrote little verses in which he contrasted Indian virtues with English failings.

The first religious songs sung in the New World were those of the Roman church. Catholic service books were published in Mexico as early as 1556. Because South America and Mexico developed as Catholic regions, the missions of the Southwest were a kind of northward extension of that culture. North America, Canada, Florida, and Louisiana reflect the same influence, as does Maryland, where a substantial number of the early settlers adhered to the Catholic faith.

Yet the main effect of this expansion of Catholicism into the New World, musically speaking, was to introduce Gregorian chant sung in Latin into the New World. That Catholic missionaries also realized the attractiveness of popular religious song is shown by Jean de Brebeuf's Huron Christmas carol, "Jesus Ahatonhia" and by the Spanish songs of the missions of the Southwest, "Qué Preciosas Mañanitas."

The musical product of the Reformation was a repertory of songs suited to congregational singing, and this "people's music" and the privilege of singing it was cherished to an extent that is difficult to understand today. The Reformation brought with it a new song. This song was in the vernacular, not in Latin, and it was sung by the entire congregation, not by the celebrant or a trained choir.

Congregational music assumed two basic forms: the chorale, which we associate with the Lutherans and Moravians, and the psalm tune, which developed among the Calvinists. The first Lutheran songbook appeared in 1524, the first collection of French psalm paraphrases in 1539. Although there were similarities and certain tunes were used by both groups, there were also differences. (One of a number of examples of a shared melody would be the wonderful DE PROFUNDIS.)

The French and English sang psalms paraphrased in meter to which they added paraphrases of other lyric passages from the Scriptures. They sang "God's word." Though the Lutherans sang texts based on the Bible ("Vater unser" is a German version of the Lord's Prayer and "Aus der Tiefe" of Psalm 130), they also welcomed devotional poems written by an individual. Luther himself wrote texts of this type, such as the Christmas song "Vom Himmel hoch." In England and America, however, there has been a long and gradual transition from songs based directly on "God's word" to devotional poems by individuals—from psalm to hymn. In this connection it is interesting to note that one of the spiritual songs included in the Sternhold and Hopkins psalter, "Give Peace in These Our Days, O Lord," was a translation of a German chorale text by Wolfgang Köpfel which was taken over with its proper tune.

The other difference was a musical one. The Lutherans and the Moravians did not reject the use of the organ or, indeed, of orchestral instruments in divine service. The Calvinists as well as the English dissenters took a more extreme position. Their church music was limited to metrical psalms sung in unison.

In 1562 the psalms of Marot and De Bèze were sung on Port Royal, an island near Charleston, South Carolina, by a party of Huguenots who had landed there. Two years later a short-lived settlement was established in Florida. We are told that the Indians there remembered two of the psalms (Pss. 128 and 130) long after the settlement was destroyed and used them as a kind of test to determine whether a white man was French (and hence friendly). They were later sung by Huguenot settlers not only in South Carolina, but also in New Rochelle and in Oxford, Massachusetts. A copy of the *Pseaulmes de David* of 1679 is still preserved in South Carolina. In New Amsterdam the worshipers joined in singing the Calvinist tunes in French and in Dutch, according to the origin of the individual.

The first psalm singing in the New World in English is recorded by Francis Fletcher, the chaplain who sailed with Sir Francis Drake in 1577. He spoke especially of the interest shown by the Indians of the West Coast, near what is now San Francisco, in the singing on ship board. Fletcher does not mention the psalmbook used, but it must have been that by Sternhold and Hopkins. The Este psalter, which contained four-part settings of Sternhold and Hopkins, was brought to Jamestown, Virginia, with those who settled there in 1607.

Except in Plymouth the English colonists "lined out" their psalms. This practice was designed to permit those who could not read, or those who had no psalter, to take part in congregational sing-

ing. The clerk or an elder read one or two lines of the appointed psalm. The congregation then joined in singing what had just been read. This alternation continued to the end of the psalm. At the best it interrupted the continuity of the psalm, and where the sense of the text was not clear by the end of the line, the effect might be disastrous. In spite of the disadvantages of the practice, congregations and the deacons who led the congregations were reluctant to give it up.

What has been said of psalmody in unison applies to the church service. For those who had some skill in music, more elaborate versions were made for domestic performance. In these the psalm tune was assigned to one voice, generally but not always the tenor, while the others sang independent parts. Allison's psalter included parts for instruments as well as voices: lute, orpharion, cittern, and bass viol. A solitary worshiper might sing a psalm accompanying himself on the lute or bass viol. (The accompaniment of Nicasius de Sille's "God Set Us Here" is based on a lute version of the French melody for Psalm 116.)

Did some of the colonists sing the psalms in harmony? The scanty evidence is of two kinds: the knowledge that they possessed harmonized psalters, and accounts which tell of singing in parts. John Endecott possessed Ravenscroft's *The Whole Booke of Psalms.* A copy of Allison's psalter belonged to William Brewster, who came here on the *Mayflower.* Samuel Sewall owned Playford's *The Whole Book of Psalms.* In Philadelphia Hopkinson owned a part-book of Giles Farnaby's, *Psalmes of David to Fower Parts for Viols and Voyces.* The *Bay Psalm Book* refers the reader to Ravenscroft for suitable tunes. When the *Bay Psalm Book* was reprinted with music, the tunes and basses were copied from Playford's *Introduction to the Skill of Music.* Obviously the engraver must have had a copy to work from. Why did the edition of 1698 include basses to the tunes if no one could sing them?

Our only direct authority for the practice of part singing is Samuel Sewall. An entry in 1698 reads: "In the new Room with the widow Gales and her daughter Sparhawk; sung the 114th Psalm. Simon catch'd us a base." In 1718 he writes of the death of a former classmate, the Rev. Daniel Gookin: "We were Fellows together at College and have sung many a Tune in Consort; hope shall sing Hallelujahs together in Heaven."

No doubt when the record is more carefully examined more evidence will be found, but perhaps not much more. Some books were brought here. At least in Sewall's circle there was some part singing. It is however important to present the polyphonic setting as well as the simple psalm tune to fully understand this movement. Even if many

circles here sang only the simple tune, it was a branch of a development which elsewhere had flowered into a rich polyphony.

That American colonists also sang ballads and folk songs might be assumed, but there are more positive indications. We know that Seaborn Cotton copied three ballads ("The Love-Sick Maid," "The Last Lamentation of the Languishing Squire," and "Two Faithful Lovers") into his notebook while he was a student at Harvard. (He graduated in 1651.) It seems unlikely that Puritan divines would have spoken so violently against ballad singing if the practice were infrequent. Benjamin Walworth complained in 1722 that "those wedded to bad Company have often a greater relish for Play-books, Romances, filthy Songs and Ballads than for the Holy Scriptures."

Not only did these offenders sing ballads; they also sang religious verses to popular tunes. George Wither rebukes those who do this: "For so impudent and irreligious are many in these Times growne, that I have heard in foolish and ridiculous Ballads (whose makers and publishers deserve whipping) the name of our blessed Saviour, invocated and sung to those roguish tunes, which have formerly served for profane jiggs; An impiety odious to a good Christian: and yet use hath made it so familiar that we can now heare it, and scarce take notice that there is ought evill therein." Yet Wither himself named A HERMIT POORE, IN SAD AND ASHIE WEEDS, and I LOVED THEE ONCE (included in Playford's *English Dancing Master*) as suitable tunes for hymns appearing in his *Halelviah* (1641).

In accordance with this practice LORD THOMAS AND FAIR ELLINOR, HOW CAN THE TREE, IN CRETE, and ESSEX'S LAST GOOD-NIGHT have been set to suitable devotional verses in our anthology. Jean de Brebeuf's Huron Christmas carol was sung to the noel UNE JEUNE PUCELLE, and Steendam's "Als ik des Heren werk" has been matched with the English "preaching tune" FORTUNE MY FOE, following his own indication.

Cotton Mather, however, suggested that the fondness of the people for ballad singing could be utilized as a means of religious instruction. "I am informed that the minds and manners of many people about the country are much corrupted by the foolish airs and ballads which the Hawkers and Peddlers carry into all parts of the country. By way of antidote I would procure poeticall composures full of Piety, and such as may have a tendency to cause Truth and Goodness to be published and scattered into all corners of the land."

Benjamin Franklin's brother Peter had written poems with a similar intention, for which he wished musical settings. Benjamin Franklin replied from London: "I think, that if you had given it to some country girl in the heart of Massachusetts, who has never heard

any other than psalm tunes or 'Chevy Chase,' 'Children in the Woods,' 'Spanish Lady,' and such old simple ditties, but has naturally a good ear, she might more probably have made a pleasing popular tune for you than any of our masters here, and more proper to the purpose."

Among the dying confessions, descriptions of natural disasters, and satirical verses versified and sold as broadsides were moralizing poems and hymns. Some of these were directed to be sung to popular tunes, and it seems probable that they would serve for sacred as well as secular verses. Among the poems included here, Wesley's "Ah Lovely Appearance of Death," Sewall's "Once More Our God Vochsafe To Shine," Tyler's "Hail to the Glorious Day," Otto's "Guter Gott! Dir ich befehle," and the anonymous "Is There No Balm in Christian Lands," were published as broadsides.

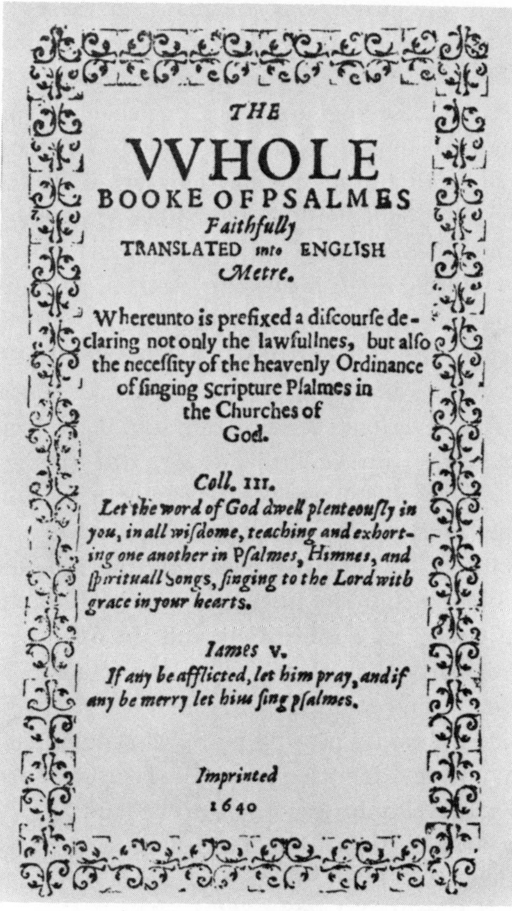

THE

VVHOLE

BOOKE OF PSALMES

Faithfully

TRANSLATED *into* ENGLISH

Metre.

Whereunto is prefixed a diſcourſe declaring not only the lawfullnes, but alſo the neceſſity of the heavenly Ordinance of ſinging Scripture Pſalmes in the Churches of God.

Coll. III.

Let the word of God dwell plenteouſly in you, in all wiſdome, teaching and exhorting one another in Pſalmes, Himnes, and ſpirituall Songs, ſinging to the Lord with grace in your hearts.

Iames V.

If any be afflicted, let him pray, and if any be merry let him ſing pſalmes.

Imprinted

1640

Title page of the 1640 *Bay Psalm Book*

The Psalters

THE PSALTER was the songbook of the Protestants. Of those which were most in use during the seventeenth century, only the *Bay Psalm Book* was the work of native scholars. The Old Version, the Scottish psalters, and that by Ainsworth were brought here.

THE OLD VERSION (STERNHOLD AND HOPKINS). The psalter of Sternhold and Hopkins was the result of a long and complicated development. It began with a group of psalms which Thomas Sternhold wrote and performed to his own organ accompaniment. His *Certayne Psalmes* (published before his death in 1549) was the earliest step. A posthumous edition contained thirty-seven paraphrases, to which seven more by John Hopkins were added in 1551. By 1562 it included all the Psalms. When Mary Tudor became queen in 1553 many Protestants fled to Geneva, and these English refugees came in contact with the French tradition. A number of French tunes thus entered the English repertory. Here too we find the beginning of the groups of "spiritual songs" at the beginning and at the end of the Psalms. Of these we have included "Our Father Which in Heaven Art," an anonymous version of the Lord's Prayer, and "Give Peace in These Our Days, O Lord," a translation by Edmund Grindal.

With the edition of 1562, the psalter of Sternhold and Hopkins may be said to have reached its final form. Most of the versions were in common or ballad meter, although others were influenced by the more complex Genevan meters. Lutheran influence was slight and largely transient, although there were tunes used by both Lutherans and the English (for example DA PACEM). There were harmonized psalters by William Daman, Thomas East, Richard Allison, Thomas Ravenscroft, and John Playford. The Ravenscroft psalter was remarkable for the number of distinguished contemporary composers who made settings for it. Aside from those by Ravenscroft himself, we have included settings by John Dowland, John Farmer, Giles Farnaby, George Kirbye, Robert William Parsons, Simeon Stubbs, and Thomas Tomkins.

Although the advent of the *Bay Psalm Book* displaced the Old Version in the Massachusetts Bay Colony in 1640, Henry Wilder Foote notes that a Book of Common Prayer, given as late as 1760 to King's

Chapel "has the Old Version bound in at the back." Episcopal churches, particularly in Virginia, Georgia, and probably North and South Carolina, used the Old Version until the close of the century. "The Lord Descended from Above" was a favorite passage, and William Billings knew it and published it with his tune MAJESTY as late as 1778.

THE SCOTTISH PSALTERS. The Scottish Presbyterians, who made many settlements in this country (such as Londonderry, N.H., and Ryegate, Vt.), and who were an important factor in others, held very strict views on the subject of church music. They were the last to give up the exclusive use of the Psalms and the most vigorous in rejecting the assistance of instruments.

The earliest Scottish psalter appeared in 1564. Of the contributors to this psalter William Kethe, whose verses had been published earlier, may have been Scottish (see his "My Soul Praise the Lord" and "Thy Mercies, Lord, to Heaven Reach"). John Craig certainly was (see his "O Hear My Prayer, Lord" and "O Lord, That Art My God and King!). The third Scotsman, Robert Pont, endeavored to write in the special meters suited to the Genevan tunes. Indeed Genevan influence was apparent in the varied meters and in the large number of French modal tunes which were included. The number of tunes was large (125). After accounting for French tunes and those taken from Sternhold and Hopkins, there remain tunes which appear in neither, and these may have been composed or arranged by native musicians.

There were evidently singers in Scotland who wished to perform the Psalms in polyphonic versions. Two sources show this development: the (manuscript) St. Andrews Psalter, 1562–1566 (see the setting of Psalm 145), and the great printed psalter of 1635. (From this we reproduce settings of Psalms 36, 143, 110, and 18.) Unfortunately, there was dissatisfaction with the texts and, after a conflict of versions, the Rous psalter displaced the earlier versions in 1650.

When Cromwell came to power Francis Rous, who was a person of importance, placed copies of a Dutch edition of his paraphrase in the hands of each member of Parliament. Though it was received with favor, it was successively referred to and revised by the Wesminster Assembly, the Scottish Church, and both houses of Parliament. Though Rous's name was still attached to it, few of his lines remained intact after such a series of revisions. This psalter was used by many Scottish-Americans. In addition to paraphrases of Psalm 12 ("Help, Lord, Because the Godly Man") and of Psalm 121 ("I to the Hills Will Lift Mine Eyes"), we have included Psalm 23 ("The Lord's My Shepherd"),

which was sung both here and in Scotland to an American folk tune called PISGAH.

Two other psalters were important, although neither was used in public worship. In the case of George Wither it was the Company of Stationers who, feeling that their rights had been violated, did not comply with the order directing them to bind Wither's psalter at the end of each Bible. The psalter of George Sandys has a special interest for us, for he was a settler in Virginia and for a time the treasurer of the colony. He was especially fortunate in his composers, for settings exist by William and Henry Lawes and by Walter Porter.

THE AINSWORTH PSALTER. The settlers who landed at Plymouth in 1620 came from Holland, and they brought with them a psalter which included suitable melodies by Henry Ainsworth. He was teacher and minister to the English there. It was also used at Salem. In its preference for a longer stanza and a more complex metrical scheme it reflected the French Calvinist tradition. The French psalm paraphrases of Marot and De Bèze had been translated into Dutch in 1566 and, although this translation had been subjected to thirty revisions, these did not simplify the meters or displace the French tunes to which they were sung. Ainsworth also included English melodies familiar to many in his congregation. He said in his preface: "Tunes for the Psalms I find none set of God; so that each people is to use the most grave, decent, and comfortable manner of singing that they know."

The one passage which describes the singing of the Pilgrims comes from Edward Winslow, who wrote of a gathering before the sailing of the *Mayflower:* "They . . . that stayed at Leyden feasted us that were to go at our pastor's house, being large; where we refreshed ourselves, after tears, with singing of psalms, making joyful melody in our hearts, as well as with the voice, there being many of our congregation very expert in music."

One would hope for evidence that Ainsworth's later paraphrase of the five books of Moses were also sung in Plymouth. It is certain that Ainsworth intended them to be sung since he suggested that his "Unto Jehovah Sing Will I" from Exodus may be sung as Psalm 113. We have also included his "Give Ear, O Heavens," from Deuteronomy. It is certain that copies existed in New England. Inventories of estates, generally vague, sometimes are helpful. "Mr. Ainsworth on the 5. books of Moses and the psalms" is one such entry in the Probate Records of Essex County. Less specific is the record of a gift of books from Mr. William Backhouse in 1629 to the Massachusetts Bay Colony which included "Ainsworth's Works in folio."

THE BAY PSALM BOOK. In 1640 appeared *The Whole Booke of Psalmes Faithfully Translated Into English Metre,* which is commonly known as the *Bay Psalm Book.* As the first book published in North America and the first version of the Psalms made by Americans and used in American churches, it has always been recognized as a historical document of the first importance. For a new settlement it was a most laborious and ambitious undertaking. There had been dissatisfaction with the Old Version. Cotton Mather later referred to this in his *Magnalia Christi:*

> Tho' they blessed God for the Religious Endeavors of them who translated the Psalms into the Meetre usually annex'd at the end of the Bible, yet they beheld in the Translation so many Detractions from, Additions to, and Variations of, not only the Text, but the very Sense of the Psalmist, that it was an Offense unto them.

In 1636 a group of "thirty pious and learned Ministers" decided to make their own translation. Especially active were Rev. Richard Mather (of Dorchester) and Rev. Thomas Welde and Rev. John Eliot (both of Roxbury). To manufacture the book a printer, press, type, and paper were necessary. They were secured largely through the efforts of Joseph (or Josse) Glover, who gave time and money and sought funds from others.

Stephen Daye, the printer, signed a contract on June 7, 1638. Glover, with his family, his servants, Stephen Daye, and three assistants set sail for New England. Glover "fell sick of a fever" and died at sea. In March, 1639, the press was set up in Cambridge, Massachusetts. The fact that Daye was later called as a witness (in the case of the heirs of Josse Glover vs. Henry Dunster) has preserved details concerning the printing of the *Bay Psalm Book.* The first edition was of 1,700 copies which were sold at 20d. each. Sales amounted to £ 141 13s. 4d.

The preface has been ascribed to Richard Mather, but Zoltan Haraszti argues persuasively that it was written by John Cotton. The preface justified the practice of singing metrical psalms in English. It discussed the question as to whether only "David and other scripture psalmes" were to be sung or whether "the psalmes invented by the gifts of godly men in every age of the church" might also be used in church. (It is to be noted that the word "psalms" is used here for what we would call "hymns.") The initial decision not to sing hymns written by individuals still left the congregation free to sing paraphrases of other passages from the Bible and these were first added to the *Bay Psalm Book* in the edition of 1647. Among them was "O Lord, Almighty God," from Revelation.

The author of the preface believed that the early spiritual songs

were received through "extraordinary gifts of the spirit," and that songs produced by an ordinary gift should not be allowed to displace those of David. Moreover not every minister was capable of extemporaneous song, although he was expected to pray extemporaneously. Even if a minister were capable of such singing, the congregation could not join in "except he that composeth a psalme, bringeth into the Church set formes of psalms of his invention; for which wee find no warrant or precedent in any ordinary offices of the Church throughout the scriptures." This is a negative argument; the practice is not specifically forbidden by the Scriptures.

Arguments against turning the psalms into English verse are answered by stating that "many verses together" in several psalms are rhymed "in the original Hebrew" and that "as all our english songs (according to the course of our english poetry) do run in metre, soe ought David's psalmes to be translated into meeter [*sic*]." As to tunes, "the truth is, the Lord hath hid from us the hebrew tunes, lest we should think ourselves bound to imitate them." Therefore "every nation without scruple might follow as the grave sort of tunes of their owne country songs, soe the graver sort of verses of their own country poetry."

Finally the preface defends and justifies a maximum literalness of translation that the ordinances of the Psalms as of the other portions of the Bible might be received "in its native purity."

Of special interest is "An admonition to the Reader" which follows Psalm 150. This deals with the meters of the paraphrases and the tunes to which they were to be sung. "The verses of these psalmes may be reduced to six kindes." These six kinds were C.M. (common meter), in which most of the Psalms were written; S.M. (short meter); L.M. (long meter); and then the special meters H.M. (hallelujah meter); L.M. six lines, and L.M.D. "The first (C.M.) may be sung in very neere fourty common tunes, as they are collected, out of our chief musicians, by *Tho. Ravenscroft.*"

Fifteen psalms were cast in S.M. (the "second kind"), and sixteen in L.M. (the "third kind"). However six of these psalms (Pss. 51, 85, 100, 117, 133, and 138) were also paraphrased in C.M. (the "first kind"). Here we note that Psalm 100 may be sung to OLD 100TH and Psalm 51 to its proper tune. The other L.M. tune is that usually used for the Ten Commandments. The tune suggested for the six texts in H.M. (the "fourth kind") was the OLD 148TH, which was to serve both for its proper psalm as well as for the remaining five. For L.M. six lines (the fifth kind"), the tune is PATER NOSTER or the OLD 112TH, but the psalms in that meter are the 85th and the 138th. Only one psalm, the

115th, was in L.M.D. (the "sixth kind"). One might expect that the tunes would be indicated in such a way as to preserve associations between given psalms and the tunes closely associated with them. It does not appear that this consideration was regarded as important since only the OLD 100TH, the OLD 148TH, and the tune for Psalm 51 were presented so as to fit the psalms for which they were named.

The success of the *Bay Psalm Book* was immediate. An English edition with some corrections appeared in 1647. John Cotton had been extremely forthright in his preface, where he stated that "We have therefore done our indeavour to make a plaine and familiar translation of the psalmes and words of David into english metre, and have not soe much as presumed to paraphrase to give the sense of his meaning in other words." He closed with the emphatic and much-quoted statement that " 'God's Altar needs not our pollishings': Ex 20. for wee have respected rather a plaine translation, than to smooth our verses with the sweetness of any paraphrase, and soe have attended Conscience rather than Elegance, fidelity rather than poetry."

Nevertheless there were objections. The following quatrain by Mr. Shepard of Cambridge was written down by Increase Mather, who evidently relished a jest at the expense of his associates. The Roxbury poets were, of course, Welde and Eliot; Richard Mather was from Dorchester.

> You Roxborough poets, take this in Time
> see that you make very good Rhyme
> And eeke to Dorchester, when you the verses lenghten
> see that you them with the words of the text doe strengthen.

Finally a revision was planned. As Cotton Mather later stated: "It was thought that a little more of art was to be employed upon them. And for that Cause, they were committed unto Mr. Dunster, who Revised and Refined this Translation; and (with some Assistance from Mr. Richard Lyon . . .) he brought it into the Condition wherein our Churches ever since have used it."

The new edition of 2,000 copies appeared in 1651: *"The Psalms Hymns and Spiritual Songs of the Old and New Testament,* faithfully translated into English meter for the use, edification, and comfort of the Saints, in publick and private, especially in New England."

Some lines were retained as they were, some were improved in expression; in others a modern turn of phrase was preferred to an archaic one. Some lines were made intelligible by themselves. This line-by-line completeness was very important where lining out was the practice. The inclusion of paraphrases of other passages from the Bible placed before and after the Psalms brought the New England version

into conformity with the Old Version. Among them were "Let Him with Kisses of His Mouth" (Song of Solomon), "The Sun and Mood So High and Bright" (Habakkuk), and "I to the Lord from Mu Distress" (Jonah).

This edition may be regarded as the definitive form of the *Bay Psalm Book.* Twenty-seven editions were printed in New England, at least twenty in England (the last as late as 1754), and six in Scotland (to 1759). Even Pilgrim churches turned from Ainsworth. A resolution by the Salem church in 1667 stated that "the Bay psalm book should be made use of together with Ainsworth." Plymouth resisted change until 1692 when the church there decided "to sing the psalms now used in our neighbor churches in the Bay." Thomas Prince's statement that the *Bay Psalm Book* was "by some eminent Congregations prefer'd to all Others in their Publick Worship" refers to English churches. The fact that over 600 lines from the *Bay Psalm Book* were utilized in the Scottish psalter of 1650 is a clear indication of the esteem felt for this American psalter.

The ninth edition (1698) of the *Bay Psalm Book* is the earliest surviving one with music. It contains music in the form of thirteen psalm tunes for treble and bass rudely printed from wooden blocks. Frédéric L. Ritter pointed out the fact that they were taken from Playford's *Brief Introduction to the Skill of Musick.*

Irving Lowens showed that the instructions were taken from the 1667 edition, the use of the letters F, S, L, M (for fa, sol, la, mi) from the edition of 1672, and the tunes with their basses from one of three identical editions, those of 1674, 1679, and 1683.

Our choice of psalms displays the "six kinds" of meters. WINDSOR, the C.M. tune, is given as it appears in the 1698 edition of the *Bay Psalm Book.* The other settings have been taken from the Ravenscroft psalter: YORK, C.M.; LONDON, S.M.; 100TH, L.M.; OLD 148TH, H.M.; PATER NOSTER or OLD 112TH, 8.8.8.D.; and OLD 113TH, L.M.D.

All these are among the thirteen tunes printed in 1698 except LONDON and OLD 112TH. The latter is mentioned as the proper tune in the edition of 1640. The short meter tune printed in 1698 was CAMBRIDGE SHORT TUNE. The 1640 edition suggests "three tunes as Pss. in 25, 50, & 67 in our English psalmbooks." LONDON appeared in Damon's *The Former Book* (1591) as the tune to Psalm 25.

Compared with the richness and variety of the Ainsworth Psalter this was admittedly a meager provision. This, however, is perhaps not a fair point of view. In Scotland the first tunes printed with the Rous psalter of 1650 were twelve in number, all in common meter, plus one solitary survivor from the earlier tradition—BON ACCORD in reports.

As Millar Patrick states: "By the end of the century these twelve were canonized as embodying the accepted and inexpandible musical tradition of the Church of Scotland." Viewed in this perspective the musical edition of the *Bay Psalm Book* must be seen as typical of its time. It was on the whole not a rich period for psalmody. The great enthusiasms of the early Reformation had waned and the little ballad meter tunes, easier to remember and congenial to English minds, had gained the ascendancy. But what was sung in Boston was probably comparable to what was sung in a parish church in England or Scotland in terms of the number of tunes sung and the quality of the performance.

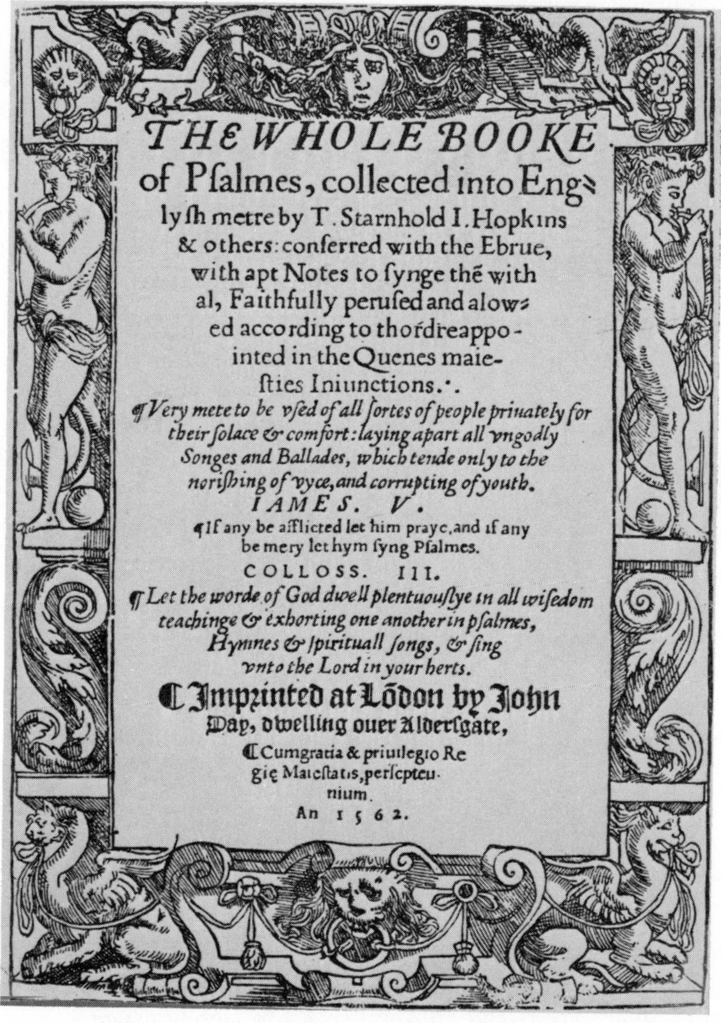

THE WHOLE BOOKE
of Pſalmes, collected into Eng-
lyſh metre by T. Starnhold I. Hopkins
& others: conſerred with the Ebrue,
with apt Notes to ſynge thē with
al, Faithfully peruſed and alow-
ed according to thordre appointed in the Quenes maie-
ſties Iniunctions.
¶ *Very mete to be vſed of all ſortes of people priuately for*
their ſolace & comfort: laying apart all vngodly
Songes and Ballades, which tende only to the
noriſhing of vyce, and corrupting of youth.
IAMES. V.
¶ If any be afflicted let him praye, and if any
be mery let hym ſyng Pſalmes.
COLLOSS. III.
¶ *Let the worde of God dwell plentuouſlye in all wiſedom*
teachinge & exhorting one another in pſalmes,
Hymnes & ſpirituall ſongs, & ſing
vnto the Lord in your herts.
¶ Imprinted at Lōdon by John
Day, dwelling ouer Alderſgate,
¶ Cum gratia & priuilegio Re-
giæ Maieſtatis, perſeptennium.
An 1562.

Title page of Sternhold and Hopkins' 1562 psalter

I LIFT MY HEART TO THEE

Ps. 25: 1, 4-9

Thomas Sternhold, before 1549

PSALM 25 S.M.D.

Frost 44

William Daman, arr. 1579

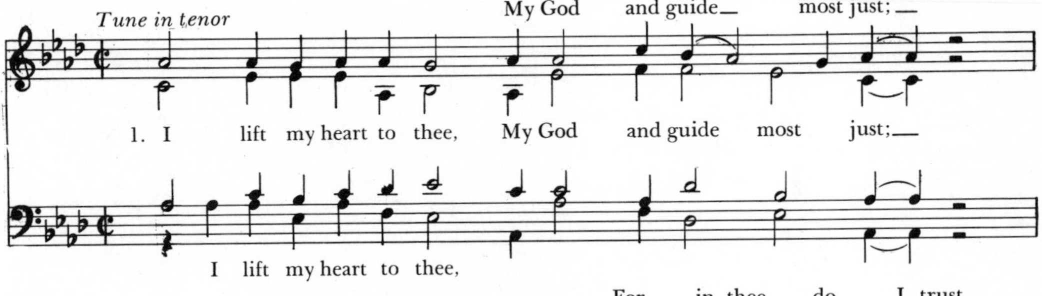
Tune in tenor
My God and guide— most just;—
1. I lift my heart to thee, My God and guide most just;—
I lift my heart to thee,

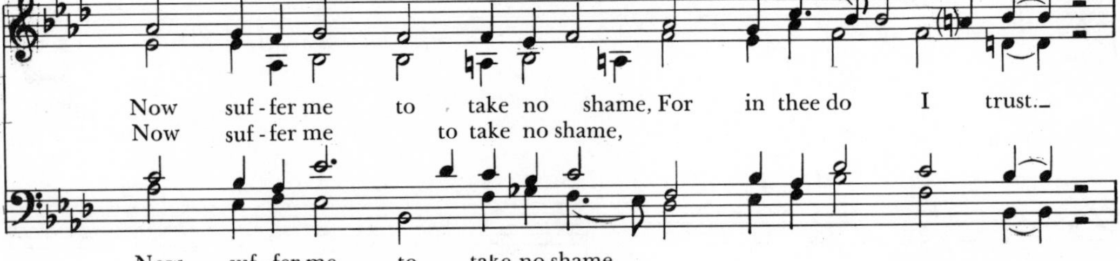
For in thee— do I trust.—
Now suf-fer me to take no shame, For in thee do I trust.—
Now suf-fer me to take no shame,
Now suf-fer me to take no shame,—

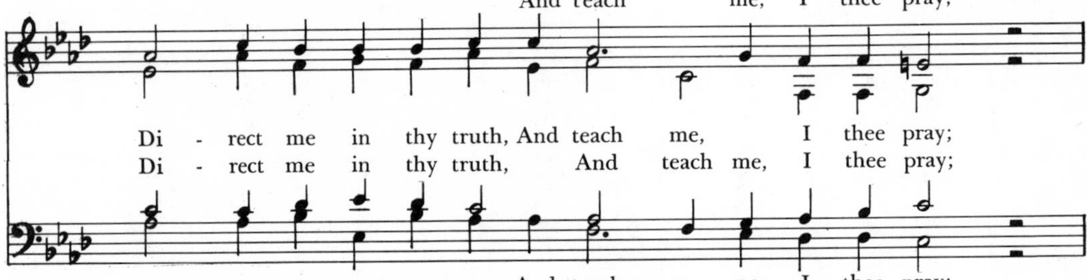
And teach me, I thee pray;
Di - rect me in thy truth, And teach me, I thee pray;
Di - rect me in thy truth, And teach me, I thee pray;
And teach me, I thee pray;

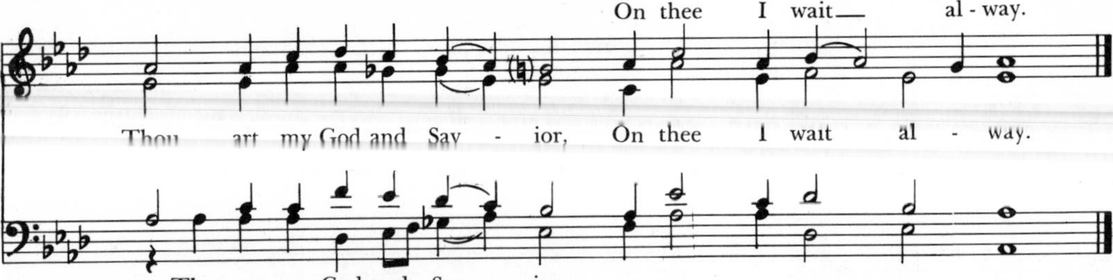
On thee I wait— al - way.
Thou art my God and Sav - ior, On thee I wait al - way.
Thou art my God and— Sav - ior,

2. Thy mercies manifold
I pray thee, Lord, remember,
And eke thy pity plentiful,
For they have been forever.
Remember not the faults
And frailty of my youth;
Remember not how ignorant
I have been of thy truth.

3. Nor after my deserts
Let me thy mercy find,
But of thine own benignity
Lord have me in thy mind.
His mercy is full sweet,
His truth a perfect guide,
Therefore the Lord will sinners teach
And such as go aside.

4. The humble he will teach
His precepts for to keep;
He will direct in all his ways
The lowly and the meek.
For all the ways of God
Are truth and mercy both
To them that keep his testament,
The witness of his truth.

NOW ISRAEL MAY SAY, AND THAT TRULY
Ps. 124: 1, 2, 5-8
William Whittingham, 1560
PSALM 124 10.10.10.10.10.
Frost 139
William Daman, arr. 1579
Tune in tenor
If that the
1. Now Is - ra - el may say, and that tru - ly, If that the
Now Is - ra - el
If that the Lord had
Lord had not our cause main-tained, If that the Lord had not
If that the Lord had
not our right sus - tained, When all the world a - gainst us fu - rious
our right sus - tained, When all the world a-gainst us fu-rious -
not our right sus - tained, When all the world a - gainst us fu-rious-
ly Made their up - roars and said we should all die.
ly Made their up - roars and said we should all die.
ly

2. The raging streams, most proud in roaring noise,
Had long ago o'erwhelmed us in the deep,
But loved be God which doth us safely keep
From bloody teeth and their most cruel voice,
Which as a prey to eat us would rejoice.

3. E'en as a bird out of the fowler's gin
Escapes away, right so it fares with us.
Broke are their nets, and we have scapèd thus.
God that made heaven and earth is our help then;
His name hath saved us from these wicked men.

GIVE PEACE IN THESE OUR DAYS, O LORD

St. 1-3

Edmund Grindal, 1561

DA PACEM 8.7.8.7.D

Frost 183; Zahn 7556

Thomas Ravenscroft, arr. 1621

Tune in tenor

1. Give peace in these our days, O Lord, Great dan - gers are__ now at hand;
2. Give us that peace that we do lack, Through mis - be - lief__ and ill life.

long slur, st. 1 and 3

Thine en - e - mies__ with one ac - cord Christ's name in ev - ery land
Thy word to of - fer thou dost not slack, Which we un - kind - ly gain - strive.

Seek to de - face, root out and rase, Thy true right wor - ship in - deed.
With fire and sword, this health - ful word Some per - se - cute and op - press.

long slur, st. 3

Be thou the stay, Lord, we thee pray, Thou helpest a - lone in all need.
Some with the mouth con fess the truth With out sin - cere god - li - ness.

3. Give peace and us thy sprite down send
With grief and repentance true;
Do piece our hearts our lives to amend,
And by faith Christ renew;
That fear and dread, war and bloodshed,
Through thy sweet mercy and grace,
May from us slide, thy truth abide,
And shine in every place.

Our Father Which in Heaven Art — The Lord's Prayer 8.6.8.6.8.6.D.

Frost 11

Anon., 1561 — John Farmer, arr. 1621

Tune in tenor
Our Fa - ther which in heav - en art, Lord, hal - lowed be thy name;
Our Fa - ther which in heav - en art, Lord, hal - lowed be thy name;
Our Fa - ther which in heav - en art, Lord, hal - lowed be thy name;
Thy king - dom come, thy will be done
Thy king dom come, thy will be done In earth, e'en as the same In heav - en is.
Thy king - dom come, thy will be done In earth, e'en as the same In heav - en is.
Give us, O Lord, Our dai - ly bread this day; As we for - give our debt - ors, so For-
Give us, O Lord, Our dai - ly bread this day; As we for - give our debt - ors, so For -
Give us, O Lord, Our dai - ly bread this day; As we for - give our debt - ors, so For -
give our debts we pray. In - to temp-ta - tion lead us not, From e - vil make us free,
give our debts we pray. In - to temp - ta - tion lead us not, From e - vil make us free,
give our debts we pray. In - to temp - ta - tion lead us not, From e - vil make us free,

For king-dom, power, and glo - ry thine, Both now and ev - er be.
For king-dom, power, and glo - ry—thine, Both now and ev - er be.
For king - dom, power, and glo - ry thine, Both now and ev - er be.
For king - dom, power, and glo - ry thine, Both now and ev - er be.

SUCH AS IN GOD THE LORD DO TRUST

HIGH DUTCH TUNE 8.8.8.8.6.6.

Ps. 125: 1-5

Frost 144

William Kethe, 1561

Giles Farnaby, arr. 1621

Tune in tenor
1. Such as in God the Lord do trust As Mount Si - on shall firm - ly stand,
2. As might - y moun - tains huge and great Je - ru - sa - lem a - bout do close,
And be re - mov - èd at no hand. The Lord will count them right and just,
So will the Lord be un - to those Who on his god - ly will do wait;
So that they shall be sure For - ev - er to en - dure.
Such are to him so dear They nev - er need to fear.

3. For though the righteous try doth he
By making wicked men his rod,
Lest they through grief forsake their God;
It shall not as their lot still be.
Give, Lord, to us thy light
Whose hearts are true and right.

O LORD, TURN NOT AWAY THY FACE — THE LAMENTATION C.M.D.

St. 1, first half of 4, first half of 5 — Frost 10

John Marckant (?), 1561 — Robert William Parsons, arr. 1621

Tune in tenor
a - way thy face From him that li - eth pros - trate,
1. O Lord, turn not a - way thy face From him that li - eth pros - trate,
From him that li - eth pros - trate,
La - ment - ing sore his sin - ful life Be - fore thy mer - cy gate.
La - ment - ing sore his sin - ful life Be - fore thy mer - cy gate.
La - ment - ing sore his sin - ful life
Be - fore thy mer - cy gate.
That do la - ment their sin;
Which gate thou o - penest wide to those That do la - ment their sin;
Which gate thou la - ment their sin;
a - gainst me, Lord, But let me en - ter in.
Shut not that gate a - gainst me, Lord, But let me en - ter in.
But let me en - ter in.

2. O Lord thou knowest what things be past
And eke the things that be,
Thou knowest also what is to come,
Nothing is hid from thee.
Before the heavens and earth were made
Thou knowest what things were then,
As all things else that have been since
Among the sons of men.

3. So come I to thy mercy gate
Where mercy doth abound,
Requiring mercy for my sin
To heal my deadly wound.
Mercy, good Lord, mercy I ask,
This is the total sum,
For mercy, Lord, is all my suit,
Lord, let thy mercy come.

THE LORD DESCENDED FROM ABOVE

MAJESTY C.M.D.

Ps. 18: 9, 10, 16, 17, 20, 21

Thomas Sternhold, 1561

William Billings, 1778

Tune in tenor

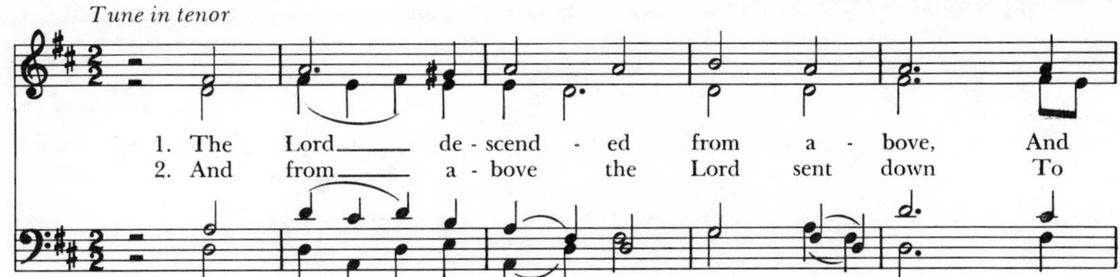
1. The Lord descend - ed from a - bove, And
2. And from a - bove the Lord sent down To

bowed the heav - ens high; And un - der - neath his feet he
fetch me from be - low, And plucked me out of wa - ters

cast The dark ness of the sky.
great That would me ov - er - flow.

Full roy - al - ly he
That would have made me
On cher - ubs and on cher - u - bims Full roy - al - ly he
And me de - liv - ered from my foes That would have made me

rode; And on the wings of all the winds Came fly - ing all a -
thrall; Yea, from such foes as were too strong For me to deal with-
rode; And on the wings of all the winds Came fly - ing all a -
thrall; Yea, from such foes as were too strong For me to deal with-

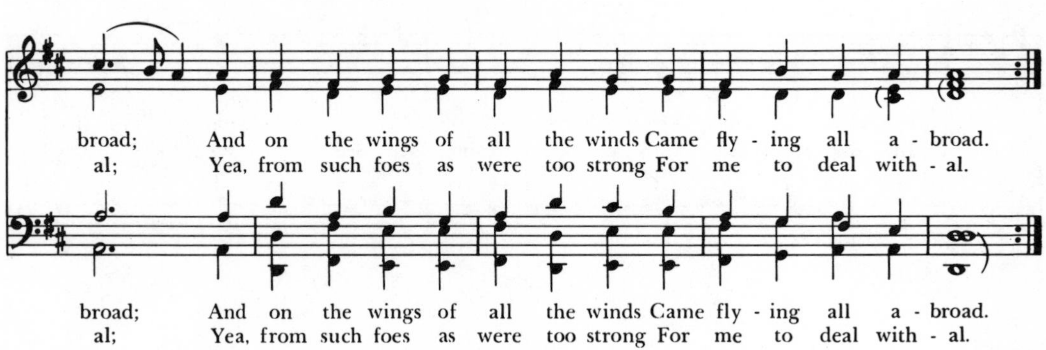
broad; And on the wings of all the winds Came fly - ing all a - broad.
al; Yea, from such foes as were too strong For me to deal with - al.
broad; And on the wings of all the winds Came fly - ing all a - broad.
al; Yea, from such foes as were too strong For me to deal with - al.

3. And as I was an innocent,
So did he me regard,
And to the cleanness of my hands
He gave me my reward.
For that I walked in his ways,
And in his paths have trod,
And have not wavered wickedly
Against my Lord and God.

MY SHEPHERD IS THE LIVING LORD — CAMBRIDGE C.M.

Ps. 23: 1-5 — Frost 42

Thomas Sternhold, 1561 — Edmund Hooper, arr. 1592

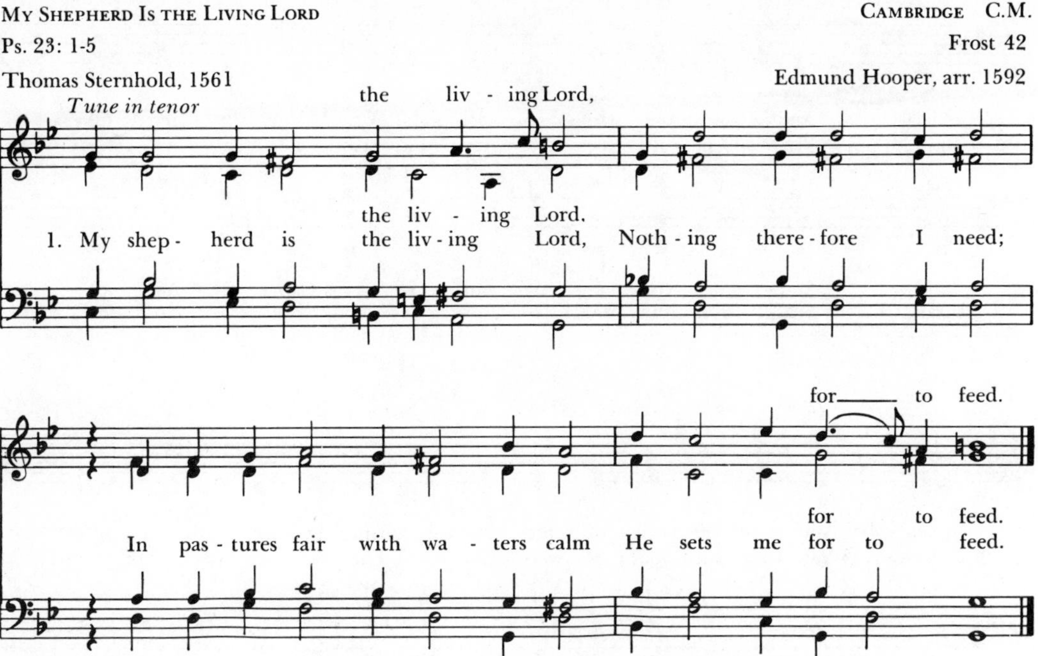
Tune in tenor
the liv - ing Lord,
the liv - ing Lord.
1. My shep - herd is the liv - ing Lord, Noth - ing there - fore I need;
for to feed.
for to feed.
In pas - tures fair with wa - ters calm He sets me for to feed.

2. He did convert and glad my soul,
And brought my mind in frame
To walk in paths of righteousness
For his most holy name.

3. Yea, though I walk in vale of death,
Yet will I fear none ill;
Thy rod, thy staff do comfort me,
And thou art with me still.

4. And in the presence of my foes
My table thou shalt spread;
Thou shalt (O Lord) fill full my cup
And eke anoint my head.

5. Through all my life thy favor is
So frankly showed to me
That in thy house for evermore
My dwelling place shall be.

THOU, LORD, HAST BEEN OUR SURE DEFENSE — FRENCH TUNE OR DUNDEE C.M.

Ps. 90: 1, 2, 4-6 — Frost 204

John Hopkins, 1562 — Thomas Ravenscroft, arr. 1621

Tune in tenor
1. Thou, Lord, hast been our sure de - fense, Our place of ease and rest,
As can - not be ex - pressed.
In all times past, As can - not be ex - pressed.
In all times past, yea, so long since As can - not be ex - pressed.

2. Or there was made mountain or hill,
The earth or world abroad,
From age to age, and always still,
Forever thou art God.

3. The lasting of a thousand years,
What is it in thy sight?
As yesterday it doth appear
Or as a watch one night.

4. So soon as thou dost scatter them
Then is their life and trade
All as asleep, and like the grass
Whose beauty soon doth fade.

5. Which in the morning shines full bright,
But fadeth by and by,
And is cut down ere it be night
All withered, dead, and dry.

THY MERCIES, LORD, TO HEAVEN REACH — PSALM 36 8.8.8.8.8.8.

Ps. 36: 5-10 — Frost 58

William Kethe, 1561 — Anon., arr. 1635

Tune in tenor
1. Thy mer - cies, Lord, to heav - en reach; Thy
2. O God! how great thy mer - cies be! The
the clouds do preach; as
do trust in thee; be
faith - ful - ness the clouds do preach; Thy right - eous - ness as
sons of men do trust in thee; With thee they shall be
moun - tains huge; no tongue can teach;
ful - ly fed, them drink full free
moun - tains huge; Thy judg - ments deep no tongue can teach;
ful - ly fed, And thou wilt give them drink full free
To man and beast thou art ref - uge.
Of pleas - ant riv - ers large - ly spread

3. The well of life is thine by right,
Thy brightness doth give us our light.
Thy favour, Lord, to such extend
As knowledge thee with heart upright;
Thy righteousness to such men lend.

O Hear My Prayer, Lord — Psalm 143 6.6.6.6.D.

Ps. 143: 1, 6, 8, 9 — Frost 168; Zahn 8187a

John Craig, 1564/65 — Anon., arr. 1635

Tune in tenor
1. O hear my pray - er Lord, And un - to my re - quest
2. With griev - ous plaint and moan Mine hands I stretch a - broad
thou think - est best,
my soul,_ O God,
To bow thine ear ac - cord, And as thou think - est best,
To thee mine help a - lone; For lo my soul, O God,
Ac - cord - ing to thy truth And for thy jus - tice sake,
Most ar - dent - ly de - sires, And long - eth aft - er thee,
an - swer_ to_ me make.
rain re - freshed to be.
O Lord, on me have ruth, And an - swer to me make.
As thirs - ty ground re - quires With rain re - freshed to be.

3. Now sith I trust in thee,
Thy clemency benign,
To hear grant unto me
When break of day doth spring.
Thy way to me descry
That I should walk and go
For I my soul on high
To thee have lifted though.

4. From all my foes me save,
And set me free, I pray:
For Lord with thee I have
Still hid my self alway.
To do thy will instruct
Me, Lord my God of might:
Let thy good sprite conduct
Me to the land of right.

O LORD, THAT ART MY GOD AND KING

PSALM 145 L.M.D.

Ps. 145: 1-3, 8-10, 15, 19

Frost 170

John Craig, 1564/65

Anon., arr. bet. 1562-1566

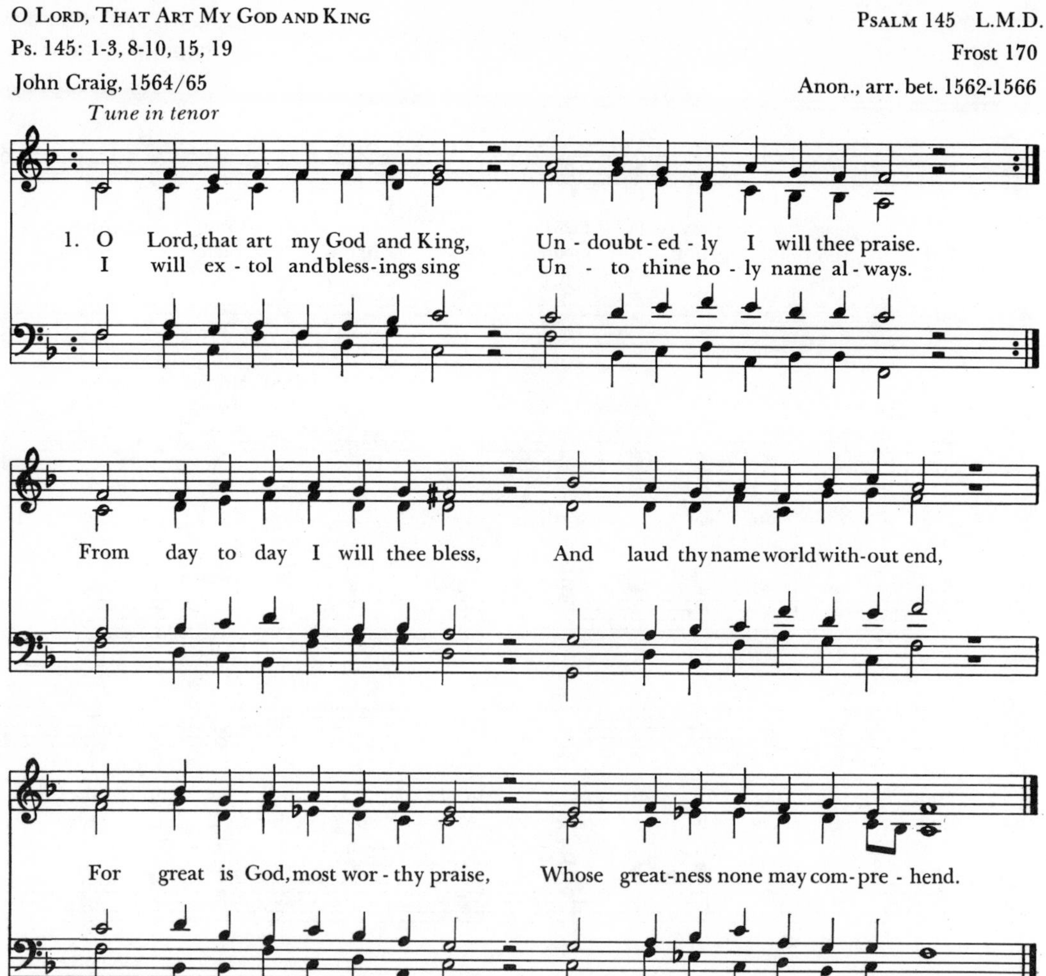
Tune in tenor
1. O Lord, that art my God and King, Un - doubt - ed - ly I will thee praise.
I will ex - tol and bless - ings sing Un - to thine ho - ly name al - ways.
From day to day I will thee bless, And laud thy name world with - out end,
For great is God, most wor - thy praise, Whose great - ness none may com - pre - hend.

2. The Lord our God is gracious
Yes, merciful is he also;
In mercy he is plenteous
But unto wrath and anger slow.
The Lord to all men is benign,
Whose mercies all his works exceed;
Thy works each one thy praises sing,
And eke thy saints thee bless indeed.

3. The eyes of all things, Lord, attend,
And on thee wait that here do live,
And thou in season due dost send
Sufficient food them to relieve.
The Lord will the desire fulfill
Of such as do him fear and dread,
And he also their cry hear will
And save them in the time of need.

Help, Lord, Because the Godly Man — Bon Accord C.M.

Ps. 12: 1, 2, 5, 6 — Frost 211

Francis Rous, 1650 — Anon., 1635

Tune in tenor
1. Help, Lord, be - cause the god - ly man Doth dai - ly fade a - way; And from a -
And

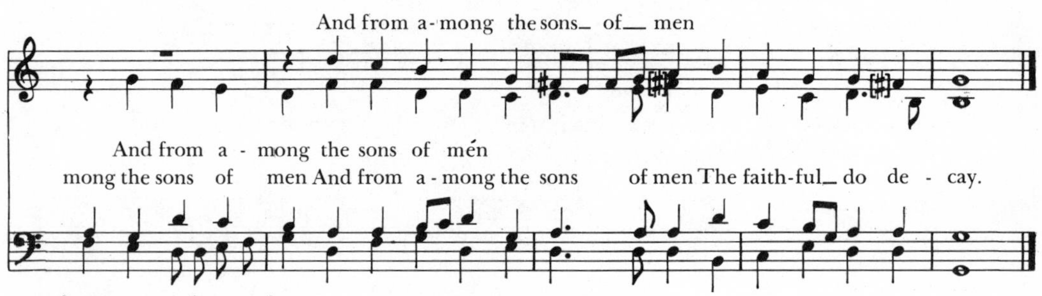
And from a - mong the sons of men
And from a - mong the sons of mén
mong the sons of men And from a - mong the sons of men The faith-ful do de - cay.
from a-mong the sons of men

2. Unto his neighbor every one
Doth utter vanity;
They with a double heart do speak,
And lips of flattery.

3. For poor oppressed, and for the sighs
Of needy, rise will I,
Saith God, and him in safety set
From such as him defy.

4. The words of God are words most pure
They be like silver tried
In earthen furnace seven times
That hath been purified.

I TO THE HILLS WILL LIFT MINE EYES

PSALM 18 C.M.D.

Ps. 121: 1-8

Frost 36

Francis Rous, 1650

Anon., arr. 1635

Tune in tenor

1. I to the hills will lift mine eyes, From whence doth come mine aid.
2. The Lord thee keeps; the Lord thy shade On thy right hand doth stay.

My safe - ty com - eth from the Lord, Who heaven and earth hath made.
The moon by night thee shall not smite, Nor yet the sun by day.

Thy foot he'll not let slide, nor will He slum - ber that thee keeps.
The Lord shall keep thy soul; he shall Pre - serve thee from all ill.

Be - hold, he that keeps Is - ra - el, He slum - bers not, nor sleeps.
Hence - forth thy go - ing out and in God keep for ev - er will.

The Lord's My Shepherd, I'll Not Want — Pisgah C.M.D.

Ps. 23: 1-6

Francis Rous, 1650 — J. C. Lowry (?), 1820

Tune in tenor
1. The Lord's my shep - herd, I'll not want, He makes me down to lie In pas - tures green; he lead - eth me The qui - et wa - ters by.
2. Yet though I walk in death's dark vale, Yet will I fear none ill; For thou art with me, and thy rod And staff me com - fort still.
My soul he doth re - store a - gain, And me to walk doth make In - to the paths of right - eous - ness, Even for his own name's sake.
My ta - ble thou hast fur - nish - ēd In pres - ence of my foes;

3. Goodness and mercy all my life
Shall surely follow me;
And in God's house forevermore
My dwelling-place shall be.
Goodness and mercy all my life
Shall surely follow me;
And in God's house forevermore
My dwelling-place shall be.

EXCEPT THE LORD, THAT HE FOR US HAD BEEN — FRENCH TUNE: PSALM 124 10.10.10.10.10.

Ps. 124: 1, 3, 4, 7-9 — Frost 139

Henry Ainsworth, 1612 — Giles Farnaby, arr. 1592

Tune in tenor
that he for us had been,
1. Ex - cept the Lord, that he for us had been, They had us
that he for us had been,
When kin - dled was their
swal - lowed up a - live even then When kin - dled was
swal - lowèd up When kin - dled was
Then had the wa - ters
an - ger a - gainst us. Then had the wa - ters
their an - ger a - gainst us. Then had the wa - ters
their an - ger a - gainst us. Then had the wa - ters
then pass - èd had the stream.
o - ver us flow - ed; O - ver our soul then pass - èd had the stream.

2. Our soul is as a bird escapèd free
From out of the entangling fowler's snare.
The snare is broke and we escapèd are.
Our succor in Jehovah's name shall be
That of the heavens and earth is the maker.

How Long, Jehovah? | The Complaint of a Sinner 6.6.6.6.6.6.6.6.
Ps. 13: 1-6 | Frost 185
Henry Ainsworth, 1612 | John Farmer, arr. 1592

Tune in tenor

1. How long, Je-ho-vah, wilt Thou me for-get for aye? How long-while wilt thou hide
2. Je-ho-vah, O my God, Be-hold me an-swer make; Il-lu-mi-nate mine eyes,

Thy face from me a-way? How long shall in my soul I coun-sels set, dai-ly
Lest sleep of death me take. Lest that my foe do say, 'Gainst him pre-vailed have I;

I coun-sels set, dai-ly
'Gainst him pre-vailed have I;

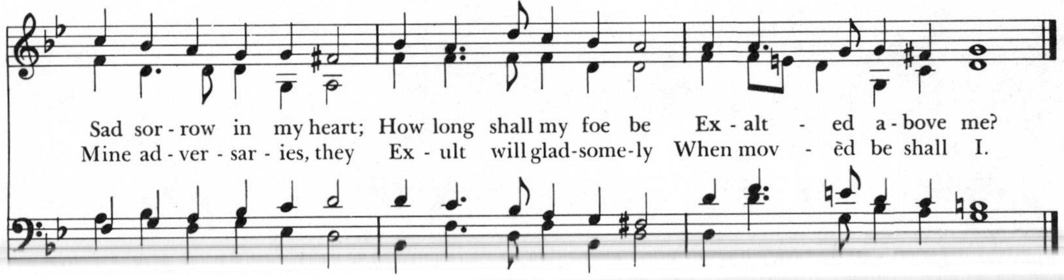
Sad sor-row in my heart; How long shall my foe be Ex-alt-ed a-bove me?
Mine ad-ver-sar-ies, they Ex-ult will glad-some-ly When mov-ēd be shall I.

3. But I do repose
Assurēd trustfulness
In thy mercy; my heart
Shall show forth gladsomeness
In my salvation;
I sing will cheerfully
Unto th' Eternal One,
For bounteously hath he
Rewarded unto me.

FIRE IN MY MEDITATION BURNED — BENEDICTUS C.M.D.

Ps. 39: 3-9, last part of 12, 13 — Frost 3

Henry Ainsworth, 1612 — Richard Allison, arr. 1599

1. Fire in my med - i - ta - tion burned; I with my tongue did speak.
Je - ho - vah, make me know my end, What my days' meas - ure eke,
What my days' meas - ure eke,
What my days' meas - ure eke,
Know let me how short lived I am. Lo, thou hast given my days
Know let me how short lived I am. Lo, thou hast given my days
Know let me how short lived I am. Lo, thou hast given my
'Fore thee as noth - ing weighs.
As hand-breadths, and my world - ly time 'Fore thee as noth - ing weighs.
'Fore thee as noth - ing weighs.

2. Sure wholly vain is every man
Though settled fast, Selah.
Sure in an image walk doth man;
Surely vain stir make they.
One heaps up goods, and knoweth not
Who shall their gatherer be;
And now, what do I look for, Lord?
My longing is for thee.

3. Free me from all my trespasses;
Fools' mockage make not me.
I dumb am, open not my mouth,
For done it is of thee.
A pilgrim as my fathers all,
Stay from me, and let me
Refresh myself; ere that I go,
And I no more shall be.

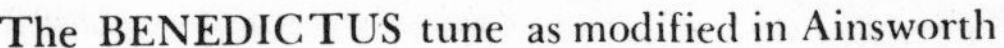

The BENEDICTUS tune as modified in Ainsworth

I Minded God

Ps. 77: 3-9, 12-14

Henry Ainsworth, 1612

French Tune: Psalms 28, 109

Frost 323

Melody from Henry Ainsworth, 1612

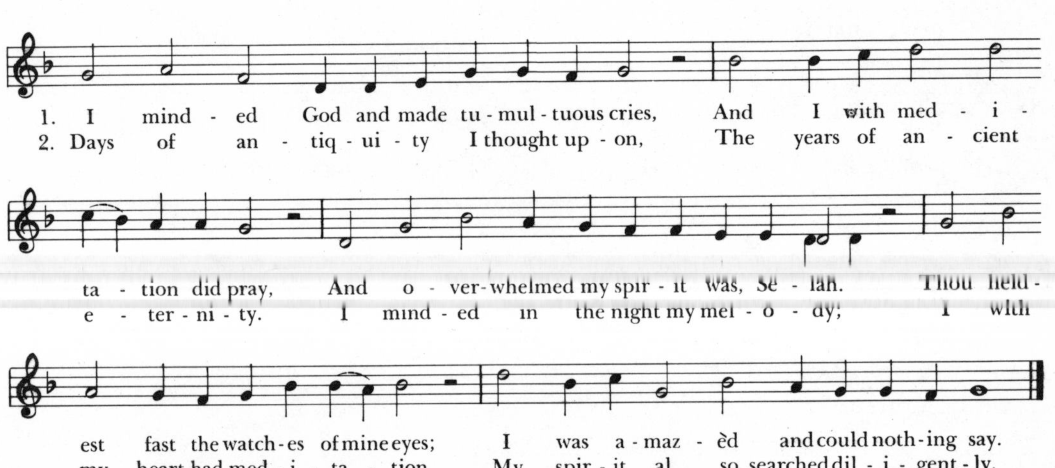
1. I mind - ed God and made tu - mul - tuous cries, And I with med - i - ta - tion did pray, And o - ver-whelmed my spir - it was, Se - lah. Thou held - est fast the watch - es of mine eyes; I was a - maz - èd and could noth - ing say.
2. Days of an - tiq - ui - ty I thought up - on, The years of an - cient e - ter - ni - ty. I mind - ed in the night my mel - o - dy; I with my heart had med - i - ta - tion, My spir - it al so searched dil - i - gent - ly.

3. Ah, will the Lord forever cast away
And add no more to accept favorably?
Is his mercy ceasèd perpetually?
Is his word ended to each age for aye?
Hath God forgot for to deal graciously?

4. Of all thy work I will eke meditate
And of thy practices discourse will I.
O God, thy way is in the sanctuary.
Who is as God so great a potentate?
Thou art the God that worketh wondrously.

I SPREAD OUT UNTO THEE MY HANDS
Ps. 143: 6, beginning of 7, 8
Henry Ainsworth, 1612

DE PROFUNDIS C.M.D.
Frost 149; Zahn 5352
Orlando di Lasso, arr. 1564

Tune in tenor
I spread out un - to thee my hands; My soul doth thirst for thee Even as the wea - ry, wea - ry land, Se - lah. Make speed, Lord, an - swer me; At morn let me thy mer - cy
I spread out un - to thee my hands; My soul, My soul doth thirst for thee Even as the wea - ry land, Se - lah. Make speed, Lord, an - swer me; At morn let me thy mer - cy
I spread out un - to thee my hands; My soul doth thirst for thee Even as the wea - ry land, Se - lah. Make speed, Lord, an - swer me; At morn let me thy mer - cy
I spread out un - to thee my hands; My soul doth thirst for thee Even as the wea - ry land, Make speed, Lord, an - swer me; At morn, At morn let me thy mer

hear, For in thee do I trust; O cause me to
hear, For in thee do I trust; O cause me
hear, For in thee do I trust; O cause me
cy hear, For in thee do I trust; O cause me

have know - ledge of The way that walk I must.
to have know-ledge of The way that walk I must.
to have know-ledge of The way that walk I must.
to have know-ledge of The way that walk I must.

IN THE DISTRESS UPON ME

Ps. 18: 7, 8, 11-13, 27-29

Henry Ainsworth, 1612

FRENCH TUNE: PSALM 23 10.10.10.D.

Frost 320; Zahn 3190

Claude Goudimel, arr. 1565

Tune in tenor
1. In the dis - tress up - on me, call did I Up - on Je - ho - vah,
2. And he did ride on cher - ub and did fly, And on wings of the
and to my God cry; And he my voice out of his pal - ace hears.
wind he flew swift - ly. He set the dark - ness for his se - cret bound,
Thy cry be - fore him came in - to his ears, And th' earth did shake and
For his pa - vil - ion a - bout him round: Dark - ness of wa - ters,
and stir rèd be for wroth was he.
clouds of the skies, be - fore his eyes.
quake, and stir - rèd be, Grounds of the mounts and shook, for wroth was he.
thick clouds of the skies, From the re-splend - ent bright-ness before his eyes.

3. Thou with the pure dost show thy purity,
And with the froward thou dost show thee wry.
For poor afflicted people save dost thou;
The lofty eyes thou also bringest low.
For thou dost make my candle to be light;
Jehovah, my God, makes my darkness bright.

FRENCH TUNE: PSALM 23 as modified in Ainsworth

יהוה

King David, the original Psalmist

WITH ALL MY HEART, JEHOVAH, I'LL CONFESS | FRENCH TUNE: PSALM 8 10.10.10.10.

Ps. 9: 1, 2, 10, 11, 13, 20 | Frost 321; Zahn 923

Henry Ainsworth, 1612 | Claude Goudimel, arr. 1565

Tune in tenor

I'll__ con - fess;
trust__ in thee;

1. With all my heart, Je - ho - vah, I'll__ con - fess; All thy works mar -
2. And they that know thy name will trust__ in thee; For thou, Lord, leav -

I will__ ex - press.
them that__ seek thee.

vel - ous I will__ ex - press. Re - joice and glad - ness show in thee
est not them that__ seek thee. Sing to Je - ho - vah that in Si -

to thy name, O most High.
show forth a - mong peo - ples.

will I; I will sing psalms to thy name, O most High.
on dwells; His prac - tic - es show forth a - mong peo - ples.

3. Jehovah, show me grace, my trouble see,
From my foes, from death's gates, uplifting me.
Jehovah, strike in them a dread dismay;
Let heathens know weak men they be. Selah.

FRENCH TUNE: PSALM 8 as modified in Ainsworth

To God Our Strength Shout Joyfully

Ps. 81: 1-6, first part of 7

Henry Ainsworth, 1612

French Tune: Psalm 100 L.M.

Frost 322 Zahn 367

Claude Le Jeune, arr. 1601

shout joy - ful - ly;
1. To God our strength shout joy - ful - ly;
To Ja - cob's God

a psalm and tim -
shout tri - um - phing. Take up a psalm and tim -
a psalm and tim -
a psalm and tim -

brel bring, The pleas - ant harp
brel bring, The pleas - ant harp with psal - te - ry.
brel bring,
brel bring,

2. Blow up the trumpet at new moon
In set time, at day of our feast,
For it to Israel is an heast,
To Jacob's God, due to be done.

3. He this in Joseph did bestow,
A witness, when as forth he fared
From land of Egypt, where I heard
A language that I did not know.

4. His back from burden I discharged;
His hands did from the basket pass;
Thou calledst in distressèd case
And I, releasing, thee enlarged.

Unto Jehovah Sing Will I
Exod. 15: 1-5, 10-13
Henry Ainsworth, 1617

French Tune: Psalm 24 8.8.8.D.
Frost 326; Zahn 2665
Claude Le Jeune, arr. 1601

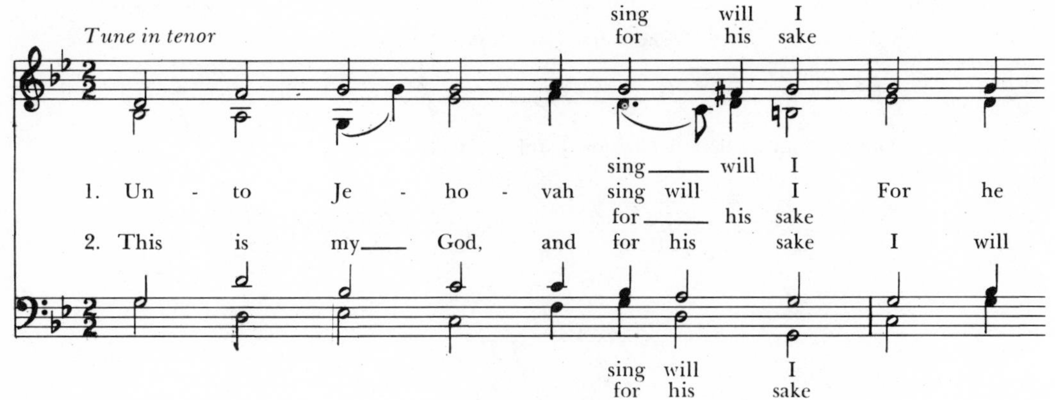
sing will I
for his sake
Tune in tenor
sing will I
1. Un - to Je - ho - vah sing will I For he
for his sake
2. This is my God, and for his sake I will
sing will I
for his sake

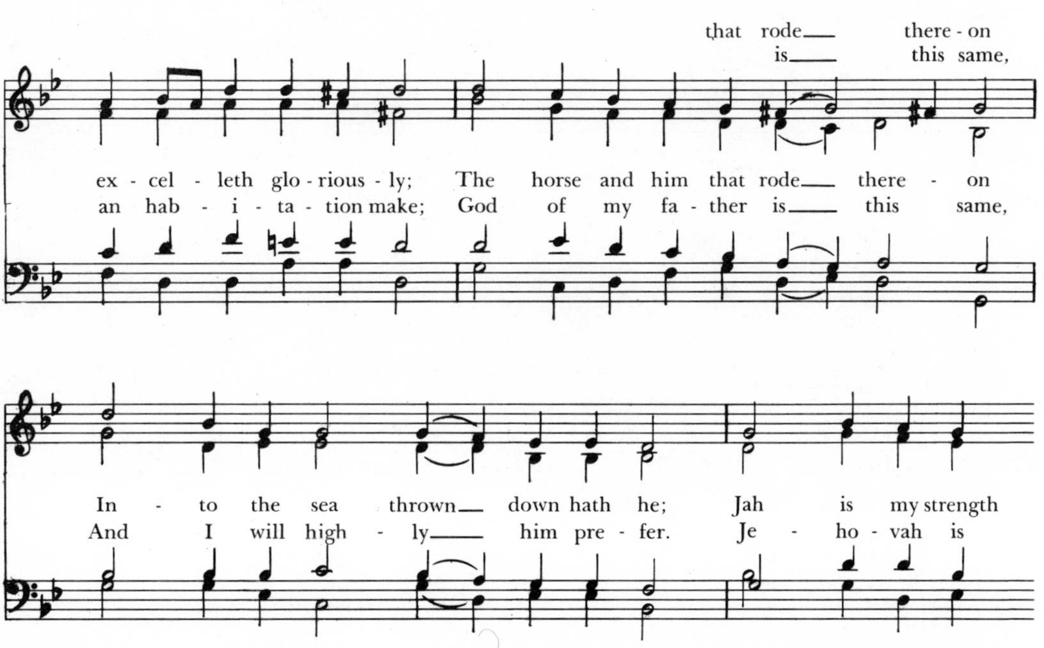
that rode there - on
is this same,
ex - cel - leth glo - rious - ly; The horse and him that rode there - on
an hab - i - ta - tion make; God of my fa - ther is this same,
In - to the sea thrown down hath he; Jah is my strength
And I will high - ly him pre - fer. Je - ho - vah is

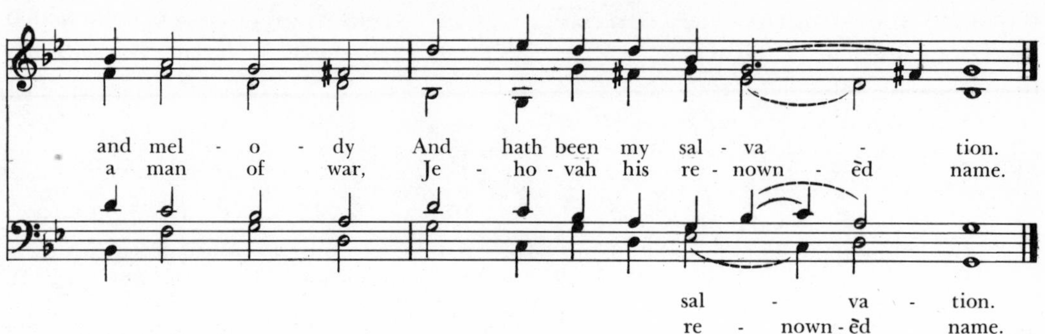
and mel - o - dy And hath been my sal - va - tion.
a man of war, Je - ho - vah his re - nown - ěd name.
sal - va - tion.
re - nown - ěd name.

3. Then with thy wind thou didest blow;
The sea them covered; they sank low
As lead in water vehement.
Among the gods who is like thee?
Lord, who like thee in sanctity,
Glorious, in praises reverent?

4. Chariots of Pharoah and his host
He down into the sea hath cast.
His captains, eke each chosen one,
He did them in the Red Sea drown.
The deeps them covered; they sank down
Into the bottoms as a stone.

FRENCH TUNE: PSALM 24 as modified in Ainsworth

GIVE EAR, O HEAVENS, TO THAT WHICH I DECLARE — FRENCH TUNE: PSALM 120 — 10.10.10.10.D.

Deut. 32: 1-3, 6, 7 — Frost 328

Henry Ainsworth, 1619 — Claude Goudimel, arr. 1565

Tune in tenor

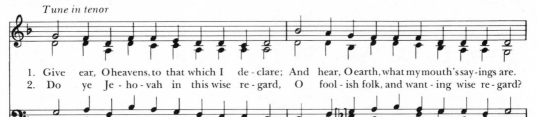

1. Give ear, O heavens, to that which I de - clare; And hear, O earth, what my mouth's say - ings are.
2. Do ye Je - ho - vah in this wise re - gard, O fool - ish folk, and want - ing wise re - gard?

Drop down as doth the rain shall my doc - trine; Dis - till as dew so shall my speech di - vine,
Thy Fa - ther, that hath brought thee, is not he? Hath he not made thee and es - tab - lished thee?

As on the ten - der herb the small rain pours, And as up - on the grass the great - er showers,
Re - mem - ber thou the days that were of old; Mind ye the years of a - ges man - i - fold;

For I Je - ho - vah's name pro - claim a - broad; O give ye great - ness un - to him our God.
Ask thou thy Fa - ther, and thee show will he; Thine eld - ers ask, and they will tell it thee.

The tune for PSALM 120 as given in Ainsworth

The Heavens Do Declare — London S.M.

Ps. 19: 1-6 — Frost 45

Anon., 1640 — Edmund Hooper, arr. 1592

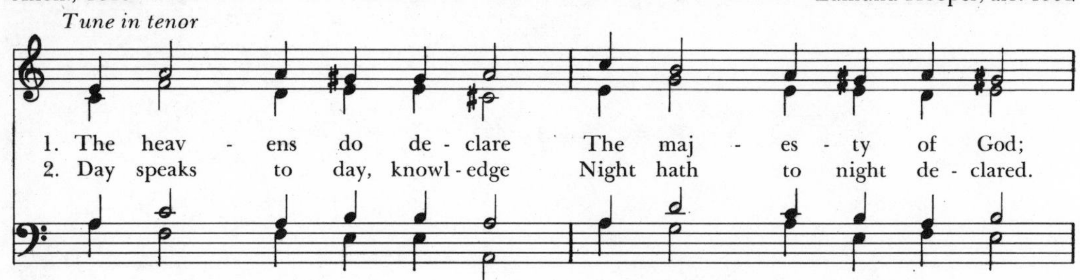
Tune in tenor
1. The heav - ens do de - clare The maj - es - ty of God;
2. Day speaks to day, knowl - edge Night hath to night de - clared.

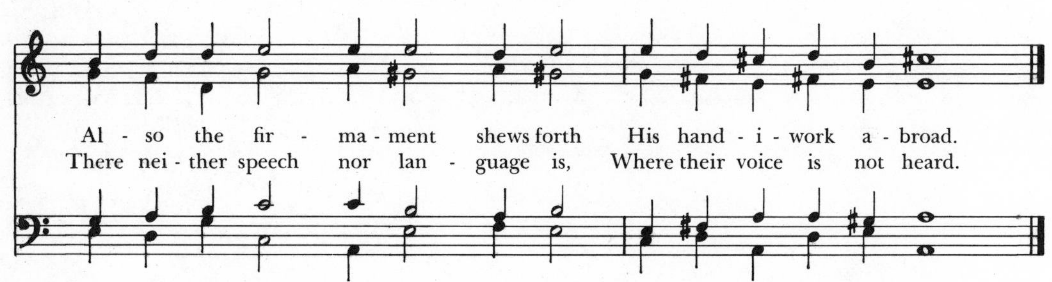
Al - so the fir - ma - ment shews forth His hand - i - work a - broad.
There nei - ther speech nor lan - guage is, Where their voice is not heard.

3. Through all the earth their line
Is gone forth; and unto
The utmost end of all the world
Their speeches reach also.

4. A tabernacle he
In them pitched for the sun
Who bridegroom-like from's chamber goes
Glad giant's race to run.

5. From heaven's utmost end,
His course and compassing
To ends of it, and from the heat
Thereof is hid nothing.

BLESSED IS EVERYONE — OLD 148TH H.M.

Ps. 128: 1-6 — Frost 174

Anon., 1640 — George Kirbye, arr. 1621

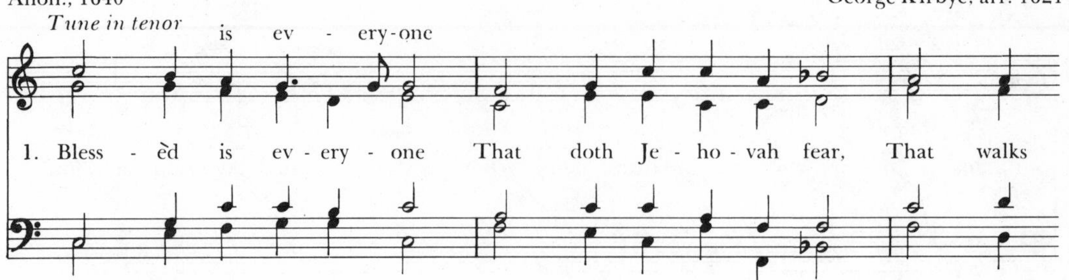

Tune in tenor
is ev - ery-one
1. Bless - ed is ev - ery - one That doth Je - ho - vah fear, That walks

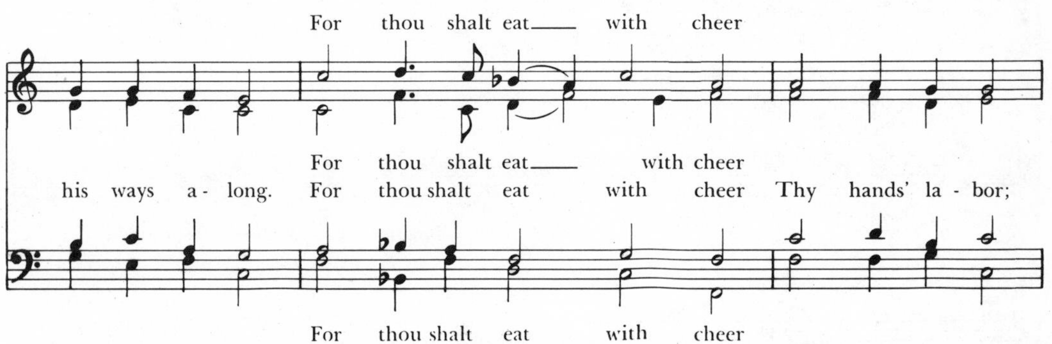

For thou shalt eat with cheer
For thou shalt eat with cheer
his ways a - long. For thou shalt eat with cheer Thy hands' la - bor;
For thou shalt eat with cheer

Shall be there-fore.
Shall be there - fore.
Blest shalt thou be, It well with thee Shall be there - fore.
Shall be there - fore.

2. Thy wife, like fruitful vine,
Shall be by thine house side;
The children that be thine
Like olive plants abide
About thy board.
Behold thus blest
That man doth rest,
That fears the Lord.

3. Jehovah shall thee bless
From Sion, and shall see
Jerusalem's goodness
All thy life's days that be,
And shalt view well
Thy children then
With their children
Peace on Israel.

NOT TO US, NOT UNTO US, LORD
Ps. 115: 1-18
Anon., 1640

OLD 113TH 8.8.8.8.8.8.D.
Frost 125; Zahn 8308
Thomas Ravenscroft, arr. 1621

Tune in tenor

1. Not to us, not un - to us, Lord, But glo - ry to thy name af - ford

For thy mer - cy, for thy truth's sake. The hea - then, where - fore should they say,

for thy— truth's sake.

The hea - then, where - fore should they say,

Where is their God now gone a - way? But heavens our God his seat doth make,

his seat— doth make,

He hath done what - so - e'er he would. Their i - dols are sil - ver and gold:

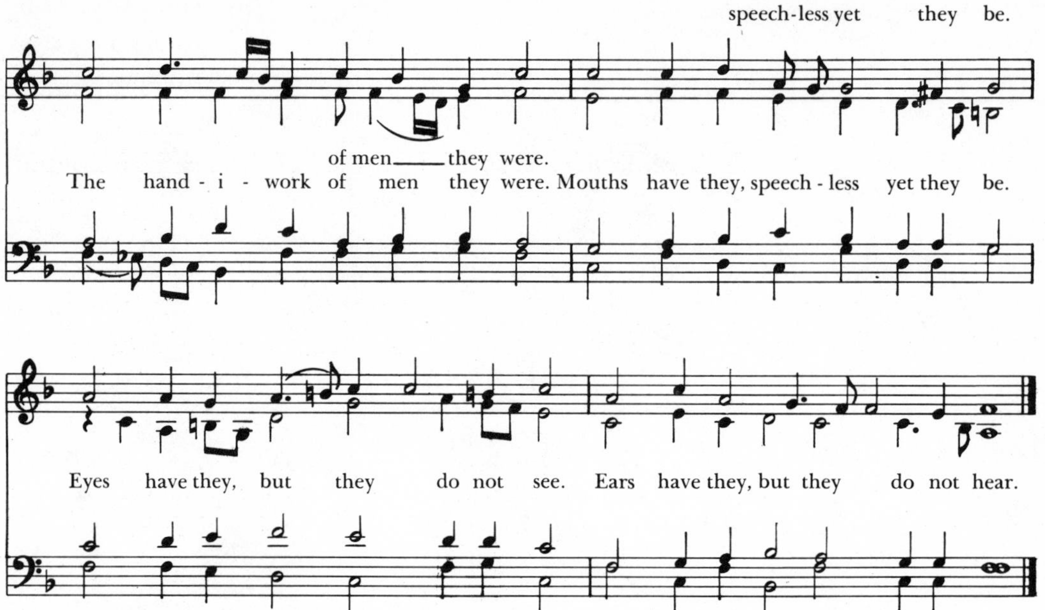
speech-less yet they be.
of men___they were.
The hand - i - work of men they were. Mouths have they, speech - less yet they be.
Eyes have they, but they do not see. Ears have they, but they do not hear.

2. Noses have they, but do not smell;
Hands have they, but cannot handle;
Feet have they, but they do not go;
And through their throat they never spake.
Like them are they that do them make,
And all that trust in them are so.
Trust in the Lord, O Israel.
He is their help, their shield as well.
O Aaron's house, the Lord trust ye;
He is their help and he their shield
Who fear the Lord, trust to him yield;
Their help also their shield is he.

3. The Lord hath mindful been of us,
He'll bless us, he'll bless Israel's house;
Blessing he'll Aaron's house afford;
He'll bless God's fearers great and small.
You and your sons he'll much increase
Increase still, you blest of the Lord
Which heaven and earth made. Heavens, heavens be
The Lord's, but th' earth men's sons gives he.
The Lord's praise dead do not afford
Nor any that to silence bow,
But we will bless the Lord both now
And ever henceforth. Praise the Lord!

Make Ye a Joyful Sounding Noise — Old 100th L.M.

Ps. 100: 1-5 — Frost 114; Zahn 368

Anon., 1640 — John Dowland, arr. 1621

Tune in tenor

a joy - ful sound - ing noise

a joy - ful sound - ing noise

1. Make ye a joy - ful sound - ing noise Un - to

Je - ho - vah,___ all the earth; Je - ho - vah___ with

Je - ho - vah,___ all the earth;

Je - ho - vah, all the earth; Serve ye Je - ho - vah with

glad - ness; Be - fore his pres - ence come with mirth.

Be - fore___ his pres - ence come with mirth.

glad - ness; Be - fore his pres - ence come with mirth.

Be - fore___his___pres - ence come___ with mirth.

2. Know that Jehovah he is God;
Who hath us formèd it is he
And not ourselves; his own people
And sheep of his pasture are we.

3. Enter into his gates with praise,
Into his courts with thankfulness;
Make ye confession unto him,
And his name reverently bless.

4. Because Jehovah he is good,
For evermore is his mercy;
And unto generations all
Continue doth his verity.

O Lord, Thou Hast Been to the Land — Pater Noster or Old 112th 8.8.8.D.

Ps. 85: 1, 2, 7-13 — Frost 180; Zahn 2561

Anon., 1640 — George Kirbye, arr. 1621

Tune in tenor

O Lord, thou hast

cap - tiv - i - ty

1. O Lord, thou hast been to the land Gra - cious; Ja - cob's cap - tiv - i - ty

(*Slurs, st. 3 and 4*)

al - so the in - iq - ui - ty___

Thou hast re - turn - èd with thy hand. Thou al - so the in - iq - ui - ty___

hast par - don-èd; Thou all their_ sin hast cov - er-èd.

Thou all their sin hast cov - er - èd.

Of thy peo - ple hast par - don - èd; Thou all their sin hast cov - er - èd.

Thou all their sin hast cov - er - èd.

2. Lord, on us show thy mercy; eke
Thy saving health on us bestow.
I'll hark what God the Lord will speak,
For he'll speak peace his folk unto
And to his saints, but let not them
To foolishness return again.

3. Surely his saving health is nigh
Unto all them that do him fear,
That in our land may dwell glory.
Mercy and truth met together;
Prosperity and righteousness
Embracing did each other kiss.

4. Truth springs out of the earth, also
From heaven looketh righteousness.
Yea, God shall that that's good bestow;
Our land eke shall give her increase.
Justice shall go before his face,
And in the way her steps shall place.

Come Harken unto Me — York C.M.

Ps. 66, third part: 16-20 — Frost 205

Anon., 1640 — Version from *Bay Psalm Book*, 1698

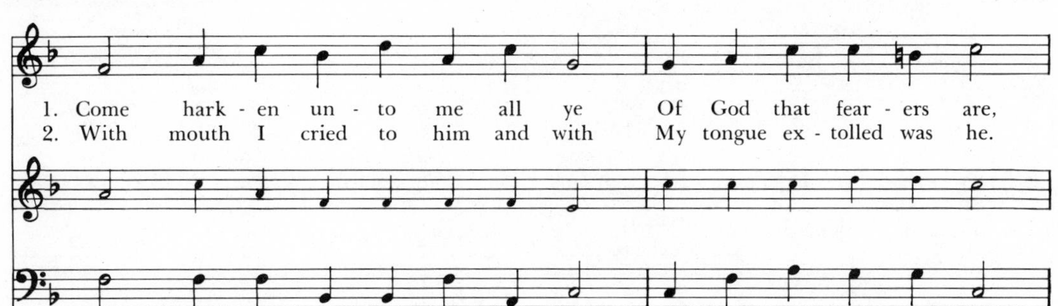
1. Come hark - en un - to me all ye Of God that fear - ers are,
2. With mouth I cried to him and with My tongue ex - tolled was he.

And what he hath done for my soul To you I will de - clare.
If in my heart I sin re - gard, The Lord will not hear me.

3. But God that is most mighty hath
Me heard assuredly;
Unto the voice of my prayer he
Listened attentively.

4. Blest be the mighty God; because
Neither my prayer hath he,
Nor yet his own benignity
Turnèd away from me.

I Love the Lord

Ps. 116: 1-7

Anon., 1640

Windsor C.M.

Frost 129

Version from *Bay Psalm Book,* 1698

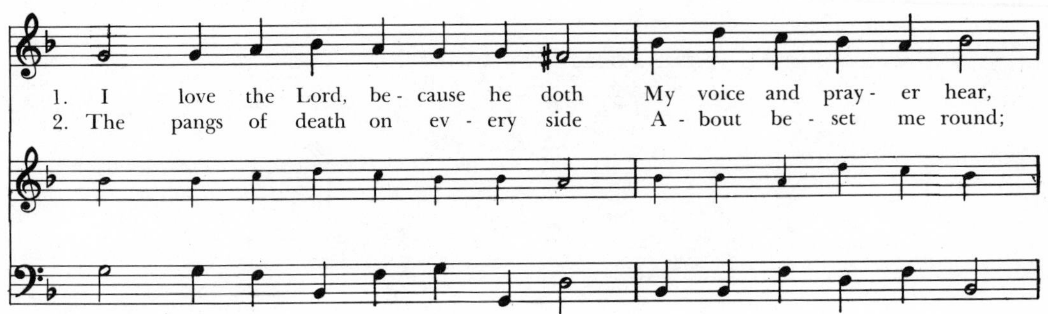
1. I love the Lord, be - cause he doth My voice and pray - er hear,
2. The pangs of death on ev - ery side A - bout be - set me round;

And in my days will call be - cause He bowed to me his ear.
The pains of hell gat hold on me, Dis - tress and grief I found.

3. Upon Jehovah's name therefore
 I callèd and did say,
 Deliver thou my soul, O Lord,
 I do thee humbly pray.

4. Gracious the Lord and just, our God
 Is merciful also.
 The Lord the simple keeps, and he
 Saved me when I was low.

5. O thou, my soul, do thou return
 Unto thy quiet rest,
 Because the Lord to thee, himself
 Hath bounteously expressed.

O LORD, ALMIGHTY GOD NUNC DIMITTIS C.M.D.

(The Song of Moses and the Lamb)

Rev. 15: 3 Frost 37

Anon., 1647 John Playford, arr. 1671

Tune in tenor

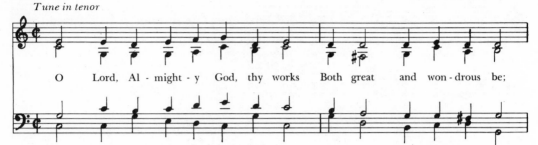

O Lord, Al - might - y God, thy works Both great and won - drous be;

Just King of Saints, and true thy ways, Who shall not rev - erence thee,

O Lord, and glo - ri - fy thy name, For ho - ly thou a - lone;

For na - tions all shall wor - ship thee, For judg - ments thine are known.

LET HIM WITH KISSES OF HIS MOUTH — OLD 119TH C.M.D.

Song of Sol. 1: 1-3 — Frost 132

Anon., 1651 — Richard Allison, arr. 1599

Let him with kiss - es of his mouth Be pleas - èd me to kiss.
pleas - èd

Be - cause much bet - ter than — the wine Thy lov - ing kind - ness is.
Be - cause much bet - ter than — the wine kind - ness is.
Be - cause much bet - ter than — the wine

Thy name as poured forth oint - ment is, Be - cause of the sweet smell
the — sweet smell
the sweet smell

Of thy good oint - ments, there - fore do The vir - gins love thee well.
Of thy good oint - ments, there - fore do The vir - gins love thee well.
there - fore do The vir - gins love — thee well.

THE SUN AND MOON SO HIGH AND BRIGHT
Hab. 3: 11-13, 17, 18
Anon., 1651

SONG 34 L.M.
Frost 362a
Orlando Gibbons, 1623

1. The sun and moon so high and bright Stood still with - in their dwell - ing sphere, Then mov - èd at Thine ar - rows light, At shin - ing of thy glit - tering spear.
2. Thou didst move through the land in wrath; The hea - then thou didst thresh in rage. Thou forth al - so didst make thy path For safe - ty of thy her - it - age.

their dwell - ing sphere,
didst thresh in rage.

thy glit - tering spear.
thy her - - it - age.

3. Though fig tree blossom not at all,
Nor any fruit in vines appear,
The labour of the olive fail,
And though the fields no meat should bear;

4. Though flocks should be cut off from fold,
In stall no herd should have abode,
Yet in the Lord rejoice I would
I'll joy in my salvation's God.

I to the Lord from My Distress — Psalm 69 C.M.D.

Jonah 2: 2-6, last part of 9 — Frost 86

Anon., 1651 — John Playford, arr. 1671

Tune in tenor

1. I to the Lord from my dis - tress Did cry and he gave ear;
2. Then did I say, I ut - ter - ly Cast from thy sight re - main.

Out of hell's bel - ly did I cry, And he my voice did hear.
Thy ho - ly tem - ple yet will I To - wards it look a - gain.

In - to the deep and midst of seas, Be - cause Thou didst me cast,
The wa - ters, ev - en to the soul, Did me en - com - pass round;

The floods me com - passed; all thy waves And bil - lows o'er me passed.
The depths me round en - closed; the weeds A - bout my head were bound.

3. To mountains' bottoms I went down,
Earth's bars me aye beset;
Yet, Lord my God, thou brought'st my life
Up from corruption's pit.
The thing I vowed and promised have,
To pay I will accord;
For all salvation wholly comes
From the almighty Lord.

Lord, Who's the Happy Man — St. David C.M.

Ps. 15: 1, 2, 5, 7

Nahum Tate and Nicholas Brady, 1696 — Daniel Purcell, arr. c.1718

1. Lord, who's the hap - py man that may
2. 'Tis he, whose ev - ery thought and deed
Unison
To thy blest courts re - pair,
By rules of vir - tue moves;
Not, stran - ger - like, to vis - it them,
Whose gen - erous tongue dis - dains to speak
But to in - hab - it there?
The thing his heart dis - proves.

3. Who to his plighted vows and trust
Has ever firmly stood;
And though he promise to his loss
He makes his promise good.

4. The man, who by his steady course
Has happiness insured,
When earth's foundation shakes, shall stand,
By providence secured.

Devotional Verse: English

MUCH seventeenth-century verse was devotional in a personal way. These texts were not isolated from the great psalters but were related to them by the familiar progression of metric patterns, and no doubt there were occasions when the words of a poet took shape as he hummed YORK or WINDSOR or even a familiar ballad tune. Indeed there is evidence in the eighteenth if not in the seventeenth century that such inspirations might be sung. Cotton Mather wrote in his diary: "When I sit alone in my languishments, unable to write or to read, I often compose little hymns, agreeable unto my present Circumstances and sing them unto the Lord." Jonathan Edwards wrote that he "used to spend abundance of my time, in walking along in the woods, and solitary places, for meditation, soliloquy and prayer, and converse with God. And it was always my manner, at such times, to sing forth my contemplations."

We have therefore concluded our selection from the seventeenth century with a number of devotional poems and contemporary tunes to which they may be sung. Among them are poems by Anne Bradstreet, our earliest poet, whose *The Tenth Muse* appeared in London in 1650. Two long narrative poems which include lyric episodes are John Wilson's "Song of Deliverance" and Michael Wigglesworth's "Day of Doom." A musician finds the "Meditations" of Edward Taylor particularly interesting because of his use of musical imagery. He would be God's trumpet to sound the praises of his creator. He thinks of himself as a virginal string turned to harmonize with divine things. A passage from Meditation 11 could be understood as a description of contrapuntal music:

> Nay had each song as many songs most sweet
> Or one intwisting in't as many,
> As all these tongues have songs most meet
> Unparalleled by any?

Benjamin Keach's "How Glorious Are the Morning Stars" has been included to represent the hymns which his Baptist congregation were singing as early as 1673.

In Pilgrim Life Our Rest

Ps. 90: selected lines

Edwin Sandys, 1615

Psalm 90 6.6.8.6.6.6.8.6.6.6.8.6.

Frost 417

Robert Tailour, 1615

Tune in upper part
1. In pil - grim life_ our rest, In thralled es - ___ tate our stay;
2. When thou - sand years_ we lived, Those thou - sand ___ in thy sight
From age to age thou, Lord, has been And_ saved us from_ de - cay.
Not more ap - peared than one day past, Than_ watch in short - est night.
Thy - self, ere_ birth to_ hills, To_ earth_ ere_ form didst_ give;
Since when, our_ dream - like_ life, As_ weak - est_ herb, soon_ dies;
Ere world hadst_ framed; from aye to_ aye All glo - rious God_ dost live.
Which morn makes_ flower, hot noon bids_ fade, Sad even mows down_ and dries.

But man, thy crea - ture fallen, Thy jus - tice doth pur - sue
What have our toils a - chieved? Through an - ger thine, our day
To dust, and saith, "ye Ad - am's sons,
Black night de - vours; our fruit - less years
Re - turn whence first ye grew."
As thought fly vain a - way.

3. And comfort, cheer us, lord,
As chastised long by thee;
Much ill our woeful eyes have seen;
Like joy so cause us see.
This joy with life shall last.
Then let thy work grow clear
Toward servants thine; on children there
Thy glory make appear.
And let God's pleased face,
Us with his beauties bless
And from our works; O Thou, our works
To happiest end address.

And Truly It Is a Most Glorious Thing — Song 24 10.10.10.D.

Selected couplets — Frost 360

William Bradford, 1623 — Orlando Gibbons, 1623

1. And tru - ly it is a most glo - rious thing Thus to hear men pray,
2. But God will still for his peo - ple pro - vide Such as be a - ble
and God's prais - es sing. O how great com - fort is it now to see
them to help and guide, If they cleave to him and do not for - sake
The church - es to en - joy full lib - er - ty, And to have the gos - pel
His laws and truth and their own ways do take. If thou hast viewed the
preach - ēd here with power, And such wolves re - pelled as [all] would else de - vour.
camp of Is - ra - el, How God in the wil - der - ness with them did dwell.

3. His great and marvelous works they here saw,
And he them taught in his most holy law.
A small emblem hereof thou mayest see
How God hath dealt with them in some degree,
For much of himself they now there have seen,
And marvellous to them his works have been.

CONFESS WE ALL, BEFORE THE LORD — LORD THOMAS AND FAIR ELLINOR C.M.

Lines 197-208, 217-228

John Wilson, 1626 — Anon., 1650

Unison
1. Con - fess we all, be - fore the Lord. His grace and mer - cy then,
2. In pres - ence of his ho - ly ones. Praise him with joy and fear,

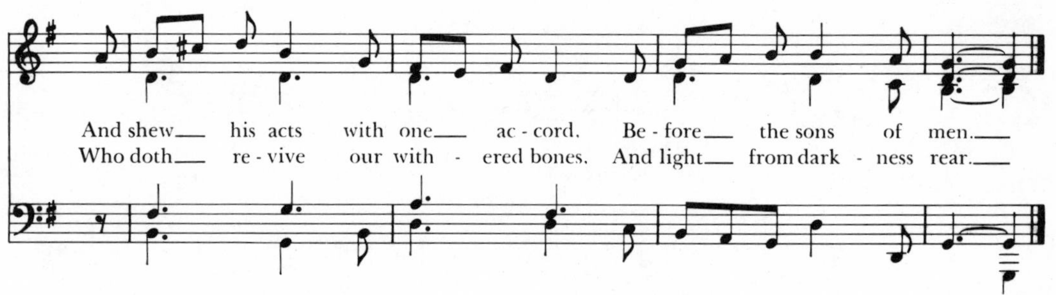
And shew his acts with one ac - cord. Be - fore the sons of men.
Who doth re - vive our with - ered bones. And light from dark - ness rear.

3. Man, woman, child, both old and young,
Rich, poor, the low and high,
Laud and extol with heart and tongue,
The highest Majesty.

4. Let all that lives confess his grace,
That saves their life and fame.
Let none by wicked life deface,
The glory of his name.

5. And thou, my Soul, remember well
The kindness of the Lord,
Cease not with thankful lips to tell
The trueness of his word.

6. Who gave thee pardon of thy sin,
And kept thee from the smart
(For all the danger thou wert in)
Of the infectious dart.

Whoso Would See This Song of Heavenly Choice

Lines 43-66

John Wilson, 1626

How Can the Tree 10.10.10.D.

Anon., 1576

1. Who - so would see this song of heaven-ly choice,— Penned by that ho - ly Shep-herd,
2. Nor shall he need to think his time mis-spent:— For what is there to Is - ra -
Is - rael's guide,— And sweet - ly ut - tered with a swan - like voice,— When
el com - mit - ted, Hath a more large and gen - er - al ex - tent,— And
here his Soul no long - er might a - bide;— Let him un - to that ho - ly
to our pres - ent times may well be fit - ted. Now is that wall of sep - a -

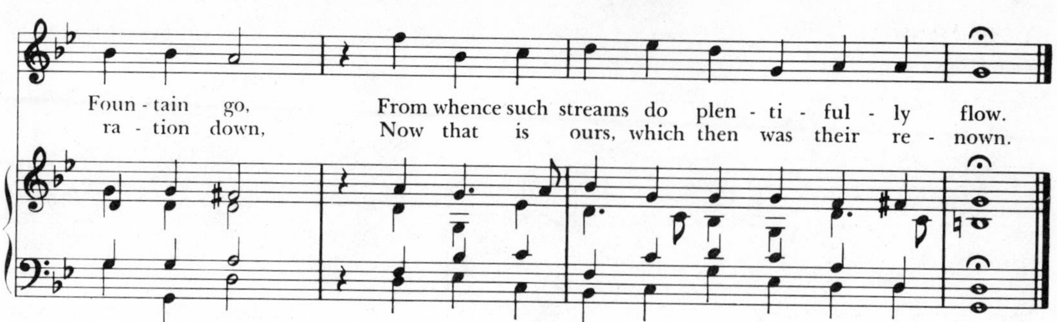
Foun - tain go, From whence such streams do plen - ti - ful - ly flow.
ra - tion down, Now that is ours, which then was their re - nown.

3. And oh, that in their holy Name alone
And other graces, we did them succeed!
Oh, that their falsehood and rebellion
Had not in us like bitter root and breed!
Oh, that by their example we might see
Such thoughts, such deeds, such sorrows, how to flee.

4. For us another Canaan is provided
Far better: better milk, and better honey,
We look our spirits should ere long be guided,
To heaven itself, where, without price or money,
We shall enjoy what here we may but taste,
A joyful, blessed life for aye to last.

JUDAH IN EXILE WANDERS

Lam. 1:3,4

George Sandys, 1634

William Lawes, 1648

Ju - dah in ex - ile wan - ders,
Ju - dah in ex -
Ju - dah in ex - ile wan - ders, Ah, sub-

Ah, sub-dued by vast af - flic - tions
ile wan - ders, Ah, sub-dued by vast af-
dued by vast af - flic - tions Ah, sub-

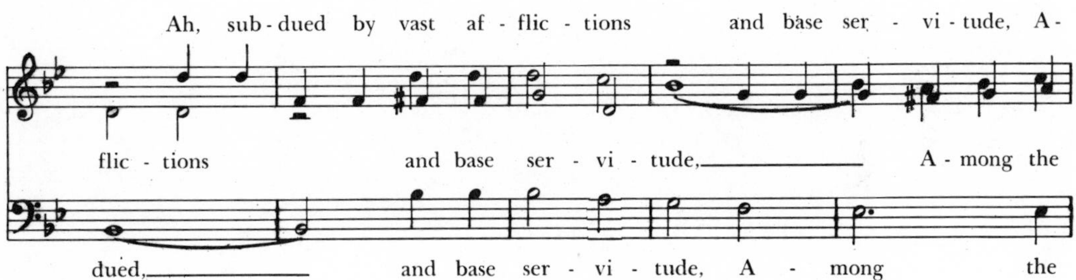
Ah, sub-dued by vast af - flic - tions and base ser - vi - tude, A-
flic - tions and base ser - vi - tude, A - mong the
dued, and base ser - vi - tude, A - mong the

mong the hea - then finds no rest. Ah!
hea - then finds no rest. Ah! see
hea - then finds no rest. Ah! see

see ___ how Si - on mourns! how Si - on
___ how Si - on mourns! how Si - on
how Si - on mourns!___ how Si - on

mourns! Her gates and ways lie un - fre- quent - ed
mourns! Her gates and ways lie un - fre- quent - ed on her sol - emn
mourns!___ Her gates and ways lie un - fre - quent - ed on her

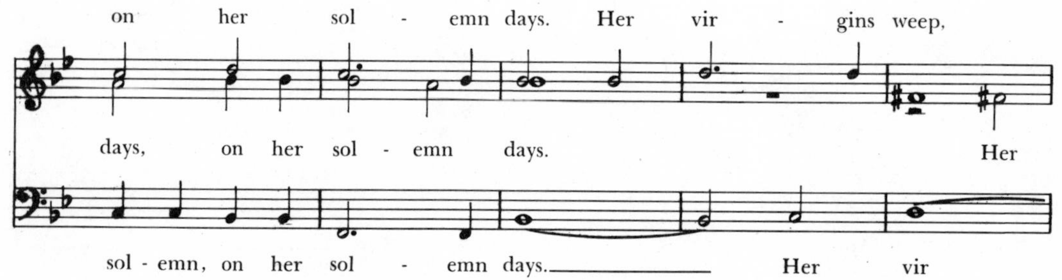
on her sol - emn days. Her vir - gins weep,
days, on her sol - emn days. Her
sol - emn, on her sol - emn days.___ Her vir

Her vir - gins weep,
vir - gins weep, Her vir - gins
- gins weep,___ Her vir - gins

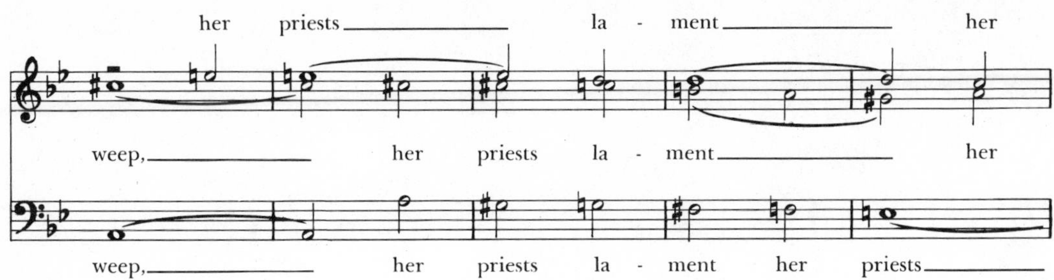
her priests la - ment her
weep, her priests la - ment her
weep, her priests la - ment her priests

fall, her priests la - ment her fall, And
fall, her priests la - ment her fall,
la - ment, her priests la - ment her fall,

all her sweets con - vert to gall, and all
And all her sweets con - vert
And all her sweets con - vert to

her sweets con - vert to gall.
to gall, con - vert to gall.
gall, all her sweets con - vert to gall.

O Blest Estate, Blest from Above

Ps. 133:1-3

George Sandys, 1636

Walter Porter, 1657

O blest es - tate! Blest from a - bove!

When breth - ren join in mu - tual love; 'Tis
When breth - ren join in mu - tual love;

like the pre - cious o - dors shed On con - se - cra - ted

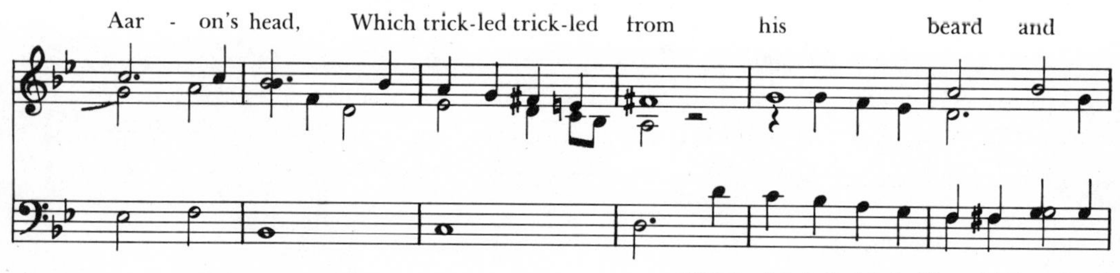
Aar - on's head, Which trick-led trick-led from his beard and
Which trick-led trick-led from his beard and

breast, Down to the bor - ders, down
breast, Down to the bor - ders, down to the

to the bor - ders of his vest. 'Tis like the pearl - y
bor - ders of his vest.

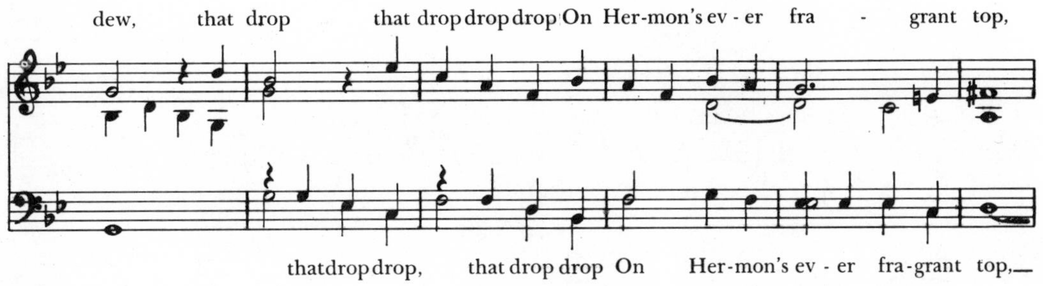
dew, that drop that drop drop drop On Her-mon's ev - er fra - grant top,
thatdrop drop, that drop drop On Her-mon's ev - er fra-grant top,

On which the smil - ing, smil - ing heavens dis - till On hap - py

Chorus
Si - on's sa - cred hill. For God hath there his fa - vors
For God hath there his fa - vors

placed And joy, and joy which shall for - ev - er last, and joy which
placed And joy, and joy which shall for - ev - er

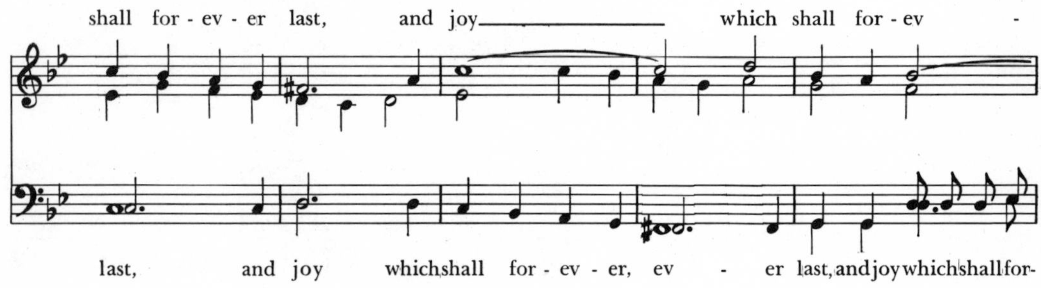
shall for - ev - er last, and joy which shall for - ev -
last, and joy which shall for - ev - er, ev - er last, and joy which shall for-

er last, which shall for - ev - er, ev - er last.
ev - er last, and joy which shall for - ev - er, ev - er last.

THE BOUNTY OF JEHOVAH PRAISE — PSALM 10 8.8.4.4.8.6.6.

Ps. 136: 1-3 — Frost 374

George Sandys, 1636 — Henry Lawes, 1638

Unison
1. The boun - ty of Je - ho - vah praise; This God of Gods all scep - tres sways.
2. Him praise who framed the arch - èd sky, Those orbs that move so or - der - ly;
Thanks to the Lord Of Lords af - ford, And his a - maz - ing won - ders blaze.
Firm earth a - bove. The floods that move, Dis - played and raised the hills on high.
For from the King of Kings E - ter - nal mer - cy springs.
For from the King of Kings E - ter - nal mer - cy springs.

3. The sun and moon informed with light,
To guide the day, and rule the night;
The fix-èd stars
And wanderers,
Created by divine foresight.
For from the King of Kings
Eternal mercy springs.

Hail, Holy Land — Song 1 10.10.10.10.D.

St. 1-3 — Frost 350

Thomas Tillam, writ. 1638 — Orlando Gibbons, 1623

Unison
1. Hail, ho - ly land, where - in our ho - ly Lord Hath plant - ed his most
true and ho - ly word. Hail, hap - py peo - ple, who have dis - pos - sessed
Your-selves of friends and means to find some rest For your poor wea - ried souls,
To you that bless - èd prom-
op-pressed of late For Je - sus' sake, with en - vy, spite, and hate.
ise tru - ly's given Of sure re - ward, which you'll re - ceive in heaven.

2. Methinks I hear the Lamb of God thus speak:
Come, my dear little flock, who for my sake
Have left your country, dearest friends, and goods,
And hazardèd your lives o'th raging floods.
Possess this country, free from all annoy.
Here I'll be with you; here you shall enjoy
My sabbaths, sacraments, my ministry
And ordinances in their purity.

3. But yet beware of Satan's wily baits!
He lurks among you! Cunningly he waits
To catch you from me; live not then secure,
But fight against sin, and let your lives be pure.
Prepare to hear your sentence thus expressed:
Come ye, my servants of my Father blessed.
Hail, holy land, wherein our holy Lord
Hath planted his most true and holy word.

Lord, Many Times Thou Pleasèd Art — Te Deum C.M.D.

St. 1, 3, 5, 11 — Frost 2

George Wither, 1641 — Thomas Ravenscroft, arr. 1621

Tune in tenor
Lord, man - y times thou pleas - èd art Thy serv - ants to com-mand

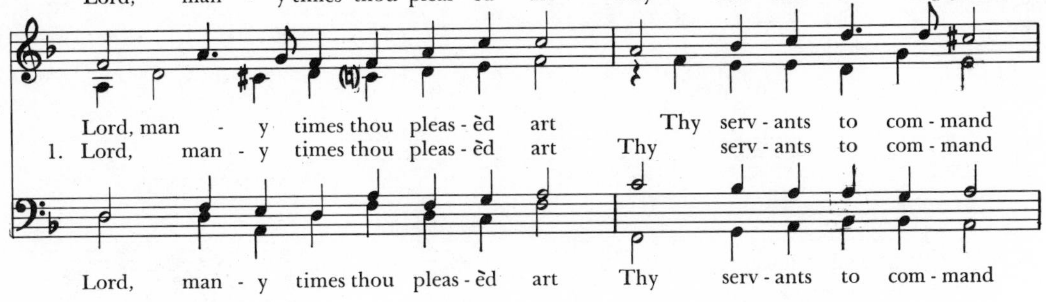
Lord, man - y times thou pleas - èd art Thy serv - ants to com - mand
1. Lord, man - y times thou pleas - èd art Thy serv - ants to com - mand
Lord, man - y times thou pleas - èd art Thy serv - ants to com - mand

From their own coun - tries to de - part In - to an - oth - er land;
From their own coun - tries to de - part In - to an - oth - er land;
From their own coun - tries to de - part In - to an - oth - er land;
From their own coun - tries to de - part In - to an - oth - er land;

That thou may'st there a dwell - ing place Up - on their seed be - stow;
That thou may'st there a dwell - ing place Up - on their seed be - stow;
That thou may'st there a dwell - ing place Up - on their seed be - stow;
That thou may'st there a dwell - ing place Up - on their seed be - stow;

Or else to bring thy sav - ing grace, To those to whom they go.
Or else to bring thy sav - ing grace, To those to whom they go.
Or else to bring thy sav - ing grace, To those to whom they go.
Or else to bring thy sav - ing grace, To those to whom they go.

2. From old acquaintance, from my kin,
And from my native home,
My life anew, here to begin,
I by thy leave am come;
And now, the place of my abode,
Appeareth unto me
Another world; yet here, Oh God!
My God thou still shalt be.

3. Oh, let the Son of Righteousness,
Thy truth, and grace divine,
Within the uncouth wilderness
With brightness also shine.

(3) That we and they whom here we find,
May live together so
That one in faith, one in mind,
We by thy grace may grow.

4. So when the course of time is run,
And God shall gather all
That lived betwixt the rising sun
And places of his fall;
Our friends that farthest from us are,
Shall meet with joy again;
And they and we, who now are here,
Together still remain.

IF BIRDS THAT NEITHER SOW NOR REAP — DUMFERMELING C.M.

St. 1-3 — Frost 206

Roger Williams, 1643 — Thomas Ravenscroft, arr. 1621

Tune in tenor
1. If birds that nei - ther sow nor reap Nor store up an - y food,
2. If man pro - vide eke for his birds, In yard, in coops, in cage,

Con - stant - ly find to them and theirs A mak - er kind and good;
And each bird spends in songs and tunes, His lit - tle time and age;

3. What care will man, what care will God
For wife and children take?
Millions of birds and worlds will God,
Sooner than His forsake.

WHEN SUN DOTH RISE

St. 1-3

Roger Williams, 1643

LANDAFFE C.M.

Frost 241

Thomas Ravenscroft, arr. 1621

Tune in tenor

Yet there's no need of light;
Yet there's no need of— light;
1. When sun doth rise the stars do set, Yet there's no need of light;

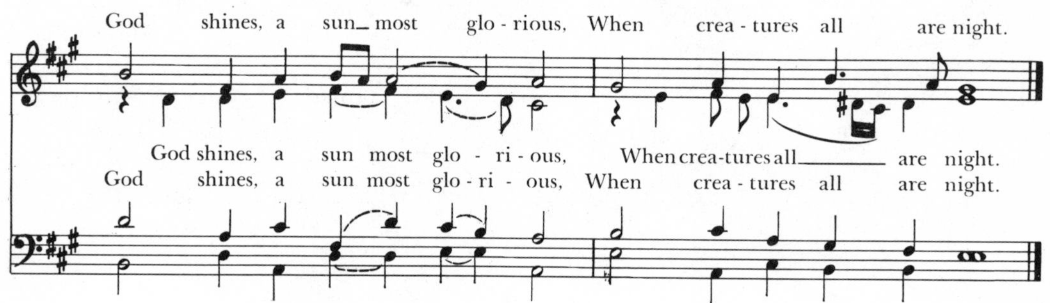

God shines, a sun— most glo - rious, When crea - tures all are night.
God shines, a sun most glo - ri - ous, When crea-tures all——— are night.
God shines, a sun most glo - ri - ous, When crea - tures all are night.

2. The very Indian boys can give
To many stars their name,
And know their course and therein do
Excel the English tame.

3. English and Indians, none enquire
Whose hand these candles hold,
Who gives these stars their names
More bright ten thousand fold.

As Spring the Winter Doth Succeed — Psalm 9 L.M.

St. 1-4 — Frost 373

Anne Bradstreet, writ. 1657 — Henry Lawes, 1638

1. As spring the win - ter doth suc - ceed, And leaves the na - ked trees do dress,

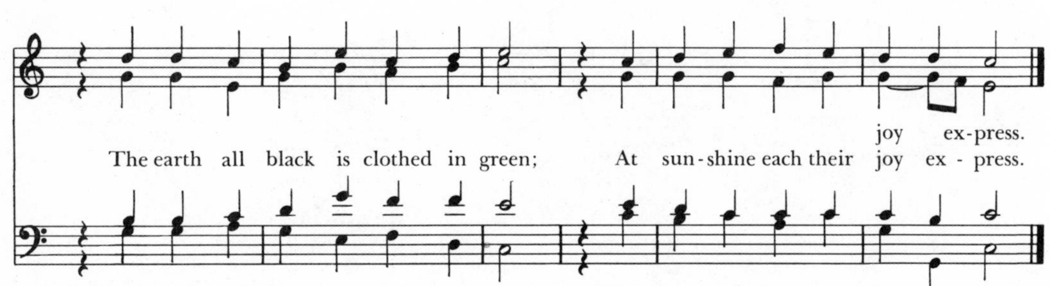
joy ex-press.
The earth all black is clothed in green; At sun-shine each their joy ex - press.

2. My winter's past, my storms are gone,
And former clouds seem now all fled;
But, if they must eclipse again,
I'll run where I was succourèd.

3. I have a shelter from the storm,
A shadow from the fainting heat;
I have access unto his throne,
Who is a God so wondrous great.

4. My Sun's returned with healing wings;
My soul and body doth rejoice;
My heart exults, and praises sings
To Him that heard my wailing voice.

O Thou Most High Who Rulest All — Song 9 C.M.

St. 1,4,6,9 — Frost 344

Anne Bradstreet, writ. 1661/62 — Anon., 1621

1. O Thou most high who rul - est all, And hear'st the prayers of thine;
2. Up - hold my heart in thee, O God, Thou art my strength and stay;

O heark - en, Lord, un - to my suit, And my pe - ti - tion sign.
Thou see'st how weak and frail I am; Hide not thy face a - way.

3. Unthankfulness for mercies past,
Impute thou not to me;
O Lord, thou knowest my weak desire
Was to sing praise to thee.

4. Remember, Lord, thy folk whom thou
To wilderness hast brought;
Let not thine own inheritance
Be sold away for nought.

If Thou Wilt Hear — Martyrs C.M.

Selected lines — Frost 209

John Grave, 1662 — Simeon Stubbs, arr. 1621

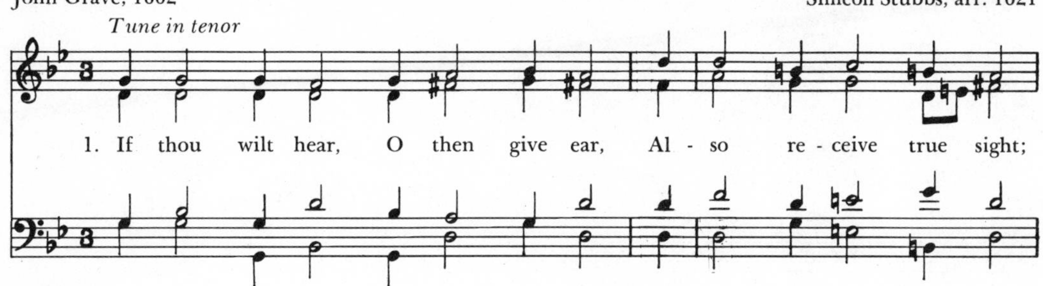
Tune in tenor
1. If thou wilt hear, O then give ear, Al - so re - ceive true sight;

be so dear to thee As Christ's most glo - rious light.
be so dear___ to___ thee As Christ's most glo - rious light.
Let noth - ing be so dear to thee As Christ's most glo - rious light.

2. Turn thine eye in and there begin
   To see its brightness shine;
   There hear the voice which may rejoice
   Thy soul in mirth divine.

3. Pure doctrine there is always near
   If thou in truth abide.
   To walk therein and cease from sin,
   And not from Christ to slide.

4. O who can guess or ought express
   How great peace such do find
   Whose hearts alway on Christ do stay
   And do him ever mind.

WELCOME, SWEET REST — PSALM 124 10.10.10.10.

St. 1-3 — Frost 140

Michael Wigglesworth, 1662 — Edward Millar, 1635

Tune in tenor
1. Wel - come, sweet rest, by me so long de - sired, Who have with sins and griefs so long_been_tired; And wel-come death, my fa - ther's mes - sen - ger, Of my fe - lic - i - ty the_ has - ten - er.
2. Wel - come good an - gels, who, for me dis - tressed, Are come to guard me to e - ter - nal_ rest. Wel - come O Christ, who hast my soul re - deemed, Whose fa - vor I_ have more than_ life_ es - teemed.
Last ending

3. Oh, do not now thy sinful soul forsake,
But to thyself thy servant gathering take.
Into thy hands I recommend my spirit,
Trusting through thee eternal life to inherit.

WHILST IN THIS WORLD I STAY — IN CRETE 10.10.10.D.

Meditations 17-20

Philip Pain, 1668 — Anon., after 1571

Unison

1. Whilst in this world I stay, some hopes have I That_ I shall reign in_
2. We are but babes of yes - ter - day, And_ we are sons and

___ heaven e - ter - nal - ly; But when my time is___ past, and_ I am gone,
daugh - ters of mor - tal - i - ty. From dust we came, to___ dust we_ must a - gain,

There's no hope left for me to build up - on. Lord, grant me full as-sur-ance
And to the grave with speed we fly a - main. Lord, let the thoughts of death pos-

(Tie, st. 3 and 4)

whilst that I Am here,___ so will - ing I shall be to___ die.
sess my heart, That so___ thee and my soul may nev - er___ part.

3. How brutish, oh, senseless are(all)those,
Who to the world do so themselves dispose,
As if there were no God to serve, no death
That's coming to deprive them of their breath?
Lord, help me so to live, that I may be
Never forgetful of my death or thee.

4. How loth, how backward are we all to leave
This transitory world? Let death bereave
Us of those mundane things, yet if we still
Resolve to live and die to Christ, what ill
Can happen to us? Lord, before I die
Let me a better kingdom far espy.

FOR JUST MEN LIGHT IS SOWN — PSALM 71 S.M.D.

St. 2, 5, 7, 9, 10 — Frost 88

Michael Wigglesworth, 1670 — Anon., arr. 1635

Tune in tenor
1. For just men light is sown (Re - ward laid up in store)
2. Thou art a pil - grim here; This world is not thy home;
Who sow in tears shall reap in joy, And af - ter mourn no more.
Then be con - tent with pil - grim's fare Till thou to heav - en come.
They'll one day wear a crown, Who now the cross sus - tain;
What if thou toss - èd art With bois - ter-ous winds and seas.
In Christ our Lord no suf - fer - ing Nor la - bor shall be vain.
Be - hold the hav - en where thou shalt En - joy long rest and ease.

3. Soldier, be strong, who fight'st
Under a captain stout;
Dishonour not thy conquering head
By basely giving out.
Endure a while, bear up,
And hope for better things;
War ends in peace, and morning light
Mounts upon midnight's wings.

4. O heaven, most holy place
Which art our country dear!
What cause have I to long for thee,
And beg with many a tear.

(4) Earth is to me a prison;
This body an useless weight;
And all things else vile, vain, and nought
To one in such ill plight.

5. O Christ, make haste, from bands
Of sin and death me free,
And to those heavenly mansions
Be pleased to carry me;
Where glorifièd saints
Forever are possessed
Of God in Christ their chiefest good,
And from all troubles rest.

Hail to the Queen — Salve Regina L.M.

St. 1-3

Anon. — Anon., arr. 18th cent.

Unison
1. Hail to the Queen who reigns a - bove, Moth - er of clem - en - cy and love. Hail Thou our hope, life, sweet - ness; we, Eve's ban - ished chil - dren, cry to Thee.
2. We from this wretch - ed vale of tears Send sighs and groans un - to thy ears; Oh! then, sweet Ad - vo - cate, be - stow A pit - ying look on us be - low.

3. After this exile let us see
Our blessed Jesus, born of Thee;
O merciful, O pious Maid,
O gracious Mary, lend thine aid.

How Glorious Are the Morning Stars — St. David's C.M.

St. 1-3, 6 — Frost 234

Benjamin Keach, 1691 — John Playford, arr. 1701

1. How glo - rious are the morn - ing stars! How doth their glo - ry shine!
2. They sang to - geth - er at the first Je - ho - vah's glo - rious praise,

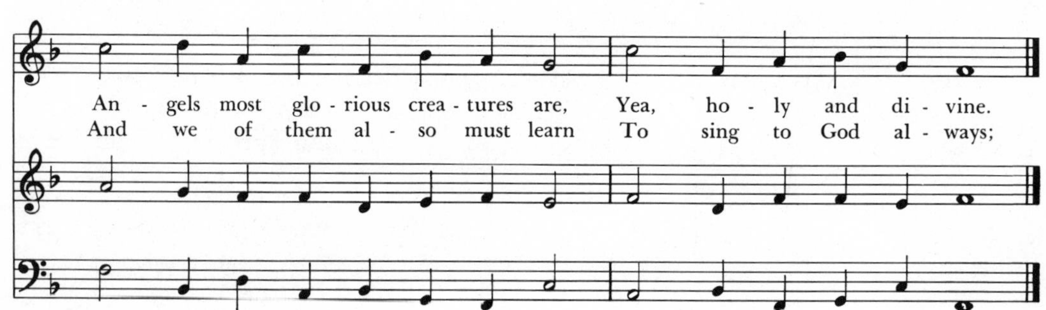
An - gels most glo - rious crea - tures are, Yea, ho - ly and di - vine.
And we of them al - so must learn To sing to God al - ways;

3. Nay, with united voices sing
In comfort, with much joy,
Since Christ has overcome our foes,
Who would our souls destroy.

4. It is his due, and it belongs
To him as his just right;
His praise to celebrate in songs
Is lovely in his sight.

LIKE TO THE GRASS THAT'S GREEN TODAY — ESSEX'S LAST GOOD-NIGHT L.M.

St. 1-3

Peter Bulkeley the Younger — Anon, 17th cent.

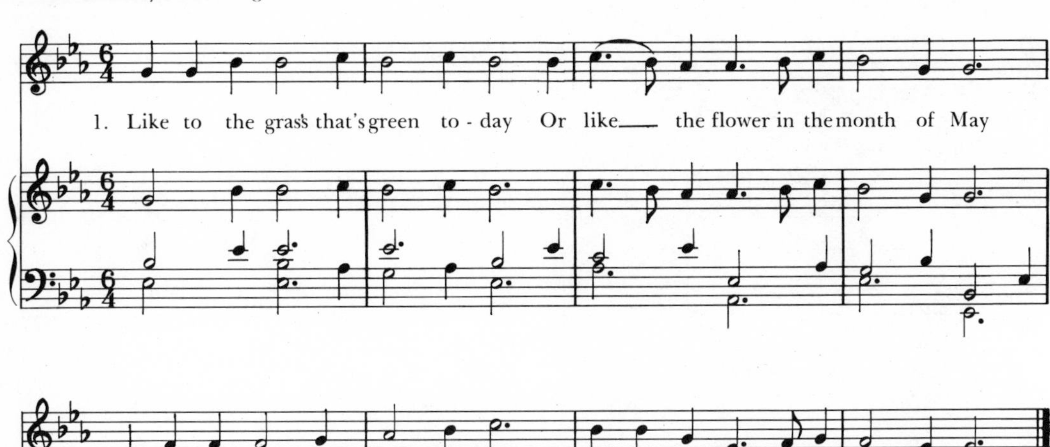
1. Like to the grass that's green to-day Or like the flower in the month of May

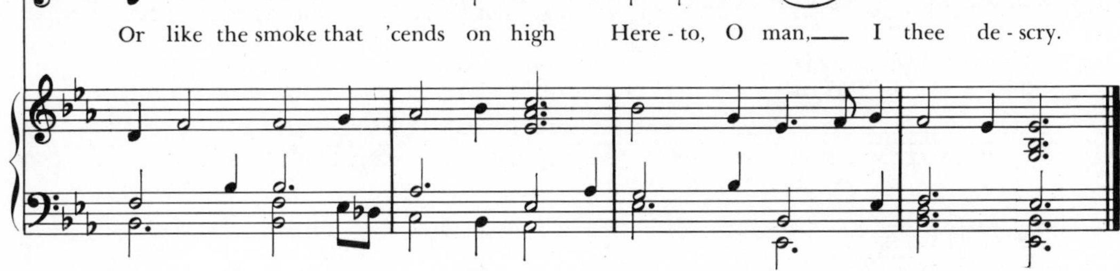
Or like the smoke that 'cends on high Here-to, O man, I thee de-scry.

2. The flower that's fresh to-day, to-mor-row dies; The grass cut down, and so it lies.

The loft-y smoke by blast of wind Is so dis-persed you can't it find.

3. They with-er, fade, con-sume a-way, No time nor art can make them stay,

Thou canst not clip the wings of time; But it may clip thee in thy prime.

Great God, Preserver of All Things — Die Helle Sonne Ist Dahin C.M.

St. 1-3, 4 (selected lines) — Zahn 206

Francis Daniel Pastorius — Laurentius Erhardi, arr. 1659

1. Great God, Pre - serv - er of all things, Most gra - cious King of Kings!
2. And where - as I, O Lord with thine Am graft - ed in the vine

Thou boun - ti - ful good hus - band - man, Canst do what no man can.
Christ Je - sus, our Re - deem - er dear, By him some fruits to bear.

3. Spare not, spare not the pruning knife,
To keep my soul alive.
The judgments of thy righteous hand
In this wild woody land.

4. Make me, God, a fruitful branch
Below here, till I launch
To thee into eternity
That time which has no end.

IN HEAVEN SOARING UP — SONG OF THE THREE CHILDREN 10.8.10.8.8.8.

St. 1-4 — Frost 363

Edward Taylor, late 17th cent. — Orlando Gibbons, c. 1660

Unison

1. In heav - en soar - ing up, I dropped an ear On earth, and oh! sweet
2. Oh! joy - ous hearts! en - fired with ho - ly flame! Is speech thus tas - sel -

mel - o - dy! And lis - tening, found it was the saints who were
ĕd with praise? Will not your in - ward fire of joy con - tain,

En - croached for heaven that sang_ for joy. For in Christ's coach
That it in o - pen flames_ doth blaze? For in Christ's coach

they sweet - ly sing, As they to_ glo - ry ride there-in.
saints sweet - ly sing, As they to_ glo - ry ride there-in.

3. And if a string do slip by chance, they soon
Do screw it up again; whereby
They set it in a more melodious tune
And a diviner harmony.
For in Christ's coach they sweetly sing,
As they to glory ride therein.

4. In all their acts, public and private, nay,
And secret too, they praise impart.
But in their acts divine, and worship, they
With hymns do offer up their heart.
Thus in Christ's coach they sweetly sing,
As they to glory ride therein.

Devotional Verse: Dutch, German, and Indian

NOT ALL our seventeenth-century poets wrote their verses in English. We have already mentioned Jean de Brebeuf's Huron Christmas carol, "Jesus Ahatonhia."

Of very special interest is the brief flowering of Dutch verse by poets associated with New Amsterdam. Jacob Steendam, merchant, traveler, and the earliest New York poet, wrote his *Complaint of New Amsterdam* in 1659. More to our purpose is *Den Distelfink* (The Goldfinch), published in 1650, which contains both religious and secular verses with tunes or the names of tunes to which they were to be sung. Among the former were "When I Admire the Greatness," and "Oh, Sing to God." Nicasius de Sille of New Utrecht freely paraphrased Psalm 116, invoking the aid of Jehovah against "the savage wild." An occasional poem by Henricius Selyns, "O Kerstnacht," is both a Christmas and a wedding song, written for a couple married by the poet in New Amsterdam in 1663.

Some poets were polylingual like Pastorius, whose treatise on bees was, as Whittier pleasantly remarked, written "in half the languages of man." Thus his "Ob Ich deiner schon vergiss" was written in German, and "Great God, Preserver of All Things" in English. Justus Falckner, the first Lutheran clergyman to be ordained in America, is remembered for one hymn, "Auf, ihr Christen, Christi Glieder."

Als Ik Des Herren Werk
When I Admire the Greatness

St. 1, 4, 8

Fortune My Foe 6.6.6.6.D.

Jacob Steendam, 1650

Adrianus Valerius, arr. 1621

1. When I ad - mire the great - ness Of the works of God,
And see how he has formed The earth on which we dwell;
2. In all thy works and deeds Thy pow - er is re - vealed;
When dark - est clouds are swept A - side and stars un - veiled.
How with his might - y arm He made the bil - lowing sea, And
Thy ven - geance falls on those Who fol - low e - vil ways; They
how he fixed its bounds That may not mov - èd be.
van - ish from our view; Their triumphs fade a - way.

3. O Lord of Lords and God
Of Gods, show us thy face;
Grant us prosperity,
Receive our heartfelt praise.
Thy righteous judgments thou
Hast shown thy faithful folk;
We pray they may be in
Every heart enthroned.

1. Als ik des Heren werk
en wonderheden groot
aanschouw en recht bemerk
hoe Hij de aarde - kloot
door zynen arm zeer sterk
op't water heeft gegrond,
en hoe Hij haar een perk
gesteld heeft in het rond;

2. Wanneer Gij's hemels macht
in alle ding beweegt,
wanneer Gij in de nacht
de lucht van wolken veegt,
Wanneer Gij pleegt met kracht
aan't boze - volk uw wraak,
wanneer Gij die belacht,
en ruimt haar zegenbaak.

3. O God, der goden Heer
die alle dingen doet
gedijen, tot uw eer,
dat men u loven moet,
die uw heilzame leer
hebt ons, uw volk, vertoond,
geeft dat die meer en meer
in onze harten woont.

LAAT ONS DEN HERRE SINGEN
OH, SING TO GOD

SEI TANTO GRATIOSA Irregular

St. 1-4

Jacob Steendam, 1650

Giovanni Ferretti, c.1580
Adrianus Valerius, arr. 1621

1. Oh, sing to God your mak - er. Your joy - ful songs and prais - es glad e'er
2. He parts the rag - ing bil - lows And leads us safe - ly through the path thus
rais - ing. Be - fore all oth - er du - ties, For
o - pened. He loosed the tem - pest's fu - ry A -
all his good - ness ne'er for - get to praise him With thank-ful tongue.
gainst the might of Phar - aoh sent to harm us. The horse-man fierce
We praise his name For all his dai - ly bless - ings; For our sal -
In full ca - reer He to the ground hath smit - ten. And in the

va - tion Which he so free - ly grants, let us ex - tol him.
bil - lows He horse and man hath ut - ter - ly de - stroy ëd.

3. Give ear O fairest virgins
In Israel born, from Abraham descended.
The Lord God worship only,
For yours the race that God the Lord has chosen.
O chosen race
His praises sing,
His greatness and his power,
Who through the billows
Did make a road and to dry land did lead you.

1. Laat ons de Here zingen,
een vrolijk lied
en zijne name loven,
Laat ons voor alle dingen
zijn goedheid niet
vergeten, noch beroven
van dankbaarhe id.
Mijn tonge zeit
Hem dank en wil Hem prijzen
voor d'hoogste zegen,
voor 't heil, van Hem verkregen,
eer bewijzen.

2. De ongestuime vleoden
keert Hij de loop
en leidt ons door haar paden
en doet ze dapper woeden
op Pharós hoop,
die ons poogde te schaden.
Want Man en paard
ook in haar vaart
heeft Hij te grond doen storten
en in de golven
des zees geheel bedolven
haat te schorten.

3. Daarom gij kuise maagden
uit Abraham,
uit Israel geboren,
die God alleen behaagden
want deze stam
is van Hem uitverkoren,
O teer geslacht
der vrouwen, tracht
Zijn goddelijke hoogheid
eeuwig te eeren,
die u door zee doet keren,
en in't broog' leidt.

God Stelt Ons Hier
God Set Us Here

French Tune: Psalm 116 10.10.10.10.

St. 1-3, 5

Frost 329; Zahn 859

Nicasius de Sille, writ. after 1657

Thysius Lute Book, arr. c. 1610

1. God set us here till sav - age rul - ers fell,
2. Pray him on us his bless - ings to be - stow,
The glo - ry of his name, we glad - ly sing,
Our lives pre - serv - ing by his sov - ereign grace,
And from the earth his prais - es forth shall bring,
Thus we no e - vil spir - it e'er shall face,
That he with us may hence - forth ev - er dwell.
And may pros - per - i - ty for - ev - er know.

3. His power with strength shall always us endow,
Our wants to meet, our cattle to increase,
Ourselves from savages and foes release;
For which to him devoutly let us bow.

4. Sinners, O Lord, we bow before thy throne,
Implore thy aid, in thee our trust we place;
Thou our protection art in our distress;
The glory, Lord, we give to thee alone.

1. God stelt ons hier tot der barbaren spijt,
tot zijnes namens eer wilt vrolijk zingen
en van harte met vrengd zijn lof voortbrengen
zo zal Hij wonen bij ons alletijd.

2. Bid dan dat Hij ons zijne zegen zendt
en ons door zijn genade wil bewaren,
zo zal geen kwaad gespook ons wederwaren,
dan zullen wij in voorspoed krijgen't end.

3. Hij zal ons sterk maken door zijne bracht,
ons van nooddruft voorzien, van vee vermeren,
barbaren en benijders van ons weren.
Daarom valt Hem te voet met alle macht.

4. Wij zondaars, Heer, vallen voor U terneer,
verzoeden U bijstand, die wij verkouwen;
onze Hoeder zijt Gij in ons benauwen,
daarom komt U, O Heer, alleen de eer.

O Kersnacht
O Christmas Night

9.9.8.D.

St. 1, 2, 4, 6

Henricus Selyns, writ. 1663
Howard Murphy, trans. 1865

Traditional

1. O Christ - mas night! day's light tran - scend - ing, Who no be - gin - ning had or end - ing Till he a man be - came, was God. Then he who ne'er be - fore was hu - man Was born in Beth - le - hem of wom - an, When nips the frost the ver - dant sod.
2. This rich - est babe comes poor in be - ing, More pearled with - in than to the see - ing With di - a - dem and roy - al power; He takes no heed of great - er plac - es, But that small spot a - lone em - brac - es, Where light il - lumes the mid - night hour.

3. This Prince, do they desire to find him?
They're worn-out swaddling clothes that bind him.
A manger, spread with hay's his bed.
His throne is higher than the highest,
Yet he among the cattle lieth;
What him to such a lot has led?

4. Now seeks he God with chaste affection
Who takes before such crib direction,
Are better than this Bethlehem,
Which Christ no resting place will give;
For they, the after-life, shall live
With him, in New Jerusalem.

1. O Kersnacht, lichter dan de dagen,
want Hij die geen begin der dagen
noch einde heeft, tot mense wordt.
God was Hij maar geen mens tevoren
en wordt tot Bethlehem geboren
als 't kruid van gure koud' verdort.

2. Dit rijhste kind komt arm ter wereld,
meer binnen, als na 't oog bepereld
met kroon en koninklijke macht,
en maakt geen werks van groote steden,
slechts met dit slechte vlek tevreden
daar 't licht schijnt midden in de nacht.

3. Want God heeft 't vlese aangenomen
en worstelt met dit hels gebroed.
een krib zijn wieg en hooi zijn bed.
zijn troon is meerder als de meeste
en wordt een mense bij de beesten,
Wat is 't Hem tot een harde wet.

4. Nu zoekt hij God met kuise minne.
Zij, die voor zulke krib beginnen
zijn beter als dit Bethlehem,
't welk Christo weigert plaats te geven,
meer dat zij leven, na dit leven
met 't kind in 't Nieuw Jerusalem.

Auf, Ihr Christen
Rise, Ye Children

Meine Hoffnung Stehet Feste 8.7.8.7.6.7.

St. 1, 5, 11

Zahn 4870

Justus Falckner, 1697
Emma Frances Bevan, trans. 1858

Christian Gregor, arr. 1784

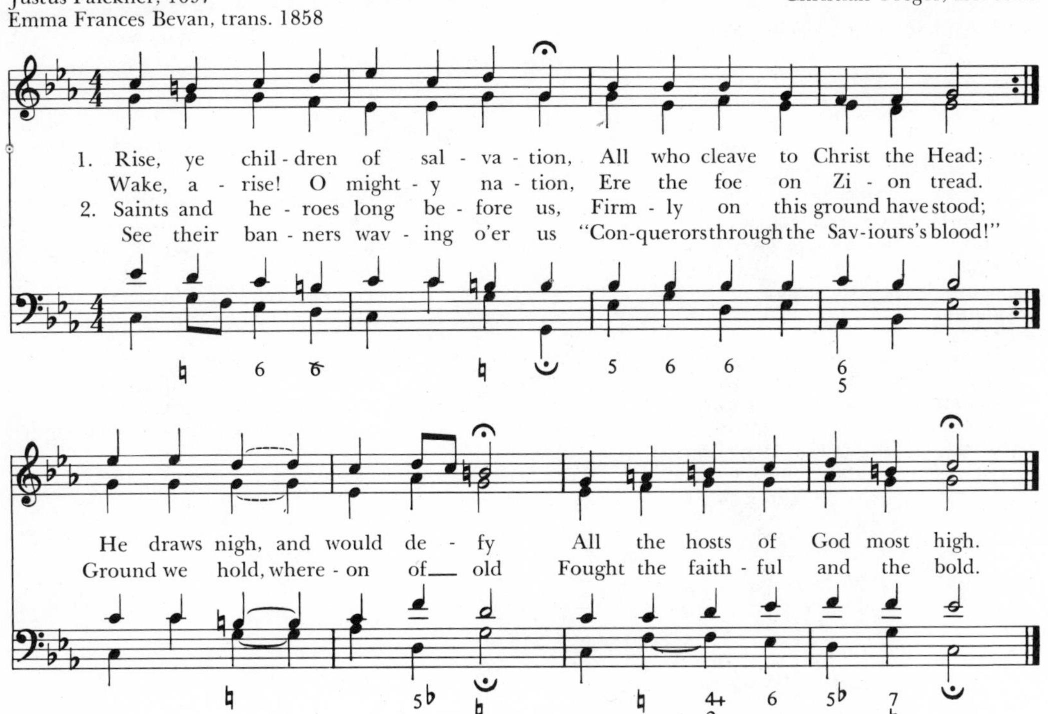
1. Rise, ye chil - dren of sal - va - tion, All who cleave to Christ the Head;
Wake, a - rise! O might - y na - tion, Ere the foe on Zi - on tread.
2. Saints and he - roes long be - fore us, Firm - ly on this ground have stood;
See their ban - ners wav - ing o'er us "Con-querors through the Sav-iours's blood!"
He draws nigh, and would de - fy All the hosts of God most high.
Ground we hold, where - on of old Fought the faith - ful and the bold.

3. When his servants stand before him
Each receiving his reward;
When his saints in light adore him,
Giving glory to the Lord —
Victory! our song shall be,
Like the thunder of the sea!

1. Auf, ihr Christen, Christi Glieder,
Die ihr noch hängt an dem Haupt,
Auf, wacht auf, ermannt euch wieder,
Eh ihr werdet hingeraubt
Satan beut an den Streit
Christo und der Christenheit

2. Dieser Sieg hat auch empfunden
Voller heilgen starker Muth,
Da sie haben überwunden
Fröhlich durch des Lammes Blut.
Sollten wir den allhier
Nicht auch streiten mit Begier?

3. Da Gott seinen treuen Knechten
Geben wird den Gnadenlohn
Und die Hütten der Gerechten
Stimmen an den Siegeston;
Da fürwahr Gottes Schar
Ihn wird loben immerdar.

Ob Ich Deiner Schon Vergiss
Though My Thoughts

Himmel, Erde, Luft und Meer 7.7.7.7.

St. 1-3

Francis Daniel Pastorius
Sheema Z. Buehne, trans. 1965

Johann Anastasius Freylinghausen, arr. 1704

1. Though my thoughts from thee — may — stray, And I of - ten lose — the — way,
2. Guide me to thy path — a - right! Grant me grace with - in — thy — sight.
And my du - ty fail to see, Lord, dear God, — turn not from — me.
When the Fiend's as - sault I flee, Lord, dear God, — turn not from — me.

3. Yet thy heart to me below
Is inclined in love, I know,
As a father's, faithfully,
And will never turn from me.

1. Ob ich Deiner schon vergiss
Und des rechten Wegs oft miss,
Auch versäume meine Pflicht,
Lieber Gott, vergiss mein nicht

2. Bring mich wieder auf die Bahn,
Nimm mich zu Genaden an;
Und, wenn mich der Feind ansieht,
Lieber Gott, vergiss mein nicht.

3. Dich ich weiss, Dein Vaterherz
Neigt in Lieb' sich niederwärts,
Ist in Treu' auf mich gericht,
Und vergiss mein nimmer nicht.

Jesous Ahatonhia
Hommes, Prenez Courage, Jésus Est Né
Let Christian Hearts Rejoice Today

Une Jeune Pucelle 8.6.8.6.8.8.6.4.7.

St. 1, 3, 6

Jean de Brebeuf, S.J., writ. 1641
Paul Picard, Fr. trans. 1913
Francis X. Curley, S.J., Eng. version 1953

Anon., 16th cent.

1. Let Chris - tian hearts re - joice to - day, Our Sav - iour, Christ, is born. To -
2. Three chiefs to - geth - er made a pact When glo - ry filled the night To
day the reign of Sa - tan ends, His King - dom's o - ver - thrown. So
fol - low where that glo - ry led And find the source of light, For
when his tempt - ing voice you hear Then quick - ly to the crib draw near Our
God to them re - vealed his plan, They has - tened towards the God - made-Man, And
Sav - iour, Christ, is there, Je - sus is there, Has - ten then to Beth - le - hem.
Je - sus wel-comed them, Je - sus the Chief, Wel-comed chiefs to Beth - le - hem.

3. The time has come for each of us
To kneel before his Lord,
He came in answer to our prayer,
Now let him be adored,
And as we kneel this holy night
For holiness and him we'll fight;
That promise now we make,
Make to our Chief,
Jesus Christ of Bethlehem.

Algonquin (approximation)

Estennialon de tson'e Jes's ahatonhia
Onna'ate'a d'oki n'an' andask'aentak
Ennonchien sk'atrihotal n'on'andilonrachatha
Jes's ahatonhia.

Hommes, prenez courage, Jesus est né,
Maintenant que le regne du diable est détruit
N'écoutez plus ce qu'il dit a vos esprits,
Jésus est né.

John Eliot preaching to the Indians

THE EIGHTEENTH CENTURY

THE EIGHTEENTH century opened with the psalm still in the ascendant. Not only were psalms woven into the fabric of the church service, they consoled, comforted, and enlivened the lives of families and of individuals. Benjamin Franklin wrote that "one could not walk through the town in an evening without hearing psalms sung in different families in every street." It is true that this was during a period of religious excitement brought on by the preaching of George Whitefield. Whitefield himself, on shipboard on his way to America in 1738, crept below after waves had swept over the hatchway "and sang psalms with, and comforted the poor wet people." In a happier situation on the way to an appointment in this country: "Night was as it were turned into day, when we rode singing through the woods."

Some of the early settlers could read music. Ainsworth's psalter included tunes, and he certainly would not have incurred the additional expense unless a reasonable proportion of his and other like-minded congregations could read music. It is also understandable that without systematic instruction this skill declined until the more difficult tunes became impossible and even easy ones hazardous. Two entries from the records of the church at Plymouth show what the situation was there.

June 19, 1692
The Pastor stayed the church after meeting and propounded that seeing many of the psalms in Mr. Ainsworth's translations, that we now sing, had such difficult tunes, that none in the church could set, that the church would consider of some way of accomodation.
August 7, 1692
When the tunes are difficult in the translation we use, we will sing the psalms now used in our neighbor churches in the Bay.

Samuel Sewall, the author of the famous diary, was the elder appointed to set the psalm tunes in the South Church, Boston. He recorded both his failures and his successes, but the former were more frequently quoted.

February 2, 1717/18 Lord's Day.
In the Morning I set York Tune, and in the 2nd going over, the Gallery carried it irresistibly to St. David's which discouraged me very much. I spoke earnestly to Mr. White to set it in the afternoon, but he declines it.

P.M. The Tune went well.

Singing Style

It has been claimed that the early psalm paraphrases were sung briskly and the terms "Beza ballads" and "Geneva jigs" have been quoted to support this view. However this might be, there were certainly New England congregations in the eighteenth century who sang their psalm tunes at a very slow tempo. Associated with these long drawn-out unison performances was a type of ornamentation which was described, and always unfavorably, by contemporary observers. A sermon on music preached in Boston puts it more briefly than most: "Many congregations here sing near one-third too long, and some syllables have been quavering."

This trend toward a florid rendering of psalm tunes is apparent in Matthew Camidges Psalmody for a Single Voice, which added graces to the simple psalm tune, but this was a mode of performance best suited to the trained solo voice rather than for congregational singing. Again our musical sermon states that "singers in the same congregation have differed one from another in the turns and flourishes of the Tune which they have sung, and have been too discordant." This type of performance became known as the "Old Way." As it became usual, it was defended as the only proper mode of performance.

It was challenged in the early part of the century by advocates of the New Way, who advocated singing by note instead of by rote, singing what was written without adding ornaments, and singing briskly in harmony rather than slowly in unison.

A competent observer who heard rural New England choirs two generations ago stated that they sang with a driving energetic rhythm with little or no flexibility and little regard to the niceties of vocal production. Recordings of the Sacred Harp Singers from the South lead to a similar conclusion.

It was clear that those who wished to have singing by note in their churches would have to provide for systematic instruction. Symmes asks the question in his *The Reasonableness of Regular Singing* (1720): "Would it not greatly tend to promote singing of psalms if singing schools were promoted?" Many clergymen and others thought that it would. Pupils in singing schools needed manuals of instruction and simple material to sing; two thin pamphlets appeared to meet this need. Both were by ministers: John Tufts of the Second Church of Newbury, Massachusetts, and Thomas Walter.

Although no copy of the first edition of Tufts's *An Introduction to the Singing of Psalm-Tunes* is known to exist, the first edition probably appeared in 1721, the year in which Walter's little treatise

was printed. The fifth edition of 1726 contained thirty-seven tunes. Thirty-one of these appeared in Playford's *Whole Book of Psalms* (1677) and also in Walter. Three of the settings came from Simon Browne's *Hymns and Spiritual Songs* (London, 1720), and one, the 100TH PSALM TUNE NEW, remains untraced and may have originated in this country. Tufts presents his tunes in a simplified notation in which the letters F, S, L, and M (fa, sol, la, and mi) are placed on the appropriate line or space of the staff. In addition to the 100TH PSALM TUNE NEW, HACKNEY and SOUTHWELL have been included here as they appear in Tufts.

The Singing Master

Americans took up the study of sight singing with enormous zest. There was a singing school in Boston in 1717. In 1721 Cotton Mather preached to a singing school on a text from Revelation "No man could learn that song"—which hardly seems likely to encourage young singers. "House was full and the Singing extraordinarily Excellent, such as hardly been heard before in Boston."

Even toward the end of the century, the study of singing was pursued with enthusiasm. The Rev. Thomas Smith of the First Church, Portland, Maine, recorded in his diary under June 20, 1785: "We are all in a blaze about singing; all flocking at 5, 10, and 4 o'clock to the meeting-house, to a Master hired (viz. Mr. Gage.)." The teacher of the singing school became a familiar figure. Such teachers were led not only to write brief digests of music theory for their students but also to compose tunes for their classes.

The dramatic rise of the singing master is one of the striking features of the musical scene of the eighteenth and early nineteenth centuries. His classes not only provided instruction but also formed a social focus for the young people of a neighborhood. The second feature often caused the church fathers to have doubts about the desirability of such gatherings.

Most of the oblong books of the eighteenth and early nineteenth centuries with their introductions that summarized the rudiments of music followed by a selection of psalm tunes, fuguing tunes, and anthems, were printed by singing masters to be sold to their classes. Such recommendations as the following from Dyer's *New York Selection of Sacred Music* have the atmosphere of their period: "The paper is stout and good, and the size sufficiently large to insure a clear and distinct appearance, which is the more necessary, as works of this kind are most commonly made use of on evenings, and of course by candle-light.

The singing master canvassed the neighborhood, assembled a class, and engaged a large room which might be a schoolhouse, a church, or a tavern. He taught the rudiments of notation, a method of beating time, and solmization. These principles were applied to psalm tunes, and the sessions terminated with an "exhibition" in which the class sang the tunes which they had learned to their assembled relatives, friends, and neighbors.

The Choir

Social status was reflected in the seating of the congregation in most of the early New England churches. We have seen that in the seventeenth century one person had set the pitch and "raised the psalm," but that the rest of the congregation had been equal as far as the musical part of the service was concerned. During the eighteenth century, the rise of a musical elite, the choir, was eventually reflected in the seating pattern within the church. Frequently a gallery was erected over the entrance vestibule, and sometimes on three sides of the church. The choir was seated there on benches set apart for them. The minister's pulpit was at the opposite end of the church, perhaps surmounted by a sounding board, and the congregation sat below in box pews closed off with doors. When the choir was to sing, the congregation turned to face it, thus turning their backs on the minister, a change not realized immediately or without conflict.

The New England choir sang in four parts soprano, counter (we would say countertenor today), tenor, and bass. The tenor sang the melody. The soprano was the only part for women, although no doubt those in the congregation who could not read music were likely to join in on the tenor part sung an octave too high. However, in such singing societies as that at Stoughton, it is clear that even the soprano part was sung either by men in falsetto or by boys, since women were not admitted to the society until 1844 (although an earlier entry, December 25, 1827, notes that three women were invited). The counter sang the part later taken by the second sopranos or altos. It was usually written in the alto clef but sometimes in the G clef an octave too high. The reign of the counter was already challenged by Amos Bull in 1795, who set some of his compositions in *The Responsary* for second trebles. Billings is not alone in insisting that the most prominent voice should be the bass.

The Composers

The compositions in a manuscript by the Pennsylvania mystic Johannes Kelpius have been claimed as the earliest music composed

in North America. A closer examination, however, has revealed that all except two can be traced to European sources. One of these, "I Love My Jesus," has been included in this collection. The one unidentified composition in the Tufts pamphlet, 100TH PSALM TUNE NEW, has already been mentioned. The *Urania* of James Lyons, published in Philadelphia in 1760, contains compositions by the compiler, while in Massachusetts, William Billings' *New England Psalm Singer* of 1770 is the first of the singing master's books. The impact of the singing master had been greatest in small towns and in the country. The more sophisticated congregations of the coastal cities remained closer to English taste.

This influence from England was felt through two different channels, the first through English tunes which were republished here, and the second through the activity on this side of the Atlantic of composers born in England and trained there. We may mention Dr. George K. Jackson, William Selby, and Raynor Taylor as English-born musicians active here.

The New England composers cultivated three types of music: the psalm tune, the fuguing tune, and the anthem. (The anthem falls outside the scope of our study.) In the psalm tune the voices tended to move together and there was little or no word repetition. The fuguing tune was in two sections. The first was more or less chordal in texture. The second began with free imitative entries in each of the voices and was repeated. Those who insisted on a clear projection of the text were disturbed by the word repetitions in the fuguing tune and by the fact that different words were sung at the same time in the imitative passages. However, these tunes were great favorites with the singers and were sung in "Old Folks" concerts and reprinted in retrospective collections long after they had been displaced as service music.

Billings' vigorous tunes were followed by those of Justin Morgan (b. 1747), Lewis Edson (b. 1748), Supply Belcher (b. 1751), Jacob French (b. 1754), Daniel Read (b. 1757), Jacob Kimball (b. 1761), Jeremiah Ingalls (b. 1764), Oliver Holden (b. 1765), and Stephen Jenks (b. 1772). On the other hand Andrew Law (b. 1748) was opposed to the fuguing tune, as were Solomon Howe and Samuel Holyoke.

In Holyoke the crudeness of the older masters has vanished, but some of the vigor of earlier examples has gone with it. His ARNHEIM enjoyed and deserved a long popularity.

Musical Instruments

Strong as was the feeling against the use of instruments in sacred music in New England there are indications that the bass viol was

used by Billings. Certainly he states that where he writes octaves for the bass part the instrument is to take the lower notes.

The prejudice against the use of instruments included the organ. An organ willed by Thomas Brattle in 1713 to the Brattle Street Church in Boston was refused, and King's Chapel, which was next offered it, allowed it to remain on the church porch for seven months before moving it inside and putting it in playing condition. Even toward the end of the century, the liberal and musical William Bentley of Salem was both indignant and discomfited when he received a ticket for a concert on the evening following Thanksgiving at which the organ was to be played. "It is singular that on a day of devotion we should be so weak as to be betrayed into a justification of an act against the practice of dissenters, not only to hear Organs in a Church, but to go on Thanksgiving Day to pay for the repairs of one for the service. This is beyond Catholic." Yet in the next year when there were too few in the choir to sing either in the morning or evening services he admits: "I shall be obliged to recant all I have said against organs from mere necessity."

Organs are recorded in Virginia for 1700. An organ and orchestral instruments were played at the installation of Justus Falchner in the Gloria Dei Church in Philadelphia in 1703.

Where an organ accompaniment is taken for granted, hymns may be composed in a different way. A unison hymn may be for figured bass and melody, relying on the organist to fill in the harmony. Such are the Charleston hymns by Peter Valton, Henry Purcell, and Jervis Henry Stevens. The organ part may be wholly or partly written out with a prelude and postlude for organ, like Carr's EROICA. How an organist might actually play a psalm tune is shown by Daniel Purcell's ST. DAVID'S TUNE and John Blow's ST. MARY HACKNEY. Both are "set full," that is, written in keyboard style and they have interludes for the organ between the lines sung by the congregation. Chorale settings might also be for melody and figured bass, or four vocal parts might be written out. In either case it was assumed that the organist would fill in the harmonies from the figured bass.

The Psalters

THE TWO most important psalters of the eighteenth century were by Tate and Brady and by Isaac Watts.

THE NEW VERSION (TATE AND BRADY). Although *The New Version of the Psalms of David, fitted to the tunes used in churches* was published in 1696, it properly belongs to the eighteenth century. The co-authors were Nahum Tate and Nicholas Brady. The former was Poet Laureate and a follower and associate of Dryden, the latter was chaplain to the king. On December 3, 1696, the king allowed publication and the version was "permitted to be used in all churches, &c., as shall think fit to receive them."

The earliest American edition of Tate and Brady (Boston, 1713) was printed especially for King's Chapel, Boston, which had voted to use this version in April of that year. The Episcopal congregations in America adopted an abridged version of Tate and Brady after the Revolution.

Our example from the New Version (included in the seventeenth-century section because of publication date) has a special interest—Thomas Jefferson owned a copy of *The Psalms set Full by Daniel Purcell* and under ST. DAVID'S TUNE he transcribed his favorite psalm: "Lord, Who's the Happy Man" (Ps. 15). The *Presbyterian Hymnal* of 1911 still contained five psalm versions derived from Tate and Brady (Pss. 34, 42, 84, 93, and 122).

Criticisms of Tate and Brady were based on the literary artifices of their version. Bishop Beveridge (1710) compared it unfavorably with the Old Version, saying it was "flourished with wit and fancy." Tate evidently felt the need of replying, which he did in his *Essay on Psalmody* (1710). Alexander Pope's slighting remark about "Tate's poor page" is well known. More important was the reaction of the common people, who felt that David "spoke plain" in the familiar lines of the Old Version.

In spite of these criticisms it was clear that the day of the literal paraphrase was past and that poetic excellence and a freer treatment of the venerable texts was sought. This trend was even more apparent in the versions of John Patrick and Isaac Watts.

THE WATTS PSALTER. *The Psalms of David Imitated in the Language of*

the New Testament And apply'd to the Christian State and Worship by Isaac Watts appeared in 1719. The first American edition (Philadelphia, 1729) was printed by Benjamin Franklin. Evidently this edition was ahead of the demand, for most of the copies were still on the shelves two years later. Franklin did not print another edition for twelve years.

From the American point of view there were two difficulties with a psalter regarded as almost sacred. The first was the fact that Watts did not paraphrase all of the Psalms. He not only omitted the imprecatory psalms (which included the moving Ps. 137) but he also preferred not to repeat himself when the psalms did. Many Americans wanted a complete psalter, since they were accustomed to read or sing the Psalms "in course," that is, in numerical order. What George C. Burgess stated at the Portland Centennial had a wider application. "The psalms were sung in regular order, without regard to the subject of the sermon, and, long or short, sung at one standing, so that the longest, say of one hundred and thirty lines, took a full half hour in the singing."

The second difficulty was that although Watts's announced intention of interpreting the Psalms in the light of the New Testament was not an obstacle to their use, his laudatory lines to Great Britain and her ruler became increasingly unacceptable as the colonies moved into opposition and finally into open rebellion. Unwilling to give up Watts, and dissatisfied with these aspects of his version, religious leaders attemped to complete Watts's version and to adapt it for American use.

A number of passages in Watts are extremely "American" in tone —the comparison "Swift as an Indian arrow flies," for example. His New England Hymn, "Where Nothing Dwelt But Beasts of Prey" was sung both in the colonies and down to the present in the South. (In spite of its title, it was a paraphrase of part of Ps. 107.)

Probably most members of congregations which sang from Watts or Tate and Brady had only the words before them and depended on the elder who led them or on their own memories for the tune. Both psalters were published in small volumes which could be carried in a pocket, and they were usually bound in calf. Those who wanted the music could obtain small collections of standard English tunes which they then had bound in at the end of the psalter.

American Psalters. There were also a number of American psalters. Thomas Prince (1758) revised the *Bay Psalm Book* but he did so with such freedom as to almost produce a new version. Cotton Mather (1718) and John Barnard (1752) produced versions of their own. John Mycall

(1775) and Joel Barlow (1785) endeavored to amend the patriotic lines in Watts and to fill the gaps which he had left. If Watts could write "The northern isles shall send the name" (Ps. 100, 2d part), Mycall was equally local when he began his version of Psalm 21 with "Our states, O Lord." Jeremy Belknap's version (1795) reflected a trend toward Unitarian views. Jacob Kimball was best known as a singing master, but his version of Psalm 65 ("Thy Praise, O God, in Zion Waits") was printed in Belknap's psalter.

THE SETTINGS. Although most American composers published their settings of psalms to lines from Watts and the New Version, they were also attracted to paraphrases by the American editors who attempted to revise Watts. Supply Belcher set Mycall's "Our States, O Lord." Barlow's version of Psalm 137 was an especial favorite. Stephen Jenks called his setting for it DESOLATION, but there were also settings by Lewis Edson, and Samuel Holyoke, as well as a later one by Elkanah Kelsey Dare. Holyoke's massive tome, *The Columbian Repository,* included tunes for all the Psalms including the Barlow additions. The *First Church Collection* (1806) adds "O God of My Salvation, Hear" to an anonymous tune called OLD BRICK.

PSALTERIUM Americanum.

The BOOK of

PSALMS,

In a Tranſlation Exactly conformed unto the ORIGINAL;

BUT ALL IN

Blank Verſe,

Fitted unto the TUNES commonly uſed in our CHURCHES. Which **Pure Offering** is accompanied with ILLUSTRATIONS, digging for *Hidden Treaſures* in it; And RULES to Employ it upon the Glorious and Various Intentions of it.

Whereto are added,

Some other Portions of the SACRED SCRIPTURE, to Enrich the CANTIONAL.

BOSTON: in *N. E.*

Printed by S. KNEELAND, for B. ELIOT, S. GERRISH, D. HENCHMAN, and J. EDWARDS, and Sold at their Shops. 1718.

Title page of Cotton Mather's psalter

Eternal God, How They're Increased — Worcester C.M.

Ps. 3: 1-3, 5, 8 — Frost 46

Cotton Mather, 1718 — John Playford, arr. 1671

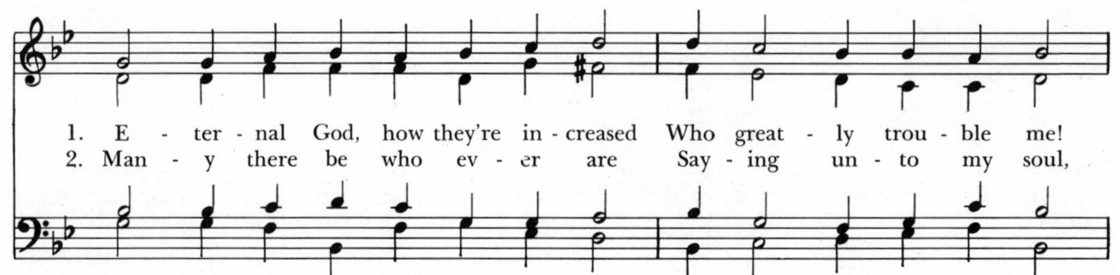
1. E - ter - nal God, how they're in - creased Who great - ly trou - ble me!
2. Man - y there be who ev - er are Say - ing un - to my soul,

How man - y are the men that stand In tri - umph o - ver me!
There's no sal - va - tion to be had For him in God at all.

3. But now about me thou'rt a shield
O thou eternal God;
Thou art my glory, and thou art
Th'uplifter of my head.

4. I laid me down, and took my sleep,
And then I did awake;
Because that the eternal God
Sustained me all along.

5. Salvation is what does belong
To the eternal God;
On those that are thy people is
Thy benediction still.

I Lift My Eyes Up to the Hills — Ixworth C.M.

Ps. 121: 1-8

Cotton Mather, 1718 — Version of 1767

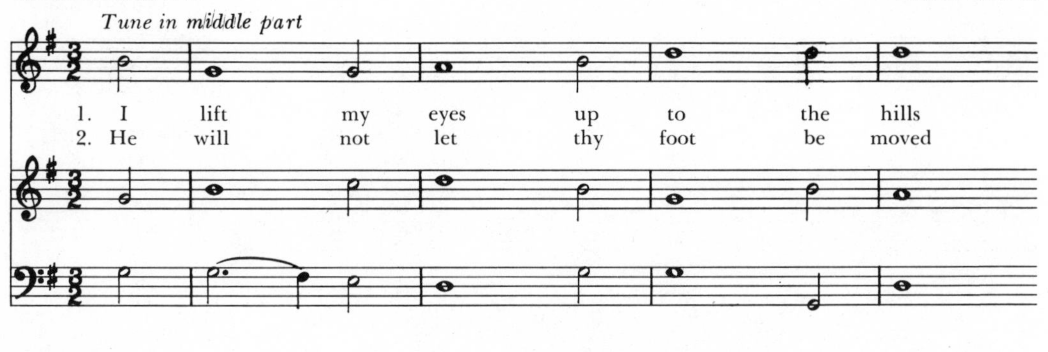
Tune in middle part
1. I lift my eyes up to the hills
2. He will not let thy foot be moved

From whence should come my help. My help's from
Thy keep - er slum - bers not. Lo, he that

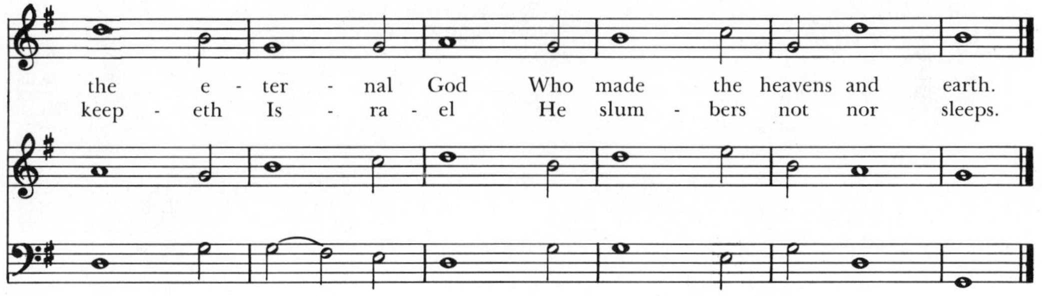
the e - ter - nal God Who made the heavens and earth.
keep - eth Is - ra - el He slum - bers not nor sleeps.

3. Th'eternal God is he who is
Thy watchful keeper still;
Th'eternal God becomes thy shade
At thy right hand he stands.

4. The sun shall not smite thee by day;
Nor shall the moon by night.
Th' Eternal keeps thee from all ill
He shall preserve thy soul.

5. Th'Eternal keeps thy going out
And keeps thy coming in.
He does it from this time, and will
Do it forever more.

Spare Us, O Lord, Aloud We Pray — Complaint L.M.

Ps. 102: st. 2-4, 6

Isaac Watts, 1719 — Parmenter, 1793

Tune in tenor
1. Spare us, O Lord, a - loud we pray, Nor let our sun go
down at noon;
Thy years are one e - ter - nal day, And
Thy
Thy years are one e - ter - nal day, And must thy
ter - nal day, And must thy chil - dren die so soon?
years are one e - ter - nal day,
must thy chil - dren die so soon? Thy years are one e -
chil - dren die so soon?
1. 2.
ter - nal day, And must thy chil - dren die so soon? soon?

2. Yet in the midst of death and grief
This thought our sorrow shall assuage:
"Our Father and our Saviour live;
Christ is the same through every age."

3. 'Twas he this earth's foundation laid;
Heaven is the building of his hand;
This earth grows old, these heavens shall fade,
And all be changed at his command.

4. Before thy face thy church shall live,
And on thy throne thy children reign;
This dying world shall they survive,
And the dead saints be raised again.

WHERE NOTHING DWELT BUT BEASTS OF PREY — WHITESTOWN L.M.

Ps. 107, "last part," st. 3-5, 7

Isaac Watts, 1718 — How'd, 1800

Tune in tenor

1. Where noth - ing dwelt but beasts of prey, Or men as fierce and wild as they, He bids th' op-pressed and poor re - pair, And builds them towns and cit - ies there.

2. They sow the fields, and trees they plant, Whose year - ly fruit sup - plies their want;

2. They sow the fields, and trees they plant, Whose year - ly fruit sup - plies their want;

2. They sow the fields, and trees they plant, Whose year - ly fruit sup - plies their want;

2. They sow the fields, and trees they plant, Whose year - ly fruit sup - plies their want;

plies their want; Their race grows up from
year - ly fruit sup - plies their want; Their race grows up from
Their race grows up from
Their race grows up from

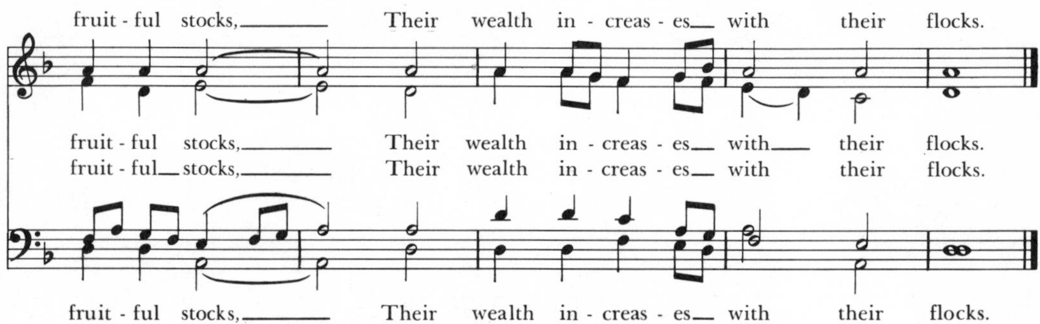
fruit - ful stocks, Their wealth in - creas - es with their flocks.
fruit - ful stocks, Their wealth in - creas - es with their flocks.
fruit - ful stocks, Their wealth in - creas - es with their flocks.
fruit - ful stocks, Their wealth in - creas - es with their flocks.

3. Thus they are blessed, but if they sin,
He lets the heathen nations in;
A savage crew invades their lands,
Their princes die by barbarous hands.

4. Yet if the humbled nation morns,
Again His dreadful hand he turns;
Again he makes their cities thrive,
And bids the dying churches live.

WHITESTOWN L. M.
119
Where nothing dwelt but beasts of prey, Or men as fierce and wild as they, He bids th' oppress'd and poor repair, And build them towns and cities there.
They sow the fields, and trees they plant, Whose yearly fruit supplies their want; Their race grows up from fruitful stocks, Their wealth increases with their flocks.

The same hymn tune in shape-note notation

NATIONS THAT LONG IN DARKNESS WALKED — MARBLEHEAD L.M.

Isa. 9: 2, 6, 7,

John Barnard, 1752 — Version from Barnard, 1752

1. Na - tions that long in dark - ness walked Have now be - held a glo - rious light;
2. For lo! the Vir - gin's Child is born; To us the Son of God is given.

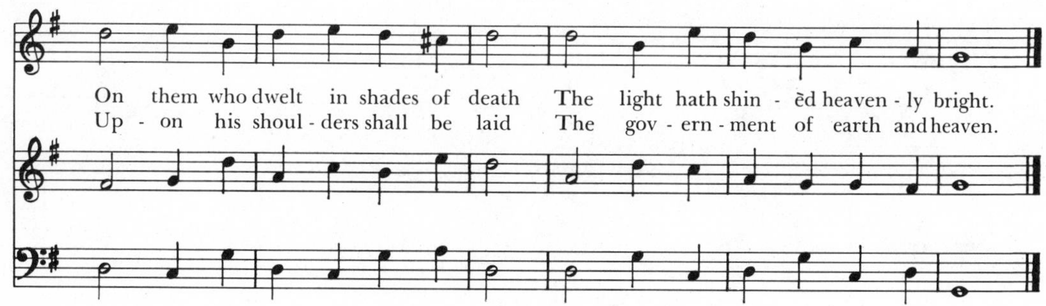
On them who dwelt in shades of death The light hath shin - ēd heaven - ly bright.
Up - on his shoul - ders shall be laid The gov - ern - ment of earth and heaven.

3. His name is callēd Wonderful,
The Counselor, the mighty God,
Eternal Father, Prince of Peace,
Peace dearly purchased with his blood.

4. His government shall know no bounds,
But far and wide o'er all extend;
And happy peace, the glorious fruits
Of his just reign, shall know no end.

5. O'er David's kingdom, on his throne
To rule, and establish it secure
With judgment clear, and justice right;
His reign forever shall endure.

THRICE BLEST THE MAN

Ps. 1: 1-6

John Barnard, 1752

100TH PSALM TUNE NEW L.M.

Version from John Tufts, 1726

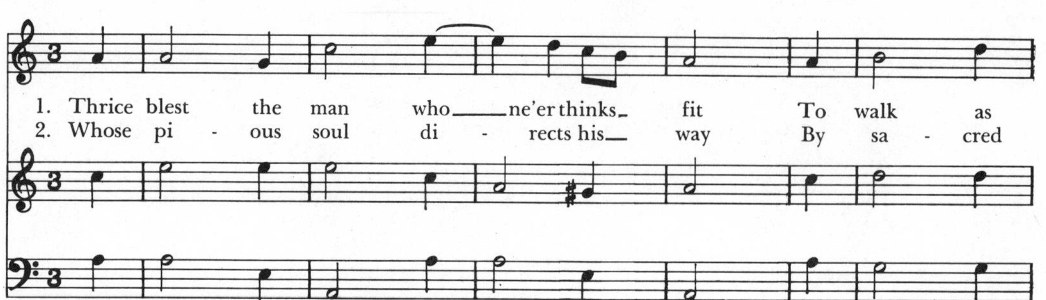
1. Thrice blest the man who ne'er thinks fit To walk as
2. Whose pi - ous soul di - rects his way By sa - cred

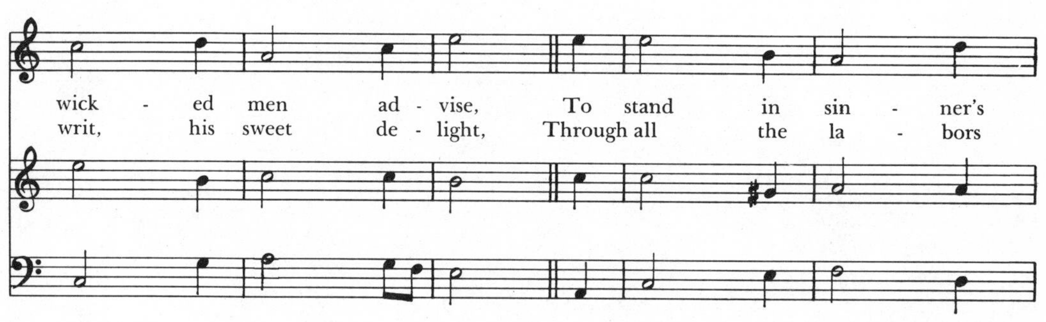
wick - ed men ad - vise, To stand in sin - ner's
writ, his sweet de - light, Through all the la - bors

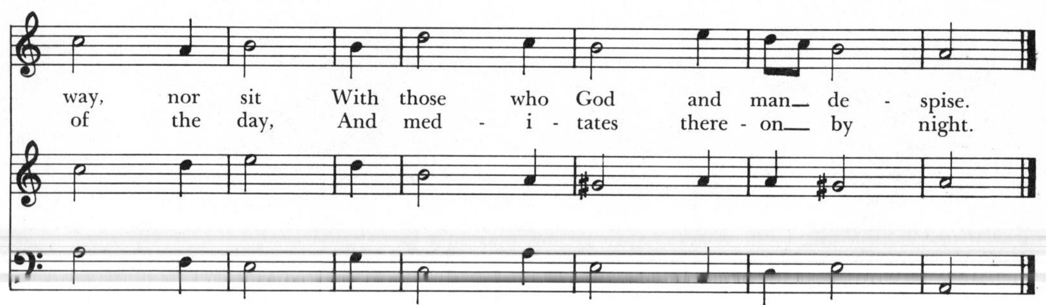
way, nor sit With those who God and man de - spise.
of the day, And med - i - tates there - on by night.

3. As planted trees by rivers' sides
Yield timely fruit a vast increase,
So in fresh verdure he abides
And God his handiwork will bless.

4. But those that spurn at sacred laws,
Shall no such favor with him find;
For God will blast them and their cause,
And whirl as chaff before the wind.

5. However in the Judgment Day
The wicked shall not stand the light;
Mix with the righteous shall not they,
Nor any formal hypocrite.

6. The Lord, who now with pleasure views,
Will then applaud the just man's way,
But who his name and word abuse
Shall feel his wrath and melt away.

GIVE EAR, O GOD, TO MY LOUD CRY

Ps. 61: 1-6

Thomas Prince, 1758

HACKNEY C.M.

Frost 333a

Version from John Tufts, 1726

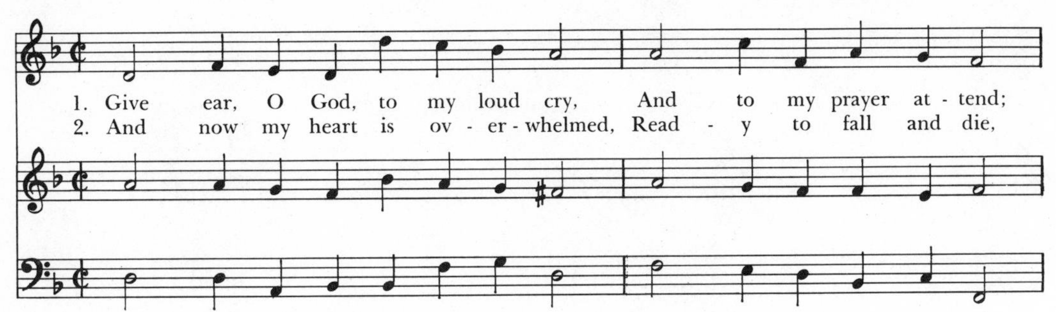
1. Give ear, O God, to my loud cry, And to my prayer at - tend;
2. And now my heart is ov - er - whelmed, Read - y to fall and die,

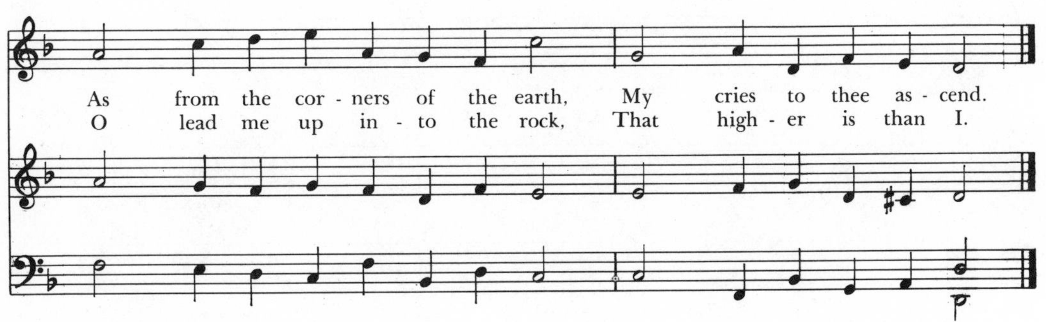
As from the cor - ners of the earth, My cries to thee as - cend.
O lead me up in - to the rock, That high - er is than I.

3. For in my danger thou hast been,
A shelter safe to me;
A tower of strength and sure defense
Against my enemy.

4. Within thy tabernacle I
Forever will abide;
And in the covert of thy wings
Will trust and safely hide.

5. For thou, O God, hast heard my vows,
As they before thee came;
And gave it me an inheritance,
With those who fear thy name.

6. O wilt thou give this to the King,
Yet many days to see;
To many generations let
His years prolongèd be.

O LORD, BOW DOWN THINE EAR — SOUTHWELL S.M.

Ps. 86: 1, 4, 7, 9-11 — Frost 45

Thomas Prince, 1758 — Version bound with Prince, 1755

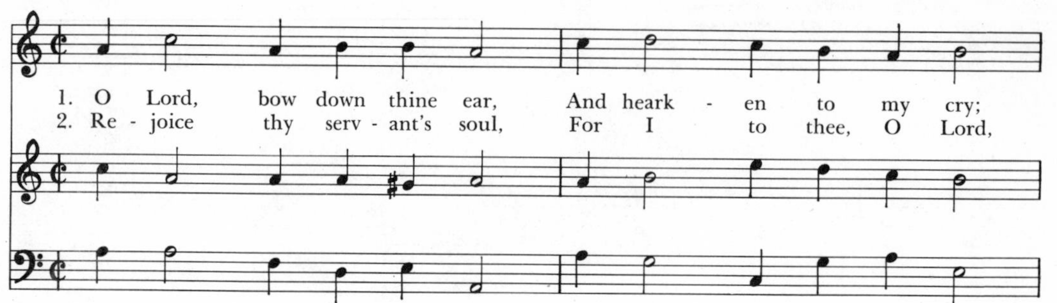
1. O Lord, bow down thine ear, And heark - en to my cry;
2. Re - joice thy serv - ant's soul, For I to thee, O Lord,

For poor and whol - ly des - ti - tute Of oth - er help am I.
Lift up my trou - bled soul, in hope That thou wilt help af - ford.

3. In days of my distress
I will to thee complain;
Because I surely know that thou
Wilt answer me again.

4. The nations all, O Lord,
Whom thy great power did frame,
Shall come before and bow to thee,
And glorify thy name.

5. For thou art high and great;
The things that thou hast done
Are truly marvelous, and show
That thou art God alone.

6. Teach me thy way of truth,
And I will walk the same;
And, Lord, to thee unite my heart,
That I may fear thy name.

OUR STATES, O LORD — UNION C.M.

Ps. 21: st. 1, 3, 6

John Mycall, 1776 — Supply Belcher, 1794

Tune in tenor

1. Our states, O Lord, with songs of praise Shall

With thy sal - va - tion

in thy strength re - joice;

With
With

With thy sal - va - tion

crowned shall raise. shall raise To heaven their cheer - ful,

thy sal - va - tion crowned shall raise To heaven their cheer - ful
thy sal - va - tion crowned shall raise To heaven their cheer - ful

crowned shall raise shall raise To heaven their cheer - ful

cheer ful voice, To heaven their cheer - ful voice.

voice, Their cheer - ful cheer - ful, cheer - ful voice.
voice, Their cheer - ful cheer - ful voice.

voice, Their cheer - ful cheer - ful, cheer - ful voice.

2. Then let our states on God alone
For timely aid rely!
His mercy which adorns his throne,
Shall all our wants supply.

3. Thus, Lord, thy wondrous power declare,
And thus exalt thy fame;
Whilst we glad songs of praise prepare
For thine almighty name.

Along the Banks

Desolation 10.10.10.10.

Ps. 137, st. 1-6

Joel Barlow, 1785

Stephen Jenks, 1791

Tune in tenor
1. A - long the banks where Ba - bel's cur - rent flows,
2. The tune - less harp that once with joy we strung,
Our cap - tive bands in deep de - spond - ence strayed,
When praise em - ployed and mirth in - spired the lay,
While Zi - on's fall in sad re - mem - brance rose,
In mourn - ful si - lence on the wil - lows hung.
And grow - ing grief pro - longed the te - dious day.

3. The barbarous tyrants, to increase the woe,
With taunting smiles a song of Zion claim;
Bid sacred praise in strains melodious flow,
While they blaspheme the great Jehovah's name.

4. But how, in heathen chains and lands unknown,
Shall Israel's sons, a song of Zion raise?
O hapless Salem, God's terrestial throne,
Thou land of glory, sacred mount of praise.

5. If e'er my memory lose thy lovely name,
If my cold heart neglect my kindred race,
Let dire destructions seize this guilty frame;
My hand shall perish and my voice shall cease.

6. Yet shall the Lord, who hears when Zion calls,
O'ertake her foes, with terror and dismay,
His arm avenge her desolated walls,
And raise her children to eternal day.

O God of My Salvation, Hear — Old Brick 8.8.8.D.

Ps. 88, st. 1-5

Joel Barlow, 1785 — Anon., 1806

Tune in tenor

1. O God of my sal - va - tion, hear My night - ly groan,

my dai - ly prayer, That still em - ploy my wast - ing

My soul de - clin - ing

breath; My soul de - clin - ing to the

My

My soul de - clin - ing to the grave,

to the grave, Im- plores thy sov - ereign power to

soul de - clin - ing to the grave, Im - plores thy sov - ereign power to

grave, Im - plores thy sov - ereign power to

Im - plores thy sov - ereign power to

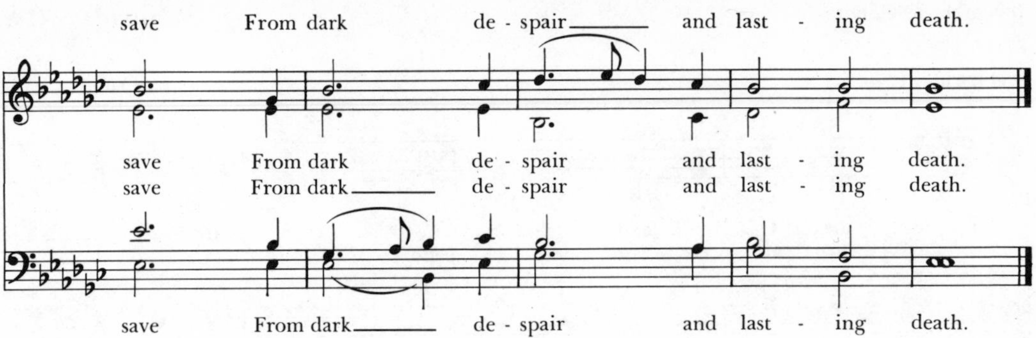
save From dark de - spair and last - ing death.
save From dark de - spair and last - ing death.
save From dark de - spair and last - ing death.
save From dark de - spair and last - ing death.

2. Thy wrath lies heavy on my soul,
   And waves of sorrow o'er me roll,
   While dust and silence spread the gloom;
   My friends beloved in happier days,
   The dear companions of my ways,
   Descend around me to the tomb.

3. As, lost in lonely grief, I tread
   The mournful mansions of the dead,
   Or to some throned assembly go;
   Through all alike I rove alone,
   While, here forgot and there unknown,
   The change renews my piercing woe.

4. And why will God neglect my call;
   Or who shall profit by my fall?
   When life departs and love expires,
   Can dust and darkness praise the Lord,
   Or wake, or brighten at his word,
   And tune the harp with heavenly quires?

5. Yet through each melancholy day,
   I've prayed to thee, and still will pray,
   Imploring still thy kind return —
   But, oh! my friends, my comforts, fled,
   And all my kindred of the dead
   Recall my wandering thoughts to mourn.

JUDGE ME, O GOD — HOPKINTON C.M.

Ps. 43: 1-4

Joel Barlow, 1785 — Oliver Holden, 1796

1. Judge me, O God, and plead my cause Against a sinful race; From vile oppression and deceit Secure me by thy grace. From vile oppression and deceit Secure me by thy grace.

2. On thee my steadfast hope depends, And am I left to mourn? To sink in sorrows and in vain Implore thy kind return? To sink in sorrows and in vain Implore thy kind return?

3. O send thy light to guide my feet
And bid thy truth appear;
Conduct me to thy holy hill
And taste thy mercies there.

4. Then to thy altar, oh my God,
My joyful feet shall rise,
And my triumphant songs shall praise
The God that rules the skies.

FAR FROM OUR FRIENDS — ST. SEPULCHRE C.M.

Ps. 137, st. 1-6

Jeremy Belknap, 1795 — William Selby, 1762

1. Far from our friends and coun - try dear
2. Our foes in - sult - ing mock our grief,
In hos - tile lands we moan; No ten - der hand
And sport with our com - plaints; No mer - cy prompts
to wipe the tear Which flows with ev - ery groan!
to give re - lief, Though lan - guid mis - ery faints.

3. In retrospective scenes employed
We think on former days;
When peaceful sabbaths we enjoyed
And all our work was praise.

4. But now, of liberty deprived
In solitude confined;
In vain we seek the word of life
To lead the starving mind.

5. To thee, O Lord, we lift our eye,
To thee, our cause commend;
Thou hearest the mourning prisoner's sigh
Thou art the sufferer's friend.

6. We seek no vengeance on our foes,
But put our trust in thee;
O let thy mercy interpose
And set thy captives free.

Thy Praise, O God, in Zion Waits — Stoneham L.M.

Ps. 65, st. 1, 3, 4, 6, 7

Jacob Kimball, 1793 — Jacob Kimball, 1793

Tune in tenor
1. Thy praise, O God, in Zi - on waits;
All flesh shall crowd thy sa - cred gates,
To of - fer sac - ri - fice and prayer And
To of - fer sac - ri -
To of - fer sac - ri - fice and prayer, And pay their will - ing
To of - fer sac - ri - fice and prayer. And pay their will - ing
pay their will - ing hom - age there And pay
fice and prayer. And pay
hom - age there, And pay their
hom - age there, And pay

1.
2.
will - ing hom - age there. there.

2. Blessed is the man approved by thee,
   And brought thy holy courts to see!
   Goodness, immense and unconfined
   Shall largely feast his longing mind.

3. Great God, by the Almighty hand,
   The everlasting mountains stand;
   And every storm, and every flood,
   Obey thy all-commanding nod.

4. From thy vast, inexhausted stores,
   The earth is blessed with kindly showers;
   And savage wilds and deserts drear,
   Confess thee, Father of the year.

5. The flocks which graze the mountains' brow,
   The corn which clothes the plains below,
   To every heart new transports bring,
   And hills and vales rejoice and sing.

Patriotic Hymns

THE SHRILL TONES of the fife and the beat of the drum resound in many of the songs of the period. Indeed, one hymn tune, MURILLO'S LESSON, was originally a fife tune which appeared in Alvin Robinson's *Massachusetts Collection of Martial Music* (1820).

We can hear echoes of the French and Indian War in Tilden's "O Heaven Indulge," of Braddock's defeat in Davies' "While O'er Our Guilty Land," of Bunker Hill in Niles' "Why Should Vain Mortals Tremble," "As Down a Lone Valley" was perhaps written by the young Timothy Dwight when he was a chaplain during the Revolution, and "Great Lord of All" by Jacob Duché, who had been obliged to take refuge in England after urging General Washington to give up the struggle against the British. Best known of all was Billings' CHESTER, which was the war hymn of the American soldiers.

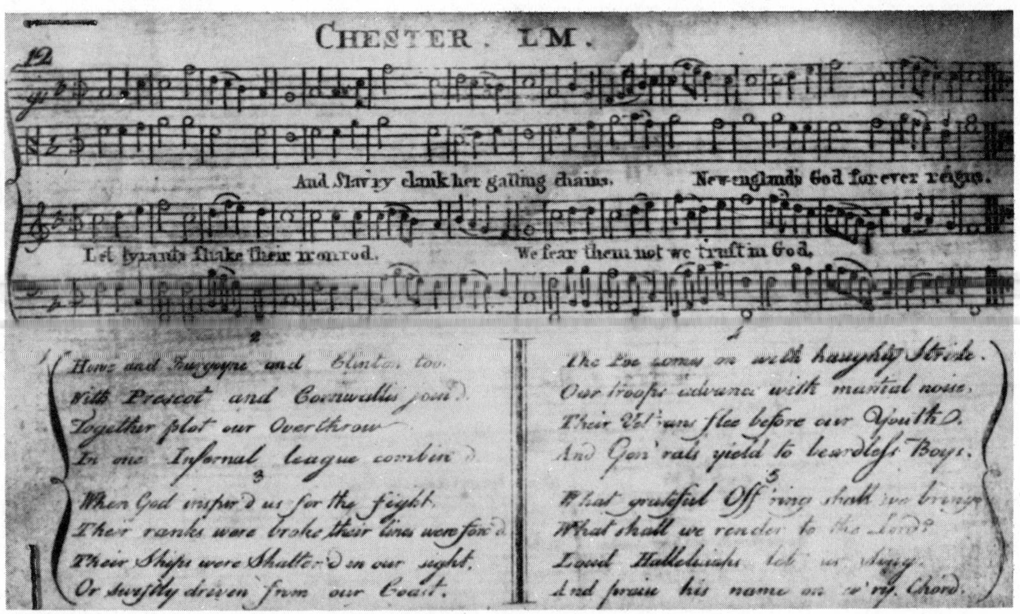
CHESTER. L.M.
And Slav'ry clank her galling chains.
New-england's God for ever reigns.
Let tyrants shake their iron rod.
We fear them not we trust in God.
Howe and Burgoyne and Clinton too
With Prescot and Cornwallis join'd
Together plot our Overthrow
In one Infernal league combin'd
When God inspir'd us for the fight
Their ranks were broke their lines were forc'd
Their Ships were Shatter'd in our sight,
Or swiftly driven from our Coast.
The Foe comes on with haughty Stride.
Our troops advance with martial noise,
Their Vet'rans flee before our Youth.
And Gen'rals yield to beardless Boys.
What grateful Off'ring shall we bring
What shall we render to the Lord?
Loud Hallelujahs let us sing,
And praise his name on ev'ry Chord.

The American Revolutionary War hymn tune

O Heaven Indulge

St. 1,2,5,6,9

Stephen Tilden, 1756

Psalm 34 8.8.8.6.D

Frost 383

Henry Lawes, 1638

1. O heaven in - dulge my fee - ble muse, Teach her what num - bers for to choose, And
2. Who made our sol - diers men of might, And taught their fin - gers how to fight, And

then my soul shall ne'er re - fuse Tri - um - phant - ly to sing Un - to that
how to aim their shafts a - right In the de - ci - sive hour. Through Him we

great and heaven - ly power, Who saved us in a gloom - y hour, When
have trod down our foe, Who all a - round en - vironed us so, And

our dire foes meant to de - vour, 'Twas heaven's e - ter - nal King.
sought our fa - tal ov - er - throw: Bless the de - liv - ering power.

3. New England's sons and daughters sing
   Triumph unto your heavenly King,
   Who did such great salvation bring
   In such a needy hour.
   Not all created powers can trace
   His glories through unbounded space,
   Nor seraph's eye behold his face
   Nor half describe his power.

4. Of old, when he was Israel's God,
   He clave the red Arabian flood,
   The watery walls like castles stood
   'Till Israel reached the land;
   But fell with most tremendous force
   On Pharoah's riders and his horse,
   'Til they were dashed, and drowned, and lost,
   And cast upon the sands.

5. He's still the same almighty God,
   He brought our fathers o'er the flood
   And scattered all their foes abroad,
   Gave them this wilderness.
   His tender mercies we must own,
   Who heard us when we made our moan;
   O might we live to him alone,
   And nevermore transgress.

To Thee the Tuneful Anthem Soars
(New England Hymn)

America 8.8.8.D.

St. 1-3

Mather Byles, 1770

William Billings, 1770

Tune in tenor
1. To Thee the tune - ful an - them soars,
2. See! how the flocks of Je - sus rise!

To Thee, our fa - thers' God, and ours; This wil - der -
See! how the face of par - a - dise Blooms through the

ness we chose our seat; To rights se - cured by
thick - ets of the wild! Here lib - er - ty e -

e - qual laws, From per - se - cu - tion's i - ron
rects her throne; Here plen - ty pours her treas - ures

claws, We here— have sought— our— calm— re - treat.
down; Peace smiles,— as heaven - ly— cher - ubs mild.

3. Lord, guard thy favors; Lord, extend
Where farther western suns descend;
Nor southern seas the blessings bound,
'Till freedom lift her cheerful head,
'Till pure religion onward spread,
And beaming, wrap the globe around.

WHY SHOULD VAIN MORTALS TREMBLE — BUNKER HILL 11.11.11.5.

St. 1-3, 8, 10, 13, 15

Nathaniel Niles, 1775 — Andrew Law, 1781

Tune in tenor

1. Why should vain mor - tals trem - ble at the sight of
2. Death will in - vade us by the means ap - point - ed,

Death and de - struc - tion in the field of bat - tle; Where blood and
And we must all bow to the King of Ter - rors; Nor am I

car - nage, Where blood and car - nage clothe the ground in
anx - ious, Nor am I anx - ious, if I am pre -

crim - son, Sound - ing with death - groans?
par - èd What shape he comes in.

1. 2.

3. Infinite goodness teaches us submission;
Bids us be quiet under all his dealings,
Never repining, but forever praising
God our Creator.

4. Now, Mars, I dare thee, clad in smoky pillars,
Bursting from bomb-shells, roaring from the cannon,
Rattling in grape-shot, like a storm of hailstones,
Torturing aether!

5. While all their hearts quick palpitate for havoc,
Let slip your bloodhounds, named the British lions,
Dauntless as death stares, nimble as the whirlwind,
Dreadful as demons!

6. Still shall the banner of the King of Heaven
Never advance where I'm afraid to follow,
While that precedes me with an open bosom,
War, I defy thee.

7. Life, for my country and the cause of freedom,
Is but a trifle for a worm to part with;
And if preserved in so great a contest,
Life is redoubled.

A Minute Man

Behold with Joy
St. 1, 2, 4, 6, 7
Elhanan Winchester, 1776

Paris L.M.
William Billings, 1781

Tune in tenor
1. Be - hold with joy the peace - ful state Of peo - ple,
2. Hap - py the land, whose rul - ers are Chose by the
where Je - ho - vah reigns, Whose wis - dom, power, and
peo - ple's voice a - lone; For such will take a
good - ness great, Their glo - rious free - dom still main - tain.
spe - cial care To save a coun - try of their own.

3. Hail happy place where freedom stands,
And liberty erects its throne;
Where fraud, and cruel slavery's bands,
And tyranny are never known.

4. Where none each other's peace annoys,
Where conscience never is oppressed;
Where each free liberty enjoys,
This is the land which God hath blessed.

5. In this free state we would rejoice,
And dwell forevermore in peace;
And praise our God with cheerful voice,
Who makes our thrall and bondage cease.

LET TYRANTS SHAKE THEIR IRON ROD

CHESTER L.M.

St. 1, 3-5

William Billings: St. 1, 1770; st. 2-4, 1778

William Billings, 1770

Tune in tenor
1. Let ty - rants shake their i - ron rod,
2. When God in - spired us for the fight
And slav - ery clank her gall - ing chains.
Their ranks were broke, their lines were forced;
We fear them not; we trust in God;
Their ships were shat - tered in our sight
New Eng - land's God for - ev - er reigns.
Or swift - ly driv - en from our coast.

3. The foe comes on with haughty stride;
Our troops advance with martial noise.
Their veterans flee before our youth,
And generals yield to beardless boys.

4. What grateful offerings shall we bring?
What shall we render to the Lord?
Loud halleluiahs let us sing,
And praise his name on every chord.

As Down a Lone Valley — Murillo's Lesson 11.11.11.11.D.

St. 1, 2

Timothy Dwight, bet. 1777 and 1783 — Morelli, 1820

Tune in tenor
1. As___ down a lone val - ley with ce - dars o'er-spread,_ From___
The___ gloom from the face___ of fair heav - en re - tired___ The___

war's___ dread con - fu - sion I pen - sive - ly strayed,
winds___ hushed their mur - murs, the thun - ders ex - pired; Per -

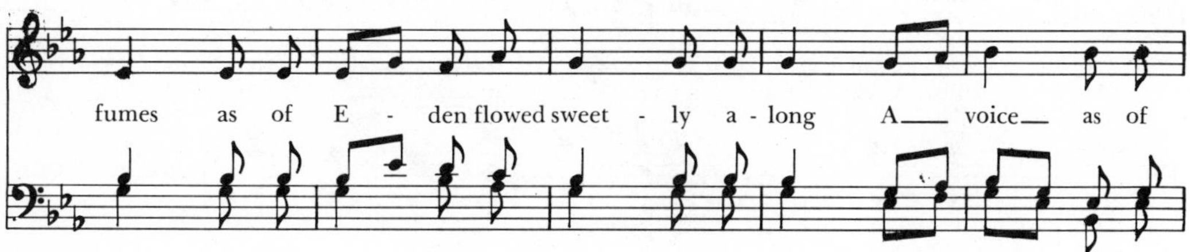
fumes as of E - den flowed sweet - ly a - long A___ voice___ as of

an - gels, en - chant - ing - ly sung,___ A___ voice___ as of an - gels en -

chant - ing - ly sung, Co - lum - bia, Co - lum - bia, to glo - ry a -

rise, The queen of the world and the child of the skies.

2. Fair science her gate to thy sons shall unbar,
And the east see thy morn hide the beams of her star.
New bards and new sages unrivalled shall soar
To fame unextinguished, when time is no more
To the last refuge of virtue designed,
Shall fly from all nations, the best of mankind,
Shall fly from all nations, the best of mankind;
To Jesus, the author of nations, will sing,
There grateful to heaven, with transport shall bring.

Denominational Hymns

ISAAC WATTS'S *Hymns and Spiritual Songs* had appeared in 1707 before his psalter. Copies of the hymns found their way to the New World. In 1711 Cotton Mather made an entry in his diary expressing delight in the copy which Watts had sent him. The first American edition (Boston, 1739) was followed by editions in Philadelphia (1742) and New York (1752). These hymns were welcomed, imitated, and used for private devotions by members of Protestant denominations in America. They were sung in churches only as they found their way into the supplements containing hymns which were added to the psalter. They became part of our common heritage and certain of them came to be associated with particular American tunes. Such were "Broad Is the Road" to Daniel Reed's WINDHAM and "Why Do We Mourn Departing Friends" to Timothy Swan's CHINA. The latter was New England's funeral hymn for generations.

Among the early Baptist hymn writers was Henry Alline, active here and in Nova Scotia, whose *Choice Hymns and Spiritual Songs* was published in 1786. Samuel Holyoke, who published his *Harmonia Americana* in 1791, included ten of Alline's hymns to his own tunes (see "Hard Heart of Mine," and "Turn, Turn, Unhappy Soul, Return"). "Amazing Sight, the Saviour Stands" was later included in a collection widely used for revival meetings, the *Village Hymns* of Asahel Nettleton (1824).

Thomas Baldwin was remembered by one hymn, "From Whence Doth This Union Arise." It was set by at least two New England composers, Samuel Holyoke and the Vermonter Jeremiah Ingalls. In the South it has been associated with a tune by Billings known there as UNION but which Billings himself called SAVANNAH. Parts of a long narrative poem on the Last Judgment by the Baptist John Peck attracted the attention both of Billings (see his SUDBURY and WEST SUDBURY) and of Elisha West. The *Divine Hymns or Spiritual Songs* by Joshua Smith and others was a favorite book among the Baptists. Many of these hymns were set to music by Jeremiah Ingalls.

John Aitken's *A Compilation of the Litanies, Vesper Hymns, and Anthems as sung in the Catholic Church* (Philadelphia, 1787) is important as the first publication of its kind in North America. The SALVE REGINA ("Hail to the Queen") is included in this volume as a hymn setting which was used in Catholic churches here during the

eighteenth century. (This hymn will be found in the seventeenth-century section, since the text reproduced in Aitken was first published in 1685).

Among the Congregationalist contributions, a New Year's hymn for the new century, "Once More Our God Vouchsafe To Shine," is by the diarist Samuel Sewall. Benjamin Coleman, an admirer of Isaac Watts, adds "God of My Life." In his *Agricola* (Boston, 1727), Cotton Mather draws religious lessons from the operations of the farmers' year. From this come "My Heart How Very Hard It's Grown" and "When the Seed of Thy Word." The witty and erudite Mather Byles wrote hymns which appear in the supplement to the edition of Tate and Brady used in his congregation as well as religious verse included in his *Poems on Several Occasions.* Thomas Prince, whose revision of the *Bay Psalm Book* has already been noted, also wrote the hymn "With Christ and All His Shining Train." "Now Let Our Hearts Their Glory Wake" with the subtitle "Settling in a New Habitation" was written by Elizabeth Scott, an Englishwoman, who was to make the long voyage to America as the wife of Elisha Williams, the former rector of Yale College.

Only at the very end of the century did the *Hartford Selection* appear. The preface refers to "the happy revival of religion in many towns in New England" and speaks of hymns suited "to the use of Christians in their closets, families, and private religious meetings." Here appeared hymns by Nathan Strong and Joseph Steward.

Although the psalter of Tate and Brady was used for congregational singing in Episcopal churches, their prayer book permitted the singing of hymns "if set forth by competent authority." Collections of hymns published within the century included those by William Duke (1790) and Andrew Fowler (1798). *A Selection of Psalms with Occasional Hymns* (Charlestown, 1792) included "Arise, My Soul, with Rapture Rise!" by Samuel J. Smith. Thomas Cradock was a Maryland clergyman whose "Ye Scattered Nations" was translated from the Latin of Buchanan. The two hymns by Jacob Duché were written when he was chaplain of an English orphan asylum after he had been obliged to leave Philadelphia because of his political views. Francis Hopkinson, a signer of the Declaration of Independence, was also poet, organist, and composer. Peter Valton, Daniel Purcell, and Jervis Stevens were musicians living in Charlestown, South Carolina. Their compositions were in English style as was that of Raynor Taylor, born in England but long an organist in Philadelphia. Benjamin Carr wrote music both for the Catholic service (see his setting of "Dies Irae") and that of the Episcopal church (see his EROICA).

The Presbyterian divine Samuel Davies was notable as a hymn writer. "Lord, I am Thine" was frequently sung by American congregations. Another early Presbyterian preacher who was active in founding the Indian school, which became Dartmouth College, was Samson Occom, a Mohican Indian, whose name is kept in mind in Hanover by Occom Pond. Occom compiled a hymnbook and is remembered for one hymn of a warning type, "Waked by the Gospel's Powerful Sound." This is the more interesting since it was associated with the tune GANGES by the American composer Chandler—a tune which was originally intended for a secular song.

Among the Universalists in this country, the earliest hymn writers were John Murray, whose first hymns were published in 1782, Silas Ballou, whose collection appeared in 1785, and George Richards, whose *Psalms, Hymns, and Spiritual Songs* appeared in 1792. Richards' "Th'Almighty Spake and Gabriel Sped" received two American settings, of which we have chosen Holden's ABERDEEN.

Awake My Soul, Betimes Awake — St. Martin's C.M.

St. 1-5

Isaac Chanler, 1745 — William Tans'ur, 1755

Tune in tenor
1. A - wake my soul, be - times a - wake,
2. To him lift up thy voice of praise

Lift up thy - self on high; Beg of thy God for
And well - tuned heart to sing A morn - ing song in

Je - sus' sake To hear thy morn - ing cry.
sa - cred lays; Thy cheer - ful trib - ute bring.

3. I laid me down and sweetly slept
In safety from all harm;
By Israel's Keeper I was kept,
Safeguarded by his arm.

4. My blessed Lord, still thou dost make
My mornings to rejoice;
Thy evening blessings I partake
And praise with joyful voice.

5. O may the dawnings of this day
New mercies usher in;
Grant me thy presence, Lord, I pray,
And keep me from all sin.

THRICE WELCOME FIRST AND BEST OF DAYS — ALL SAINTS L.M.

St. 1-4, 6, 7

Isaac Chanler, 1745 — William Knapp, 1760

Tune in tenor

1. Thrice wel - come first and best of days;
2. God's Sab - bath my de - light I'll call

Un - to__ my soul__ thy morn - ing rays
Of oth - er days__ the best__ of all;

Re - splend - ent shines and__ warms my breast;
From world - ly la - bor__ I'll ab - stain,

O 'tis__ a__ day of ho - ly rest.
And serve__ my__ God with might__ and main.

3. All earthly cares I'll bid stand by,
Whilst to my God I do draw nigh;
My tongue shall sing his praises great;
With joy I'll worship at his seat.

4. Unto his sacred courts I'll go,
That I his holy will may know;
O may my Jesus meet me there
And say, "Dear soul be of good cheer."

5. Dear Jesus, when wilt thou remove
My soul unto thy courts above,
That I a Sabbath then may keep
Quite free from slumber and from sleep?

6. Haste, my dear Lord, and come away;
On eagles wings make no delay,
And fetch my longing soul on high,
That I may sing eternally.

Jesus, Master, O Discover | Helmsley 8.7.8.7 with chorus

St. 1, 2, 5, 6

Anon., before 1770 | Thomas Olivers, 1765

Tune in middle part
1. Je - sus,_ Mas - ter,_ O___ dis - cov - er Pleas - ure in us, now_ we_ stand___
2. Make this_ stream,_ like_ Jor - dan,_ bless - ēd. Lep - rous Naa - mans en - ter_ in.___
On this_ bank of Schuyl - kill_ Riv - er, To o - bey thy great_ com - mand.___
Rise, saith_ Je - sus, be___ bap - tiz - ēd, And you wash a - way_ your_ sin.___
Chorus
Pleas - ure_ in us, pleas - ure_ in__ us, pleas - ure_ in__ us, To o - bey thy great com - mand.
Be_ bap - tiz - ēd, be_ bap - tiz - ēd, be_ bap - tiz - ēd, And you_ wash a - way your sin.

3. Help us, thou baptizēd Jesus!
What we vowēd to fulfill.
Of our fears of failing ease us,
Form and mould us to thy will.
Chorus
Help us Jesus, help us Jesus, help us Jesus,
What we vowēd to fulfill.

4. Hence we go our way rejoicing
Conscious of our pleasing God,
Following Jesus still proposing
In the paths his feet have trod.
Chorus
Go rejoicing, go rejoicing, go rejoicing,
Conscious of our pleasing God.

HERE IS A SONG
(A Poem on Death)

St. 1, 2, 8, 9, 14, 15

John Peck, 1773

WEST SUDBURY C.M.D.

William Billings, 1794

Tune in tenor

1. Here is a song which doth_ be - long_ To_ all the hu - man race, Con -

cern - ing death, who steals the breath, And blasts_ the_ come - ly face.

2. Come lis - ten all un - to the call Which I do make_ to - day; For

And_ pass from hence_ a - way,_

And pass from hence a - way, and pass from

you must die as well_ as_ I,_ And_ pass_

And pass from_ hence a - way, and pass from_

from hence a - 1.way. 2. way.
hence, from hence a - way. way.
from hence a - way. way.
hence, from hence a - way. way.

3. The princes high and beggars die,
   And mingle with the dust,
   The rich and brave, the Negro slave,
   The wicked and the just.

4. Come let us hark, and now remark
   The mortal's dying day;
   Behold how death doth stop the breath,
   And change the flesh to clay.

5. And when the sound does echo round,
   The living mortals must
   Prepare a bed to lodge the dead,
   And cover it with dust.

6. Here in this place the human face
   Deep in oblivion lies,
   Till Christ on high shall rend the sky,
   And bid the dead arise.

What If the Saint Must Die
(A Poem on the Resurrection)

Sudbury S.M.D.

St. 1, 2, 8, 9, 14, 15

John Peck, 1773

William Billings, 1794

Tune in tenor

1. What if the saint must die And lodge a - mong the
3. The res - ur - rec - tion day Shall crown the saints with

tombs, He need not mourn, he shall re - turn, Re -
joy, When Christ shall come to fetch them home And

joic - ing as he comes.
all their griefs de - stroy.

2. Though death shall hold him down, With bands and might - y
4. Now will they sing for joy, When they in beau - ty

bars,
Yet he shall rise a - bove the skies And
rise!
Their songs a - round the plan - ets sound. As

1.
2.
sing a - bove the stars.
they as - cend the skies.

5. Eternal joy indeed
With them is now begun.
They walk in white, and shine more bright
Than the meridion sun.

6. Behold the blessèd Lamb
Their songs shall ever sound.
The angels join, and all combine
To spread their anthems round.

From Whence Doth This Union Arise? Savannah L.M.

St. 1-3, 6

Thomas Baldwin, writ. c.1780 William Billings, 1778

Tune in tenor
1. From whence doth this un - ion a - rise, That
2. It can - not in E - den be found, Nor
ha - tred is con - quered by love?
yet in a Par - a - dise lost;
It fast - ens our
It grows on Im -
souls with such ties,
man - u - el's ground,
That dis - tance and time can't re - move.
And Je - sus' dear blood it did cost.

3. My friends once so dear unto me,
Our souls so united in love;
Where Jesus is gone we shall be,
In yonder blest mansions above.

4. With Jesus we ever shall reign,
And all his bright glories shall see;
We'll sing Alleluia, Amen!
Amen! even so let it be.

Amazing Sight! The Saviour Stands — Newmark C.M.

St. 1-4

Henry Alline, 1785 — Amos Bull, 1795

Tune in tenor
1. A - maz - ing___ sight! the Sav - iour stands,
2. "Be - hold!" he___ saith, "I bleed___ and die

And___ knocks at___ ev - ery door; Ten thou - sand bless - ings
To___ bring you___ to my rest; Hear, sin - ners! while I'm

in his hands, To sat - is - fy the___ poor.
pass - ing by, And be___ for - ev - er___ blessed."

3. "Will you despise my bleeding love,
And choose the way to hell?
Or, in the glorious realms above,
With me, forever dwell?"

4. "Say, will you hear my gracious voice,
And have your sins forgiven?
Or will you make that wretched choice,
And bar yourselves from heaven?"

Hard Heart of Mine — Sunbury C.M.

St. 1, 2, 4-6

Henry Alline, 1785 — Samuel Holyoke, 1791

Tune in tenor
1. Hard heart of mine, O that the Lord Would
2. I hear the heaven - ly pil - grims tell Their

this hard heart sub - due! O come thou blest life -
sins are all for - given; And while on earth their

giv - ing word, And form my soul a - new.
bod - ies dwell, Their souls en - joy a heaven.

3. The Christians sing redeeming love,
And talk of joys divine;
And soon they say in realms above,
In glory they shall shine.

4. But, ah! 'tis all an unknown tongue,
I never knew that love;
I cannot sing that heavenly song,
Nor tell of joys above.

5. I want, O God, I know not what!
I want what saints enjoy;
O let their portion be my lot,
Their work be my employ.

NOW BEHOLD THE SAVIOUR PLEADING — PLEADING SAVIOUR 8.7.8.7.D.

St. 1-4

John Leland, 1791 — William Hauser, arr. 1878

1. Now be - hold the_ Sav - iour plead - ing At the_ sin - ner's_ bolt - ed heart;
Now in_heaven he's_ in - ter - ced - ing, Un - der - tak - ing_ sin - ner's part.
2. Sin - ners,_ hear your_ God and Sav - iour; Hear his_ gra - cious_ voice to - day.
Turn from_ all your_ vain be - hav - ior, Oh! re - pent, and_ turn, and pray.
Sin - ner_ can you hate the_ Sav - iour? Will you_ thrust him from your_ arms?
Oh! be_ wise, be - fore you_ lan - guish On the_ bed of dy - ing_ strife;
Once he_ died for_ your be - hav - ior, Now he_ calls you_ to his arms.
End - less_ joy, or_ dread - ful an - guish, Hangs on_ the e - vents of life.

3. Now he's waiting to be gracious;
Now he stands and looks on thee:
See what kindness, love, and pity,
Shine around on you and me!
Open now your hearts before him;
Bid the Saviour welcome in;
Now receive him; Oh, adore him;
Take a full discharge from sin.

4. Come, for all things now are ready;
Yet there's room for many more:
O ye blind, ye lame, and needy,
Come to wisdom's boundless store.
Sinner, wilt reject the Saviour?
Wilt thou thrust him from thy arms?
Once he died for thy behavior,
Now he calls thee to his arms.

TURN, TURN, UNHAPPY SOULS, RETURN

CYRENE C.M.

Henry Alline, 1791

Samuel Holyoke, 1791

Tune in tenor
Turn, turn, un - hap - py souls, re - turn,
Ac - cept e - ter - nal peace; Why will you at the
Sav - iour spurn, Who of fers you his grace?

O Could I Find from Day to Day — Bethel C.M.

St. 1, 2, 3 (altered), 4

Benjamin Cleavland, 1792 — Hibbard, 1800

Tune in tenor
1. O could I find from day to day A near - ness to my God;
Then should my hours glide
Then should my hours glide swift a -
Then should my hours glide swift a - way And
should my hours glide swift a - way And
swift a - way, Then should my hours glide swift a - way And
way Then should my hours glide swift a - way And
lean
lean up on his word word
lean
1.
2.

2. Lord, I desire with thee to live,
Anew from day to day;
In joys the world can never give
Nor ever take away.

3. O Jesus, come and rule my heart
And make me wholly thine,
That I may never more depart,
Nor grieve thy love divine.

4. Thus, till my last expiring breath,
Thy goodness I'll adore;
And when my flesh dissolves in death
My soul shall love thee more.

THE DAY IS PAST AND GONE — EVENING SHADE S.M.

St. 1-5

John Leland, 1792 — Stephen Jenks, 1805

Tune in tenor
1. The day is past and gone The
eve - ning shades ap - pear;
O may I ev - er
O may I ev - er keep in mind,
may I ev - er keep in mind, O may I ev - er
keep in mind, O may I ev - er
O may I ev - er
keep in mind, The night of death draws 1. near. 2. near.
keep in mind, The night of death draws near. near.
keep in mind, The night of death draws near. near.

2. I lay my garments by,
   Upon my bed to rest;
   So death will soon remove me hence,
   So death will soon remove me hence,
   And leave my soul undressed.

3. Lord, keep me safe this night,
   Secure from all my fears;
   May angels guard me while I sleep,
   May angels guard me while I sleep,
   Till morning light appears.

4. And when I early rise,
   To view th'unwearied sun,
   May I set out to win the prize,
   May I set out to win the prize,
   And after glory run.

5. And when my days are past,
   And I from time remove,
   Lord, may I in thy bosom rest,
   Lord, may I in thy bosom rest,
   The bosom of thy love

Once More, Our God, Vouchsafe to Shine!
St. 1-3, 6
Samuel Sewall, writ. 1700

Veni Creator L.M.
Frost 197 Zahn 367
John Playford, arr. 1671

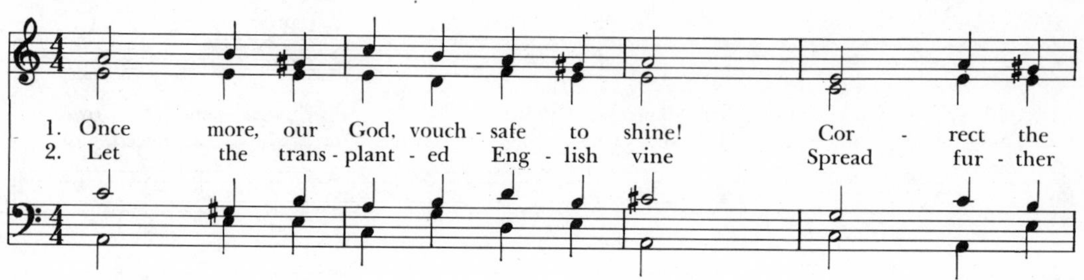
1. Once more, our God, vouch - safe to shine! Cor - rect the
2. Let the trans - plant - ed Eng - lish vine Spread fur - ther

cold - ness of our clime; Make haste with thy im - par - tial
still, still call it thine; Prune it with skill, for yield it

light And ter - mi - nate this long dark night.
can More fruit to Thee the Hus - band - man.

3. Give the poor Indians eyes to see
The Light of Life, and set them free;
That they religion may profess,
Denying all ungodliness!

4. So false religions shall decay,
And darkness fly before bright day;
So men shall God in Christ adore,
And worship idols vain no more.

God of My Life! — Standish C.M.

St. 1-3, 6

Benjamin Colman, 1711 — Version from John Tufts, 1726

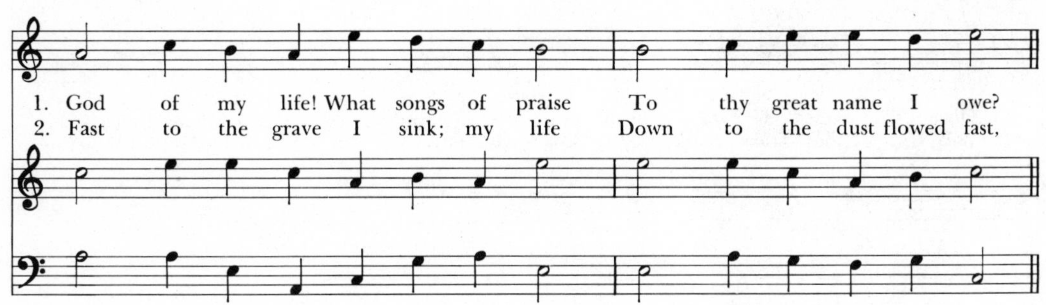
1. God of my life! What songs of praise To thy great name I owe?
2. Fast to the grave I sink; my life Down to the dust flowed fast,

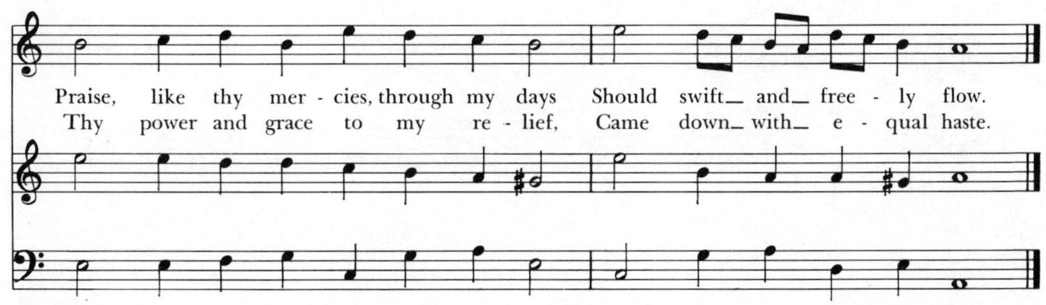
Praise, like thy mer - cies, through my days Should swift_ and_ free - ly flow.
Thy power and grace to my re - lief, Came down_ with_ e - qual haste.

3. Thy word which kills and makes alive
Rebuked the mortal foe;
My Saviour came, bid me revive,
Take up my bed and go.

4. Lord to thy praise I consecrate
My spared renewèd time;
Take hence my life an happier date
More heavenly, more sublime.

My Heart, How Very Hard It's Grown! Cambridge C.M.
(Singing at the Plough)

St. 1-5

Cotton Mather, 1727 John Playford, arr. 1677

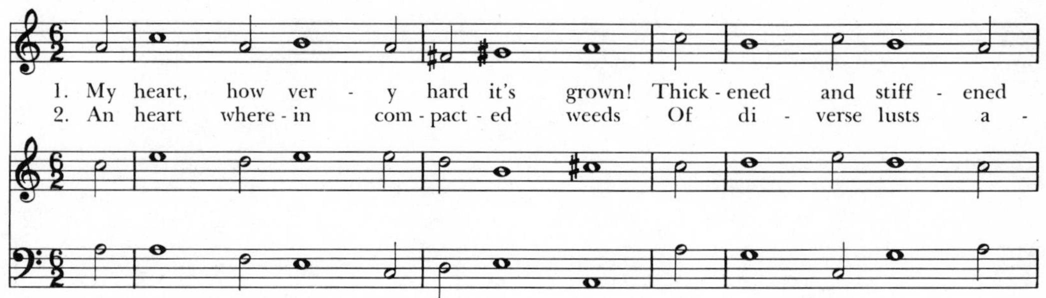
1. My heart, how ver - y hard it's grown! Thick - ened and stiff - ened
2. An heart where - in com - pact - ed weeds Of di - verse lusts a -

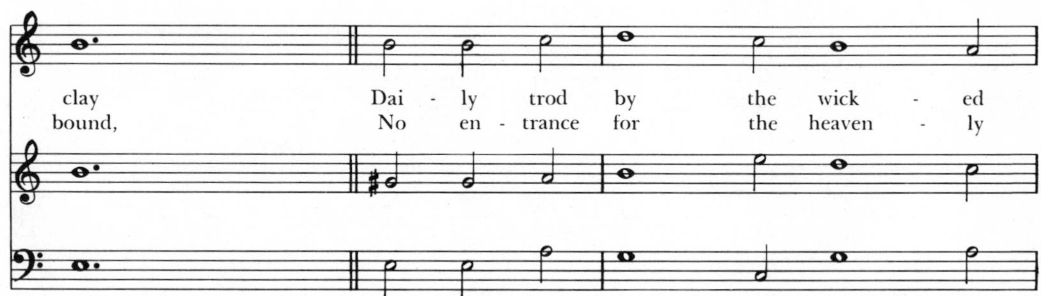
clay Dai - ly trod by the wick - ed
bound, No en - trance for the heaven - ly

one. Of sin the beat - en way.
seeds Fall - ing on such a ground!

3. O my almighty Saviour, come!
Thy word's a wondrous plow,
And let thy spirit drive it home;
This heart, oh break it so!

4. Lord, let my broken heart receive
Thy truth with faith and love;
May it a just reception give
To what falls from above.

5. Will my God plow upon a rock?
Change thou the soil, my Lord!
My heart, once by thy plowshare broke,
Will entertain thy word.

When the Seed of Thy Word Is Cast
(The Sower a Singer)

Psalm 41 C.M.D.

St. 1-4

Cotton Mather, 1727

John Playford, arr. 1677

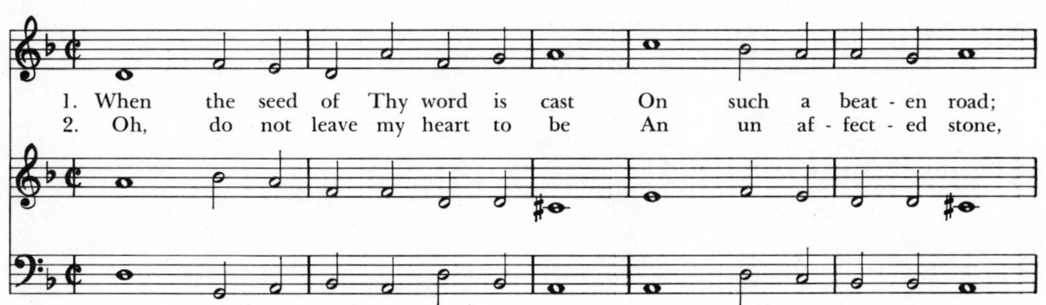
1. When the seed of Thy word is cast On such a beat - en road;
2. Oh, do not leave my heart to be An un af - fect - ed stone,

Let not the fruit of all be lost, Nor un - der foot be trod.
Where heav - en's eye no fruit will see, But what will soon be gone.

May't be no un - at - ten - tive heart, When there my les - sons fall;
Let there be found of pi - e - ty In me a root so deep

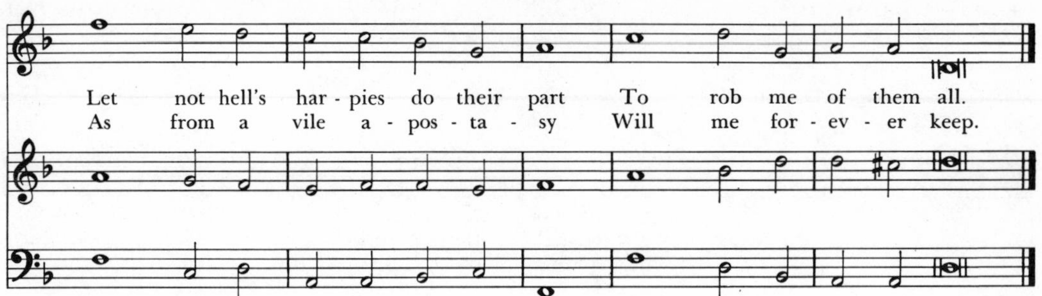
Let not hell's har - pies do their part To rob me of them all.
As from a vile a - pos - ta - sy Will me for - ev - er keep.

3. Lord, let not worldly lusts and cares
   Thy work in me annoy;
   Choke all good fruit, and prove the snares
   That shall my soul destroy.
   Ye cursed thorns I deprecate
   All your entanglements.
   My Saviour, let not these defeat
   Thy gospel's' kind intents.

4. O Glorious Christ of God, from whom
   Does all my fruit proceed;
   Let thy sweet influences come,
   And quicken thou the seed.
   With fruits make me a blessèd field,
   More precious things than gold;
   With fruits of thy good spirit filled,
   More than a hundred-fold.

GREAT GOD, THY WORKS
(Hymn at Sea)

ARNHEIM L.M.

St. 1-5

Mather Byles, writ. 1732, pub. 1744

Samuel Holyoke, 1791

Moderato
Tune in tenor
1. Great God, thy works our won - der
2. Thy power pro - duced this might - y

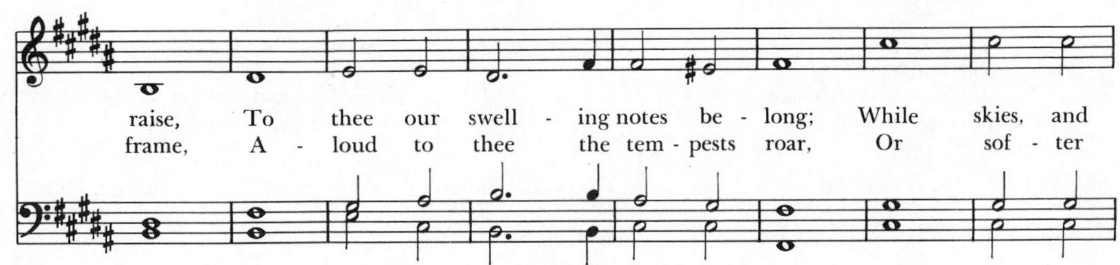
raise, To thee our swell - ing notes be - long; While skies, and
frame, A - loud to thee the tem - pests roar, Or sof - ter

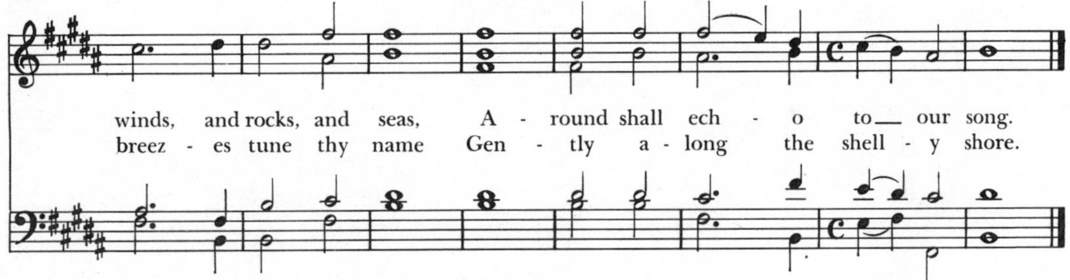
winds, and rocks, and seas, A - round shall ech - o to our song.
breez - es tune thy name Gen - tly a - long the shell - y shore.

3. 'Round thee the scaly nation roves,
Thy op'ning hands their joys bestow,
Through all the blushing coral groves,
Those silent, gay retreats below.

4. See the broad sun forsake the skies,
Glow on the waves, and downward slide!
Anon, heaven opens all its eyes,
And star-beams tremble o'er the tide.

5. Each various scene, or day or night,
Lord, points to thee our ravished soul;
Thy glories fix our whole delight,
So the touched needle courts the pole.

See How the Rising Sun
St. 1-3, 5-7
Elizabeth Scott, 1806

Sutton S.M.
Anon., 1812

Tune in middle part
1. See how the ris - ing sun Pur - sues his
2. Thus would my ris - ing soul Its heaven - ly

shin - ing way; And wide pro - claims his
par - ent sing; And to its great o -

tr
Mak - er's praise, With ev - ery bright - ening ray.
rig - i - nal, The hum - ble trib - ute bring.

3. Serene I laid me down
   Beneath his guardian care;
   I slept, and I awoke, and found
   My kind preserver near!

4. O how shall I repay
   The bounties of my God?
   This feeble spirit pants beneath
   The pleasing, painful load.

5. Dear Saviour, to thy cross
   I bring my sacrifice;
   By thee perfumed it shall ascend
   With fragrance to the skies.

6. My life I would anew
   Devote, O Lord, to thee;
   And in thy presence I would spend
   A long eternity.

Now Let Our Hearts Their Glory Wake
(Settling in a New Habitation)

Variety C.M.

St. 1-5

Elizabeth Scott, 1806

Stephen Jenks, 1800

Tune in tenor
1. Now let our hearts their glory wake, The sacred song to raise;

And ev - ery tune-ful
And every tune - ful power com - bine, To shout Je - ho - vah's praise,
And To
And ev - ery tune - ful power com - bine, To shout Je - ho - vah's

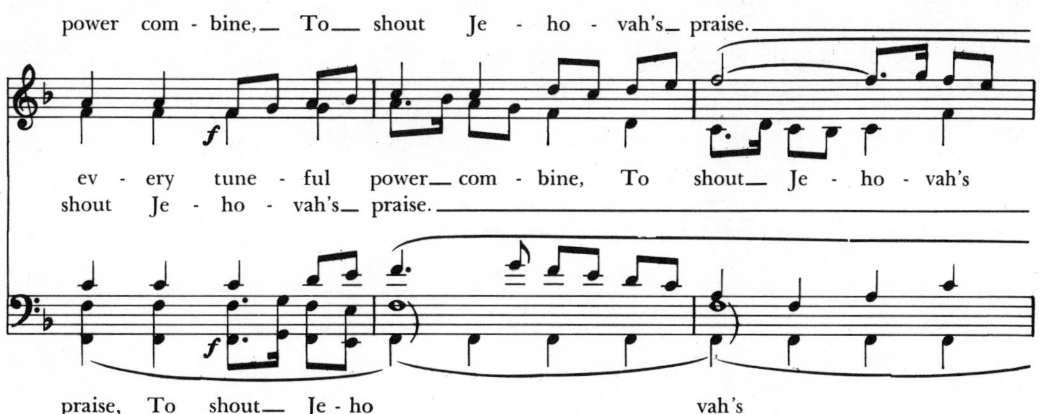
power com - bine, To shout Je - ho - vah's praise.
f
ev - ery tune - ful power com - bine, To shout Je - ho - vah's
shout Je - ho - vah's praise.
f
praise, To shout Je - ho vah's

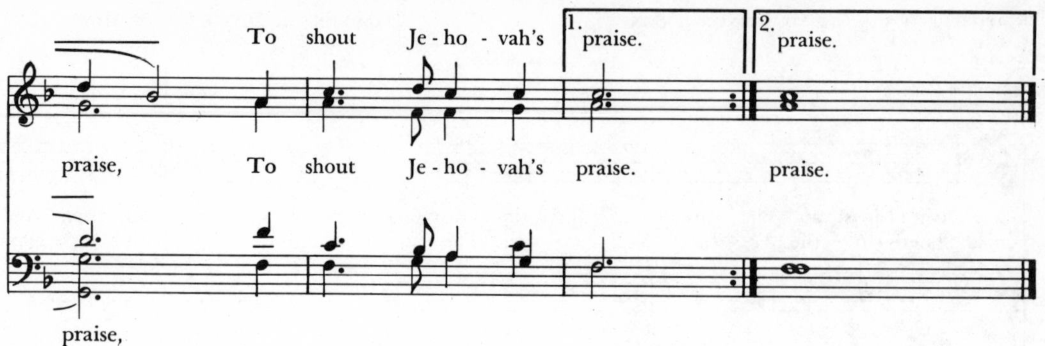
To shout Je - ho - vah's
1.
praise.
2.
praise.
praise,
To shout Je - ho - vah's praise.
praise.
praise,

2. To us a goodly heritage
His providence assigns,
And in a safe and pleasant place,
Marks out our happy lines.
And in a safe and pleasant place,
Marks out our happy lines.

3. Come, let us to his holy name
A grateful altar raise;
And be this habitation styled
The house of prayer and praise,
And be this habitation styled
The house of prayer and praise.

4. Here may his secret breathings fan
Devotion to a flame,
And faith and love and zeal inspire,
T'adorn the Christian name,
And faith and love and zeal inspire,
T'adorn the Christian name.

5. Thus with thy visits, smiles and grace,
May this abode be blest;
And here, O great Jehovah, fix
Thy pleasant, lasting rest.
And here, O great Jehovah, fix
Thy pleasant, lasting rest.

With Christ and All His Shining Train — Hymn on the Divine Use of Music L.M.

St. 1-3 — Frost 201

Thomas Prince, 1758 — John Playford, arr. 1677

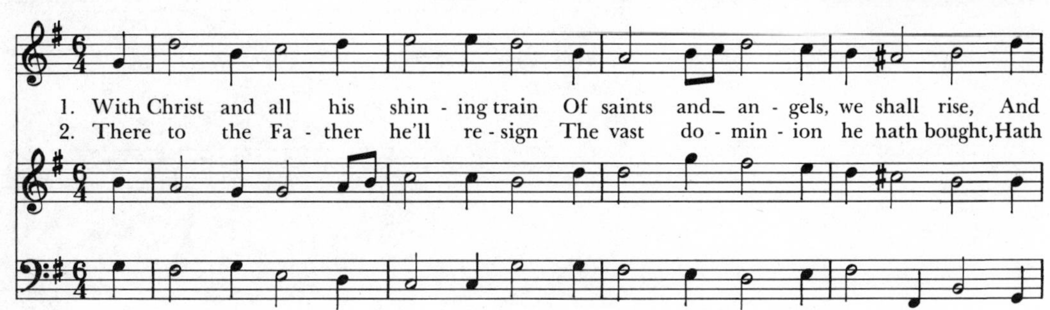
1. With Christ and all his shin - ing train Of saints and_ an - gels, we shall rise, And
2. There to the Fa - ther he'll re - sign The vast do - min - ion he hath bought, Hath

pass the glit - tering worlds a - round, While heaven wide o - pens to our eyes.
by his spir - it formed and ruled, And then to full pro - tec - tion brought.

3. There glorious services we'll do;
And he'll unveil his wond'rous ways,
His love and glories ever show;
And filled with joy, we'll ever praise.

Great God, How Frail a Thing Is Man — Thomas-Town C.M.D.

St. 1, 2

Mather Byles, 1744 — William Billings, 1781

Tune in tenor
1. Great God, how frail a thing is man, How swift his min - utes pass;

His age con - tracts with - in a_span,_He blooms_ and_dies_like grass.

2. And must my_mo - ments thus de - cline, And must I sink to death?

To thee my spir - it I re - sign, Thou mak - er_ of my_breath.

WHEN WILD CONFUSION WRECKS THE AIR
(The God of Tempest)

HACKNEY C.M.

St. 7, 8, 11, 14

Mather Byles, 1795

John Blow, c.1718?

Unison
1. When wild con - fu - sion wrecks the air
2. A - mid the hur - ri - cane I'll stand,
And tem - pests rend the skies,
And strike a tune - ful song,
Whilst blend - ed ru - in, clouds, and fire
My harp all trem - bling in my hand,
In harsh dis - or - der rise;
And all in - spired my tongue.

3. Let the earth totter on her base,
Clouds heaven's wide arch deform;
Blow, all ye winds, from every place,
And breath the final storm.

4. O Jesus, haste the glorious day
When thou shalt come in flame;
And burn the earth, and waste the sea,
And break all nature's frame.

5. Come quickly, blessèd hope, appear,
Bid thy swift chariot fly;
Let angels tell thy coming near,
And snatch me to the sky.

6. Around thy wheels, in the glad throng
I'd bear a joyful part;
All hallelujah on my tongue,
All rapture in my heart.

Our Kind Creator

Charity L.M.

St. 1, 3, 5, 6

Solomon Howe, 1799

Solomon Howe, 1799

Piano
Tune in tenor
1. Our kind Cre - a - tor formed our voice, To speak his praise in grate - ful joys; His saints on earth and saints a - bove, Con - cord - ant sing his bound - less love.
2. Mu - sic, with all its heaven - ly charms, In - vites us to our Sav - iour's arms; Where mil - lions par doned by his blood, In sweet - est praise a - dore their God.
* In original
† In original

3. When parents lead in sacred songs,
Children pursue with cheerful tongues;
'Till true harmonic chords excite
The whole to joy's sublime delight.

4. For heaven itself consists in praise,
Expressed the most delightful ways;
There, saints, in love's most rapturous flame,
In music, praise Messiah's name.

To Thee, O God — Bridgewater L.M.

St. 1-6

Abiel Holmes, 1796 — Lewis Edson, 1782

Tune in tenor

1. To thee, O God, I of - fer praise,___ Whose hand sus -

tained my in - fant_days,___ To thee, whose

To thee, whose kind pa - ter - nal

To thee, whose kind pa - ter - nal_ care My

To thee, whose kind pa -

kind pa - ter - nal care My child - hood saved from

care My child - hood saved from ev - ery snare. My

child - hood saved___ from ev - ery snare.

ter - nal care My child - hood saved from ev - ery snare.

ev - ery snare, My child - hood saved from ev - ery snare.

child - hood saved from ev - ery snare.

2. Thy hand my youthful steps upheld,
And threatening dangers oft repelled;
When I the years of manhood gained,
The guardian hand my strength sustained,
The guardian hand my strength sustained.

3. Thou didst my natal place prepare,
Where first I breathed the vital air;
By thee the best of parents given,
Early I learned the way to heaven,
Early I learned the way to heaven.

4. Amid the ills that life betide,
Thy hand hath all my wants supplied;
And oft in large profusion shed
Thy richest blessings on my head,
Thy richest blessings on my head.

5. What time I saw the cloud arise,
Darkening with death my cheerful skies,
The storm but followed thy command;
I saw, and owned, thy guiding hand,
I saw, and owned, thy guiding hand.

6. My God! through each succeeding day,
Sustain my steps, and guide my way;
And, when my evening hour shall come,
O may thy hand conduct me home!
O may thy hand conduct me home!

Who Here Can Cast His Eyes Abroad — Invitation L.M.

St. 1-5

Abiel Holmes, 1796 — Jacob Kimball, 1793

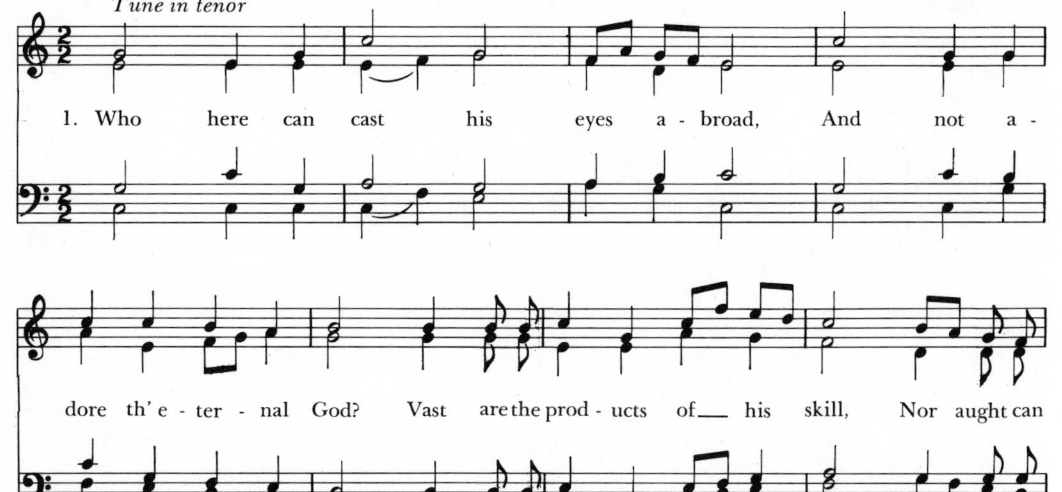
Tune in tenor
1. Who here can cast his eyes a - broad, And not a -
dore th' e - ter - nal God? Vast are the prod - ucts of his skill, Nor aught can

Vast are the
stay his sov - ereign will. Vast are the prod - ucts of his
Vast are the prod-ucts of his skill, Nor aught can

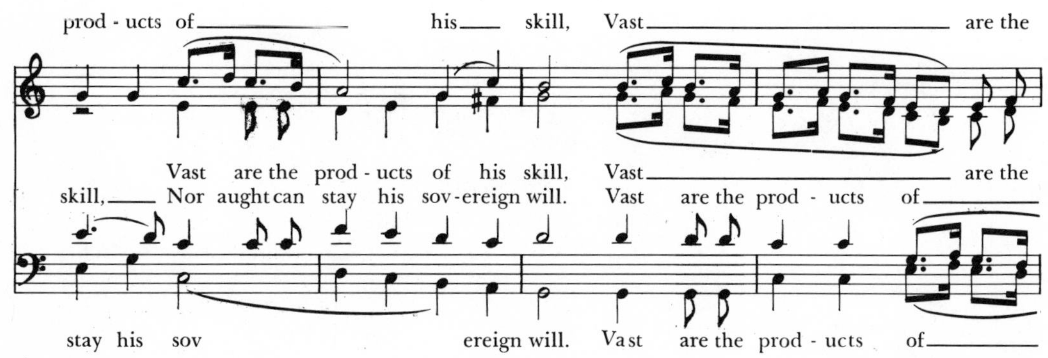
prod - ucts of his skill, Vast are the
Vast are the prod - ucts of his skill, Vast are the
skill, Nor aught can stay his sov-ereign will. Vast are the prod - ucts of
stay his sov ereign will. Vast are the prod - ucts of

prod-ucts_ of his skill, Nor aught can stay his sov - ereign_ will.
3
prod-ucts of his skill, Nor aught can stay his sov - ereign will.
his skill, Nor aught can stay his sov - ereign will.
his skill, Nor aught can stay his sov - ereign will.

2. What being framed those lofty skies?
   Whose fiat bade this ocean rise?
   Who fixed its spacious bounds, and said
   Here shall thy proudest waves be stayed?
   Who fixed its spacious bounds, and said
   Here shall thy proudest waves be stayed?

3. What hand omnipotent can bind
   The rage and fury of the wind?
   Whose sovereign word the storm can raise,
   Or quell the tumult of the seas?
   Whose sovereign word the storm can raise,
   Or quell the tumult of the seas?

4. Great God! thy power and matchless skill
   These great and wondrous works fulfill;
   The sea and skies thy night display,
   And winds and storms thy voice obey.
   The sea and skies thy might display,
   And winds and storms thy voice obey.

5. Here then accept my humble song,
   O thou, to whom all worlds belong!
   To thee my tuneful voice I raise,
   To thee I consecrate my praise.
   To thee my tuneful voice I raise,
   To thee I consecrate my praise.

God from His Throne with Piercing Eye — Russia L.M.

St. 1-6

Joseph Steward, 1799 — Daniel Read, 1793

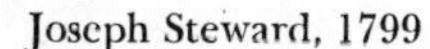
Tune in tenor

1. God from his throne with pierc - ing eye, Nak - ed does ev - ery

But
But nev - er till we
heart be - hold; But nev - er till_ we come to die,_ But
But nev - er till_ we come to die, But_ nev - er till we_

nev - er till we_ come to die To us will such a view un - fold.
come to die, To us will_such a view un - fold.
nev - er till_ we_ come to die,_ To us_will_such a_ view un - fold.
come to die, To us will such a view un - fold.

2. Should sin, in naked form, appear,
 Just as it rises in the heart,
 And others know and see it there,
 In every feeling, every thought:

3. The fire of hell must kindle soon,
 How envy and revenge would flame!
 One heart would urge another on,
 Till rage and vengeance want a name!

4. Sin in its nature would appear
 A living death to form a hell;
 The worst of miseries creatures fear,
 The worst of plagues the tongue can tell.

5. Unveiled and naked every heart
 Before the judgment seat must stand;
 Sin act no more a double part,
 But meet a death from its own hand.

6. The fiery lake must hotter grow,
 From the fierce clash of sinful souls;
 Each bosom, like a furnace, glows,
 Nor God the rage or fire control.

My Soul Would Fain Indulge a Hope — Aberford C.M.

St. 1-6

Joseph Steward, 1799 — G. K. Jackson, 1804

1. My soul___ would fain in - dulge___ a hope
2. That when___ I shall be - hold___ the Lamb,
To reach___ the heaven - ly shore; And when___ I drop___ this
Who once___ for sin___ was slain, But rose___ tri - um - phing
dy - ing flesh, That I___ shall sin___ no more.
o'er___ the grave, And on___ his throne___ doth reign.

3. I hope to hear and join the song
That saints and angels raise;
And while eternal ages roll,
To sing eternal praise.

4. But, oh, this dreadful heart of sin!
It may deceive me still;
And while I look for joys above,
May plunge me down to hell.

5. The scene must then forever close,
Probation at an end;
No gospel grace can reach me there,
No pardon there descend.

6. Come then, O blessēd Jesus, come,
To me thy spirit give;
Shine through a dark, benighted soul,
And bid a sinner live.

SWELL THE ANTHEM, RAISE THE SONG

ASCENSION 7.7.7.7.

St. 1-6

Nathan Strong, 1799

Jacob French, 1802

Tune in tenor

1. Swell the an - them, raise the song, Prais - es__ to our God be - long;
3. Lo! the trem - bling na - tions stand, Smote__ by__ thy a - veng - ing hand;

p Saints__ and an - gels join__ to sing, *f* Praise__ to__ heaven's Al - might - y King.
O'er__ their wide - ex - tend - ed plains, Aw - ful__ des - o - la - tion reigns.

2. Bless - ings from his lib - eral hand,____ Pour a - round this hap - py land;
4. Yet, to thee our joys as - cend,____ Thou hast been our heaven - ly friend;

Let____ our hearts____ be - neath his sway, *p* Hail the bright tri -
Guard - ed by____ thy__ might - y power Peace and free - dom

f
um - phant day. Hail the bright tri - um - phant day.
bless our shore, Peace and free - dom bless our shore.
f

5. Here beneath a virtuous sway,
Subjects cheerfully obey;
Here we feel no tyrant's rod,
Here we own and worship God.

6. Hark! The voice of nature sings
Praises to the King of kings;
Let us join the choral song,
And the heavenly notes prolong.

THE SUMMER HARVEST SPREADS THE FIELDS — STRATFIELD L.M.

St. 1-5

Nathan Strong, 1799 — Goff, 1793

Tune in tenor

1. The sum - mer har - vest spreads ___ the fields, Mark how the whiten - ing

Be - hold them to the

hills ___ are turned! Be - hold them to the reap - ers

Be -

Be - hold them to the reap - ers yield Be -

reap - ers yield; Be - hold them_ to the reap - ers yield;

hold them to the reap - ers yield; the reap - ers yield; The

yield; Be - hold them to the reap - ers yield;

hold them to the reap ers yield;

The wheat is saved, the tares are burned.

wheat is saved, the tares are burned. The wheat is saved, the tares are

The wheat is saved, the

The wheat is saved, the tares ___ are

The wheat is saved, the tares are
1. burned.
2. burned.
burned. The wheat is saved, the tares are burned. burned.
tares are burned. The wheat is saved, the tares are burned. burned.
burned. The wheat is saved, the tares are burned. burned.

2. Thus the great Judge with glory crowned,
Descends to reap the ripened earth!
Angelic guards attend him down,
The same who sang his humble birth.
Angelic guards attend him down,
The same who sang his humble birth.

3. In sounds of glory hear him speak,
"Go search around the flaming world;
Haste — call my saints to rise, and take
The seats from which their foes were hurled.
Haste — call my saints to rise, and take
The seats from which their foes were hurled.

4. Go, burn the chaff in endless fire,
In flames unquenched, consume each tare;
Sinners must feel my holy ire,
And sink in guilt — to deep despair.
Sinners must feel my holy ire,
And sink in guilt — to deep despair."

5. Thus ends the harvest of the earth,
Angels obey the awful voice;
They save the wheat, they burn the chaff;
All heaven approves the sovereign choice.
They save the wheat, they burn the chaff;
All heaven approves the sovereign choice.

Almighty Sovereign of the Skies! Psalm 97 L.M.

St. 1, 3-5, 8

Nathan Strong, 1799 William Tuckey, arr. 1761

Tune in tenor
1. Al - might - y Sov - ereign of the skies!
2. From thee our choic - est bless - ings flow,
To thee let songs of glad - ness rise;
Life, health, and strength thy hands be - stow;
Each grate - ful heart its trib - ute bring,
The dai - ly good, thy crea - tures share,
And ev - ery voice thy good - ness sing.
Springs from thy prov - i - den - tial care.

3. The rich profusion nature yields,
The harvest waving o'er the fields,
The cheering light, refreshing shower,
Are gifts from thy exhaustless store.

4. At thy command the vernal bloom
Revives the world from winter's gloom,
The summer's heat the fruit matures,
And autumn all her treasures pours.

5. Let every power of heart and tongue,
Unite to swell the grateful song;
While age and youth in chorus join
And praise the majesty divine.

What Glorious Vision — Song 12 10.10.10.10.

St. 1, 2, 7, 10, 11 — Frost 347

Thomas Cradock (?), writ. c.1759 — Anon., 1621

1. What glo - rious vi - sion breaks up - on my eyes?
2. Sure heaven now o - pens to my long - ing heart,
Colle 8va
What heaven - ly pros - pect charms my rap - tured mind?
And gives a fore - taste of those fu - ture joys,
What won - drous beau - ties sud - den round me rise
Which its high mon - arch will to all im - part,
Colle 8va
As if pate my
Who make their lives one grate - ful sac - ri - fice.

3. What rapture, O my soul! the melody
Of seraph and of cherub strikes my ears,
Amid the tuneful choir I seem to be,
And listen to the music of the spheres.

4. And does my God this place for me prepare?
And will these heavenly pleasures all be mine?
Shall I the glories of immortals share?
O blest beneficence of love divine!

5. Strive, O my soul, with all thy efforts strive,
To please that gracious being who provides
These bright rewards, to him then only live,
And scorn to fix thy views on aught beside.

Ye Scattered Nations — **Symphony** 10.10.10.10.D.

Ps. 66: 1-3

Thomas Cradock, trans. 1754 — Justin Morgan, 1798

Tune in tenor
1. Ye scat - tered na - tions, sing in tune - ful lays, In loft - iest

strains your great Cre - a - tor's praise; Sing, sing the hon - ors

of thy ho - ly name, Ex - tol his glo - ry, and his power pro-

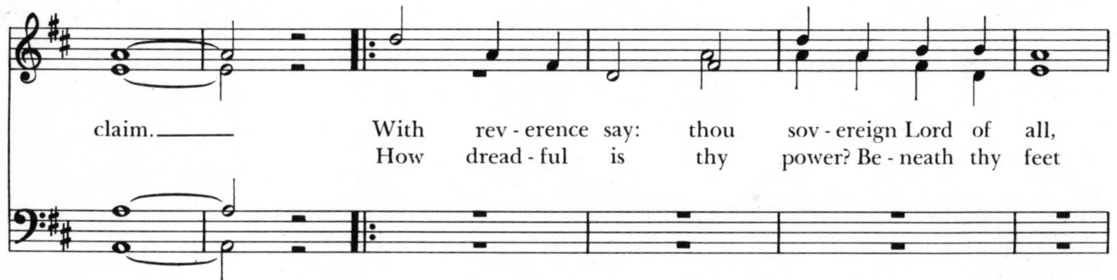

claim.
With rev - erence say: thou sov - ereign Lord of all,
How dread - ful is thy power? Be - neath thy feet

Who madst yon heavens and this ter - res - trial ball?
Crouch thy proud foes, and to thy rule sub - mit.

2. To thee the earth shall pious homage pay,
Sing to thy name, thy glorious name display.
Approach and hear the wonders of our God;
With his stupendous works the world he awed;
He drove the waters from their oozy bed,
And on firm ground his favored people led;
With joy they walked,their God their feet sustain;
With joy they viewed, as on a flowery plain.

3. O'er all, o'er all, he holds eternal sway,
His eyes the nations of the earth survey;
Hear this, ye wicked, and rebel no more,
Lest you too late your wretched pride deplore.
Approach, attend, who your creator fear,
To me his wondrous goodness I'll declare.
Gracious he heard when prostrate I implored;
(And be the God that hears our prayers adored.)

To Thee, Then, Let All Beings Bend — Eroica L.M.

Ps. 145, selected lines

Nathaniel Evans, 1772 — Benjamin Carr, 1820

Maestoso
Tromba

tr
Tutti

1. To Thee, then, let all be - ings bend, And shouts of joy the
2. Till all con - fess thy glo - rious fame, And trem - bling - ly a -

e - ther rend, And chief - ly let thy saints on high Laud the great sov - ereign
dore thy name; Thus ev - er shall thy reign en - dure In end - less maj - es -

of the sky.
ty se - cure.
Tromba

3. When trouble sinks us to the dust
To thee, for aid, O Lord, we trust,
'Tis thine to heal affliction's smart,
And raise from death the languid heart.

4. Bless then, my soul, his sacred name,
And let all nature join the theme;
All nature to its God shall cry,
Who lives through vast eternity.

CHILLED BY THE BLASTS OF ADVERSE FATE

HYMN ON THE EXCELLENCY OF THE BIBLE C.M.

St. 1-4

Jacob Duché, c.1785

Thomas Spence Duché, 1801

1. Chilled by the blasts of ad - verse fate, Op - pressed by sor - row's gloom, The sooth - ing voice of par - ent love All hushed with - in the tomb.
2. With - out us, want his vig - ils kept, With - in us, si - lent woe; Our in - fant minds in fear - ful thought Made ev - ery shade a foe.
6 6 [4 3]
6 4 [7] 6 7 ♯ 6
6 5 4 2 6 5 6 6 4 7

3. God's pitying eye our trouble saw,
And instantly, relief
Broke through the wintry clouds of woe
And scattered every grief.

4. Beneath his heavenly wings we find
A calm and safe retreat.
O then let every orphan breast
With grateful transport beat.

Great Lord of All, Whose Work of Love — Hymn for Whitsunday L.M.

St. 1, 2, 4-6

Jacob Duché, c.1785 — Thomas Spence Duché, 1801

1. Great Lord of all, whose work of love Cre - a - tion's bound - less realms dis - play, Help us to join the choirs a - bove, And hail thy prov - i - den - tial sway.
2. Stern death pro - nounced the dread de - cree, En - tailed on all of wom - an born, From sor - row set our par - ents free, But left us help - less and for - lorn.

3. Dark was the color of our fate
Till thy benignant mercy shown,
Redeemed us from our wretched state,
And made the fatherless thine own.

4. Our hopes revive, our fears are fled,
Our joyless days and nights are o'er.
Our mortal frames are clothed and fed,
Our minds informed with virtue's lore.

5. Blest guardian whose fraternal care
With bounteous hand our want supplies,
O may our ceaseless praise and prayer
To thy bright throne as incense rise.

Arise, My Soul! With Rapture Rise! — Hereford L.M.D.

St. 1-5

Samuel J. Smith, 1792 — Henry Purcell, 1809

1. A - rise, my soul! With rap - ture rise! And, filled with
3. But can it be that power di - vine Whose throne is
love and fear, a - dore The aw - ful Sov - ereign
light's un - bound - ed blaze, While count - less worlds and
of the skies, Whose mer - cy lends me one day more.
an - gels join To swell the glo - rious song of praise.
2. And may this day, in - dul - gent power! Not i - dly
4. Will deign to lend a fa - voring ear. When I, poor

pass, nor fruit - less be, But may each swift - ly
ab - ject mor - tal pray? Yes, bound - less good - ness!
6 5 6 6 6

fly - ing hour Ad - vance my soul more nigh to thee.
He will hear, Nor cast the mean - est wretch a - way.
7 6 5 6 6 6 6 8 7
4 3 4

5. Then let me serve thee all my days,
   And may my zeal with years increase.
   For pleasant, Lord, are all thy ways,
   And all thy paths are paths of peace.

Arise and See the Glorious Sun — Philadelphia C.M.

St. 1, 3, 7, 9-11

Francis Hopkinson, 1792 — Francis Hopkinson, 1816

(Organist is to play all notes in upper stave and the bass part.)

Soprano
1. A - rise and see the glo - rious sun Mount
2. How fresh the health - ful morn - ing air, What
Tenor
Bass

3
in the east - ern sky; See with what maj - es -
fra - grance breathes a - round! New lus - ter paints each

3
ty he comes, What splen - dor strikes the eye.
open - ing flow'r, New ver - dure clothes the ground.

3. The trees that shade its flowery banks
Are nourished by the flood,
Whilst from their branches songsters sweet
Re-echo through the wood.

4. Oh! Let us then with souls sincere
Adore that power divine;
Who makes that orb move thus complete,
Who makes His rays to shine.

5. Who causes every rising day
In beauty to return;
And bids the suns meridian height
With brighter glories burn.

6. Who morning, noon, and evening too,
Has with His blessing blest;
And kindly gives the nights still shades
For wearied man to rest.

At Length the Busy Day Is Done — St. Michael's L.M.

St. 1-4, 12

Francis Hopkinson, 1792 — Peter Valton, c.1770

1. At length the bus - y day is done, And yon bright orb, the glo - rious sun, Deep in the west re - clines his head, Where mis - ty cur - tains shroud his bed
2. Oh, God of hosts, with this day's close, How man - y sleep in death's re - pose? And with the sink - ing sun's de - cline, To their flee - ing souls re - sign.

3. Hark! 'Tis the tolling bell I hear,
And slow and dull it strikes mine ear;
E'en whilst I tune my pensive song,
The solemn funeral moves along.

4. He whom this night th' expecting tomb,
Shall wrap within the dreary gloom,
At yester-morn, devoid of care,
Up rose and breathed the healthful air.

5. Therefore, my soul, thy thoughts employ
O God, thy glory, wealth, and joy;
Virtue alone is stable here,
Nought but religion is sincere.

Awake, My Soul! In Grateful Songs — Hymn 6 C.M.

St. 1-3

Andrew Fowler, 1793 — John C. Bechler, c.1813

Con spirito
Unison
1. A - wake, my soul! in grate - ful songs, And all thy powers em - ploy; To
2. For us he left his Fa - ther's throne, And laid his glo - ries by; For

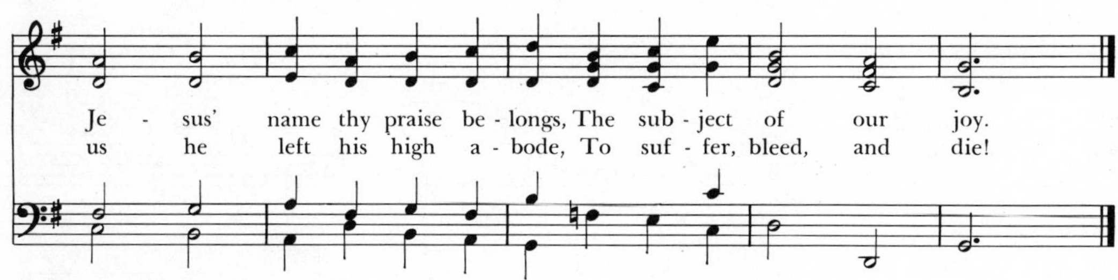
Je - sus' name thy praise be - longs, The sub - ject of our joy.
us he left his high a - bode, To suf - fer, bleed, and die!

3. Amazing love! Surprising grace!
   That Jesus thus should come
   To make us heirs of heavenly peace,
   And bring us wanderers home.

O Gracious Jesus, Blessēd Lord! — Church Street L.M.

St. 1-3

Andrew Fowler, 1793 — Jervis Henry Stevens, comp. 1783/84

1. O gra - cious Je - sus, bless - ēd Lord! With ho - ly
2. A wed - ding gar - ment we de - sire, To clothe our
trem - bling, ho - ly fears, We now ap - proach thy
souls with ho - li - ness; O grant a spark of
sa - cred board To taste the feast thy love pre - pares.
heaven - ly fire, And fit us all for hap - pi - ness.

3. Worthy receivers of thy blood,
May we continue through thy grace;
That when we hear the last loud trump,
We may awake to see thy face.

Hail Our Incarnate God! Tigris S.M.

St. 1-5

William Duke, 1790 Raynor Taylor, 1822

1. Hail our in - car - nate_ God! Let heaven_ and_ earth re - sound;_
2. Of the Re - deem - er's_ birth, An - gels_ the_ news pro - claim;_

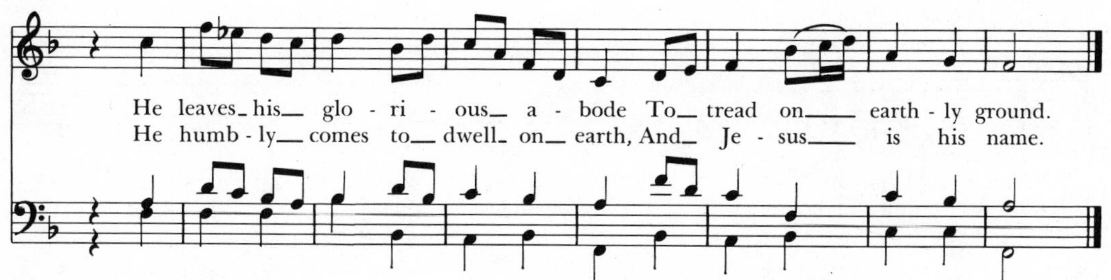
He leaves_ his_ glo - ri - ous_ a - bode To_ tread on_ earth - ly ground.
He humb - ly_ comes to_ dwell_ on_ earth, And_ Je - sus_ is his name.

3. Tidings of joy and peace
Are spread in his great name;
He is the Lord of Righteousness,
Almighty to redeem.

4. The shepherds long to know
The mystery profound;
With haste to Bethlehem they go,
And there the Saviour found.

5. Now Lord, effect the end
Of thy humility;
Into our waiting hearts descend,
Our perfect Saviour be.

Jesu, to Thee My Heart I Bow

St. 1-6

Nicolaus L. Zinzendorf, 1721
John Wesley, trans. 1737

Lob sey dem allmächtiger Gott L.M.

Zahn 346

Johann D. Mueller, arr. 1754

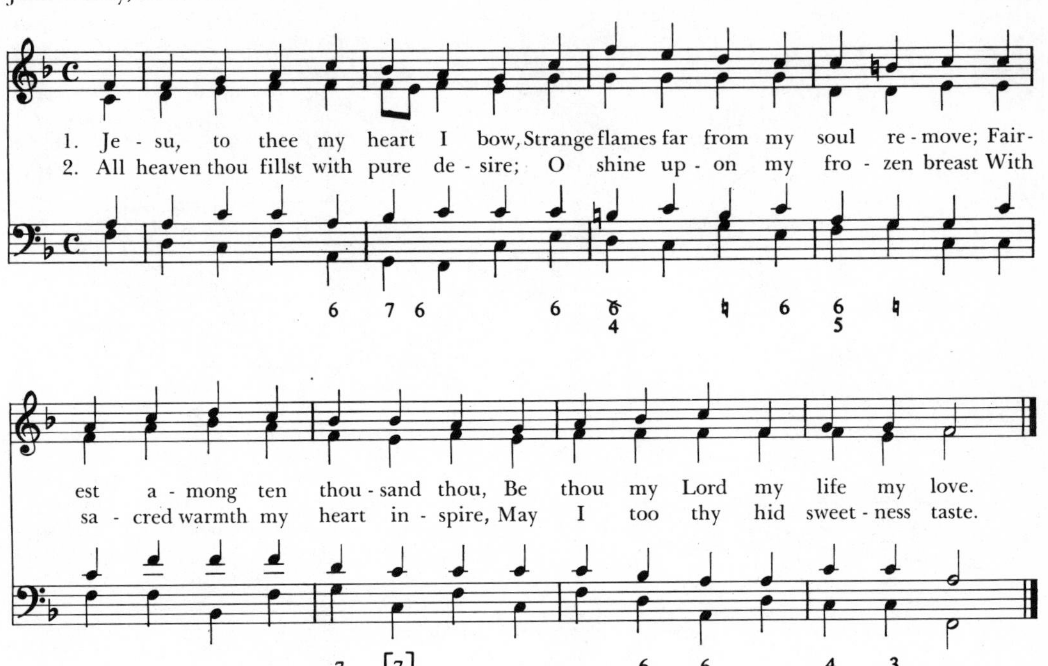
1. Je - su, to thee my heart I bow, Strange flames far from my soul re - move; Fair - est a - mong ten thou - sand thou, Be thou my Lord my life my love.
2. All heaven thou fillst with pure de - sire; O shine up - on my fro - zen breast With sa - cred warmth my heart in - spire, May I too thy hid sweet - ness taste.

3. I see thy garments rolled in blood,
Thy streaming head, thy hands, thy side;
All hail, thou suffering, conquering God!
Now man shall live; for God hath died.

4. O kill in me this rebel sin,
And triumph o'er my willing breast;
Restore thy image Lord, therein,
And lead me to my Father's rest!

5. Ye earthly loves be far away,
Saviour, be thou my love alone;
Ne'er more may mind usurp the sway,
But in me thy great will be done!

6. Yea, thou, true witness, spotless lamb,
All things for thee I count but loss;
My sole desire, my constant aim,
My only glory be thy cross!

MY SOUL BEFORE THEE PROSTRATE LIES — ZEUCH MEINEN GEIST L.M.

St. 1, 3, 5, 6, 9, 11

C. F. Richter, 1704 — Johann Christoph Kühnau, arr. 1786
John Wesley, trans. 1737

1. My soul__ be - fore__ Thee pros - trate lies, To thee__ her
2. Je - su,__ vouch - safe__ my heart and will With thy__ meek

source__ my spir - it flies; My wants__ I mourn,__ my
low - li - ness to fill; No more__ here power__ let

chains I see; O let__ thy pres - ence set me free.
na - ture boast, But in__ thy will__ may mine be lost.

3. In life's short day let me yet more
Of thy enlivening power implore;
My mind must deeper sink in thee,
My foot stand firm from wandering free.

4. And well I know thy tender love,
Thou never didst unfaithful prove;
And well I know thou standst by me,
Pleased from myself to set me free.

5. Already springing hope I feel,
God will destroy the power of hell.
God from the land of wars and pain
Leads me where peace and safety reign.

6. When my warmed thoughts I fix on thee
And plunge me in thy mercy's sea,
Then even on me thy face shall shine,
And quicken this dead heart of mine.

The God of Bethel Heard Her Cries — New Britain C.M.

St. 1-3

Richard Allen, 1793 — Anon., 1835

Tune in tenor

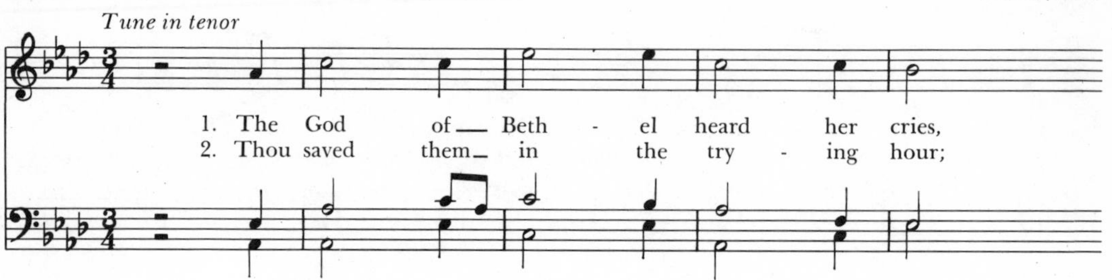
1. The God of Beth - el heard her cries,
2. Thou saved them in the try - ing hour;

He let his power be seen; He stopped the proud op -
Min-is-ters and coun - cils joined, And all stood read - y

1. 2.
pres - sor's frown, And proved him - self a king.
to re - tain That help - less church of thine.

3. Bethel surrounded by her foes,
But not yet in despair;
Christ heard her supplicating cries,
The God of Bethel heard.

Ah! Lovely Appearance of Death! — Stockholm L.M.D.

St. 1-3, 7, 11, 12

Charles Wesley, 1746 — Jacob Kimball, 1793

1. Ah! love - ly ap - pear - ance of death! No sight up - on earth is so fair; Not
3. How blest is our broth - er, be - reft Of all that could burth - en his mind! How
all the gay pag - eants that breathe Can with a dead bod - y com - pare.
eas - y the soul, that hath left This wea - ri - some bod - y be - hind!
2. With sol - emn de - light I sur - vey The corpse when the spir - it is fled; In
4. This lan-guish - ing head is at rest, Its think - ing and ach - ing are o'er; This

love with the beau - ti - ful clay, And long - ing to lie in its stead.
qui - et im - mov - a - ble breast Is heaved by af - flic - tion no more.

5. To mourn and to suffer is mine,
While bound in a prison I breathe,
And still for deliverance pine,
And press to the issues of death.

6. What now with my tears I bedew,
O! might I this moment become!
My spirit created anew,
My flesh be consigned to the tomb.

WHILE O'ER OUR GUILTY LAND, O LORD — DELHI L.M.D.

St. 1, 2, 4-6, 8

Samuel Davies, writ. 1755 — Samuel Holyoke, 1791

1. While o'er our__ guilt - y land, O Lord, We view the ter - rors of thy sword;
3. On thee, our__ guard - ian God, we call, Be - fore thy throne of grace we fall,

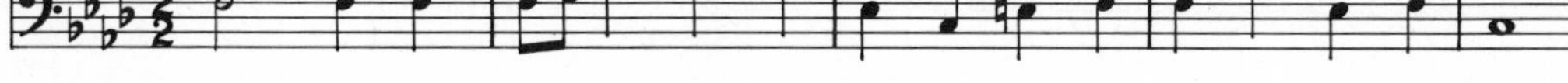

While heaven its__ fruit - ful showers de - nies, And na - ture round us fades and dies;
And is there__ no de - liv - erance there? And must we per - ish in des - pair?

Soft

2. While clouds col - lec - ting o'er our head Seem charged with wrath to smite__ us dead,
4. See, we re - pent, we weep, we mourn, To our for - sak - en God__ we turn;

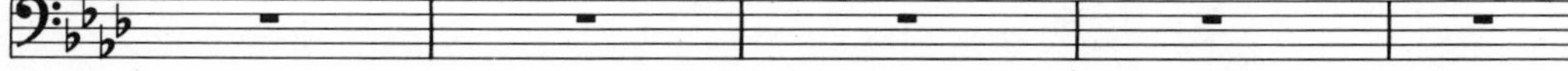

Loud

Oh! Whith - er__ shall the help - less fly? To whom but thee di - rect their cry?
O spare__ our__ guilt - y coun - try, spare The church which thou hast__ plant - ed here.

5. Revive our withering fields with rain,
Let peace compose our land again,
Silence the horrid noise of war!
O spare a guilty people, spare!

6. These pleas, by faith urged at thy throne,
Have brought ten thousand blessings down
On guilty lands in helpless woe;
Let them prevail to save us too!

Eternal Spirit, Source of Light — Psalm 104 8.8.8.D.

St. 1-4

Samuel Davies, 1769 — James Lyon, 1761

Solo
1. E - ter - nal Spir - it, source of light, En - liv - ening, con - se - cra - ting fire, De - scend, and with ce - les - tial heat Our dull, our fro - zen hearts in - spire.
2. In our cold breasts O strike a spark Of the pure flame which ser - aphs feel, Nor let us wan - der in the dark Or lie be - numbed and stu - pid still.
Chorus
Our souls re - fine, our dross con - sume! Come, con -
Come viv - i - fy - ing Spir - it, come, And make our hearts thy con - stant home!

3. Whatever guilt and madness dare,
We would not quench the heavenly fire;
Our hearts as fuel we prepare,
Though in the flame we should expire.
Our breasts expand to make thee room,
Come purifying Spirit, come!

4. Let pure devotion's fervors rise!
Let every pious passion glow!
O let the raptures of the skies
Kindle in our cold hearts below!
Come, condescending Spirit, come,
And make our souls thy constant home!

Lord, I Am Thine

St. 1, 4, 5, 7

Samuel Davies, 1769

Bath L.M.

Version from James Lyon, 1761

Tune in tenor
1. Lord, I am thine, en tire - ly thine,
2. Thine would I live, thine would ___ I die,
Pur - chased and saved by blood di - vine;
Be thine through all e - ter - ni - ty;
With full con - sent thine I would be,
The vow is past be - yond re - peal,
And own thy sov - ereign right in me.
Now will I set the sol - emn seal.

3. Be thou the witness of my vow,
Angels and men attest it, too,
That to thy board I now repair
And seal the sacred contract there.

4. Do thou assist a feeble worm
The great engagement to perform;
Thy grace can full assistance lend,
And on that grace I dare depend.

Hark! 'Tis the Saviour of Mankind

St. 1, 2, 4, 5

John Murray, 1782

Jordan C.M.D.

William Billings, 1781

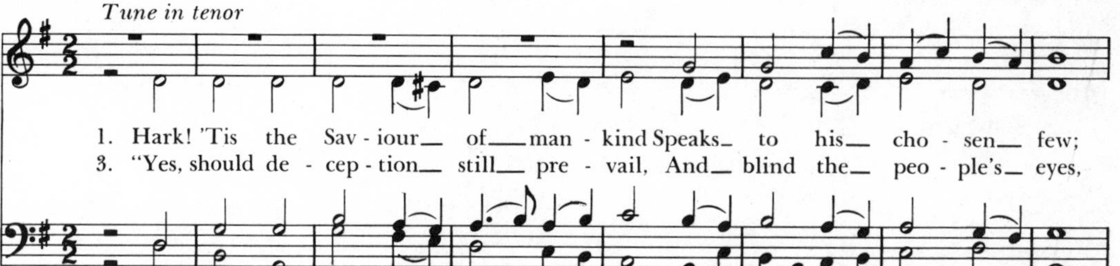
Tune in tenor
1. Hark! 'Tis the Sav - iour of man - kind Speaks to his cho - sen few;
3. "Yes, should de - cep - tion still pre - vail, And blind the peo - ple's eyes,

'Tis he who leads the wan - dering blind In ways they could not know.
In my great day I'll rend the veil From all be - neath the skies.

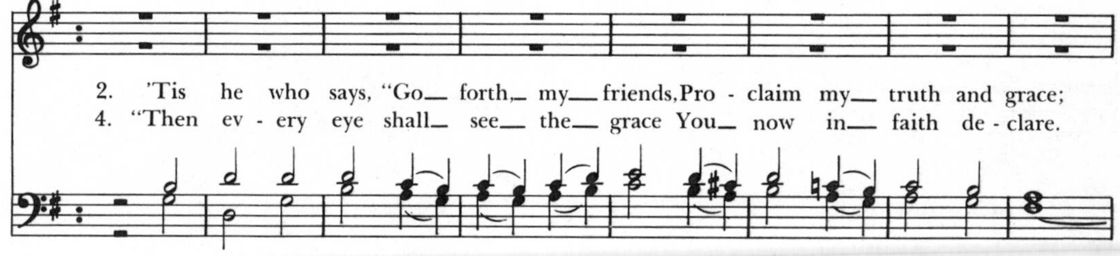
2. 'Tis he who says, "Go forth, my friends, Pro - claim my truth and grace;
4. "Then ev - ery eye shall see the grace You now in faith de - clare.

In - form each soul my love ex - tends To all of Ad - am's race.
And I my - self, from ev - ery face, Will wipe off ev - ery tear."

All-Knowing God, 'Tis Thine To Know

Lang L.M.

St. 1-5

Anon., 1783

James Hewitt, 1812

Tune in tenor

1. All - know - ing God, 'tis thine to___ know The springs whence
2. Who a - mong men, high Lord of___ all Thy serv - ants

wrong o - pin - ions___ flow; To judge from prin - ci -
to his bar may___ call, De - cide of her - e -

ples with - in,___ Where frail - ty___ errs, and where we___ sin.
sy, and shake___ A broth - er___ o'er the flam - ing___ lake?

❋ *In original*

† *In original*

3. Who with another's eye can read,
Or worship by another's creed?
Revering thy command alone,
We humbly seek and use our own.

4. If wrong, forgive, accept if right;
While faithful we obey our light,
And cens'ring none, are zealous still
To follow as to learn thy will.

5. When shall our happy eyes behold
Thy people fashioned in thy mold,
And charity our language prove
Derived from thee, O God of love?

While I Am Young

Happy Choice 8.8.6.6.D.

St. 1-4

Silas Ballou, 1785

Jeremiah Ingalls, 1805

Tune in tenor
1. While I am young and in my youth, Teach me to know thy ways of truth. And love and fear thy name, And love and fear thy name;
2. Stretch out thine arm of match-less grace Con-duct my feet in wis-dom's ways, Oh, Son of Right-eous-ness, Oh, Son of Right-eous-ness;
And fol-low thee with all my heart, And nev-er from thy ways de-part Thou ev-er-last-ing Lamb, Thou ev-er-last-ing Lamb.
If thou wilt grant me this in-deed, There's noth-ing shall my course im-pede Nor hin-der my prog-ress, Nor hin-der my prog-ress.

3. Thy presence is a paradise;
The beauties of thy face and eyes
Can never be expressed,
Can never be expressed;
Could I before thy presence come,
I could not seek a better home,
Nor find a sweeter rest,
Nor find a sweeter rest.

4. Teach me to live in thine embrace,
'Till I have spent my fleeting days
Then send a convoy down,
Then send a convoy down;
On wings of love, oh let me rise,
And soar and reach the heav'nly prize,
My mansion and my crown,
My mansion and my crown.

Almighty God in Being Was — Solemnity C.M.D.

St. 1, 3, 4-9

Silas Ballou, 1785 — Eliakim Doolittle, 1798

Tune in tenor
1. Al - might - y God in be - ing was Be - fore the
2. He called the wa - ters to their place, And gave the

world be - gun, And Wis - dom, he dwelt
deep its bound; The wa - ters he pro -

with him there, And was his on - ly son.
nounc - ēd seas, And earth he named the ground.

Then gloom - y dark - ness bore the sway, Till he cre -
Now let the ver - dant grass a - rise, And herbs bring

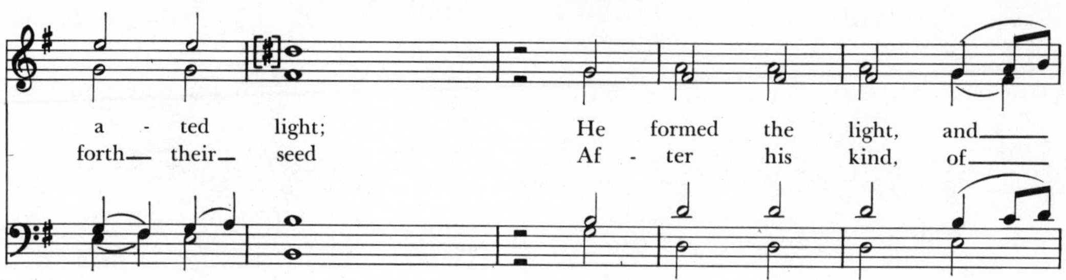
a - ted light; He formed the light, and
forth their seed Af - ter his kind, of

called it day, And called the dark - ness night.
ev - ery size, And so it was in - deed.

3. Now in the firmament appears
The lights which he hath given,
For signs and seasons, days and years,
To us beneath the heaven.
He made the sun to rule the day,
Which gives the moon her light;
He made the moon and stars, and they
Were made to rule the night.

4. He formèd every creeping thing,
And fish of every size,
And beast, and fowl of every wing,
And everything that flies.
And so God blessed them all indeed
With innocence and food,
And bid each multiply his seed,
For he pronounced them good.

LONG AS THE DARKENING CLOUD ABODE — FAIRLEE L.M.

St. 1-5

George Richards, 1792 — Oliver Holden, 1793

Tune in tenor
1. Long as the dark - ening cloud a - bode, So long did
2. Fa - ther of spir - its! light of light! Lift up the

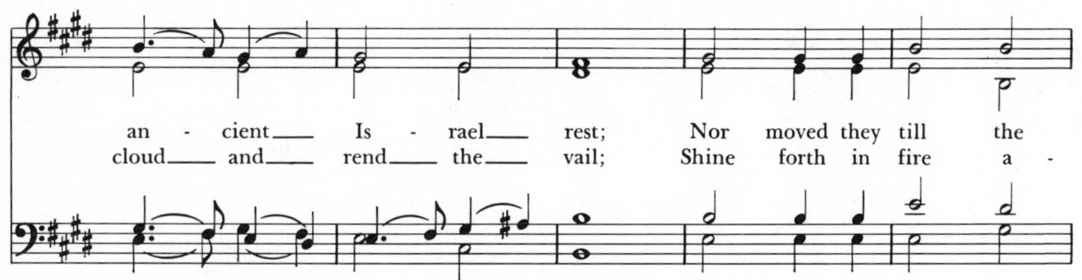
an - cient Is - rael rest; Nor moved they till the
cloud and rend the vail; Shine forth in fire a -

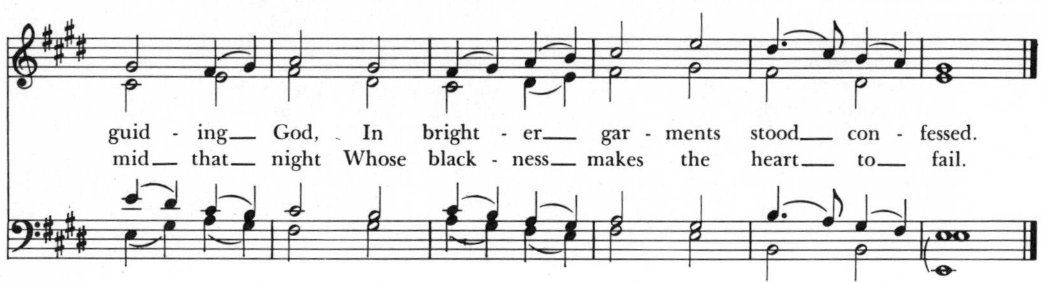
guid - ing God, In bright - er gar - ments stood con - fessed.
mid that night Whose black - ness makes the heart to fail.

3. 'Tis done! to Christ the power is given.
His death — it rent the vail away.
Our great forerunner enters heaven,
And opes th'eternal gates of day.

4. Nor shall those mists that brood o'er time,
Forever blind the mental eye;
They backward roll, and light sublime.
Beams glory from the God on high.

5. Adoring nations hail his dawn;
All kingdoms bless the noontide beam.
And light unfolding life's full morn.
Is vast creation's deathless theme.

TH' ALMIGHTY SPAKE, AND GABRIEL SPED — ABERDEEN 8.6.8.8.6.

St. 1, 3, 4, 6

George Richards, 1792 — Oliver Holden, 1793

Tune in tenor
1. Th'Al - might - y spake, and Ga - briel sped, Up - borne on wings of light;
2. One note of peace was heard on high, Glad tid - ings rolled a - round;

Je - ho - vah's glo - ry round him spread, Je - ho - vah's glo - ry round him
Ten thou - sand thou - sand left the sky, Ten thou - sand thou - sand left the
1.
2.
spread, And changed to day the night. night.
sky, To catch sal - va - tion's sound. sound.

3. Shout, shout for joy; rejoice, O earth;
Hail, hail this glorious morn;
Rejoice! Rejoice in Jesus' birth!
Rejoice! Rejoice in Jesus' birth!
Today are nations born.

4. He comes! He comes! The Saviour God!
Good will, peace, joy for men.
Glad tidings shout to all abroad,
Glad tidings shout to all abroad,
So be it, Lord, Amen.

Let All Created Things — Lenox H.M.

St. 1-3

Artis Seagrave, 1792 — Lewis Edson, 1782

Tune in tenor
1. Let all cre - a - ted things Their cheer - ful voic - es raise,
And own the King of kings, With thank - ful songs of praise.
Cre - a - ting love Should loud be sung, Through
Cre - a - ting love Should
Cre - a - ting love Should loud be sung, Through ev - ery world, By
Cre - a - ting love Should loud be sung, Through ev - ery world, By ev - ery tongue. Through
ev - ery world, By ev - ery
1. tongue.
2. tongue.
loud be sung, Through ev - ery world, By ev - ery tongue. tongue.
ev - ery tongue. Through ev - ery world, By ev - ery tongue. tongue.
ev - ery world, By ev - ery tongue. tongue.

2. Let angels round the throne,
In joyful ranks above,
His power and goodness own,
And his preserving love.
With thankful tongues
His praise proclaim,
And drop their crowns
To shout his name.

3. Let all old Adam's race,
Wherever they may be,
Shout the redeemer's grace,
And to him bow the knee.
He died for all,
And to restore
All things, he rose
To die no more.

Thus Spake the Saviour | Alhallows Tune L.M.

St. 1-3, 5, 7

Jeremy Belknap, 1795 | William Selby, 1762

1. Thus spake the Sav - iour, when he sent His min - is - ters to preach his word; They through the world o -
2. "Go forth, ye her - alds, in my name, Bid the whole earth my grace re - ceive, The gos - pel ju - bi -

6 6/4 6 ♮ 6 6/4 ♮ 6

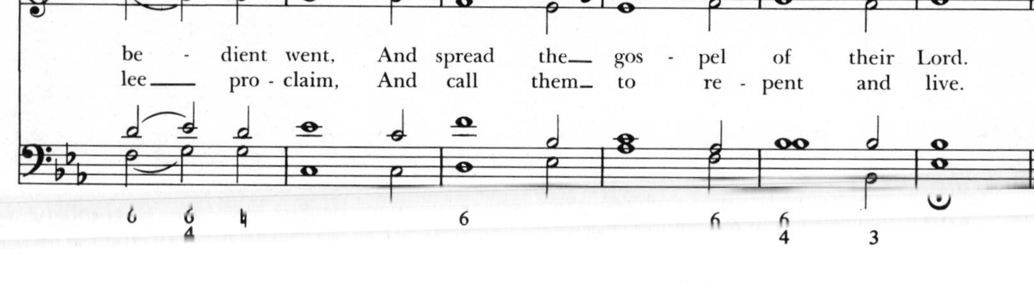

be - dient went, And spread the gos - pel of their Lord.
lee pro - claim, And call them to re - pent and live.
6 6/4 ♮ 6 6 6/4 3

3. "The joyful news to all impart,
And teach them where salvation lies;
Bind up the broken bleeding heart,
And wipe the tear from weeping eyes.

4. "Freely from me ye have received,
Freely in love to others give;
Thus shall your doctrines be believed,
And by your labors, sinners live."

5. Happy those servants of the Lord,
Who thus, their master's will obey!
How rich, how full is their reward,
Reserved until the final day!

Lord of the Worlds Below! — Worship H.M.

St. 1-5

James Freeman, 1799 — Hans Gram, 1802

Tune in tenor
1. Lord of the worlds be - low! On earth thy glo - ries
2. Forth in the flow - ery spring, We see thy beau - ty
shine; The chang - ing sea - sons show Thy skill and
move; The birds on branch - es sing Thy ten - der -
power di - vine. In all we see A God ap -
ness and love; Wide flush the hills; The air is
pears; The roll - ing years Are full of thee. thee.
balm; De - vo - tions calm Our bos - om fills. fills.
1.
2.

3. Then come, in robes of light,
The summer's flaming days;
The sun, thine image bright,
Thy majesty displays;
And oft thy voice
In thunder rolls;
But still our souls
In thee rejoice.

4. In autumn, a rich feast
Thy common bounty gives
To man, and bird, and beast,
And everything that lives.
Thy liberal care
At morn, and noon,
And harvest moon,
Our lips declare.

5. In winter, awful thou!
With storms around thee cast;
The leafless forests bow
Beneath thy northern blast.
While tempests lower,
To thee, dread King,
We homage bring,
And own thy power.

Devotional Verse and Singing Masters' Tunes

Many religious poems of the century were not intended for psalm- or hymnbook. Yet they share the familiar meters, they repeat familiar themes, and they help us to see the period as a whole. Some were intended for music, like Royall Tyler's "Hail to the Joyous Day," which was sung at Claremont, New Hampshire, in 1793. It seems strange that Claremont was to sing a Christmas hymn at a time when many in Massachussetts and Connecticut opposed the practice. John Wilson's "For Lo My Jonah How He Slumpt" is a ballad-like poem applying the trials and the deliverance of Jonah to the case of William Thompson, minister of Braintree, who had been afflicted with a black melancholy. In "Praise Ye the Lord," we have a Nantucket whaler's version of the De Profundis. Volumes of verse contain paraphrases of single psalms. Philip Freneau's "By Babel's Streams" (Ps. 137) may be compared with Joel Barlow's "Along the Banks," another treatment of the same psalm. Martha Brewster's "The Stately Structure of This Earth" is a very free paraphrase of Psalm 24.

Broad Is the Road

St. 1-4

Isaac Watts, 1707-1709

Windham L.M.

Daniel Read, 1785

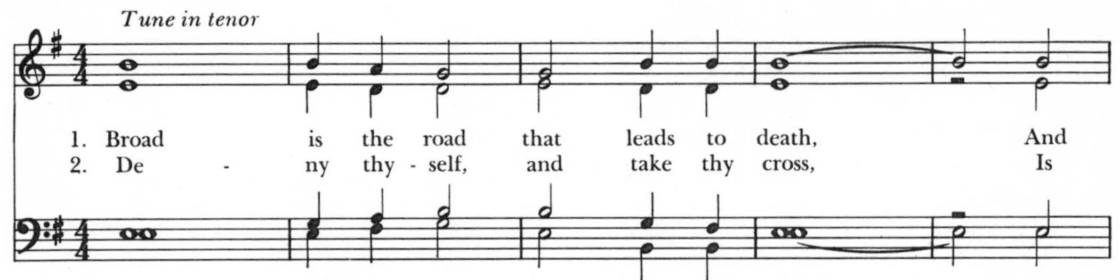
Tune in tenor
1. Broad is the road that leads to death, And
2. De - ny thy - self, and take thy cross, Is

thou - sands walk to - geth - er there, But wis - dom shews
the Re - deem - er's great com - mand! Na - ture must count

a nar - row path, With here and there a trav - el - er.
her gold but dross, If she would gain this heaven - ly land.

3. The fearful soul that tires and faints,
And walks the ways of God no more,
Is but esteemed — almost a saint,
And makes his own destruction sure.

4. Lord, let not all my hopes be vain,
Create my heart entirely new;
Which hypocrites could ne'er attain,
Which false apostates never knew.

WHY DO WE MOURN DEPARTING FRIENDS? CHINA C.M.

St. 1, 3, 5, 6

Isaac Watts, 1707 Timothy Swan, 1801

Tune in tenor
1. Why do we mourn de - part - ing friends, Or
2. Why should we trem - ble to con - vey Their

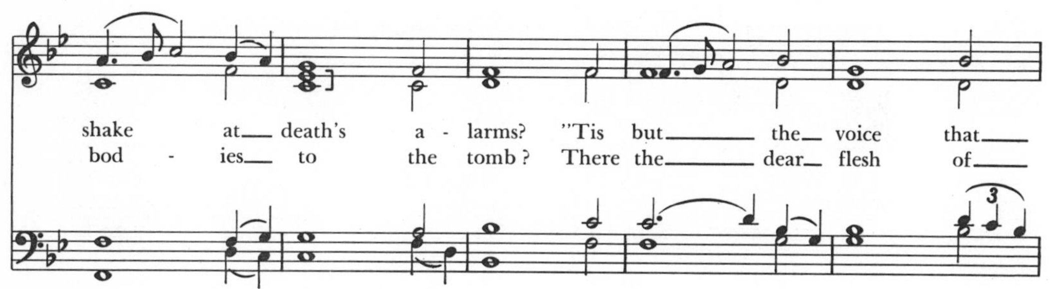
shake at death's a - larms? 'Tis but the voice that
bod - ies to the tomb? There the dear flesh of
3

Je - sus sends, To call them to his arms.
Je - sus lay, And left a long per - fume.
3

3. Thence he arose, ascending high,
And showed our feet the way;
Up to the Lord our flesh shall fly
At the great rising day.

4. Then let the last loud trumpet sound,
And bid our kindred rise:
Awake ye nations under ground;
Ye saints, ascend the skies.

For Lo! My Jonah How He Slumped — Canterbury C.M.

Anagram 2, St. 1-4, 6, 8

John Wilson, copied bet. 1712 and 1723 — John Playford, arr. 1677

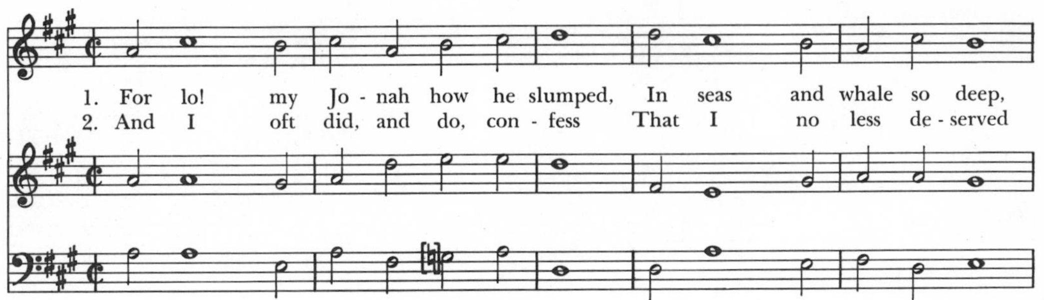
1. For lo! my Jo - nah how he slumped, In seas and whale so deep,
2. And I oft did, and do, con - fess That I no less de - served

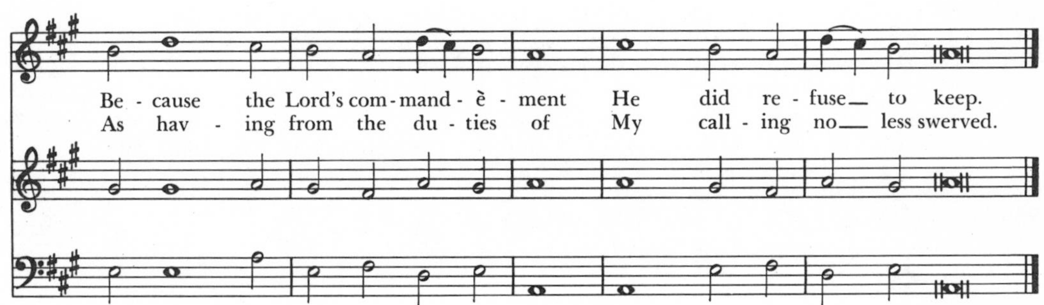
Be - cause the Lord's com - mand - ĕ - ment He did re - fuse__ to keep.
As hav - ing from the du - ties of My call - ing no__ less swerved.

3. No marvel then that I was cast
Into the sea and whale,
And that such horrid, hellish darts
Against me did prevail.

4. But Jonah in those woeful depths
Did pray unto his God,
And so have I done, often-times,
Under his heavy rod.

5. Yet, O dear brethren that survive
Do not account me lost,
Whom Christ redeemĕd by his blood,
And at so great a cost.

6. With Jonah now I'm cast ashore;
The whale could not me keep,
But in my saviour Jesus Christ,
I sweetly fell asleep.

THE ANGELS SUNG A CAROL — SONG 4 10.10.10.D.

St. 1, 6-9 — Frost 352

Edward Taylor, 1712 — Orlando Gibbons, 1623

1. The an - gels sung a car - ol at thy birth, My Lord, and thou thy-self
2. Joy stands on tip - toes all the while thy guests Sit at thy ta - ble,read-
didst sweet - ly sing An ep - i - ni- ci -on at thy death on earth, And or -
y forth to sing Its hal - le - lu - jahs in sweet mu - sic's dress, Wait - ing
derst thine, in mem - ory of this thing, Thy Ho - ly Sup - per, clos - ing it
for or - gans to em - ploy here - in. Here mat - ter is al - lowed to all,

at last Up with an hymn, and chokst the foe thou hast.
rich, high, My Lord, to tune thee hymns me - lo - dious - ly.

3. Oh! make my heart thy pipe; the Holy Ghost
The breath that fills the same and spiritually.
Then play on me, thy pipe, that is almost
Worn out with piping tunes of vanity.
Wind music is the best, if thou delight
To play the same thyself, upon my pipe.

4. Hence make me, Lord, thy golden trumpet choice,
And trumpet thou thyself upon the same,
Thy heart enravishing hymns with sweetest voice.
When thou thy trumpet soundst, thy tunes will flame.
My heart shall then sing forth thy praises sweet,
When sounded thus will thy sepulchre reach.

5. Make too my soul thy cittern, and its wires
Make my affections; and rub off their rust
With thy bright grace; and screw my strings up higher,
And tune the same to tunes thy praise most just.
I'll close thy supper then with hymns most sweet,
Bur'ing thy grave in thy sepulchre's reach.

Praise Ye the Lord, O Celebrate His Fame — Babylon 10.10.10.10.

Selected stanzas

Peleg Folger, after 1755 — Jacob French, 1802

Tune in tenor
1. Praise ye the Lord, O cel - e - brate his fame, Praise

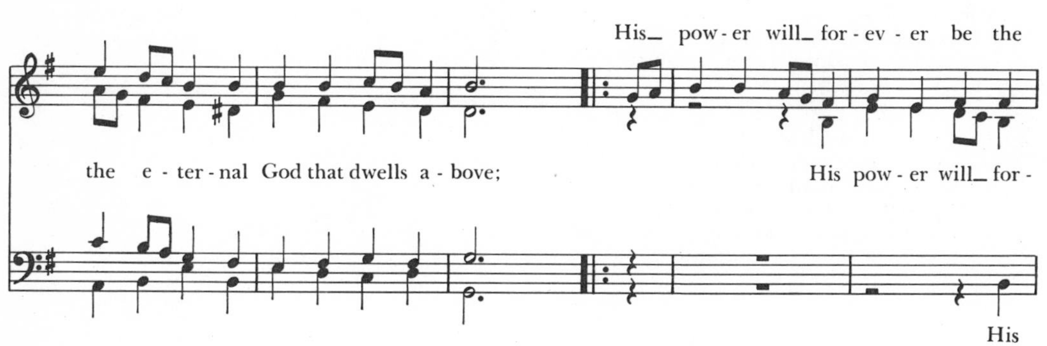
His pow - er will for - ev - er be the
the e - ter - nal God that dwells a - bove; His pow - er will for -
His

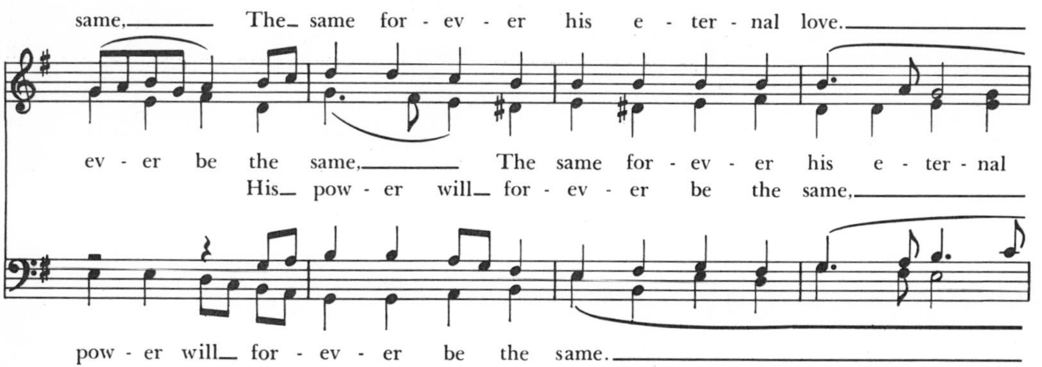
same, The same for - ev - er his e - ter - nal love.
ev - er be the same, The same for - ev - er his e - ter - nal
His pow - er will for - ev - er be the same,
pow - er will for - ev - er be the same.

The same for - ev - er his e - ter - nal
1. love.
2. love.
love. The same for - ev - er his e - ter - nal love. love.
The same for - ev - er his e - ter - nal love. love.

2. Ye sailors, speak, that plow the watery main,
Where raging seas and foaming billows roar,
Praise ye the Lord, and in a lofty strain,
Sing of his wonder-working love and power.

3. Thou didst, O Lord, create the mighty whale,
That wondrous monster of a mighty length;
Vast is his head and body, vast his tail,
Beyond conception his unmeasured strength.

4. But, everlasting God, thou dost ordain,
That we poor feeble mortals should engage
(Ourselves, our wives and children to maintain)
This dreadful monster with a martial rage.

5. And, though he furiously doth us assail,
Thou dost preserve us from all dangers free;
He cuts our boat in pieces with his tail,
And spills us all at once into the sea.

6. I twice into the dark abyss was cast,
Straining and struggling to retain my breath,
Thy waves and billows over me were past,
Thou didst, O Lord, deliver me from death.

7. Thou savedst me from the dangers of the sea,
That I might bless thy name for ever more.
Thy love and power the same will ever be
Thy mercy is an inexhausted store.

8. And when I shall this earthly ball forsake,
And leave behind me frail mortality,
Then may my soul her nimble journey take
Into the regions of eternity.

THE STATELY STRUCTURE OF THIS EARTH — PLAINFIELD C.M.D.

Ps. 24: st. 1, 3, 6, 7

Martha Brewster, 1757 — Jacob Kimball, 1800

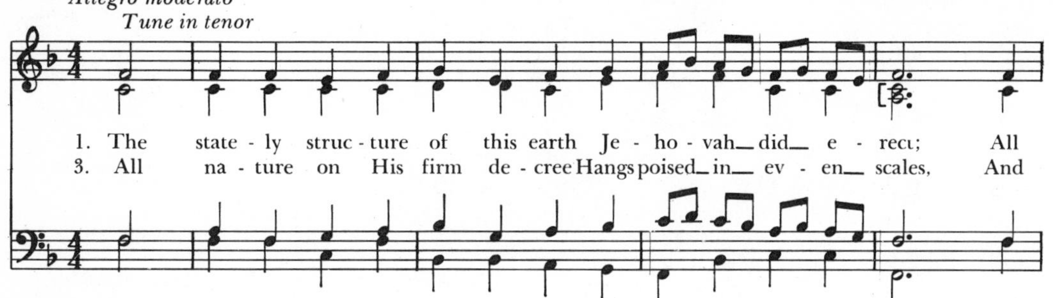
Allegro moderato
Tune in tenor
1. The stately structure of this earth Jehovah did erect; All
3. All nature on His firm decree Hangs poised in even scales, And

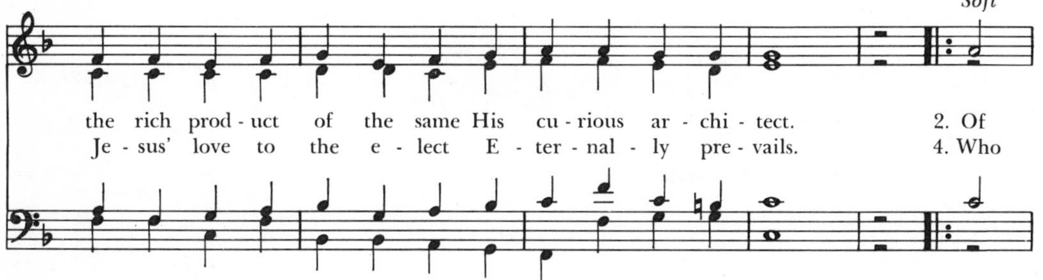
Soft
the rich product of the same His curious architect. 2. Of
Jesus' love to the elect Eternally prevails. 4. Who

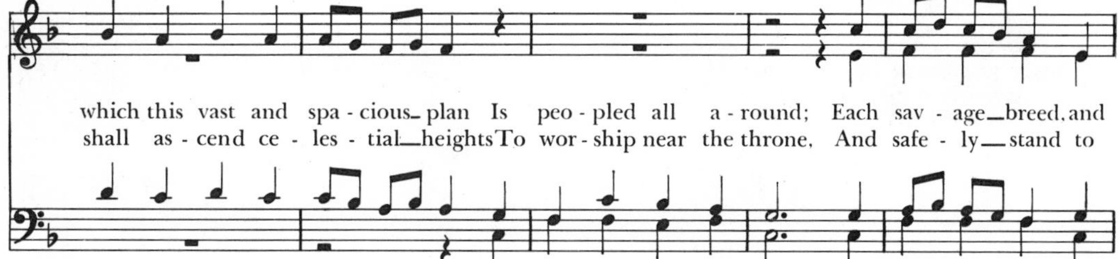
Loud
which this vast and spacious plan Is peopled all around; Each savage breed, and
shall ascend celestial heights To worship near the throne, And safely stand to

1.
2.
tamer herd, And man their ruler crowned, And man their ruler crowned. crowned.
hear their Judge Pronounce the sweet well done? Pronounce the sweet well done? done?

Permit Us, Lord, To Consecrate — Sullivan L.M.

St. 2, 4, 6, 9-11

Joseph Green, 1766 — William Billings, 1778

Tune in tenor
1. Per - mit us, Lord, to con - se - crate Our
2. All earth - ly be - ings here who move Ex -
first ripe fruits of ear - ly days To
pe - rience thy pa - ter - nal care, And
Thee, whose care to us is great, Whose
feel the in - fluence of thy love, Which
love de - mands our con - stant praise.
sweet - ens life from year to year.

3. Our morn of years which smile in bloom,
And those arrived at eve of age,
Must bow beneath thy sovereign doom,
And quit this frail, this mortal stage.

4. Conduct us safe through each event
And changing scene of life below,
Till we arrive where days are spent
In love which can no changes know.

5. Lord, in thy service us employ,
And when we've served thee here on earth,
Receive us hence to realms of joy,
To join with those of heavenly birth.

6. May we from angels learn to sing
The songs of high seraphic strain;
Then mount aloft on cherubs' wings,
And soar to worlds that cease from pain.

BY BABEL'S STREAMS

Ps. 137: st. 1-4

Philip Freneau, writ. bet. 1768 and 1794

PSALM 46 8.8.8.D.

Amos Bull, 1793

1. By Ba - bel's streams we sat and wept,____ When Si - on bade our sor - rows flow;____ Our harps on lof - ty wil - lows slept That near those dis - tant__ wa - ters grow____ The wil - lows high, the wa - ters clear,____ Be - held our toils and sor - rows there.
2. The cru - el foe, that cap - tive led____ Our na - tion from their na - tive soil,____ The ty - rant foe, by whom we bled, Re - quired a song, as__ well as toil:____ "Come, with a song your sor - rows cheer,____ "A song, that Si - on loved to hear."

3. How shall we, cruel tyrant, raise
A song on such a distant shore?
If I forget my Sion's praise,
May my right hand assume no more
To strike the silver sounding string
And thence the slumbering music bring.

4. If I forget that happy home,
My perjured tongue, forbear to move!
My eyes be closed in endless gloom
My joy, my rapture, and my love!
No rival grief my mind can share,
For thou shalt reign unrivalled there.

Wherein Consists the High Estate | Dukes Tune C.M.
Question 28, st. 1-5 | Frost 203
Ebenezer Dayton, 1769 | Thomas Ravenscroft, arr. 1621

Question (Teacher)

1. Where - in con - sists the high es - tate Of Christ's ex - al - ta - tion?

To which he's now ar - rived of late, What's his high - est sta - tion?

Answer (Students)
Tune in tenor

2. The third day doth these ti - dings bring, By break of day he rose,
3. Je - sus he rose and left the dead And van-quished sin and hell;

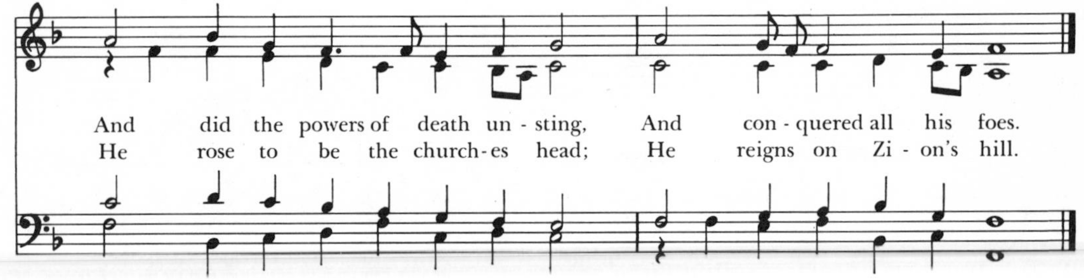
And did the powers of death un - sting, And con - quered all his foes.
He rose to be the church- es head; He reigns on Zi - on's hill.

4. Our Lord ascends above the sky,
From whence he did descend;
Jesus he reigns in majesty,
And doth his church defend.

5. A Potentate, or King of kings,
All worlds do Christ obey;
Praise to his name all nature sings,
His godhead shines through clay.

Hail to the Joyous Day

St. 1, 3, 4, 7, 10

Royall Tyler, 1793

Amherst H.M.

William Billings, 1770

Tune in tenor
1. Hail to the joy - ous day, On which our Lord was born; Lift high the vo - cal lay, And sing the bliss - ful morn. Your voic - es raise! To hail the morn On which was born The Lord of grace.
2. He o'er the track - less waste Our pi - ous fa - thers led; And though in des - ert placed, He them with bless - ings fed. Your voic - es raise! To him who binds The waves and winds, Be end - less praise.

3. He crowned fair freedom's cause,
He made our nation great;
The leader of our wars,
He raised to rule our states.
Your voices raise!
To him who brings
To earth proud kings,
Be deathless praise.

4. Here where the savage foes,
Their deathful war-song sung,
Sweet peace her olive shows,
And joy on earth is sung.
Your voices raise!
Let all accord
To praise the Lord,
The Lord of grace.

5. Let solemn organs sound,
And sweetest chords combine.
Swell the full notes around,
With grateful voices join.
Your voices raise!
On every wing,
In transport sing
The Saviour's praise.

DEAR BRETHREN, ARE YOUR HARPS IN TUNE? NEWTON C.M.D.

St. 1-4, 10, 13

Eunice Smith, 1798 Samuel Babcock, 1795

Tune in tenor

1. Dear breth - ren, are your_ harps in tune? Come,_ then, and let us sing A_
3. Who - ev - er tast - ed_heaven-ly love Should_ sing the heaven-ly song, Un -

song of hon - our and of praise To Zi - on's love - ly king.
til our souls shall join a - bove With all the heaven - ly throng.

2. Dear sis - ters,_ al - so come and_join And let our hearts be one, To
4. Be - hold the_love - ly lamb of_God De - scend - ing from a - bove! Be

1. 2.

try to send a note_ of_praise To God's be lov ĕd Son! Son!
hold what pains he un - der - went To man - i - fest his love! love!

5. Come, then, and let us watch and pray,
And fight the monster, sin;
Through Jesus, our victorious king,
We shall the victory win.

6. Oh! may I spend each day I live
In praising of my king,
Until He call my soul away,
Eternal praise to sing!

Dear Happy Souls

Rich Provision C.M.D.

St. 1, 3, 6, 8

Eunice Smith, 1798

Jeremiah Ingalls, 1805

Tune in tenor
1. Dear hap - py souls who have be - gun The joy - ful work of praise, Oh, do not stop, but ev - er run The bless - ed Chris - tian race.
3. Let Je - sus be your joy and strength; Re - ly on him a - lone; Oh, nev - er stop and you at length Shall shine be - fore the throne.
2. When world - ly cares be - set you round To turn your feet a - stray, Oh,
4. There you may join the shin - ing throng, The God of heaven to praise; And
a - stray, a - stray,
to praise, to praise,

do not stop on earth - ly ground, But run the heaven - ly way.
nev - er stop your joy - ful song To ev - er - last - ing days.

(Or, if desired, sing the last 3 measures thus:)

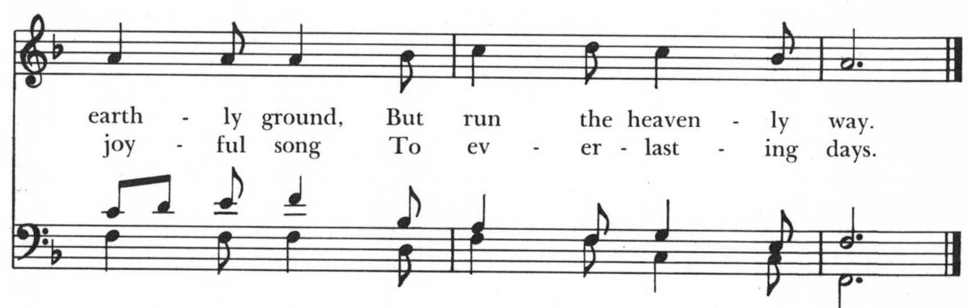
earth - ly ground, But run the heaven - ly way.
joy - ful song To ev - er - last - ing days.

Hymns in Swedish, Dutch, and German

THE TOLERANT policies of William Penn made Pennsylvania a refuge for German-speaking religious groups, many of which had been persecuted in Europe: Pietists (Johannes Kelpius, Johann A. Gruber), Dunkers (Alexander Mack I), German Seventh Day Baptists (Johann Conrad Beissel), Schwenkfelders (Caspar Kriebel, Balthasar Hoffman), Lutherans (Andrew Rudman, Conrad Weiser), Moravians (Anna and David Nitschmann, Johann C. Pyrlaeus, Nicholaus L. Zinzendorf), and Mennonites (Christopher Dock). They brought with them a voluminous literature of hymns. Indeed, it was only in this country that the Schwenkfelders were able to print their hymns (which they had previously preserved in manuscripts) since the use of the printing press had been denied them in Europe. Although most of this literature was created in Europe, we have chosen our examples from poems written in Pennsylvania.

Nor was Pennsylvania lacking in musicians. Johann Conrad Beissel was a prolific composer as well as a poet and the choir he formed at Ephrata attracted the attention of visitors. There were notable composers among the Moravians among whom Christian Gregor, John Antes, and John Bechler are represented here. The Lutherans and the Moravians sang chorales rather than psalm tunes, and where a native composition was not available to us, we have chosen suitable chorale tunes from eighteenth-century collections.

The chorale tunes of this period were often published in two parts, the melody which the congregation sang, and an instrumental bass provided with figures which guided the organist in realizing the accompaniment. The use of the organ was thus taken for granted.

It was soon evident, except in the most closed groups, that a move must be made toward a liturgy in English. The first attempts by the Dutch and the Lutherans took place within the eighteenth century. In New York the Reformed Dutch Church commissioned Francis Hopkinson to adapt the version of Tate and Brady to fit the longer phrases of the Dutch psalm tunes. It was also in New York that the Lutherans published their first hymnbook in English in 1795 which contained original hymns by John E. Kunze, John F. Ernst, and George Strebeck, as well as translations from the German.

NÄR VIL DU, JESU, MIN ELÄNDES VANDRING BESLUTA?
WHEN SHALL MY PILGRIMAGE, JESUS MY SAVIOUR, BE ENDED?

LOBE DEN HERREN 14.14.4.7.8.

St. 1-3, 5

Andrew Rudman (?), c.1700
Ernest Edwin Ryden, trans. 1970

Anon., 1665

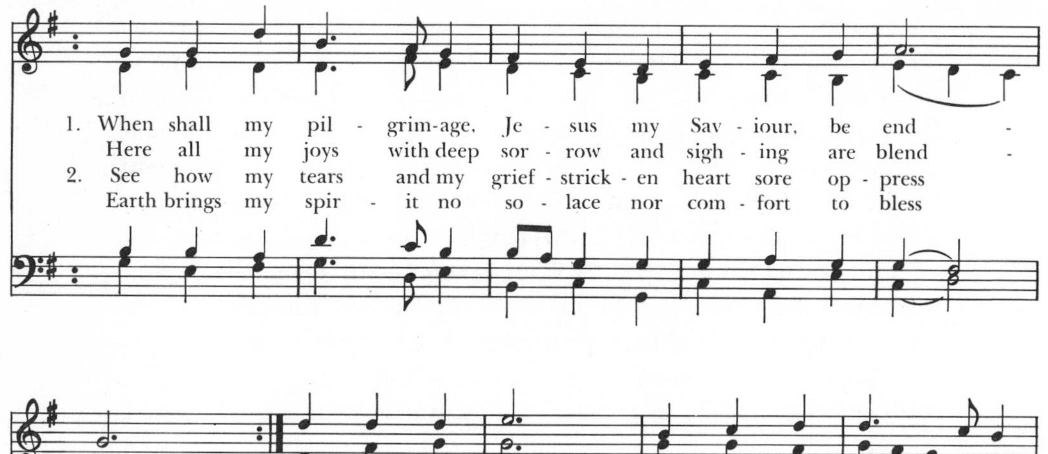
1. When shall my pil - grim-age, Je - sus my Sav - iour, be end -
Here all my joys with deep sor - row and sigh - ing are blend -
2. See how my tears and my grief - strick - en heart sore op - press
Earth brings my spir - it no so - lace nor com - fort to bless

ed?
ed, When shall my soul, Cleansed from all sin and made
me;
me. Sa - tan's dark guile, Car - nal temp - ta - tions and

whole, Fol - low thee where thou'rt as - cend - ed?
vile Hind - er my soul to con - fess thee.

3. Lo, how the darkening tempests of life are descending,
Bringing me poverty, sorrow and cares never ending!
Earth knows no rest;
Heav'n is my home ever blest.
Thither my spirit is tending.

4. Farewell, O earth, and now welcome, thou homeland supernal,
Where with the angels and saints I shall find joys eternal;
And with that host,
To Father, Son, Holy Ghost,
Join in their anthems immortal.

1. När vill du, Jesu, min eländes vandring besluta,
Där jag måst stundelig tårar av ögonen gista.
När skall dock visst,
Jesu, min själ utan brist
Himmelska glädjen åtnjuta.

2. Se huru tårar och sorger mitt hjärta betaga;
Världen här slätt ingen tröst som kan själen behaga.
Djävulens list,
Köttet och svagheters brist,
Vilja mig städs' från dig draga.

3. Ja, detta timliga, torftiga, flyktiga livet
Är med sorg, möda och omak allt städse omgivet.
Här är oro,
Men hos dig lyfter mig bo:
Där är bekymmer fördrivet.

4. Ade, O värld, och välkommen.O himmelska gamman!
Jag får här efter med helgonen glädjas tillsamman.
Lov i sin tron
Vare Gud Fader och Son,
Helge And' sammaleds! Amen.

Ich liebe Jesus noch allein
I Love My Jesus Quite Alone

The Best Choice 8.9.8.9.8.9.7.

St. 1, 6-8

Johannes Kelpius, writ. before 1705
Christopher Witt, trans. before 1705

Anon., before 1705

Unison
1. I love my Je - sus quite a - lone. The bride the bride-groom of my
2. The mag-net - nee-dle err - ing goes. When from when from the pole dis -
spir - it; No oth - ers shall my heart. no none. Through love through
tract - ed. And take be - fore quite no re - pose. Till he, till
lov - ing more in - her - it. No man can do at once for two. For
he has her at - tract - ed. And since my heart with thy love dart Is
one's for one's will and for t'oth - ers: There - fore I'll leave all oth - ers.
touched is touched by its flam - ing e - ther. There - fore. they haste to - geth - er.

3. And though thou art like the North Star
In heav – in heaven altified
And I on earth so distant far
I'll fol – I'll follow undenied.
Still thee my light.
And my eye-sight.
Shall still – shall still be turned to Thee
From every place, and woo Thee.

4. At distance yet, I hear Thy voice
When my – when my heart can but reach Thee:
And I again observe the choice
Which thy – which thy dear mouth does teach me.
And though thou'rt known in heaven's throne
From me – from me at such a distance.
Thou'rt present with assistance.

1. Ich liebe Jesum mir allein
Den Brautgam {deiner / meiner} Seelen;
Kein andrer soll mein Herzelein
Durch Liebe mir abstehlen.
Niemand kan Zwei
Mit gleicher Treu
Zu einer Zeit umfassen,
Drum will ich Andrer lassen.

2. Mein Ohr allein nur deine Stim
Mit Andacht soll anhören.
Wann einer Fremdem ich vernim
Lass ich mich drum nicht stören.
Mann kann ja nicht
Mit treuer Pflicht
Zwei widrigen anhören;
Meiner Jesus soll mich lehren.

3. Die Magnet Nadel irrn geht
Wann sie vom Pol verrücket ist;
Auch gar nicht ehe stille steht
Bis ihr sie zu süss zücket.
Und weil mein Herz
Dein liebes Herz
Berufet mit ihren Flammen.
Drum eilen sie zusammen.

4. Gehörsam hör ich deine Stim
Wann mein Herz zu dir fahret.
Und ich hin wiederum vernim
Was mich dein Mund da lehret;
Drum ob du schon
Ins Himmel's Thron
So weit bist abgelegen.
Bist mir doch zugegen.

Die kleine Heerde zeugen
This Flock So Small

O Welt, sieh hier dein Leben 7.7.6.7.7.8.

St. 1-3

Zahn 2298

Anna Nitschmann, 1742
Sheema Z. Buehne, trans. 1965

Christian Gregor, 1784

1. This flock so small_now kneel - ing. At - test - ing and ap - peal - ing. Is
2. Tears flow as I,_Thy serv - ant, Sense long - ing, deep and fer - vent, When
6 6 7 7 5 6 5 7 # 5 6 5 # 6 5
called the sin - ner's band. If tes - ti - mo - ny sole - ly Must
I the Lord re - quest To hold me in his keep - ing, As
6 6 5 6 7 7
vouch for good souls whol - ly, Scant few will then be - fore Thee stand.
in my cham - ber weep - ing I feel such woe in heart and breast.
6 7 7 6 3 6 6 5 6 5

3. O Lamb, Thy people greet Thee;
O hear as I entreat Thee,
As I weep in Thy sight.
In what I find that claims me,
There is so much that shames me
Before Thy saints in radiant light.

1. Die kleine Heerde zeugen,
die sich vorm Creutze beugen,
nennt mann die Sünderschaft;
der guten Seelen Menge
sitzt nicht sehr im Gedränge,
so bald nichts als die Zeugniss haft't.

2. Das kost't mich manche Thränen,
manch innigliches Sehnen,
wenn ich des Herren Hut
bestell in meiner Kammer,
und mir mein eigner Jammer
so weh an meinem Herzen thut.

3. Ach Lamm, du Gott der deinen!
erhöre doch mein Weinen
vor deinem Angesicht,
ich finde so viel Sachen,
die mich beschämet machen
vor deinen heiligen im Licht.

A Moravian wedding

Glückselger ist uns doch keine Nacht
For Us No Night Can Be Happier

Nun bitten wir

St. 1, 6, 9

Zahn 2029a

Nicolaus L. Zinzendorf, improvised 1742, pub. 1743
John Gambold (?), trans. 1754

Christian Gregor, 1784

Unison
1. For us no night can be hap - pi - er filled, Than that which
4
2
6
5

brought forth that won - drous Child, Which in mean
6
6
5

clothes wrapped was in a man - ger (Hard sure for
6
4
3
6
5
4
3
6
5

child of some beg - gar stran - ger!) Laid down to sleep.
6
4
3
6
6
6
4
5
#
6

2. Yea, what would think now all Chris - ten - dom, If in our
time— an - y— one— should come With such
signs, re - quir - ing all to re - ceive— him, And the true
God in this plight be - lieve— him; Would— they be - lieve it?
3. But those with - out,— they con-cern— us not; Praise to
him,— who— on— us— has wrought, That with
full as - sent we to think are a - ble, That the poor
Babe in home-ly rags and sta - ble Is— the Lord God.

1. Glückselger ist uns doch
keine Nacht, als die
uns das Wunder-kind hat
Gebracht, das in einer Krippe,
(das ist gewisslich vor eines
Bettelmanns Kind verdriesslich)
in lümplein lag

2. Was dächte die heutige
Christenheit, wenn einer käme
zu ihrer zeit mit dergleichen
Zeichen, ihr vorzuschreiben,
sie solte einen Gott
aus ilm gläuben, gläubten
sie es wohl?

3. Aber was gehn uns die
draussen an? Lob sey dem,
der das an uns gethan, dass
wir gläuben können: das
schmutz'ge Kindel in der zer-
rissenen Bettel-windel ist unser
Gott.

LAMM GOTTES ABGESCHLACHTET
SLAIN LAMB OF GOD

NUN RUHEN ALLE WÄLDER 7.7.6.7.7.8.

St. 1, 4, 9, 11

Zahn 2293a

Nicolaus L. Zinzendorf, writ. 1742
Sheema Z. Buehne, trans. 1965

Johann M. Spiess, arr. 1745

1. Slain Lamb of God,_ so mourned here, Thou, King, so deep-ly_scorned here,
2. As thine, O Shep-herd, name us! As thine, we pray thee,_ claim us,
6 7 5 3 6 6 6 7 6
Prince of the blest, on high; Guide our small con-gre-ga-tion On
Poor or-phans that we are! Our hearts are thine_ to own here; We
5 6 4 3 7 5 3 6 7 6
earth, thine own cre-a-tion, Cease not thy flock_ to_ mul-ti-ply.
would be lost a-lone here, Mere drops in man-kind's_ sea we are.
6 6 7 6♮ 5 6 4 3 6 6 5 4 3

3. O let there be ignited
Love's tapers brightly lighted
Within our hearts for thee.
Rejoice in our flames burning!
From thee they come — returning
Unto thy spirit ardently.

4. Now this we plead: O hear us,
Thou, Sovereign, ever near us!
Make thou thy presence known.
Pour thy heart's sweetness o'er us,
And wash our feet. Restore us,
And sanctify us as thine own.

1. Lamm Gottes abgeschlachtet,
   Du König tief verachtet,
   Doch Fürst der seligen,
   Und Haupt der kleinen Heerde
   Auf dieser deiner erde,
   Ach mach uns zu unzähligen!

2. Erkenn uns, unser Hüter!
   Uns kindliche Gemühter,
   Uns armen Waysen-volk,
   Das sich sonst nirgends wüste,
   Wenns selber etwas müste,
   Uns tropfen von dem grossen Volk.

3. So lass in unsern Herzen
   Die lichten Liebes-kerzen
   Dir sanft entgegen wehn;
   Und freu dich unsrer Flammen,
   Die hier aus dir zusammen
   Und wieder in dein Feuer gehen.

4. Nun diss ist unsre Bitte,
   Du Fürst in unsrer Mitte!
   Zeig deine Gegenwart;
   Mach uns dein Herze süsse;
   Und wasch uns unsre Füsse;
   Und heil'ge unsre ganze Art.

Ein Lämmlein Geht
On Earth There Is a Lamb So Small

Hör liebe Seele 8.7.8.7.

St. 1, 2, 8, 13

Zahn 252

Nicolaus L. Zinzendorf, 1742
Sheema Z. Buehne, trans. 1965

Balthasar Schmid arr., 1748

1. On— earth there is— a Lamb so small, So pa - tient - ly it tar - ries; The— im - age— of— poor sin - ners all, The whole world's guilt— it— car - ries.
2. O— might - y King— up - on this globe. Yet might - ier wast thou nev - er Than— in— thy— blood - y mar - tyr's robe; My song praise Thee— for - ev - er!
[6] 6 5 3 [6] 6 6 5
6 5 6 6 6
[6] 6 6 5 4 3

3. O little Lamb, so small art thou,
With longing I behold thee;
Ineffable my anguish now,
Until I may enfold thee.

4. O my dear Saviour, grant this grace
To thy poor child, that duly
It may behold thy holy face
And all its radiance truly.

1. Ein Laemmlein geht und traegt die Schuld
der Welt und ihrer Kinder;
es geht und wird mit viel Gedult
das Bildniss armer Suender.

2. Ach Koenig gross zu aller Zeit!
doch niemals mehr und groesser,
als in dem blutgen Marter-kleid;
besanng ich dich nur besser!

3. O Laemmlein Jesu noch so klein!
nach dir kan einem bange
und unausprechlich aengstlich seyn,
bis dass man dich umfange.

4. Mein lieber Heiland mache nur,
gib deinem armen Kinde,
das es die eigentliche Spur
von deinem Antlitz finde.

Jesu, komm herein — Seelenbrautigam, Jesu Gottes Lamm 5.5.8.8.5.5.
Jesu, Come on Board
(Hymn of the Second Sea Congregation)

St. 1, 4, 12, 19 — Zahn 3255b

Johann C. Pyrlaeus, writ. 1743
Sheema Z. Buehne, trans. 1965 — Johann D. Mueller, arr. 1754

1. Je - su, come on board This small ship, O Lord! Though the waves mount with each mo-tion,
2. O small com-pa - ny! Live on this wild sea Joy - ous - ly, and wa - ver nev - er;

6
4 3
6 6

We are sail - ing on thy o - cean, Nev - er ter - ri - fied; Thou turnst death a - side.
Stead - fast in the Lamb's blood ev - er. Kiss the dear hand nailed, On the cross im - paled.

#
#
6
6 6
4 3

3. Jesus crucified
Sails with us as guide,
Vigor in our men instilling,
Sense of duty, quick and willing.
Thank thee, spirit, whence
Comes our diligence.

4. Thus our way we wing;
Songs of praise we sing.
Jesus rocks us through the waters
To the other sons and daughters
Whom he sanctified,
Soldiers on his side.

1. Jesu! komm herein
in dem Schiffelein;
so mags Meer die Well'n erhohen,
fahr'n wir doch in deinen Seen,
furchten keine Noth,
du warst fur uns todt.

2. Leb, o kleines Heer!
auf dem wilden Meer
frohlich, bey des Lammes sünden
unverrukt zu allen Stunden;
kuss die theure Hand
an dem Baum gespannt.

3. Jesu Creutzes-lehr
folgt uns übers Meer:
unsre Manner sind lebendig
und zum dienste sehr behandig;
Geist! wir danken dir,
der von Fleiss gibt hier.

4. So geht unser Gang
unter Lob-gesang;
Jesus wiegt uns durch die Wellen
zu den andern Kampf-gesellen,
die er sich geweiht
und zum Streit bereit.

REINE LIEBE SUCHT NICHT SICH SELBER
LOVE THAT'S PURE, ITSELF DISDAINING

WO IST WOHL EIN SÜSSER LEBEN 8.7.8.7.6.6.7.7.

St. 3, 6, 8

Zahn 6519

Johann A. Gruber, 1748
Sheema Z. Buehne, trans. 1965

Johann Balthasar König, 1738

1. Love that's pure, it - self dis - dain - ing, Will the Loved One's cause em - brace,
Seeks no gold - en calf, main - tain - ing Meek - ness, bear - ing Christ's dis - grace;
2. O you souls, you who are deem - ing, You are what you ought to be
In your fame, your work, your seem - ing, Learn first right - ly naught to be.
Ev - er un - as - sum - ing, Glad - ly un - pre - sum - ing, Al - ways
Glad - ly in all ac - tions Give up sat - is - fac - tions. Cher - ish
hum - ble, nev - er vain, Much though it a - chieve and gain.
meek ob - scur - i - ty! Self - love grows too read - i - ly.

3. Could you learn to bide in stillness
And relinquish self, straightway
Then would every pain and illness,
On that unknown judgment day,
Liberate and ease you,
Profit and appease you;
And your heart and house would be
From within swept clean and free.

1. Reine Liebe sucht nicht sich selber,
Sondern des Geliebten Sach,
Sucht noch macht nicht guldene Kalber,
Liebt in Einfalt Christi Schmach;
Will zu allen Zeiten
Gerne nichts bedeuten;
Dunckt sich je nicht gros noch gut,
Ob sie gleich viel Thaten thut.

2. O ihr Seelen, die ihr meynet,
Ihr seyd, was es musse seyn,
Das ihr leuchtet, wircket, scheinet,
Lernet doch erst recht nichts seyn.
Lasset bey allen Sachen
Gern nichts aus euch machen:
Liebt die Klein Verborgenheit!
Eigenlieb sich gern ausbreit.

3. Lerntet ihr sein stille werden,
Und verlassen euer Ich:
O, so wurden die Beschwerden,
Und das fremde Knechts-Gericht
Bald zu eurem frommen
Auf eich selber kommen,
Und ihr euer Hertz und Haus
Reinigen von innen h'raus.

JEHOVAH, HERR UND MAJESTÄT
JEHOVAH, LORD AND MAJESTY

NUN FREUT EUCH, LIEBEN CHRISTEN GMEIN 8.7.8.7.8.8.7.

St. 1, 2, 12, 13

Zahn 4427

Conrad Weiser, writ. 1753
Sheema Z. Buehne, trans. 1964

Balthasar Schmid, arr. 1748

1. Je - ho - vah, Lord, and Maj - es - ty! Thy chil - dren stand im - plor - ing:
In - cline thine ear un - to the plea Of mul - ti - tudes a - dor - ing
2. This house to - day we sanc - ti - fy In cov - e - nant with thee,— Lord.
O let thy glo - ry from on high De - scend— for us to see,— Lord,
Be - fore thy ra - diant, ho - ly face. Scorn not— our prayer, but
And in a cloud, this house em - brace; Dis - pel— all e - vil
grant us grace. For thy name's— sake, O hear— us!
from this place. For thy name's— sake, O hear— us!

3. And grant us, highest Majesty
In heav'n, earth, sea, and air,
That we may offer here to thee
Our thanks, pleas, praise, and prayer
For all the ranks of Christendom,
That in eternity to come
Thy name may be adorèd.

4. From war, from drought, from fire's breath,
O keep this house securely,
That, after we meet blessèd death,
Our children will know surely
That we have loved the true God, thee,
And by thy word lived steadfastly.
For thy name's sake, O hear us.

1. Jehovah, Herr und Majestät!
Hör unser kindlich Flehen:
Neig Deine Ohren zum Gebet
Der Schaaren, die da stehen
Vor Deinem heiligen Angesicht:
Verschmähe unsere Bitte nicht,
Um Deines Namens willen!

2. Dies Haus wird heute eingeweiht
Von Deinem Bundes-Volke:
Lass uns, Herr, Deine Herrlichkeit
Hernieder in der Wolke,
Dass sie erfülle dieses Haus
Und treibe alles Böse aus,
Um Deines Namens willen!

3. Gieb endlich, höchste Majestät
Des Himmels und der Erden,
Dass Fürbitt, Dank, Preis und Gebet
Mag hier geopfert werden
Für jeden Stand der Christenheit,
Damit in alle Ewigkeit
Dein Nam' geehret werde!

4. Vor Feuer, Krieg und Wassers-Noth
Wollst Du dies Haus bewahren!
Damit nach sel'gem Tod
Die Nachkommen erfahren,
Dass wir Dich, wahren Gott, geliebt
Und uns in Deinem Wort geübt,
Um Deines Namens willen!

Die Sonn ist wieder aufgegangen
The Sun Now Risen

9.9.8.8.

St. 1, 8, 20

Johann Conrad Beissel, 1747
Johann Conrad Beissel, 1747
1. The sun_now ris - en, splen - did and bright, Hath_bathed all_the world in ra-diant light.
2. His hand_my fee - bler steps is guid - ing; He_chang - es_sor - row to re - joic - ing.
Now must my_in - most soul re - joice, For - got - ten now is sor - row's voice.
He brought me_to_the right - eous way From_which I nev - er-more_will stray.

3. No longer will he leave me grieving,
His sheltering love all doubts relieving,
His presence will my soul sustain
In days of deepest grief and pain.

1. Die Sonn ist wieder aufgegangen
im Lichtenpracht mit grossen Prangen,
drum freuet sich mein Geist und Hertz
dass ich vergesse allen Schmertz.

2. Doch da ich mich so thäte beugen,
Könt er mirs länger nicht verschweigen,
und zeigte mir sogleich mit an,
dass ich gewichen von der Bahn.

3. Da könt er mich nicht länger lassen,
und thäts mich in Lieb umfassen:
versprach hinfort bei mir zu seyn
auch in dem grösten Schmertz und Pein.

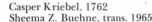

Nun schlaff du liebes Kindelein
Now Sleep My Little Child So Dear

Lobt Gott ihr Christen Allzugleich 8.6.8.6.6.

St. 1, 5-7

Zahn 199

Casper Kriebel, 1762
Sheema Z. Buehne, trans. 1965

Balthasar Schmid, arr. 1748

1. Now sleep, my lit - tle child so ___ dear, Rest peace - ful - ly a - new. Dear God, your guar - dian, ___
2. For you are sin - ful and de - filed By na - ture and by birth. But God's will makes of ___

3 6 3 6 6 3

will be ___ here; He'll send his an - gels, too, ______ That no harm come to you.
you his ___ child, A be - ing new on earth, ______ Good, pure, and full of worth.

6 6 5 6 6 5 3 6 6 5 3

3. Hence did a sinless child appear,
Born frail like you, and weak.
We call him little Jesus dear.
Chosen was he, the meek,
What had been lost to seek.

4. He wants to care for you on earth,
That you his heir may be;
He brought redemption ere your birth,
Before in infancy
The world you first did see.

1. Nun schlaff, du liebes Kindelein!
In still und sanffter Ruh:
Der lieb Gott will dein Hüter seyn;
sendt die Sein Englein zu,
dass dir nichts schaden thu

2. Denn du selbst bist voll Wust und Sünd,
von Geburt und Natur,
Gott's will ab'r ist: Aus Dir Sein Kind,
und neue Creatur,
zu machen gut und pur.

3. Drum, dir gleich, ward ein Kindlein klein,
Heilig ohn Sünd gebohr'n;
Es heisst das liebe Jesulein,
so dazu auserkohrn,
zu suchen was verlohrn.

4. Es will sich um dich nehmen an,
dass du Sein Erb mögst seyn;
Es hat für Dich Lösung gethan,
Eh Du ein Kindlein klein,
in die Welt trattest ein.

GEBENEDYT SEY ALLZEIT
BE GLORIFIED ETERNALLY

ALLEIN GOTT IN DER HÖHE 8.7.8.7.8.8.7.

St. 1, 2, 5, 8

Zahn 4457

Balthasar Hoffman, 1762
Sheema Z. Buehne, trans. 1965

Balthasar Schmid, arr. 1748

1. Be glo - ri - fied e - ter - nal - ly. Be praised__ and hon - ored du - ly;
The to - tal sa - cred trin - i - ty. The scrip - tures teach,__ is tru - ly One be - ing, one di - vin - i - ty And un - di -
2. The Fa - ther is to be ac-claimed As true__ a God__ in be - ing;
A true God must his Son be named, Born man__ by his__ de - cree - ing. The Ho - ly Ghost must be pro - fessed, Like-wise, true

[6] 6 6

5 6 6 6 6 ♮ # [6]

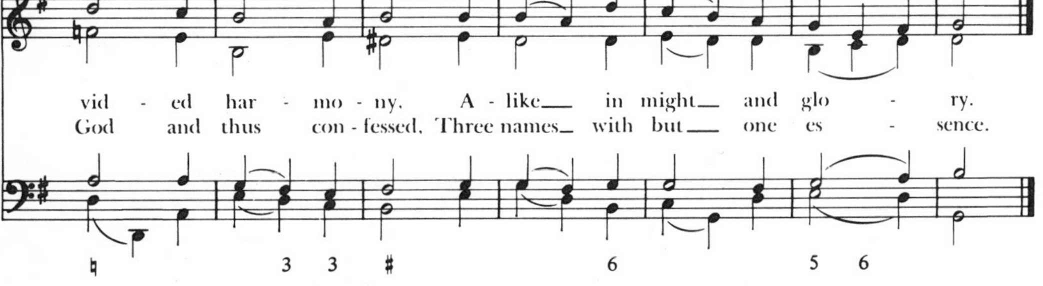
vid - ed har - mo - ny. A - like__ in might__ and glo - ry.
God and thus con - fessed. Three names__ with but__ one es - sence.
♮ 3 3 # 6 5 6

3. Oh, let us all with one accord
Our hymns of praise now sing him
Who has his throne in heav'n, the Lord.
Acclaim and thanks we bring him.
Let us with hearts rejoicing sing,
And God, our Lord, all honor bring,
Who dwells on high in heaven.

4. O Lord, our God, Almighty King,
We honor and adore thee.
Now at this hour, to thee we sing,
With thanks we come before thee.
To thee all glory, honor, praise
We'll offer up, through endless days
Eternally resounding.

1. Gebenedeyt sey allezeit,
Gelobet und geehret.
Die gantze heilige Dreyheit,
Die, wie die Schrifft uns lehret,
Eins Wesens ist, Eine Gottheit,
Und unzertheilte Einigkeit,
In gleicher Macht und Ehren.

2. Der Vater ist ein wahrer Gott,
Im Wesen zu bekennen.
Der Sohn Den Er gebohren hat,
Ist wahrer Gott zu nennen.
Desgleichen der Heilige Geist,
Ein wahrer Gott auch ist und heisst:
Drey Namen nur Ein Wesen.

3. Eja, so lasst uns nun zugleich,
Dem Herren auch lobsingen,
Der sein Thron hat im Himmelreich;
Lob und Danck vor Ihn bringen.
Lasst uns Ihm froelich singen gern,
Als unsren Gott und Herrn Ihn ehr'n,
Der hoch im Himmel wohnet.

4. Herr Gott! Der Du allmaechtig bist,
Dich wir ehrn und anbeten.
Wir singen Dir zu dieser Frist,
Mit Dancken vor Dir tretten:
Dir sey Gloria, Lob und Ehr,
Von jetzt fortan und immer mehr,
Bisz in Ewigkeit, Amen.

Ach Kinder wollt ihr lieben?
O Children, Would You Cherish?

St. 1, 9, 11, 13

Christopher Dock, after 1764
Samuel W. Pennypacker, trans. 1883

Ihr Sünder kommt gegangen 7.6.7.6.6.6.7.6.

Anon.

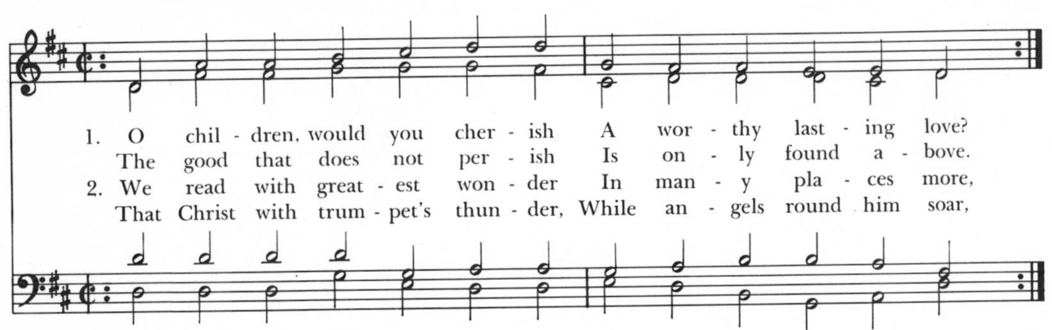
1. O chil - dren, would you cher - ish A wor - thy last - ing love?
The good that does not per - ish Is on - ly found a - bove.
2. We read with great - est won - der In man - y pla - ces more,
That Christ with trum - pet's thun - der, While an - gels round him soar,

Seek God, the high - est goal. With spir - it and with soul,
Will come up - on that day, The Ho - ly Scrip - tures say,

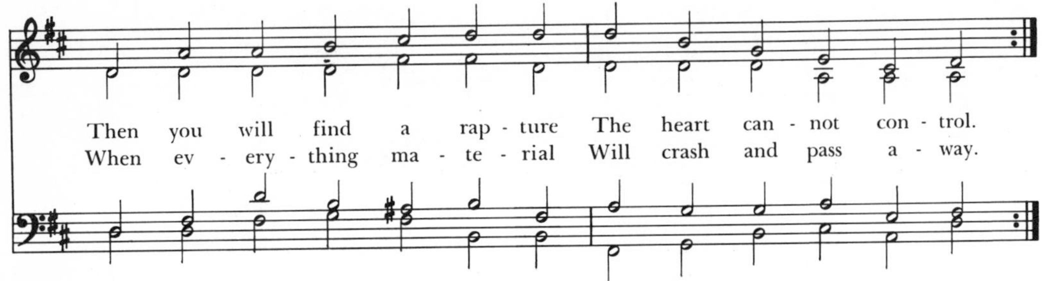
Then you will find a rap - ture The heart can - not con - trol.
When ev - ery - thing ma - te - rial Will crash and pass a - way.

3. Our secret inclinations
Will then be open thrown,
Our strongest aspirations
Will in the light be shown;
And he who then with heed
The Book of Life can read,
And find his name there written.
Is fortunate indeed.

4. While bells are softly ringing,
The angel music choir
With chanting and with singing,
Will enter through the door
To Zion's golden town,
On mortals looking down,
And every lamb of Jesus
Shall then receive his crown.

1. Ach Kinder, wolt ihr lieben,
So liebt was liebens werth,
Wollt ihr ja Freude üben,
So liebt was Freude werth;
Liebt Gott, das höchste Gut,
Mit Geist, Herz, Seel, und Muth,
So wird euch solche Liebe
Erquicken Herz und Muth

2. Man liesset mit Erstaunen
An andern Orten mehr,
Dass Christus mit Posaunen,
Mit seinem Engels Heer,
Wird kommen zum Gericht,
Wie Gottes Wort ausspricht,
Da alles wird vergehen
Mit Krachen, was man sieht.

3. Die Bücher der Gewissen
Werden dort aufgethan,
Worauf man hier beflissen,
Wird es dort zeigen an,
Das Buch des Lebens dann,
Wird auch da aufgethan,
Wer darin wird gefunden,
Der ist recht glüklich dran.

4. Ach da wird lieblich klingen,
Der Engel Musick-Chor,
Mit Jauchzen und mit Singen,
Wird gehen durch die Thor,
In Zions Stadt hinein,
Was Christi Schäflein seyn,
Wo ewig Freud und Wonne
Auf ihrem Haupt wird seyn.

O Lord, How Lovely Is the Place

Psalm 84 L.M.D.

Ps. 84: 1-3

Francis Hopkinson, adapted 1767

Version from Claude Goudimel, 1774

1. O Lord, how love - ly is the place, Where thou vouch-safst to show thy face,
2. O Lord of Hosts! how blest are they, Who in thine house thy praise dis - play,
In glo - ry, ev - er bright ar - rayed; My soul faints for thy blest a - bode,
Whose hopes in thee are firm - ly placed; Who with a pi - ous zeal do tread
My heart cries out to see her God With lus - tre un - ob-scured dis-played.
The ways that to thy tem - ple lead; For they shall nev - er be dis-graced.
The birds a - round thy tem - ple throng, And there they build and hatch their young.
In parch - ēd vales they know no want, For thou re - fresh-ing rain shall grant.

Use the bass notes added in parentheses for a more satisfactory musical effect.

* Line 3 as it appeared in 1774.

3. Thus, they proceed free from all fear,
From strength to strength, 'till all appear
On Sion's mount, forever blessed.
Lord, let my humble prayer be heard,
My soul's sincere desires regard;
To thee, O Jacob's God! addressed;
To us thy sure protection bring,
And look on thine, annointed King.

Ich bin ein Herr
I Am the Lord

Psalm 4 8.8.7.4.4.7.

St. 1-3

Zahn 4170

Alexander Mack I, 1774
Sheema Z. Buehne, trans. 1965

Heinrich Schütz, 1628

1. I am the Lord who sins for - gives, The Lord whose love un
2. Each sin I cast in - to the sea, And wipe it from my
chang - ing lives; The Son of Man I gave you. 'Tis fin - ished. See!
mem - o - ry, That it for - ev - er per - ish. My blood pro - fessed
How ten - der - ly My sac - ri - fice will save you.
Makes all things blessed; I gave it you to cher - ish.

3. Yea, walk before my countenance;
Be pious, loyal, with no glance
To right or left directed.
Heed my decree,
Show love for me,
Your cause shall be protected.

1. Ich bin ein Herr, der Sünd vergiebt,
Ich bin, der unverändert liebt,
Ich, Gott und Menschen-Sohne!
Es ist vollbracht,
Mein Opfer macht,
Dass ich nun deiner schone.

2. Die Sünde werf ich in das Meer,
So dass sie nimmer wiederkehr,
Und nicht mehr gedenke.
Mein theures Blut
Macht alles Gut,
Nur darum ich dirs schenke.

3. Doch wandle vor mein'm Angesicht,
Sey fromm, getreu, und weiche nicht
Zur Linken noch zur Rechten;
Gieb acht auf dich,
Und liebe mich,
Man wird dein Recht verfechten.

GUTER GOTT! DIR ICH BEFEHLE
LORD, DEAR GOD! TO THY ATTENDING

VON DEM TROST AUS JESU LEIDEN 8.8.7.7.

St. 1-3, 7, 8

Zahn 1376

Heinrich Otto, 1785
Sheema Z. Buehne, trans. 1965

Tune from Christian Gregor, 1784

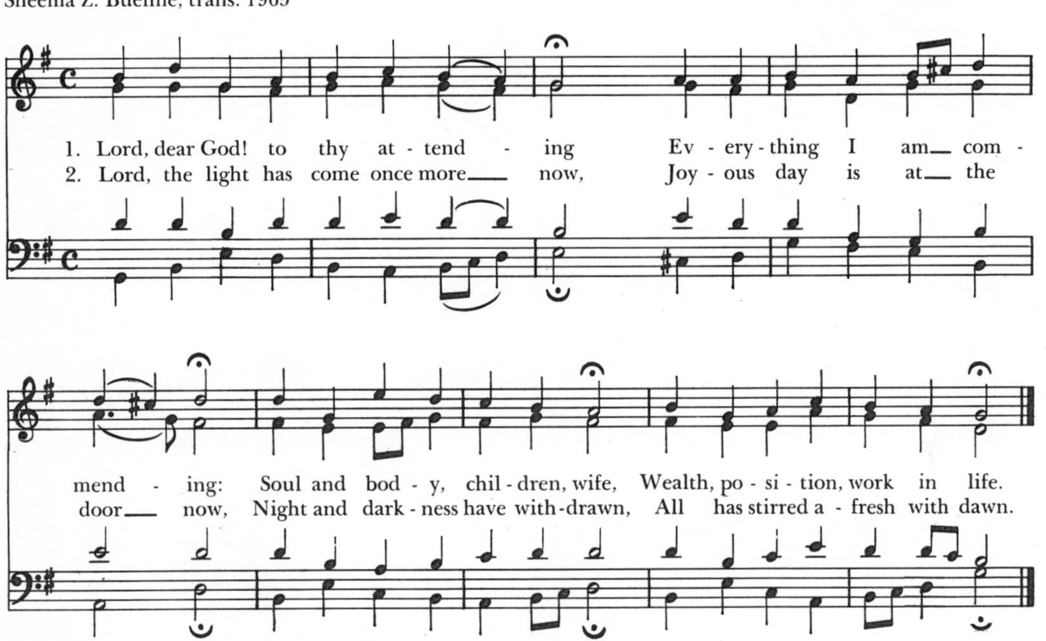
1. Lord, dear God! to thy at - tend - ing Ev - ery - thing I am — com - mend - ing: Soul and bod - y, chil - dren, wife, Wealth, po - si - tion, work in life.
2. Lord, the light has come once more — now, Joy - ous day is at — the door — now, Night and dark - ness have with - drawn, All has stirred a - fresh with dawn.

3. Thank thee for our lives defending,
Lightning, dread, and terror ending;
Thank thy angels watching bright
'Gainst dark Satan's wiles and might.

4. Let thy radiant grace descending
Shine on me and mine unending;
Bless me where in life I stand;
Bless the labor of my hand.

1. Guter Gott! Dir ich befehle,
Weib und Kinder, Leib und Seele,
Hab und Guter Werck und Stand,
Alles sey in deiner Hand.

2. Herr! das Licht ist Neu enstanden,
Und der frohe Tag vorhanden,
Nacht und Dunckel ist vorbey,
Alle Welt ist Munter neu.

3. Danck sei dir fur dein Beschützen,
Wieder Schrecken Furcht und Blitzen,
Danck fur deiner Engel-Wacht,
Wider Satans List und Macht.

4. Ueber mich und all die meinen,
Spurte deiner Gnaden-Scheinen,
Segne mich in meinem Stand,
Segne meine Werck und Hand.

O welch ein Licht
What Splendid Rays

8.6.7.6.

St. 1-4

Christian Gregor
Anon., Eng. trans. 1789

John Antes, late 18th cent.

St. 2, 3, and 4 revised by
Kenneth G. Hamilton, 1957

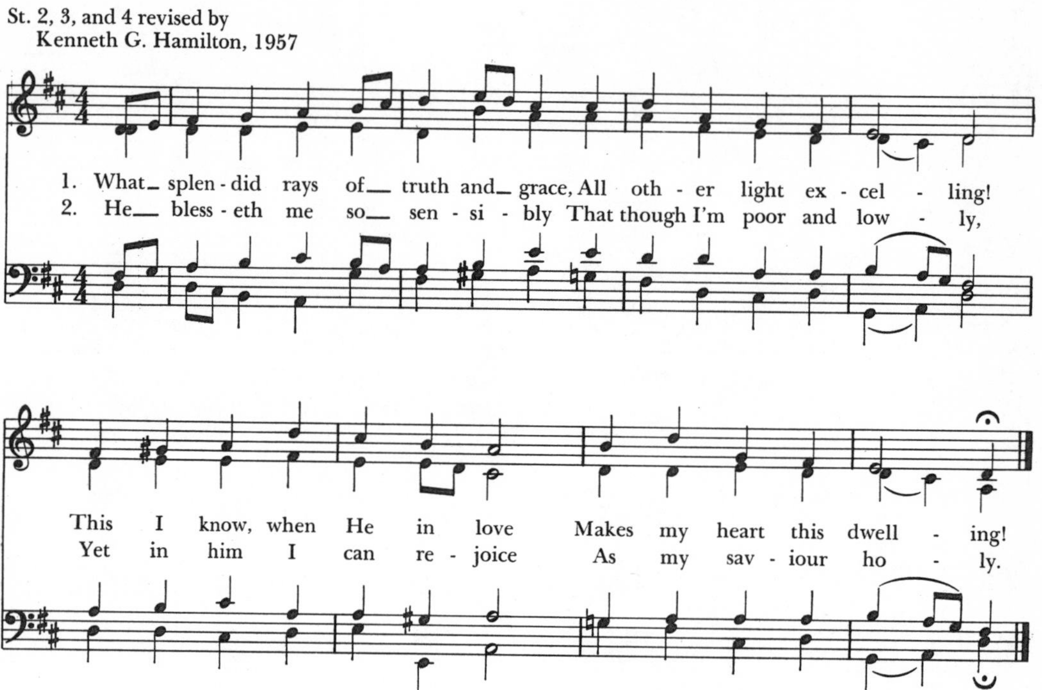
1. What_ splen - did rays of_ truth and_ grace, All oth - er light ex - cel - ling!
2. He_ bless - eth me so_ sen - si - bly That though I'm poor and low - ly,
This I know, when He in love Makes my heart this dwell - ing!
Yet in him I can re - joice As my sav - iour ho - ly.

3. Had I the grace to seek his face
In any trying hour!
Help from none will he withhold
Who implores his power.

4. Therefore I pray, while here I stay
And look to him with yearning:
Fixed in him may I abide,
Kept from ever turning.

A Joyful Sound It Is — Lobt Gott ihr Christen allzugleich 8.6.8.6.6.

St. 1, 4, 5, 7 — Zahn 199

George Strebeck, 1795 — Johann M. Spiess, arr. 1745

1. A joy - ful sound it is, the voice Of Je - sus to his friends, A sound that makes their hearts re - joice, And con - so - lates their minds, And con - so - lates their minds.

2. Its pre - cepts teach hu - mil - i - ty It leads the soul to God; By it the pris - oner is set free, Through the a - ton - ing blood, Through the a - ton - ing blood.

3. Oh! may I know the blessedness,
To dwell with Jesu's heirs.
Exalted in his righteousness,
Which this sweet sound declares,
Which this sweet sound declares.

4. So shall I in thy name rejoice;
I'll praise thee all my days;
Through all eternity my voice
Shall never cease to praise,
Shall never cease to praise.

O JESUS CHRIST, TRUE LIGHT OF GOD — HERR JESU CHRIST DICH ZU UNS WEND L.M.

St. 1, 4-6

John F. Ernst, 1795 — Version from John Christian Jacobi, 1732

1. O Je - sus Christ, true light of God, En - light - en
2. To all deaf grant an o - pen ear, The dumb an

such as know thee not, And bring them in - to
ut - terance with - out fear, Free - dom, to such, who

thy sheep - fold There - by to save their pre - cious soul.
would con - fess Their faith con - cern - ing right - eous - ness.

3. Beguilēd souls do undeceive,
Bring all back who mean thee to leave;
Them who are scattered congregate,
Convince those in a doubtful state.

4. Then, Lord! due praises shall be giv'n
On earth below, above in heaven
By all of thy redeemēd race
To thee for all thy love and grace.

YOKE SOFT AND DEAR | ACH GOTT UND HERR 8.7.8.7.
St. 1, 3, 10
John C. Kunze, 1795 | Adapted from the version of J. G. Schmauk, 1847

1. Yoke soft and dear, that brings me here To join in sweet em - brac - es,
2. Thee, thee a - lone as head we own, On Je - sus lips de - pend - ing,

The choir that sings its glo - rious King Un - ut - ter - a - ble prais - es.
We learn and hear with list - ening ear Words sweet and con - de - scend - ing.

3. Come Spirit, God, fill thy abode
With grace and supplication.
Send from above harmonious love
And joy and consolation.

THE NINETEENTH CENTURY

THE SEVENTEENTH and eighteenth were psalm-singing centuries. The nineteenth century became the century of the hymn and of the denominational hymnal. Earlier congregations had interpreted the ancient texts in the light of their own experiences. Now a new song developed, speaking the language of the period and reflecting its aspirations. The order of service was planned to give the congregational hymn its due place.

The Congregational Hymn

A brief sketch by T. S. Arthur called "The Circuit Preacher" describes a Methodist itinerant attempting to maintain an order of service, including hymn singing under primitive conditions. Mr. Odell, the subject of the story, had been transferred to a new circuit and was about to address his congregation, numbering about thirty, for the first time. "The preacher rose and gave out a hymn, but there was no one to raise the tune. . . . Odell was not much of a singer, but he had practised on 'Old Hundred' so much that he could lead that air very well; and the hymn happening, by good luck, to be set to a long metre tune, he was able to start it." Then followed a prayer and a Bible reading, after which Odell seated himself. "It is customary for the choir, if there is one, to sing an anthem during this pause; or, where no singers are set apart, for some member to strike up an appropriate hymn." On this occasion nothing was done and the preacher, after a brief pause, read the text of his sermon. The meeting closed with a final hymn.

A local tradition of Alstead, New Hampshire, concerns an unusual way of singing the opening hymn.

> The Slade brothers with their families and farm hands are singing as they trudge along the country road to attend the little white church on Sunday. The women and children are packed into the ox cart in front, the men walking behind, all singing hymns with strong voices as they walk the four miles to church. It is customary for the village folks to wait in front of the church for the Slades to arrive before ringing the last bell and then to join them as they march into church singing.

Many devout families not only sang hymns at Sunday service, they also made the hymn a regular part of morning worship at home. Such a family was that of Lyman Beecher, father of Henry Ward

Beecher and Harriet Beecher Stowe. A letter pictures him as "persevering in the hymn at family prayers during those years after his singing boys and girls were all gone away."

In the nineteenth century sopranos sang the tune—not the tenors, as in earlier times. When the older settings were reprinted they were rearranged to give the soprano the melody. This was true of Father Kemp's *Old Folks' Concert Tunes* and of the group of old tunes appended to the *Hymnal of the Methodist Episcopal Church* of 1878.

The countertenor lingered on into the century. In Harriet Beecher Stowe's *Oldtown Folks,* one of the various accomplishments of Sam Lawson was singing counter. In real life we read of the Reverend Buckminster, who delighted in taking the alto part when the altos in the choir were absent. The trend, however, was toward the second soprano or alto, and we hear little of the countertenor until the present century, when the artistry of such singers as Alfred Deller and Russell Oberlin made the voice familiar again.

It had been the duty of the clerk or of a designated deacon or elder to establish the pitch and set the tune. When church choirs occupied the singing seats this function passed to the choir leader. Harriet Beecher Stowe describes the process in her *Mayflower.*

> He [the choir leader] was a little man, whose fiery-red hair, brushed straight up on the top of his head, had an appearance as vigorous and lively as real flame; and this, added to the ardor and determination of all his motions, had obtained for him the surname of the "Burning Bush." With what an air did he sound the important fa sol la in the ears of the waiting gallery, who stood with open mouths ready to seize their pitch, preparatory to their general *set to* !

The use of a tuning fork or pitch pipe helped to prevent the mishaps which occurred when the pitch set was too high or too low. Yet because of the continuing prejudice against musical instruments, it sometimes seemed more decorous to disguise even so modest an instrument as the pitch pipe, so that to a casual observer it resembled a psalmbook.

Musical Instruments

As in the eighteenth century, the bass viol was commonly employed as an accompanying instrument. It was normally a cello with a short neck. Its introduction caused violent controversies and schisms. In one instance, where a member of the congregation refused to attend public worship as long as the obnoxious instrument was played, the church fathers decided that the viol was not to be played at stated services so that the aggrieved member might not be deprived altogether of the benefits of the Sunday service. The "great bass viol" or double

bass was sometimes used in church, and the choir in Barnard, Vermont, was accompanied by both forms. To this foundation instrument others were added.

In the East Church at Salem the clarinet and violin were first played in Christmas Day, 1792. Mr. Gardner was requested to play the counter part on his flute October 28, 1795, and on the following day a bass viol was purchased. The pastor, the Reverend William Bentley commented that "the fondness for instrumental music in the churches so increases that the inclination is not to be resisted." In 1814 in the Park Street Church, Boston, the singing was supported by flute, bassoon, and cello. Ryan, the clarinetist of the Mendelssohn Quinet, played his instrument at the Hanover Street Church in the same city with ophicleide and double bass for two years after 1845.

Similar instrumental groups were used in small country churches in England. Thomas Hardy's grandfather, for example, played cello in the church at Stinsford from 1801 or '02 to his death in 1837, and his two sons continued to play until c.1842. Thomas Hardy has left a drawing showing the position of the performers (c.1835). The instrumental performers at this time were four in number: three violins and cello. In general such groups simply doubled vocal parts, but in Lowell Mason's *The Hallelujah* (1854) and Isaac Woodbury's *The Cythara* (1854) interludes are provided which might be played on instruments. Indeed Mason composed them for church ensembles rather than for the organ since capable organists could improvise their own interludes.

The organ was gradually accepted as a proper instrument for the church. Dr. Bentley, in an entry of February 28, 1798, noted that a thousand dollars had been subscribed for an organ in his own church at Salem and thus was led to list the organs already in use. He knew of four in Boston, one recently acquired for Newburyport, and a small one in Charlestown. The old church in Salem had commenced a subscription with the intention of acquiring one. All of these were in New England and all but one were in Congregational churches. This gives a useful view of the local situation at the turn of the century.

The small organs of that period were, of course, pipe organs, but churches who delayed in installing a keyboard instrument might buy a reed organ or melodion. Indeed some country congregations still sing hymns to the accompaniment of a reed organ.

Choirs

Churches with sufficient means and a highly developed liturgy tended to establish professional choirs or at least choirs strengthened with professional singers. Where the use of male voices was mandatory,

as in the Roman Catholic Church, or preferred, as it was in many Episcopal churches, schools for choir boys to sing the soprano and alto parts had to be established. Churches which did not support a choir frequently hired a professional quartet of singers and an organist. There was a tendency in Episcopal churches in the large cities to seek English organists. Edward Hodges at Trinity Church is an early instance and T. Tertius Noble at St. Thomas is a more recent one in New York City.

Hymnbooks

Many of the New England churches moved toward the hymnbook by way of the psalm paraphrases of Watts, with a supplement of hymns. In an earlier preface we have traced the attempts to complete the psalm paraphrases of Isaac Watts and to make them suitable for use in American churches. One of these, published in 1801, was the work of Timothy Dwight. It enjoyed a substantial success and contained one paraphrase that has been sung in American churches to the present day: "I Love Thy Kingdom, Lord," based on part of Psalm 137.

Dwight's collection was followed in 1815 by Samuel Worcester's *Christian Psalmody*. Worcester, however, had curtailed some of Watts's versions and omitted others. These improvements were not regarded as such by his contemporaries and the protests were so vehement that Worcester felt obliged to restore the missing portions in his *Watts and Select* of 1819. Among the Baptists "Winchell's Watts" appeared in 1818–19.

The Convention of the Universalists of New England held in 1807 had instructed Hosea Ballou, Abner Kneeland, and Edward Turner to compile a hymnbook. What was actually published in 1808 as *Hymns composed by different authors* was perhaps unique for its period, first, because it was a hymnbook, not a psalmbook with a supplement, and second, because it was a denominational hymnbook that contained only American hymns written by the editors.

Among the clergymen of the Protestant Episcopal Church, Rev. William A. Mühlenberg was so zealous for hymn singing that he first wrote *A Plea for Christian Hymns* (1821) and then compiled a collection called *Church Poetry* (1823), which he used in his own church. A result of this pioneer effort was the appointment of a committee to prepare a hymnal by the General Convention of 1823. The committee, submitted a collection for approval in 1826, and it was published in the following year as *Hymns of the Protestant Episcopal Church of the United States of America*. It included American hymns by Mühlenberg, Onderdonk, George Washington Doane, and Eastburn.

Tune Books

Although members of the choir in the earlier part of the century had a volume containing the texts, they also needed a tune book containing appropriate music. Oblong books that were used in singing schools were carried into the gallery to meet this need.

The organist found this system inconvenient. As late as 1855 Richard Storrs Willis could write that "he must read the music before him, and follow the words in the hymn-book by the side of the music." An early collection which attempted a solution of the problem was the *Valuable Collection of Sacred Music* (Exeter, 1818). The text was printed above, the music below, with the page slit apart between them. Thus the pages of text and music could be turned independently and any tune could be associated with any text.

Two features in such books as the *Boston Academy Collection* (1822 and later) point to the growing acceptance of the organ in church. One is the order in which the vocal parts are printed, the other the appearance of figures below the bass part.

The older New England singing masters printed their vocal parts in order of pitch—soprano on top followed by counter, tenor, and bass. Mason's order is tenor, alto, soprano, and bass, reckoning from top to bottom. The purpose of the arrangement is to place the melody and the supporting bass part next to each other. Thus the organist of limited ability could play the two lowest lines in the score; a more skillful performer could play all four vocal parts at the keyboard.

As mentioned before, figures below the bass part represent a continuation of a kind of shorthand to represent intervals and chords that was usual in the Baroque period. The organist was expected to be able to improvise an accompaniment with only the figured bass before him. It hardly seems necessary to add figures where all four parts of the score are on the page, yet it was done in a number of collections (for example the popular *Bridgewater Collection*) showing that some organists preferred to play from the figures.

Printing the inner parts in small notes between the soprano and bass parts simplified the task of the organist. When Darley and Standbridge state that their *Cantus Ecclesiae* is "provided" with an accompaniment for the Organ or Piano Forte," they refer to an arrangement of this kind. Finally the parts were compressed on two staves, soprano and alto above, tenor and bass below, as in twentieth-century hymnals.

Information as to which tune books were used in choirs is scanty. A pamphlet by Edward Heaton entitled *A Brief History of the Post*

Mills Congregational Church gives an unusually complete list of tune books used in conjunction with *Watts and Select,* including:

The Village Harmony	1813
Handel and Haydn Society	1822
Bridgewater Collection	1826
The Choir	1832
Church Harmony	1833
New Hampshire Collection	1833
Ancient Harmony Revised	1843
The Psaltery	1846
The Dulcimer	1850

Many of the tunes in nineteenth-century books are not original compositions but arrangements from works by European composers. Although arrangements (other than arrangements of folk tunes) are in general not included in this collection, there are two which may serve to represent the type. One is Mason's HAMBURG, which is of special interest because it is a meeting between the New England hymn tune and a Gregorian chant. It is true that Mason's tonal harmonies and regular barring have completely altered the character of his source. The other is the tune which is sometimes called MERCY, sometimes GOTTSCHALK after its composer.

The adaptation of classic themes to hymn meters was due to an Englishman, William Gardiner. Lowell Mason's adoption of the practice is described in the preface to the *Boston Academy Collection,* where he claims that his earlier *Handel and Haydn Society Collection* was the first to introduce such arrangements to American singers.

Tune books of this period sold in thousands where the earlier books sold in hundreds. The Boston *Handel and Haydn Society Collection* sold 50,000 copies in the period from 1822 to 1858. Luther Orlando Emerson, in the preface of his *Ideal,* claimed that his *Harp of Judah, Jubilate,* and *Choral Tribute* had sold 50,000 copies each. The more successful musicians became teachers of teachers at conventions and editors and promoters of their books. Thus William O. Perkins was able to announce in the preface of *The Chorister* (1870) that "the success of the editor's previous works has induced him to abandon the business of teaching (except in Conventions) and devote himself exclusively to authorship." As congregational hymnbooks with music appeared, tunes by Lowell Mason and by other American composers of the period were included. Many of them were almost universally known in Protestant churches through most of the nineteenth

century and to a lesser degree into the present century. It was probably our most American period in terms of the congregational hymn tune.

Hymnbooks with Music

We have traced in outline the appearance of collections of hymn texts adapted to congregational use. We have also shown that the development of tune books was largely due to individual enterprise and that these books were designed for singing-school classes, church choirs, and eventually for the organist. The convenience of having the music closely associated with the words is obvious to us. Actually the first books to do this were designed, not for use in the regular Sunday services, but for revival meetings. They appeared in the second and third decade of the century. Most church members knew and could sing a limited number of the standard tunes, but revivals brought in a new repertory of tunes which they wished to learn.

The congregational hymnal with words and music together appeared after the mid-century. The words might be under the tune on the same page. Sometimes several texts were given with one tune and, if this were so, the tune and the chosen text might be on facing pages. Most convenient of all was the plan in which one or more stanzas were printed between the staves. These volumes were in the upright form which has been usual to the present day. Some were produced by individuals, some by publishers. In instances where the hymns but not the tunes were authorized by the denomination, there might be several hymnals with the same texts but with different music. Thus there were five musical editions of the *Protestant Episcopal Hymnal* of 1871–74 and six of that of 1886.

If we turn to inquire what musical influences superseded those exerted by Lowell Mason and those who came after him we must consider an Anglican hymnal, the *Hymns Ancient and Modern,* which was published in 1861. The more chromatic harmony, the freedom with which transient modulations were used, all seemed to contemporaries to represent an advance on the tunes in our own churches. Its effect here was to reduce the number of older American tunes in American hymnals and to inspire later American composers to imitate more or less closely what we may call the "English cathedral style." Its influence however was broader than this. It reflected a tendency toward the rites and the music of the Middle Ages, a tendency which was stimulated by the Oxford Movement and which resulted, for example, in the introduction of the Office Hymns with their melodies.

Such a broadening of view may be noted earlier in Henry Ward Beecher's "discovery" (for such it seemed to him) of the evangelical

zeal reflected in medieval Latin hymns. Another Congregationalist, Ray Palmer, was perhaps equally known for his original hymns and for his translations from Latin sources. Though we have not in general included translations by Americans in this volume, we have sought to suggest this trend by reproducing Palmer's "Behold, the Shade of Night Is Now Receding," which is a translation of Gregory's "Ecce iam noctis."

The initial impact, as was natural, was felt in the Protestant Episcopal Church. The American edition of *Hymns Ancient and Modern* appeared in 1866, was adopted by a number of Episcopal churches in this country, and was generally greeted with enthusiasm.

A church choir with melodeon

Hymns of War and Peace

Poets of the early nineteenth century looked back at the struggle which made us a nation with a sense of achievement.

> No more beneath th' oppressive hand of tyranny we groan.
> Behold the smiling, happy land that freedom calls her own.

The Civil War, the tragic and inescapable fact of the century, was rich in songs. Stanzas which are sometimes omitted from Longfellow's "I Heard the Bells on Christmas Day" show how deeply he was affected by the conflict. It is impossible to read the lines of Julia Ward Howe's "Battle Hymn of the Republic" without hearing in one's mind the jubilant and confident strains of "John Brown's Body," yet if we could separate such lines as "He is trampling out the vintage where the grapes of wrath are stored" and "He has loosed the fateful lightning of his terrible swift sword," they might convey a different meaning.

Poets took sides in the conflict as well as soldiers. George N. Boker, who spoke for the North, is represented by his "God, To Thee We Humbly Bow." Among the poets who espoused the Southern cause was Henry Timrod, who at other times wrote in a more militant vein, but in the poems chosen here writes of the Southerners who gave up their lives for a lost cause.

Walt Whitman, who had served as a nurse during the Civil War, wrote a new kind of hymn, a hymn to our pioneers. It is true that "All the Past We Leave Behind," although written in 1865, did not enter our hymnbooks until the twentieth century.

At the First Peace Jubilee, organized by Patrick Gilmore in 1869, a gargantuan chorus sang a new poem by Oliver Wendell Holmes, "Angel of Peace, Thou Hast Wandered Too Far." The tune to which it was sung, Matthias Keller's American Hymn, was composed for Keller's own text "Speed Our Republic, O Father on High." The theme is repeated in hymns of the twentieth century: "Give Peace, O God, the Nations Cry" (John W. Norris, 1940); "God of Peace, in Peace Preserve Us" (Ernest W. Olson, 1958); and "From Countless Hearts" (Gail Brook Burket, 1955).

Samuel F. Smith, in lines familiar to most Americans from childhood ("My country, 'tis of thee") celebrated America as a land of freedom. In a not dissimilar vein (and in the same meter) Theodore Chickering Williams wrote "My Country, to Thy Shore" (1912). The

idea of America as a refuge for "eager peoples flocking to be free" is stressed in Walter Russell Bowie's "God of the Nations."

There were poets who sang of the beauty of our land. "O beautiful for spacious skies" by Katherine Lee Bates immediately comes to mind, but Frederick Lucian Hosmer sounded a similar note in his "O Beautiful My Country."

The ideals of Christianity had always exceeded national boundaries, but national hymns by definition celebrated the glories of one nation. Few, however, would take as local a view as William Billings, who wrote "New England's God forever reigns." It is characteristic of the twentieth century that hymns appear which are international in appeal. Thus Frederick Lucian Hosmer wrote his "Hear, Hear, O Ye Nations," with its appeal for a "world triumph of peace and good will."

A singing master teaching a singing school

No More Beneath the Oppressive Hand — Liberty C.M.

Anon., 1800 — Stephen Jenks, 1800

Tune in tenor
No more be-neath th' op-pres-sive hand Of tyr-an-ny we groan.
Be-
Be-hold the smil-ing,
Be-hold the smil-ing, hap-py land, Be-
Be-hold the smil-ing, hap-py land, Be-hold the smil-ing,
hold the smil-ing, hap-py land, Be-hold the smil-ing, hap-py land, That
hap-py land, Be-hold the smil-ing, hap-py land, That free-dom calls her
hold the smil-ing, hap-py land, That free-dom calls her own,
hap-py land, That free-dom calls her own,
free-dom calls her own,
That free-dom calls her 1. own. 2. own.
That free-dom calls her own. own.
That free-dom calls her own. own.
That free-dom calls her 1. own. 2. own.
in original

Columbia, Trust the Lord — Columbia 10.10.10.D.

Anon., 1801 — Abraham Maxim, 1804

Tune in tenor
Co - lum - bia, trust the Lord, thy foes in vain At - tempt thy ru - in
and en - force their reign. Had they pre - vailed, dark - ness had closed our days,
And death and si - lence had for - bid his praise; But we are
saved and live, let songs a - rise! Co - lum - bia, bless the God who built the skies.

God of Our Fathers, Bless This Our Land 5.4.5.4.5.4.5.4.5.5.5.5.

St. 1-4

John Henry Hopkins, Jr., 1862 Dudley Buck, 1894

1. God of our fa - thers, Bless this our land; O - cean to o - cean
2. Lord God of Sab - bath, Might - y in war, Bound - less and num - ber - less
Own - eth thy hand. Home of all na - tions From far and near,
Thine ar - mies are. Thy right hand con - quer - eth All that op - pose;
Give, to u - nite us, Thy faith and fear. God of our fa - thers,
Launch forth thy thun - der - bolts. Smite down our foes; Lord God of Sab - a - oth,
Fail - ing us nev - er, God of our fa - thers, Be ours for - ev - er.
Fail - ing us nev - er, Lord God of Sab - a - oth, Fight for us ev - er.

3. Lord God our Saviour,
Thy love o'erflows,
Making our wilderness
Bloom as the rose.
Thou with true liberty,
Makest us free,
Knowing no master,
No king but thee,
Lord God our Saviour,
Failing us never,
Lord God our Saviour,
Reign thou forever.

4. Spirit of unity,
Crown of all kings,
Find us a resting place
Under thy wings.
By thine own presence,
Thy will be dóne,
Millions of free men,
Banded as one.
Lord God almighty,
Failing us never,
Thine be the glory,
Now and forever.

MINE EYES HAVE SEEN THE GLORY — THE BATTLE HYMN OF THE REPUBLIC — 15.15.15.6., with chorus

St. 1-4

Julia Ward Howe, 1862 — William Steffe, 1852

1. Mine___ eyes have seen the glo - ry of the com - ing of the Lord;
2. I have seen him in the watch - fires of a hun - dred cir - cling camps;

He is tram - pling out the vin - tage where the grapes of wrath are stored;
They have build - ed him an al - tar in the eve - ning dews and damps;

He hath loosed the fate - ful light - ning of his ter - ri - ble swift sword;
I can read his right - eous sen - tence by the dim and flar - ing lamps,

His truth is march - ing on.
His day is march - ing on.

Chorus

Glo - ry! Glo - ry! Hal - le - lu - jah! Glo - ry! Glo - ry! Hal - le-
Glo - ry! Glo - ry! Hal - le - lu - jah! Glo - ry! Glo - ry! Hal - le-

lu - jah! Glo - ry! Glo - ry! Hal - le - lu - jah! His truth is march - ing on.
lu - jah! Glo - ry! Glo - ry! Hal - le - lu - jah! His day is march - ing on.

3. He has sounded forth the trumpet that shall never sound retreat;
He is sifting out the hearts of men before his judgment seat;
O be swift, my soul to answer him; be jubilant, my feet!
Our God is marching on.

Chorus
Glory! Glory! Hallelujah!
Glory! Glory! Hallelujah!
Glory! Glory! Hallelujah!
Our God is marching on.

4. In the beauty of the lilies Christ was born across the sea,
With a glory in his bosom that transfigures you and me;
As he died to make men holy, let us die to make men free!
While God is marching on.

Chorus
Glory! Glory! Hallelujah!
Glory! Glory! Hallelujah!
Glory! Glory! Hallelujah!
While God is marching on.

FAINT FALLS THE GENTLE VOICE
St. 1-3

BETTEVER'S CHANT L.M.

Henry Timrod, writ. 1864

Benjamin H. Everett, 1871

1. Faint falls the gen - tle voice of prayer In the wild sounds that fill the air, Yet,
2. Thine ear, thou ten - der one, is caught, If we but bend the knee in thought; No
Lord, we know that voice is heard, Not less than if thy throne it stirred.
cho - ral song that shakes the sky Floats far - ther than the Chris - tian's sigh.

3. Not all the darkness of the land
Can hide the lifted eye and hand;
Nor need the clanging conflict cease,
To make thee hear our cries for peace.

God To Thee We Humbly Bow | Imperial 7.7.7.7.D.

St. 1, 2, 4, 5

George H. Boker, 1864 | C. M. Wyman, 1868

Joyfully
1. God, to thee we hum-bly bow, With hand un-armed and na-ked brow;
2. Of our-selves we noth-ing know;—— Thou, and thou a-lone, canst show,
Mus-ket,— lance, and— sheath-èd sword At thy feet we— lay, O Lord!
By the— fa-vor— of thy hand, Who has drawn the— guil-ty brand.

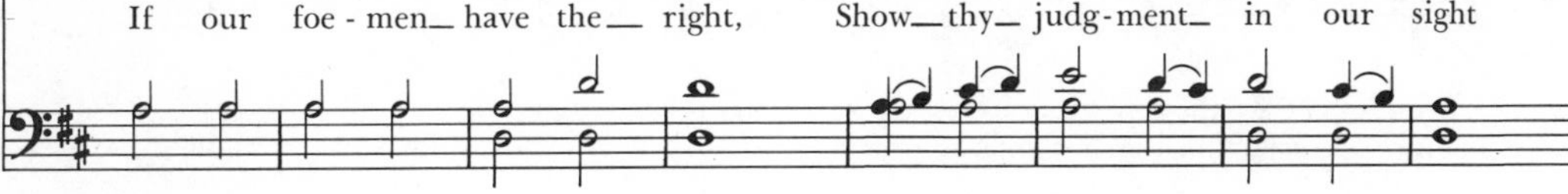
Gone is all the— sol-dier's— boast In—the— val-or— of the host;
If our foe-men— have the— right, Show—thy— judg-ment— in our sight

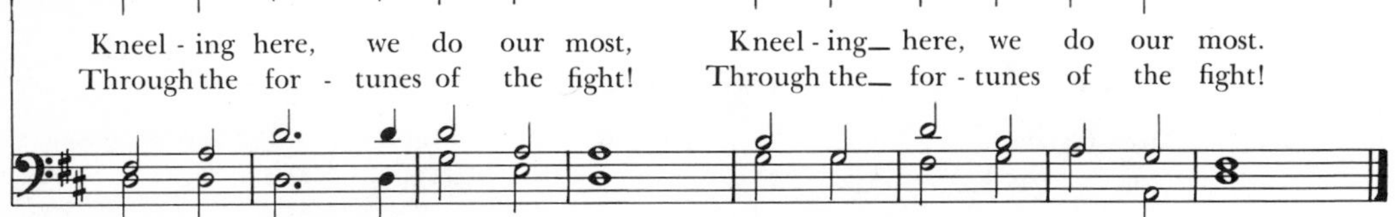
Kneel-ing here, we do our most, Kneel-ing— here, we do our most.
Through the for-tunes of the fight! Through the— for-tunes of the fight!

3. God of mercy, some must fall
In thy holy cause. Not all
Hope to sing the victor's lay,
When the sword is laid away.
Brief will be the prayers then said;
Falling at thy altar dead,
Take the sacrifice instead!
Take the sacrifice instead!

4. Now, O God, once more we rise,
Marching on beneath thy eyes;
And we draw the sacred sword
In thy name and at thy word.
May our spirits clearly see
Thee, through all that is to be,
In defeat or victory!
In defeat or victory!

SLEEP SWEETLY

St. 1-3, 5

Henry Timrod, 1866

THE PILGRIM'S LOT 8.8.8.6.D.

Andrew Gramblin, 1835

Tune in tenor
1. Sleep sweet - ly in your hum - ble graves, Sleep, mar - tyrs of a fal - len cause;
3. Mean - while be-half the tar - dy years Which keep in trust your sto - ried tombs,
Though yet no mar - ble col - umn craves The pil - grim here to pause.
Be - hold! your sis - ters bring their tears, And these me - mo - rial blooms.
2. In
4. Stoop,
seeds of lau - rel in the earth The blos - som of your fame is blown,
an - gels, hith - er from the skies! There is no ho - lier spot of ground
And some - where, wait - ing for its birth, The shaft is in the stone!
Than where de - feat - ed val - or lies, By mourn - ing beau - ty crowned!

ANGEL OF PEACE, THOU HAST WANDERED TOO LONG — AMERICAN HYMN 10.10.10.10.D.

St. 1-3

Oliver Wendell Holmes, 1869 — Matthias Keller, 1866

1. An - gel of Peace, thou hast wan-dered too long! Spread thy white wings to the sun - shine of love!
2. Broth-ers we met, on this al - tar of thine, Min-gling the gifts we have ga-thered for thee,
Come while our voic - es are blend - ing in song, Fly to our ark like the storm beat - en dove!
Sweet with the o - dors of myr - tle and pine, Breeze of the prair - ie, and breath of the sea,
Fly to our ark on the wings of the dove! Speed o'er the far sound-ing bil-lows of song,
Mea-dow and moun-tain and for - est and sea! Sweet is the fra-grance of myr - tle and pine,
Crowned with thine ol - ive leaf gar-land of love, An - gel of Peace, thou hast wait - ed too long!
Sweet - er the in - cense we of - fer to thee, Broth-ers once more round this al - tar of thine!
cresc.

3. Angels of Bethlehem, answer the strain!
Hark! a new birthsong is filling the sky!
Loud as the storm wind that tumbles the main,
Bid the full breath of the.organ reply,
Let the loud tempest of voices reply,
Roll in long surge like the earth - shaking main!
Swell the vast song till it mounts to the sky!
Angels of Bethlehem, echo the strain!

All the Past We Leave Behind | Paumanok 7.8.8.8.7.7.
St. 1-4

Walt Whitman, 1882 | Philip James, cop. 1964

Voices in Unison
Voices in Harmony
1. All the past we— leave be-hind: We take up the— task e-ter-nal, And the bur-den and the— les-son, Con-quering, hold-ing, dar-ing,—ven-turing, So we go the un-known ways,— Pi-o-neers! O Pi-o-neers!
2. Not for de-lec-ta-tions sweet, Not the rich-es— safe and pall-ing, Not for us the tame en-joy-ment; Nev-er must you be— di-vid-ed, In our ranks you move u-nit-ed, Pi-o-neers! O Pi-o-neers!

3. All the pulses of the world,
All the joyous, all the sorrowing,
These are of us, they are with us,
We today's procession heading,
We the route for travel clearing,
Pioneers! O Pioneers!

4. On and on the compact ranks,
With accessions, ever waiting,
We must never yield or falter,
Through the battle, through defeat,
Moving yet and never stopping,
Pioneers! O Pioneers!

O Beautiful My Country
St. 1-3
Frederick Lucian Hosmer, 1884

Salve Domine 7.6.7.6.D.
Lawrence W. Watson, 1909

1. O beau - ti - ful, my coun - try! Be thine a no - bler care
2. For thee our fa - thers suf - fered, For thee they toiled and prayed;
Than all thy — wealth of com - merce, Thy har - vests wav - ing fair.
Up - on thy — ho - ly al - tar Their will - ing lives they laid.
Be it thy pride to lift up The man - hood of the poor;
Thou hast no com - mon birth - right, Grand mem - ories on thee shine;
Be thou to the op - press - èd Fair free - dom's o - pen door!
The blood of pil - grim na - tions Com - min - gled flows in thine.

3. O beautiful, our country!
Round thee in love we draw;
Thine is the grace of freedom,
The majesty of law.
Be righteousness thy scepter,
Justice thy diadem;
And on thy shining forehead
Be peace the crowning gem!

Folk Hymns and Spirituals

Folk Hymns

The "all-day singing" was a Southern institution. Singers gathered at the county courthouse with their lunch baskets and their yellowed copies of the *Sacred Harp* or *Southern Harmony*. After sounding their notes, fa, sol, la, mi, they sang the first hymn through the syllables, then with the words in a brisk uninflected tempo. After a hearty picnic lunch on the grounds they returned to the auditorium for more hymn singing. As the number of singers diminished, scholars, and notably the late George Pullen Jackson, became interested in what they sang, and the real beauty of the Southern folk hymn was recognized.

The folk hymn is known by its musical character. The melody, and it is usually assigned to the tenor, is often in one of the ancient modal scales. Certain tones are omitted or less conspicuously employed, giving the impression of a gapped scale with five or six notes. The settings of these hymns were evidently made by local editors and singing masters in a style that has many points of resemblance with that of the early New England school. There is some indication of a shift from three- to four-voice writing.

One type of folk hymn is closely related to the ballads which Cecil Sharp and others collected in the Southern Appalachians. These religious ballads are the spiritual equivalent of the doleful broadsides containing the supposed confessions of convicted criminals. "Remember, Sinful Youth" is associated with a tune in the special meter which had served for a ballad on the fate of the famous pirate Captain Kidd. Another and later hymn of the same type is Samuel Wakefield's " 'Go Bring Me,' Said the Dying Fair," which deals with the sad end of a young woman who was too fond of jewelry and fine apparel.

Many of the favorite texts are anonymous. This is true of the familiar "What Wondrous Love Is This," which has found its way into denominational hymnals. Others are the work of camp meeting preachers. The Baptist John Leland wrote "Now Behold the Saviour Pleading," the Western poet John A. Granade, "Come, All Ye Mourning Pilgrims" and "Sweet Rivers of Redeeming Love," and Caleb Jarvis Taylor, "O Jesus, My Saviour." "Where Are the Hebrew Children" is often attributed to Peter Cartwright. Still other texts were taken from Northern or English writers. A good example is the missionary hymn "Wake, Isles of the South" by William B. Tappan,

which William Hauser arranged in folk style. Especially curious is Timothy Dwight's "As Down a Lone Valley," associated with a brisk fife tune by Morelli which was taken over by Southern singers.

Early accounts of Southern folk singing are rare indeed. A passage in Peter Cartwright's autobiography is of special interest. He had reached "the spurs of the Alleghany Mountains." He wished a place to stay to avoid traveling on the Sabbath and was directed to a house where they invited him to preach. At the conclusion of his sermon Cartwright "called on our kind local preacher to conclude. He rose and began to sing a mountain song, and pat his foot, and clap his hands, and ever and anon would shout at the top of his speech, 'Pray brethren.' In a few moments the whole house was in an uproarious shout."

Of the folk hymns included, "High O'er the Hills," "Our Bondage, It Shall End," "Oh When Shall I See Jesus," "Remember, Sinful Youth," "The Time Is Swiftly Rolling On," and "Where Are the Hebrew Children" come from *Southern Harmony*. The hymns from *Sacred Harp* are "O Jesus, My Saviour," "Our School Now Closes Out," "Oh When Shall I See Jesus," "Sweet Rivers of Redeeming Love," "The Happy Day Will Soon Appear," and "What Ship Is This." From William Hauser's *Olive Leaf* come "Now Behold the Saviour Pleading," and "Come All Ye Mourning Pilgrims." It also seemed appropriate to choose a Southern tune, THE PILGRIM'S LOT for Henry Timrod's elegy to the Confederate dead, "Sleep Sweetly."

When modern choral groups sing these hymns they are generally reharmonized. We give "What Wondrous Love Is This" and "Where Are the Hebrew Children" here as they appear in the Southern books and also in arrangements by Mrs. Annabel Morris Buchanan.

Spirituals

Created in slavery, the spiritual was recorded only after the Civil War. Yet it had long been clear that the slaves brought here from Africa had an uncommon aptitude for music. "A torrent of sacred harmony poured into my chamber and carried my mind away to heaven"—it is in these terms that Samuel Davies describes the singing of Negroes who in 1756 spent the night in his house. But what the Negroes sang were the psalm tunes of the whites. When religious revivals swept through the country the Negroes heard and remembered the camp meeting hymns. Peter Cartwright, when he stopped at a farm house on the Cumberland River, preached to white and to black. "I sung and prayed, took my text, and preached to them about an hour as well as I could. The colored people wept, the white people wept, the

man of the house wept; and when I closed he said, 'Do leave another appointment, and come and preach to us, for we are sinners and greatly need preaching.' " That the slaves remembered the music of Africa is certain. Those who heard them sing in the New World describe their performances as different and strange. What finally emerged as the spiritual was the expression of a people torn violently from one tradition and thrust against their will into another.

Though some texts were printed earlier, the first important book containing both words and music was *Slave Songs of the United States,* which appeared in 1867. The wide dissemination of the collections which followed was due to the desperate need for Negro education in the South in the period following the Civil War and to the discovery that tours by groups of student singers were an effectual way of raising funds.

Jubilee Songs contained the repertory of the group sent out from Fisk. The group was rehearsed by George L. White, who became a schoolteacher and eventually the treasurer of Fisk University. Although "he had never had any musical instruction himself, his schools were famous for the good singing which he had the knack of getting out of his pupils." The songs "had been written out for the first time by Theodore F. Seward, the distinguished teacher and composer," who states that these melodies "spring from the white heat of religious fervor during some protracted meeting in church or camp." He points to the complicated and "sometimes strikingly original" rhythm, the preference for duple meters, which he relates to the "beating of the foot and the swaying of the body," and the use of a scale with the "fourth and seventh tones omitted." The manner in which these touring groups performed was evidently modified to suit the white audiences for which they performed. E. M. Cravath was speaking of the Jubilee Singers when he remarked that they "have become familiar with much of our best sacred and classical music, and this has modified their manner of execution."

The songs selected for the present anthology have been chosen to represent the important collections. From *Slave Songs* we have taken "Hurry On, My Weary Soul"; from the *Jubilee Singers and Their Songs,* "Didn't My Lord Deliver Daniel" and "When Israel Was in Egypt's Land"; from *Cabin and Plantation Songs* (the later edition of 1918), "He Raise a Poor Lazarus." The John W. Work collection is the source for "Calvary," "I'm Agoing to Lay Down My Sword," and "O Mary, Don't You Weep, Don't You Mourn," while "Nobody Knows de Trouble I've Seen" and "Roll, Jordan, Roll" come from the R. Nathaniel Dett collection. "Don't You Be Like the Foolish Virgin" is from

Slave Songs of the Georgia Sea Islands by Lydia Parrish. It was largely through the arrangements of Harry T. Burleigh that the spiritual entered the song recital. Here we have included an arrangement of "Let Us Cheer the Weary Traveler," written to celebrate Burleigh's thirtieth year as soloist in the choir of St. George's Church, New York.

It is only in the twentieth century that denominational hymnbooks have included spirituals. They thus become part of a common heritage. Winifred Douglas' arrangement of "Were You There" was included in *The Hymnal 1940*. "Let Us Break Bread Together" comes from the *Presbyterian Hymnal* of 1953, while "Lord, I Want To Be a Christian" was arranged by R. Nathaniel Dett for the *African Methodist Episcopal Zion Hymnal* of 1957.

A Southern family singing folk hymns

Remember, Sinful Youth | Solemn Thought 12.9.12.12.9.

St. 1-5

Anon., early 19th cent. | F. Price, arr. 1854

Tune in Middle Part
1. Re - mem-ber, sin - ful youth, you must die, you must die, Re - mem-ber, sin - ful youth, you must die; Re - mem - ber, sin - ful youth, who hate the way of truth And in your pleas - ures boast, you must die, you must die; And in your pleas - ures boast, you must die.
2. Un - cer - tain are your days here be - low, here be - low, Un - cer - tain are your days here be - low, Un - cer - tain are your days, for God hath man - y ways To bring you to your graves here be - low, here be - low, To bring you to your graves here be - low.

3. The God that built the sky, great I am, great I am,
The God that built the sky, great I am;
The God that built the sky, hath said (and cannot lie),
Impenitents shall die, and be damned, and be damned,
Impenitents shall die, and be damned.

4. And, O my friends, don't you, I entreat, I entreat,
And, O my friends, don't you, I entreat;
And, O my friends, don't you your carnal mirth pursue,
Your guilty souls undo, I entreat, I entreat,
Your guilty souls undo, I entreat.

5. Unto the Saviour flee, 'scape for life!
'scape for life!
Unto the Saviour flee, 'scape for life!
Unto the Saviour flee, lest death eternal be
Your final destiny, 'scape for life!
'scape for life!
Your final destiny, 'scape for life!

The Happy Day Will Soon Appear
St. 1, 2

Sweet Morning 8.11.8.11., with chorus

Anon., early 19th cent.

H. S. Reese, arr. 1859

Tune in tenor
1. The happy day will soon appear, And we'll all shout together in that morning;
When Gabriel's trumpet you shall hear, And we'll all shout together in that morning.
Chorus
Sweet morning, Sweet morning, And we'll all shout together in the morning.

2. Behold the righteous marching home.
   And we'll all shout together in that morning.
   And all the angels bid them come.
   And we'll all shout together in that morning.
   Chorus

What Wondrous Love Is This — Wondrous Love 12.9.12.12.9.

St. 1-3, 5, 7

Anon., early 19th cent. — Anon., 1854

Tune in Middle Part
1. What won-drous love is this, O my soul! O my soul! What won-drous love is this, O my soul! What won-drous love is this that caused the Lord of bliss To bear the dread-ful curse, for my soul, for my soul, To bear the dread-ful curse, for my soul.
2. When I was sink-ing down, sink-ing down, sink-ing down, When I was sink-ing down, sink-ing down; When I was sink-ing down, be-neath God's right-eous frown, Christ laid a-side his crown, for my soul, for my soul, Christ laid a-side his crown, for my soul.

3. Ye wingèd seraphs, fly! Bear the news! Bear the news!
Ye wingèd seraphs fly! Bear the news
Ye wingèd seraphs fly, like comets through the sky,
Fill vast eternity with the news, with the news,
Fill vast eternity with the news!

4. Come, friends of Zion's king, join the praise, join the praise,
Come, friends of Zion's king, join the praise!
Come, friends of Zion's king, with hearts and voices sing,
And strike each tuneful string, in his praise, in his praise,
And strike each tuneful string in his praise!

5. Yes, when to that bright world we arise, we arise,
Yes, when to that bright world we arise;
When to that world we go, free from all pain and woe,
We'll join the happy throng, and sing on, and sing on,
We'll join the happy throng, and sing on.

What Ship Is This? — Old Ship of Zion — Irregular, with chorus

St. 1-4

Samuel Hauser (?), c.1800 — Thomas W. Carter, arr. 1844

Tune in tenor
1. What ship is this that will take us all home, O glory hal-le-lu-jah,
And safe-ly land us on Ca-naan's bright shore? O glory hal-le-lu-jah.
Chorus
'Tis the old ship of Zi-on, hal-le-lu, hal-le-lu, 'Tis the old ship of Zi-on, hal-le-lu-jah.

2. The winds may blow and the billows may foam,
O glory hallelujah,
But she is able to land us all home,
O glory hallelujah.

Chorus

3. She landed all who have gone before,
O glory hallelujah,
And yet she is able to land still more,
O glory hallelujah.

Chorus

4. If I arrive there, then, before you do,
O glory hallelujah,
I'll tell them that you are coming up, too,
O glory hallelujah.

Chorus

Come All Ye Mourning Pilgrims

Pilgrim 8.6.8.6.7.6.8.6.

St. 1,3,5,6

John A. Granade, writ. c.1801

William Hauser, arr. 1878

1. Come all ye mourn-ing pil - grims dear, Who're bound for Ca - naan's land;
Take cour - age and fight val - iant - ly, Stand fast with sword in hand!
Our Cap - tain's gone be - fore us, Our Fa - ther's on - ly son;
Then— pil - grims dear, pray do not fear, But let us fol - low on.

2. We have a howling wilderness
To Canaan's happy shore,
A land of drought, and pits, and snares,
While chilling winds do roar,
But Jesus will be with us
And guard us by the way;
Though enemies examine us,
He'll teach us what to say.

3. The pleasant fields of Paradise
Are glorious to behold;
The vales are clad in living green,
The city paved with gold,
The trees of life with heavenly fruit
Behold how rich they stand!
Blow, gentle gales, and bear my soul
Away to Canaan's land!

4. Already to my raptured sight
The blissful fields arise,
And plenty spreads her smiling stores
Inviting to my eyes.
O sweet abode of endless rest,
I soon shall travel there;
Nor earth, nor all her empty joys
Shall long detain me here.

Oh, When Shall I See Jesus? Morning Trumpet, 7.6.7.6.D.

St. 1-5

Anon., 1805 Benjamin Franklin White, arr. 1854

Tune in tenor
1. Oh___ when shall I see Je - sus, And reign with him a - bove?
And___ from the flow - ing foun - tain, Drink ev - er - last - ing love?
When___ shall I be de - li - ver'd From this vain world of sin?
And___ with my bless - ed Je - sus Drink end - less plea - sures in?
And shall hear the trum - pet sound___ in that morn - ing.
And shall hear the trum - pet sound___ in that morn - ing.
Chorus
Shout,___ O___ glo - ry! for I shall mount a - bove the skies,
When I hear the trum - pet sound___ in that morn - ing.

2. But now I am a soldier,
My Captain's gone before;
And shall hear the trumpet sound in that morning.
He's given me my orders,
And bids me ne'er give o'er;
And shall hear the trumpet sound in that morning.
His promises are faithful
A righteous crown he'll give,
And shall hear the trumpet sound in that morning.
And all his valiant soldiers
Eternally shall live.
And shall hear the trumpet sound in that morning.

Chorus

3. Through grace I feel determined
To conquer, though I die,
And shall hear the trumpet sound in that morning.
And then away to Jesus,
On wings of love I'll fly:
And shall hear the trumpet sound in that morning.
Farewell to sin and sorrow,
I bid them both adieu!
And shall hear the trumpet sound in that morning.
And O my friends, prove faithful,
And on your way pursue,
And shall hear the trumpet sound in that morning.

Chorus

4. Whene'er you met with troubles
And trials on your way,
And shall hear the trumpet sound in that morning.
Then cast your care on Jesus,
And don't forget to pray.
And shall hear the trumpet sound in that morning.
Gird on the gospel armour
Of faith, and hope, and love,
And shall hear the trumpet sound in that morning.
And when the combat's ended,
He'll carry you above.
And shall hear the trumpet sound in that morning.

Chorus

5. Oh do not be discouraged,
For Jesus is your friend;
And shall hear the trumpet sound in that morning.
And if you lack for knowledge,
He'll not refuse to lend.
And shall hear the trumpet sound in that morning.
Neither will he upbraid you,
Though often you request,
And shall hear the trumpet sound in that morning.
He'll give you grace to conquer,
And take you home to rest.
And shall hear the trumpet sound in that morning.

Chorus

SWEET RIVERS OF REDEEMING LOVE — SWEET RIVERS C.M.D.

St. 1,2,4,6,7

John A. Granade, 1814 — William Moore, 1859

Tune in tenor
1. Sweet riv - ers_ of re - deem - ing_ love Lie just_ be - fore_ my eyes,
Had I the_ pin - ions_ of a_ dove, I'd to_ those re - gions rise;
2. While I'm im - pris - oned_ here be - low, In an - guish, pain,_ and smart,
Some - times those_ trou - bles_ I fore - go, When love sus - tains_ my heart;
I'd rise su - pe - rior to_ my_ pain, With joy out - strip the_ wind,
In dark - est shad - ows of_ the_ night, Faith mounts the up - per_ sky,
I'd cross proud Jor - dan's swell - ing_ flood, And leave_ the world be - hind. hind.
I then be - hold my heart's_ de - light, And would_ re - joice to_ die. die.
1.
2.

3. A few more days or years at most
My troubles will be o'er;
I hope to join the heavenly host,
On Canaan's happy shore.
My raptured soul shall drink and feast,
In love's unbounded sea;
The glorious hope of endless rest
Is ravishing to me.

4. O come, my Saviour, come away,
And bear me to the sky,
Nor let thy chariot long delay,
Make haste and bring it nigh.
I long to see thy glorious face,
And in thine image shine,
To triumph in victorious grace,
And be forever thine.

5. Then will I tune my harp of gold
To my eternal king;
Through ages which can ne'er be told,
I'll make thy praises ring.
All hail eternal Son of God!
Who died on Calvary,
Who bought me with his precious blood,
From endless misery.

O Jesus, My Saviour, I Know Thou Art Mine — Expression 11.11.11.11.

St. 1-3

Caleb J. Taylor, 1814 — Anon., 1844

Tune in tenor
1. Oh, Je - sus, my Sav - iour, I know thou art mine;
2. Thou art my rich treas - ure, my joy and my love.
For thee all the pleas - ures of earth I re - sign.
(None rich - er pos - sessed by the an - gels a - bove);
Of ob - jects most pleas - ing, I love thee the best;
For thee all the pleas - ures of sense I fore - go.
With - out thee I'm wretch - ed, but with thee I'm blessed.
And wan - der a pil - grim de - spis - èd be - low.

3. Thy Spirit first taught me to know I was blind,
And taught me the way of salvation to find.
For when I was sinking in dreadful despair,
My Jesus relieved me and bid me not fear.

High O'er the Hills

French Broad L.M.

St. 1, 2, 4-6, 8

William Walker, writ. 1831

William Walker, comp. 1831

Slow
Tune in tenor
1. High o'er the hills the_moun-tains rise, Their sum - mits tow - er_toward the skies;
2. Oh, God! for - bid that_ I should fall And lose my ev - er - last - ing all;
1.
2.
But far a - bove them I must dwell, Or sink be - neath the_flames of hell. flames of hell.
But may I rise on wings of love, And soar to the blest_world a - bove. world a - bove.

3. There it must lie till that great day,
When Gabriel's awful trumpet shall say,
Arise, the judgment day is come,
When all must hear their final doom.

4. If not prepared, then I must go
Down to eternal pain and woe,
With devils there I must remain,
And never more return again.

5. But if prepared, oh, blessed thought!
I'll rise above the mountain's top,
And there remain for evermore
On Canaan's peaceful, happy shore.

6. Then will I sing God's praises there,
Who brought me through my troubles here
I'll sing, and be forever blest,
Find sweet and everlasting rest.

Where Are the Hebrew Children? — The Hebrew Children 7.7.7.6.8.8.8.6.

St. 1-3

Anon., often attributed to Peter Cartwright, 1835 — David Walker, arr. 1841

Tune in tenor
1. Where are the_ He - brew chil - dren? Where are the_ He - brew chil - dren?
2. Where are the_twelve a - pos - tles Where are the_ twelve a - pos - tles?
Where are the He - brew chil - dren? Safe in the_ prom - ised land.
Where are the twelve a - pos - tles? Safe in the_ prom - ised land,
Though the fur - nace_ flamed a - round them, God, while in their_ trou - bles found them,
They went up through pain and sigh - ing. Scoff - ing, scourg - ing,_ cru - ci - fy - ing,
He with love and mer - cy bound_them, Safe_____ in the prom - ised land.
No - bly for their mas - ter dy - ing, Safe_____ in the prom - ised land.

3. Where are the holy Christians?
Where are the holy Christians?
Where are the holy Christians?
Safe in the promised land.
Those who've washed their robes and made them
White and spotless pure and laid them
Where no earthly stain can fade them,
Safe in the promised land.

OUR BONDAGE IT SHALL END
St. 1-3, 5, 6
Anon., attributed to Peter Cartwright, 1835

SAINTS BOUND FOR HEAVEN Irregular
J. King and William Walker, arr. 1854

Tune in tenor
1. Our bond-age it shall end, by and by, by and by, Our bond-age, It shall end, by and by. From E-gypt's yoke set free; Hail the glo-rious ju-bi-lee, And to Ca-naan we'll re-turn, by and by, by and by, And to Ca-naan we'll re-turn, by and by.
2. Our De-liv-er-er will come, by and by, by and by, Our De-liv-er-er, will come, by and by. And our sor-rows have an end, With our three-score years and ten, And vast glo-ry crown the day, by and by, by and by, And vast glo-ry crown the day, by and by.

3. Though our enemies are strong, we'll go on, we'll go on,
Though our enemies are strong, we'll go on.
Though our hearts dissolve with fear,
Lo! Sinai's God is near,
While the firey pillar moves, we'll go on, we'll go on,
While the firey pillar moves, we'll go on.

4. And when to Jordan's flood, we are come, we are come,
And when to Jordan's flood, we are come.
Jehovah rules the tide,
And the waters he'll divide,
And the ransom'd host shall shout, "We are come, we are come."
And the ransom'd host shall shout, "We are come."

5. Then friends shall meet again who have loved, who have loved,
Then friends shall meet again who have loved.
Our embraces will be sweet
At the dear Redeemer's feet,
When we meet to part no more, who have loved, who have loved.
When we meet to part no more, who have loved.

The Time Is Swiftly Rolling On — Hicks' Farewell C.M.

St. 1, 3, 5, 6, 9, 10

Berryman Hicks, 1835 — William Walker, 1854

Tune in tenor

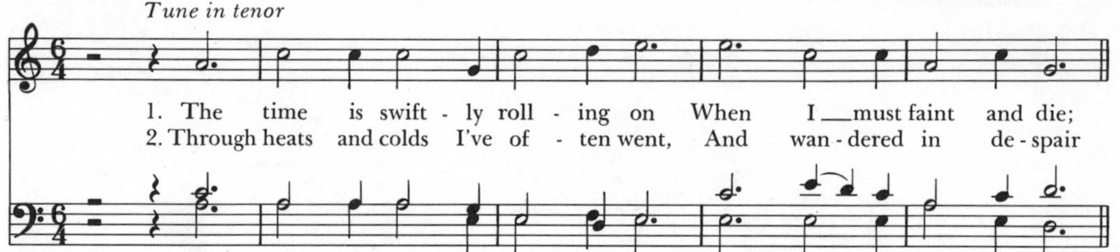
1. The time is swift - ly roll - ing on When I — must faint and die;
2. Through heats and colds I've of - ten went, And wan - dered in de - spair

My bo - dy to the dust re - turn, And there for - got - ten lie.
To call — poor sin - ners to re - pent, And seek the Sav - iour dear.

3. My brother preachers, fare you well,
Your fellowship I love;
In time no more I shall you see,
But soon we'll meet above.

4. My little children near my heart,
And nature seems to bind,
It grieves me sorely to depart,
And leave you all behind.

5. My loving wife, don't grieve for me,
Neither lament nor mourn;
For I shall with my Jesus be,
When you are left alone.

6. How often you have looked for me,
And ofttimes seen me come;
But now I must depart from thee,
And never more return.

OUR SCHOOL NOW CLOSES OUT

THE TEACHER'S FAREWELL S.M., with chorus

St. 1-3

Edmund Dumas, 1858

Edmund Dumas, 1858

Tune in tenor
1. Our school now clos - es out, And we to - day must part. How sad the thought to part with you; I hope we'll meet a - gain.
Chorus: Oh let us meet in heaven, The Christ - ians hap - py home. The house a - bove, when all is love There'll be no part - ing there.

2. You've been so kind to me;
How can I bear the thought,
To part with you, it grieves my heart
Perhaps to meet no more.

Chorus

3. Wherever you may go,
Dear students, think of me.
Oh, pray for me wherere you go,
That we may meet in heaven.

Chorus

REMEMBER THY CREATOR NOW PRIMROSE C.M.

St. 1-4

Peter Long, 1878 Aaron Chapin, 1878

1. Re - mem-ber thy Cre - a - tor now, While in the days of youth;
2. For they who seek Him young, shall find Par - don for ev - ery sin;
To your Di - vine Re - deem - er bow, And seek the ways of truth.
A calm of con - science; peace of mind, And end - less glo - ry win.

3. But they who slight his voice so sweet,
And wait for better years,
Shall but increasing troubles meet,
And sad, perplexing cares.

4. Then come to Jesus, while you may;
Obey the gospel sound:
Youth is the day, the precious day,
When mercy may be found.

HURRY ON, MY WEARY SOUL

St. 1, 3-5

Traditional, version from *Slave Songs,* 1867

Hur - ry on, my wea - ry soul, And I heard_from heav-en to - day, Hur - ry
on, my___ wea - ry soul, And I heard___ from heav-en to - day.
1. My___ sin is for-giv-en and my soul___ set free, And I heard_from heav-en to - day, My
2. De___ trum - pet___ sound___ in de od-er_bright land, And I heard_from heav-en to - day, De
sin is for - giv-en, and my soul___ set free, And I heard___ from heav - en to - day.
trum - pet___ sound___ in de od - er bright land, And I heard___ from heav - en to - day.

3. Hurry on, my weary soul,
   And I heard from heaven today,
   Hurry on, my weary soul,
   And I heard from heaven today.

   My name is called and I must go,
   And I heard from heaven today,
   My name is called and I must go,
   And I heard from heaven today.

4. Hurry on, my weary soul,
   And I heard from heaven today,
   Hurry on, my weary soul,
   And I heard from heaven today.

   De bell is a - ringin' in de oder bright world,
   And I heard from heaven today,
   De bell is a - ringin' in de oder bright world,
   And I heard from heaven today.

Didn't My Lord Deliver Daniel

St. 1-4

Traditional, version from *Jubilee Songs*, 1872

Chorus
Did-n't my Lord de-liv-er Dan - iel,— d'liver Dan - iel,— d'liver Dan - iel, Did-n't
my Lord de - liv - er Dan - iel,— And why not a ev - er - y man?
Fine
1. He de - liv-ered Dan-iel from the li - on's den, Jo-nah from the bel-ly of the whale, And the
He - brew child-ren from the fie - ry fur-nace, And why not ev - er - y man?
Did-n't my Lord de-liv-er Dan - iel,— d'liver Dan - iel,— d'liver Dan - iel, Did-n't
my Lord de - liv - er Dan - iel,— And why not a ev - er - y man?
2. The moon run down in a pur-pl. - stream, The sun for - bear to shine, And
D. C. "Didn't My Lord."
ev - er - y star— dis - ap - pear,— King Je - sus shall— be mine.
3. The wind blows East, and the wind blows West, It blows like the judg-ment day, And
D. C. "Didn't My Lord."
ev - ery poor soul— that nev - er did pray.— will be glad to pray— that day
4. I set my foot on the Gos - pel ship, And the ship it be-gin to sail. It
D. C. "Didn't My Lord."
land-ed me o - ver on Ca - naan's shore,— And I'll nev - er come back— a - ny more.

**Go on without pause, leaving out two beats of the measure.*

When Israel Was In Egypt's Land

St. 1-3, 17, 18

Traditional, version from *Jubilee Songs*, 1872

1. When Is - rael was in E - gypt's land, Let my peo - ple go;
2. Thus saith the Lord, bold Mo - ses said, Let my peo - ple go;
Op - pressed so hard they could not stand, Let my peo - ple go.
If not I'll smite your first - born dead, Let my peo - ple go.
Chorus
Go down, Mo - ses, Way down in E - gypt land,
Tell ole Pha - roh, Let my peo - ple go.

3. No more shall they in bondage toil,
Let my people go;
Let them come out with Egypt's spoil,
Let my people go.
Chorus

4. O let us all from bondage flee,
Let my people go;
And let us all in Christ be free,
Let my people go.
Chorus

5. We need not always weep and moan,
Let my people go;
And wear these slavery chains forlorn,
Let my people go.
Chorus

He Raise a Poor Lazarus

St. 1-3

Traditional, pub. 1918

1. Oh, He raise a poor Laz - a - rus, (raise him up), He raise him from de dead, (I
2. He give heal un - to de sick, (yes, he did,)[He]give sight un - to de blin', (I
tol' ye so), While man - y were stand - in' by,
know he did,)[He]done a - ble de crip - ple to walk,
Je - sus loos - en' de man from un - der de groun' An' tell him "Go
Oh, he raise de dead from un - der de groun' An' give dem per -
proph - e - sy." An' tell him "Go proph - e - sy."
mis - sion to talk. An' give dem per - mis - sion to talk.
pp
(Bass hum with closed lips)

3. Oh, moan along, moan along,
Oh, ye moanin' souls! ye moanin' souls,
[Oh] Heaven is my home.
Jesus been here one time; Lord, he's comin' agin,
Git ready and let us go home.
Git ready and let us go home.

O Ride On, Jesus
Version of Natalie Curtis Burlin, 1918
St. 1-4
Traditional, pub. 1918
Adapted by R. Nathaniel Dett, 1927
♩= 60 – 70
Chorus
Solo
Marcato
Tutti
molto marcato
O ride on, Je - sus, Ride on, Je - sus, Ride on,
con - quer - in' King!_ I want t' go t' heb - b'n in de mo'n - in'. O
ride on, Je - sus, Ride on, Je - sus, Ride on, con-quer-in' King!_ I
want t' go t' heb - b'n in de mo'n - in'.
Fine

Solo
declamato
1. Ef yo' see my Moth - er,
2. Ef yo' see my Fa - ther,
3. Ef yo' see my sis - ter,
4. Ef yo' see my broth - er,
Jes' tell her fo' me, For t'
(him)
f Tutti
O yes! O yes!
meet me t'-mor-row in Gal - i - lee: Want t' go t'heb - b'n in de mo'n - in'. O
Want t' go t'heb - b'n in de mo'n - in'.

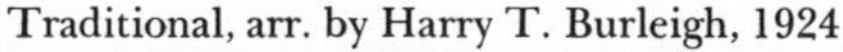

Let Us Cheer the Weary Traveler

St. 1, 2

Traditional, arr. by Harry T. Burleigh, 1924

Adagio *Voices in unison* *very broadly*

Organ

mf

Let us cheer the wea - ry trav-el - er, cheer the wea - ry trav-el - er, Let us cheer the wea - ry trav - el - er, a - long the heav - en - ly way.

Voices in harmony, steady and stately

1. I'll take my gos - pel trum - pet And I'll be - gin to blow, And if my Sav - iour helps me I'll blow where - ev - er I go. Let us

2. And if you meet with cross - es And tri - als on the way, Just keep your trust in Je - sus, And don't for - get to pray. Let us

1. helps me
2. Je - sus,

1. blow where -
2. don't for -

cheer the wea - ry trav - el - er, cheer the wea - ry trav - el - er, Let us
cheer the wea - ry trav - el - er, cheer the wea - ry trav - el - er, Let us
Organ
1.
cheer the wea - ry trav - el - er, a - long the heav - en - ly way.
cheer the wea - ry trav - el - er, a - long the heav - en - ly
2.
way. A - long the heav - en - ly way.
f
f

Nobody Knows de Trouble I've Seen

St. 1, 2

Traditional, pub.1927 R. Nathaniel Dett, arr. 1927

Andante molto espress. ♩ = 60

Chorus

Oh, no-bod - y knows de trou-ble I've seen, No-bod - y knows but Je - sus,

No-bod y knows de trou-ble I've seen, Glo - ry, Hal - le - lu - jah!

Fine

Duet
patetico

mp

1. Some - times I'm up, some - times__ I'm down, Oh, yes, Lord;
Al - though you see me go-in' long so, Oh, yes, Lord;
2. One day when I was walk-in' a - long, Oh, yes, Lord,
I nev - er shall for - get__ dat day, Oh, yes, Lord,

Duet
patetico

mp

rit. *a tempo*

D. C. al Fine

Some - times__ I'm al - most__ to de groun', Oh, yes, Lord.__
I have__ my tri - als__ here be - low, Oh, yes, Lord.__
De el-e-ment o-pened, an' de Love came down, Oh, yes, Lord.__
When Je - sus washed__ my__ sins a - way, Oh, yes, Lord.__

Roll, Jordan, Roll
St. 1-4
Traditional, pub.1927

R. Nathaniel Dett., arr. 1927

♩ = 52

f

Roll, Jor - dan, roll, Roll, Jor - dan, roll. I want to go to heav - en when I die, To hear Jor - dan roll.

Fine

mf

1. O broth - er, you ought t'have been there,
2. O sis - ter, you ought t'have been there,
3. O preach - er, you ought t'have been there,
4. O sin - ners, you ought t'have been there,

cresc.

Yes, my Lord! A - sit - ting in the king - dom To hear Jor - dan roll.

mf *cresc.* *D. C.*

I'M AGOING TO LAY DOWN MY SWORD

St. 1-3

Traditional, pub. 1940

John W. Work, arr. 1940

1. I'm a-going to lay down my sword and shield Down by the riv-er side, down by the riv-er side, down by the riv-er side, Going to lay down my sword and shield, Down by the riv-er side, Ain't going to' stud-y war no more.
2. I'm a-going to put on my long white robe Down by the riv-er side, down by the riv-er side, down by the riv-er side. Going to put on my long white robe Down by the riv-er side. Ain't going to stud-y war no more.

Chorus

Ain't going to stud-y war no more, Ain't going to stud-y war no more, Ain't going to

stud - y war no more, Ain't going to stud - y war no more, Ain't going to
stud-y war no more

stud - y war no more, Ain't going to stud - y war no more.

3. I'm a - going to talk with the Prince of Peace,
Down by the river side, down by the river side, down by the river side.
Going to talk with the Prince of Peace,
Down by the river side.
Ain't going to study war no more.
Chorus

CALVARY

St. 1-4

Traditional, pub. 1940 John W. Work, arr. 1940

Very slowly
Chorus
Cal - va - ry, Cal - va - ry, Cal - va - ry Cal - va - ry
Fine
Cal - va - ry, Cal - va - ry, Sure - ly he died on Cal - va - ry
1. Ev - ery time I think a-bout Je - sus, Ev - ery time I think a-bout Je - sus,
2. Sin - ner, do you love my Je - sus? Sin - ner, do you love my Je - sus?
D. C.
Ev - ery time I think a-bout Je - sus, Sure - ly he died on Cal - va - ry.
Sin - ner, do you love my Je - sus? Sure - ly he died on Cal - va - ry.

Chorus

3. We are climbing Jacob's ladder,
We are climbing Jacob's ladder,
We are climbing Jacob's ladder,
Surely he died on Calvary.

Chorus

4. Every round goes higher and higher,
Every round goes higher and higher,
Every round goes higher and higher,
Surely he died on Calvary.

O Mary, Don't You Weep, Don't You Mourn

St. 1-3

Traditional, pub. 1940

John W. Work, arr. 1940

Chorus
f
O Mar - y, don't you weep, don't you mourn, O Mar - y, don't you weep, don't you mourn;
Phar - oh's ar - my got drown - dèd, O Mar - y, don't you weep.
Fine
1. Some of these morn - ings bright and fair, Take my wings and cleave the air.
2. When I get to hea - ven goin' to sing and shout, No - bod - y there for to turn me out.
Phar - oh's ar - my got drown - dèd O Mar - y don't you weep.
D.C.

Chorus

3. When I get to heaven goin' to put on my shoes,
Run about glory and tell all the news.
Pharoh's army got drowndèd
O Mary don't you weep.

Don't You Be Like the Foolish Virgin

St. 1, 3, 4, 7

Traditional, pub. 1942

Andante
p
1. Don't you be like the fool - ish vir - gin When the bride - groom come, Don't you
4. We will en - ter in - to the mar - riage When the bride - groom come, We will
be like the fool - ish vir - gin When the bride - groom come.
en - ter in - to the mar - riage When the bride - groom come.
Chorus
O Zi - on, Zi - on, O Zi - on, Zi - on, O Zi - on, When the
mf
O Zi - on O Zi - on When the
bride - groom come.
Fine
2. Keep your lamp trimmed and burn - in' When the
3. Five were wise an' five were fool - ish When the
bride - groom come.

bride - groom come, Keep your lamp_trimmed and burn- in' When the bride - groom come.
bride - groom come, Five were wise an' five were fool - ish When the bride - groom come.
Chorus
For St. 4 D. C. al Fine
O Zi - on, Zi - on, O Zi - on, Zi - on, O Zi - on, When the bride - groom come.
O Zi - on, When the bride - groom come.

Singing congregation, Washington, D.C.

Were You There

St. 1-3

Traditional

Winfred Douglas, arr. 1940

With deep reverence

1. Were you there when they cru - ci - fied my Lord? Were you
2. Were you there when they nailed him to the tree? Were you

there when they cru - ci - fied my Lord? Oh! ________
there when they nailed him to the tree? Oh! ________

Some - times it caus - es me to trem - ble, trem - ble, trem - ble.
Some - times it caus - es me to trem - ble, trem - ble, trem - ble.

Were you there when they cru - ci - fied my Lord?
Were you there when they nailed him to the tree?

3. Were you there when they laid him in the tomb?
Were you there when they laid him in the tomb?
Oh! Sometimes it causes me to tremble, tremble, tremble.
Were you there when they laid him in the tomb?

Let Us Break the Bread Together — 7.3.7.3., with chorus

St. 1-3

Traditional — Harmonized 1953

1. Let us break bread to-geth-er, On our knees, on our knees;
2. Let us drink wine to-geth-er, On our knees, on our knees;
Let us break bread to-geth-er, On our knees, on our knees.
Let us drink wine to-geth-er, On our knees, on our knees.
Chorus
When I fall on my knees, with my face to the ris-ing sun, O Lord, have mer-cy on me.

3. Let us praise God together,
On our knees, on our knees;
Let us praise God together,
On our knees, on our knees.
When I fall on my knees, with my face to the rising sun,
O Lord, have mercy on me.

Lord, I Want To Be a Christian

St. 1-5

Traditional, transcribed by R. Nathaniel Dett

R. Nathaniel Dett, arr. 1957

Solo *Chorus*

1. Lord, I want to be a Chris - tian,
2. Lord, I want to be more lov - ing,
3. Lord, I want to be more ho - ly, In - a my heart, in - a my
4. I don't want to be like Ju - das,
5. But I want to be like Je - sus,

heart; Lord, I want to be a Chris - tian, In - a my

In - a my heart, In - a my heart

heart. In - a my heart, In - a my

heart, Lord, I want to be a Chris - tian, In - a my heart.

Missionary Hymns

THE CONVERSION of the American Indian had been zealously sought in the Colonial period. The labors of John Eliot, the "Apostle to the Indians," the Catholic missions among the St. Francis Indians, the California Missions, the work of Nicolaus Zinzendorf and other Moravians—all these testify to the extent and the duration of the effort. The workers in the field found that converts were eager to sing psalms and hymns. This was true of the "praying Indians" whom John Endecott observed in 1651 singing a psalm "chearfully and prettie tunablie" to an English tune. However what the converts sang in their own language was what the white settlers sang, and the tunes were generally European tunes. Attempts to adapt an Indian melody to a devotional text were rare. Only in the Southwest did popular religious songs in Spanish develop and persist.

The dramatic surge of interest in foreign missions in the early nineteenth century was due to several factors, including reports from the successful mission at Serampore, India, established by English Baptists, and the persuasive eloquence of Frank Nathan Daniel Buchanan whose sermon "The Star in the East" was reprinted here. (Catherine Beecher states that it was Buchanan's *Travels in the East* "that first woke the religious world to the spirit of missions.") A group of American students, fired by missionary zeal, sought support and the formation of the (Congregational) Board of Commissioners for Foreign Missions in 1810 was a response to their appeal. Accepting the command "go ye into all the world, and preach the gospel to every creature," American missionaries set sail to Burma, to India, to the Pacific Islands, and to Africa. Church members in the United States met and prayed together, collected contributions for the support of missionaries, and sang hymns.

Leonard Bacon's "Wake the Song of Jubilee" appeared in 1823 in his *Hymns and Songs for the Monthly Concert.* The sailing of a ship carrying missionaries was a dramatic event, since both those on shipboard and those on shore knew that this might be a final parting. William B. Tappan's "Wake, Isles of the South" was sung in 1823 on the wharf at New Haven where a ship carrying missionaries to the Sandwich Islands was about to sail. Lowell Mason's famous tune MISSIONARY HYMN also dates from 1823. Though it was written for Bishop Heber's "From Greenland's Icy Mountains," it was also used

for Thomas Hastings' "Now Be the Gospel Banner." This hymn, as well as Thomas Hastings' "Hail to the Brightness" appeared in *Spiritual Songs for Social Worship* (1832). Samuel F. Smith had hoped to become a missionary himself. He did write a missionary hymn which was widely sung, "The Morning Light Is Breaking," which has been closely associated with a spirited American tune by George Webb. A similar note was sounded after the midcentury by A. Cleveland Coxe with his "Saviour, Sprinkle Many Nations" (1869). Samuel Wolcott's "Christ for the World We Sing" (1869) and Mary A. Thomson's "O Sion Haste" (1892) complete this section.

The departure of missionaries in February 1812

Wake, Isles of the South — Isles of the South 11.11.11.11.11.

St. 1-4

William B. Tappan, 1822 — William Hauser, 1848

Tune in tenor
1. Wake, Isles of the South! your re-demp-tion is near, No long-er re-
2. The bil-lows that girt you, the wild waves that roar, The zeph-yrs that
pose in the bor-ders of gloom; The strength of his cho-sen in
play where the o-cean-storms cease, Shall bear the rich freight to your
love shall ap-pear, And light shall a-rise on the verge of the tomb,
des-o-late shore, Shall waft the glad ti-dings of par-don and peace,
And light shall a-rise on the verge of the tomb.
Shall waft the glad ti-dings of par-don and peace.

3. On the islands that sit in the regions of night,
The lands of despair, to oblivion a prey,
The morning will open with healing and light,
The glad star of Bethlehem brighten today,
The glad star of Bethlehem brighten today.

4. The heathen will hasten to welcome the time,
The day-spring, the prophet in vision once saw,
When the beams of Messiah will 'lumine each clime,
And the isles of the ocean shall wait for his law,
And the isles of the ocean shall wait for his law.

HAIL TO THE BRIGHTNESS OF ZION'S GLAD MORNING — WESLEY 11.10.11.10.

St. 1-4

Thomas Hastings, 1832 — Lowell Mason, 1832

1. Hail to the bright - ness of Zi - on's glad morn - ing;
2. Hail to the bright - ness of Zi - on's glad morn - ing,
Joy to the lands that in dark - ness have lain;
Long by the proph - ets of Is - rael fore - told;
Hushed be the ac - cents of sor - row and mourn - ing
Hail to the mil - lions from bond - age re - turn - ing;
Zi - on in tri - umph be - gins his glad reign.
Gen - tiles and Jews the blest vi - sion be - hold.

3. Lo, in the desert rich flowers are springing;
Streams ever copious are gliding along;
Loud from the mountain-tops echoes are ringing;
Wastes rise in verdure, and mingle in song.

4. See, from all lands, from the isles of the ocean,
Praise to Jehovah ascending on high;
Fallen are the engines of war and commotion;
Shouts of salvation are rending the sky.

Now Be the Gospel Banner — Missionary Hymn 7.6.7.6.D.

St. 1,2

Thomas Hastings, 1832 — Lowell Mason, comp. 1823/24, pub. 1829

1. Now be the gos - pel ban - ner In ev - ery land un - furled;
2. Yes, thou shalt reign for - ev - er, O Je - sus, King of kings!
6 4 6 4 2 6 4 3 6 4 5 3
And be the shout ho - san - na Re - ech - oed through the world;
Thy light, thy love, thy fa - vor, Each ran - somed cap - tive sings.
6 4 6 6 4 5 ♮
Till ev - ery isle and na - tion, Till ev - ery tribe and tongue,
The isles for thee are wait - ing, The des - erts learn thy praise,
6 4 3 6 4 3 6 5 6 4 5 3
Re - ceive the great sal - va - tion, And join the hap - py throng.
The hills and val - leys greet - ing, The song re - spon - sive raise.
6 4 6 6 6 4 5 3

The Morning Light Is Breaking

Webb 7.6.7.6.D.

St. 1-4

Samuel Francis Smith, 1832

George J. Webb, 1837

1. The morn - ing light is break - ing, The dark - ness dis - ap - pears,
2. Rich dews of grace come o'er us, In many a gen - tle shower,
The sons of earth are wak - ing To pen - i - ten - tial tears.
And bright - er scenes be - fore us, Are open - ing ev - ery hour;
Each breeze that sweeps the o - cean Brings tid - ings from a - far,
Each cry to heav - en go - ing, A - bun - dant an - swers brings,
Of na - tions in com - mo - tion Pre - pared for Zi - on's war.
And heaven - ly winds are blow - ing, With peace up - on their wings.

3. See heathen nations bending
Before the God of love,
And thousand hearts ascending
In gratitude above;
While sinners now confessing
The gospel call obey,
And seek the Saviour's blessing,
A nation in a day.

4. Blest river of salvation,
Pursue thy onward way,
Flow thou to every nation,
Nor in thy riches stay,
Stay not till all the lowly
Triumphant reach their home;
Stay not till all the holy
Proclaim "The Lord is come."

ONWARD, ONWARD, MEN OF HEAVEN HALL 8.7.8.7.D.

St. 1-3

Lydia H. Sigourney, 1833 Abner Jones, 1836

1. On - ward, on - ward, men of heav - en! Bear the gos - pel's ban - ner high;
Rest not, till its light is giv - en, Star of ev - ery pa - gan sky.
2. Where the Arc - tic o - cean thun - ders, Where the trop - ics fierce - ly glow,
Broad - ly spread its page of won - ders, Bright - ly bid its ra - diance flow.
1. Send it where the pil - grim stran - ger Faints be - neath the tor - rid ray;
2. In - dia marks its lus - tre steal - ing; Shiver - ing Green - land loves its rays;
Bid the red - browed for - est ran - ger Hail it, ere he fades a - way.
Af - ric, 'mid her des - erts kneel - ing, Lifts the un - taught strain of praise.

3. Rude in speech, or grim in feature,
Dark in spirit, though they be,
Show that light to every creature —
Prince or vassal, bond or free.
Lo! they haste to every nation,
Host on host the ranks supply;
Onward! Christ is your salvation,
And your death is victory.

Fling Out the Banner! Banner L.M.D.

St. 1-6

George Washington Doane, writ. 1848, pub. 1860 G. B. Lissart, 1894

♩ = 88
f
1. Fling out the ban - ner! Let__ it__ float Sky - ward and sea - ward, high and wide,
3. Fling out the ban - ner! Hea - then__ lands Shall see from far the glo - rious sight,
f

The sun__that__lights its shin - ing__folds, The Cross on which the Sav - iour__died.
And na - tions,__crowd - ing to__ be__born, Bap - tize their spir - its in its__light.

mf
dim.
p
2. Fling out the ban - ner! An - gels__bend In anx - ious si - lence__ o'er the sign;
4. Fling out the ban - ner! Sin - sick__souls That sink and per - ish__ in the strife,

mf
dim.
p

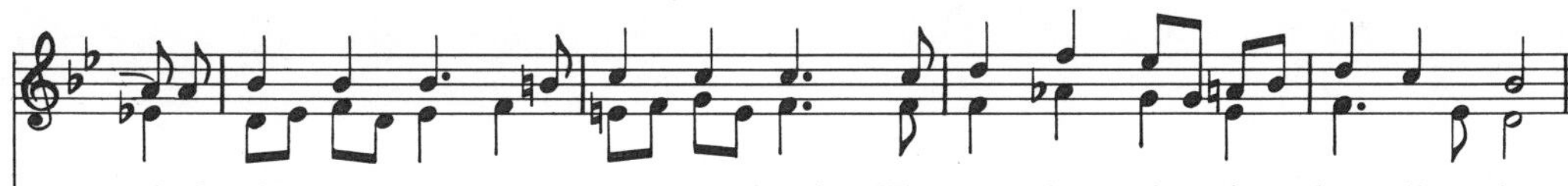
And vain - ly seek to com - pre - hend The won - der of__ the__ love di - vine.
Shall touch in faith its ra - diant hem, And spring im - mor - tal__ in - to life.

5. Fling out the banner! Let it float
Skyward and seaward, high and wide,
Our glory, only in the Cross,
Our only hope, the Crucified!

6. Fling out the banner! Wide and high,
Seaward and skyward, let it shine
Nor skill, nor might, nor merit ours,
We conquer only in that sign.

Saviour, Sprinkle Many Nations — Faben 8.7.8.7.D.

St. 1-3

Arthur Cleveland Coxe, 1851 — John Henry Wilcox, 1849

1. Sav - iour, sprin - kle man - y na - tions, Fruit - ful let thy sor - rows be; By thy pains and con - so - la - tions, Draw the Gen - tiles un - to thee. Of thy cross the won - drous sto - ry, Be it to the na - tions told; Let them see thee in thy glo - ry, And thy mer - cy man - i - fold.
2. Far and wide, though all un - know - ing, Pants for thee each mor - tal breast; Hu - man tears for thee are flow - ing, Hu - man hearts in thee would rest; Thirst - ing, as for dews of ev - en, As the new - mown grass for rain, Thee they seek, as God of heav - en, Thee, as man for sin - ners slain.

3. Saviour, lo! the isles are waiting,
Stretched the hand, and strained the sight
For thy Spirit, new creating
Love's pure flame and wisdom's light;
Give the word, and of the preacher
Speed the foot, and touch the tongue,
Till on earth by every creature
Glory to the Lamb be sung.

CHRIST FOR THE WORLD! WE SING

MACEDON 6.6.4.6.6.6.4.

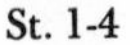

St. 1-4

Samuel Wolcott, 1869

Frederick Field Bullard, 1904

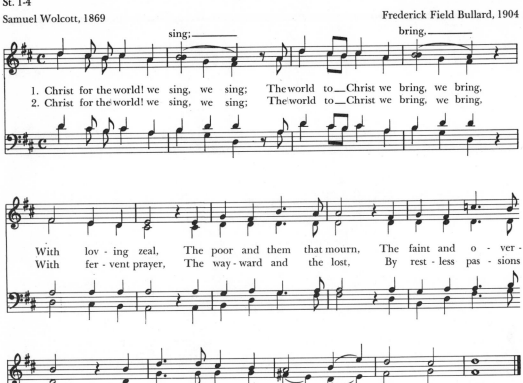

sing;
bring,
1. Christ for the world! we sing, we sing; The world to Christ we bring, we bring,
2. Christ for the world! we sing, we sing; The world to Christ we bring, we bring,

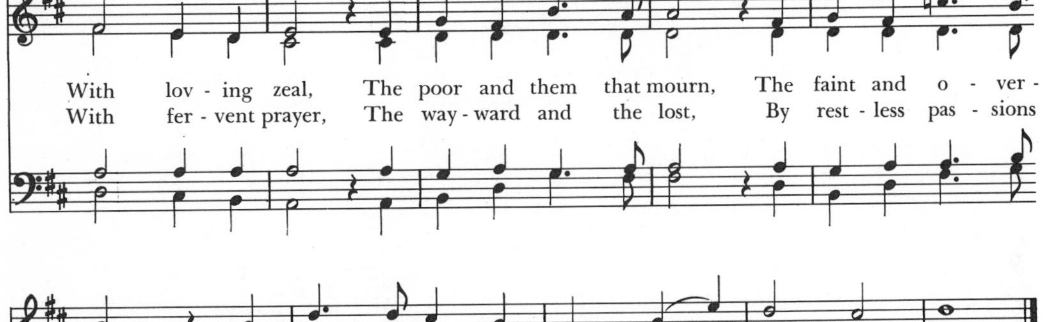
With lov - ing zeal, The poor and them that mourn, The faint and o - ver -
With fer - vent prayer, The way - ward and the lost, By rest - less pas - sions

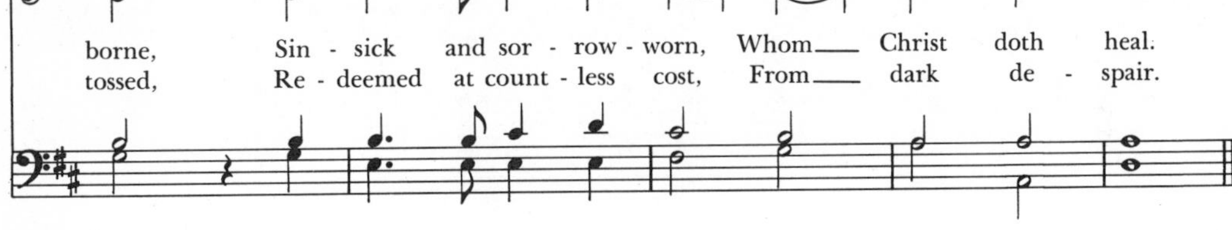
borne, Sin - sick and sor - row - worn, Whom Christ doth heal.
tossed, Re - deemed at count - less cost, From dark de - spair.

3. Christ for the world! we sing;
The world to Christ we bring,
With one accord,
With us the work to share,
With us reproach to dare,
With us the cross to bear,
For Christ our Lord.

4. Christ for the world! we sing;
The world to Christ we bring,
With joyful song,
The new-born souls whose days,
Reclaimed from error's ways,
Inspired with hope and praise,
To Christ belong.

O Sion, Haste, Thy Mission High Fulfilling — O Sion Haste 11.10.11.10., with chorus

St. 1-6

Mary A. Thomson, 1892 — Henry J. Storer, 1894

With spirit
mf
1. O Si - on, haste, thy mis - sion high ful - fill - ing, To tell to all the
2. Be - hold how man - y thou - sands still are ly - ing Bound in the dark - some
world that God is Light; That he who made all na - tions is not
pri - son - house of sin, With none to tell them of the Sav - iour's
dim.
will - ing One soul should per - ish, lost in shades of night
dy - ing Or of the life he died for them to win.
Chorus
piu mosso
cresc.
Pub - lish glad
ti - dings, Ti - dings of peace; Ti - dings of Je - sus, Re - demp - tion and re - lease.
f

3. 'Tis thine to save from peril of perdition
The souls for whom the Lord his life laid down;
Beware lest, slothful to fulfill thy mission,
Thou lose one jewel that should deck his crown.
Chorus

4. Proclaim to every people, tongue and nation
That God, in whom they live and move is love;
Tell how he stooped to save his lost creation,
And died on earth that man might live above.
Chorus

5. Give of thy sons to bear the message glorious;
Give of thy wealth to speed them on their way,
Pour out thy soul for them in prayer victorious;
And all thou spendest Jesus will repay.
Chorus

6. He comes again — O Sion, ere thou meet him,
Make known to every heart his saving grace;
Let none whom he hath ransomed fail to greet him,
Through thy neglect, unfit to see his face.
Chorus

Christmas Carols

As we have seen, the earliest recorded Christmas song in North America must surely be the Huron carol "Jesus Ahatonhia" by Jean de Brebeuf if we accept the story of its origin. It was on Christmas Night, 1742, that Count Zinzendorf improvised "For Us No Night Can Be Happier" in the new settlement of Bethlehem, Pennsylvania. Caspar Kriebel's "Now Sleep My Little Child" is a Schwenkfelder Christmas song of 1762.

Many early settlers in New England, however, looked with stern disapproval on the celebration of Christmas. Samuel Sewall had noted on December 25, 1685, that "Carts come to Town and shops open as is usual." Even at a much later period Harriet Beecher Stowe pictured the white Congregational Church as dark and empty on Christmas Eve while the neighboring Episcopal church was decorated with greenery, lighted with candles, and filled with the sound of the "Te Deum."

Yet even in the latter part of the eighteenth century this attitude must have softened. William Billings composed at least one Christmas carol and Nahum Tate on occasion wrote in the Christmas tradition. The inhabitants of Claremont, New Hampshire, were willing to raise their voices in singing Royal Tyler's "Hail to the Joyous Day" on December 25, 1793.

In the following century a number of American carols became almost universally known. John Henry Hopkins Jr. wrote both the words and the music of "We Three Kings of Orient Are." Henry Wadsworth Longfellow's "I Heard the Bells on Christmas Day" was better known as a poem than as a song. "O Little Town of Bethlehem" by Phillips Brooks, on the other hand, has always been associated with the tune St. Louis, which his organist, Lewis Redner, wrote for it. Sears's "Calm on the Listening Ear of Night" has been sung less than his "It Came upon the Midnight Clear" because the latter has been matched with the tune Carol, which fits it so well. "Morning Star, O Cheering Sight!" with music by Francis F. Hagen, was long a favorite Christmas song among the Moravians.

The twentieth century has its characteristic carols and among them are Ferdinand Q. Blanchard's "O Child of Lowly Manger Birth," Earl Marlatt's "Through the Dark the Dreamers Came," Anna Hoppe's "Precious Child, So Sweetly Sleeping," and Harry Webb Farrington's "I Know Not How That Bethlehem's Babe." Among the contemporary

composers who were invited to contribute settings to *American Hymns Old and New,* three chose to compose Christmas texts. Norman Della Joio wrote his LULLABY to Anna Elizabeth Bennett's "Hush Thee, Princeling." John Jacob Niles created the text as well as the music for "In All the Magic of Christmastide," and Virgil Thomson composed the music for Amanda Benjamin Hall's "It Seems That God Bestowed Somehow."

All may be found in the appropriate sections of this book.

Young carolers

Calm, on the Listening Ear of Night — Gould C.M.

St. 1-6

Edmund Hamilton Sears, 1834 — John E. Gould, 1846

1. Calm, on the listen - ing ear of night, Come heaven's me - lo - dious strains,
2. Ce - les - tial choirs, from courts a - bove, Shed sa - cred glo - ries there;
Where wild Ju - de - a stretch - es far Her sil - ver - man - tled plains.
And an - gels, with their spark - ling lyres, Make mu - sic on the air.

3. The answering hills of Palestine
Send back the glad reply;
And greet, from all their holy heights,
The Dayspring from on high.

4. O'er the blue depths of Galilee
There comes a holier calm;
And Sharon waves, in solemn praise,
Her silent groves of palm.

5. "Glory to God!" the sounding skies
Loud with their anthems ring;
"Peace to the earth, good will to men,"
From heaven's eternal King!

6. Light on thy hills, Jerusalem!
The Prince of Peace is born!
And bright, on Bethlehem's joyous plains,
Breaks the first Christmas morn.

It Came Upon the Midnight Clear

St. 1-3

Edmund Hamilton Sears, writ. 1849, pub. 1850

Carol C.M.D.

Richard S. Willis, 1850

Brightly
1. It came up - on the mid - night clear, That glo - rious song of old,
2. Still through the clo - ven skies they come With peace - ful wings un-furled,
From an - gels bend - ing near the earth To touch their harps of gold
And still their heav - en - ly mu - sic floats O'er all the wea - ry world;
"Peace on the earth, good will to men, From heav-en's all - gra - cious King."
A - bove its sad and low - ly plains They bend on hov - er - ing wing,
The world in sol - emn still - ness lay To hear the an - gels sing.
And ev - er o'er its Ba - bel sounds The bless - èd an - gels sing.

3. Yet with the woes of sin and strife
The world has suffered long;
Beneath the heavenly strain have rolled
Two thousand years of wrong;

And man, at war with man, hears not
The tidings which they bring;
O hush the noise, ye men of strife,
And hear the angels sing!

I Heard the Bells on Christmas Day — Christmas Bells L.M.

St. 1-3,6,7

Henry Wadsworth Longfellow, 1864 — J. T., 1910

Unison
1. I heard the bells on Christ - mas day Their old fa - mil - iar car - ols play, And
2. And thought how, as the day had come, The bel - fries of all Chris - ten - dom Had
wild and sweet the words re - peat, Of "Peace on earth, good will to men!"
rolled a - long the un - bro - ken song, Of "Peace on earth, good will to men!"

3. Till ringing, singing on its way,
The world revolved from night to day,
A voice, a chime, A chant sublime,
Of "Peace on earth, good will to men!"

4. And in despair I bowed my head;
"There is no peace on earth," I said,
"For hate is strong And mocks the song
Of 'Peace on earth, good will to men!"

5. Then pealed the bells more loud and deep:
"God is not dead; nor doth he sleep!
The wrong shall fail, The right prevail,
With Peace on earth, good will to men!"

We Three Kings of Orient Are — Kings of Orient 8.8.8.6., with chorus

St. 1-5

John Henry Hopkins Jr., writ. 1857, pub. 1863 — John Henry Hopkins Jr., writ. 1857, pub. 1863

Joyously

1. We three kings of O - ri - ent are, Bear - ing gifts we trav - erse a -
2. Born a King on Beth - le - hem's plain, Gold I bring to crown him a -

1. We three kings of O - ri - ent are, Bear - ing gifts we trav - erse a -
2. Born a King on Beth - le - hem's plain, Gold I bring to crown him a -

1. We three kings of O - ri - ent are, Bear - ing gifts we trav - erse a -
2. Born a King on Beth - le - hem's plain, Gold I bring to crown him a -

far Field and foun - tain, moor and moun - tain, Fol - low - ing yon - der star.
gain, King for - ev - er, ceas - ing nev - er O - ver us all to reign.

far Field and foun - tain, moor and moun - tain, Fol - low - ing yon - der star.
gain, King for - ev - er, ceas - ing nev - er O - ver us all to reign.

far Field and foun - tain, moor and moun - tain, Fol - low - ing yon - der star.
gain, King for - ev - er, ceas - ing nev - er O - ver us all to reign.

Chorus
O___ star of won - der, star of night Star with roy - al beau - ty bright;
West - ward lead - ing, still pro - ceed - ing, Guide us to thy per - fect light!
Interlude

3. Frankincense to offer have I,
   Incense owns a Deity nigh,
   Prayer and praising, all men raising,
   Worship him, God on high.
   Chorus

4. Myrrh is mine; its bitter perfume
   Breathes a life of gathering gloom;
   Sorrowing, sighing, bleeding, dying,
   Sealed in the stone cold tomb.
   Chorus

5. Glorious now behold him arise,
   King, and God, and Sacrifice,
   Heaven sings Alleluia; Alle-
   luia the earth replies.
   Chorus

O LITTLE TOWN OF BETHLEHEM — ST. LOUIS 8.6.8.6.7.6.8.6.

St. 1-5

Phillips Brooks, writ. 1868 — Lewis H. Redner, comp. 1868

In moderate time
1. O lit - tle town of Beth - le - hem, How still we — see thee lie!
2. For Christ is born of Ma - ry, And gath - ered — all a - bove,
A - bove thy deep and dream - less sleep The si - lent — stars go by;
While mor - tals sleep, the an - gels keep Their watch of — won - d'ring love.
Yet in thy dark streets shin - eth The ev - er - last - ing Light;
O morn - ing stars, to - geth - er Pro - claim the ho - ly birth!
The hopes and fears of all the years Are — met in thee to - night.
And prais - es sing to God the King, And — peace to men on earth.

3. How silently, how silently,
The wondrous gift is giv'n!
So God imparts to human hearts
The blessings of his heav'n.
No ear may hear his coming,
But in this world of sin,
Where meek souls will receive him still
The dear Christ enters in.

4. Where children pure and happy
Pray to the blessed Child,
Where misery cries out to thee,
Son of the mother mild;
Where charity stands watching
And faith holds wide the door,
The dark night wakes, the glory breaks,
And Christmas comes once more.

5. O holy Child of Bethlehem!
Descend to us, we pray;
Cast out our sin and enter in,
Be born in us to-day.
We hear the Christmas angels
The great glad tidings tell;
O come to us, abide with us,
Our Lord Emmanuel!

MORNING STAR, O CHEERING SIGHT! — MORNING STAR 7.7.6.7.

St. 1-4

Anon., c. 1870 — Francis F. Hagen, comp. 1842

1. Morn - ing Star, O cheer - ing sight! Ere Thou cam'st how dark earth's
2. Morn - ing Star, thy glo - ry bright Far ex - cels the sun's clear
night! Je - sus mine, in me shine; In me shine; Je - sus
light. Je - sus be, con - stant - ly, Con - stant - ly, Je - sus
mine, Fill my heart with light di - vine.
be, More than thou - sand suns to me.
Solo
Chorus
Solo
Chorus

3. Thy glad beams, thou Morning Star,
Cheer the nations near and far;
Thee we own, Lord alone,
Man's great Saviour, God's dear Son.

4. Morning Star, my soul's true light,
Tarry not, dispel my night;
Jesus mine, in me shine,
Fill my heart with light divine.

AWAY IN A MANGER | MUELLER 6.5.6.5.D.

St. 1, 2

Anon. Lutheran, 1885 | James R. Murray, 1887

Unison

1. A - way in a man - ger, No crib for his bed, The lit - tle Lord
2. The cat - tle are low - ing, The poor ba - by wakes, But lit - tle Lord

Je - sus Laid down his sweet head; The stars in the sky____ Looked
Je - sus, No cry - ing he makes. I love thee, Lord Je - sus, Look

down where he lay, The lit - tle Lord Je - sus, A - sleep on the hay.
down from the sky, And stay by my side Un - til morn - ing is nigh.

Sunday School Hymns

THREE DIFFERENT activities might be included under the heading Sunday School. One was the attempt to teach the neglected children of poor families the rudiments of reading and writing. The schools established by Robert Raikes in 1780 were of this kind. Earlier than this was the Sabbath School at the Ephrata Cloister in Pennsylvania, where Ludwig Hocker taught both secular and religious subjects for forty years from c.1739. There were attempts to teach groups of children the catechism, thus preparing them to answer the questions asked by the pastor on Sunday. Finally there was the Sunday School as we understand it today, with opening exercises including the singing of appropriate hymns, as well as Bible study groups organized by age.

In German and Dutch communities, the schoolmaster was often the precentor on Sunday, and school children were taught religious songs as part of their classwork. "Ach Kinder, wollt ihr lieben" is an original hymn for children written by the pioneer Mennonite schoolteacher Peter Dock. Children were taught the catechism by their fathers and were later tested by the pastor. In some communities, however, the schoolmaster devoted Saturday to religious instruction. Ebenezer Dayton, who had been a schoolteacher in Newport, turned the Shorter Catechism into a cycle of hymns "in the Form of a Question and Answer; and fitted to the several Metres, and suitable to be sung in Families and private Meetings of Societies." Silas Ballou included a children's hymn "While I Am Young" in his *New Hymns on Various Subjects* (1785).

The Sunday School movement in the United States dates from 1791 when the First-Day School Society of Philadelphia organized a Sunday School. Lowell Mason, who went to Savannah in 1812, organized and was the superintendant of a Sunday School there. The American Sunday School Union was founded in 1824. As the name implies, this was a joint effort by Protestant churches to establish Sunday Schools where they were needed.

The full development of the American Sunday School hymn was to come later past the mid-century. Sunday School superintendants, composers, and publishers were quick to realize that the singing of simple hymns could be an attractive feature of these schools. Sunday School hymns of this period have much in common with the gospel hymn—the use of the chorus, the animated and frequently marchlike

rhythms, and the novel meters. The fatal ease with which rudimentary jingles and tunes could be manufactured and the emergence of a new mass market led to the production of a plethora of juvenile songsters, most of them of little real interest. That these weaknesses were evident to critical contemporary observers is shown by an anonymous article in *The Aldine* (Vol. VII, No. 9, Sept. 1874).

Children have not been vouchsafed the respect due to them. The disposition has been to underrate their intelligence and capacity for appreciation. Authors and composers have fallen into the error of writing *down* to a level below the average intellect instead of drawing the mind up by a grade of words and music higher than that average.

Some Sunday School songs were adaptations like "Kind Words Can Never Die" by Abby Hutchinson, which was published for solo voice and piano in 1855. It was arranged as a hymn in *Songs for the Sabbath School and Vestry* in 1859. We have selected "Who Has Our Redeemer Heard" and "When Our Earthly Sun Is Setting" from the hymns which Stephen Collins Foster composed for the *Athenaeum* (1863). A number of hymns intended for the Sunday School were taken up as gospel hymns. This was true of Sylvanus Dryden Phelps's "Saviour, Thy Dying Love," which first appeared in a Sunday School songster called *Pure Gold.* A similar course was followed by "We Bring No Glittering Treasures" by Harriet C. Phillips. Written for a Sunday School festival, it was later included in the Methodist hymnals of 1849 and 1878.

A Sunday School class

A LITTLE KINGDOM I POSSESS C.M.D.

St. 1-4

Louisa May Alcott, writ. c. 1846 A. P. Howard, cop. 1873

Unison
1. A lit - tle king - dom I pos - sess, Where thoughts and feel - ings dwell, And ver - y hard I find the task Of gov - ern - ing it well; For pas - sion tempts and trou - bles me, A way - ward will mis - leads, And self - ish - ness its shad - ow casts On all my will and deeds.
2. How can I learn to rule my - self, To be the child I should, Hon - est and brave, nor ev - er tire Of try - ing to be good? How can I keep a sun - ny soul To shine a - long life's way? How can I tune my lit - tle heart, To sweet - ly sing all day?

3. Dear Father, help me with the love
That castest out my fear!
Teach me to lean on thee and feel
That thou art very near.
That no temptation is unseen,
No childish grief too small,
Since thou, with patience infinite,
Dost soothe and comfort all.

4. I do not ask for any crown
But that which all may win;
Nor try to conquer any world
Except the one within.
Be thou my guide until I find,
Led by a tender hand,
Thy happy kingdom in myself
And dare to take command.

The Morning Bright, with Rosy Light — Morning C.M.

St. 1-3

Thomas O. Summers, writ. c. 1846 — Anon., 1861

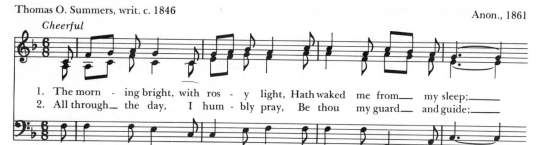

Cheerful
1. The morn - ing bright, with ros - y light, Hath waked me from my sleep;
2. All through the day, I hum - bly pray, Be thou my guard and guide;

Fa - ther, I own thy love a - lone Thy lit - tle one doth keep.
My sins for - give, and let me live, Blest Je - sus, near thy side.

3. Oh, make thy rest within my heart,
Great Spirit of all grace;
Make me like thee, then shall I be
Prepared to see thy face.

We Bring No Glittering Treasures — Miriam 7.6.7.6.D.

St. 1-3

Harriett C. Phillips, writ. c. 1848, pub. 1849 — Joseph P. Holbrook, 1865

1. We bring no glit - tering treas - ures, No gems from earth's deep mine;
2. The dear - est gift of heav - en, Love's writ - ten word of truth,
Fine
(1.) We come, with sim - ple meas - ures, To chant Thy love di - vine.
Fa - ther, ac - cept our of - fering, Our song of grate - ful praise.
(2.) To us is ear - ly giv - en, To guide our steps in youth;
We read of homes in glo - ry, From sin and sor - row free.
D. S.
Chil - dren, thy fa - vors_ shar - ing, Their voice of thanks would raise;
We hear the won - drous_ sto - ry, The tale of Cal - va - ry;

3. Redeemer, grant thy blessing!
O teach us how to pray,
That each, thy fear possessing,
May tread life's onward way;
Then, where the pure are dwelling
We hope to meet again,
And, sweeter numbers swelling,
Forever praise thy name.

Kind Words Can Never Die — 6.4.6.4.6.6.6.4., with chorus

St. 1-4 — B. W. Williams, arr. 1859

Abby Hutchinson, 1855 — Abby Hutchinson, 1855

1. Kind words can nev-er die, Cher - ished and blest, God knows how deep they lie
2. Child - hood can nev - er die; Wrecks of the past, Float o'er the mem - o - ry,
Rall.
Stored in the breast; Like child-hood's sim - ple rhymes, Said o'er a thou - sand times,
Bright to the last. Man - y a hap - py thing, Man - y a dai - sy spring
Tempo
Age in all years and climes Dis - tant and near.
Float o'er time's cease-less wing, Far, far a - way.
Chorus
Kind words can nev - er die,
nev - er die, nev - er die, Kind words can nev - er die, no, nev - er die.

3. Sweet thoughts can never die,
Though like the flowers
Their brightest hues may fly,
In wintry hours.
But when the gentle dew
Gives them their charms anew,
With many an added hue,
They bloom again.
Chorus

4. Our souls can never die,
Though in the tomb
We may all have to lie,
Wrapped in its gloom.
What though the flesh decay,
Souls pass in peace away,
Live through eternal day
With Christ above.
Chorus

Jesus a Child His Course Begun — Ernan L.M.

St. 1-5

Margaret Fuller, 1859 — Lowell Mason, 1850

Gently, softly
1. Je - sus a child his course be - gun:
2. His Fa - ther's busi - ness was his care;
How ra - diant dawned his heaven - ly day!
Yet in man's fa - vor still he grew:
And those who such a race would run
O might we learn by thought and prayer,
As ear - ly should be on their way.
Like him a work of love to do!

3. For all mankind he came, nor yet
An infant's visit would deny;
Nor friend nor mother did forget
In his last hour of agony.

4. O children, ask him to impart
That spirit clear, that temper mild,
Which made the mother in her heart
Keep all the sayings of her child.

5. Bless him who said, of such as you
His Father's kingdom is; and still,
His yoke to bear, his work to do,
Study his life to learn his will.

Jesus Loves Me, This I Know — Jesus Loves Me 7.7.7.7., with chorus

St. 1-4

Anna B. Warner, 1859 — William Batchelder Bradbury, 1862

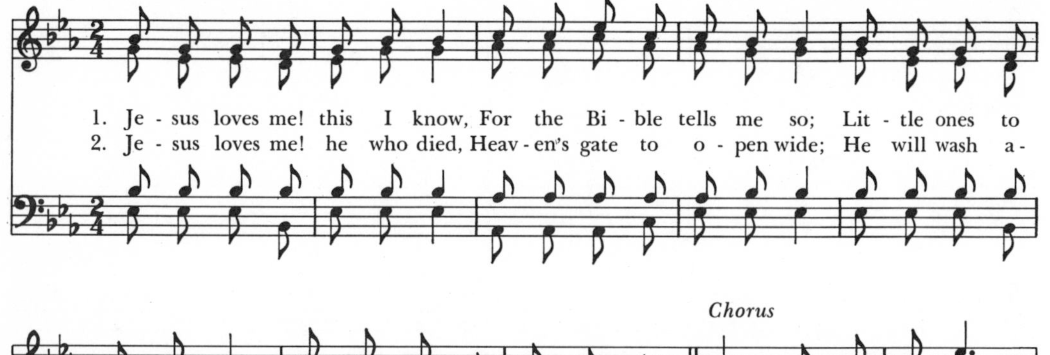
1. Je - sus loves me! this I know, For the Bi - ble tells me so; Lit - tle ones to
2. Je - sus loves me! he who died, Heav - en's gate to o - pen wide; He will wash a -

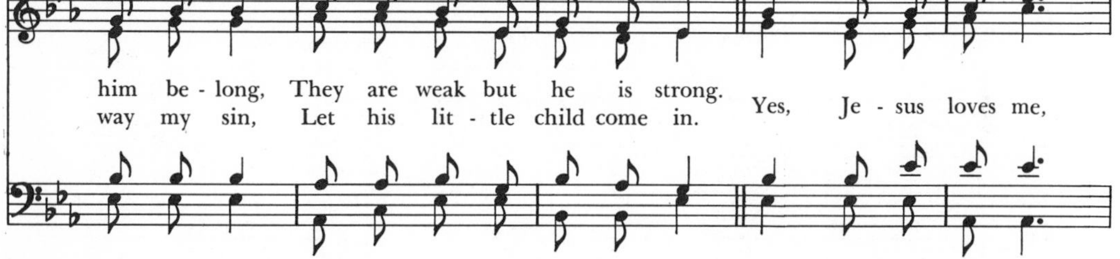
Chorus
him be - long, They are weak but he is strong.
way my sin, Let his lit - tle child come in.
Yes, Je - sus loves me,

Yes, Je - sus loves me, Yes, Je - sus loves me, The Bi - ble tells me so.

3. Jesus loves me! loves me still,
Though I'm very weak and ill;
From his shining throne on high,
Comes to watch me where I lie.
Chorus

4. Jesus loves me! he will stay,
Close beside me, all the way;
If I love him, when I die
He will take me home on high.
Chorus

WHEN OUR EARTHLY SUN IS SETTING

8.7.8.7., with chorus

St. 1-4

Edwin H. Nevin, 1863

Stephen C. Foster, 1863

1. When our earth - ly sun is set - ting, And its glo - ry fad - ing fast;
When our life's long looked for eve - ning With its shad - ows comes at last.
2. When the tear - drops fast are flow - ing, And our hearts are torn with grief;
When for all our sor - rows, vain - ly We at - tempt to find re - lief.
Chorus
Oh! 'tis glo - rious, Oh! 'tis glo - rious, To en - ter in the sweet re - frain, Oh! 'tis
glo - rious, Oh! 'tis glo - rious, To know we'll meet a - gain.

3. When the cold sweat of the dying
Hangs in drops upon our face;
And a secret voice assures us
We have almost run our race.
Chorus

4. When the friends we love are standing
Round our lonely, dying bed,
And we take our farewell parting
Ere the spark of life has fled.
Chorus

Who Has Our Redeemer Heard

7.6.7.6., with chorus

St. 1-4

Stephen C. Foster, 1863

Stephen C. Foster, 1863

Duett, with accompaniment
1. Who has our Re - deem - er heard, Whose voice was good and kind?
2. Come with gen - tle, con - trite heart, And seek the Sav - iour's grace,
Thus he spoke in ho - ly word: Seek and ye shall find.
Come, that when from earth we part, We'll meet him face to face.
Chorus
Ask and it shall be giv - en, Seek and ye shall find,
Ev - ery prayer is heard in heav-en That is breathed from a truth - ful mind.

3. Every prayer is heard above
That we sincerely feel,
Every sigh received with love,
When we repenting kneel.
Chorus

4. Life to all our Lord has shown,
Then be to hope resigned,
When around you doubts are thrown,
"Seek and ye shall find."
Chorus

Revival and Gospel Hymns

Revival Hymns

As settlers pushed westward they moved beyond the influence of the established churches. They were served by a new race of preachers, born on the frontier, or at least familiar with pioneer life. Many of them had little formal education, but they possessed the ability to sway and convince their audiences. They preached wherever a group could be assembled.

No hymns portray the life of the itinerant more vividly than those by Samuel Wakefield. "The Music of His Steps" portrays the family of a circuit rider waiting in vain for his return.

Camp meetings might last several days and attracted hearers from a larger area. Families had to bring food and live in their wagons (the women sleeping inside and the men underneath) or in improvised shelters. Peter Cartwright describes such a gathering in his autobiography. "The church would not hold the tenth part of the congregation, accordingly the officers of the Church erected a stand in a contiguous shady grove, and prepared seats for a large congregation. . . . The power of God was wonderfuly displayed; scores of sinners fell under the preaching, like men slain in mighty battle; Christians shouted aloud for joy." Camp meeting hymns like "I Have Some Friends Before Me Gone" were easy to learn, since only two lines changed from stanza to stanza. Even these could be sung by a leader leaving the congregation to join in the chorus. These choruses were often sung at a point in the meeting when the exhortations of the preacher had roused his hearers. Favorite choruses led an independent life and might be sung after the stanzas of any appropriate hymn. The closing morning of a camp meeting was the time for a hymn of farewell as preachers and people parted "never to meet again in this world." An example of a farewell hymn is "Our School Now Closes Out."

Some revival hymns like "The Lord into His Garden Came" are of unknown authorship. "You Will See Your Lord A-Coming" was associated with the Millerites, who believed in the imminent second coming of Christ.

Revivals occurred in the settled communities and in the churches as well as on the frontier. Books like the *Hartford Selection* (1799) and Nettleton's *Village Hymns* (1824) were published to meet this need. Both contain American verse, the former hymns by Joseph

Steward and Nathan Strong, the latter hymns by Phoebe Brown, Abby Bradley Hyde, and William B. Tappan.

It was evidently this need for new tunes to match the new texts that led to the publication of books containing both words and music. One of the most important of these was Joshua Leavitt's *The Christian Lyre* (1831). No less than nine hymns by Jared Bell Waterbury appeared in this work, including "I Have Fought the Good Fight," and "Sinner, Is Thy Heart at Rest." "When Shall We All Meet Again" is said to have originated with three Indian students at Dartmouth College, who planned a reunion after graduation.

A rival volume which was intended to supply the same need was the *Spiritual Songs for Social Worship* of Thomas Hastings and Lowell Mason. Two famous missionary hymns made their appearance here, Samuel F. Smith's "The Morning Light Is Breaking" and Hasting's "Hail to the Brightness of Zion's Glad Morning." Ray Palmer's "My Faith Looks Up to Thee" was first published here with the tune OLIVET, which Mason wrote for it.

Joseph Hillman, a merchant and a Methodist layman of Troy, New York, not only established a camp meeting ground at Round Lake but also traveled in New York state and New England with a "praying band" which he organized. It is said that hymns which he later included in his *Revivalist* (1868) were first printed on separate sheets which were passed out to those in attendance. *The Revivalist* contains hymns of a folk type like "Come, Precious Soul," camp meeting choruses like "I Have Some Friends Before Me Gone," and gospel hymns like "Let Me Go Where Saints Are Going" by the music editor Lewis Hartsough.

Gospel Hymns

The gospel hymn was developed to meet the needs of revival and prayer meetings. The camp meeting hymn was frequently the work of anonymous singers; the gospel hymn was created by individual writers and musicians. The camp meeting hymn was characteristic of the frontier and of rural areas; the gospel hymn of the great cities.

To an unusual degree the gospel hymn was popularized by one man—Dwight Moody. Unmusical himself (he was unable to carry a tune), he had a keen appreciation of the possibilities of music in connection with his services. He made hymn singing a major feature of his meetings. He also had a clear idea of the kind of musician he needed. His meeting with Ira Sankey in 1870 in Indianapolis was the beginning of an association that was to make a kind of double personality

of them. People said "Moody and Sankey" when they thought of gospel hymns.

The mood of the text might be optismistic ("Blessed Assurance, Jesus Is Mine") or pleading ("Almost Persuaded"); the music was tuneful and easy to grasp. The rudimentary harmonies, the use of the chorus, the varied metric schemes, and the motor rhythms were characteristic. A marchlike movement as in "Shall We Gather at the River" was especially typical. The device of letting the lower parts echo rhythmically a motive announced by the sopranos became a mannerism which was abused by later writers (see the chorus of "There's a Land That Is Fairer than Day").

The gospel hymn developed its own manner of performance. The engravings which show a solo singer of gospel songs like Philip Phillips looking at a filled auditorium over a reed organ on which he accompanied himself seem strange indeed. Sankey preferred such an instrument to accompany the choir, even when the meeting was in a church which had a pipe organ, on the ground that the organ was likely to dominate the voices. He opposed the professional quartet choir and the practice of placing the singers back of the minister and behind a screen. He organized choruses utilizing members of the choir and the best singers in the congregation and placed them near the minister and in front of the congregation.

Among the earlier composers was George F. Root (1820–1895), whose THE BEAUTEOUS DAY ("We Are Watching, We Are Waiting") belongs to this type. Peter Phillips (1834–1895) began his career as a musical farm boy who wandered from house to house selling copies of songs which he had composed and published (see his "In Some Way or Other the Lord Will Provide"). Paul Bliss (1838–1876) was active chiefly in the Middle West. Beginning as a compiler of Sunday School hymns, he published his *Gospel Songs* (1874), afterwards joining Sankey in compiling the first volume of *Gospel Hymns* (1875), a title which became a household word. Bliss's "Almost Persuaded" appeared in *Gospel Songs.*

Although Robert Lowry, a Baptist clergyman, was a writer and compiler of Sunday School hymns (his "Shall We Gather at the River" is sometimes so classified), he also wrote music for "Saviour, Thy Dying Love" and "Five Were Foolish." From the pen of his associate, William Doane, we have selected NEAR THE CROSS ("Jesus, Keep Me Near the Cross"). Hubert P. Main, a member of the publishing firm of Bigelow and Main, was a composer of gospel hymns and an ardent collector of hymnbooks. (See his tune for "In the Silent Midnight Watches.")

Completing our group of gospel hymns are Gould's PILOT ("Jesus,

Saviour, Pilot me"), Mrs. Joseph P. Knapp's tune for "Blessed Assurance" to a text by Fanny Crosby, John Stockton's tune STOCTON for "Come, Every Soul," Edgar Stites's BEULAH LAND ("I've Reached the Land of Corn and Wine"), and William Tomer's GOD BE WITH YOU ("God Be With You Till We Meet Again"). Similar songs were sung by Swedish settlers ("Med Gud och hans vanscap") and by German-speaking singers ("O seid im arnscht"). The best of the gospel hymns have a direct simplicity which has appealed to singers ever since the appearance of the first gospel hymnals. Some of them have been included in recent hymnals published by denominational authority. Their enormous popularity (Sankey stated that a volume used in their English visit had sold not less than 5 million copies) stimulated a voluminous production of imitations which continues to the present day, especially in the Southern states.

A Camp Meeting

THE LORD INTO HIS GARDEN COMES | GARDEN HYMN 8.8.6.6.D.

St. 1-6

Anon., 1805 | Anon., version of 1866

1. The Lord in - to his gar - den comes; The spic - es yield a rich per - fume, The
2. O that this dry and bar - ren ground In springs of wa - ter may a - bound, A
lil - ies grow and thrive; The lil - ies grow and thrive.
fruit - ful soil be - come! A fruit - ful soil be - come!
Re - fresh - ing showers of grace di - vine, From Je - sus flow to ev - e - ry vine, Which
The des - ert blos - soms as the rose, When Je - sus con - quers all his foes, And
makes the dead re - vive, Which makes the dead re - vive.
makes his peo - ple one, And makes his peo - ple one.

3. The glorious time is rolling on,
The gracious work is now begun,
My soul a witness is,
My soul a witness is.
I taste and see the pardon free,
For all mankind as well as me
Who come to Christ may live,
Who come to Christ may live.

4. The worst of sinners here may find
A Saviour pitiful and kind,
Who will them all receive!
Who will them all receive!
None are too late who will repent;
Out of one sinner legions went;
Jesus did him relieve,
Jesus did him relieve.

5. Come, brethren, ye who love the Lord,
And taste the sweetness of his word,
In Jesus' ways go on;
In Jesus' ways go on.
Our troubles and our trials here,
Will only make us richer there,
When we arrive at home,
When we arrive at home.

6. Amen, amen, my soul replies,
I'm bound for realms of Paradise,
To claim my mansion there;
To claim my mansion there.
Now here's my heart, and here's my hand,
To meet you in the heavenly land,
Where we shall part no more,
Where we shall part no more.

THE WORLD, THE DEVIL, AND TOM PAINE

St. 1-3

Anon., 1807

COME AND GO ALONG WITH ME L.M.

Anon., 1868

1. The world, the dev - il, and Tom Paine, Have tried their force, but all in vain;
2. They pray, they sing, they preach the best, And do the Dev - il most mo - lest;
They can't pre-vail, the rea - son is The Lord de-fends the Meth - o - dist.
If Sa - tan had his vi - cious way, He'd kill and damn them all to - day.

3. They are despised by Satan's train,
Because they shout and preach so plain;
I'm bound to march in endless bliss,
And die a shouting Methodist.

A circuit rider

Let Thy Kingdom — Nettleton 8.7.8.7.D.

St. 1-3,6

Anon., version of 1831 — Anon., version of 1858

Fine
1. Let thy king - dom, bless - èd Sa - viour, Come and bid our jar - rings cease,
Come, O come, and reign for - ev - er, God of love, and Prince of Peace;
D.C. Day and night thy lambs are cry - ing, Come, good shep - herd, feed thy sheep.
D.C. al Fine
Vis - it now poor bleed - ing Zi - on, Hear the peo - ple mourn and weep,

2. Some for Paul, some for Apollos,
Some for Cephas—none agree;
Jesus, let us hear thee call us,
Help us, Lord, to follow thee.
Then we'll rush through what encumbers,
Over every hindrance leap,
Undismayed by force or numbers;
Come, good shepherd, feed thy sheep.

3. Lord, in us there is no merit,
We've been sinners from our youth;
Guide us, Lord, by thy good spirit,
Which shall teach us all the truth.
Oh, the gospel word we'll venture,
Till in death's cold arms we sleep,
Love our Lord and Christ our Saviour,
O good shepherd, feed thy sheep.

4. Christ alone, whose merit saves us,
Taught by him we'll own his name,
Sweetest of all names is Jesus,
How it doth our souls inflame!
Glory, glory, glory, glory,
Give him glory, he will keep,
He will clear your way before you,
The good shepherd feeds his sheep.

WHEN SHALL WE ALL MEET AGAIN? PARTING FRIENDS 7.7.7.7.7.7.

St. 1-3

Anon., 1831 Anon., 1831

Unison
1. When shall we all meet a-gain? When shall we all meet a-gain?
2. Though in dis-tant lands we sigh, Parched be-neath the hos-tile sky;
Oft shall glow-ing hope as-pire, Oft shall wea-ried love re-tire,
Though the deep be-tween us rolls, Friend-ship shall u-nite our souls;
Oft shall death and sor-row reign, Ere we all shall meet a-gain.
And in fan-cy's wide do-main, There shall we all meet a-gain.

3. When the dreams of life are fled,
When its wasted lamps are dead,
When in cold oblivion's shade,
Beauty, wealth, and fame are laid
Where immortal spirits reign,
There may we all meet again.

O Turn Ye, O Turn Ye — Expostulation 11.11.11.11.

St. 1-5

Josiah Hopkins, 1831 — Anon., 1831

1. O turn ye, O turn ye, for why will ye die, When
2. How vain the de - lu - sion, that while you de - lay Your
God in great mer - cy is com - ing so nigh? Now
hearts may grow bet - ter by stay - ing a - way! Come
Je - sus in - vites you, the Spir - it says, "Come!" And
wretch - ed, come starv - ing, come just as you be, While
an - gels are wait - ing to wel - come you home.
streams of sal - va - tion are flow ing so free.

3. And now Christ is ready your souls to receive;
O how can you question, if you will believe?
If sin is your burden, why will you not come?
'Tis you he bids welcome; he bids you come home.

4. In riches, in pleasures, what can you obtain,
To soothe your affliction or banish your pain?
To bear up your spirit when summoned to die,
Or waft you to mansions of glory on high?

5. Why will you be starving and feeding on air?
There's mercy in Jesus, enough and to spare;
If still you are doubting, make trial and see,
And prove that his mercy is boundless and free.

I Have Fought the Good Fight

The Death Song 12.12.12.12.

St. 1-6

Jared B. Waterbury, 1831

Anon., 1831

1. I have fought the good fight, I have fin - ished my race, And thee, O my Sa - viour, I soon shall em-brace; They may tor - ture this bod - y, my spir - it is free, And the bil - lows of death shall but waft it to thee.
2. Let thy strength, Lord, but gird me, thy smile be but mine, And my soul on thy faith - ful - ness, firm - ly re - cline; The dun - geon, the sword, or the stake, I can dare, And in trans - ports ex - pire, if my Je - sus be there.

3. Did my Lord feel the scourge? Did the
   thorns pierce his brow?
   In the darkness of death, on the cross did he bow?
   All this didst thou suffer, my Saviour, for me?
   Then welcome the fetters, that link me to thee.

4. United in sufferings, the promise is clear,
   I shall with my Jesus in glory appear;
   Out of great tribulation in triumph I go,
   With my robe washed in blood,
   and made whiter than snow.

5. I go to my Savior, I go to my God,
   I tread the same path my Redeemer once trod;
   Unworthy, my Jesus, unworthy am I,
   E'en to fall in thy cause, for thy truth e'en to die.

6. Lo! on my clear vision, the seats of the blessed
   Seem calmly to shine, and invite me to rest;
   Then unshaken my soul on the promise relies;
   "Though I die, I shall live; though I fall, I shall rise."

Sinner, Is Thy Heart at Rest? — Fairfax 7.7.7.7.

St. 1,2,4,5

Jared B. Waterbury, 1831 — Anon., 1831

1. Sin - ner, is thy heart at rest?
2. Can ___ this world af - ford thee bliss?
Is thy bos - om ___ void of fear?
Can it chase ___ a - way thy gloom?
Art thou ___ not by guilt ___ op - pressed? ___
Flat - tering, ___ false, and vain ___ it ___ is; ___
Speaks not con - science ___ in thine ear?
Trem - ble at ___ the ___ world - ling's doom.

3. Think, O sinner, on thy end;
See the judgment day appear!
Thither must thy spirit wend;
There thy righteous sentence hear.

4. Wretched, ruined, helpless soul,
To a Saviour's blood apply;
It alone can make thee whole;
Fly to Jesus, sinner, fly!

THE GLOOMY NIGHT OF SADNESS

St. 1-4

Anon., 1834

GEORGE 7.6.7.6.D.

Abraham Down Merrill, 1834

1.
2.
Fine
D. C. al Fine
1. The gloom - y night of sad - ness, Be - gins to flee a - way, The
glow - ing tinge of morn - ing, Pro - claims the ris - ing day; That wel - come day of prom - ise, When Christ shall claim his right, And on the world in dark - ness, Pour forth a flood of light.
2. Now truth, un-veiled, is shin - ing, With beams of sa - cred light, The
mourn - ing pil - grims won - der, And leave the paths of night. Their glow - ing hearts in rap - ture, All filled with joy di - vine, Burst forth in shout - ing glo - ry, And like their Mas - ter shine.

3. Come let's begin the anthems
And join the choir above,
To praise our blessed Jesus,
And bless the God we love.
All honor, praise and glory,
Salvation to our God;
Hosanna to our Jesus,
Who washed us in his blood.

4. The courts of heaven are ringing,
With songs of highest strains,
And ceaseless praise is rolling,
Along the flowery plains.
O could we rise triumphant,
And join with those above,
To shout and sing forever,
Free grace and dying love.

My Days Are Gliding Swiftly By — Shining Shore 8.7.8.7., with chorus

St. 1-4

David Nelson, writ. 1835 — George F. Root, 1856

1. My days are glid - ing swift - ly by, And I, a pil - grim stran - ger,
2. Our ab - sent King the watch-word gave, "Let ev - ery lamp be burn - ing;"
Would not de - tain them as they fly, Those hours of toil and dan - ger
We look a - far, a - cross the wave, Our dis - tant home dis - cern - ing
Chorus
For now we stand on Jor - dan's strand, Our friends are pass - ing ov - er,
And just be - fore the shin - ing shore, We may

3. Should coming days be dark and cold,
We will not yield to sorrow;
For hope will sing, with courage bold,
"There's glory on the morrow."
Chorus

4. Let storms of woe in whirlwinds rise,
Each cord on earth to sever,
There — bright and joyous in the skies,
There — is our home forever.
Chorus

In the Silent Midnight Watches 8.5.8.5.D.

St. 1-3

Arthur Cleveland Coxe, 1842 Hubert P. Main, 1877

1. In the si - lent mid-night watch-es, List, thy bo - som door! How it knock-eth,
2. Death comes down with reck-less foot - step, To the hall and hut! Think you death will
knock-eth, knock-eth, Knock - eth ev - er - more! Say not 'tis thy pulse is beat - ing,
stand a - knock - ing Where the door is shut? Je - sus wait - eth, wait - eth, wait - eth;
'Tis thy heart of sin; 'Tis thy Sav-iour knocks, and cri - eth, "Rise, and let me in!"
But thy door is fast! Grieved, a - way thy Sav - iour go - eth, Death breaks in at last.

3. Then 'tis thine to stand entreating
Christ to let thee in;
At the gate of heaven beating,
Wailing for thy sin.
Nay, alas! thou foolish virgin,
Hast thou then forgot?
Jesus waited long to know thee,
But he knows thee not.

You Will See Your Lord A-Coming — Old Churchyard — Irregular

St. 1-3,5,7,9

Anon., 1843 — Anon., 1849

1. You will see your Lord a - com - ing, You will see your Lord a - com - ing, You will see your Lord a - com - ing, From the old church-yards. Hear the band of mu - sic, Hear the band of mu - sic, Hear the band of mu - sic Which is sound - ing through the air.
2. Ga - briel sounds his might - y trum - pet, Ga - briel sounds his might - y trum - pet, Ga - briel sounds his might - y trum - pet, Through the old church-yards, While the band of mu - sic, While the band of mu - sic, While the band of mu - sic, Shall be sound - ing through the air.

3. He'll awake all the nations,
He'll awake all the nations,
He'll awake all the nations,
From the old church-yards,
While the band of music,
While the band of music,
While the band of music
Shall be sounding through the air.

4. O sinner, you will tremble,
O sinner, you will tremble,
O sinner, you will tremble,
At the old church-yards,
While the band of music,
While the band of music,
While the band of music
Shall be sounding through the air.

5. You will see the saints arising,
You will see the saints arising,
You will see the saints arising,
From the old church-yards,
While the band of music,
While the band of music,
While the band of music
Shall be sounding through the air.

6. Then we'll shout, our sufferings over,
Then we'll shout, our sufferings over,
Then we'll shout, our sufferings over,
From the old church-yards,
While the band of music,
While the band of music,
While the band of music
Shall be sounding through the air.

Joyfully, Joyfully Onward I Move — Joyfully, Joyfully 10.10.10.10.D.

St. 1-3

William Hunter, 1843 — Abraham Down Merrill, 1845

1. Joy - ful - ly, joy - ful - ly on - ward I move, Bound for the land of bright spir - its a - bove;
An - gel - ic chor - ist - ers sing as I come, "Joy - ful - ly, joy - ful - ly, haste to thy home."
2. Friends fond - ly cher - ished have passed on be - fore; Wait - ing, they watch me ap - proach-ing the shore;
Sing - ing, to cheer me through death's chill-ing gloom, "Joy - ful - ly, joy - ful - ly, haste to thy home."

Soon with my pil-grim - age end - ed be - low, Home to the land of bright spir - its I'll go;
Sounds of sweet mel - o - dy fall on my ear; Harps of the bless - ed! your voic - es I hear;

Pil - grim and stran-ger no more shall I roam, Joy - ful - ly, joy - ful - ly rest - ing at home.
Ring with the har - mo - ny heav - en's high dome, "Joy - ful - ly, joy - ful - ly, haste to thy home."

3. Death, with thy weapons of war lay me low;
Strike, king of terrors, I fear not thy blow:
Jesus hath broken the bars of the tomb;
Joyfully, joyfully, will I go home.
Bright will the morn of eternity dawn;
Death shall be banished, his sceptre be gone
Joyfully then shall I witness his doom;
Joyfully, joyfully, safely at home.

"Go Bring Me," Said the Dying Fair — The Dying Backslider C.M.D.

St. 1-4

William Hunter, 1854 — Samuel Wakefield, 1854

1. "Go, bring me," said the dy - ing fair, With anguish in her tone,
"My cost - ly robes and jew - els here, Go, bring them ev - ery one."
2. "With glo - rious hopes I once was blest, Nor feared the gap - ing tomb;
With heaven al - read - y in my breast, I looked for heaven to come.
They strewed them on her dy - ing bed, Those robes of prince - ly cost; "Fa -
I heard a Sav - iour's par-doning voice, My soul was filled with peace; Fa -
ther," with bit - ter - ness she said, "For these my soul was lost."
ther, you bought me with these toys, I bar - tered heaven for these."

3. "Take them — they are the price of blood,
For these I lost my soul;
For these, must bear the wrath of God,
While ceaseless ages roll.
Remember, when you look on these,
Your daughter's fearful doom,
That she, her pride and thine to please,
Went quaking to the tomb."

4. "Go, bear them from my sight and touch,
Your gifts I here restore;
Keep them with care, they cost you much,
They cost your daughter more.
Look at them every rolling year,
Upon my dying day,
And drop for me the burning tear,"
She said, and sunk away.

THE MUSIC OF HIS STEPS

THE ITINERANT'S DEATH L.M.

St. 1-4

Samuel Wakefield, 1854

Samuel Wakefield, 1854

1. The mu - sic of his steps was sought, His time had come, and *he* came not;
His lit - tle ones were wont to greet The sound of his re - turn - ing feet.
2. He was a faith - ful man of God, And in his Sav-iour's foot - steps trod;
Stern du - ty bade him of - ten stray From those who near his bos - om lay.
They wait - ed long were wait - ing still, To see him has-tening o'er the hill,
But when from anx - ious toils re-turned, Kind hearts with strong af - fec - tion burned;

A - cross the brook, and to the door, His man - ly face with joy spread o'er.
The hus-band's and the fa - ther's voice, In ev - ery ear poured rich - est joys.

3. But ah! those ears no more shall hear
That voice to wife and children dear;
Those eyes of love shall never more
Look on that face with joy spread o'er;
Shall never see their loved one come,
To cheer their hearth and bless their home.
Low lies his form beneath the sod;
High lives his spirit with his God.

4. Yet still they look with glistening eye,
Till lo! a herald hastens nigh;
He comes the tale of woe to tell,
How he, their prop and glory, fell;
How died he in a stranger's room,
How strangers laid him in the tomb,
How spake he with his latest breath,
And loved and blessed them all in death.

My Latest Sun Is Sinking Fast — The Land of Beulah C.M., with chorus

St. 1-4

Jefferson Haskell, 1860 — William Batchelder Bradbury, 1862

1. My latest sun is sinking fast, My race is nearly run;
My strongest trials now are past My triumph is begun.
2. I know I'm nearing the holy ranks Of friends and kindred dear,
For I brush the dews on Jordan's banks, The crossing must be near.
Chorus
O, come, angel band, come and around me stand, O,
bear me away on your snowy wings To my immortal home, O,
bear me away on your snowy wings To my immortal home.

3. I've almost gained my heavenly home,
My spirit loudly sings;
The holy ones, behold, they come!
I hear the noise of wings.
Chorus

4. O bear my longing heart to Him
Who bled and died for me;
Whose blood now cleanses from all sin
And gives me victory.
Chorus

He Leadeth Me, O Blessed Thought
St. 1-4
Joseph Henry Gilmore, 1862

He Leadeth Me L.M., with chorus
William Batchelder Bradbury, 1864

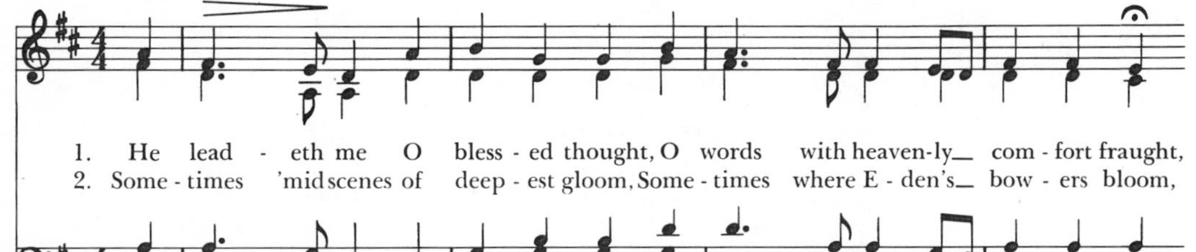
1. He lead - eth me O bless - ed thought, O words with heaven-ly_ com - fort fraught,
2. Some - times 'mid scenes of deep - est gloom, Some - times where E - den's_ bow - ers bloom,

What - e'er I do, wher - e'er I be, Still_ 'tis God's hand that_ lead - eth me.
By wa - ters still, o'er trou - bled sea, Still_ 'tis his hand that_ lead - eth me.

Chorus

f He lead - eth me, he lead - eth_ me, By his own hand_ he_ lead - eth me;

His faith ful fol - lower I would_ be, For by his hand_ he_ lead - eth me.

3. Lord, I would clasp thy hand in mine,
Nor ever murmur nor repine;
Content, whatever lot I see,
Since 'tis my God that leadeth me.
Chorus

4. And when my task on earth is done,
When, by thy grace, the victory's won,
E'en death's cold wave I will not flee,
Since God through Jordan leadeth me.
Chorus

Watchman, Tell Me | Buchanan 8.7.8.7.D.

St. 1-3, 6

Anon., 1863 | Anon., version of 1866

Fine
1. Watch-man, tell me, does the morn - ing Of fair Zi - on's glo - ry dawn?
Have the signs that mark its com - ing Yet up - on thy path - way shone?
Gird thy bri - dal robes a - round thee, Morn - ing dawns! a - rise! a - rise!
D. C. al Fine
Pil - grim, yes! a - rise! look round thee Light is break - ing in the skies!

2. Watchman, has the tribulation
Of the cruel man of sin
Ceased his bloody persecution?
Will it not return again?
Pilgrim, no! his times have ended,
Never shall the monster reign;
Tekel on his brow is written
Soon he will consume in flame.

3. Watchman, were there signs attending
At the ending of the time?
With the closing moments pending,
Did the sun refuse to shine?
Pilgrim, yes; the sun was shrouded
In a veil of gloom that day;
Nature was in darkness clouded
On that nineteenth day of May.

4. Watchman, see! the land is nearing,
With its vernal fruits and flowers!
On! just yonder, O, how cheering,
Bloom forever Eden's bowers.
Hark! the choral strains there ringing,
Wafted on the balmy air!
See the millions! hear them singing!
Soon the pilgrims will be there!

Let Me Go Where Saints Are Going — 8.7.8.7.D., with chorus

St. 1-5

Lewis Hartsough, writ. 1861, pub. 1867 — Lewis Hartsough, writ. 1861, pub. 1867

1. Let me go where saints are go - ing To the man - sions of the blest; Let me go where my re - deem - er Has pre - pared his peo - ple's rest. I would gain the realms of bright - ness, Where they dwell for - ev - er - more, I would join the friends that wait me O - ver on the oth - er shore.
2. Let me go where none are wea - ry, Where is raised no wail of woe, Let me go and bathe my spir - it In the rap - tures an - gels know, Let me go, for bliss e - ter - nal Lures my soul a - way, a - way, And the vic - tor's song tri - um - phant Thrills my heart, I can - not stay.

Chorus
Let me go, 'tis Je - sus calls me; Let me gain the realms of day; Bear me
o - ver an - gel pin - ions, Longs my soul to be a - way.

3. Let me go, why should I tarry?
What has earth to bind me here?
What, but cares and toils and sorrows?
What, but death and pain and fear?
Let me go, for hopes most cherished
Blasted round me often lie,
O I've gathered brightest flowers
But to see them fade and die.
Chorus

4. Let me go where tears and sighing
Are forevermore unknown,
Where the joyous songs of glory
Call me to a happier home.
Let me go — I'd cease this dying,
I would gain life's fairer plains,
Let me join the myriad harpers,
Let me chant their rapturous strains.
Chorus

5. Let me go, O speed my journey,
Saints and seraphs lure away,
O I almost feel the raptures
That belong to endless day.
Oft methinks I hear the singing
That is only heard above,
Let me go, O speed my going,
Let me go where all is love.
Chorus

Shall We Gather at the River?

St. 1-4

Robert Lowry, writ. 1864, pub. 1865

Beautiful River 8.7.8.7., with chorus

Robert Lowry, writ. 1864, pub. 1865

1. Shall we gath - er at the riv - er, Where bright an - gel feet have trod,
2. On the mar - gin of the riv - er, Wash - ing up its sil - ver spray,
With its crys - tal tide for - ev - er Flow - ing from the throne of God?
We shall walk and wor - ship ev - er, All the hap - py, gold - en day.
Chorus
Yes, we'll gath - er at the riv - er, The beau - ti - ful, the beau - ti - ful riv - er,
Gath - er with the saints at the riv - er That flows from the throne of God.

3. On the bosom of the river,
Where the Saviour King we own,
We shall meet and sorrow never,
'Neath the glory of the throne.
Chorus

4. Soon we'll reach the shining river,
Soon our pilgrimage will cease;
Soon our happy hearts will quiver
With the melody of peace.
Chorus

I'm on My Way to Canaan — Way to Canaan C.M.D.

St. 1-4

Anon., c.1866 — Anon., 1866

1. I'm on my way to Ca - na - an, I bid this world fare - well. Come
2. I'll blow the gos - pel trum - pet loud, And on the na - tions call; For

on, my fel - low trav - el - ers, In spite of earth and— hell. Though
Christ hath me com - mis - sion - èd To say he died for— all. Come

Sa - tan's ar - my rag - es hard, And all his hosts com - bine, Yet
try his grace, come prove him now, You shall the gift ob - tain; He

st. 4

scrip - ture doth en - gage the— sword, And strength of love di - vine.
will not send you emp - ty a - way, Nor let you come in vain.

3. My soul looks up and sees him smile,
While he the blessing sends,
And I am thinking all the while –
"When will this journey end?"
I contemplate it can't be long
Till he will come again,
Then I shall join that heavenly throng,
And in his kingdom reign.

4. "But stop," says Patience, "wait awhile,
The crown's for those who fight,
The prize for those who run the race
By faith and not by sight."
Then Faith doth take a pleasing view,
Hope waits. Love sits and sings,
Desire flutters to be gone,
But Patience clips her wings.

THERE'S A LAND THAT IS FAIRER THAN DAY | SWEET BY-AND-BY 9.9.9.9., with chorus

St. 1-3

S. Fillmore Bennett, writ. 1867 | J. P. Webster, comp. 1867

1. There's a land that is fair - er than day, And by faith we can see it a - far; For the Fa - ther waits o - ver the way, To pre - pare us a dwell - ing place there.
2. We shall sing on that beau - ti - ful shore The me - lo - di - ous songs of the blest, And our spir - its shall sor - row no more, Not a sigh for the bless - ing of rest.

Chorus

In the sweet by - and - by, We shall meet on that beau - ti - ful shore, In the sweet by - and - by, We shall meet on that beau - ti - ful shore.

In the sweet by-and-by by-and-by by - and - by, by - and - by, by - and - by,

3. To our bountiful Father above,
We will offer our tribute of praise,
For the glorious gift of his love,
And the blessings that hallow our days.
Chorus

Come, Precious Soul — Calvary or Gethsemane — Irregular

St. 1,2,10,13

Anon., version of 1868 — Anon., melody pub. 1868

Unison

1. Come pre - cious soul, and let us take A walk be - com - ing you and me,
2. O Cal - va - ry is a moun - tain high; 'Tis much too hard a task for me,

And whith - er, my friend, shall we our foot - steps bend, To Cal - va - ry or to
And I had ra - ther stay in the broad and plea - sant way Than to walk in the gar - den of

Geth - se - ma - ne? 3. O con - science! thou art ev - er mak - ing a noise, I
Geth - se - ma - ne. 4. O tar - ry not in all the plain, Lest it

can - not en - joy an - y peace for thee, There is time e - nough yet, and the
prove a dan - ger - ous snare to thee, But look up to the man who was

jour - ney's not so great, I can soon climb the moun - tain Cal - va - ry.
bruised for thy sin, And he'll help thee climb up Cal - va - ry.

I HAVE SOME FRIENDS BEFORE ME GONE A HOME UP YONDER 8.8.6.D., with chorus

St. 1, 4-6

Anon., 1868 Anon., version sung by Rev. B. I. Ives, 1868

1. I have some friends be - fore me gone For a few days,
And I'm re - solved to fol - low on, For a few days,
D.C. For I have a home up yon - der, For a few days,
Fine
for a few days, For I am go - ing home.
for a few days, For I am go - ing home.
for a few days, And I am go - ing home.
Chorus
D.C. al Fine
For I have a home up yon - der, Glo - ry Glo - ry

2. My suffering time will soon be o'er,
For a few days, for a few days
For I am going home.
Thus I shall sigh and weep no more!
For a few days, for a few days,
For I am going home.
Chorus

3. Fight on ye conquering souls, fight on,
For a few days, for a few days,
For I am going home.
Until the conquest you have won,
For a few days, for a few days,
For I am going home.
Chorus

4. Farewell vain world, I'm going home,
For a few days, for a few days,
For I am going home.
My Saviour smiles and bids me come,
For a few days, for a few days,
For I am going home.
Chorus

WE ARE WATCHING, WE ARE WAITING — THE BEAUTEOUS DAY 8.7.8.7., with chorus

St. 1-4

William O. Cushing, 1868 — George F. Root, 1868

Slow
1. We are watch-ing, we are wait - ing For the bright, pro-phet - ic day; When the shad - ows, drear - y shad-ows, From the world shall roll a - way.
2. We are watch-ing, we are wait - ing For the beau-teous King of day; For the chief - est of ten thou-sand, For the Light, the Truth, the Way.
Chorus
We are wait - ing for the morn-ing, When the beau - teous day is dawn - ing, We are wait - ing for the morn - ing, For the gold - en

3. We are watching, we are waiting
For the time so long foretold,
When with saved ones of all ages,
We shall walk the streets of gold.
Chorus

4. We are watching, we are waiting
For an earth made free from strife,
Then the power of Satan ended,
We shall have eternal life.
Chorus

Come, Friends and Neighbors, Come — The Pastor's Appeal 6.4.6.4.6.6.6.4.

St. 1-5

Lewis Hartsough, 1868 — Lewis Hartsough, arr. 1868

1. Come, friends and neigh-bors, come, Sal - va - tion's free, Come, gain in heav'n a home, And hap - py be; This world's a world of sin, And aims your souls to win; From end - less fear and pain A - rouse and flee!
2. Your time at most is short Ah! Death is near; Your cru - el foe's a - lert, Should you not fear? O flee from his em - brace, For heaven be - gin the race; 'Tis Christ will give you grace, And save you here.

3. O fly to Jesus' side —
No longer stay;
His arms are open wide,
He is the way.
To-morrow's sun may ne'er
Again shine on you here;
O how will you appear
On Judgment day?

4. O listen while you may —
'Tis mercy's hour;
Begin to weep and pray,
An heavenly power
Will bring a helper nigh,
Who will not pass you by.
'Till you are saved on high
Forever more.

5. How can we say, farewell!
And leave you all
To make your way to hell,
'Mid terrors all?
How can we give you up,
To fill your fearful cup
Of ruin, drop by drop?
Heed Mercy's call.

COME, EVERY SOUL

STOCKTON C.M., with chorus

St. 1-4

John H. Stockton, 1868

John H. Stockton, 1868

1. Come, ev - ery soul by sin op-pressed, There's mer - cy with the Lord;
2. For Je - sus shed his pre - cious blood Rich bless - ings to be - stow;
And he will sure - ly give you rest, By trust - ing in his word.
Plunge now in - to the crim - son flood That wash - es white as snow.
Chorus
On - ly trust — him, on - ly trust him, On - ly trust him now;
He will save — you, he will save you, He will save you now.

3. Yes, Jesus is the truth, the way,
That leads you into rest;
Believe in him without delay,
And you are fully blest.
Chorus

4. Come then, and join this holy band,
And on to glory go,
To dwell in that celestial land,
Where joys immortal flow.
Chorus

JESUS, KEEP ME NEAR THE CROSS

St. 1-4

Fanny J. Crosby, 1869

NEAR THE CROSS 7.6.7.6., with chorus

William Howard Doane, 1869

1. Je - sus, keep me near the cross, There a pre - cious foun - tain
2. Near the cross, a trem - bling soul, Love and mer - cy found me;
Free to all — a heal - ing stream, Flows from Cal - vary's moun - tain.
There the bright and morn - ing star Sheds its beams a - round me.
Chorus
In the Cross, in the Cross, Be my glo - ry ev - er;
Till my rap - tured soul shall find Rest be - yond the riv - er.

3. Near the Cross! O Lamb of God,
Bring its scenes before me;
Help me walk from day to day,
With its shadows o'er me.
Chorus

4. Near the Cross I'll watch and wait,
Hoping, trusting ever,
Till I reach the golden strand,
Just beyond the river.
Chorus

One More Day's Work for Jesus

7.6.10.6.10., with chorus

St. 1-3, 5

Anna B. Warner, 1869

Robert Lowry, 1869

1. One more day's work for Je - sus; One less of life for me! But heaven is
2. One more day's work for Je - sus; How glo - rious is my King! 'Tis joy, not
near - er, And Christ is dear - er, Than yes - ter - day to me; His love and
du - ty, To speak his beau - ty; My soul mounts on the wing At the mere
Chorus
light Fill all my soul to-night.
thought How Christ my life has bought.
One more day's work for Je - sus, One more day's work for
Je - sus, One more day's work for Je - sus, One less of life for me.

3. One more day's work for Jesus;
How sweet the work has been.
To tell the story, to show the glory,
When Christ's flock enter in!
How it did shine in this poor heart of mine!
Chorus

4. Oh, blessed work for Jesus!
Oh, rest at Jesus' feet!
There toil seems pleasure. My wants are treasure.
And pain for him is sweet.
Lord, if I may, I'll serve another day.
Chorus

Almost Persuaded | Almost Persuaded 9.9.6.6.6.4.

St. 1-3

Philip Bliss, 1871 | Philip Bliss, 1871

1. "Almost persuaded," Now to believe;
"Almost persuaded," Christ to receive,
Seems now some soul to say,
"Go, Spirit, go thy way,
Some more convenient day
On thee I'll call."

2. "Almost persuaded," Come, come today;
"Almost persuaded," Turn not away,
Jesus invites you here,
Angels are lingering near,
Prayers rise from hearts so dear;
O wanderer, come.

3. "Almost persuaded," harvest is past!
"Almost persuaded," doom comes at last!
"Almost" can not avail;
"Almost" is but to fail!
Sad, sad, that bitter wail—
"Almost—*but lost!*"

Jesus, Saviour, Pilot Me

Pilot 7.7.7.D.

St. 1-3

Edward Hopper, 1871

John E. Gould, 1871

1. Je - sus, Sav - iour, pi - lot me O - ver life's tem - pest - uous sea;
2. As a moth - er stills her child, Thou canst hush the o - cean wild;
Un - known waves be - fore me roll, Hid - ing rock and treach-erous shoal;
Boist - erous waves o - bey thy will When thou sayest to them, "Be still."
Chart and com - pass came from thee; Je - sus, Sav - iour, pi - lot me.
Won - drous Sov - ereign of the sea, Je - sus, Sav - iour, pi - lot me.

3. When at last I near the shore,
And the fearful breakers roar
'Twixt me and the peaceful rest,
Then, while leaning on thy breast,
May I hear thee say to me,
"Fear not, I will pilot thee."

Saviour, Thy Dying Love — 6.4.6.4.6.6.6.4.

St. 1-4

Sylvanus D. Phelps, 1871 — Robert Lowry, 1871

1. Sav - iour! thy dy - ing love thou__ gav - est me,____ Nor should I
2. At the blest mer - cy - seat, Plead - ing for me,____ My fee - ble
aught with - hold, Dear__ Lord, from thee; In love my soul would bow,
faith looks up, Je - sus, to thee. Help me the cross to bear,

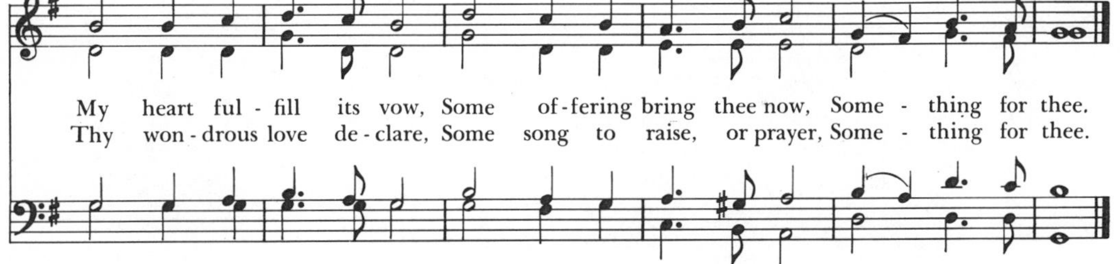
My heart ful - fill its vow, Some of - fering bring thee now, Some - thing for thee.
Thy won - drous love de - clare, Some song to raise, or prayer, Some - thing for thee.

3. Give me a faithful heart,
Likeness to thee;
That each departing day
Henceforth may see
Some work of love begun,
Some deed of kindness done,
Some wanderer sought and won,
Something for thee.

4. All that I am and have
Thy gifts so free;
In joy, in grief, through life,
Dear Lord, for thee!
And when thy face I see,
My ransomed soul shall be,
Through all eternity,
Something for thee.

IN SOME WAY OR OTHER THE LORD WILL PROVIDE THE LORD WILL PROVIDE 11.6.6.6.5., with chorus

St. 1-4

Mrs. M. A. W. Cook, 1873 Philip Phillips, 1875

1. In some way or oth - er the Lord will pro - vide; It may not be
2. At some time or oth - er the Lord will pro - vide; It may not be

my way, It may not be *thy* way; And yet, in his *own* way, "The—
my time, It may not be *thy* time; And yet, in his *own* time, "The—

Lord will pro - vide."
Lord will pro - vide."

Chorus

Then, we'll trust in the Lord, and he will pro -

vide; Yes, we'll trust in the Lord, And— he will— pro - vide.

3. Despond then no longer, the Lord will provide;
And this be the token—
No word he hath spoken
Was ever yet broken.
"The Lord will provide."
Chorus

4. March on then right boldly; the sea shall divide.
The pathway made glorious,
With shoutings victorious,
We'll join in the chorus,
"The Lord will provide."
Chorus

BLESSED ASSURANCE, JESUS IS MINE

9.10.9.9., with chorus

St. 1-3

Fanny J. Crosby, 1873

Mrs. Joseph F. Knapp, 1873

1. Bless - ed as - sur - ance, Je - sus is mine! O what a fore - taste of glo - ry di - vine! Heir of sal - va - tion, pur - chase of God, Born of his Spir - it, washed in his blood.
2. Per - fect sub - mis - sion, per - fect de - light, Vi - sions of rap - ture burst on my sight; An - gels de - scend - ing, bring from a - bove, Ech - oes of mer - cy, whis - pers of love.
Chorus
This is my sto - ry, this is my song, Prais - ing my

Sav - iour all the day long; This is my sto - ry this is my
song, Prais - ing my Sav - iour all the day long.

3. Perfect submission, all is at rest,
   I in my Saviour am happy and blest,
   Watching and waiting, looking above,
   Filled with his goodness, lost in his love.
   Chorus

BEHOLD
I BRING YOU
WHICH SHALL BE

A Moody and Sankey revival, January 1876

I've Reached the Land of Corn and Wine

Beulah Land L.M., with chorus

St. 1-4

Edgar P. Stites, writ. c.1875

John R. Sweney, comp. c.1875

1. I've reached the land of corn and wine, And all its rich - es free-ly mine; Here shines un-dimmed one bliss - ful day, For all my night has passed a - way.
2. The Sav-iour comes and walks with me, And sweet com-mun-ion here have we; He gen - tly leads me with his hand, For this is heav - en's bor - der-land.
Chorus
O Beu-lah land, sweet Beu - lah land, As on thy high - est mount I stand, I look a - way a - cross the sea, Where man-sions are pre - pared for me. And view the shin - ing glo - ry shore, My heaven, my home for - ev - er-more.

3. A sweet perfume upon the breeze
Is borne from ever vernal trees,
And flowers that never fading grow
Where streams of life forever flow.
Chorus

4. The zephyrs seem to float to me,
Sweet sounds of heaven's melody,
As angels, with the white-robed throng,
Join in the sweet redemption song.
Chorus

FIVE WERE FOOLISH — THE DOOR WAS SHUT L.M., with chorus

St. 1-4

Arthur J. Hodge, 1880 — Robert Lowry, 1880

1. Five were fool-ish, and five were wise, All were wait-ing with heav - y eyes;
2. Who are fool-ish, and who are wise, Wait - ing wait-ing with heav - y eyes?
Five were read - y, and five were not, Five re-mem-bered, and five for - got.
Who are read - y, and who are not? Who re-mem-bered, and who for - got?
Chorus
Their lamps were not filled, The wicks were not cut; The bride-groom went in, And the door was shut.

3. These are foolish, and those are wise,
Waiting, waiting with heavy eyes;
Some are doubting, and cling to sin,
Some are trusting, and enter in.
Chorus

4. You, the foolish, hear wisdom's cry,
Days of waiting pass quickly by;
God is gracious, but know you not,
Foolish sleepers will be forgot!
Chorus

God Be with You Till We Meet Again

God Be with You 9.8.8.9., with chorus

St. 1-4

Jeremiah E. Rankin, writ. 1882

William G. Tomer, comp. 1882

1. God be with you till we meet a - gain! By his coun-sels guide, up - hold you,
2. God be with you till we meet a - gain! 'Neath his wings se - cure - ly hide you,
With his sheep se - cure - ly fold you; God be with you till we meet a - gain!
Dai - ly man - na still pro - vide you; God be with you till we meet a - gain!
Chorus
Till we meet! Till we meet! Till we meet at Je - sus' feet;
Till we meet! Till we meet a-gain! Till we meet!
Till we meet! Till we meet! God be with you till we meet a - gain!
Till we meet! Till we meet a - gain!

3. God be with you till we meet again!
When life's perils thick confound you,
Put his arms unfailing round you;
God be with you till we meet again!
Chorus

4. God be with you till we meet again!
Keep love's banner floating o'er you,
Smite death's threatening wave before you;
God be with you till we meet again!
Chorus

MED GUD OCH HANS VANSCAP — ACK, SALIGA STUNDER 11.11.11.6.6.11.

WITH GOD AND HIS MERCY

St. 1-5

Carl Olof Rosenius — Oscar Ahnfelt, 185 (?)

Unison
1. With God and his mer - cy, his spir - it, and Word, And lov - ing com-mun - ion at
2. In per - il - ous times, a - mid tem - pests and night, A band press - es on through the
al - tar and board, We meet with as - sur - ance the dawn of each day: The
gloom to - ward light; Though hum - ble, and meek, and dis - owned by the world, They
Shep-herd is with us, The Shep - herd is with us, To lead and pro-tect us, and teach us the way.
fol - low the Sav-iour, They fol - low the Sav-iour, And march on to glo - ry, with ban - ners un-furled.
3

3. While groveling worldlings with dross are content,
And ever on sin and transgression are bent,
I follow, victorious hosts, at your word,
And march on to glory,
And march on to glory,
We march on to glory, our captain the Lord.

4. The sign of the cross I triumphantly bear,
Though none of my kindred that emblem may wear;
I joyfully follow the champions of right,
Who march on to glory,
Who march on to glory,
Who march on to glory, with weapons of might.

5. O Shepherd, abide with us, care for us still,
And feed us and lead us and teach us thy will;
And when in thy heavenly fold we shall be
Our thanks and our praises,
Our thanks and our praises,
Our thanks and our praises we'll render to thee.

1. Med Gud och hans vanskap, hans Anda och ord,
Samt broders gemenskap och nadenes bord,
De osedda dagar vi mote med trost.
Oss foljer ju Herden,
Den trofaste Herden,
Den trofaste Herden, Vi kane hans rost!

O Seid Im Arnscht

O Earnest Be

8.7.9.7., with chorus

Recorded by Don Yoder, 1951

Chorus (unison)
O ear - nest be, O ear - nest be, O hal - le - o, hal - le - lu - jah, We
O seid im Arnscht, O seid im Arnscht, O hal - le - o, hal - le - lu - jah! Wir
Fine
trav - el towards e - ter - ni - ty, O hal - le - o, hal - le - lu - jah!
rei - sen nach der Ew - ich - keit, O hal - le - o, hal - le - lu - jah!
Verse
It is a wea - ry wil - der - ness Where we must so - journ long - er, There
Es iss ein gros - si Wil - der - ness, Da mis - sen wir noch dar - ich, Da
D. C. al Fine
taste the heav - en - ly man - na sweet, O nev - er be faint heart - ed.
schmackt des him - mel - isch Man - na siess, O wer - det nur nicht nar - risch.

Hymns of Reform

THE MORE ENLIGHTENED spirits of the nineteenth century strove for a more humane world. Eric Routley's statement that "the English Christians of the nineteenth century are at their most powerful and influential in their social and reforming work" was equally true of the United States. This movement manifested itself in the extension and improvement of medical care, in the development of methods of teaching the handicapped, in better treatment for the retarded and the mentally ill, in the temperance movement, and in the struggle to establish the rights of oppressed groups: the black slaves, working people, and women. We find a varied repertory of songs related to the activities of these groups. Some are gathered here, others will be found in other sections.

Gallaudet's hymn, "Jesus, in Sickness and in Pain," comes from the pen of a man who devoted his life to the education of the deaf. An important step forward was the establishment of urban hospitals, some of them under denominational auspices like St. Luke's Hospital in New York, founded by William A. Mühlenberg, who also wrote both hymn texts and tunes. (See his "I Would Not Live Alway," and "Saviour, Who Thy Flock Art Feeding.") The attempt to make hospitalization more bearable is shown in the hospital visitation hymn by Arthur C. Coxe, "Father, Who Mak'st Thy Suff'ring Sons."

Many songs of reform were not hymns; many churches differed in the nineteenth century, as they still do, as to the extent to which songs advocating reform might be sung in church and, more particularly, in a church service. Many felt that the church service must be directed to the praise of God. Nevertheless, there were churches and hymnbooks which admitted hymns of reform. Such was the Universalist *Hymns for Christian Devotion* (Boston, 1871), which contained a section headed "Philanthropic Subjects." Some of these have to do with charitable enterprises, others with temperence, slavery, and peace.

Two of the movements of the nineteenth century are hardly represented even in hymnbooks intended for less formal meetings. Churches administered by male deacons were not likely to sing of the rights of women. Hymns addressed to workers mostly belong to the twentieth century rather than the nineteenth. Indeed, workers struggling to form unions might regard the attitude of the local preacher with some skepticism. Joe Hill's "Long-haired preachers come out

every night/Try to tell you what's wrong and what's right," and ending with the promise that "you'll eat pie in the sky bye and bye" was based on the gospel hymn "There's a Land That is Fairer than Day" ("In the sweet bye and bye").

Temperance songs borrowed tunes from popular songs of the day or some, like "Come, Happy Children," were sung to revival tunes. There was no doubt as to the seriousness of the problem, and the fact that temperance hymns like Mrs. Sigourney's "We Praise Thee If One Ransomed Soul" were included in denominational hymnals shows that this was recognized.

If slavery was built into the fabric of our country, so was the conviction that it was a shameful violation of the law of God. The songs concerning slavery divide between those written by whites and those sung by the black slaves. "Is There No Balm in Christian Lands" appeared as a broadside. Though the sentiments expressed are those of the black slave, it was probably written by some Northern sympathizer. John Greenleaf Whittier was the poet of the movement, and his "O Thou Whose Presence Went Before" was written for an antislavery meeting held in 1834. Eliza Lee Follen's Prayer for the Slave, "Lord Deliver, Thou Can'st Save" appeared in 1836. The slave songs themselves employ scriptural imagery to express their longing for freedom. "Go Down, Moses" is a wonderful example with its refrain, "Let my people go."

An Easter observance

O Thou! Whose Presence Went Before — Dedication Chant L.M.

St. 1-5

John Greenleaf Whittier, writ. 1834, pub. 1844 — Leonard Marshall, 1842

Dolce
1. O Thou! whose pres - ence went be - fore Our fa - thers in their wea - ry way, As with thy cho - sen moved of yore The fire by night the cloud by day!
2. When from each tem - ple of the free, A na - tion's song as - cends to heaven, Most ho - ly Fa - ther! un - to thee, May not our hum - ble prayer be given.
7 5 ♯6
6 6 4 7 ♯
6 5 6

3. For those to whom this day can bring,
   Not, as to us, the joyful thrill;
   For those, who, under freedom's wing,
   Are bound in slavery's fetters still.

4. And grant, O Father! that the time
   Of earth's deliverance may be near,
   When every land, and tongue, and clime,
   The message of thy love shall hear.

5. When smitten, as with fire from heaven,
   The captive's chain shall sink in dust,
   And to his fettered soul be given
   The glorious freedom of the just.

Is There No Balm in Christian Lands?

St. 1-4

Anon., 1834

On the Death of a Child C.M.

Anon., 1849

1. Is there no balm in Chris - tian lands, No kind phy - si - cian there,
3. Must vile op - pres - sion's reck - less form Still beat up - on my soul,
To heal a bro - ken heart and save A broth - er from de - spair?
No sun of free - dom ev - er dawn, To make my spir - it whole?
2. Is there no love in Chris - tian hearts, To pit - y griefs like mine,
4. Just God, be - hold the Ne - gro's woe; The white man's sins for - give;
No ten - der sym - pa - thet - ic art Sweet mer - cy to en - shrine?
O - pen his heart thy love to know, And bid his bro - ther live.

LORD, DELIVER, THOU CANST SAVE — TAPPAN 7.7.7.7.

St. 1-5

Eliza Lee Follen, 1836 — Charles Zeuner, 1845

Moderato
1.
cresc.
1. Lord! de - liv - er; Thou canst save; Save from e - vil
Hear, O hear the kneel - ing slave,

2.
might - y God!
cresc.
dim.
Break, O break th'op - pres - sor's rod.

2. May the captive's pleading fill
   All the earth and all the sky;
   Every other voice be still,
   While he pleads with God on high.

3. He whose ear is everywhere,
   Who doth silent sorrow see,
   Will regard the captive's prayer,
   Will from bondage set him free.

4. From the tyranny within,
   Save thy children, Lord! we pray;
   Chains of iron, chains of sin,
   Cast, forever cast away.

5. Love to man, and love to God,
   Are the weapons of our war;
   These can break th'oppressor's rod,
   Burst the bonds that we abhor.

WE PRAISE THEE, IF ONE RESCUED SOUL

MEINECKE L.M.

St. 1-4

Lydia H. Sigourney, 1846

Anon., 1848

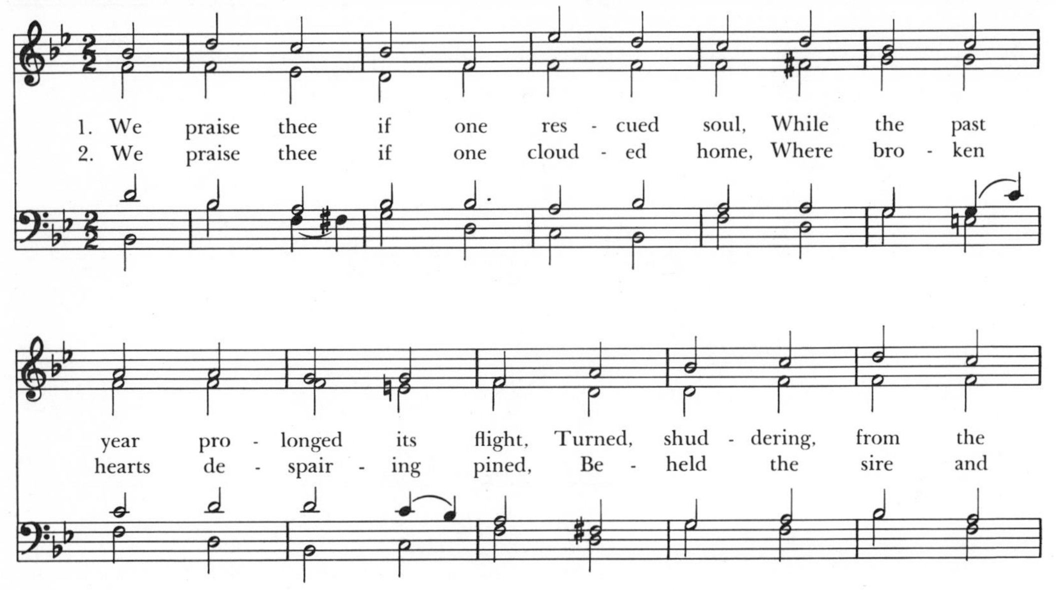
1. We praise thee if one res - cued soul, While the past
2. We praise thee if one cloud - ed home, Where bro - ken
year pro - longed its flight, Turned, shud - dering, from the
hearts de - spair - ing pined, Be - held the sire and

poi - sonous bowl To health, and lib - er - ty, and light.
hus - band come E - rect and in his per - fect mind.

3. No more a weeping wife to mock,
Till all her hopes in anguish end;
No more the trembling child to shock,
And sink the father in the fiend.

4. Still give us grace, almighty king,
Unwavering at our posts to stand,
Till grateful to thy shrine we bring
The tribute of a ransomed land.

Come, Happy Children

St. 1, 2

Anon., 1864

Canaan 8.7.8.7.D., with chorus

Traditional, used here from c.1820

1. Come, hap - py chil - dren, let__ us__ sing In__ praise of__pure__cold wa - ter,
That gush - es forth from well__ and__spring, To__ ev - ery__ son__ and daugh - ter.

From__ riv - er, lake, and might - y sea The clouds on__ high drink wa - ter; Then__
shout a - loud, in joy - ful__strains, The__ prais - es__ of__cold wa - ter.

Chorus Wa - ter! bright wa - ter! The crys - tal__stream of wa - ter; 'Tis__
na-ture's__ drink from hand__ di - vine; O,__ then give__me__cold wa - ter.

2. Let others sing in Bacchus' praise;
Its votaries shout with laughter;
The dearest treasure that I hail
Is a cup of sparkling water.

The mighty hills, the towering woods,
With flowers in beauty blending,
And happy birds with plumage fair,
All quaff the drops descending.

Chorus

Denominational Hymns

DURING THE NINETEENTH century, the tendency was to bring both music and texts under denominational control and to depend on committee judgment rather than on individual initiative. The *Baptist Chorale* was published in 1859. *The Psalmist,* an important Baptist hymnal, was issued without music in 1843, and published in a musical edition in 1860.

Among the Congregationalists the pioneer efforts were due to Henry Ward Beecher. The congregational singing in his Plymouth Church in Brooklyn was famous, and two books were designed for use there: Darius E. Jones's *Temple Melodies* (1851) and the more widely used *Plymouth Collection* (1855).

Although there were a number of books intended for the use of Episcopalian churches which included music, the earliest with both text and music issued by denominational authority was that of 1918. The Methodists published their *Hymns for the Use of the Methodist Episcopal Church* in 1857. The Unitarian *Hymn and Tune Book* appeared in 1868.

The vernacular hymn played a secondary role in Catholic churches since congregational singing was limited to novenas and other occasions outside of the prescribed liturgy. Hymnals were compiled by an individual or for use in a given religious community or church. Nevertheless hymn singing was varied, ranging as it did from the Spanish hymns sung by the Indians in the missions of the Southwest, to the hymns with organ accompaniment composed by Benjamin Carr for St. Peter's Church in Philadelphia. (See his setting of "That day of wrath.") "O Mother dear, O pray for me" was a devotional song adapted to a popular American tune. Alfred Young's setting of "Holy God, we praise thy name" comes from the hymnal which he compiled for the Paulist church.

The music of the orthodox synagogue falls outside the scope of a collection which in general limits itself to hymns which originated in the United States. The Reform movement first appeared in Germany and the first Reform congregation in the United States was in Charleston, South Carolina. The remarkable Penina Moise compiled the first hymnbook for this congregation, which was published in 1843 (see her "God Supreme, to Thee We Pray"). A number of hymnals issued by individuals were followed by the *Union Hymnal,* compiled by the

Central Conference of American Rabbis, which is now in its third edition.

The summary just concluded can do no more than suggest when hymnals of modern type were authorized and issued by several of the many denominations.

A singing congregation

How Sweet Is the Language of Love — Suncook L. M. D.

St. 1-4

Oliver Holden, 1806 — Samuel Holyoke, 1804

1. How sweet is the lan - guage of love, Which dwells on the pen - i-tents'tongue! The
3. Im - man - u - el's glo - ry the theme, Our hearts are in - flamed with de - sire; Or
theme of their heav - en - ly joys, The notes of Im - man - u - el's song!
while of his suf - fering we tell, We won - der, re - pent, and ad - mire.
2. 'Twas thus with the con - verts of old, Though pris - ons and chains were their lot; At
4. O lov - ing Re - deem - er, we come, With pant - ing and long - ing to be As -
mid - night, when Je - sus ap - peared, They sang, and their bands were for - got.
sured of sweet par - don and peace, And whol - ly con - form - èd to thee.

Weeping Sinner, Dry Your Tears — Keswick 7.7.7.7.

St. 1, 3, 7, 8

Oliver Holden, 1806 — Samuel Holyoke, 1804

1. Weep - ing sin - ner, dry your tears, Je - sus
2. Pit - y brought him from on high; Us he

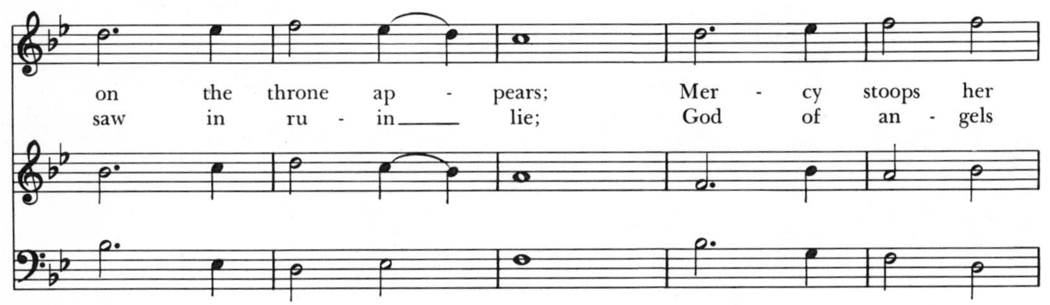
on the throne ap - pears; Mer - cy stoops her
saw in ru - in lie; God of an - gels

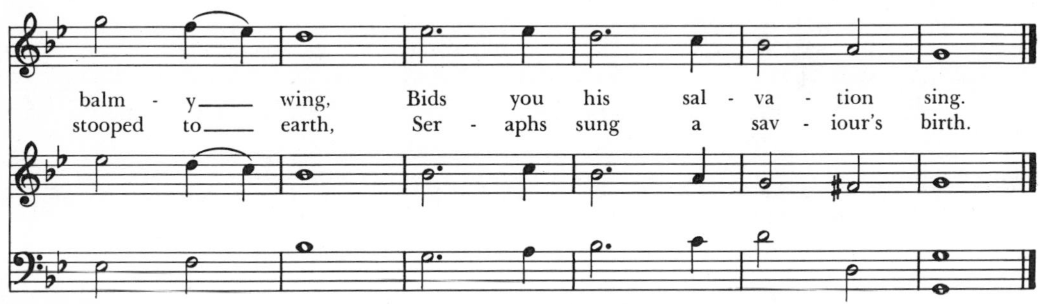
balm - y wing, Bids you his sal - va - tion sing.
stooped to earth, Ser - aphs sung a sav - iour's birth.

3. Weeping sinner, dry your tears;
Jesus in the heavens appears;
Once he hung upon the tree,
There he died for you and me.

4. Peace he brings you by his death,
Peace he speaks with every breath;
Can you slight such heavenly charms?
Flee, O flee to Jesus' arms.

WITHIN THESE DOORS ASSEMBLED NOW — CORONATION C.M.D.

St. 1-4

Oliver Holden, before 1808 — Oliver Holden, 1793

Tune in tenor
1. With - in these doors as - sem - bled now, We wait thy bless - ing, Lord!
Ap - pear with - in the midst we pray, Ac - cord - ing to thy word.
2. May some sweet prom - ise be— ap - plied When we at - tempt to— read; For
this a - lone can give— sup - port In all our times— of need.

3. O breathe upon our lifeless souls,
And raise our drooping hearts,
That we may see thy smiling face
Ere we from hence depart.

4. And now, dear Saviour, when we pray,
Be thou thyself so near,
If Satan fright our trembling souls,
Thy mercy may appear.

LORD, IN THY PRESENCE HERE

St. 1, 5, 6, 9

Jesse L. Holman, 1825

LIBERTY HALL C. M.

Anon., 1820

Tune in tenor

1. Lord, in thy pres - ence here we meet, May
2. With har - mo - ny and un - ion bless, That

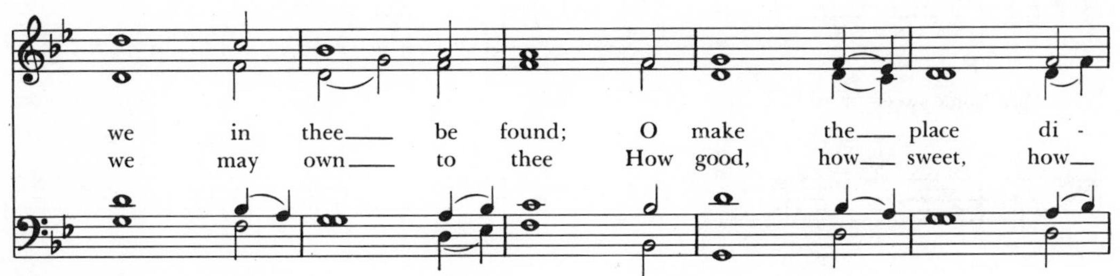

we in thee be found; O make the place di -
we may own to thee How good, how sweet, how

vine - ly sweet, O let thy grace a - bound.
pleas - ant 'tis When breth - ren all a - gree.

3. May Zion's good be kept in view,
And bless our feeble aim,
That all we undertake to do,
May glorify thy name.

4. Work in us by thy gracious sway,
And make thy work appear,
That all may feel, and all may say,
The Lord indeed is here.

Our Father, God | Cottage C. M.

St. 1-3

Adoniram Judson, writ. 1825, pub. 1853 | George F. Root, 1860

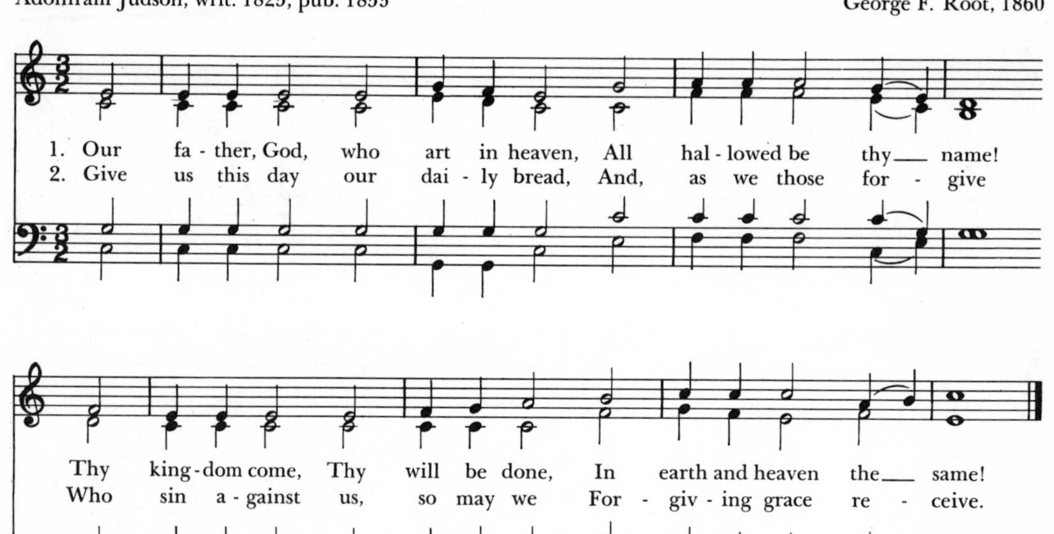
1. Our fa - ther, God, who art in heaven, All hal - lowed be thy__ name!
2. Give us this day our dai - ly bread, And, as we those for - give
Thy king - dom come, Thy will be done, In earth and heaven the__ same!
Who sin a - gainst us, so may we For - giv - ing grace re - ceive.

3. Into temptation lead us not;
From evil set us free;
And thine the kingdom, thine the power
And glory, ever be.

Help Thy Servant — Warning Voice 7.6.7.6.7.7.7.6., with chorus

St. 1, 2

Andrew Broaddus, 1828 — Anon., 1860

Tune in tenor
1. Help thy serv - ant, gra - cious Lord, Who comes in Je - su's name;
On - ly thou canst strength af - ford, Thy gos - pel to pro - claim.
Grant his soul a heaven - ly ray, Fill his heart with ho - ly fire,
Chorus O, for sanc - ti - fy - ing grace! O, for love's in - spir - ing power!
Help thy serv - ant, Lord, we pray, Re - gard our souls' de - sire.
Lord, we beg, for Je - sus' sake A sweet re - fresh - ing shower.

2. Give us to receive the word,
With love, and joy, and fear;
Grant thy quickening grace, O Lord,
On all assembled here.

Seal the truth on all today;
All our hearts will heaven inspire;
Help thy servant, Lord, we pray,
Regard our soul's desire.

Chorus

HITHER WE COME, OUR DEAREST LORD — HOLINESS L.M.

St. 1,2,4,6

Enoch W. Freeman, 1829 — David Paine, 1839

1. Hith - er we come, our dear - est Lord, O - be - dient
2. Here ranged a - long the wa - ter's side, Where gent - ly

to thy sa - cred word, 'Tis thou hast called our hearts to
rolls the si - lent tide, O what on earth can sweet - er

flee From sense__ and sin and__ fol - low thee.
be, Than thus__ to come and__ fol - low thee.

3. When darkness did our souls enshroud,
And o'er our heads the storm was loud,
We saw no way from wrath to flee,
But to obey and follow thee.

4. Thou wast immersed beneath the wave,
The emblem of thy future grave:
O while the way so plain we see,
What can we do but follow thee.

Proclaim the Lofty Praise — **Eldridge** S.M.D.

St. 1-4

Sarah Judson, 1829 — Thomas Hastings, 1847

1. Pro - claim the loft - y — praise Of him who once was slain, But — now is risen, through end-less days, In bliss, to live and reign. He lives and reigns on high, Who bought us with his blood, En - throned a-bove the farth-est sky, Our Sav-iour, Lord, and God.
2. The — Son of God a - dore; Ye ran-somed! spread his fame; With — joy and glad-ness, ev - er-more Ex - tol his glo-rious name. Let ev - ery tongue con-fess That Je - sus Christ is Lord, And — ev - ery crea - ture join to bless The great in - car - nate Word.
Final stanza
Our Sav - iour, God, and King.

3. All honor, power, and praise,
To Jesus' name belong;
With hosts seraphic, glad, we raise
The joy-inspiring song:
"Worthy the Lamb," they cry,
"That on the cross was slain,
But now, ascended up on high,
Lives evermore to reign."

4. He lives to bless and save
The souls redeemed by grace,
And rescue from the dreary grave
His chosen ransomed race;
And soon we hope, above,
A louder strain to sing,
With all our powers to praise and love
Our Saviour, God, and King.

Gracious Saviour, We Adore Thee **Fenwick** 8.7.8.7.4.7.

St. 1,2

Sewall Sylvester Cutting, 1832

Anon., 1845

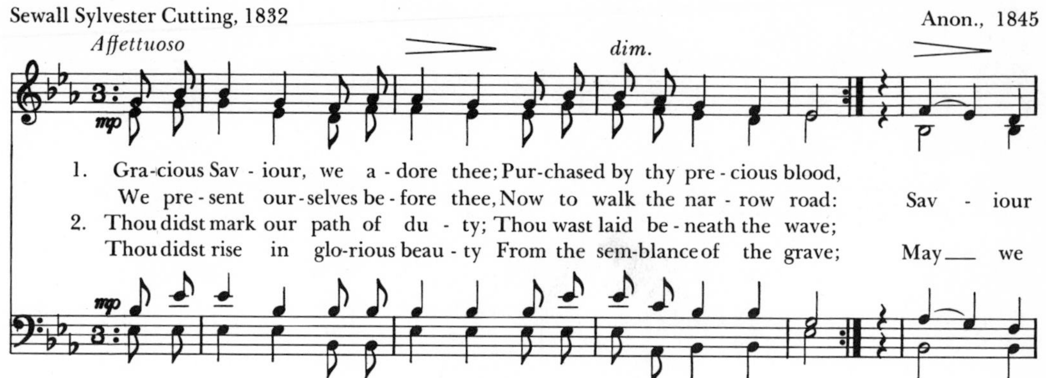
Affettuoso
dim.
mp
1. Gra-cious Sav - iour, we a - dore thee; Pur-chased by thy pre - cious blood,
We pre - sent our-selves be - fore thee, Now to walk the nar - row road: Sav - iour
2. Thou didst mark our path of du - ty; Thou wast laid be - neath the wave;
Thou didst rise in glo-rious beau - ty From the sem-blance of the grave; May__ we
mp

cresc.
dim.
guide us, Guide us to our heaven - ly home.
fol - low In the same de - light - ful way.

A baptismal scene

Come Holy Spirit, Dove Divine — Benevolent Street L.M.

St. 1-4

Adoniram Judson, 1832 — Oliver Shaw, 1815

Tune in middle voice
1. Come, Ho - ly Spir - it, Dove di - vine On these bap - tis - mal wa - ters shine, And teach our hearts, in
2. We love thy name, we love thy laws, And joy - ful - ly em - brace thy cause; We love thy cross, the

high - est strain, To praise the Lamb, for sin - ners slain.
shame, the pain, O Lamb of God, for sin - ners slain.

3. We sink beneath thy mystic flood;
O bathe us in thy cleansing blood;
We die to sin, and seek a grave,
With thee, beneath the yielding wave.

4. And as we rise, with thee to live,
O let the Holy Spirit give
The sealing unction from above
The breath of life, the fire of love.

Down to the Sacred Wave — Ferguson S. M.

St. 1-3

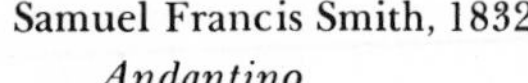

Samuel Francis Smith, 1832 — George Kingsley, 1843

Andantino

1. Down to the sacred wave The Lord of life was led; And he who came our souls to save In Jordan bowed his head.

2. He taught the solemn way; He fixed the holy rite; He bade his ransomed ones obey, And keep the path of light,

3. Blest Saviour, we will tread
In thy appointed way;
Let glory o'er these scenes be shed,
And smile on us today.

Softly Fades the Twilight Ray — Holley 7.7.7.7.

St. 1-5

Samuel Francis Smith, writ. 1832, pub. 1843 — George Hews, 1835

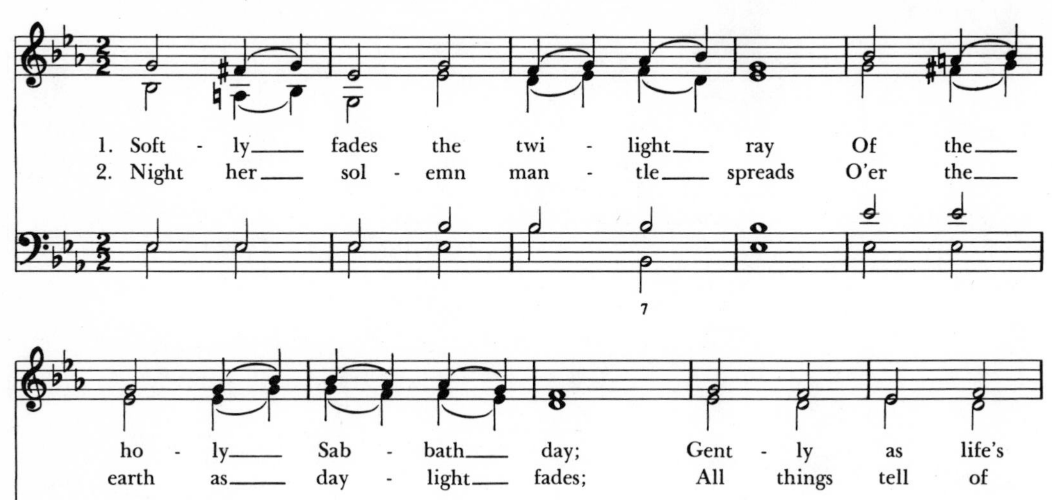
1. Soft - ly fades the twi - light ray Of the
2. Night her sol - emn man - tle spreads O'er the
7
ho - ly Sab - bath day; Gent - ly as life's
earth as day - light fades; All things tell of
[6 5] [7]

set - ting sun, When the Chris - tian's course is run.
calm re - pose At the ho - ly Sab - bath's close.
6 6 7 ♮ 6 6 4 5 3

3. Peace is on the world abroad;
'Tis the holy peace of God –
Symbol of the peace within,
When the spirit rests from sin.

4. Still the Spirit lingers near,
Where the evening worshipper
Seeks communion with the skies,
Pressing onward to the prize.

5. Saviour, may our Sabbaths be
Days of peace and joy in thee,
Till in heaven our souls repose,
Where the Sabbath ne'er shall close.

THE TIME WILL SURELY COME — CONCORD 6.6.8.8.6.

St. 1-4

Robert T. Daniel, 1833 — Oliver Holden, 1793

Tune in tenor
1. The time will sure - ly come, When all the ran - somed race,
With an - gels shall go shout - ing home, With
With an - gels shall go shout - ing home,
With an - gels shall go shout - ing home, With
With an - gels shall go shout - ing home, With
an - gels shall go shout - ing home, To meet their Sav - iour's face. face.
an - gels shall go shout - ing home, To meet their Sav - iour's face. face.
an - gels shall go shout - ing home, To meet their Sav - iour's face. face.
an - gels shall go shout - ing home, To meet their Sav - iour's face. face.
1.
2.

2. The church of God on earth,
As well as those above,
Are sheltered from the storms of wrath,
Are sheltered from the storms of wrath,
In robes of dying love.

3. No trials that they meet
Shall rob them of their rest;
For Jesus makes them all complete
For Jesus makes them all complete
In his own righteousness.

4. All hail, thou conquering King!
Come quickly from above,
And all thy chosen race shall sing
And all thy chosen race shall sing
Thy free, redeeming love.

As Flows the Rapid River

Passaic 7.6.7.6.D.

St. 1-3

Samuel Francis Smith, 1833

William Batchelder Bradbury, 1851

1. As flows the rap - id riv - er, With chan - nel broad and free,
2. As moons are ev - er wan - ing, As hastes the sun a - way,
Its wa - ters rip - pling ev - er, And hast - ing to the sea,
As storm and winds, com - plain - ing, Bring on the win - try day,
So life is on - ward flow - ing, And days of of - fered peace,
So fast the night comes o'er us, The dark - ness of the grave;
And man is swift - ly go - ing Where calls of mer - cy cease.
And death is just be - fore us; God takes the life he gave.

3. Say, hath thy heart its treasure
Laid up in worlds above?
And is it all thy pleasure
Thy God to praise and love?
Beware, lest death's dark river
Its billows o'er thee roll,
And thou lament forever
The ruin of thy soul.

Here, Lord, Retired, I Bow in Prayer — Lawrence L. M.

St. 1-4

Matthew Bolles, 1836 — Deodatus Dutton Jr., 1834

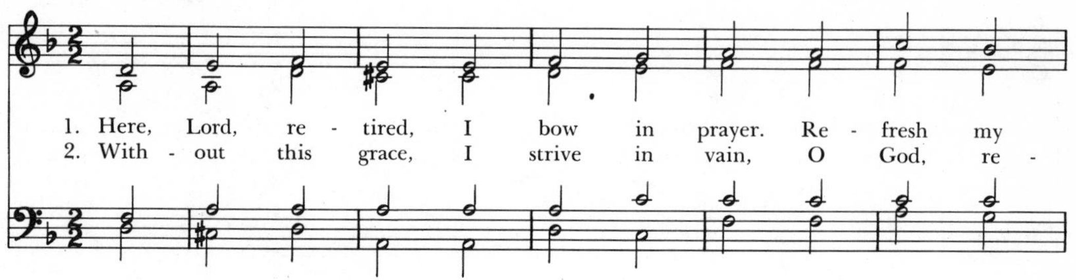
1. Here, Lord, re - tired, I bow in prayer. Re - fresh my
2. With - out this grace, I strive in vain, O God, re -

soul — my heart pre - pare To preach thy— word with
vive thy saints a - gain; Con - vince poor— sin - ners

power di - vine; If I suc - ceed, the praise be thine.
of their case, Cause them to seek thy par - doning grace.

3. Draw thousands to thy mercy seat;
Their hearts renew — their sins remit,
Fill them with joy of faith and love
To serve on earth, to praise above.

4. In tears I sow the precious seed;
Cause it to spring — my work succeed.
With souls reward my work of love;
Then take me to thyself above.

LABORERS OF CHRIST! ARISE KEITH S.M.

St. 1-4

Lydia Sigourney, 1836 Thomas Loud, 1838

1. La - borers of Christ! a - rise, And gird you
2. Go where the sick re - cline, Where mourn - ing
for the toil; The dew of prom - ise,
hearts de - plore; And, where the sons of

from the skies, Al - read - y cheers the soil.
sor - row pine, Dis - pense your hal - lowed store.

3. Be faith, which looks above,
With prayer, your constant guest;
And wrap the Saviour's changeless love
A mantle round your breast.

4. So shall you share the wealth,
That earth may ne'er despoil;
And the blessed gospel's saving health
Repay your arduous toil.

Tell Us, Ye Servants of the Lord — Syme C. M.

St. 1, 3-5

William Staughton, 1836 — Edward Hamilton, 1857

Choral
1. Tell us, ye serv - ants of the Lord, Where's your great mas - ter found?
2. We would see Je - sus, does not he Bid con - trite sin - ners come?
Him would we see, whose power - ful word Can heal our ev - ery wound.
And to such guilt - y souls as we Pro - claim, "There yet is room."

3. Millions have hastened to his arms,
And now resound his name;
Him would we see whose endless charms
Our anxious hearts inflame.

4. We would see Jesus, for his saints
May lean upon his breast;
Pour out with confidence their plaints,
And find celestial rest.

Almighty God, Thy Constant Care

Rolland 8.8.8.8.8.

St. 1-4

Henry S. Washburn, writ. 1841, pub. 1843

William Batchelder Bradbury, 1851

1. Al - might - y God, thy con - stant care Hath been our sure sup - port and
2. Ac - cept our vows: in hum - ble trust This house we con - se - crate to
stay, And hith - er glad - ly we re - pair, Our
thee. O, may thy prom - ise to the just For -
ear - ly sac - ri - fice to pay, Our ear - ly sac - ri - fice to pay.
ev - er, Lord, our por - tion be, For - ev - er, Lord, our por - tion be.

3. And may that stream which maketh glad
The city of our God below,
Revive the drooping, cheer the sad,
As still its healing waters flow,
As still its healing waters flow.

4. So let thy people here enjoy
The blessings which thy grace hath given,
That they may hail with purer joy,
The unseen, perfect bliss of heaven,
The unseen, perfect bliss of heaven.

God of the World, Thy Glories Shine — Succoth L. M.

St. 1-4

Sewall Sylvester Cutting, 1843 — Anon., 1835

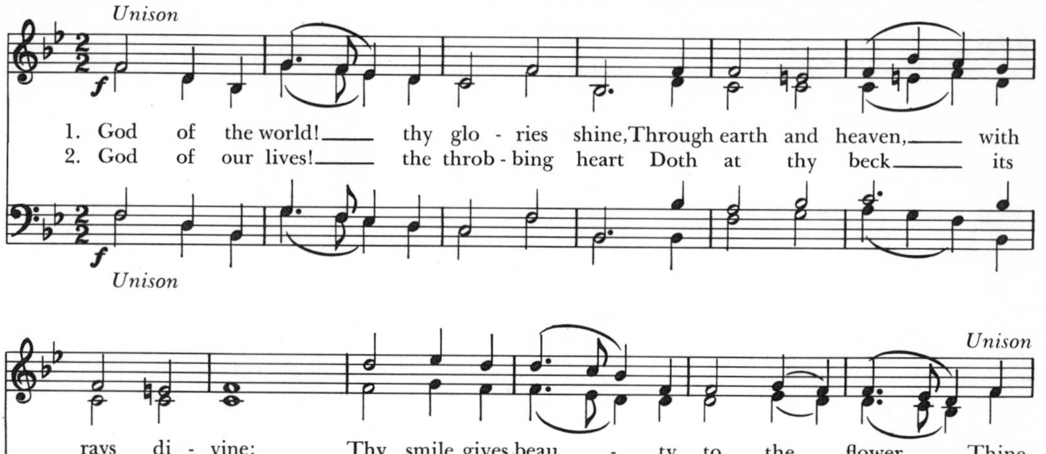
Unison
1. God of the world! thy glo - ries shine, Through earth and heaven, with
2. God of our lives! the throb - bing heart Doth at thy beck its
Unison
rays di - vine; Thy smile gives beau - ty to the flower Thine
ac - tion start, Throbs on, o - be - dient to thy will, Or
Unison
Unison

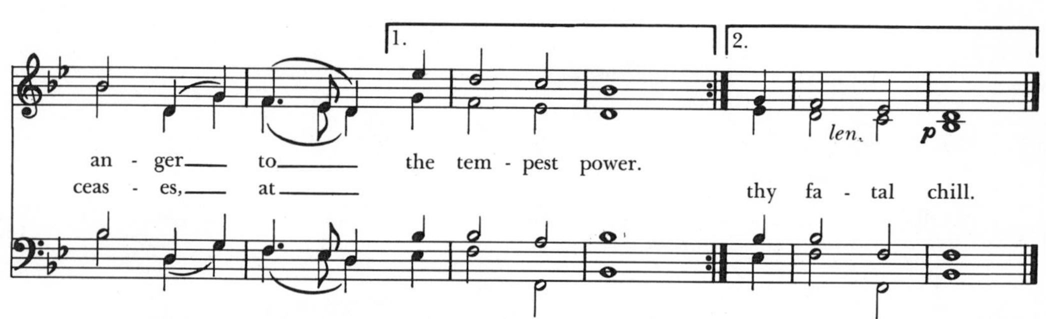
1.
2.
an - ger to the tem - pest power.
ceas - es, at thy fa - tal chill.
len.

3. God of eternal life! thy love
Doth every stain of sin remove;
The cross, the cross – its hallowed light
Shall drive from earth her cheerless night.

4. God of all goodness! to the skies
Our hearts in grateful anthems rise;
And to thy service shall be given
The rest of life – the whole of heaven.

O God, Though Countless Worlds of Light — Northfield C. M.

St. 1-5

James D. Knowles, 1843 — Jeremiah Ingalls, 1805

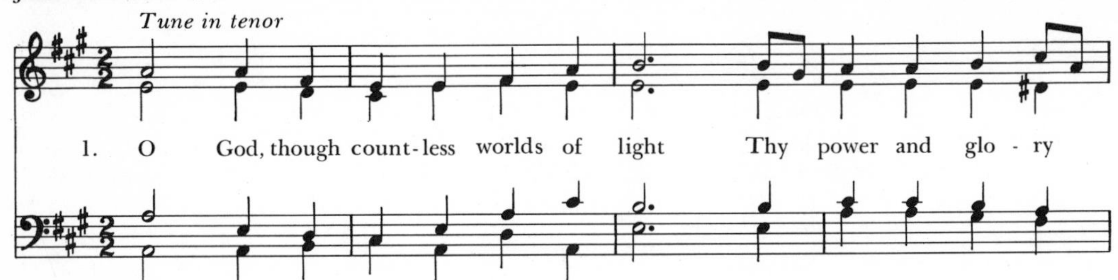
Tune in tenor
1. O God, though count-less worlds of light Thy power and glo - ry

Though
show, Though round thy throne a -
Though round thy throne a - bove all hight, Im -
Though round thy throne a - bove all hight, Though round thy throne a -

round thy throne a - bove all hight, Im - mor - tal ser - aphs glow.
bove all hight, Im - mor - tal ser - aphs glow.
mor - tal ser - aphs glow. Im - mor - tal ser - aphs glow.
bove all hight, Im - mor - tal ser - aphs glow.

2. Yet oft to men of ancient time
Thy glorious presence came,
And in Moriah's fane sublime
Thou didst record thy name.

3. And now, whene'er thy saints apart
Are met for praise and prayer,
Wherever sighs a contrite heart,
Thou, gracious God, art there.

4. With grateful joy thy children rear
This temple, Lord, to thee;
Long may they sing thy praises here,
And here thy beauty see.

5. Here may thy truth fresh triumphs win.
Eternal Spirit, here,
In many a heart now dead in sin,
A living temple rear.

THERE IS A LAND MINE EYE HATH SEEN

St. 1-4

Gurdon Robins, 1843

ALTITUDE L. M.

Leonard Marshall, 1852

1. There is a land mine eye hath seen In vi - sions
2. A land up - on whose bliss - ful shore There rests no
of en - rap - tured thought, So bright that all which
sha - dow, falls no stain; There those who meet shall
spreads be - tween Is with its ra - diant glo - ry fraught.
part no more, And those long part - ed meet a - gain.

3. Its skies are not like earthly skies,
With varying hues of shade and light;
It hath no need of suns to rise
To dissipate the gloom of night.

4. There sweeps no desolating wind
Across that calm, serene abode;
The wanderer there a home may find
Within the paradise of God.

When Thickly Beat the Storms of Life

Zephyr L. M.

St. 1-4

Gurdon Robins, 1843

William Batchelder Bradbury, 1844

Gently
1. When thick - ly beat the storms of life, And heav - y
2. What hope dis - pels the spir - it's gloom, When sink - ing
is the chas - tening rod, The soul, be - yond the
'neath af - flic - tion's shock? Faith, through the vis - ta
waves of strife, Views the e - ter - nal rock — her God.
of the tomb, Points to the ev - er - last - ing Rock.

3. Is there a man who cannot see
That joy and grief are from above?
O let him humbly bend the knee,
And own his Father's chastening love.

4. Hope, Grace, and Truth, with gentle hand,
Shall lead a bleeding Saviour's flock,
And show them, in the promised land,
The shelter of th'eternal Rock.

Holy Spirit, Faithful Guide 7.7.7.7.D.

St. 1-3

Marcus Morris Wells, 1858 Marcus Morris Wells, 1858

1. Ho - ly Spir - it, faith - ful guide, Ev - er near the Chris - tian's side;
2. Ev - er pre - sent, tru - est Friend, Ev - er near thine aid to lend,
Fine
Gent - ly lead us by the hand, Pil - grims in a des - ert land;
D.S. Whis - pering soft - ly, wan - derer, come! Fol - low me, I'll guide thee home.
Leave us not to doubt and fear, Grop - ing on in dark - ness drear,
D.S. Whis - pering soft - ly, wan - derer, come! Fol - low me, I'll guide thee home.
D.S. al Fine
Wea - ry souls for - e'er re - joice, While they hear that sweet - est voice
When the storms are rag - ing sore, Hearts grow faint, and hopes give o'er,

3. When our days of toil shall cease,
Waiting still for sweet release,
Nothing left but heaven and prayer,
Wondering if our names were there;
Wading deep the dismal flood,
Pleading nought but Jesus' blood;
Whispering softly, wanderer, come!
Follow me, I'll guide thee home!

Qúe Preciosas Mañanitas

Dawning Fair, Morning Wonderful

Traditional

Traditional

Unison
Dawn - ing fair, morn - ing won - der - ful, When the in - fant
Christ was born; Tid - ings brought by hum - ble shep - herds,
Child be - lov - èd, child a - dored, Child be - lov - èd, child a - dored.

Qúe preciosas mañanitas,
Cuando el Niño Dios nació.
Le decían los pastorcitos:
Niñito, y a amane ció.
Niñito, y a amane ció.

Dies Irae, Dies Illa
That Day of Wrath, That Direful Day

L. M.

St. 1-3, 8

Thomas of Celano, 13th cent.
Anon., trans.

Benjamin Carr, 1805

Larghetto
Sempre piano
1. That day of wrath, that dire - ful day, Shall all the world in ash - es lay, As Da - vid and Sy - bil - la say, As Da - vid and Sy - bil - la say.
2. How shall poor mor - tals quake with fears, When their im - par - tial judge ap - pears, Who all their caus - es strict - ly hears, Who all their caus - es strict - ly hears.
Organ

3. His trumpet sounds a dreadful tone,
The noise through all the graves is blown,
And calls the dead before his throne,
And calls the dead before his throne.

4. O dreadful God! O glorious King!
Who dost the savèd freely bring,
To bliss; save me, O mercy's spring,
To bliss; save me, O mercy's spring.

WHAT HAPPINESS CAN EQUAL MINE L.M.D.

St. 1-4

John David, 1840 John David, 1840

Unison
1. What happiness can equal mine; I've found the object of my love;
2. I am my love's, and he is mine; In me he dwells, in him I live;
My Jesus dear, my King divine, Is come to me from heaven above.
What greater treasure could I find? And could ye, heavens, a greater give?
He chose my heart for his abode, He there becomes my daily bread,
O sacred banquet, heavenly feast! O everlasting source of grace,
There on me flows his healing blood, There, with his flesh my soul is fed.
Where God the good, and man the guest, Meet and unite in sweet embrace.

3. Ye angels, lend your heavenly tongues,
Come, and with me in praises join;
Come, and unite, in thankful songs,
Your sweet immortal voice to mine.
O, that I had your burning hearts,
To love my God, my spouse most dear!
O that he would with flaming darts,
Raise in my heart a heavenly fire!

4. Dear Jesus! now my heart is thine;
O may it from thee never fly!
Hold it with chains of love divine,
Make it be thine eternally;
Vain objects! that seduced my soul,
I now despise your fleeting charms;
In vain temptation's billows roll,
I lie secure in Jesus' arms.

Holy God, We Praise Thy Name — 7.8.7.8.7.7.

St. 1-7

Clarence A. Walworth, 1858 — Alfred Young, 1884

1. Ho - ly God, we praise thy Name! Lord of all, we bow be - fore thee!
2. Hark! the loud ce - les - tial hymn An - gel choirs a - bove are rais - ing!
All on earth thy scep - tre claim, All in heaven a - bove a - dore thee;
Cher - u - bim and Ser - a - phim, In un - ceas - ing cho - rus prais - ing,
In - fi - nite thy vast do - main, Ev - er - last - ing is thy reign.
Fill the heavens with sweet ac - cord: Ho - ly, Ho - ly, Ho - ly Lord!

3. Lo! the Apostolic train
Join, thy sacred name to hallow!
Prophets swell the loud refrain,
And the white-robed martyrs follow!
And from morn to set of sun,
Thro' the Church the song goes on.

4. Holy Father, Holy Son,
Holy Spirit, three we name thee,
While in essence only one
Undivided God, we claim thee;
And adoring bend the knee,
While we own the mystery.

5. Thou art King of Glory, Christ!
Son of God, yet born of Mary;
For us sinners sacrificed,
And to death a tributary;
First to break the bars of death,
Thou hast opened heaven to faith.

6. From thy high celestial home,
Judge of all, again returning,
We believe that thou shalt come,
On the dreadful doomsday morning,
When thy voice shall shake the earth,
And the startled dead come forth.

7. Spare thy people, Lord! we pray,
By a thousand snares surrounded;
Keep us without sin today,
Never let us be confounded.
Lo! I put my trust in thee,
Never, Lord, abandon me.

MOTHER DEAR, O! PRAY FOR ME — 7.6.8.6.D., with chorus

St. 1-3

Anon.: St. 1, 1863; St. 2, 3, 1867 — Isaac B. Woodbury, 1850

Unison

1. Moth - er dear, O! pray for me, Whilst far from heaven and thee I
2. Moth - er dear, O! pray for me, Should pleas - ure's sir - en lay, E'er

wan - der in a fra - gile bark O'er life's tem - pes - tuous sea; O
tempt thy child to wan - der far From vir - tue's path a - way, When

Vir - gin Moth - er, from thy throne, So bright in bliss a - bove, Pro -
thorns be - set life's de - vious way, And dark - ling wa - ters flow, Then

tect thy child and cheer my path With thy sweet smile of love.
Ma - ry, aid thy weep - ing child, Thy - self a moth - er show.

Chorus
Moth - er dear, re - mem - ber me; And nev - er cease thy care,
'Till in heaven e - ter - nal - ly, Thy love and bliss I share.

3. Mother dear, O! pray for me,
When all looks bright and fair,
That I may all my danger see,
For surely then 'tis near,
A mother's prayer how much we need
If prosperous be the ray
That paints with gold the flowery mead,
Which blossoms in our way.

Interior of a mission church

O'er Waiting Harp-Strings of the Mind

Norton 8.4.8.4.

St. 1-7

Mary Baker Eddy, cop. 1887

Lyman Brackett, cop. 1887

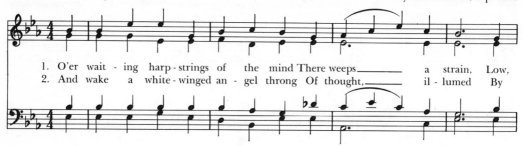

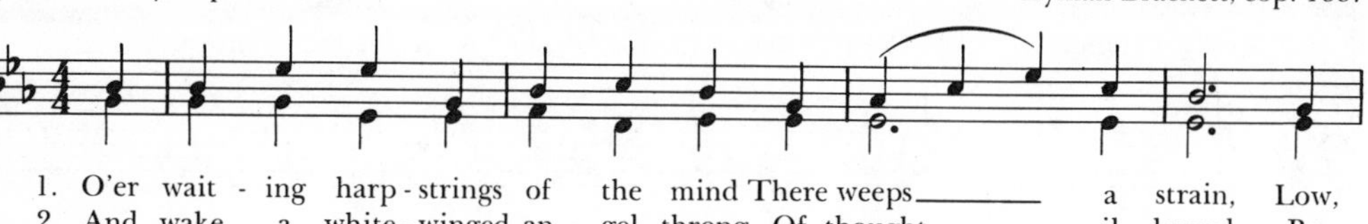
1. O'er wait - ing harp - strings of the mind There weeps a strain, Low,
2. And wake a white - winged an - gel throng Of thought, il - lumed By

sad, and sweet, whose meas - ures bind The pow - er of pain,
faith, and breathed in rap - tured song, With love per - fumed.

3. Then His unveiled, sweet mercies show
Life's burdens light.
I kiss the cross, and wake to know
A world more bright.

4. And o'er earth's troubled, angry sea
I see Christ walk,
And come to me, and tenderly,
Divinely talk.

5. Thus Truth engrounds me on the rock,
Upon life's shore,
'Gainst which the winds and waves can shock,
Oh, nevermore!

6. From tired joy and grief afar,
And nearer thee,
Father, where thine own children are,
I love to be.

7. My prayer, some daily good to do
To thine, for thee;
An offering pure of love, where to
God leadeth me.

Shepherd, Show Me How To Go — Guidance 7.5.7.5.D.

St. 1-3

Mary Baker Eddy, cop. 1887 — Lyman Brackett, cop. 1887

1. Shep - herd, show me how to go O'er the hill - side steep,
2. Thou wilt bind the stub - born will, Wound the cal - lous breast,
How to gath - er, how to sow, How to feed thy sheep.
Make self - right - eous - ness be still, Break earth's stu - pid rest.
I will lis - ten for thy voice, Lest my foot - steps stray;
Stran - gers on a bar - ren shore, La - boring long and lone,
I will fol - low and re - joice All the rug - ged way.
We would en - ter by the door, And thou knowest thine own.

3. So, when day grows dark and cold,
Tear or triumph harms,
Lead thy lambkins to the fold,
Take them in thine arms.
Feed the hungry, heal the heart,
Till the morning's beam;
White as wool, 'ere they depart,
Shepherd, wash them clean.

I Love Thy Kingdom, Lord — St. Thomas S.M.

Ps. 137, second part: 1, 2, 5-8

Timothy Dwight, 1800 — Aaron Williams, 1770

Tune in tenor
1. I love thy king - dom, Lord, The house of thine a - bode, The Church our blest Re - deem - er saved With his own pre - cious blood.
2. I love thy Church, O God: Her walls be - fore thee stand, Dear as the ap - ple of thine eye, And grav - en on thy hand.

3. For her my tears shall fall,
For her my prayers ascend;
To her my cares and toils be given,
Till toils and cares shall end.

4. Beyond my highest joy
I prize her heavenly ways,
Her sweet communion, solemn vows,
Her hymns of love and praise.

5. Jesus, thou friend divine,
Our Saviour and our King,
Thy hand from every snare and foe
Shall great deliverance bring.

6. Sure as thy truth shall last,
To Zion shall be given
The brightest glories earth can yield,
And brighter bliss of heaven.

SING TO THE LORD MOST HIGH — NEW MILFORD 6.6.8.6.4.4.4.4.

Ps. 100: st. 1-4

Timothy Dwight, 1800 — Japhet Coombs Washburn, c.1804

Tune in tenor

1. Sing to the Lord most high; Let ev - ery voice a - dore;
2. En - ter his courts with joy; With fear ad - dress the Lord;

With grate - ful voice make known His good - ness and his power. Let cheer - ful songs de -
He formed us with his hand And quick - ened by his word. With wide com - mand he

clare his ways, Let cheer - ful songs de - clare his ways, And let his praise in -
spreads his sway With wide com - mand he spreads his sway O'er ev - ery sea and

de - clare his ways,
he spreads his sway

1. 2.

spire your tongues, And let his praise in - spire your tongues.
ev - ery land, O'er ev - ery sea and ev - ery land.

3. His hands provide our food
And every blessing give;
We feed upon his care
And in his pastures live.
With cheerful songs declare his ways,
With cheerful songs declare his ways,
And let his praise inspire your tongues,
And let his praise inspire your tongues.

4. Good is the Lord our God;
His truth and mercy sure;
While earth and heaven shall last,
His promises endure.
With bounteous hand he spreads his sway
With bounteous hand he spreads his sway
O'er every sea and every land,
O'er every sea and every land.

SHALL MAN, O GOD OF LIGHT — WASHINGTON L.M.

Ps. 88, Second part: st. 1-4

Timothy Dwight, 1800 — Timothy Olmstead, 1805

Largo affetuoso

1. Shall man, O God of light and life For - ev - er moul - der in the grave? Can'st thou for - get thy glo - rious work, Thy prom - ise, and thy power to save?

2. But in those si - lent realms of night Shall peace and hope no more a - rise? No fu - ture morn - ing light the tomb, Nor day - star gild the dark - some skies?

Chorus

In death's ob - scure ob - li - vious realm, No truths are taught nor won - ders

sung. No mer - cy beams to warm the heart, Thy
name un - sung, thy grace un - known. No mer - cy
beams to warm the heart, Thy name un -
sung, thy grace un - known. known.
1.
2.

3. Cease, cease, ye vain, desponding fears;
When Christ, our lord, from darkness sprang,
Death, the last foe, was captive led,
And heaven with praise and wonder rang.
Chorus

4. Him, the first fruits, his chosen sons
Shall follow from the vanquished grave;
He mounts his throne, the King of Kings,
His church to quicken and to save.
Chorus

Sinners, Will You Scorn the Message? — Brandywine 8.7.8.7.8.7.

St. 1-6

Jonathan Allen, 1801 — Dr. Robert Rogerson, 1786

Largo maestoso
1. Sin - ners, will you scorn the mes - sage, Sent in mer - cy from a - bove?
2. Hear the her - alds of the gos - pel, News from Zi - on's King pro - claim,
Ev - ery sen - tence — O how ten - der! Ev - ery line is full of
To each re - bel sin - ner par - don, Free for - give - ness in his
Piano
love. Lis - ten to it, lis - ten to it Lis - ten
name, How im - por - tant! How im - por - tant! How im-
Lis - ten to it
How im - por - tant!
Spirituoso
to it, lis - ten to it Ev - ery line is full of love.
por - tant! How im - por - tant! Free for - give - ness in his name.

3. Tempted souls, they bring you succour,
Fearful hearts, they quell your fears;
And with news of consolation,
Chase away the falling tears.
Tender heralds, tender heralds,
Tender heralds, tender heralds,
Chase away the falling tears.

4. False professors, grovelling worldlings,
Callous hearers of the word,
While the messengers address you,
Take the warnings they afford,
We entreat you, we entreat you.
We entreat you, we entreat you.
Take the warnings they afford.

5. Who hath our report believĕd?
Who received the joyful word?
Who embraced the news of pardon,
Offered to you by the Lord!
Can you slight it? Can you slight it?
Can you slight it? Can you slight it?
Offered to you by the Lord!

6. O ye angels hovering round us,
Waiting spirits speed your way,
Hasten to the court of heaven,
Tidings bear without delay.
Rebel sinners, rebel sinners,
Rebel sinners, rebel sinners,
Glad the message will obey.

I Love to Steal Awhile Away — Monson C.M.

St. 1-5

Phoebe Hinsdale Brown, writ. 1818, pub. 1824 — Samuel R. Brown, 1842

1. I love to steal a - while a - way From ev - ery cum - bering care. And spend the hours of set - ting day, In hum - ble, grate - ful prayer.
2. I love in sol - i - tude to shed The pen - i - ten - tial tear, And all his prom - i - ses to plead, Where none but God can hear.

3. I love to think on mercies past,
And future good implore,
And all my cares and sorrows cast
On him whom I adore.

4. I love by faith to take a view
Of brighter scenes in heaven;
The prospect doth my strength renew
While here by tempests driven.

5. Thus, when life's toilsome day is o'er,
May its departing ray
Be calm as this impressive hour,
And lead to endless day.

THERE IS AN HOUR OF PEACEFUL REST — TAPPAN 8.6.8.8.6.

St. 1-4

William B. Tappan, 1818 — George Kingsley, 1838

1. There is an hour of peace-ful rest, To mourn-ing wan - derers given; There is a joy for souls dis-tressed, A balm for ev - ery wound-ed breast: 'Tis found a-bove, in heaven.
2. There is a home for wea-ry souls, By sin and sor - row driven, When tossed on life's tem-pest - uous shoals, Where storms a-rise, and o-cean rolls, And all is drear, but heaven.

3. There faith lifts up her cheerful eye
To brighter prospects given;
And views the tempest passing by,
The evening shadows quickly fly,
And all serene, in heaven.

4. There fragrant flowers immortal bloom,
And joys supreme are given;
There rays divine disperse the gloom;
Beyond the confines of the tomb
Appears the dawn of heaven!

'Tis Midnight and on Olive's Brow — Olive's Brow L.M.

St. 1-4

William B. Tappan, 1822 — William Batchelder Bradbury, 1853

1. 'Tis mid-night, and on Ol-ive's brow The star is dimmed that
2. 'Tis mid-night; and from all re-moved, The Sav-iour wres-tles
late-ly shone; 'Tis mid-night; in the gar-den,
lone with fears; E'en that dis-ci-ple whom he
now, The suf-fering Sav-iour prays a-lone.
loved Heeds not his Mas-ter's grief and tears.
6 4 5 3
6 5 8 7 ♮ 7
4 [2] 6 — 6 4 5 3 7

3. 'Tis midnight; and for others' guilt
The Man of Sorrows weeps in blood;
Yet, he that hath in anguish knelt
Is not forsaken by his God.

4. 'Tis midnight; and from ether-plains
Is borne the song that angels know;
Unheard by mortals are the strains
That sweetly soothe the Saviour's woe.

Trembling Before Thine Awful Throne

St. 1-3, 7

Augustus L. Hillhouse, 1822

Confidence L.M.

Samuel Holyoke, 1804

1. Trem - bling, be - fore thine aw - ful throne, O
3. Earth has a joy un - known in heaven, The
Lord! in dust my sins I own: Jus - tice and mer - cy
new - born peace of sins for - given: Tears of such pure and
for my life Con - tend; Oh! smile,_ and heal the_ strife.
deep de - light, Ye an - gels! nev - er dimmed your_ sight.
Soft
2. The Sav - iour smiles; up - on my soul New tides of hope tu -
4. But I a - mid your choirs shall shine, And all your knowl - edge_

Soft
His voice pro - claims my par - don found; Se -
Ye on your harps must lean to hear A
mul - tuous roll;
shall be mine;
raph - ic trans - port wings the sound!
se - cret chord that mine will bear.
Loud
His voice pro - claims my
Ye on your harps must
par - don found; Se - raph - ic trans - port wings the sound!
lean to hear A se - cret chord that mine will bear.

WAKE THE SONG OF JUBILEE

AMBOY 7.7.7.7.D.

St. 1-3

Leonard Bacon, 1823

Lowell Mason, 1845

Joyful, animated
f
1. Wake the song of ju - bi - lee, Let it ech - o o'er the sea.
Now is come the prom-ised hour; Je - sus reigns with sov - ereign power!
6 7
mf
2. All ye na - tions, join and sing, "Christ, of lords and kings, is King,"
3. Now the des - ert lands re - joice, And the is - lands join their voice;
Let it sound from shore to shore, Je - sus reigns for - ev - er - more!
Joy, the whole cre - a - tion sings, "Je - sus is the King of Kings!"
6

Welcome, Ye Hopeful Heirs of Heaven — **Elm Street** 8.8.8.8.8.

St. 1-4

Phoebe Hinsdale Brown, 1824 — A. Eastman, 1835

1. Wel - come, ye hope - ful heirs of heaven, To this rich
2. How great the bless - ing, thus to meet A - round the
feast of gos - pel love. This pledge is but the
sa - cra - men - tal board, And hold by faith com -
pre - lude given To that im - mor - tal feast a -
mun - ion sweet, With Christ our dear and com - mon
Lord, With Christ our dear and com mon Lord.

3. And if so sweet this feast below,
What will it be to meet above,
Where all we see, and feed, and know,
Are fruits of everlasting love,
Are fruits of everlasting love.

4. Soon shall we tune the heavenly lyre
Whilst listening worlds the song approve;
Eternity itself expire,
Ere we exhaust the theme of love,
Ere we exhaust the theme of love.

The Ransomed Spirit to Her Home — Webster L.M.D.

St. 1-3

William B. Tappan, 1824 — George Kingsley, 1844

Allegretto

1. The__ ran - somed spir - it to her home, The clime of cloud - less
2. The__ cher - ub near the view - less throne Hath smote the harp with

beau - ty flies; No__ more on storm - y seas to roam, She
trem - bling hand; And__ one with in - cense - fire hath flown, To

hails__ her ha - ven in__ the__ skies But__
touch__ with flame__ the an - gel - band. But__

cheer - less are those heaven - ly fields, The cloud - less clime no
tune - less is the quiv - ering string, No mel - o - dy can

pleas - ure yields, There is no bliss in bowers a - bove, If
Ga - briel bring, Mute are its ar - ches when a - bove The
6 6 5 6
thou art ab - sent, Ho - ly Love!
harps of heaven wake not to Love!
4 3 9 6 4 8 8 7 6 4 7

3. Earth, sea and sky one language speak,
In harmony that sooths the soul;
'Tis heard when scarce the zephyrs wake,
And when on thunders, thunders roll
That voice is heard and tumults cease,
It whispers to the bosom peace;
O, speak, Inspirer! from above,
And cheer our hearts, Celestial Love!

AND CANST THOU, SINNER, SLIGHT

STATE STREET S.M.

St. 1-4

Abby Bradley Hyde, 1824

Jonathan C. Woodman, 1844

1. And canst thou, sin - ner, slight The call of love di - vine?
2. Wilt thou not cease to grieve The Spir - it from thy breast,

Shall God with ten - der - ness in - vite, And gain no thought of thine?
Till he thy wretch - ed soul shall leave, With all thy sins op - pressed?

3. Today, a pardoning God
Will hear the suppliant pray;
Today, a Saviour's cleansing blood
Will wash thy guilt away.

4. But, grace so dearly bought
If yet thou wilt despise,
Thy fearful doom, with vengeance fraught,
Will fill thee with surprise.

Dear Saviour, If These Lambs Should Stray — Woodworth L.M.

St. 1-4

Abby Bradley Hyde, 1824 — William Batchelder Bradbury, 1849

6
4
1. Dear Sav - iour, if these lambs should stray, From thy se - cure en -
2. Re - mem - ber still that they are thine, That thy dear sa - cred
clo - sure's bound, And, lured by world - ly joys a - way, A -
name they bear, Think that the seal of love di - vine, The
mong the thought - less crowd be found.
sign of cov - enant grace they wear.

3. In all their erring, sinful years,
Oh, let them ne'er forgotten be;
Remember all the prayers and tears,
Which made them consecrate to thee.

4. And when these lips no more can pray,
These eyes can weep for them no more,
Turn thou their feet from folly's way,
The wanderers to thy fold restore.

My Faith Looks Up to Thee

St. 1-4

Ray Palmer, writ. 1830, pub. 1832

Olivet 6.6.4.6.6.6.4.

Lowell Mason, 1832

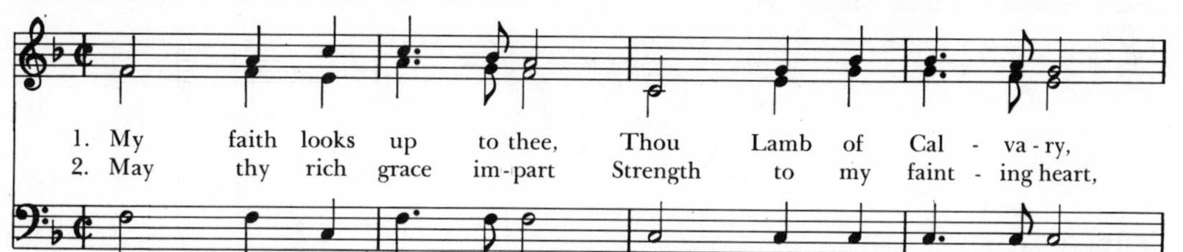
1. My faith looks up to thee, Thou Lamb of Cal - va - ry,
2. May thy rich grace im - part Strength to my faint - ing heart,

Sav - iour Di - vine: Now hear me while I pray, Take all my
My zeal in - spire; As thou hast died for me, O may my

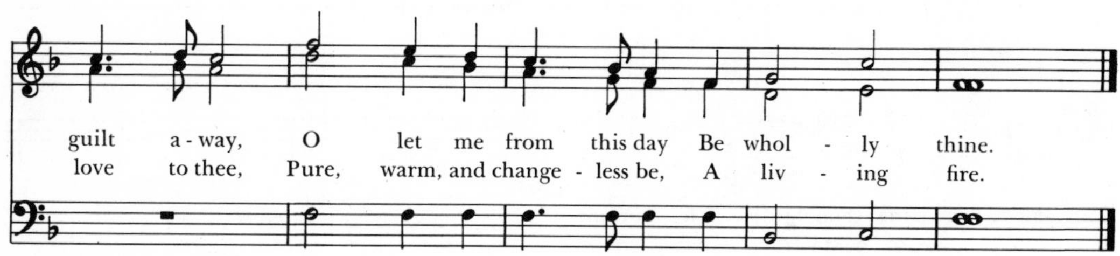
guilt a - way, O let me from this day Be whol - ly thine.
love to thee, Pure, warm, and change - less be, A liv - ing fire.

3. While life's dark maze I tread,
And griefs around me spread,
Be thou my guide;
Bid darkness turn to day,
Wipe sorrow's tears away,
Nor let me ever stray
From thee aside.

4. When ends life's transient dream,
When death's cold, sullen stream
Shall o'er me roll;
Blest Saviour, then, in love,
Fear and distrust remove;
O, bear me safe above,
A ransomed soul.

O God, Beneath Thy Guiding Hand — Baltimore L. M.

St. 1-4

Leonard Bacon, writ, 1833 — Christopher Meinecke, 1831

Adagio
1. O God, be - neath thy guid - ing hand
2. Thou heardst, well - pleased, the song, the prayer;
Our ex - iled fa - thers crossed the sea;
Thy bless - ing came; and still its power
And, when they trod the win - try strand,
Shall on - ward through all a - ges bear
With prayer and psalm they wor - shipped thee.
The mem - ory of that ho - ly hour.

3. Laws, freedom, truth, and faith in God
Came with those exiles o'er the waves;
And where their pilgrim feet have trod,
The God they trusted guards their graves.

4. And here thy name, O God of love,
Their children's children shall adore,
Till these eternal hills remove,
And spring adorns the earth no more.

Hallelujah! Praise the Lord — Hallelujah 7.6.7.6.7.7.7.7.

St. 1-3

Edwin Francis Hatfield, writ. 1837, pub. 1872 — Samuel Prowse Warren, comp. 1871, pub. 1872

1. Hal - le - lu - jah! praise the Lord; Sing Mes - si - ah's glo - ry;
2. Praise him with the trum - pet's tongue, Far and wide re - sound - ing;
Heaven and earth with one ac - cord, Shout the won - drous sto - ry;
Praise him with the harp well - strung, While your hearts are bound - ing;
Praise him for his might - y deeds; Praise ye him, whose grace ex - ceeds
Praise him with the sweet - toned lyre; Let his praise the lute in - spire;
All that heaven in songs con - cedes; Worlds of bliss his praise re - cord.
Praise him in a might - y choir; Let his praise be loud - ly sung.

3. Praise him with the viol's strings,
Waking joyous feeling;
While the vault of glory rings
With the organ's pealing;
Let the cymbals ring his praise,
Wake the clarion's grandest lays,
Praise the Lord through endless days,
Him the wide creation sings.

Brother, Though from Yonder Sky — Fulton 7.7.7.7.

St. 1-5

James Henry Bancroft, writ. 1842, pub. 1843 — William Batchelder Bradbury, 1847

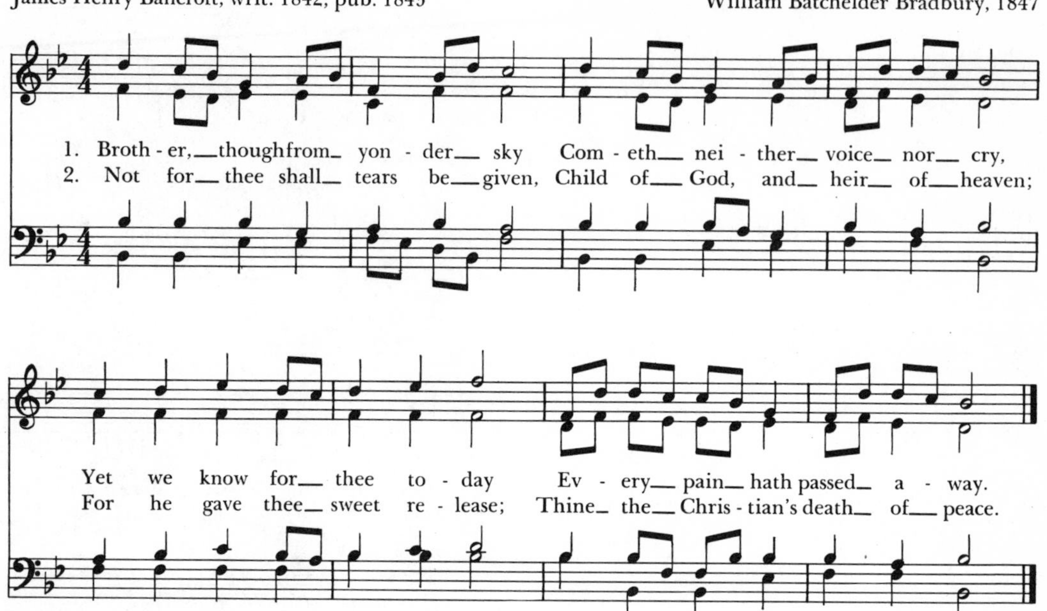
1. Broth - er, thoughfrom yon - der sky Com - eth nei - ther voice nor cry,
2. Not for thee shall tears be given, Child of God, and heir of heaven;
Yet we know for thee to - day Ev - ery pain hath passed a - way.
For he gave thee sweet re - lease; Thine the Chris - tian's death of peace.

3. Well we know thy living faith
Had the power to conquer death;
As a living rose may bloom
By the border of the tomb.

4. Brother, in that solemn trust
We commend thee, dust to dust;
In that faith we wait till risen
Thou shalt meet us all in heaven.

5. While we weep as Jesus wept,
Thou shalt sleep as Jesus slept;
With thy Saviour thou shalt rest,
Crowned, and glorified, and blest.

By Vows of Love Together Bound — Ira C.M.

St. 1-5

Eleazar Thompson Fitch, 1845 — Charles Zeuner, 1845

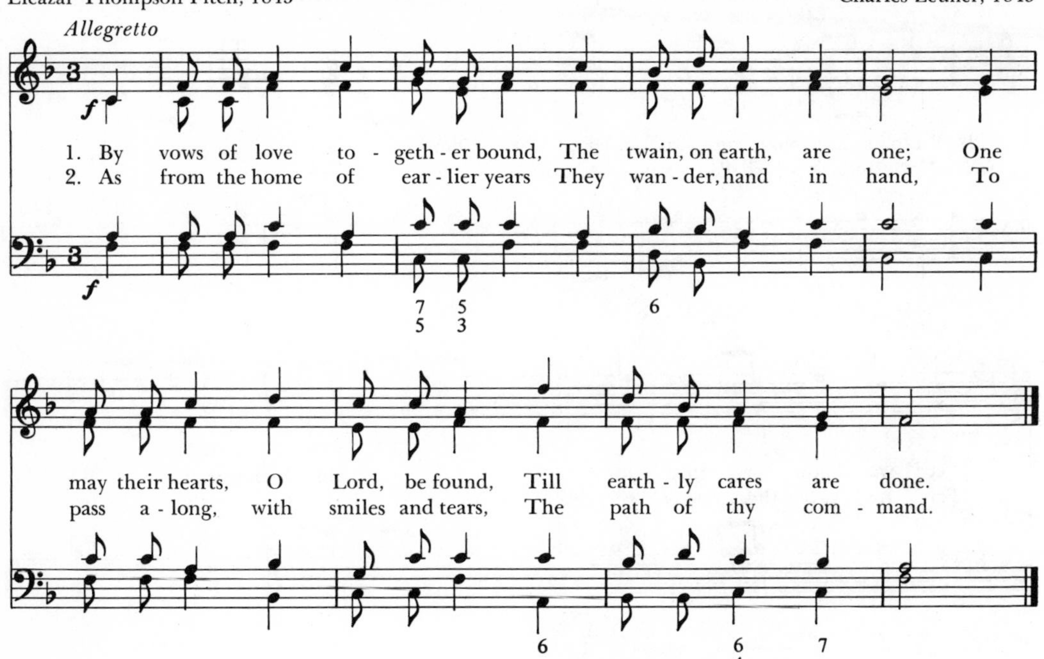
Allegretto
f
1. By vows of love to - geth - er bound, The twain, on earth, are one; One
2. As from the home of ear - lier years They wan - der, hand in hand, To
f
7 5
5 3
6
may their hearts, O Lord, be found, Till earth - ly cares are done.
pass a - long, with smiles and tears, The path of thy com - mand.
6
6 7
4

3. With more than earthly parents' care,
   Do thou their steps attend;
   And with the joys or woes they share,
   Thy loving kindness blend.

4. O let the memory of this hour
   In future years come nigh
   To bind, with sweet, attractive power,
   And cheer them till they die.

5. And to that blessèd, fadeless land,
   Where partings may not be,
   Lead them — a happy household band —
   Forever near to thee.

HAIL, TRANQUIL HOUR OF CLOSING DAY — CORINTH C.M.

St. 1-5

Leonard Bacon, 1845 — Anon., 1831

1. Hail, tran - quil hour of clos - ing day! Be - gone, dis - turb - ing
2. How sweet the tear of pen - i - tence Be - fore his throne of
care! And look, my soul, from earth a - way To
grace, While, to the con - trite spir - it's sense,
Him who hear - eth prayer.
He shows his smil - ing face!
1.
2.

3. How sweet, through long-remembered years,
His mercies to recall,
And, pressed with wants, and griefs, and fears,
To trust his love for all!

4. How sweet to look, in thoughtful hope,
Beyond this fading sky,
And hear him call his children up
To his fair home on high!

5. Calmly the day forsakes our heaven
To dawn beyond the west;
So let my soul, in life's last even,
Retire to glorious rest.

Lord, at This Closing Hour

Knowlton S.M.

St. 1-4

Eleazar Thompson Fitch, 1845

Charles Zeuner, 1845

Moderato
1. Lord, at this clos - ing hour, Es - tab - lish ev - ery heart Up - on thy word of truth and power, To keep us when we part.
2. Peace to our breth - ren give; Fill all our hearts with love; In faith and pa - tience may we live, And seek our rest a - bove.

3. Through changes bright or drear,
We would thy will pursue;
And toil to spread thy kingdom here,
Till we its glory view.

4. To God, the Only Wise,
In every age adored,
Let glory from the Church arise
Through Jesus Christ our Lord.

Thy Loving Kindness, Lord, I Sing — Winthrop L.M.

St. 1-5

George Barrell Cheever, writ. 1845, pub. 1851 — Anon., 1849

1. Thy loving kindness, Lord, I sing, Of grace and life the sacred spring; The spring o'erflowing, rich, and free, In precious blood, once shed for me.
2. I to thy mercy-seat repair, And find thy loving-kindness there; And when to thy sweet word I go, Thy loving kindness there I know.

3. Each evening, from the world apart,
Thy loving kindness cheers my heart,
And when the day salutes mine eyes,
I see thy loving kindness rise.

4. Lord, from the moment of my birth,
I've nothing known but love on earth;
By day, by night, where'er I be,
Thy loving kindness follows me.

5. From daily sin and daily woe
Thy loving kindness saves me now:
And I will praise, for sins forgiven,
Thy loving kindness all, in heaven.

To Thee, O God, the Shepherd Kings — Woodstock C.M.

St. 1-6

John G. C. Brainard, 1845 — Deodatus Dutton Jr., 1829

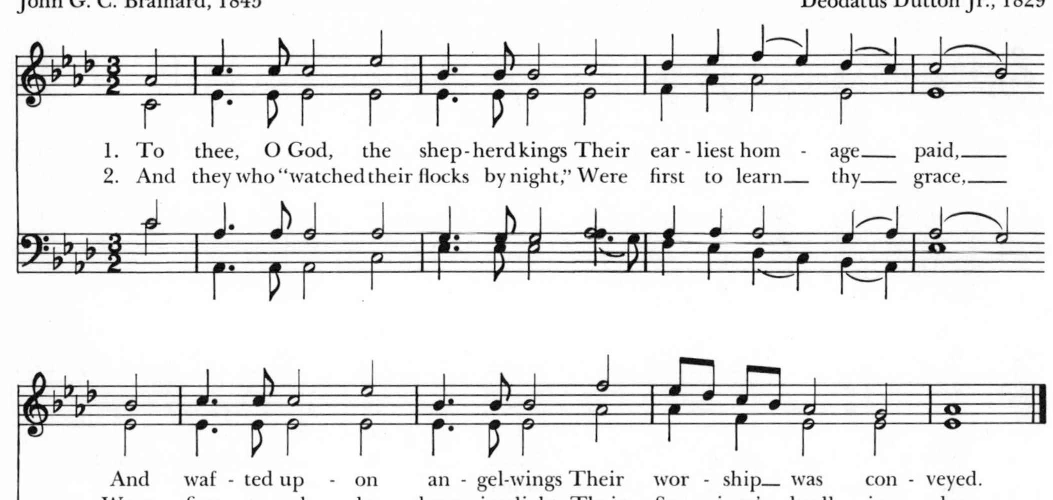
1. To thee, O God, the shep-herd kings Their ear - liest hom - age___ paid,___
2. And they who "watched their flocks by night," Were first to learn___ thy___ grace,___
And waf - ted up - on an - gel-wings Their wor - ship___ was con - veyed.
Were first to seek by dawn - ing light, Their Sav - iour's_dwell - ing place.

3. The hills and vales, the woods and streams,
The fruits and flowers, are thine;
Where'er the sun can send its beams
Or the mild moon can shine.

4. By thee, the spring puts forth its leaves,
By thee, comes down the rain,
By thee, the yellow harvest sheaves
Stand ripening on the plain.

5. When winter comes in storm and wrath,
Thy soothing voice is heard;
As round the farmer's peaceful hearth
Is read thy holy word.

6. Thus are we fostered by thy care,
Supported by thy hand;
Our heritage is rich and fair,
And this thy chosen land.

Just As Thou Art
St. 1-3
Russell Sturgis Cook, 1850

Woodworth L.M.
William Batchelder Bradbury, 1849

1. Just as thou art, with-out one trace Of love, or joy, or in - ward grace, Or meet - ness for the heaven - ly place, O
2. Thy sins I bore on Cal - va-ry's tree; The stripes, thy due, were laid on Me, That peace and par - don might be free; O

guilt - y sin - ner, come, O come.
wretch - ed sin - ner, come, O come.

3 Come, leave thy burden at the cross,
Count all thy gains but empty dross;
My grace repays all earthly loss;
O needy sinner, come, O come.

Blest Be the Wondrous Grace

St. 1-3

George Barrell Cheever, 1851

St. Louis 6.6.8.6.6.8.

Joseph Emerson Sweetser, 1849

1. Blest be the won - drous grace, That gives my soul a place With - in the man - sions of thy love! That par - dons all my sin, And makes me pure with - in, And writes my name in heaven a - bove.
2. All good de - sires I owe, And mer - cies here be - low, And thoughts of grace, and hopes of heaven, To Him, whose suf - fering breath Still prayed for me in death, Whose pre - cious blood for me was given.

3. Lord, bind me to thy sway,
And keep me every day,
Weaned from the world by thy dear cross,
May I, redeemed by grace,
Behold thy glorious face
And count all other things but loss.

One Sweetly Solemn Thought — Nearer Home S.M., with chorus

St. 1-3, 7 alt.

Phoebe Cary, writ. 1852 — Philip Phillips, 1876

1. One sweet - ly sol - emn thought Comes to me o'er and o'er; I'm
2. Near - er my Fath - er's house, Where man - y man - sions be; Near-
near - er home to - day, to - day, Than I have been be - fore.
er the great white throne to - day, Near - er the cryst - al sea.
Chorus
Near - er my home, near - er my home, Near - er my home today, to - day, Than I have been be - fore.

3. Nearer the bound of life,
Where burdens are laid down;
Nearer to leave the cross today,
And nearer to the crown.
Chorus

4. Be near me when my feet
Are slipping o'er the brink;
For I am nearer home today,
Perhaps than now I think.
Chorus

Tarry with Me, O My Saviour

Kidron 8.7.8.7.

St. 1-4

Caroline Sprague Smith, writ. 1852

William Mason, comp. 1845, pub. 1848

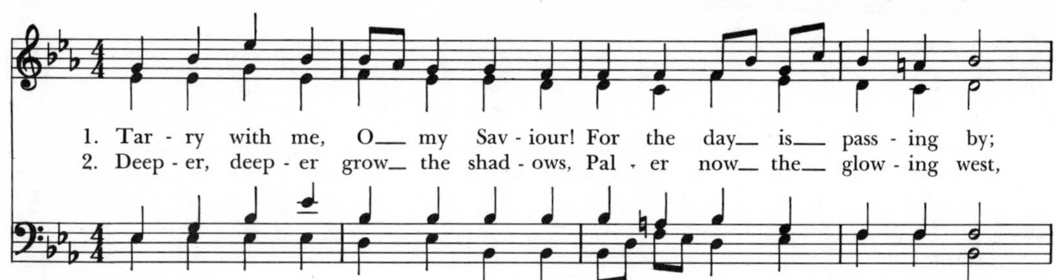
1. Tar - ry with me, O— my Sav - iour! For the day— is— pass - ing by;
2. Deep - er, deep - er grow— the shad - ows, Pal - er now— the— glow - ing west,

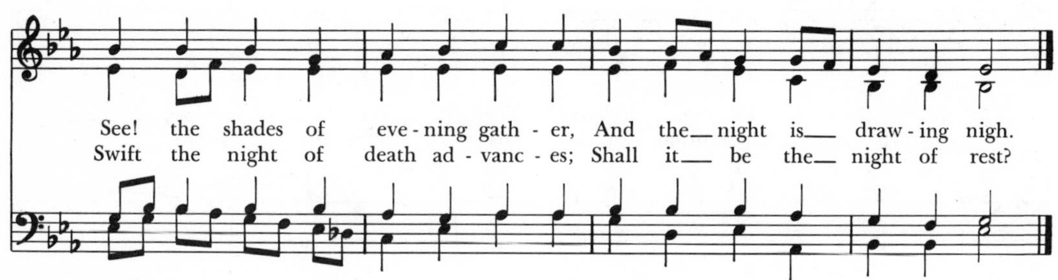
See! the shades of eve - ning gath - er, And the— night is— draw - ing nigh.
Swift the night of death ad - vanc - es; Shall it— be the— night of rest?

3. Feeble, trembling, fainting, dying,
Lord, I cast myself on thee;
Tarry with me through the darkness;
While I sleep, still watch by me.

4. Tarry with me, O my Saviour!
Lay my head upon thy breast,
Till the morning; then awake me,
Morning of eternal rest!

Abide in Me, O Lord, and I in Thee — Cuba 10.10.10.10.

St. 1 (new), 2, 3, 5, 6

Harriet Beecher Stowe, 1855 — Anon., 1853

1. A - bide in me, O Lord, and I in thee, From
2. A - bide in me; o'er shad - ow by thy love Each
this good hour, oh, leave me nev - er - more; Then
half - formed pur - pose and dark thought of sin; Quench
shall the dis - cord cease, the wound be healed, The
ere it rise each self - ish, low de - sire, And
life - long bleed - ing of the soul be o'er.
keep my soul as thine, calm and di - vine.

3. As some rare perfume in a vase of clay,
Pervades it with a fragrance not its own,
So, when thou dwellest in a mortal soul,
All heaven's own sweetness seems around it thrown.

4. Abide in me; there have been moments blest,
When I have heard thy voice and felt thy power;
Then evil lost its grasp; and passion, hushed,
Owned the divine enchantment of the hour.

5. These were but seasons beautiful and rare;
Abide in me, and they shall ever be;
Fulfill at once thy precept and my prayer,
Come, and abide in me, and I in thee.

Laboring and Heavy Laden — Collyer 8.7.8.7.

St. 1-4

Jeremiah E. Rankin, writ. 1855 — Leonard Marshall, 1852

1. La - bor - ing and heav - y - lad - en With my
2. Make my stub - born spir - it will - ing To o -

sins, O Lord, I roam, While I know thou hast in -
bey thy gra - cious voice, At the cross to leave its

vit - ed All such wan - derers to their home.
bur - den, And de - part - ing to re - joice.

3. Thy sweet yoke I'd take upon me,
And would learn, O Lord, of thee;
Thou art meek in heart, and lowly,
Teach me like thyself to be.

4. Laboring and heavy-laden,
Lord, no longer will I roam.
Here I fix my habitation,
In thy sheltering love at home.

We Are on Our Journey Home

Mt. Blanc Irregular

St. 1-5

Anon., version of Charles Beecher, 1855

Anon., version of Charles Beecher, 1855

1. We are on our jour - ney home, Where_ Christ our Lord is gone;
2. We can see that dis - tant home, Though_ clouds rise dark be - tween,
We shall meet a - round his throne, When he makes his peo - ple one
Faith__ views the ra - diant dome, And a lus - ter flash - es keen
In the new,_____ In the new_____ Je - ru - sa - lem.
From the new,_____ From the new_____ Je - ru - sa - lem.
In the new Je - ru - sa - lem.
From the new Je - ru - sa - lem

3. A glory shining far
From the never setting Sun!
O trembling morning star!
Our journey's almost done
To the new,
To the new Jerusalem.

4. O holy, heavenly home!
O, rest eternal there!
When shall the exiles come,
Where they cease from earthly care,
In the new,
In the new Jerusalem.

5. Our hearts are breaking now
Those mansions fair to see;
O Lord! thy heavens bow
And raise us up with thee
To the new,
To the new Jerusalem.

When Winds Are Raging | Rest 11.10.11.10.

Still, Still with Thee

St. 1-5, St. 1-6

Harriet Beecher Stowe, 1855 | Charles Beecher, 1855

1. When winds are rag - ing o'er the up - per o - cean, And
2. Far, far be - neath, the noise of tem - pests di - eth, And
bil - lows wild con - tend with an - gry roar, 'Tis said, far down, be -
sil - ver waves chime ev - er peace - ful - ly, And no rude storm, how
neath the wild com - mo - tion, That peace - ful still - ness reign - eth ev - er - more.
fierce so e'er it fli - eth, Dis - turbs the Sab - bath of that deep - er sea.

3. So to the heart that knows Thy love, O Purest!
There is a temple, sacred evermore,
And all the babble of life's angry voices
Dies in hushed stillness at its peaceful door.

4. Far, far away, the roar of passion dieth,
And loving thoughts rise calm and peacefully,
And no rude storm, how fierce so e'er it flieth,
Disturbs the soul that dwells, O Lord, in Thee.

5. O Rest of rests! O Peace, serene, eternal!
Thou ever livest, and Thou changest never;
And in the secret of Thy presence dwelleth
Fullness of joy, for ever and for ever.

1. Still, still with Thee–when purple morning breaketh,
When the bird waketh, and the shadows flee;
Fairer than morning, lovelier than the daylight,
Dawns the sweet consciousness, I am with Thee!

2. Alone with Thee–amid the mystic shadows,
The solemn hush of nature newly born;
Alone with Thee in breathless adoration,
In the calm dew and freshness of the morn.

3. As in the dawning, o'er the waveless ocean,
The image of the morning star doth rest,
So in this stillness, Thou beholdest only
Thine image in the waters of my breast.

4. Still, still with Thee! as to each new-born morning
A fresh and solemn splendor still is given,
So doth this blessed consciousness awaking,
Breathe, each day, nearness unto Thee and Heaven.

5. When sinks the soul, subdued by toil, to slumber,
Its closing eye looks up to Thee in prayer,
Sweet the repose beneath Thy wings o'er-shading,
But sweeter still, to wake and find Thee there.

6. So shall it be at last, in that bright morning,
When the soul waketh, and life's shadows flee;
Oh! in that hour, fairer than daylight dawning,
Shall rise the glorious thought — I am with Thee.

O Saviour of a World Undone — Westfield 8.8.8.D.

St. 1-3

Leonard Withington, 1857 — Anon., 1845

Slowly and plaintively
cresc.
1. O — Sav - iour of a world un - done! Whose dy - ing sor - rows blot the sun,
Whose — pain-ful groans and bow-ing head Could rend the vail and wake the dead,
Ten.
dim.
Say, from that ex - e - crat - ed tree De - scends the rud - dy tide for me?

2. For me did he who reigns above,
The object of paternal love,
Consent a servant's form to bear
That I a kingly crown might wear?
Is his deep loss my boundless gain,
And comes my victory from his pain?

3. O, let me own the deep decree
That wounded him and rescued me!
His death, his cross, his funeral sleep,
Instruct repentance how to weep;
He poured for me the vital flood;
My tears shall mingle with his blood.

WHILE WE LOWLY BOW BEFORE THEE | ALVAN 8.7.8.7.4.7.

St. 1-3

Daniel C. Colesworthy, 1857 | Lowell Mason, 1854

1. While we low - ly bow before thee, Wilt thou, gra - cious Sav - iour, hear?
We are poor and need - y sin - ners, Full of doubt and full of fear;
Gra - cious Sav - iour, Gra - cious Sav - iour,

Make us hum - ble and sin - cere.

2. Fill us with thy Holy Spirit;
Sanctify us by thy grace;
Oh, incline us more to love thee,
And in dust our souls abase.
Hear us, Saviour, Hear us, Saviour,
And unveil thy glorious face.

3. None in vain did ever ask thee
For the spirit of thy love;
Hear us, then, dear Saviour, hear us;
Grant an answer from above;
Blessed Saviour, Blessed Saviour,
Hear and answer from above.

Jesus, These Eyes Have Never Seen — Boston C.M.

St. 1-5

Ray Palmer, 1858 — Uzziah C. Burnap, 1869

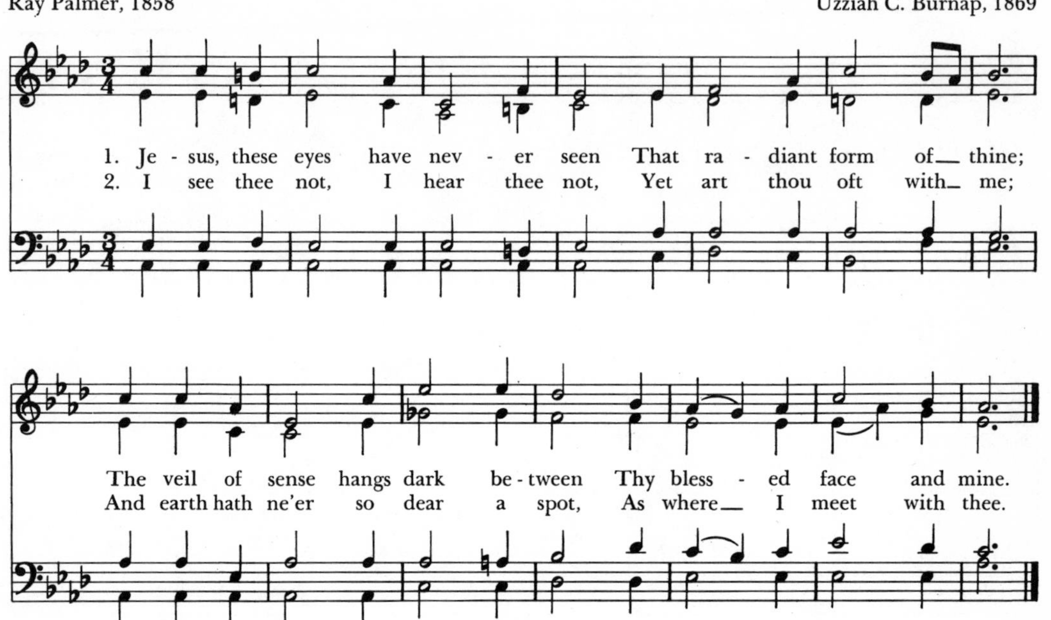
1. Je - sus, these eyes have nev - er seen That ra - diant form of — thine;
2. I see thee not, I hear thee not, Yet art thou oft with — me;
The veil of sense hangs dark be - tween Thy bless - ed face and mine.
And earth hath ne'er so dear a spot, As where — I meet with thee.

3. Like some bright dream that comes unsought
When slumbers o'er me roll,
Thine image ever fills my thought,
And charms my ravished soul.

4. Yet though I have not seen, and still
Must rest in faith alone,
I love thee, dearest Lord, and will,
Unseen, but not Unknown.

5. When death these mortal eyes shall seal,
And still this throbbing heart,
The rending veil shall thee reveal,
All-glorious as thou art.

Lord, My Weak Thought in Vain Would Climb — Louvan L.M.

St. 1-5

Ray Palmer, 1858 — Virgil Corydon Taylor, 1846

1. Lord, my weak thought in vain would climb To search the star - ry vault pro - found; In vain would wing her flight sub - lime, To find cre - a - tion's out - most bound.
2. But weak - er yet that thought must prove To search thy great e - ter - nal plan; Thy sov - ereign coun - sels, born of love Long a - ges ere the world be - gan.
cresc.

3. When my dim reason would demand
Why that, or this, thou dost ordain,
By some vast deep I seem to stand,
Whose secrets I must ask in vain.

4. When doubts disturb my troubled breast,
And all is dark as night to me,
Here, as on solid rock, I rest;
That so it seemeth good to thee.

5. Be this my joy, that evermore
Thou rulest all things at thy will:
Thy sovereign wisdom I adore,
And calmly, sweetly, trust thee still.

My Soul, Weigh Not Thy Life — Laban S.M.

St. 1-4

Leonard Swain, 1858 — Lowell Mason, 1854

1. My soul, weigh not thy life A - gainst thy heaven - ly crown;
2. With prayer and cry - ing strong, Hold on the fear - ful fight,
Nor suf - fer Sa - tan's dead - liest strife
And let the break - ing day pro - long
To beat thy cour - age down.
The wrest - ling of the night.

3. The battle soon will yield,
If thou thy part fulfill;
For strong as is the hostile shield,
Thy sword is stronger still.

4. Thine armor is divine,
Thy feet with victory shod;
And on thy head shall quickly shine
The diadem of God.

HAPPY, SAVIOUR, WOULD I BE — TRUST 7.7.7.D.

St. 1-3

Edwin H. Nevin, 1858 — George F. Root, 1880

1. Hap - py, Sav - iour, would I be, If I could but trust in thee;
2. Trust thee as the on - ly light In the dark - est hour of night;

𝄋

Fine

Trust thy wis - dom me to guide; Trust thy good - ness to pro - vide;
Trust in sick - ness, trust in health; Trust in pov - er - ty and wealth;

D.S. al Fine

Trust thy sav - ing love and power; Trust thee ev - ery day and hour:
Trust in joy and trust in grief; Trust thy prom - ise for re - lief:

3. Trust thy blood to cleanse my soul;
Trust thy grace to make me whole;
Trust thee living, dying, too;
Trust thee all my journey through;
Trust thee till my feet shall be
Planted on the crystal sea.
Trust thee living, dying, too;
Trust thee all my journey through.

Saints in Glory, We Together — Sing of Jesus 8.8.8.5.

St. 1-6

Nehemiah Adams, 1864 — Luther O. Emerson, 1863

1. Saints in glo - ry, we to - geth - er Know the
2. Theme of Ad - am, when for - giv - en, Theme of

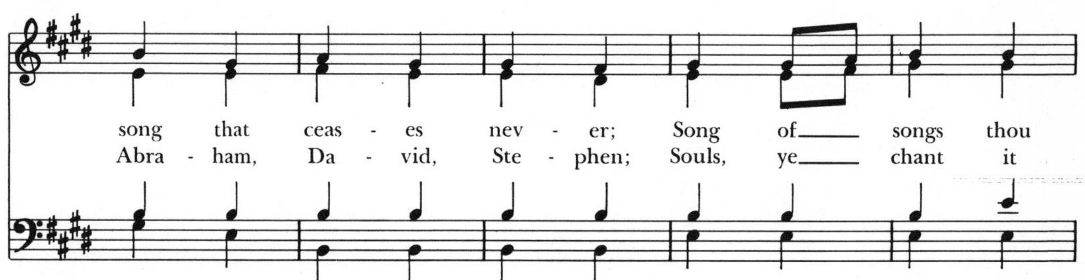
song that ceas - es nev - er; Song of songs thou
Abra - ham, Da - vid, Ste - phen; Souls, ye chant it

art, O Sav - iour, All that end - less day.
en - tering heav - en, Now, hence - forth, al - way.

3. O the God-man! O Immanuel!
Cloud by day! Jehovah-Angel!
Fire by night! He led his Israel,
So he leads us home.

4. Come, ye angels, round us gather,
While to Jesus we draw nearer;
In his throne he'll seat forever
Those for whom he died.

5. Underneath his throne a river,
Clear as crystal, flows forever,
Life his fullness, failing never,
Hail, enthroned Lamb!

6. O the unsearchable Redeemer!
Shoreless Ocean, sounded never!
Yesterday, today, forever,
Jesus Christ, the same.

If I Can Stop One Heart from Breaking — Charity Irregular

St. 1, 2

Emily Dickinson, writ. c.1864, pub. 1890 — Peter C. Lutkin, comp. 1927, pub. 1928

1. If I can stop one heart from break - ing, I shall not live in vain;
2. If I can keep one spir - it sing - ing, I shall not live in vain;

If I can ease one life the ach - ing, Or cool one pain,
Or send one twink - ling vi - sion wing - ing Through fog and rain,

Or help one faint - ing rob - in In - to his nest a - gain,___
Or lead one grop - ing pil - grim In - to the light a - gain,___

I shall not live in vain, I shall not live in vain.
I shall not live in vain, I shall not live in vain.

Father! I Own Thy Voice — Aspiration 6.6.8.6.6.

St. 1-5

Samuel Wolcott, writ. 1868, pub. 1869 — Luther O. Emerson, 1869

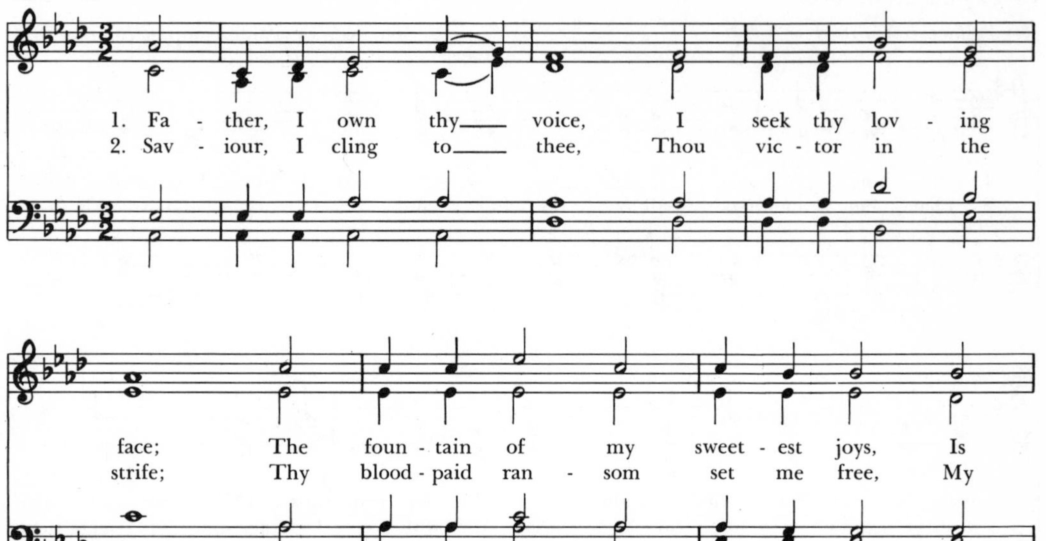
1. Fa - ther, I own thy voice, I seek thy lov - ing
2. Sav - iour, I cling to thee, Thou vic - tor in the
face; The foun - tain of my sweet - est joys, Is
strife; Thy blood - paid ran - som set me free, My

thine a - bound - ing grace, Is thine a - bound - ing grace.
peace, my hope, my life, My peace, my hope, my life.

3. Father, behold thy child,
Guide me, and guard from ill:
In dangers thick, through deserts wild,
Be my protector still,
Be my protector still.

4. Saviour, gird me with power
For thee the cross to bear;
Victorious in temptation's hour,
Safe from the secret snare,
Safe from the secret snare.

5. Ancient of days, to thee
By love celestial drawn,
My soul thy majesty shall see,
And greet her glory's dawn,
And greet her glory's dawn.

Behold, the Shade of Night Is Now Receding
Ecce Iam Noctis
St. 1-3
Gregory the Great, 6th cent.
Ray Palmer, trans. 1869

Devotion 11.11.11.5.
John Knowles Paine, comp. 1873, pub. 1874

1. Be - hold, the shade of night is now re - ced - ing, Kin - dling with
2. That he, our God, will look on us in pi - ty, Send strength for
splen - dors fair the dawn is glow - ing, With fer - vent hearts, O let us all im -
weak - ness, grant us his sal - va - tion, And with a Fa - ther's pure af - fec - tion
plore him, Rul - er Al - might - y.
give us Glo - ry e - ter - nal.

3. This grace O grant us, Godhead ever blessèd,
Of Father, Son, and Holy Ghost in union,
Whose praises be through earth's most distant regions
Ever resounding.

FEAR NOT, POOR WEARY ONE DANVERS S.M.

St. 1-4

Thomas Cogswell Upham, writ. 1872, pub. 1874 William Oscar Perkins, 1867

Legato
1. Fear not, poor, wea - ry one; But strug - gle brave - ly yet; Toil on un - til thy task is done, Un - til thy sun is set.
2. Though man - y are thy cares, And man - y are thy fears, The lov - ing Christ thy bur - den shares, And wipes a - way thy tears.

3. No distant Christ is he,
And one that doth not know;
But watches close and constantly
The path which thou dost go.

4. 'Tis when thy heart is tried,
'Tis in thine hour of grief,
He standeth ever at thy side,
And ever brings relief.

O MASTER, LET ME WALK WITH THEE — GLADDEN L.M.

St. 1-4

Washington Gladden, 1879 — Charles L. Ziegler, cop. 1902

1. O Mas - ter, let me walk with thee In low - ly paths of ser - vice free,
2. Help me the slow of heart to move By some clear, win-ning word of love,
Tell me thy se - cret, help me bear The strain of toil, the fret of care.
Teach me the way - ward feet to stay, And guide them in the home - ward way.

3. Teach me thy patience; still with thee
In closer, dearer company,
In work that keeps faith sweet and strong,
In trust that triumphs over wrong.

4. In hope that sends a shining ray
Far down the future's broadening way,
In peace that only thou canst give,
With thee, O Master, let me live.

Unto Our God Most High We Sing — Plymouth L.M.

St. 1-3

John Vance Cheney, 1879 — Simeon Pease Cheney, 1879

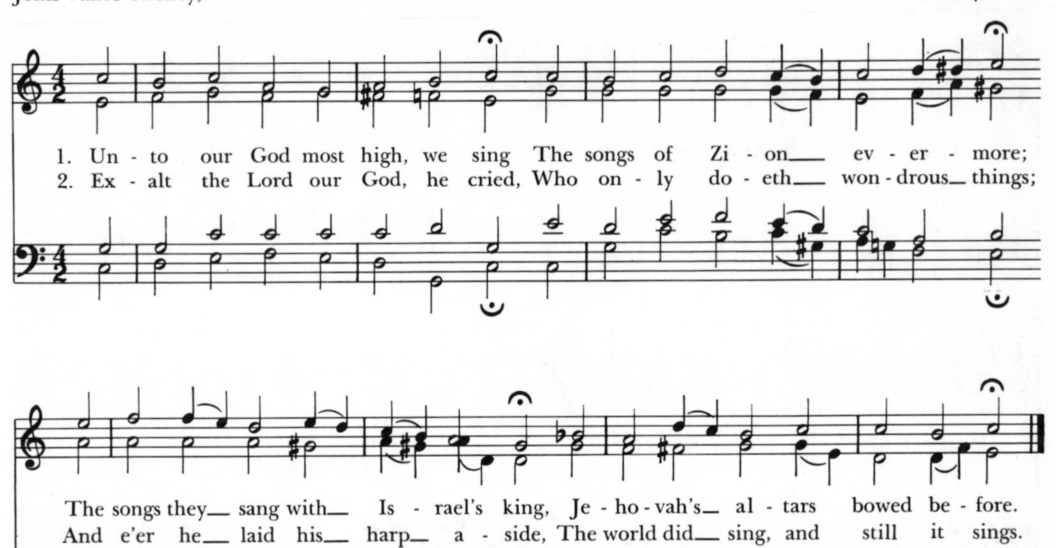
1. Un - to our God most high, we sing The songs of Zi - on ev - er - more;
2. Ex - alt the Lord our God, he cried, Who on - ly do - eth won - drous things;
The songs they sang with Is - rael's king, Je - ho - vah's al - tars bowed be - fore.
And e'er he laid his harp a - side, The world did sing, and still it sings.

3. O blessèd by his glorious name,
Till sun and stars be dark again;
Let earth awide with glory flame,
Forever, ever and amen.

Lead On, O King Eternal — Rex Aeternus 7.6.7.6.D.

St. 1-3

Ernest W. Shurtleff, writ. 1887, pub. 1888 — Charles L. Ziegler, 1904

1. Lead on, O King E - ter - nal, The day of march has come;
2. Lead on, O King E - ter - nal, Till sin's fierce war shall cease,
Hence - forth in fields of con - quest Thy tents shall be our home.
And ho - li - ness shall whis - per The sweet A - men of peace!
Through days of prep - a - ra - tion Thy grace has made us strong,
For not with swords, loud clash - ing, Nor roll of stir - ring drums,
And now, O King E - ter - nal, We lift our bat - tle song.
But deeds of love and mer - cy, The heaven - ly king - dom comes.

3. Lead on, O King Eternal, We follow, not with fears,
For gladness breaks like morning where'er thy face appears.
Thy cross is lifted o'er us; We journey in its light;
The crown awaits the conquest; Lead on, O God of might.

MASTER, NO OFFERING

St. 1-4

Edwin Pond Parker, writ. 1888, pub. 1889

LOVE'S OFFERING 6.4.6.4.6.6.4.4.

Edwin Pond Parker, writ. 1888, pub. 1889

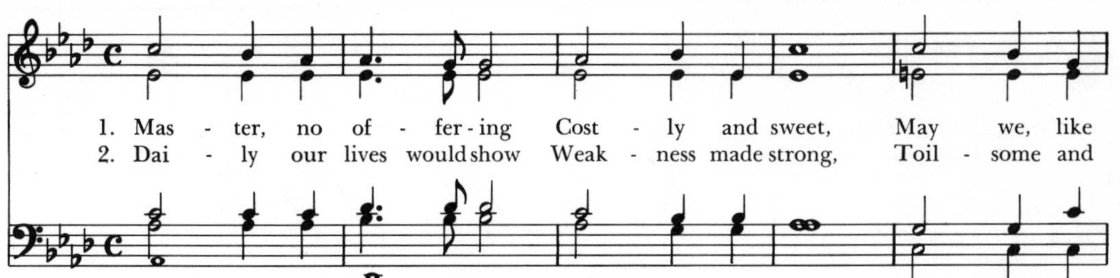
1. Mas - ter, no of - fer - ing Cost - ly and sweet, May we, like
2. Dai - ly our lives would show Weak - ness made strong, Toil - some and

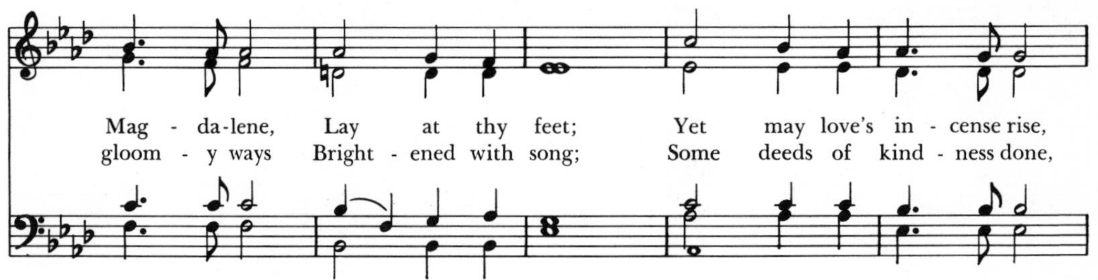
Mag - da-lene, Lay at thy feet; Yet may love's in - cense rise,
gloom - y ways Bright - ened with song; Some deeds of kind - ness done,

Sweet - er than sac - ri - fice, Dear — Lord, to thee, Dear Lord, to thee.
Some souls by pa - tience won, Dear — Lord, to thee, Dear Lord, to thee.

3. Some words of hope for hearts
Burdened with fears,
Some balm of peace for eyes
Blinded with tears,
Some dews of mercy shed,
Some wayward footsteps led,
Dear Lord, to thee,
Dear Lord, to thee.

4. Thus in thy service, Lord,
Till eventide
Closes the day of life,
May we abide;
And when earth's labors cease,
Bid us depart in peace,
Dear Lord, to thee,
Dear Lord, to thee.

O Lord of Life — Greylock C.M.D.

St. 1-3

Washington Gladden, 1897 — Waldo S. Pratt, 1927

1. O Lord of Life, to thee we lift Our hearts in praise for those,
2. Shine forth, O Light, that we may see With hearts all un - a - fraid,
Thy pro - phets, who have shown thy gift Of grace that ev - er grows;
The mean - ing and the mys - ter - y Of things that thou hast made;
Of truth that spreads from shore to shore, Of wis - dom's wide - ning ray,
Shine forth, and let the dark - ling past Be - neath thy beam grow bright!
Of light that shin - eth more and more Un - to thy per - fect day.
Shine forth, and touch the fu - ture vast With thine un - cloud - ed light!

3. Light up thy Word, the fettered page
From killing bondage free;
Light up our way; lead forth this age
In love's large liberty!
O Light of Light, within us dwell,
Through us thy radiance pour,
That word and life thy truth may tell
And praise thee evermore!

HILLS OF GOD, BREAK FORTH IN SINGING

PACIFIC 8.7.8.7.7.7.7.7.

St. 1-3

John Wright Buckham, writ. 1898, pub. 1904

Henry J. Storer, comp. 1903, pub. 1904

1. Hills of God, break forth in__ sing - ing; Winds, breathe balm on ev - ery shore;
2. Van - ish, war - fare, from the__ na - tions; Cease, all cries of pain and grief;

Stars your glit - tering_ gems far fling - ing, Lead to Je - sus__ ev - er - more;
Hush, drear sighs and__ la - men - ta - tions; Je - sus comes_ to__ bring re - lief.

Whis - per, pines where tem - pests__ sweep; Gleam, white lus - ter of__ the__ snow;
Sing, O si - lent tongue_ of__ dumb; Leap, O lame man, as__ the__ hart;

Palms, by an - gels stirred from sleep, Je - sus__ comes in love bend low.
Joy to poor, to bruised, to bond! Je - sus__ comes to bear your part.

3. Chant high praises, young man, maiden;
Age, your songs are not all sung;
Children, with glad hearts love-laden,
Sing the Child who makes all young:
Haste, O messengers of peace,
Swift through all the wide world run,
Gladness speak, love, hope, release;
Joy! for Christ the Lord is come.

O FOR THE HAPPY HOUR

FIRTH 6.6.8.6.6.

St. 1-6

George Washington Bethune, 1843

Sylvanus Billings Pond, 1841

With earnestness
1. O for the hap - py hour When God will hear our cry, And send, with a re - viv - ing power, His Spir - it from on high, His Spir - it from on high.
2. We meet, we sing, we pray; We lis - ten to the word In vain; we see no cheer - ing ray, No cheer - ing voice is heard, No cheer - ing voice is heard.

3. Our prayers are faint and dull,
And languid all our songs;
When once with joy our hearts were full,
And rapture tuned our tongues,
And rapture tuned our tongues.

4. While many crowd thy house,
How few around thy board
Meet to record their solemn vows,
And bless thee as their Lord!
And bless thee as their Lord!

5. Thou, thou alone can'st give
Thy gospel sure success;
Can'st bid the dying sinner live
Anew in holiness,
Anew in holiness.

6. Come, then, with power divine,
Spirit of life and love:
Then shall our people all be thine,
Our church, like that above,
Our church, like that above.

I AM WEARY OF STRAYING — PRESCOTT 12.11.11.11.

St. 1-5

Sarah E. York, 1847 — George Oates, 1832

1. I am wea - ry of stray - ing; Oh! fain would I rest
2. I am wea - ry of hop - ing; where hope is un - true,
In the far dis - tant land of the pure and the blessed,
As fair, but as fleet - ing, as morn - ing's bright dew.
Where sin can no lon - ger her blan - dish - ments spread,
I long for that land, whose bless-ed prom - ise a - lone
And tears and temp - ta - tions for - ev - er have fled.
Is change - less, and sure, as E - ter - ni - ty's throne.

3. I am weary of sighing o'er sorrows of earth.
O'er joy's glowing visions, that fade at their birth;
O'er the pangs of the loved, which we cannot assuage,
O'er the blightings of youth, and the weakness of age.

4. I am weary of loving what passes away;
The sweetest, the dearest, alas! may not stay;
I long for that land, where these partings are o'er,
And death and the tomb can divide hearts no more.

5. I am weary, my Saviour, of grieving thy love;
Oh! when shall I rest in thy presence above?
I am weary; but oh! let me never repine,
While thy word, and thy love, and thy promise are mine.

THERE IS NO NAME SO SWEET ON EARTH

SWEETEST NAME 8.7.8.7, with chorus

St. 1-3

George Washington Bethune, 1858

William Batchelder Bradbury, 1861

1.
2.
Fine
1. There is no name so sweet on earth, No name so sweet in heav - en,
The name be - fore his won-drous birth, To Christ the Sav - iour giv - en.
D. C. For there's no word ears ev - er heard So dear, so sweet as Je - sus.
Chorus
D. C. al Fine
We love to sing a - round our King, And hail him bless - ed Je - sus.

2. And when he hung upon the tree,
They wrote this name above him,
That all might see the reason we
For evermore must love him.
Chorus

3. So now, upon his Father's throne,
Almighty to release us
From sin and pains, he ever reigns,
The Prince and Saviour Jesus.
Chorus

JESUS, SHEPHERD OF THY SHEEP

BETHUNE 7.7.7.7.D.

George Washington Bethune, 1863

Anon., 1863

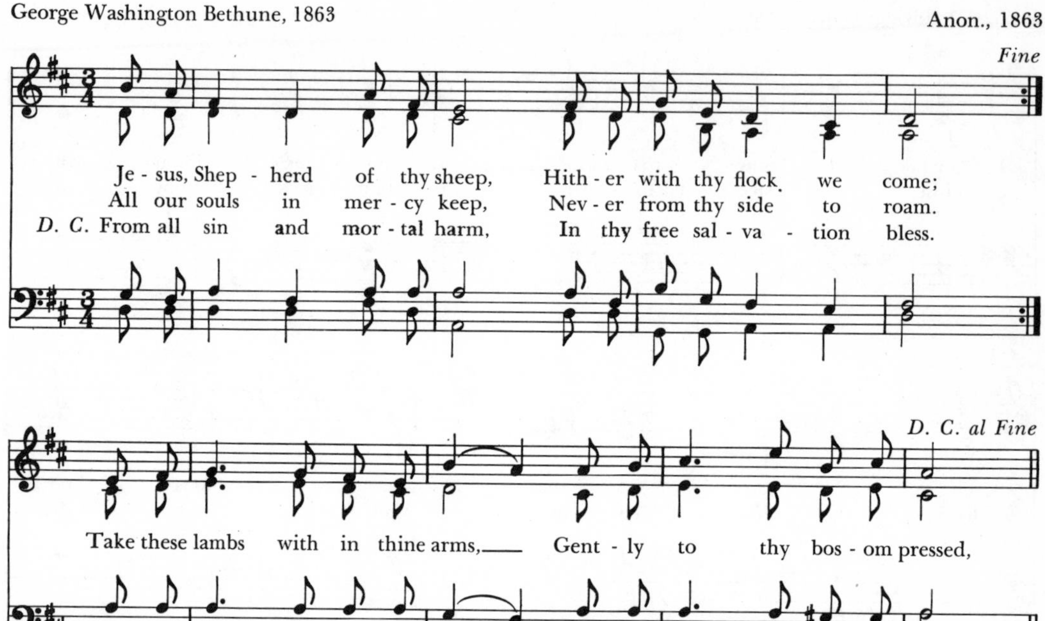
Fine
Je - sus, Shep - herd of thy sheep, Hith - er with thy flock we come;
All our souls in mer - cy keep, Nev - er from thy side to roam.
D. C. From all sin and mor - tal harm, In thy free sal - va - tion bless.
D. C. al Fine
Take these lambs with in thine arms, Gent - ly to thy bos - om pressed,

Lord, I Know Thy Grace Is Nigh Me — Rathbun 8.7.8.7.

St. 1-5

Hervey Doddridge Ganse, 1864 — Ithamar Conkey, comp. 1847, pub. 1851

1. Lord, I know thy grace is nigh me, Though thy -
2. While I sit in wea - ry blind - ness, Long - ing

self I can - not see; Je - sus Mas - ter,
for the bless - ed light, Man - y taste thy

pass not by me; Son of Da - vid, pit - y me.
lov - ing - kind - ness; "Lord, I would re - ceive my sight."

3. I would see thee and adore thee,
And thy word the power can give;
Hear the sightless soul implore thee:
Let me see thy face and live.

4. Ah, what touch is this that thrills me?
What this burst of strange delight?
Lo, the rapturous vision fills me!
This is Jesus! this is sight!

5. Room, ye saints that throng behind Him!
Let me follow in the way;
I will teach the blind to find Him
Who can turn their night to day.

FLOODS SWELL AROUND ME, ANGRY, APPALLING
St. 1-4
Zachary Eddy, 1869

SCHELL 10.10.11.12.
Uzziah C. Burnap, 1869

1. Floods swell a - round me, an - gry, ap - pall - ing!
2. Faith is o'er - cloud - ed, cour - age is fail - ing,
Bil - lows go o'er me, deep to deep call - ing!
Hope dies with - in me, doubts are pre - vail - ing,
Help - less, de - ject - ed, o'er - whelmed, bro - ken - heart - ed — O
Con - science up - braids me, and Sa - tan ac - cus - es, While
God of my life, is thy mer - cy de - part - ed?
Je - sus the to - kens of fa - vor re - fus - es.

3. Oh, by thy fasting and bitter temptation!
Oh, by thy passion, the price of salvation!
Mighty Redeemer, of help the sole giver,
Now hasten, oh hasten, my soul to deliver!

4. Glory to God! he regardeth my crying;
Life hath he sent to the soul sick and dying;
Hope once again in my bosom is springing;
All praise to Jehovah, with gladness and singing!

Jesus, Enthroned and Glorified — **Meribah** 8.8.6.8.8.6.

St. 1-4

Zachary Eddy, 1869 — Lowell Mason, 1839

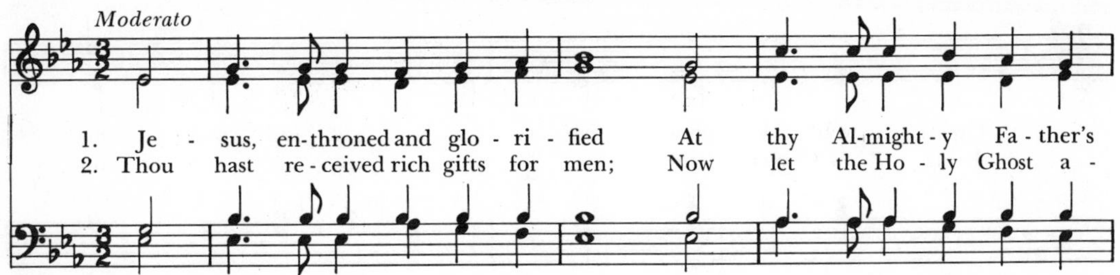
Moderato
1. Je - sus, en-throned and glo - ri - fied At thy Al-might - y Fa - ther's
2. Thou hast re - ceived rich gifts for men; Now let the Ho - ly Ghost a -

side, Thy peo - ple's prayer in - spire!
gain On all thy Church de - scend.

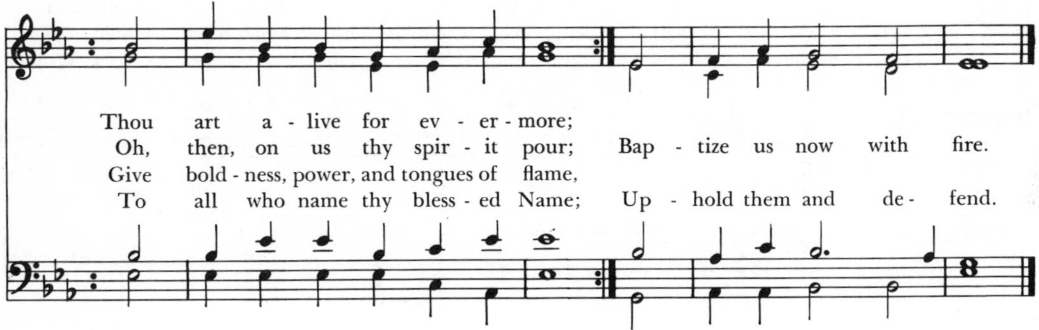
Thou art a - live for ev - er - more;
Oh, then, on us thy spir - it pour; Bap - tize us now with fire.
Give bold - ness, power, and tongues of flame,
To all who name thy bless - ed Name; Up - hold them and de - fend.

3. The fullness of thy life bestow
On us thy members here below;
Revive each fainting heart;
Each sick and wounded spirit heal,
Thy beauty to our souls reveal,
Thy light and love impart.

4. Blest Comforter, celestial Dove,
Thou Lord of Life, Thou Fount of Love,
Be thou our inward guest;
Illumed and sanctified by thee,
Thy living temples let us be,
Thine everlasting rest.

Wayfarers in the Wilderness | Shining Shore 8.7.8.7., with chorus

St. 1-4

Alexander R. Thompson, 1869 | George F. Root, 1856

1. Way - far - ers in the wil - der - ness, By morn, and noon, and e - ven,
2. By day the cloud be - fore us goes, By night the cloud of fire,
Day af - ter day, we jour - ney on With wea - ry feet towards heav - en.
To guide us o'er the track - less waste, To Ca - naan ev - er nigh - er.
Chorus
Oh, land a - bove! oh, land of love! The glo - ry shin - eth o'er thee;
O Christ our King, in mer - cy bring Us thith - er we im - plore thee!

3. Each morning find we, as he said,
The dew of daily manna;
And ever when a foe appears,
Confronts him Christ our Banner.
Chorus

4. The sea was riven for our feet,
And so shall be the river;
And by the King's highway brought home,
We'll praise his name forever.
Chorus

TODAY BENEATH BENIGNANT SKIES — CENTENNIAL HYMN 8.8.8.D.

St. 1-4

Denis Wortman, 1881 — John Knowles Paine, 1876

1. To - day be - neath be - nig - nant skies, 'Mid scenes Thy fa - vor beau - ti - fies, Our hopes and prayers to thee we raise, And found a tem - ple to thy praise, Our hum - ble work pro - pi - tious own As now we lay this cor - ner - stone.
2. Ex - cept the Lord the house do build, Ex - cept with grace the work be filled, All la - bor's vain. O, Christ, im - part Thy lov - ing spir - it to each heart: By thee, to thee, on thee a - lone, We build, thou fair - est cor - ner - stone!

3. Here may the truth and right grow strong,
Here love prevail thy saints among,
Here sinners feel thy quickening grace,
And seek with hasting joy thy face;
And thousands gladly make thee known
As their eternal corner-stone.

4. Build thou the walls! Make them so glow
With glory, we on earth below
The eternal splendors shall foresee;
Grander than Salem's may they be
All luminous with grace thine own,
From topmost peak to corner-stone!

God of the Prophets! Bless the Prophets' Sons — Assurance 10.10.10.10.

St. 1-6

Denis Wortman, 1884 — William Fiske Sherwin, 1878

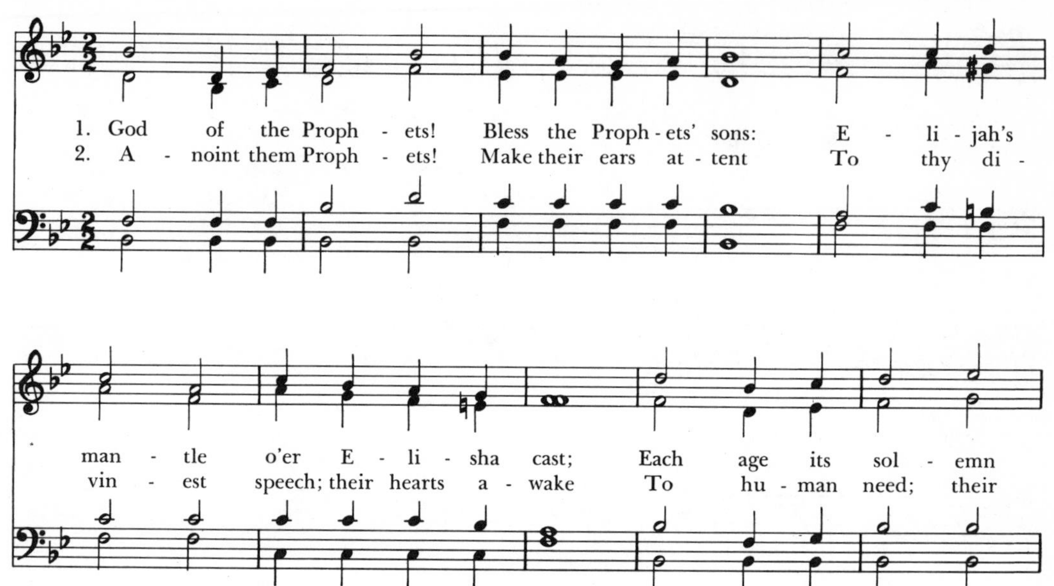
1. God of the Proph - ets! Bless the Proph - ets' sons: E - li - jah's
2. A - noint them Proph - ets! Make their ears at - tent To thy di -
man - tle o'er E - li - sha cast; Each age its sol - emn
vin - est speech; their hearts a - wake To hu - man need; their

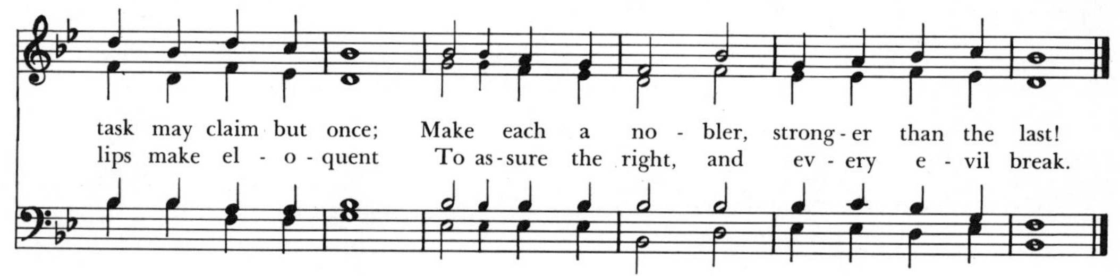
task may claim but once; Make each a no - bler, strong - er than the last!
lips make el - o - quent To as - sure the right, and ev - ery e - vil break.

3. Anoint them Priests! Strong intercessors they
For pardon, and for charity and peace!
Ah, if with them the world might pass astray
Into the dear Christ's life of sacrifice!

4. Anoint them Kings! Aye, kingly kings, O Lord!
Anoint them with the Spirit of thy Son:
Their's, not a jeweled crown, a blood-stained sword;
Their's, by sweet love, for Christ a kingdom won.

5. Make them Apostles! Heralds of thy cross,
Forth may they go to tell all realms thy grace;
Inspired of thee, may they count all but loss,
And stand at last with joy before thy face.

6. O mighty age of prophet-kings, return!
O truth, O faith, enrich our urgent time!
Lord Jesus Christ, again with us sojourn;
A weary world awaits thy reign sublime!

Lord of Life, All Praise Excelling

St. 1-4

Clement Clarke Moore, 1808

Grafton Street 8.7.8.7.

P. K. Moran, 1828

1. Lord of life, all praise ex - cel - ling,
2. As thy love, through all cre - a - tion,
Thou, in glo - ry un - con - fined,
Beams like thy dif - fu - sive light;
Deignst to make thy hum - ble dwell - ing
So the high and hum - ble sta - tion
With the poor of hum - ble mind.
Both are e - qual in thy sight.

3. Thus thy care, for all providing,
Warmed thy faithful prophet's tongue;
Who, the lot of all deciding,
To thy chosen Israel sung.

4. When thy harvest yields thee pleasure,
Thou the golden sheaf shalt bind;
To the poor belongs the treasure
Of the scattered ears behind.

O Holy, Holy, Holy Lord

Brighton L.M.

St. 1-4

James Wallis Eastburn, writ. 1815, pub. 1826

Alling Brown, 1823

1. O ho - ly, ho - ly, ho - ly Lord, Bright in thy deeds and in thy name, For - ev - er be thy name a - dored, Thy glo - ries let the world pro claim.
2. O Je - sus, Lamb once cru - ci - fied To take our load of sins a - way, Thine be the hymn that rolls its tide A long the realms of up per day.

3. O Holy Spirit from above,
In streams of light and glory given,
Thou source of ecstasy and love,
Thy praises ring through earth and heaven.

4. O God Triune, to thee we owe
Our every thought, our every song;
And ever may thy praises flow
From saint and seraph's burning tongue.

Softly Now the Light of Day — Preparation 7.7.7.7.

St. 1-4

George Washington Doane, writ. 1824 — Abner Jones, 1834

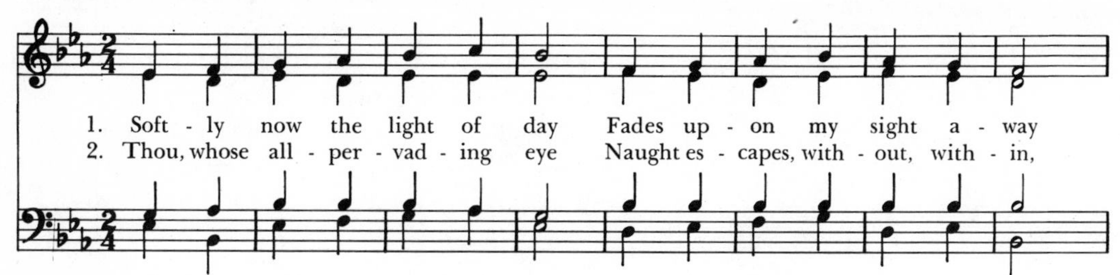
1. Soft - ly now the light of day Fades up - on my sight a - way
2. Thou, whose all - per - vad - ing eye Naught es - capes, with - out, with - in,

Free from care, from la - bor free, Lord, I would com - mune with thee.
Par - don each in - fir - mi - ty, O - pen fault and se - cret sin.

3. When for me the light of day
Shall for ever pass away,
Then, from sin and sorrow free,
Take me, Lord, to dwell with thee.

4. Thou who sinless yet hast known
All of man's infirmity;
Then, from thine eternal throne,
Jesus, look with pitying eye.

Thou Art the Way — Atkinson C.M.

St. 1-4

George Washington Doane, 1824 — John Cole, 1839

1. Thou art the way,— to thee— a - lone From sin— and death we flee;
2. Thou art the truth,— thy word— a - lone True wis - dom can im - part;

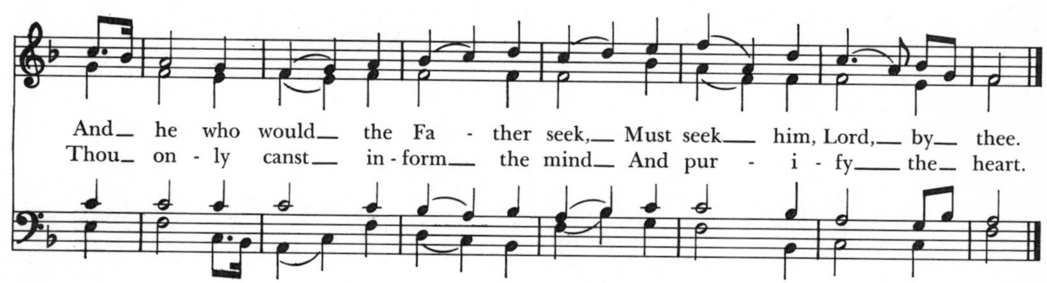

And— he who would— the Fa - ther seek,— Must seek— him, Lord,— by— thee.
Thou— on - ly canst— in - form— the mind— And pur - i - fy— the— heart.

3. Thou art the life, the rending tomb
Proclaims thy conquering arm,
And those who put their trust in thee
Nor death nor hell shall harm.

4. Thou art the way, the truth, the life;
Grant us that way to know,
That truth to keep, that life to win,
Whose joys eternal flow.

I Would Not Live Alway

St. 1-4

William Augustus Mühlenberg, writ. 1824, pub. 1826

Frederick 11.11.11.11.

George Kingsley, 1838

1. I___ would not live al - way; I___ ask not to stay, Where storm aft - er storm___ ris - es dark o'er the way. The___ few lu - cid morn - ings that dawn on us here, Are e - nough for life's woes,___ full e - nough for its cheer.
2. I___ would not live al - way; no___ wel - come the tomb, Since Je - sus has lain there, I___ dread not its gloom; There,___ sweet be my rest, till he bid me a - rise To___ hail him in tri - umph de - scend - ing the skies.

3. Who, who would live alway, away from his God;
Away from yon heaven, that blissful abode,
Where the rivers of pleasure flow o'er the bright plains,
And the noontide of glory eternally reigns;

4. Where the saints of all ages in harmony meet,
Their Saviour and brethren transported to greet;
While the anthems of rapture unceasingly roll,
And the smile of the Lord is the feast of the soul.

LIKE NOAH'S WEARY DOVE S.M.

St. 1-5

William Augustus Mühlenberg, 1826 John Henry Hopkins, Jr., 1882

1. Like No - ah's wea - ry___ dove, That soared the earth a - round,
2. O cease, my wan - dering___ soul, On rest - less wing to___ roam;

But not a rest - ing place a - bove The cheer - less wa - ters found.
All the wide world to ei - ther pole, Has not for thee a home.

3. Behold the ark of God,
Behold the open door;
Hasten to gain that dear abode,
And rove, my soul, no more.

4. There, safe thou shalt abide,
There, sweet shall be thy rest,
And every longing satisfied,
With full salvation blest.

5. And, when the waves of ire
Again the earth shall fill,
The ark shall ride the sea of fire,
Then rest on Sion's hill.

Saviour, Who Thy Flock Art Feeding — Philadelphia 8.7.8.7.7.

St. 1-4

William Augustus Mühlenberg, 1826 — Benjamin Carr, 1828

Moderato
1. Saviour, who thy flock art feeding, With the shepherd's kindest care,
2. Now, these little ones receiving, Fold them in thy gracious arm;
Unison
All the feeble gently leading, While the lambs thy bosom share,
There, we know, thy word believing, Only there, secure from harm,
While the lambs thy bosom share.
Only there, secure from harm.

3. Never from thy pasture roving,
Let them be the lion's prey;
Let thy tenderness, so loving,
Keep them all life's dangerous way,
Keep them all life's dangerous way.

4. Then, within thy fold eternal,
Let them find a resting-place;
Feed in pastures ever vernal,
Drink the rivers of thy grace,
Drink the rivers of thy grace.

On Zion and on Lebanon — Quebec Chapel C.M.

St. 1-6

Henry Ustic Onderdonk, 1826 — John Paddon, 1828

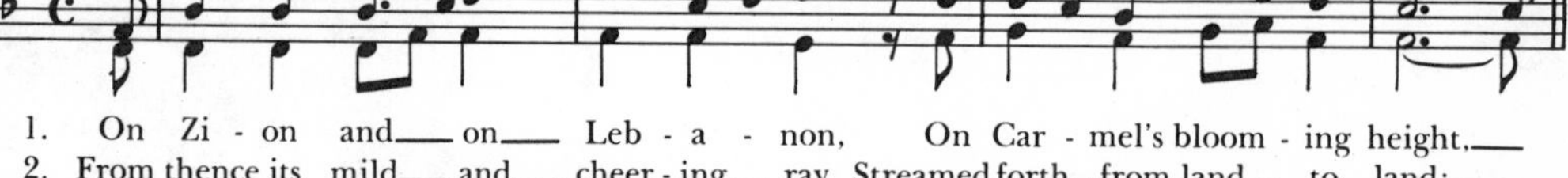
1. On Zi - on and— on— Leb - a - non, On Car - mel's bloom - ing height,—
2. From thence its mild— and— cheer - ing— ray Streamed forth— from land— to land;—

On Shar - on's— fer - tile plains, once—shone—The— glo - ry, pure and bright.—
And em - pires— now be - hold its— day;—And— still its beams ex - pand.—
On Shar - on's— fer - tile plains, once shone The glo-ry, pure and bright.—
And em - pires— now be - hold its day; And still its beams ex - pand.—

3. Its brightest splendors, darting west,
Our happy shores illume;
Our farther regions, once unblest,
Now like a garden bloom.

4. But ah! our deserts deep and wild
See not this heavenly light;
No sacred beams, no radiance mild,
Dispel their dreary night.

5. Thou, who didst lighten Zion's hill,
On Carmel who didst shine,
Our deserts let thy glory fill,
Thy excellence divine.

6. Like Lebanon, in towering pride,
May all our forests smile;
And may our borders blossom wide
Like Sharon's fruitful soil.

THE SPIRIT IN OUR HEARTS

St. 1-4

Henry Ustic Onderdonk, 1826

UTICA S.M.

Charles Zeuner, 1834

Andantino
1. The Spir - it in our hearts, Is whis - pering, sin - ner, come;
2. Let him that hear - eth say To all a - bout him, come.

The Bride, the Church of Christ, pro - claims To all his chil - dren, come.
Let him that thirsts for right - eous - ness To Christ, the foun - tain, come.

3. Yes, whosoever will,
O let him freely come,
And freely drink the stream of life;
'Tis Jesus bids him come.

4. Lo, Jesus, who invites,
Declares, I quickly come.
Lord! even so, I wait thy hour;
Jesus, my Saviour, come.

THOUGH I SHOULD SEEK — HARMONIA L.M.

St. 1-5

Henry Ustic Onderdonk, 1826 — Anthony Philip Heinrich, 1832

Majestic with spirit
1. Though I should seek to wash me clean In wa - ter of the driv - en snow, My soul would yet its spot re - tain, And sink in con - scious guilt and woe.
2. The Spir - it, in his power di - vine, Would cast my vaunt - ing soul to earth, Ex - pose the foul - ness of its sin, And show the vile - ness of its worth.
8va
8
8

3. Ah! not like erring man is God,
That men to answer him should dare;
Condemned, and into silence awed,
They helpless stand before his bar.

4. There, must a Mediator plead,
Who, God and man, may both embrace;
With God, for man to intercede,
And offer man the purchased grace.

5. And, lo! the Son of God is slain
To be this Mediator crowned;
In him, my soul, be cleansed from stain,
In him thy righteousness be found.

Where there are octaves, the basses always sing the upper notes.

The lower notes and the figurations in eighth notes are for the accompanying instrument.

ONCE MORE, O LORD

CALVARY C.M.D.

St. 1-3

George Washington Doane, writ. 1827

Christopher Meinecke, 1827

Slow and solemn
1. Once more, O Lord, thy sign shall be Up - on the heavens dis - played,
And earth and its in - hab - i - tants Be ter - ri - bly a - fraid.
2. The ter - rors of that aw - ful day, O who can un - der - stand?
Or who a - bide, when thou in wrath Shall lift thy ho - ly hand?
Duo
For not in weak - ness clad thou com'st, Our woes, our sins to bear,
The earth shall quake, the sea shall roar, The sun in heaven grow pale;
Tutti
But girt with all thy Fa - ther's might, His judg - ment to de - clare.
But thou hast sworn, and wilt not change, Thy faith - ful shall not fail.

3. Then grant us, Saviour, so to pass
Our time in trembling here,
That when upon the clouds of heaven
Thy glory shall appear,
Uplifting high our joyful heads,
In triumph we may rise,
And enter, with thine angel train,
Thy palace in the skies.

LORD! LEAD THE WAY THE SAVIOUR WENT — BRISTOL C.M.

St. 1-4

William Crosswell, writ. 1831, pub. 1860 — Edward Hodges, 1848

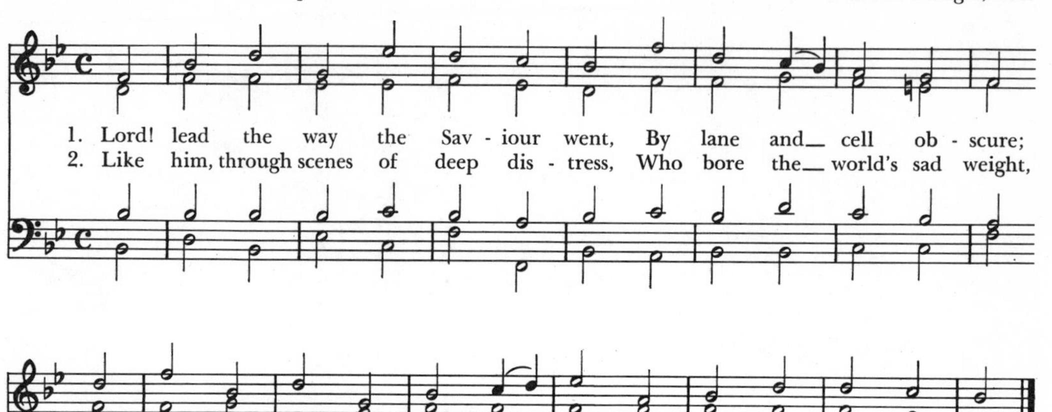
1. Lord! lead the way the Sav - iour went, By lane and— cell ob - scure;
2. Like him, through scenes of deep dis - tress, Who bore the— world's sad weight,

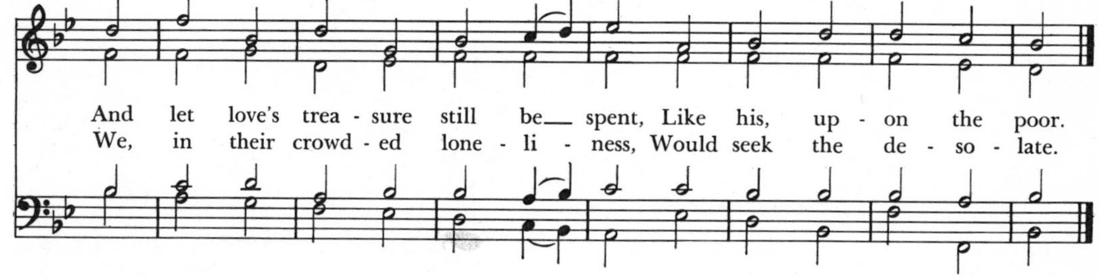
And let love's trea - sure still be— spent, Like his, up - on the poor.
We, in their crowd - ed lone - li - ness, Would seek the de - so - late.

3. For thou hast placed us side by side,
In this wide world of ill;
And, that thy followers may be tried,
The poor are with us still.

4. Mean are all offerings we can make;
Yet thou hast taught us, Lord!
If given for the Saviour's sake,
They lose not their reward.

Our Father in Heaven — Bazetta 6.5.6.5.D.

St. 1, 2

Sarah Josepha Hale, 1831 — Lowell Mason, 1845

Plaintive

1. Our Fa - ther in heav - en, We hal - low thy name! May thy king - dom
2. For - give our trans - gres - sions, And teach us to know That hum - ble com -

ho - ly On earth be the same! Oh, give to us dai - ly Our
pas - sion Which par - dons each foe. Keep us from temp - ta - tion, From

por - tion of bread; It is from thy boun - ty That all must be fed.
weak - ness and sin, And thine be the glo - ry For - ev - er, A - men.

Holy Father, Great Creator — Abercrombie 8.7.8.7.D.

St. 1-4

Alexander V. Griswold, 1835 — C. Hommann, 1844

1. Ho - ly Fa - ther, great cre - a - tor, Source of mer - cy, love, and peace,
2. Ho - ly Je - sus, Lord of glo - ry, Whom an - gel - ic hosts pro - claim,
Look up - on the Me - di - a - tor, Clothe us with his right - eous - ness;
While we hear thy won - drous sto - ry, Meet and wor - ship in thy Name,
p
Heaven - ly Fa - ther, Heaven - ly Fa - ther, Through the Sav - iour hear and bless;
Dear Re - deem - er, dear Re - deem - er, In our hearts thy peace pro - claim,
Organ
f
Heaven - ly Fa - ther, Heaven - ly Fa - ther, Through the Sav - iour hear and bless.
Dear Re - deem - er, dear Re - deem - er, In our hearts thy peace pro - claim.
f

3. Holy Spirit, Sanctifier,
Come with unction from above,
Raise our hearts to raptures higher,
Fill them with the Saviour's love!
Source of comfort, source of comfort,
Cheer us with the Saviour's love,
Source of comfort, source of comfort,
Cheer us with the Saviour's love.

4. God the Lord, through every nation
Let thy wondrous mercies shine!
In the song of thy salvation
Every tongue and race combine!
Great Jehovah, great Jehovah,
Form our hearts and make them thine,
Great Jehovah, great Jehovah,
Form our hearts and make them thine.

Jesus Spreads His Banner o'er Us — Rockwell 8.7.8.7.D.

St. 1, 2

Roswell Park, 1836 — Anon., 1845

Moderato
Fine
1. Je - sus spreads his ban - ner o'er us, Cheers our fam - ished souls with food;
He the ban - quet spreads be - fore us Of his mys - tic flesh and blood.
D. C. May we taste it, kind - ly giv - en, In re - mem-brance, Lord, of thee.
D.C. al Fine
dim.
cresc.
rit.
Pre - cious ban - quet, bread of heav - en; Wine of glad - ness, flow - ing free;

2. In thy holy incarnation,
When the angels sang thy birth;
In thy fasting and temptation;
In thy labors on the earth;
In thy trial and rejection;
In thy sufferings on the tree;
In thy glorious resurrection;
May we, Lord, remember thee.

Come unto Me, When Shadows Darkly Gather — Henley 11.10.11.10.

St. 1-3

Catharine H. Watterman, 1839 — Lowell Mason, 1854

1. Come un - to me, when shad - ows dark - ly gath - er, When the sad
2. Large are the man - sions in thy Fa - ther's dwell - ing, Glad are the
heart is wea - ry and dis - tressed, Seek - ing for com - fort
homes that sor - rows nev - er dim; Sweet are the harps in
from your heaven-ly Fa - ther, Come un - to me, and I will give you rest.
ho - ly mu - sic swell - ing, Soft are the tones which raise the heaven-ly hymn.

3. There, like an Eden blossoming in gladness,
Bloom the fair flowers the earth too rudely pressed;
Come unto me, all ye who droop in sadness,
Come unto me, and I will give you rest.

The Harvest Dawn Is Near | Leighton S.M.

St. 1, 2

George Burgess, 1839 | Henry Wellington Greatorex, 1849

1. The har - vest dawn is near, The year de - lays not long;
2. Sad to his toil he goes, His seed with weep - ing leaves;

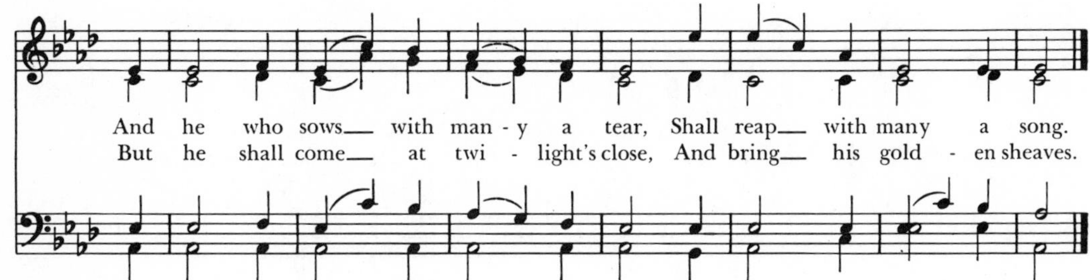
And he who sows— with man - y a tear, Shall reap— with many a song.
But he shall come— at twi - light's close, And bring— his gold - en sheaves.

WHILE O'ER THE DEEP THY SERVANTS SAIL — HARTFORD L.M.

St. 1-4

George Burgess, 1845 — Jonathan Mayhew Wainwright, 1830

1. While o'er the deep thy serv - ants sail,
2. If on the morn - ing's wings they fly,
Send thou, O Lord, the pros - perous gale;
They will not pass be - yond thine eye.
And on their hearts wher - e'er they go,
The wan - derer's prayer thou bendst to hear,
O let thy heaven - ly breez - es blow.
And faith ex - ults to know thee near.

3. When tempests rock the groaning bark,
O hide them safe in Jesus' ark;
When in the tempting port they ride,
O keep them safe at Jesus' side.

4. If life's wide ocean smile or roar,
Still guide them to the heavenly shore;
And grant their dust in Christ may sleep,
Abroad, at home, or in the deep.

Jesus, in Sickness and in Pain

Pitt C.M.

St. 1-4

Thomas H. Gallaudet, 1845

Anon., 1845

Supplicatory con affetto
1. Je - sus, in sick-ness and in pain, Be near to suc-cor me,
2. When cares and sor-rows thick - en round, And noth - ing bright I see,

To thee I turn, to thee.
pp
cresc.
dim.
My sink - ing spir - it still sus-tain; To thee I turn, to thee.
In thee a - lone can help be found; To thee I turn, to thee.

3. Should strong temptations fierce assail,
As if to ruin me,
Then in thy strength will I prevail,
While still I turn to thee.

4. Through all my pilgrimage below,
What e'er my lot may be,
In joy or sadness, weal or woe,
Jesus, I'll turn to thee.

God of Our Fathers, Whose Almighty Hand — National Hymn 10.10.10.10

St. 1-4

Daniel C. Roberts, writ. 1876, pub. 1892 — George W. Warren, 1892

Voices Alone
ff
ff
Trumpets, before each verse.
1. God of our fa - thers, whose al - might - y hand
2. Thy love di - vine hath led us in the past,
With Organ
cresc.
Leads forth in beau - ty all the star - ry band
In this free land by thee our lot is cast;
Of shin - ing worlds in
Be thou our rul - er,
ff
splen - dor through the skies,
guard - ian, guide, and stay,
Our grate - ful songs be - fore thy throne a - rise.
Thy word our law, thy paths our cho - sen way.

3. From war's alarms, from deadly pestilence,
Be thy strong arm our ever sure defense;
Thy true religion in our hearts increase,
Thy bounteous goodness nourish us in peace.

4. Refresh thy people on their toilsome way,
Lead us from night to never-ending day;
Fill all our lives with love and grace divine,
And glory, laud, and praise be ever thine.

Alleluia! Christ Is Risen Today — 9.11.9.11. D., with chorus

St. 1-5

John Henry Hopkins Jr., 1863 — John Henry Hopkins Jr., 1863

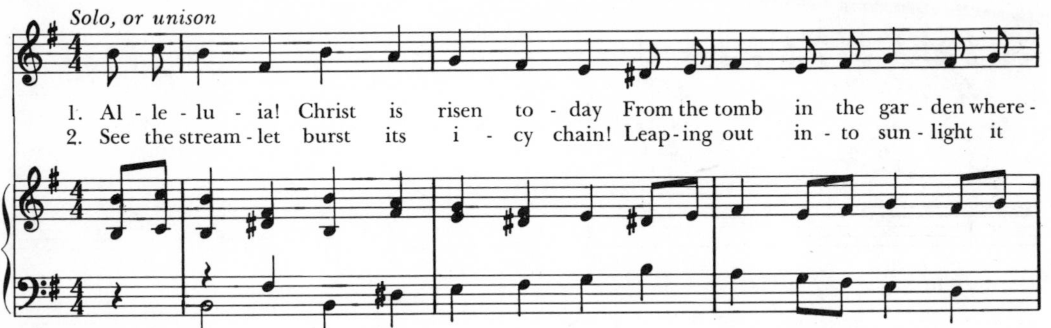
Solo, or unison
1. Al - le - lu - ia! Christ is risen to - day From the tomb in the gar - den where -
2. See the stream - let burst its i - cy chain! Leap - ing out in - to sun - light it

in he lay; Shin - ing an - gels raise their shout on high, And on
seeks the plain, And its joy in li - quid tones it tells To the

Chorus
earth we ex - ult - ing - ly make re - ply:
rocks and the woods and the wind - ing dells:
Al - le - lu - ia, Al - le -
Al - le - lu - ia, Al - le -

Solo, or Unison
lu - ia, Al - le - lu - ia, A - men.
Na - ture too, that, through long
Gi - ant pines, whose broad, up
lu - ia, Al - le - lu - ia, A - men.

drear - y gloom, Lay em - balmed in the shroud of her win - try tomb, Ris - es
reach - ing arms Bore the frosts and the snows of the north - ern storms, To the

now to meet her ris - ing Lord, And in my - ri - ad e - cho re -
balm - y breez - es blow - ing now Give a mur - mur - ing whis - per on

Chorus
peats the word:
ev - 'ry bough:
Al - le - lu - ia, Al - le - lu - ia, Al - le - lu - ia, A - men.
Al - le - lu - ia, Al - le - lu - ia, Al - le - lu - ia, A - men.

3. Little birds, that flew so far away,
Now return with a sweet, merry roundelay;
Through the shady grove, in soft refrain,
Lo, the voice of the turtle is heard again:
Chorus
In the old church-tower the swallows build,
And their nests with the tenderest young are filled;
And they join the chaunting when they hear
Both the organ and choir swelling loud and clear:
Chorus

4. Now the primrose greets the daffodil,
And the daisy is winking on every hill,
And the pansy drinks the light of day,
And the breath of the violet seems to say:
Chorus

(4) Now the Rose of Sharon opens wide,
On the sunshiny banks of the mountain side;
And the lily of the valley blooms,
Filling every vale with its rich perfumes:
Chorus

5. While the fields are clothed in beauty rare,
Shall the altar of Jesus be cold and bare!
Shall the church no loving token show
That the Risen above is to rise below!
Chorus
Round the altar let bright flowers be seen,
With the fresh-budding branches of evergreen;
Let the earth, with us, her incense bring,
And the trees of the forest rejoice and sing:
Chorus

FATHER, WHO MAK'ST THY SUFF'RING SONS — HOSPITAL SUNDAY HYMN 8.8.8.D.

St. 1-4

Arthur C. Coxe, writ. 1883 — George W. Warren, comp. 1883, pub. 1888

Andante con espressione
mp
1. Fa - ther, who mak'st thy suf - f'ring sons thy min - is - ters to strong - er ones, To light love's ho - ly flame with - in, De - pos - ing self, a - bas - ing sin, Oh, teach my soul, con - fid - ing still, To suf - fer or to do thy will.
2. If in this world of mys - ter - y, Un - e - qual fa - vors fall on me, While broth - ers, bet - ter far than I, Are called to lan - guish or to die, Help me in turn their ills to share, Their wounds to heal, their load to bear.
poco rit.

3. Blest is their task, 'mid human woe
Thy gifts on others who bestow;
For suffering lies at plenty's door,
And God appeals when cries the poor.
His law ordains, for all that live,
What sorrow lacks let mercy give.

4. The day shall come when veils remove,
And all shall see that God is love.
Then he himself all tears shall dry,
And show of pain the reason why,
And theirs shall be the great reward
Who in his poor beheld their Lord.

ANCIENT OF DAYS, WHO SITTEST THRONED IN GLORY — ANCIENT OF DAYS 11.10.11.10.

St. 1-5

William Croswell Doane, writ. 1886, pub. 1892 — J. Albert Jeffery, comp. 1886, pub. 1892

With marked rhythm *Voices*

1. An - cient of Days, who sit - test throned in glo - ry,
2. O Ho - ly Fa - ther, who hast led thy chil - dren

Introduction 1st stanza

Accomp.

To thee all knees are bent, all voic - es pray; Thy love has blest the
In all the a - ges, with the fire and cloud, Through seas dry - shod, through

wide world's won - drous sto - ry With light and life since E - den's dawn - ing day.
wea - ry wastes be - wild - 'ring; To thee, in rev - erent love, our hearts are bowed.

3. O Holy Jesus, Prince of Peace and Saviour,
To thee we owe the peace that still prevails,
Stilling the rude wills of men's wild behavior,
And calming passion's fierce and stormy gales.

4. O Holy Ghost, the Lord and the Life Giver,
Thine is the quickening power that gives increase;
From thee have flowed, as from a pleasant river,
Our plenty, wealth, prosperity, and peace.

5. O Triune God, with heart and voice adoring,
Praise we the goodness that doth crown our days;
Pray we that thou wilt hear us, still imploring
Thy love and favor, kept to us always.

O KING OF SAINTS, WE GIVE THEE PRAISE AND GLORY — WITNESSES 11.10.11.10.

St. 1-5

Mary A. Thomson, 1892 — William H. Walter, comp. 1889, pub. 1892

1. O King of saints, we give thee praise and glo - ry
2. And for thy hid - den saints, our praise a - dor - ing,
For the bright cloud of wit - ness - es un - seen,
Fount of all sanc - ti - ty, to thee we yield,
Whose names shine forth like stars, in sa - cred sto - ry,
Who in thy treas - ure - house on high art stor - ing
Guid - ing our steps to realms of light se - rene.
Jew - els whose lus - ter was, on earth, con - cealed.

3. Thine arm sustained them all in conflict mortal
With sin, the world, and all the powers of hell;
Thy hand hath opened for all, the shining portal
To realms where peace and joy forever dwell.

4. There are the throned and white-robed elders casting
Before the King of kings their crowns of gold;
And there are crowns and mansions everlasting,
And palms and harps for multitudes untold.

5. Though, in thy service, we too oft have slumbered,
Like the ten virgins, foolish ones and wise;
Yet with thy saints, may we at last be numbered,
And at thy call with burning lamps arise.

HAIL THE GLORIOUS GOLDEN CITY 8.7.8.7.
St. 1-3

Felix Adler, writ. 1878 Jacob Weinberg, 1932

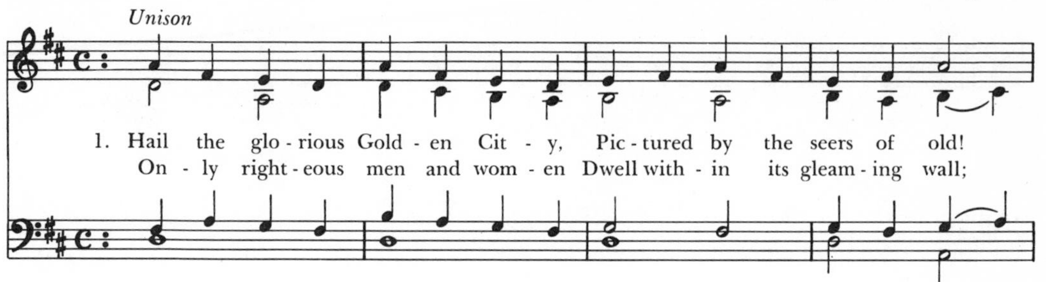
Unison
1. Hail the glo - rious Gold - en Cit - y, Pic - tured by the seers of old!
On - ly right - eous men and wom - en Dwell with - in its gleam - ing wall;

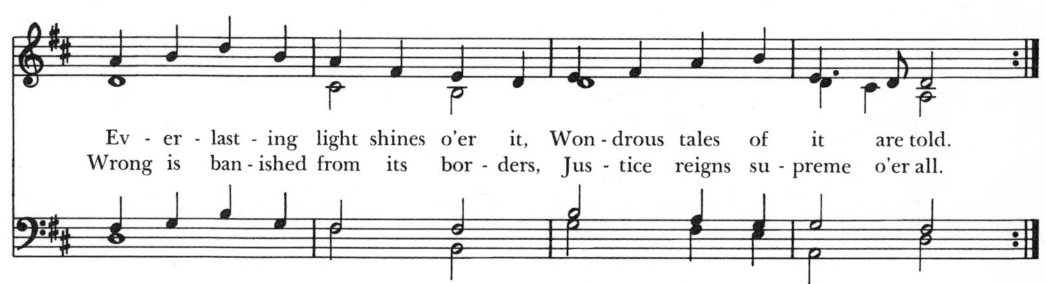
Ev - er - last - ing light shines o'er it, Won - drous tales of it are told.
Wrong is ban - ished from its bor - ders, Jus - tice reigns su - preme o'er all.

2. We are builders of that city;
All our joys and all our groans
Help to rear its shining ramparts;
All our lives are building stones.
Whether humble or exalted,
All are called to task divine;
All must aid alike to carry
Forward one sublime design.

3. And the work that we have builded,
Oft with bleeding hands and tears,
Oft in error, oft in anguish,
Will not perish with our years.
It will live and shine transfigured
In the final reign of right;
It will pass into the splendors
Of the City of the Light.

JESUS, I LIVE TO THEE — LAKE ENON S.M.

St. 1-4

Henry Harbaugh, writ. c. 1860, pub. 1861 — Isaac B. Woodbury, 1854

1. Je - sus, I live to thee, The love - li - est and best;
2. Je - sus, I die to thee, When - ev - er death shall come;

My life in thee, Thy life in me, In thy blest love I rest.
To die in thee is life to me In my e - ter - nal home.

3. Whether to live or die,
I know not which is best;
To live in thee is bliss to me,
To die is endless rest.

4. Living or dying, Lord,
I ask but to be thine;
My life in thee, Thy life in me,
Makes heaven forever mine.

Salve Jesu Pastor Bone
Wide Open Are Thy Hands
St. 1-3
Bernard of Clairvaux
Charles P. Krauth, trans. 1870

Salve Jesu S.M.D.
Harold Lewars, comp. 1914, pub. 1917

1. Wide o - pen are Thy hands, Pay - ing with more than gold
2. Wide o - pen are Thine arms, A fall - en world to em - brace;
The aw - ful debt of guilt - y men, For - ev - er and of old.
To take to love and end - less rest Our whole for - sak - en race.
Ah, let me grasp those hands, That we may nev - er part,
Lord, I am sad and poor, But bound - less is Thy grace;
And let the pow - er of their blood Sus - tain my faint - ing heart.
Give me the soul - trans - form - ing joy For which I seek Thy face.

3. Draw all my mind and heart
Up to Thy throne on high,
And let Thy sacred Cross exalt
My spirit to the sky.

To these, Thy mighty hands,
My spirit I resign;
Living, I live alone to Thee,
Dying, alone am Thine.

HERALDS OF CHRIST

St. 1-4

Laura S. Copenhaver, 1894

PRO PATRIA 10.10.10.10.

Horatio Parker, 1914

1. Her - alds of Christ, who bear the King's com - mands,
2. Through des - ert ways, dark fen, and deep mo - rass,
Im - mor - tal ti - dings in your mor - tal hands, Pass
Through jun - gles, slug - gish seas, and moun - tain pass, Build
on and car - ry swift the news ye bring:
ye the road, and fal - ter not, nor stay;
Make straight, make straight the high - way of the King.
Pre - pare a - cross the earth the King's high - way.

3. Where once the crooked trail in darkness wound
Let marching feet and joyous song resound,
Where burn the funeral pyres, and censers swing,
Make straight, make straight the highway of the King.

4. Lord, give us faith and strength the road to build,
To see the promise of the day fulfilled,
When war shall be no more and strife shall cease
Upon the highway of the Prince of Peace.

Ein von Gott Geborner Christ

Every Christian Born of God

St. 1-5

Anon., 1829

Christe Wahres Seelenlicht 7.6.7.6.D.

Johann Anastasius Freylinghausen, arr. 1704

1. Ev - ery Chris - tian born of God Must the love em - bod - y
That from God the Fa - ther flows True to him re - main - ing.
If he God in truth does love, Could he then find hate - ful
What the Fa - ther calls his own? He could not, you an - swer.

2. When a child of holy God
Looks upon a people
Who in truth God's children are,
Then will grow and flourish
In the new-created mind
Sweet and pure devotion.
He to them inclines his mind
With the purest feelings.

3. When God crowns with holy grace
One of his disciples,
Others too will find a share
For their own remaining.
Everyone must be prepared
Help to all to offer,
Only peace and unity
Flourishes among them.

4. Lord pour down thy holy balm
On the earth below thee;
One in heart and one in soul
Make thy chosen people.
Conquer ill-will, scorn, and pride,
Which our joy may stifle;
Let us hear no sound of strife
In our band of brothers.

1. Ein von Gott geborner Christ
Wird auch herzlich lieben,
Was von Gott gezeuget ist,
Und ihn treu verblieben.
Wer den Vater liebt und ehrt,
Sollte der wohl hassen
Was den Vater angehört?
Das wird er wohl lassen.

To Show How Humble — Mear C.M.

St. 1-4

Anon., 1877 — Anon., 1720

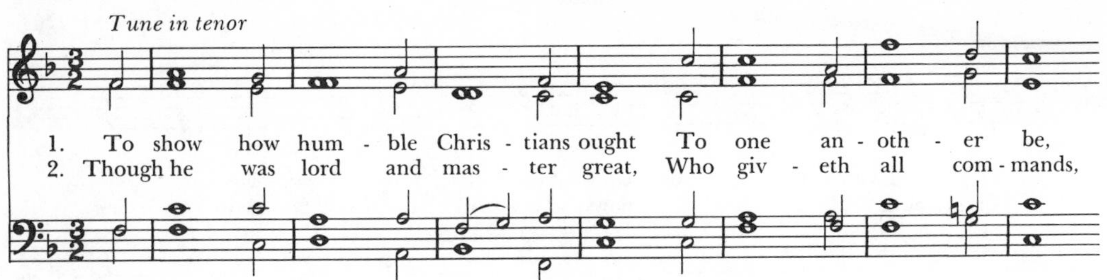
Tune in tenor
1. To show how hum - ble Chris - tians ought To one an - oth - er be,
2. Though he was lord and mas - ter great, Who giv - eth all com - mands,

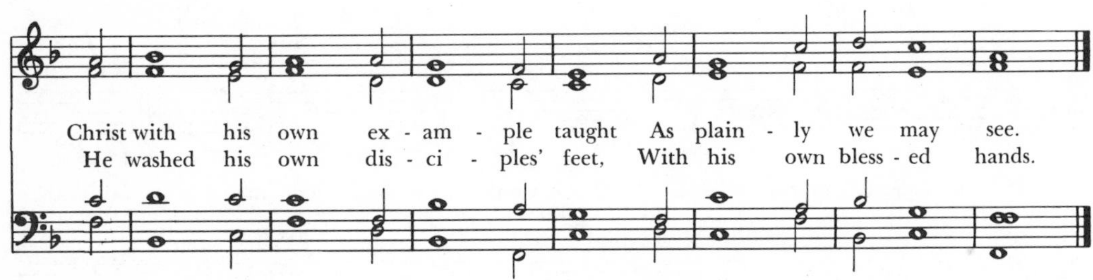
Christ with his own ex - am - ple taught As plain - ly we may see.
He washed his own dis - ci - ples' feet, With his own bless - ed hands.

3. When thus their master with them dealt,
And proved his love to them,
How must their drooping hearts have felt
To meet with such esteem.

4. May they who worldly honor seek
Learn what it is to be
Like Jesus, humble, truly meek,
From self-applauses free.

"To show how humble. . ."

YOU THAT HAVE BEEN OFTEN INVITED

OSCEOLA 11.11.11.11.

Anon., 1845

Thomas Commuck, melody 1845, Thomas Hastings, arr. 1845

You that have been of - ten in - vit - ed to come To heav - en's great sup - per, while yet there is room; The voice of the Sav - iour now hear and o - bey; O bow to his scep - ter while it's called to - day.

COME, LET US TUNE OUR LOFTIEST SONG — WHITEFIELD L.M.

St. 1-4

Robert A. West, 1849 — R. N., 1849

1. Come,— let us tune our loft - iest— song, And raise to—Christ our— joy - ful strain;
2. His— sov-ereign power our bod - ies—make; Our souls are— his im - mor - tal breath;
Wor - ship and thanks to him be - long, Who— reigns, and shall— for - ev - er reign.
And when his crea - tures sinned, he— bled, To— save us from— e - ter - nal death.

3. Burn every breast with Jesus' love;
Bound every heart with rapturous joy;
And saints on earth, with saints above,
Your voices in his praise employ.

4. Extol the Lamb with loftiest song,
Ascend for him our cheerful strain;
Worship and thanks to him belong,
Who reigns, and shall forever reign.

The Lord Our God Alone Is Strong — Camp L.M.

St. 1-5

Caleb T. Winchester, writ. 1871 — Peter C. Lutkin, 1905

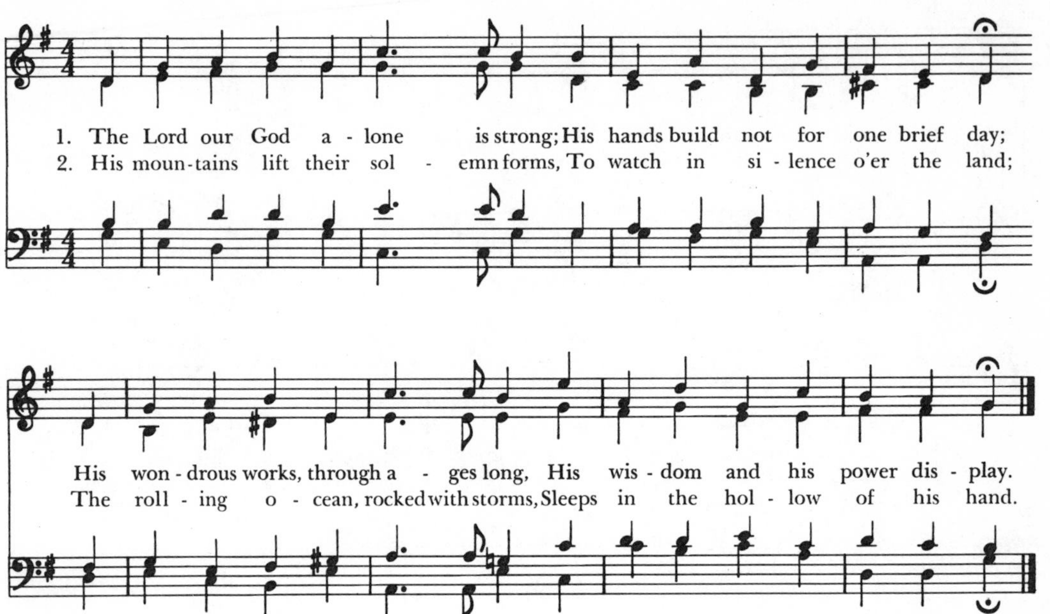
1. The Lord our God a - lone is strong; His hands build not for one brief day;
2. His moun-tains lift their sol - emn forms, To watch in si - lence o'er the land;
His won - drous works, through a - ges long, His wis - dom and his power dis - play.
The roll - ing o - cean, rocked with storms, Sleeps in the hol - low of his hand.

3. Beyond the heavens he sits alone,
The universe obeys his nod;
The lightning-rifts disclose his throne,
And thunders voice the name of God.

4. Thou sovereign God, receive this gift
Thy willing servants offer thee;
Accept the prayers that thousands lift,
And let these halls thy temple be.

5. And let those learn, who here shall meet,
True wisdom is with reverence crowned,
And science walks with humble feet
To seek the God that faith hath found.

I SHALL NOT WANT: IN DESERTS WILD

LOWRY L.M.

St. 1-4

Charles F. Deems, writ. 1872, pub. 1874

Anon., 1849

Moderato
1. I shall not want: in des - erts wild Thou spreadst thy ta - ble for thy child; While grace in streams for thirst - ing souls, Through earth and heaven for - ev - er rolls.
2. I shall not want: my dark - est night Thy lov - ing smile shall fill with light; While prom - is - es a - round me bloom, And cheer me with di - vine per - fume.
T.S.

3. I shall not want: thy righteousness
My soul shall clothe with glorious dress;
My blood-washed robe shall be more fair
Than garments kings or angels wear.

4. I shall not want: whate'er is good
Of daily bread or angel's food,
Shall to my Father's child be sure,
So long as earth and heaven endure.

Break Thou the Bread of Life | Bread of Life 6.4.6.4.D.

St. 1-2

Mary Artemisia Lathbury, writ. 1877 | William Fiske Sherwin, comp. 1877

1. Break thou the bread of life, Dear Lord, to me,
2. Bless thou the truth, dear Lord To me, to me,
As thou didst break the loaves Be - side the sea;
As thou didst bless the bread By Gal - i - lee;
Be - yond the sa - cred page I seek thee, Lord;
Then shall all bond - age cease, All fet - ters fall;
My spir - it pants for thee, O liv - ing Word!
And I shall find my peace, My All - in - All.

Day Is Dying in the West
St. 1, 2
Mary Artemisia Lathbury, writ. 1877

Chautauqua 7.7.7.7.4., with chorus
William Fiske Sherwin, comp. 1877

1. Day is dy - ing in the west; Heaven is touch - ing earth with rest;
2. Lord of life, be - neath the dome Of the u - ni - verse, thy home,

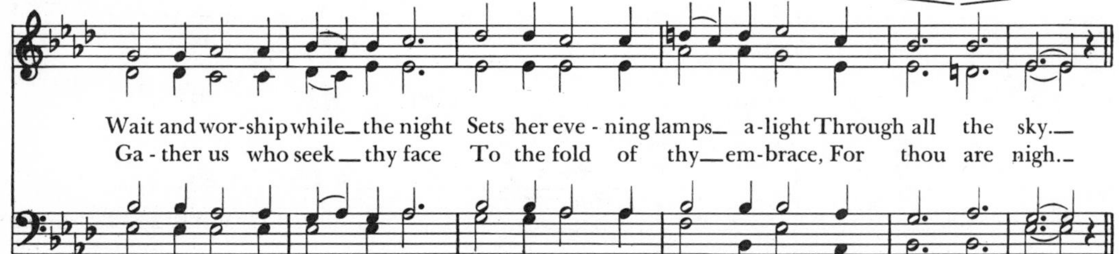
Wait and wor-ship while the night Sets her eve - ning lamps a-light Through all the sky.
Ga - ther us who seek thy face To the fold of thy em-brace, For thou are nigh.

Chorus
p
Ho - ly, ho - ly, ho - ly Lord God of Hosts! Heaven and earth are

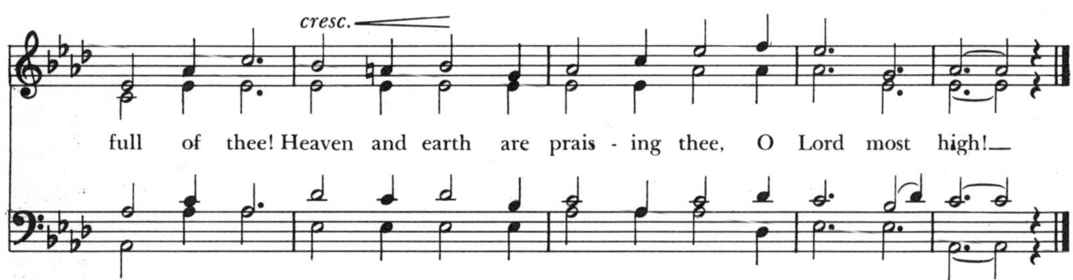
cresc.
full of thee! Heaven and earth are prais - ing thee, O Lord most high!

I Worship Thee, O Holy Ghost — Cooling C.M.

St. 1-4

William F. Warren, writ. 1877, pub. 1878 — Alonzo J. Abbey, 1858

1. I___ wor - ship thee, O Ho - ly Ghost, I___ love to wor - ship thee;___
2. I___ wor - ship thee, O Ho - ly Ghost, I___ love to wor - ship thee;___

My___ ris - en Lord for aye were lost But___ for thy com - pa - ny.
I___ grieved thee long, a - las! thou know'st It___ grieves me bit - ter - ly.

3. I worship thee, O Holy Ghost,
I love to worship thee;
Thy patient love, at what a cost
At last it conquered me!

4. I worship thee, O Holy Ghost,
I love to worship thee;
With thee each day is Pentecost,
Each night Nativity.

THE CHOSEN THREE, ON MOUNTAIN HEIGHT — TAMAR C.M.

St. 1-4

David H. Ela, 1878 — Isaac B. Woodbury, 1850

1. The chos - en three, on moun - tain height, While
2. And lo! with the trans - fig - ured Lord, Lead -

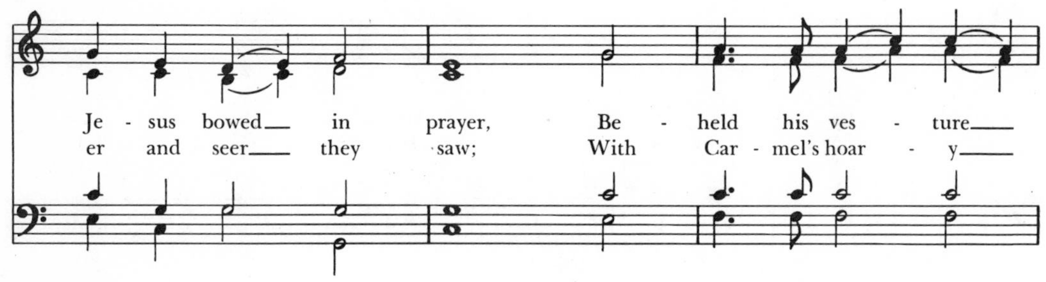
Je - sus bowed in prayer, Be - held his ves - ture
er and seer they saw; With Car - mel's hoar - y

glow with light, His face shine won - drous fair.
proph - et stood The giv - er of the law.

3. From the low-bending cloud above,
Whence radiant brightness shone,
Spake out the Father's voice of love,
"Hear my beloved Son!"

4. Lord, lead us to the mountain height,
To prayer's transfiguring glow;
And clothe us with the Spirit's might
For grander work below.

Defend Us, Lord, from Every Ill — Joshua L.M.

St. 1-3

John Hay, writ. 1896 — Peter C. Lutkin, 1905

Unison
1. De - fend us, Lord, from ev - ery ill; Strength - en our hearts to do thy — will;
2. O let us hear the in - spir - ing word Which they of old at Ho - reb — heard;
In all we plan and all we — do, Still keep us to thy — serv - ice true.
Breathe to our hearts the high com - mand, "Go on - ward and pos - sess the land!"

3. Thou who are light, shine on each soul!
Thou who are truth, each mind control!
Open our eyes and make us see
The path which leads to heaven and thee!

Arise, Ye Saints of Latter Days — Meribah 8.8.6.8.8.6.

St. 1-5

Anon., 1845 — Lowell Mason, 1839

Moderato

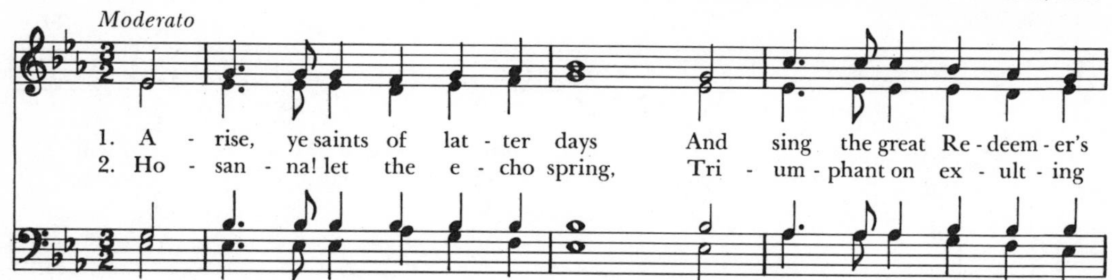
1. A - rise, ye saints of lat - ter days And sing the great Re - deem - er's
2. Ho - san - na! let the e - cho spring, Tri - um - phant on ex - ult - ing

praise, With joy - ful hearts a - rise.
wing, A - bove the powers of hell;

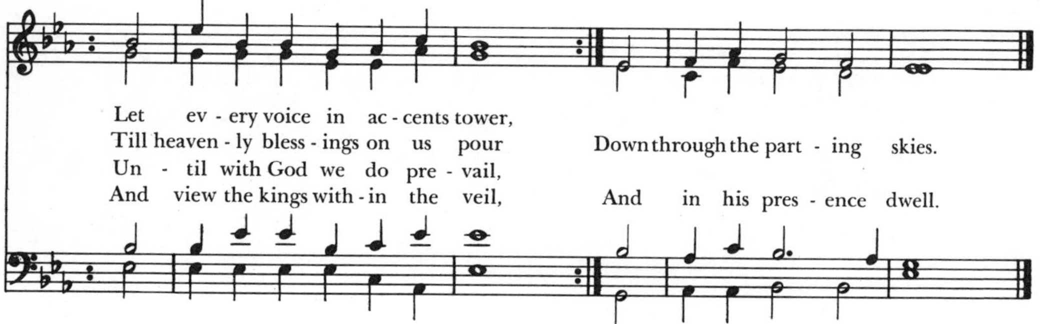
Let ev - ery voice in ac - cents tower,
Till heaven - ly bless - ings on us pour Down through the part - ing skies.
Un - til with God we do pre - vail,
And view the kings with - in the veil, And in his pres - ence dwell.

3. Hosanna, let the angels say
Who dwell in realms of endless day
With Enoch's perfect band;
Amen, amen, let earth resound,
And all the saints where'er they're found
Repair to Zion's hill.

4. Go forth, ye hirelings of our God
Proclaim his gospel far abroad
In every foreign clime.
Go, visit lands and isles unknown
In every realm, in every zone,
Till time with you shall end.

5. Then rise and join the hallowed throng
Who sing the everlasting song
In an eternal strain:
O! "Holy, holy, King of kings,
Who wast and art" — while heaven rings
And seraphs shout, Amen!

Arise, O Glorious Zion
St. 1-4
William G. Mills, 1851

Arise, O Glorious Zion 7.6.7.6.D.
George Careless, 1889

Brightly
1. A - rise, O glo - rious Zi - on, Thou joy of lat - ter days, Whom
2. Let faith - ful saints be rear - ing The cit - y of our Lord, On
count - less Saints re - ly on To gain a rest - ing place. A -
moun - tain tops ap - pear - ing, Ac - cord - ing to his word. A
rise and shine in splen - dor A - mid the world's deep night, For
sought - out hab - i - ta - tion By men of truth and faith, A
God, thy sure de - fend er, Is now thy life and light
con - vert of sal - va - tion From ig no - rance and death.

3. The temple long expected
Shall stand on Zion's hill,
By willing hearts erected,
Who love Jehovah's will.
Let earth her wealth bestowing,
Adorn his holy seat,
For nations great shall flow in
To worship at his feet.

4. What though the world in malice
Despise these mighty things,
We'll build the royal palace
To serve the King of kings,
Where holy men annointed
To know his sovereign will,
Each ordinance appointed
To save us, will reveal.

THINK NOT WHEN YOU GATHER TO ZION 9.8.9.8.D.

St. 1-4

Eliza R. Snow, 1856 John Tullidge, 1857

Brightly
1. Think not when you gath - er to Zi - on, Your trou - bles and tri - als are through, That
2. Think not when you gath - er to Zi - on, That all will be ho - ly and pure; That
noth - ing but com - fort and pleas - ure Are wait - ing in Zi - on for you. No,
fraud and de - cep - tion are ban - ished, And con - fi - dence whol - ly se - cure. No,
no, 'tis de - signed as a fur - nace, All sub - stance, all tex - tures to try, To
no, for the Lord our Re - deem - er Has said that the tares with the wheat Must
burn all the "wood, hay, and stub - ble," The gold from the dross pur - i - fy.
grow till the great day of burn - ing Shall ren - der the har - vest com - plete.

3. Think not when you gather to Zion,
The saints here have nothing to do
But to look to your personal welfare,
And always be comforting you.
No, those who are faithful are doing
What they find to do with their might;
To gather the scattered of Israel
They labor by day and by night.

4. Think not when you gather to Zion,
The prize and the victory won.
Think not that the warfare is ended,
The work of salvation is done.
No, no, for the great prince of darkness
A tenfold exertion will make,
When he sees you go to the fountain,
Where freely the truth you may take.

Waked by the Gospel's Powerful Sound — Ganges 8.8.6.8.8.6.

St. 1, 3, 6-8

Samson Occom, 1801 — S. Chandler, 1798

Tune in tenor Moderato
1. Waked by the gos - pel's power - ful sound, My soul in sin and thrall I found Ex - posed to dread - ful woe;
2. I to the law then ran for help, But still I felt the weight of guilt, And no re - lief I found;
E - ter - nal truth did loud pro - claim The sin - ner must be born a - gain Or down to ru - in go. go.
While sin my bur - dened soul did pain, The sin - ner must be born a - gain, As loud as thun - der sound. sound.
1.
2.

3. But as my soul with dying breath,
Lay gasping near eternal death,
Christ Jesus I did see;
Free grace and pardon he proclaimed,
I trust I then was born again
In gospel liberty.

4. Not angels in the world above,
Nor saints could glow with greater love
Than what my soul enjoyed
My soul did mount on faith her wings,
And glory, glory did I sing
To Jesus, my dear Lord.

5. Now with the saints I'll join to tell
How Jesus saved my soul from hell,
And sing redeeming love;
Ascribe the glory to the Lamb,
The sinner now is born again,
To dwell with Christ above.

Blest Is the Man Whose Tender Breast — New Jersey L.M.

Ps. 41: 1-4

Abijah Davis, 1813 — Ishmael Spicer, 1788

Tune in tenor
1. Blest is the man whose tender breast, Has for the suf-fering mourn-er felt, And while his hand re - lieves th'op-pressed, He feels his soul with pit - y melt.
2. His heart con-trives for their re - lief, More good than thou-sands could per-form, This man in times of gen-eral grief, Shall find a shel - ter from the storm.

3. The Lord shall keep his soul alive,
Long shall he live, the blest of earth,
And like a plant celestial thrive,
Amid the pestilence and dearth.

4. When sick, the Lord shall stir his bed,
And make the hard affliction soft,
Shall raise and cheer his drooping head,
Or bear his willing soul aloft.

Blessed Comforter Divine — **Loudon** 6.6.8.6.6.

St. 1-4

Lydia Sigourney, 1824 — Timothy Olmstead, 1805

Tune in tenor
1. Blessed Com - fort - er Di - vine! Whose rays of heaven - ly
2. Thou! who with "still small voice," Does stop the sin - ner's

love A - mid our gloom and dark - ness shine, And
way, And bid the mourn - ing saint re - joice, Though

point our souls a - bove, And point our souls a - bove;
earth - ly joys de - cay; Though earth - ly joys de - cay.
And point our souls a - bove;
Though earth - ly joy de cay.

3. Thou! whose inspiring breath
Can make the cloud of care,
And e'en the gloomy vale of death,
A smile of glory wear;
A smile of glory wear.

4. Thou! who dost fill the heart
With love to all our race,
Blest Comforter! to us impart
The blessings of thy grace,
The blessings of thy grace.

Jesus, I Come to Thee — Luther 6.6.8.6.6.

St. 1-6

Nathan S. S. Beman, 1832 — Thomas Hastings, 1836

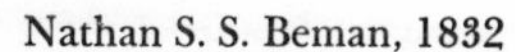

Vigoroso
1. Je - sus, I come to thee, A sin - ner doomed to die;
2. Can mer - cy reach my case, And all my sins re - move?

dim.
My on - ly ref - uge is thy cross, Here
Break, O my God, this heart of stone, And

f
at thy feet I lie, Here at thy feet I lie.
melt it by thy love, And melt it by thy love.

3. Too long my soul has gone
Far from my God astray;
I've sported on the brink of hell,
In sin's delusive way,
In sin's delusive way.

4. But, Lord, my heart is fixed,
I hope in thee alone;
Break off the chains of sin and death,
And bind me to thy throne,
And bind me to thy throne.

5. Thy blood can cleanse my heart,
Thy hand can wipe my tears;
Oh, send thy blessēd Spirit down
To banish all my fears,
To banish all my fears.

6. Then shall my soul arise,
From sin and Satan free;
Redeemed from hell and every foe,
I'll trust alone in thee,
I'll trust alone in thee.

O Sing to Me of Heaven — No Sorrow There S.M., with chorus

St. 1-4

Mary Stanley Bunce Dana, 1840 — William Batchelder Bradbury, 1860

1. Oh, sing to me of heaven, When I am called to die,
2. When cold and slug - gish drops Roll off my mar - ble brow;
Sing songs of ho - ly ec - sta - sy, To waft my soul on high.
Break forth in songs of joy - ful - ness, Let heaven be - gin be - low.
Chorus
There'll be no sor - row there, There'll be no sor - row there,
In a - bove, where all is love, There'll be no sor row there.

3. When the last moment comes,
Oh, watch my dying face;
To catch the bright, seraphic gleam,
Which o'er my features plays.
Chorus

4. Then to my raptured soul,
Let one sweet song be given,
Let music cheer me last on earth,
And greet me first in heaven.
Chorus

Day of God! Thou Blessēd Day — Berlin 7.7.7.7.

St. 1-4

Hannah Flagg Gould, 1841

Josiah Osgood, 1867

1. Day— of— God! thou bless - ēd— day,— At— thy— dawn— the— grave gave way
2. Thine— the— ra - diance to— il - lume— First,— for— man,— the— dis - mal tomb,

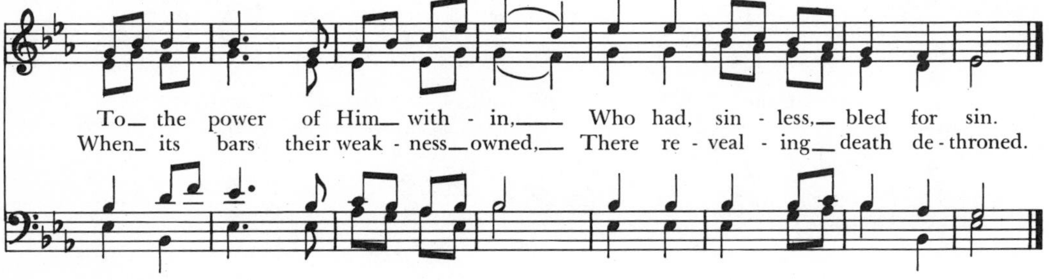
To— the power of Him— with - in,— Who had, sin - less,— bled for sin.
When— its bars their weak - ness—owned,— There re - veal - ing—death de - throned.

3. Then the Sun of righteousness
Rose, a darkened world to bless,
Bringing up from moral night
Immortality and light.

4. Day of glory, day of power,
Sacred be thine every hour,
Emblem, earnest, of the rest
That remaineth for the blest.

Complete in Thee, No Work of Mine — Ware L.M.

St. 1-5

Aaron R. Wolfe, 1850/1851 — George Kingsley, 1838

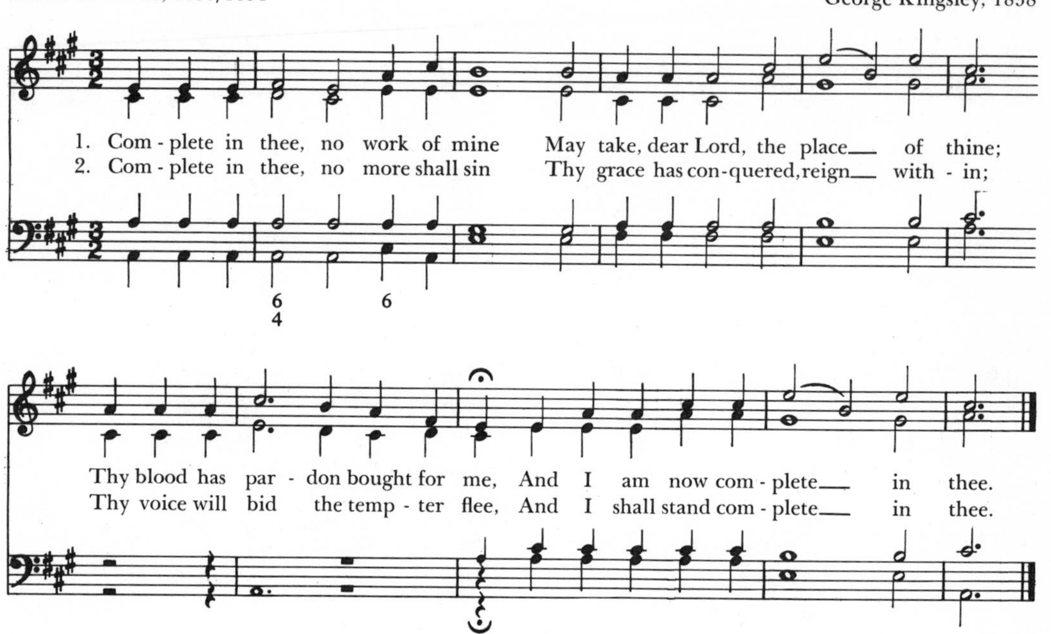
1. Com - plete in thee, no work of mine May take, dear Lord, the place— of thine;
2. Com - plete in thee, no more shall sin Thy grace has con-quered, reign— with - in;
6
4
6
Thy blood has par - don bought for me, And I am now com - plete— in thee.
Thy voice will bid the temp - ter flee, And I shall stand com - plete— in thee.

3. Complete in thee, each want supplied,
And no good thing to me denied,
Since thou my portion, Lord, wilt be,
I ask no more, complete in thee.

4. Dear Saviour, when before thy bar
All tribes and tongues assembled are,
Among thy chosen may I be
At that right hand, complete in thee.

5. Complete in thee, forever blest,
Of all thy fullness, Lord, possessed,
Thy praise throughout eternity,
Thy love I'll sing, complete in thee.

NOW FROM LABOR AND FROM CARE

TOPLADY 7.7.7.D.

St. 1-3

Thomas Hastings, 1850

Thomas Hastings, comp. 1830, pub. 1832

Fine
1. Now from la - bor and from care Eve - ning hours have set me free,
D. C. O be - hold me from a - bove, Fill me with a Sav-iour's love.

D. C. al Fine
In the work of praise and prayer, Lord, I would con-verse with thee,

2. Sin and sorrow, guilt and woe
Wither all my earthly joys;
Nought can charm me here below,
But my Saviour's melting voice,
Lord, forgive, thy grace restore,
Make me thine for evermore.

3. For the blessings of this day,
For the mercies of this hour,
For the gospel's cheering ray,
For the Spirit's quickening power,
Grateful notes to thee I raise,
O accept the song of praise.

We Would See Jesus — Kermode 11.10.11.10.

St. 1-4

Anna B. Warner, 1852 — Luther O. Emerson, 1872

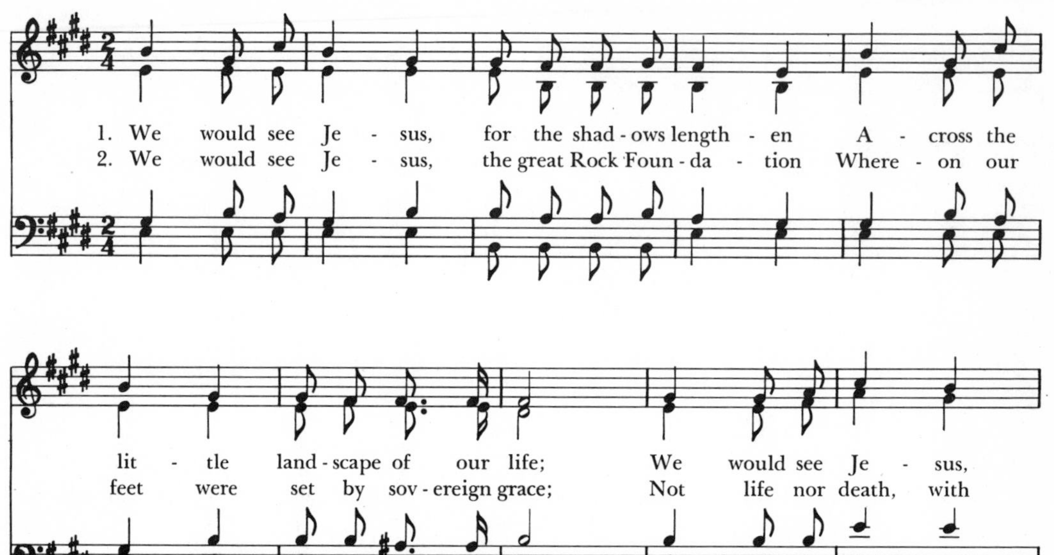
1. We would see Je - sus, for the shad - ows length - en A - cross the
2. We would see Je - sus, the great Rock Foun - da - tion Where - on our
lit - tle land - scape of our life; We would see Je - sus,
feet were set by sov - ereign grace; Not life nor death, with

our weak faith to strength - en For the last wea - ri - ness, the fi - nal strife.
all their ag - i - ta - tion Can thence re - move us, if we see his face.

3. We would see Jesus, sense is all too blinding
And heaven appears too dim, too far away;
We would see thee, to gain a sweet reminding
That thou hast promised our great debt to pay.

4. We would see Jesus, this is all we're needing,
Strength, joy, and willingness come with the sight;
We would see Jesus, dying, risen, pleading;
Then welcome day, and farewell mortal night.

MORE LOVE TO THEE, O CHRIST

BETHANY 6.4.6.4.6.6.6.4.

St. 1-4

Elizabeth Payson Prentiss, writ. c. 1856, pub. 1869

Lowell Mason, 1859

1. More love to thee, O Christ, More love to thee; Hear thou the prayer I make On bend - ed knee. This is my ear - nest plea: More love, O Christ, to thee, More love, O Christ, to thee, More love to thee.
2. Once earth - ly joy I craved, Sought peace and rest; Now thee a - lone I seek, Give what is best. This all my prayer shall be: More love, O Christ, to thee, More love, O Christ, to thee, More love to thee.

3. Let sorrow do its work,
Come grief or pain;
Sweet are thy messengers,
Sweet their refrain.
When they can sing with me:
More love, O Christ, to thee,
More love, O Christ, to thee,
More love to thee.

4. Then shall my latest breath
Whisper thy praise;
This be the parting cry,
My heart shall raise.
This still its prayer shall be:
More love, O Christ, to thee,
More love, O Christ, to thee,
More love to thee.

A PARTING HYMN WE SING — BRAINARD S.M.

St. 1-4

Aaron R. Wolfe, 1858 — James Flint, 1849

1. A part - ing hymn we sing A - round thy
2. Here have we seen thy face, And felt thy
6 7

ta - ble, Lord; A - gain our grate - ful
pres - ence here; So may the sa - vor
6 5 4 — 3 6 7 6 — 5

trib - ute bring, Our sol - emn vows re - cord.
of thy grace In word and life ap - pear.
6 6 6 4 7 5 — —

3. The purchase of thy blood,
By sin no longer led
The path our dear Redeemer trod,
May we rejoicing tread.

4. In self - forgetting love
Be our communion shown,
Until we join the church above,
And know as we are known.

JESUS, MERCIFUL AND MILD! ALSEN 7.7.7.7.

St. 1-5

Thomas Hastings, 1858 Frederick L. Abel, 1822

Largo
1. Je - sus, mer - ci - ful and mild! Lead me as a help - less child; On no oth - er arm but thine, Would my wea - ry soul re - cline.
2. Thou canst fit me, by thy grace, For the heaven - ly dwell - ing place; All thy prom - is - es are sure, Ev - er shall thy love en - dure.

3. Then what more could I desire,
How to greater bliss aspire?
All I need, in thee I see,
Thou are all in all to me.

4. Jesus, Saviour all divine!
Hast thou made me truly thine?
Hast thou bought me by thy blood?
Reconciled my heart to God?

5. Hearken to my tender prayer,
Let me thine own image bear;
Let me love thee more and more,
Till I reach heaven's blissful shore.

Stand Up, Stand Up for Jesus | Webb 7.6.7.6.D

St. 1-4

George Duffield Jr., 1858 | George J. Webb, 1837

1. Stand up, stand up for Je - sus, Ye sol - diers of the cross, Lift high his roy - al ban - ner, It must not suf - fer loss; From vic - tory un - to vic - tory His ar - my he shall lead Till ev - ery foe is van - quished, And Christ is Lord in - deed.
2. Stand up, stand up for Je - sus, The trump - et call o - bey Forth to the might - y con - flict, In this his glo - rious day; Ye that are men now serve him A - gainst un - num - bered foes. Let cour - age rise with dan - ger, And strength to strength op - pose.

3. Stand up, stand up for Jesus
Stand in his strength alone
The arm of flesh will fail you,
Ye dare not trust your own.
Put on the gospel armor,
Each piece put on with prayer;
Where duty calls, or danger
Be never wanting there.

4. Stand up, stand up for Jesus,
The strife will not be long;
This day the noise of battle
The next the victor's song.
To him that overcometh
A crown of life shall be;
He with the King of Glory
Shall reign eternally.

At the Door of Mercy Sighing — Talmar 8.7.8.7.

St. 1-4

Thomas Mackellar, 1872 — Isaac B. Woodbury, 1850

1. At the door of mer - cy sigh - ing With the bur - den of my sin,
2. Wait - ing 'mid the dark - ness drear - y, Stretch-ing out my hands to thee,

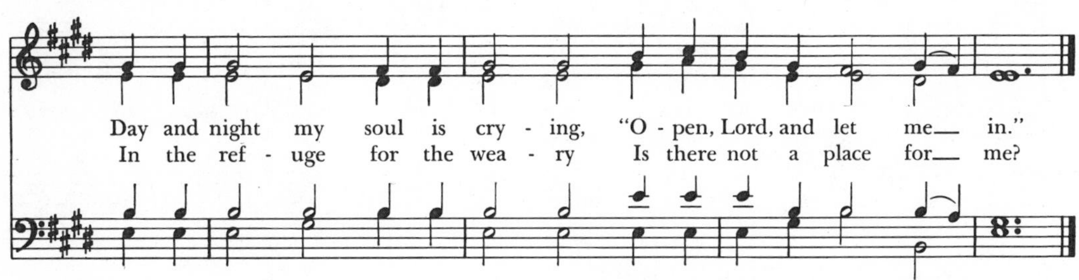
Day and night my soul is cry - ing, "O - pen, Lord, and let me___ in."
In the ref - uge for the wea - ry Is there not a place for___ me?

3. Hark, what sounds my ear receiveth,
Sweet as songs of seraphim!
"He that in the Lord believeth
Life eternal hath in him."

4. At the outer door why staying?
Nothing, soul, hast thou to pay.
Christ in love to thee is saying,
"Weary child, come in today."

THEY PRAY THE BEST WHO PRAY AND WATCH — BISHOP L.M.

St. 1-4

Edward Hopper, writ. 1873, pub. 1874 — Joseph P. Holbrook, 1874

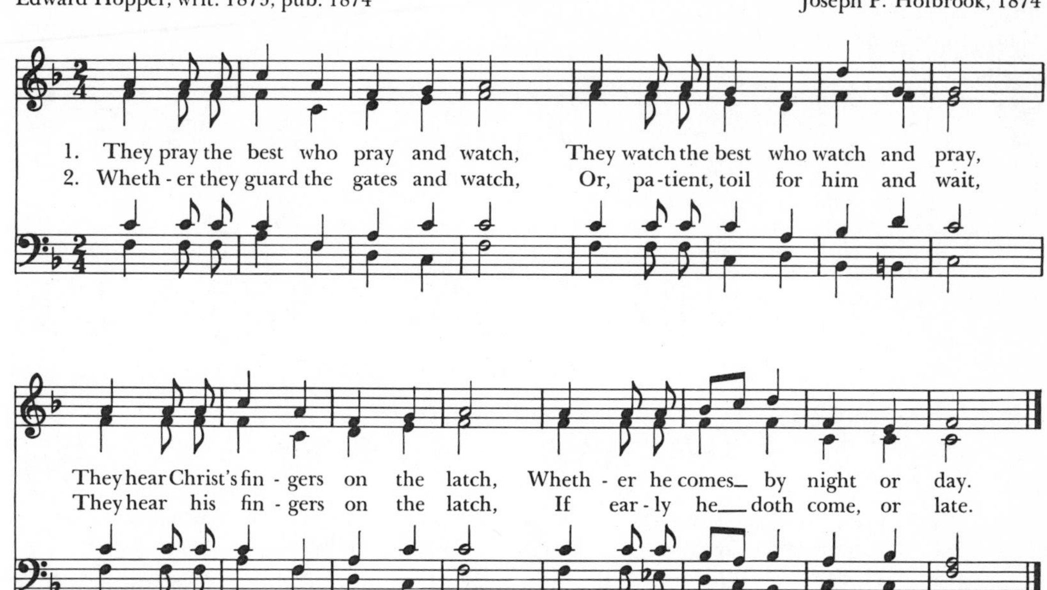
1. They pray the best who pray and watch, They watch the best who watch and pray,
2. Wheth - er they guard the gates and watch, Or, pa-tient, toil for him and wait,
They hear Christ's fin - gers on the latch, Wheth - er he comes by night or day.
They hear his fin - gers on the latch, If ear - ly he doth come, or late.

3. With trembling joy they hail their Lord,
And haste his welcome feet to kiss,
While he, well pleased, doth speak the word
That thrills them with unending bliss:

4. "Well done, my servants, now receive,
For faithful work, reward and rest,
And wreaths which busy angels weave
To crown the men who serve me best."

INTO THE WOODS MY MASTER WENT

(A Ballad of Trees and the Master)

St. 1, 2

Sidney Lanier, writ. 1880

LANIER Irregular

Peter C. Lutkin, 1905

mp
1. In - to the woods my Mas - ter went, Clean for - spent, for - spent;
2. Out of the woods my Mas - ter went, And he was well con - tent;
mp
In - to the woods my Mas - ter came, For - spent with love and shame. But the
Out of the woods my Mas - ter came, Con - tent with death and shame. When
ol - ives they were not blind to him, The lit - tle gray leaves were kind to him, The
death and shame would woo him last, From un - der the trees they drew him last, 'Twas
cresc.
rit.
thorn - tree had a mind to him, When in - to the woods he came.
on a tree they slew him last, When out of the woods he came.

God of Our Fathers

St. 1-3

Melancthon W. Stryker, 1889

Ithaca 9.9.9.9.

William Piutti, 1884

1. God of our fa - thers, our God to - day, Deep are thy
2. Heal - er of na - tions! Life - giv - ing God! Pu - ri - fy,
coun - sels, high is thy hand! Still for thy guid - ance
chas - ten, keep by thy grace, Show us thy par - dons,
hum - bly we pray; Spare thou the peo - ple, save thou the land!
shat - ter thy rod, Gath - er and hold us in thine em - brace.

3. Stand thou above us, Sun, Lord, and Shield!
March thou before us, Pillar of Flame!
Earth then her increase gladly shall yield,
Yea, all her peoples shout to thy name.

O RISEN LORD UPON THE THRONE

O RISEN LORD L.M.

St. 1-4

Louis F. Benson, 1895

Uzziah C. Burnap, comp. 1898, pub. 1925

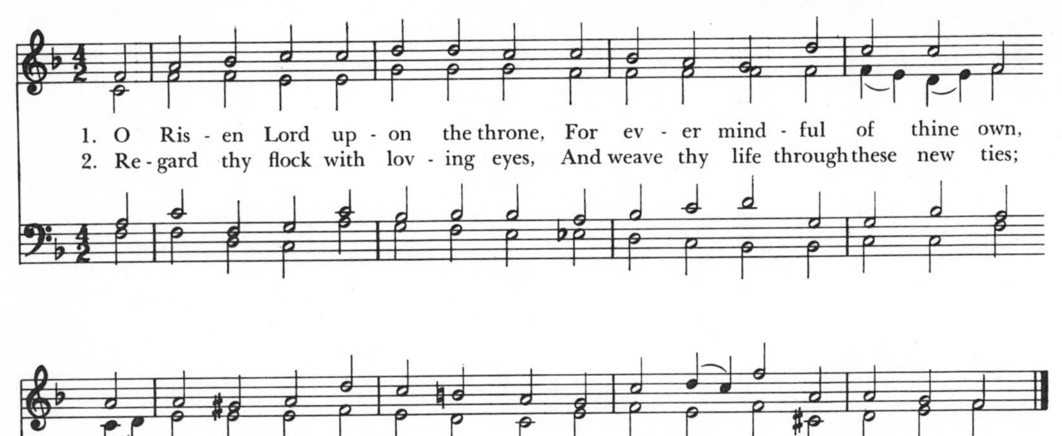
1. O Ris - en Lord up - on the throne, For ev - er mind - ful of thine own,
2. Re - gard thy flock with lov - ing eyes, And weave thy life through these new ties;

Now seal with thy right hand of power The coven - ants_ of this ho - ly hour.
Our faith re - new, our hearts re - claim; Re - call thy_ way - ward sheep by name.

3. O lead us, Saviour; only thou
Canst be the shepherd's Shepherd now;
Reveal the path of life, and we
Will follow where he walks with thee.

4. By thee alone our toils are blest;
Thine arms enfold thy flock at rest;
When day begins, till labors cease,
Refresh us from thy wells of peace.

O Thou Whose Feet Have Climbed Life's Hill — Log College C.M.

St. 1-5

Louis F. Benson, writ. 1894, pub. 1895 — George W. Warren, comp. 1894, pub. 1895

1. O thou whose feet have climbed life's hill, And trod the path of youth,
2. The call is thine: be thou the Way, And give us men, to guide;

Our Sav - iour and our Broth - er still, Now lead us in - to truth.
Let wis - dom broad - en with the day, Let hu - man faith a - bide.

3. Who learn of thee, the truth shall find;
Who follow, gain the goal
With reverence crown the earnest mind,
And speak within the soul.

4. Awake the purpose high which strives,
And, falling, stands again;
Confirm the will of eager lives
To quit themselves like men.

5. Thy life the bond of fellowship,
Thy love the law that rules;
Thy name, proclaimed by every lip,
The Master of our schools.

Almighty Lord, with One Accord

Patten C.M.

St. 1-4

Melancthon W. Stryker, 1896

Peter C. Lutkin, cop. 1902

1. Al - might - y Lord, with one ac - cord We of - fer thee our youth,
2. Thy cause doth claim our souls by name, Be - cause that we are strong;

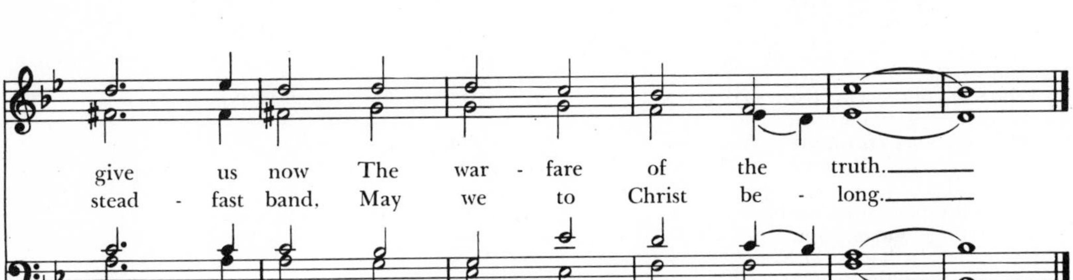
And pray that thou wouldst give us now The war - fare of the truth.
In all the land, one stead - fast band, May we to Christ be - long.

3. Let fall on every college hall
The luster of thy cross,
That love may dare thy work to share
And count all else as loss.

4. Our hearts be ruled, our spirits schooled
Alone thy will to seek;
And when we find thy blessèd mind,
Instruct our lips to speak.

Why Linger Yet upon the Strand?

St. 1-4

Louis F. Benson, writ. 1897, pub. 1925

Wider Ways C.M.

Uzziah C. Burnap, comp. 1898, pub. 1925

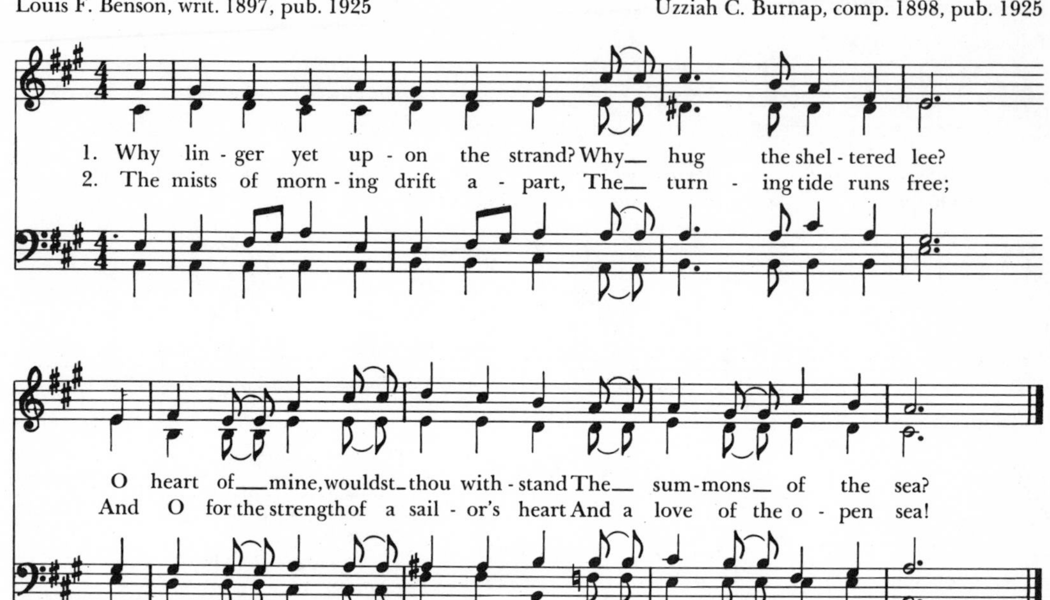
1. Why lin - ger yet up - on the strand? Why__ hug the shel - tered lee?
2. The mists of morn - ing drift a - part, The__ turn - ing tide runs free;
O heart of__ mine, wouldst_ thou with - stand The__ sum-mons__ of the sea?
And O for the strength of a sail - or's heart And a love of the o - pen sea!

3. What wider ways that God has planned
Bode any ill to thee,
If in the hollow of his hand
He holds the unknown sea ?

4. When winds are wild and waters riven,
And his waves gone over thee,
Unshaken is the throne of heaven;
Thy God still rules the sea.

God Supreme! To Thee We Pray

7.7.7.7.7.

St. 1-4

Penina Moise, 1840, St. 1, 2

Edward N. Calisch, St. 3, 4

Joseph Achron, 1932

Andante (unison)
p
1. God su - preme! to thee we pray; Let our lips be taught to say,
2. What thy wis - dom may dic - tate, Let thy serv - ant vin - di - cate,
3
p
Wheth - er good or ill may flow,
Though it may our hopes o'er-throw,
Chorus
Heav - en - ly Fa - ther
be it so, Heav - en - ly Fa - ther be it so.

3. Thou alone dost best decide
Whatsoe'er shall us betide;
Be our station high or low,
Heavenly Father be it so,
Heavenly Father be it so.

4. When our sky is overcast,
When our life-work's o'er at last,
When thou call'st for us to go
Heavenly Father be it so,
Heavenly Father be it so.

Come, O Sabbath Day 7.7.7.7.6.

St. 1-3

Gustav Gottheil, 1887 Abraham W. Binder, 1932

Larghetto
mf
1. Come, O Sab - bath day, and bring Peace and heal - ing on thy wing;
2. Earth - ly long - ings bid re - tire, Quench the pas - sions' hurt - ful fire;
mf

And to ev - ery trou - bled breast Speak of the di - vine be - hest:
To the way - ward, sin op - pressed, Bring Thou thy di - vine be - hest:

Thou shalt rest, thou shalt rest!
Thou shalt rest, thou shalt rest!

3. Wipe from every cheek the tear,
Banish care and silence fear;
All things working for the best,
Teach us the divine behest:
Thou shalt rest, thou shalt rest.

How Goodly Is Thy House — L.M.

St. 1-3

Henry S. Jacobs, 1887 — Jacob Weinberg, c. 1947

Very slowly (unison)
1. How good - ly is thy house, O Lord! With - in its courts we turn— to thee, Who
2. We hith - er come to praise thy name, And hum - bly seek thy gra - cious face; Thy
ritard
a tempo
art by Is - rael's sons— a - dored As God to all e - ter - ni - ty.
truth and great - ness to— pro - claim In this, thy ho - ly dwell - ing place.

3. Accord us, then thy tender love;
Unto our prayerful words give ear;
Grant them acceptance from above,
And to our plaint be ever near.

Kindle the Taper
10.10.10.10.
St. 1-3
Emma Lazarus, 1889
Jacob Singer, 1932
Maestoso (unison)
1. Kin - dle the ta - per like the stead - fast star A- blaze on___ eve - ning's
2. Clash, Is - ra - el, the cym - bals, touch the lyre, Blow the___ loud trum -
fore - head o'er__ the earth; Send through the night its lus - ter till a - far,
pet and harsh-tongued horn; Chant psalms of vic - tory till the heart take fire,
An eight - fold splen - dor shine a - bove the hearth.
The Mac - ca - be - an spir - it leap new - born.

3. Still ours the dance, the feast, the glorious Psalm,
The mystic lights of emblem and the Word.
Where is our Judah? Where our five-branched palm?
Where are the lion warriors of the Lord?

IN MERCY, LORD, INCLINE THINE EAR C.M.

St. 1-4

Isaac M. Wise, 1897 Abraham W. Binder, 1932

Andante
f
1. In mer - cy, Lord, in - cline thine ear To Zi - on's faith - ful band;
2. Re - veal once more ce - les - tial light O'er Zi - on's ho - ly tents,

In__ love and grace__ our__ plead - ings hear, Re - veal thy might - y hand.
Dis - pel the clouds__ and__ end the night, Let truth per - vade all lands.

3. To truth be laid this cornerstone,
Be reared these massive walls;
To thee, Most High, and only One,
Be arched these sacred halls.

4. Pour down thy grace in sunny rays,
Let Judah's temple be
The house of praise to teach thy ways,
Devoted, Lord, to thee.

HARK, AND HEAR MY TRUMPET SOUNDING

THREE O'CLOCK TRUMPET 8.7.8.7.D

Anon, early 19th cent.

Anon., early 19th cent.

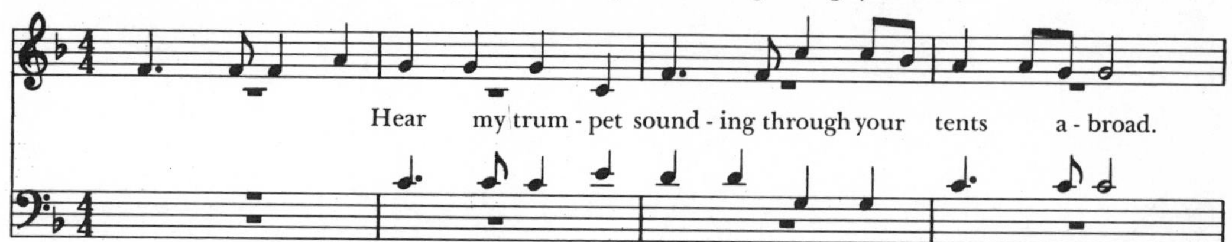
Hark, and hear my trum - pet sound - ing, Sound - ing through your tents a - broad.
Hear my trum - pet sound - ing through your tents a - broad.

Hear my voice of sol - emn warn - ing, Hear it ech - o through the crowd.
Hear my voice of warn - ing, Hear it ech - o through the crowd.
Hear it ech - o through the crowd.

Tune your hearts where God is call - ing, Seek his ho - ly love and fear;
While his sol - emn truths are roll - ing, Know ye 'tis his word we hear.

We Read of a People

St. 1-3, 5

Anon., 1852

Gospel Liberty 11.8.11.8.D.

Anon., 1852

1. We___ read of a peo - ple in a - ges long past, Who wish - ed their neigh - bors no ill;
2. The___ Lord was not deaf to his peo-ple's com-plaints, When in for - mer a - ges op-pressed,
Yet___ were per - se - cu - ted and dai - ly har - assed, And driv - en from moun - tain to hill:
But___ gra-cious-ly prom - ised his in - no - cent saints, A day of sal - va - tion and rest.
These___ in - no - cent souls had no law - ful de - fense, But if per - se - cu - tors now say
When___ this bless - ed sea - son has tru - ly be - gun, And God puts an end to the fray,
"A - ban - don your faith or we'll ban - ish you hence," In rea - son we an - swer them, *Nay.*
Must peac - a - ble men to the wil - der - ness run? Each prom-ise of God an - swers, *Nay.*

3. We have not the laws of a Nero to face,
Nor the horrid edicts of Rome;
This dispensation has altered the case,
And fixed us a peaceable home.
While men of sound reason are widely awake,
Asserting the rights of the day,
Must harmless believers their country forsake?
The good constitution says, *Nay.*

4. The law and the gospel do now harmonize,
And each has its work to perform;
To root out the gospel if wicked men rise,
The law has to scatter the storm
The gospel does honor the laws of the land,
The law does the gospel survey;
Then ask if this gospel may lawfully stand,
The law has to answer us, *Yea.*

More Love

Anon., 1876 Anon., 1876

More love, more love; The heavens are blessing, The angels are calling, O Zion, more love.
If ye love not each other In daily communion, How can ye love God, Whom ye have not seen?

'Tis the Gift To Be Simple

Traditional

Aaron Copland, arr. 1950

Quietly flowing
legato, simply
mp (2nd time f)
'Tis the gift to be sim - ple 'tis the
f (very plain)
mf
mp (2nd time f)
gift to be free 'Tis the gift to come down where you ought to be And
[2nd time play small notes]
p
hold back a trifle
when we find our - selves in the place just right 'Twill be in the val - ley of
hold back a trifle
[2nd time to Coda]
love and de - light.
When true sim - pli - ci - ty is gained To
mf (plainly)
f
mf

mp
bow and to bend we shan't be a-shamed To turn, turn will be our de-light 'Till by
mf
mp
p
turn - ing, turn-ing we come round right.
f
'Tis the
p
f
CODA
(rit. _ _ _ _ _)
p
p
pp
(dreamily)

Trust in Me

Anon., 1876 Anon., 1876

Unison
Trust in me, trust in me, I am a - ble to im - part Strength ac - cord - ing
to your day, As you jour-ney on - ward. I'll sus - tain with my right hand When you pass the
des - ert land; A pil - lar of fire shall light the way While you jour - ney heav - en - ward.

My God, I Thank Thee — Dunbarton L.M.

St. 1-4

Andrews Norton, 1809 — William Selby, 1802

1. My God, I thank thee! may no thought E'er
2. Thy mer - cy bids all na - ture bloom; The
deem thy chas - tise - ments se - vere; But
sun shines bright, and man is gay. Thine
may this heart, by sor - row taught, Calm
e - qual mer - cy spreads the gloom That
each wild wish, each
i
dle fear.
dark - ens o'er his lit - tle day.

3. Full many a throb of grief and pain
Thy frail and erring child must know;
But not one prayer is breathed in vain,
Nor does one tear unheeded flow.

4. Thy various messengers employ,
Thy purposes of love fulfil;
And, mid the wreck of human joy,
Let kneeling faith adore thy will.

Lift Your Glad Voices in Triumph on High — **Trumpet** 10.11.11.11.12.11.10.11.

St. 1, 2

Henry Ware Jr., 1817 — Isaac B. Woodbury, 1854

Very spirited

1. Lift_your_glad_ voic - es in tri - umph on high, For Je - sus_hath_ ris - en, and
D.C. Loud_was_the_ cho - rus of an - gels on high: "The Sav - iour_hath_ ris - en, and

man can - not die; *Fine* Vain were the ter - rors that gath - ered a - round him, And
man can - not die."

short the do - min - ion of death and the grave, He burst from the fet - ters of

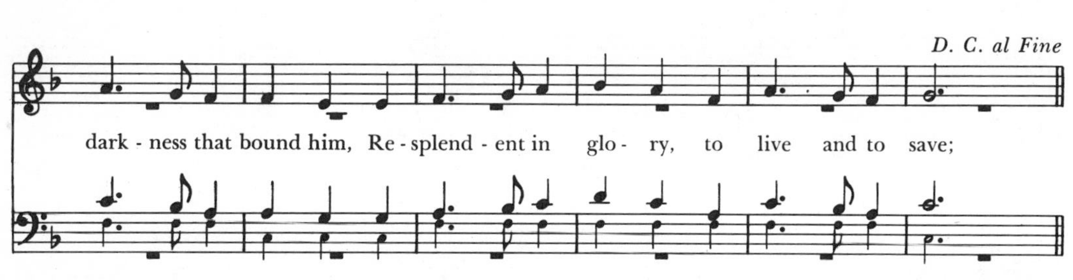
D. C. al Fine
dark - ness that bound him, Re - splend - ent in glo - ry, to live and to save;

2. Glory to God, in full anthems of joy!
The being he gave us death cannot destroy!
Sad were the life we must part with tomorrow,
If tears were our birthright, and death were our end;
But Jesus hath cheered the dark valley of sorrow,
And bade us, immortal, to heaven ascend.
Lift, then, your voices in triumph on high,
For Jesus hath risen, and man shall not die.

Great God, the Followers of Thy Son — Woodstown L.M.

St. 1-4

Henry Ware Jr., writ. 1819, pub. 1868 — Benjamin Holt, 1822

♪ = 100
1. Great God, the fol - lowers of thy Son, We bow be -
2. O grant thy bless - ing here to - day! O give thy

fore thy mer - cy seat, To wor - ship thee, the
peo - ple joy and peace! The to - kens of thy

Ho - ly One, And pour our wish - es at thy feet.
love dis - play, And fa - vor that shall nev - er cease.

3 We seek the truth which Jesus brought;
His path of light we long to tread.
Here be his holy doctrines taught,
And here their purest influence shed.

4 May faith and hope and love abound;
Our sins and errors be forgiven;
And we, in thy great day, be found
Children of God and heirs of heaven!

O God, Accept the Sacred Hour — Communion C.M.

St. 1-3

Samuel Gilman, 1820 — S. Hill, 1834

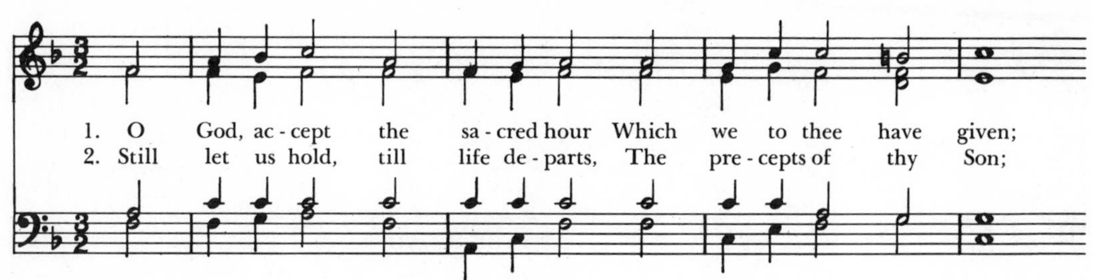
1. O God, ac - cept the sa - cred hour Which we to thee have given;
2. Still let us hold, till life de - parts, The pre - cepts of thy Son;

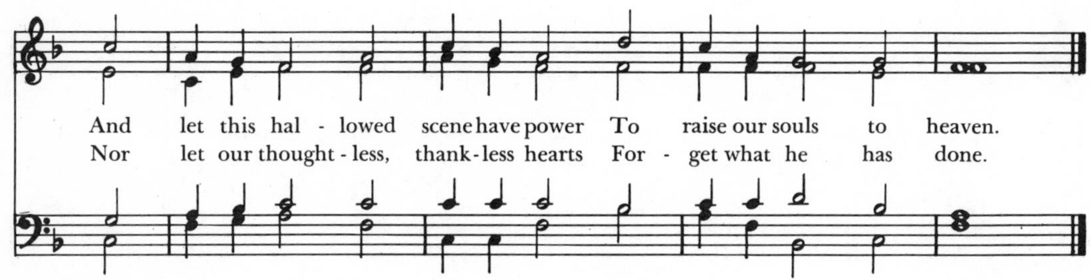
And let this hal - lowed scene have power To raise our souls to heaven.
Nor let our thought - less, thank - less hearts For - get what he has done.

3. His true disciples may we live,
From all corruption free;
And humbly learn, like him, to give
Our powers, our wills, to thee.

SLOWLY, BY GOD'S HAND UNFURLED — KNISELY 7.7.7.7.

St. 1-4

William Henry Furness, writ. 1825, pub. 1840 — George Frederick Bristow, 1865

1. Slow - ly, by God's hand un - furled, Down a -
2. Might - y Ma - ker, ev - er nigh, Work in
round the wea - ry world Falls the dark - ness;
me as si - lent - ly; Veil the day's dis -

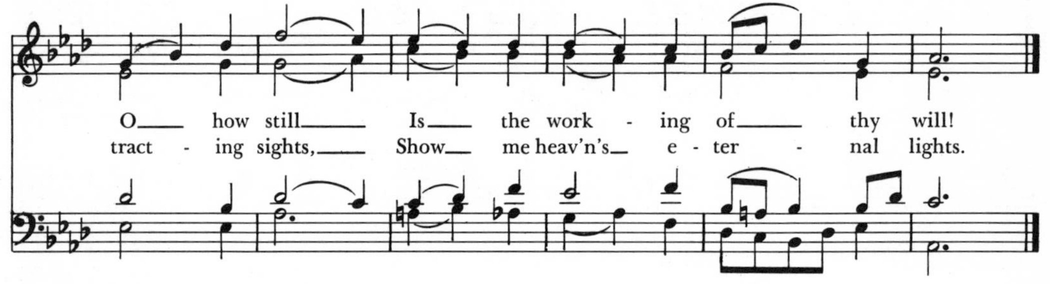
O how still Is the work - ing of thy will!
tract - ing sights, Show me heav'n's e - ter - nal lights.

3. Living worlds to view be brought
In the boundless realms of thought;
High and infinite desires,
Flaming like those upper fires.

4. Holy truth, eternal light,
Let them break upon my sight;
Let them shine, serene and still,
And with light my being fill.

O God Whose Presence Glows in All

St .1-4

Pilesgrove L.M.

Nathaniel L. Frothingham, writ. 1828

Nahum Mitchell, 1812

1. O God whose pres - ence glows in all With - in, a -
2. That truth be with the heart be - lieved, Of all who

round us, and a - bove! Thy word we bless, thy
seek this sa - cred place; With power pro - claimed, in

name we call, Whose word is truth, whose name is love.
peace re - ceived, Our spir - its' light, thy Spir - it's grace.

3. That love its holy influence pour,
To keep us meek and make us free,
And throw its binding blessing more
Round each with all, and all with thee.

4. Send down its angel to our side;
Send in its calm upon the breast;
For we would know no other guide,
And we can need no other rest.

SOVEREIGN AND TRANSFORMING GRACE — LEVERETT 7.7.7.7.

St. 1-4

Frederic Henry Hedge, writ. 1829, pub. 1853 — Henry Kemble Oliver, comp. 1842, pub. 1875

1. Sov - ereign and trans - form - ing Grace! We in - voke thy quick - ening power; Reign the spir - it of this place, Bless the pur - pose of this hour.
2. Ho - ly and cre - a - tive Light! We in - voke thy kind - ling ray; Dawn up - on our spir - its' night, Turn our dark - ness in - to day.

3. To the anxious soul impart
Hope all other hopes above,
Stir the dull and hardened heart
With a longing and a love.

4. Work in all; in all renew,
Day by day, the life divine;
All our wills to thee subdue,
All our hearts to thee incline.

HAIL TO THE SABBATH DAY COMPTON S.M.

St. 1-5

Stephen Greenleaf Bulfinch, 1832 E. K. Prouty, 1835

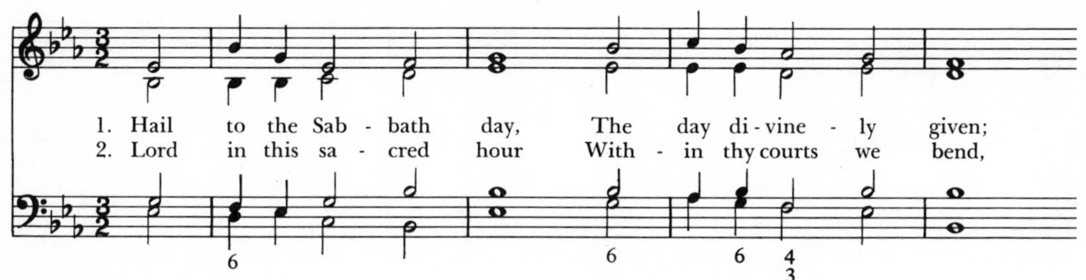
1. Hail to the Sab - bath day, The day di - vine - ly given;
2. Lord in this sa - cred hour With - in thy courts we bend,
6 6 6 4 3

When men to God their hom-age pay, And earth draws near to heaven.
And bless thy love, and own thy power, Our Fa - ther and our Friend.
6 6 6 6 6 4 7

3. But thou art not alone
In courts by mortals trod;
Nor only is the day thine own
When man draws near to God.

4. Thy temple is the arch
Of yon unmeasured sky;
Thy Sabbath, the stupendous march
Of grand eternity.

5. Lord, may that holier day
Dawn on thy servants' sight;
And purer worship may we pay
In heaven's unclouded light.

We Love the Venerable House — Hermon C.M.

St. 1-6

Ralph Waldo Emerson, 1833 — Lowell Mason, 1839

Slow and soft
1. We love the ven - er - a - ble house Our fa - thers built to God;
2. Here ho - ly thoughts a light have shed From many a rad - iant face,
In heaven are kept their grate-ful vows, Their dust en - dears the sod.
And prayers of hum - ble vir - tue spread The per - fume of the place.

3. And anxious hearts have pondered here
The mystery of life,
And prayed th' Eternal Light to clear
Their doubts and aid their strife.

4. From humble tenements around
Came up the pensive train,
And in the church a blessing found,
That filled their homes again;

5. For faith, and peace, and mighty love,
That from the Godhead flow,
Showed them the life of heaven above
Springs from the life below.

6. They live with God their homes are dust;
Yet here their children pray,
And in this fleeting lifetime trust
To find the narrow way.

O THOU WHOSE OWN VAST TEMPLE STANDS — ARMENIA C.M.

St. 1-4

William Cullen Bryant, writ. 1835 — Sylvanus Billings Pond, 1841

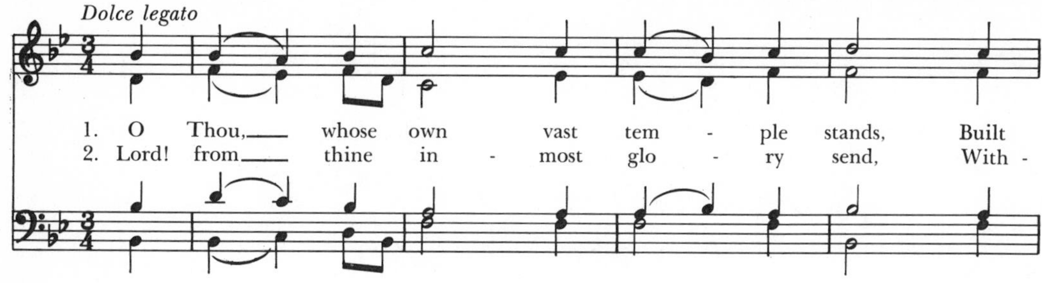
Dolce legato
1. O Thou, whose own vast tem - ple stands, Built
2. Lord! from thine in - most glo - ry send, With -

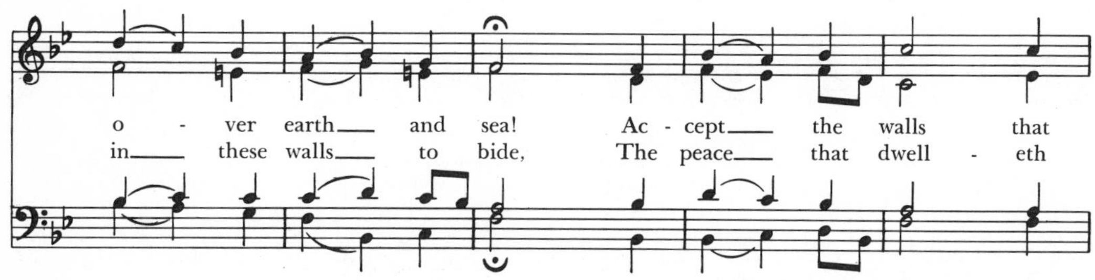
o - ver earth and sea! Ac - cept the walls that
in these walls to bide, The peace that dwell - eth

hu - man hands Have raised to wor - ship thee.
with - out end, Se - rene - ly by thy side!

3. May erring minds that worship here
Be taught the better way;
And they who mourn, and they who fear,
Be strengthened as they pray.

4. May faith grow firm, and love grow warm,
And pure devotion rise,
While, round these hallowed walls, the storm
Of earth-born passion dies.

TELL ME NOT IN MOURNFUL NUMBERS — JACINTH 8.7.8.7.D.

(Psalm of Life)

St. 1-6

Henry Wadsworth Longfellow, 1839 — Charles Beecher, 1855

1. Tell me not, in mourn - ful num - bers, Life is but an emp - ty dream;
For the soul is dead that slum - bers, And things are not what they seem.
2. Life is real! life is ear - nest! And the grave is not its goal;
Dust thou art, to dust re - turn - est, Was not spo - ken of the soul!

3. Not enjoyment, and not sorrow,
Is our destined end and way;
But to act, that each tomorrow
Find us further than today.

4. Lives of true men all remind us
We can make our lives sublime,
And, departing, leave behind us
Foot-prints on the sands of time;

5. Footprints which perhaps another,
Sailing o'er life's solemn main,
A forlorn and shipwrecked brother,
Seeing, shall take heart again.

6. Let us, then, be up and doing,
With a heart for any fate;
Still achieving, still pursuing,
Learn to labor and to wait.

Wilt Thou Not Visit Me? — Vingrove 6.10.6.10.

St. 1-5

Jones Very, 1839 — Henry Kemble Oliver, 1860

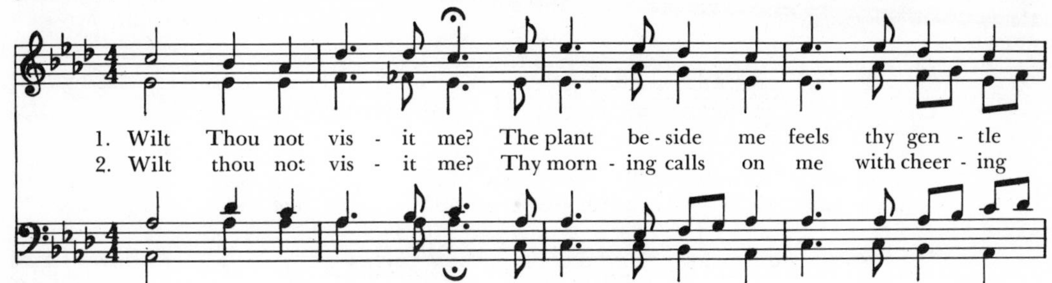
1. Wilt Thou not vis - it me? The plant be - side me feels thy gen - tle
2. Wilt thou not vis - it me? Thy morn - ing calls on me with cheer - ing

dew; Each blade of grass I see From thy deep
tone; And ev - ery hill and tree Lend but one

earth its quick - ening mois - ture drew.
voice, the voice of thee a - lone.

3. Come! for I need thy love,
More than the flower the dew, or grass the rain;
Come, like thy holy dove,
And let me in thy sight rejoice to live again.

4. I will not hide from them,
When thy storms come, though fierce may be their wrath;
But bow with leafy stem,
And strengthened follow on thy chosen path.

5. Yes, thou wilt visit me;
Nor plant nor tree thy eye delights so well
As when, from sin set free,
Man's spirit comes with thine in peace to dwell.

MIGHTY ONE, BEFORE WHOSE FACE | LAYON 7.7.7.7.

St. 1-3

William Cullen Bryant, 1840 | John Zundel, 1855

1. Might - y One, be - fore whose face Wis - dom
2. Source of truth, whose rays a - lone Light the
had her glo - rious seat, When the orbs that peo - ple
might - y world of mind! God of love, who from thy
space Sprang to birth be - neath thy feet!
throne Kind - ly watch - est all man - kind!

3. Shed on those who in thy name
Teach the way of truth and right,
Shed that love's undying flame,
Shed that wisdom's guiding light.

IN PLEASANT LANDS HAVE FALLEN THE LINES — WALLINGFORD L.M.

St. 1-4

James Flint, writ. 1840, pub. 1845 — Benjamin F. Baker, 1854

Andante
1. In pleas - ant lands have fallen the lines That bound our
2. What thanks, O God, to thee are due, That thou didst

good - ly her - i - tage; And safe be - neath our
plant our fa - thers here; And watch and guard them

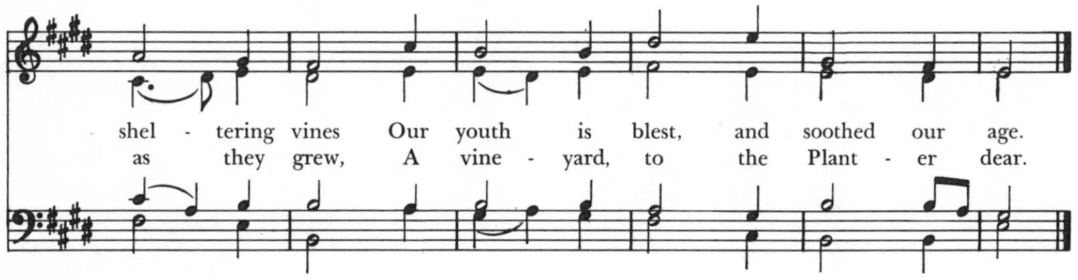
shel - tering vines Our youth is blest, and soothed our age.
as they grew, A vine - yard, to the Plant - er dear.

3. The toils they bore our ease have wrought;
They sowed in tears, in joy we reap;
The birthright they so dearly bought,
We'll guard till we with them shall sleep.

4. Thy kindness to our fathers, shown
In weal and woe through all the past,
Their grateful sons, O God, shall own,
While here their name and race shall last.

In the Morning I Will Pray — Benson 7.7.7.7.

St. 2-6

William Henry Furness, 1840 — Lowell Mason, 1830

1. In the morn - ing I will pray For God's bless - ing on the day; What this day shall be my lot, Light or dark - ness, know I not.
2. Should it be with clouds o'er - cast, Clouds of sor - row gath - ering fast, Thou, who giv - est light di - vine, Shine with - in me, Lord, oh, shine!
4 3 6 4 3 6 5 6 3 7 — 4 9 3 8 #4 2
6 6 6 4 7 # 4 2 6 — 4 3
6 4 5 3 4 2 6 6 5 6 5 8 7

3. Show me, if I tempted be,
Needed strength to find in thee,
And a perfect triumph win
Over every bosom sin.

4. Keep my feet from hidden snares,
And my eyes, O God, from tears;
Every step thy grace attend,
And my soul from death defend.

5. Then, when fall the shades of night,
All within shall still be light;
Thou wilt peace around diffuse,
Gently as the evening dews.

Send Forth, O God, Thy Light and Truth — Holden C.M.D.

St. 1, 2

John Quincy Adams, 1841 — Thomas Whittemore, 1841

1. Send forth, O God, thy light and truth, And let them lead me still,
2. O why, my soul, art thou cast down? With-in me why dis-tressed?
Un-daunt-ed, in the paths of right, Up to thy ho-ly hill.
Thy hopes the God of grace shall crown; He yet shall make thee blessed.
p.
Then to thy al-tar will I spring, And in my God re-joice;
To him, my nev-er-fail-ing Friend, I bow, and kiss the rod;
f.
And praise shall tune the trem-bling string, And grat-i-tude my voice.
To him shall thanks and praise as-cend, My Sav-iour and my God.

Brother, Hast Thou Wandered Far — Martyn 7.7.7.7.D.

St. 1-4

James Freeman Clarke, 1844 — Simeon B. Marsh, 1834

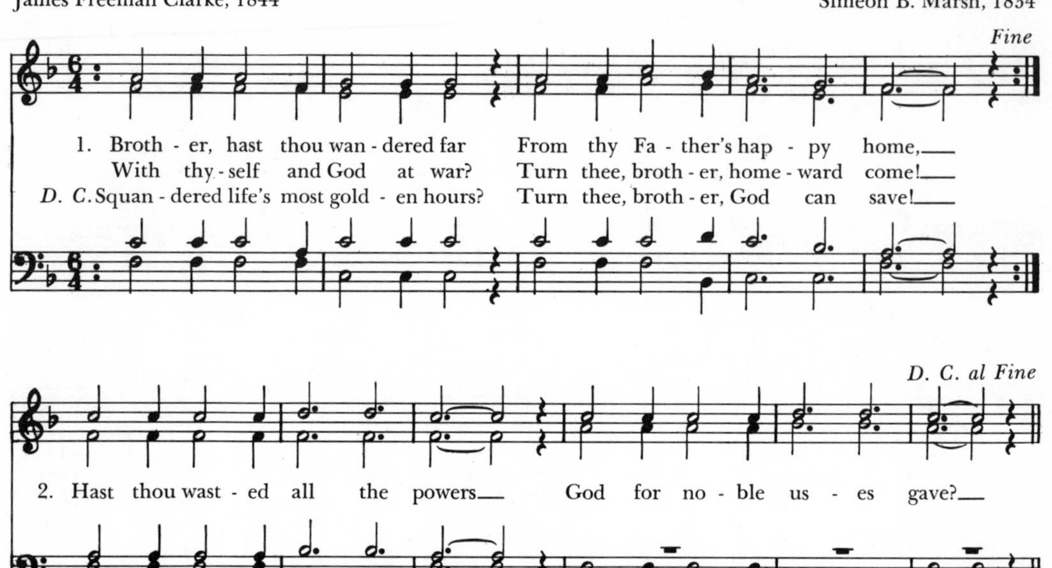
Fine
1. Broth - er, hast thou wan - dered far From thy Fa - ther's hap - py home,
With thy - self and God at war? Turn thee, broth - er, home - ward come!
D. C. Squan - dered life's most gold - en hours? Turn thee, broth - er, God can save!
D. C. al Fine
2. Hast thou wast - ed all the powers God for no - ble us - es gave?

3. Is a mighty famine now
In thy heart and in thy soul?
Discontent upon thy brow?
Turn thee, God will make thee whole!

4. Fall before him on the ground,
Pour thy sorrow in his ear;
Seek him, for he may be found;
Call upon him; He is near.

THOU LORD OF HOSTS, WHOSE GUIDING HAND

MISSIONARY CHANT L.M.

St. 1-5

Octavius Brooks Frothingham, 1846

Charles Zeuner, 1834

Vivace
1. Thou Lord of hosts, whose guid - ing hand Hath brought us here, be -
2. Those spir - its lay their no - blest powers, As of - ferings on thy

fore thy face; Our spir - its wait for thy com -
ho - ly shrine. Thine was the strength that nour - ished

mand, Our si - lent hearts im - plore thy peace.
ours; The sol - diers of the Cross are thine.

3. While watching on our arms at night,
We saw thine angels round us move;
We heard thy call, we felt thy light,
And followed, trusting to thy love.

4. Send us where'er thou wilt, O Lord!
Through rugged toil and wearying fight,
Thy conquering love shall be our sword,
And faith in thee our truest might.

5. Send down thy constant aid, we pray;
Be thy pure angels with us still;
Thy truth, be that our firmest stay;
Our only rest to do thy will.

The Past Is Dark with Sin and Shame — Baden L.M.

St. 1-5

Thomas Wentworth Higginson, 1846 — Thomas Hastings, 1855

1. The past is dark with sin and shame, The fu - ture dim with doubt and fear;
2. For man has striv - en, a - ges long, With fal-tering steps, to come to thee;

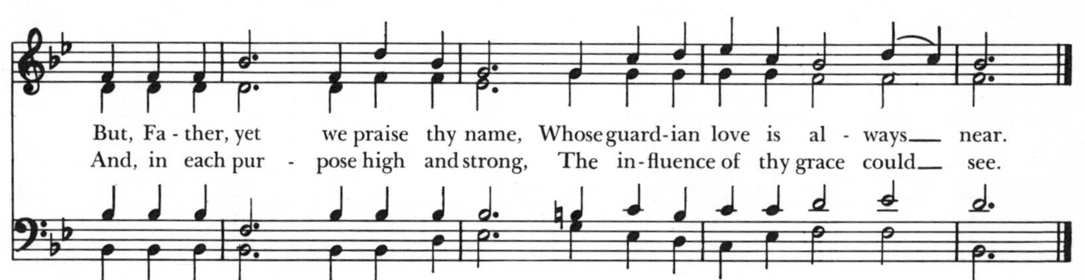
But, Fa - ther, yet we praise thy name, Whose guard-ian love is al - ways near.
And, in each pur - pose high and strong, The in-fluence of thy grace could see.

3. He could not breathe an earnest prayer,
But thou wast kinder than he dreamed,
As age by age brought hopes more fair,
And nearer still thy kingdom seemed.

4. But never rose within his breast
A trust so calm and deep as now:
Shall not the weary find a rest?
Father, Preserver, answer thou!

5. 'Tis dark around, 'tis dark above,
But through the shadow streams the sun;
We cannot doubt thy certain love,
And man's true aim shall yet be won!

To Thine Eternal Arms, O God — Hamburg L.M.

St. 1-4

Thomas Wentworth Higginson, 1846 — Lowell Mason, arr. 1825

Slow, gentle, smooth Sotto voce
cresc.
1. cresc.
mp
1. To thine e - ter - nal arms, O God, Take us, thine err - ing
From dan-gerous paths too bold - ly trod,
2. Those arms were round our child - hood's ways, A guard through help - less
O leave not our ma - tur - er days!
2.
dim.
chil - dren in;
From wan-dering thought and dreams of sin.
years to be;
We still are help - less with - out thee.

3. We trusted hope and pride and strength;
Our strength proved false, our pride was vain,
Our dreams have faded all at length,
We come to thee, O Lord, again!

4. A guide to trembling steps yet be!
Give us of thine eternal power!
So shall our paths all lead to thee,
And life still smile, like child-hood's hour.

FATHER, IN THY MYSTERIOUS PRESENCE KNEELING — WHITE 11.10.11.10.

St. 1-4

Samuel Johnson, 1846 — T. B. White, 1877

1. Fa - ther, in thy mys - ter - ious pres - ence kneel - ing,
2. Lord, we have wan - dered forth through doubt and sor - row,
Fain would our souls feel all thy kind - ling love;
And thou hast made each step an on - ward one;
For we are weak, and need some deep re - veal - ing,
And we will ev - er trust each un - known mor - row,
Of trust and strength and calm - ness from a - bove.
Thou wilt sus - tain us till its work is done.

3. In the heart's depths a peace serene and holy
Abides; and when pain seems to have its will,
Or we despair, oh, may that peace rise slowly,
Stronger than agony, and we be still!

4. Now, Father, now, in thy dear presence kneeling,
Our spirits yearn to feel thy kindling love.
Now make us strong, we need thy deep revealing
Of trust and strength and calmness from above.

Lord of All Being, Throned Afar — Federal Street L.M.

St. 1-5

Oliver Wendell Holmes, writ. 1848, pub. 1859 — Henry Kemble Oliver, comp. 1832, pub. 1835

1. Lord of all be - ing,— throned a - far, Thy glo - ry
2. Sun of our life, thy— quick - ening ray Sheds on our
6
4
6
4
7
7

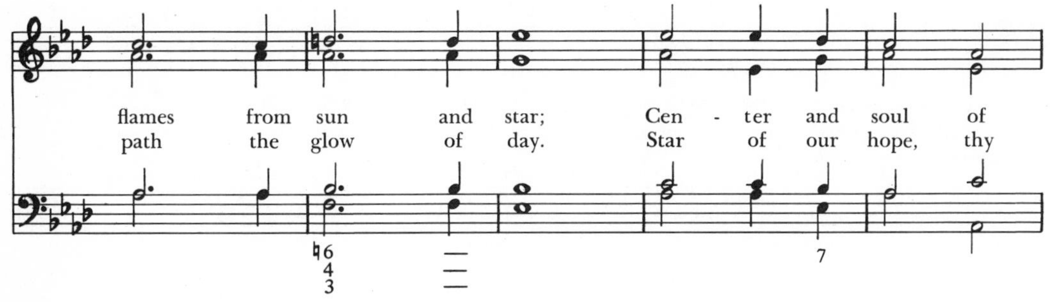
flames from sun and star; Cen - ter and soul of
path the glow of day. Star of our hope, thy
♮6
4
3
7

ev - ery— sphere, Yet to each lov - ing heart how near!
sof - tened— light Cheers the long watch - es of the night.
3 4 5 6 7
8 2 3 4 5
6
6
4
7

3. Our midnight is thy smile withdrawn,
Our noontide is thy gracious dawn;
Our rainbow arch, thy mercy's sign,
All, save the clouds of sin, are thine.

4. Lord of all life, below, above,
Whose light is truth, whose warmth is love,
Before thy ever-blazing throne
We ask no luster of our own.

5. Grant us thy truth to make us free,
And kindling hearts that burn for thee,
Till all thy living altars claim
One holy light, one heavenly flame.

Dear Friend, Whose Presence in the House — Downs C.M.

St. 1-5

James Freeman Clarke, 1852 — Lowell Mason, 1832

1. Dear Friend! whose pres - ence in the house, Whose gra - cious word be - nign, Could once, at Ca - na's wed - ding feast, Change wa - ter in - to wine,
2. Come vis - it us, and when dull work Grows wea - ry, line on line, Re - vive our souls, and make us see Life's wa - ter glow as wine. And wa - ter changed to wine.
1.
2. Use for last stanza only
6 4 5 3 6 7 6 6 6 4 7 ♯
8 6 7 5 6 4 5 3 6 4 3
6 6 4 8 7 6 4

3. Gay mirth shall deepen into joy,
Earth's hopes shall grow divine,
When Jesus visits us, to turn
Life's water into wine.

4. The social talk, the evening fire,
The homely household shrine,
Shall glow with angel-visits when
The Lord pours out the wine.

5. For when self-seeking turns to love,
Which knows not mine and thine,
The miracle again is wrought,
And water changed to wine.

THOU GRACE DIVINE, ENCIRCLING ALL

HEBER C.M.

St. 1-5

Eliza Scudder, writ. 1852, pub. 1857

George Kingsley, 1838

1. Thou— Grace Di - vine, en - cir - cling all, A shore - less, sound - less— sea,
2. When— o - ver diz - zy heights we go, One soft hand blinds— our— eyes,

Where - in at last our souls must fall, O love of God— most— free!
The— oth - er leads us safe and slow, O love of God— most— wise!

3. And though we turn us from thy face,
And wander wide and long,
Thou holdest us still in thine embrace,
O love of God most strong!

4. The saddened heart, the restless soul,
The toil-worn frame and mind,
Alike confess thy sweet control,
O love of God most kind!

5. And, filled and quickened by thy breath,
Our souls are strong and free
To rise o'er sin and fear and death,
O love of God, to thee!

IMMORTAL LOVE, FOREVER FULL — ABBY C.M.

St. 1-6

John Greenleaf Whittier, 1856 — S. Allen, 1845

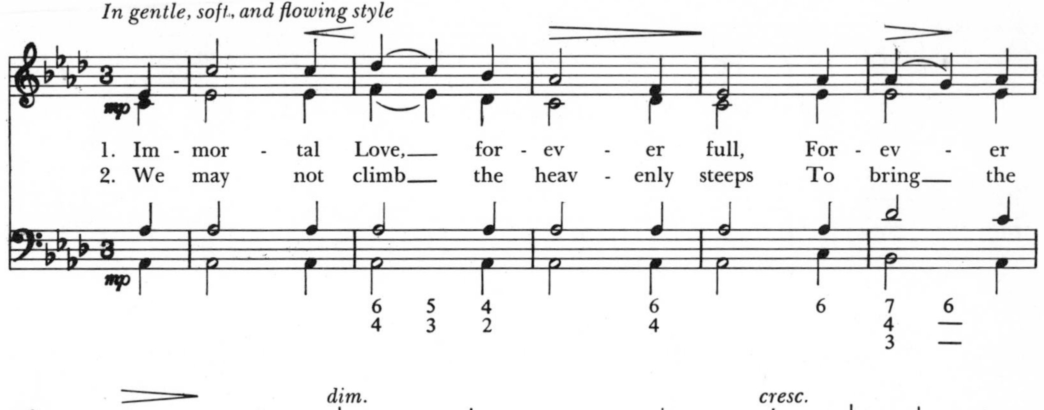
In gentle, soft, and flowing style
1. Im - mor - tal Love, for - ev - er full, For - ev - er
2. We may not climb the heav - enly steeps To bring the

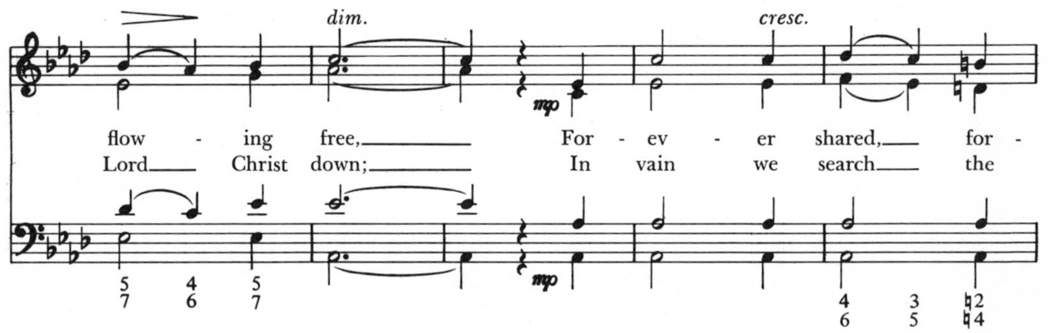
dim.
cresc.
flow - ing free, For - ev - er shared, for -
Lord Christ down; In vain we search the

cresc.
ev - er whole, A nev - er - ebb - ing sea!
low - est deeps, For him no depths can drown.

3. But warm, sweet, tender, even yet
A present help is he;
And faith has still its Olivet,
And love its Galilee.

4. The healing of his seamless dress
Is by our beds of pain.
We touch him in life's throng and press,
And we are whole again.

5. Through him the first fond prayers are said,
Our lips of childhood frame;
The last low whispers of our dead
Are burdened with his name.

6. O Lord and Master of us all,
What'er our name or sign,
We own thy sway, we hear thy call,
We test our lives by thine.

O LOVE DIVINE, THAT STOOPED TO SHARE — CROWN POINT L.M.

St. 1-4

Oliver Wendell Holmes, 1859 — Henry Kemble Oliver, comp. 1873

1. O Love di - vine, that stooped to___ share Our
2. Though long the wea - ry way we___ tread, And

sharp - est pang, our bit - terest tear,___
sor - row crown each lin - gering year,___

On thee we cast___ each earth - born___ care;
No path we shun,___ no dark - ness___ dread;

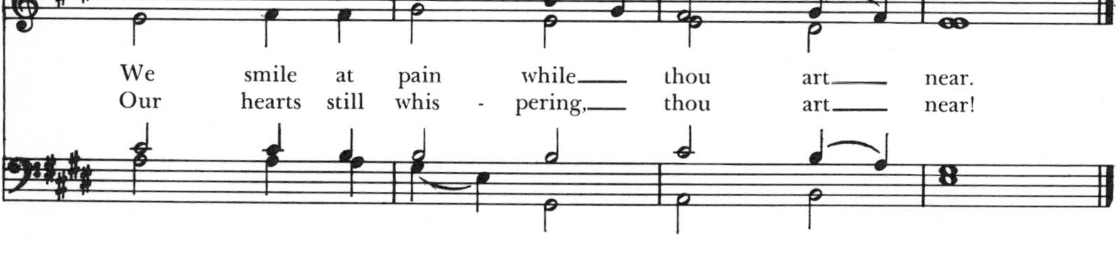
We smile at pain while___ thou art___ near.
Our hearts still whis - pering,___ thou art___ near!

3. When drooping pleasure turns to grief,
And trembling faith is changed to fear,
The murmuring wind, the quivering leaf,
Shall softly tell us, thou art near!

4. On thee we fling our burdening woe,
O Love divine, forever dear!
Content to suffer while we know,
Living and dying, thou art near.

Again As Evening's Shadow Falls

St. 1-4

Samuel Longfellow, 1859

Selena L.M.

Isaac B. Woodbury, 1850

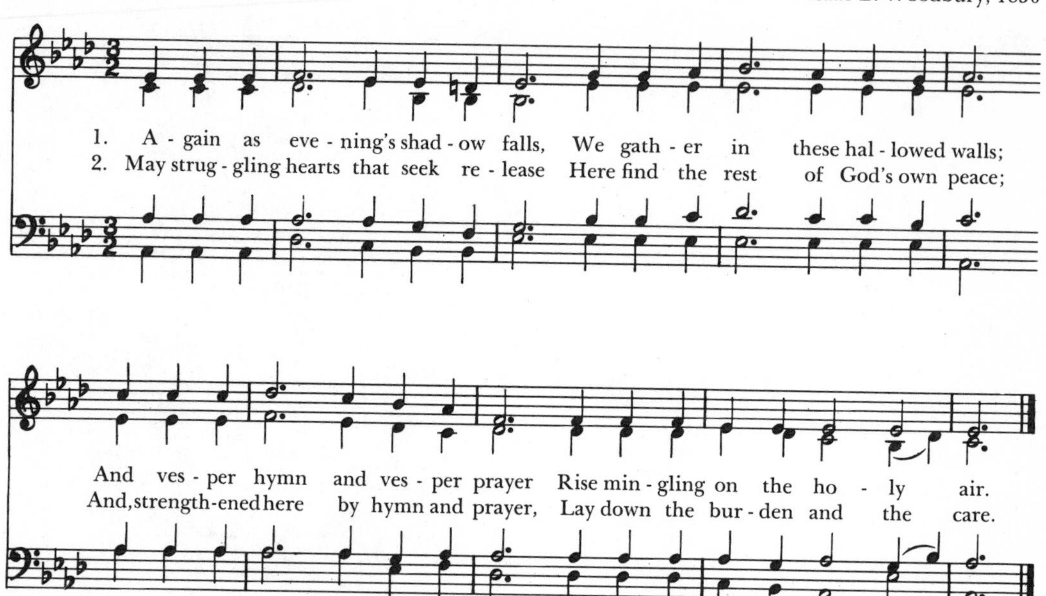
1. A - gain as eve - ning's shad - ow falls, We gath - er in these hal - lowed walls;
2. May strug - gling hearts that seek re - lease Here find the rest of God's own peace;
And ves - per hymn and ves - per prayer Rise min - gling on the ho - ly air.
And, strength-ened here by hymn and prayer, Lay down the bur - den and the care.

3. O God, our light! to thee we bow;
Within all shadows standest thou;
Give deeper calm than night can bring;
Give sweeter songs than lips can sing.

4. Life's tumult we must meet again,
We cannot at the shrine remain;
But in the Spirit's secret cell
May hymn and prayer forever dwell.

Father, Hear the Prayer We Offer — Stockwell 8.7.8.7.

St. 1-4

Love Maria Willis, pub. 1859, alt. 1864 — Darius Eliot Jones, 1851

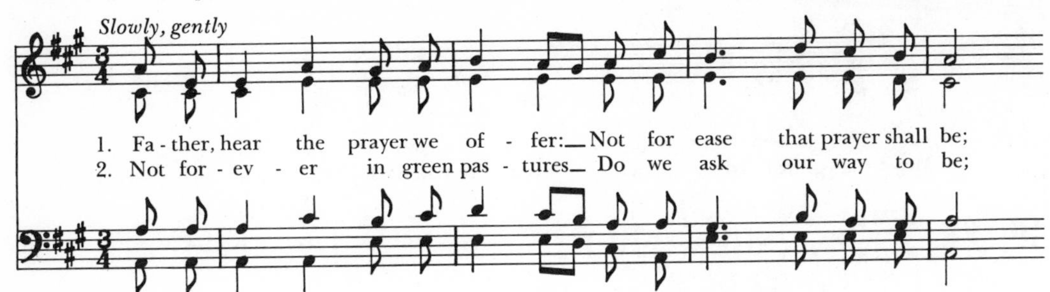
Slowly, gently
1. Fa - ther, hear the prayer we of - fer:_ Not for ease that prayer shall be;
2. Not for - ev - er in green pas - tures_ Do we ask our way to be;

But for strength, that we may ev - er Live our lives cou - ra - geous - ly.
But the steep and rug - ged path - way May we tread re - joic - ing - ly.

3. Not forever by still waters
   Would we idly quiet stay;
   But would smite the living fountains
   From the rocks along our way.

4. Be our strength in hours of weakness;
   In our wanderings, be our guide;
   Through endeavor, failure, danger,
   Father, be thou at our side!

THOU LONG DISOWNED, REVILED, OPPRESSED — GEER C.M.

St. 1-5

Eliza Scudder, writ. 1860, pub. 1864 — Henry Wellington Greatorex, 1849

1. Thou long dis - owned, re - viled, op - pressed, Strange
2. How late thy bright and aw - ful brow Breaks

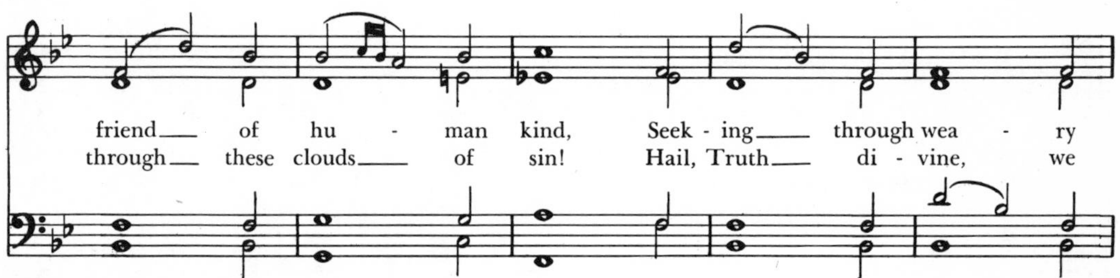
friend of hu - man kind, Seek - ing through wea - ry
through these clouds of sin! Hail, Truth di - vine, we

years a rest With - in our hearts to find,
know thee now; An - gel of God, come in!

3. Come, though with purifying fire
And desolating sword!
Thou of all nations the desire,
Earth waits thy cleansing word.

4. Struck by the lightning of thy glance,
Let old oppressions die;
Before thy cloudless countenance
Let fear and falsehood fly.

5. Flood our dark life with golden day,
Convince, subdue, enthrall;
Then to a mightier yield thy sway,
And love be all in all!

I BLESS THEE, LORD, FOR SORROWS SENT

ROCKPORT L.M.

St. 1-4

Samuel Johnson, 1864

August Kreissman, 1854

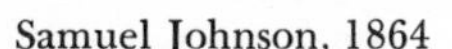

Soft and slow

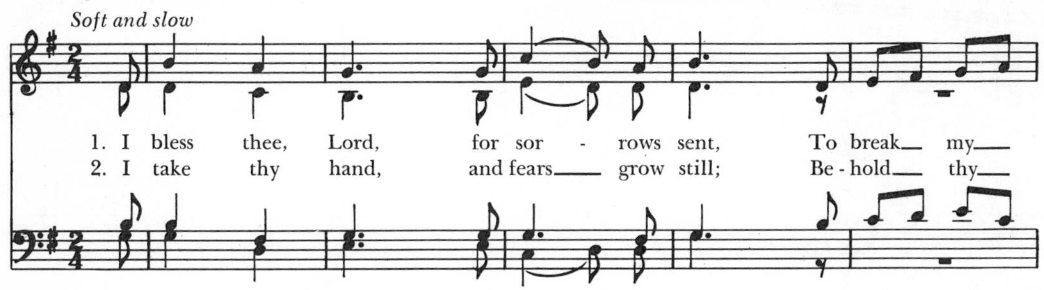
1. I bless thee, Lord, for sor - rows sent, To break my
2. I take thy hand, and fears grow still; Be - hold thy

dream of hu - man power; For now, my shal - low
face, and doubts re - move; Who would not yield his

cis - terns spent, I find thy founts, and thirst no more.
wa - vering will To per - fect truth and bound - less love?

3. That love this restless soul doth teach
The strength of thine eternal calm;
And tune its sad and broken speech
To join, on earth, the angels' psalm.

4. O be it patient in thy hands,
And drawn, through each mysterious hour,
To service of thy pure commands,
The narrow way to love and power.

LIFE OF AGES, RICHLY POURED

SOLITUDE 7.7.7.7.

St. 1-5

Samuel Johnson, 1864

Lewis Thompson Downes, 1877

1. Life of ag - es, rich - ly_ poured, Love of_ God, un - spent and free,
2. Nev - er was to chos - en_ race That un - stint - ed tide con - fined.
Flow - ing in the proph - et's_ word And the peo - ple's lib - er - ty!
Thine is ev - ery time and_ place, Foun - tain sweet_ of heart and mind!

3. Breathing in the thinker's creed,
   Pulsing in the hero's blood,
   Nerving simplest thought and deed,
   Freshening time with truth and good;

4. Consecrating art and song,
   Holy book and pilgrim track;
   Hurling floods of tyrant wrong
   From the sacred limits back;

5. Life of ages, richly poured,
   Love of God, unspent and free,
   Flow still in the prophet's word
   And the people's liberty!

HOLY SPIRIT, TRUTH DIVINE

MERCY 7.7.7.7.

St. 1-4

Samuel Longfellow, 1864

Louis Moreau Gottschalk, comp. 1840
Edwin Pond Parker, arr. 1867

Not too fast
1. Ho - ly Spir - it, truth di - vine, Dawn up - on this soul of mine; Word of God, and
2. Ho - ly Spir - it, love di - vine, Glow with - in this heart of mine; Kin - dle ev - ery

in - ward light, Wake my spir - it, clear my sight.
high de - sire; Per - ish self in thy pure fire.

3. Holy Spirit, power divine,
Fill and nerve this will of mine;
By thee may I strongly live,
Bravely bear, and nobly strive.

4. Holy Spirit, right divine,
King within my conscience reign;
Be my law, and I shall be
Firmly bound, forever free.

MYSTERIOUS PRESENCE! SOURCE OF ALL — CATON L.M.

St. 1-4

Seth Curtis Beach, writ. 1866 — Henry Kemble Oliver, comp. 1866, pub. 1875

1. Mys - ter - ious Pres - ence, source of all, The world with -
2. Thou breath - est in the rush - ing wind, Thy spir - it
out, the soul with - in, Foun - tain of life, O
stirs in leaf and flower; Nor wilt thou from the
hear our call, And pour thy liv - ing wa - ters in.
will - ing mind With - hold thy light and love and power.
3

3. Thy hand unseen to accents clear
Awoke the psalmist's trembling lyre,
And touched the lips of holy seer
With flame from thine own altar fire.

4. That touch divine still, Lord, impart,
Still give the prophet's burning word;
And, vocal in each waiting heart,
Let living psalms of praise be heard.

Lead Us, O Father, in the Paths of Peace

Willow 10.10.10.10.

St. 1-4

William Henry Burleigh, 1868

John Zundel, 1855

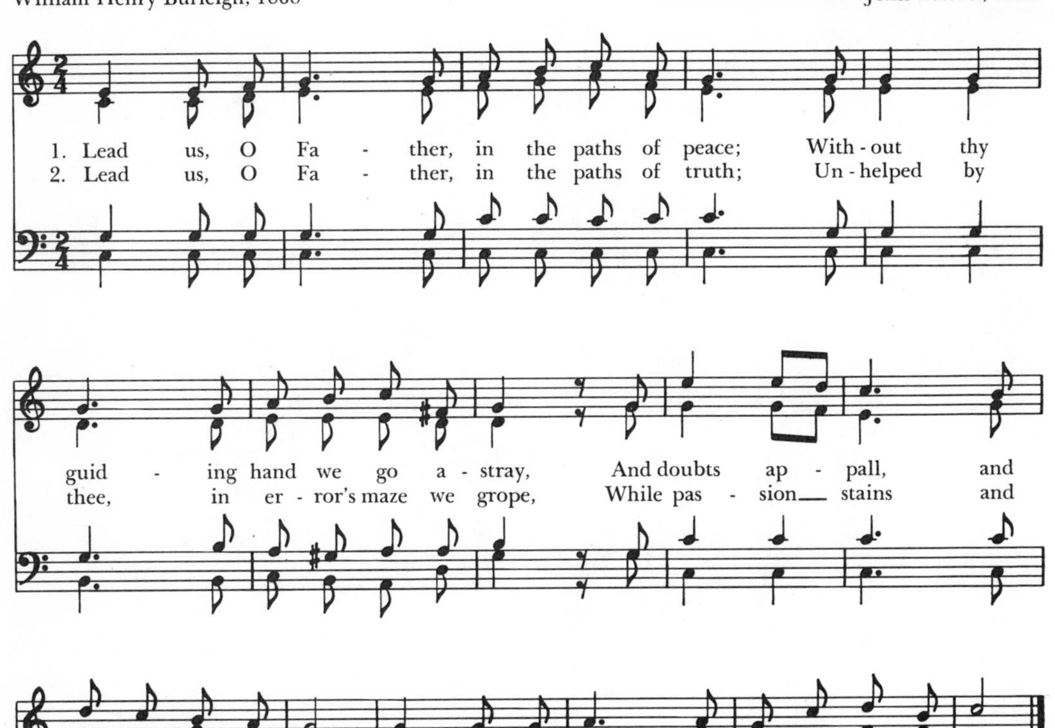
1. Lead us, O Fa - ther, in the paths of peace; With - out thy
2. Lead us, O Fa - ther, in the paths of truth; Un - helped by
guid - ing hand we go a - stray, And doubts ap - pall, and
thee, in er - ror's maze we grope, While pas - sion stains and

sor - rows still in - crease; Lead us through Christ, the true and liv - ing way.
fol - ly dims our youth, And age comes on un - cheered by faith or hope.

3. Lead us, O Father, in the paths of right;
Blindly we stumble when we walk alone,
Involved in shadows of a darkening night;
Only with thee we journey safely on.

4. Lead us, O Father, to thy heavenly rest,
However rough and steep the pathway be,
Through joy or sorrow, as thou deemest best,
Until our lives are perfected in thee.

Abide Not in the Realm of Dreams

St. 1, lines 1, 2; St. 2, lines 3, 4; St. 4, 6, 7, 10

William Henry Burleigh, 1871

East Hayes L.M.

Thomas Comer, 1840

Andante
1. A - bide not in the realm of dreams, O man, how - ev - er fair it seems; But with clear eye the pres - ent scan, And hear the call of God and man.
2. Think not in sleep to fold thy hands, For - get - ful of thy Lord's com - mands; From du - ty's claim no life is free; Be - hold, to - day hath need of thee.

3. Thrust in thy sickle, nor delay
The work that calls for thee today;
Tomorrow, if it come, will bear
Its own demands of toil and care.

4. The present hour allots thy task;
For present strength and patience ask;
And trust his love whose sure supplies
Meet all thy needs as they arise.

5. While the day lingers, do thy best!
Full soon the night will bring its rest;
And, duty done, that rest shall be
Full of beatitudes to thee.

Dear Lord and Father of Mankind

Woodland 8.6.8.8.6.

St. 1-5

John Greenleaf Whittier, writ. 1872

Nathaniel D. Gould, 1832

1. Dear Lord and Fa - ther of man-kind, For - give our fool - ish
2. In sim - ple trust like theirs who heard, Be - side the Sy - rian

ways; Re - clothe us in our right - ful mind; In
sea, The gra - cious call - ing of the Lord, Let

pur - er lives thy serv - ice find, In deep - er rev - erence, praise.
us, like them, with - out a word, Rise up and fol - low thee.

3. O Sabbath rest by Galilee!
O calm of hills above!
Where Jesus knelt to share with thee
The silence of eternity,
Interpreted by love.

4. Drop thy still dews of quietness,
Till all our strivings cease;
Take from our souls the strain and stress,
And let our ordered lives confess
The beauty of thy peace.

5. Breathe through the heats of our desire
Thy coolness and thy balm;
Let sense be dumb, let flesh retire;
Speak through the earthquake, wind, and fire,
O still small voice of calm.

As Shadows Cast by Cloud and Sun — Sydney C.M.

St. 1-4

William Cullen Bryant, writ. 1874, pub. 1877 — Henry Kemble Oliver, comp. 1858, pub. 1875

1. As shad - ows cast by cloud and sun, Flit o'er the sum - mer grass, So, in thy sight, Al - might - y One! Earth's gen - er - a - tions pass.
2. And while the years, an end - less host, Come press - ing swift - ly on, The bright - est names that earth can boast Just glis - ten, and are gone.

3. Yet doth the star of Bethlehem shed
A lustre pure and sweet;
And still it leads, as once it led,
To the Messiah's feet.

4. O Father, may that holy star
Grow every year more bright,
And send its glorious beams afar
To fill the world with light.

O LIFE THAT MAKETH ALL THINGS NEW — ROSEHILL L.M.

St. 1-4

Samuel Longfellow, writ. 1874, pub. 1876 — Joseph Emerson Sweetser, 1856

With dignity
1. O Life that mak - eth all things new, The bloom - ing earth, the thoughts of men! Our pil - grim feet, wet with thy dew, In glad - ness hith - er turn a - gain.
2. From hand to hand the greet - ing flows, From eye to eye the sig - nals run, From heart to heart the bright hope glows; The seek - ers of the light are one.

3. One in the freedom of the truth,
One in the joy of paths untrod,
One in the soul's perennial youth,
One in the larger thought of God;

4. The freer step, the fuller breath,
The wide horizon's grander view,
The sense of life that knows no death,
The life that maketh all things new.

Thou One in All, Thou All in One — Clonberne L.M.

St. 1-4

Seth Curtis Beach, 1884

Henry Kemble Oliver, writ. 1873, pub. 1875

1. Thou One in all, thou All in one,
2. We bless thee for the life that flows,
Source of the grace that crowns our days,
A pulse in ev - ery grain of sand,
For all thy gifts 'neath cloud or sun,
A beau - ty in the blush - ing rose,
We lift to thee our grate ful praise.
A thought and deed in brain and hand.

3. For life that thou hast made a joy,
For strength to make our lives like thine,
For duties that our hands employ,
We bring our offerings to thy shrine.

4. Be thine to give and ours to own
The truth that sets thy children free,
The law that binds us to thy throne,
The love that makes us one with thee.

From Heart to Heart — Clovelly C.M.

St. 1-4

William Channing Gannett, writ. 1875, pub. 1885 — Horatio Parker, 1903

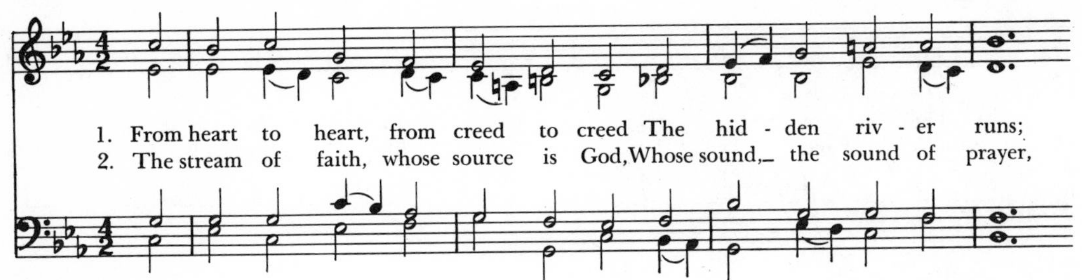
1. From heart to heart, from creed to creed The hid - den riv - er runs;
2. The stream of faith, whose source is God, Whose sound,— the sound of prayer,

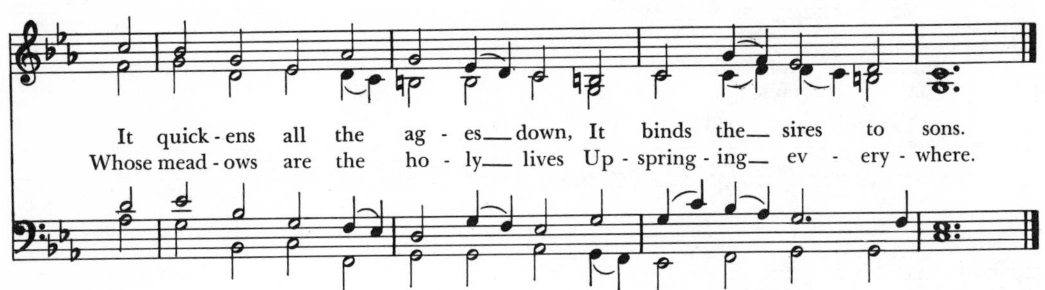
It quick - ens all the ag - es— down, It binds the— sires to sons.
Whose mead - ows are the ho - ly— lives Up - spring - ing— ev - ery - where.

3. And still it moves, a broadening flood,
And fresher, fuller grows
A sense as if the sea were near,
Towards which the river flows.

4. O thou who art the secret source
That riseth in each soul,
Thou art the ocean, too, and thine,
That ever deepening roll!

From Age to Age They Gather — Hosmer — Irregular

St. 1-4

Frederick Lucian Hosmer, writ. 1891, pub. 1894 — Frederick Field Bullard, 1902

1. From age to age they gath - er, all the brave of heart and strong, In the
2. "In this sign we con - quer:" 't is the sym - bol of our faith, Made
strife of truth with er - ror, of the right a-gainst the wrong; I can see their gleam-ing
ho - ly by the might of love tri - um - phant o - ver death; "He finds his life who
ban - ner, I can hear their tri-umph song: The truth is march - ing on!
los - eth it," for - ev - er - more it saith; The right is march - ing on!

3. The earth is circling onward out of shadow into light;
The stars keep watch above our way, however dark the night;
For every martyr's stripe there glows a bar of morning bright,
And love is marching on!

4. Lead on, O cross of martyr faith, with thee is victory;
Shine forth, O stars and redd'ning dawn, the full day yet shall be;
On earth his kingdom cometh, and with joy our eyes shall see;
Our God is marching on!

When Thy Heart with Joy O'erflowing — Woodlawn 8.5.8.3.

St. 1-5

Theodore Chickering Williams, 1891 — Robert L. Sanders, 1934

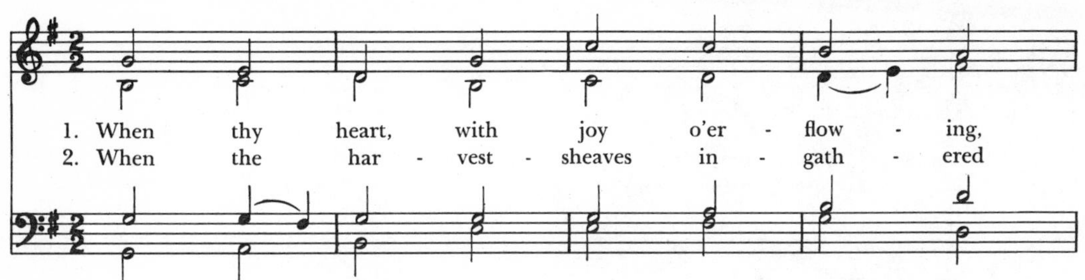
1. When thy heart, with joy o'er - flow - ing,
2. When the har - vest - sheaves in - gath - ered

Sings a thank - ful prayer, In thy joy, O
Fill thy barns with store, To thy God and

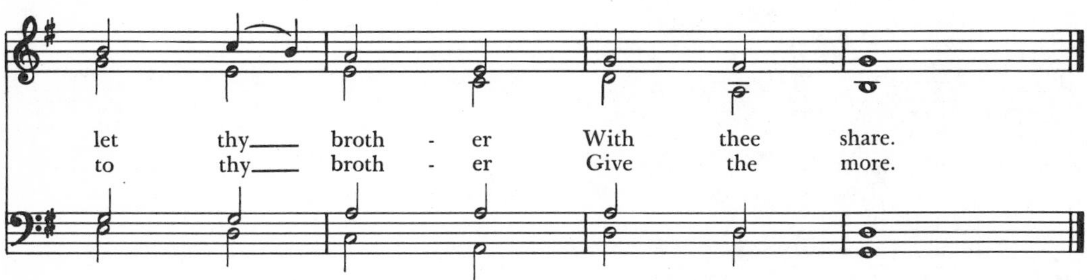
let thy___ broth - er With thee share.
to thy___ broth - er Give the more.

3. If thy soul, with power unlifted,
Yearn for glorious deed,
Give thy strength to serve thy brother
In his need.

4. Hast thou borne a secret sorrow
In thy lonely breast?
Take to thee thy sorrowing brother
For a guest.

5. Share with him thy bread of blessing,
Sorrow's burden share;
When thy heart enfolds a brother,
God is there.

He Hides Within the Lily — Resurrection 7.6.7.6.D.

St. 1-4

William Channing Gannett, 1893 — Alice Nevin, 1879

Jubilantly
1. He hides with - in the li - ly A strong and ten - der care, That
2. We lin - ger at the vig - il With him who bent the knee To
wins the earth - born at - oms To glo - ry of the air; He
watch the old - time li - lies In dis - tant Gal - i - lee; And
weaves the shin - ing gar - ments Un - ceas - ing - ly and still, A -
still the wor - ship deep - ens And quick - ens in - to new, As
long the wa - ters, In the hill.
es God's thrill - eth through.

3. O Toiler of the lily,
Thy touch is in the man!
No leaf that dawns to petal
But hints the angel-plan.
The flower-horizons open,
The blossom vaster shows;
We hear thy wide worlds echo,
'See how the lily grows!'

4. Shy yearnings of the savage,
Unfolding thought by thought,
To holy lives are lifted,
To visions fair are wrought.
The races rise and cluster,
And evils fade and fall,
Till chaos blooms to beauty,
Thy purpose crowning all!

Our Father! While Our Hearts Unlearn

Capen C.M.

St. 1-6

Oliver Wendell Holmes, 1893

Leo R. Lewis, 1898

1. Our Fa - ther! while our hearts un - learn The creeds that wrong thy name,
2. Not by the light - ning - gleams of wrath Our souls thy face shall see,

Still let our hal - lowed al - tars burn With faith's un - dy - ing flame!
The star of love must light the path That leads to heav'n and thee.

3. Help us to read our Master's will
Through every darkening stain
That clouds his sacred image still,
And see him once again,

4. The brother man, the pitying friend,
Who weeps for human woes,
Whose pleading words of pardon blend
With cries of raging foes.

5. If, mid the gathering storms of doubt
Our hearts grow faint and cold,
The strength we cannot live without
Thy love will not withhold.

6. Our prayers accept; our sins forgive;
Our youthful zeal renew;
Shape for us holier lives to live
And nobler work to do!

When God Descends with Men To Dwell — **Corinth** 8.8.8.8.8.

St. 1-5

Hosea Ballou I, 1808 — Amos Blanchard, 1798

1. When God de-scends with men to dwell, And all cre-a-tion wakes a-new, What tongue can half the won-ders tell? What eye the dazz-ling glo-ries view? What eye the dazz-ling glo-ries view? view?
2. Zi-on, the des-o-late, a-gain Shall see her lands with ros-es bloom; And Car-mel's mount, and Shar-on's plain Shall yield their spic-es and per-fume, Shall yield their spic-es and per-fume. fume.
Soft
Loud
1.
2.

3. Celestial streams shall gently flow;
The wilderness shall joyful be;
Lilies on parchèd ground shall grow;
And gladness spring on every tree,
And gladness spring on every tree.

4. The weak be strong, the fearful bold,
The deaf shall hear, the dumb shall sing.
The lame shall walk, the blind behold;
And joy through all the earth shall ring,
And joy through all the earth shall ring.

5. Monarchs and slaves shall meet in love;
Old pride shall die, and meekness reign,
When God descends from worlds above
To dwell with men on earth again,
To dwell with men on earth again.

Dear Lord, Behold Thy Servants Blue Hill L.M.

St. 1-5

Hosea Ballou I, 1808 Daniel Belknap, 1800

Tune in tenor
1. Dear Lord, be - hold thy serv - ants, here From

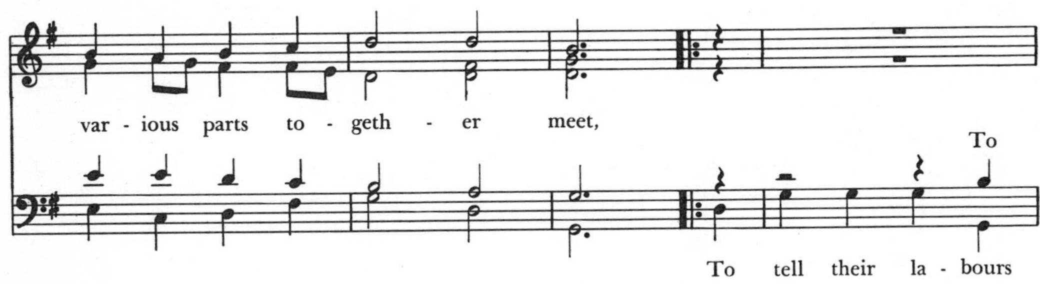
var - ious parts to - geth - er meet,
To
To tell their la - bours

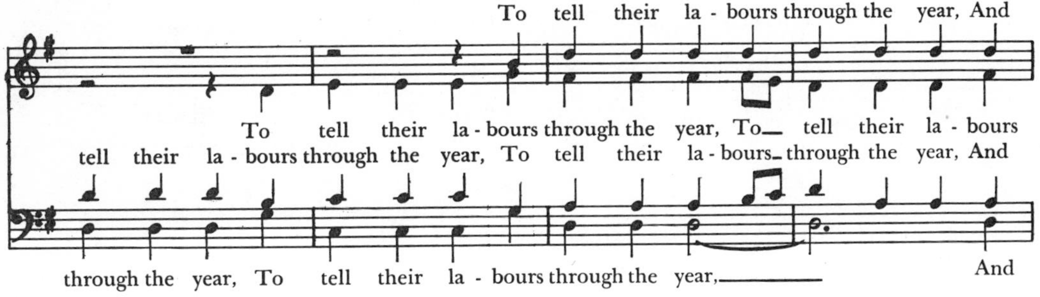
To tell their la - bours through the year, And
To tell their la - bours through the year, To tell their la - bours
tell their la - bours through the year, To tell their la - bours through the year, And
through the year, To tell their la - bours through the year,
And

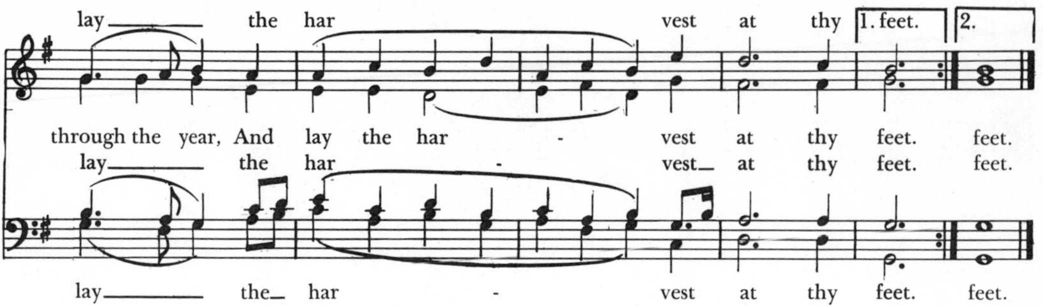
lay the har vest at thy 1. feet. 2.
through the year, And lay the har - vest at thy feet. feet.
lay the har - vest at thy feet. feet.
lay the har - vest at thy feet. feet.

2. In thy wide fields and vineyards, Lord,
We've toiled and wrought with watchful care;
Thy wheat doth flourish by thy word,
Thy love consumes the choking tare.

3. The reapers cry, thy fields are white,
And ready to be gathered in;
The labourer shouts with sweet delight,
This is the day to finish sin!

4. O bless us while we still remain;
With holy love thy servants fill;
O may thy doctrine drop like rain,
And like the silent dew distill.

5. While we attend thy churches' care,
O grant us wisdom from above;
With cautious steps and humble prayer,
May we fulfil the works of love.

In God's Eternity — Thornton S.M.

St. 1-4

Hosea Ballou I, 1821 — John G. Adams, 1841

1. In God's e - ter - ni - ty There shall a
2. As night be - fore the rays Of morn - ing

day a - rise When all the race of
flees a - way, Sin shall re - tire be -

man shall be With Je - sus in the skies.
fore the blaze Of God's e - ter - nal day.

3. As music fills the grove
When stormy clouds are past,
Sweet anthems of redeeming love
Shall all employ at last.

4. Redeemed from death and sin,
Shall Adam's numerous race
A ceaseless song of praise begin,
And shout redeeming grace.

Ye Realms below the Skies — Spring Street 6.6.6.6.8.8.8.

St. 1-4

Hosea Ballou II, 1829 — Thomas Whittemore, 1841

1. Ye realms be-low the skies, Your Mak-er's prais-es sing; Let bound-less hon-ors rise, To heaven's e-ter-nal King. O bless his name, whose love ex-tends, Sal-va-tion to the world's far ends, Sal-va-tion to the world's far ends.
2. 'Tis he the moun-tains crowns With for-ests wav-ing wide; 'Tis he old o-cean bounds, And heaves her roar-ing tide; He swells the tem-pests on the main, Or breathes the zeph-yr o'er the plain, Or breathes the zeph-yr o'er the plain.
f
ff

3. Still let the waters roar,
As round the earth they roll;
His praise forevermore
They sound, from pole to pole.
'Tis nature's wild unconscious song,
O'er thousand waves, that float along,
O'er thousand waves, that float along.

4. His praise, ye worlds on high,
Display with all your spheres,
Amid the darksome sky,
When silent night appears.
O, let his works declare his name,
Through all the universal frame,
Through all the universal frame.

Lo, What Enraptured Songs of Praise | Persia L.M.

St. 1-4

Sebastion Streeter, 1829 | Thomas Whittemore, 1841

Re-sound through heaven to
1. Lo, what en - rap - tured songs_ of_ praise Re-sound through heaven to
Re-sound through heaven,
Re-sound through heaven, Re-sound through heaven to

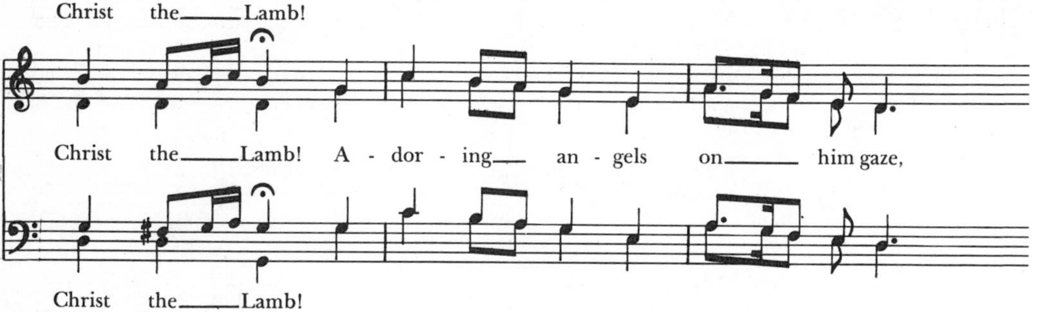
Christ the_ Lamb!
Christ the_ Lamb! A - dor - ing_ an - gels on_ him gaze,
Christ the_ Lamb!

And swell the gold - en trump of fame.
And swell the gold - en trump of fame, And swell the gold - en trump of fame.
And swell the gold - en trump of fame.

2. Amid his smiles and glories bright
Transported millions round him bend,
And, robed in life's primeval light,
The honours of his cross extend.

3. Salvation to the Lamb, they cry,
That sits upon the shining throne,
Who once for sinful men did die,
That he might seek and bring them home.

4. Hosanna! all have joined the song,
In heaven, in earth, and in the seas;
Salvation sounds from every tongue
In swelling notes of ceaseless praise.

A King Shall Reign in Righteousness — Wyeford L.M.

St. 1-4

Sebastian Streeter, 1829 — Henry Kemble Oliver, 1848

1. A King shall reign in right - eous - ness,
2. In him the na - ked soul shall find
And all the kin - dred na - tions bless;
A hid - ing - place from chill - ing wind;
He's King of Sa - lem, King of peace,
Or, when the rag - ing tem - pests bear,
shall his spread - ing king dom cease.
warm, a safe re - treat.

3. In burning sands, and thirsty ground,
He like a river shall be found;
Or lofty rock, beneath whose shade
The weary traveller rests his head.

4. The dimness gone, all eyes shall see
His glory, grace, and majesty;
All ears shall hearken, and obtain
The words of life from Christ the Lamb.

As Gentle Dews Distill — Watkin S.M.

St. 1, 2

George Rogers, 1845 — Thomas Whittemore, 1841

Moderato
1. As gen - tle dews dis - still, At qui - et
2. So from our God shall flow His sweet re -
eve - ning hour, And with re - fresh - ing
fresh - ing grace, To make our Chris - tian
mois - ture fill Each thirst - y herb and flower;
vir - tues grow, And fill our hearts with praise.

Heaven Is Here — **Eden** 8.7.8.7.

St. 1-4

John G. Adams, 1845 — Josiah Osgood, 1849

1. Heaven is here, where hymns of glad - ness Cheer the toil - er's rug - ged way, In this world where clouds of sad - ness Of - ten change to night our day.
2. Heaven is here, where mis - ery light - ened Of its heav - y load is seen, Where the face of sor - row bright - ened, By the deed of love hath been.
6
4
6 6
4 7 7 6
7 6
4 7 6 6
4 7

3. Where the sad, the poor, despairing,
Are uplifted, cheered and blest,
Where in others' labors sharing,
We can find our surest rest,

4. Where we heed the voice of duty,
Tread the path that Jesus trod,
This is heaven, its peace, its beauty,
Radiant with the love of God.

O Thou, Who Didst Ordain the Word — Chadwick C.M.

St. 1-3

Edwin Hubbell Chapin, 1846 — Henry Kemble Oliver, 1835

1. O Thou, who didst or - dain the Word, And
To this young war - rior of the cross, Who

its strong her - alds send. We draw the ho - ly
takes his sta - tion here. Be thou a teach - er

veil of prayer, And in thy pres - ence bend,
and a guide, And be thy spir - it near.

2. A pure disciple, let him tread
The ways his master trod,
Giving the weary spirits rest,
Leading the lost to God;
Stooping to lend the sufferer aid,
Crushed sorrow's wail to hear,
To bind the widow's broken heart,
And dry the orphan's tear.

3. For war with error, make him strong,
And sin, the soul's dark foe,
But let him humbly seek for truth,
Where'er its waters flow.
And when, O Father, at the grave
He lays his armor down.
Give him the victor's glistening robe,
The palm-wreath and the crown.

Hark! Hark! with Harps of Gold — Caton S.M.D.

St. 1-4

Edwin Hubbell Chapin, 1846 — Anon., 1846

Con spirito
1. Hark! hark! with harps of gold, What an-them do they sing?
2. "Glo-ry to God!" re-peat The glad earth and the sea;
The ra-diant clouds are back-ward rolled, And an-gels smite the string.
And ev-ery wind and bil-low fleet, Bears on the ju-bi-lee.
Glo-ry to God; bright wings, Spread glist-ening and a-far,
Where He-brew bard hath sung, Or He-brew seer hath trod,
And on the hal-lowed rap-ture rings, From cir-cling star to star
Each ho-ly spot hath found a tongue, "Let glo-ry be to God."

3. Soft swells the music now,
Along the shining choir,
And every seraph bends his brow,
And breathes above his lyre.
What words of heavenly birth,
Thrill deep our hearts again
And fall like dew drops to the earth,
"Peace and good will to men."

4. Soft! yet the soul is bound
With rapture, like a chain;
Earth,vocal, whispers them around,
And heaven repeats the strain.
Sound, harps, and hail the morn,
With every golden string;
For unto us this day is born,
A Saviour and a King.

Cast Thy Bread upon the Waters

Agawam 8.7.8.7.

St. 1-4

Phoebe A. Hanaford, 1852

Thomas Whittemore, 1841

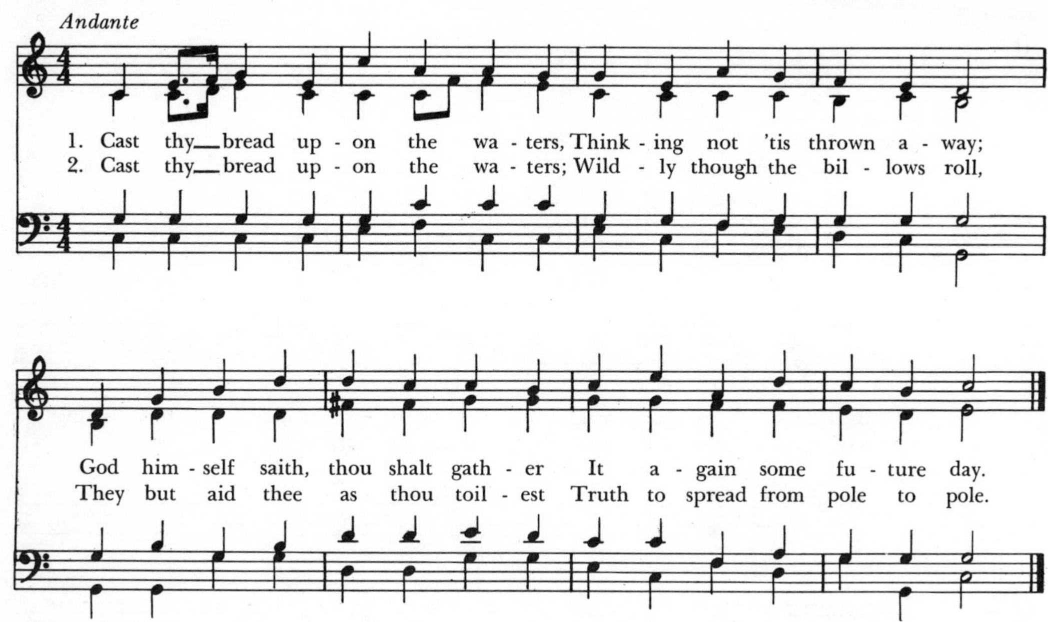
Andante
1. Cast thy bread up - on the wa - ters, Think - ing not 'tis thrown a - way;
2. Cast thy bread up - on the wa - ters; Wild - ly though the bil - lows roll,
God him - self saith, thou shalt gath - er It a - gain some fu - ture day.
They but aid thee as thou toil - est Truth to spread from pole to pole.

3. As the seed, by billows floated,
To some distant island lone,
So to human souls benighted,
That thou flingest may be borne.

4. Cast thy bread upon the waters;
Why wilt thou still doubting stand?
Bounteous shall God send the harvest,
If thou sowest with liberal hand.

THE TWENTIETH CENTURY

EVERY SUNDAY the sound of hymn singing rises from thousands of churches across the United States. Many of these hymns, written a century or more ago, still serve to express the beliefs and the hopes of the singers; many written within the twentieth century join in the same chorus of hope and praise. They are, however, sung in a changing world and our hymnbooks also contain other hymns that deal with problems of our time or with age-old longings, like the search for peace, which are given special urgency by the circumstances of our own period.

A Lutheran conductor and composer, Dr. Daniel T. Moe, has advocated "disposable or situation hymnody . . . something appropriate for one occasion that will be discarded for the next. . . . I hope that such hymns would add things which are currently lacking—namely concern for urban living, technology, the problems of war in a nuclear age."

"Where Cross the Crowded Ways of Life," "The City, Lord, Where Thy Dear Life," and "Not Only Where God's Free Winds Blow" are hymns of the city. It was the black slaves who shaped and sang the spirituals; a century later our black citizens, still not free from discrimination, sang a new song as they marched in the South—"We Shall Overcome." The early painters liked to picture Christ helping Joseph in the carpenter shop: "O Master Workman of the Race" sings of Christ as a craftsman who shapes the lives of men.

In a century ravaged by two world wars and a succession of bloody but more local conflicts, the voice of peace is less confident than it was a hundred years ago. Yet a number of hymns do express our common longing for peace: "The Prince of Peace His Banner Spreads," "Give Peace, Oh God, the Nations Cry," and "God of Peace, in Peace Preserve us."

In earlier pages, we have presented hymns in Huron, in Dutch, in German, and in Swedish. English has replaced each language as children and grandchildren adopt the language of their neighbors. The earlier hymns in Spanish were sung in the Southwest, where missions were established in an area which was later included in the United States. The recent movement of Spanish-speaking people to the United States is by no means confined to border areas. In Catholic churches in New York hymns are sung and masses celebrated in Spanish. A Spanish Baptist hymn much sung in this country is "Si feliz quieres ser."

The Denominational Paradox

A New England village street with the steeples of four or five churches rising above the shade trees, each barely supported by a faithful few, is a symbol of the tendency of Protestantism to divide and to persist in division. Yet the twentieth century has witnessed a striking reversal of that trend and this in turn has had a very definite effect on hymnody.

In 1939 three groups of Methodists reunited as the Methodist Episcopal Church. In 1957 the Evangelical and Reformed Church (which itself represented a merger of two denominations) joined with the Congregational Christian Church as the United Church of Christ. In 1961 the Unitarian and Universalist denominations were associated as one church.

This spirit of cooperation had already been apparent in the field of hymnody. Three divisions of the Methodist church cooperated to make the *Methodist Hymnal* (1935) possible. The Unitarians and Universalists have had a common hymnal since *Hymns of the Spirit* (1937). Four Presbyterian groups issued their *Hymnbook* (1955). Eight synods of the Lutheran Church joined to make their hymnbook of 1958 possible.

Such moves toward unity have not been achieved without some loss of local and regional flavor. In some instances it would appear that elements in a musical tradition have not always been valued as highly as they might have been. For example, in general the fine psalm tunes sung by the early English-speaking settlers have been neglected by their descendants. Some twentieth-century hymnbooks lack a sense of valued and continuous tradition.

Therefore, it would seem safe to argue that many twentieth-century hymnbooks are planned to serve a denominational need and are the product of a committee rather than of an individual. One reason for this trend is the increase in publication costs and the economic advantage of a large edition. Another is the probability that a committee chosen from a denomination would contain more highly qualified specialists than would be available in a single congregation. The very fact that such books are committee products means that the contents represent in some instances a consensus, in others a compromise between opposing views. Such a procedure is likely to produce a book which is generally acceptable but it is not favorable to innovation.

Recent changes in the Catholic Church, on the other hand, have had a profound effect on its music and liturgy. The mass as well as the ancient hymns which have become a part of that rite were sung in

Latin. Now the mass may be sung in the vernacular and provision is made for a choice of hymns to be sung by the congregation. Not only has this involved translating the ancient texts; it has also involved the selection of suitable hymns, some chosen from the Protestant repertory, as well as the creation of new ones. With this step congregational hymnody, which had been restricted to nonliturgical devotions, has assumed an important part in the mass. If Catholic hymnody has now become ecumenical in the sense that Protestant hymns are now sung, Protestant congregations have for a longer span been singing hymns of Catholic origin.

The Music

Many tune books of the nineteenth century were abundantly supplied with original compositions by the compiler. The role of the composer is much more restricted in most denominational hymnals. Frequently the new tunes are in special meters. The reasons for this are simple enough. Only a limited number of tunes in the basic meters can be included in a denominational hymnal, and there are more than that number of tunes of proven usefulness. In some Episcopalian hymnals second and even third tunes are provided for certain texts in an attempt to satisfy both those who wish to sing the usual tunes as well as those who are willing to learn new ones. On the other hand members of the committee may wish to introduce a hymn in a less usual meter and fail to find a suitable tune. In that event they are likely to turn to the music editor to ask for a new one.

In a preceding preface we told of the enthusiasm with which *Hymns Ancient and Modern* was received in this country. The results were twofold. The richer harmonic and modulatory schemes made the simplicity of American tunes of the Lowell Mason school seem insipid, and American composers began to compose in a more elaborate style. This trend is perhaps best exemplified in the hymn tunes of Horatio Parker.

The Oxford Movement, of course, originated in England in the middle of the last century, but it was not until the present century that the renewed interest in Gregorian song that followed had an effect on American composers. Although Lowell Mason's HAMBURG (q.v.) is based on a Gregorian melody, Mason was not concerned with the rhythmic freedom or the character of the modal scales in which they developed.

There were plain chant melodies in *Hymns Ancient and Modern* and, in our own country, scholars like Winifred Douglas edited and published editions of Gregorian song with English text. However the

final effect in Protestant circles has been not so much to stimulate the wider use of the ancient melodies as to inspire American composers to compose tunes which have something of the modal flavor, the rhythmic freedom, and the traditional cadences appropriate to them.

One of the more arresting facts of recent musical life is the growing interest in the music of Johann Sebastian Bach, which has gradually extended to include his contemporaries and his predecessors. Bach not only enriched the Lutheran church with original chorale tunes but harmonized many traditional chorale tunes, some of them several times. This influence has been felt in the churches, and not exclusively in the Lutheran church where these tunes were a natural heritage.

In the *Hymnal for Colleges and Schools* (1956) twenty-two different tunes bear Bach's name, either as composer or arranger. This does not count chorales harmonized by other masters. Although this trend is very characteristic of the present, there are few twentieth-century chorales. Irving Fine's setting of "That We May Worship Thee" might be considered an example. The example of Bach has, however, been one of the influences which has spurred composers to give melodic life and interest to each voice and particularly to the inner ones.

It was early in this century that Ralph Vaughan Williams became a folk-song collector. He thus took an active part in the revival of interest in folk song with other musicians such as Cecil Sharp and Percy Grainger. Vaughan Williams, however, combined an interest in folk songs with an active interest in hymns. As editor of *The English Hymnal* (1906) he introduced folk melodies into a congregational hymnbook with notable success. The *Oxford Book of Carols,* which he edited with Martin Shaw, was equally important in its special field.

Americans had been in the curious position of having sung folk hymns throughout the nineteenth century without being very conscious of that fact. Although this was truer of the South, singers in the North, where folk hymnody was first apparent, did not altogether abandon the practice. Folk hymns may be found in such a collection as the *Revivalist* (published in Troy, New York, in 1868) and even in denominational hymnbooks where they were called "Southern" or "Western" tunes. It was not, however, until the publication of George Pullen Jackson's *White Spirituals in the Southern Uplands* (1933) that Americans became conscious of what some of them had been singing all along. Spirituals also began belatedly to appear in denominational hymnbooks. The tune McKee, arranged by Harry Burleigh, appeared

in *The Hymnal* of 1940, *The Pilgrim Hymnal* of 1956 has seven, and there are nine grouped as a special section in the *African Methodist Zion Hymnal* of 1957.

One aspect of this change has gained prominence only in the very recent past. Folk music is no longer confined to isolated enclaves, but reaches a national audience through the personal appearances and the recordings of such singers as Burl Ives, Woody Guthrie, Peter Seeger, Bob Dylan, and Joan Baez. At the same time the repertory sung has changed in a very basic fashion. Rock music has reached the status of a cult, and rock festivals attract thousands of young people.

Thus, there is a new literature of devotional song. Much is published in the form of small pamphlets with symbols for guitar chords. In some contemporary publications, verses are set to the tunes of spirituals or familiar folk songs. Some of the original tunes are derived for folk, blues, jazz, or rock. In the *People's Mass Book* there are simple songs, some old and some new, which are to be used as service music (see Joseph Wise's "Glory"). There have been jazz masses. Duke Ellington has performed in churches, and St. Peter's Lutheran Church in New York has instituted jazz vesper services. Recordings like those of the Singing Nun, of *Jesus Christ Superstar,* and revivals of old Southern folk hymns like "Amazing Grace" have attained wide popularity.

Since many black musicians were entertainers, the spirituals were also influenced by a variety of pop styles. Some of these reveal a willingness to exploit the spirituals to entertain white audiences. Some are the product of musicians who have grown up as jazz or blues performers and who find it natural to perform the spirituals in the way in which they perform other songs. Clarence Joseph Rivers, a Negro priest of Cincinnati, has tried to write in the spirit of American Negro music in his American Mass Program.

The black people of America are searching for their African roots. This is shown in music as in the visual arts. Such compositions as the Congolese *Missa Luba* (long available as a recording) and the *Royal Mass of Mogho* (performed at St. Patrick's Cathedral April 25, 1971) reveal a fusion of African and European influences. The *Royal Mass* featured West African drummers in addition to chorus, orchestra, and organ. Neither composition is of American origin. Both come from cultures that American blacks wish to claim as their own.

The Methodist Commission on Worship has urged churches to employ "All the sources of music, both traditional and contemporary" and Bishop Lance Webb has stated that this includes "jazz, folk music, guitars, drums, trumpets, and other wind and string instruments."

Some of these innovations are an effort on the part of young ec-

clesiatics and of musicians who have grown up in the atmosphere of pop music. Some of them are the work of still younger people who have preferred to make up their own songs. Some churches have endeavored both to keep the old and to welcome the new. The Church of St. Baptiste, New York, for example, had two midnight masses on Christmas Night, 1971, one in the church, the other in a smaller room.

Two teen-agers in bulky sweaters and faded corduroy pants strode in. "You must be looking for the bongo mass," Father Hebert said. "Yeah," they answered. Father Hebert took them back to an adjacent auditorium where seventy-five people were sitting on folding chairs and buzzing among themselves, waiting for the formal mass to begin.

At the rear a young priest was going over the songs with some musicians. "O.K." he said to them, "let's get rolling." Then he marched to the altar, put on his vestments, and welcomed everyone to the mass.

The musicians began a version of "Greensleeves." In the darkened auditorium the wistful cool music of guitar and recorder sounded more medieval then contemporary. Those who object to the guitar as a sacred instrument should remember that the first performance of "Silent Night" was accompanied by guitar, and that psalm singing to the lute was a usual feature of domestic music in the seventeenth century.

This brings us to the difficult problem of the nature of ecclesiastical style in music. If we take a careful look at the past, we find that church music has been repeatedly attacked for frivolity, for excessive display, for operatic traits—criticisms which may be justly applied to certain hymns of the past. There have been hymns in waltz tempo, there have been hymns arranged from well-known operatic arias. While it is true that many composers found the use of passages in an older style to be better suited to church music, it is also true that church music of past periods was in general conformity with the secular music of that period. If there is an ecclesiastical style, it has varied as secular music has, barring archaisms which usually do not affect basic character.

The more serious aspect of the situation is the question of values. To many older observers, some of these recent experiments lack the essential qualities that the finest psalm and hymn tunes possess, lack the literary and musical substance which can make them worthy to express the aspirations of mankind. Yet one should realize that compromises between discrepant musical styles have been made within the walls of the church before now.

It is possible that our rich heritage of congregational hymns from the past may be related to the new experiments much as the camp

meeting hymn and the gospel hymn in the past were related to the older graver and more sedate congregational hymns sung on Sunday morning at public worship, satisfying somewhat different needs and sung on different occasions and by different voices.

CHRIST'S LIFE OUR CODE

St. 1-5

Benjamin Copeland, 1900

COPELAND L.M.

Karl P. Harrington, 1905

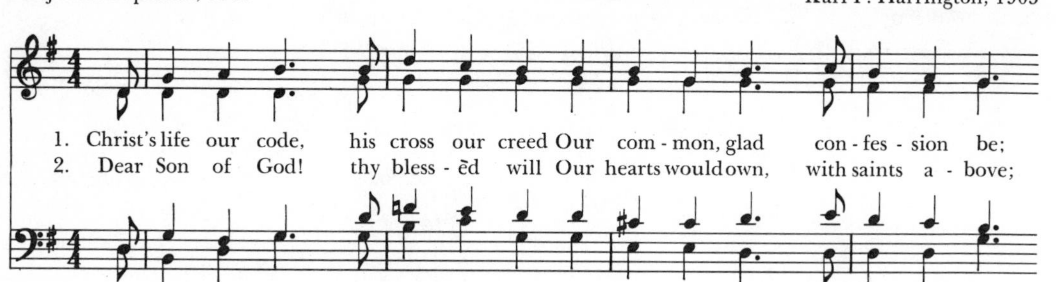
1. Christ's life our code, his cross our creed Our com - mon, glad con - fes - sion be;
2. Dear Son of God! thy bless - ēd will Our hearts would own, with saints a - bove;

Our deep - est wants, our high - est aims, Find their ful - fill - ment, Lord in thee.
All life is larg - er for thy law, All serv - ice sweet - er for thy love.

3. Thy life our code! in letters clear
We read our duty, day by day,
Thy footsteps tracing eagerly,
Who art the truth, the life, the way.

4. Thy cross our creed! thy boundless love
A ransomed world at last shall laud,
And crown thee their eternal King,
O Lord of Glory! Lamb of God!

5. 'Til then, to thee our souls aspire
In ardent prayer and earnest deed,
With love like thine, confessing, still
Christ's life our code! his cross our creed!

Our Fathers' God

St. 1-5

Benjamin Copeland, 1903

Puritan L.M.

Henry M. Dunham, 1905

Slow
1. Our fa - thers' God, to— thee we raise, In— cheer - ful—song, our grate - ful praise;
2. In - cline our hearts with— god - ly fear To— seek— thy— face, thy word re - vere;

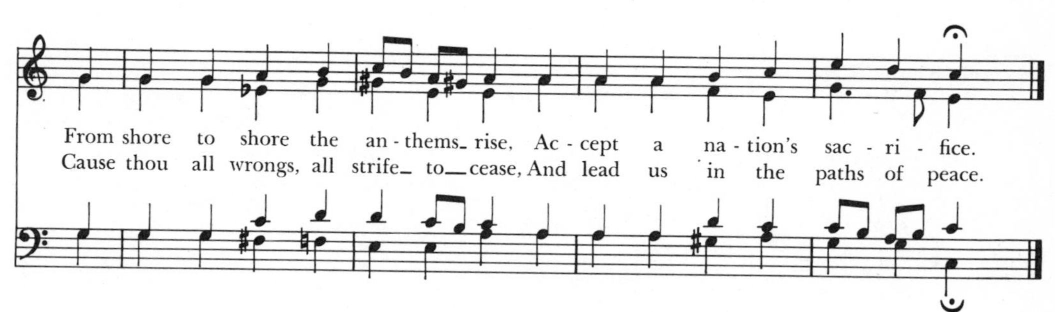
From shore to shore the an - thems— rise, Ac - cept a na - tion's sac - ri - fice.
Cause thou all wrongs, all strife— to—cease, And lead us in the paths of peace.

3. Here may the weak a welcome find,
And wealth increase with lowly mind;
A refuge, still, for all oppressed,
O be our land forever blest!

4. Thy wisdom, Lord, thy guidance lend,
Where'er our widening bounds extend;
Inspire our wills to speed thy plan:
The kingdom of the Son of man!

5. Through all the past thy truth we trace,
Thy ceaseless care, thy signal grace;
O may our children's children prove
Thy sovereign, everlasting love.

Be Strong! We Are Not Here To Play — Fortitude Irregular

St. 1-3

Maltbie Davenport Babcock, 1901 — David S. Smith, 1905

1. Be strong! We are not here to play, to dream, to— drift, We have hard work to do, and—
2. Be strong! Say not the days are e - vil—who's to—blame? And fold the hands and ac - qui -

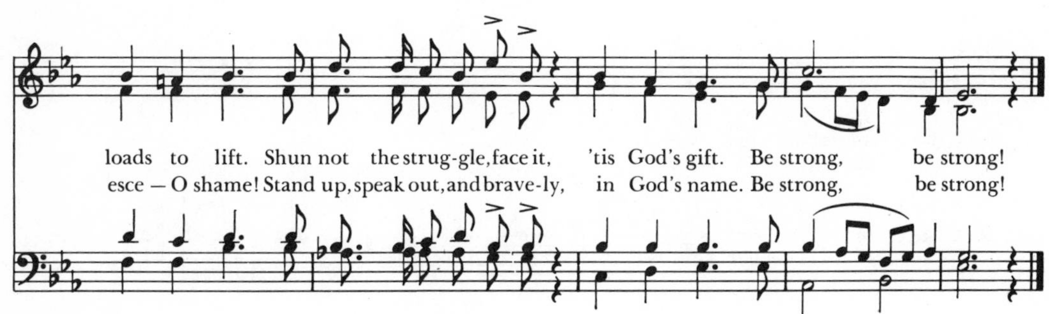
loads to lift. Shun not the strug-gle, face it, 'tis God's gift. Be strong, be strong!
esce — O shame! Stand up, speak out, and brave-ly, in God's name. Be strong, be strong!

3. Be strong!
It matters not how deep intrenched the wrong,
How hard the battle goes, the day, how long;
Faint not, fight on! Tomorrow comes the song.
Be strong, be strong!

This Is My Father's World — Terra Patris S.M.D.

St. 1-3

Maltbie Davenport Babcock, 1901 — Franklin L. Sheppard, arr. 1915

In moderate time

1. This_ is my Fa - ther's world, And_ to my lis - tening ears All
2. This_ is my Fa - ther's world; The_ birds their car - ols raise; The

na - ture sings, and_ round me rings The mu - sic of the_ spheres.
morn - ing light, the_ lil - y white, De - clare_ their Mak - er's_ praise.

This is my Fa - ther's world; I_ rest me in the thought Of_
This is my Fa - ther's world; He_ shines in all that's fair; In the

rocks and trees, of_ skies and seas, His hand_ the_ won - ders_ wrought.
rust - ling grass I_ hear him pass, He speaks_ to_ me ev - erywhere.

3. This is my Father's world,
O let me ne'er forget
That though the wrong seems oft so strong,
God is the Ruler yet.
This is my Father's world;
Why should my heart be sad?
The Lord is King, let the heavens ring;
God reigns, let the earth be glad!

Hast Thou Heard It, O My Brother

Panoply of Light 8.7.8.7.D., with chorus

St. 1-3

Theodore Chickering Williams, 1902

Leonard Parker, 1926

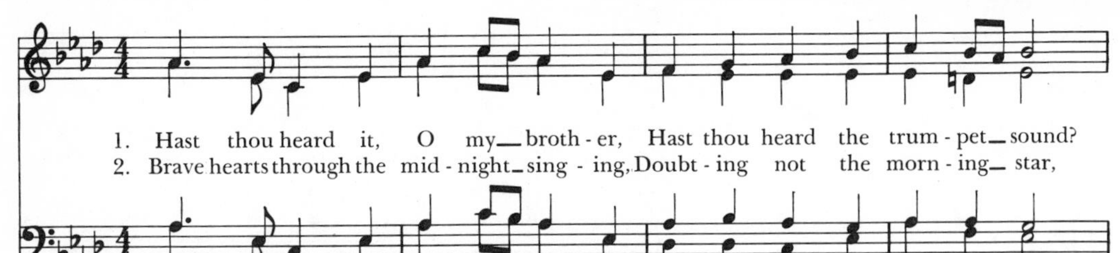
1. Hast thou heard it, O my — broth - er, Hast thou heard the trum - pet — sound?
2. Brave hearts through the mid - night — sing - ing, Doubt - ing not the morn - ing — star,

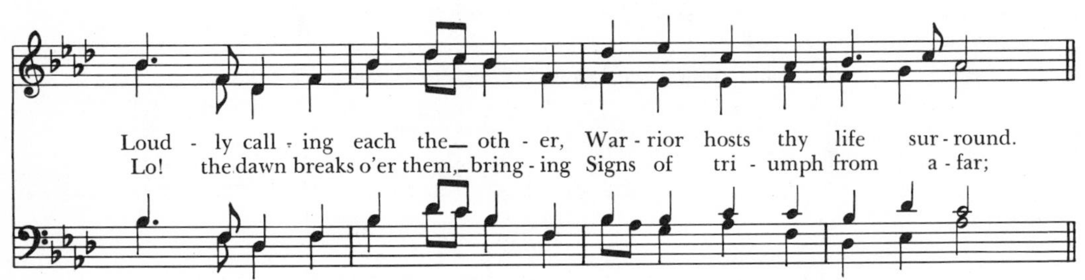
Loud - ly call - ing each the — oth - er, War - rior hosts thy life sur - round.
Lo! the dawn breaks o'er them, — bring - ing Signs of tri - umph from a - far;

Hark, the tides of bat - tle — roll - ing Fill the wide — world like a sea,
Scorn - ing fear, the dark - ness — scorn - ing, While thy brow — of youth is bright,

Star - ry powers, the tides con - trol - ling, Lift up faith - ful — hearts and free.
Set the fore - head to the morn - ing! Wear thy pan - o - ply of light!

Chorus
Gird thee, gird thee, O my—broth - er, We will march in close ar - ray,
Trust - ing God and in each oth - er, We are chil - dren— of the day.

3. O the ancient earth is calling
For such life as thine may be!
Ages gone were stumbling, falling,
Toward the light thine eyes shall see.
Though the old, heroic story
Glow with noble deed sublime,
There shall be a greater glory
In the coming golden time.

Chorus

To Thee, Eternal Soul, Be Praise — Gilder L.M.

St. 1-5

Richard W. Gilder, writ. 1903, pub. 1905 — Arne Oldberg, 1905

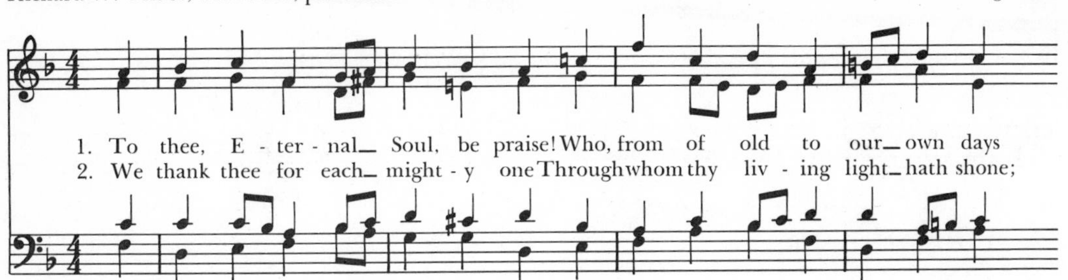
1. To thee, E - ter - nal Soul, be praise! Who, from of old to our own days
2. We thank thee for each might - y one Through whom thy liv - ing light hath shone;

Through souls of saints and proph - ets, Lord, Hast sent thy light, thy love, thy word.
And for each hum - ble soul and sweet That lights to heaven our wan - dering feet.

3. We thank thee for the love divine
Made real in every saint of thine;
That boundless love itself that gives
In service to each soul that lives.

4. We thank thee for the word of might
Thy Spirit spake in darkest night,
Spake through the trumpet voices loud
Of prophets at thy throne who bowed.

5. Eternal Soul, our souls keep pure,
That like thy saints we may endure;
Forever through thy servants, Lord,
Send thou thy light, thy love, thy word.

God of the Strong, God of the Weak — Godwin L.M.

St. 1-4

Richard W. Gilder, writ. 1903, pub. 1910 — William G. Blanchard, comp. 1934, pub. 1935

1. God of the strong, God of the weak, Lord of all
2. In suf - fering thou hast made us one, In might - y

lands and our own land, Light of all souls, from
bur - dens one are we. Teach us that low - liest

thee we seek Light from thy light, strength from thy hand.
du - ty done Is high - est serv - ice un - to thee.

3. Teach us, great Teacher of mankind,
The sacrifice that brings thy balm.
The love, the work that bless and bind;
Teach us thy majesty, thy calm.

4. Teach thou, and we shall know indeed
The truth divine that maketh free;
And knowing, we may sow the seed
That blossoms through eternity.

CREATION'S LORD, WE GIVE THEE THANKS — SEABURY L.M.

St. 1-4

William deWitt Hyde, 1903 — Claude Means, 1941

In moderate time
1. Cre - a - tion's Lord, we give thee thanks That this thy world is in - com - plete;
2. That thou hast not yet fin - ished man; That we are in the mak - ing still,

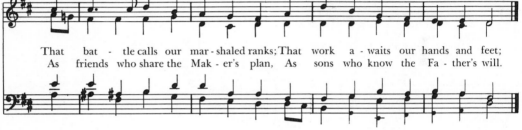

That bat - tle calls our mar - shaled ranks; That work a - waits our hands and feet;
As friends who share the Mak - er's plan, As sons who know the Fa - ther's will.

3. What though the kingdom long delay,
And still with haughty foes must cope?
It gives us that for which to pray,
A field for toil and faith and hope.

4. Since what we choose is what we are,
And what we love we yet shall be,
The goal may ever shine afar;
The will to win it makes us free.

O DAY OF LIGHT AND GLADNESS | LAUFER 7.6.7.6.D.

St. 1-3

Frederick Lucian Hosmer, writ. 1903, pub. 1904 | Emily Swan Perkins, 1924

1. O day of light and glad - ness Of proph - e - cy and song,
2. Earth feels the sea - son's joy - ance; From moun - tain range to sea,
What thoughts with - in us wak - en, What hal - lowed mem - ories throng!
The tides of life are flow - ing, Fresh, man - i - fold and free.
The soul's ho - ri - zon wid - ens, Past, pres - ent, fu - ture blend;
In val - ley and on up - land, By for - est path - ways dim,
And
that hath no end,
All na - ture lifts in
tion hymn .

3. O Lord of life eternal,
To thee our hearts upraise
The Easter song of gladness,
The Passover of praise.
Thine are the many mansions,
The dead die not to thee,
Who fillest from thy fullness
Time and eternity.

HEAR, HEAR, O YE NATIONS — GORDON 11.11.11.11.

St. 1-5

Frederick Lucian Hosmer, writ. 1909, pub. 1914 — Adoniram J. Gordon, 1872

1. Hear, hear, O ye na - tions, and hear - ing o - bey
2. Lo, dawns a new e - ra tran - scend - ing the old,
The cry from the past — and the call of to - day!
The po - et's rapt vi - sion, by proph - et fore - told!
Earth wea - ries and wastes — with her fresh — life out - poured, —
From war's grim tra - di - tion, it mak - eth ap - peal —
The glut of the can - non, the spoil — of the sword.
To serv - ice of all — in a world's — com - mon - weal.

3. Home, altar, and school, the mill, and the mart,
The workers afield, in science, in art,
Peace-circled and sheltered, shall join to create
The manifold life of the firm-builded state.

4. Then, then shall the empire of right over wrong
Be shield to the weak and a curb to the strong;
Then justice prevail and, the battle-flags furled,
The high court of nations give law to the world.

5. And thou, O my country, from many made one,
Late-born among nations, at morning thy sun,
Arise to the place thou art given to fill,
And lead the world-triumph of peace and good will.

THROUGH WILLING HEART AND HELPING HAND

St. 1-5

Frederick Lucian Hosmer, 1909

THEODORE L.M.

Peter C. Lutkin, 1905

1. Through will - ing heart and help - ing hand, Be - hold a -
2. Be wel - comed here the old, the young, The rich, the

chieved our long de - sire! And gath - ered here, a
poor, the prince and thrall. Be Je - sus' mot - to

house - hold band,___ We light to - night___ the___ house - hold fire.
high up - hung:___ Who serv - eth most___ is___ chief of all.

3. Here mirth and pastime speed the hour,
The lighter moods that ease our care;
Here graver themes through lips of power,
Give guidance to the ways we fare!

4. May human fellowship here take
A radiance from the altar's glow,
And kindlier hearts, here quickened, make
From purer founts its worship flow!

5. O Thou whose service, wide and free,
Is inward strength and light and cheer,
Be that our bond of unity
And fire the souls that gather here!

O GOD, GREAT FATHER, LORD, AND KING — BAPTISM L.M.

St. 1-5

E. Embree Hoss, 1903 — Peter C. Lutkin, 1905

1. O God, great Fa - ther, Lord, and King! Our chil - dren un - to thee we bring;
2. Thy cov - enant kind - ness did of old Our fa - thers and their seed en - fold;

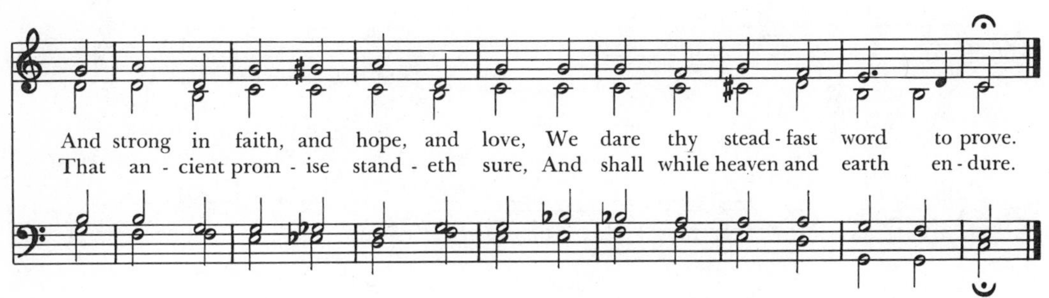
And strong in faith, and hope, and love, We dare thy stead - fast word to prove.
That an - cient prom - ise stand - eth sure, And shall while heaven and earth en - dure.

3. Look down upon us while we pray,
And visit us in grace today;
These little ones in mercy take
And make them thine for Jesus' sake.

4. While they the outward sign receive,
Wilt thou thy Holy Spirit give;
And keep and help them by thy power
In every hard and trying hour.

5. Guide thou their feet in holy ways,
Shine on them through the darkened days;
Uphold them till their life be past,
And bring them all to heaven at last.

WHERE CROSS THE CROWDED WAYS OF LIFE — KIEL L.M.

St. 1-6

Frank Mason North, writ. 1903 — Peter C. Lutkin, 1905

1. Where cross the crowd - ed ways of life, Where sound the cries of race and clan, A -
2. In haunts of wretch - ed - ness and need, On shad - owed thresh - olds dark with fears, From

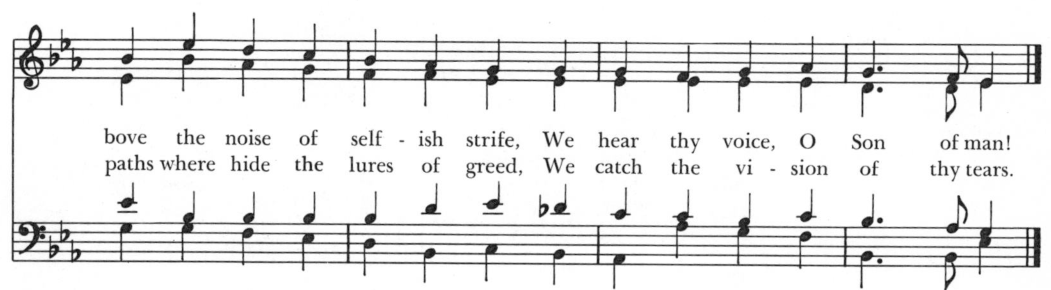
bove the noise of self - ish strife, We hear thy voice, O Son of man!
paths where hide the lures of greed, We catch the vi - sion of thy tears.

3. From tender childhood's helplessness,
From woman's grief, man's burdened toil,
From famished souls, from sorrow's stress,
Thy heart has never known recoil.

4. The cup of water given for thee
Still holds the freshness of thy grace;
Yet long these multitudes to see
The sweet compassion of thy face.

5. O Master, from the mountain side,
Make haste to heal these hearts of pain;
Among these restless throngs abide,
O tread the city's streets again.

6. Till sons of men shall learn thy love,
And follow where thy feet have trod;
Till, glorious from thy heaven above,
Shall come the city of our God!

JEHOVAH, GOD, WHO DWELT OF OLD — TEMPLE C.M.

St. 1-6

Lewis R. Amis, writ. 1904, pub. 1905 — Maro L. Bartlett, 1905

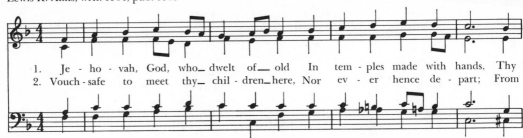

1. Je - ho - vah, God, who_ dwelt of_ old In tem - ples made with hands, Thy
2. Vouch - safe to meet thy_ chil - dren_here, Nor ev - er hence de - part; From

power dis - play, thy truth un-fold, Where this new_ tem - ple stands.
sor - row's eye wipe ev - ery tear, And bless each_ long - ing heart.

3. The rich man's gift, the widow's mite
Are blended in these walls;
These altars welcome all alike
Who heed God's gracious calls.

4. From things unholy and unclean,
We separate this place;
May naught here ever come between
This people and thy face!

5. Now with this house we give to thee
Ourselves, our hearts, our all,
The pledge of faith and loyalty,
Held subject to thy call.

6. And when at last the blood-washed throng
Is gathered from all lands,
We'll enter, with triumphant song,
The house not made with hands.

Lord, Thou Hast Promised — Belleville L.M.

St. 1-4

Samuel K. Cox, 1905 — Peter C. Lutkin, 1905

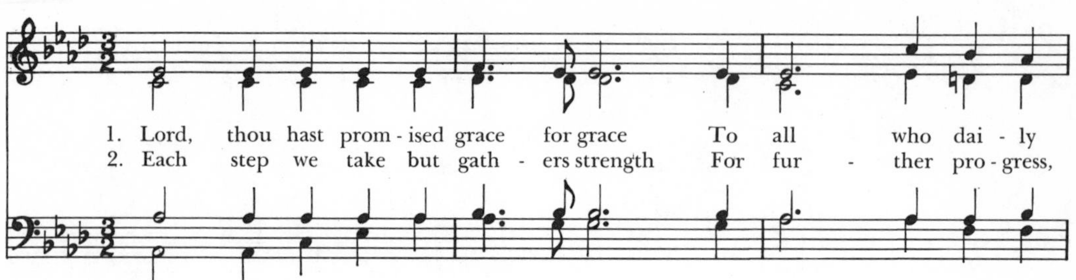
1. Lord, thou hast prom - ised grace for grace To all who dai - ly
2. Each step we take but gath - ers strength For fur - ther pro - gress,

seek thy face; To them who have, thou giv - est more
till at length, With ease the high - est steeps we gain,

Out of thy vast, ex - haust - less store.
And count the moun - tain but a plain.

3. Who watch, and pray, and work each hour,
Receive new life and added power,
A power fresh victories to win
Over the world, and self, and sin.

4. Help us, O Lord, that we may grow
In grace as thou dost grace bestow;
And still thy richer gifts repeat
Till grace in glory is complete.

O CHILD OF LOWLY MANGER BIRTH

EATON L.M.

St. 1-5

Ferdinand Q. Blanchard, writ. 1906, pub. 1909

George W. Chadwick, comp. 1888, pub. 1895

1. O Child of low - ly man - ger birth On whose low cry the a - ges wait,
2. O Je - sus, youth of Naz - a - reth, Pre - par - ing for the bit - ter strife,

Lead us thy way, and ev - ery day Guide us to see what made thee great.
Wilt thou im - part to ev - ery heart Thy per - fect pur - i - ty of life?

3. O Christ whose words made dear the fields
And hillsides green of Galilee,
Grant us to find, with reverent mind,
The truth thou saidst should make us free.

4. O suffering Lord on Calvary,
Whom love led on to mortal pain,
We know thy cross is not a loss,
If we thy love shall truly gain.

5. O Master of abundant life
From natal morn to victory's hour,
We look to thee, heed thou our plea,
Teach us to share thy ageless power.

Lord God of Hosts | Faithful Legions 11.10.11.10

St. 1-4

Shepherd Knapp, writ. 1907, pub. 1912 | Edward Shippen Barnes, comp. 1936, pub. 1937

Unison
1. Lord God of hosts, whose pur - pose, nev - er swerv - ing, Leads toward the
2. Strong Son of God, whose work was his that sent thee, One with the
day of Je - sus Christ thy son, Grant us to march a - mong thy faith - ful
Fa - ther, thought and deed and word, One make us all, true — com - rades in thy
le - gions, Armed with thy cour - age, till the world is won.
serv - ice, And make us one in thee with God the Lord.

3. O Prince of peace, thou bringer of good tidings,
Teach us to speak thy word of hope and cheer —
Rest for the soul, and strength for all man's striving,
Light for the path of life, and God brought near.

4. Lord God, whose grace has called us to thy service,
How good thy thoughts toward us, how great their sum!
We work with thee, we go where thou wilt lead us,
Until in all the earth thy kingdom come.

Not Only Where God's Free Winds Blow — Eternal Light 8.6.8.8.6.

St. 1-5

Shepherd Knapp, writ. 1908, pub. 1937 — Kenneth E. Runkel, 1941

In moderate time

1. Not on - ly where God's free winds blow, Or in the
2. Dear God, the sun whose light is sweet On hill and

si - lent wood, But where the cit - y's rest - less flow Is
plain and sea, Doth cheer the cit - y's bus - y street; And

nev - er still, his love we know, And find his pres - ence good.
they that pass with wea - ry feet Give thanks for light from thee.

3. Thy bounties from the field and mine
Come at the city's call;
The fire upon the hearth is thine,
And home, where lights of kindness shine,
The dearest gift of all.

4. More near than outward gifts art thou,
O Father of mankind;
Yea, those, who under burdens bow
Of toil and care, thou dost endow
With riches of thy mind.

5. But in the city's grief and shame
Dost thou refuse a part?
Oh, no, for burneth there the flame
Of human help in Christ's dear name;
There, most of all, thou art.

LET THERE BE LIGHT L.M.D.

St. 1-4

William M. Vories, 1909 Jacob Singer, 1932

Maestoso

f

1. Let there be light, Lord God of Hosts! Let there be wis - dom on the earth!
3. Give us the peace of vi - sion clear To see our broth - ers' good our own,

f

Let broad hu - man - i - ty have birth! Let there be deeds, in - stead of boast!
To joy and suf - fer not a - lone: The love that cast - eth out all fear!

2. With - in our pass - ioned hearts in - still The calm that end - eth strain and strife;
4. Let woe and waste of war - fare cease, That use - ful la - bor yet may build

Make us thy min - is - ters of life; Purge us from lusts that — curse and kill!
Its homes with love and laugh - ter filled! God, give thy way - ward — chil - dren peace!

AT LENGTH THERE DAWNS THE GLORIOUS DAY — CORWIN 8.6.8.6.6.D.

St. 1-3

Ozora S. Davis, writ. 1909, pub. 1912 — J. W. Lerman, 1908

1. At length there dawns the glo - rious day By proph - ets long fore - told;
2. For what are sund - ering strains of blood, Or an - cient caste and creed?

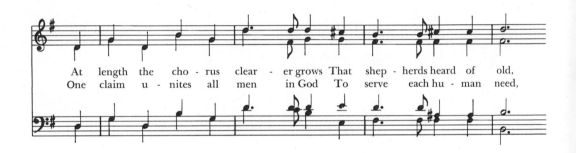

At length the cho - rus clear - er grows That shep - herds heard of old,
One claim u - nites all men in God To serve each hu - man need,

That_ shep - herds heard of old. The day of dawn - ing Broth - er-hood
To_ serve each hu - man need. Then here to - geth - er, broth - er-men,

Breaks on our ea - ger eyes, And hu - man ha - treds flee be - fore
We pledge the Lord a - new Our loy - al love, our stal - wart faith,

The ra - diant east - ern skies, The ra - diant east - ern skies.
Our serv - ice strong and true, Our serv - ice strong and true.

3. One common faith unites us all,
We seek one common goal,
One tender comfort broods upon
The struggling human soul,
The struggling human soul.
To this clear call of brotherhood
Our hearts responsive ring;
We join the glorious new crusade
Of our great Lord and King,
Of our great Lord and King.

Not Alone for Mighty Empire — Geneva 8.7.8.7.D.

St. 1-4

William Pierson Merrill, writ. 1909, pub. 1910 — George Henry Day, 1940

Unison
1. Not a - lone for might - y em - pire Stretch - ing far o'er land and sea,
2. Not for bat - tle - ship and for - tress, Not for con - quests of the sword,
Not a - lone for boun - teous har - vests, Lift we up our hearts to thee.
But for con - quests of the spir - it Give we thanks to thee, O Lord:
Stand - ing in the liv - ing pres - ent, Mem - o - ry and hope be - tween,
For the her - i - tage of free - dom, For the home, the church, the school,

Lord, we— would with deep— thanks - giv - ing Praise thee— most for— things un - seen.
For the— o - pen door— to— man - hood In a— land the— peo - ple rule.

3. For the armies of the faithful,
Souls that passed and left no name;
For the glory that illumines
Patriot lives of deathless fame;
For our prophets and apostles,
Loyal to the living word,
For all heroes of the spirit,
Give we thanks to thee, O Lord.

4. God of justice, save the people
From the clash of race and creed,
From the strife of class and faction,
Make our nation free indeed;
Keep her faith in simple manhood
Strong as when her life began,
Till it find its full fruition
In the brotherhood of man!

RISE UP, O MEN OF GOD — FESTAL SONG S.M.

St. 1-4

William Pierson Merrill, writ. 1911, pub. 1912 — William H. Walter, 1894

With spirit
1. Rise up, O men of God! Have done— with less - er things;
2. Rise up, O men of God! His king - dom tar - ries long;

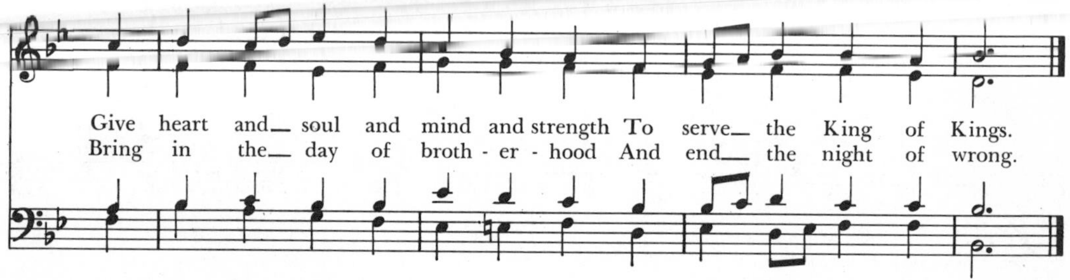
Give heart and— soul and mind and strength To serve— the King of Kings.
Bring in the— day of broth - er - hood And end— the night of wrong.

3. Rise up, O men of God!
The Church for you doth wait,
Her strength unequal to her task;
Rise up and make her great!

4. Rise up, O men of God!
Tread where his feet have trod;
As brothers of the Son of Man,
Rise up, O men of God!

JESUS, THOU DIVINE COMPANION — LOVE DIVINE 8.7.8.7.D.

St. 1-3

Henry Van Dyke, writ. 1909 (altered), pub. 1910 — George F. Le Jeune, 1887

1. Je - sus, thou di - vine com - pan - ion, By thy low - ly hu - man birth,
2. Where the man - y toil to - geth - er, There art thou a - mong thine own;
Thou hast come to join the work - ers, Bur - den - bear - ers of the earth.
Where the tired work - man sleep - eth, There art thou with him a - lone:
Thou, the car - pen - ter of Naz - areth, Toil - ing for thy dai - ly food,
Thou, the peace that pass - eth knowl - edge, Dwell - est in the dai - ly strife;
By thy pa - tience and thy cour - age, Thou hast taught us toil is good.
Thou, the bread of heaven art bro - ken In the sac - ra - ment of life.

3. Every task, however simple,
Sets the soul that does it free;
Every deed of love and kindness
Done to man is done to thee.
Jesus, thou divine companion,
Help us all to work our best;
Bless us in our daily labor,
Lead us to our Sabbath rest.

O Lord Our God, Thy Mighty Hand — America Befriend C.M.D.

St. 1-4

Henry Van Dyke, 1912 — William Pierson Merrill, 1912

With spirit
1. O Lord our God, thy might - y hand Hath made our coun - try free;
2. The strength of ev - ery state in-crease In un - ion's gold - en chain;
From all her broad and hap - py land May wor - ship rise to thee.
Her thou - sand cit - ies fill with peace, Her mil - lion fields with grain.
Ful - fill the prom - ise of her youth, Her lib - er - ty de - fend;
The vir - tues of her min - gled blood In one new peo - ple blend;
By law and or - der, love and truth, A - mer - i - ca, A - mer - i - ca be - friend!
By u - ni - ty and broth - er - hood, A - mer - i - ca, A - mer - i - ca be - friend!

3. O suffer not her feet to stray,
But guide her untaught might
That she may walk in peaceful day,
And lead the world in light.
Bring down the proud, lift up the poor,
Unequal ways amend;
By justice, nationwide and sure,
America, America befriend!

4. Through all the waiting land proclaim
Thy gospel of good will;
And may the joy of Jesus' name
In every bosom thrill.
O'er hill and vale, from sea to sea,
Thy holy reign extend;
By faith and hope and charity
America, America befriend!

I KNOW NOT HOW THAT BETHLEHEM'S BABE — OUR CHRIST C.M.

St. 1-3

Harry Webb Farrington, writ. 1910, pub. 1921 — Oscar R. Overby, comp. 1926, pub. 1932

1. I know not how that Beth - lehem's babe Could in the
2. I know not how that Cal - vary's cross A world from

God - head be; I on - ly know the
sin could free; I on - ly know the

man - ger child Has brought God's life to me.
match - less love Has brought God's love to me.

3. I know not how that Joseph's tomb
Could solve death's mystery;
I only know a living Christ,
Our immortality.

LORD JESUS CHRIST, WE HUMBLY PRAY — SURSUM CORDA L.M.

St. 1-5

Henry Eyster Jacobs, 1910, pub. 1933 — Luther Reed, 1910, pub. 1933

1. Lord Je - sus Christ, we hum - bly pray That we may
2. The chas - tened peace of sin for - given, The fil - ial

feed on thee to - day; Be - neath these forms of
joy of heirs of heaven, Grant, as we share this

bread and wine, En - rich us with thy grace di - vine.
won - drous food, Thy bod - y bro - ken and thy blood.

3. Our trembling hearts cleave to thy word.
All thou hast said thou dost afford;
All that thou art we here receive,
And all we are to thee we give.

4. One bread, one cup, one body, we,
United by our life in thee;
Thy love proclaim till thou shalt come
To bring thy scattered loved ones home.

5. Lord Jesus Christ, we humbly pray
To keep us steadfast to that day,
That each may be thy welcomed guest,
When thou shalt spread thy heavenly feast.

O HOLY CITY SEEN OF JOHN

RANGELEY 8.6.8.6.8.6.

St. 1-5

Walter Russell Bowie, 1910

Henry M. Dunham, 1909

1. O Ho - ly Cit - y seen of John, Where Christ, the Lamb, doth reign,
2. Hark, how from men whose lives are held More cheap than mer - chan - dise,

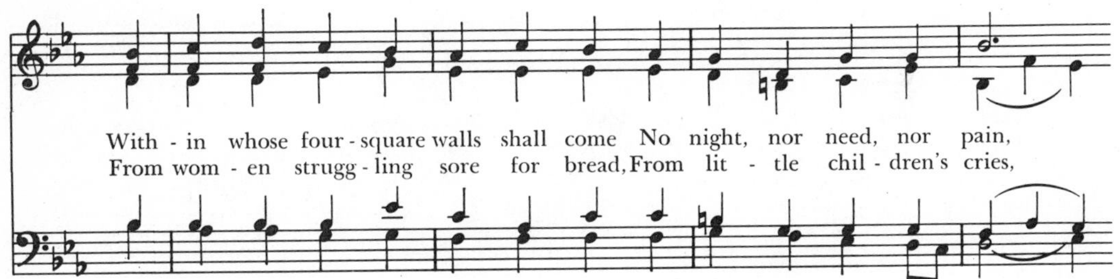
With - in whose four - square walls shall come No night, nor need, nor pain,
From wom - en strugg - ling sore for bread, From lit - tle chil - dren's cries,

rall.
And where the tears are wiped from eyes That shall not weep a - gain.
There swells the sob - bing hu - man plaint That bids thy walls a - rise.

3. O shame to us who rest content
While lust and greed for gain
In street and shop and tenement
Wring gold from human pain,
And bitter lips in blind despair
Cry, "Christ hath died in vain!"

4. Give us, O God, the strength to build
The City that hath stood
Too long a dream, whose laws are love,
Whose ways are brotherhood,
And where the sun that shineth is
God's grace for human good.

God of the Nations — Pro Patria 10.10.10.10.

St. 1-4

Walter Russell Bowie, writ. 1913, pub. 1914 — Horatio Parker, 1894

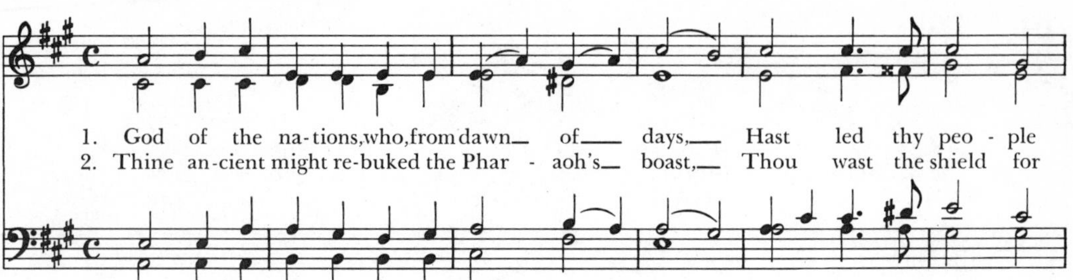
1. God of the na-tions, who, from dawn of days, Hast led thy peo - ple
2. Thine an-cient might re-buked the Phar - aoh's boast, Thou wast the shield for

in their wide-ning ways, Through whose deep pur - pose stran - ger thou - sands
Is - rael's march-ing host, And all the a - ges through, past crumb - ling

stand Here in the bor - ders of our prom - ised land.
throne And bro - ken fet - ter, thou hast brought thine own.

3. Thy hand has led across the hungry sea
The eager peoples flocking to be free,
And from the breeds of earth, thy silent sway
Fashions the nation of the broadening day.

4. Then, for thy grace to grow in brotherhood,
For hearts aflame to serve thy destined good,
For faith and will to win what faith shall see,
God of thy people, hear us cry to thee.

God of the Nations, Near and Far — Holmes C.M.

St. 1-6

John Haynes Holmes, writ. 1911, pub. 1914 — Edward Shippen Barnes, writ. 1936, pub. 1937

Unison
1. God of the na - tions, near and far, Rul - er of all man-kind,
2. The clash of arms still shakes the sky, King bat - tles still with king;

Bless thou thy peo - ple as they strive The paths of peace to find.
Wild through the fright - ed air of night The blood - y toc - sins ring.

3. But clearer far the friendly speech
Of scientists and seers,
The wise debate of statesmen and
The shouts of pioneers.

4. And stronger far the claspèd hands
Of labor's teeming throngs,
Who in a hundred tongues repeat
The common creeds and songs.

5. From shore to shore the peoples call
In loud and sweet acclaim;
The gloom of land and sea is lit
With pentecostal flame.

6. O Father, from the curse of war
We pray thee give release,
And speed, O speed the blessèd day
Of justice, love, and peace.

THE VOICE OF GOD IS CALLING — MISSION 7.6.7.6.D.

St. 1-4

John Haynes Holmes, writ. 1913, pub. 1914 — Horatio Parker, 1894

1. The voice of God is call - ing Its sum - mons un - to men;
2. I hear my peo - ple cry - ing In cot and mine and slum;
As once he spake in Zi - on, So now he speaks a - gain.
No field or mart is si - lent, No cit - y street is dumb.
Whom shall I send to suc - cor My peo - ple in their need?
I see my peo - ple fall - ing In dark - ness and des - pair.
Whom shall I send to loos - en The bonds of shame and greed?
Whom shall I send to shat - ter The fet which they bear?

3. We heed, O Lord, thy summons,
And answer: Here are we!
Send us upon thine errand!
Let us thy servants be!
Our strength is dust and ashes,
Our years a passing hour;
But thou canst use our weakness,
To magnify thy power.

4. From ease and plenty save us,
From pride of place absolve;
Purge us of low desire,
Lift us to high resolve.
Take us, and make us holy,
Teach us thy will and way.
Speak, and, behold! we answer,
Command, and we obey!

O'ER CONTINENT AND OCEAN PATMOS 7.6.8.6.D.

St. 1-3

John Haynes Holmes, 1917 Henry J. Storer, 1891

1. O'er con - ti - nent and o - cean, From cit - y, field, and wood,
2. We hear, O Lord, these voic - es And hail them as thine own,
Still speak, O Lord, thy mes - sen - gers Of peace and broth - er - hood.
They speak as speak the winds and tides On plan - ets far and lone.
In Ath - ens and Be - na - res, In Rome and Gal - i - lee,
One God, the Life of A - ges One rule, his will a - bove,
They front - ed kings and con - quer - ors, And taught man - kind of thee.
One realm our wide hu - man - i - ty, One law, the law of love.

3. The tribes and nations falter
In rivalries of fear;
The fires of hate to ashes turn,
To dust the sword and spear.
Thy word alone remaineth;
That word we speak again;
O'er sea and shore and continent,
To all the sons of men.

WE PRAISE THEE, GOD, FOR HARVESTS EARNED — PIXHAM L.M.

St. 1-5

John Coleman Adams, writ. 1911, pub. 1914 — Horatio Parker, comp. 1901, pub. 1903

1. We praise thee, God, for har - vests earned, The fruits of
2. We praise thee for the har - bor's lee, And moor - ings

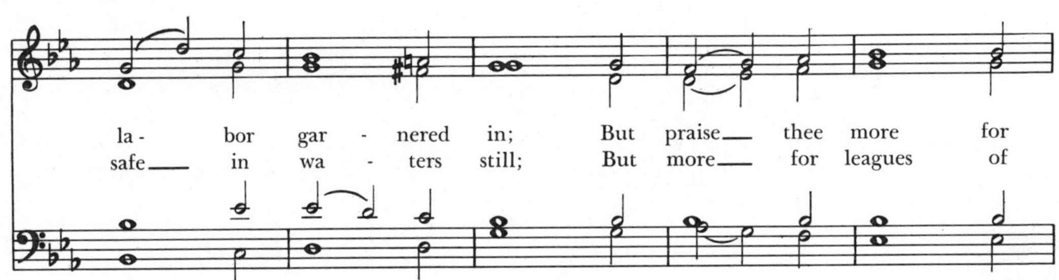
la - bor gar - nered in; But praise thee more for
safe in wa - ters still; But more for leagues of

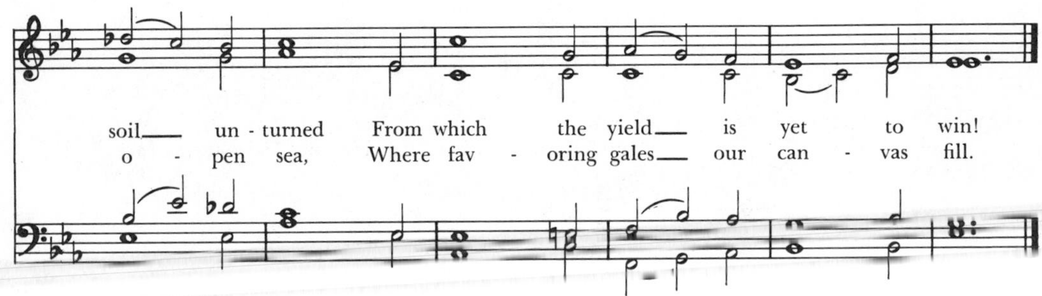
soil un - turned From which the yield is yet to win!
o - pen sea, Where fav - oring gales our can - vas fill.

3. We praise thee for the journey's end,
The inn, all warmth and light and cheer;
But more for lengthening roads that wend
Through dust and heat to hilltops clear.

4. We praise thee for the conflicts won,
For captured strongholds of the foe;
But more for fields whereon the sun
Lights us when we to battle go.

5. We praise thee for life's gathered gains,
The blessings that our cup o'erbrim;
But more for pledge of what remains
Past the horizon's utmost rim!

Touch Thou Mine Eyes — Lanherne 11.10.11.10.

St. 1-3

Marion Franklin Ham, writ. 1911, pub. 1914 — Henry Hayman, 1904

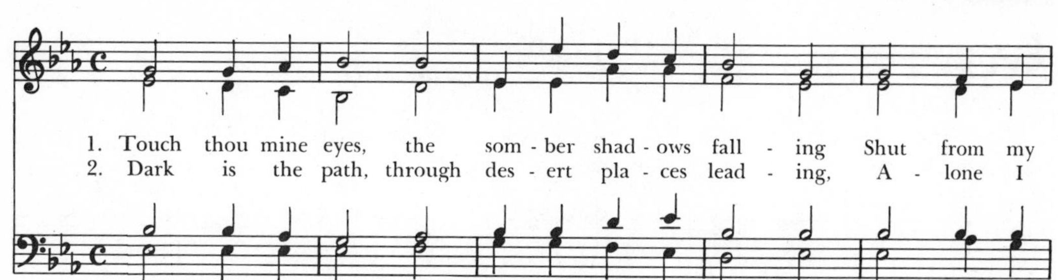
1. Touch thou mine eyes, the som - ber shad - ows fall - ing Shut from my
2. Dark is the path, through des - ert pla - ces lead - ing, A - lone I

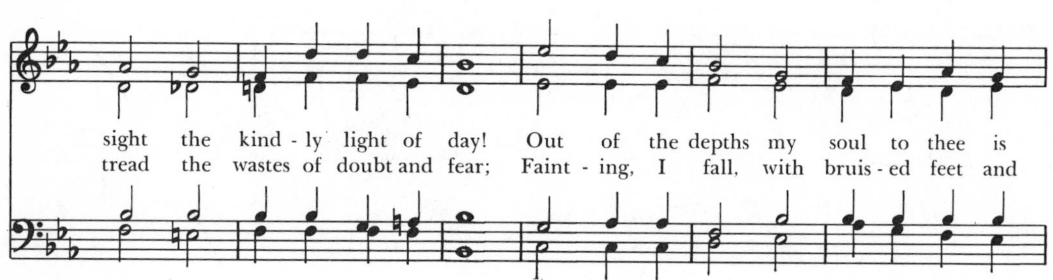
sight the kind - ly light of day! Out of the depths my soul to thee is
tread the wastes of doubt and fear; Faint - ing, I fall, with bruis - ed feet and

call - ing, Touch thou mine eyes, I can - not see the way!
bleed - ing, O touch mine eyes, that I may know thee near!

3. Fain would I see, as in the olden story,
Thy shining hosts encamped on every side;
Angels of light, armed with thy power and glory,
To guard my steps, whatever may betide.

O Thou Whose Gracious Presence Shone — Pixham L.M.

St. 1-4

Marion Franklin Ham, writ. 1912, pub. 1914 — Horatio Parker, comp. 1901, pub. 1903

1. O thou whose gra - cious pres - ence shone A light to bless thy fel - low men, To thee we fond - ly turn a - gain, As to a friend that we have known.
2. Thy grace and truth, thy life that shed Un - dy - ing ra - diance through all time, Thy ten - der love, thy faith sub - lime, Re - mem - bering these, we break the bread.

3. And lo! again we seem to hear
Thy blessing on the loaf and cup;
The presence that was lifted up
Again to loving hearts brought near.

4. Our lesser lives, thus touching thine,
Are joined, with all the pure and good,
In truer, nobler brotherhood
That lifts the world to realms divine.

My Country, to Thy Shore — Macedon 6.6.4.6.6.6.4.

St. 1-5

Theodore Chickering Williams, 1912 — Frederick Field Bullard, 1902

1. My coun-try, to thy shore Far wan-dering pil - grims pour,
2. In thy wide wa - tered plains, Thy moun-tains' lib - eral veins,
To build in thee A new re - pub - lic's plan, New truth of loft - ier
And for - ests fair, Large, gold - en gifts are found; And in thy gar - den
span, New broth - er-hood of man, And lib - er - ty.
ground, Earth's proud - est fruits a - bound, For all to share.

3. Thy cities, strong and wise,
Shall lift to cloudless skies
Fraternal towers.
What toil and genius gave
To serve men, not enslave,
In thee shall help and save
Man's noblest powers.

4. Young heroes smiling died;
True hearts have sanctified
Long life for thee.
Heirs of a free-born land,
Free may our children stand,
And God's almighty hand,
Their guidance be.

5. May freedom clothed in light
Obey th' Eternal Right
From sun to sun;
And to all lands display
Her blest and righteous way,
Until, in God's own day,
Mankind be one.

O God, in Whose Great Purpose — Neilson 7.6.8.6.D.

St. 1, 2

James G. Gilkey, writ. 1912 — John H. Gower, 1894

Unison

1. O God, in whose great pur - pose An age is but a day,
2. A - gain with vi - sion kin - dled, We sons of lat - ter days

Who watch - est sun give place to sun And plan - ets burn a - way;
Lift ea - ger hands as here we wait Be - side the part - ing ways.

Harmony

In thee our fa - thers trust - ed, For thee they dared the sea,
A - cross thine earth we scat - ter To meet the tasks of men.

And thou didst teach their fee - ble hands To shape a world for thee.
O God of strength, be thou to us Our fa - thers' God a - gain!

OUTSIDE THE HOLY CITY

PATMOS 7.6.8.6.D.

St. 1-4

James G. Gilkey, writ. 1915

Henry J. Storer, 1891

1. Out - side the Ho - ly Cit - y Un - num - bered foot - steps throng,
2. Once more be - side a cit - y The Son of Dav - id waits,
And crowd - ed mart and streets of trade Fling back a swell - ing song.
Once more the chil - dren throng to bring A wel - come at the gates.
The voic - es ech - o near - er, In flam - ing hope they sing;
With - in are hearts sore bur - dened And feet that go a - stray;
"Throw down your branch - es at his feet! Ho - san - na to the King!"
O Christ of God, come near and walk Our cit - y streets to - day!

3. The branches that we offer
Are no unmeaning sign;
Take thou the hands we lift on high
And make them wholly thine.
No songs of shallow welcome
Are these we raise to thee;
O give us faith to face the cross
And set thy city free!

4. A distant music mingles
With all our songs today,
The chorale from a city fair
Where sin has passed away.
There rides the Christ triumphant
And victory song ring clear;
O God, give us the strength to build
With Christ that city here!

O SON OF MAN, THOU MADEST KNOWN — SUTHERLAND L.M.

St. 1-4

Milton S. Littlefield, writ. 1916, pub. 1920 — Emma L. Ashford, 1905

1. O Son of Man, thou mad - est known, Through qui - et work in shop and home
2. O Work-man true, may we ful - fill In dai - ly life thy Fa - ther's will;

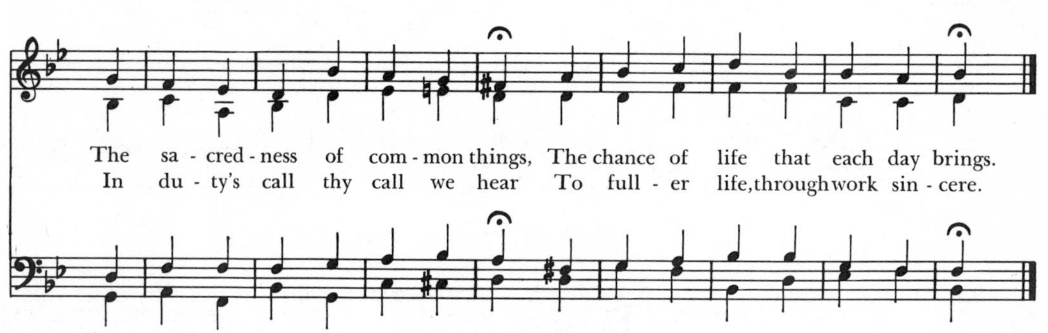
The sa - cred - ness of com - mon things, The chance of life that each day brings.
In du - ty's call thy call we hear To full - er life, through work sin - cere.

3. Thou Master Workman, grant us grace
The challenge of our tasks to face;
By loyal scorn of second best,
By effort true, to meet each test.

4. And thus we pray in deed and word,
Thy kingdom come on earth, O Lord;
In work that gives effect to prayer
Thy purpose for thy world we share.

O Master Workman of the Race — Mount Sion C.M.D.

St. 1-3

Jay T. Stocking, 1912 — Horatio Parker, comp. 1886, pub. 1894

With joy, in stately rhythm
1. O Mas - ter Work - man of the race, Thou man of
2. O Car - pen - ter of Naz - a - reth, Build - er of

Unison
Gal - i - lee, Who with the eyes of ear - ly youth
life di - vine, Who shap - est man to God's own law,

Harmony
E - ter - nal things didst see, We thank thee for thy
Thy - self the fair de - sign, Build us a tower of

boy - hood faith That shone thy whole life through; "Did ye not
Christ - like height, That we the land may view, And see, like

know it is my work, My Fa - ther's work to do?"
thee, our no - blest work, Our Fa - ther's work to do.

3. O thou who does the vision send
And givest each his task,
And with the task sufficient strength,
Show us thy will, we ask;
Give us a conscience bold and good,
Give us a purpose true,
That it may be our highest joy,
Our Father's work to do.

On a Hill Far Away
The Old Rugged Cross

St. 1-4

George Bennard, 1913

The Old Rugged Cross 12.8.12.8., with chorus

George Bennard, 1913

1. On a hill far a - way stood an old rug - ged cross, The
2. Oh, that old rug - ged cross, so de - spised by the world, Has a

em - blem of suf - fering and shame; And I love that old cross, where the
won - drous at - trac - tion for me; For the dear Lamb of God left his

dear - est and best For a world of lost sin - ners was slain.
glo - ry a - bove To bear it to dark Cal - va - ry.

Chorus
So I'll cher - ish the old rug - ged cross, Till my
cross, the old rug - ged cross,

tro - phies at last I lay down; I will cling to the old rug - ged
cross, the

cross, And ex - change it some day for a crown.
old rug - ged cross,

3. In the old rugged cross, stained with blood so divine,
 A wondrous beauty I see;
 For 'twas on that old cross Jesus suffered and died
 To pardon and sanctify me.
 Chorus

4. To the old rugged cross I will ever be true,
 Its shame and reproach gladly bear;
 Then he'll call me some day to my home far away,
 Where his glory forever I'll share.
 Chorus

O GOD, I CRIED, NO DARK DISGUISE — RENASCENCE L.M.

St. 1-5

Edna St. Vincent Millay, 1917 — Hugh Porter, 1927

Unison

1. O God, I cried, no dark dis - guise Can e'er here - af - ter hide from me
2. Thou canst not move a - cross the grass But my quick eyes will see thee pass,
4. The world stands out on ei - ther side, No wi - der than the heart is wide;

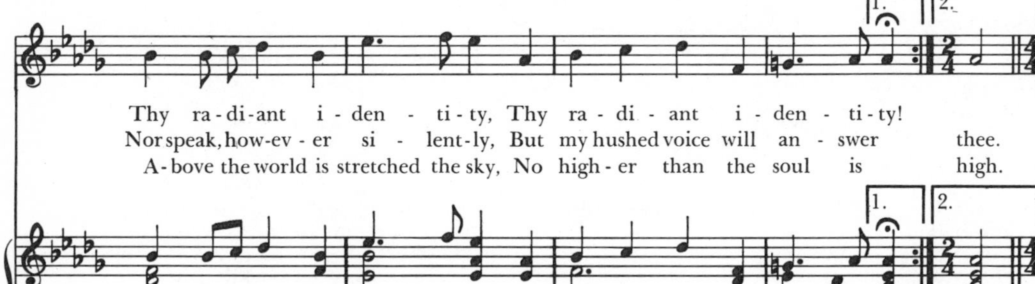
1.
2.
Thy ra - di - ant i - den - ti - ty, Thy ra - di - ant i - den - ti - ty!
Nor speak, how - ev - er si - lent - ly, But my hushed voice will an - swer thee.
A - bove the world is stretched the sky, No high - er than the soul is high.

3. I know the path that tells the way Through the cool eve of ev - ery day.
5. The heart can push the sky and land Far - ther a - way on ei - ther hand;

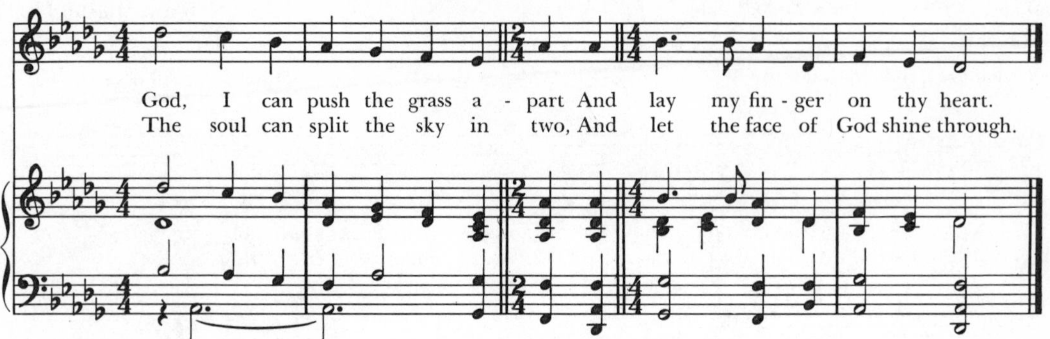
God, I can push the grass a - part And lay my fin - ger on thy heart.
The soul can split the sky in two, And let the face of God shine through.

TAKE THOU OUR MINDS, DEAR LORD

HALL 10.10.10.10.

St. 1-4

William H. Foulkes, writ. 1918

Calvin W. Laufer, comp. 1918

1. Take thou our minds, dear Lord, we hum - bly pray;
2. Take thou our hearts, O Christ, they are thine own;
Give us the mind of Christ each pass - ing day.
Come thou with - in our souls and claim thy throne.
Teach us to know the truth that sets us free;
Help us to shed a - broad thy death - less love;
Grant us in all our thoughts to hon - or thee.
Use us to make the earth like heaven a - bove.

3. Take thou our wills, Most High! hold thou full sway;
Have in our inmost souls thy perfect way.
Guard thou each sacred hour from selfish ease;
Guide thou our ordered lives as thou dost please.

4. Take thou ourselves, O Lord, heart, mind, and will;
Through our surrendered souls thy plans fulfill.
We yield ourselves to thee — time, talents, all;
We hear, and henceforth heed, thy soverign call.

THOUGH FATHERLAND BE VAST — AMERICA THE BEAUTIFUL C.M.D.

St. 1-4

Allen Eastman Cross, 1918 — William W. Sleeper, 1908

1. Though Fa - ther - land be vast and fair, Though heaven be e'er so near,
2. So, while we face the com - mon sun Up - on this an - cient star,
Yet there's a land, a land, a land, That is to God more dear!
And dawn and dusk swing o - ver us, We'll hail our dreams a - far;
There is no gulf, there is no sea, And shore is touch - ing shore,
We'll greet the glo - ry of a land Where love shall nev - er tire,
And moun - tains bow and bor - ders blend, And ha - treds are no more.
We'll light a flame, a flame, a flame, To set the world on fire.
And moun - tains bow and bor - ders blend,
We'll light a flame, a flame, a flame,

3. O land of lands, dear brotherland,
The country of our dream,
The home of fealty and faith,
How marvelous you seem!
Your rivers flow in shining peace,
Your trees have healing worth,
Your stones are gentleness and grace,
Your mercy fills the earth.

4. O Christ of freedom and of faith,
O Flame of Pentecost,
Thou hast a name o'er every name
To lead the marching host,
Till wrong be bound, and peace be crowned,
And love be on the throne,
Thou hast a name, a name, a name,
To make the stars thine own.

YOUNG AND RADIANT, HE IS STANDING

SON OF MAN 8.7.8.7.D.

St. 1-4

Allen Eastman Cross, 1921

Louis Adolphe Coerne, 1921

1. Young and ra - diant, he is stand - ing As he stood at Sa - lem's shrine;
2. I can see him hum - bly kneel - ing, As he knelt up - on the hill;
Just a lad, a lad for - ev - er, With a look and grace di - vine!
While the wa - ters hushed their mu - sic, And the night glow bright and still
"Tell me, how it is ye sought me? Wist ye not my Fa - ther's plan?
"Broth-ers tell me why ye sought me? Wist ye not my Fa - ther's plan?
I must be a - bout his busi - ness, Would I be a Son of Man."
He must grow in grace and wis - dom, Who would be a Son of Man."

3. Like a flame his soul is striking
In his wrath at greed and shame;
"Ye have made a den of robbers
Of the temple to his name;
Know ye not his equal justice?
Wist ye not my Father's plan?
He must bathe his sword in heaven
Who would be a Son of Man."

4. I can see him dying, loving
Unto death on Calvary;
His dear hands still pleading, praying,
Worn and torn for you and me!
"Brothers, will ye scorn and leave me?
Wist ye not my Father's plan?
He must wear a crown of sorrow
Who would be a Son of Man."

The Gray Hills Taught Me Patience — Manchester 7.6.7.6.

St. 1-3

Allen Eastman Cross, 1926 — G. Waring Stebbins, 1927

Unison
1. The gray hills taught me pa - tience, The wa - ters taught me prayer; The
2. The calm skies made me qui - et, The high stars made me still; The

flight of birds un - fold - ed The mar - vel of thy care.
bolts of thun - der taught me The light - ning of thy will!

3. Thy soul is on the tempest,
Thy courage rides the air!
Through heaven or hell I'll follow;
I must, and so I dare!

I Know a Flower So Fair and Fine — Flowers of Love 8.7.8.4.7.

St. 1-3

Nicolai F. S. Grundtvig
Olav Lee, trans. 1919

F. Melius Christiansen, 1919

1. I know a flower so fair and fine, So fra - grant and so cheer - ing; With life - blood clear as pur - est wine, And leaf - let fine, Like rose - leaves all ap - pear - ing.
2. This flower so fair and fine is love; God's hand with art it mold - ed. Un - seen on earth, but not a - bove, Is growth of love, Till fair it is un - fold - ed.

3. Upon this earth but wild it grows;
Not so in new earth's Eden,
Where stream of life serenely flows;
It buds and blows,
Delightful fragrance breathing.

We Thank Thee, Lord — Field 10.10.10.10.

St. 1-4

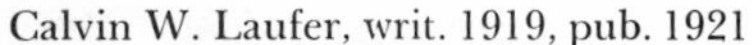

Calvin W. Laufer, writ. 1919, pub. 1921 — Calvin W. Laufer, writ. 1919, pub. 1921

In moderate time

1. We thank thee, Lord, thy paths of serv - ice lead To bla - zoned heights and down the slopes of need; They reach thy throne, en - com - pass land and sea, And he who jour - neys in them walks with thee.

2. We've sought and found thee in the se - cret place, And mar - veled at the ra - diance of thy face; But of - ten in some far - off Gal - i - lee, Be - held thee fair - er yet while serv - ing thee.

3. We've felt thy touch in sorrow's darkened way,
Abound with love and solace for the day;
And 'neath the burdens there, thy sovereignty,
Has held our hearts enthralled while serving thee.

4. We've seen thy glory like a mantle spread
O'er hill and dale in saffron flame and red;
But in the eyes of men, redeemed and free,
A splendor greater yet while serving thee.

Let the Deep Organ Swell — L.M.D.

St. 1, 2

Constantine Pise, 1851 — Nicola A. Montani, 1920

Marcato
1. Let the deep or - gan swell the lay, In hon - or of this fes - tive day;
2. Then from the world's be - wil - dering strife, In peace she spent her ho - ly life,
Let the har - mo - nious choirs pro - claim Ce - cil - ia's ev - er bless - ed name.
Teach - ing the or - gan to com - bine With voice, to praise the Lamb di - vine. Ce -
Rome gave the vir - gin mar - tyr birth, Whose ho - ly name hath filled the earth; And
cil - ia with a two - fold crown A - dorned in heaven, we pray look down Up -
from the ear - ly dawn of youth, She fixed her heart on God and truth.
on thy fer - vent vo - tories here, And heark - en to their hum - ble prayer.

703

True Son of God, Eternal Light — L.M.

St. 1, 2, 4, 5

P. J. Cormican, 1920
Cyr de Brant, 1953
Unison
1. True Son of God, E - ter - nal Light, Come down to earth, il - lume the night! Can - cel the curse of par - a - dise, Haste thou to pay re - demp - tion's price!
2. O Lord, de - sired of na - tions, haste! Lo, de - mons lay thy king - dom waste; See hands out - stretched for help in vain, Hear cries of woe, de - spair, and pain!
A - men.

3. O Lord of Hosts, we pray thee, come!
Put down the powers of heathendom;
Rise up, in all thy matchless might,
Drive back the troops of hell in flight!

4. God's kingdom come, his will be done!
May all men serve the Triune One;
Sing hymns of thanks, thou sainted host,
To Father, Son, and Holy Ghost.

Now Help Us, Lord (The Collection) 8.6.8.6.6.

"Stanzas from old hymns," 1, 2 Charles E. Ives, comp. 1920

In moderate time
Organist
mp
Ped.
Soprano
1. Now help us, Lord, Thy yoke to wear, and joy to
2. O has - ten, Lord, the prom - ised days, when all the
mp
do Thy will; Each oth - er's bur - dens glad - ly bear, and love's sweet
na - tions shall re - joice; And Jew and Gen - tile join in praise, with one u -

law fulfill, And love's sweet law fulfill.
ni - ted voice! With one u - ni - ted voice!
p
p
Response by village choir
1. And love's sweet law ful - fill.
2. With one u - ni - ted voice!
mf
2d Verse ad lib.
D.C. for it

THOU ART, O GOD, THE GOD OF MIGHT

BURG 8.7.8.7.

St. 1-4

Emily Swan Perkins, 1921 (altered)

Emily Swan Perkins, 1921

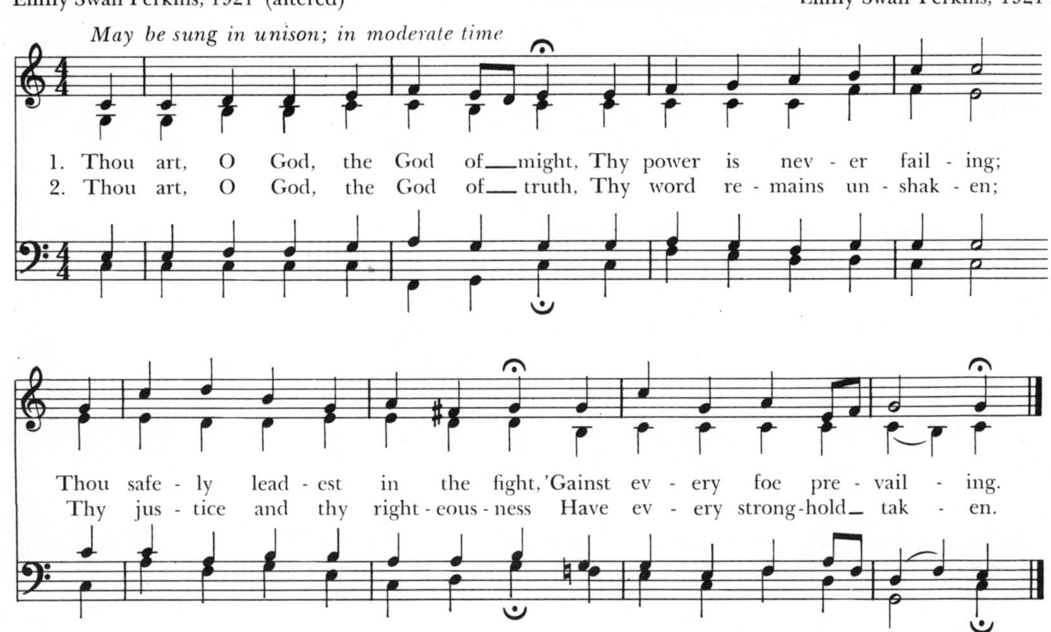
May be sung in unison; in moderate time
1. Thou art, O God, the God of__might, Thy power is nev - er fail - ing;
2. Thou art, O God, the God of__truth, Thy word re - mains un - shak - en;
Thou safe - ly lead - est in the fight, 'Gainst ev - ery foe pre - vail - ing.
Thy jus - tice and thy right - eous - ness Have ev - ery strong-hold_ tak - en.

3. Thou art, O God, the God of love,
Thy mercy is unending;
Thou guardest us with tender care,
Each day our souls defending.

4. Thou art, O God, the God of grace,
Though sin our hearts hath hardened;
Thy grace can wash away the stain,
And heaven receive us pardoned.

I KNOW NOT WHERE THE ROAD WILL LEAD — LARAMIE C.M.D.

St. 1-6

Evelyn Atwater Cummins, writ. 1922, pub. 1940 — Arnold G. H. Bode, comp. 1941

1. I know not where the road will lead I fol - low day by day,
3. And some I love have reached the end, But some— with me may stay,
Or where it ends, I on - ly know I walk the—King's high - way.
Their faith and hope still guid - ing me I walk the—King's high - way.
2. I know not if the way is long, And no one else can say;
4. The way is truth, the way is love, For light and strength I pray,
But rough or smooth, up hill or down, I— walk the—King's high - way.
And through the year of life, to God, I— walk the—King's high - way.

5. The countless hosts lead on before,
I must not fear nor stray;
With them, the pilgrims of the faith,
I walk the King's highway.

6. Through light and dark the road leads on,
Till dawns the endless day,
When I shall know why in this life,
I walk the King's highway.

O LOVE THAT LIGHTS THE EASTERN SKY

VITTEL WOODS C.M.

St. 1-4

Louis F. Benson, writ. 1923, pub. 1924

Bradley Keeler, comp. 1924, pub. 1925

1. O Love that lights the east - ern sky And shrouds the eve - ning rest,
2. O life, con - tent be - neath the blue! Or, if God will the gray,

From out whose hand the swal - lows fly, With - in whose heart they nest!
Then tran - quil yet, till light breaks through To melt the mist a - way!

3. O death that sails so close to shore
At twilight! From my gate
I scan the darkening sea once more,
And for its message wait.

4. What lies beyond the afterglow?
To life's new dawn how far?
As if an answer, spoken low,
Love lights the evening star.

The Lone Wild Fowl

St. 1, 2

H. R. MacFayden, writ. 1923, pub. 1927

Cwmafan L.M.

Philip James, 1927

Adagio con calore
1. The lone, wild fowl in loft - y flight Is still with thee, nor leaves thy sight. And I am thine! I rest in thee. Great Spir - it, come and rest in me.
2. The ends of earth are in thy hand, The sea's dark deep and no man's land. And I am thine! I rest in thee. Great Spir - it, come and rest in me.

THEY CAST THEIR NETS IN GALILEE

GEORGETOWN C.M.

St. 1-4

William A. Percy, 1924 (altered)

David McK. Williams, 1941

In unison, with movement
1. They cast their nets in Gal - i - lee Just off the hills of brown;
2. Con - tent - ed, peace - ful fish - er - men, Be - fore they ev - er knew

Such hap - py, sim - ple fish - er - folk, Be - fore the Lord came down.
The peace of God that filled their hearts Brim - ful, and broke them too.

3. Young John who trimmed the flapping sail,
Homeless, in Patmos died.
Peter, who hauled the teeming net,
Head down was crucified.

4. The peace of God, it is no peace,
But strife closed in the sod.
Yet, brothers, pray for but one thing –
The marvelous peace of God.

O GRACIOUS FATHER OF MANKIND

CREEVELEA C.M.D.

St. 1-4

Henry Hallam Tweedy, writ. 1925

Arthur Davis, 1927

1. O gra - cious Fa - ther of man - kind, Our spir - its' un - seen friend,
2. Thou hear - est these—the good and ill— Deep bur - ied in each breast;
Lord of the skies, our hearts' dear guest, To thee our prayers as - cend.
The se - cret thought, the hid - den plan, Wrought out or un - ex - pressed.
Thou dost not wait till hu - man speech Thy gifts di - vine im - plore;
O cleanse our prayers from hu - man dross! At - tune our lives to thee,
im - plore;
to thee,
Our dreams, our alms, our work, our lives Are prayers thou lov - est more.
Un - til we la - bor for those gifts We ask on bend - ed knee.

3. Our best is but thyself in us,
Our highest thought thy will;
To hear thy voice we need but love,
To listen, and be still.
We would not bend thy will to ours,
But blend our wills to thine,
Not beat with cries on heaven's doors,
But live thy life divine.

4. Thou seekest us in love and truth
More than our minds seek thee;
Through open gates thy power flows in
Like floodtides from the sea.
No more we seek thee from afar,
Nor ask thee for a sign,
Content to pray in life and love
And toil, till all are thine.

THE TWILIGHT SHADOWS ROUND ME FALL

CECILE C.M.D.

St. 1-3

Ernest Edwin Ryden, 1925

Peter Johnson, 1925

Quietly
1. The twi - light shad - ows round me fall, And night comes steal - ing on;
2. My life is but a fleet - ing day, My race how quick - ly run!
But thou dear Lord art ev - er near, My day when day is gone,
The dawn and noon - day glo - ry fade With yon - der set - ting sun.
Thy wings in love o'er - shad - ow me, The night with thee is light;
A stran - ger and a pil - grim here In un - known paths I roam;
I rest in thee, thou change - less one, And wait the morn - ing bright.
Lord, let thy glo - ry light the way That leads me to my home.

3. By faith I see the better land,
Where falls no earthly night,
Where thou dost shine, a radiant sun,
The everlasting Light.
Then grant me, Lord, to walk with thee,
And keep me thine alway,
That with the morn I may awake
Unto the perfect day.

Spirit of Life, in This New Dawn — De Pauw L.M.

St. 1-5

Earl B. Marlatt, writ. 1926, pub. 1928 — Robert G. McCutchan, comp. 1928, pub. 1930

1. Spir - it of Life, in this new dawn, Give us the
2. Spir - it Cre - a - tive, give us light, Lift - ing the

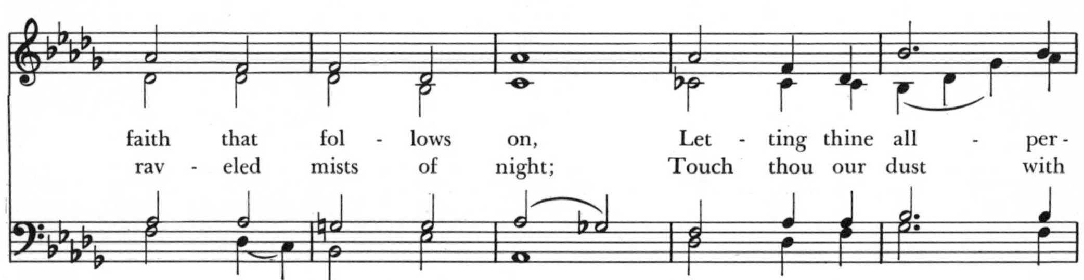
faith that fol - lows on, Let - ting thine all - per -
rav - eled mists of night; Touch thou our dust with

vad - ing power Ful - fill the dream of this high hour.
spir - it - hand, And make us souls that un - der - stand.

3. Spirit Redeeming, give us grace
When crucified, to seek thy face;
To read forgiveness in thine eyes
Today with thee in Paradise.

4. Spirit consoling, let us find
Thy hand when sorrows leave us blind;
In the gray valley let us hear
Thy silent voice, "Lo, I am near."

5. Spirit of Love, at evening time,
When weary feet refuse to climb,
Give us thy vision, eyes that see,
Beyond the dark, the dawn and thee.

Through the Dark the Dreamers Came — Dreamers — Irregular

St. 1-3

Earl B. Marlatt, writ. 1927, pub. 1928 — Mabel W. Daniels, comp. 1927, pub. 1928

1. Through the dark the dream - ers came, Mel - chi - or, Bal - tha - sar,
2. But the way did not seem Shad - ow - y or long.
Cas - par, fol - low - ing the flame Of a star. Vi - a,
It was bright - ened by a dream And a song. Glo - ri - a!
Softly
vi - a, De pro - fun - dis vi - a!
glo - ri - a! In ex - cel - sis glo - ri - a!
Organ

3. It was worth the journeying
To the weary end;
For they found their dream, a King
And a friend.
Maxima, maxima,
Gloria Dei maxima

BRAVING THE WILDS ALL UNEXPLORED MARCUS WHITMAN 8.8.8.10.8.8.

St. 1-4

Robert Freeman, writ, 1927, pub. 1928 William Pierson Merrill, comp. 1927, pub. 1928

In march rhythm

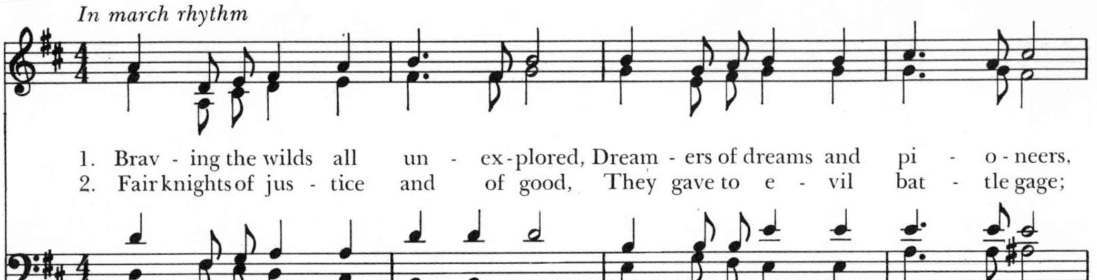
1. Brav - ing the wilds all un - ex-plored, Dream - ers of dreams and pi - o-neers,
2. Fair knights of jus - tice and of good, They gave to e - vil bat - tle gage;

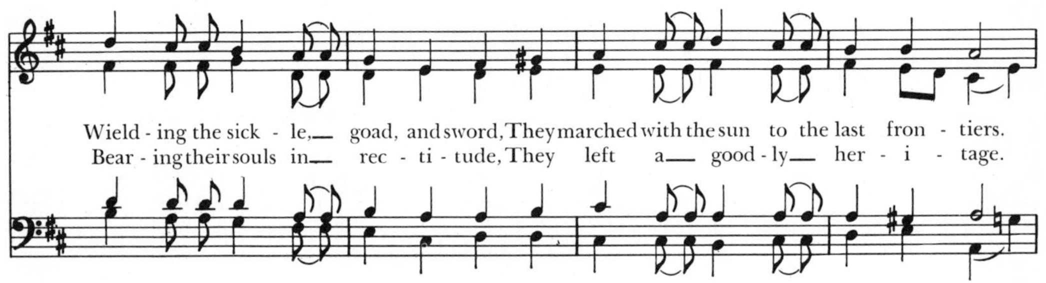
Wield - ing the sick - le, goad, and sword, They marched with the sun to the last fron - tiers.
Bear - ing their souls in rec - ti - tude, They left a good - ly her - i - tage.

God of the val - iant, grant that we, Their sons, do fol - low val - iant - ly!
God of the right - eous, grant that we, Their sons, do fol - low right - eous - ly!

3. Guards of the sacred altar flame,
Bringers of learning and of faith,
They lumined life in the blessed Name,
And hope they flared in the day of death.
God of the faithful, grant that we,
Their sons, do follow faithfully!

4. Theirs was the Presence ever sure,
Theirs was the all-abounding grace,
Theirs was the passion ever pure
To honor the Lord in all their ways.
God of the Christlike, grant that we
Do follow, follow worthily!

PRECIOUS CHILD, SO SWEETLY SLEEPING — PRECIOUS CHILD 8.7.8.7.7.7.

St. 1-4

Anna Hoppe, writ. 1928, pub. 1932 — Oscar R. Overby, arr. 1931, pub. 1933

1. Pre - cious Child, so sweet - ly sleep - ing In a vir - gin's fond_ em - brace,
2. An - thems joy - ous now are ring - ing In the skies_ of Beth - le - hem;

Heaven - ly hosts their watch are keep - ing O'er thy hum - ble dwell - ing place.
An - gels their sweet song are sing - ing, "Peace on earth, good will_ to men."

Blest Mes - si - ah, new - born king, Let_ my heart_ its trib - ute bring.
Pre - cious Je - sus, at_ thy birth Hea - ven's peace_ is brought_ to earth.

3. Thou hast come to bring salvation
To this sin - cursed world below,
That thy blood redeemed creation,
Thine abounding love might know.
Enter each believing heart;
Pardon, grace, and peace impart.

4. Take my humble adoration
While on earth below I dwell.
Let my songs in exultation
Of thy boundless goodness tell.
Till in heaven above, my King,
Endless hymns of praise I sing.

Where Is Our Holy Church? OXNAM S.M.

St. 1-5

Edwin H. Wilson, writ. 1928, pub. 1937 Robert G. McCutchan, 1930

1. Where is our ho - ly church? Where race and class u - nite
2. Where is our ho - ly writ? Wher - e'er a hu - man heart

As e - qual broth - ers in the search For beau - ty, truth, and right.
A sa - cred torch of truth has lit, By in - spi - ra - tion taught.

3. Where is our holy man?
A mighty host respond;
For good men rise in every land
To break the captive's bond.

4. Where is our holy land?
Within the human soul,
Wherever strong men truly seek
With character the goal.

The City, Lord, Where Thy Dear Life — Brooklyn C.M.

St. 1-5

William E. Dudley, 1929 — Frank Kasschau, 1929

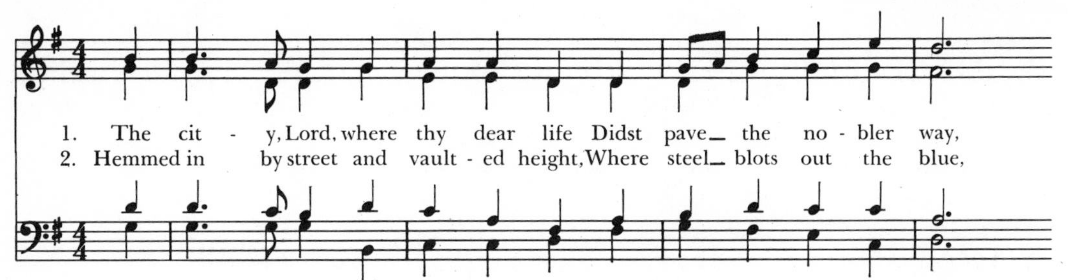
1. The cit - y, Lord, where thy dear life Didst pave the no - bler way,
2. Hemmed in by street and vault - ed height, Where steel blots out the blue,

Save it from grief and self - ish strife For this, O Lord, we pray.
Thy peo - ple, Lord, look up for light; Thou art the light; shine through.

3. Where move the weak and strong,
   Who toil in market, shop, and lane,
   Make swift thy promise, evil foil;
   Speak Lord, and save again.

4. Though iron must rust and spires decay,
   And splendored pomp turn dust,
   Let faith foresee the glad new day
   When men of earth are just.

5. So, Lord, the city bless and save;
   Where press the throngs, forgive;
   Bring heaven to earth, so long delayed;
   God, make thy people live.

THE SABBATH DAY WAS BY — DEXTER STREET S.M.

Stanzas 1,2,4,6,7

Howard Chandler Robbins, 1929 — Winfred Douglas, comp. 1940

Joyously
1. The Sab - bath day was by, The light was
2. Sad Ma - ry, dry thine eyes, And cease thy

in the sky, When on the first day of the
woe - ful cries; It is no gard - ner, but thy

week The Prince of life drew nigh.
Lord Who brings thee glad sur - prise.

3. Simon, thy Lord knows all;
He doth forgive thy fall,
And sends thee forth to feed the sheep
That heed the Shepherd's call.

4. So did the Lord draw near
To his disciples dear,
When he came back from death and hell,
And to them did appear.

5. Blest were the eyes of yore
That saw their friend once more,
And blessed we, who have not seen,
But love him and adore.

AND HAVE THE BRIGHT IMMENSITIES TREGARON C.M.D.

St. 1, 2

Howard Chandler Robbins, 1931 Philip James, 1941

Triumphantly
1. And have the bright im - men - si - ties Re - ceived our ris - en___ Lord, Where
2. The heaven that hides him from our sight Knows nei - ther near___ nor___ far. An
Organ

light - years frame the Plei - a - des And point___ O - ri - on's sword? Do
al - tar can - dle sheds its___ light As sure - ly___ as a star; And

flam - ing suns his foot - steps trace Through cor - ri - dors sub - lime, The
where his lov - ing peo - ple meet To share the gift di - vine, There

Lord of in - ter - stel - lar space And con - quer - or___ of___ time?
stands he with un - hur - rying feet; There heaven - ly splen - dors___ shine.

Put Forth, O God, Thy Spirit's Might — Chelsea Square C.M.

St. 1-4

Howard Chandler Robbins, 1937 — Howard Chandler Robbins, comp. 1941; Ray Francis Brown, arr. 1941

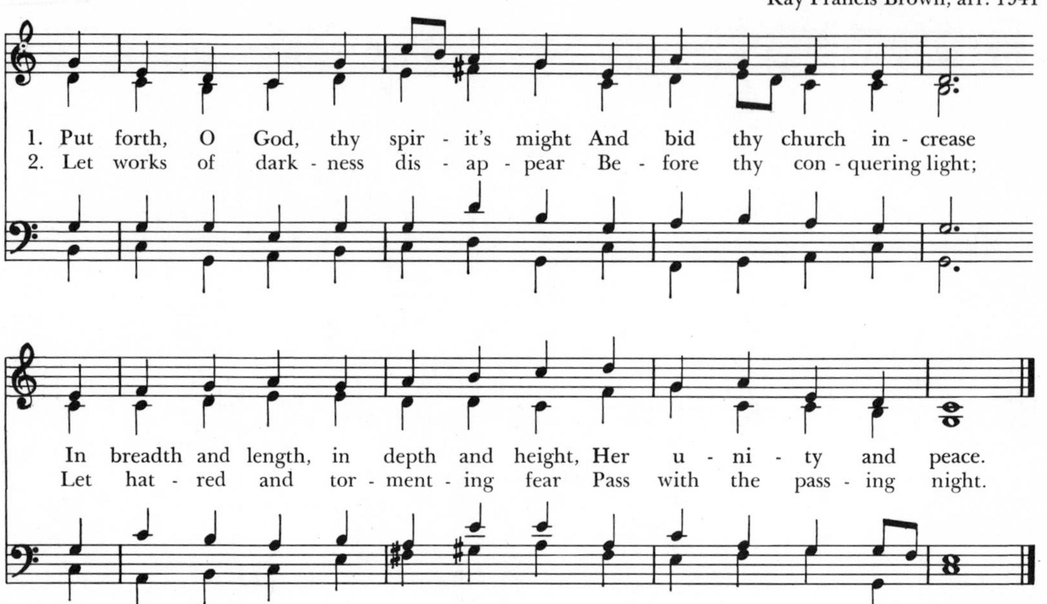
1. Put forth, O God, thy spir - it's might And bid thy church in - crease
2. Let works of dark - ness dis - ap - pear Be - fore thy con - quering light;
In breadth and length, in depth and height, Her u - ni - ty and peace.
Let hat - red and tor - ment - ing fear Pass with the pass - ing night.

3. Let what apostles learned of thee
Be ours from age to age;
Their steadfast faith our unity,
Their peace our heritage.

4. O Judge divine of human strife,
O vanquisher of pain!
To know thee is eternal life,
To serve thee is to reign.

O Young and Fearless Prophet — Comrades of the Cross 7.6.7.6.D.

St. 1-6

Samuel Ralph Harlow, writ. 1931, pub. 1935 — Edward Shippen Barnes, 1927

1. O young and fear - less Proph - et Of an-cient Gal - i - lee, Thy
2. We mar - vel at the pur - pose That held thee to thy course, While

life is still a sum - mons To serve hu - man - i - ty. To
ev - er on the hill - top Be - fore thee loomed the cross; Thy

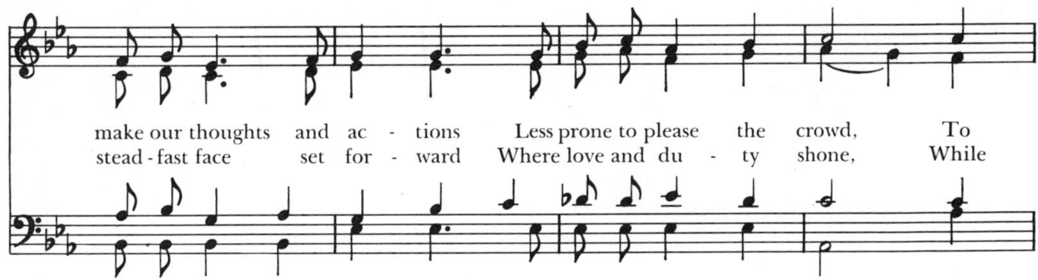
make our thoughts and ac - tions Less prone to please the crowd, To
stead - fast face set for - ward Where love and du - ty shone, While

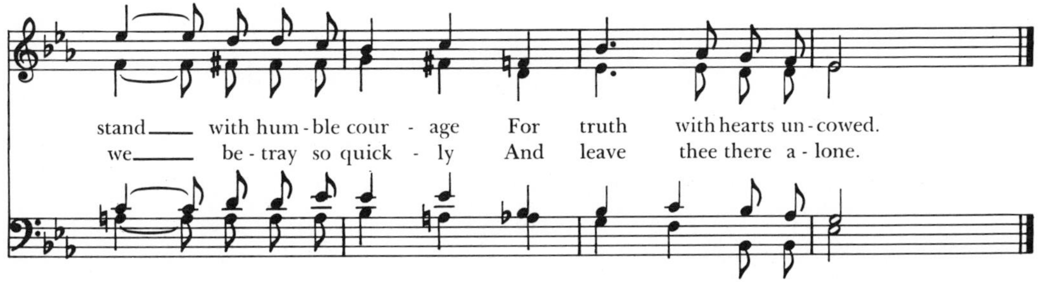
stand with hum - ble cour - age For truth with hearts un - cowed.
we be - tray so quick - ly And leave thee there a - lone.

3. Stir up in us a protest
Against unearnèd wealth,
While men go starved and hungry,
Who plead for work and health;
Whose wives and little children
Cry out for lack of bread,
Who spend their years o'erweighted
Beneath a gloomy dread.

4. O help us stand unswerving
Against war's bloody way,
Where hate and lust and falsehood
Hold back Christ's holy sway;
Forbid false love of country,
That blinds us to his call,
Who lifts above the nation
The Brotherhood of all.

5. Create in us the splendor
That dawns when hearts are kind
That knows not race nor station
As boundaries of mind.
That learns to value beauty,
In heart, or brain, or soul,
And longs to bind God's children
Into one perfect whole.

6. O young and fearless Prophet,
We need thy presence here
Amid our pride and glory
To see thy face appear.
Once more to hear thy challenge
Above our noisy day
Triumphantly to lead us
Along God's holy way.

As Tranquil Streams — Grace L.M.

St. 1-5

Marion Franklin Ham, writ. 1933, pub. 1937 — Charles L. Ziegler, 1902

1. As tran - quil streams that meet and merge And flow as one to seek the sea,
2. Free from the bands that bind the mind To nar - row thought and life - less creed;
Our kin - dred fel - low - ships u-nite To build a church that shall be free.
Free from a so cial code that fails To serve the cause of hu man need.

3. A freedom that reveres the past,
But trusts the dawning future more;
And bids the soul, in search of truth,
Adventure boldly and explore.

4. A freedom, subject still to law,
That seeks its wisdom from above;
And fighting zealously for right,
Still tempers all its blows with love.

5. Prophetic Church, the future waits
Thy liberating ministry;
Go forward in the power of God,
Proclaim the truth that makes men free.

The Prince of Peace His Banner Spreads — All Saints C.M.D.

St. 1-4

Harry Emerson Fosdick, writ. 1931, pub. 1937 — Henry S. Cutler, 1872

1. The Prince of Peace his ban - ner spreads, His way - ward folk to lead
2. Lead on, O Christ! That haunt - ing song No cen - tu - ries can dim,
From war's em - bat - tled hates and dreads, Its bul - warked ire and greed.
Which long a - go the heaven - ly throng Sang o - ver Beth - le - hem.
O mar - shal us, the sons of sires Who braved the can - non's roar,
Cast down our ran - cor, fear and pride, Ex - alt (all) good - will a - gain!
To ven - ture all that peace re - quires As they dared death for war.
Our wor - ship doth thy name de - ride, Bring we not peace to men.

3. Thy pardon, Lord, for war's dark shame,
Its death-strewn, bloody fields!
Yet thanks to thee for souls aflame
We dared with swords and shields;
O Christ, who died to give men life,
Bring that victorious hour,
When man shall use for peace, not strife,
His valor, skill, and power.

4. Cleanse all our hearts from our disgrace—
We love not world, but clan!
Make clear our eyes to see our race
One family of man.
Rend thou our little temple veils
That cloak the truth divine;
Until thy mighty word prevails,
That cries, "All souls are mine."

Where Now Are the Hebrew Children? 8.8.8.6.D.

St. 1-4

Traditional — Annabel Morris Buchanan, arr., cop. 1934

Moderato ♩=96
1. Where now are the He - brew chil - dren? Where now are the He - brew chil - dren?
2. Where now are the twelve a - pos - tles? Where now are the twelve a - pos - tles?
mf
Where now are the He - brew chil - dren? Safe in the prom - ised land.
Where now are the twelve a - pos - tles? Safe in the prom - ised land.
Though the fur - nace flamed a - round them, God, while in their troub - les, found them,
They went through the flam - ing fire, Trust - ing in the great Mes - si - ah,
f
p
He with love and mer - cy bound them Safe in the prom - ised land.
Ho - ly grace did raise them high - er, Safe in the prom - ised land.

3. Where now are the holy martyrs?
Where now are the holy martyrs?
Where now are the holy martyrs?
Safe in the promised land.
Those who washed their robes and made them
White and spotless pure and laid them
Where no earthly stain could fade them,
Safe in the promised land.

4. Where now are the holy Christians?
Where now are the holy Christians?
Where now are the holy Christians?
Safe in the promised land.
There our souls will join the chorus,
Saints and angels sing before us,
While all heaven is beaming o'er us,
Safe in the promised land.

WHAT WONDROUS LOVE IS THIS 12.9.12.12.9.

St. 1-4

Traditional — Annabel Morris Buchanan, arr., cop. 1934

Andante semplice ♩= 80
1. What won - drous love is this, O my soul, O my soul! What
2. When I was sink - ing down, sink - ing down, sink - ing down; When
won - drous love is this O my soul, my soul! What
I was sink - ing down, sink - ing, sink - ing down. When
soul!
down.
sing.
on.
won - drous love is this That caused the Lord of bliss To
I was sink - ing down Be neath God's right - eous frown Christ
bear the dread - ful curse for my soul, for my soul; To
laid a - side his crown for my soul, for my soul; Christ

soul.
soul.
sing.
on.
bear the dread - ful curse for my soul, for my soul.
laid a - side his crown for my soul, for my soul.

3. To God and to the Lamb
I will sing, I will sing;
To God and to the Lamb,
I will sing,
To God and to the Lamb
Who is the great I Am
While millions join the theme
I will sing, I will sing;
While millions join the theme
I will sing, I will sing.

4. And when from death I'm free,
I'll sing on, I'll sing on,
And when from death I'm free
I'll sing on,
And when from death I'm free,
I'll sing and joyful be,
And through eternity
I'll sing on, I'll sing on;
And through eternity
I'll sing on, I'll sing on.

O God of Youth — Lynne 13.10.11.10.

St. 1-4

Bates G. Burt, writ. 1935, pub. 1940 — Bates G. Burt, 1940

In unison, spirited
1. O God of youth, whose spir - it in our hearts is stir - ring
2. Fill thou our hearts with zeal in ev - ery brave en - deav - or
Hope and de - sire for no - ble lives and true,
To right the wrongs that shame this mor - tal life;
Keep us, we pray thee, stead - fast and un - err - ing;
Give us the val - iant spir - it that shall nev - er
With light and love di - vine our souls en - due.
Fal - ter or fail, how - ev - er long the strife.

3. Teach us to know the way of Jesus Christ, our Master;
Give us his clear-eyed faith, his fearless heart;
And through life's darkness, danger, and disaster,
O may we never from his side depart.

4. May we be true to him, our Captain of salvation,
Bearing his cross in service glad and free,
Winning the world to that last consummation
When all its kingdoms shall his kingdom be.

PEACE IS THE MIND'S OLD WILDERNESS — SURSUM CORDA 10.10.10.10.

St. 1-4

John Holmes, writ. 1937, pub. 1943 — Alfred Morton Smith, comp. 1941

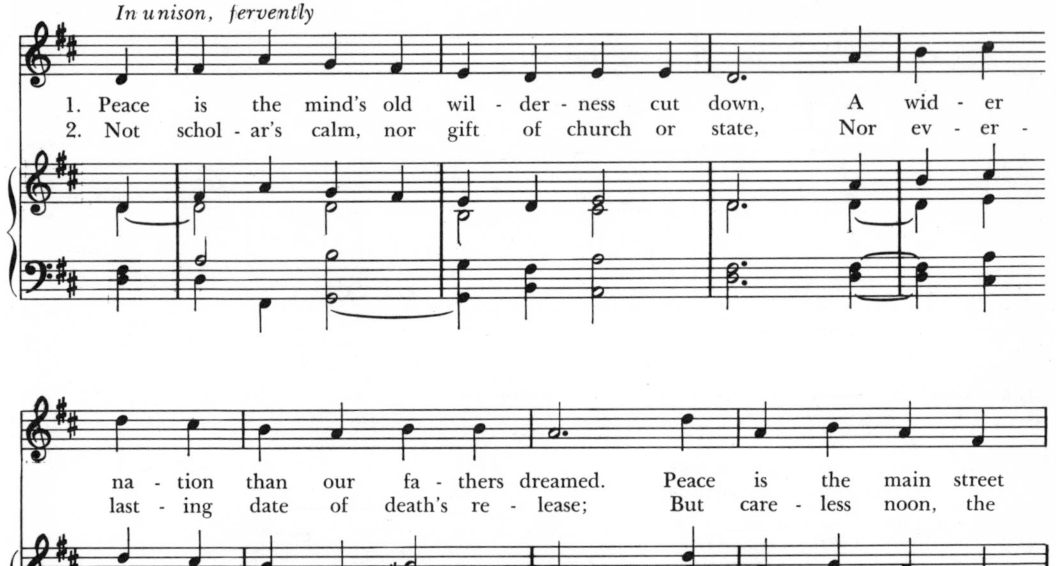
In unison, fervently
1. Peace is the mind's old wil - der - ness cut down, A wid - er
2. Not schol - ar's calm, nor gift of church or state, Nor ev - er -
na - tion than our fa - thers dreamed. Peace is the main street
last - ing date of death's re - lease; But care - less noon, the

in a coun - try town; Our chil - dren named; our fa - ther's lives re - deemed.
hous - es light - ed late, Har - vest and hol - i - day; the peo - ple's peace.

3. The peace not past our understanding falls
Like light upon the soft white tablecloth
At winter supper warm between four walls,
A thing too simple to be tried as truth.

4. Days into years, the doorways worn at sill,
Years into years, the plans for long increase
Come true at last for men of God's good will;
These are the things we mean by saying, Peace.

All Praise to Thee — Deed 10.10.10.4.

St. 1-5

F. Bland Tucker, writ. 1938, pub. 1940 — Daniel Gregory Mason, comp. 1927, pub. 1928

1. All praise to thee, for thou, O King di - vine, Didst yield the glo - ry that of right was thine, That in our dark - ened hearts thy grace might shine. Al - le - lu - ia! Al - le - lu - ia!
2. Thou cam'st to us in low - li - ness of thought; By thee the out - cast and the poor were sought, And by the death was God's sal - va - tion wrought. Al - le - lu - ia! Al - le - lu - ia!

3. Let this mind be in us which was in thee,
Who was a servant that we might be free,
Humbling thyself to death on Calvary.
Alleluia!

4. Wherefore, by God's eternal purpose, thou
Art high exalted o'er all creatures now,
And given the name to which all knees shall bow.
Alleluia!

5. Let every tongue confess with one accord
In heaven and earth that Jesus Christ is Lord;
And God the Father be by all adored.
Alleluia!

Our Father, by Whose Name — King of Glory 6.6.6.6.8.8.8.

St. 1-3

F. Bland Tucker, writ. 1939, pub. 1940 — Horatio Parker, 1894

1. Our Fa - ther, by whose name All fa - ther - hood is known,
2. O Christ, thy - self a child With - in an earth - ly home,
Who dost in love pro - claim Each fam - i - ly thine own,
With heart still un de - filed, Thou didst to man - hood come;
Bless thou all par - ents, guard - ing well, With con - stant love as sen - ti - nel,
Our chil - dren bless, in ev - ery place, That they may all be - hold thy face,
The homes in which thy peo - ple dwell.
And know - ing thee may grow in grace.

3\. A Spirit, who dost bind
Our hearts in unity,
Who teachest us to find
The love from self set free,
In all our hearts such love increase,
That every home, by this release,
May be the dwelling place of peace.

Now Evening Puts Amen to Day

St. 1-4

Paul Horgan, pub. 1942

Ernst Bacon, comp. 1942

Fairly slow
p
1. Now eve - ning puts a - men to day,
2. Eve - ning is e - ter - nal rest,
accompaniment
sempre legato

Calm is the cloud up - on the hill;
Soft the sound from in the rill.
We are com - fort - ed in our way,
Love is day - light in the breast;

Won - drous is God's sov - ereign will.
Won - drous is God's sov - ereign will.
cresc.
3. Tree is down but seed is deep, The

child a sire will soon ful - fill,
Branch will rise while root's a - sleep,
dim.

Won - drous is God's sov - ereign will.
4. Aft - er the rain the
riv - ers flood, Thanks from the hum-ble heart do spill, All things whis - per
poco cresc.
pp
p
in the blood, Won - drous is God's sov - ereign will.

GIVE PEACE, O GOD, THE NATIONS CRY — VERMONT C.M.

St. 1-5

John W. Norris, 1940 — Anne Langdon Miller, 1941

1. Give peace, O God, the na - tions cry, From e - vil man and deed;
2. Yet not thy peace, O God, they ask, The peace that grace be - stows;
Their voic - es, ris - ing to the sky, Pro - claim a hu - man need.
The peace which hal - lows care and task, That makes us friends, not foes.

3. But peace, they ask, from war's alarms,
Surcease from earthy care,
And peace that rests on fighting arms
Of land and sea and air.

4. We need the peace of heart and mind
In men from hate set free,
Who by their love for human kind
Show deeper love for thee.

5. O cleanse all hearts of pride and greed,
Remove all lust and sin,
That man from chains of wrath be freed,
Eternal peace to win.

WE SHALL OVERCOME 10.7.9.7.

Selected lines

Anon., sung before 1947

1. We shall o - ver - come, we shall o - ver - come,
2. We'll walk hand in hand, we'll walk hand in hand,
We shall o - ver - come some day; Oh,
We'll walk hand in hand some day; O,
deep in my heart, I do be - lieve
deep in my heart, I do be - lieve
I know that shall o - ver - come.
walk hand in hand.
We shall o - ver - come some day.
We'll walk hand in hand some day.
shall o - ver - come.
walk hand in hand.

3. We shall live in peace, we shall live in peace,
We shall live in peace some day;
Oh, deep in my heart, I do believe
We shall live in peace some day.

4. We shall all be free, we shall all be free,
We shall all be free some day;
O, deep in my heart, I do believe
We shall all be free some day.

5. The Lord will see us through, the Lord will see us through,
The Lord will see us through some day;
Oh, deep in my heart, I do believe
The Lord will see us through some day.

REJOICE, LET ALLELUIAS RING

C.M., with chorus

St. 1-3, 6

Sister M. Cherubim Schaefer, O.S.F., 1951

Sister M. Cherubim Schaefer, O.S.F., 1951

Animato ♩ = 96–100
1. Re - joice! let al - le - lu - ias ring This bright and
2. The foes of Christ re - joiced in vain When on the
glo - rious day; For risen is Christ, our Lord and
cross he died; For us the Pas - chal Lamb was
King, May heaven re - sound the lay.
slain To stem sin's woe - ful tide.
Chorus
Then

al - le-lu - ia let us sing, For ris - en is our Lord and King! Al-le-
lu - ia, al-le-lu - ia, al - le - lu - ia.
f

3. The tomb was but a resting place
For limbs all bruised and torn,
To rise again ere gone three days,
On blessed Easter morn.
Chorus

4. Triumphant Saviour, Thee we praise;
Our faith is not in vain.
O Shepherd of a ransomed race,
Thy death is all our gain.
Chorus

SI FELIZ QUIERES SER
IF YOU HAPPY WOULD BE

10.9.10.9., with chorus

St. 1-3

Abraham Fernández, cop. 1955

Cosme C. Cota, 1955

1. If you hap-py would be, come to Je - sus, When af - flic - ted with sad - ness and pain;
2. If you hap-py would be, come to Je - sus, Ev - en death can-not cause you to quail.
3. If you hap-py would be, come to Je - sus And en - joy blest and tran - quil re - pose;
Trust-ing al - ways in Christ, al - ways hap - py, Find in him end-less com - fort and gain.
Lift your spir - its and trust in his mer - cy, And the Lord will il - lu - mine your souls.
Oh how sweet and how wel-come the sum - mons: Come ye blest, find your prom-ised re - ward!
Chorus
If you hap - py would be, come to Je - sus, In this choice sure-ly blest you will be;
Join with cour - age the train of his peo - ple, Sure to win in his name vic - to - ry.

1. Si feliz quieres ser, ven a Cristo,
Cuando tengas tristeza y dolor;
Hallarás a Jesús siempre listo
Para darte consuelo y amor.

Coro

Si feliz quieres ser, ven a Cristo.
Y dichosa tu alma será;
Que siguiendo al valiente caudillo
Siempre, siempre del mal triunfarás.

2. Si feliz quieres ser, ven a Cristo,
Ni la muerte que infunde terror
Causará leve espanto a tu alma,
Si ilumina tu senda el Señor.
Coro

3. Si feliz quieres ser, ven a Cristo,
Y reposo bendito hallarás;
Oh! cuán dulce es la voz que te llama;
Ven, si quieres la dicha gozar.
Coro

Come, All Ye People

Festal Day L.M.

St. 1-6

George R. Seltzer, comp. 1956, pub. 1958

Ralph P. Lewars, comp. 1956, pub. 1958

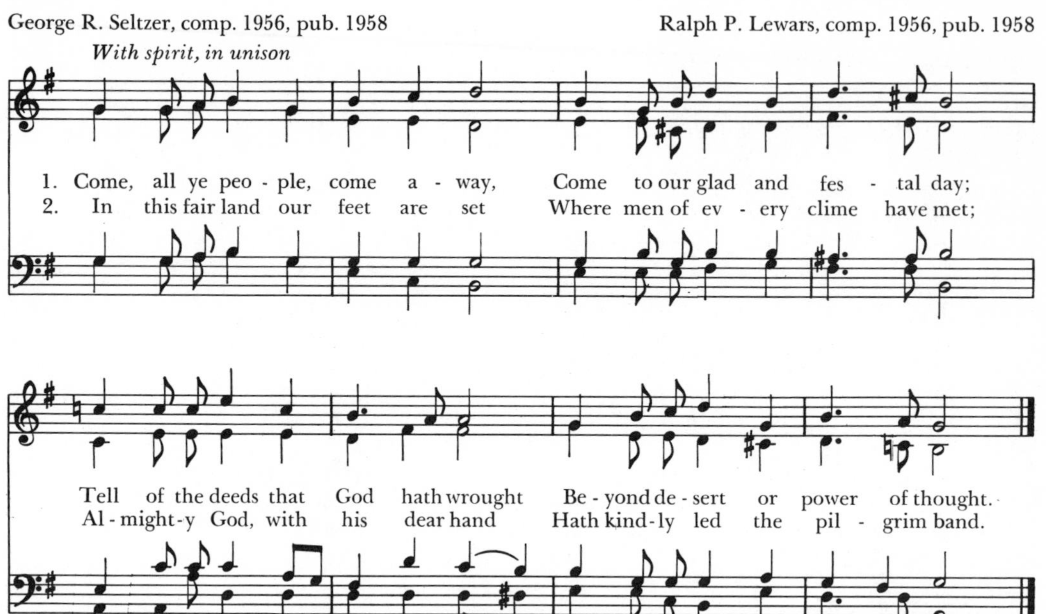
With spirit, in unison
1. Come, all ye peo - ple, come a - way, Come to our glad and fes - tal day;
2. In this fair land our feet are set Where men of ev - ery clime have met;
Tell of the deeds that God hath wrought Be - yond de - sert or power of thought.
Al - might-y God, with his dear hand Hath kind-ly led the pil - grim band.

3. Throughout our life his truth and light
Have been our beacon in the night;
Know we in war and peace his care
Of loved ones far away and near.

4. O God, to thee we bring the meed
Of praise, for help in times of need,
For mercies given by thy Son,
For joys which make our cup o'er-run.

5. Grant us, throughout our earthly day.
To love and serve thee all the way;
To labor for thy kingdom's spread,
For Christ our Lord, for Christ our Head!

6. Father and Son and Spirit blest,
To thee be every prayer addressed,
Who art in threefold name adored,
From age to age, the only Lord.

God of Peace, in Peace Preserve Us

Pax 8.7.8.7.7.7.

St. 1-3

Ernst W. Olson, 1958

Clive Harold Kilgore, 1958

1. God of peace, in peace_ pre - serve us, Hear us, mer - ci - ful Lord God!
2. God of love, if foe - men_ face us Armed with wea - pons forged in hate,
Let no lust for pow - er swerve us From the way our Mas - ter trod.__
Let not pride nor greed de - base us; All our ef - forts con - se - crate__
Guard - ed by thy might - y__ hand, Safe and free our peo - ple stand.
That the wrong shall be__made_ right In thy spir - it, by thy might.

3. God of mercy, bid the terrors
Of inhuman strife to cease;
Overrule our grievious errors
By thy scepter, Prince of Peace.
Let thine angels speak again,
Peace on earth, good will toward men.

Within the Shelter of Our Walls

Hearthside 8.6.8.8.6.

St. 1-3

Elinor Lennen, cop. 1961

Shirley L. Brown, 1970

Unison
1. With - in the shel - ter of___ our walls, Be pres - ent, Lord,___ to
2. Trans - form our spir - its as___ we learn Thy lov - ing dis - ci -

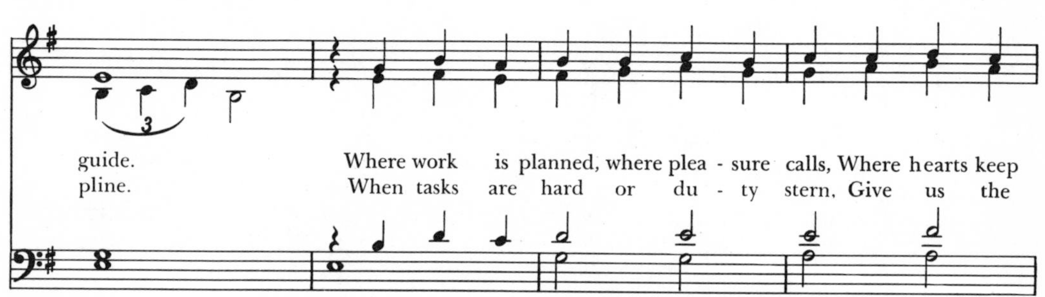
guide. Where work is planned, where plea - sure calls, Where hearts keep
pline. When tasks are hard or du - ty stern, Give us the

ho - ly fes - ti - vals, Find wel - come, and___ a - bide.
wis - dom to___ dis - cern Thy com - rad - ship___ with - in.

3. Make daily bread a sacrament
Which thou, O Lord, might share.
Give conversation high intent;
Our daily strength for thee be spent
With thought and loving care.

Praise Now Your God — 11.11.10.10., with chorus

St. 1-3

H. P. Brucker, S.J., 1964 — Jan Kern, 1964

Unison
1. Praise now your God, all ye peo - ples and na - tions!
2. Hail, great Re - deem - er, whose life giv - ing sac - ri - fice

Speak to your sons and to all gen - er - a - tions,
Freed us from sin, mid the pains of the suf - fering Christ.

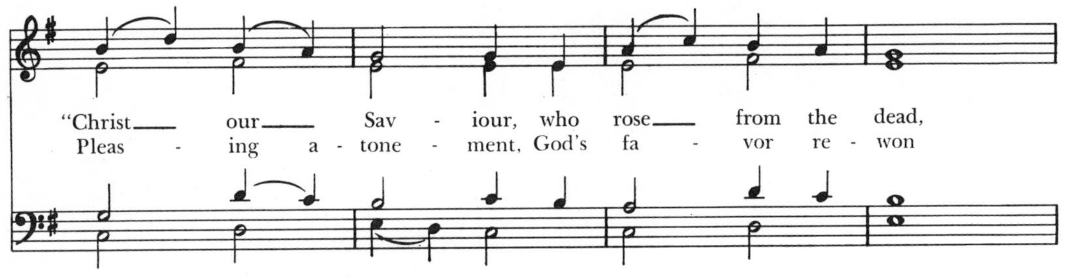
"Christ our Sav - iour, who rose from the dead,
Pleas - ing a - tone - ment, God's fa - vor re - won

Dwells with us now, in the shad - ow of bread."
Thanks to the Fa - ther's o - be - di - ant Son.
Al -

le - lu - ia, Great is God! Al -

le - lu - ia, Al - le - lu - ia!

3. Christ is our manna that clothes his divinity.
Christ is our food that hides his humanity.
All may receive him, in union divine.
Blessèd am I then, when Jesus is mine.
Alleluia, Great is God!
Alleluia, Alleluia!

O God, Send Men

St. 1-4

Elizabeth Burrowes, 1966

Hughes Hall 11.10.11.10.

Wilbur Held, 1970

Unison
1. O God, send men whose pur - pose will not fal - ter,
2. Not to be served but ev - er to be serv - ing,
Who dare to walk where Christ has set his feet,
Feed - ing the hun - ger in the hearts of men;
Who know the Church as bea - con and as al - tar,
To know the love that waits not man's de - serv - ing,
Where need of men and thine a - bun - dance meet.
Giv - ing and giv - ing but to give a - gain.

3. Empires have come and flourished and departed,
But lives thy Church as witness to thy way,
Our hope in darkness, light of the true-hearted,
Calling to action those feet would stay.

4. O God, send men in whom thy heart rejoices,
Men who have heard the call that makes us free,
With eager hearts and jubilating voices,
Each making answer, Here am I, send me.

GLORY

St. 1-4

Joseph Wise, cop. 1967

Joseph Wise, cop. 1967
Refrain
Dm(Am) F(C) Dm(Am) F(C) Dm(Am) Gm(Dm) F(C)
Glo(ho - ho)-ry (hee), glo (ho - ho)-ry (hee), Glo-ry sing to the Lord;
Dm(Am) F(C) Dm(Am) F(C) Dm(Am) C7(G7)
1. F(C) 2. F(C) *last time* F(C)
Glo(ho-ho)-ry(hee), glo(ho - ho)-ry(hee) Glo - ry sing to the___ Lord. Lord. Lord.
Verses
Dm(Am) F(C) Dm(Am) F(C)
1. Well his peo - ple were___ lone - ly,___ So he sent them a___ Sav - iour,___
2. He___ took lit - tle___ chil - dren,___ And he set them on his knee___
3. Well, he died, and he___ bore him - self Deep in this___ earth;___
4. Well I wake up ev - ery morn - ing,___ And I kiss the sun hel - lo;___
Dm(Am) F(C) Dm(Am) F(C)
Glo - ry, sing to the Lord. A man who could___ whis - tle___
Glo - ry sing to the Lord. And kissed them and ca-ressed them___ Till they
Glo - ry sing to the Lord. Now all of cre - a - tion___ Gets up
Glo - ry sing to the Lord. And one of these___ days___ It's gon-na
Repeat refrain after
Dm(Am) F(C) Dm(Am) C7(G7) F(C) *each verse*
Walk, and talk, and sing___ Glo - ry sing to the___ Lord.
did - n't want to leave him.___ Glo - ry sing to the___ Lord.
with him in the morn - ing.___ Glo - ry sing to the___ Lord.
be the Son of God.___ Glo - ry sing to the___ Lord.

And the Cock Begins to Crow

St. 1-4

Richard K. Avery, cop. 1970 — Donald S. Marsh, cop. 1970

Chorus

Gm
Dm
Gm

And the cock be- gins to crow, oh - h - h,

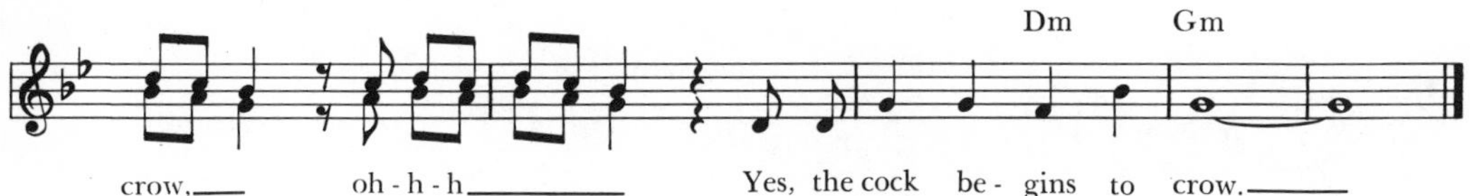
Dm
Gm

crow, oh - h - h Yes, the cock be- gins to crow.

Gm
Gm
D7

1. Poor Pe - ter did - n't know him - self at all (not at all) Poor, poor Pe - ter!
2. Poor Pe - ter heard his Lord and Mas - ter say (Mas - ter say) "Poor, poor Pe - ter!
3. Poor Pe - ter set a real - ly aw - ful trend (aw - ful trend) Poor, poor Pe - ter!
4. Poor Pe - ter, what a quan - dary to be in (to be in) Poor, poor Pe - ter!

Gm
Gm
D7

So cer - tain he would nev - er, nev - er fall (nev - er fall) Poor, poor Pete! Do you re -
You'll fail me just be - fore the break of day (break of day)" Poor, poor Pete! Well, af - ter
He taught us how to hurt your clos - est friend (clos - est friend) Poor, poor Pete! We know that
He did it 'cause he had to save his skin (save his skin) Poor, poor Pete! We know that

Gm
F6
E♭6
Dm
Gm
D7

mem - ber how up - set he got when Je - sus told him: "Pe - ter, you'll de - ny me"? Poor, poor Pete! His face got
Je - sus got ar - rest - ed Pe - ter had an op - por - tu - ni - ty to show him Poor, poor Pete! But then to
if your friend's in trou - ble and he needs you ve - ry bad - ly stand - ing by him Just like Pete! But you re-
if the world is blam - ing Christ - ians 'cause it's not a bet - ter place to live in We're like Pete! We'd be like

Gm
F6
E♭6
Dm
D7

red and he got an - gry and he shout - ed: "No, I won't, my Lord, just try me!" Poor, poor Pe - ter! And the
peo - ple who kept ask - ing: "Aren't you one of them?" he an - swered: "I don't know him" Poor, poor Pe - ter! And the
fuse to stand by him it's just like Pe - ter and the Lord 'cause you de - ny him. Poor, poor Pe - ter! And the
Pe - ter if in - stead of say - ing "Right, and I must change it!" we would give in. Poor, poor Pe - ter! And the

The Commissioned Hymns

A NUMBER of hymnbook editors in the twentieth century sought out American and other poems of high literary quality which originally were not written to be sung. Perhaps this trend is most clearly marked in a series of hymnals edited by H. Augustine Smith. An instance is the use of poems by Emily Dickinson and Edna St. Vincent Millay as hymns (see "If I Can Stop One Heart from Breaking" and "O God, I Cried, No Dark Disguise"). This was an attempt to satisfy students and others who might respond more readily to felicity of expression and poetic imagery than to hymns with a more didactic turn of expression.

In planning the section of hymns commissioned for this volume, we have pursued a similar search, including poems by Bliss Carmen, Robert Frost, Edwin Markham, Emily Dickinson, e.e. cummings, Langston Hughes, and Mark Van Doren. A number of contemporary American poets were helpful in pointing out poems from their works that were suitable for hymns. Two of the composers, John Jacob Niles and David Diamond, preferred to write their own texts. John St. Edmunds, Gardner Read, William Grant Still set poems written by their wives under the names Beatrice Quickender, Vail Read, and Verna Arvey. Another valuable source of verse for setting has been the series of pamphlets containing hymns on topics chosen by the Hymn Society of America as part of their program to stimulate the writing of contemporary hymns.

It was with the hope of bridging the growing gap between the professional composer and the hymn that contemporary tunes were sought from many distinguished American composers. Some of their contributions fall more properly into the category of choir hymns or short anthems rather than true congregational hymns. We present these here, assuming the privilege (which was quite usual in early American tune books) of closing our volume with music suitable for the choir. Others are true congregational hymns.

We may note the austere diatonic tune by Daniel Pinkham. The tune by Edward Lawton is almost equally diatonic. Since Professor Lawton has his own views on the qualities of a good church tune, we will let him speak for himself.

1. The tune should be melodically strong enough to stand on its own feet, independent of any harmonic setting. Accordingly I composed each of these first as a melody, and only then considered the setting.

2. There should be in the setting enough rhythmic activity so that the organist can kick it along, so to speak, and keep the congregation moving.
3. The setting, while not ostentatiously aggressive, should sound as if the composer has been living in the twentieth century with his ears open.

A folk spirit combined with skilled musical craftmanship lies behind the apparently simple Christmas song of Virgil Thomson. Henry Cowell chose an early New England text rather than a modern one for his setting and his tune was perhaps composed with a Southern folk hymn in mind. John Jacob Niles, long known as a collector and singer of folk songs and ballads, has also contributed both the words and the music of a carol. Smoothly melodious, and perhaps a little Latin in style, is the tune by Norman Dello Joio. There are echoes of Broadway in William Schuman's setting of Langston Hughes. Closer to the conventional congregational hymn are those by Seth Bingham, Quincy Porter, Gardner Read, and Douglas Moore. Howard Hanson's tune is modal in coloring. Irving Fine's contribution is a present-day chorale, while that by Herbert Inch is sharply dissonant. Quite a different path is taken by Alan Hovhanness, who uses fundamental triads in unusual relationships. Such are some of the directions taken by the composers represented here.

No one would wish to see the fine hymns in the current hymnals discarded, except as the passage of time and the gradual shifts in taste make it necessary. Nor in an increasingly ecumenical world can we ever again be American or regional in any narrow or parochial sense. Yet the American contribution to religious song has been extensive and influential in the past and, in the hope that it may continue so in the future, we have closed with American contemporary verse set to music by American composers of our own day.

O God, Above the Drifting Years

Forefathers L.M.

St. 1-4

John Wright Buckham, 1916

Seth Bingham, submitted 1957

May be sung in unison

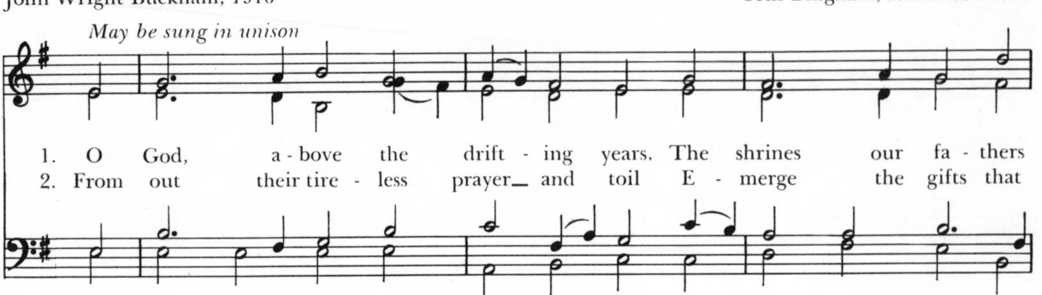
1. O God, a - bove the drift - ing years, The shrines our fa - thers
2. From out their tire - less prayer and toil E - merge the gifts that

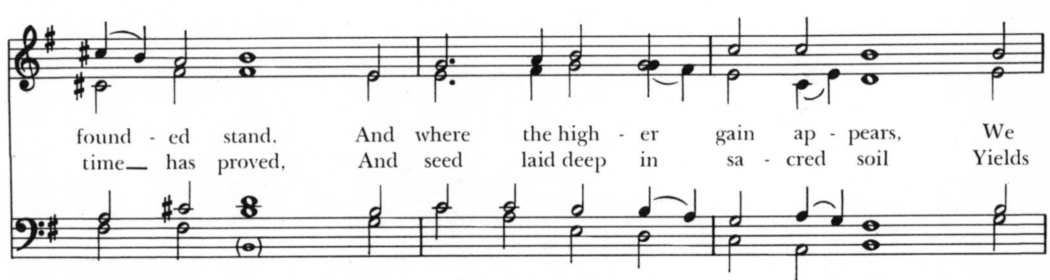
found - ed stand, And where the high - er gain ap - pears, We
time has proved, And seed laid deep in sa - cred soil Yields

trace the work - ing of thy hand.
har - vests rich in last - ing good.

3. The torch to their devotion lent,
Lightens the dark that round us lies;
Help us to pass it on unspent,
Until the dawn lights up the skies.

4. Fill thou our hearts with faith like theirs,
Who served the days they could not see;
And give us grace, through ampler years,
To build a kingdom yet to be.

LORD OF MY HEART'S ELATION

ADVENT 7.6.7.6.D.

St. 1-3

Bliss Carman, 1894

Seth Bingham, submitted 1957

Unison
1. Lord of my heart's e - la - tion, Spir - it of things un - seen, Be thou my as - pi - ra - tion Con - sum - ing and se - rene! Bear up, bear out, bear
2. As the foam-heads are loos - ened And blown a - long the sea, Or sink and merge for - ev - er In that which bids them be, I, too, must climb in

on - ward! This mor - tal soul a - lone, To self - hood and ob -
won - der, Up - lift at thy com - mand; Be one with my frail
liv - ion In - cred - i - bly thine own.
fel - lows Be - neath the wind's strong hand.

3. A fleet and shadowy column
Of dust or mountain rain,
To walk the earth a moment
And be dissolved again.
Be thou my heart's elation
Or fortitude or mien,
Lord of the world's elation,
Thou breath of things unseen.

O Day of God, Draw Nigh — Day of God S.M.

St. 1-5

Robert B. Y. Scott, writ. 1937 — Howard Boatwright, comp. 1956

1. O Day___ of God,_ draw_ nigh In beau - ty and in power, Come
2. Bring to___ our trou - bled_ minds, Un - cer - tain and a - fraid, The

with thy time - less_ judg - ment now To match our pres - ent hour.
qui - et of a_ stead - fast faith, Calm of a call o - beyed.

3. Bring justice to our land,
That all may dwell secure,
And finely build for days to come
Foundations that endure.

4. Bring to our world of strife
Thy sovereign word of peace,
That war may haunt the earth no more
And desolation cease.

5. O Day of God, draw nigh
As at creation's birth,
Let there be light again, and set
Thy judgments in the earth.

Green Plumes of Royal Palms — Palm Sunday 10.10.10.10.D.

St. 1, 2

LeRoy V. Brant, 1930 — Annabel Morris Buchanan, comp. 1955

With dignity and breadth
1. Green plumes of roy - al palms the high - ways pave, The Son of
2. Oh, Son of God, thou fac - est Cal - va - ry, Un - to the
The Son
Un - to
God sets forth on fi - nal quest To meet the
dregs wilt drink its bit - ter wine. Yet on thou
last, the last and great - est test End - ing with -
rid - est to thy des - ti - ny Sav - ing man -
3
in a gar - den cir - cled grave. A - mid ho -
kind by sac - ri - fice di - vine. The tri - umph
a gar - den cir - cled grave.
by sac - ri - fice di - vine.

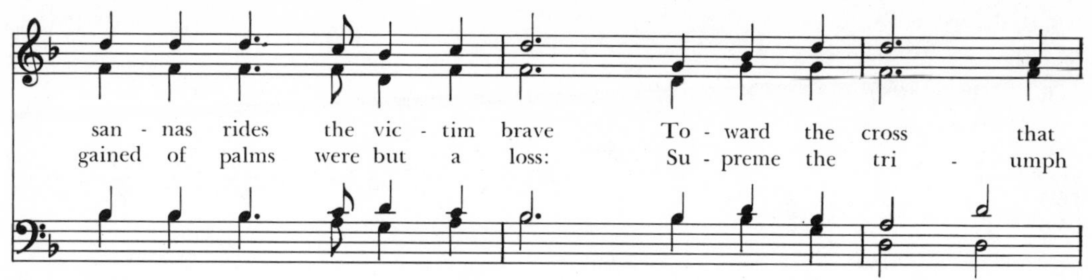
san - nas rides the vic - tim brave To - ward the cross that
gained of palms were but a loss: Su - preme the tri - umph

shad - ows all the West; To - ward the sting - ing scourge, more sting - ing
gained up - on the cross! The tri - umph gained of palms were but a

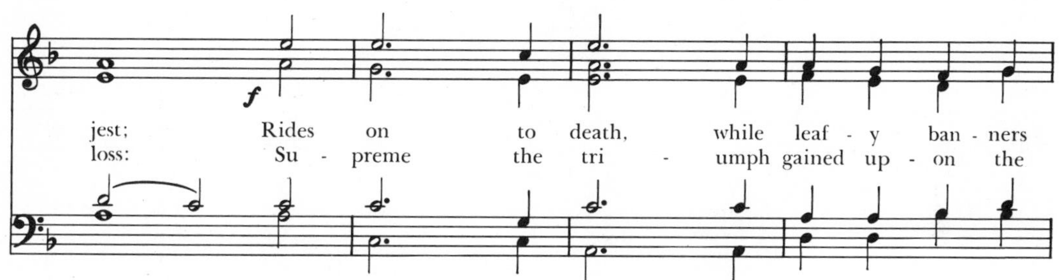
f
jest; Rides on to death, while leaf - y ban - ners
loss: Su - preme the tri - umph gained up - on the

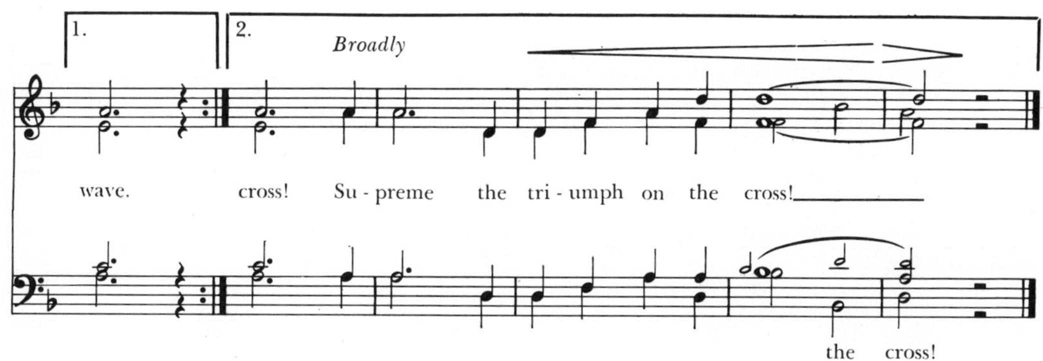
1.
2.
Broadly
wave. cross! Su - preme the tri - umph on the cross!
the cross!

Oh, Day of Days

St. 1-4

LeRoy V. Brant, 1930

Day of Days 10.10.10.10.

Annabel Morris Buchanan, comp. 1955

Simply, joyously

1. Oh, Day of days, when cen - tu - ries a - go _____ A
2. Light - ened, the sky; and on the plains be - low_____
3. From Beth - lehem's plain the light has long since fad - ed,
4. Hark! Hear we still from far the an - gel choirs,_____

babe was born with - in a sta - ble bare
Shep - herds, and kings with cost - ly gifts and rare
Yet, from that shin - ing, myr - iad, al - tar flames
See! Shin - ing still the sweet star's ho - ly fires.

While o - ver - head the an - gels filled the air With
Drew near to see the ten - der babe so fair. Oh,
Kind - led, whose light through roll - ing years have aid - ed Men
Hark! Hear we still from far the an - gel choirs, See!

Verses 1.–3.
sing - ing, with sing - ing and mys - tic ra - diant glow.
day of days, two thou - sand years a - go.
rev - erent - ly to seek the name of names.
Shin - ing still the sweet star's ho - ly

Verse 4.
fires. See! Shin - ing still the sweet star's ho - ly fires.

Oh, Give Us Pleasure in the Flowers Today

St. 1-4

Robert Frost, 1913

Thomas Canning, comp. 1957

Simply, devoutly
p
1. Oh, give us pleas - ure in the flowers to - day; And
2. Oh, give us pleas - ure in the or - chard white, Like

give us not to think so far a - way As the un - cer - tain har - vest;
noth - ing else by day, like ghosts by night; And make us hap - py

keep us here All sim - ply in the spring - ing of the year.
in the hap - py bees, The swarm di - la - ting round the per - fect trees.

3. And make us happy in the darting bird
That suddenly above the bees is heard,
The meteor that thrusts in with needle bill,
And off a blossom in mid air stands still.

4. For this is love and nothing else is love,
The which it is reserved for God above
To sanctify to what far ends he will,
But which it only needs that we fulfill.

Mary Lifted from the Dead 7.7.7.7.D.

St. 1-6

William Alfred, writ. 1956 Theodore Chanler, comp. 1956

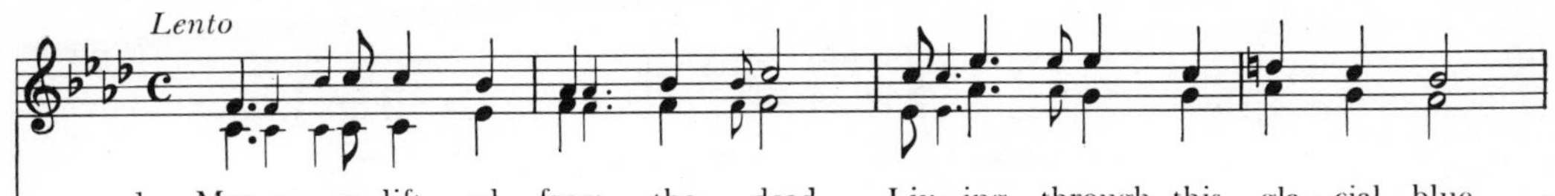
Lento

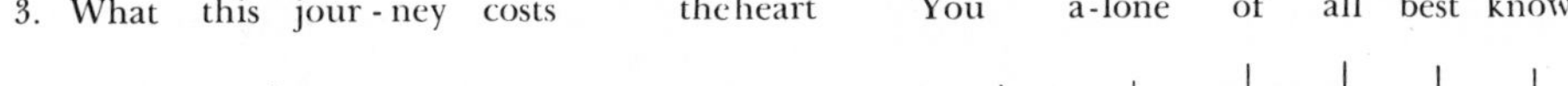
1. Mar - y lift - ed from the dead Liv - ing through this gla - cial blue
3. What this jour - ney costs the heart You a - lone of all best know.

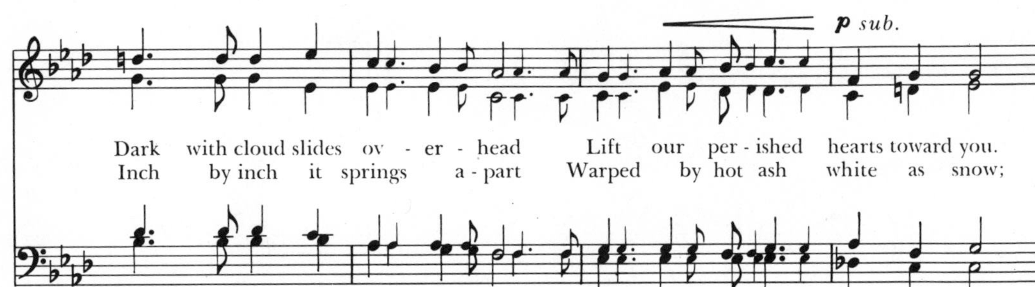
p sub.
Dark with cloud slides ov - er - head Lift our per - ished hearts toward you.
Inch by inch it springs a - part Warped by hot ash white as snow;

cresc.
f

2. When the win - ter grew this stern And heav - en there like Ev - er - est, What
4. Still the mind can see no path Still the soul as cold as ice

dim.
p
p sub.
was there we had left to burn But the heart with - in the breast.
Hud - dles fro - zen half to death In this ditch near Par - a - dise.

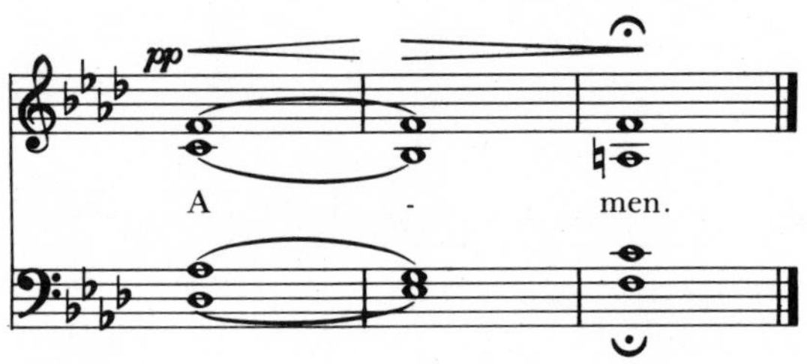
pp
A - men.

5. Past the beacon of the sun
   Set to light us on our way,
   Past the watch-fire of the moon
   That holds the beasts of night at bay.

6. Mary lifted from the dead
   Living through this glacial blue
   Dark with cloud shines overhead
   Lifted our perished hearts toward you.

THOU ART THE TREE OF LIFE

St. 9, 10

Edward Taylor, 1703

TREE OF LIFE 10.10.10.D.

Henry Cowell, comp. 1955

Con moto

Thou art the Tree of Life ___ in Par - a - dise, Whose

live - ly branch - es are ___ with clus - ters hung Of

love - ly fruits, and flowers ___ more sweet than spice Bend

down to us, and do ___ out - shine the sun. De -

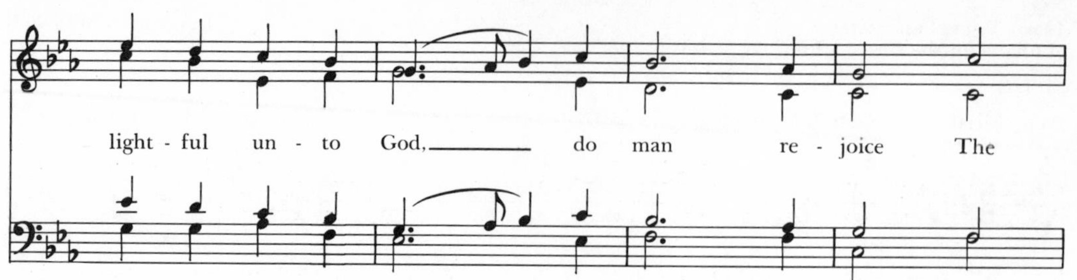
light - ful un - to God, do man re - joice The

pleas - ant'st fruits in all God's Par - a - dise.

Hush Thee, Princeling
(Lullaby for the Christ Child)

Lullaby 10.10.10.9.

St. 1, 2

Anna Elizabeth Bennett, writ. 1940

Norman Dello Joio, comp. 1956

Tenderly ♩. = 60
1. Hush thee, prince - ling, love - ly lit - tle Je - sus, Moth-er's lull - a - bye
is the on - ly sound.
Night is
fold - ing ov - er sheep and shep - herds; Hush thee, dar - ling, love en-folds thee
round.
2. Hush thee, Je - sus.

gen - tle lord of heav - en. Stars flock to the sky soft - ly one by one.
They are sing - ing, prais - ing God, in glo - ry. Hush thee, prince - ling,
God's own bless - èd Son.

We Will Not Fear

David Diamond, 1955

David Diamond, 1955

Decisively ♩ = 108
mf
cresc.
f
We will not fear though the earth should change, Though the moun-tains shake And the
mp
cresc.
mf
cresc.
sea with an - ger roar and foam. We will not fear, we will not
f
ff
fear. It is thy law that we be-hold these won-drous things,
p
pp
Fear - ful though they be, fear - ful though they be.

WHY, LORD?

St. 1-3

Mark Van Doren, 1935

WHY, LORD 10.10.10.

Anthony Donato, comp. 1957

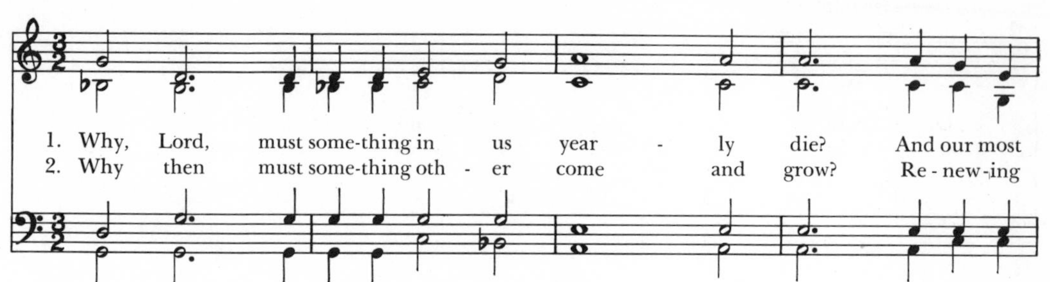
1. Why, Lord, must some-thing in us year - ly die? And our most
2. Why then must some-thing oth - er come and grow? Re - new-ing

true re - mem - brance of it lie? Un - til the pure for - get - ting
us for noth - ing, save the slow Up-build - ing of this bed of

by and by.
nee - dles, so. A - men.

3. Why is the soil not bitter where we stand?
Whose, Lord, upon our roots the sweetening hand?
For so it is: we love no shallower land.

O CHRIST OF BETHLEHEM S.M.

St. 1-4

H. Glenn Lanier, writ. 1954, pub. 1955 Richard Donovan, comp. 1956

In moderate time, in unison

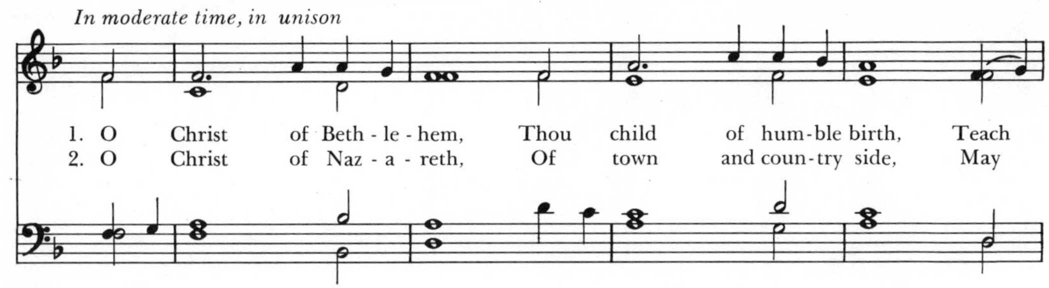
1. O Christ of Beth - le - hem, Thou child of hum-ble birth, Teach
2. O Christ of Naz - a - reth, Of town and coun-try side, May

us to hon - or all the folk Who fill the fruit-ful earth.
all the peo - ple ev - ery-where With - in thy love a - bide.

3. O Christ of Galilee,
Whose friends were toilers there,
May thy great Church in vale and town
The laborer's burden share.

4. O Christ of Bethany,
Where love and friendship shone,
The blessing of thy holy Name
Grace every village home.

Word of God, Across the Ages — Word of God 8.7.8.7.D.

St. 1-3

Ferdinand Q. Blanchard, 1952 — Richard Donovan, comp. 1956

With movement
1. Word of God, a - cross the a - ges Comes thy mes - sage to our life
2. Sto - ry of man's won - drous jour - ney From the shad - ows of the night
Source of hope, for ev - er pres - ent In our toil and fears and strife
Gar - nered truth of sage and proph - et Guid - ing for - ward in - to light
Con - stant wit - ness to God's mer - cy Still our grace what - e'er be - fall
Words and deeds of Christ our mas - ter Point - ing to the life and way
ter - nal Of - fered free - ly to us all.
Still ap - peal - ing, still in - spir - ing 'Mid the strug - gles of to - day.

3. In the tongues of all the peoples
May the message bless and heal,
As devout and patient scholars
More and more its depths reveal.
Bless, O God, to wise and simple,
All thy truth of ageless worth
Till all lands receive the witness
And thy knowledge fills the earth.

So Touch Our Hearts with Loveliness — Worship C.M.

St. 1-3

Gail Brook Burket, writ. 1955 — Irving Fine, comp. 1955

1. So touch our hearts with love-li-ness That we may wor-ship thee For
all the beau-ty of the earth, The bound-less sky and sea. 2. So
touch our hearts with ho-li-ness That we may wor-ship thee For
right-eous truth and up-right lives Of staunch in-teg-ri-ty. 3. So

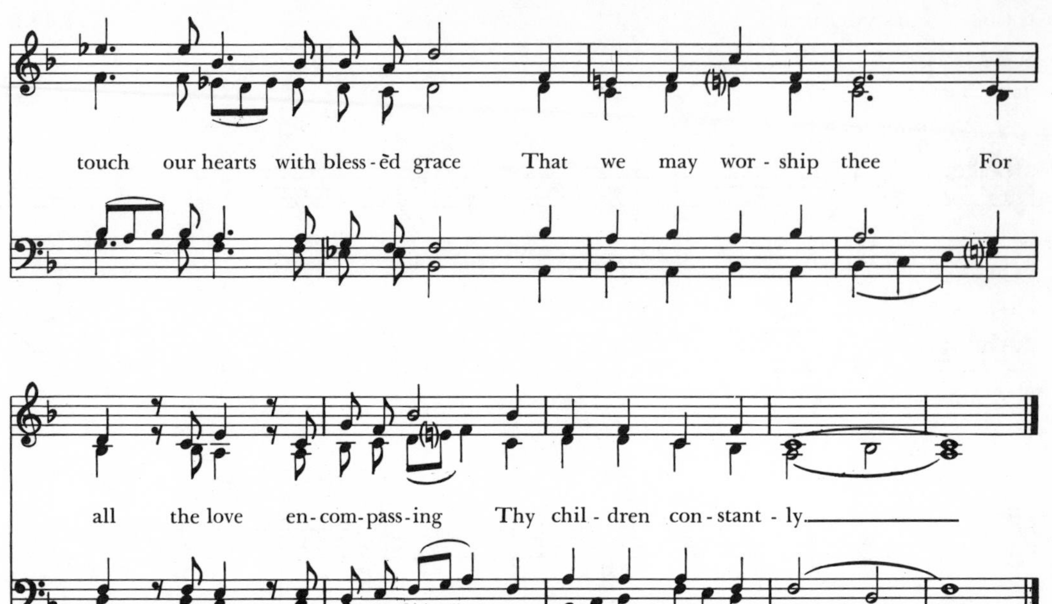
touch our hearts with bless-ĕd grace That we may wor-ship thee For
all the love en-com-pass-ing Thy chil-dren con-stant-ly.

O God of Stars and Distant Space 8.8.8.D.

St. 1-3

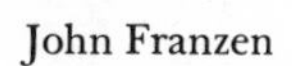
John Franzen Edwin Gerschefski, comp. 1971

Andante 𝅗𝅥 = 69
mp espress.
1. O God of stars and dis - tant space And
2. Thy word to life didst beau - ty bring As -

cresc. poco a poco
mys - ter - ies and end - less grace, Re - new this day each
sist us now thy praise to sing. Thy Spir - it broods o'er

f
wea - ry mind En - large our faith and make us
all the earth Keep strong the pur - pose of our

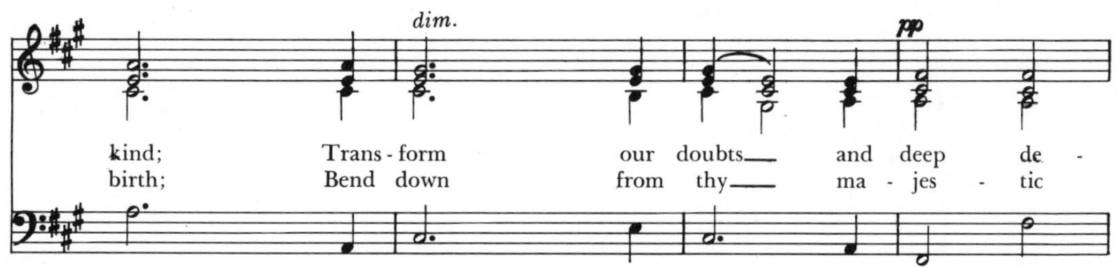
dim.
pp
kind; Trans - form our doubts and deep de -
birth; Bend down from thy ma - jes - tic

mf
p
First two stanzas
Last stanza
spair O God of love, hear thou our prayer. all.
height Cre - a - tor, God, please lead us right.

3. O God of earth and sky and sea,
Pour Holy Spirit into me.
Drench me with light from stars and sun
Help me the race of life to run;
And when the evening shadows fall
Bestow thy blessing on us all.

CREATOR OF INFINITIES L.M.

St. 1-3

Chadwick Hansen, writ. 1958 Howard Hanson, comp. 1956

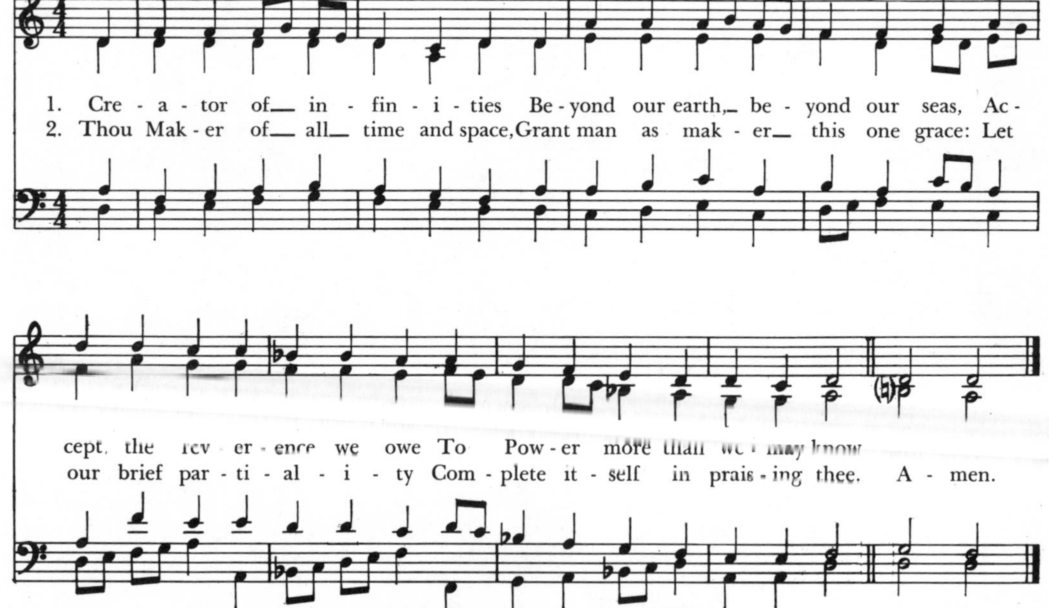
1. Cre - a - tor of in - fin - i - ties Be - yond our earth, be - yond our seas, Ac -
2. Thou Mak - er of all time and space, Grant man as mak - er this one grace: Let
cept, the rev - er - ence we owe To Pow - er more than we may know
our brief par - ti - al - i - ty Com - plete it - self in prais - ing thee. A - men.

3. May our wills, joined to honor thee,
Find joy in such a harmony;
From sea to sea, from sun to sun,
In gladness may thy will be done.

READ, SWEET, HOW OTHERS STROVE 11.10.10.10

St. 1, 2

Emily Dickinson, writ. c. 1861, pub. 1891 Roy Harris, comp. 1956

1. Read, sweet, how oth - ers strove till we are stout - er,
(8va Basso if needed — This part can be sung 4 part a Cappella or with organ)
What they re - nounced till we are less a - fraid,
How man - y times they bore the faith - ful - ness,
Till we are helped as though a king - dom cared.

2. Read then of faith that shone a - bove the fag - ot,
Clear strains of hymns the riv - er could not drown,
Brave names of men and ce - les - tial wom - en
Passed out of rec - ord in - to re - nown.

Our Tense and Wintry Minds S.M.

Hayden Carruth, writ. 1955 Roy Harris, comp. 1956

Congregation
1. Our tense and win - try minds Good friends, our trou - bled night
2. And hear! Be - neath the star That gleams a - cross the earth,
Organ

For unison (octave congregation or men unison, or women unison)

Are filled this hour with all Man-kind's most pure and pla - cid light.
Soft voi - ces sing - ing from a - far Praise this ex - ult - ant birth.

3. Minds fevered, minds forlorn,
All minds oppressed by hate,
Tonight the peace of Christ is born
And joy inviolate.

O God, in Whom the Flow of Days — L.M.

St. 1-4

Donald C. Babcock, writ. 1956 — Bernhard Heiden, comp. 1956

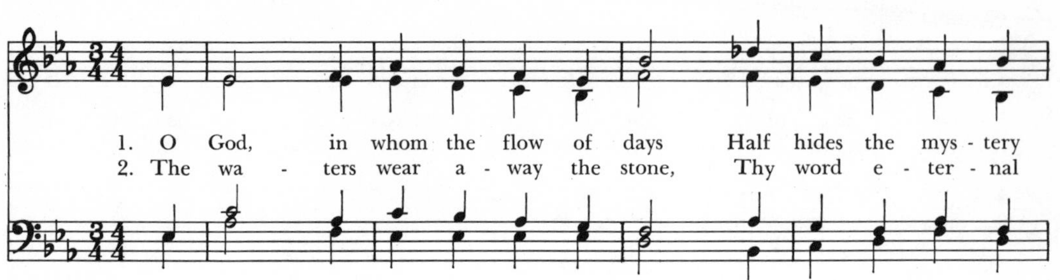
1. O God, in whom the flow of days Half hides the mys - tery
2. The wa - ters wear a - way the stone, Thy word e - ter - nal

of thy ways, And half re - veals the pa - tient
stands a - lone, The law whose roots un - hur - ried

love With - in whose pulse we live and move.
range Through all the con - stan - cy of change.

3. As certain as the break of dawn
The good unto the Good is drawn,
And many a trivial deed is bent
Unto the form of thine intent.

4. O God, to whom the flight of years
Fulfillment of thy will appears,
Forbid that we should vainly rove
Beyond the freedom of thy love.

CHRISTIAN, BE UP 10.10.10.6.

St. 1-4

Robert Nathan, 1940 Everett Helm, comp. 1959

Resolutely

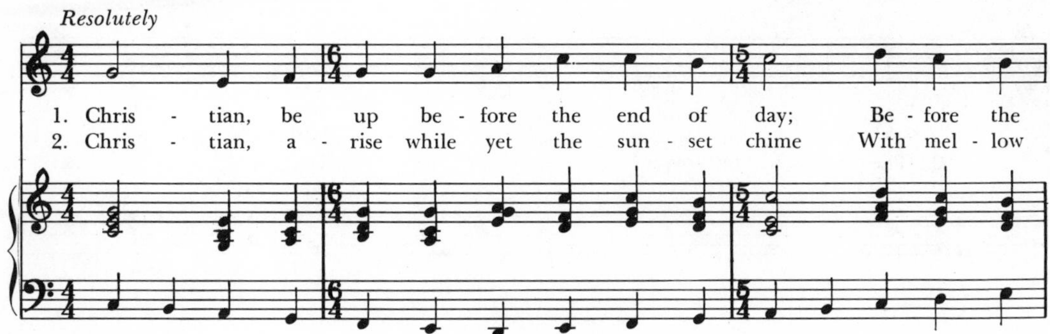
1. Chris - tian, be up be - fore the end of day; Be - fore the
2. Chris - tian, a - rise while yet the sun - set chime With mel - low

last, the fad - ing hour dies; Sleep not un - til the
mu - sic all the dis - tance fills, And while God walks, as

light has fled a - way, And night's black trum - pet cries.
in an old - er time, In beau - ty on the hills.

3. Lie not so long with dim, unmindful eye;
Sleep not so late while others wake and hark;
There is a grief of voices in the sky,
An evil in the dark.

4. Christian, awake and watch upon the height;
The day is dying in the darkening air.
There is but little time before the night;
There is but time for prayer.

There Is a High Place
(One Music)

10.10.10.10.

St. 1, 2

Edwin Markham, 1915

Alan Hovhaness, comp. 1957

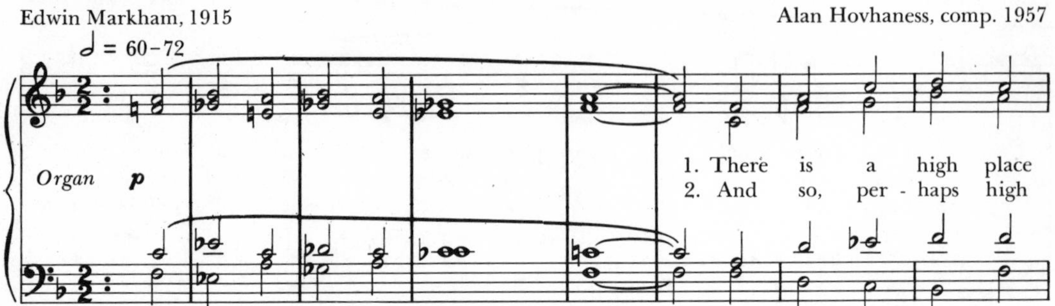

𝅗𝅥 = 60–72
Organ
p
1. There is a high place
2. And so, per - haps high

in the up - per air, So high that all the jar - ring sounds of
o - ver worm and clod There is an un - im - ag - i - na - ble

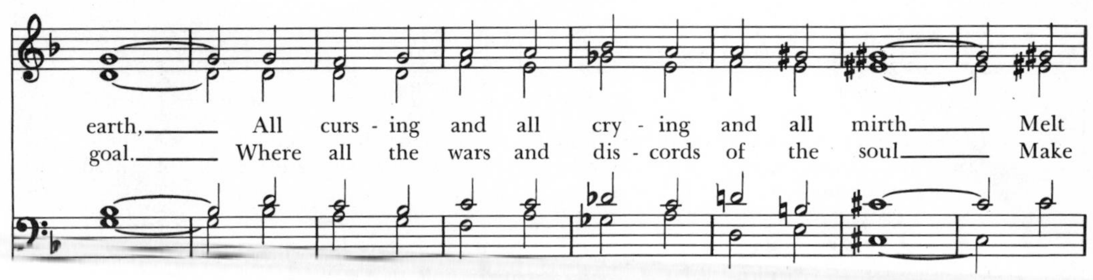

earth, All curs - ing and all cry - ing and all mirth Melt
goal. Where all the wars and dis - cords of the soul Make

to one mur - mur and one mu - sic there.
one still mu - sic to the heart of God.

LORD OF EACH SOUL 8.8.8.8.8.8.

St. 1-3

Paul Engle, writ. 1957 Harriett Johnson, comp. 1958

Lento
1. Lord of each soul and each plain thing, The heart of man and heart of bread, You are the one to whom we sing, Lord of our hand and Lord of head,
2. From you we take our life and death, De - light and dread for all our days. Wheth - er with proud or pain - ful breath, Still we thank you, still we praise,
3. Great gal - ax - ies of hea - ven drift, Like clouds of dust a - cross your eyes. Here, with our hu - man voice, we lift To you our lit - tle liv - ing cries,
Verses 1.-2.
Lord of our hand and Lord of head.
Lord of our hand and Lord of head.

Verse 3. only
Lord of our hand and Lord of head. A - men.

THROUGH WARMTH AND LIGHT OF SUMMER SKIES C.M.
(Summertide)

St. 1-4

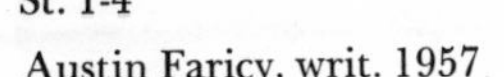

Austin Faricy, writ. 1957 Harriett Johnson, comp. 1958

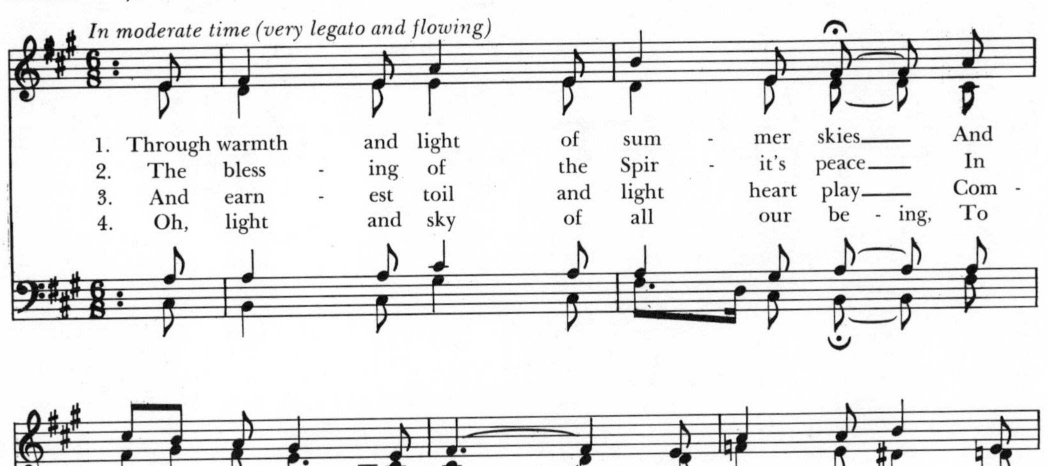
In moderate time (very legato and flowing)
1. Through warmth and light of sum - mer skies And
2. The bless - ing of the Spir - it's peace In
3. And earn - est toil and light heart play Com -
4. Oh, light and sky of all our be - ing, To

length - en - ing of days, Through song of bird and
sum - mer's peace made flesh Se - ren - i - ty of
bine in sun - lit joy To lift us up with
Fa - ther and to Son, Be love and prayer for -

Verses 1, 2, 3. only
hue of flower Re - sounds our Fa - ther's praise.
limbs re - pose To sleep and to re - fresh.
full - est sense That Ho - ly Ghost in One.

Descant for fourth verse only
With Ho - ly Ghost in One.
ev - er more With Ho - ly Ghost in One.

A - men.
A - men.

'Tis Winter Now

L.M.

St. 1-4

Samuel Longfellow, 1864

Lockrem Johnson, comp. 1955

Andante
1. SOPRANI: 'Tis win - ter now; the fal - len snow Has left the
2. SOPRANI And yet God's love is not with-drawn; His life with -
ed ALTI:

heavens all cold - ly clear; Through leaf - less boughs the
in the keen air breathes; His beau - ty paints the

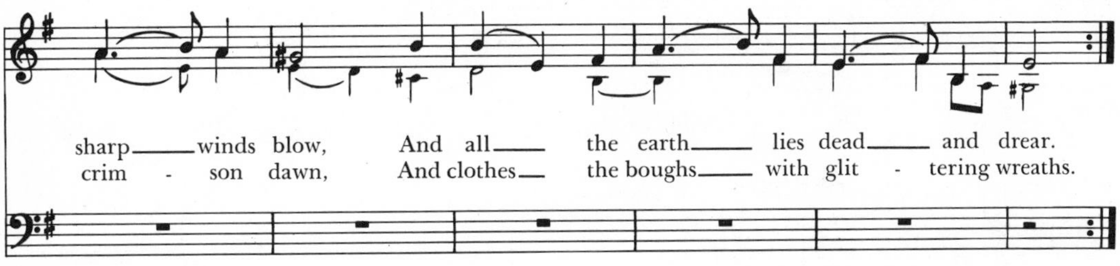
sharp winds blow, And all the earth lies dead and drear.
crim - son dawn, And clothes the boughs with glit - tering wreaths.

3. And though a - broad the sharp winds blow, And skies are

chill and frosts are keen, Home clos - er draws her
cir - cle now, And warm - er glows her light with - in.
4. O God! who givest the win - ter's cold, As well as
sum - mer's joy - ous rays, Us warm - ly in thy love en -

fold, And keep us through life's win - try days.

Not Only Where God's Free Winds Blow — 8.6.8.8.6.

St. 1-5

Shepherd Knapp, 1908 — Edward Lawton, comp. 1957

= 76 – 80

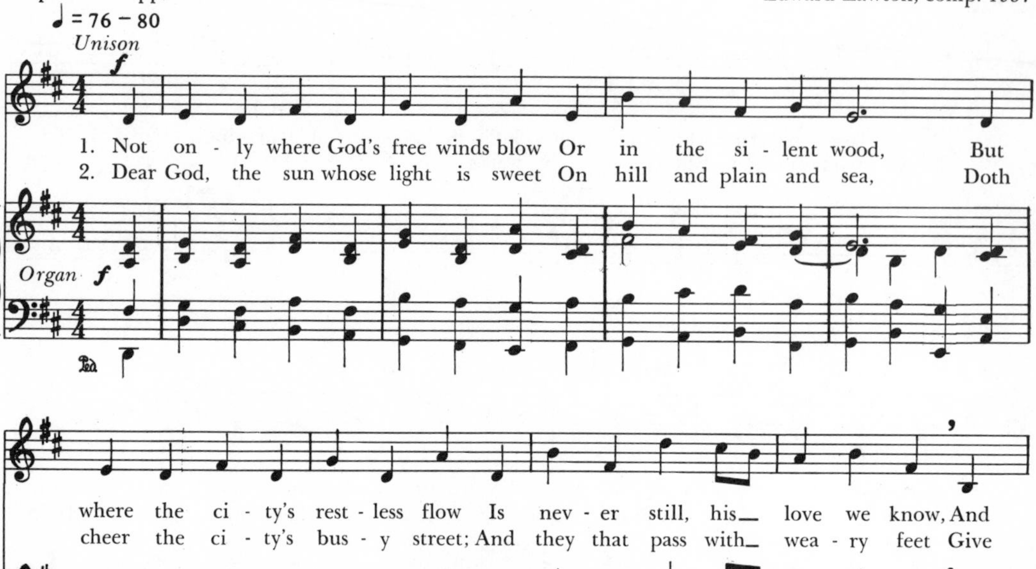

Unison

1. Not on - ly where God's free winds blow Or in the si - lent wood, But where the ci - ty's rest - less flow Is nev - er still, his love we know, And find his pres - ence good.
2. Dear God, the sun whose light is sweet On hill and plain and sea, Doth cheer the ci - ty's bus - y street; And they that pass with wea - ry feet Give thanks for light from thee.

1.–4. | 5. art. A - men.

Organ

3. Thy bounties from the field and mine
Come at the city's call;
The fire upon the hearth is thine
And home, where lights of kindness shine,
The dearest gift of all.

4. More near than outward gifts art thou,
O Father of mankind;
Yea, those, who under burdens bow
Of toil and care, thou dost endow
With riches of thy mind.

5. But in the city's grief and shame
Dost thou refuse a part?
Ah, no; for burneth there the flame
Of human help in Christ's dear name;
There, most of all, thou art.

Eternal God, Whose Power Upholds

St. 1-5

Henry Hallam Tweedy, 1929

Eternal God C.M.D.

Douglas Moore, comp. 1957

Majestically
1. E - ter - nal God, whose power up - holds Both flower and flam - ing star, To
2. O God of love, whose spir - it wakes In ev - ery hu - man breast, Whom

whom there is no here nor there, No time, no near nor far, No
love, and love a - lone, can know, In whom all hearts find rest, Help

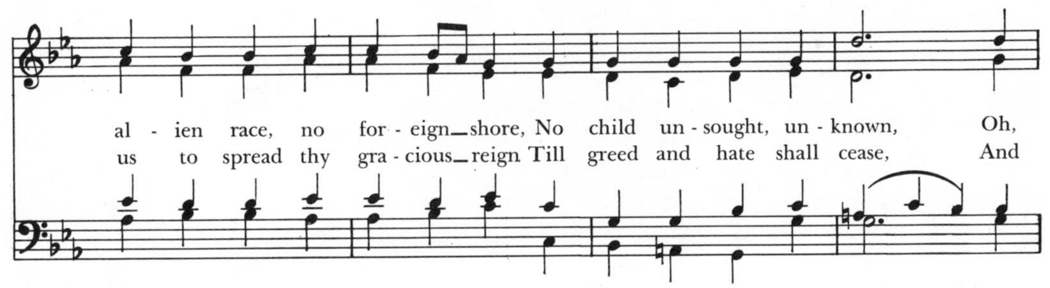
al - ien race, no for - eign shore, No child un - sought, un - known, Oh,
us to spread thy gra - cious reign Till greed and hate shall cease, And

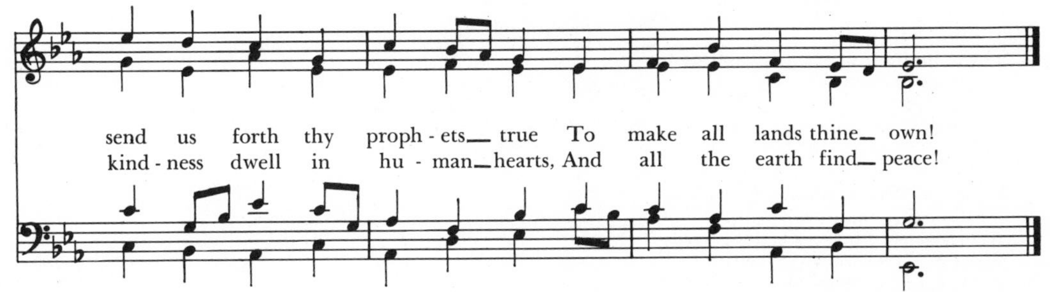
send us forth thy proph - ets true To make all lands thine own!
kind - ness dwell in hu - man hearts, And all the earth find peace!

3. O God of truth, whom science seeks
And reverent souls adore,
Who lightest every earnest mind
Of every clime and shore,
Dispel the gloom of error's night,
Of ignorance and fear,
Until true wisdom from above
Shall make life's pathway clear!

4. O God of beauty, oft revealed
In dreams of human art,
In speech that flows to melody,
In holiness of heart,
Teach us to ban all ugliness
That blinds our eyes to thee,
Till all shall know the loveliness
Of lives made fair and free!

5. O God of righteousness and grace,
Seen in the Christ, thy son,
Whose life and death reveal thy face,
By whom thy will was done,
Inspire thy heralds of good news
To live thy life divine,
Till Christ be formed in all mankind
And every land be thine.

In All the Magic of Christmas-Tide — Magic Night L.M.

St. 1-3

John Jacob Niles, 1955 — John Jacob Niles, 1955

1. In all the mag - ic of Christ - mas - tide There is no mag - ic that can a - bide A -
2. When Ma - ry brought this child to light, It was up - on a star - lit night; And
gainst the birth of Christ our King, Of whom the an - gels bright - ly sing.
see how shep - herds crowd the stall With and ass and cat - tle all.

3. It was against the winter sky,
The heavenly hosts in splendor fly
And gentle Mary, mother mild,
Did comfort Christ, the blessèd child.

From Countless Hearts
(A Prayer for Peace)

8.8.7.10.

St. 1-3
Gail Brook Burket, submitted 1955
Paul Nordoff, comp. 1955
Fervently (Allegro)
f Unison
1. From count - less hearts these words a - rise, Like in - cense waft - ed toward the skies, O dear Fa - ther of man - kind, We pray for peace to bless our lives to - day.
2. In na - tions scourged by war and hate, The an - guished peo - ple watch and wait. O, dear Fa - ther of man - kind, We pray for peace to bless our lands to - day.
p
cresc.
f
Slower
dim.
1.

2.
3. The soul of all hu - man - i - ty Cries out to God un -
ceas - ing - ly; O, dear Fa - ther of man - kind, We pray for peace
to bless the world to - day. A - men.
Slower ff

HEAVEN, HEAVEN, HEAVEN IS THE PLACE
(Children's Hymn)

Langston Hughes, writ. 1955

Paul Nordoff, comp. 1955

Joyfully
p
cresc.
f
Heav - en, heav - en, heav - en is the place where Hap - pi - ness is
f
Heav-en is the place where Hap - pi - ness is
ev - ery-where, ev - ery - where, ev - ery - where. An - i-mals and birds,
mf
ev - ery-where, ev - ery-where, ev - ery-where.
an - i-mals and birds sing, sing, sing, sing As does ev - ery-thing,
ev - ery-thing,
ev - ery - thing, ev - ery - thing. To each stone "How do you do?"
3
ev - ery-thing, ev - ery-thing.
3

cresc.
Stone an-swers back, "Well! And you? And you? And you?" (And you?") And the streets of,
cresc.

and the streets of, and the streets of gold so bright To my soul af-
And the streets of gold so bright af-ford my

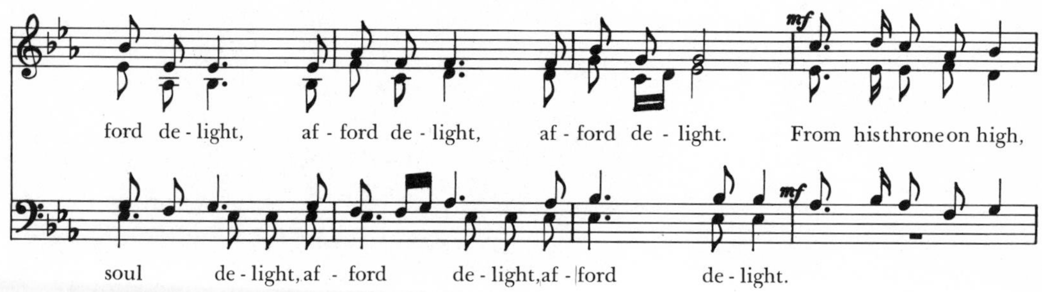
ford de-light, af-ford de-light, af-ford de-light. From his throne on high,
soul de-light, af-ford de-light, af-ford de-light.

from his throne on high a-bove, -bove, -bove God be-stows e-ter-nal love, e-
e-ter-nal love, e-

p
ter - nal love, e - ter - nal love. All who find him, he will bless
p
ter - nal love, e - ter - nal love.

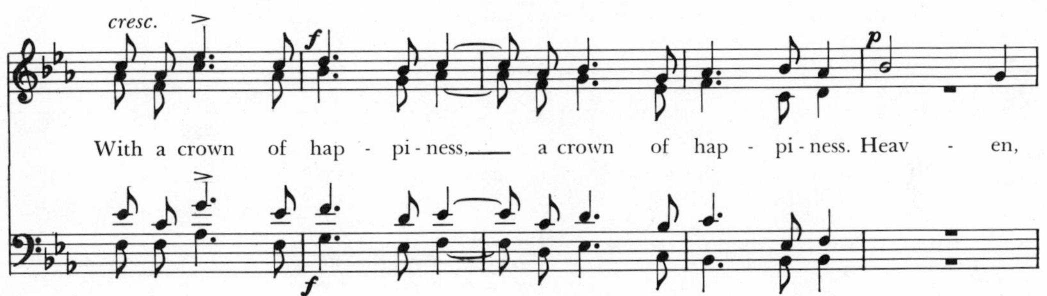
cresc.
f
p
With a crown of hap - pi - ness, a crown of hap - pi - ness. Heav - en,
f

cresc.
f
heav - en, heav - en is the place where Hap - pi - ness is ev - ery - where,
f
Heav - en is the place where Hap - pi - ness is ev - ery - where,

p
ev - ery
ev - ery - where, ev - ery, ev - ery, ev - ery - where. A - men.
p
ev - ery - where, ev - ery - where.

purer than purest pure

STAR

e. e. cummings, 1950

Vincent Persichetti, 1956

In unison, gently
1. pur - er than pur - est pure whis - per of whis - per so, so (big with in - no-cence) for - giv-ing-ly a once of ea - ger glo - ry, no more mir - a - cle may grow
2. child - ful - ly se - ri - ous flow - er of ho - li - ness a pil - grim from be-yond, be - yond the fu-ture's fu - ture; im - me-di-ate like new, like some new - ly re-mem - bered dream.
3. flam - ing a cool-ly bell touch - es most mere un - til (e - ter-nal-ly) with (now) with (now) with lu-mi-nous the shad-ow of love him-self: who's we nor can you die or i
Last time only
4. and ev - ery world be - fore si - lence be - gins a star. A - men.

Bow Down, Mountain

St. 1, 2

Norma Farber, writ. 1955

Daniel Pinkham, comp. 1955

Cheerfully
1. Bow down, moun - tain, to hear the glad - ness is - su - ing From every source and foun - tain. Flow down, riv - er, to let the cur - rent joy - ous - ly The hap - py news de - liv - er. Bend down, morn - ing, to seek a Ba - by born, In a
2. Fly up, pin - ion, to find the farth - est reach - es Of his peace - a - ble do - min - ion. Sing up, for - est, from ev - ery tree The tid - ings of Na - tiv - i - ty are cho - rused. Rise up, heav - en, raise up the wing of love, While the

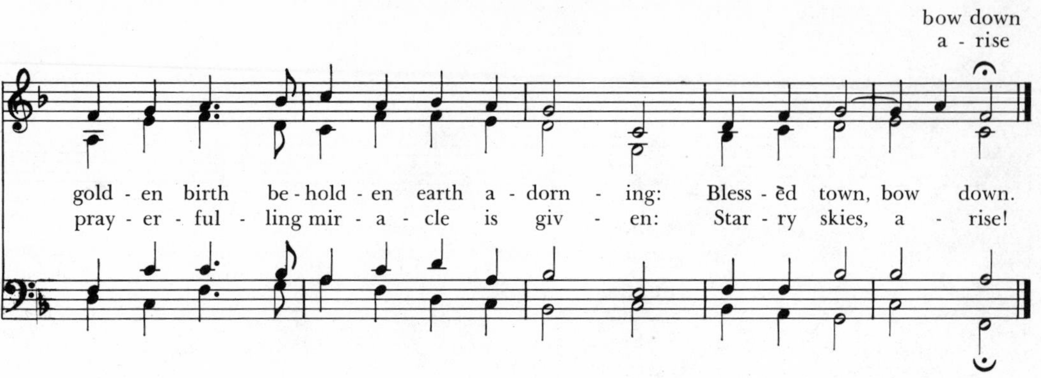
bow down
a - rise
gold - en birth be - hold - en earth a - dorn - ing: Bless - ēd town, bow down.
pray - er - ful - ling mir - a - cle is giv - en: Star - ry skies, a - rise!

ETERNAL GOD, WHOSE POWER UPHOLDS

POWER C.M.D.

St. 1-5

Henry Hallam Tweedy 1929

Quincy Porter, comp. 1956

f
1. E - ter - nal God, whose power up-holds Both flower and flam - ing star, To
2. O God of love, whose spir - it wakes In ev - ery hu - man breast, Whom
f

dim.
p
whom there is no here nor there, No time, no near nor far, No
love, and love a - lone, can know, In whom all hearts find rest, Help
p

cresc.
a - lien race, no for - eign shore, No child un - sought, un - known, Oh
us to spread thy gra - cious reign Till greed and hate shall cease, And

f
send us forth thy pro - phers true To make all lands thine own!
kind - ness dwell in hu - man hearts, And all the earth find peace!
f

For stanzas 3 to 5 see setting by Douglas Moore.

I STOOD WITHIN THE HEART OF GOD 8.8.8.6.D.

St. 1-6

William Vaughn Moody Quincy Porter, comp. 1956

p
mf
1. I stood with - in the heart of God; It seemed a place that I had known (I
3. I saw the spring and sum - mer pass, The trees grow bare, and win - ter come; All
dim.
p
was blood - sis - ter to the clod, Blood - broth - er to the stone.) 2. I
was the same as once it was Up - on my hills at home. 4. Then
cresc.
found my love and la - bor there, My house, my rai - ment, meat and wine, My
sud - den - ly in my own heart I felt God walk and gaze a - bout; He
f
dim.
mp
an - cient rage, my old de - spair,—Yea, all things that were mine.
spoke; his words seemed held a - part With glad - ness and with doubt.

5. "Here is my meat and wine," He said,
"My love, my toil, my ancient care;
Here is my cloak, my book, my bed,
And here my old despair.

6. "Here are my seasons: winter, spring,
Summer the same, and autumn spills
The fruits I look for; everything
As on my heavenly hills."

THIS NEW DAY — NEW DAY 8.7.8.7.

St. 1-4

Vail Read, writ. 1955 — Gardner Read, comp. 1955

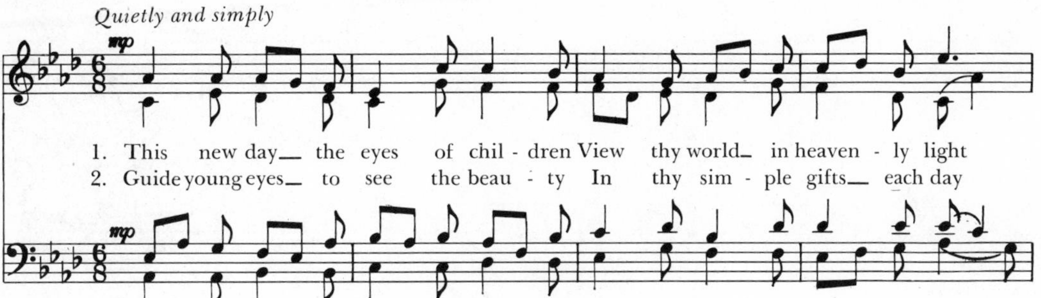
Quietly and simply
mp
1. This new day the eyes of chil - dren View thy world in heaven - ly light
2. Guide young eyes to see the beau - ty In thy sim - ple gifts each day
mp

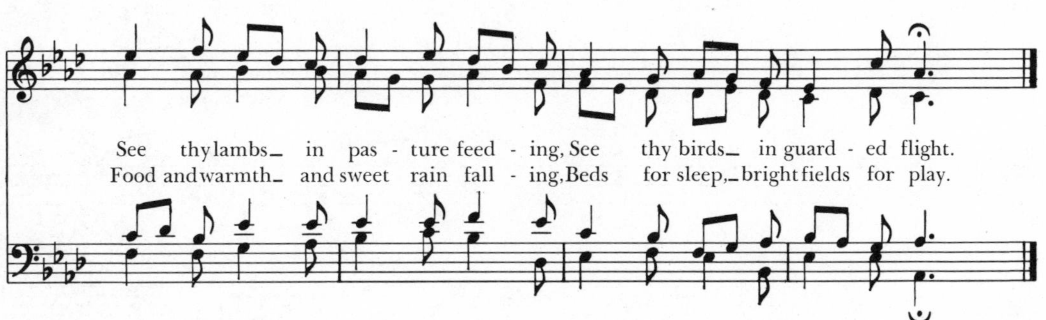
See thy lambs in pas - ture feed - ing, See thy birds in guard - ed flight.
Food and warmth and sweet rain fall - ing, Beds for sleep, bright fields for play.

3. Guide young ears to hear thy music
In the voices of our time;
Through thy church to find God's pattern
In each conquest of the mind.

4. Guard young souls, where'er thy future,
Folded dark, shall take their flight;
Let them feel thy hand upon them,
Walk the moon, but see thy light.

SING, MY SOUL

SING, MY SOUL 7.7.7.7.

St. 1-4

Anon., 1805

Ned Rorem, comp. 1955

Moderato, molto tranquillo

p espr.
1. Sing, my soul, his won - drous love, Who, from yon bright throne a - bove,
p espr.

dim.
Ev - er watch - ful o'er our race. Still to man ex - tends his grace.

mp
mf
2. Heaven and earth by him were made; All is by his scep - tre swayed;
mp

mp
p
What are we that he should show So much love to us be - low?

pp
p
3. God, the mer - ci - ful and good, Bought us with the Sav - iour's blood;
mf
mp
And, to make our safe - ty sure, Guides us by his spir - it pure.
f
4. Sing, my soul, a - dore his name! Let his glo - ry be thy theme
mf
mp
rit.
p
Praise him till he calls thee home; Trust his love for all to come.

Hail, Oh Hail to the King — Stevenson 12.10.12.4.

St. 1-3

Beatrice Quickenden, writ. 1957 — John St. Edmunds, comp. 1957

Unison
1. Hail, oh hail to the king who does in glo - ry reign, Praise his
2. Loud, oh, loud may the sil - ver trum - pet's voice be heard, Brisk and

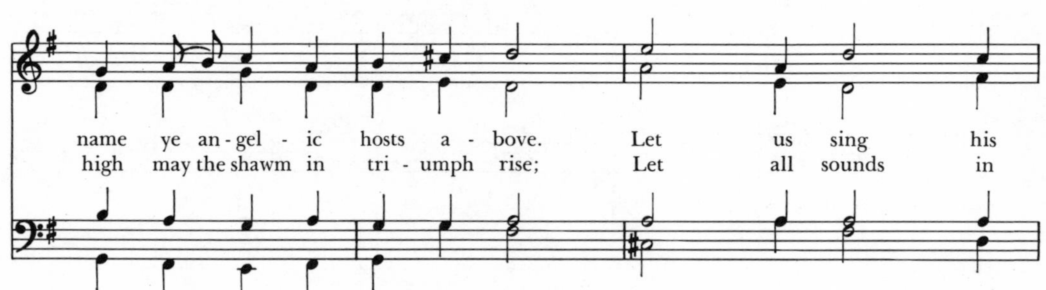
name ye an - gel - ic hosts a - bove. Let us sing his
high may the shawm in tri - umph rise; Let all sounds in

praise that the earth with joy - ous song May ech - o long.
one sub - lime har - mo - nious choir Hon - or our Sire.

3. Sun and moon show forth the splendor of his law,
Land and sea reflect his mighty power,
All that live upon the teeming earth his fame
Ever proclaim.

The Lord Has a Child

St. 1, 2

Langston Hughes, writ. 1955

William Schuman, comp. 1956

Moderato ♩ = circa 100
Voices
The Lord has a child. That
Organ or Piano
mf
child I know is me. Ev - en when I'm not all I ought to be
His lov - ing care guides me on my way
1st time only
continue from ✻
Ev - ery place, ev - ery-where, ev - ery day.

2d time only
continue from ❋
Last time only
day.
day.
ev - ery day.
❋
1. Some - times I'm lost,
Some - times I'm lone.
2. Wea - ry this world,
Heav - y my load.
Some - times there's no one to call my own; But the
Bur - dens I hear on this rock - y road; But the

As I Went Down to David's Town — The Shepherds — Irregular

St. 1-6

George Craig Stewart, 1934 — Leo Sowerby, comp. 1956

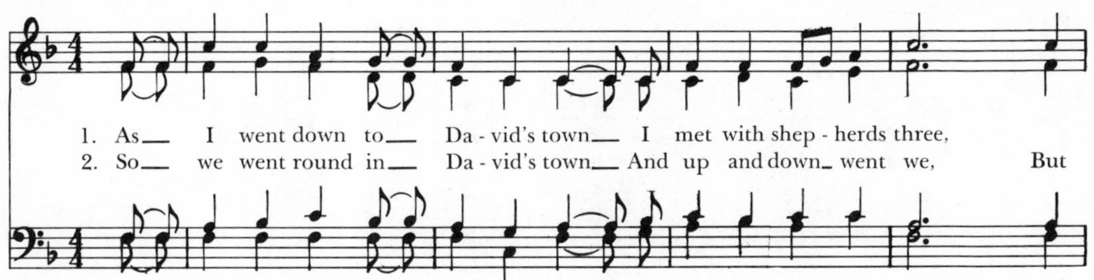
1. As— I went down to— Da-vid's town— I met with shep-herds three,
2. So— we went round in— Da-vid's town— And up and down— went we, But

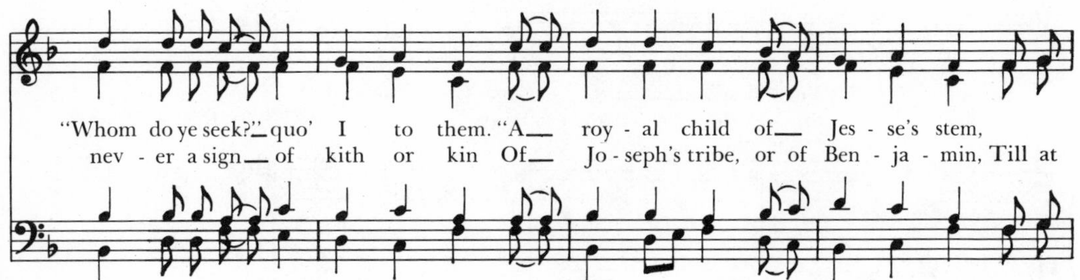
"Whom do ye seek?"— quo' I to them. "A— roy-al child of— Jes-se's stem,
nev-er a sign— of kith or kin Of— Jo-seph's tribe, or of Ben-ja-min, Till at

He shall be born in— Beth-le-hem,"— Thus— they an-swered— me.
last we— came to a crowd-ed inn,— I and the shep-herds— three.

3. And there we found in a stable, bound
In swaddling clothes, the King.
Oh, he was bonny and he was fair,
And a light shone from him everywhere,
So we knelt and offered our duty there,
And we pledged him everything.

4. And as I came up from David's town,
I beheld the shepherd's three,
The first was stolèd half around
And the next was clad in a surpliced gown,
And the last he wore a cross and a crown,
And all were full of glee.

5. So David's town hath great renown,
For all the shepherds three
Have told to the world the wondrous sight
Holy Lumen Lumine, Light of Light,
God of God, that Christmas night
Come to you and me.

6. Now may this town King Jesus crown
And ye who shepherd men,
Find in him your staff and stay,
And the light and joy of Christmas Day
Shine upon you all the way
Till Christmas comes again!

All That I Am

Verna Arvey, writ. 1955 William Grant Still, comp. 1955

All that I am, All I ev-er can be I owe to you, Lord, For you have mold-ed me.
All that I am, All I ev-er have been, Tells of the growth of truth with - in.
You are the source of light Source of ev - ery bless - ing To your last - ing kind-ness I
find my-self con-fess - ing. You are the source of love, Love that binds in broth-er-hood; In

your be - nign wis - dom You give us all that's good. All that I am,

3
All I ev - er can be; This I sur - ren - der, Oh, my Lord, to thee.
3

It Seems That God Bestowed Somehow C.M.
(Song for the Stable)

St. 1-5

Amanda Benjamin Hall, 1938 Virgil Thomson, comp. 1955

1. It seems that God be - stowed some - how, The night his son was born, An
seems he blessed the sheep, the small A - pos - tle of the fold. Oh,

For 2d stanza only
was that first cry scrip-tur-al That
Stanzas 1–4
Last stanza
in - no - cence up - on the cow, Mild crea - ture of the horn. 2. It
rang a - cross the cold? 3. Or
was that first cry scrip-tur-al That
For 2d stanza only

3. Or did the new Babe drowse and dream,
His mother's breast his sphere?
High-roosting on your dusky beam,
What saw you, chanticleer?

4. What saw you, kind and clumsy mule,
What heard you, ox and ass,
Upon that first and distant Yule
When wonder came to pass?

5. What vision far beyond your ken,
Remembered, marks you so?
I ask you, Sirs, what thought you then
On Christmas long ago?

PRAISE HIM WHO MAKES US HAPPY — NEVER ANOTHER 7.6.7.6.

St. 1-5

Mark Van Doren, 1953 — Virgil Thomson, comp. 1955

3. And
4. Re -
1. Praise Him who makes us hap-py When not an - oth - er would; There
2. Praise Him who waits all morn-ing, All aft - er - noon, all night, All

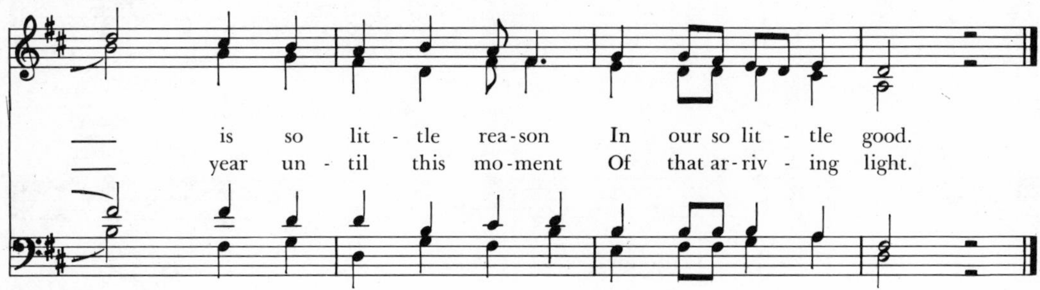
(Soprano)
1. There
2. All
3. move
4. mem - bers
5. Praise
is so lit - tle rea-son In our so lit - tle good.
year un - til this mo-ment Of that ar-riv - ing light.

3. Praise Him who sends it dancing,
Praise Him who lets us see,
And move with it, and listen,
And sing, soberly.

4. Praise Him who when we lose it,
And twilight thickens round,
Remembers where we slumber;
Marks this nether ground.

5. And waits upon our waking
As ne'er another would;
Praise Him who is the reason,
Praise Him, the only good.

INDEXES

First Lines/Titles

Authors and Composers

Tunes

Meters

Bible Verses

Acknowledgments

It is a pleasure to make grateful acknowledgment to the following authors, composers, and copyright proprietors for their permission to reproduce in this volume texts and tunes to which they hold the rights, the location of which in the preceding pages is indicated by the page numbers enclosed in parentheses following either the hymn or tune title.

Abingdon Press: FORTITUDE (652) (copyright renewed 1933 by the Methodist Book Concern, owner).

American Peace Society: "Let There Be Light" (669), originally published in *Advocate of Peace* (February 1909), vol. 121, no. 2.

A. S. Barnes: "The City, Lord, Where Thy Dear Life" (718), from *The New Church Hymnal.*

Baptist Spanish Publishing House: "If You Happy Would Be" (738).

F. M. Barton: "O Gracious Father of Mankind" (711), from *The Expositor.*

Beacon Press: WOODLAWN (626), "O Day of Light and Gladness" (659), "Hear, Hear, O Ye Nations" (660), "Through Willing Heart and Helping Hand" (661), "Touch Thou My Eyes" (684), "Where Is Our Holy Church?" (text only) (717), "As Tranquil Streams" (723), from *Hymns of the Spirit* (copyright 1937 by the Beacon Press); "My Country, to Thy Shore" (686), from *Hymn and Tune Book* (copyright 1914 by the Beacon Press); "O Thou Whose Gracious Presence Shone" (685), from *Hymns for the Celebration of Life* (copyright © 1964 by Unitarian Universalist Association).

Belwin-Mills: "Where Now Are the Hebrew Children?" (725) and "What Wondrous Love Is This" (726), both from *Folk Hymns of America* (copyright 1934 by J. Fischer; copyright renewed © 1962 by J. Fischer).

Boosey & Hawkes: "What Splendid Rays" (267), from *Twelve Moravian Chorales,* by John Antes (copyright 1957 by Boosey & Hawkes); " 'Tis the Gift To Be Simple" (582), from *Old American Songs* (copyright 1950 by Boosey & Hawkes).

Brandt and Brandt: "O God, I Cried, No Dark Disguise" (694) (copyright 1912, 1940 by Edna St. Vincent Millay).

Elizabeth Davis Burford, "At Length There Dawns the Glorious Day" (670).

Central Conference of American Rabbis: tune to "Hail the Glorious Golden City" (535); texts and tunes to "God Supreme! To Thee We Pray" (574), "Come, O Sabbath Day" (575), "How Goodly Is Thy House" (576), "Kindle the Taper" (577), "In Mercy, Lord, Incline Thine Ear" (578), and "Let There Be Light" (669), from the *Union Hymnal* published by the Conference.

Church of Jesus Christ of Latter-day Saints: "Arise, O Glorious Zion" (551), "Think Not When You Gather to Zion" (552).

The Church Pension Fund: SEABURY (658), ETERNAL LIGHT (668), GENEVA (672); and the Rt. Rev. John H. Burt: "O God of Youth" (728); and Mrs. Alexander G. Cummins: "I Know Not Where the Road Will Lead" (707); and Mrs. Winifred Douglas: DEXTER STREET (719); and Philip James: TREGARON (720); and Anne L. Miller: VERMONT (734); and the Rev. John W.

Norris: "Give Peace, O God, the Nations Cry" (734); and the Rev. F. Bland Tucker: "All Praise to Thee" (730), "Our Father by Whose Name" (731); and Mrs. Howard Chandler Robbins: "The Sabbath Day Was By" (719), "And Have the Bright Immensities" (720), "Put Forth, O God, Thy Spirit's Might" (721); and David McK. Williams: GEORGETOWN (710).

Francis X. Curley, S.J.: "Let Christian Hearts Rejoice Today" (102).

Elinor F. Downs: "The Prince of Peace His Banner Spreads" (724).

Elkan-Vogel: STAR (793), reprinted from *Hymns and Responses for the Church Year* by Vincent Persichetti (copyright 1956, Elkan-Vogel, Philadelphia). Text used by permission.

Farrar, Straus, & Giroux: "Don't You Be Like the Foolish Virgin" (326), from *Slave Songs of the Georgia Sea Islands* by Lydia Parrish (copyright 1942 by Lydia Parrish, copyright renewed © 1969 by Maxfield Parrish, Jr.).

Fortress Press: "I Know a Flower So Fair and Fine" (700), "Precious Child So Sweetly Sleeping" (716).

Funk and Wagnalls and H. R. McFadyen: "The Lone Wild Fowl" (709).

G.I.A. Publications: "Let the Deep Organ Swell" (702), from the *St. Gregory Hymnal* (copyright 1920 by Nicola Montani (copyright 1940 by the St. Gregory Guild).

James Gordon Gilkey: "O God, in Whose Great Purpose" (687), "Outside the Holy City" (688).

Gregorian Institute of America: "Praise Now Your God" (742), from the *Hymnal of Christian Unity.*

Hampton Institute: "He Raise a Poor Lazarus" (315), from *Cabin and Plantation Songs* (ed. 1918); "O Ride On, Jesus" (316), "Nobody Knows de Trouble I've Seen" (320), "Roll, Jordan, Roll" (321), all arranged by R. Nathaniel Dett, from *Religious Folk Songs of the Negro* (1927); "Lord, I Want To Be a Christian" (330), transcribed and arranged by R. Nathaniel Dett, from the *African Methodist Episcopal Hymnal 1957.*

S. Ralph Harlow: "O Young and Fearless Prophet" (722).

Harper and Row: "O Holy City Seen of John" (678), from *Hymns of the Christian Life* (copyright 1910 by Harper & Row).

John Haynes Holmes: "O'er Continent and Ocean" (682).

Roger W. Holmes: "Peace Is the Mind's Old Wilderness" (729).

Mrs. George Pelham Hyde: "Creation's Lord, We Give Thee Thanks" (658).

Hymn Society of America: "I Know Not How That Bethlehem's Babe" (676); "Within the Shelter of Our Walls" (741), from *Thirteen New Marriage and Family Life Hymns;* "O God, Send Men" (744), from *Ten New Hymns on the Ministry;* "O Christ of Bethlehem" (766), from *Fourteen New Rural Hymns* (copyright 1955 by the Society); "Word of God, Across the Ages" (767), from *Ten New Hymns on the Bible* (copyright 1953 by the Society).

Philip James: PAUMANOK (291), CWMAFAN (709), TREGARON (720).

Robert F. Jeffreys: "O Risen Lord" (570), "Why Linger Yet Upon the Strand?" (573).

Ludlow Music: "We Shall Overcome" (735); new words and music arrangement by Zilphia Horton, Frank Hamilton, Guy Carawan, and Pete Seeger (TRO copyright © 1960, 1963 by Ludlow Music, New York, N.Y.).

Lutheran Commission on the Liturgy and Hymnal: text and music of "Lord Jesus Christ, We Humbly Pray" (677), "The Twilight Shadows Round Me Fall" (712), "Come All Ye People" (739), and "God of Peace in Peace Preserve Us" (740), and the tunes Lobe den Herren (240) and Our Christ (676), from the *Lutheran Service Book and Hymnal;* Salve Jesu (537), from the *Lutheran Common Service Book.*

H. C. Lutkin: Charity (488), Camp (543), Joshua (549), Lanier (568), Patten (572), Theodore (661), Kiel (663), and Belleville (665).

McLaughlin & Reilly, Evanston, Ill.: "True Son of God, Eternal Light" (703), from *The Pius X Hymnal* (copyright 1953 by McLaughlin & Reilly; all rights reserved); "Rejoice, Let Alleluias Ring" (736), from *The Alverno Hymnal and Choir Book,* Book 2 (copyright 1950 by McLaughlin & Reilly; all rights reserved).

Earl Bowman Marlatt: "Through the Dark the Dreamers Came" (714).

Maryland Historical Society: "What Glorious Vision" (189) and "Ye Scattered Nations" (190), from the original in the Cradock Papers (MS 196) in the Maryland Historical Society, Baltimore.

Ernest Merrill: "Not Alone for Mighty Empire" (672).

Musical Quarterly: "Dawning Fair, Morning Wonderful" (440), from Anne Blanche McGill, "Old Mission Music" (1938), vol. 24.

Arne Oldberg: "To Thee, Eternal Soul, Be Praise" and Gilder (656).

LeRoy A. Percy: "They Cast Their Nets in Galilee" (710).

C. F. Peters Corporation: Sing, My Soul (799) (copyright © 1962 by Henmar Press), by permission of C. F. Peters, sole selling agents.

Pilgrim Press: "O Master Workman of the Race" (690), reprinted from *New Worship and Song* and the *Pilgrim Hymnal.*

Mrs. George R. Potter: Copeland (650).

The Presbyterian Outlook: "Rise Up, O Men of God" (673).

Theodore Presser: "The Lord Has a Child" (802) (copyright © 1957 by Merion Music; Langston Hughes text used by permission).

Proclamation Productions: "And the Cock Begins to Crow" (746) from *More, More, More,* by Richard K. Avery and Donald S. Marsh (copyright © 1970 by Richard K. Avery and Donald S. Marsh), used by permission of Proclamation Productions, Orange Square, Port Jervis, N.Y.

Fleming H. Revell: Faithful Legions (667), Holmes (680), Dreamers (714), from the *New Church Hymnal;* "O Child of Lowly Manger Birth" (666), from *Hymns for the Living Age;* Renascence (694), from *New Hymnal for American Youth.*

Rodeheaver: "The Old Rugged Cross" (692) (copyright 1913 by George Bennard; copyright renewed 1941 Rodeheaver).

G. Schirmer, Inc.: "O Ride On, Jesus" (316), from *Religious Folk-Songs of the Negro,* Book 1 (1927), from recording by Natalie Curtis Burlin (copyright 1918 by G. Schirmer).

Scribner's: "Jesus, Thou Divine Companion" (674), from *The Toiling of Felix,* by Henry Van Dyke.

William A. Sleeper: America the Beautiful (697).

Trustees under the Will of Mary Baker Eddy: "O'er Waiting Harp-Strings of the Mind" (446) and "Shepherd, Show Me How To Go" (447), from the *Christian Science Hymnal.*

United Church Press: "O Master Workman of the Race" (690), reprinted from *New Worship and Song* and *The Pilgrim Hymnal* (words copyright 1912 by Congregational Sunday-School and Publishing Society).

The United Presbyterian Church Board of National Missions: "Braving the Wilds All Unexplored" (715).

George A. Vondermuhl: "Lord God of Hosts" (667), "Not Only Where God's Free Winds Blow" (668, 785).

Walter Weinberg: tune to "How Goodly Is Thy House" (576).

Westminster Press: "Let Us Break Bread Together" (329), from *The Hymnbook* (1955).

World Library Publications: "Glory" (745), from the *People's Mass Book,* reproduced by permission of the copyright owner, World Library Publications, Cincinnati, Ohio.

Don Yoder: "O Earnest Be" (406), from Don Yoder, *Pennsylvania Spirituals* (1961), no. 111.